Migrants and Religion: Paths, Issues, and Lenses

Migrants and Religion: Paths, Issues, and Lenses

*A Multi-disciplinary and Multi-sited Study
on the Role of Religious Belongings
in Migratory and Integration Processes*

Edited by

Laura Zanfrini

BRILL

LEIDEN | BOSTON

Copyright 2020 by the authors. Published by Koninklijke Brill NV, Leiden, The Netherlands. Koninklijke Brill NV incorporates the imprints Brill, Brill Hes & De Graaf, Brill Nijhoff, Brill Rodopi, Brill Sense, Hotei Publishing, mentis Verlag, Verlag Ferdinand Schöningh and Wilhelm Fink Verlag. Koninklijke Brill NV reserves the right to protect this publication against unauthorized use.

Cover illustration: Mexico–United States barrier at the border of Tijuana, Mexico and San Diego, USA. The crosses represent migrants who died in the crossing attempt. Some identified, some not. Surveillance tower in the background. 1 May 2006. © Tomas Castelazo, www.tomascastelazo.com, Wikimedia Commons, CC BY-SA 4.0.

Library of Congress Cataloging-in-Publication Data

Names: Zanfrini, Laura, editor.
Title: Migrants and religion : paths, issues, and lenses. A multi-disciplinary and multi-sited study on the role of religious belongings in migratory and integration processes / edited by Laura Zanfrini.
Description: Leiden ; Boston : Brill, [2020] | Includes bibliographical references and index.
Identifiers: LCCN 2020030436 (print) | LCCN 2020030437 (ebook) | ISBN 9789004429444 (hardback) | ISBN 9789004429604 (ebook)
Subjects: LCSH: Emigration and immigration--Religious aspects--Case studies. | Religious refugees--Social conditions--Case studies. | Immigrants--Religious life--Case studies. | Freedom of religion. | Belonging (Social psychology)
Classification: LCC JV6107 .M57 2020 (print) | LCC JV6107 (ebook) | DDC 305.6086/91--dc23
LC record available at https://lccn.loc.gov/2020030436
LC ebook record available at https://lccn.loc.gov/2020030437

Typeface for the Latin, Greek, and Cyrillic scripts: "Brill". See and download: brill.com/brill-typeface.

ISBN 978-90-04-42944-4 (hardback)
ISBN 978-90-04-42960-4 (e-book)

Copyright 2020 by the authors. Published by Koninklijke Brill NV, Leiden, The Netherlands.
Koninklijke Brill NV incorporates the imprints Brill, Brill Hes & De Graaf, Brill Nijhoff, Brill Rodopi, Brill Sense, Hotei Publishing, mentis Verlag, Verlag Ferdinand Schöningh and Wilhelm Fink Verlag. Koninklijke Brill NV reserves the right to protect this publication against unauthorized use.

This book is printed on acid-free paper and produced in a sustainable manner.

Contents

PART 5
Migrations, Intergenerational Relations and Families

PART 6
Religious Diversity in Italian Schools

Figures and Tables

Figures

Tables

Notes on Contributors

Mario Antonelli

is a Priest of the Archdiocese of Milan. At the Pontifical Gregorian University, he took his doctorate in Theology with a thesis about the *Action* by Maurice Blondel. He started teaching in 1989. Until 2018, he was Professor of Fundamental Theology at the Seminary of the Archdiocese of Milan, with the occasional teaching of Trinitary Theology and Ecclesiology. He was sent as *fidei donum* to the area of Belém (Brazil) where he also taught Theological Anthropology, Trinitary Theology and Christology from 2004 to 2010. He is a collaborator of the missionary Pastoral and of the pastoral Care of Migrants, and since 2018 he has been Episcopal Vicar for Education and Celebration of Faith in the Archdiocese of Milan.

Fr. Fabio Baggio

is a member of the Missionaries of St. Charles Borromeo. He gained a doctorate in Church History at the Pontifical Gregorian University in 1998. Fr. Baggio worked as a pastor in Santiago de Chile from 1995 to 1997 and was also advisor for migrations to the Chilean bishops' conference (INCAMI). Afterwards, until 2002, he served as Director of the Department for Migration of the Archdiocese of Buenos Aires. From 1999–2010, he taught at the Universidad del Salvador in Buenos Aires as well as at the Ateneo de Manila and at the Maryhill School of Theology at Quezon City in the Philippines, where he was Director of the Scalabrini Migration Center (SMC). Since the year 2000, he was also Professor at the Scalabrini International Migration Institute (SIMI), which is incorporated into the Theology Faculty of the Pontifical Urban University in Rome. He became Director of the Institute in 2010. Since January 1, 2017 he has been Under-Secretary of the Refugees and Migrants Section, Dicastery for the Promotion of Integral Human Development (Holy See).

Paola Barachetti

graduated in Political and Social Science. She has had a long career in a nonprofit organization offering social welfare services, including those devoted to migrants and refugees. She is currently affiliated with the Università Cattolica del Sacro Cuore of Milan, where she is serving as Teaching Assistant. Her research interests include intercultural psychology and social practice; acculturation and integration in migrant families and children; the influence of religious values in the process of social inclusion.

Alessandro Bergamaschi

has an international French-Italian Ph.D. in Sociology and is Associate Professor at the University of the Côte d'Azur. His research focuses on the manifestations of xenophobia among adolescents and on the role of formal education in the prevention of interethnic intolerance. He is a member of the "Migrations et société" research unit (CNRS 8245 – IRD 205) and fellow at the Institut Convergences Migrations – INED Paris.

Olga Bernad-Cabero

is a Postdoctoral fellow of the Department of Pedagogy at the University of Lleida, Catalonia, Spain. Her research lines focus on the sociology of education, family and school relations, migration and cultural diversity. She has carried out research at the University of Montreal and at the University of Dakar. She is a trainer and consultant at educational centers and has given numerous lectures, communications and consultations for various institutions. In recent years, she has published articles and book chapters in prestigious publishing houses. She is part of the GR-ASE research group "Educational and Social Analysis" of UdL.

Catherine Blaya

is Professor of Education Sciences at the University for Teachers' Education in Lausanne (Switzerland). She teaches at the Special Education Needs unit and is Co-Director of its Research Centre for the Prevention of School Dropout (LASALE). She is member of the Research Unit on Migrations and Society (UMR CNRS 8245-IRD 205), specialized in the study of migrations and interethnic relations at the University Nice Sophia Antipolis. She has been dedicating her academic career to researching issues that might affect young people's lives, such as dropping out of school, school climate, cyberbullying, and cyberhate.

Lucia Boccacin

Ph.D. in sociology, is currently Full Professor of Cultural Sociology in the Faculty of Education, Università Cattolica del Sacro Cuore, Milan. Chair of National Scientific Qualification in Sociology of the Cultural and Communicative Processes, Scientific Sector 14/C2, years 2016–2018. Her research focuses on the third sector, partnership models among the third sector and other social macro-players, social policies and social services, family and intergenerational relations.

Paolo Bonetti

is Associate Professor of Constitutional Law at the University of Milano-Bicocca, where he teaches Institutions of Public Law and Immigration Law in undergraduate and postgraduate degrees. Among other things, he conducts research on the organization of jurisdiction and fundamental rights, on social and family rights and on the principles of equality, the conditions of foreigners and the right to asylum. He has collaborated with ISMU Foundation – Initiatives and Studies on Multi-ethnicity and with ORIM (the Regional Centre for immigration supported by the Lombardy Regional Council) on the collection, analysis and processing of regulatory and judicial data regarding immigration and asylum applications from a constitutional perspective. He also collaborated with the Inter-University Research Centre on Service of Public Utility for the Individual (CRISP) on a report about the situation of undocumented foreigners in Italy for the EU Fundamental Rights Agency (FRA). He took part in and coordinated the working group for the research on "Administrative Judges and Constitutional Rights" that ended with the convention held at the University of Trento (2011), where he delivered an introductory lecture on the independence and impartiality of the administrative judge.

Donatella Bramanti
is Full Professor of Sociology of the Family and Sociology of Personal Services at the Università Cattolica del Sacro Cuore of Milan. She has conducted a number of studies on the themes of family and of ageing population. She has also participated in numerous research projects. She has collaborated with the National Observatory of the Family with a research on "Self-sufficient Seniors and Family Friendly Services". She is the author and co-author of over 100 monographs and articles concerning social policies, personalized services and good practices, social and cultural family transformations, impact evaluation in the field of personalized services and educational processes.

Luca Bressan
has been Presbyter of the Diocese of Milan since 1987. At the Archiepiscopal Seminary of Milan, he teaches Homiletics and Pastoral Theology. He is a permanent Professor at the Theological Faculty of Northern Italy (Milan). Since June 2012, he has been Episcopal Vicar for Culture, Charity, Mission and Social Action.

Maddalena Colombo
is Full Professor of Sociology of Cultural and Communicative processes; she teaches Sociology of Education, Sociology of Educational Policy and Sociology of Inequalities and Differences at the Faculty of Education, Università Cattolica del Sacro Cuore of Milan and of Brescia. She is the Director of the CIRMiB (Centre of Initiatives and research on Migration – Brescia) and of the Laris (Laboratory of Research and Intervention on Society). She is a

member of the Scientific Board of several journals in Italy. She co-ordinates the AIS-Education section. At the Milan campus of UCSC, she co-ordinates the Jean Monnet Module IDEAL (Intercultural Dialogue in Europe and Active poLicies) (a.y. 2016/2019). Her most recent publication is "The impact of Ethnicity on school life: a cross-national post-commentary", *Italian Journal of Sociology of Education* (3) 2018.

Jordi Garreta-Bochaca

holds a degree and a doctorate in Sociology from the Autonomous University of Barcelona and is currently teaching at the University of Lleida. He has carried out research on educational sociology and sociology of migrations and is Director of GR-ASE research group "Educational and Social Analysis" of UdL. As well as presenting his work in conventions, he has published articles in national and international journals and books (https://lleida.academia.edu/JordiGarretaBochaca). He has carried out various research visits at the Centre d'Études Ethniques at the University of Montreal (1996, 1998, 2000 and 2009) and the École des Hautes Études en Sciences Sociales in Paris (1997, 1998, 2007, 2010 and 2020).

Cristina Giuliani

is an academic researcher and serves as Assistant Professor of Social Psychology at the Faculty of Linguistic Sciences, Università Cattolica del Sacro Cuore of Milan. She is also member of the Family Studies and Research University Centre. Her main issues of research are the following: critical family transition and resiliency processes, migration processes, acculturation process and family relationship transformations in post-migration, Muslim immigrant families.

Paolo Gomarasca

Ph.D. , is an Associate Professor in Moral Philosophy at the Faculty of Political and Social Sciences – Università Cattolica del Sacro Cuore of Milan, where he currently teaches Social Philosophy, Philosophy of Intercultural Dialogue, Ethics of Care, Ethics and Professional Conduct for Social Work and Global Ethics. At the Università Cattolica del Sacro Cuore of Milan, he is a member of the Doctoral Board of Ph.D. "Social Work and Personal Social Services", a member of Research Centre of Relational Social Work (RSW) and a member of the Transdisciplinary Research On Food Issues Centre (TROFIC). He is also an external collaborator in the international project "Emotional culture and identity", Instituto Cultura y Sociedad, Universidad de Navarra, Pamplona (Spain). His areas of study and research are the following: care ethics for social work, gender studies, studies on refugees, and food ethics.

Núria Llevot-Calvet

is Professor in the Department of Pedagogy at the University of Lleida, Catalonia, Spain (Serra Hunter Programme of the Generalitat of Catalonia). Her lines of research focus on mediation and intercultural education, religious diversity, ethnic minorities and cooperation between Africa and Europe. She has carried out several research stays at universities such as Sherbrooke, Quebec, Montreal, Paris, Mostar, Dakar, Padua, Rome; she has given lectures and training courses in various centers and has published articles in journals, as well as book chapters and books. She is a member of the Board of Directors in the Research Institute "INDEST" and in the Research Group GR-ASE "Educational and Social Analysis" of UdL.

Rosangela Lodigiani

Ph.D. , is an Associate Professor of Sociology of Economics at the Faculty of Political and Social Sciences – Università Cattolica del Sacro Cuore of Milan, where she currently teaches Employment relations and active labor market policies, European Social Policies, and General Sociology. She is member of the WWELL (Work, Welfare, Enterprise and Lifelong Learning) Research Centre's Steering Board at the Department of Sociology, and member of the Scientific Committee of the Ph.D. Course in "Sociology, Organizations, Cultures" at the same University. Her research interests are focused on labor market, lifelong learning and activations policies, as well as on Italian and European active welfare system's reform and innovation, in a comparative perspective. On these issues, she has carried out and managed many field-research projects and published several essays and papers.

Vera Lomazzi

received her Ph.D. in Sociology and Social Research Methods in 2015. She is a Senior Researcher at the Data Archive for Social Sciences at GESIS – Leibniz Institute for Social Sciences in Cologne, Germany, and Secretary of the Executive Committee of the European Values Study. Her substantive research mainly focuses on the cross-cultural study of gender equality and gender role attitudes, youth engagement, and collective identities. She has a specific interest in the quality of the instruments adopted by large cross-sectional survey programs and on their measurement equivalence. Before joining GESIS, she took part as trainer and consultant in a UNICEF-funded project in South Lebanon (2014–2015) and was research fellow at the University of Aberdeen, where she was involved in the EC-funded project "Arab Transformations".

Linda Lombi

Ph.D. in Sociology, is Assistant Professor at the Università Cattolica del Sacro Cuore of Milan, where she teaches Sociology and Methods (Faculty of Education Science). Her research interests are around welfare policies, health sociology, and digital research.

Paolo Maggiolini

is Research Fellow at the Università Cattolica del Sacro Cuore of Milan, Faculty of Political and Social Sciences, and Adjunct Professor of Regional Studies – Middle East and History of Islamic Asia, Faculty of Linguistic Sciences and Foreign Literatures.

Monica Martinelli

is Associate Professor of Sociology at the Università Cattolica del Sacro Cuore of Milan and a member of the Centre for the Anthropology of Religion and Cultural Change (ARC). Her scientific research focuses on the study of the sociological classics and their questions about the relationship between the individual and society, applied to contemporary socio-cultural transformations.

Stefania Giada Meda

is a sociology researcher at the Università Cattolica's Centre for Family Studies and Research. Her main research topics are in the field of sociology of the family, ageing, and social policies. She was awarded a Marie Curie Actions fellowship for international mobility and research.

Alessia Melcangi

is Tenure Track Assistant of Contemporary History of North Africa and Middle East and Globalization and International Relations at the Sapienza University of Rome, Department of Social Sciences and Economics (DiSSE), Non-Resident Senior Fellow at the Atlantic Council, Rafik Hariri Center for the Middle East, Washington D.C., and collaborates with the Centre of Research on the Southern System and the Wider Mediterranean (CRiSSMA–Università Cattolica del Sacro Cuore).

Giulia Mezzetti

has recently obtained a Ph.D. in Sociology. She is Researcher and project Officer at ISMU Foundation – Initiatives and Studies on Multiethnicity, a research institute on migration and integration. Her research interests concern children of Muslim migrants' religiosity, activism and visibility, contemporary forms of jihadist radicalization and the religion-integration nexus.

Beatrice Nicolini

has a degree in International Relations and Comparative Government from Harvard University, U.S.A. and graduated in Political Sciences from Università Cattolica del Sacro Cuore of Milan. She obtained a Ph.D. in History of Africa from Siena University, Italy. She is Full Professor of History and Institutions of Africa, Religions, Conflicts and Slavery, Indian Ocean World, Faculty of Political and Social Sciences at the Università Cattolica del Sacro Cuore of Milan. Expert for Zanzibar V-Dem – Varieties of Democracy Project, Oslo University, Norway. She has received grants and recognition for her research from Italy, from the Sultanate of Oman and from the UK. She has released more than 110 publications, most of which in English, and a number of them have been translated into Arabic.

Andrea Plebani

is Associate Fellow at the Università Cattolica del Sacro Cuore of Milan and Adjunct Professor in Geopolitics, Faculty of Linguistic Sciences and Foreign Literatures.

Riccardo Redaelli

is the Director of the Center for Research on the South and the Wider Mediterranean System (CRiSSMA) and Director of the Master in Middle Eastern Studies (MIMES) of the Università Cattolica del Sacro Cuore of Milan, and Full Professor of History and Institutions of Asia. He also teaches Post Conflict and Emergency Management. Member of the Observatory on Religious Minorities in the World and the Respect for Religious Freedom of the Italian Ministry of Foreign Affairs, since 2004 he has been coordinating a plurality of Track-two programs of national reconciliations, international cooperation and knowledge transfer in the Middle East. He published more than 100 monographs, edited books, essays and articles on the history and contemporary politics of the Middle East.

Camillo Regalia

is Full Professor of Social Psychology at the Faculty of Education, Director of the Ph.D. program in Social and Developmental Psychology at the Università Cattolica del Sacro Cuore of Milan, and member of the executive committee of the Family Studies and Research University Centre. His main issues of research are the following: psychological integration of first and second generation of immigrants; cultural identity and family processes; Muslim migration in the West.

Giovanna Rossi

has been a Full Professor of Sociology of the Family, Faculty of Psychology, and Head of the Centre for Family Studies and Research, Università Cattolica del Sacro Cuore of Milan, since 1997. She is also Member of the ESA (European Sociological Association) Advisory Board of Research Network 13 "Sociology of Families and Intimate Lives". She has carried out extensive and documented research focusing on family, social policy, and third sector. She is author and co-author of many books and over 130 scientific contributions on national and international journals, editor of *Studi di Sociologia* (Sociology Studies) and of *Sociologia e Politiche sociali* (Sociology and Social Policy), Co-Director of *Studi interdisciplinari sulla Famiglia* (Interdisciplinary Studies on Family) and *Politiche sociali e servizi* (Social Policy and Services).

Giancarlo Rovati

was Full Professor of Sociology at the Università Cattolica del Sacro Cuore of Milan from 2003 to 2018, teaching General Sociology and Sociology of Development in the Faculty of Political and Social Sciences. He has been involved in several national research projects, supported by CNR and MIUR and in multinational research projects on Values System change (in the context of European Values Study program), cultural enterprises (in the context of the European Community ADAPT program), international cooperation programs with Russia, Azerbaijan, Ukraine (in the context of Tempus-Tacis program); development cooperation programs (in the context of the Orphan Vulnerable Children – OVC program managed by AVSI and supported by USAID in Kenia, Rwanda, Uganda, Ivory Coast). He was member of the national board of the Italian Sociological Association (1996–1998); President of the national Inquiry Commission on Social Exclusion – CIES (2002–2007), member of EVS Theory Group and Italian Director of the IV and V wave of the European Values Survey (EVS-Italy 2008 and 2017) coordinated by University of Tilburg. His main fields of theoretical and empirical researches are the following: cultural institutions, social-economic elites, social stratification, change in religious, moral and political values, development and globalization, poverty and social exclusion.

Mariagrazia Santagati

is Assistant Professor of Sociology of Education in the Faculty of Education at the Università Cattolica del Sacro Cuore of Milan, as well as Scientific Secretary of the CIRMiB. She is the head of the Department for Education of the ISMU Foundation (Initiatives and Studies on Multiethnicity) and, since 2010, she has been the editor of the annual "Report on students with non-Italian citizenship", promoted by the Ministry of Education and ISMU. Her main scientific interests deal with the connections between education and migration (ethnic inequalities; successful students with an immigrant background; interethnic and interreligious relationships; intercultural policies). Last publication on the topic: "The (im)possible success of disadvantaged students. Reflections on education, migration and social change" in Arxius de Ciències Socials, (40) 2019.

Andrea Santini

is Associate Professor of European Union Law at the Faculty of Political and Social Sciences of the Università Cattolica del Sacro Cuore of Milan, where he also coordinates the Bachelor course in Political Sciences and International Relations and is a member of the Ph.D. School of Institutions and Policies. He has recently published, with Ugo Draetta and Francesco Bestagno, the handbook *Elementi di diritto dell'Unione europea – Parte istituzionale*, Giuffrè Francis Lefebvre, Milan, 2018.

Annavittoria Sarli

Ph.D. in Anthropology, collaborates as a researcher and expert in migration studies with the WWELL (Work, Welfare, Enterprise Lifelong Learning) Centre of the Università Cattolica del Sacro Cuore of Milan and with ISMU Foundation – Initiatives and Studies on Multi-ethnicity in Milan. Author of several scientific publications, she has collaborated in various national and international research projects.

Monica Spatti

Ph.D. in International, Supranational and European Institutions at the University of Teramo, is a researcher of European Law at the Faculty of Political and Social Science at the Università Cattolica del Sacro Cuore of Milan. Her main research subjects concern the international and European system of protection of human rights, especially regarding migration, privacy, freedom of expression and religious rights.

Giovanni Giulio Valtolina

educated in Padua, Milan and Chicago, is currently affiliated with the Università Cattolica del Sacro Cuore of Milan, where he is serving as Associate Professor of Developmental Psychology. At the Università Cattolica del Sacro Cuore, he is also member of the faculty board of the Ph.D. program in Relational Social Work and Personal Social Services.

His research interests are the following: intercultural psychology and social practice; migrant children; acculturation and psychosocial adaptation in migrant families. Since 2000, he has been a member of the editorial committee of the Ismu Italian Report on Migrations and since 2009 he has also been serving as Head of the Child and Family Department at Ismu Foundation – Initiatives and Studies on Multiethnicity in Milan.

Laura Zanfrini

Ph.D. in Sociology, is Full Professor at the Università Cattolica del Sacro Cuore of Milan, where she teaches Sociology of Migrations and Interethnic Relations and Organizations, Environment and Social Innovation. She is the Scientific Director of the research center WWELL (Work, Welfare, Enterprise and Lifelong Learning); the coordinator of the Board of Professors of the Master's Degree in Labor and Business Management; and the Scientific Director of the Summer School "Human Mobility and Global Justice". She is Head of the Economic and Labor Department, as well as the scientific supervisor of the Documentation Center (CeDoc) at ISMU Foundation – Initiatives and Studies on Multiethnicity, the most important Italian scientific institution studying international migrations and intercultural relations. She is member of several editorial boards, scientific networks, and consultative bodies; she took part and coordinated various international research project. She is the author of about 400 publications, including books, essays, articles and research reports, published both in Italy and abroad. Among these, the first Sociology of Migration and Sociology of Interethnic Coexistence handbooks ever published in Italy and several dictionary and encyclopedia entries.

PART 1

Migrations and Religious Belongings: from Periphery to Core, for a New Humanism

∴

CHAPTER 1

Introduction: General Description of the Study, Key Issues, and Provisional Conclusions

Laura Zanfrini

1 Migrants and Religion: a Challenging Couple for European Contemporary Societies

There has been an extraordinary surge in international migration in recent years, both in the volume of flows and in their composition.[1] Within this complex scenario, Europe has become the first destination in the world in terms of migrants' arrivals and, in the last years, it has faced the most dramatic refugee crisis since the end of World War II. In a more patent way than ever, newcomers are obliging Europe to confront with the multi-faceted religious landscape of migrants' sending countries. Dramatic circumstances such as the growing influence of Boko Haram in Nigeria –and of its foolish attempt to "purify Islam" and society as a whole–, the increasing intolerance towards Christians in Egypt –a sort of "spill-over" effect of terrorism in Iraq and Syria (Open Doors, 2019)–, or the upsurging of religious nationalism in India are now irrupting in European society, through the arrival of people claiming protection or, at times, accused of corrupting "our" –European– religious identity, or even of importing the virus of religious intolerance and religious radicalism to Europe.

While forcing European societies to become aware of the tremendous religious-based violations and persecutions that are characterizing the contemporary global scenario, new arrivals are challenging the main distinction on which European migration regimes have been traditionally based: the discrimination between voluntary and forced migrants. For this reason, all along the book we will put the adjective "forced" within brackets, in order to emphasize the porous and disputable character of this concept. More deeply, paraphrasing Sayad's well-known concept (1999), new arrivals "disturb" Europe and its systems of refugee protection, whereas asylum seekers' religious affiliations seem to represent, in themselves, an "embarrassing" variable that discloses the

---

[1] https://www.un.org/development/desa/en/news/population/international-migrant-stock-2019.html.

© LAURA ZANFRINI, 2020 | DOI:10.1163/9789004429604_002

weaknesses and pitfalls of these systems, since the latter were built in a geo-political context that was very distant from the contemporary one.

As a matter of fact, religious-based claims mirror the extraordinary enlarge-ment of the concept of forced mobility, once circumscribed by the definition provided by the Geneva Convention. However, today it has been progressively extended to include new categories of individuals, situations, and agents of persecution. Yet, because of their nature, both complex and intimate, this kind of claim easily feeds the suspect of the recurrence of "bogus" requests (as we will describe in Chapter 11), thus contributing to the delegitimization of the asylum institute. Finally, asylum's procedures and practices face while being influenced by them, preconceptions and distorted convictions about the dif-ferent religious groups, and about the relations among them. As is shown by the Middle Eastern region –the cradle of the three main monotheistic faiths, chosen as one of the focuses of the present study–, current analyses are often dominated by opposite understandings, unable to comprehend the "turbu-lent" situations of Europe' peripheries, but also unable to grasp what is really at stake.

To cite one example, while accusing humanitarian channels and reception services of becoming an instrument for the attraction of (Muslim) (fake) refu-gees, European public opinion seems to disregard how these same channels provide a possibility of survival for many Christians currently "under attack".[2] Not to mention the case of those migrants –Muslims and not Muslims– preju-dicially perceived as "enemies" only because they come from given "Islamic" undemocratic countries. Ultimately, a debate dominated by concerns of a cultural and security nature ends up obscuring the other implications of the migration-religion link; first of all, the importance of the religious factor in the genesis of migration. In this context, European religious identity has been repeatedly evoked as a vessel to be wielded in order to protect "Europe" from arrivals, depicted as a menace. One of the most shocking examples was the *Rozaniec do Granic*, the Rosary on border boundaries: a collective prayer that took place on October 7, 2017, involving an impressive number of people along the over-3,100-kilometre Polish borders, creating an ideal human chain. The official motivation of the event was that of imploring the intercession of the Mother of God "to save Poland and the world", on the occasion of the feast of Our Lady of the Rosary, "established after the great battle of Lepanto, where

---

2 As a matter of fact, according to the reports produced every year by "Aiuto alla Chiesa che soffre", the persecution of Christians has been producing significant outflows of people try-ing to escape, to the extent of putting into question the very survival of some of the oldest Christian churches of the world, thus compromising the multi-religious composition of the sending societies (Aiuto alla Chiesa che soffre, 2019).

the Christian fleet defeated the much larger fleet of Muslim society, thus saving Europe from Islamization".

Finally, European public opinion looks at current migration as something from which "to defend itself", and is worried about not only the economic, but also the cultural impact of incoming flows, particularly when they are composed of migrants presumed to be Muslims (Mavelli, Wilson, 2016). Both economic and humanitarian migrations are perceived as an "identity challenge", since they are forcing the symbolic borders of European nations, shaped by their "Christian roots". In this manner, they "miss" the key point: policies for the granting of asylum and other forms of humanitarian protection represent a conscious way of affirming principles, values and worldviews. In the end, they should be an opportunity for societies to reflect on the values on which they are based and deserve to be handed down as a legacy to future generations, and an extraordinary –if not prophetic– opportunity of self-reflection and of display of "our" own culture. The goal of contributing to raising the general awareness of this concept is one of the main reasons behind the present study: as it often happens, migration proves to be a "mirror" that permits to grasp and discuss key issues and emerging challenges.

Indeed, as exemplified by the experience of (forced) migrants intercepted thanks to the research on which the present book is based, religious rights and religious freedom represent a "litmus test" of the quality of a democracy. On the one hand, their systematic violation dramatically gives evidence of the lack of democracy in many sending countries, and marks the limit beyond which it is not possible to accept any abuses, thus forcing victims to opt for the "exit strategy" represented by migration. On the other hand, they offer European citizens the opportunity to realize the importance of religious rights at both individual and collective level, shaking them from the inertia that sometimes seems to characterize European societies, not to mention the temptation to encourage authoritarian turns. Finally, the experience of people who have migrated for religious motives, which encourages reflection about the importance of religion in both private –individual and family– life and public life; particularly in Europe, where this dimension has been traditionally expulsed from the public sphere and it is now more and more reduced to its "identitarian" dimension (Roy, 2019). As we will analyze in depth, the contemporary "post-secular" scenario proves to be particularly stimulating for this kind of reflection since, alongside the insistent secularization, a more composite, not easily defined picture is emerging. Religion today is closely connected with cultural and social transformations involving contemporary Europe, but it is also the borderline where contradictory pressures and, in some cases, thorny questions relating to the coexistence between people with different religious traditions interweave.

At the same time, since contemporary (forced) migrations are perceived as more and more unpredictable in their dimension and internal composition, they are obliging Europe to come to terms with the full and long-standing legacy represented by its relationship with immigration and the "diversity" – including religious – that immigration brought with it. According to our interpretation (Zanfrini, 2019), as institutionalized during the post-war period, the European migration regime contained in itself the reasons for cultivating the illusion of the temporary nature of migration, discouraging the stable settlement of immigrant families and communities, and defining migration as a pure economic phenomenon; that is a phenomenon unable to change the political and identity borders of European national communities. Nevertheless, the unpredicted settlement of the post-World War II "guest workers" and their progressive inclusion in the citizens' community, the huge number of family reunions, the implosion of the Soviet empire and the subsequent redefinition of the internal States' borders, as well as the arrival of millions of asylum seekers following the crises in various regions of the world (from Latin America to South-East Asia, from the Balkans to the Middle East) have contributed to the formation of ethnic and religious minorities. Their presence and their "visibility", also in the public space, represent an unexpected –if not an unwelcomed– phenomenon; a phenomenon definitely inconsistent with the myth of the ethnic, cultural and religious homogeneity on which the European nations have been founded.

Indeed, in recent times, the main societal institutions have been profoundly challenged by the settlement of people with different cultural and religious background (Vilaça *et al.*, 2014); even more so when these people not only expect to be treated as "equals", but ask to be acknowledged as "diverse". National school systems –another of the topical issues chosen by the present study–, invested by the task of socializing new generations to the role of future citizens, have therefore become a key actor: the presence of students with a (minority) religious background challenges them through the request of recognition; what is more, it offers a unique opportunity to grasp the concepts of democracy and citizenship, without avoiding the confrontation with the dimension of conflict inevitably present in every pluralistic and truly democratic context. Finally, among the other consequences, the permanent settlement of migrant families and migrant communities has transformed European States into multi-religious societies, thus offering them the opportunity "to test" the principle of religious freedom.[3]

---

3 For a brief review of the issues and possible solutions concerning the governance of post-immigration religious diversity see: Modood, Sealy, 2019.

Another point deserving our attention is that the migrants' condition of structural disadvantage –in its turn, a "natural" inheritance of a migratory regime that has traditionally attracted a "poor" migration, useful to enter the lowest ladders of the occupational stratification (see again Zanfrini, 2019)– has amplified the perception of a social and cultural distance between migrants and natives. In other words, it has fed anxiety about the "diversity" embedded in the population with a migratory background, starting exactly from their religious diversity. Religious affiliations, particularly Islamic affiliations, have therefore turned to be viewed as an element of vulnerability, if not as a barrier inhibiting the integration process and the relations with the native population. Not to mention that, according to available data, low levels of socio-economic inclusion tend to be correlated with a higher involvement in religious practices. Lastly, the transformation of an economic process –as immigration was originally conceptualized– into a political process, has catapulted at the core of the political agenda issues and problems related with the "identity" (included the "religious identity") of European societies. Not surprisingly, the religion of refugees has become a noticeable issue (Schmiedel, Smith, 2018), definitively denying the prophecy of a decline in the importance of religion in the public sphere that has accompanied the modernization of European societies. At the height of the refugee crisis, religion has even been identified as a useful filter to select, among potential asylum seekers, those individuals who should be able to cross the symbolic and cultural boundaries of European national communities. "Anti-migrants" actors make an open and sometimes violent use of religion in order to endorse securitarian and selective approaches in the management of migratory flows. What is even more embarrassing, "pro-migrants" narrative sometimes evokes the low percentage of Muslim migrants as a supposed reassuring argument for public opinion, thus implicitly reaffirming the problematic character of religious diversity. All this is in line, after all, with the historical European approach to the subject, which has been traditionally shared by both policy makers and social researchers. As is well known, once confronted with the "ideal-type" of immigration country (the US), Europe not only has a different migration history, but it has also suffered from the different role and meaning traditionally attributed to religious affiliations. In the seminal volume *Protestant, Catholic, Jew* (1955), W. Herberg stated that it is precisely through religion that immigrants, and even their children and grandchildren, have found an identifiable place in American life; even today, in a much more diversified scenario, many immigrants "become Americans" thanks to the participation in the religious and the community activities of churches, mosques and Jewish temples (Alba, 2009). Furthermore, the American population is much more "religious" than the European population (according to available statistics), so as to perceive less distance from the immigrant

communities, usually more inclined (or supposed to be more inclined) to religious practice. However, even more than the actual data, it is the interpretation that social sciences have provided that illuminates the different meaning
of religious practice. Until recently, religiosity has been eventually depicted, by
European social researchers, as a "refugee" and a balm for the soul, an instrument to enforce intra-community solidarity and to contrast individual frustration and isolation, but also as a possible source of self-segregation, reactive
identification, and potential conflict with the mainstream institutions. Thus,
while in the American context many sociologists are inclined to see in religious affiliations a factor supporting integration, in Europe religiosity has often
been described as the indicator of a lack of integration in the framework of an
a prioristically-defined secularized society –as well as a factor negatively affecting interethnic relations (the French experience is indeed typical in this
regard)–. The same public discourse has often tended to underestimate the
role that religious affiliations and organizations can play not only in supporting integration, but also in the process of identity building, by favoring the internalization of values oriented towards the common good and some peaceful
coexistence. Finally, by reflecting the common tendency to confine religion in
the private sphere, European studies have tended to emphasize the "bonding"
component of the religious capital of migrants; that of the "bridging" type,
more emphasized in the American tradition, in Europe has a potential that is
not only underused, but also largely neglected by academic research. Just as
much evidence of how the role of religion –and of the migrant religion nexus–
is socially constructed.

Finally, there are several reasons behind both the misunderstanding and the
underestimation of the role of religion in migratory and integration processes.
However, as it will be deeply analyzed, migrants' religious affiliations have become increasingly visible also in the public space and, despite religion's marginality in the mainstream analysis of the integration processes, religion today
has being more and more acknowledged as a significant component in the
construction of migrants' individual and collective identity, in (peaceful or
conflicting) interconnection with the other actors of society. In this way, the
religion of migrants is set to be one of the relevant themes in the debate on the
so-called post-secularized society.

Given this background, the study-project on which this book is based –
*Migrations and religious belongings. From the periphery to the core, for a new
humanism*– supported by Università Cattolica del Sacro Cuore of Milan and
developed in 2016–2018, has aimed to contribute to filling significant knowledge gaps, and to provide both theoretical analysis and empirical evidence on

the relationship between migrants and religion. This phenomenon has been studied by using the concept of religion in its broader meaning, including:

a)   individual and collective religious affiliations, belongings, beliefs, identities, and practices;

b)   religious-based organizations and institutions, as well as interreligious initiatives;

c)   religious rights' violation, religious-based discriminations and conflicts.

Furthermore, it has been inquired by different disciplinary perspectives –from philosophy to law, from sociology to psychology, from political sciences to theology– and has been focusing on different levels of analysis –macro, meso and micro–. Finally, from a methodological point of view, as subsequently illustrated, the study has made use of a variety of methods –including literature review, key-informants' interviews, and focus groups discussion (FGDs)– described in detail within each thematic part.

While ensuring a scientific approach to the subject, the study has been based on a clear cultural and ethical option: the need to acknowledge and illustrate how religious-based belongings, identities, and institutions affect both the genesis of contemporary migrations and the development of migration and integration processes – and, as a further implication, the opportunity to activate religion-related potential in order to support migrants' integration and social cohesion, as well as in order to improve the global governance of (forced) migrations and the efficacy of the protection system.

More in detail, two key hypotheses have encouraged the present study, and guided both the speculative analysis and the collection of empirical evidence.

First of all, *the denial of religious rights –in its overall meaning– is one of the main drivers of contemporary (forced) migration, usually in interconnection with other social, political and economic factors.* The current global scenario witnesses a dramatic recurrence of situations of religious rights' violation and even of open persecution towards minority groups or single believers. Just to cite one of the most dramatic examples, during the timespan of this study, the international community has helplessly witnessed the forced expulsion from Myanmar of hundreds of thousands of Rohingya, a long-standing discriminated Muslim minority. This is only one of the many emergencies involving religious minorities and single believers –or non-believers escaping from "pre-secularized" States–, which have been producing millions of displaced people, asylum seekers, and "voluntary" migrants. All this notwithstanding, the relationship between religion and migration choices and strategies has still been studied insufficiently. More precisely, our hypothesis was that the factors connected with religious affiliations and belongings play a much more significant role than what is shown by available data on refugees for religious reasons, not to mention the common (improper) perception of their effective importance. Indeed, despite the growing concern for the religion of migrants and refugees, there is scarce evidence on the role it played and plays in the life of people who try to penetrate the European Fortress. Besides the possible shortfalls of the legislation in force, our hypothesis was that a multiplicity of factors concurs to a general under-evaluation of this issue, including the existence of religious-based biases and anti-religious sentiments. In order to analyze this point, we have closely studied the situation of the contemporary Middle Eastern region, chosen as a representative to investigate the processes which generate (forced) migrations (Part 2); as well as a clear example of how current analyses are often dominated by opposite understandings, unable to comprehend the "turbulent" situations of Europe's peripheries (but also unable to grasp what really is at stake, as suggested above). Moreover, we have collected plenty of evidence from migrants who have escaped because of religious-based persecutions (or, in more general terms, from migrants for whom religion has played a significant role both in the decision to migrate and in its subsequent developments) and from different kinds of key informants (Part 3). Finally, a selected group of families, adolescents and children have been included in the study in order to grasp the relationship between religion and migration culture also along intergenerational links (Part 5).

Related to this latter point, the second key hypothesis at the basis of the study was that *religious institutions, religious affiliations and religious values are crucial factors not only in structuring migration patterns and practices, but also in supporting the adaptation of newcomers –particularly in the case of (forced) migrants and asylum seekers– and the integration processes of first- and second-generation migrants –especially through the mediation of the family and faith-based organizations* (from now on: FBOS)–, *thus positively impacting on the social cohesion and the common good.* Recent contributions, from sociological (Part 4), psychological (Part 5) and theological (Ahn, 2019) studies, offer new insights that help us to grasp the (positive) role of spirituality, religious belongings and interreligious dialogue, thus contributing to fill the traditional knowledge gap on the issue. Besides providing a systematic review of this literature, our study emphasizes how the emerging "post-secularized" Europe offers a revitalized scenario in which to analyze their role and their future evolutionistic prospects. This hypothesis has been tested through different kinds of analyses, focused on migrants and asylum seekers (Part 3), families (Part 5), FBOS (Part 4) and public schools (Part 6).

As explained in detail in the remaining chapters of Part 1, the discussion on these two hypotheses has been conducted in the light of a philosophical, sociological, and judicial theoretical framework which provides suggestions for:

a)   a perspective to "deinstrumentalize religion" and to "rehumanize" migrants and asylum seekers (Chapter 2);

b)   the unexpected vitality of the religious phenomenon currently emerging as a result of a continuous intersection of long processes and secularizing influences, as well as of responses reacting to those processes and those influences, not without new dilemmas and conflict (Chapter 3);

c)   the opportunities and the limitations that follow the interpretation of the relationship between the violation of religious rights and the status of protection granted by international judicial and quasi-judicial organs (Chapter 4).

2   The Book's Content

The book is articulated in six parts, each composed of four chapters (except for Part 6, which is composed of five chapters).

Part 1 (Migrations and Religious Belongings: from Periphery to Core, for a New Humanism), after the general description of the study's aims and contents, and the presentation of its provisional conclusions (object of the present *Chapter 1*), illustrates the philosophical, socio-cultural, and legislative frames that constitute the research background.

Chapter 2 starts with a description of the unethical ambivalence of the dominant narratives about migration and (forced) displacement. On the one hand, refugees are criminalized and targeted as a threat to border security. On the other hand, counter-narratives portray refugees as innocent, vulnerable victims. The paradox is that these two stereotyped images of (forced) displacement are two faces of the same unethical process of dehumanization: in both cases, refugees are the objects of other people's interpretations and actions. Moreover, in this process of dehumanization, religion is often politicized and plays an instrumental role in justifying two opposite narratives and political solutions. Given this picture, the author develops the proposal of a new "ethics of hospitality", based on two conditions: (*a*) de-instrumentalizing religion, in order to analyze the real, multi-dimensional role of religion in refugees' experience (as both a root cause of displacement and as a source of resiliency and support); (*b*) returning refugees their human subjectivity, which means enabling them to express their subjective outlook on their own experience of (forced) displacement and on the importance of their religious belonging. The political effect of this "post-secular" hospitality is a discursive act that creates a public space, where social ties can be (re-)built. Religion, in this context of re-humanization, can be an integral part of refugees' public space making, along four main lines of research:

1)   *identity*, which focuses on the individual and collective processes of (re-) shaping some forms of self-definition, based on religious beliefs and values;

2)   *religious freedom*, which legitimizes the pluralistic involvement of (religious) identities in public life;

3)   *citizenship*, which is not tied to rigid national territoriality, but includes fluidity of borders and multiple (religious) identities and loyalties;

4)   *common good*, i.e. a multi-religious social capital, generated by the new citizens and their desire to participate in their new society of settlement.

Moving from the perspective of the sociology of religion, *Chapter 3* intends to outline the main characteristics of the so-called (European) "post-secular society". Although a vast literature from the second half of the 20th century announced the imminent end of the religious phenomenon, in Europe –as well as in other regions of the world– a different scenario has been unfolding: religion is still present, even if it is in crisis, as it has increasingly been relegated to the intimate sphere and set free from institutional set-ups, reinvented in content and contaminated by secularization factors. Moreover, in many cases, this presence is strengthened precisely in relation to the migration phenomenon.

Consequently, the European scenario cannot be explained by simply choosing between two options: "secularization *versus* non-secularization". There is a much more articulated and complex picture, certainly from a geographical and national point of view, but in general also because of the singular forms it assumes: these elements are the result of a continuous intersection of secularizing thrusts and responses that oppose them –not without this leading to new dilemmas and, sometimes, to real conflicts–. It is therefore evident that we are living in a different time than that defined as completely "secularized". As a matter of fact, the post-secular society constitutes the socio-cultural context which migrants enter when arriving in Europe, often bearing forms of religious belonging considered to be significant for the construction of their identity in interconnection with the other actors of society, whether it is a peaceful or conflictual interconnection.

Finally, *Chapter 4*, authored by two law scholars, aims to verify the relationship between the right to freedom of religion and the status of refugee considering, in particular, the applications of these institutes given by the international judicial and quasi-judicial organs.

Freedom of religion is a fundamental right recognized in many acts within international and European law. It includes the right for everyone to have, to change and to manifest one's religion. Serious violations of this right could be ascertained as a form of persecution, thus giving rise to the possibility, for those who escape from places where this right is not respected, to obtain the recognition of the status of refugee, according to the Geneva Convention of 1951, and to the EU directive 2011/95/EU concerning the recognition of international protection to refugees. However, following the pronouncements of the European Court of Human Rights and of the Court of Justice of the European Union, a violation of freedom of religion or belief does not automatically grant the right to receive protection, which is obligatorily reserved only to those individuals who are exposed to serious breaches of their fundamental rights. Finally, as clearly illustrated by the empirical study presented in Part 3, the "space" of religion within the system of international protection is subject of different interpretations and negotiations.

Part 2 (Where (Forced) Migrations Are Generated) focuses the attention on one of the most turbulent word-wide regions, which is particularly explanatory with reference to the study's main topics.

The multiple crises that, especially from 2001 onward, inflamed the wider Middle East dramatically altered the geopolitical equilibriums of a region that has always played a crucial role in the international arena. Affected by heightening levels of violence and widespread destabilization, the area became increasingly associated with processes of radicalization and socio-political fragmentation destined to redefine the very foundations of a system whose roots can be traced back to the end of the Great War. The arch of crises that came to bisect the region largely contributed to project the image of a Middle Eastern region "endemically" marred by divisions and instability and destined to be partitioned according to apparently undeniable ethno-sectarian fault lines. In this framework, Middle East ethno-linguistic and religious diversity has become the focal point of two different and opposite arguments. On the one hand, diversity has been considered as the victim of the rising polarization, manipulated and politicized in order to impose a specific political agenda. On the other, it has been listed as one of the drivers or sources of present instability in a region experiencing its own Thirty Years' War, as Europe did in the 16th century.

The authors of *Chapter 5*, thanks to their specific background as experts in the contemporary history of the Middle East, aim to maintain distance from both understandings, reconsidering the contemporary history of the Middle East and of state- and nation-building process in the region according to the image of multiple geographies. Instead of proposing once again the idea of the Middle East as a mosaic, the chapter aims to offer an account of the role of diversity in the region. Through the idea of multiple geographies, the chapter explains why diversity in the Middle East has always played a crucial role. Middle East does not stand out only for its diversity *per se*, but because the features that compose and define its diversity and "multi-vocality" often strongly intertwine and overlap, thus giving birth to social fabrics that are far more complex and branched than usually represented. In this spirit, the analysis ends by showing how a more precise understanding of the Middle East's diversity, of its significance and its role can help to demystify today's sectarian narratives and tackle instability and violence in the region.

This perspective is paradigmatically developed in *Chapter 6*, whose aim is to offer a dynamic account of Christians' presence in the Middle East, of their contribution and position in the contemporary history of the region. In this regard, the historical vicissitude of the Coptic community is helpful to focus more clearly on the challenges, issues and ambitions that have influenced Christians' historical vicissitudes from the beginning of the contemporary state- and nation-building process in the contemporary Middle East until today. Firstly, the chapter focuses on the multi-vocal dimension of the Christian presence in the Middle East – a feature that needs to be taken into account to fully understand its position and condition within the different States in the region; the study helps to reconsider how the interplay between international, regional and local interests affected and shaped the political and institutional presence of Christians within the region. Then the authors analyze the dynamics of sectarian violence and persecution of Christians in the Middle East. In particular, they focus on contemporary Egypt, from the 1950s until the 2011 Uprisings, taking the specific case of the Egyptian Christian Copts (also the subject of the qualitative study presented in the Part 5 of the book) as a case study.

The remaining chapters of Part 2 offer a general picture of cultural orientations in the Middle East and a special focus on attitudes about women's role.

Chapter 7, authored by a researcher with long experience in the study of societal values and world-views, provides a sociological analysis of data produced by the Arab Barometer. This latter constitutes an important source for monitoring the cultural and social dynamics in the countries of the region, since it provides longitudinal surveys supporting comparisons over a long time frame (from 2006 to 2018) in 14 Arab-speaking countries. The data that emerges shows what the heterogeneous Arab public thinks about key issues related to social coexistence, among which religious beliefs and belongings have a fundamental relevance. Beyond the official representations of the strong relations between religion and the political system inside the Arab countries, the focus of this contribution is to check how people perceive their religious affiliations, in order to understand their level of openness toward different religious identities, and so far toward a more tolerant and pacific coexistence. Some people's attitudes give support to this desirable transition, but many other changes ought to happen inside civil laws and political system.

Chapter 8 focuses on the interpretation of Shari'a law in relation to women's rights in countries of the Middle East and North Africa (MENA). In particular, the study deals with the transformation of people's beliefs and values as far as the role of women over the Arab Uprisings of 2011 is concerned. These have often been considered, especially by Western observers, as drivers of social change leading to democratization processes that would enhance the value of equality. In addition to the theoretical review of the topic, the study provides empirical evidence of different forms of feminism existing in this region. By using data from the Arab Barometer (2010, 2018) and the Arab Transformation Project (2014), the study combines elements of secularization versus radicalization in people's support for Shari'a and for women's rights. It also aims to define four typologies of feminism, which are differently distributed across countries: Islamism, Islamic Reformism, Islamic feminism, and Secular Feminism.

Parts 3–6 are devoted to presenting and discussing the empirical evidence collected during the study. With few exceptions, the data presented refer to Italy. Two major aspects make the country an interesting place in which to analyze the role of religion in migratory and integration processes. Firstly, as it is well known, the country is one of the most involved in the recent refugee crisis, as well as in the violent debate based on the two opposite narratives described above. Since it is one of the main European countries of first arrival, according to the highly disputed "Dublin agreement", it plays a very critical role in the evaluation of asylum demands, that is on defining the distinction between voluntary and forced migrants. Incidentally, that the assessment procedures are presumed to be highly discretionary has contributed to the recent –and violently discussed– frequent and opposing legislative reforms. Secondly, Italy is commonly portrayed as a Catholic country, and until recently it has had a relatively homogeneous population from a religious point of view; this circumstance makes it the ideal place to analyze the transition towards an increasingly heterogeneous society, also population from a religious point of view. The same reception system is here described as a space strongly challenged by this evolution; a space in which it is possible to detect the emergence of prejudices on a religious basis, but also to experience the coexistence of people of different religions; to analyze individual spiritual needs, but also the importance of educating people about religious pluralism, understood as a constitutive condition of a democratic society.

The aim of *Part 3* (*The Religion's Dimension in the Trajectories of (Forced) Migrants Directed to Italy*) is to explore the role of religion as a root cause of (forced) migrations addressed to Italy, as well the "place" of religion in the context of the Italian asylum seekers' reception system.

Chapter 9 –written by an influential member of the Italian association of immigration lawyers–, traces the legislative and procedural framework in force in Italy, which was the object of recent significant changes, some of which directly impact on the issues here discussed. Moreover, it examines the discipline of the religious dimension of everyone's life, which can also be applied to the foreigners who have been forced to migrate to Italy (and, of course, who have voluntarily chosen to migrate). In particular, in addition to the description of the legislation on the prevention and combating of discrimination, the chapter focuses on the legislative rules about the State's relations with the different religious denominations, as well as on some crucial aspects of family law, school legislation –for the part that concerns the teaching of religion (a topic that will then be deepened in the empirical study presented in Part 6 of the volume)–, and the discipline of religious assistance in health facilities and prisons. Throughout the chapter, the presentation of current legislation is enriched by the reporting of pertinent jurisprudential judgments.

Chapters 10, 11 and *12* present the results of original research, based on data and suggestions from different sources: five FGDs, which have globally involved around 40 key informants (selected among executives, officials and operators of the reception system for asylum seekers; spiritual leaders and pastoral agents of different religions; representatives of Italian and international organizations and associations involved in the reception of asylum seekers; managers and members of the assessment commissions for asylum applications; local administrators; executives and officials of police stations and prefectures); six semi-structured interviews with religious leaders and pastoral operators belonging to different Catholic organizations involved in the reception of migrants and asylum seekers; 20 in-depth interviews with migrants and asylum seekers who, regardless of the entry channel and of their current legal status, have been significantly influenced by their religious belongings, with regard to both their decision to migrate and the development of migration and insertion processes.

Chapter 10, after a general introduction to the role of religious belongings and institutions as both push and pull factors in the Italian immigration experience, focuses on the role of religion as a factor contributing to defining the distinction between forced and voluntary migrations. Moving from the current political and ethical debate about the increasing "porosity" of this distinction, the author –thanks to her rich experience in the field of migration studies– discusses how the evidence from the fieldwork can help to describe and understand the role of the two key concepts represented by

Religious Identity and Religious Liberty. Furthermore, on the basis of the testimonies provided by the interviewed migrants and the key experts, the chapter offers a classification of cases in which religion turns out to be a direct or indirect cause of migration.

Chapter 11 is devoted to analyzing the role of religion within the procedure for the scrutiny of asylum applications. Given the legislative framework in force in Italy, the author discusses how the actual implementation of rules and procedures allows (or does not allow) for the emergence and the acknowledgment of those aspects variously connected with asylum seekers' religious belongings. Here, religiosity has emerged as both an obscured and a sensitive issue.

Thirdly, *Chapter 12* explores the "space" dedicated to the religious dimension and to the spiritual needs of migrants, also during the delicate phase of first reception and re-elaboration of the migratory distress. Thanks to the involvement of a theology scholar as co-author, the chapter also investigates the "functions" and meanings that (forced) migrants for religious reasons attribute to religion and spirituality, seen both in their individual and communitarian declinations. Finally, following the approach suggested in Chapter 2, through a de-instrumentalization of religion and the acknowledgment of migrants' human subjectivity, the authors discuss the results of the study through the concepts of identity, religious freedom, citizenship, and common good.

Part 4 (Religion, Faith-Based Organizations, Integration and Social Cohesion) is devoted to exploring the relationship among religion, FBOs, migrants' integration and social cohesion through different levels of analysis: a critical review of European social research on this subject; a qualitative sociological study on a selected sample of FBOs; a theological reflection about the role of interreligious dialogue; and a "chronicle" of the Synod recently launched by the world's largest Catholic Diocese, solicited by its demographic transformation into a multi-ethnic and multi-religious social space.

Chapter 13 provides a critical review of the international sociological literature, focusing the attention on the role of religion as a factor that hampers or fosters migrants' integration. As it is largely acquired –and as we have already observed–, this issue has been tackled through rather opposite perspectives in Europe and in the US – taking the latter as a paradigmatic immigration country. Moving from the analysis of this divergent path and of its historical and social reasons, the chapter focuses on the European approach, which has traditionally understood religion as a barrier to integration. The authors examine how migrants' religion has been approached by European social researchers, and highlight the circular dynamic interlinking this approach with public opinion's concerns. Finally, the chapter hints at some recent trends in the

European discourse on religion and integration. These trends mostly regard policy-making practices and, to a certain extent, applied social sciences – also as an answer to recent phenomena of religious radicalization, which has encouraged a rethink of the role of religion and FBOS in integration processes.

Chapter 14 –authored by sociologists with expertise in the field of non-profit organizations and civil society's initiatives– focuses on the migrants' reception practices offered by a selected sample of FBOS, mainly located in Italy. The analyses, performed on four qualitative case studies, show the difficulty of bringing out the theme of religious persecution as one of the explicit motives that led to the migration choice. Despite such critical point, the authors show how the empirical findings lend support to the claim that the religious dimension affects the migratory processes in different modes.

Chapter 15, authored by the Under-Secretary of the Refugees and Migrants Section, Dicastery for the Promotion of Integral Human Development of the Holy See, offers a series of suggestions concerning the potential role of religion in the governance of human mobility. Mainly based on the analysis of documents produced by Catholic Church's teaching and on the personal experience of the author –who has performed his pastoral mission in different regions of the world–, this chapter moves from a basic assumption: because of the very fact that a vast majority of the world population declare adherence to a given religion, the governance of human mobility, as well as any other political process, should include religion as an essential component of human well-being and self-achievement. The presumed superiority of laicism and the political-ideological instrumentalization of religion have helped to dispute the relevance of religion in human achievement, and to expel it from the public sphere. While facing this scenario, it is imperative that religion regains its fundamental role. Moreover, according to the author, since different religious traditions offer an inestimable patrimony of values and principles, it would be desirable to look into them in order to build a common platform for a global ethic. Finally, beyond the role that religions and FBOS play in supporting migrants in their processes of mobility and integration, the inclusion of religions in the public space and debate can help to identify and disseminate principles and values indispensable to guarantee peaceful cohabitation.

Chapter 16 (co-authored by the book's editor and the president of the commission in charge of the coordination of the 2018 "Synod from the Peoples"), provides a selection of the suggestions that emerged from the consultative phase of this pioneer initiative promoted by the Archdiocese of Milan. The empirical base of the analysis, then, consists of reports, consultations, FGDS, and bottom-up contributions collected from the local Church and its various institutions and stakeholders (among which are parishes, religious orders, associations, charities, public schools, and individual citizens, including non-believers).

Launched immediately after the peak of the refugee crisis, which invested Milan with the arrival of thousands of asylum seekers, the Synod aimed to support an evolution of the local Church, in line with the tremendous transformation of the demographic composition of the diocesan space. As stressed by the authors, from a Catholic perspective the Synod can be understood as a "prophetic enterprise", as much as the social transformation of the city can be approached as a "prophetic challenge".

More in detail, the growing presence of Muslims represents both an identity challenge and a chance for the development of interreligious dialogue, just as the presence of many Christian Orthodox believers constitutes a spiritual challenge and a chance for the development of ecumenism; lastly, the significant number of Catholics with a migratory background embodies both a pastoral challenge and a chance to develop a self-reflective ability. To sum it up, it is by managing these challenges and chances that the Milanese Church – as well as any other local Church– will be able to fulfill its authentic "catholicity", while positioning itself in the global society and in the universal Church.

As previously reported, according to the study's initial assumptions, the family represents –together with FBOS– a crucial medium through which religion contributes to structuring migration and integration practices. *Part 5* of the book (*Migrations, Intergenerational Relations and Families*), deals with this topic, once again through both theoretical and empirical contents.

Chapter 17 provides a critical review of the sociological and psychological literature devoted to religion in families' migratory history, and more specifically to the intergenerational transmission of (religious) values and practices. Two macro-themes emerge from international literature and empirical inquiries: the relationship between family and society and the dynamics within generations. The main themes that emerge, and the challenges migrant families face in the relationship with the younger generation, are then re-proposed.

The following chapters of this part (*Chapters 18, 19,* and *20*) focus on the paradigmatic case of Coptic families belonging to the Diaspora community "escaped" from Egypt to Italy. Indeed, despite the relevance of the Christian Diaspora in the world, little scholarly attention has been paid to Middle Eastern Christians' migration to Europe, in particular to the Coptic Diaspora in Europe. This circumstance makes the study particularly suggestive.

Chapter 18, substantially based on a literature review and a desk analysis (and on the research background of the author, who is an expert in the field of African and Diaspora studies), provides the basic information and analysis regarding the history and the characters of the Coptic Diaspora in Italy, which today is supposed to represent around 70,000 people scattered along the territory – the exact number remains quite obscure partly because of the religious

menaces and attacks received by those who migrated from Egypt. The majority
are concentrated around the Milan area, where our study has been developed.
The role of this religious community is very important: the Copts not only give
aid to their parishioners, but they also offer shelter to local communities, valorizing the churches and the territories where they pray and live. The chapter
tries to give a short overview of the presence of this religious community, with
testimonies from its exponents.

Chapter 19, authored by two experts in the field of social psychology of the
family, aims to explore how Coptic Orthodox families who migrated from Egypt
to Italy define and negotiate their identity within the resettlement society. Ten
households and 30 people (10 fathers, 10 mothers, and 10 adolescent children)
were involved in the study and gave their views through in-depth semi-
structured interviews. Thematic analysis carried out on the interview transcripts allowed several themes to be identified, thus revealing the complexity
that characterizes Coptic families' post-migration experience in Italy: the acculturative challenges faced by parents and children, parental norms and expectations, the role played by the Churches in sustaining heritage identity and
faith across generations, not to mention the meaning associated with Christians' persecution, martyrdom, and migration.

Even rarer are studies specifically addressed to minors with a (forced) migratory background. Trying to fill this gap, *Chapter 20* illustrates and discusses the results of a qualitative study based on four FGDs with Coptic
minors living in Milan, both Orthodox and Catholic. A total of 18 adolescents were involved in the research, daughters and sons of Egyptian parents
who migrated to Italy because of harsh conditions in their home country,
characterized –according to their storytelling– by discriminations, inequity
and violence against Christians. Moving from the developmental and intercultural psychology's perspective, the authors depict a portrait of their psychological needs, expectations, and hitches. The condition of being a migrant child is often burdensome, especially in the case of (forced) migration,
and the combined effects of this experience can lead to problematic consequences for the mental health of minors and for the parent–child interaction. The study aims to identify the acculturative challenges faced by these
minors, and the role played by Churches in sustaining heritage identity and
faith across generations.

Part 6 (Religious Diversity in Italian Schools) deals with the multi-ethnic
and multi-religious transformation of Italian public schools, and with the
role of religious education. Religious diversity is a largely neglected topic in
educational studies, despite the fact that education is one of the most sensitive fields engaged with religion. The latter represents a crucial resource

for many immigrants, but can also be a source of conflict, and is sometimes perceived –as we have already observed– as a threat for European cohesion and identity, with an intuitive impact on the school space. Drawing from this ambivalent scenario, this part investigates the role of religion in multi-cultural schools.

By exploring the nexus immigration-religion-education, the study has aimed to update our understanding of the Italian situation, often stereotypi-cally depicted as a mono-confessional environment, fairly reluctant to recog-nize pluralism. The whole study, authored by experts in the field of sociology of education, was based on 14 FGDs, globally involving 69 adults (teachers, schools' managers and students' parents) and 74 minor students. The partici-pation of different generations and ethnic groups has offered the opportunity to compare diverse points of view on religious diversity, religious belonging, and religious freedom in public school, and to identify strategies to prevent and resolve religious conflicts.

Chapter 21 discusses some institutional, relational and strategic issues re-lated to the religious dimension in so-defined "plural" schools. The role of religions within public schooling is presented, together with the "space" of reli-gion education in the contemporary frame of multi-ethnicity. The chapter also includes a general appraisal of the European and Italian legislative and cultur-al frame on the subject. Finally, the author presents the different approaches to prevent and contrast religious conflicts involving students and parents with different religious backgrounds, and the methods for enhancing intercultural and interreligious dialogue.

In *Chapter 22*, by focusing on the basic concepts of religious freedom and citizenship, the author explores youth religious beliefs, spirituality and athe-ism in a context of "weak secularization" and illustrates how the school can be deemed a public space to test religious plurality. The latter is portrayed as a deep challenge to the school, intended as a secular and open place, and as producing opposite reactions, from neutralization of religion to the promotion of its cultural dimensions. Finally, interreligious and intercultural dialogue are proposed as a training ground for democratic citizenship, since issues that were thought to have been secularized –finding a peaceful solution in the dif-ferentiation of private, civil and religious spheres– come back in the school debate (e.g.: how protecting the right to freedom of expression, which are the boundary of parental authority over children's education).

Chapter 23 faces the issue of interreligious conflicts and integration in multi-cultural schools. After a description of the state of art emerging from the inter-national literature, the author illustrates the hypotheses of the research and then describes and discusses the study's results related to some specific topics.

Interreligious conflicts are analyzed from the point of view of adults (teachers, school managers, parents), as well as from the students' point of view. School narrative about religious radicalism is also analyzed, together with the role of religion in the integration process in schools.

The last section of this part, compiled thanks to the involvement of researchers based in France and Spain, explores the question of religions and *laïcité* in the French republican school (*Chapter 24*) and the manner through which Spanish public schools cope with the multi-religiosity and religious freedom of students and school professionals (*Chapter 25*).

3   From the Periphery to the Core: Key Issues and Provisional
         Conclusions

As can be gleaned from the description of the content of the single chapters, our study has provided a rich collection of both speculative analysis and empirical evidence in order to improve our knowledge of the role of religion in the genesis of contemporary (forced) migrations and as a relevant (supportive) variable in the processes of migration and integration in the society of destination, particularly through the mediation of the family, the school, and FBOs. In this section, we will discuss some of the key issues emerging from the whole project, and we will offer some provisional conclusions, articulating them according to the theoretical schema described in Chapter 2, that is assuming religion as an integral part of migrants' and refugees' public space making, along four main concepts: identity, religious freedom, citizenship, and common good.

Confirming our initial hypotheses, the study has revealed that not only does the understanding of these issues suffer from their extraordinary complexity and from still insufficient research investments; but a widespread ideological bias has traditionally prevented adequate analysis of and understanding of the role of religion within migration and interethnic coexistence. If this is true at general level, it is even more pertinent in the case of Europe, for reasons related to both its historical relationship with immigration and its self-representation in terms of a secularized society.

Concerning the first point, an initial option for the "temporary labor model" –characterized by a "reluctance" toward accepting the prospective of migrants' stable settlement– has marked European attitudes toward migration (Zanfrini, 2019). To the point that the contemporary multi-ethnic and multi-religious society can be understood as an unexpected (and largely unwelcomed) outcome, due to the normative and institutional foundations of the European democracies, which impose serious limits on governments' ability to restrict immigration and immigrants' rights (including the right to settle permanently, to reunite family members, and to ask for asylum) (see, among others: Cornelius *et al.*, 1994; Hampshire, 2013).

Concerning the second point (Chapter 3), the concept of secularization – which since the late 1800s, was strongly endorsed by European sociologists– has until recently benefited from an undisputed hegemony. The theses of a progressive decline (and of a final disappearance) of the religious phenomenon has strongly influenced both the scientific and the political approach to the issue, particularly encouraging religion retreat from the public sphere. What is more, this assumption has deeply affected the manner in which both social sciences and politics have approached the issue of migrants' religiosity (Chapters 3, 13, and 17).

As analytically described in the following parts of the book, in the context of contemporary "post-secular" Europe, renewed attention to the role of religion, even within the public sphere, characterizes the social sciences and encourages civil society's activism. Across European countries, both institutions (at different levels) and civil society have started considering religious leaders and communities as potential allies in facilitating integration and in promoting social cohesion, thus possibly getting past the idea that religion is intrinsically an obstacle to integration. This, in turn, may open further directions for research, producing a rapprochement with the American experience, traditionally more attentive to the bridging function carried out by religion and religious organizations (Chapter 13), as we have already pointed out. Within this promising scenario, our study –conceived to enhance academic and political debate on the ethical implications of contemporary migratory policies and practices– has actually been based on a clear cultural option: the opportunity to give evidence and illustrate how religious-based belongings, identities, and institutions affect both the genesis of contemporary migrations, and the development of migration and integration processes. As a further implication, the researchers involved share the belief about the opportunity to activate religions-related potential in order to manage migrations and support migrants' integration and social cohesion. This clear set of values has not invalidated the academic nature of the results, although it has certainly guided the choice of themes, problems and possible developments on which to focus attention.

The study was conceived in 2015, at the height of the largest refugee crisis that Europe has had to face since the end of World War II. Besides other consequences, our continent has been challenged by the question of (re)defining the "borders" of forced mobility (Chapter 10), in order to distinguish between "true" and "bogus" asylum seekers – this operation, in its turn, is fundamental in order to guarantee the political and financial sustainability of the reception system, which faces mounting public concern. As described in Chapter 4, international and European law clearly establishes that the right of freedom of religion or belief covers a very wide number of situations and can be limited only in few cases; however, this legislation does not automatically protect everybody who cannot effectively exercise this right in the country of origin, and who decides, for this reason, to migrate abroad. Therefore, to choose who must be welcomed and protected represents an extraordinary challenge, in both political and ethical terms. What is more, religious-based claims (or potential claims) are an extraordinary litmus test for analyzing the capacity of our protection systems to remain faithful to the principles on which European democracies are funded.

This study makes clear that (see in particular Part 3) reception and protection systems are certainly ruled by a detailed legislative discipline, as meticulously described in Chapter 9. However, these systems are also embedded in a particular socio-cultural and political context, which results to be strongly influenced by negative and positive bias about the role of religion, particularly when the latter is related to the migration phenomenon.

Today, dominant narratives about religious seekers are prisoners of antithetical ambivalences, as illustrated in Chapter 2: on one hand, migrants and refugees are criminalized and targeted as a dangerous threat to border security, particularly if they are "religiously others". On the other hand, they are portrayed as helpless and passive victims, particularly if they are allegedly persecuted for religious (anti-Christians) motives. According to our interpretation, these two stereotyped narratives are the two faces of the same unethical process of dehumanization; what is more, in this process of dehumanization, religion is often politicized and plays an instrumental part in justifying the opposite narratives. In order to overcome this unethical paradox, two conditions are needed. Firstly, we need to de-instrumentalize religion and analyze the real, multi-dimensional role of religion in refugees' experience: the role as a root cause of displacement, in the countries of departure; and the role as a source of resiliency and as a key factor, which can both facilitate (and eventually hamper) integration processes in the countries of arrival. Secondly, we need to give back to the refugees their human subjectivity, which means enabling them "to enter the discourse" and express their subjective outlook on their own experience of (forced) displacement and on the importance of their religious belonging.

As we have already illustrated, these conditions have been tested through both theoretical analysis and a rich spectrum of original empirical evidence collected thanks to this study. In what follows, we will anticipate and discuss some of the key points emerged, organizing the examination around our four main lines of research.

3.1   *Identity*

As we have already illustrated, during the recent and dramatic refugee crisis, the issue of religious identity has been frequently evoked as a reason to protect "Europe" from arrivals depicted as a menace for "our way of life". While millions of (Christian) faithful are everyday engaged in welcoming asylum seekers and migrants, "anti-migrants" actors, in a more and more explicit manner, use religious symbols as strong argument to endorse securitarian migration policies, as well as discriminatory schemes for the access to welfare provision and to religious rights (for example, when it comes to hindering the construction of mosques and minarets). As a matter of fact, their arguments are in line with the contemporary tendency to "culturalize" religion, intended here as a strategy to restrict rights and opportunities of non-Christian groups, while formally maintaining the liberal State's commitment to neutrality in religious matters (Chapter 3, §4.2; Brubaker, 2016).

All this sounds paradoxical: not only because this kind of solution is difficult to reconcile with basic Christian principles (epitomized in the expression "I was a stranger and you welcomed me"); but also because, according to existing estimations,[4] Europe is the only continent in which the number of Christian faithful is expected to decrease in the coming years. More than the growing of the Muslim community –through new arrivals and new births–, it is the decreasing percentage of "native" Europeans who define themselves as Christians that will provoke a new equilibrium in the religious composition of the European population. In this landscape, the concept of religious identity clearly risks being emptied of its religious content, and reduced to a cultural construct and an instrumental argument (Roy, 2019).

Academic reflection on this topic is clearly aware of this tendency, which is not really resolved by the emerging post-secular scenario (Chapter 3). Our study offers a complementary perspective from which to analyze the phenomenon, looking at asylum seekers and migrants as subjects able to challenge the concept of religious identity, in both its individual and collective declination.

In line with the first theoretical premise, our study has illustrated the prospect of de-instrumentalizing religion, by choosing the Middle East region as a representative place to analyze a "super-diverse" society from an ethnolinguistic and a religious point of view; as well as a region endemically represented as marred by divisions and instability exactly because of this

---

4   https://worldchristiandatabase.org/.

plural composition. The regional socio-political spectrum is here described (Chapter 5) as the result of multiple geographies of power which have historically subordinated the role of civic society and of any form of autonomous organizations. According to our interpretation, the entropic spread of violence that destabilizes today's Middle East, threatening the survival of its populations beyond religious or ethnic affiliations –and producing large flows of (forced) migrants–, can be understood without the need for subscribing to a culturalist approach, that is the idea of an intrinsically anarchic Middle East shaped by primordial identities. On the contrary, it is the most recent manifestation of a matrix, established at the turn of the 20th century, which has fostered a struggle for authority and legitimacy taking place at intra- and interstate levels. In this framework, the controversial spread of sectarian violence and its destructive effects over the wider Middle East have to be considered as an integral part of an historical continuum whose roots cannot be tracked to the beginning of the 21th century alone, and that have further been exacerbated by competing geopolitical agendas. Accordingly, the exploitation of sectarian forms of violence represents other forms of struggle for supremacy within national and supranational political fields, where the religious, along with other features, have become particularly manipulated for developing new political meaning out of the regional multiple geographies. Egypt, the sending country of the Coptic Diaspora in Italy studied in the Part 5 of the book, is a case in point. Indeed, within the multi-vocal character of this country, even Christians are not at all a homogenous subject, not even where they suffer a condition of minority and oppression (Chapter 6). Local, regional and denominational distinctions make them a plural presence, as well as a living testimony of a two-thousand history of a religion embodied in the true life of peoples and communities. By renouncing to acknowledge this plural composition – and essentializing their condition of fragility and discrimination (and their inevitable emigration)– we risk stereotyping their faith as an impediment to full integration into a socio-political fabric inspired by Islam. On the other hand, according to a second type of common narrative, Christians are invested with the role of mediators in conflicts and crisis, thus making their Muslim neighbors aware of the usefulness of their presence. In both cases, Christians' identity is denied, together with its "multi-vocal" character, which implies that each voice possesses a distinctive ecclesiastical identity, biography and local history to tell. On the contrary, it is exactly their presence that expresses the history, and the *identity*, of their countries; to the point that some components of the Christian population exactly refuse to be identified as a "minority", since they consider themselves as a constitutive part of historic Egypt. Moreover, since the 1980s, Christians in Egypt have elaborated new theological thinking and understanding about their minority condition and conflict and crisis in the region, bringing them to the conclusion that they are not religions that have provoked Middle Eastern instability, but the lack of social justice and the political struggle.

In line with the second basic theoretical premise –that is, the need to give back to the migrants their human subjectivity– a central part of our study has consisted in the collection of a significant number of interviews with (forced) migrants. This prospect is also in line with the Global Approach on Migration and Mobility (GAMM) –the overarching framework of the European Union's external migration policy– and its *migrant-centered* approach thus synthesized: "In essence, migration governance is not about 'flows', 'stocks' and 'routes', it is about people. In order to be relevant, effective and sustainable, policies must be designed to respond to the aspirations and problems of the people concerned" (European Commission, 2011: 6).

"From flows to people": we have decided to take this fundamental shift seriously, and that is why our study has strongly emphasized the role of migrants' narratives – as well of a "lived religion", unavoidably shaped by a multiplicity of biographical variables (Cadge, Howard Ecklund, 2007). We are aware of the methodological and ethical problems involved in "listening" to migrants' voices. As Bhabha suggests, "it's never adequate to say their voices must be heard as voices, because none of their voices is just an innocent voice, their voices are mediated through the dialogue they have with the questioner, through their own sense of what it means to represent themselves, through their own ideologies, so they are also framed voices, if you like, and produced voices. But, in just that sense, they are testimonies of the construction of a changing identity, of a changing polity, of a changing transnational community" (Bhabha, 1994: 199). This kind of testimonies are exactly the concrete empirical results arising from the fieldwork: biographical journeys marked by sufferance and oppression, but also by resilience and hope, where religious belonging plays a vital role, as a factor of either empowerment or disempowerment during the process of migrations, asylum application and its aftermath.

From the interviewed migrants' perspective, religious identity represents a source of resistance and resilience, but it is also the limit beyond which it is not possible to accept any violations. The concept of religious identity provides a meaning to the decision to migrate – even for those who have discovered this concept only after having migrated to another country, where they first experienced a context of religious freedom. Therefore, together with this latter concept (religious freedom), religious identity provides the *lexicon* through which to understand migratory choices and strategies (Chapter 10), well beyond what emerges from the common perception of the quantitative importance of religious-based asylum demands, and offers new elements to be considered when it comes to trace the distinction between voluntary and forced migration (we will return on this point later). Finally, migrants are often "more religious" compared to non-migrants, not only because most of them come from pre-secularized States (with all the ambivalences that this circumstance may involve), but also because they often find in religion a source of self-identity and a balm for the soul.

Given the extraordinary relevance of this concept in the experience of (forced) migrants, it is easy to understand that one of their main expectations, once landed in a democratic context, is that of being acknowledged as members of a given religious community, and witnesses of its history and of its turbulences. This point too has clearly emerged from the migrants' narratives. As we could expect, Muslim migrants suffer from what they perceive as a stereotyped representation of Islam, and even more so from the destructive image produced by "Islamic" terrorism and attacks. Asylum seekers asking for protection towards persecutions carried out by religious authorities, regardless of what their religious affiliation is, lament the incapacity of the commissioners to grasp the complexity of the religious landscape of their sending community, particularly in the case of Muslims escaping from what in Italy are commonly depicted as Islamic countries (Chapter 11). But even more thought-provoking is the experience of Christian migrants, who remark with sufferance and resentment the widespread unfamiliarity of Italian people with regard to traditions different from (Roman) Catholicism. Proud of their identity –particularly in the case of migrants belonging to "religious enclaves"–, they find themselves dealing with those who do not know the variety of ritual and religious traditions. Copts are a case in point: while their presence constitute an ancient reality in Italy, today the majority of Italians are substantially ignoring them; the striking lack of recent sources and information, compared to the richness of Middle Eastern sources of such a lively religious reality, is a symptom of the need for further research (Chapter 18), but also of the social invisibility of this community, which does not create any problems (surely, and paradoxically, also thanks to its strong religiosity).

Particularly when they had been victims of persecutions because of their religious affiliation, and after having accepted to be persecuted in the name of their Christianity –according to the concept of martyrdom (Chapter 19)– it is easy to understand the frustration that migrants feel every time they encounter misconceptions among the hosting society. The Coptic teenagers described in Chapter 20 are used to experiencing that not only their schoolmates, but also their teachers, label them as "Muslims" just because they (or their parents) come from Egypt, thus realizing Italians' ignorance about the very existence of

Christians in Egypt. Their experience is similar to that of many others, who are depicted as "Muslims" (or as "Arabs", that in the contemporary Italian *milieu* is virtually a synonymous of Muslims), after having escaped from an Islamic country that harassed them in the name of religion. This widespread "confusion" is clearly perceptible in the school environment, where young students tend to attribute improper affiliations to their foreign classmates, while parents and teachers rather tend to "neutralize" religious identities, reducing them to socio-economic data (Chapter 23), thus depriving migrants of a fundamental element of their individual and communitarian identity.

To a certain degree, this widespread misinterpretation seems to reproduce the stereotypical way in which we portray the religious scenario of the sending country. Our multi-situated study has provided interesting insights on this regard, particularly through the analysis of one of the regions in which contemporary (forced) migrations are generated (Part 2). As clearly illustrated, once more, by the experience of Christians in Egypt, it is very easy to stereotype faiths and religious-based identities. On the contrary, the analysis provided in Chapter 6 suggests that, through their theological reflection, they have elaborated a sort of *lexicon* that can be applied to the same European context, in order to contrast the misleading use (and abuse) which often is made of the concept of Christian identity (see again Roy, 2019). The risk that we have to avoid is that of reproducing what has happened in Egypt in the last decade, where religion has replaced nationalism; and where matters that should be governed by the law have been managed as identity politics. We are speaking of the kind of risk that has materialized during the last refugee crisis, when the need to protect European identity has been repeatedly evoked in order to hide the lack of effective migration management (Zanfrini, 2019).

Finally, a fundamental indication emerging from the research is that *the recognition of the (religious) identity of migrants is an essential condition for the process of re-humanization on which to build a new ethics of hospitality* (and, as it is easy to understand, for allowing them to take part in a virtuous manner to the building of the common good). However, to satisfy this condition, it is necessary to deal with a sort of "educational emergency" represented by a situation of widespread illiteracy on religious matters; not only about "other" religious traditions, made visible through the presence of migrants coming from abroad; but also about "our" religious tradition.

As suggested by the international literature, the actual acknowledgment of the right to freedom of religion represents one of the basic conditions in order to create a favorable context where to reconfigure one's own religious identity, thus avoiding reactive solutions and behaviors (Chapter 2). Our study suggests that, before and beyond the formal recognition of the freedom to believe and practice one's religious belief, what migrants experience is the lack of recognition, both at the cultural level and through daily interactions, of their religious identity. Italians' "religious illiteracy" ends up constituting a factor – invisible and certainly undervalued– hindering the processes of integration and mutual acculturation. What's more, religious leaders and pastoral operators are also involved in the problem. According to what has emerged from the key experts involved in the study, during their education career, not even Catholic pastors receive an adequate preparation regarding the richness of Christians' and Catholics' history, since school programs are focused on the Latin Church; not to mention the lack of knowledge about non-Christians religions. A fortiori, those who cover key roles in the processes of integration and cohabitation –teachers, public officials, cultural animators, etc. –, often perceive precisely through the presence of faithful from elsewhere how the knowledge they possess, sometimes reduced to stereotypical descriptions, is completely inadequate to interpret the complex contemporary religious scenario.

In the same line of thinking, the evidence provided by the study suggests that *"regaining" the awareness of "our" religious identity –here intended as the majoritarian religion in Italy (as in Europe)– is a precondition to meet and confront with the "others"*, and to manage possible conflicts produced by the cultural distance. Not incidentally, Italian and European (Christian) scholars sometimes openly speak of the challenge of Europe's "rechristianization" (see Chapter 16). As a matter of fact, plenty of data coming from our research prove the tendency to reduce religion to a mere type of culture, losing the connection with both its transcendent dimension and with the essence of a religion "embodied" in the lives of Christians. This clearly emerges within the school context, also through the vantage point of religion teachers (Chapter 22). Significantly, this socio-cultural framework even influences the setting of the interviews with asylum seekers: still reflecting its invisibility in the public sphere, the religion dimension turns out to be largely "invisible" in the interview's setting; worried about the possible reactions of the commissioners, aprioristically perceived as agnostic, some asylum claimants declare that they tend to gloss over the elements of their personal and migratory trajectory linked with their religious belonging, and even denounce a positive discrimination favoring migrants who declare other kinds of "diversity", such as homosexuality; sometimes, and even more paradoxically, the hegemony attributed to Islam in the public discourse inhibits the concern towards other religious traditions (and towards the variety of Islamic traditions as well), through a game of mutual "compliance" between commissioners and asylum seekers (Chapter 11). Finally, this aspect is also clearly apparent from a critical analysis of the current global governance system of migration which, as we will explore later, radically underestimates how the religious/spiritual dimension is constitutive of every human being (Chapter 15).

In this context, *migration proves to be a sort of "prophetic" challenge for a society –such as the European and the Italian one– which would claim to be founded on Christian roots.* Migrants often perceive themselves as more "religious" than the hosting society, which is sometimes recognized as even anomic and threatening (Chapter 12). Migrant families with a strong religious identity –as in the case of the Copts– look at the Italian environment with apprehension, since religion and faith seem to be forgotten by many people (Chapter 19); even their children suffer the charm of a society that they describe as without any beliefs or ethics: the deep sense of belonging to a religious tradition contributes to the lack of apparent signs of psychological distress and to the gratitude for the parents' efforts to give them a better future, but it makes them distant from the society in which they grow up (Chapter 20). By explicitly using the concept of martyrdom, these migrants proudly affirm their belonging to a thousand-year-old Church, and identify in suffering a constitutive element of their religious identity: the furthest from the loose and tepid ways in which we live today, in Italy, the experience of an increasingly intimate faith (Chapter 3). Sometimes this kind of perception is shared by the same religious leaders and pastoral operators, who represent migrants as those who recall them the true substance of their faith and spiritual essence (Chapter 12) and who challenge pastoral and liturgical practices (Chapter 16). Finally, school teachers discover that pupils belonging to minority groups and recently arrived migrants have more familiarity with the religious sphere compared with the increasingly agnostic manifestation of the (Spanish) indigenous population (Chapter 25).

As it can be read between the lines in various chapters of the present book, Christian people (and, in a certain way, the entire "Christian" Italian society) could decidedly gain from a valorization of the typical feature of Christianity, represented by "reflexivity" (Magatti, 2018). Just to cite some example, local communities of faithful can even rediscover the essence of their spiritual lives, when confronted with the faithful of other religions, or with the faithful of their own religion who have come from elsewhere, custodians of other liturgical and spiritual traditions (Chapter 16). Migrant (and not migrant) families involved in the transmission of their faith to the younger generation end up being an exception in contemporary Europe, where it is exactly the declining religious socialization leading to the phenomenon of religious disaffiliation, in its turn, the main driver of the new religious scenario. But they can also offer an important example for parents (believers and agnostics), called to educate their children in an "ethically neutral" society, as contemporary society is perceived and described by social scientists (Chapter 18). Teachers in charge with religion education –among the other teachers– can find in Christianity and in its cultural heritage a lever for curriculum enrichment and for promoting constructive dialogue skills among pupils (Chapter 22). However, teachers feel definitely not prepared to manage interreligious classes and classroom discussions about all the topics and issues related to religion(s) within the legal system and the cultural context of reference. Grown up within a context commonly represented as mono-religious, they have firstly "met" the religion issue through the arrival of migrant students, and therefore they have tended to overlap the intercultural dynamics with the interreligious ones. Socialized in the 1960s, most Italian teachers mainly emphasize the material socio-economic nature of the conflicts between students, since they grew in a political era in which the main reference was class or gender conflict (Chapter 23). In their view, religion is downgraded as a pretext for the conflict, that is the most visible aspect, legitimized and culturally accepted, to justify the division between groups: thus doing, they underestimate the question of the religious identity, its relevance in the process of the students' identity development, but also its potential in terms of religious agency to be activated for the common well-being.

Finally, and once again, migrants prove to be a "mirror" through which to grasp critical processes and risks involving society as a whole. The vicissitudes of migrants in search of emancipation tell us of how religion can become oppressive also for the majority group, when it marries a fundamentalist interpretation of religious dictates, or even incoherent with the sacred texts themselves. On the other side of the Mediterranean –that is in Italy–, growing discrimination and intolerance are among the possible outcomes of marginalization of Christians in the public sphere. Marginalization impacts on their civil rights, thus inhibiting their freedom to express their thoughts, to exercise conscientious objection, and to contest, within the democratic deliberative process, solutions aprioristically defined as "progressive" although conflicting with religious values. Also for this reason it is important to take the rights of religious minorities seriously, since they are nothing but the other side of the coin of the "majority" rights (for a deeper analysis of the phenomenon of the erosion of religious freedom see: Durhan, Thayer, 2019). Ultimately, as it will emerge throughout the book, there is a strict link between religious liberty and liberty more generally; that is between religious liberty and human dignity.

3.2   *Religious Freedom*

The prospect of rehumanization of asylum seekers and migrants, that is the willingness to listen to their voices and narratives, has also made it possible to grasp the strict link between religious freedom and personal freedom, between the respect for religious rights and the concept of democracy. Moreover, it has made clear that these concepts are not only a theoretical argument, but they are embodied in the real lives of people, different from each other (Chapters 10–12; 19–20).

In many cases, the experience of migrating –particularly for those who migrate for religious motives, but also in all the cases in which the religious dimension breaks the scene before, along, and after the migration process–, is exactly linked to the need to protect the human openness towards the transcendent, in front of the possible absorption operated by political, social, and familial structures; sometimes even by religious structures, when they instrumentally pursue goals far from their own nature. So, the concept of religious freedom, once applied to the (forced) migrants' experience, shows how "freedom" is a necessary attribute of religion, i.e. an intimate expectation of any believer, which therefore mirrors individual characters and feels.

As a matter of fact, not only religious diversity intermingles with other "diversities", relating to the political, cultural, linguistic, spatial, and kin-family background, and reflecting the "multi-vocal" character of the sending societies (Chapter 5), as well as the socio-economic status acquired in the destination society (Chapters 20 and 23). These variables also combine with personal characters such as gender, age, and cohort. Once again, this plurality can be grasped by hearing migrants' voices and narratives.

Gender, intended in its sociological meaning –that is as a product of a process of social construction– has emerged as a crucial variable, particularly in the case of migrants coming from Muslim-majority countries. As it is well known, the relationship between Islam and the concept of gender equality (or more precisely the woman condition) is currently intended as crucial. According to a common Western perspective, Islamic countries are characterized by patriarchal gender norms, to the point of making their women in need "to be saved", exactly because they are supposed to be deprived of their personal freedom. Actually, evidence collected during this study seems to prove a positive discrimination toward female asylum seekers when they come from given countries, perceived as prey to Islamist regimes (Chapter 11). On this regard, the analysis provided in Chapter 8 endorses the hypothesis that Islamist authoritarian drifts tend to associate with a patriarchal reading of Shari'a, but it also introduces the variety of gender cultures existing in Muslim-majority countries, the different levels of gender equality in the domestic legislations, and the different way in which people conceive the influence that religion should have in politics and legislation. Furthermore, it discusses how, alongside a secular perspective that considers theocracy as a limit for gender equality, forms of feminism combining the quest for women's rights with the support for the Shariʿa law are possible (or, in any case, envisaged by a significant percentage of the population). Here again, the choice of giving back to migrants their own subjectivity has proved to be profitable in permitting the emergence of new insights. Among the many testimonies collected, there are Muslim women who do not contest the Shariʿa's influence on the everyday life of men and women, but the way in which the Islamic law is (mis)understood and imposed in their country of origin. As a matter of fact, the process of radicalization, which currently involves various countries, implies a regression in the field of women's rights and condition, often interpreted as an opposition to the Western model of life. Revolving this kind of reading, some (female) migrants have described the "true" essence of Islam, that some of them declare having discovered only in Italy (Chapter 12), thus realizing the misleading interpretation of religion by religious leaders who had transformed it into an instrument to exercise power and social control.

Passing to consider another biographical character, the same commissioners in charge with the assessment of asylum demands are aware of the different meanings assigned to religion by people of different ages, particularly if coming from countries recently involved in radical political and social changes (Chapter 11). So, together with the chronological age, cohort's belonging is another crucial variable influencing the way in which to interpret and live religion, as well as the concept of religious freedom. Basing on this circumstance, we can try to understand some bizarre data emerged from the study. As discussed in Chapter 7 –based on the analysis of the last Arab Barometer surveys–, the relationship between the individual age and the way of understanding religion and its role in the public sphere is ambivalent; in other words, youngest interviewed are not necessarily less "traditionalist" than the older ones. Passing to consider a completely different context, within the Italian school system, interreligious relations and religious-based conflicts are read and interpreted in very different ways by young students and adults. For the latter, religion is just a pretext for a conflict that has to do with a socio-economic divide, resulting from the migrants' weak economic fragility. For the students, instead, the question of (religious) identity and belonging to the (religious) group is the most important, and the religious dimension is the bullet that deeply hurts identity dimensions linked to personal, familial, and communitarian elements (Chapter 23).

The individual way of experiencing the faith, as a consequence of the personal and family background, is another relevant variable. The study of Coptic families and their children (Chapters 19 and 20) describes a completely unique way of experiencing faith also through the succession of generations, making it a fundamental anchor of identity and a protective resource in the process of adaptation, but also a possible obstacle to full membership in the destination society. However, it also happens that, through the teaching and the example of parents, the faith becomes the catalyst for a feeling of openness, capable of transforming the experience of suffering into a motivation for the commitment to the common good, and the sense of captivity in something that sets the real religious sentiment free (Chapter 12). Finally, it also happens that one's faith is hardly declared as one of the main reasons to escape, for fear of retaliation against family members left behind or threats and pressures internal and external to their groups (Chapter 14), thus making it difficult to elaborate one's own experience in a context of religious freedom.

Significantly, in the personal biographies of (forced) migrants, the link between religious freedom and individual freedom has emerged, from time to time, as a crucial node in the decision to migrate, or as an awareness acquired *ex post*, once arrived in a democratic context. This awareness is the yardstick with which migrants measure the gap between the country of origin and European democracy; but also the gap between their expectations and real life conditions in the destination country –in this case, Italy– which are not always up to the promises of freedom and equality on which the European democracies claim to be founded. As a matter of fact, these concepts represent a sort of litmus-test of the quality of a democracy.

On the one hand, migrants asking for protection "vote with their foots", by opting for an exit strategy in front of the violation of their (religious) rights, or of the counterfeit interpretation of religious duties imposed to the same majority members. For those who escape from places where religious rights are not guaranteed, the possibility to obtain a status of protection because of this is a first and crucial test. On this regard, the research has revealed the existence of both technical-procedural and cultural-political biases which, more or less deliberately, influence the relationship between commissioners and asylum seekers, giving opacity to the treatment of religious arguments (Chapter 11). The emergence of this issue suffers from various aspects: the instrumental recur to religious motives, particularly in the context of reiterated chronicles, which concurs to delegitimize all religious-based claims; the complexity of the contemporary religious scenario in many sending countries, which makes it very arduous for the commissioners to mature an adequate level of knowledge and competence; the tendency to negatively or positively "pre-categorize" on the basis of well-known situations; the role of the media, which defines the semantic framework within which, in a less or more deliberate way, the different actors involved in the process construct their personal perceptions; the media hype reserved to given situations, together with the neglecting of others, despite their gravity.

On the other hand, European democracies are challenged by the heterogeneity of individual experiences, which provide many insights useful to think about the distinction between voluntary and forced migrants. Indeed, religious-based claims are particularly useful to illustrate the difficulty to process through standardized procedures –such as the procedures regulating the acknowledgment of a status of protection– the extraordinary complexity of contemporary (forced) human mobility. The stories of our interviewees (Chapter 10) illustrate how the violation of individual rights and dignity often passes through subtle practices, which hide behind the appearance of legality. Since vulnerability is part of the everyday life of some religious minorities' members – regardless of whether or not they directly suffered persecution–, once adopting a humanistic perspective (that is a perspective targeted to the governance of "migrants", not of "flows") it becomes quite impossible to clearly distinguish between voluntary and forced migration; particularly when this distinction is linked to the dimension of religion and its relationship with personal identity and personal freedom. Should the concept of forced migration be limited to the situations in which individual survival and integrity is seriously in danger? Or should it be extended to every situation of serious limitation of individual freedom and lack of democracy?

State-borders have a clear political dimension, strongly emphasized by current debate. However, through the adoption of a prospect of rehumanization of asylum seekers, another critical dimension of borders has clearly emerged: the ethical one. The management of borders, often reduced to a security language, has appeared here as a "filter" through which we decide the right to move and cross national boundaries; to obtain protection; to fly from a condition of subordination and dearth –or eventually of "captivity"– variously intermingled with religions variables; to freely benefit from individual freedom and manifest one's religious beliefs; to make visible, also in the European public space, particularistic belongings, particularly those connected with different religious background.

Defining the contours of involuntary mobility is an indispensable operation to guarantee the sustainability of protection systems, as we have had the opportunity to anticipate. However, listening to the voices of migrants should make us more aware of the possible effects, on the *real* life of human beings, of certain political choices, such as the policies of externalization of borders' control, that leave the responsibility to "play rough" with extra-EU countries (Zanfrini, 2019). Significantly, exactly in the days in which we are closing this book, the Italian government has approved a new list of "Safe Third Countries", which includes States that do not offer, according to our study (Chapter 9), a sufficient level of protection towards the risk of being persecuted and discriminated because of religious motives. Finally, in the light of the narratives we have gathered, the arbitrary character of this type of operation appears to be evident more than ever.

What is more, through the experiences of asylum seekers and migrants coming from countries that deny both religious freedom and religious pluralism, European societies can appreciate the importance of these concepts, and their strict link with the concept of democracy (Chapter 10); ultimately, they have given the opportunity to test if their everyday functioning is coherent with the promises of equality and inclusion. In this regard, a first focus of attention is represented by the gap separating fundamental principles asserted by their constitutional codes and the rules and procedures regulating specific matters, besides those specifically addressed to process religious-based protection's demands. Among the many concerned fields, our research has concentrated on the role of religion and religious pluralism in the context of the reception system (Chapter 11) and on the role of religion teaching within the public school (Chapter 22). In both cases, what has emerged is, on the one hand, an inclusive attitude –which shapes the professional cultures of many operators and teachers, and sometimes stimulates their creativity in experimenting innovative practices and solutions– and, on the other hand, the persistence of weaknesses at both legislative and organizational level. As a matter of fact, in the context of contemporary (post)secularized society, religious freedom seems to be acknowledged and proclaimed more than an evidence-based experience: since the migrants often represent the main religious minorities in their receiving country, it is exactly their arrival that has permitted to gain the awareness of this gap. The fulfilment of personal needs (including the spiritual ones) by respecting the individual cultural and religious traditions is in principle guaranteed within the asylum seekers' reception system, although with some limitations (particularly when it comes to the centers for repatriation) (Chapter 9). However, despite the importance quite unanimously attributed, by our experts and key informants, to the religious/spiritual sphere in the process of adaptation, the solutions adopted are different, reflecting the heterogeneity of approaches that distinguish the Italian reception system –largely entrusted with the initiative of the actors of the civil society– and producing a situation of clear lack of homogeneity in the access to spiritual assistance and in the possibility of participating in religious rites and interreligious initiatives (§12.2). In its turn, the fieldwork conducted within public schools provides significant evidence of this gap, starting from the students' scarce ability to identify moments and contexts in which they take advantage from this freedom. What is more, this phenomenon is common to both Italian (Catholic) students and foreign (non-Catholic) ones. Among the minority groups there

could be the habit to keep religion belonging to the foreground, in order to reduce contrasts and possible stigmatizations, if not the risk to be excluded.
Whereas among Italian students who claim to be Catholics there is little awareness that religious belonging may represent a means for their self-affirmation
or self-definition (Chapter 22). Finally, they are exactly the migrants –
particularly if they emigrated for reasons linked to the violation of their religious rights–, who can provide the importance of religious rights and –as repeatedly highlighted– their connection with the concept of personal freedom
and the quality of the democracy.

In this regard, a substantially neglected aspect in the interventions that accompany the path of reception of migrants and asylum seekers is education to
religious pluralism. Within the framework of European democracies, this concept tends to be considered as self-evident, and therefore not problematized.
*Educating for mutual recognition and respect between religious groups is instead
of particular importance if we are to lay the foundations for peaceful and constructive coexistence.* All the more so, if we consider that immigration is composed to a significant extent by citizens of countries still far from the principles
of authentic democracy and who have mainly experienced their religious
identity as an antagonistic marker. Countries in which, if not the law, at least
the practice acts in a discriminatory manner towards certain religious groups,
and disavows their equal dignity. In this regard, differently from what one can
sometimes think –and although religious freedom and religious pluralism are
sometimes represented as Western constructs–, it cannot be said that there is
a priori hostility towards them in the Muslim world. Significantly, indeed, in
the course of our research work, the urge to promote education in religious
pluralism for newcomers derived precisely from a Muslim Imam (Chapter 11):
this is one of the areas in which it would be desirable to strengthen cooperation between government institutions and FBOs. Here, again, *it emerges the
need to invest in training initiatives directed both to religious leaders and operators and to public officials* (Chapter 15). The former must be made more aware
of all the facilities and opportunities that can be activated to support migrants,
but also of the legal framework that is expected to regulate both migrants' arrivals and integration, and must be solicited to diffuse correct information to
both migrants and would-be migrants (thus discouraging them, for example,
from improper and instrumental exploitation of the protection's measures).[5]

---

5 See, on this regard, the project report realized by the IOM – International Organization for
   Migration, *Integration: A Multi-faith Approach*, aimed at working with migrant religious leaders to help migrant communities better understand the expectations and norms of host communities in relation to their own cultural and religious values.

The latter, in turn, need to be trained on the characters and contents of each individual religion, especially with regard to those aspects that can have a greater impact on social life, or that can be activated in integration and inter-religious programs. Furthermore, the provision of education programs addressed to religious leaders and pastoral agents of different religions can be a way to promote the mutual confidence and the common engagement, and possibly to encourage the launch of shared programs.

Concerning these points, it is acknowledged that the social and political context of the host country has an important influence on making religion a divisive cleavage or, alternatively, a source of unity and solidarity. At the same time, different religions and religious groups exhibit different approaches, not necessarily oriented to support a full integration and a sense of belonging to the new society. Consistent with some classical contributions of sociological thought on migration and integration pathways (Chapter 3), the collected evidence proves that religious affiliation, by its cosmopolitan nature, allows the migrants to adapt to the new context while maintaining its cultural specificity, and passing it on to new generations (Chapter 20). However, it also shows how the perception of the outside world as threatening can produce the risk of an introverted tendency and of displaying reactive solutions and behaviors, thus making it more complicated to identify the common good that human migration can promote (Chapter 19).

On this regard, the study directed to analyze the "space" of religion within the reception system (Chapter 11) suggests that the first phases of the reception and settlement process are definitely crucial in shaping newcomers' feelings and behaviors, as well as the evolution of interreligious relations. *Within the framework of a holistic approach in the reception of asylum seekers –that is the mostly envisaged approach by both academic experts and institutional statements–, religion and spirituality must be officially acknowledged as basic human needs, as well as a lever able to support the individual adaptation*, the respect for the other people, and the personal engagement in the common good. The insights emerged from the qualitative study on FBOs (Chapter 14) suggest, in this regard, the crucial importance of the operators' ability to establish with (forced) migrants reciprocal, trusting and stable relationships, based on a personalized approach and contiguous under the cultural and symbolic profile.

One last aspect to be mentioned concerns the relationship between the migration of believers persecuted because of their faith and the future of minority communities in various sending countries. Religious organizations sometimes play as push and pull actors, facilitating the transnational mobility of their affiliated (Chapter 10). However, sometimes they are also worried about the departure of their members, and engaged in the attempt to prevent their emigration, appealing to an effort of resilience. As a matter of fact, the international dimension of the problem must be taken into serious account: all kinds of religious rights' violations must be covered by systems of protection (Chapter 15); but we must also be aware that the asylum system can become the instrument to facilitate the expulsion of religious minorities, thus paving the way to realize the criminal goal of a monoreligious society (Aiuto alla Chiesa che soffre, 2019). As it easy to grasp, we are dealing with a topic that solicits a stronger direct involvement of FBOs, following the very important steps already taken along the road of interreligious dialogue (see below), to aim at the construction of a society which, together with the equal dignity of every human being, also recognizes the right to freedom of faith in all its forms.

3.3   *Citizenship*

In the tradition of many European States, based on a principle of isomorphism between the people, the nation, and the territory in which sovereignty is exercised –in turn, delimited by state boundaries–, and belonging defined by citizenship (Wimmer, Glick Schiller, 2003), religion is one of the elements that contribute to defining the homogeneity of the population of a nation-State. Not by chance, as it has already been pointed out, migrants' "religious diversity" is one of the main factors used in the representation of immigration as an identity challenge (or even as an identity threat), although this implies the disavowal of religious pluralism as a constitutive trait of the European population, present well before the arrival of immigrants in the last decades. Still, this circumstance would be enough to understand how suggestive it is to investigate the relationship between immigration, religion and citizenship. Moreover, as it is well known today, the process of invention of the nation-States took advantage of the concept of "methodological nationalism", that is the tendency to assume national borders as the "natural" ones, within which to analyze societal phenomena. Thus disregarding both the existence of transnational processes and links and the various kinds of transnational belongings, particularly those connected with the membership to ethnic/religious groups and diasporic communities. As a matter of fact, as it is illustrated in Chapter 2, in the experience of (forced) migrants, citizenship is "naturally" not tied to rigid national territoriality, but includes fluidity of borders and multiple (religious) identities and loyalties. This point makes migrants a paradigmatic subject to rethink the concept of citizenship –by definition, a national and "closed" institution– in the context of contemporary globalized and interconnected society (see, among others: Carens, 2013; Kymlicka, 2001; Walzer, 1983; Zanfrini, 2007).

In general terms, it is easy to understand that religion, in the migrants' experience –and even more so for those who escaped for reasons related to their religious affiliations– often becomes a marker of demarcation and distinction, sometimes in a racialized and antagonistic way, sometimes in a dialectical and potentially cooperative way (Chapter 2). Our research has actually provided examples of both outcomes. Interviewed (forced) migrants (Chapter 12) sometimes are able to transform their experience of sufferance and discrimination in a generative way, engaging themselves in the social, cultural and political life of the hosting society, according to a participative idea of the citizenship. Significantly, in some cases, it is exactly the spiritual rethinking of their experience that, by breaking down the logic of rancor, provides the (forced) migrants with the emotional and psychological resources useful to support their pro-active and altruistic engagement, and their feeling part of the hosting society – without this signifying the renunciation of other forms of affiliation and belonging, even of a transnational or universal type, as is typical of religious affiliations. However, it also happens that migrants cultivate a very negative attitude towards other religious groups, and they interpret the possibility of living in a democratic country as a sort of "compensation" for the wrongs suffered in the past, in any case a possibility not able to alleviate wounds that are still open, and which seem to prevent them from really feeling like citizens of the polis and citizens of the world.

In this regard, a very interesting case is offered by Copts coming from Egypt. As a mirror of their condition in the homeland –where suffering had become an "ordinary" character of their daily-life, the only possible destiny which relegate the Christians to this marginal minority status (Chapter 6)–, Coptic migrants risk to reproduce, also in Italy, a passive and sometimes rancorous posture. Their strong religious identity is self-portrayed as an indelible marker, and perfectly functions as an instrument of resilience and of intergroup cohesion; however, it does not endorse neither the sense of belonging to the Italian society, nor the motivation to get out of the boundaries of the ethnic community. At the opposite, their strong sense of belonging to a minoritarian community seems to work as boundary marker, thus reproducing the condition of (self) isolation experienced in Egypt (Ha, 2017). Unilaterally insisting on their condition of sufferance and exclusion in the home country, and of subalternity in the hosting one (where many of them have experienced downward mobility), Coptic migrants renounce to trespass the borders of their protective community. As discussed in Chapter 19, this option may become challenging for younger generations born in Italy, invested with a mandate which requires them to preserve their cultural and religious heritage, prioritizing the latter over the opening towards the new society. At the same time, it involves the risk of an introverted tendency and of displaying reactive solutions and behaviors.

We have already pointed out that the lack of preparation of Italians in recognizing the specificity of this religious tradition (and its full membership in

Christianity) is a factor that negatively influences Coptic migrants' sense of belonging to the Italian society. At the same time, we have to point out the critical role of the religious leaders and of the Coptic Church (both Orthodox and Catholic) in the hosting society. As a matter of fact, according to what emerged from the study (Chapter 20), the latter supports a form of transnationalism and selective acculturation, by keeping Egyptian and Coptic identity alive among the Diaspora's members (included the youngest) and facilitating the adaptation to the host society, perceived as very different in terms of values and customs. But current adaptation's outcomes –surely facilitated by the high adaptability of the first generation, who "sacrifice" themselves in order to offer their offspring the possibility to leave Egypt– would need to be re-examined – as suggested by the chapter's authors– after a long period of time, through third and fourth generations. Ultimately, this community, strongly linked to its *bounding* function, lacks a *bridging* function, that is of the ability to really support its members in "entering" the new society and feeling part of it.[6]

Actually, it is exactly through the "intrusion" of religious identities and practices within public space that we are solicited to shift our focus from citizenship as a legal status, to performances of citizenship, i.e. creative enactments that negotiate membership, re-inventing ways of living together (see again Chapter 2). This shift is today acknowledged also at institutional level. The same European Integration Agenda[7] has encouraged, since 2005, migrants' involvement in mainstream institutions through various kinds of "active citizenship" (Vogel, Triandafyllidou, 2006) intended to stimulate migrants to take part in the participative and deliberative processes (e.g.: Morales, Giugni, 2011). However, besides the legal provisions and the EU recommendations, the initiative promoted and supported by the civil society are of particular relevance. All across Europe, actors such as voluntary associations, Unions, and cultural organizations have been engaging in the promotion of a "generative" form of citizenship. The latter is intended as a participative citizenship, linking all those people living in the same *polis* –notwithstanding their nationality or their migratory status– meeting their desire of belonging, and enhancing their contribution for the common well-being.

---

6 An interesting analysis of the relation between religious practices and group's identity is provided by Stroup, 2017. Here the author distinguishes among a universalizing role, a negotiating role, and a differentiating role. In the case of the Copts we studied, religion seems play a differentiaging role, by setting apart on ethno-religious group from an "outsider other".

7 Communication from the Commission to the Council, the European Parliament, the European Economic and Social Committee and the Committee of the Regions, *A Common Agenda for the Integration of Third-Country Nationals in the European Union*, COM (2005) 389 final.

In this perspective, initiatives sustained by FBOs are particularly relevant. If not because they defy the idea that religious affiliations are likely to obstacle migrants' integration and social cohesion. Indeed, religious organizations are surely important agents in supporting migrants' inclusion in the new society, and in offering them the possibility to recover from the migration trauma and to "feel at home". What is more, in many occasions they have proved to be able to involve newcomers in common projects, emphasizing the mutual enrichment gained by reciprocity and cooperation. As has been repeatedly stated, the image of a secularized Europe –in which religion is relegated to the private sphere– and the same concern about the religious diversity embodied in immigration, have contributed to overshadowing the potential of the binomial "religion–integration". This has strengthened, on the one hand, the tendency to make (one's) religion (more or less practiced) a bulwark of identity for those who are "in-group" with respect to "others", whose religion constitutes a destabilizing threat; on the other hand, the tendency to consider religion as a secondary factor for the purposes of integration and "citizenship's construction". However, today there are signs that show a different attitude in considering the potential of this couple of concepts. They go in the direction of both containing fundamentalist thrusts, adopting measures not only to combat them, but also assisting migrants and promoting interreligious dialogue, and to highlight the positive aspects of the role of religion in the processes of integration of migrants (as emerges, for example, from various special programs adopted by some European countries and/or coordinated by the European Commission as well as by international bodies).

The qualitative study contained in the book (Chapter 14) –albeit in an embryonic/limited form and, however, significant for the processes indicated by the interested stakeholders themselves (whether they are migrants and refugees and/or referents of established organizations and groups)–, identify some paths along which the role of the FBOs unfolds disseminating actions that support social integration in the broad sense. In particular, their main and first task is that of taking care of the needs and problems migrants and refugees are facing in the new context. This action concerns both the answering to their material needs of first necessity and, together with them, the need for a more integral accompaniment of the person (to cure invisible wounds on a psychic and spiritual level), and the implementation of actions which concern support for religious freedom, especially when faced with forced migration which, among push factors, include religious persecutions. This last element is often intertwined with others, such as the existence of serious social and political conditions, the spread of violence and conflicts, existential precariousness, so that the religious factor becomes –as underlined by different operators– "an additional factor". In any cases, among the needs of migrants, there is also the spiritual one (this point is deeply analyzed in Chapter 12). In this sense, the FBOs are also the context within which spiritual support is offered that allows migrants to continue to live their faith together with others, both compatriots and/or belonging to the same religion, and autochthonous where local religious communities start walking of encounter and mutual knowledge. In many cases, these places are characterized by a strong transnational configuration (maintaining close ties with the same diasporic communities). However, the long-term outcomes of these processes are influenced by the orientations of host societies: where migrations are seen as a merely transitory phenomenon and religion is considered as a parallel element with respect to personal experiences, vicious circles are triggered whose repercussions can lead to identity closures and to the instrumentalization of religion.

Here we meet a second basic task played by FBOs, that is that of providing capacity building for the integration and the acceptance of diversity. When they place the person of the migrant/refugee at the center of their actions, FBOs can facilitate their empowerment, by enabling the abilities of each one and awakening, in particular, the constructive orientation towards the destination society, thus contributing to triggering the processes of positive integration. At the same time, these organizations work on the reception field, in such a way as to broaden the meaning of "integration" well beyond its unilateral reading that only engages the immigrant component. The religious theme offers a particularly significant starting point in this regard, recalling, both on the side of migrants and on the side of those who are expected to welcome them, aspects of personal and social life that require everyone a renewed awareness of the role and contribution that religions can offer not only to the formation of personal identity, but also to the civil coexistence of a democratic country. In this way, they try to overcome emerging hostility and intolerance both from fundamentalist positions, often associated with immigrant religious groups (but, nevertheless, to closed indigenous groups), and from forms of "exclusive humanism" characterizing the secularized context of Western countries (Chapter 3).

More generally, the intervention on the front of personal capacity refers, on both fronts, to the work (wide-ranging cultural and educational) for the acceptance of the diversity of each person: in fact, the religious element often becomes the catalyst for other aspects considered problematic and less explicit. A suggestive illustration of all these processes –and of their both complex and "prophetical" nature– is provided in Chapter 16, through the analysis of the first steps of the "Synod from the people", launched in January 2018 by the Diocese of Milan – the largest Catholic Church world-wide. The aim of the consultative phase described in the chapter was that of collecting suggestions in order to improve foreign migrants' inclusion in the everyday life of the local Church, together with the capacity of the latter to answer the needs of a multi-ethnic and multi-religious population. Going well beyond these expectations, emerged results clearly show how this challenge mirrors many other critical issues involving the life of the Church and of the local society. According to a theological perspective, this challenge constitutes an extraordinary opportunity to test –and possibly achieve– the true meaning of the "catholicity", described in the Scriptures as "unity in diversity". But in this way, the Church can contribute to provide the *lexicon*, the semantic framework, and the procedures through which redefining the concept of citizenship –in its multiple dimensions– in a more and more pluralistic society, while maintaining a strong attachment to those basic values which define this concept as it has been forged in the European democracies.

In the end, our study confirms *the need to rethink, besides the current citizenship regimes –in most cases still based on an ethnic conception of the membership–, the very idea of citizenship*, going beyond the "contractualistic" approach followed by many countries through different kinds of "integration agreements" (Joppke, 2007) and according to a new prospective that gives particular emphasis to its participatory dimension. All this in order to valorize the contribution of each person to the construction of citizenship "from below", through the confrontation of different –cultural, ideological, religious, experiential– perspectives, giving new life to the basic principles of European civilization: the principle of the indissoluble dignity of each human being and the principle of institutionalized solidarity, intended also as an expression of the human anthropological vocation to build relations of reciprocity and solidarity (Zanfrini, 2013).

In this framework, one of the basic issues concerns the safeguarding and support of pluralism which constitutes a social value within Western democratic societies. Moreover, pluralism in its more specific declination of the "religious", on the one hand belies the classical hypotheses of an extinction of religion in secularized contexts, on the other it constitutes a challenge for the religions themselves, with respect to their vocation to the encounter with the other. In this regard, among some other topics, our research has deeply explored (Chapter 22) how the Italian school copes with religious plurality, and finds strategies to deals the challenge that it poses to the school day life, curriculum, and family-school relationships: to protect the freedom of expression with regards to religious plurality, in compliance with the school's "*laïcité*" and the rules (and limits) of the democratic, liberal society. Here again, beyond the description of the legislative and institutional framework and of its ambivalences (Chapters 9 and 21), our study has mainly focused on the direct experience of migrants', migrants' offspring, and the (Italian) people they meet in the everyday life, according to the prospect of returning them their own subjectivity. One of the most relevant issues emerged from the analysis concerns the blurring borders between the private and the public spheres at school, due to the students', families' and teachers' daily behaviors and choices. The legal protection of religious freedom assured by the Italian (and European) laws and citizenships rights, while providing a crucial leverage for social integration, triggers claims for the recognition of the legitimacy of each religious belief and practice within the school life. Hence, religious and civic loyalties may come into conflict. The request from some students (and their families) to different treatments (in order to meet the values, the customs, and the practices relating to their religion affiliation) prove the inner "power dimension" of school relationships and the religion's role in shaping people's "world vision", that is an idea of what constitutes a good citizen, of how it should be the "right order" of society. Hence, it is difficult to establish, once and for all, the boundaries between different orders of law, and between beliefs and practices. In other words, the request for recognition of religious freedom (to *believe* and *practice* one's own faith) at school turns out to have, not only a cultural and religious dimension, but also a political one. Compelled to face these challenges, students, families, and teachers find a profitable way to overcome barriers and to build reciprocal trust through practices of dialogue, negotiations, argumentations: in so doing, their self-reflexivity and awareness of being part of a pluralistic scenario increases. What's more, the interreligious and intercultural dialogue developed within the school become a training ground for democratic citizenship, ensuring the school not to be a "neutral space", but a "safe space" for dialogue (Jackson, 2014), where inclusion and mutual respect are promoted within a given framework of rules, rights and duties. In this wake, religious education reveals an extraordinary "learning potential", for curriculum enrichment and for promoting constructive dialogue skills among pupils (Chapter 22).

3.4   *Common Good*

This final point introduces us to the fourth main line of research, represented by the common good, that is by the idea that migrants and refugees can contribute, through their competences, abilities, sensitiveness, and experiences, to build the social fabric of the communities in which they live. Here, again, the prospect is that of the emergence of a "new-generation" citizenship: a generative form of citizenship linking citizens as they live together within the *polis* intended as a shared space and a shared time which becomes, in turn, a place of reciprocity of rights and duties (Martinelli, 2013). We are speaking about a type of "responsible" citizenship, which manifests itself within a scenario of freedom, the latter conceived according to a relational perspective, thus connecting the creativity and innovation potential of social actors with their aspiration to belong and feel included.

As a matter of fact, this prospect implies, first of all, a paradigmatic shift with respect to the economistic model on which the European approach has been traditionally based, in order to valorize the "Diversity Value" (Zanfrini, 2015) which migration bring with it. Instead of enhancing migrants' adjustment to European society and labor market (by means of selective migration schemes and of standardized procedures defined from the top), this new paradigm is focused on how to valorize migrants' competences and experiences in view of promoting European economic, social and institutional development – with a special focus on those skills acquired thanks to migratory trajectories and to the migrants' condition of dual belonging. In addition, according to this perspective, the emphasis on the dimension of self-realization and personal achievement –stressed by the current individualistic culture and targeted by most policies and programs–, must be complemented by a renewed attention to the dimension of individual responsibility for the construction of the common well-being. Furthermore, together with that of governments and local administrations, the role of civil society's actors must be acknowledged and valorized, since it is crucial in determining the "quality" of the integration processes and of interethnic cohabitation. Finally, this shift requires the willingness to recognize pluralism –including religious pluralism– as a constitutive character of contemporary and future European democracies, overcoming not only nationalistic narratives which pretend to affirm a strictly ethnic conception of the political community, but also a pro-migrant discourse which recur to arguments such as the low share of Muslim migrants (thus implicitly restating the problematic character of Muslims' presence) or "our" need for the migrants' cheap labor force (thus reaffirming the image of a dualistic society, which assign to migrants a subordinate position). As a matter of fact, according to this perspective, the real challenge is not to welcome migrants, but to portray them as full members of a pluralistic society in which the opportunity is acknowledged to keep transnational links and multiple identities and belongings.

Within this picture, in this study we have focused the attention on those migrants' contributions linked to their religious affiliations; that is, on their potential in terms of "religious agency" as part of (forced) migrants' public space making, here intended both as an individual resource and as a resource which can be activated through the mediation of associative bodies, in particular the FBOS.

Starting from the individual level (Chapter 12), interviewed migrants offer a lot of examples about the role of religion in providing the spiritual and psychological resources able to transform past sufferance into a generative behavior. Many migrants –particularly in the case of (forced) ones, strongly stained by their religious background–, often cultivate a form of transnational membership, and self-represent them as the members of an international (if not a universal) community; a community to which they are bound by obligations of mutual support (Bahá'i are a case in point). Therefore, the transnational or diasporic characters of many religious communities offer the migrants the possibility to experience a concept of brotherhood that translates into a form of mutual support and protection able to reproduce itself in every place, overcoming the barriers represented by socio-economic status, States' borders, geographic and time distance. Finally, the activating power of religion also operates through the testimonies of many believers that, through their involvement in migrants' reception and welcoming, instill in newcomers the motivation to engage themselves, in their turn, in helping other people in need and work for the common good (Chapter 12).

This point introduces as to the role of FBOs. As illustrated in Chapter 10, the social capital embedded into religious-based institutions and networks often turns out to be a driver of migration, permitting people to escape from intolerable conditions and gain the opportunity to achieve personal and family well-being – although its role sometimes feeds disputable migratory cultures and patterns. Furthermore, from our analysis it has emerged that, beyond the institutional apparatus in charge with the reception of asylum seekers and the evaluations of their claims, FBOs play a crucial role not only in welcoming new comers and support their adaptation, but also in preparing and accompanying them all along the official procedure. In so doing, they contribute to re-humanizing asylum seekers, and to humanizing the reception system, thus stimulating a positive attitude toward the new society. Spirituality can also have a "therapeutic" impact, when it comes to dealing with traumatized people; therefore, spiritual assistance can be of crucial importance in order to recover an emotional balance and a working capacity, to the point that spiritual and religious assistance is often mixed up with different forms of social assistance and empathetic sustain. Not only many FBOs have implemented, independently from the official reception system, various initiatives specifically addressed to (forced) migrants and refugees; what is more, every step of the migration journey is supported by FBOs that are engaged in answering migrants' basic everyday needs. Often, FBOs provide the possibility to attend the celebrations in the migrants' mother tongue, to meet and spend free time in spaces provided by their places of worship, and to implement initiatives to support the inclusion process (language courses, matching with the labor demand, social assistance...). By taking care of migrants without any kind of selection or discrimination based on the religious affiliation, FBOs fuel their attitude to "give back" what one has been given for free –without expecting anything in return–, to "assist" instead of just "being assisted", and to commit to the common good. Finally, FBOs are involved in the building of a coordinated interreligious dialogue and cooperation. This line of action involves specific activities –particularly the support offered to the victims of religious intolerance–, as well as the promotion of religious freedom and of solidarity relations among communities of different religions – for example, through the provision of initiatives of civic education and peace.

This point deserves specific attention. As deeply discussed in Chapter 3, current global scenario provides unexpected conditions for a recovery of the presence of religion(s) in the public sphere, and the search of (transcendent) ethical norms that must be placed at the basis of socio-economic and political life. Following the fundamental contribution of J. Habermas (2005), the idea that religion is a *public good*, not just a private good (Modood, Sealy, 2019), is now increasingly acknowledged. Moreover, cooperation between religious groups and traditions has become increasingly common, so much so to speak of a "multi-religious approach to integration" (Lick-Bowen, Owen, 2019). As a matter of fact, the aforementioned contribution proves that multi-religious collaboration can help counter some of the problems associated with religion acting as a barrier to integration, by expanding social networks, countering negative stereotypes and perceptions through opportunities for engagement, and encouraging migrants to look beyond potentially exclusive religious and ethnic communities and identities. The pressures and fears on host societies and communities should also not be lightly dismissed; and there is good indication that multi-religious collaborations can also benefit existing inhabitants in many ways. Given this picture, our study has developed this suggestive perspective by investigating in particular the role of interreligious dialogue – intended as a confrontation among different conception of values, but also as the search of those principles which made up a heritage of values for all and for the common good, thus formulating a sort of "global ethics" (Chapter 15). In particular, among the principles largely shared by the different religions, the study has identified the following: the primacy of the common good towards the individual one; the universal destination of the hearth's resources, and consequently the duty of solidarity; the duty of welcoming foreigners and hosting them; the good administration of the planet and the environment's protection; the concept of a transnational citizenship. Contrasting the common tendency to neglect how any law and rule is always embedded in a given structure of values –be the latter explicitated or not–, this approach identifies in different religions the custodians of the values that are most closely-related to human nature; at the same time, overcoming the ambiguities and prejudices that accompanied the secularization process, this approach recognizes how religiosity must become a qualifying component not only of the "human", but also of the "social" (Chapter 14). Finally, it envisages the rediscovery of the essence of the European Christian roots (Roy, 2019), by refocusing the attention on the issue of values, and on the need to inscribe them in the society and its main institutions.

In recent times, despite the aggravation of conflicting issues –such as the Ukrainian crises–, significant steps have been taken in the field of interreligious dialogue at institutional level, following the meeting (Havana, February 2016) between Pope Francis and the Patriarch of Moscow and all the Russias, Kiril. Just to cite an example, the European Orthodox-Catholic Forum involves representatives of both local Catholic Churches and Orthodox Churches with the aim of solving common social problems, such as poverty, the crisis of the family and the need to ethicize economic behaviors. Christians' persecution in the Middle East is one of the topics of common interest –as strongly emphasized by the final declarations of the Havana meeting–, which will be able to gain from this new era of cooperation: exactly this problem was the focus of the yearly conference organized in 2018, again following the Cuba event. As stressed in Chapter 7, another crucial divide is represented by the recent meeting (4 February 2019) between Pope Francis and the Grand Imam of Al-Azhar Ahamad al-Tayyib, which ended with the signing of the Document "Human Fraternity for World Peace and Living Together", encouraging all persons who have faith in God to work together for promoting a culture of mutual respect, tolerance, coexistence and peace, and warn from any political manipulation of religion, particularly as a means to perpetrate violence, hostility, extremism, oppression. Following these institutional steps, we can expect a further development of the initiatives launched at both national and local level. As a matter of fact, well beyond its concrete outcomes and realizations, *interreligious dialogue offers a methodology useful for the identification of new ways of living together and for the construction of the well-being of the entire human family*. Finally, relegated to the private sphere by the secularization's narrative and the secularization's ideology, religion today reappears a resource that can be activated for the common good.

What we have discussed in this introductory chapter certainly cannot give reason for the richness of this wide and articulated research. However, we think it is sufficient to give evidence of how the religious dimension can play a crucial role not only in enriching the analysis of migratory and integration processes, but also in stimulating profound processes of social transformation, through the provision of creative principles and an enriched awareness (Chapter 3). There is one last point which deserves our attention: recognizing and promoting the role that religiosity –in both its individual and community declinations– and religious organizations can play in the governance of human mobility and in planning paths of peaceful coexistence goes exactly in this same direction. As stressed in Chapter 2, the "intrusion" of religious identities and practices within public space –through the activism of different FBOS– stimulates us to shift our focus from citizenship as a legal status to "performances of citizenship", able to reinvent ways to live together while facing the major challenges that are unfolding on the horizon of European and Italian society. Among these challenges, there is certainly the search of sustainable ways to manage human mobility, in front of the strong and growing inequalities at global level.

As a matter of fact, as the refugee crisis has dramatically shown, this issue suffers from the lack of sufficiently shared and ethically founded criteria. Having reduced migration and border management to a technocratic task, measured in terms of economic costs and efficiency, and substantially aimed to restrain migration flows and reduce the number of refugee/asylum applications, Europe has discovered that it lacks convincing, persuasive and ethically based criteria through which to manage the complexity of contemporary human mobility (Chapter 11); that is for distinguishing between "authentic" and "fictitious" refugees. People with different national and religious backgrounds, together with FBOS, have to be involved in the debate, which is exactly a manifestation of a "performing" citizenship, anchored in participatory and negotiation practices, and aimed at giving shape to an inclusive and integrated society. As I have suggested elsewhere (Zanfrini, 2019), the need to identify new criteria and solutions through which to manage asylum seekers' reception, the exam of asylum applications, and the initiatives in support of their integration could represent a remarkable test-bench for experiencing this kind of participative *agora*. In a certain degree, this wish was endorsed also by the final text of the recent "Global Compact on Refugees",[8] which has included FBOS among the relevant stakeholders to be considered in the sharing of responsibilities. Not to mention that the shared moral values by different religious traditions provide strong arguments for the legal empowerment of migrants and asylum seekers. Despite all this, the reference to the religious and faith dimension in the major documents enacted by international organizations about migration policies and programs is quite scarce, if not inexistent. In this way, a substantial dimension of the migratory and integration processes is neglected, as well as a substantial dimension of human realization (Chapter 15), a significant

---

8 https://www.unhcr.org/the-global-compact-on-refugees.html.

ingredient for both personal and social life which should be included in all the policies and actions involved in the migration governance.

Religion has historically offered a valuable contribution to various civilizations, as demonstrated by the numerous achievements in the economic, cultural, educational and artistic fields, which arose precisely thanks to the values, ideals and religiously connoted actions of individuals and groups. However, contrary to the tendency to reduce religion to a cultural construct, it refers to something that distinguishes the human being: that is, his/her constitutive openness to the mystery, to the transcendent, to beyond what is immediately controllable. For this reason, the religious dimension cannot be excluded from the debate that intends to consider social life in its properly human dimension. Furthermore, as we have repeatedly remarked, religion is combined with freedom, which derives from the very high dignity with which every human being is endowed, who, despite being social, is never fully assimilable and/or deducible from the social context in which he/she is inserted (Martinelli, Magatti, 2016). Significantly, in many cases, the experience of migrating is linked precisely to the need to protect the openness of the man/woman to the transcendence from the possible absorption by the political, social, familial and sometimes even religious structures – when the latter pursue aims far from their own nature (Chapter 10). *Only by taking seriously the prospect of focusing on migrants, not on flows, it is possible to grasp the regenerative function that religion can play not only for the single believers, but also for society as a whole.* As it has clearly emerged from this study, the religious dimension, in fact, brings into play the crucial importance of the meaning of collective coexistence: the latter does not stand only on instrumentality and functionality, saturating every space of personal and social life by means of efficient technical devices and reassuring bureaucratic procedures – thus reinforcing the individualization and isolation of the subjects, on the one hand, and the absolutization of the techno-economic systems, on the other, and pushing for a merely technical integration at the expense of the social and cultural one (Martinelli, forthcoming). Repositioning at the center of attention the meanings (cultural, social, personal) that nurture collective coexistence is good for all, believers (of various religions) and non-believers, since this option safeguards the human and social values that constitute the heritage of every culture and set in motion the most vital dimension of the human flourishing. For this reason, the challenge that confronts local societies as well as the international community and its institutional bodies concerns the correct consideration of the religious dimension within the debates, documents and actions undertaken in relation to the migration phenomenon. Since the latter is not merely constituted by "flows", but by persons.

The Uncanny "Religious" Refugee: a Post-Secular Perspective on Ethics of Hospitality

Paolo Gomarasca

The aim of this chapter is to show and analyze the unethical ambivalence of the dominant narratives about the events of migration, especially in the case of (forced) displacement. On the one hand, refugees are criminalized and targeted as a dangerous threat to border security. Refoulement practices and concentration camp-like conditions in some refugee camps are the "zoopolitical" effect of this paranoid rhetoric. On the other hand, counter-narratives portray refugees as helpless, passive victims. The effect of this idealized rhetoric is associated with a wide range of relief actions, such as safe zones, humanitarian entry visas, resettlement in solidarity, residency permits and other forms of what some theorists call biopolitical care. The paradox is that these two stereotyped imaginaries of forced displacement are the two faces of the same unethical process of dehumanization: in both cases, refugees are objects of other people's interpretations and actions. But the key point is that, in this process of dehumanization, religion is often politicized and plays an instrumental part in justifying the two opposite narratives: the dangerous refugee is a (bad) Muslim, who threatens Christian civilization; the vulnerable refugee is a (good) victimized Christian or a (good) poor Muslim, who wait patiently in camps for Western salvation.

An ethics of hospitality is possible only under two conditions. Firstly, we need to de-instrumentalize religion and analyze the real, multi-dimensional role of religion in refugees' experience: the role as a root cause of displacement, in the countries of departure; and the role as a source of resiliency and as a key factor, which can both facilitate and impede integration processes in the countries of arrival. Secondly, we need to give back to the refugees their human subjectivity, which means enabling them to enter the discourse and express their subjective outlook on their own experience of forced displacement and on the importance of their religious belonging.

The political effect of this post-secular hospitality is a discursive act that creates a public space, where social ties can be (re-)built. Religion, in this context of re-humanization, can be an integral part of refugees' public space making, along four main lines of research:

1)   *identity*, that focuses on individual and collective processes of shaping and reshaping some forms of self-definition, based on religious beliefs and values;

2)   *religious freedom*, which legitimizes the pluralistic involvement of (religious) identities in public life;

3)   *citizenship*, which is not tied to rigid national territoriality but includes fluidity of borders and multiple (religious) identities and loyalties;

4)   *common good*, i.e. a multi-religious social capital, generated by the new citizens and their desire to participate in their new society of settlement.

1   Agents of Transgression

The first ethical step to be taken when talking about refugees is to acknowledge the transgressive character of their arrival: displaced persons, especially in the case of religious refugees, cross the border by force, they explore all avenues to negotiate (with border guards, smugglers, fishermen, and other actors (Mainwaring, 2016) and finally break in, under the effect of the terror of persecution. Their sudden appearance on the European scene unleashes anxiety. Religious refugees embody danger, they are perceived as carriers of trauma, which is associated with "a simplistic trope about violence: yesterday's victim may become tomorrow's perpetrator" (Varvin, 2017: 360). The Syrian flux in 2015 is representative: an incredibly effective right-wing message has framed the immigration crisis as a "Muslim threat" (Forlenza, Turner 2018: 28), perhaps because too many Europeans (and Americans) know that most of ISIS's victims are Muslim, not only Shia, as would have seemed logical (Flescher, 2017: 175).[1] It is not by chance that the vast majority of the refugees registered by UNHCR are Sunni Muslims (Eghdamian, 2015). Of course, it could be argued that Sunni are not, in a strict legal sense, religious refugees.[2] Besides, they are not a

---

1   With respect to the Syrian conflict, it is worth pointing out that it is precisely a conflict with ancient religious roots, as Tomass argued: "for more than a millennium, the tradition of attributing infidelity (*takfīr*) and apostasy (*irtidād*) to religious communities that did not conform to the dominant Sunni orthodoxy led, in the best case, to the marginalization of those communities" (Tomass, 2016: 5).

2   It is worth mentioning that, while the law is clear that religious persecution constitutes grounds for asylum, applications on these grounds are very few. Partly because religious minorities are generally reluctant to denounce religious discriminations: "fearing for their safety, they often hide their identities to avoid reprisal attacks based on sectarian tensions" (Eghdamian, 2015). Partly because UNHCR tends to prioritize refugee claims based on basic human needs. Things do not change, even if the Muslim "invaders" decide to convert to Christian faith: when applying for asylum, they may be treated with suspicion, because "the

minority, as in the case of Christian, Druze, Ismaili and other Muslim and non-Muslim minority religious people and families fleeing Syria. But the truth is that religious persecution is following them and waiting for them at Europe's borders. An interesting case-study relates to Bulgarian vigilantes, patrolling the borders of the EU, between 2014 and 2016. Among these far-rights activists and defenders of Europe, there was an unexpected "hero", a Bulgarian Muslim who explained his rationale, during an interview: "we want to stop an Islamic invasion" (Rexhepi, 2018: 2223).

All this seems to confirm our starting point: the religious refugee is inseparable from the theme of the (unexpected) trespasser, which materializes as an "illegal body", to be carefully controlled (Ajana, 2013; Lindskov Jacobsen, 2017). As Nancy would point out, this trauma of intrusion is intrinsically bind to the stranger in general: "there must be something of the *intrus* in the stranger; otherwise, the stranger would lose its strangeness" (Nancy, 2002: 1). However, this evidence is not as simple as it appears at first sight and that is why it deserves a further exploration.

2   Too Much Like Us

Let us consider now the famous scene of intrusion in *The Uncanny Guest*, an early tale by Hoffmann, originally published in 1819:

> Into a quiet happy group of friends, just when supernatural matters were forming the subject of conversation, there suddenly came a stranger, who struck everyone as being uncanny and terrifying, notwithstanding his apparent everydayness, and seeming belonging to the common level. (Hoffmann, 1892: 141)

In his analysis, Freud explained the shocking effect triggered by the Hoffmannian guest with the ambivalence of his entrance, reaching the conclusion that the uncanny (*Unheimlich*) is in some way or another a sub-species of familiar

---

genuineness of their conversion is often called into question" (Bielefeldt *et al.*, 2016: 62). Christian convert asylum-seekers (but also Christians) are asked detailed factual "Bible trivia" questions, such as: "Can you name the twelve apostles?" "When is Pentecost?" "What fruit did Adam eat?" (APPG and AAG, 2016: 3). Moreover, "extraditions of converts to their countries of origin, even in the face of obvious risks of persecution, have at times been justified with the cynical recommendation that they could simply "conceal" their new faith" (Bielefeldt *et al.*, 2016: 62).

TABLE 2.1   Countries where nationalist political parties or politicians targeted religious
             groups in 2016, and religious groups that were targeted

Country	Region	Targeted religious group
United States	Americas	Muslims
Burma (Myanmar)	Asia-Pacific	Muslims
India	Asia-Pacific	Christians, Muslims, Hindus
Nepal	Asia-Pacific	Christians
New Zealand	Asia-Pacific	Muslims
Philippines	Asia-Pacific	Jews, Christians
Sri Lanka	Asia-Pacific	Christians, Muslims, Non-Buddhists
Austria	Europe	Muslims
Bulgaria	Europe	Christians
Denmark	Europe	Muslims
Estonia	Europe	Muslims
Finland	Europe	Muslims
France	Europe	Muslims
Germany	Europe	Muslims, Jews
Greece	Europe	Muslims, Jews
Hungary	Europe	Muslims
Italy	Europe	Muslims
Netherlands	Europe	Muslims
Poland	Europe	Muslims, Jews, Non-Christians
Slovakia	Europe	Muslims
Sweden	Europe	Muslims, Jews
Switzerland	Europe	Muslims

SOURCE: PEW RESEARCH CENTER ANALYSIS OF EXTERNAL DATA (PEW RESEARCH, 2016)

(*Heimlich*) (Freud, 1919: 232). More specifically, the unexpected visitor arouses
horror because of the uncomfortable sense of the unfamiliar within the familiar. This blurring of the boundaries between everydayness and strangeness
makes the uncanny especially applicable to debates on forced displacement.
Symptomatically, the refugees' arrival involves a creeping feeling of familiarity

with people whose lives are distant from our own. Briefly, they are people just like us – "perhaps too much like us" (Macdonald, 2015).

What happens, then? The answer depends on the direction of oscillation between the familiar and the unfamiliar. If the "too much" prevails, repugnance arises. For example, when refugees are perceived and judged to be excessively similar, to the point of becoming "more like ourselves than we" (Žižek, 2008: 72), an unconscious claim of superiority will try to "refoul" the stifling commonalties with them. That sounds remarkably close to what our Muslim vigilante claimed: "We, the Bulgarian Muslims, cannot accept jihadist and islamists, people who violate our culture; we are used to living by European standards and by Bulgarian standards" (Rexhepi, 2018: 2223). This narcissistic defense against the perceived excess of equality can be paraphrased like this: all things considered, they should really not be like us, perhaps they are not even human (and then inhumane behavior and cruelty may be justified).

On the contrary, when refugees are interpreted as "just" like us, thus neutralizing the shock of intrusion, a sense of romantic closeness can prompt a reaction of compassion and care. Take, for example, the first executive order of Trump's presidency, the travel ban, that barred citizens of seven mostly Muslim nations from entering America: many protesters expressed solidarity by carrying placards bearing such messages as "We Are All Muslims Now" and "Let Them In" (*The Economist*, 2017: 15).

We can explain this unconditional sympathy as follows: all things considered, we are all foreigners. And we can go further, as Kristeva has done: "If I am a foreigner, then there are no foreigners" (Kristeva, 1991: 192).[3]

As we can easily imagine, this repugnance/compassion dialectic results in the current ambivalence of narratives about religious asylum seekers: on the one hand, religious refugees are demonized and targeted as a dangerous threat to border security; on the other hand, counter-narratives portray religious refugees as innocent victims. Religion, properly manipulated, plays therefore a pivotal role in reinforcing these two stereotypes, and in justifying two opposite

---

3 We agree with Kristeva in arguing that the antidote of xenophobia can occur when we recognize our "internal uncanniness". Freud's discovery of unconscious can be explained with the idea that the constituent portion of the human psyche amounts to a sort of "strangeness" within ourselves. Nevertheless, her idealistic claim of disappearance of strangeness by self-effacement ("there are no foreigners") seems to contradict the premise ("I am a foreigner"). Besides, if the stranger would lose its strangeness – Nancy would say – what are we talking about?

policies: in one case, refoulement practices and concentration camp-like conditions in some refugee camps or detention centers; in the other case, humanitarian camps, safe zones, resettlements in solidarity and other forms of relief actions. This oscillation between aggressive closure and humanitarian openness has been visible in Europe's Janus-faced handling of the 2015 refugee crisis, as argued by Zanfrini (2019).

Let's start by investigating the demonizing narrative: first of all, we will examine the zoopolitics, i.e., the use of animalized metaphors and imagery that pervade the rhetoric of "irregular" migrants and the violent de-humanization of refugees (§3); secondly, our focus will be on Islamophobia (§4); thirdly, we will delve into the experience of discrimination in aid, suffered by Christian asylum seekers (§5).

3   Caged Animals

Yarl's Wood is the UK's main immigration detention center. In 2014, the treatment of detainees was revealed in exclusive footage obtained by a Channel 4 News investigation. The 15-minute video revealed racism and animalization, combined with sexist objectification: to give an insight, one guard refers to detained women as "beasties" and "caged animals", suggesting that his colleague "take a stick in with you and beat them up". In another scene, a guard states nonchalantly that "these Black women... they're fucking horrible" (Canning, 2017: 56).

How is it possible to imagine this de-humanization of persecuted[4] people, in a country, by the way, which is often represented as a champion of human rights?

The Hoffmannian guest helps us to understand the case of Yarl's Wood: the terrifying everydayness of detained women is their obvious precariousness. That does not mean that refugees are innocent, passive victims: this is, as we will see (§6), the typical Left-liberal litany, which stands in opposition to the demonizing narrative. Precariousness is simply the basic aspect of human condition: life, all human life, is vulnerable and, therefore, ethics begins when we recognize that all lives are worth living and worth protecting.[5]

---

4   This is not to say that all refugee women have experienced sexual violence. Nevertheless, as Women for Refugee Women reported, out of 46 female interviewees who had been held in detention in the UK, 33 had been raped in their home country (Girma *et al.*, 2014: 5–6).

5   As Butler rightly suggested, "precarity cuts across identity categories as well as multi-cultural maps" (Butler, 2009: 32).

Conceived along these lines, it seems difficult to deny that precariousness is the truth that drives us to say: all things considered, "these Black women" are people just like us. The problem is when this radical familiarity becomes, for some people, "too much". More specifically, the problem is when we try to repudiate our own precariousness, this common truth that refugees, by just being there, remind us. If "these Black women" are nothing but the projective apparition of our disturbing, intolerable precariousness, then they must not be human like us.[6] They are horrible caged animals.

This fetishist vilification is possible through an unconscious mechanism of abjection[7] and usually takes the brutal form of control: Yarl's Wood is a clear example of what Berlant has termed "hygienic governmentality" (Berlant, 1997: 175), a defensive strategy underpinned by the narrative that an abject population threatens the common good and must be rigorously governed and monitored by all sectors of society.

This zoopolitics (Vaughan-Williams, 2015: 70)[8] can be particularly aggressive, especially when it is combined with the paranoid fantasy that "the only good Muslim is the bad Muslim" (Akil, 2016: 111). And that is how we arrive to measure the fear of the uncanny religious refugee: Islam is the "principal

---

6 As Arendt noticed (Arendt, 1976: 190), this claim of superiority is well depicted in a famous passage from Conrad's *Heart of Darkness*: "The earth seemed unearthly. We are accustomed to look upon the shackled form of a conquered monster, but there – there you could look at a thing monstrous and free. It was unearthly, and the men were... No, they were not inhuman. Well, you know that was the worst of it – this suspicion of their not being inhuman. It would come slowly to one. They howled and leaped and spun and made horrid faces, but what thrilled you was just the thought of their humanity – like yours – the thought of your remote kinship with this wild and passionate uproar. Ugly. Yes, it was ugly enough, but if you were man enough you would admit to yourself that there was in you just the faintest trace of a response to the terrible frankness of that noise, a dim suspicion of there being a meaning in it which you – you so remote from the night of first ages – could comprehend" (Conrad, 1988: 37–38).

7 "The abject – Butler argues – designates here precisely those "unlivable" and "uninhabitable" zones of social life which are nevertheless densely populated by those who do not enjoy the status of the subject, but whose living under the sign of the "unlivable" is required to circumscribe the domain of the subject. This zone of uninhabitability will constitute the defining limit of the subject's domain; it will constitute that site of dreaded identification against which –and by virtue of which– the domain of the subject will circumscribe its own claim to autonomy and to life. In this sense, then, the subject is constituted through the force of exclusion and abjection, one which produces a constitutive outside to the subjected, an abjected outside, which is, after all, "inside" the subject as its own founding repudiation" (Butler, 1993: 3).

8 Vaughan-Williams gives the shocking example of the transformation of the former zoo in Tripoli into a detention centre for predominantly Ghanaian, Nigerian, and Chadian migrants destined to Europe. Research undertaken by NGOs in Tripoli zoo, but also across Libyan processing centres, suggests the same animalization process that we have discovered in Yarl's

catalyst" (Wilson, Mavelli, 2017: 3) for increasingly harsh immigration policies and growing exclusionary discourses.

4 Muslim Intruders

A 2016 infamous cover of the Polish magazine *wSieci* showed a crude representation of what we can call a demonizing narrative of religious refugees, portrayed as hypersexualized predators (Fiddian-Qasmiyeh, 2017): a naked white blond woman, wrapped in the flag of Europe and screaming in fear, being grabbed by dark-skinned hands, with the headline "Islamic Rape of Europe" (Hart, 2017: 32). According to Pew Research Center, the use of such rhetoric is especially common in Europe: "about a third of European countries (33%) had nationalist parties that made political statements against religious minorities, an increase from 20% of countries in 2015" (Pew Research Center, 2016: 7).[9] A clear example is what happened in 2015, when Hungary erected a 170-kilometre razor-wire fence along its border with Serbia. This first act was later revealed as a part of a complex plan of hygienic governmentality: Hungary further adopted two legal measures that created the category of "illegal migrant".[10] The Prime Minister Viktor Orbán explained in a commentary for *Frankfurt Allgemeine Zeitung* his line of argument: "those arriving have been raised in another religion, and represent a radically different culture. Most of them are not Christians, but Muslims. This is an important question, because Europe and European identity is rooted in Christianity. Is it not worrying in itself that European Christianity is now barely able to keep Europe Christian?

Wood: "They (the guards) don't even enter our room because they say that we smell and that we have illnesses. They constantly insult us, and call us: 'you donkey, you dog'. When we are moving in their way, they look disgusted and slap us sometimes" (Amnesty, 2013: 14).

9   Obviously, anti-refugee views and ideologies are not limited to governments and politicians. The number of European countries where nongovernmental nationalist organizations targeted religious groups also increased in 2016 (Pew Research Center, 2016: 10).

10   "The first was an amendment to Hungary's penal code, stating that persons entering the country without authorization –by forcing the frontier fence after September 15, 2015– are committing transgression liable to punishment by expulsion or imprisonment from one to three years. The second measure was taken by the Parliament of Hungary on September 12. At this time, a law was adopted which stipulated that military forces and police can use rubber bullets, teargas and various pyrotechnic devices to support action against migrants. Altogether, Parliament adopted a resolution providing that, in cases of emergency, authorities are entitled to make use of any kind of available measure to protect the borders of Hungary" (Kantor, Cepoi, 2018: 156).

There is no alternative, and we have no option but to defend our borders" (Metykova, 2016: 2).

Not surprisingly, this kind of Christian fundamentalism correlates strongly
with right-wing authoritarianism (Koopmans, 2015: 38).[11] As it is known, all
four Visegrad countries refused EU quotas on refugees and proclaimed the demise of Schengen (Matlary, 2018: 110–111). But the same paranoid rhetoric is
pervasive across Europe. We only need to look at the list of countries where
religious groups have been targeted (Pew Research, 2016: 7) to see the "elephant
in the room" (Betts, 2016).

Perhaps this Islamophobic backlash can be statistically correlated (Pew Research, 2018)[12] to a sort of reactive Christianity, or, should we better say, "Christianist secularism" (Brubaker, 2016):[13] because they are (bad) Muslims, they
cannot be like us. And if they are bad, dangerous Muslims, then we, Europeans,
must be, in some sense, Christians, and good Christians, perhaps not perfect,
but superior to them.

That being the case, what happens to Christian refugees? Apparently, they
are entitled to a better fate than that of Muslim invaders. However, the reality
is quite different.

5   Christian Refugees = Muslim Terrorists

As we have just seen, the "violent Muslim invader" narrative reinforces a "toxic
cocktail" (Hurd, 2017: 106) of nationalism, racism and anti-Muslim zoopolitics.
During the 2016 US election, this cocktail was visible in Republican primary
candidates' demonizing rhetoric about a potential threat of Syrian refugees.
Two candidates, Jeb Bush and Ted Cruz, suggested that the United States
should admit only Christian refugees, because "there is no meaningful risk of
Christians committing acts of terror" (Meral, 2018: 5). Besides, they deserve

---

11   As for the Polish clergy, we need to point out that the situation is more complex: some
      urge the Polish Catholic Church to follow the instructions of their Pope; but others are
      eager to align themselves with the right-wing government's rhetoric around Muslim refu-
      gees, invasion and fear of terrorism (Narkowicz, 2018: 363).
12   This is what emerges from a 15-country survey done by the Pew Research Center, span-
      ning 15 Western European: both church-attending and non-practicing Christians are
      more likely than religiously unaffiliated adults to express anti-immigrant views. This is
      not to say that most Christians in Europe oppose immigration or want to keep Muslims
      out of their countries: "the survey data show a statistical correlation – not a clear relation-
      ship of cause and effect" (Pew Research, 2018: 78).
13   For a detailed account on the debate about secularism, see Chapter 3.

priority, if only we consider that "Christians are the most widely targeted religion". And this is certainly true, although Muslims are not exactly that much better (Pew Research Center, 2016: 26).

But the demonizing narrative claims that Christian's suffering is deeper, and ultimately unique. Precariousness should be differentially allocated, because not all lives are worth protecting.[14]

An issue, however, arises whether the heralded "preference" for Christians involves a real intention to help the most persecuted religious group in the world or not. As rightly noticed by Song (2019: 124), Trump's tough line on refugees from mostly Muslim countries has also closed the door to Christians and other religious minorities. Not surprisingly, the number of Christian refugees granted entry into the US has fallen dramatically, even though Christians account for a far larger share of refugees admitted than Muslims the first half of fiscal 2018 (63% *vs* 17%), according to a Pew Research Center analysis of State Department data (Konnor, Krogstad, 2018).

The situation in Europe is possibly worse than in US. Take, for example, the case of Pakistani Christians. A qualitative research conducted between June and December 2015 by Madziva and Lowndes (2018) gives us an understanding of Christian asylum seekers' experiences in the UK, which is, by the way, a "Christian country", if we believe the then PM Cameron (Oliva, Hall, 2017: 54). Among the interviewees, there was a male asylum seeker who explained:

> As a Christian asylum seeker from a Muslim majority country you face many obstacles in putting forward your case. The major obstacle is the place where you come from and the way you look – these are things that you can't change. Because of the way we look, immigration officials don't trust us. (…) They don't tell you openly that they are suspicious of you (…) but through their actions and body language, you can tell that you are a suspect. The problem is you can't easily separate Christians from Muslims, as we all look the same. (…) I am a Christian, but when people see me, they just conclude that I am a Muslim. So they think I have come to bomb their country. (Madziva, Lowndes, 2018: 80)

This equation of Pakistanis with bad Muslims makes it more difficult for Pakistani Christians to establish their Christian identity, and to prove their

---

14   As Akil argued, this instrumentalization becomes a disavowal of the meaning of suffering itself, because it denies the universal and shared precariousness: "one could assert that the singularization of one's suffering as unique and unrepeatable could also function as a repudiation of the suffering of all others" (Akil, 2016: 138).

well-founded fear of persecution.[15] That means, once again, that the rhetorical bias for Christianity is instrumental to criminalize refugees, on the whole. And this is nothing compared to what happens when Pakistani Christians come to Thailand and seek UN protection from persecution. The problem here is that Thailand has not signed the 1951 UN Refugee Convention and therefore considers all refugees to be illegal immigrants. A BBC investigation has revealed that Thai officials routinely arrest and detain Christian asylum seekers, sometimes chaining them like dogs (Rogers, 2016).

And with this, we are back to where we started: how can we escape from the horrific dehumanization of zoopolitics?

An easy way is to mobilize compassion towards refugees, as opposed to demonization (El Sheikh, 2017). But is this counter-narrative a real solution? That is what we need to address now. We begin with the left liberal litany "we are all human (refugees)" and its secularist indifference to the religious belonging of refugees (§6); we will proceed to show two dehumanizing effects of seeing refugees as helpless creatures and camping them in "humanitarian spaces":

a)   the underestimation of the risks of religiously motivated attacks in refugee camps, especially against non-Muslim minorities (§7);

b)   the "zombification" of refugees, or the underestimation of the "agency of refugees" (Parekh, 2017) (§8).

6   Beautiful Souls

During the so-called long summer of migration of 2015, a great variety of campaigners[16] have opposed human rights abuses and injustice against refugees. In explaining their decision to support the migrant cause, several activists framed it as a moral duty rooted in humanitarian motivations: "It is humanity. You cannot just pass by. We are all victims of a system. This feeling of injustice and insecurity harms all of us" (Milan, Pirro, 2018: 145).

As we can immediately see, "We are all victims" is the exact antithesis of "They are all Muslim intruders". In this counter-narrative, the uncanny nature of intrusion has disappeared and refugees are romantically interpreted as "just like us". Clearly, we are not arguing that mobilizations and protests, from civil disobedience to solidarity actions towards refugees (Lahusen, Grasso, 2018),

---

15   The truth is that Home Office tends to paint "a broad picture of Pakistanis as fraudulent and opportunistic cheats, and hence potentially bogus claimants" (Madziva, Lowndes, 2018: 87–88).

16   Supporters include many NGOs, church-based charities, established migrant organisations, left-wing academics and artists, as well as some groups within trade unions and political parties (Ataç et al., 2015: 8).

are purely rhetorical exhibitions. On the contrary, resistance and rebellion against injustice, as we will see (§8), is of crucial importance from an ethical point of view. The problem is that the "We are all victims" frame is easily exploitable, especially when it becomes a typical left-wing strategy against populism or the litany of the "greatest hypocrites", as Žižek polemically likes to call those who advocate for open borders and unconditional hospitality:

> secretly, they know very well this will never happen, for it would trigger an instant populist revolt in Europe. They play the Beautiful Soul, which feels superior to the corrupted world while secretly participating in it: they need the corrupted world as the only terrain where they can exert their moral superiority. (Žižek, 2016: 8)

What is relevant for our analysis is that this idealizing narrative is not only potentially hypocrite, but also indifferent to the religious dimension of forced displacement. We can identify this undervaluation of religion using the drama triangle,[17] as shown in the version provided by Ruard Ganzevoort (2017: 19–20).

We have seen that the demonizing (typically right-wing) narrative frames Muslim refugees in the role of perpetrator, as a national security threat. Even if they are persecuted, their religious background takes precedence in the framing. Christian refugees are –in stark contrast– framed as innocent victims. And obviously the right-wing populists define themselves as the rescuers, claiming to be the only group that can offer the solution to stop the threat: the securitization and progressive closure of borders and the creation of detention centers to accelerate the deportation of irregular migrants.

In response, left-wing Beautiful Souls apply the drama triangle quite differently. They see their right-wing opponents as the real perpetrators, threatening and sometimes committing violence against refugees, which are now considered as victims, whether they are Muslims or Christians: they are all suffering from various discriminations, first from oppressive regimes and cruel opponents, then from traffickers and harsh immigration policies, and finally from the anti-immigration movements. The focus, therefore, is not on the religious dimension of displacement, but instead on the humanitarian one: "It is humanity", said the previously mentioned activist. And as you would expect, the (left-wing) "Beautiful Souls" cast themselves in the same role as their (right-wing) counterpart: the rescuer that takes the side of the sufferers. The relief strategy, in this case, is the production and management of hospitable spaces, such as humanitarian camps.

---

17   The "Drama triangle" is a model of social interaction and conflict, originally described by Karpman (1968), using the terms "perpetrator", "rescuer" and "victim".

TABLE 2.2   The "Drama triangle"

Rescuer	Perpetrator	Victim
Right-wing populists	Muslim intruders	Persecuted Christians
Left-wing 'Beautiful Souls'	Right-wing populists	All refugees

Paradoxically, though, this secularized humanitarian narrative, along with its humanitarian camping strategies, can have severe dehumanizing consequences, thus proving that it is not a real alternative to the zoopolitical drift. Let us look at why this happens.

7   Re-persecuted (non-Muslim) Refugees

The ignorance of the importance of religious belonging in the humanitarian narrative and in the practice of refugee protection, is not difficult to identify. Eghdamian (2016), who conducts a research about the minority Syrians in Jordan, has revealed a considerable lack of statistics on religious experiences, particularly those on religious minorities, in refugee camps. When he asked why the UNHCR staff he interviewed in Jordan did not take religion seriously in their understanding and assessment of Syrian refugees' needs, José Riera[18] referred to the continued dominance of the secular line of thought among humanitarian actors:

> It's my own view that because of the secular mind-set and the reality that many United Nations officials come from societies where faith has been pushed out of the public sphere and into a corner somewhere, we are supposed to be "blind" to faith. (Eghdamian, 2016: 453–454)

Interestingly, even a Caritas staff activist showed the same neutral position:

> UNHCR does not shed light on Christians because it's a general crisis. Who is the most vulnerable? A refugee is a refugee. They (UNHCR) are

---

18   José Riera is senior advisor to the director of international protection, UNHCR headquarters, Geneva.

neutral. We should all be neutral. It's what our work should be. (Eghdamian, 2016: 455)

So, where is the problem? The problem is that religious minorities could be
vulnerable to reprisal attacks based on sectarian lines in refugee camps or asylum centers (USCIRF, 2013: 6). Consequently, a religious-blind position is unable to assess needs and vulnerability among refugee population and to prevent discrimination that can emerge in displacement contexts. The cases of
Sweden and Germany are tragically representative: as reported by Kino,[19]
Christians are persecuted in the Middle East and re-persecuted in asylum centers by their Muslim counterparts:

> Christians are slaughtered because of their faith in Syria and Iraq. The
> ones that are escaping to the neighboring countries cannot be in the refu-
> gee centers because they are persecuted there as well. If they make it to
> Sweden and Germany they risk to be persecuted again, this time in the
> countries' asylum centers. (Quoted in Abdelhady, Malmberg, 2019: 120)

The situation in the rest of Europe is not much better and this motion for a
resolution, tabled by Unhurian (2017) and other members of the Parliamentary
Assembly of the Council of Europe, is a sign of serious concern:

> (...) Regrettably, many refugees have continued to suffer from discrimina-
> tion, violence and sometimes death because of their minority beliefs
> even after reaching Europe, in many cases at the hands of fellow refugees.
> In Resolution 2050 (2015), the Parliamentary Assembly highlighted cases
> where Christians have been thrown out of boats crossing the Mediterra-
> nean. There are also widespread reports of cases where refugees have
> been attacked for their beliefs in reception centers and refugee camps
> across Europe – in a 2016 report, Open Doors for instance documented
> hundreds of religiously motivated attacks on Christians and Yazidis in
> German refugee shelters. As member States are working to implement
> best practices to care for refugees and migrants in accordance with the
> core values of the Council of Europe, including equality and the

---

19   Nuri Kino is an award-winning Assyrian-Swedish journalist of Turkish origin who focuses
      on minority rights in the Middle East. In 2014, he started an organization, A Demand for
      Action, which attempts to provide aid to Christians in Iraq and Syria. He is also active in
      the Assyrian Orthodox Church.

protection of minorities, the Assembly should closely examine this challenging reality and propose recommendations aimed at effectively protecting minorities having fled religiously motivated violence, and upholding freedom of thought, conscience and religion in reception centers and refugee camps.

It seems therefore clear that, despite the commitment for non-discrimination and care for all migrants, a secular form of hospitality could turn out to be really harmful for some religious refugees. And this is not the only dehumanizing effect of the humanitarian narrative.

8   Zombipolitics

Let us consider now the representation of refugees as helpless creatures. This reduction of refugees to "Muselmänner"[20] is obviously functional to emphasize the moral superiority of humanitarian rescuers: if refugees are nothing but "zombies",[21] they are definitely in need of a providential savior. Obviously, the sense of desperation and helplessness is not uncommon to most refugees.[22]

---

20   The "Muselmann" appears in Primo Levi's account of his experience of the concentration camp: this slang term was used by concentration camp inmates to categorize fellow inmates who were reduced to the status of zombie, having lost "all consciousness and all personality" (Agamben, 1998: 185).

21   The thought of describing the life of refugees in refugee camps as the life of the "living dead" occurred to Bauman in 2002: "Having abandoned or been forced out of their former milieu, refugees tend to be stripped of the identities that milieu defined, sustained and reproduced. Socially, they are 'zombies': their old identities survive mostly as ghosts – haunting the nights all the more painfully for being all but invisible in the camp's daylight" (Bauman, 2002: 347). Interestingly, such alignment of refugees and zombies eventually became a common trope in pro-migrant narratives and accusations of dehumanisation and disregard of fellow human beings, "to the point that these lives become disposable" (Oktem, 2016). And the same plot device is used even outside academic circles: a famous Slovenian comic, Klemen Slakonja, plays Angela Merkel in a YouTube video, where the German chancellor dances with refugees made up to resemble zombies. "Refugees coming to Europe ... don't have the opportunities that they should get, so they are like the living dead here", Slakonja explained to Reuters (Reuters, 2017).

22   It is known that "refugees experiencing long transitional periods in which they are refused *refugee* status can develop disabling sociosomatic reaction, as exemplified by the *Uppgivenhetssyndrom* ("resignation syndrome") that is observed in Sweden, where hundreds of refugee children have fallen unconscious, after being informed that their families will be expelled from the country" (Ventevogel *et al.*, 2019: 107).

But the point is: are we sure that the life in humanitarian camps is perfectly equivalent to the life in concentration camps?

It is true that these temporary, exceptional spaces, where refugees are kept indefinitely in a "frozen transience" (Bauman, 2002: 345), come close to Goffmann's ideal type of "total institution". The ambivalent case of Zaatari camp in Jordan is telling. On the one hand, this camp typifies the negative conceptual representation of a camp: "it is an extraterritorial space of exclusion, exception, segregation, and control" (Kikano, Lizarralde, 2019: 39). On the other hand, its occupants cannot be considered as walking corpses. It is undeniable, indeed, that the camp has evolved into a city-like space, displaying a remarkable resilience. There is even an office for employment, set up in coordination with the Government of Jordan, in order to facilitate access to formal work opportunities across Jordan for refugees living in the camp (ILO, 2017).

It is impressive, but let us not deceive ourselves, Zaatari is not a wonderful haven, certainly not for young girls, increasingly targets of harassment, sexual assault, and early forced marriages. Once again, however, even these young victims are not bodies in complete submission, or a voiceless "biopolitical mass of bare life" (Bulley, 2017: 40). The story of Omaima Hoshan, a teenage Syrian refugee in Zaatari, proves it: this Malala-inspired girl is campaigning against child marriage in her refugee camp, encouraging other girls to fight the practice (Dunmore, 2016).

Briefly, it is true that humanitarian camps are sites in which refugees are closed and their bodies are potentially "abjected"; but camps are also sites of counter-conduct, in which forced displaced persons choose to stage protest activities and make use of a language of rights against the language of dehumanization.[23] And fortunately, these fundamental processes of defiance are in place not only in humanitarian camps, but also in detention centers, where refugees –as we have previously commented (§3)– are exposed to horrific animalization. Let us go back for a moment to Yarl's Wood Immigration Removal

---

23   It is no coincidence that, for example, there is a right to appeal against a refused asylum application. Without this fundamental right, "the state may apply its coercive power arbitrarily since this application will not be critically examined" (Kritzman-Amir, Spijkerboer, 2013: 26). In this context, the landmark case of MSS v Greece and Belgium (2011) is instructive. In its verdict, the European Court of Human Rights ruled against Greece and Belgium for "inhuman and degrading treatment" in respect of their arrangements for the detention of asylum seekers, "the first time in legal history that an EU Member State was found in breach of international humanitarian law. Moreover, the ruling was used by the ECtHR to further warn all EU national governments of the need to comply with international human rights legislation in respect of conditions of detention" (Vaughan-Williams, 2015: 26).

Centre: in February 2018, more than 100 women have gone on hunger strike over "inhumane" conditions at the facility (Bulman, 2018).[24]

These micro-tactics of resistance are decisive, because they are undeniable symptoms of subjectivity: refugees are not passive victims; sometimes, they prove to be agents of rebellion against their subaltern condition. And sometimes, this open dissent can assume a political vibrancy, especially when these acts of protest become "creative breaks" (Isin, Nielsen, 2008) that re-invent ways of living together. This participatory vitality rejects the double hegemonic discourse of zoopolitics and zombipolitics, helping us to understand that the only good narrative is the narrative that refugees tell about themselves, i.e. a narrative that re-establishes their status as *auctori* and claimants of justice: as Bauman reminds us, refugees are "fully fledged actors in the life-drama; people, like all of us, endowed with motives that reach beyond the instinct of survival and purposes that transcend the breadline, and who engage in interaction or decline interaction, weave networks of social bonds or tear them apart" (Bauman, 2002: 343–344).

This anti-hegemonic narrative of engagement/decline of social bonds is not an easy task: it demands an ethics of "hostipitality" (Derrida, 2002: 356),[25] where the tension between the unfamiliar and the familiar of refugees is never finally resolved, neither in favor of violent repulsion, nor in favor of romantic compassion. Needless to say, this ethics is possible if, and only if, we proceed on a provisional hypothesis concerning the role of religion in refugees' narrative and in their political decision to reconfigure (Sennett, 2018: 288) a livable place in exile. Our hypothesis relies on the undeniable fact that the emergence of refugee question is inseparable from, and sometimes coextensive with, religion. Suffice it to consider, as argued by Hollenbach, that "humanitarian emergencies fracture the taken-for-granted worlds of the displaced, shattering and reshaping the relationships that give meaning to the routines of ordinary life. Such crises also affect those seeking to help, who have to face the suffering of those they assist in a way that can lead to secondary trauma and burnout. Thus, humanitarian crises and forced migration–Hollenbach concludes–often raise questions about the ultimate meaning that are, in essence, religious. Is continuing to struggle pointless in the face of loss, or can one trust, however tentatively, that there is a deeper source of hope?" (Hollenbach, 2014: 454).

---

24   Besides, this is not the first time: in 2007 more than 100 women were involved in a hunger strike at Yarl's Wood centre and was "propelled by abusive treatment by detention centre stuff" (Conlon, 2016: 137).

25   Derrida invents the neologism of "hostipitalité" (hostipitality) in order to illustrate that hostility (which is, in Hoffmaniann terms, the structural aspect of intrusion of the "uncanny guest") is intimately intertwined with hospitality.

Let us sketch, then, in conclusion, a four-dimensional frame for this post-secular ethics of displacement.

9   Asylum Speakers

In 1981, on the occasion of forming the International Committee Against Piracy, Foucault delivered a speech entitled *Confronting Governments: Human Rights* at the UN in Geneva. Addressing "all members of the community of the governed", he argued that the "suffering of men must never be a silent residue of policy. It grounds an absolute right to stand up and speak to those who hold power" (Foucault, 2000: 474).[26]

If we agree that refugees have the fundamental right to be heard, we automatically admit their ability to construct themselves as subjects through narrative (Shemak, 2011: 3–4). Briefly, at stake here is their crafting of one's self. *Identity* then is our first keyword that requires us to de-instrumentalize the role of religion.

Religious belonging is not reducible to a discriminatory label (bad Muslim/ good Christian refugee). When we really listen to life stories, we immediately realize that beliefs and religious affiliations are powerful signifiers for identity-building strategies. Furthermore, religion, especially in the case of forced displacement, becomes more and more important as a marker of demarcation and distinction from others, sometimes in a racialized and antagonistic way, sometimes in a dialectical and potentially cooperative way (Pickel, 2018: 35). That means that beliefs and religious values operate in competing ways, as they both facilitate and impede integration processes. It is therefore impossible to guarantee that religious refugees will avoid reactive solutions and behaviors, in the process of coping with uprooting and the additional burden of adaptation to a new way of life (Goździak, Shandy, 2002: 131). However, what should be guaranteed, and fostered by the States, is the favorable context in which they can express, exercise and eventually reconfigure their religious identities. This legal context is formally opened by the right to *freedom of religion*, which is our second keyword.

True freedom of religion must protect the fundamental aspiration of persons to gather and flourish in communities. As democratic theorists argue, the freedom of religious communities to operate in civil society serves as a crucial basis for democratic governance (Hertzke, 2013). It is also true that freedom of

---

26   As it is known, Foucault was referring to the specific suffering of the Vietnamese asylum seekers who had left their country after the fall of Saigon.

religion is subject to a diversity of interpretations in its meaning and application, around the world. But from this complexity it does not follow that the concept is a Western construct, without universal meaning. The proof is that this human right is present in the Muslim world and Islam is not inherently hostile to it (Philpott, 2019).

Freedom of religion is obviously crucial in determining the refugee status. This is an interesting sentence, passed on 5 September 2012: the Court of Justice of the European Union (CJEU, 2012) points out that, "given the concept of religion also includes participation in formal worship in public, the prohibition of such participation may constitute a sufficiently serious act within the meaning of Article 9(1)(a)".[27] What is important is that the Luxembourg Court rejects the common European practice of granting asylum for religious motives only in case of extreme persecution, and recognize that the freedom of religion includes the right to manifest one's faith in public and collectively (see Chapters 4 and 9).

Finally, this fundamental religious agency is highly relevant in refugees' social integration in the host society. Integration is a two-way process and can only be successfully pursued by refugees when the host society is truly hospitable to the impact of the uncanny (Robila, 2018: 2). It seems therefore clear that "government protections of religious freedom and social acceptance of diverse religious identities provide crucial leverage for inclusion of newcomers" (Hertzke, 2018: 513–514).[28] And that is how we arrive at the third keyword: *citizenship*.

If we accept that religious agency is an integral part of refugees' public space making (Horstmann, Jung, 2015: 1), we must then ask ourselves: what happens when "non-citizens with extremely precarious status assert themselves as political by publicly making claims about rights and membership, freedom and equality?" (Nyers, 2008: 161). This "intrusion" of religious identities and practices

---

27 "Everyone has the right to freedom of thought, conscience and religion; this right includes freedom to change his religion or belief and freedom, either alone or in community with others and in public or private, to manifest his religion or belief, in worship, teaching, practice and observance" (European Convention for the Protection of Human Rights and Fundamental Freedoms, art. 9(1)(a)).

28 From this inclusive point of view, the idea to prioritize the resettlement of certain religious refugees over members of other religious groups does not seem justifiable, as recently stated by the Special Rapporteur on freedom of religion and belief: "States are reminded of their obligation to provide protection to refugees and migrants, regardless of their specific religion or belief. The pretext that refugees and migrants would erode the traditional religious make-up of a country amounts to a 'territorialization' of religion, which violates the spirit and the letter of the universal right to freedom of religion or belief" (Shaheed, 2018: 19).

within public space forces us to shift our focus from citizenship as a legal status (which tends to neglect the importance of identities, participation and belonging) to performances of citizenship, i.e. creative enactments that negotiate membership, re-inventing ways of living together (Isin, Saward, 2013). The case of religious communities of Muslim immigrants in Norway is typical. Immigrants bring with them religious faith and practice from their countries of origin, but "the Norwegian context offers them and their offspring the opportunity to develop and choose alternative forms of associational life" (Nyhagen Predelli, 2008: 256). Consider, for example, Muslim women: they are increasingly invited to participate in the mosque, which is traditionally considered as "men's arena". This new religious performance has visibly a political impact: it is no accident if Muslim women in Norway have made public calls for the reinterpretation of the Qur'an in ways that are more inclusive towards women.

It is not arbitrary, all things considered, to conclude by arguing that "migration is part of our cultural heritage" (EU, 2015: 14): "migratory peoples bring with them skills, knowledge, ideas, new approaches, entrepreneurship and cultural practices that enrich the social fabric of the communities they become part of". With this in mind, the fourth and final keyword stands out immediately: *common good*.

In his 1963 letter *Peace on Earth*, Pope John XXIII argued that "civil authority exists not to confine men within the frontiers of their own nations, but primarily to protect the common good of the State, which certainly cannot be divorced from the common good of the entire human family" (John XXIII, 1963: n. 98). That is why the Pontiff focuses on the unfairness and ill-treatment suffered by refugees, because their "incredible sufferings" (John XXIII, 1963: n. 103) are bound to have impact on both the common good of the State and the common good of the entire human family. As Hollenbach rightly points out, the marginalization of refugees' voice puts the common good in trouble: "when millions of people are forced to live under plastic sheeting and to face the dangers of cholera and other serious diseases, oftentimes for years on end, individual countries and the global human community itself are gravely wounded" (Hollenbach, 2008: 12).

Clearly, no one can offer ready-made solutions at hand. Perhaps, we need to review the assumptions of our global system. In the meantime, religious "asylum speakers" claim to be heard, and challenge the limited horizons of a state-based conception of citizenship. What is to be done? Hos(ti)pitality, surely. Not unconditionally, though. The common good criterion suggests here a necessary counterbalance to the excessive claims of rights. Indeed, we know that refugees are obliged to comply with the laws of their host country, because –as Rawls would suggest– there is "a duty of fair play": if refugees have accepted and intend to continue to accept the benefits of just institutions, they must do their part and not take advantage of these benefits by not cooperating (Rawls, 1999: 117). But that alone is not enough: our basic hypothesis forces us to reasonably imagine requiring refugees to share civic burdens and responsibilities, with their creative religious agency.

Without this duty to contribute to the common good of their host country, their weak, suffering voices, with their indignant claims, would remain merely lyrical, bound to disappear once again in the realm of rhetoric. But, above all, they will never become truly human storytellers of a transformative, even poetic (Derrida, 2000), public space.

CHAPTER 3

Religion in Secularized and Post-Secularized Europe

Monica Martinelli

1 Introduction: the Frame of Reference

Viewed by anyone wondering about the role of religion in Europe today, the phenomenon of migration cannot fail to arouse a certain degree of interest.

In the second half of the 1900s, when an extensive literature announced the imminent end of the religious phenomenon, in Europe –as in other parts of the world– a different scenario continued to unfold: a religiosity certainly in crisis, increasingly relegated to the personal sphere and detached from institutional structures, reinvented in its content and influenced by some factors of secularization, but nevertheless present. In many cases the presence of religion, especially in its more traditional and collective forms, takes on significant characteristics precisely in relation to the migration phenomenon, since for many immigrants belonging to a religion is by no means a secondary dimension of their identity.

In itself, the European scenario is a composite, plural one, which cannot be explained simply by choosing between two options: "secularization" *versus* "non-secularization". It is a much more articulated, complex phenomenon, certainly geographically and nationally but, more in general, for the vitality of the religious phenomenon and of the individual forms that it adopts: elements that are the result of a continuous intersection of long processes and secularizing influences as well as of responses reacting to those processes and those influences – not without new dilemmas and conflicts.

What seems evident is that we are living in a different epoch from the one defined as completely secularized. In it, new challenges are emerging; indeed, if we are not convinced of a definitive disappearance of religion, we cannot ignore the possibility that the process of moving away from religious practices and the mistrust or even neglect of the contents of faith can progressively intensify. The end-point of this process is no longer only atheism as a strong position taken up towards faith, but concerns all the alternative forms to believing which qualify our times, ranging from interpretations of agnosticism and laicism, which express a certain indifference towards questions of faith, to new forms of spirituality, up to the emergence of a fluctuating religiosity, often completely modelled and withdrawn into the subject, but sometimes maintaining some reference to a traditional religion in the background. In this panorama, however, we also find the more traditional expressions of the religious experience, connected with historic Churches or new groups, along with the emergence of the phenomenon of religious radicalization, which takes the form of fundamentalism in its multi-faceted expressions.

In the varied and stratified religious composition of society described as "post-secular", new problems open up as do new opportunities for renewal for the religions themselves; the religious meaning continues to be spread, even if with profoundly different demands and according to profoundly different modes from the past.

In the present chapter we shall dwell first of all on the debate about secularization, taking up its salient features: it developed, as is known, mainly in a western context and received a strong impulse from the European sociologists of the late 1800s and early 1900s. A polysemic concept, the term "secularization" has lent itself to many different interpretations with the risk of not capturing important nuances of reality, especially where its use has claimed to entirely represent an epoch, according to a subtractive view of history. From this point of view, the change in outlook within that debate provides an important passage to understanding more about the complexity of western society and of individual life in terms of religious experience.

After tracing the main lines of this debate, we shall pinpoint some processes concerning religion within the context of post-secular society: alongside the insistent secularization a more composite, not easily defined picture emerges where, on the one hand, religion is closely connected with cultural and social transformations within the European countries, but on the other hand becomes the borderline where contradictory pressures and, in some cases, thorny questions relating to the coexistence between people with different religious traditions interweave. These questions, well beyond the religious contents in the strict sense, threaten to bring about the collapse of these very contents onto problems of another kind, which would need to be treated differently.

Finally, we shall try, within the cross pressures to which the religious experience is subjected and from which it takes shape in post-secular society, to highlight the challenge of pluralism and the role of religion within our time, also in relation to migratory phenomena.

2   The Theses of Secularization

2.1   The "Prophecies" of the Classics of Sociology

In the debate that opened up in the social sciences, the long-dominant theses of secularization argued that a progressive advancement of modernity would inevitably be followed by a decline in the religious phenomenon, which would eventually disappear altogether. This religious eclipse was supposed to involve a progressive retreat of religion from the public sphere and social life and the exclusion of the dimension of transcendence from the domain of the personal conduct of life (Ferrara, 2009). In other words, secularization would be followed by a single possible effect: the transformation of religion, following the processes linked to modernity, would coincide with the end of the religious experience, both in the forms of the associated living and in the subjective sphere, in the direction of a predominance of the immanent dimension of life.

Those theses of secularization start from an interpretation of the celebrated prophecies of Weber and Durkheim.

According to Weber, the unceasing advance of rationalization and disenchantment of the world –typical processes of western modernity– provokes, on the one hand, the emptying of the secular spheres of any religious reference and, on the other hand, the declassing of the religious sphere itself, deprived of any claim to truth and to definition of the meaning of collective living in relation to transcendence. The modern individual gradually becomes insensitive to what is sacred and religious. The progressive abandonment of what is magical and religious is accompanied by an ever-greater appropriation by man of the control of the forces of nature and of the ways in which he relates to them. The resulting dispersion of religion in the pluralism of faiths is further weakened and deprives man of supreme values, condemning him to live in an age without God and without prophets (Weber, 2017).

E. Durkheim, unlike Weber, considers religion as a complex fact, of social origin and nature, with the function of stabilizing coexistence and integration, creating a homogeneous system of shared meanings within society. Like Weber, he nevertheless appears equally peremptory when he states that, with the advance of modernity, God abandons men and their controversies (Durkheim, 1962). With traditional religion left behind, society ends up celebrating the cult of itself, becoming the creator of religion to guarantee, on its own, that connective tissue which is generated precisely by the religious phenomenon and ensures the widest social integration. It is as if society, having moved away from God, had to seek the foundations of its own existence within itself. Indeed, according to Durkheim, societies become creators of the divine by means of a projective mechanism whereby religion comes onto the scene to justify the symbolic universe that a given society builds for itself. In this way, it avoids the danger of finding itself at the mercy of single individuals. In other terms, the absence of a religious framework leads to a veritable "cult of the individual" (Durkheim, 1972). For Durkheim it is a process, which presents some highly problematical aspects. He is aware that secularization and individualization are in certain respects inevitable. And he does not call for any return to the predominance of traditional religion. He rather fears that the liberation and emancipation of individuals from religious institutions, in the name of their autonomy, can go to the point of distancing oneself also from society, which he describes as a moral entity, a producer of solidarity.

Both these authors, each in one's own particular outlook on the religious phenomenon, leave an indelible mark on subsequent theories of secularization. The thesis of privatization of religion, for example, inherits both Weber's considerations on the rationalization and the differentiation of the secular spheres from the religious sphere and Durkheim's diagnosis as to the cult of the individual typical of modernity and the hypothesis that religion is a social (and, after Durkheim, individual) construct. Many scholars – although from different points of view – have shared the diagnoses of the two classical sociologists.

2.2 Subsequent Studies

The heirs of those prophecies have therefore sustained the thesis of secularization as a loss in importance of religion in social life and have often exasperated the eclipse of the religious phenomenon, excluding the latter's metamorphic character. In this view, religion tends to be made to coincide with one of the stages in the march of western civilization, a stage that is subsequently eliminated by other phases, such as the advent of the scientific revolution. Within this approach, one concentrates above all on what, in secularization, has been lost, without explaining the complexity of the reality that bears witness, sometimes weakly and other times even violently, to the persistence of religion also within modern society. Modernity and religion are considered as mutually exclusive realities: the prevailing of the former inevitably implies the exit of the latter (Yinger, 1957).

In this perspective we find an internally varied and articulated thread of studies that asserted itself especially from the 1960s in the western context. These studies developed different attentions and accentuations, but in the background of each was the common approach of the theses on secularization. We can subdivide these analyses around the following paths:

i)   there are studies that postulate a progressive privatization of religion;

ii)   others concentrate their attention on the desacralization and desecra-
        tion of religion;

iii)   also the transposition of religion to the secular sphere is the subject of
        analysis of the theories of secularization, as

iv)   the interpretation of secularization as a process of liberation from re-
        ligion and its binding dogmas.

We shall take up the essential features of these ramifications in summary
form.

i) According to the hypothesis of the progressive privatization of religion,
modernity is characterized by the passage of religion from the public sphere,
where it constituted a shared interest of the community, to the private sphere,
thus losing significance in social terms. Luckmann talks, in this connection,
of "invisible religion" (1967; 1973), underlining with this adjective the non-
institutionalized character of the religious phenomenon. For Luckmann, the
subjective conscience acquires a greater centrality: the individual must learn
to seek the ultimate meanings for himself. Religion thus becomes a "subjective
construction" (1973) which is separate from every belonging and connection.[1]
Hervieu-Léger (1986) is positioned on the same line when he talks of "de-
institutionalization of religion", while Davie (1994) uses the well-known
expression "believing without belonging" to reinforce the reduction of religion
to an exclusively individual matter and the loss of any claim to truth by a sacred cosmos and the social institutions correlated to it.

In agreement with Luckmann, Berger argues for the emergence of a subjective secularization, indicating also in this case the transfer of religion to the
private sphere. He highlights the advent of pluralism given the "collapse in
plausibility of the traditional religious descriptions of reality" (Berger, 1973:
197). On the one hand, according to Berger (and also Luckmann) there is a
progressive differentiation of the secular spheres from the religious sphere, as
Weber had already indicated for that matter; on the other hand, in the intimate
sphere religion continues to exercise an important role, even though "privatized", so that it becomes the subject of an individual choice or preference.
However, it loses its function of social integration, until it is included in the
dynamics typical of the modern market economy, becoming at most one of
many possible objects of consumption.

---

1   Luckmann writes: "once religion is defined as a private matter, the individual can choose as
    best he pleases among an assortment of ultimate meanings – guided only by preferences
    determined by his social biography. An important consequence of this situation is that the
    individual builds not only his personal identity but also his own individual system of ulti-
    mate significance" (1973: 139).

Among the theorists of the privatization of religion we find, although in a different form, the idea of the end of religion in modernity: the religion that they trace in the private and "invisible" spheres no longer shapes the conduct of life in the social sphere and no longer touches the experience of the transcendent or, as the historians of religion Otto and Eliade would say, of the sacred. It is rather a question of a subjective religion – in Luckman's sense – thus understood not so much because it is lived by the subject starting in any case from some shared collective reference (within a group or a Church) but because it is built by him/her to his/her liking.

ii) Another line of study has focused attention on the process of "desacralization" (Wilson, 1969) and "desecration" (Acquaviva, 1992) to explain secularization. With Weber, Wilson shares the theses of emancipation of the secular spheres from religion: the religious becomes, if anything, a refuge now at the margins of personal experience. The advance of the process of rationalization and technicalization contributes to this loss of monopoly of wide spheres of social life by religion, which, at that point, loses significance and credibility. A loss that concerns, more in general, the sense of the sacred at both an individual and a social level: it is in this view that he speaks of "desacralization".

Acquaviva insists on this loss stating that, more than secularization, we should speak of a process of "worldliness and desecration" already within the Churches (1973: 167), a typical process of industrialized societies.[2] In this case, it is the Churches themselves that, in their wish to modernize, renounce the experiences of the sacred. Acquaviva looks on this road with concern, although he points to a positive aspect where the experience of the sacred is provoked to free itself from the scaffoldings that tend to suffocate it.

According to these authors, it is the experience of the sacred that withdraws from social and personal life. In this case, secularization invests not only the secular spheres, depriving them of a religious reference, but religion itself, going within it to empty the rites of their significance, with the failure of the central and indispensable element for every religion. Thus, once again, traditional religions lose their strength within modernity, significantly weakening their ability to aggregate around shared practices able to orient the individual conduct of life.

iii) In the multi-faceted sea of the theories of secularization, there is also a thread of studies that sustains the complete transposition of religion to the secular sphere. Bellah, who agrees with Weber (secularization is understood as

---

2 The term "sacred" –notes Acquaviva– indicates the place where the meeting between the subject and the "radically other" takes place; this experience constitutes the founding element of religion.

a differentiation of the secular spheres from the religious one), does not embrace the latter's view of an inexorable decline. Following in the tracks of the American sociologist Parsons, who puts forward a view of secularization as the institutionalization of Christian values within modern society, religion – as Durkheim had already stated – is definable above all for its socially unifying and integrating function. Therefore, where such values are effective, that is where they are institutionalized in a positive manner, we have a "civil religion" (Bellah, 1967, 1970).

Civil religion is a shared set of values derived from the Christian tradition, although the former distinguishes itself from the latter. In fact, the god of civil religion refers much more to order, law and rights than to salvation and love (*Ibidem*, 1967).[3]

To place the branch of studies that has developed around civil religion among the theories of secularization would certainly require a more thorough in-depth analysis. It is enough to point out that what Bellah calls "religion" makes little reference to the experience of the sacred and the transcendent and is more connected to the "secular" dimension, thus once more reinforcing the perspective of the theories of secularization.

iv) We will now discuss the last branch of studies, which has gathered wide consensus. Secularization is here considered as a process of liberation of man from the yoke of religion, of its dogmas and worldviews. There are numerous scholars who fall within this branch, with reference to various disciplines.[4] Let us remember that at the end of the 19th century, the *Deutsche Gesellschaft für Ethische Kultur* (the German society that dealt with the Prussian government's 1892 Education Bill) proposed to create a technocratic view of social life, placing all its faith in the power of scientific reason, promoting a civil morality independent of religion. In the British context there had been the *Secular Society* founded by Holyoake in 1846, which called for the possibility that the rights of the citizen should not be conditioned by a Christian confession: the successors decidedly pursued the project of creating a society free of every theological and religious reference (Lübbe, 1965).

---

3   As is known, in particular in the United States, the reference to this religion has meant impressing, in various stages of the history of that country, a new thrust to secular society, by mobilising people around national aims of a more cultural and political than religious nature.

4   It would be enough to cite modern philosophy and psychoanalysis, which, in various ways, insist on the authoritarian, oppressive role of religion within social life and on the negative implications exercised on individuals' life conduct.

In the furrow of these views emerged a secularistic vision: in a laicistic society, it is useful and opportune that there should be a retreat of the influence of religion from the claim to want to guide human action. The aim of this manifesto is to guarantee the progress of man and the extension of his individual freedom.

Within this branch of research, rather than putting the accent on the differentiation of the secular from the religious sphere, or on the eclipse of the sacred, or on the privatization of religion, secularization coincides with the passage that leads mankind out of its minority condition to guide it along the illuminated ways of rationality that are strengthened by the scientific revolution, with its technological applications. This is what the founder of sociology, A. Comte (1864), indicated in the early 1800s, as an evolution of the human species by its exit from the theological stage to arrive, after passing through the metaphysical stage, at the finally positive and scientific one.

3   The Change of Perspective: towards a Post-Secular Society?

3.1   *Indications from the Literature*

The studies of secularization, although with different emphases, all adopt a view of history as a progressive succession of phases marked by breaks. The phase of modernity marks the arrival at a stage in which religion is counterposed with the characteristics of an epoch. Concentrating principally on what has been lost, these studies have difficulty in grasping the fact that, in reality, religion and the religious experience do not disappear from the modern scene.

Significantly, those theses are subsequently questioned by their own supporters, who have realized that reality offers a profoundly different scenario from what appeared as an inexact and even "ideological" interpretation of secularization (Martin, 1973: 198; 2005).

Exemplary among others is the case of Cox who, twenty years after publishing a book entitled *The Secular City* (1966) –which sustained the evidence of the secularization taking place–, published a new book in 1984, entitled *Religion in the Secular City: Toward a Postmodern Theology*, where the author argues that we are entering a post-modern era of religious reawakening and return to the sacred.

Also the title of Berger's well-known text *A Rumor of Angels* (1969) was already eloquent in this sense: he speaks of a murmur, to indicate that interest in the sacred and the transcendental dimension has not completely disappeared, and is represented metaphorically as a barely perceptible whispering of angels.

However, it is especially his text *The Desecularization of the World*, written in 1999, that suggests the most decisive change in outlook.

Casanova too, in his famous text entitled *Public Religions in the Modern World* (1994), describes a passage to a subsequent phase, beyond secularization, speaking of a de-privatization of the religious phenomenon. Going away from the predictions developed within a purely illuminist cultural framework, he alludes to the attempt of the great religions to counter the process of marginalization to which they have been subjected by the advent of modernity. The religious traditions refuse to limit their range of action to the simple care of souls but attempt to show the close connection between the importance of ethical-religious questions and the economic-political life of the various national contexts. Added to this are two other tendencies that confirm the change in relation to the expectations: faced with the progressive differentiation between religion and the other social systems, religion tends in any case to play a preponderant role in society; in addition, the decline in faith and religious practice in a strict sense does not affect all the contexts in the same way, so the picture relating to contexts other than the European need to be analyzed better.[5] The effects of this investment of the religions in the public field are two: a re-politicization of the public and private religious sphere (for which, for example, among some active minorities there is a return to thinking that religion must function as an inseparable element of social integration); a pressing appeal to the existence of transcendent ethical norms that must be placed at the basis of socio-economic and political life.

Starting from a similar assumption to Casanova's, Beyer (1994) states that globalization favors the conditions for a recovery of the presence of religion in the public sphere, speaking of a "global civil religion". A presence that, according to Kurtz (1995), involves questions considered as universally important, as for example the advent of biotechnologies, defense of the environment, global conflicts.

In these authors' line of thought, religion is thus considered as a phenomenon able to mobilize energies within society, playing a crucial public and political role. And if on the one hand the change of perspective that starts to be discussed, enables us to describe the signals of a reality that the theories of secularization were in danger of losing, on the other hand it often tends to

---

5 Concerning this last aspect, also Martin (2005), criticising the idea of a disappearance of religion, states that on the contrary it shows symptoms of evident vitality, for example with reference to Christianity in Latin America, Africa, Asia. These symptoms lead one to think that secularization limited itself to looking at just a particular social context, i.e. Europe, where the indicators of continuous decline of religion were indeed very marked.

consolidate a mental habit whereby, also in the presence of significant religious phenomena, one continues to think according to the model of the "disappearance" and, possibly, of the "return", of the "death" and the "triumph" of religion.

The hypothesis of a "return" of religion is explained by the need for an order within the chaos of cultural and social complexity, of a direction of sense for the individual conducts of life: it can also bring with itself a different god from that of the historic European religions (Graf, 2004; Kepel, 1991; Shah *et al.*, 2012).

Revisiting the theories of secularization, the hypothesis we assume in these pages goes in the direction of considering the latter as such a jagged, complex process that already includes dynamics of a religious nature within itself. Hence, "post-secular" society should be understood not as a phase subsequent to that of secularization.[6] From a closer examination, the same process of secularization originates precisely from a religious phenomenon, namely the Protestant Reformation, given that the latter also includes the social and civil dimension in its moral project, favoring an anthropocentric turn and an immanent pluralistic orientation in its unforeseen effects, as pointed out by Gregory (2012).

The hypothesis is that secularization does not necessarily exclude religion and religiosity: in this way, the religious experience can probably be understood as an experience that does not contradict secularized contemporary society, even though its position and its social and individual role are very different from the past. It is rather a matter of grasping the changes that it has encountered and how the conditions of the contexts of adherence to the faith have changed. If secularization and religious phenomenon have long been understood, manifestly or implicitly, as contradictory, the point becomes trying to consider them rather as opposite poles that do not annul each other but that are in constant tension between them. And it is precisely from this tension that the contemporary religious experience of individuals and organized groups takes shape, highlighting the fact that both the former (secularization) and the latter (religious experience) are non-linear phenomena, and yet intense and involving given that they concern numerous dimensions. Secularization involves all the levels of existence and social life, taking on, as we have seen, different definitions and features. And religious experience can be considered as

---

6   Terminologically, the expression "post-secular society" is intended to express a "change in consciousness" with respect to the terms in which the process of secularization was previously described and studied (Ballestrem, 2009: 267). For an analytical reconstruction of the question, see the Doctoral Thesis by Nicoli (a.y. 2017/2018).

a constant of the human being, observable in all historic ages and different civilizations, according to many different modes of expression (Eliade, 1957; Ries, 2007; Hart 2013).

As Rémond (1999) has effectively pointed out, the long description of the progress of secularization over two hundred years has been able to describe only a part of the events; it says nothing about other forms of presence and the perennial nature of the religious fact. To stop only at the religious decline would forget that also in the most secularized society statistically the religious fact remains very important and that it is by far the most massive social fact of a voluntary nature.

3.2   *Some Empirical Observations*

Rémond's statement finds further confirmation in the data of the Gallup Foundation (relating to 2016), according to which 62% of people in the world define themselves as "religious" and many of them are also engaged in activities of a religious nature; 71% declare that they believe in God and consider the religious dimension as an important reference point in their daily life; 25% define themselves as "non-religious", while the number of atheists is around 9%.[7] If in some contexts –such as Latin America and sub-Saharan Africa– the religious experience is strongly felt and is expressed through belonging to institutionalized historic Churches and/or to groups often born of the various evangelical ramifications, or –as often occurs particularly in Asia– it takes shape with reference to local spiritualities (Buddhism, Hinduism etc.) and, for the Arab countries, in relation to Islam, in Europe we observe a high level of secularization which is accompanied, however, by the declaration of feeling in any case "religious" by tradition and culture. We shall shortly return to the contents and ambivalences of these declarations.

Research and data on the European context in fact confirm the persistence and the complex structure of the religious phenomena. This happens both because adherence to a religion is an option increasingly "thought-out" and chosen (often unconventionally), and due to the growing religious pluralism configured by reason not only of the historic presence of the great traditional

---

7   The data quoted here are taken from the 2017 report by Gallup International: *End of Year 2016. Global Report on Religion*, which covers 68 countries (http://gallup.com.pk/wp-content/up-loads/2017/04/Global-Report-on-Religion-2.pdf). Among the various information, the report confirms the connection, which has emerged for some time, between religiousness and socio-demographic characteristics (such as age, income and education: in general, as education and income levels grow higher, religiosity levels tend to diminish).

religions in their internal structure (in particular, the different Christian confessions), but for the growing coexistence of persons and groups bringing different faiths.

In a text edited by P. Berger *et al.* (2008), the authors posed the question of
whether Europe is really as secularized as people say and think, especially with
reference to the United States of America considered as a religious nation.[8]
According to Lehmann, on the one hand, precisely for its development, secularization would seem to be a typically European process, therefore a sort of
"exceptional" process of a portion of the world. On the other hand –in the face
of some far-reaching social changes, including globalization and international
migrations– it is necessary to better understand whether secularization has
been only a transitory phase in European history or whether the profoundly
secularized continent will align itself with the other continents where religion
continues to be important; *or* whether the other continents, like the people
who arrive in Europe with a different religious and cultural background, will
adapt to the European cultural-religious frame (Lehmann, 2004).

Although estimates of the number of believers and the mapping of religious affiliations are not easy to construct, they led Berger (1999, 2001) to
assume that Europe is affected by a certain de-secularization. In the perspective adopted in these pages, rather than de-secularization, we prefer to
speak of coexistence, within a post-secular society, of secularizing tendencies with forms of adherence to religion as tendencies that do not contradict each other but coexist. In this framework, states Pace (2011), the European socio-religious geography appears as a picture in movement; on one
side, three quarters of Europeans say that they feel religious, that they resort
to some form of prayer, that they feel the need to give a meaning to their
action with reference to some form of prayer, in addition to a link to an
institutional frame. In relation to traditional religions, both in countries
with a Catholic majority and those with a Protestant majority, the reference
to the religious dimension takes in a varied range of feelings and actions in
terms of belonging, of active participation or generic acknowledgment, of

---

8   According to various researchers, until the 1970s, the United States and Europe seemed to be
    proceeding in step in the secularization process (Inglehart, Norris, 2004), but then the USA's
    destiny seems to have changed, given that American churches have tended to move as com-
    petitors within a crowded market, positioning themselves on emerging needs. Thus, within
    what has been defined as the "spiritual turn", not only has there been a change in the ways of
    believing of people seeking their own "spiritual way of life" that makes them feel well, but
    also in the religious offer of goods and services by the religious institutions (Roof, 1993). The
    debate about spirituality and the relationship between religion and spirituality is very wide,
    both in the USA and in Europe; for a useful introduction see Giordan (2007, 2016).

total or partial affiliation to the contents of faith. On another side, alongside the substantial nucleus in Europe that continues to define itself as Christian or belonging to the historic Jewish minorities, we see a growth –as a result of the grafting of new cultural and religious stocks through the migratory processes– of forms of Christianity referring to new Churches, of mainly Asian, African, and Latin American origin, which build on a spirituality mainly without dogmas and apparatus.[9] Alongside this is an increasingly important presence of Islam, though not so marked in absolute numerical terms: the estimated presence of Muslims in the countries of the European Union does not on average exceed 3% of the population of the principal countries with large-scale immigration (*Ibidem*).[10]

In general, the social and cultural environment of many European societies is still marked by the presence of the historical religions, although new forms of religion seem to emerge alongside them. If we wish to trace "an ideal map of religiosity of Europeans, on the one hand, the different meridians and parallels tend to show the long history of the religions that civilized this or that area of Europe, and on the other to highlight a morphology of the religious terrain which is still fed by a common humus, but which is dotted with many gardens and vegetable patches cultivated directly by individuals" (*Ibidem*: 65–89).

The data of the Pew Research Center, too, confirm that the majority of Europeans (about 70%) continue to consider themselves as Christians even though they do not regularly attend the Church they belong to (only 22% say they are

---

9   Pace refers to the data of the European Values Study (EVS): prudent estimates state that about 37 million Europeans belong either to Pentecostal churches of protestant matrix or to new charismatic and neo-Pentecostal churches that have arrived through immigrants. See also Halman *et al.* (2008, 2005).

10   The 2018 Report of the Pew Research Center, referring only to the countries of Western Europe, gives an estimate of 4.9% (including Norway and Switzerland, with the highest peak values in France – 8.8%, UK – 6.3% and Germany – 6.1%). As is known, however, there is an objective difficulty in measuring the presence of the different religions in Europe. Often the reference consists of the residence permit of the immigrants who, in this case, are the principal bringers of the Islamic religion (apart from some European regions where Islam is a historically rooted local presence): this is evidently a vague figure as geographical origin cannot be taken as a secure source for stating automatically that all the inhabitants coming from countries with a predominant Muslim tradition adhere to that religion and/or are practicing believers (whether in their homeland or where they have emigrated to); in addition, the minorities also living in these countries should be considered; in some cases, they emigrate precisely by reason of their different religious affiliation from the official one (in this connection see Chapters 6, 10 and 14).

practicing).[11] The non-practicing[12] form the majority in all the Western European countries, with particularly high peaks in the Nordic Countries (reaching, for example, 68% in Finland against 9% practicing; 55% in Denmark against 10% practicing), with the exception of Italy (where the percentage of non-practicing and practicing is equal, at about 40%).

Although Europe appears as a secularized region, in many of the countries studied in the survey the non-practicing believers far exceed those who state they are non-believers (atheists, agnostics or, more in general, the so-called "nones"). And also, even with the recent immigrations from the Middle East and North Africa, there are in any case more non-practicing Christians than people of other religions, considered all together. According to the Pew Research Center, these figures are explained by the fact that what remains particularly rooted in the individual life experience is the Christian identity as the cultural badge in Western Europe, an identity not in a merely nominal sense.

Furthermore, although there has been, for some time, a strong tendency towards a decline of Christianity in various countries (e.g. Belgium, Finland, Ireland, Holland, Spain and Portugal), other countries, at the same time, exhibit a relative stability or a more modest decline. The process of secularization varies considerably from country to country.[13] It should then be defined also in the light of the various historical vicissitudes of the different nations and of the relationship that each country has maintained with the religion or religions present within its territory in the phase of construction of the modern State.[14]

---

11   The report is available at http://www.pewforum.org/2018/05/29/being-christian-in-western-europe/. The data refer to a survey carried out in the period April-August 2017 in 15 countries of Western Europe, through 24,000 telephone interviews administered to adults. The processes identified have been continuing for some time also in the countries of Eastern Europe, as for example in Romania where, already ten years ago, there was a very high percentage, with almost 98%, of people declaring themselves to be "Orthodox" with 30% practicing (Kosela, 2007).

12   Those are considered as such who define themselves as Christian but attend the places and activities of worship only a few times in a year. Those who attend at least once a month are considered "practicing".

13   In this connection it should also be pointed out that in some cases (e.g. Germany, Sweden, Denmark, France, UK) the smaller decline recorded over recent years starts from an already fairly high level of secularization.

14   In fact, in some cases religion has contributed historically to the formation of the national identity, rooting itself in people's experience beyond the declared affiliation. In other contexts, freeing from dictatorial regimes has meant distancing oneself also from the dominant religion which, with respect to those regimes, had adopted ambiguous attitudes, while in yet other cases religion has played exactly the opposite role, acting as a critical

And if, in general, the religious phenomenon seems to have become more problematic and fragile than in the past, this does not mean that it has lost all significance in relation to personal biographical paths. This is evident, for example, in the frequent visits to sacred sites, as testified by the widespread phenomenon of pilgrimages in many regions of Europe (Cipriani, 2012; Damari, 2016)[15] and to places of worship (also those less institutionalized) or in the persistence of the demand for solemnization of certain decisive moments of existence.[16] This finds confirmation in the case of Italy, which occupies a particular position in the Western European panorama, as indicated: empirical research shows a structured, complex, and vital co-presence of secularizing tendencies and forms of religiosity.[17] If for example we observe the religious practices, with reference to Catholicism, we note that the bond between the Italians and the Church has been loosened but has not been broken (Garelli, 2011). This is well confirmed by the request for sacraments even by the more uncertain and hesitant believers.[18] The religious sense continues to be widespread among Italians who do not completely renounce turning to the Catholic Church, even if in different ways than in the past. In fact, although personal discretion is widespread as regards the choice of timing, manner and forms of participation (Diotallevi, Allievi, 2004), it is not possible to talk of a definitive abandonment of religious practice, but rather of a religiosity seeking new

---

element towards the system, gathering around itself the resilient forces (consider, for example the case of Spain with the Franco dictatorship and the case of Poland before the fall of the Berlin Wall).

15   When the Council of Europe in 1987 recognised the importance of the religious and cultural paths running through various European regions, a new season opened up for adherence to these itineraries (see, for example, what happened with the "Way of St. James").

16   We refer, more precisely, to the so-called "rites of passage" i.e. those that mark the three cardinal moments of existence, solemnising birth (with Baptism in the Christian tradition), the union between two persons (marriage) and death (funeral).

17   See in this connection the various studies and sociological researches in Italy: among others, Garelli (1995, 2003, 2011); Gattamorta (2009); Abbruzzese (2009, 2010); Pollini (2012); Berzano (2017a, 2017b).

18   Sacraments constitute the heart of Italian religiosity –and, more generally, of Catholic religion– as evidenced by the persistence of their celebration also by those who consider the faith only as a cultural tradition. In addition, if sacraments risk losing their specificity – that of being the meeting point between immanence and transcendence and of linking the individual to the community– they represent one of the major challenges for the Catholic Church because of their importance among people even in the secularizing pressures. The importance of sacraments emerged also from a recent research in Italy carried out by a group of researchers of ARC, Center for the Anthropology of Religion and Cultural Change, Catholic University of Milan, and the Italian Episcopal Conference during 2015–2016 (cfr. the Survey Report drawn up by ARC, 2016).

modes of expression, which are able to make greater use of the individual's contribution within a traditional, communitarian frame.

The European picture is therefore in movement. The question of secularization is more complex than it had been presented initially by the different branches of study: in fact, within the category of those who define themselves as believers there appear the "intermittent" and the "doubtful" who, unlike the atheists and agnostics, do not abandon their path of faith. In other words, the fact that the religious experience in secularized society is profoundly crossed by doubt does not seem to preclude the possibility of a spiritual and religious search by those who manifest it.

At the same time, from the research there also emerges a more "disenchanted" view of reality, which expresses itself for example in the gradual abandonment of some fundamental beliefs: the existence of life after death, the divine judgement of history, the role of original sin. This phenomenon reflects some typically modern secularizing dynamics, linked to the oblivion of topics that bring great questions, such as death, evil and good, which influence the religious representations of believers and adhesions to given contents of faith, profoundly modifying them.[19]

3.3   The "Secular Age", Secularized and Religious

The evidence of the complex relationship between secularization and religiousness has led a number of researchers to associate with the term "post-secular society" a wider meaning than that which aims to record simply the passage from one historical age to another, indicating rather how religion persists within an increasingly secularized frame.[20] The "dialectics of secularization" –as discussed by Habermas and Ratzinger (2005)– would show the ambivalence of the processes of secularization: on the one hand, in the name of emancipation from religion –and from its dogmas, values and meanings, from its truths, moral authorities, institutional forms– it was expected to disappear; on the other hand, however, this eclipse has not occurred.

In clarifying Casanova's thesis, Habermas (2005) maintains that religious communities persist also within a more secularized horizon. For the German thinker, religion continues to exert an influence in the public spheres of the single countries, as well as signaling the phenomenon of pluralism of forms of

---

19   In reality, these are questions set aside decidedly by contemporary culture in general (see for example the eclipse of the question of death for the contemporary man: among others, cfr. Bauman, 1992).

20   On the notion of post-secular society understood in a broad sense see, among others: Habermas (2006); Belardinelli (2006); Ferrara (2009); and especially Taylor (2007).

life following especially the processes of immigration. This opens up new challenges in terms of the necessary mediations by the religious authorities with the social contexts, on one side, and of opening towards religious thought by post-secular societies on the other.

In the change of outlook on post-secular societies, secularization can ultimately be defined as a complex process, which, while causing breaks with the past, does not entail incompatibility with the religious phenomenon, so that there would not be a phase after secularization of returning of religion as if it had disappeared for a period from social and individual life. The religious phenomenon, despite transformed with respect to the traditional forms, and although fragmented and sometimes contradictory, remains even within the secularized contexts. This interpretation enables a widening of the scenario in which to investigate the phenomenon of religiousness, posing new questions that start from the recognition of a co-presence of secularizing tendencies and religious inclinations.

As stated by C. Taylor –one of the most authoritative researchers into religious phenomena–,

> The whole culture experiences cross pressures, between the draw of the narratives of closed immanence on one side, and the sense of their inadequacy on the other, strengthened by encounter with existing milieux of religious practice, or just by some intimations of the transcendent. The cross pressures are experienced more acutely by some people and in some milieux, but over the whole culture, we can see them reflected in a number of middle positions, which have drawn from both sides. (2007: 595)

This scenario is well expressed by the metaphor, suggested by H. Joas, of the sea in a storm: like the sea, our history is marked by strong secular waves but also by religious back-currents that often revitalize religious traditions or facilitate new religious options (2014).

In this perspective, the view of history adopted by Taylor is not subtractive but additive: the turn of historical events is conceived as an uninterrupted succession of events, however non-linear it may be, that also presents some constant nuclei, although subject to change. Among these nuclei, there is precisely the phenomenon of religion and religiosity. Recognizing how secularization has undoubtedly exerted a powerful influence on the religious phenomenon, he shows how this has nevertheless not caused its disappearance: the religious motivation "was and is evident in the creation of new forms, replacing those disrupted or rendered unviable by these 'secularizing' agents. The vector of this whole development does not point towards a kind of heat death of faith" (Taylor, 2007: 437).

Thus, despite the weakening of the faith, secularization causes a new position of the sacred and the spiritual in relation to the individual and social life and challenges religion to examine its contents to verify what its message is regarding a historical period. And this "new placement is now the occasion for the reorganization of spiritual life in new forms, and for new ways of existing both in and out of the relation to God" (*Ibidem*).

Significantly, Taylor's text analyzing these changes is entitled, as we have said, *A Secular Age*, inviting us to go beyond the more diffuse term "*post-secular*" unless we use it taking into account the complexity of reality. Also, for Joas the secular age is an epoch that is not marked by the absence of religion and faith but by the mixing of religious and non-religious elements, with a greater complexity of personal experiences.

Starting from this awareness and keeping in the background the idea of secularization as "a change from a society where believing in God is unchallenged and indeed, unproblematic, to one in which it is one option among others, and frequently not the easiest one to embrace" (Taylor, 2007: 3), in the next section we shall try to reinterpret European post-secular society as an interweaving of "cross pressures" on religious experience and within which it moves.

4   Post-Secular Society: an Interweaving of "cross pressures"

The most evident trends in the process of secularization that give rise to "cross pressures" on the experience of belief, to the point of changing the conditions of the context in which it takes shape, are those that Weber expressed with the two terms of "disenchantment" of the world and "rationalization". These are two closely interconnected movements that influence each other and affect both the societal structural factors and personal experience.

Disenchantment of the world, as already mentioned, consists in the gradual loss of the magical-sacral reference, which goes in step with the growing belief of human beings that they can control the forces of nature by means of a calculating rationality. These processes, in late-modernity, constitute an indisputable fact. Disenchantment and rationalization produce multiple effects on reality, but not all these effects are necessarily negative as Weber argued.[21]

On the one hand, having removed every magical-sacral reference, the disenchanted man finds himself effectively less constrained by external forces and

---

21   The discussion that follows is based primarily on the already-mentioned reflection by Taylor in *A Secular Age*, where the phenomenon of disenchantment is reinterpreted, in its positive and negative aspects, starting from the focus on the experience of modern man.

able to manage his existence and his relationship with the world by himself; in short, he becomes more autonomous. In parallel with this process, a new subjective demand opens up, for understanding, participation and action, which in modernity becomes increasingly important. The disenchanted man is no longer satisfied with being a passive spectator in the experiences that mark his life –which include the religious experience– but demands the possibility of participating actively, of becoming their protagonist.[22]

On the other hand, in order to be able to happen, disenchantment requires an assumption to be satisfied: that is to say, it is necessary for the subject to make a veritable break with respect to the link between himself and the world, which only from that moment can be perceived as an objective, separate and external reality and only as such controllable. According to an effective metaphor of Taylor's, the self, from "porous", becomes "buffered", separate from everything and everyone (Taylor, 2007: 38; Taylor, Dotolo, 2012). This break with the world takes on various forms in reality.

The first form directly concerns the link between the self and the deity which, following the break, undergoes a veritable "uprooting"[23] from the earthly world: there is thus a passage from a world where everything refers to a god, i.e. to a meaning other than and external to the self, to a world in which the signs of the deity disappear and the idea that the divine reveals itself in our world appears even incomprehensible (Scruton, 2015).

The second form of break concerns the link between the self and the community, that is to say that social space where the individual defined his identity by virtue of his belonging to a group, which in turn qualified itself in the light of a sacred and divine foundation. The community guaranteed the condition of a belief shared among its members and sustained the biographical paths of the latter. Thus, if the distancing of the individual from the community, which has occurred in the disenchantment, has on the one hand enabled the modern man to recognize himself and assert himself as a single, unique individual, on

---

22   These are aspects amply discussed by Habermas (1986). According to the author, the decentralization of the religious vision of the world, and the freeing of the vital world from a highly dogmatic dimension, open for the individual the possibility of clarifying and verifying in first person the reasons on which the various "claims to validity" rest, thus allowing the production of a criticisable understanding. Disenchantment of the world thus has the merit of opening up a new potential of rationality in the vital world; a positively qualified rationality which is distinguished from the instrumental one by the fact of being oriented to understanding and founded on an interpersonal relationship.

23   The term takes up A. Bilgrami's expression "*deus deracinus*", which puts the accent on the act of eradicating the divine roots from the world, which, as a result, becomes an ugly, desacralized place (Warner *et al.*, 2013).

the other hand it has transformed the construction of the identity into a burdensome task, to be achieved in spite of the dissolution of the community.

A third form concerns the link between the self and the other person, in other words the social relationship. Disenchantment, in fact, if taken to its extreme consequences, requires total autonomy from the "buffered" self, which must erect barriers against everything that escapes its control. The link with the other becomes devoid of usefulness in the eyes of a person who considers reality from the point of view of a calculating rationality; thus, in the majority of cases, the other ends up as an obstacle to modern man's project of autonomy and independence.

The process of rationalization intertwines with disenchantment. It consists in a movement of a historical nature towards a progressive predomination of the instrumental, calculating attitude, with respect to action oriented to value and meanings.

In other words, among all the possible ways of relating to reality, what is progressively affirmed in modernity is a rational view of the world, based principally on scientific knowledge and technological control (Inglehart, Norris, 2004). At this point, it appears evident that modern man, moved by that quest for comprehension, participation and action that has been freed in disenchantment, chooses to avail himself of this worldview, which rationally explains every event, including those linked to the religious phenomenon. With the consequent refusal of all contents and meanings that do not fall within the criteria of instrumental rationality in the strict sense, and which in the eyes of the disenchanted man therefore appears devoid of meaning: in the case of religion, the dimensions of mystery and grace, which by definition cannot be explained in rational terms, are excluded.

From the process of disenchantment and rationalization "cross-pressures" unfold, which influence the religious experience. We shall dwell in particular on some of them: the subjectivization of this experience, with its positive and the more problematic aspects; the question of social bonds; the change of the relationship between transcendence and immanence.

4.1 The Challenge of Subjectivity and the Question of the Fluctuating Religion

In many European countries, as already mentioned, the disenchantment of the world has implied a loss of significance of traditional religions or, in some cases, a sort of ex-culturation of Christianity (e.g. in France) as stated by Hervieu-Leger (1986) or, more in general, a sort of de-Christianization of the European context (Lehmann, 1997). The shrinking of the space occupied by the more institutionalized religions has been accompanied by a widening of the space in which individuals, with different levels of freedom, have renegotiated their religious beliefs, in favor of a less strong bound to dogmas and social ties.

These processes pose some challenges, in particular to religious institutions, to the way in which they propose religious practice, to their ability to seek mediations between the more institutionalized dimension and the more subjective one of belief, considering that religion continues to be an important point of reference. At the same time, however, also at a level of religious experience we see the same loosening and weakening of bonds that runs through the wider social life, and individuals often abandon themselves to the continuous fluctuation of things, up to the experience of insignificance that leads them to pursue consistent reasons for going forward by resorting to the numinous. So if on the one hand there emerges a quest for greater subjectivity in living the religious experience also with reference to more traditional forms of affiliation, on the other hand, what is sought continuously within religious experience is the uniqueness of one's own self, its sacrality, according to individualized paths also in the direction of "alternative spiritualities".

As far as the first aspect is concerned –the relationship between the institutionalized dimension and the more subjective dimension of faith– we are dealing with an equilibrium that is always difficult to maintain. It concerns the relationship between "religion" and "religiosity". In this respect, it is useful to refer to another classical sociologist, G. Simmel, who –unlike his contemporaries Weber and Durkheim– more than focusing on the modern process of secularization, approaches religion starting precisely from the personal experience that individuals make of it. For Simmel, religiosity is the space in which the subject gathers himself with respect to the mystery, it is the place where the center of the individual safeguards itself, i.e. the opening towards the transcendence; religion instead is the objectivated historic form that emerges from the continuous interaction over time of a plurality of persons. Religion is therefore concerned with the collective cultural translation of religiosity; it takes shape through the organizational modes of religiosity.[24]

A problematic aspect of religion is, in Simmel's view, the tendency to unify the religious behaviors of its adepts around norms considered universal to be applied homogeneously to everyone. This has led, over time, to ignore all the more personal dimension of religious experience and –in the more specific case of Christianity– of the concept of salvation, i.e. of the dimension

---

24   Simmel overturns the usual concept, whereby religion must already be present in order for religiosity to arise, and states that "religion does not create religiosity but religiosity creates religion" (1997: 150).

questioning individuality. And it has led to a failure to consider adequately the importance of cultivating one's own talent, demanding uniform behavior from all instead of drawing on the uniqueness of each person. According to Simmel, if God, for the believer, is placed at the center of existence of the human being, then He is not counterposed to his individuality. Therefore, religiosity constitutes a space where the subject protects his experience of transcendence even from the possible absorption of religious structures. Subjectivity is always a subjectivity in relation to another you, beyond self, the world, history, the divine.[25] For Simmel, safeguarding the person does not in fact mean opting for the absence of organized forms. With reference to the religious sphere, he points out that one of the functions formerly carried out by the Church was to assert the value of the person as unmistakably unique. The point is that, as happens for all instituted social forms, also religious ones can threaten to monopolize the people, thus pushing them to realize their identity outside them. This has negative implications for religion itself: the latter –as Simmel predicted in the early 1900s– risks retreating into the private, losing the possibility of representing a "*Heimat*" for even the most individualized believer. In this way, the Churches themselves, as institutions placed at the service of the perpetuation of the faith over time, and the mediation of the contents of belief are weakened, as they are sustained by believing persons.

Religiosity and religion interpenetrate, in a constantly dynamic equilibrium: religiosity constitutes the beginning of renewal of religion that remains a significant source of symbolic values also for social life. In order to prevent the breakup of religion, Simmel considers it as necessary to create spaces where the heritage of tradition is placed more in relation to the recipients, to their needs, thus recognizing the possibility of a personal, creative contribution.

So on the one hand, disenchantment causes us to continually rethink the relationship between the more institutionalized dimension of belief and subjective experience, so that the two poles coexist and supplement each other, but on the other, disenchantment that absolutizes and strengthens itself in the increasingly technical, nihilistic and fragmented cultural frame of contemporary societies, may lead to the construction of that "God of one's own" of which Beck speaks. With this definition he indicates a religious where "a God of one's own might well be template for a life or a space of one's own" allowing the

---

25   Simmel is in fact critical towards the absolutization of the modern process of individualization that leads to the impoverishment of the subject because the subject comes to find himself without bonds, without the world – an abstract Ego. This dualism that runs through the modern subject threatens to eclipse its original duality; the subject is, for Simmel, a "whole man", i.e. both an individual in himself, peculiar, and an individual projected outside himself, social (Martinelli, 2014).

subject to construct his own "sacred canopy" (Beck, 2010: 14, 16).[26] The "God of one's own" is, in fact, a god with whom one intimately interacts into the daily experience of human life, beyond the religious dictates and dogmas. However, this "God of one's own" tends to become "a commonplace, banal and trivial. It has been devalued by endless repetition. No distinction is made any longer between God and idols. We move in a world of multi-faith quotations whose source and meaning we do not know"; it is sufficient to look through "a catalogue destined for the New Age market – for the God of our own choosing has become venal" (*Ibidem*: 13). That "God of one's own" becomes a god filtered by the awareness about our own life, knowledge, a god similar to us and reflecting our own image: it is the individual that builds his own religious cover and decides his own faith. This is an attitude that does not exclude the adherence to a doctrine or a Church: the individualistic forms of affiliation to religion are in fact numerous, as long as subjectivity desired. This shapes a fluctuating religiosity, where religious faith can freely be conveyed, like any other content, provided that it does not require any privileges. In the *mare magnum* of cultural resources made available in the mediatized aesthetic space, there is also the religion as a symbolic resource equivalent to many others.

Heelas and Woodhead (2005), in considering the relationship between religion and spirituality –which in Europe, unlike the USA, implies a progressive marginalization of religion by spirituality– argue that, despite the indicators of secularization, the sacred does not disappear but is redefined in tune with the massive "subjective turn" of modern culture described then by Taylor: this "subjective turn" is a turn to subjective-life, a life lived in deep connection with the unique experience of the self in relation to one's own emotions and passions, which shape a subjective life-spirituality.

Within this orientation, it is not to be excluded that a breach may open to the return of the numinous (Casement, Tracey, 2006), until religious experience undergoes torsions approaching the neo-magical. Paradoxically, the disenchantment is countered by forms of re-enchantment with the world. The neo-magical attitude uses religious forms to promote an optimistic relationship with reality.[27] Magic has its own functionality, because it reintegrates the

---

26   The term "sacred canopy" used by Beck is taken from a famous Berger's text (Berger, 1967).
27   As Malinowski wrote, "the function of magic is to ritualize man's optimism to enhance his faith in the victory of hope over fear. Magic expresses the greater value for man of confidence over doubt, of steadfastness over vacillation, of optimism over pessimism" (1948: 70).

individual into some system of values without binding it to Churches (De Martino, 1962): each one tries in fact to propitiate the positive forces to his own advantage. In this frame, contemporary individualism marries easily with neo-magical attitudes while religion tends to produce communities. In full conformity with the contemporary consumeristic culture, the reference to magic satisfies the need for immediate solutions and a low acceptance of normativity. It dissolves the complex link of the relationship with God, with the other and the community, paradoxically reinforcing the technical-rational dimension of collective life, within which the otherness becomes abstract.

In conclusion, disenchantment produces cross pressures, sometimes contradictory ones, on the religious experience: on the one hand, it pushes for a useful revision of the relationship between the personal experience of the faith *and* the order of instituted forms; on the other hand, a greater subjectivization of the religious experience can mean a total unbalancing on the individual side which produces by itself what to believe in, within a fluctuating, basically immanent religion.

4.2   *Reconstruction of Bonds and Emergence of Closed Communities*

The weakening of bonds brought about by disenchantment produces unexpected side effects. On the one hand, the "buffered Self" becomes effectively able to keep under control, even manipulate and construct, wider and wider portions of reality, but on the other there grows a sense in him of insecurity and disorientation, produced precisely by the different forms of break carried out. In fact, the bond, while forming a constraint in some senses, is in other senses a promise of support to the individual in his biographical path.

Not relying, instead, on a network of bonds (whether with the deity, the community or the other) that confers a meaning to existence, the modern man, disorientated, exposes himself to numerous options that post-secular society places before him: "at one moment, we understand our situation as one of high tragedy, alone in a silent universe, without intrinsic meaning, condemned to create value (...) a flattened world, in which there aren't very meaningful choices because there aren't crucial issues" (Taylor, 1991: 68).

In this disorientation, a question of rooting emerges: it often goes in the opposite direction to systematic eradication, to eclectic nomadism, to the aimless wandering and pure universalism celebrated by contemporary culture. It expresses a need of identification with something: a demand that goes in the direction of communities considered to be salvific. Not by chance, in the age of individualism, which already the classics of sociology thought to become more and more unbridled, there is an increase in the fusional forms of community and the so-called "gated communities".[28] The more the process of demolition of the real and of meanings advances, the more a space is created for the search for a new foundation, understood as something solid to be subtracted from the discussion and from the insubstantiality to which the whole existence seems to be subjected. In this line, religion – together with other references, such as territory, ethnicity and tradition – belongs to those distinctive elements that are not suspected of being affected by the virus of fragmentation: religion becomes a powerful bond, able to contain and counter the crumbling of social bonds and cultures. It becomes a particularly strong reference for reaffirming some roots that allow some form of personal and collective identification, in the face of relativism and chaos.

Thus, wishing to recover what has been lost, it is done with the idea of ordering the world in a fundamental difference between a "we" and a "you", between an inside and an outside. And when the "sacred" comes on the scene, religion can even acquire radical, fundamentalist features, without excluding violence through organized groups.[29]

Religion is once again subjected to cross pressures: on the one hand it can provide that "*Heimat*" that the believer seeks in order to be able to give a meaningful direction to his experience, but on the other hand it lends itself easily to being made to coincide with a reassuring element for the individual identity and a fundamental answer to the need for protection from the threat of insignificance. And if religion has often surfaced in forms of creative and collective resilience to the problems produced by the dominant model of development or of critical protest for a forward-projected social redemption, it is here evoked as a compensatory refuge, functioning as a protected technique mediating values (De Martino, 1958). In this frame, the values that religion serves to mediate are those originating particularly from tradition. Religion is thus reduced to becoming a bulwark to keep itself firmly in the past, even though it competes with other repertories that contradict it (in particular the media), with no concern over the fact that the values of which it makes itself a bearer are often only affirmed in words but belied in facts.

---

28   Among others, refer to Bauman (2001) who defines this kind of aggregation "peg communities", i.e. spaces where people seek pegs on which they can together hang their fears and anxieties.

29   The relationship between the sacred and religion is, as is known, a theme that recurs constantly in literature as in social life; it is particularly delicate because, precisely in the name of the sacred, religion takes on and justifies violent features (among others, see in particular the work of R. Girard, for example 1972, 1982; for a recent research into the matter, with reference to the European context, see Lanzetti, 2018).

According to the data mentioned before provided by Pew Research Center and concerning Europe, a tendency emerges to use religion as a symbolic repertoire useful to assert an (alleged) identity and to oppose what is "different" (the latter typically represented by the immigrant). The data show, for example, a greater frequency of negative opinions among believers (both practicing and non-practicing) towards other religions, especially Islam. This raises a number of thorny questions, such as the one relating to the meaning of "Christian identity" and, consequently, to the role of religious contents and the relationship between religion and culture.[30]

In this connection, Brubaker (2016) speaks of a "reactive Christian identity" to indicate how the topic of Christian religious identity has become a question around which many other questions raise in secularized Europe – such as the defense of individual rights (freedom of expression, individual autonomy, gender equality, toleration of homosexuality etc.) that are perceived to be threatened by the settling in one's own territory of cultural and religious groups considered to be anti-modern.[31] Those who consider themselves as believing Christians and, in particular, non-practicing, call for a reduction in immigration to Europe more easily than do the "nones", especially if they come from the Middle East and sub-Saharan Africa. Brubaker sees an "assertive secularism" which, unlike the "militant secularism" understood historically as opposition to institutional power and the influence of the authority of the Church, is now aimed against Muslim immigrants and their descendants: this is a tendency which, in the author's view, concerns especially some populist movements, which appeal to religion in defense of the West, although what they are interested in is not religious values in the strict sense.

As it has often happened in history, religion becomes a cultural badge used in defense of questions that in reality are not closely connected with religious contents (in this case, the Christian ones). The process of "culturalization" of religion is pursued, again according to Brubaker, for a dual gain. On the one hand, it allows Christianity to have a position of privilege as "culture" within a context –the secularized European one– in which it has lost that privilege as a religion, given the liberal State's commitment to neutrality in religious matters. On the other, it enables minority religious practices, redefined as cultural, to be restricted in a way that would not be possible, given the option of liberal States toward religious freedom.

---

30   For a detailed account of related ethical issues, see Chapter 2.
31   The encounter, or the confrontation, between Christianity and Islam is often reduced to a pair of concepts: liberal and illiberal, individualistic and collectivist, democratic and authoritarian, modern and retrograde, secular and religious.

Roy (2016) takes up a similar position when he states that European Christianity, from being a faith with its rites and practices, has become a mere cultural badge that easily risks degenerating into a neo-ethnic badge with closures towards the outside. In this frame, the continuity between Christianity in Europe and modern secularism is no longer based on values considered universal and felt to be common to both positions. If we wish to speak of continuity, this is built, if anything, around the idea of identity: the Christian identity is understood in a merely "cultural" sense, excluding the religious values in the strict sense from those that are instead defined as "European values", made to coincide mostly with individual rights.

As highlighted by various scholars of religion, where religion, for one reason or another, has been historically "culturalized", in reality it is no longer a religion, but something else, thus also compromising the conditions for a balanced religious pluralism, given that religions end up competing miserably with one another rather than allying themselves around common, shared questions, therefore nurturing the fundamentalist traits that are hidden in each of them (Soeffner, 2014).

The questions are very complex. The breaking of intersubjective and social bonds produces cross-pressures on the religious experience, in the direction of exasperating the search for strong bonds, reassuring identity, not without the danger that religious groups take on radical traits. On the other hand, however, this shows that the individual without ties is an abstraction and that he therefore seeks a position within significant relational networks.

In this sense, the search for ties finds, in belonging to religious groups, a pertinent response to this need, given that the religious dimension is a profound element of the believer's identity and lifestyle, with positive effects on social coexistence when the form of these aggregations is peaceful. It would suffice to mention, among the many experiences of this kind, the case of the so-called "ethnic" communities and missions made up of immigrants, present in many European cities with reference to the Christian context or, in the case of the other religions, the numerous places of worship and the cultural associations that have an explicit reference to religion. In particular, the ethnic missions have a long history in Europe following the large-scale migrations in the second post-war period: suffice it to think of the case of the Italian, Spanish and Portuguese migrants in the cities of Central and Northern Europe where, in many cases, they favored routes of integration not counterposed with the local host society.[32] Their role is to provide places of worship but also of

---

32   Among the numerous studies on the subject, see: Prencipe, 2010 and, with reference to
       the European case as a whole Tassello *et al.*, 2011. For the Italian case, see, among others:
       Golinelli, 2011; Ambrosini, 2016; Ambrosini *et al.*, 2018.

assistance, education, solidaristic commitment and production of culture.[33] These structures can carry out an important task of "ferrying" into the local ecclesial communities, after offering the possibility, for an initial or more prolonged period, of expressing themselves in their own language and according to the traditions of their communities of origin. As to the risk of a possible retreat within their ethnic, cultural and religious communities, there is also a tendency, if and where present in the arrival society, to consider migrations as a transitory phenomenon and religion as a parallel element in relation to the immigrants' experiences. In this case, the result is often a limited adaptation and a poor inclusion by the migrants into the structures of the host society. On the contrary, where the presence and religious experience of the migrants are considered as structural phenomena of the host society and as a vital and vitalizing part of the activity of the Churches and local religious groups, virtuous processes are set in motion with positive side effects, insisting on the value of the religion in relation also to broader social ties.[34]

4.3   *Transcendence and Immanence*

The effect of the interweaving between disenchantment and rationalization is the detachment between immanence and transcendence. If indeed the man of the Middle Ages or, as Taylor puts it, the man of Latin Christianity considered the two polarities only simultaneously, because every immanent occurrence could not have an autonomous significance but had a transcendent foundation, for the disenchanted man this co-presence has become inconceivable. The disenchanted view of the world is based on the assumption that no immanent phenomenon can at the same time have a transcendent foundation, because otherwise it would escape the control of man; on the contrary, it must be possible to explain everything rationally.

The gradual unfolding of a technical society pushes decidedly towards the immanent option. This type of society –leaning on individualization and fragmentation of social bonds, economic and financial expansion, technological progress and bureaucratization, detachment between functions and meanings– has legitimized itself thanks to its capacity to increase the possibilities in a constant, ever-greater manner, together with the predictability of what occurs, and to overcome the limits posed by the institutions and the culture with their constraints of place, memory, meanings and values. In this model, on the one hand there arises the individual; on the other, the increasingly

---

33   See in this connection the research as to the role of religion in the process of integration of migrants into the new cultural context contained in Part 4, where it is also stated how religion-, faith-based organizations contribute to integration and social cohesion.

34   Refer to the experience described in Chapter 16.

systemic organization that responds to the growing demand for individualization. For the system, the individual is a bearer of needs to be satisfied: for the
individual, the system is the interlocutor that must guarantee the maximum
individualization by reducing social obligations to the minimum. As in a circuit that continuously feeds itself, individualization reinforces the process of
technicalization of society. The growing demand for subjectivity coming from
individuals in the advanced societies is satisfied (at least this is the dominant
assumption) through the increase in the systemic power, able to broaden the
instruments infinitely, beyond the meanings.

The technical element is one of the factors that give shape to post-secular
society by acting within it; it is what has been increasingly raised to a system
shaping a technical society (Magatti, 2018). Disenchantment and rationalization thus reach unheard levels in the age of techno-science, where the pervasive
capacity to increase the possibilities without limit requires the individuals to
remain continually open. Transcendence is exchanged precisely with this unconditional opening to new possibilities here and now.[35] It is as if the opening
of man to the beyond were shifted onto a completely horizontal axis, nevertheless able to play this immanence in a highly dynamic way. It is indeed an insistent immanence that candidates itself to give rapid, relevant answers regarding
people's existence, if we think of the role acquired by consumption, and of the
capacity of technical systems to give solutions to day-to-day problems and to
the possibilities of optimization and manipulation of reality (and life), up to the
hypothesis of overcoming the fragility and mystery because they are in contradiction with the efficiency, predictability, performativity required by contemporary capitalism. Significantly, already W. Benjamin defined modern capitalism
as a "religion" because it "serves essentially to allay the same anxieties, torments,
and disturbances to which the so-called religions offered answers" (2103: 59).

In this frame, the strong material component is more and more preponderant. All this, however, has increased the need to draw on an immaterial dimension. In part, this need has been intercepted and incorporated by capitalism
itself which, above all, with marketing, has understood how to recover a sort of
reference to the immaterial (Baudrillard, 1976), in order to respond apparently
to the "spiritual" needs of individuals, but transforming them into something
else, more in line with its own project.[36]

---

35   Past and future are swallowed up in an eternal present celebrated as the only time exist-
      ing: the perception of continuity, that is of the dynamic and processual nature of time,
      breaks down. As argued by Hervieu-Léger, in contemporary society we observe a situation
      brought about by the pure and simple disappearance of every memory that is not imme-
      diate and functional (1993).

36   As stated by Boltanski and Chiapello (1999), what distinguishes capitalism is its ability to
      intercept the reactions towards it by transforming them so as to be able to incorporate

Beyond consumption, the thrusts in the direction of the immaterial are channeled into other orientations, such as the myth of the "return to origins" which animates some of today's ecological movements, or the logic of giving and sharing proposed in various forms in contemporary societies, especially through the use of Web platforms.

On the more strictly religious front, we may think of the moments of ritual that persist even though they seem out of time in the eyes of contemporary culture. Often considered to be the heart of religiosity, such practices – inevitable exposed to the cross pressures that we are discussing– are in danger of losing their specificity, that is their being the possible point of encounter between immanence and transcendence, and of posing, by virtue of this nature, a correspondence between daily life and faith, between an earthly time and an eternal one, between the single person and the community. Different scholars have documented the crisis of such rites and religious practices, reduced to mechanisms emptied of meaning. On closer examination, however, this crisis is actually present but is only one side of the coin. The other side suggests that we investigate more thoroughly, what it means to live religious practice today with all its complement of reference beyond the immanence that envelops daily life, demanding directly to the only person who can speak of such a personal experience: the one who lives it in the first person.[37]

Each of these phenomena of orientation to the immaterial is one of those signs of transcendence and constitutes a laceration of that immanent framework which, according to Taylor, overshadows post-secular society. The complete realization of that framework would lead to what Taylor calls "a purely self-sufficient humanism (...) a humanism accepting no final goals beyond human flourishing, not any allegiance to anything else beyond this flourishing. Of no previous society was this true" (2007: 31).

Between immanentistic and disenchanted tendencies, on the one hand, and re-enchantment phenomena on the other, the search for an immaterial dimension (expressed in different ways) and the persistence of the religious phenomenon in its appeal to transcendence contribute to keeping the immanent framework open and not saturated. If this were not so, societies would implode and people would be impoverished of that freedom that arises from distancing themselves from the saturation typical of technical societies, regulated by the logic of functionality: through this distance, individuals are able to access universes of meaning.

---

them. And, significantly, Pine and Gilmore speak of an "economy of experiences" to underline how also the emotional component is incorporated in the ambits susceptible to entering into the circuit of economic valorisation (2000).

37   Useful in this direction is the work described in Parts 3, 4, and 5 of this book.

5   Conclusive Considerations: Some Issues Related to the Migration
         Processes

In this chapter, starting from the literature and from some empirical observations, we have analyzed the secularizing tendencies at work in modernity and
contemporaneity, in the light of some effects produced by them within society.
More in particular, we focused on "post-secular society" – a society in which
the religious experience finds itself in the midst of disenchanting tendencies
without, however, definitively succumbing to them. What has changed in it are
the conditions of belief and the ways in which we have access to the contents
of faith.

We have thus spoken of the emergence of a new demand for subjectivity
within the religious experience, which represents a challenge for the religious
institutions in their knowing how to place themselves in our time, and simultaneously provokes problematic torsions at the limit of religion itself. We have
then focused on the weakening of social bonds, which exposes the individual
to new forms of religious aggregation with closed and sometimes radical traits,
whilst bringing with itself the need for community inherent in the individual.
And we have seen the tendency to adopt a rationalized view of reality that
questions the dimension of meaning and conflicts with the religious view in its
opening to the transcendence.

The outlook of "post-secular" society suggests that we do not consider such
tendencies as a sign indicating an eclipse of religion from social and individual
life and, consequently, its possible return after a period of absence: the real
circumstance, the starting point for the present reflection about secularization, suggests considering that secularization and religious experience, in other terms modernity (or late-modernity) and religion, do not completely exclude one another.

The scenario of European "post-secular societies", that complex set of secularizing pressures and tendencies moving in the opposite direction as well as
cross pressures within it affecting religious experience, subjecting it to new
challenges whose conclusion is not foregone, constitutes the frame within
which immigration takes place and within which Europe itself is challenged. It
is challenged also by migrations to overcome the unresolved, ambivalent tension between the techno-economicism of its politics (especially those related
to the migration of labor) and its philosophy of rights (among which there is
religious freedom) and solidarity embedded in its foundation project.[38]

---

38   For a useful analysis of the challenge of migration "in a Janus-Faced Europe", and the os-
      cillation of Europe between positions of openness and closure, pluralism and uniformity,
      see Zanfrini, 2019.

In some respects, the plural scenario of the European post-secular societies is shaped also by the presence of migrants: the believers with a migration background contribute to shaping the variegated religious landscape, and to the reconsideration of questions set aside following the processes of secularization, even if only for the fact that they make the religious phenomenon more "visible" within European societies by placing at the center issues linked to freedom and human rights.

In the final stage, we shall mention two questions emerging in post-secular society, solicited *also*, though not only, by the presence of migrants. We refer in particular to religious pluralism and the role of religion in the public area. These are nodes around which unsolved questions and ambivalences of globalization and secularization condense, but also complex challenges in the direction of a re-opening of the horizon with respect to a society that wishes to question itself, beyond the mere technical function, on meanings of human coexistence.

5.1 The Challenge of Religious Pluralism

Religious pluralism constitutes the proof that the dream –fed by globalizing tendencies– of a world without differences has not come true. All the migrations –closely connected with the phenomenon of globalization– have contributed to profound changes from a cultural and religious point of view. Not, however, in the sense of a fusion that homologates singularities but in the sense of a coexistence of different religious alternatives. In fact, although the nation States have for a long time tried to impose some homogeneity also from a religious point of view, so as to guarantee social cohesion, the international migratory processes have sustained religious pluralism (Saunders *et al.*, 2016). This is particularly true in the case of Europe, where diversity based on religion is one of the most challenging (Zanfrini, 2019).

If we wished to find a point of contact between religious pluralism and the aspirations of globalization, it would concern the deconstruction of dominant value references. From this point of view, religious pluralism lends itself well to a society where the individual dimension is increasingly preponderant over the collective dimension. Although every religion always tries to meet a need for belonging, the plurality of alternatives has been interpreted as a way to satisfy the need of individuals, especially of the contemporary individuals, to choose – Berger defines this need as "heretical imperative" (Berger, 1979) – and to shape with one's own hands one's personal spiritual and religious path. In this regard, often pluralism is simply confused with a veritable "do-it-yourself religion" (Lucà Trombetta, 2004) put together by the individual who draws on different religious options: it runs the risk of ambiguity, overlapping with relativism.

In the framework of European religious pluralism, migrants themselves can undergo the influences of the tendencies of individualism and subjectivism. One's religious orientation –which in the case of migrants is often decisive in defining personal and social identities– can therefore weaken, or radicalize by reaction, or can be renegotiated with the context and take on a new form.

On the front of the processes of secularization, religious pluralism produces two effects. On the one hand it belies the "classical" hypotheses of secularization whereby the religious phenomenon, reacting to changes in modernity and in the globalizing dynamics, would simply wither away – or, in the more normative theses would *have to* wither away. On the other hand, pluralism constitutes a challenge for the more traditional kinds of religion and for the characteristics presented by such religions: the integrity and solidity given by the internal consistency and by the constancy of individual paths; the presence of a strong collective and community dimension, and of dogmas and doctrines stable over time, of a univocal truth bringing salvation, and a consolidated ritual dimension. Also in this case there emerges an underlying ambiguity of religious pluralism, which on the one hand nourishes the religious impulses, but on the other undermines the more traditional forms. This ambiguity cannot be resolved on a theoretical level but must be observed in the concrete of the experiences of individuals and groups. Undoubtedly, some European contexts form an interesting framework for analyzing these processes, because they are contexts with the strong presence of a historical religion (Christianity) in its most evident institutional form. At the same time, they are challenged to rediscover more deeply the contents of their faith, which often contemplates, already in itself, a dimension of opening and plural encounter. This, for historical events (not least the difficulty precisely in facing modernity) and for contingent needs, has been put in the background with the danger, moreover, of weakening the potentialities inherent to religion itself. Pluralism therefore also constitutes a chance where it becomes a reason for a deeper knowledge of its own religious contents.[39]

In addition to the more traditional religions, it is important to acknowledge the presence of other religions, such as the oriental ones –Buddhism and Hinduism–, New Age and the New Religious movements. These, too, reflect the role of migrations and, although their diffusion varies from country to country, their presence is evident also because of media support – an example is the renowned achieved by the Soka Gakkai or by Scientology in the media sphere.

---

39   Significant in this sense is the Synodal process experienced in the Diocese of Milan: it has contributed to the deeper understanding by believers (both native and immigrants) of the content of their faith (see again Chapter 16).

These religions are different from the traditional western ones and can often be translated into forms of alternative spirituality rather than true paths of faith – in some cases, in the concrete of the experience of the single individuals, they can be reduced to simple practices or philosophies of life. In this sense, they are difficult to perceive as a menace for Europeans, who on the contrary are curious about these currents running through the pluralism of the western world.

In considering the possible configurations of the relations between Europeans and migrants, it therefore becomes necessary to specify first of all what types of religion enter into relation with one another through people. In addition, the "Christian" population is in reality very varied internally, as an effect of the dynamics above outlined which shape multiple paths: there are those who feel they simply belong to a cultural form; those who adhere for personal belief; those who declare themselves to be convinced Christians but practice intermittently; those who say they are Christian in their own way and adhere to Christianity selectively.[40]

And if, on the one hand, Europeans consider the increase in religious pluralism as a source of cultural enrichment, on the other hand pluralism is interpreted as a cause of conflict if not as even a threat to the identity, especially in relation to Islam – a religion which, though limited in percentage terms, has seen a growing diffusion as a result of migratory flows. The level of mistrust has increased following terrorist attacks in Europe. However, on a different level, the difficulties in reconciling radically different worldviews and ways of thinking of individual and social life often reach public debate: the possibility of building mosques, whether or not to remove the crucifix from state schools, the use of the veil are some such examples. In these debates, religion– differently from expectations– enters significantly into the public scene. And the public sphere takes on a crucial role in shaping the integration processes of migrants; it can direct the interpretations but above all the states of mind towards immigrants, just as it can decide to throw light on some phenomena and leave others in the shadow – for example, the fact that in the European territory there are integrated second generations of immigrants, just as there are native Europeans who have converted to Islam.

In the plural religious framework, the encounter and/or the confrontation occur within a context that, in the wake of disenchantment and rationalization,

---

40   See, for example, for the case of Italy and Catholicism, the research on young generations realized by Bichi and Bignardi (2015); and with reference to migrations (with a high Christian and Catholic internal component) and, more in particular, to the second generation, see Bichi *et al.* (2018).

has accentuated some aspects of collective life, at the expense of other dimensions. And, in this context, religion can acquire a crucial position because it is not equivalent to functional and technocratic views of reality but raises questions of meaning regarding social life and the human condition.

5.2   Religions as "Anti-environments"

J. Habermas, in his extensive research into the public sphere, has come to identify precisely in religion the models of language and meaning that allow us to name experiences, relationships, history, the world, and hence interpret what otherwise would probably remain unexpressed.

This leads us to the point on the *role of religion* in the public sphere, which calls into question, more broadly, the meaning of "*laïcité*", on the one hand, and the task of religion in general, on the other.

As far as "*laïcité*" is concerned, the French Revolution has bequeathed to us the notion of *laïcité* to be understood as that condition in which non-religious thought finds its place and legitimacy in a world dominated by the stance defined by the institutionalized Church. From here, given the formation of the State according to the idea of *laïcité*, what takes shape is the effort to retain the influence of religion within well-defined borders, by relegating it to the private space. However, the question arises whether, in a social world organized around the global technical system and surrounded by an "a purely self-sufficient humanism", where the human dimension of social life is marginalized, it is the right time to review the conception of *laïcité*, as it often ends in "laicism".

The French philosopher Henri Bergson focused on the ways in which religion, precisely because it is embodied in historical processes, experiences the internal dialectic between openness and closure, between conservation and prophecy. This dialectic, while continuously threatening to render religion organic with the status quo, also enables the continuous evocation of new energies for critical and creative innovation.

In such a direction, religion represents one of the few experiences able to oppose the "purely self-sufficient humanism" that is deeply embedded in our times. A useful idea to capture the potential role of religion is that of the "anti-environment" – a concept used by McLuhan (1964, 1967), which we adapt here to our subject. Within a social context deeply marked by the pervasiveness of rationalization and disenchantment, combined with technical systems constituting the "environment" of our whole individual and social life, "anti-environments" are worth a lot, as they shape a space able to activate some antidotes to the technocratic, homologating colonization of human life. Religion could be one of these "anti-environments"; others are certainly conceivable (i.e. education, arts, etc.).

By reopening the question of meaning in relation to existence together with the meanings and forms of the human condition, this "anti-environment" is extremely relevant for the freedom of everyone, believers and non-believers. In a world that threatens to collapse on itself, in which technique has no counterweights and reality is confused with individualized points of view, this environment is a valuable bulwark of freedom precisely in redesigning the reference to "transcendence" – a term which describes not only the human openness to a God, a divine otherness, but also a domain of awareness, of openness to the mystery of the other or of creative principles that humans can access in order to receive guidance in relation to sense-making. Transcendence allows us to distance ourselves from historical configurations that are built on an "a purely self-sufficient humanism" pestered by the expansion of technocracy. That idea about transcendence can play a crucial role in stimulating profound processes of social transformation. In such a frame, religion could be considered as a "sacred space of the infinite", as it is able to safeguard human openness to the unexpected and the otherness, and to shape humanly-practicable paths, interweaving the material dimension with the sense-making demands, the finite and the infinite (Magatti, Martinelli, 2012).

Therefore, starting from the important recognition of keeping open the question of meaning, which is strongly related to freedom, it is possible to redefine the issue that historically has gone under the name of "*laïcité*", going beyond the "immanent frame" which shaped –as Taylor highlights– the social imaginary that arose during the Enlightenment, as people started trying to conceptualize society in self-subsistent terms, which is to say in a way that does not presuppose the existence of a transcendent spiritual reality and does not admit the human possibility to be resilient to defined social patterns.

The assertion of secularization, according to which religion is only a private matter, denies the fact that all societies –even though in different ways– have questioned themselves about the issue of the infinite. Simply because such a question –whatever the answer– concerns the human condition. Of course, this opens up important questions regarding the public sphere and its reorganization. The history of modernity bequeaths to us the awareness that no religion (as well as no ideology, culture or tradition) can reasonably expect to exhaust the universal breadth of human experience. And yet, this does not mean that it is not worth taking into account the great religious traditions as worthy spaces for building a richer social world and, therefore, one more suitable for human condition. The recognition of the collective value of the "sacred space of the infinite", for example, may create a more favorable condition for the development of the intercultural and interreligious dialogue that is a current human imperative of our time and that may be deployed not only horizontally – among different conceptions of values– but also vertically, namely by considering the structural openness of the human being to transcendence as an unavoidable feature. It is an openness to which every culture and religion offers answers and different realizations.

This "sacred space of the infinite" includes the religious dimension within the public life not as a compensatory receptacle of those problematic consequences of socio-economic development models that succeed over time. If it were such a receptacle (as it often is), it would be unable to distance itself from the principles of those models. Rather, the "sacred space of the infinite" – precisely through a new understanding of "*laïcité*"– becomes a valuable "anti-environment" that allows us to always reopen the issue of sense about collective living and the plurality of human achievements. Its potentiality comes into play both in challenging dogmatisms that even in a free society eventually rise, and in fighting fundamentalism of religions that becomes more likely the higher the demand for meaning raised by religion is censored.

In conclusion, post-secular society expresses the emergence of a new epoch in relation to the epoch of secularization, a time in which the religious phenomenon is affected by profound changes and does not at all seem doomed to disappear. The challenge is rather to recognize, on the one hand, the new risks punctuating the religious experience and, on the other, to capture the signals, often formless and not yet institutionalized, that open up in post-secular societies, by going in the direction of considering religion –understood as a possible "anti-environment" and a "sacred space of the infinite"– as a sphere that can safeguard dimensions of the human (opening towards transcendence, the central role of meanings, the uniqueness and dignity of the person, the cruciality of bonds and the recognition of the other, the importance of questions such as justice, peace, the safeguard of creation, etc.) which make up a heritage of value for all.

CHAPTER 4

Migration and Religious Freedom: the Legislative and Judicial Framework at International and European Level

Andrea Santini and Monica Spatti

1 Introduction

Despite being a fundamental human right, freedom of religion is still violated in many parts of the world today.* The violation of this right can take on different forms. Sometimes, it simply consists of preventing people from choosing their own religion. More frequently, there are abuses. In some countries people belonging to religious minorities are discriminated and are prohibited to exercise some basic rights such as participating in public elections, applying for jobs or freely circulating in the country. Sometimes religious minorities are subject to detention, torture or other cruel treatments.

These persecutions, which can be of different kind, represent, as described in Chapters 5 and 10, a driving factor of emigration. Indeed, oppressed people try to migrate to a place where they hope to live in peace. Once they left their country of origin, they try to apply to some form of protection from the State they emigrated to. The purpose of this contribution is to verify the conditions under which legal protection can be granted to those individuals who have left their country of origin due to religious persecutions. The research will focus on both international and European law, as well as the relevant case law on the matter. Accordingly, it will be necessary to understand first what freedom of religion is from the point of view of international and European law. Secondly, it will be analyzed what kind of protection can be granted to those people who are leaving their country due to a violation of their freedom of religion.

2 Freedom of Religion or Belief in International and European Law

Freedom of religion or belief is a fundamental right recognized in several sources of international law. It was first proclaimed in art. 18 of the Universal

---

* Although this chapter is the result of common reflections and work, sections 1, 2 and 3 have been drafted by Monica Spatti and sections 4 and 5 by Andrea Santini.

Declaration of Human Rights and then enshrined in several legal acts both binding and not binding, regional[1] and universal.[2] It is worth to recall, in particular, art. 18 of the International Covenant on Civil and Political Rights (ICCPR),[3] and art. 9 of the European Convention on Human Rights (ECHR).[4]

Commonly known as "freedom of religion or belief", the full definition of this human right is "freedom of thought, conscience, religion or belief". Accordingly, it recognizes not only the right to have any religion or belief, but also the right not to profess anyone.[5] The inclusion of freedom of thought and conscience in the definition has the purpose to cover also atheism and not only strictly religious convictions (Evans, 2001: 40). The formula adopted in many legal acts is so wide to include also the right not to reveal religious convictions or beliefs to anyone.[6]

International law does not define what "religion" is. Normally international courts and other bodies in charge of the protection of human rights interpret it in a broad sense. More precisely, the concept of religion cannot be limited to established confessions or those "with institutional characteristics or practices analogous to those of traditional religions".[7] For this reason, international

---

1   Among the human rights regional treaties recognising the right to freedom of religion or belief see: American Convention on Human Rights, San José, 22 November 1969, art. 12; African Charter on Human and People Rights, Nairobi, 27 June 1981, art. 8.

2   Among the universal binding acts see, for example: Convention relating to the Status of Refugees, Geneva, 28 July 1951, art. 4; Convention on the Rights of the Child, New York, 20 November 1989, art. 14; International Convention on the Protection of the Rights of All Migrant Workers and Members of Their Families, New York, 18 December 1990, art. 12. Among the other international acts see, *inter alia*: the Declaration on the Elimination of All Forms of Intolerance and of Discrimination based on Religion of Belief, proclaimed by General Assembly resolution No. 36/55 of 25 November 1981; the Declaration on the Rights of Persons Belonging to National or Ethnic, Religious and Linguistic Minorities, adopted by General Assembly resolution No. 47/135 of 18 December 1992.

3   New York, 16 December 1966.

4   Rome, 4 November 1950.

5   See General Comment No. 22, adopted by the Human Rights Committee on 30 July 1993, para 5. See the following judgements of the European Court of Human Rights: *Kokkinakis v. Greece*, 25 May 1993, par. 31; *Buscarini and others v. San Marino* (GC), 18 February 1999, par. 34; *Alexandridis v. Greece*, 21 February 2008, par. 32.

6   General Comment No. 22, cit., par. 3. See also the European Court of Human Rights' judgements *Sinan Isik v. Turkey*, 2 February 2010, par. 49–52, and *Dimitras and others v. Greece*, 3 June 2013, par. 35.

7   General Comment No. 22, cit., par. 2. The European Court of Human Rights has recognized the guarantees coming from art. 9 ECHR to traditional religions as Alevism (judgement *Izzettin Doğan and others v. Turkey* (GC), 26 April 2016, par. 114), Buddhism (judgement *Jakóbski v. Poland*, 7 December 2010), Hinduism (judgement *Kovalkovs v. Latvia*, 31 January 2012), Islam (judgement *Hassan et Tchaouch v. Bulgaria* (GC), 26 October 2000), Taoism (decision *X. v. United Kingdom*, 18 May 1976), Sikhism (decision *Jasvir Singh v. France*, 30 June 2009), but also

human rights bodies do not distinguish between "religion" and "sect". The European Court of Human Rights has applied art. 9 ECHR regardless any qualification coming from national authorities.[8] The term "belief" has also been interpreted in a wide sense in order to include convictions of non-religious nature, such as pacifism,[9] anti-abortion convictions[10] and vegetarianism.[11] At the same time, the concept of belief is not so broad to include any personal preference. According to the European Court of Human Rights, in order to be protected by the Convention, the personal conviction must have "a certain level of cogency, seriousness, cohesion and importance"[12] (Bielefeldt, 2015: 16–17).

Once defined what freedom of religion or belief is, it is possible to identify two dimensions where it applies: the *forum internum* and the *forum externum*. The *forum internum* regards the internal sphere of the individual and consists of the right to have a freely chosen religion or belief. Accordingly, it cannot be subject to any coercion. The *forum externum* instead consists of the freedom to profess a certain religion or belief. As it may have consequences on the others, it can be subject to limitations. Therefore, freedom of religion is not an unconditional and absolute principle, such as the prohibition of torture and slavery or freedom of opinion. Freedom of religion or belief as prescribed by international law simply implies the prohibition of coercion: no one can be forced to have or adopt a religion against their will.[13]

The right to change religion is the most controversial component of freedom of religion or belief. The *travaux préparatoires* of several treaties reveal that State representatives had passionate debates on the opportunity to recognize the right to change religion. Some countries were openly against it by arguing that it may encourage unwelcome proselytism and undermine national

---

to more recent religions as Aumism of Mandaron (judgement *Association de Chevaliers du Lotus d'Or v. France*, 31 January 2013), Osho (judgement *Mockuté v. Lithuania*, 27 February 2018, par. 121), Mormonisme (judgement *The Church of Jesus Christ of Latter-Day Saints v. United Kingdom*, 4 March 2014), the Raelian movement (decision *F.L. v. France*, 3 November 2005), Jehovah's Witnesses (judgement *Jehovah's Witnesses of Moscow and others v. Russia*, 10 June 2010).

8   The European Court of Human Rights has not excluded from the guarantees coming from art. 9 groups as Scientology (decision *X. and Church of Scientology v. Sweden*, 5 May 1979), druidism (decision *Chappell v. United Kingdom*, 14 July 1987), the "Divine Light Zentrum" (decision *Omkarananda and Divine Light Zentrum v. Switzerland*, 19 March 1981), without investigating their qualifications.

9   European Court decision *Arrowsmith v. United Kingdom*, 16 May 1977.

10   European Court decision *Knudesn v. Norway*, 3 March 1985.

11   European Court decision *w.c. v. United Kingdom*, 10 February 1993.

12   European Court judgement *Campbell and Cosans v. United Kingdom*, 22 March 1983, par. 293.

13   General Comment No. 22, cit., par. 5.

cohesion[14] (Bielefeldt *et al.*, 2016: 57–58). For this reason, while the right to change religion was expressly mentioned in the Universal Declaration on Human Rights and in the ECHR, the ICCPR adopted the more nuanced formula of "religion or belief of one's choice". Despite this reticence, the right to change religion constitutes a necessary component of freedom of religion as underlined by the Human Rights Committee in the General Comment No. 22.

The right to change or abandon a religion is not granted in every country yet. While few governments punish this behavior through criminal sanctions, other countries foresee some other consequences, such as limiting access to education, employment, as well as the right to travel and vote (Bielefeldt *et al.*, 2016). This happens in particular in those States that have an official religion (Bielefeldt *et al.*, 2016). Quite interestingly, international law does not prohibit States to choose an official religion, even if this choice may increase the risk of discriminations and persecutions against minorities.[15] As pointed out by the Human Rights Committee "the fact that a religion is recognized as a State religion (…) or that its followers comprise the majority of the population, shall not result in any impairment of the enjoyment of any of the rights under the Covenant".[16]

The *forum externum* of freedom of religion or belief consists of the right to manifest any religion or belief. This freedom has a private as well as a community dimension, as it protects the manifestation of belief "in worship, observance, practice and teaching" both in public and in private (Clark, Durham, 2015). The collective aspect of freedom of religion or belief gives communities the right to perform "acts integral to the conduct by religious groups of their basic affairs",[17] this including the right to establish places for worship,[18] select and train leaders,[19] establish religious schools, etc. More generally, the right to profess a religion or belief does potentially include a broad range of acts, such as the use of ritual formulas, observance of holidays and of dietary regulations, as well as wearing distinctive clothing.[20]

---

14   The recognition of the right to change religion in art. 18 of the Universal Declaration on Human Rights is the main reason for the abstention of Saudi Arabia at the vote. See A/C.3/SR.289, par. 40–47.

15   According to H. Bielefeldt, 2015: 20 "Freedom of religion or belief, understood as a human right for all without discrimination, can thus become a powerful argument for establishing secular constitutions and secular legal orders".

16   General Comment No. 22, cit., par. 9.

17   Ivi, par. 4.

18   See the judgement of the European Court of Human Rights *Association for Solidarity with Jehovah Witnesses and others v. Turkey*, 24 May 2016, par. 104–108.

19   European Court of Human Rights judgement *Hasan and Chaush v. Bulgaria* (GC), 26 October 2000, par. 85–89.

20   General Comment No. 22, cit., par. 4.

As it has already been said, the right to manifest a religion or belief can be subject to limitations. According to art. 18 (3) ICCPR and art. 9 (2) ECHR, legitimate restrictions must be prescribed by the law and pursue a legitimate aim, such as public safety, public order, health, moral or the protection of rights and freedom of others. Moreover, the restriction is legitimate as long as it is necessary to achieve the defined aim, thus requesting an evaluation of the proportionality of the measure.

Freedom of religion or belief is also recognized within the European Union legal system. From a EU law perspective, this right is directly connected to the values on which the Union is based –such as democracy, the rule of law and respect of human rights– as it contributes to their achievement.[21] In particular, art. 10 of the Charter of Fundamental Rights (CFR) of the European Union presents the same formulation of freedom of religion outlined in art. 9 ECHR.[22] However, art. 10 of the Charter does not provide a specific discipline on the possible limitations of freedom of religion. This depends on the decision of the drafters to introduce a general provision in art. 52 CFR allowing limitations to all rights and freedoms provided by the Charter. According to par. 3 of this provision, in particular, when the Charter contains rights which correspond to the rights guaranteed by the ECHR, "the meaning and scope of those rights shall be the same as those laid down" by the ECHR. As clarified in the explanations relating to the EU Charter of Fundamental Rights, as the right guaranteed in art. 10 (1) CFR corresponds to the right guaranteed in art. 9 of the ECHR, limitations should also comply with the discipline that the latter provision provides on the matter in par. 2.

3 Refugees and the Principle of Non-refoulement

Another important treaty for the protection of freedom of religion or belief is the Geneva Convention on the status of refugees adopted in 1951 (hereinafter: Geneva Convention).[23] It represents the only global treaty protecting people who are escaping from their country of origin due to the risk of serious

---

21 See the EU Guidelines on the promotion and protection of freedom of religion or belief, adopted by the Council of the European Union, 24 June 2013, par. 1.

22 Charter of Fundamental Rights of the European Union, Strasbourg, 12 December 2007.

23 The Geneva Convention is integrated by the Protocol of New York, adopted the 31 January 1967, that removed, for those States that have ratified it, the geographical and temporal restrictions established in the Convention according to which the Geneva Convention applied only to persons who became refugees as a result of events occurring before 1 January 1951 in Europe.

violations of their fundamental rights, including freedom of religion or belief. According to art. 1 (A) (2) of the Geneva Convention, a refugee is someone who

> owing to well-founded fear of being persecuted for reasons of race, religion, nationality, membership of a particular social group or political opinion, is outside the country of his nationality and is unable or, owing to such fear, is unwilling to avail himself of the protection of that country.

The people falling under this definition may obtain the status of refugee if the country where they ask protection has ratified this Convention.[24]

Also the European Union takes care of people obliged to escape from their country of origin. More precisely, Directive 2011/95/EU recognizes two kinds of protection: the "refugee status" and the "subsidiary protection".[25] The definition of refugee outlined in art. 2 (*d*) of the Directive recalls the same formulation adopted by the Geneva Convention, which focuses on the risk of persecution. At the same time, the Directive is more precise as it specifies in details the requirements to be considered a refugee. For example, aside from defining explicitly what acts can be qualified as "persecution" (see *infra* par. 4), art. 10 also explains the possible reasons behind such behavior. Furthermore, it is also interesting for the purpose of this research the fact that art. 10 (1) (*b*) provides a definition of religion: this consisting of "the holding of theistic, nontheistic and atheistic beliefs, the participation in, or abstention from, formal worship in private or in public, either alone or in community with others, other religious acts or expressions of view, or forms of personal or communal conduct based on or mandated by any religious belief". The definition is clearly very wide in accordance with the approach adopted by the treaties on the protection of human rights mentioned above.

Quite interestingly, EU law also clarifies who the actors of the persecution may be. This is something the Geneva Convention has left rather nuanced, by simply stating that the refugee "is unable (…) or unwilling, to avail himself of the protection" of his country of origin. From this formulation, it has been possible to deduce that refugees are "unwilling" when the persecution comes

---

24   145 States have ratified the Convention. See https://www.unhcr.org/protect/PROTEC
      TION/3b73b0d63.pdf.

25   Directive 2011/95/EU of the European Parliament and of the Council of 13 December 2011
      on standards for the qualification of third-country nationals or stateless persons as beneficiaries of international protection, for a uniform status for refugees or for persons eligible for subsidiary protection, and for the content of the protection granted, in *oj* L 337,
      20 December 2011, pp. 9–26.

directly from the State, and "unable" when the country of origin is not able not protect them from persecution coming from others. Art. 6 of Directive 2011/95/EU supports this interpretation, as it explains that the actors of persecution include not only States but also parties or organizations that control the territory of the State, totally or for a substantial part, and non-state actors when the authorities don't want, or are unable to, provide protection.[26]

Directive 2011/95/EU regulates also another situation, which has been ignored in the Geneva Convention: the possibility to become refugees after having left the country of origin. Better known as refugees "*sur place*", this phenomenon is particularly important for the purpose of this research because it covers the issue of those who change their religion after having left their country. Accordingly, art. 5 of the Directive clearly states that the fear of being persecuted may be also based "on events which have taken place since the applicant left the country of origin".[27]

Subsidiary protection takes care of those who are escaping from their country not due to the risk of persecution but for other reasons. According to art. 2 (*f*) of Directive 2011/95/EU, a person is eligible for subsidiary protection when he or she "does not qualify as refugee but in respect of whom substantial grounds have been shown for believing that the person concerned, if returned to his or her country of origin, or in the case of a stateless person, to his or her country of former habitual residence, would face a real risk of suffering serious harm (...) and is unable, or, owing to such risk, unwilling to avail himself or herself of the protection of that country". This kind of protection focuses on the risk of suffering serious harm in the country of origin. As clarified in art. 15 of the Directive, serious harm may consist of death penalty, torture, inhuman or degrading treatments, and punishments in the country of origin or, again, "serious and individual threat to a civilian's life or person by reason of indiscriminate violence in situations of international or internal armed conflict". The subsidiary protection can therefore have a very wide application.

The recognition of the status of refugee implies a series of guarantees expressly established in the Geneva Convention, including the right to access housing, labor market, freedom of movement within the territory of the State, right to obtain travel documents, etc. The same guarantees are also provided by Directive 2011/95/EU in favor of those who have obtained either the status of refugees or the subsidiary protection.

---

26   Art. 6 also applies in relation to the subsidiary protection. Between the European Court of Human Rights judgements see *H.L.R. v. France*, 29 April 1997, par. 32, and *Ahmed v. Austria*, 17 December 1997, par. 44.

27   Art. 5 also applies in relation to the subsidiary protection.

The most important form of protection for refugees is provided by the principle of *non-refoulement* outlined in art. 33 of the Geneva Convention and extended by EU law also to the beneficiaries of subsidiary protection. According to art. 33 (1) "No Contracting State shall expel or return (*'refouler'*) a refugee in any manner whatsoever to the frontiers of territories where his life or freedom would be threatened on account of his race, religion, nationality, membership of a particular social group or political opinion". Therefore, those who have obtained the status of refugee cannot be expelled or returned to a country where there is a risk of persecution. Within the Geneva Convention the principle of *non-refoulement* is not absolute, as art. 33 (2) establishes that "(t)he benefit of the present provision may not, however, be claimed by a refugee whom there are reasonable grounds for regarding as a danger to the security of the country in which he is, or who, having been convicted by a final judgment of a particularly serious crime, constitutes a danger to the community of that country". Similar provisions are provided in art. 21 of Directive 2011/95/EU.

The principle of *non-refoulement* has been recognized in many international and regional treaties[28] and its content has developed in accordance with the evolution of international law on human rights. An important contribution in this regard was given by the case law of the European Court of Human Rights. In the well-known case *Soering v. United Kingdom* of 1989,[29] the European Court claimed that States parties cannot expel, return, extradite or reject any person towards countries where they risk being subject to torture and degrading or inhuman treatments and punishment (all these behaviors being illegal in accordance with art. 3 of the Convention). It should be noticed that the ECHR does prevent States from expelling or rejecting people towards countries where there is a well-founded risk that the individual may be subject to a punishment or inhuman treatment.[30] The risk must be real and regard specifically the person subject to expulsion, thus excluding a situation of general risk concerning either an entire community or other people presenting a similar

---

28   AU Convention Governing the Specific Aspects of Refugee Problems in Africa, Addis Abeba, 10 September 1969, art. 2 (3); American Convention on Human Rights, cit., art. 22 (8); Convention against Torture and Other Cruel, Inhuman or Degrading Treatment or Punishment, New York, 10 December 1984, art. 3; Charter of Fundamental Rights of the European Union, art. 19 (2).

29   Judgement of 7 July 1989.

30   See, *inter alia*, the European Court judgements *Cruz Varas and others v. Sweden*, 20 March 1991, par. 75, *Chahal v. United Kingdom*, 15 November 1996, par. 74, and *H.L.R. v. France*, cit., par. 33–34.

status or background.[31] However, in cases of extreme violence, it is not necessary to demand specific evidence of an individual risk, as the latter is implied in the general context.[32]

Similarly, art. 2 ECHR, on the right to life, has been applied in a way to prevent States from expelling, returning, extraditing or rejecting anyone towards a country where there are substantial grounds to believe that their life is at risk.[33]

Clearly, the case law of the European Court does not focus specifically on refugees. The ECHR protects all human beings, regardless the personal status of the beneficiaries. It is remarkable that the European Court granted protection regardless any consideration on the danger the right-holders may represent for the country or the community where they live.[34] Indeed, the prohibition of torture and inhuman treatments, as well as the right to life cannot be balanced with other interests or rights.[35] According to the Court, governments have sufficient instruments to limit dangers for the security of the community, i.e. applying imprisonment after a due trial.

In addition to the evolution "*rationae personae*", the principle of *non-refoulement* has also evolved "*rationae materiae*". While art. 33 of the Geneva Convention prohibits expulsion and return, the rejection at the frontier is not expressly contemplated. Looking at the preparatory works of the Convention, it is quite clear that the contracting States did not want to regulate this situation (Aga Khan, 1976; Goodwin-Gill, 1996). Nowadays, however, the gap has been filled: it is generally acknowledged that the principle of *non-refoulement* does prevent rejection at the frontier (Coleman, 2003; Stenberg, 1989).[36]

---

31 European Court judgements *Vilvarajah and others v. United Kingdom*, 30 October 1991, par. 111, and *H.L.R. v. France*, cit., par. 41.

32 European Court judgements *Salah Sheekh v. The Netherlands*, 11 January 2007, par. 148, and *NA. v. United Kingdom*, 17 July 2008, par. 115–117.

33 European Court decisions *A.A. v. Norway*, 21 October 1993, *Sinnarajah v. Switzerland*, 11 May 1999, and judgements *Bahaddar v. the Netherlands*, 19 February 1998, par. 75–78, and *Kaboulov v. Ukraine*, 19 November 2009, par. 99.

34 In the judgement *Chahal v. United Kingdom*, cit., par. 80, the European Court has affirmed that "the activities of the individual in question, however undesirable or dangerous, cannot be a material consideration. The protection afforded by Article 3 is thus wider than that provided by Articles 32 and 33 of the United Nations 1951 Convention on the Status of refugees". See also judgements *Ahmed v. Austria*, cit., par. 41 and *Saadi v. Italy*, 28 February 2008, par. 127.

35 *Saadi v. Italy*, cit., par. 140.

36 See: Declaration on Territorial asylum, adopted by General Assembly resolution No. 2312(XXII), 14 December 1967, art. 3 (1); Committee of Ministers of the Council of Europe, resolution No. (67) 14 on Asylum to persons in danger of persecution, 29 June 1967, par. 2; Directive 2013/33/EU of the European Parliament and of the Council of 26 June 2013

The evolution of the principle of *non-refoulement* triggered by the case law of the European Court has influenced international law as a whole. The Human Rights Committee for example, as well as the Committee against Torture, have repeatedly recognized that "the principle of 'non-refoulement' of persons to another State where there are substantial grounds for believing that they would be in danger of being subjected to torture" or inhuman or degrading punishment or treatment, or would be in a danger for their life, is absolute (Bouziri, 2003; Phuong, 2007; Weissbrodt, Hörtreiter, 1999).[37]

4   Religious Persecutions

As seen above, the notion of refugee can be deduced from the one of persecution. This is indeed the situation which allows to access the status of refugee. While the Geneva Convention does not provide any definition of persecution, EU law is more precise. Art. 9 (1) of Directive 2011/95/EU states that an act of persecution must: (*a*) be sufficiently serious by its nature, or because it is repeated, "as to constitute a severe violation of basic human rights"; (*b*) or "be an accumulation of various measures, including violations of human rights which is sufficiently severe as to affect an individual in a similar manner as mentioned in point (a)". The notion of persecution is therefore defined by an objective criterion, meaning "the nature and intrinsic severity of the act or the situation experienced as well as the consequences suffered by the person concerned in his country of origin".[38]

Art. 9 (1) specifies that the most relevant affected human rights are those which cannot be derogated according to art. 15 (2) ECHR, and therefore are considered absolute. These are: right to life (art. 2); prohibition of torture and degrading or inhuman treatments and punishments (art. 3); prohibition of slavery (art. 4 (1)); *nulla poena sine lege* (art. 7). The concept of persecution as established in the Directive is consistent with the case law of both the European Court of Human Rights and the Human Rights Committee: as it was already explained, these authorities have already clarified that States cannot

---

laying down standards for the reception of applicants for international protection, in *OJ* L 180, 29 June 2013, pp. 96–116, art. 3.

37   See Human Rights Committee, General Comment No. 20, par. 9 and 12, and Committee against Torture, General Comment No. 4 (2017), par. 9–11.

38   Opinion of Advocate General Bot, 19 April 2012, joined cases C-71/11 and C-99/11, *Bundesrepublik Deutschland v. Y and Z*, par. 53.

expel, return, extradite or reject people towards countries where they risk being subject to torture and degrading or inhuman treatments and punishment or to be deprived of their life.

Art. 9 (2) of Directive 2011/95/EU gives some examples of acts of persecution. These are, first of all, "acts of physical or mental violence", thus including torture, inhuman and degrading treatment and punishment.[39] Other examples recalled in art. 9 (2) are: "legal, administrative, police, and/or judicial measures which are in themselves discriminatory or which are implemented in a discriminatory manner", "prosecution or punishment which is disproportionate or discriminatory", and, again, "denial of judicial redress resulting in a disproportionate or discriminatory punishment". These examples focus on the concept of discrimination and disproportion. At the same time, a mere discrimination does not lead to a persecution. Par. 2 must be read in conjunction with par. 1: a discrimination does not necessarily lead to a persecution, especially if it doesn't also cause some serious violation of human rights.

When focusing on freedom of religion, it is necessary to verify what behaviors may be qualified as a religious persecution. As seen above, persecution is a personal attack, which may undermine the most essential rights. Accordingly, only serious violations of the right to freedom of religion or belief could be considered as a form of persecution. This has been already clarified by the European Court of Human Rights and the Court of Justice of the European Union in two important cases regarding the expulsion of asylum seekers towards countries where they may have been persecuted because of their religious affiliation. The European Court of Human Rights in the case *Z. and T. v. United Kingdom*,[40] and the Court of Justice of the European Union in the case *Bundesrepublik Deutschland v. Y and Z*,[41] stated that the mere violation of freedom of religion or belief does not constitute a persecution, even if there is a radical ban to practice the religion of own choice. A violation of the right to freedom of religion or belief may represent a persecution (thus allowing the

---

39 About the distinction between "inhuman" and "degrading", the European Court has stated that "inhuman" is a premeditated treatment, which "was applied for hours at a stretch and caused either actual bodily injury or intense physical and mental suffering", while a treatment can be considered "degrading" when it is "such as to arouse in its victims feelings of fear, anguish and inferiority capable of humiliating and debasing them and possibly breaking their physical or moral resistance" (see judgement *Jalloh v. Germany*, 11 July 2006, par. 68). Torture, instead, is an aggravated form of inhuman or degrading treatment.

40 Decision of 28 February 2006.

41 Judgement of 5 September 2012, joined cases C-71/11 and C-99/11.

possibility to obtain the status of refugee) only when the person, "as a result of exercising that freedom in his country of origin, runs a genuine risk of, inter alia, being prosecuted or subject to inhuman or degrading treatment or punishment" or being tortured or killed.[42] Therefore, the violation of freedom of religion or belief does not automatically allow the possibility to obtain protection (Labayle, 2012). It is instead necessary to look at the consequences coming from that violation. Only if the violation consists of acts of torture or degrading and inhuman treatments, or a threat to life or, again, a risk of being prosecuted for religious affiliation, the claimant can obtain protection. The Human Rights Committee adopted the same view. The case *X. c. Denmark* concerned an asylum seeker who refused returning to his country of origin where he risked incarceration without trial and torture in detention due also to his refusal to undertake military service on the basis of conscience.[43] The Committee declared that the allegations were founded and stated that the deportation would constitute a violation of art. 7 of the ICCPR, which is the norm recognizing the prohibition of torture and degrading and inhuman treatments and punishments (Bielefeldt *et al.*, 2016: 411–413).[44]

The judgement *Bundesrepublik Deutschland v. Y and Z* of the Court of Justice of the European Union is interesting under another point of view. The national judge asked the Court to consider whether the fear of persecution –which prevents expulsion only if it is supported by evidence– exists even if the person could prevent the persecution "by abstaining from certain religious practice" in the country of origin.[45] The Court answered that none of the rules of the Directive states that "it is necessary to take account of the possibility open to the applicant of avoiding the risk of persecution by abstaining from the religious practice".[46] Accordingly, a State cannot allow an expulsion when the person concerned may be safe simply by abstaining from a religious practice or hiding an affiliation. According to the Court of Justice, "where it is established that, upon his return to his country of origin, the person concerned will follow a religious practice which will expose him to a real risk of persecution, he should be granted refugee status".[47]

---

42   See: decision of the European Court of Human Rights *Z. and T. v. United Kingdom*, cit., and judgement of the Court of Justice of the European Union, *Bundesrepublik Deutschland v. Y and Z*, cit., par. 66–67.

43   Decision of 26 March 2014.

44   Ivi, par. 8.4 and 9.3.

45   Par. 73.

46   Par. 78.

47   Par. 79.

5   Concluding Observations

Everyone in the world must be able to benefit from a series of fundamental rights, which are inherent in the essence of human being. Freedom of religion or belief is certainly one of them. As established in international and European law, and better clarified by international courts and treaty bodies, this right covers a very wide number of situations and can be limited only in few cases. Unfortunately, many countries do not respect freedom of religion, this having a negative impact on the conferral of other fundamental rights. It is therefore understandable that people oppressed for their religion decide to move to another country in order to find a place where they can freely express themselves. In the host State, they ask, first, the right to practice their religion or belief and, second, the right not to be sent back to the country of origin. At the same time, international and European laws on immigration do not automatically protect everybody who cannot effectively exercise their rights in their country of origin. As clearly explained by the European Court of Human Rights and the Court of Justice of the European Union, protection must be reserved to those individuals who are exposed to serious breaches of their fundamental rights. Therefore, a violation of freedom of religion or belief does not automatically grant the right to receive protection.

References to Part 1

Abbruzzese, S. (2009). *Verso una società post-secolare: secolarizzazione e disincanto laico*. In S. Belardinelli, L. Allodi, & L. Gattamorta (Eds), *Verso una società post-secolare?* Soveria Mannelli: Rubettino, pp. 187–212.

Abbruzzese, S. (2010). *Un moderno desiderio di Dio*. Soveria Mannelli: Rubbettino.

Abdelhady, D., Malmberg, G.F. (2019). Swedish Media Representation of the Refugee Crisis: Islam, Conflict and Self-Reflection. In E. O'Donnell Polyakov (Ed.), *Antisemitism, Islamophobia, and Interreligious Hermeneutics. Ways of Seeing the Religious Other*. Lieden, Boston: Brill Rodopi, pp. 107–136.

Acquaviva, S. (1973). *Irreligione e secolarizzazione*. In S. Acquaviva, & G. Guizzardi (Eds), *La secolarizzazione*. Bologna: Il Mulino, pp. 167–186.

Acquaviva, S. (1992). *L'eclisse del sacro nella civiltà industriale*. Milano: Mondadori.

Aga Khan, S. (1976). Legal Problems Relating to Refugees and Displaced Persons. In *Collected Courses of the Hague Academy of International Law*, vol. 149, pp. 287–352.

Agamben, G. (1998). *Homo Sacer: Sovereign Power and Bare Life*. Stanford: Stanford University Press.

Ahdar, R., & Leigh, I. (2013). *Religious Freedom in the Liberal State*. Oxford: Oxford University Press.

Ahn, I. (2019). *Theology and Migration*. Leiden, Boston: Brill.

Aiuto alla Chiesa che soffre (2019). *Libertà religiosa nel mondo. Rapporto 2018*. Königstein: Aid to the Church in Need International.

Ajana, B. (2013). *Governing through biometrics: the biopolitics of identity*. Basingstoke, Palgrave Macmillan.

Akil, H.N. (2016). *The Visual Divide between Islam and the West. Image Perception within Cross-Cultural Contexts*. New York: Palgrave Macmillan.

Alba, R. (2009). *Blurring the Color Line: The New Chance for a More Integrated America*. Cambridge: Harvard University Press.

Ambrosini, M. (2016). *Protected but Separate: International Immigrants in the Italian Chatholic Church*. In D. Pasura, & M. Bivand Erdal (Eds), *Migration, Transnationalism and Catholicism: Global Perspective*. London: Palgrave-Macmillan, pp. 317–335.

Ambrosini, M., Bonizzoni, P., & Molli, S. (2018). Immigrati cristiani a Milano: esperienze di partecipazione, aggregazione, integrazione sociale. *Annali di Scienze Religiose, 11*, 113–140.

Amnesty International. 2013. 'Scapegoats of Fear: Rights of Refugees, Asylum-Seekers and Migrants Abused in Libya'. Available online at: http://www.amnesty.org/en/library/info/MDE19/007/2013/en.

APPG (All-Party Parliamentary Group for International Freedom of Religion or Belief) and AAG (Asylum Advocacy Group) (2016). *Fleeing Persecution: Asylum Claims in the*

UK on Religious Freedom Grounds? http://statewatch.org/news/2016/jun/uk-ap pg-religious-freedom-asylum-report.pdf.

ARC-Center for the Anthropology of Religion and Cultural Change (2016). *"Già e non ancora". Il sacramento tra trascendenza e immanenza oggi. Una ricerca sui sacramenti in Italia.* Università Cattolica, Milano: Research Report.

Arendt, H., (1976). *The Origins of Totalitarianism (1951).* New York: A Harvest Book.

Ataç, I., Kron, S., Schilliger, S., Schwiertz, H. and Stierl, M. (2015). Kämpfe der Migration als Un-/Sichtbare Politiken. Movements. *Journal für kritische Migrations- und Grenzregimeforschung*, *1*(2), 1–18.

Ballestrem, K.G. (2009). *Religione e politica nell'Europa post-secolare.* In S. Belardinelli, L. Allodi, & L. Gattamorta, *Verso una società post-secolare?* Soveria Mannelli: Rubettino, pp. 260–279.

Batnitzky, L., & Dagan, H. (Eds) (2017). *Institutionalizing Rights and Religion.* Cambridge: Cambridge University Press.

Baudrillard, J. (1976). *La società dei consumi.* Bologna: Il Mulino.

Bauman, Z. (1992). *Mortality, Immortality and Other Life Strategies.* Redwood City: Stanford University Press.

Bauman, Z. (2001). *Missing Community.* Cambridge: Polity Press.

Bauman, Z. (2002). In the lowly nowherevilles of liquid modernity. Comments on and around Agier. *Ethnografy*, *3*(3), 343–349.

Beck, U. (2010). *A God of One's Own.* Cambridge: Polity Press.

Belardinelli, S. (2006). *Religione.* In S. Belardinelli, & L. Allodi, *Sociologia della cultura.* Milano: FrancoAngeli, pp. 237–252.

Bellah, R.N. (1967). *Civil Religion in America.* Reprinted by Daedalus, Journal of the American Academy of Arts and Sciences, from the Issue entitled "Religion in America", Vol. 96, No. 1, pp. 1–21.

Bellah, R.N. (1970). *Beyond Belief: Essays on Religion in a Post-Traditional World.* New York: Harper & Row.

Benjamin, W. (2013). *Il capitalismo come religione.* Genova: Il Melangolo.

Berger, P.G., & Davie, G., & Fokas, E. (2008). *Religious America, Secular Europe?: A Theme and Variations.* Farnham: Ashgate Publishing.

Berger, P.L. (1967). *The Sacred Canopy: Elements of a Sociological Theory of Religion.* Garden City, N.Y.: Doubleday.

Berger, P.L. (1969). *A rumor of Angels: Modern Society and the Rediscovery of the Supernatural.* Garden City, N.Y.: Doubleday.

Berger, P.L. (1973). *Secolarizzazione e plausibilità della religione.* In S. Acquaviva, & G. Guizzardi (Eds), *La secolarizzazione.* Bologna: Il Mulino, pp. 107–131.

Berger, P.L. (1979). *The Heretical Imperative: Contemporary Possibilities of Religious Affirmation.* Garden City, N.Y.: Anchor Books/Doubleday.

Berger, P.L. (1999). *The Desecularization of the World: Resurgent Religion and World Politics*. Grand Rapids: Ethics and Public Policy Center and Ww. B. Eerdmans Publishing Co.

Berger, P.L. (2001). *Le réenchantement du monde*. Paris: Bayard.

Berlant, L. (1997). *The Queen of America goes to Washington. Essays on Sex and Citizenship*. Durham&London: Duke University Press.

Berzano, L. (2017a). *Quarta secolarizzazione. Autonomia degli stili*. Milano: Mimesis.

Berzano, L. (2017b). *Spiritualità. Moltiplicazione delle forme nella società secolare*. Milano: Editrice Bibliografica.

Betts, A. (2016). The elephant in the room. Islam and the Crisis of Liberal Values in Europe. *Foreign Affairs*, https://www.foreignaffairs.com/articles/europe/2016-02-02/elephant-room.

Beyer, P. (1994). *Religion and Globalization*. London: Sage.

Bhabha, H. (1994), Between identities (interview with Paul Thompson). In R. Benmayor, & A. Skotnes (Eds), *Migration and Identity, International Yearbook of Oral History and Life Stories*, Vol. III, Oxford: Oxford University Press.

Bichi, R., & Bignardi, P. (Eds) (2015). *Dio a modo mio. Giovani e fede in Italia*. Milano: Vita e Pensiero.

Bichi, R., Introini, F., & Pasqualini, C. (Eds) (2018). *Di generazione in generazione. La trasmissione della fede nelle famiglie con background migratorio*. Milano: Vita e Pensiero.

Bielefeldt, H. (2015). Privileging the 'Homo Religiosus'? Towards a Clear Conseptualization of Freedom of religion or Belief. In M.D. Evans, P. Petkoff, & J. Rivers (Eds), *The Changing Nature of Religious Rights under International Law*, Oxford: Oxford University Press, pp. 9–24.

Bielefeldt, H., Ghanea, N., & Wiener, M. (2016). *Freedom of Religion or Belief. An International Law Commentary*. Oxford: Oxford University Press.

Bloom, I., Martin, J.P., & Proudfoot, W. (Eds) (1996). *Religious diversity and human rights*. New York: Columbia University Press.

Boltanski, L., & Chiapello, E. (1999). *Le nouvel esprit du capitalisme*. Paris: Éditions Gallimard.

Bouziri, N. (2003). *La protection des droits civils et politiques par l'O.N.U. L'œuvre du Comité des droits de l'homme*. Paris: L'Harmattan.

Brubaker, R. (2016). A New "Christianist" Secularism in Europe. *The Immanent Frame*. https://tif.ssrc.org/2016/10/11/a-new-christianist-secularism-in-europe/.

Bulley, D. (2017). *Migration, Ethics and Power: Spaces Of Hospitality In International Politics*. London: Sage.

Bulman, M. (2018). More than 100 women in Yarl's Wood detention centre go on hunger strike over 'inhumane' conditions. *Indipendent*, February, 22. Available at https://

www.independent.co.uk/news/uk/home-news/yarls-wood-women-immigration-detention-centre-hunger-strike-home-office-a8223886.html.

Butler, J. (1993). *Bodies That Matter: On the Discursive Limits of Sex*. New York: Routledge.

Butler, J. (2009). *Frames of War*. London/New York: Verso.

Cadge, W., & Howard Ecklend, E. (2007). Immigration and Religion. *Annual Review of Sociology, 33*, 359–379.

Canning, V. (2017). *Gendered Harm and Structural Violence in the British Asylum System*. London and New York: Routledge.

Carens, J. (2013). *The Ethics of Immigration*. Oxford: Oxford University Press.

Casanova, J. (1994). *Public Religion in the Modern World.* Chicago: The University of Chicago Press.

Casement, A., & Tracey, D. (Eds) (2006). *The idea of the numinous. Contemporary Jungian and psychoanalytic perspectives.* Oxford: Routledge.

Cipriani, R. (2012). *Sociologia del pellegrinaggio*. Milano: FrancoAngeli.

Clark, E.A., & Durham, W.C. (2015). The Emergence of Corporate Religious Freedom. In M.D. Evans, P. Petkoff, & J. Rivers (Eds), *The Changing Nature of Religious Rights under International Law*, Oxford: Oxford University Press, pp. 256–285.

Coleman, N. (2003). Non-Refoulement Revised Renewed Review of the Status of the Principle of Non-Refoulement as Customary International Law. *European Journal of Migration Law*, 23–68.

Comte, A. (1864). *Cours de philosophie positive (1830–1842)*. Paris: J.B. Baillière & fils.

Conlon, D. (2016). Hungering for Freedom: Asylum Seekers Hunger Strikes. Rethinking Resistance as Counter-Conduct. In D. Moran, N. Gill, & D. Conlon (Eds), *Carceral Spaces: Mobility and Agency in Imprisonment and Migrant Detention*. London, New York: Routledge, pp. 133–148.

Conrad, J. (1988). *Heart of Darkness* (1902). Edited by R. Kimbrough. New York: Norton & Company.

Cornelius, W.A., Martin, P.L., & Hollifield, J.F. (1994). Introduction: The Ambivalent Quest for Immigration Control. In W.A. Cornelius, P.L. Martin, & J.F. Hollifield (Eds), *Controlling Immigration: A Global Perspectives*. Stanford: Stanford University Press, pp. 3–41.

Court of Justice of the European Union (CJEU) (2012). C-71/11 and C-99/11 Germany v Y and Z, 05-09-2012. Available at http://www.asylumlawdatabase.eu/en/content/cjeu-c-7111-and-c-9911-germany-v-y-and-z.

Cox, H. (1966). *The Secular City: Secularization and Urbanization in Theological Perspective*. Harmondsworth: Penguin Books.

Cox, H. (1984). *Religion in the Secular City: Toward a Postmodern Theology*. New York: Simon and Schuster.

Damari, C. (2016). *Religione e devozione. Epoche e forme del pellegrinaggio.* Milano: FrancoAngeli.

Davie, G. (1994). *Religion in Britain since 1945. Believing without belonging.* Oxford: Blackwell.

De Martino, E. (1958). *Morte e pianto rituale nel mondo antico.* Torino: Einaudi.

De Martino, E. (Ed.) (1962). *Magia e civiltà.* Milano: Garzanti.

Derrida, J. (2000). *Of Hospitality.* Trans. by R. Bowlby. Stanford: Stanford University Press.

Derrida, J. (2002). Hostipitality. In G. Anidjar (Ed.), *Acts of religion*, London: Routledge, pp. 356–420.

Diotallevi, L., & Allievi, S. (2004). *Le religioni degli italiani.* In G. Amendola (Ed.). *Anni in salita. Speranze e paure degli italiani.* Milano: FrancoAngeli, pp. 202–226.

Dunmore, C. (2016). Too Young to Be a Bride. *UNHCR Tracks*, April, 12. Available at http://tracks.unhcr.org/2016/04/too-young-to-be-a-bride/.

Durham Jr., W.C., & Thayer, D.D. (2019) (Eds). *Religion, Pluralism and Reconciling Differences.* London: Routledge.

Durkheim, E. (1962; ed. or. 1893). *La divisione del lavoro sociale.* Milano: Edizioni di Comunità.

Durkheim, E. (1972; ed. or. 1898). *L'individualismo e gli intellettuali.* In Durkheim, E. *La scienza sociale e l'azione.* Milano: Il Saggiatore, pp. 290–291.

Eghdamian, K. (2015). Refugee Crisis: Syria's Religious Minorities Must Not Be Overlooked. *The Conversation* https://theconversation.com/refugee-crisis-syrias-religious-minorities-must-not-be-overlooked-47448.

Eghdamian, K. (2016). Religious identity and experiences of displacement: An examination into the discursive representations of Syrian refugees and their effects on religious minorities living in Jordan. *Journal of Refugee Studies, 30*(3), 447–467.

El Sheikh, S. (2017). Dehumanizing Refugees: between Demonization and Idealization. *Refugee Hosts.* Available at https://refugeehosts.org/2017/12/13/dehumanizing-refugees-between-demonization-and-idealization/?blogsub=subscribed#blog_subscription-3.

Eliade, M. (1957). *Das Heilige und das Profane. Vom Wesen des Religiösen.* Reinbeck bei Hamburg: Rowohlt.

European Commission (2011). Communication from the Commission to the European Parliament, The Council, the European Economic and Social Committee and the Committee of the Regions. The Global Approach to Migration and Mobility. Brussels. http://eur-lex.europa.eu/legal-content/EN/TXT/PDF/?uri=CELEX:52011DC0743&from=en.

Evans, C. (2001). *Freedom of Religion Under the European Convention on Human Rights.* Oxford: Oxford University Press.

Feller, E., Türk, V., & Nicholson, F. (Eds) (2003), *Refugee Protection in International Law*. Cambridge: Cambridge University Press.

Ferrara, A. (2009). *Religione e politica nella società post-secolare*. Roma: Meltemi.

Fiddian-Qasmiyeh, E. (2017). The Faith-Gender-Asylum Nexus: An Intersectionalist Analysis of Representations of the 'Refugee Crisis'. In L. Mavelli & E.K Wilson (Eds), *The Refugee Crisis and Religion: Secularism, Security and Hospitality in Question*. London: Rowman & Littlefield International, pp. 207–222.

Flescher, A. (2017). The ethics of war and peace in the contemporary era. In W.H. Wiist & S.K. White (Eds), *Preventing War and Promoting Peace: A Guide for Health Professionals*. Cambridge University Press: Cambridge, pp. 169–179.

Forlenza, R., & Turner, B. (2018). Res Publica Christiana: Europe's three religious borders, in D.L. Machado, B.S. Turner, & T. Eiliv Wyller, *Borderland Religion: Ambiguous practices of difference, hope and beyond*. London: Routledge, pp. 27–43.

Foucault, M. (2000). Confronting governments: Human rights, eng. trans. by R. Hurley *et al.*, in James D. Faubion (Ed.), *Essential Works of Foucault 1954–1984, vol. 3: Power*. New York: The New Press, pp. 474–475.

Freud, S. (1919). *Das Unheimliche* (Gesammelte Werke, Band XII, 229–268). Leipzig: Wien, Frankfurt am Main. (Fisher. *The uncanny*. Standard Edition, 17, 217–252, London: Hogarth).

Gallup International (2017). *End of Year 2016. Global Report on Religion*. http://gallup .com.pk/wp-content/uploads/2017/04/Global-Report-on-Religion-2.pdf.

Garelli, F. (1995). *Credenze ed esperienza religiosa*. In V. Cesareo (Ed.), *La religiosità in Italia*. Milano: Arnoldo Mondadori Editore, pp. 19–67.

Garelli, F. (2003). *L'esperienza e il sentimento religioso*. In F. Garelli (Ed.), *Un singolare pluralismo*. Bologna: Il Mulino, pp. 77–114.

Garelli, F. (2011). *Religione all'italiana*. Bologna: Il Mulino.

Gattamorta, L. (2009). *Le ricerche empiriche sui valori e la religione degli italiani*. In S. Belardinelli (Ed.), *Verso una società post-secolare?* Soveria Mannelli: Rubbettino, pp. 281–313.

Giordan, G. (2007). *Spirituality: From a religious concept to a sociological theory*. In K. Flanagan, & P.C. Jupp (Eds), *A sociology of spirituality*. Farnham: Ashgate, pp. 161–180.

Giordan, G. (2016). *Spirituality*. In D. Yamane (Ed.), *Handbook of Religion and Society*. New York: Springer, pp. 197–216.

Girard, R. (1972). *La Violence et le sacré*. Paris: Éditions Bernard Grasset.

Girard, R. (1982). *Le bouch émissaire*. Paris: Éditions Bernard Grasset.

Girma, M., Radice, S., Tsangarides, N., & Walter, N. (2014), *Detained: Women Asylum Seekers Locked Up in the UK*, London: Women for Refugee Women.

Golinelli, M. (2011). Il valore delle appartenenze religiose in una società multietnica. *Studi Emigrazione/International Journal of Migration Studies, 48*(181): 5–23.

Goodwin-Gill, G.S. (1996). *The Refugee in International Law.* Oxford: Oxford University Press.

Gowllands-Debbas, V. (Ed.) (1996). *The Problem of Refugees in the Light of Contemporary International Law Issues.* The Hague – London – Boston: Martinus Nijhoff Publishers.

Goździak, E. & Shandy, D. (2002). Editorial Introduction: Religion and Spirituality in Forced Migration. *Journal of Refugee Studies, 15*(2), 129–135.

Graf, F.W. (2004). *Die Wiederkehr der Götter. Religion in der modernen Kultur.* München: C.H. Beck Verlag.

Gregory, B. (2012). *The Unintended Reformation. How a Religious Revolution Secularized Society.* Cambridge: Harvard University Press.

Gruetters, C., & Dzananovic, D. (Eds) (2018), *Migration and Religious Freedom. Essays on the Interaction between Religious Duty and Migration.* Nijmegen: Wolf Legal Publishers.

Ha, H.I. (2017). Emotions of the weak: violence and ethnic boundaries among Coptic Christians in Egypt. *Ethnic and Racial Studies, 40*(1), 133–151.

Habermas, J. (1986; or. 1981). *Theorie des kommunikativen Handelns* (2 Vol.). Berlin: Suhrkamp.

Habermas, J. (2005). *Zwischen Naturalismus und Religion.* Berlin: Suhrkamp.

Habermas, J. (2016). Religion in the public sphere. *European Journal of Philosophy, 14*(1), 1–25.

Habermas, J., & Ratzinger, J. (2005). *Dialektik der Säkularisierung. Über Vernunft und Religion.* Freiburg i. Br.: Herder Verlag.

Halman, L., Inglehart, R., Diez-Medrano, J., Luijkx, R., Moreno, A., & Basáñez, M. (Eds) (2008). *Changing Values and Beliefs in 85 Countries.* Leiden: Brill.

Halman, L., Luijkx, R., & Van Zundert, M. (Eds) (2005). *Atlas of European Values.* Leiden: Brill.

Hampshire, J. (2013). *The Politics of Immigration: Contradictions of the Liberal State.* Oxford: Polity Press.

Hart, D.B. (2013). *The Experience of God: Being, Consciousness, Bliss.* New Haven: Yale University Press.

Hart de, B. (2017). Sexuality, race and masculinity in Europe's refugee crisis. In C. Grütters, S. Mantu, & P. Minderhoud (Eds), *Migration on the Move: Essays on the Dynamics of Migration.* Leiden, Boston: Brill, pp. 27–53.

Hashemi, K. (2008). *Religious Legal Traditions, International Human Rights Law and Muslim States.* Leiden: Martinus Nijhoff Publishers.

Heelas, P., & Woodhead, L. (2005). *The spiritual revolution. Why religion is giving way to spirituality.* Oxford: Blackwell.

Herberg, W. (1955). *Protestant-Catholic-Jew. An Essay in American Religious Sociology.* Chicago: The University of Chicago Press.

Hertzke, A.D. (2013). *The Future of Religious Freedom: Global Challenges.* Oxford: Oxford University Press.

Hertzke, A.D. (2018). Religious Agency and the Integration of Marginalized People. In P. Donati (Ed.), *Towards a Participatory Society: New Roads to Social and Cultural Integration.* Vatican City: Libreria Editrice Vaticana, pp. 499–529.

Hervieu-Léger, D. (1986). *Vers un nouveau christianisme: introduction à la sociologie du christianisme occidental.* Paris: Edition du Cerf.

Hervieu-Léger, D. (1993). *La religion pour mémoire.* Paris: Cerf.

Hoffmann, E.T.A. (1892). "The Uncanny Guest" (1819), in *The Serapion Brethren*, trans. by A. Ewin, vol. II. London: George Bell & Sons.

Hollenbach, D. (2008). *The Rights of Refugees in a Globalizing World.* Dayton: University of Dayton Press.

Hollenbach, D. (2014). Religion and Force Migration. In E. Fiddian-Qasmiyeh *et al.* (Eds), *The Oxford Handbook of Refugee and Forced Migration Studies.* Oxford: Oxford University Press, pp. 447–459.

Horstmann, A., & Jung, J.H. (2015). Introduction. Refugees and Religion. In A. Horstmann, & J.H. Jung, *Building Noah's Ark for Migrants, Refugees, and Religious Communities.* New York: Palgrave Macmillan, pp. 1–20.

Hurd, E.S. (2017). Muslims and Others. The Politics of Religion in the Refugee Crisis. In L. Mavelli, & E.K. Wison (Eds), *The Refugee and Religion. Secularism, Security and Hospitality in Question.* London, New York: Rowman&Littlefield, pp. 97–108.

Inglehart, R., & Norris, P. (2004). *Sacred and Secular. Religion and Politics Worldwide.* Cambridge: Harvard University Press.

International Labour Organization (ILO). (2017). Jordan's first job centre for Syrian refugees opens in Zaatari camp. Press release, August, 21. Available at https://www.ilo.org/beirut/media-centre/news/WCMS_570884/lang--en/index.htm.

International Organization for Migration (IOM). (2019). *Integration: A Multi-Faith Approach.* Project Report.

Isin, E.F., & Saward, M. (Eds) (2013). *Enacting European Citizenship.* Cambridge: Cambridge University Press.

Jackson, R. (2014). *Signposts – Policy and practice for teaching about religions and non-religious world views in intercultural education,* Council of Europe, Strasbourg. https://www.academia.edu/29035890/Signposts_Policy_and_practice_for_teaching_about_religions_and_non-religious_world_views_in_intercultural_education.

Joas, H. (2014). *Faith as an option: possible futures for Christianity.* Redwood City: Stanford University Press.

John XXIII, Pope (1963). *Pacem in Terris.* Encyclical of Pope John XXIII, On Establishing Universal Peace in Truth, Justice, Charity, and Liberty. April 11, 1963. Available at http://w2.vatican.va/content/john-xxiii/en/encyclicals/documents/hf_j-xxiii_enc_11041963_pacem.html.

Joppke, C. (2007). Transformation of Immigrant Integration: Civic Integration and antidiscrimination in The Netherlands, France, and Germany. *World Politics*, *59*(2), 243–273.

Kantor, I.A., & Cepoi, V. (2018). From Neglect to Crime. The Role of Media in the 2015 European Migration Crisis. A Comparative Study in Three ECE Countries: Romania, Hungary and Slovenia. In E. Balica & V. Marinescu (Eds), *Migration and Crime. Realities and Media Representations*. New York: Palgrave Macmillan, pp. 139–166.

Karpman, S. (1968). Fairy tales and script drama analysis. *Transactional Analysis Bulletin*, *7*(26), 39–43.

Kepel, G. (1991). *La revanche de Dieu*. Paris: Seuil.

Kikano, F., & Lizarralde, G. (2019). Settlement Policies for Syrian Refugees in Lebanon and Jordan: An Analysis of the Benefits and Drawbacks of Organized Camps. In A. Asgary (Ed.), *Resettlement Challenges for Displaced Populations and Refugees*. Cham: Springer, pp. 29–40.

Konnor, P. & Krogstad, J.M. (2018). The number of refugees admitted to the U.S. has fallen, especially among Muslims. Pew Research Center. Available at http://www.pe wresearch.org/fact-tank/2018/05/03/the-number-of-refugees-admitted-to-the-u-s-has-fallen-especially-among-muslims/.

Koopmans, R. (2015). Religious Fundamentalism and Hostility against Out-groups: A Comparison of Muslims and Christians in Western Europe. *Journal of Ethnic and Migration Studies*, *41*(1), 33–57.

Kosela, Z. (Ed.) (2007). *John Paul II in the eyes of Poles*. Varsavia: Centre for Thought of John Paul II.

Kristeva, J. (1991). *Strangers to ourselves*. Trans. by L.S. Roudiez. New York: Columbia University Press.

Kritzman-Amir, T., & Spijkerboer, T.P. (2013). On The Morality and Legality of Borders: Border Policies and Asylum Seekers. *Harvard Human Rights Journal*, (*26*), 1–38.

Kurtz, L.R. (1995). *Gods in the Global Village. The World's Religions in Sociological Perspective*. Thousand Oaks: Pine Forge Press.

Kymlicka, W. (2001). Territorial boundaries: A liberal egalitarian perspective. In D. Miller, & S. Hashmi (Eds), *Boundaries and Justice: Diverse Ethical Perspectives*. Princeton: Princeton University Press, pp. 249–275.

Labayle, H. (2012). *Le droit d'asile devant la persecution religieuse: la Cour de justice ne se dérobe pas*. ELSJ (http://www.gdr-elsj.eu/2012/09/09/asile/le-droit-dasile-devant-la-persecution-religieuse-la-cour-de-justice-ne-se-derobe-pas).

Lahusen, C., & Grasso, M.T. (2018). *Solidarity in Europe: Citizens' Responses in Times of Crisis*. New York: Palgrave Macmillan.

Lanzetti, C. (2018). L'umanesimo europeo di fronte ai problemi della secolarizzazione, del terrorismo e della sacralizzazione dei conflitti: la prospettiva religiosa. *Annali di scienze religiose*, *11*, 17–59.

Lehmann, H. (Ed.) (2004). *Säkularisierung. Der europäische Sonderweg in Sachen Religion?* Göttingen: Wallstein Verlag.

Lehmann, H. (1997). *Säkularisierung, Dechristianisierung, Rechristianisierung im neuzeuitlichen Europa.* Göttingen: Vandenhoeck & Ruprecht.

Lyck-Bowen, M., & Owen, M. (2019). A multi-religious response to the migrant crisis in Europe: A preliminary examination of potential benefits of multi-religious cooperation on the integration of migrants. *Journal of Ethnic and Migration Studies, 45*(1) 21–41.

Lindkvist, L. (2017). *Religious Freedom and the Universal Declaration of Human Rights.* Cambridge: Cambridge University Press.

Lindskov Jacobsen, K. (2017). On Humanitarian Refugee Biometrics and New Forms of Intervention. *Journal of Intervention and Statebuilding, 11*(4), 529–551.

Lübbe, H. (1965). *Säkularisierung: Geschichte eines ideenpolitischen Begriffs.* Freiburg: Verlag Karl Alber.

Lucà Trombetta, P. (2004). *Il bricolage religioso: sincretismo e nuove religiosità.* Bari: Edizioni Dedalo.

Luckmann, T. (1967). *The Invisible Religion. The Problem of Religion in Modern Society.* New York: Macmillan.

Luckmann, T. (1973). *Fine della religione istituzionale.* In S. Acquaviva, & G. Guizzardi (Eds), *La secolarizzazione.* Bologna: Il Mulino, pp. 133–144.

Macdonald, H. (2015). The human flock. *New York Times,* Dec. 2.

Machnyikova, Z. (2007). Religious Rights. In M. Weller (Ed.), *Universal Minority Rights. A Commentary on the Jurisprudence of International Courts and Treaties Bodies.* Oxford: Oxford University Press, pp. 179–202.

Madziva, R., & Lowndes, V. (2018). What counts as evidence in adjudicating asylum claims? Locating the monsters in the machine: an investigation of faith-based claims. In B. Nerlich, S. Hartley, S. Raman, & A. Smith, *Science and the politics of openness. Here be monsters.* Manchester: Manchester University Press, pp. 75–93.

Magatti, M. (2018). *Oltre l'infinito. Storia della potenza dal sacro alla tecnica.* Milano: Feltrinelli.

Magatti, M., & Martinelli, M. (2012). The Potential Role of Religion in the Public Sphere. Considerations by Means of the Contemporary Imaginary. *Global Journal of Human Social Science History and Anthropology 12*(10), pp. 11–21.

Mainwaring, Ċ. (2016). Migrant agency: Negotiating borders and migration controls. *Migration Studies, 4*(3), 289–308.

Malinowski, B. (1948). *Magic, Science and Religion and Other Essays.* USA: Free Press.

Martin, D. (1973). *Negare validità al concetto di secolarizzazione.* In S. Acquaviva, & G. Guizzardi (Eds), *La secolarizzazione.* Bologna: Il Mulino, pp. 187–198.

Martin, D. (2005). *On Secularization.* Burlington: Ashgate.

Martinelli, M., (2013). Cittadini e nuove forme di appartenenza: esperienze in discussione. *Studi Emigrazione/International Journal of Migration Studies, 50*(189) 125–151.

Martinelli, M. (2014). *L'uomo intero. La lezione (inascoltata) di Georg Simmel.* Genova: Il Melangolo.

Martinelli, M. (2019). Die Freiheit der Freien im technisch-ökonomischen Zeitalter. Eine offene Herausforderung. *Limina*, 2, pp. 1–34.

Martinelli, M., & Magatti, M. (2016). Modern individualism and Christian schism: why what we miss is important. *International Review of Economics, 63*(1), 51–75.

Matlary, J.H. (2018). *Hard Power in Hard Times: Can Europe Act Strategically?* New York: Palgrave Macmillan.

Mavelli, L., & Wilson, E. (Eds) (2016). *Refugee Crisis and Religion, Secularism, Security and Hospitality in Question.* London: Rowman & Littlefield International.

McDonald, D. (2016). Escaping the Lions: Religious Conversion and Refugee Law. *Australian Journal of Human Rights, 22*(1), 135–158.

McGoldrick, D. (2017). Religious Rights and the Margin of Appreciation. In P. Agha (Ed.), *Human Rights Between Law and Politics. The Margin of Appreciation in Post-National Contexts.* Oxford: Hart Publishing, pp. 145–168.

McLuhan, M. (1964). *Understanding Media: The Extension of Man.* Berkeley: Gingko Press.

McLuhan, M. (1967). *The Medium is the Message.* New York: Random House.

Meral, Z. (2018). *How Violence Shapes Religion: Belief and Conflict in the Middle East and Africa.* Cambridge: Cambridge University Press.

Metykova, M. (2016). *Diversity and the media.* New York: Palgrave Macmillan.

Milan, C., & Pirro, L.P.A. (2018). Interwoven Destinies in the 'Long Migration Summer': Solidarity Movements Along the Western Balkan Route. In D. della Porta (Ed.), *Solidarity. Mobilizations in the 'Refugee Crisis'. Contentious Moves.* New York: Palgrave Macmillan, pp. 125–154.

Modood, T., & Sealy, T. (2019). *Secularism and the Governance of Religious Diversity.* Concept Paper. GREASE Project (https://www.grease.eui.eu). May.

Morales, L., & Giugni, M. (Eds) (2011). *Social Capital, Political Participation and Migration in Europe. Making multicultural democracy work?* London: Palgrave Macmillan.

Nancy, J.-L. (2002). L'Intrus. *The New Centennial Review 2*(3).

Narkowicz, N. (2018). Refugees Not Welcome Here': State, Church and Civil Society Responses to the Refugee Crisis in Poland. *International Journal of Politics, Culture, and Society, 31*(4), 357–373.

Nicoli, B. (2017/2018). *Le questioni ultime nella società secolare. Un'analisi della comunicazione pubblica della scienza.* Milano: Università Cattolica del Sacro Cuore, PhD Dissertation.

Nyers, P. (2008). No One Is Illegal Between City and Nation. In E.F. Isin & G.M. Nielsen (Eds), *Acts of Citizenship.* London: Zed Books, pp. 160–181.

Nyhagen Predelli, L. (2008). Religion, citizenship and participation: A case study of immigrant Muslim women in Norwegian mosques. *European Journal of Women's Studies*, 15(3), 241–260.

Oktem, K. (2016). Zombie politics: Europe, Turkey and the disposable human. Open Democracy, March, 19. Available at https://www.opendemocracy.net/kerem-oktem/zombie-politics-europe-turkey-and-disposable-human.

Oliva, J.G., & Hall, H. (2017). *Religion, Law and the Constitution. Balancing Beliefs in Britain*. London, New York: Routledge.

Open Doors (2019). World Watch List – Global Trends in 2018 (online) disponibile su www.opendoorsuk.org/persecution/trends/.

Pace, E. (2011). La nuova geografia socio-religiosa in Europa: linee di ricerca e problemi di metodo. *Quaderni di Sociologia LV*(55), 65–89.

Parekh, S. (2017). *Refugees and the Ethics of Forced Displacement*. London, New York: Routledge.

Pew Research Center. (2016). *Global Uptick in Government Restrictions on Religion in 2016*. Available at http://www.pewforum.org/2018/06/21/global-uptick-in-government-restrictions-on-religion-in-2016/.

Pew Research Center (2018). *Being Christian in Western Europe*. Washington DC. Available at http://www.pewforum.org/2018/05/29/being-christian-in-western-europe/.

Philpott, D. (2019). *Religious Freedom in Islam. The Fate of a Universal Human Right in the Muslim World Today*. Oxford: Oxford University Press.

Phuong, C. (2007). Minimum Standards for return Procedures and International Human Rights Law. *European Journal of Migration and Law*, 105–125.

Pickel, G. (2018). Perceptions of Plurality: The Impact of the Refugee Crisis on the Interpretation of Religious Pluralization in Europe. In U. Schmiedel, & G. Smith (Eds), *Religion in the European Refugee Crisis*. New York: Palgrave Macmillan, pp. 15–38.

Pine, B.J., & Gilmore, J.H. (2000). *L'economia delle esperienze*. Milano: Etas Libri.

Pollini, G., Pretto, A, & Rovati, G. (Eds) (2012). *L'Italia nell'Europa: i valori tra persistenze e trasformazioni*, Milano: FrancoAngeli.

Prencipe, L. (2010). La religione dei migranti: tra ripiegamenti ghettizzanti e possibilità di nuova coesione sociale. *Studi Emigrazione/International Journal of Migration Studies,* 47(178), 265–290.

Rawls, J. (1999). Legal obligations and the duty of fair play. In S. Freeman (Ed.), *John Ralws. Collected Papers*. Cambridge, London: Harvard University Press, pp. 117–129.

Reidpath, D. (2019). *The Health of Refugees: Public Health Perspectives from Crisis to Settlement*. Oxford University Press: Oxford.

Rémond R. (1999; or. 1996). *La secolarizzazione. Religione e società nell'Europa contemporanea*. Roma-Bari: Laterza.

Reuters (2017). Slovenian comic's parody has Merkel dancing with 'zombie' refugees. July 3. Available at https://www.reuters.com/article/us-merkel-parody-idUSKBN19O127.

Rexhepi, P. (2018). Arab others at European borders: racializing religion and refugees along the Balkan Route, *Ethnic and Racial Studies*, 41(12): 2215–2234.

Ries, J. (2007). *L'uomo religioso e la sua esperienza del sacro*. Milano: Jaca Book.

Robila, M. (2018). *Refugees and Social Integration in Europe*. United Nations Expert Group Meeting, New York 15–16 May 2018. United Nations Department of Economic and Social Affairs (UNDESA) Division for Social Policy and Development.

Robinson, N. (1953). *Convention Relating to the Status of Refugees. Its History, Contents and Interpretation*. New York: Institute of Jewish Affairs.

Rogers, C. (2016). The Christians held in Thailand after fleeing Pakistan. *BBC News Magazine*. Available at https://www.bbc.com/news/magazine-35654804.

Roof, W.C. (1993). *A generation of seekers: The spiritual journey of the baby boom generation*. San Francisco: HarperCollins.

Roy, O. (2016). *Rethinking the place of religion in European secularized societies: the need for more open societies*. http://hdl.handle.net/1814/40305.

Roy, O. (2019). *L'Europe est-elle chrétienne?*. Paris: Editions du Seuil.

Ruard Ganzevoort, R. (2017). The Drama Triangle of Religion and Violence. E. Aslan, & M. Hermansen (Eds), *Religion and Violence. Muslim and Christian Theological and Pedagogical Reflections*. Wiesbaden: Springer, pp. 17–30.

Saunders, J.B., Fiddian-Qasmiyeh, E., & Snyder, S. (2016). *Intersections of Religion and Migration. Issues at the Global Crossroads*. New York: Palgrave Macmillan.

Sayad, A. (1999). *La double absence. Des illusions de l'émigré aux souffrances de l'immigré*. Paris: Seuil.

Schmiedel, U., & Smith, G. (Eds) (2018). *Religion in the European Refugee Crises*. London: Palgrave Macmillan.

Scruton, R. (2015). *La tradizione e il sacro*. Milano: Vita e Pensiero.

Sennett, R. (2018). *Building and Dwelling. Ethics for the City*. New York: Ferrar, Straus and Giroux.

Shah, T.S., Stepan, A., & Toft, M. (2012). *Rethinking religion and world affairs*. New York: Oxford University Press.

Shaheed, A. (2018). *Report of the Special Rapporteur on freedom of religion and belief*. (Focus: State-Religion Relationships and their Impact on Freedom of Religion or Belief). A/HRC/37/49. Available at: https://documents-dds-ny.un.org/doc/UN DOC/GEN/G18/052/15/PDF/G1805215.pdf?OpenElement.

Shemak, A.A. (2011). *Asylum Speakers: Caribbean Refugees and Testimonial Discourse*. New York: Fordham University Press.

Simmel, G. (1997; or. 1906/1912). *Essays on Religion*. Ed. and transl. by Helle, H.J. New Haven: Yale University.

Soeffner, H.G. (2014). *Fragiler Pluralismus*. In H.G. Soeffner, & T.D. Boldt (Eds). *Fragiler Pluralismus*. Wiesbaden: Springer, pp. 207–224.

Song, S. (2019). *Immigration and Democracy*. Oxford: Oxford University Press.

Stenberg, G. (1989). *Non-Expulsion and Non-Refoulement*. Uppsala: Iustus Förlag.

Stroup, D.R. (2017). Boundaries of belief: religious practices and the construction of ethnic identity in Hui Muslim communities. *Ethnic and Racial Studies, 40*(6), 988–1005.

Tassello, G., Deponti, L., & Proserpio, F. (2011). *Kirche sein im Zeichen der Migrationen.* Basel: Studienzentrum für Migrationsfragen-Cserpe.

Taylor, C. (2007). *A Secular Age.* Cambridge: The Belknap Press of Harvard University Press.

Taylor, C., & Dotolo, C. (2012). *Una religione disincantata. Il cristianesimo oltre la modernità,* Padova: Edizioni Messaggero.

Taylor, C. (1991). *The Ethics of Authenticity.* Cambridge, Massachusetts and London, England: Harvard University Press.

The Economist (2017). America first and last: What the visa ban shows about American foreign policy. http://www.economist.com/news/briefing/21716079-divided-nation-seeks-divided-world-what-visa-ban-shows-about-american-foreign-policy.

Tomass, M. (2016). *The Religious Roots of the Syrian Conflict: The Remaking of the Fertile Crescent.* New York: Palgrave Macmillan.

Unhurian, P., *et al.* (2017). *Violence and discrimination against religious minorities in refugee camps across Europe.* Motion for a resolution. Parliamentary Assembly of the Council of Europe. Available at http://www.assembly.coe.int/nw/xml/XRef /Xref-XML2HTML-en.asp?fileid=24226&lang=en#

United States Commission On International Religious Freedom (USCIRF) (2013). Factsheet Syria: Syria's Refugee Crisis and its Implications. Available at http://www.uscirf.gov/images/Syria%20Factsheet%20-%20July%2018.pdf.

Varvin, S. (2017). Our Relations to Refugees: Between Compassion and Dehumanization. *The American Journal of Psychoanalysis,* 77, 359–377.

Vaughan-Williams, N. (2015). *Europe's Border Crisis Biopolitical Security and Beyond.* Oxford: Oxford University Press.

Ventevogel, P., Cavallera, V., Jones, L., & Weisbecker, I. (2019). Mental health in complex emergencies. In A. Kravitz (Ed.), *Oxford Handbook of Humanitarian Medicine.* Oxford: Oxford University Press , pp. 117–153.

Vilaça, H., Pace, E., Furseth, I., & Pettersson, P. (Eds) (2014). *The Changing Soul of Europe. Religions and Migrations in Northern and Southern Europe.* London: Routledge.

Vogel, D., & Triandafyllidou, A. (2006). *Civic activation of immigrants – An introduction to conceptual and theoretical issues.* POLITIS-Working paper No. 1 (http://www.politis-europe.uni-oldenburg.de/download/WP1_POLITIS_VogelTriandafyllidou _2005).

Walzer, M. (1983). *Spheres of Justice: A Defence of Pluralism and Equality.* New York: Basic Books.

Warner, M., VanAntwerpen, J., & Calhoun, C.J. (2013). *Varieties of Secularism in a Secular Age*. Cambridge: Harvard University.

Weber, M. (2017; or. 1917). *Wissenschaft als Beruf*. Berlin: Verlag Matthes & Seitz.

Weissbrodt, D., & Hörtreiter, I. (1999). The Principle of Non-Refoulement: Article 3 of the Convention Against Torture and Other Cruel, Inhuman or Degrading Treatment or Punishment in Comparison with the Non-Refoulement Provisions of Others International Human Rights Treaties. *Buffalo Human Rights Law Review*, 1–73.

Wilson, B.R. (1969). *Religion in Secular Society*. Baltimore, Md.: Penguin Books.

Wilson, E., & Mavelli, L. (2016). The Refugee Crisis and Religion: Beyond Conceptual and Physical Boundaries. In E. Wilson, & L. Mavelli (Eds), *The Refugee Crisis and Religion: Secularism, Security and Hospitality in Question*. London: Rowman and Littlefield, pp. 1–22.

Wimmer, A., & Glick Schiller N. (2003). Methodological Nationalism, the Social Sciences, and the Study of Migration: An Essay in Historical Epistemology. *International Migration Review*, *XXXVII*(3), 576–610.

Yinger, J.M. (1957). *Religion, Society and the Individual*. New York: McMillan Co.

Zanfrini, L. (2007). *Cittadinanze. Ripensare l'appartenenza e i diritti nella società dell'immigrazione*. Roma-Bari: Laterza.

Zanfrini, L. (2013). Lo scenario contemporaneo: ripensare la cittadinanza nella società globale. *Studi Emigrazione/International Journal of Migration Studies*, *50*(189), 30–51.

Zanfrini, L. (Ed.) (2015). *The Diversity Value. How to Reinvent the European Approach to Immigration*. Maidenhead, UK: McGraw-Hill Education.

Zanfrini, L. (2019). *The Challenge of Migration in a Janus-Faced Europe*. London: Palgrave Macmillan.

Žižek, S. (2016). *Against the Double Blackmail: Refugees, Terror and Other Troubles with the Neighbours*. London: Penguin Random House.

Žižek, Z. (2008). *Enjoy Your Symptom!*. London: Routledge.

Zucca, L. (Ed.) (2015). *Religious Rights*. London: Routledge.

PART 2

Where (Forced) Migrations Are Generated

∵

No One Size Fits All: Diversity, State and Politics in the Contemporary Middle East

Paolo Maggiolini, Andrea Plebani and Riccardo Redaelli

1 Introduction

Especially since 2001, the multiple crises inflaming the wider Middle East have dramatically altered the geopolitical equilibriums of a region that has always played a crucial role in the international arena. Affected by heightening levels of violence and widespread destabilization, the area became increasingly associated with processes of radicalization and socio-political fragmentation allegedly destined to redefine the very foundations of a system whose roots can be traced back to the end of the Great War.

The arch of crises that came to bisect the region largely contributed to projecting the image of a Middle Eastern region "endemically" marred by divisions and instability and destined for partition according to apparently undeniable ethno-sectarian fault lines. In this framework, Middle Eastern ethno-linguistic and religious diversity has become the focal point of two different and opposite arguments. On the one hand, diversity has been considered the victim of increasing polarization, manipulated and politicized in order to impose specific political agendas. On the other, it has been listed as one of the drivers or sources of present instability in a region experiencing its own Thirty Years' War, as Europe did in the 16th century.

The chapter aims to take a distance from both understandings, reconsidering the contemporary history of the Middle East and of state- and nation-building in the region based on the image of multiple geographies. Instead of again proposing the idea of the Middle East as a mosaic, the chapter aims to offer an engaged account of the role of diversity in the region, analyzing the multiple features that have characterized and composed it. Through the idea of multiple geographies, the chapter will explain why diversity in the Middle East has always played a crucial role. The Middle East stands out not only for its diversity *per se*, but because the features that compose and define its diversity and multi-vocality often strongly intertwine and overlap, giving birth to social fabrics far more complex and branched than usually represented.

In this spirit, after delineating some of the main features defining the Middle East diverse socio-political fabric, the chapter focuses on contested visions of state and nation that have developed especially in the Arab world since the turn of the 20th century. It analyzes the most prominent features and elements of a debate waving across supra-national, trans-national and national visions and orientations of how to represent and organize diversity in accordance to a modern State framework. On these bases, the third part of the analysis places the above-mentioned dynamics in a historical continuum tracking its roots in the post first world war order. The chapter then concludes by showing how a more precise understanding of the Middle East's diversity, of its significance and role can help to demystify today's sectarian narratives and tackle instability and violence in the region.

By focusing on contested visions of State and nation and the role diversity plays within these fields, the analysis does not intend to downplay the influence exerted by geopolitics over the regional scenario. Especially since 2001, the wider Middle East has become the epicenter of a heightening competition between (and among) state and non-state actors able to project their influence well beyond the boundaries of their polities and to alter the equilibriums of the area in ways and modalities that would have been impossible even to conceive only a few years before. While geopolitical dynamics have always played a crucial role in the area, their incidence escalated dramatically during the course of the 21st century. Far from being confined to the mere security level, these phenomena invested the socio-political, economic and even cultural dimensions favoring a growing interplay among the international, regional, national and local domains that has become the specific focus of a significant part of the most recent academic literature. By stressing the role diversity, State and politics play in contemporary Middle East the current analysis aims also at reaffirming the necessity to recur to a holistic approach able to take in due consideration the multiple nuances of a region that has always had in its diversity one of its most defining features.

2   A Diverse Social Fabric Defined by Multiple (and Variable) Geographies

Widely perceived well before the beginning of the 21st century as a highly unstable area subject to cyclical outbursts of violence and lingering instability, the wider Middle East has witnessed in the past two decades one of the most critical phases of its history. From North Africa to the Persian Gulf and beyond, the region has been invested by a series of crises that impacted dramatically on its equilibriums.

The war on terror launched after the 9/11 attacks and Operation Iraqi Freedom in particular, came to be seen as the defining moment of a new historical
phase marking the passage from a US dominated world to an international
system increasingly characterized by its multi-polarity. And it was in the Middle East that the unipolar moment emerged after the Cold War began to crum-
ble: as described by several analysts and media pundits alike, it was as if a new
Pandora's box had been opened, thus setting free evils ready to wreak havoc
well beyond the region's disputed boundaries. Old prejudices combined with
self-fulfilling prophecies foreseeing heightening East *vs* West confrontations
and images of unending violence, brutality and gross violations of human
rights contributed to surreptitiously transform the area in as a sort of "onto-
logical Other" socio-politically (but –interestingly– not economically, militar-
ily and geopolitically) detached from its most immediate neighbors, Europe
and the West *in primis* (Tuastad, 2010).

The scale of the destabilization that invested the region and the consequences it had over the international system spurred an intense debate aimed
at assessing the root causes of the phenomenon. Particularly important was in
this sense the crisis that affected the Iraqi State from 2003 onwards and the
analytical frameworks adopted to describe it. While several studies focused on
the responsibilities of the US-led international coalition, the shortcomings of
the Iraqi reconstruction process and the disillusion stemming from the inability to cope with the huge expectations generated by the fall of the Ba'thist regime, other recurred to different interpretative paradigms focusing on the allegedly inherent weakness of the Iraqi State. According to such visions, the
causes of the difficulties post-2003 Iraq had to cope with were to be found in a
sort of "original sin" marring the history of the Iraqi State since its inception:
the decision to create an artificial State in line with British imperial desiderata
yet not in line with the aspirations of its diverse population. Accordingly, priority had not to be given to the deficiencies of the post 2003 reconstruction process but to the apparently unavoidable polarization of the Iraqi political system along sectarian[1] lines.

According to such visions, the deepening polarization of the Iraqi socio-
political fabric represented the proof that alleged "primordial" identities, despite having been marginalized by the consolidation of the modern State,
maintained the potential to mobilize significant strata of the population and
to influence both State and regional politics. The emergence of non-state actors largely defined by overtly sectarian agendas, their ability to provide basic

---

1   While in studies related to the Middle Eastern region the term tends to refer to Sunni – Shia
    competition, the term is here employed in its broader sense, referring to ethnic, linguistic,
    religious and confessional related processes and features.

services to populations largely neglected by their governments coupled with the fragmentation of the Iraqi political spectrum and the inability of state institutions to reassert their primacy all contributed to threaten the very foundations of the Iraqi polity.

Even more important, the heightening destabilization of the wider Middle East registered from 2011 onwards and the emergence of similar phenomena all over the area increasingly questioned state-centered representations of the region making sectarian paradigms attractive well beyond the Iraqi borders.

Loyalties based on sect, kin and different forms of local particularisms gradually acquired an academic dignity of their own and were increasingly entrusted with a symbolic dimension far exceeding the contours of the debates between "primordialist" and "modernist" schools (Hinnebusch, 2016; Al-Qarawee, 2013).

Reimagined through such lenses, the wider Middle East came again to be increasingly represented as a mosaic of different communities defined by clear-cut fault-lines constrained in a regional framework dominated by "artificial states". Sectarian conflicts in the region were then largely considered as manifestations of ancient ethnic hatreds and struggles symbolized by an archetypal approach of We *vs* Others.

The process reached its apex between 2014 and 2016 spurring a debate centered around the possible overcoming of an a-historical and often mythicized "Sykes-Picot" order accused of having been framed according to the needs of Western colonial powers and hence of being disconnected from the "natural" equilibriums of the area (Kamel, 2016a, 2016b). Curiously enough, some of these positions seemed to partially reflect the propaganda of the "Islamic State" organization that in June 2014, after extending its grip over most of the Jazira region, announced the erasing of the Syria-Iraq borders and the beginning of a new era destined to cancel the legacy of a century of humiliation.

> It was 98 years ago that the Allies of WWI forged a secret agreement to carve up the territories of the Muslim lands. This arrangement, referred to since as the Sykes-Picot agreement, mapped out parts of the Middle East and designated them as being under the influence or control of either France or the United Kingdom in anticipation of the subsequent conquest of the region. (...) Years after the agreement, invisible borders would go on to separate between a Muslim and his brother, and pave the way for ruthless, nationalistic *tawaghit* (impious tyrant) to entrench the ummah's division rather than working to unite the Muslims under one imam carrying the banner of truth. (...) As the operation to capture Ninawa and advance towards Baghdad and the Radi strongholds to the south

was underway, the lions succeeded in taking control of the border region between Wilayat Al-Barakah in Sham, and Wilayat Ninawa in Iraq, and in demolishing the barriers set up to enforce the crusader partitions of the past century. (Islamic State Report, 2014: 2-4)

Jihadist proclaims apart, the calls for a complete redefinition of existing Middle East boundaries found a significant echo in the West albeit being met, expect for a few notable exceptions, by stiff local opposition (Plebani, 2018). Particularly interesting are, in this regard, the positions expressed by Robin Wright who proposed to replace the current regional order with a new one based on the creation of fourteen new States presenting a higher level of religious and ethno-linguistic homogeneity (Wright, 2013, 2016).

Questioning the validity of such schemes does not pertain to the scope of the present analysis. Much more significant is, instead, analyzing the theoretical assumptions underpinning them and, in particular, the essence of the sectarian boundaries claimed to define the groupings slated to become the constituent units of such a re-imagined Middle East.

While no shared socio-political taxonomy of the phenomenon exists – with the term itself being the focus on an intense debate (Haddad, 2017; Hinnebusch, 2016) – sectarian conflict and polarization are generally created out of imagined boundaries set at the linguistic and religious levels, with kinship, regionalisms and local particularisms playing lesser albeit important roles.

Broadly speaking, the primary marker of group identity tends to be set at the (ethno-)linguistic level. While the wider Middle East has always been characterized by the compresence of multiple groups, Arabic is by far the main regional language, with Turkish, Persian, Kurdish and Hebrew communities following suit. Yet, such groupings represent only part of the extremely diverse Middle Eastern linguistic spectrum. Other communities inhabiting the area include Amazighs, Circassians, Assyrians, Armenians, Turkmen, Azeris, Baluchis, and Pashtuns, just to mention some of the most demographically relevant. Iran, Iraq and Afghanistan represent typical examples of such linguistic "melting-pots". Furthermore, the region is characterized by a high-level of intra-linguistic diversity with each key group presenting significant internal variety and marked differences. Such a situation is evident when considering Arabic dialects spoken in North Africa and the Levant but the same holds true even at country level. Iraq, for example, is the home of at least three Arabic dialects (Jaziran, Mesopotamian, and of the Marshes) and of three Kurdish vernaculars (Kurmanji, Sorani and Pehlewani).

A second fault-line is generally represented by religion. While Islam is undisputedly the most practiced faith, the region is home to a wide array of non-Muslim groups of whom Christians, Jews, Zoroastrians, Sabians-Mandeans, Yazidis, Kalashas represent some of the most known examples. Such variety is further increased by the presence of different sects and denominations within the main religious communities. Beyond Sunni-Shia differentiation, Islam presents a significant internal diversity. Although today less relevant than in the past, Sunni Islam has traditionally encompassed a precise number of "schools" of interpretation (Hanafi, Maliki, Shafi, Hanbali). At the same time, it has always been characterized by the presence of Sufi orders that played a crucial role in bridging the gap with realities characterized by extremely diverse socio-political, cultural and economic fabrics. In this regard, Naqshbandi Sufi order's influence in both Iraq and Turkey is illuminating. Similarly, Sunni Islam is today strongly influenced by different orientations in the way of experiencing and practicing its message in private and public life. The role of Salafism at the local, regional and international levels explains not only a strict and puritanical approach toward Sunni Islam, but also how the same orientations can foster diverse attitudes distinguishing between quietists, politics-oriented, and militant-activists (Wiktorowitz, 2006).

Shia Islam is also internally diverse, with many sub-confessional groups such as Alevi in Turkey, Alawites and Ismailis in Syrian or Zaydis in Yemen. In this framework, Ibadites and Druze differently distance from such a picture. The former represents a sort of third path toward Islam, while Druze maintains a certain distance and autonomy, strongly defending their community boundaries, albeit being connected with the history of Islam in the region. With Christians, the situation further complicates, because in the Middle East, one can find multiple confessions and rites. The region is the homeland of Eastern and Oriental Christianity (for example, Orthodox, Syrians and Copt), but it also sees the presence of Catholics of different rites (such as Latin, Melkite, Maronite) and of different manifestations of Reformed Christianity (for instance: Anglican, Lutheran, Evangelists, Adventist). In all these cases, the religious factor can variably intertwine with the ethno-linguistic dimension producing a very nuanced image of the Middle Eastern socio-cultural fabric and of its multiple and variable geography. Religious diversity can enrich an ethno-linguistic sphere, dividing people speaking the same languages between different religion, confessions and rite. This is particularly evident within the Arab-Speaking domain where one can find Sunnis and Shiites (of different schools, orientations and sub-confessions) and Christians, equally diverse in their belonging and professions. But it also manifests with Kurds, predominantly belonging to Sunni Islam, but also to Shia Islam and Yezidism. Turks and Kurds also differentiate between Sunni Islam and Alevi, with the latter generally considered part of the Shia world. Furthermore, religious affiliations can become a vector through which expressing a different (quasi)ethno-linguistic independent identity. It is the case of Assyrians in Iraq, but also of Druze in Israel.

Kinship and family ties too tend to be considered as factors further contributing to shape the *weltanschauung* and the realm of possibilities of single individuals and communities. Such a perception becomes particularly relevant when considering the influence exerted by tribal norms and power structures over different areas and in different times. The concept of tribe remains highly contested due to past tendencies to read a broad array of socio-political dynamics in exclusively tribal terms and to reify power dynamics inherently fluid and subject to changes (Dodge, 2003). Yet, tribal networks keep being considered important players contributing to determine local equilibriums and dynamics. Traditionally considered to be built along segmented structures largely (albeit not exclusively) defined in terms of kinship (Evans-Pritchard, 1940; Emanuel Marx, 1977; Khoury, Kostiner, 1991), tribes can be described as forms of mutual-aid association aimed at preserving internal order, defending the group from external threats and maximizing its resources. Competition among the different sub-units of the archetypal tribe (confederation, tribe, clan, segment, etc.) and with external opponents activate forms of in-bound solidarity that may expand up to the ladder of the tribal system or be mitigated by mediation processes rooted in forms of collective responsibility (Gellner, 1983; Gellner, 1990; Lindholm, 1986). Far from being limited to specific (and largely peripheral) areas and from being insulated from state apparatuses, tribal dynamics have tended to overlap with different layers of power and authority succeeding in exerting significant influence *vis-à-vis* the State.

This capacity and potential have endured state- and nation-buildings processes. Although attacked and subject to different pressures from the central power, tribalism has entertained a strict relationship with the state power. While tribes have certainly represented hinders to the ambitions of central rule, they have also represented in time of need a resource to be exploited (through selected cooptation) to increase the legitimacy of a regime. At the same time, tribalism has distinguished itself for its resilience, especially when the centralizing logics of the States entered in phases of structural crisis losing its absolute monopoly over power. Paradigmatic, in this sense, are Saddam Hussein's tribal policies enacted after the Gulf War (Baram, 1997) as well as the case of the Hashemite Kingdom of Jordan that since the 1970s has promoted Bedouin traditions with the aim of consolidating the national identity fabric and the legitimacy of the its regime (Massad, 2011).

Regional identities and forms of local particularisms complete the set of fault-lines associated with the already-mentioned sectarian visions. Albeit less considered than other layers of differentiation, these factors played an important role in articulating alternative visions of unity within the State (promoting autonomist and federal schemes), in supporting the redefinition of the existing order (projects advocating partitioning or union of different areas) or in inoculating local power dynamics within state institutions. The predominance of Tikritis within the upper echelons of the Iraqi administration during Saddam Hussein's tenure is a good example of the latter (Baram, 2003; Zeidel, 2007), while the former is well represented by Benghazi's longstanding pleas for autonomy within the Libyan system or Basra bids for self-government (Visser, 2005; Isakhan, Mulherin, 2018).

While the above-mentioned layers of differentiation unequivocally influence the equilibriums governing the Middle Eastern socio-political spectrum, they do not represent any sort of "prime movers" able to shape regional dynamics and equilibriums alone. Looking at the Middle East as a mosaic of "gated communities" largely autonomous, independent and based on a set of largely fixed (primordial) elements does not reflect the complexity and the fluidity of socio-political frameworks characterized by the overlapping of mutually influencing factors and by a constant competition (Roy, 2018). A feature, the latter, well represented by the old tribal saying "me against my brother. Me and my brother against my cousin. Me, my brother and my cousin against the outsider".

Even ethno-linguistic boundaries, while representing an important element of differentiation and one of the fault-lines more prone to be politicized, cannot be considered unsurmountable walls inevitably destined to separate different communities and to determine their political stances. Especially in times of crises, transversal ties tend to be rediscovered and differences put aside. The case of the alliances forged between the Kurdish peshmerga and tribal units of Arab Sunni descent to face the threat posed by the "Islamic State" organization in northern Iraq is a clear example. The same holds true at the religious level, as demonstrated by significant cases of interfaith solidarity taking place even at the apex of the Iraqi civil war, and at the tribal level, where it is still far from uncommon to find components of a single tribe belonging to different confessions and even religions.[2] The very fact that the term sectarian/sectarianism (today's *ta'ifiyya*) is largely perceived as derogatory in countries like Syria and Iraq (which used to be considered as the countries most characterized by the presence of mixed families) and that local populations

---

2   Significant, in this sense, are the case of the Iraqi Muntafiq confederation (led till the beginning of the 20th century by the Sunni al-Sadoun clan but mainly made of sub-units of Shia descent) and the tribal allegiances centered around al-Karak and al-Salt witnessing forms of Christian-Muslim solidarity (Maggiolini, 2010).

have been the most vocal in opposing to projects aimed at partitioning the region along sectarian lines (Plebani, 2018) largely attests to this stance.

Instead of looking at the region through sectarian lenses and mosaic-inspired analytic prisms that, despite their alleged theoretical purity, present multiple deficiencies and rigidities, the diverse socio-political fabric of the Middle East seems to be better served by an approach taking in consideration the strong interaction and the mutual influence characterizing the different souls of its societies. In doing so, it is impossible not to consider the crucial role played by state agencies in imaging, articulating and dealing with diversity in all its forms. Artificial or not, Middle Eastern modern States have contributed to shape regional dynamics and equilibriums in ways and modalities that cannot be ignored.

Building on such considerations, the regional socio-political spectrum could then be described as the result of multiple geographies of power that, while competing among each other, contribute to influence the environment they operate in and by doing so get influenced by it. It is in this framework that, as described in the second part of this chapter, the theories elaborated by Jean Pierre Bourdieu can represent a particularly useful asset.

3   Contested Visions of State and Nation

The study of the Middle East multiple and variable geographies holds an important double role for understanding how state- and nation-building processes have developed in this region since the turn of the 20th century. On the one hand, it delineates the features and elements out of which "State" and "nation" have been imagined, projected and transformed. On the other, it is the subject through which alternative visions of "State" and "nation" have been developed, inevitably becoming one of the arenas on which geopolitical and regional competitions took place and are still developing.

The analysis of the features and parabolas of state- and nation-building processes in the contemporary Middle East has been always a focal thread in studies of the region and in tracing the reconfiguration of its diverse socio-political fabrics from the dissolution of the Ottoman Empire until today, both from a theoretical perspective and from a historical one. This started from and has advanced according to different contextual conditions, political interests and ideological orientations, each providing important clues for reconsidering why the Middle East has witnessed the development of multiple, contested visions of State and nation.

Such a history still speaks out with the name that is employed to describe the area. Elaborated around the mid-19th century according to Western colonial projections within the Ottoman Empire and then imposed during the Mandate period, the term Middle East is a geographical notion intrinsically imbued with geopolitical meanings. It substantially conveys a specifically north-western European perspective of the role and position of the region in world geography. In fact, this definition historically depended on Europe's conceptualization of itself and others, where the others (the Middle East) are described as a region essentially contended by diverse and conflicting understandings of its borders and identities (Zubaida, 2011).

This kind of understanding continues to vehicle the conviction of a sort of inadequateness of the Middle Eastern social-political fabric to fully conform to the modern State ideal and to adopt categories such as that of nation, because historically imposed from above and outside. The Middle East becomes the region of "States without nations" (Vatikiotis, 2016) or a geographic mosaic of different minorities fluctuating in an Islamic continuum.

Accordingly, this analysis takes its distance from these orientations. In doing so, it does not question either the presence, saliency, and role of the manifold and diverse Middle East identity and community landscapes or the importance of Islam in politics and society or the complex political and security situation that has undermined and still challenges the condition of many minorities, communities and groups in the region. Rather, it proposes to focus on the politicization and reconfiguration of regional identity spheres for pursing political projects, especially in the field of state- and nation-building processes. The question is not whether and why state- and nation-building processes developed or failed, but how they have been conceived out of regional diversity, affecting their conditions and roles. At the same time, exactly because the acritical imposition of the idea of nation according to a narrow Western understanding has been problematic, given the composite Middle Eastern landscapes, the historical exploration of its development still stands out as an important thread in regional politics.

In essence, the history of the Middle East shows that identity designations can be selectively manipulated and reconfigured either by a central regime to project its authority and legitimacy or by local communities to resist or establish solid relationships of cooperation with central powers, but also with external actors, to defend themselves or extract revenues. The colonial past has mattered, the role of Islam is grounded in history, diversity has always played an important role, and the competition between external and regional powers has always played a crucial role in orienting state- and nation-building processes.

All these elements need to be taken into consideration in exploring and understanding socio-political engagements and disengagements within and from the region. Nevertheless, the Middle East is much more than a mosaic composed of distinct tiles that dominate or are dominated. Politics in the region is not simply the result of linear and univocal behaviors, postures and strategies developed by homogenous, coherent and monolithic ethno-linguistic and religious communities or kin groups. As said above, this image needs to be reconsidered, looking at regional diversity according to the idea of variable geographies unevenly distributed over this wide territory. State and nation have been developed according to these variable geographies and through a complex matrix of contestation, cooperation and competition at the local, regional and international levels. Instability and turmoil, which affected the region well before the end of Great War, have not broken out because the concepts of "modern State" and "nation" have simply been refused *per se*. Rather, conflicts, unrest and wars need to be analyzed as the symptoms or manifestations of a deeper quest for meaning, legitimacy, authority and power. This process has been developing since the late 19th century. State and nation have been thus the arena and subject of this struggle, drawing new political contents out of regional diversity and inevitably pervading the realms of citizenship, community affiliation, the role of religion in public space and the political quest for identity. This is one of the reasons why the Middle East has witnessed the elaboration of a number of contested visions of it; a dynamic that today has entered into a new phase following the 9/11 attacks, the 2011 uprisings and the explosion of an all-out geopolitical regional competition. In this framework, diversity in all its attributes has been an actor and not just a scapegoat or victim.

4   State and Nation in the Middle East: an Analytical Assessment

Moving to the level of theories and approaches, State and nation in the Middle East have been analyzed according to different concerns and interests.

On the one hand, there are studies that have predominantly focused on exploring the origin of nations. In this regard, the central question that has substantiated such analyses is why ethnicity has become a dominant force in modern politics and a political fact in the life of States (Bengio, Ben-Dor, 1999). Primordialists espouse the idea that ethnic groups have an authentic existence that endures from generation to generation (Geertz, 1967). They are not simply ascriptive, but able to bypass and overcome other forms of belonging and identification. Modernists take their distance from such an understanding, pointing out that the modernization process has transformed traditional societies. Modernization has exacerbated ethnic conflicts, but it has also laid the basis for the creation of new entities and, thus, new States beyond premodern identities (Gellner, 1990; Anderson, 1991). In this regard, mass communication, education and modern technologies are fundamental for understanding this process of "imagining" the nation. Ethno-symbolism seems positioned between these two poles, suggesting the importance of recognizing the ethnic origin of modern nations without ignoring the importance of the process of reconfiguring and transmitting ethnic symbols (Smith, 1989, 1999, 2003). Therefore, phenomena such as Political Islam and its relationship with national ideals in the Middle East can be understood in a totally different manner according to each perspective. Primordial approaches often point out that the Western ideal of nation is substantially undermined by the persistent and pervasive relationship between politics and religion (Vatikiotis, 2016). Accordingly, Islam would represent a dominant force inherently inclined to transcend boundaries and spheres of territorial modern States. Therefore, nations in the Western sense cannot fully emerge in the region. In this framework, non-Muslim communities are considered to be inevitably destined to remain minorities in the fullest meaning. Modernists and ethno-symbolists can variably consider Political Islam as one of the products of modernity. According to these visions, the phenomenon would not represent the most authentic expression of the traditional religious culture, but it would convey new understandings of its role in the public sphere through the construction or revival of symbols and meanings (Zubaida, 2001). Nevertheless, beyond their evident differences, all approaches subscribe to the conviction of the importance of analyzing ethnicity, its attributes and features for understanding Middle Eastern politics and the relationship between majorities and minorities in the region.

On the other hand, one can find studies more clearly focused on analyzing the history of the different ideologies and political systems that have developed in the Middle East since the end of the 20th century.

From an ideological standpoint, the main divide has been the contraposition between secularists/liberals and Islamists (the idea of a secular State *vs* an Islamic State). These two orientations have also assumed different perspectives, dividing those supporting nationalist/patriotic orientations (e.g. Syrian, Egyptian, Lebanese nationalisms or manifestations of irredentism as in the case of the Kurds, but also Islamist activism focusing on the national level such as in Jordan) from those promoting supranational projects (e.g. the pan-Arab; pan-Iranian; pan-Turkish or pan-Islamic).

From this standpoint, it is interesting to point out that after the Arab uprisings these opposing poles tended to converge on the concept of "civil State" or "civil government" (*dawla madaniyya*). Although it is widely considered to possess indubitably positive connotations, this notion is still subject to debate, lacking clear-cut definitions. *Dawla madaniyya* seems basically to convey the idea of the need for a democratic regime and the opportunity to avoid playing identity politics, prioritizing the development of an inclusive society despite the fact that it is not clear if the essence of society, State and nation that such a vision seeks to promote conforms to liberal/secular or Islamist ideals (Bahlul, 2018). While it is still premature to consider it an orientation, it is worth mentioning because it elucidates the state of the art of such a debate.

Historically, whatever the content of the various political projects that have developed since the end of the 20th century, the ideological competition concerning State and nation has initially entailed a reconfiguration of the traditional ethno-linguistic and religious designations of the Ottoman epoch, transforming the manner of conceiving and understanding regional diversity and projecting it toward its modern and contemporary forms. This is one of the first elements that need to be taken into account for analyzing the transformation of regional identity spheres and boundaries through state- and nation-building processes.

In fact, it was between the late 19th and early 20th centuries that words such as "Turk" and "Arab" lost their past connotations. Previously referring to rough local communities and tribal peoples, they became honorable and patriotic expressions of nations in search of independence (Zubaida, 2001). The Kemalist State and its muscular secularism elevated the word "Turk", to which was associated a Sunni Muslim character, to the key parameter for guiding state- and nation-building in the country, relegating non-Sunni Muslim and non-Turkish speaking communities to the margins because considered inherently alien. It is important to point out that the reference to Sunni Islam was interpreted as part of the cultural attribute of being Turk in a process of nation-building expressly secular in its stance. In the case of the "Arab" ideal, the dynamic has been much more contested, and still is, although regional competition has ceased to be predominantly played out on this kind of rhetorical discourse. It has constantly oscillated between approaches focused on stressing the existence of a single Arab nation, with a common language and culture but also with multiple religious manifestations (predominantly Islam and Christianity) and those supporting the intrinsic association of "Arabness" with Islam. In both cases, such orientations have varied, oscillating between different territorial configurations despite sharing the same conviction of the need to question the Mandate systematization. At the same time, other forms of nationalism have been developed with a clear patriotic stance, downsizing or refusing the saliency of Arabness, such as in the case of the Maronites in Lebanon or of Egypt during the inter-war period.

Similar developments also occurred in the Iranian context, culminating in the 1930s with Tehran's official request to avoid use of the word "Persian" in diplomacy, deeming the term "Iranian" more appropriate for communicating the "authentic" pluri-millennial culture and traditions of this territory and its populace.

This plurality of orientations and outlooks, even within the same identity field as in the case of Arabness, should not be considered peculiar or exceptional. The multiple forms and platforms through which nationalist ideals have been promoted is the clearest expression of the variable socio-cultural geographies that cut across this region, depicting many possible landscapes with shifting boundaries and spheres. Accordingly, the history of the Middle East and its countries offers further evidence that nationalism is never a unified and homogeneous phenomenon (Owen, 2013).

At the state-building level, such diverse ideological orientations have been variously elaborated and contextualized. Nevertheless, there have been two main models of political system that have been followed. These are monarchies (either centered on a family such as in Jordan and Morocco or dispersed and extended like in Saudi Arabia) and republics. These two models of political system implicitly differ in their approaches to diversity. For instance, the case of Jordan shows how monarchies have more frequently promoted a sort of "fuzzy" nationalism (Frisch, 2002), maintaining a certain ambiguity in their discourses in order to separate and selectively recompose or organize local diversity according to an idea of "nation" similar to that of one big family united around the ruling crown. At the same time, between the 1930s and the 1950s, the Hashemite crown of Iraq proved how such an image can also be instrumental to developing a more pronounced discourse based on Arab nationalism.

Republics have, instead, been more obvious and outspoken in their assimilatory ideals, directly entering the field of nation-building with the aim of making a "strong" nation the condition of their existence and the path through which to fulfil promises of independence and progress, due also to the discomfort that political elites have in the Middle East with the idea of federalism or identity plurality within the state structure. In essence, they have more frequently embarked on identity politics. This is not to say that monarchies have been distinctive for a gentler or softer approach than republics in their strategy to manage and deal with diversity or that they have shown less interest in nation-building, but to underline some basic, and very general, differences in their stances and struggles for legitimacy through state- and nation-building processes. At the same time, there is no intention here to over-simplify, ignoring that regimes changed over time, sometimes preserving nationalist rhetoric while developing it in its essence and scope. An eloquent example is provided by Ba'thist Syria and how it transformed with Hafiz Al Assad and then after the ascendancy of his son, Bashar. While preserving the same rhetoric of Arabism, Al Assad's Ba'thist regime overcame part of its traditional secularist stance, reintroducing references to Islam in the constitution. In essence, he sought to promote his own idea of Arab nationalism, transitioning it from the role of ethnic kinship to a principle centered on cultural affinity, with the aim of quelling sub-national identities and manipulating minority issues. Bashar Al Assad then concentrated on promoting an idea of Syria as the "safe-haven" for minorities dwelling in the country. The regime and political system remained stable, but their ideological content structurally changed through manipulation of Syrian diversity (Rabo, 2012). This evolution elucidates how diversity can be both actor and subject in state- and nation-building processes, serving as the basis for developing new coalitions of power or becoming a victim of political projects.

Therefore, without the ambition of being exhaustive, this brief systematization offers some initial clues for looking at the complex political continuum within which Middle Eastern regimes positioned or transitioned since the defeat of the Ottoman Empire. Clearly, the intertwining between the various ideological orientations and their different forms of contextualization produced different forms of rulers, each proposing their specific understanding of State and nation, and how to create them out of local diversity.

In this regard, it is worth pointing out that differences and analogies between such experiences also depended on or were affected by other two factors, namely authoritarianism and rentierism. Both factors played and still play a fundamental role in defining rulers and regimes in the region and in influencing their contextual approach towards diversity in state- and nation-building processes. They should be taken as attributes that further complicate the intertwining between the ideological and systemic levels. For example, authoritarianism was manifest both in the case of Nasserist Egypt through its single party system and in the Hashemite monarchy of Jordan between the 1960s and the end of the 1980s, when parliamentary life in the country was suspended. Regarding such countries, it is still employed, albeit adding the attribute of "hybrid", to describe a regime that tolerates and somehow promotes procedural forms of democracy but does not fully subscribe to it. Therefore, authoritarianism should not be simply considered as equivalent to strong, severe or repressive regimes or political systems. In this field, authoritarianism can be viewed as a distinctive position and method of engaging and dealing with society and diversity via state- and nation-building processes. Its frequency and ubiquitousness have been widely explained according to culturalism.

Nevertheless, authoritarianism should be reconsidered according to a precise historical parabola. After the Second World War, state- and nation-building processes were widely launched and developed under the pressure of traumatic transformations, first with the aim of taking revenge on European colonial projections and then to forestall the effects of recurring political and military failures. On the one hand, the trauma of colonization was reprocessed considering it the result of internal fragmentation and weaknesses. According to such an understanding, colonization in the heart of the Middle East had been possible because of the inadequateness of political leaderships and the presence of internal fifth columns. On the other, with the exception of North African countries and the Islamic Republic of Iran, the Middle East region has frequently witnessed the foundation and emergence of new political systems and regimes more because of revolts, civil wars and coup d'états than as the culmination of popular revolutionary movements and popular national struggles for independence.

The intertwining between these factors has not only infused into state- and nation-building processes a sense of urgency and anxiety, but it has also encaged them in a sort of securitization syndrome, subjecting Middle Eastern society to the authoritarian dilemma. State and nation were essentially considered weak and authoritarianism became the posture to make them strong out of their fragility. In order to strengthen state foundations there has been a tendency to "overstate" state role and structures, as pointed out by Ayubi (Ayubi, 1996). Although Middle Eastern countries already existed on the map, the colonial legacy consolidated the idea of the need to establish "authentic" States and nations out of past manipulations and impositions. At the same time, such projects were considered in need of being defended against a number of different challenges and possible enemies at the local, regional and the international levels. This situation became the hotbed that fostered the emergence of the military against civil rule. In fact, already during the interwar period, two *coup d'état* took place in Iraq with Sidqi-Sulayman (1936) and later on with al-Kaylani and the officers of the "Golden Square" (1941) (Marr, al-Marashi, 2017). In this framework, shortly after defeat at the hands of Israel in 1948, Syria witnessed the first post-Mandate era military coup with Husni Al Za'im deposing Shukri Al Quwatli with the support of the population (Salibi, 1998) and a few years after, the Free Officers in Egypt (1952) became a model. The military entered regional politics, mobilizing their populaces and presenting itself as the only actor capable of taking the State and the nation to real independence. The role of the military and the constant tension between them and civilian rulers are factors determinant to understanding an important part of the history of state- and nation-building processes in the region.

In essence, authoritarian regimes in the Middle East are distinctive for prioritizing the direct and constant mobilization of people, bypassing representative institutions and political participation. They are also characterized by their focus on political forms of control both of society and of the economy. The Middle Eastern authoritarian State has not simply governed society, but has claimed to control all spheres in the life of their States and societies, showing no tolerance for forms of autonomous organization (Zubaida, 1993). Civil society has thus become an extension of the regime-state and of its bureaucracy. In cases such as that of Kemalist Turkey and Pahlavi Iran (1920s) or Nasserist Egypt (1950s-1960s), nationalism combined with authoritarianism expressing the will to create both "State" and "nation" at the same time, reconfiguring society according to rigid categories imposed from above.

In this framework, rentierism helps to elucidate how authoritarianism has established its resilience in Middle Eastern politics and how the State has been developed as a mechanism of distribution and patronage. To a large extent, rentierism has been and still is more important for understanding the history of States and regimes in the region than the previous categories and orientations. In fact, rentierism explains important attributes of Middle Eastern authoritarian States and regimes. In particular, it describes why they have been essentially immanent, intrusive and invasive, but not capable of penetrating society as in the case of totalitarianism (Owen, 2013). These features are not simply useful for appreciating the scope of authoritarianism in the Middle East, but reveal the essence of the relationship between regimes and societies. Although forms of rentier State existed already during the inter-war period, such as, for example, the case of the Emirate of Transjordan and its dependence on the revenues provided by London, this model has been developed since the 1970s, during the oil crisis. Rentierism has been employed to explore and explain the role of patronage and distributive policies in modern Middle Eastern States and regimes (Beblawi, Luciani, 1987). Well described by the principle of "no taxation, no representation", rentierism has allowed regimes to "buy" their legitimacy, imposing themselves on societies and cultivating their loyalty without the need to pervade them through taxation and other forms of extraction. Rentierism has thus been a critical resource for regimes seeking stability and legitimacy, but it has also been an endemic weakness for States and regimes in the region. Such a condition has amplified a State's dependency on a distributive and exchange relationship. The State appeared to be strong, but this attribute was achieved to the detriment of society, intentionally weakening it (Migdal, 1988). At the same time, rentierism has provided the State with power and leverage, but has also precluded hegemony (Ayubi, 1996). Accordingly, authority, legitimacy and sovereignty are imposed from above and depend on enduring acts of distribution and patronage. Beyond these, regimes intrinsically lack substantial recognition. This condition has undermined state- and nation-building processes in their essence. While the focus on ideological orientations and models of political system is fundamental for guiding the analysis, an excessive concentration on them can distract, losing sight of the transformation and dynamism of Middle Eastern politics over the decades. The State can be interpreted as a sort of coherent political architecture while the nation turns into the product of single actors and specific ideologies (Mitchel, 1991). In order to overcome such a risk, a more effective analytical approach seems the one looking at State and nation as a field. The State becomes a "national field" from which the nation can be imagined, "promoted" or represented according to the accumulation or exclusion of the diverse elements that compose a socio-cultural fabric within a given territory (Zubaida, 1993; Owen, 2013). This approach contemplates all previous remarks. But it also criticizes the notion of the State as a unified actor, distinctive from society. Therefore, the State *per se* becomes a field and an arena for re-orienting and re-directing all assumptions of power toward its political center as opposed to the traditional transboundary relationships of the pre-modern epoch. In its Middle Eastern articulation, the national political field determinates advantages and distributes resources on the basis of individuals, families and communities, whether village, religious or kin-group. The actors involved in the field compete for resources and influence through cooperation or contestation, inevitably infusing new political meanings. Therefore, it is through this matrix of relationships that the political field can transform and change. In essence, the analysis of state- and nation-building processes can become the study of this field and its evolution through the multiple relationships between its inhabitants. State, nation and society are thus integrated into one single field, which through its functioning can selectively vehicle either inclusion, participation and co-optation or exclusion, marginalization and even alienation. At the same time, it can be transformed in an arena within which external influences are projected in order to orienting its functioning, providing with extra support specific actors with the aim of making them prevail in the internal competition for recognition, legitimacy and authority.

5   The Struggle to Create State and Nation Out of Middle Eastern Diversity

The contemporary history of the Middle East shows that the above-mentioned orientations and models have not simply been contextualized in a number of different manners, but have also been experienced with very ambiguous and contrasted stances. This seems particularly clear looking at Arab countries, the focus of this overview.

In the Middle East, state- and nation-building processes have been always developed under the pressure of overlapping solidarity-group, patriotic/national and supranational influences (Roy, 2007). Different forms of loyalties have not simply competed for leadership and for orienting and guiding these processes, but have often developed in synchrony, with strong overlapping. Such a dynamic placed diversity under contrasting tensions, making it actor and subject of continuous political interplays (Zubaida, 2002). Pan-Arabism and pan-Islamism (in both the Shiite and Sunni versions) have been the leading supranational ideologies that inspired a number of political platforms, groups and movements in the region. They have largely represented the main political utopias through which it has been dreamt to reconfigure the fragmented Middle Eastern geography and dissolve the international boundaries imposed in the 1920s (Roy, 2007). At the same time, each orientation has proposed a distinctive vision of regional diversity and of its political saliency.

While a supranational utopia has constantly provided a fundamental point of reference, concrete politics have been always developed according to a "national" framework. This was manifest in the uneasy relationship between Ba'thist Syria and Nasserist Egypt at the time of the United Arab Republic (1958–1961), which failed because perceived by Syrians as a form of assimilation and not the fulfilment of Arabism (Owen, 2013). The same could be said about the strained relationship between Syria and Iraq since the 1960s, with the two Ba'thist declinations competing for leadership in the region. Even the Muslim Brotherhood established its presence in the region through national chapters (Boulby, 1999). This soon proved to be far more than a simple functional strategy. Since the 1950s, and especially during the ban on the Brotherhood's parent branch in Egypt, each chapter has taken root in its respective country, developing specific local orientations. This occurred without questioning any aspects of the supranational pan-Islamist vision promoted by the Brotherhood. In this regard, indicative is the different positioning of the Kuwaiti and Jordanian branches during the Gulf war in 1991, with the former supporting prompt intervention and the latter opposing the US' coalition (Moaddel, 2002). This episode also elucidates another aspect of the importance of the national dimension for actors usually considered inspired by a supranational vision. Their history shows that each chapter has most frequently looked at regional politics according to the perspective of their territory, country and regime, and not vice-versa. It was by associating with the national framework that they conveyed and articulated their utopic supranational vision (Roy,

2007). Another example is provided by the most recent events occurring after the Arab uprisings and, in particular, following the ousting of Muhammad Morsi in Egypt (Milton-Edwards, 2017). If one looks at the fragmentation process experienced by the Jordanian Muslim Brotherhood, it becomes clear how national visions and interests have taken the upper hand over supranational orientation. In Jordan, the Brotherhood's division into three different branches is neither solely the result of manipulation, co-optation and selective repression nor a consequence of their survival strategy, but confirms how the national dimension (the national political field) remains key in concrete politics.

Nevertheless, to complicate the situation, this "national" focus is not unchallenged. Quite the contrary, it is constantly undermined by multiple internal divisions (ethnic, religious and kin-group) which can either destabilize the country fabric or increase the ambiguity of concrete politics.

Ethnic divisions tend to be most significant "challengers" of the State and of its territorial dimensions and territorial space (such as the Kurds in Iraq or Turkey) (Bengio, Ben-Dor, 1999). At the same time, radical or existential forms of competition can develop also within the same ethnic dimension not simply for controlling the State and its resources, but for advancing contrasting visions of the identity of State and nation (e.g. Fatah and Hamas in their search for a Palestinian State) (Sayigh, 2011) to the point of breaking out into open conflict for control of the national political field. This is also the case of ethnic and religious rivalries that compete for their position within the State (e.g. the ethnic and religious rivalries in Lebanon and Iraq). At the same time, they can also transgress a State's international boundaries, reconnecting with supranational ideologies while still posing as a national actor (e.g. Hizb Allah and Iran) or they can associate with supranational utopianists to reinforce their political leverage, status and transboundary networks (e.g. the relationship that developed between the Islamic State organization and some tribes in the area of the Jazeera between Syria and Iraq) (Collombier, Roy, 2018).

This is the complex matrix of relationships and contrasting influences that describe the development of concrete politics in the region, fostering multiple visions of State and nation. As said before, the mechanics and grammar of this complex interplay are defined by variable regional geographies.

In this regard, history shows that such a matrix mainly due to a series of specific traumatic events (Roy, 2007) that contributed to reshuffling balances of power and alignments in the region. In literature, these have been traditionally described according to the following tripartition: the demise of a great Arab kingdom from the Mediterranean to Mesopotamia; the Arab States' defeats at the hand of Israel (1948, 1967, 1973), and the Iranian Revolution from which emerged the Islamic Republic of Iran (Roy, 2007). The present crisis and conflicts in the Middle East can be understood on the basis of such a legacy, with most recent events being part of a process of transformation and reconfiguration that had begun at the end of the 20th century.

The first trauma explains the conditions and rationales on which national political fields have been developed. The aftermath of the First World War produced different effects on Middle Eastern geographies.

At the regional systemic level, the disintegration of the Ottoman Empire opened this space to the contextualization and imposition of the modern state ideal according to the Western vision. From then on, this became the "compulsory model" inspiring all debates and confrontations beyond specific orientations and ideals. At the political level, the expulsion of Faysal from Damascus in 1920 attested to the drastic failure of the war strategy espoused by part of Arab nationalist leaderships, namely those who had decided to fight against Istanbul, supporting London and Paris. Instead of a united Arab State at the heart of the Middle East, as the Sharif of Mecca had tentatively negotiated with London in exchange for its support against Istanbul, the two European countries (backed in a second moment by Russia and Italy) opted for partitioning the region according to the (in)famous Sykes-Picot agreement (1916). The foundation of modern Middle Eastern States was realized on the basis of a selective re-interpretation of the Ottoman past and according to French and British geopolitical interests (Rogan, 2012).

London supervised the organization of the Mandate in Palestine, making sure that the Balfour Declaration guaranteeing a "Jewish Homeland" was included in the texts. It created the Emirate of Transjordan from a remote periphery of the old provinces of Damascus and it offered its administration to one of the sons of its ally, Sherif Husayn of Hijaz. At the same time, London promoted the foundation of the Kingdom of Iraq merging the three Ottoman provinces of Baghdad, Basra and (eventually) Mosul, and recognizing its crown to Faysal, another son of Sherif Husayn. Such a systematization was considered perfectly suited to London's geopolitical interests in the area and its colonial empire.

In turn, Paris obtained control of the rest of the Ottoman Sham, promoting the foundation of a "smaller Syria" and of a "wider Lebanon". Syria was formed by the unification of the Aleppo and Damascus areas plus the Jabal Druze and the plain of Latakia. The Sanjak of Alexandretta was instead detached and recognized as part of modern Turkey. "Greater Lebanon" was created by merging the Mountain with the Ottoman districts of Tripoli, Sidon and the Bekaa Valley.

This picture of the configuration of the contemporary Middle East was completed by Turkish and Iranian stabilization of their State boundaries and regimes (both of which adopted the secularization process of their societies as a path to consolidate the state structure) in the early 1920s and by the Al Saud triumph in their struggle to form a State, fulfilled with the conquest of Medina and Mecca that allowed them to found today's Saudi Arabia.

In the short term, the price of this process was essentially paid by the Armenians, Kurds and Assyrians who saw their independence ambitions totally frustrated. The new inter-war regional outlook developed according to a precise politicization of ethno-linguistic distribution and minority status. In essence, at a macro level, the regional balances of power were defined according to the tripartition between the Arab (divided into distinct countries), Turkish and Iranian dimensions. Non-Arab/Turkish/Iranian groups were thus ignored as well as heterodox Muslim groups, while non-Muslims were integrated as religious minorities. Regarding the heterodox Muslims, their position was essentially fragile (such the Alevi in Turkey or Bahá'is in Iran) and this is still the case today since they have no access to concrete politics. The foundation of the colonial State was decisive in framing national political fields. It fostered the organization of (supra)national camps.

At the national systemic level, each country was involved in direct "negotiation" with the Mandate power for establishing local balances of power and the new political centers of authority (Khoury, 2003, 2014). In essence, London and Paris were able to capitalize the support of a part of local leaderships establishing precise *modus vivendi*, exploiting variable local geographies. Generally, both powers designed the national political field through the combination of a selective political discourse centered on patriotic and ethno-national features (being Syrian, but also Arab) and the re-interpretation of the traditional Ottoman instruments for dealing with non-Muslim communities, now understood according the framework of the protection of religious minorities. This occurred explicitly, for example in Iraq with the Declaration of Guarantees (1932) (Müller-Sommerfeld, 2016), or indirectly, such as in Transjordan's institutionalizing the role of the Church in the field of education and personal status (Maggiolini, 2015). In Mandate Palestine, Britain's strategy was clearly ambiguous in its stance, also giving contrasting ambitions to the impracticability of harmonizing Jews and Arabs. Divide and rule selectively played with ethno-linguistic and religious designations. It avoided giving political or legal content to terms such as Palestinian or Arab-speaking in favor of the adoption of religious categories, Muslims and Christians. In substance, Palestinians were not recognized as a nation and they were classified in Mandate administration according to their religious affiliations (Robson, 2011).

In the post-war period, London's strategy to define State and nation in the Middle East thus followed the model of the Treaty of Lausanne signed by Turkey. Non-Arab ethno-linguistic groups were ignored, being considered fragments to be assimilated within the three above-mentioned majoritarian designations. Religious factors were taken into account in the name of the Ottoman past.

In the area under French control, the reconfiguration of variable local geographies was much more strident, at least apparently. While the Maronites' ambitions were welcomed, establishing their leadership in the newly founded "Greater Lebanon", the fusion of Ottoman districts with a considerable Muslim presence assured Paris the role of arbiter in national politics. In Syria, Paris was more "creative" (Dueck, 2010). While France consolidated the external international borders according to the Mandate treaty, internally the country was recurrently divided. Initially, the Mandate administration recognized three ministates (Aleppo, Damascus and that of the Alawites), followed by a fourth, the Jabal Druze. In 1925, Damascus and Aleppo were then merged, becoming the backbone of the future "united" State of Syria. This subdivision was inspired by an ambiguous understanding of Syrian diversity, promoting a political accommodation based on local distinctiveness (Aleppo and Damascus) and quasi ethnic-religious designations (Druze and Alawite that never before had been recognized as such within the Ottoman Empire) (White, 2007). At the same time, Christians were granted specific protection status as non-Muslim minorities. This divide and rule strategy endured until the 1940s. Although in use for less than a couple of decades, its effects produced a controversial legacy, politicizing and spatializing identities in the country.

Inevitably, the demiurgic Mandate policy did not develop unchallenged. Rebellions and protests recurrently broke out, especially in Palestine as a consequence of the rising tension between Jews and Arabs. At the same time, it is also important to point out that the Mandate vision was substantially considered acceptable by a large part of the local political leaderships. Patriotic orientations concentrated on the territorial State recently founded. They contested or collaborated on the basis of achieving the independence of their newly founded countries. Nationalists inspired by supranational ideals opposed foreign presences and their visions, but they also found a part of such systematization acceptable because inherently subscribing to Arabism (White, 2012). Accordingly, the issue was overcoming the international boundaries dividing the Arab nation, not conveying a different vision of the identity of the region. On the basis of such understanding, the interwar period became a hotbed for nationalist/patriotic platforms (e.g. the Lebanese nationalist movement inspired by the Maronite intellectuals of the Revue Phénicienne; the Egyptian Wafd party of Saad Zaghloul Wassef Boutros Ghali, pan-nationalist movements such as the 1932 Syrian Social Nationalist Party of the Greek-Orthodox Antoun Saadeh and the 1947 Ba'th Party of Michel Aflaq and Muhammad Al

Bitar). But in Egypt in 1928 the first modern pan-Islamist movement, the Muslim Brotherhood, also emerged. The Brotherhood was the sole actor taking a distance from the ideal of the secular national State and that of "Arabness", focusing on the need to promote an Islamic approach towards the state- and nation-building processes in the region. At the same time, it is also interesting to point out the manifestation of another form of pan-Islamist orientation. In early 1931, following the first congresses of Mecca and Cairo dedicated to discussing the necessity to re-establish the Caliphate in the Arab world, the Muslim Supreme Council in Palestine organized the first Islamic Congress with the aim of conveying in the same place representative from all Muslim countries. Although the Congress was widely ostracized by official authorities, such as those of Turkey and Egypt, it expressed this desire of unity and solidarity beyond the imposed categories and boundaries. It is also indicative because the Congress, predominantly attended by Sunni, was opened by a Shiite Imam. Today, this can sound strange giving the predominance of the Sunni-Shi'a sectarian predicament, but it was perfectly fitting the search for unity of those decades.

The second trauma pertains to the Arab States' defeats at the hand of Israel (1948, 1967 and 1973), thus embracing the phase of independence, the secular nationalist movement in the region and the reconfiguration of regional balances of power and national political orientations that culminated in the separate peace between Egypt and Israel (Camp David 1978) and the revolution in Iran (1979). This was a very intense and dynamic period in the history of the region, characterized by transformations and transitions at the local, regional and international levels. While immersed in a world shaped by Cold War logic, the Middle East embarked on a complex struggle for defining State and nation, regional balances of power and its role at the international level. In this struggle for power, leadership and meanings, the Middle East's variable geographies played a crucial role.

The 1950s and 1960s were the decades of Arab nationalist triumph, which became the leading ideal in state- and nation-building processes. It was during this period that the tension between patriotic and supranational orientations were clearer. At the same time, becoming progressively more evident during those years was the above-mentioned ambiguity in the relationship between utopian and concrete politics in the Arab nationalist sphere. In this regard, the Mandate legacy and the 1948 defeat of the Arab front against Zionism and the newly founded State of Israel were determinant.

The nationalist movement had multiple voices. While all shared the same conviction about the need to promote development and progress from above and about State intervention in society and the economy, they promoted different visions and strategies. Arabism became a contested ideal disputed between different nationalist currents (e.g. Ba'thist *vs* Nasserites) as well as between national parties subscribing to the same ideology (Syrian Ba'thists *vs* Iraqi Ba'thists). However, competition also developed through the rivalry between monarchies and republics, with the two branches of the Hashemite family in Iraq and Jordan proposing a path toward Arabism through the fulfilment of the united Arab State promised by London, and Nasserists promoting the pan-Arabist vision as the solution to Arab weaknesses (Rogan, 2012).

At the country level, post-war nationalism produced contrasting effects. For those subscribing to the Arabist ideal, the nationalist movement offered inclusion and participation in national fields. On the other hand, the non-Arab ethnic groups were further marginalized, being forced to surrender to assimilation by the various nationalist regimes ruling in the region. But secular nationalism imposed a price also on non-Muslim Arab-speaking communities. In fact, in the spirit of national unity and equality, they were asked to renounce most of the guaranties and autonomies recognized by Mandate authorities, proving their loyalty to the State and nation. In the early 1950s in Syria, for example, Colonel Shishakli publicly championed the need to eliminate religious minorities' reserved seats in parliament (Picard, 2012). In Iraq, the military coup in 1958–1959 by Qasim and his second-in-command 'Arif was only rhetorically presented as a solution to "national" minority issues (Rassam, 2006; Donabed, 2015). The promises of integrating Iraqi diversity were subordinated to the primary concern of defending the State and the regime in power. While containing or quelling any attempts requesting recognition of non-Arab identities, the Ba'th party in Syria and Iraq concentrated on depoliticizing the role of religious affiliations.

State and nation were recomposed in the image of the ruling party that imposed itself as the sole reference in charge of representing the people, mobilizing them and managing national, political and economic life in the country. It is not a coincidence that, in these countries, the Christian establishments (charities and schools) were generally nationalized, thus reducing the maneuver space of Christian leaderships.

But such dirigisme in state- and nation-building processes not only put pressure on ethnic and religious designations through the imposition of a majoritarian perspective, but also sought to create political identity in the image of the ruling power. An indicative example in this regard was in Jordan between 1950 and 1967, when the Hashemite rulers sought to develop a totally new expression of "national" identity (Massad, 2008). The "Jordanian" designation was created with the objective of legitimizing Hashemite rule over the East and West Banks. Therefore, it was initially created from the Trans-Jordanian and Palestinian outlooks. This strategy was very ambiguous in its stance, also because the Hashemite sought to develop it within the broader framework of Arabism. In fact, it was opposed and contested by both the left leaning supporters of pan-Arabism and the Palestinians involved in organizing their national resistance movement.

In essence, with the independence of the Arab countries, the struggle for State and nation put great pressure on Middle Eastern diversity. The variable regional geographies were substantially overshadowed in the name of the ideal of the "strong State" and "homogenous nation", ambiguously declined by different combinations of supranational ideologies and concrete politics (Mahmood, 2015).

In the early 1970s, Middle Eastern politics began to change. Pan-Arabism movements and leaderships were suffering a crisis of legitimacy and political credibility. The defeats by Israel and intra-Arab competition for regional leadership was exposing their internal ambiguities and weaknesses. This opened the space for elaborating new political projects and reconfiguring previous balances of power. It was in this context that progressively developed the so-called "return of religion in politics", namely the re-introduction of Islam into constitutions and States (where before it had been either given a marginal position, such as in Syria, or subjected to the modernizing political ambition of the regime, like in Nasser's Egypt), the co-optation of religion by political leadership to find new legitimacy and, finally, the (re)emergence of different Islamic actors in the public arena, from Islamist political activists and radical militants to the first currents of the contemporary Salafist vision under the inspiration of personalities such as Al Albani. In this framework, the most representative event was surely the revolution in Iran and the triumph of Khomeini – as it will be explained below, the third trauma in the history of defining "Arabness" in state – and nation-building processes. Nevertheless, it is important to point out that the "return of religion" was also expressed in the non-Muslim dimension with reconfiguration of the role of the Church and its ecclesiastical institutions in the community and public spheres (McCalloum, 2012). Nevertheless, at a closer glance, this decade represented a much more complex historical intersection than a simple phase of transition towards the revival of Islam in politics, in its multiple manifestations. In this regard, the civil war in Lebanon of 1975 is indicative, coalescing in a single conflict multiple polarizing factors, at the religious (e.g. Christian-Muslim), national/supranational (e.g. Maronite nationalism-pan-Arabism and Palestinian nationalism) and geopolitical levels (e.g. Syrian and Israeli interventions). The Lebanese civil war has been a real crucible of Middle East fault-lines, anticipating their future political developments. The foundation of Hizb Allah provides the clearest evidence of the newly developing configuration of the intertwining between solidarity-group, patriotic/national and supranational levels. Hizb Allah emerged in the midst of the civil war as a militant Islamist movement equally dedicated to a plurality of goals: defending the Lebanese Shiite community in the country; advancing the ideal of direct involvement of the Shiite clergy in politics (the *al-wilayat al-faqih* doctrine), while informally serving the interests of the Islamic Republic of Iran in the region; and striking back at Israel and Zionism for the sake of the Palestinians and Islam.

Therefore, the 1970s can be described as a decade of different political temporalities in the search for establishing State and nation on a solid new basis, with traditional secular orientations fighting to defend their role and authority in the attempt to recover from the failures of the 1960s, and new forms of political engagement emerging on the basis of different visions of identities and boundaries in the region. These dynamics developed according to multiple contextual configurations, transforming regional balances of power and logics of alignment in the whole Middle East. On the one hand, the so-called "return of religion to politics" did not entail making polity and society more "religious" (Mahmood, 2015), but described a potent mechanism of politicizing community identities that progressively appeared at the local and regional levels, also through the re-ethnicization and re-activation of religious boundaries. On the other, nationalism and ethno-nationalism continued to play a central role. The 1970s also saw the revival of traditional forms of ethic-irredentism, such as with the case of the Kurds and Assyrians in Iraq, and continuation of the Arab nationalist struggle for State and nation.

In this framework, the Iraq-Iran war well represents the complexity of this period of transformation. At the contextual level, the ascendancy of Saddam Hussein in Iraq fostered a new phase of muscular state- and nation-building processes. Diversity was confined and contained (Sassoon, 2012). Arabization and Ba'thification were the main objectives to be pursued on the basis of Saddam Hussein's personality cult (Donabed, 2015). Diversity was only tolerated if conforming to such a vision. It was not opposed *per se*, but it was subject to functional considerations of its contribution to achieving the regime's objectives. More generally, diversity was considered something to be kept private if not to be fully assimilated through acculturation, political negation and indoctrination. The rhetoric of the unity and indivisibility of the State predominated over any group or community's distinct perspective. It was in this framework that the Kurdish struggle for autonomy gained new momentum.

At the regional level, the war between Ba'thist Iraq and Khomeini's Iran was much more than an inter-state conflict for leadership in the region or control of the contested border of the Shatt Al-Arab. It can be considered as the muscular reaction to the third traumatic event in the history of defining the political meaning of "Arabness", namely the revolution in Iran and the foundation of the first Islamic Republic in the history of the region.

Although the Iraqi-Iranian border is one of the most vivid expressions of the variable geographies in the Middle East, with Arabs, Turkmen and Kurds, either Sunni or Shiite, on both sides, it has always served as a sort of psychological political frontier dividing the visions of two Empires –in one of their last historical manifestations, the Ottoman and the Safavid– and their heirs. In the course of the centuries, this political division also acquired a political-religious implication, beyond strict demographic facts, defining the separation between a field where Sunni Islam was undoubtedly ruling, no matter the faith of its subjects, and a context where Shiism was dominating, according to the same understanding. This psychological frontier was then essentially interiorized, remaining latent (Roy, 2007). The post-Empire configuration of the Middle East substantially respected such an understanding, as the tripartition between Turkish, Arab and Iranian spheres explains. Without subscribing to perennialism, after 1979, this cultural specialization became open to contestation especially within the so-called Arab world, with the possibility of negating – in essence– the ideal of State and nation as it had been developed until then. The reason lay in the above-mentioned tensions between national and supra-national. Although explicitly advocating pan-Islamism, the Islamic Republic of Iran adopted instead a clear nationalistic posture, and it openly called into question not only the continued existence of such a psychological border (the separation between the realm of Sunnism and that of Shiism, according to a sectarian understanding), but also the very existence of an Arab Iraq, implicitly Sunni (an Iraq defined according to the Ba'thist ideal of Arabness). The Islamic Republic of Iran was perceived as inherently predisposed to entertaining a strong relationship with Middle Eastern Shiite communities, menacing Arab solidarity in the region, overstating the real importance of relations of those ties for Tehran (which always subordinated them to its geopolitical interests). In essence, the Islamic Republic of Iran was considered a challenge to the very fabric of Iraq, a menace that could have subverted "national" hierarchies by negating the "Arab" character of Shiism in the country. With this in mind, and considering the predominance of Shiism on a demographic level, such subversion could have threatened the very foundations of the Iraqi socio-political field.

Accordingly, the Iraq-Iran war (which on the contrary demonstrated the weakness of the sectarian paradigm, as well demonstrated by the loyalty shown to Baghdad by Iraqi soldiers of Shiite descent) was not simply a conflict between two regional rivals representing structurally different identities and orientations, but also a struggle for State and nation in both countries. In fact, in the midst of the war and throughout it, both regimes were fully dedicated to state- and/or nation-building processes, Iran to establishing the Islamic Republic over an already solid "national State" frame and Iraq to securitizing and welding "national borders" of its political field. Moreover, beyond concerns and fears, the Iraqi "national" political field fought compactly against Iran, without showing signs of internal fragmentation. The same occurred in the opposite camp.

With this in mind, the foundation of the Islamic Republic of Iran and the Iraqi-Iran war offer important clues for understanding part of present conflicts' logics and root causes because it provides a field in which to explore the impact of politicization processes outside of variable regional geographies. In fact, the Iraq-Iran war, in all its implications, cannot be understood only according to one analytical lens. This is also the case for the conflicts and crises in today's Middle East. It requires an appreciation of the tensions between national, supranational and local-contextual levels; geopolitical rivalries; the potential of ethnic and religious factors as well as the protracted contraposition between secular and Islamist orientations (and within them). The use of multiple interpretative lenses helps us understand the function of variable geographies, subjects and actors in this political struggle for State and nation. It also suggests taking a distance from essentialist and monolithic interpretations of the issues and challenges at stake, reconsidering engagement and disengagement in the region as the result of the intertwining of multiple factors and not simply the implementations of decisions taken by individual united and coherent actors.

Therefore, the Iraq-Iran war is an important episode for looking at how regional politics progressively began to change and transform during the last two decades of the 20th century, with multiple dynamics of politicization and revival of political content in the broader field of identities. In fact, if one looks at the Middle East between the 2003 military operations in Iraq that signaled the end of Saddam Hussein's regime and the recent uprisings, it clarifies the manifold features and multiple pull-factors that are fueling present turmoil, severely testing diversity. Without suggesting any connections between them or offering reductionist explanations of dynamics essentially having multiple significances, these two events put into the spotlight the development of an intricate dynamic of contestation and construction of new meanings of State and nation, intertwining concrete politics, geopolitics and utopian orientations. On the one hand, the fall of Saddam's regime and the uneven path of the Iraqi reconstruction process mobilized Iraq's variable geographies in the campaign to define the logics, contents and balances of power in the "new" national political field (Zubaida, 2012). In essence, the military operation drastically opened room for making a new political field, redrawing boundaries both internally and internationally as well as exposing the Iraqi system to multiple external influences. It also destabilized the capacity of the Iraqi State to resist external influences. In fact, preservation of the territorial scope of the Iraqi State has been subject to multiple pressures and tensions regarding its regime, political system and the very existence of the country as such. The image of variable ideologies helps again to elucidate the situation. The fall of Saddam's regime inherently weakened the psychological frontier between (Arab) Shiism and (Iranian) Shiism (Roy, 2007). Obviously such a divide did not disappear, but somehow moved within the Iraqi polity, questioning both the concept of being "Arab" and "Iraqi", ascribing new meanings to Sunni and Shi'a designations, and making the state- and national-building process acquire a geopolitical role in its fullest meaning, for the country and the region. Such a process becomes particularly evident when considering the different positions have emerged at the political level within the Iraqi Arab Shia community, with actors maintaining extremely close relations with Iran and other focused on a more Iraq-centric vision. In this sense, even the civil war that reached its peak between 2006 and 2008, usually labelled as a sectarian struggle between Arab Sunnis and Shiites, can speak in favor of such an understanding if considered as a fight for supremacy over State and nation (namely the Iraqi national political field).

At the same time, the post-Saddam state- and nation-building process created enough maneuver room for Kurds, and somehow for the Assyrians, to project their own idea of the Iraqi political system, oscillating between the demand for full independence and that for pronounced autonomy. Moreover, the Kurds' autonomist or separatist ambitions have not only challenged the traditional territorial configuration of Iraq, but have also potentially created the possibility of setting a new frontier between a Kurdish and a non-Kurdish world well beyond Iraq and across other countries in the region, namely Syria and Turkey. In fact, it is now perceived as running into Syria, where Turkey is engaged to neutralize it.

On the other hand, by overthrowing regimes that had been ruling for decades in countries such as Egypt, Libya and Tunisia, the Arab uprisings opened a new chapter in the history of state- and nation-building processes in the region. The final results are still contended. It is exactly this state of affairs that is fueling the present turmoil. In Syria, the uprisings quickly turned into a civil war and a geopolitical confrontation that now is approaching a tentative solution that seems to be working in favor of the Assad regime. In a country like Egypt, the balance of power suddenly changed, triggering a phase of strong confrontation between military and civil rule, liberalists-secularists and Is-lamists, inevitably involving the spheres of community identity in complex dynamics of negotiating places and roles within a newly developing configuration of the national political field. In the case of Libya, the national political field essentially collapsed under the pressures of contrasting parochial and tribal interests and solidarities, despite the fact that the territorial configuration is not questioned in its international boundaries.

It is in the heart of such complex dynamics of polarization and politicization that the Islamic State (IS) developed and expanded, unilaterally proclaiming itself a caliphate in Mosul (2014). Beyond the specific features of this organization, its code of conduct and strategy, IS most vividly evidences the political potential of the Middle East's variable geographies and the multiple possible configurations of the intertwining between solidarity-group, patriotic/national and supranational influences. IS has positioned itself in the midst of Iraqi-Syrian geographies, politicizing them on the basis of its utopic vision (Hughes, 2017). It has exploited the rhetoric of the psychological frontier between an Arab Sunni and Iranian Shiite world, ambiguously playing with "national" and sectarian polarizations and tensions on the ground. At the same time, it has sought to co-opt local kin-group solidarities and their transboundary potential to challenge existing international boundaries and consolidate in rural and remote contexts (Collombier, Roy, 2018). This operation was not simply imposed from above, but worked out by developing an alternative path through the intertwining between local, national and supranational concerns. This has made its utopian vision resound in the region and internationally. The historical vicissitudes of IS can also be considered a testament to the controversial consequences produced by using diversity and variable regional geographies as strategic military resources at the disposal of political agendas for the state- and nation-building process.

6   Conclusion

The entropic spread of violence that destabilizes today's Middle East, threatening the survival of its populations beyond religious or ethnic affiliations, can be clearly understood without the need for subscribing to a culturalist approach. The protracted instability in Iraq, the civil wars in Syria, Libya and Yemen, the political crises that Egypt experienced from the uprising until the election of Al Sisi as president and, finally, the emergence of the Islamic State organization between Syria and Iraq are not demonstrations of an intrinsically anarchic Middle East shaped by primordial identities. They are the most recent developments of a matrix, established at the turn of the 20th century, which has fostered a struggle for authority and legitimacy taking place at intra- and inter-state levels. In this framework, the controversial spread of sectarian violence and its destructive effects over the wider Middle East have to be considered as an integral part of an historical continuum whose roots cannot be tracked to the beginning of the 21th century alone and that have further been exacerbated by competing geopolitical agendas. Accordingly, the "new Middle Eastern Cold war" apparently centered around the Sunni-Shia divide and the development, the imposition and the exploitation of sectarian forms of violence represent other forms of the struggle for supremacy within national and supranational political fields, where the religious, along with other features, as seen before, have become particularly manipulated for developing new political meaning out of the regional multiple geographies.

CHAPTER 6

Christians Navigating through Middle East Turbulences: the Case of the Copts in Egypt

Alessia Melcangi and Paolo Maggiolini

The aim of the chapter is to offer a dynamic account of the Christian presence within the Middle East, of its contribution to and position in the contemporary history of the region. In this regard, the historical vicissitudes of the Coptic community will be helpful to focus on the challenges, issues and ambitions that have influenced Christians' history in the region from the beginning of the contemporary state- and nation-building process in the contemporary Middle East until today.

In the first part, the chapter will focus on the multi-vocal dimension of the Christian presence in the Middle East, a feature that needs to be taken into account to fully understand its position and condition within the different States in the region. In the second part, the chapter will analyze the dynamics of sectarian violence against and persecution of Christians in the Middle East. In particular, it will focus on contemporary Egypt from the 1950s until the 2011 uprisings, taking the specific case of the Egyptian Christian Copts as a case study. In recent years, communalism has inflamed Egypt, weakening national cohesiveness and unity.

1 The Multi-vocal Christian Presence in Today's Middle East

The history of Christians in the contemporary Middle East is an account that speaks with multiple languages and many vocabularies, sketching a number of multifarious images of their present and future condition in the region. These representations can be either rich and many-branched or monolithic and axiomatic.

If one looks at the perspectives and orientations through which Christians in the region have been considered and narrated, most of the representations can be enclosed within a continuum defined by two only apparently contradictory but, in reality, often complementary discourses. These poles can be briefly summarized according to the following formulations and discourses.

A first discourse tends to approach Christians as a homogenous subject, without showing specific interest in exploring local, regional or denomination- al distinctions (Makari, 2014). Accordingly, such an outlook often points out that the common features of their presence in today's Middle East are the fra- gility of their condition and their almost inevitable emigration. At the heart of such an understanding one can find the implicit idea that, because of their faith, Christians cannot fully integrate into a socio-political fabric inspired by Islam, unless by accepting to be a sort of second-class citizen. This image is a product of a more general description of the Middle East as an anarchic and radical space (Malak, Salem, 2015; Korany, 2015). This perception had matured already in the 19th century, but has consolidated since the 1970s with the Islam- ization of Middle Eastern politics and public discourse (Robson, 2011). Al- though such a perspective can be substantiated by concrete evidence, it can pose the risk of essentializing and stereotyping their condition through their sufferings and challenges. And so the demise of most of the Arab uprisings' promises and the conflicts in Iraq and Syria have increased such an under- standing. In reality, the decline of Christians' presence is not a phenomenon of today. It began at the turn of the 20th century, when Christians represented 14% of the region's population (7 million) (Johnson, Zurlo, 2015). Since then, emigration and a declining birth-rate progressively eroded their numbers, but it was by the mid-1970s that the pace of this dynamic considerably accelerated. In the 1970s, Christians had already decreased to 7% (12 million in 1975) and today they are 5% (25 million in 2015). In 2050, they will be likely 25 million, namely 3% of the population (Johnson, Zurlo, 2015). While Egypt continues to have the largest Christian population in the region (8 million), countries such as Iraq have witnessed a dramatic decline in their number. First the 2006 civil war and then the emergence of the Islamic State tragically accelerated the pace of their decline. At the end of 2013, from a population of more than a mil- lion, Christians in Iraq were estimated to be no more than 300,000 to 500,000, with approximately 80% of their religious establishments destroyed or dam- aged and abandoned (Salloum, 2013). Their decline is almost turning into an- nihilation. Such an outlook is only partially mitigated by the fact that the Christian population is increasing in countries such as Saudi Arabia (4%), Ku- wait (10%) or the United Arab Emirates (14%). In fact, this trend is fostered by the arrival of a significant number of Christian migrant workers from South and Southeast Asia (Johnson, Zurlo, 2015). Therefore, it does not directly affect the scope of the historic Churches of the Middle East.

Nevertheless, numbers alone cannot explain the various points of tensions that affect the situation of Christians in today's Middle East. They are not able to fully communicate their diverse issues and approaches to the ongoing

regional instability. In fact, by making their sufferings and demographic decreases the main if not the sole parameter for understanding their condition
and presence, this discourse risks overlooking the complexity of the challenges
and positions at stake. While Christian leaderships loudly exhort the international community to recognize their plight, which is real and evident, they also
resist being simply portrayed as a detached or passive minority distinct from
the rest of the social fabric of the countries where they live, condemned to surrender by remaining at the margins or heading abroad (Rowe, 2014). Such a
position is particularly clear with the case of Christians in Iraq or Egypt.

Without underestimating Christians' present challenges and fragility, a second discourse tends to look at Christians in the region according to their functional potential (McGahern, 2012). Accordingly, since they have played a central role in the history of the modern Middle East as intellectual vanguards of
Arabism and cultural and spiritual bridges between the West and the East, today Christians can perform a new positive role in the region. Because they are
subjects or victims and not a direct part of present struggles, they can serve
today's Middle East by aiding in the mediation of a resolution to the ongoing
conflicts. While such an understanding tries to project a creative role for Christians in the Middle East, it encages them within a sort of "identity and role
syndrome" (Kattan, 2012: 51). Although it recognizes an agency to them, such
an ideal type of discourse tends to evaluate their presence according to their
capacity to perform a role. In essence, they become compelled to perform a
sort of recurring duty of persuading their Muslim neighbors of the benefits
and usefulness of their presence in the region. Such an understanding risks
essentializing Christians in the Middle East by removing them from the heart
of the ongoing conflicts or considering only what they can offer to both the
West and the East. This approach is frequently employed in the case of the
Israeli-Palestinian conflict and was proposed again in Iraq after 2003. In this
framework, Christians' passive role is only apparently redeemed, while their
identity and suffering risk being implicitly denied, becoming secondary to the
roles of mediator and/or of a bridge between cultures and civilizations. It is not
surprising that local Christian communities have frequently resisted this func-
tionalist discourse, advocating for full recognition of their right to live in the
region and to be recognized as full citizens in the different Middle Eastern
States without being compelled to prove their values and the "profitability" of
their presence. As said above regarding the first discourse, this is not to negate
that Christians have such potential and role to play, but their presence should
be explored, recognizing them as an integral part of the ongoing conflicts and
crises with full rights to have a voice beyond what they can offer. This holds
particularly true today when the present turbulences in the region are fostered

by disagreements and conflicts between Muslims that do not *per se*, or always, result in attacks against Christians because of their faiths or that configure for them a specific role to play. They are integrally part of the ongoing conflicts and crises not simply because they have been targeted and have suffered from the conflict, but because the issues at stake concern the nature of the State, the notion of rights and duties, the concept of public space and that of welfare from which the Christians should not be excluded.

In essence, while both discourses clearly point out critical factors and elements for understating the present challenges to Christians' presence in today's Middle East, they need to be cautiously endorsed to avoid the risk of misreading Christians' attitudes, overlooking their behaviors and strategies. On the one hand, the sole focus on their sufferings denies Christians agency. On the other, the sole acknowledgment to Christians of a role as mediators in conflicts and crises deprives them of the right to be recognized as a full part of and voice in the ongoing dynamics beyond the function that they can perform.

Now looking at the multiple landscapes which describe and distinguish the diverse configurations of Christians' presence in the Middle East, it is important to recognize that Christians' multi-vocal character implies that each voice possesses a distinctive ecclesiastical identity, biography and local history to tell.

In this framework, Christian multi-vocality can be variously described and appreciated. On the one hand, it can be approached by focusing on the diverse stances adopted by Christians in the Middle East both in local and regional politics and in their relationship with the West. It can be explored by considering two distinct "orientations", "outlooks" or "discourses" developed by Christians in the Middle East since the turn of the 20th century. Labelled by Sabra as "Arab Christian" and "Eastern Christian" outlooks (Sabra, 2006: 44), these two perspectives define a sort of wide continuum of shifting and evolving positions portraying the different Christians' understandings of their role and position within the region. Arab Christian orientation tends to attach great value to Arab culture and identity, including Islamic civilization. This position has been openly supported by intellectuals such as Michel 'Aflaq, the founder of the Ba'ath party, but also by various Christian personalities in Iraq and the Palestinian territories. In this framework, although is not the rule, the relationship with the West can sometimes be uneasy and critical with the specific aim of countering the image of Middle Eastern Christians as the natural allies of the West or, worse, as one of its fifth columns in the region because of their faith. Eastern Christian orientation extends their sight beyond the limits of the Arab dimension with the aim of embracing the multiple expressions of Christianity in the Middle East, thus including all non-Arab Christian communities, such as the Armenians or Assyrians. In doing so, the word "Eastern" posits a distance from Islam and Islamic culture and civilization as well as from the Arab cultural milieu (Sabra, 2006). Such a distance can vary in its lengths, but this orientation expresses a general agreement on the need to prioritize Christian identity and establish a solid relationship with the West for the sake of protecting local Christian communities.

Therefore, Arab Christian orientations evidently support the idea that their distinct religious affiliation does not contradict their solid roots in Arab culture (for instance, the Christians in Palestine and Jordan). Eastern Christian perspectives can take on different forms. Coalescing religious and ethno-linguistic features to stand out from the majoritarian Arab milieu, it can manifest a local patriotic or national sense of belonging (such as the Copts in Egypt) or an autonomous ethno-nationalist pride (such as the Assyrians in Iraq and the Maronites with the Phoenician ideal in Lebanon). Although such orientations should be considered ideal types, they are useful in exploring the different Christians positions towards local politics and/or understanding their choice to emigrate, going beyond the simple category of fragile minority and persecuted subjects and appreciating their dynamism.

On the other hand, Christians' multi-vocality can be described by considering how it locally changes, intertwining the ecclesiastical, community and ethno-linguistic dimensions. It can also be understood on the basis of how Christian demography is unevenly distributed within the different Middle Eastern States, with some communities and Churches strongly concentrated within specific countries while others are distinctive for being essentially disseminated or "trans-boundary". The socio-economic factor is of equal importance in understanding their position within a specific country.

Looking at the Israeli-Palestinian contexts, the manifold implication of Christians' trans-boundary presence speaks out *per se*. While being 2% of the population both in Israel and under the Palestinian National Authority, Christians are divided between the jurisdictions of three Patriarchates (Greek Orthodox, Armenian and Latin), five archbishops (the Church of the East, Syrian Orthodox, Coptic Orthodox and Ethiopian) and two Reformed bishoprics (Anglican and Lutheran). In the case of the Latin and Greek Orthodox Patriarchate, these two ecclesiastical institutions exert their authority over most of the Christians in Jordan. Although the vast majority of Christians in Israel-Palestine are Arab natives – with the exception of foreigners and Hebrew-speaking Christians (both Roman Catholic and Russian Orthodox) in Israel – this plurality exists in a very fragmented landscape with each ecclesiastical institution having distinct orientations and identities (O'Mahony, 1999). Christians in the Israeli-Palestinian context clearly show how multi-vocality can also mean ecclesial fragmentation (O'Mahony, 2005); a condition that Christian religious leaderships seek to confront by fostering ecumenical dialogue. This is a challenge for both Christians in the Middle East and to one's searching for a univocal explanation of their position in daily politics and society. Furthermore, Christians in Israeli-Palestinian territories are part of two different political fields in conflict. While they are a minority in both contexts, their contextual socio-political positions significantly change. Conflict and contextual minority conditions increase the complexity of their positioning, presenting considerable divergences in their outlooks and orientations. For those living in Israel, Christians as well as Muslims are faced with all the challenges of being part of the Arab speaking minority in a non-Arab country, especially after the recent developments in promoting the Jewish character of Israel, epitomized by the removal of Arabic as an official language of the country. This pressure is amplified by ongoing conflict and the tension between different designations (Arab-speaking minority, non-Muslim and non-Jewish religious minority) and in their relationship with their Palestinian brethren living under the Palestinian National Authority. Moreover, their position is challenged by the increasing role that religion plays in local politics, which tends to single out Christians as irrelevant if not for their international networks, marginalizing or removing their presence in a confrontation that predominantly involves Jews and Muslims. Regarding the case of the Palestinian territory, Christians have been directly part of the Palestinian national movement since the beginning, supporting the idea of an independent secular Palestinian State to achieve the status of full citizens as Arab and Palestinian. They have both participated in secular political platforms and developed new understandings of their presence and role as a non-Muslim religious community integrally part of the Palestinian nation. At the same time, the growing influence of Hamas and the Palestinian Islamic Jihad has posed a challenge to such a commitment (Andezian, 2008). The Islamization of local politics and of the national resistance keeps on posing the risk of marginalizing their role, encaging them within the sole dimension of religious minority.

On the other hand, the case of Iraq offers useful insight to appreciate the different outlooks that Christians can promote in a situation of relative concentration within a single country. The Christian landscape in Iraq (1% of the population) (Johnson, Zurlo, 2015) appears fragmented and multi-vocal as it is within the other Middle Eastern countries. Christians are divided between the Syriac Orthodox, Syriac Catholics, Chaldean Catholics, the Church of the East (ecclesiastically also known as the Assyrian Church of the East), and finally Latin (Roman Catholic) and Reformed communities (O'Mahony, 2004). In this framework, Assyrians and Chaldeans differ in their positions towards the idea of Iraq and thus in regard to how they conceive of their presence in the country (Zubaida, 2002). Their outlooks are deeply grounded in the history of the modern Middle East since the turn of the 20th century; orientations and positions that have been accentuated even more after the 2006 civil war and the emergence of the Islamic State. The Chaldean Church have always been devoted to developing Christian minority status as a resource for protecting the community and, at the same time, positioning it as an integral part of the wider Iraqi social fabric. Accordingly, they concentrate on avoiding that their minority status could be turned into political marginalization. On the other hand, the Assyrians have always sought to reunite local Christians to demonstrate an ethnic-linguistic identity distinct from that of an Arab Iraqi. In this framework, the recognition of ethnic-linguistic minority status or achievement of the right to autonomy in a localized province within the country was considered necessary to confirm their own political dignity and rights as a distinct nation. Such divergences between Chaldeans and Assyrians have thus directly influenced their stances towards Baghdad, dividing local Christians between integrational and separatist or autonomist orientations (Maggiolini, 2018). In the case of the Assyrians, this attitude has come at a tragic cost. Persecution and open confrontation by the central authorities have pushed them out of the country, consolidating in their diaspora a strong sense of uniqueness.

Finally, similarity in the trajectories of the Assyrians, Maronites and Copts offers another two important examples of the complexity of being both Christians and part of the Middle East. Their concentration in territories that are homelands of their community and original seats of their Churches has developed a solid relationship with these contexts so that they perceive their presence and existence as the most vivid and authentic expression of the history, tradition and thus identity of their countries (McCallum, 2010). In these cases, concentration has favored a process of full identification with and projection of a specific idea of State and nation, where they consider themselves not only a part of the project but also an essential if not core component. It is somehow possible to say that in these cases the Church is lived as an institution that was already manifesting the existence of a "nation" before the launch of the nation- and state-building process at the turn of the 20th century. Focusing on the case of the Copts, such a position has constantly developed two different, albeit intertwined, dialectic approaches (Mahmood, 2016). One component of the community has focused on reconfiguring the distinctive Coptic religious character into an autonomous ethnic category, as a national minority. On the other hand, the vast majority of the community has refused such a discourse, emphasizing that the Copts are the original voice of historic Egypt and therefore never a minority by definition.

Nevertheless, Christian multi-vocality also appears through the intertwining of socio-economic and geographic conditions. Copts in Egypt show how these factors are more determinant in explaining the marginality of a part of the community than the mere religious factors. This also explains how Muslims and Christians defined a common ground, expressing the same frustration during the uprisings. Similarly, Christians' concentrations in specific towns and villages and their predominant presence in professional sectors are important for understanding how the community divided between supporters and opposers of Al Assad's regime during the protests in 2011 (Farha, Mousa, 2015; Fahmi, 2018).

To conclude this section, multi-vocality is an intrinsic feature of Christian communities in the region and it appears under different configurations cutting across multiple dimensions and discourses. It also represents a challenge that Christians have tried to face by both participating in secular platforms and by developing new theological and ecclesiastical thinking through ecumenism and interfaith dialogues. But multi-vocality is not simply important for understanding Christians living within the Middle East – it is also a critical factor to be taken into account in exploring the manifold and diverse motivations that induce Christians to emigrate or seek refuge abroad.

2   Christians in Middle Eastern Politics

Christians' multi-vocality is not only the most vivid expression of the rich ecclesiastical and theological patrimony of Eastern Christianity and its millennial history, but it is also the product of the different contextual configurations that Christians have experienced in the region.

Histories of Christians in the contemporary Middle East traditionally begun focusing on the last century of the Ottoman Empire's rule in the region. Given the scope of such a chapter, it is not the case here to explore this period in their history in detail. What it is useful to take into consideration is that precisely during this century were laid the bases on which later the orientations described before developed, first during the Mandate period (from the 1920s to the 1940s) and then in the course of the first two decades of the Middle Eastern States' independence (in the 1950s and 1960s). The 19th century is the period of the colonial encounter between the West and the East (Makdisi, 2000).

With the image of the colonial encounter can be portrayed the development of an intricate relationship of influence, conditioning, cooperation and reaction that directly influenced the history of what would become the contemporary Middle East (Mitri, 2012). It was exactly from this period that

Christian multi-vocality began to acquire a political scope. Religious spheres arose as one of the first fields through which to participate in the life of the Empire or challenge Ottoman authority (Makdisi, 2000). Christians in the Empire began to be described in the West as a fragile minority doomed to be persecuted by an intolerant Islam. At the same time, local Christian communities began to distinguish between different orientations, namely the "Arab" and "Eastern". One component became the vanguard of Arabism, with the aim of promoting a secularist interpretation of the concept of the Arab "nation", stressing the need for Muslims and Christians to reunite in a single nation because they shared a common language and culture (Cragg, 1991). In this framework, the triumph of Arabism would make it possible to overcome religious divides and politicization, emancipating from Ottoman rule and resisting European interference. Other communities started to claim their right to live according to their cultural and religious heritage in a homogeneous autonomous space. Therefore, in the course of the 19th century Christians emerged as dynamic actors in the life of the Empire, contributing to the reinvention of the political significance of the different regional localities belonging to the Ottoman State, as citizens of Istanbul's polity, supporters of Arabism or distinct ethno-linguistic communities searching for their full recognition (Roussos, 2014).

With these premises, the period between the two World Wars was a phase both of disillusion and hope. Christians dedicated themselves to pursuing different political programs aimed at fulfilling the promises of independence and emancipation previously elaborated. The establishment of modern Middle Eastern States under the Mandates projected the Christians presence towards three different, albeit frequently intertwined, political paths. First, the Mandate powers kept on with their strategies of cultivating relationships with minority communities. Depending on the specific socio-political balances of each territory and the different French and British colonial strategies, Christians in the post-Ottoman Middle East were integrated into the new States under the double guise of citizens and protected minority. The protection of minorities became one of the facets of the colonial strategy of divide and rule and a source of legitimization for the Mandate system (White, 2007). Christians were invited to develop their community institutions as distinctive social units on the basis of their minority status. On the one hand, such an accommodation of Middle Eastern non-Muslim diversity consolidated a specific, homogeneous image of "Christians in the Middle East", overlooking their contextual ethnic and denominational differences as well as their political aspirations. On the other, Christian constituencies fragmented. Christians either concentrated on consolidating their community borders and spheres, as a religious minority, or on overcoming the post-Ottoman configurations promoted by Paris and London. It was exactly in this framework that the Assyrians focused their efforts in the struggle to be recognized as an autonomous nation, ethnically and religiously distinct. However, their project dramatically failed. Left alone by London, the Iraqi State showed no tolerance for what was perceived as a threat to the ideal of the Arab nation (Zubaida, 2002). The Assyrians were first repressed and then forced to accept their minority status as a part of the non-Muslim minorities living in the country, with no recognition of their ethnic-linguistic demands. Similarly, in Egypt the Copts refused minority discourses and the quota system proposed by London in the early 1920s. Their specific religious affiliation was considered the most authentic proof of their belonging to the Egyptian nation (Mahmood, 2016). In essence, during these decades the process of diversification of Christians' orientations developed, along with that of their Muslim brethren, dividing between different notions of the scope and role of community, nation and State. While Christians generally promoted the ideal of a secular State and nation on the bases of a shared language, history and culture, these positions oscillated between pan-nationalist movements (e.g. the 1932 Syrian Social Nationalist Party of the Greek-Orthodox Antoun Saadeh and the 1947 Ba'ath Party of Michel Aflaq) and nationalist ideals (e.g. the Lebanese nationalist movement inspired by the Maronite intellectuals of the *Revue Phénicienne*; the Egyptian Wafd party with Wassef Boutros Ghali) (Robson, 2011).

With the end of the Second World War and the independence of the Middle Eastern States, Arabism and pan-Arabism increased their momentum, becoming the leading ideologies for developing nation- and state-building processes in the region. Ideals and aspirations theorized during the inter-war period became thus not only viable, but imposed as the core ideologies for achieving full independence from the past colonial influence. In reality, most of the Mandate systematization of majority-minority relationships and the condition of Christians in politics remained almost untouched. Arabism and pan-Arabism did not take the form of liberal regimes, but of muscular political projects authoritarian in their stance. Nonetheless, Christians fully participated in these projects, because essentially secular.

However, the ideal of a national unity to be defended against any kind of divisive pressure, both external and internal, imposed a precise code of conduct on Christians. By embracing such orientations, Christians and their religious institutions were granted the right to access public space. But they were also "invited" to privatize their identities as Christians for the sake of nations and states designed in the spirit of Muslim majorities (Mahmood, 2016). In essence, assimilation was the most practiced strategy for managing diversity in the region.

The pan-Arabist movement lasted for almost two decades, progressively encountering crises after the Six-Day War and the defeat of the Arab front by Israel in 1967 and again in 1973. In this framework, the 1970s represented a disorienting awakening, setting the condition of a new systematization of regional politics that today, after the 2011 uprisings, is still looking for new positive directions. The liturgies and rhetoric of the previous decades were somehow kept alive by almost all regimes in the region, but the Arab States entered into what afterwards became a prolonged period of internal crises only partially allayed by the temporary rise in oil prices between the mid-1970s and early 1980s. In essence, while nationalist programs were being progressively dismissed, their place was taken by strong regimes imposed on their societies. In particular, an event and a dynamic proved that previous Christians' orientations were going to be confined to the margins of regional politics.

First, the Lebanon civil war (1975–1990) led to a drastic discontinuity in the traditional balances of power of this country, the sole non-authoritarian regime with a political system dominated by non-Muslims in the region (MacCallum, 2010). The civil war diminished and fragmented Christian leverage, in particular that of the Maronites. It dissolved their primacy within the new power-sharing system and polarized Maronite political elites between the Sunni and Shiite fronts. At the same time, while Maronite nationalists were encountering a severe defeat on the ground, Church religious leaders, and especially the Maronite Patriarch, re-emerged as leading authorities for the local community. The Maronite Patriarch increased his political role by devoting himself to the mission of representing the interests of the entire Christian community within the framework of multi-faith Lebanon.

Secondly, while the Lebanese civil war was breaking out, Islam's institutional and political appeal began to rise in the region, pushing Christian communities to reconfigure their role and presence. The progressive Islamization of Middle Eastern politics, well epitomized by the course of the revolution in Iran (1979), represented a real turning point. It came about through growing Islamist activism in political and radical militant groups. At the same time, it occurred through the development of "formal" or "institutionalized" Islam, even in countries such as Egypt or Syria that until then had defined their regimes and political systems as essentially secular. As the chapter will point out, this development worsened the conditions of Christians in Egypt between the 1970s and early 1980s. It also formed the basis for reconfiguring the political balances of power in what would become the Syria of Hafiz al-Assad and his

son Bashar, again making religious and ethnic discourses instrumental to legitimizing rulers or contesting the regime in power (Rabo, 2012).

In essence, from the late 1970s and increasingly during the 1980s Christians
experienced a double dynamic, only apparently contradictory. On the one
hand, they witnessed a lessening of their manoeuvre room in regional and national politics, in some circles fostering adoption of an introverted attitude and
a clustering around Church institutions and leaderships (Roussos, 2014). Such
a stance developed further at the end of the 1980s while Arab States entered
into what would become a prolonged period of economic difficulty and legitimacy crisis, concealed only by the presence of strong regimes in most of the
countries of the region. It is not surprising that an increasing number of Christians begun to emigrate, seeking career opportunities abroad. On the other,
such a conditioned retreat pushed them to reconnect with their religious dimension, fostering a new exploration of the significance of being Christian in
the Middle Eastern institutional, political, social and national dimensions. The
Islamization of regional politics led Christian Churches to revive and re-launch
their activities for the sake of a new, active and creative role in the region (Mc-
Callum, 2010). While the idea of their inevitable decline in an increasingly Islamized Middle East was developing at the international level, Christian ecclesiastical institutions dedicated themselves to internal reforms with the aim of
rejecting such a predicament (Robson, 2011). By the mid-1980s, Christians thus
focused on elaborating new theological thinking and understanding about
their minority condition, and conflict and crisis in the region, describing such
challenges as essentially fostered by a lack of social justice and an ongoing
political struggle. In essence, they refused the religious hypothesis as the main
driver of Middle Eastern instability.

The intertwining between this double dynamic found the most vivid representation in what has been called the "authoritarian dilemma". This dilemma
has compressed the Christian presence between two extremes: appealing to
the strong or fierce regime in power for the sake of defending their community,
prioritizing stability and security, or mobilizing for change and reform of both
political systems and regimes, accepting the risk of being involved in a difficult
transition with no guarantees of improvements for Christian conditions (Mc-
Callum, 2012).

This dilemma describes the complex continuum within which Christians
continuously oscillated until and during the Arab uprisings in 2011. It should be
recognized that security was more frequently prioritized by Church and community leaderships. Accommodating the regimes in power gave Christian establishments the benefit of the support of state administration, acting as representatives for their communities and minimizing the impact of sectarian

tensions within their own countries (Rowe, 2014). This *modus vivendi* was the case with Saddam Hussein in Iraq, Mubarak in Egypt, as the chapter will show, and Hafez and Bashar al-Assad in Syria. With the case of Syria, this configuration has taken a very controversial outlook that the ongoing civil war is contributing to reinforce. In a country where ethnic and linguistic features can transcend and cut across absolute religious classifications (see Chapter 5), sectarian politics has been always a resource in the hands of the regimes in power. With Hafez and Bashar al-Assad, the idea of a Syrian "safe haven" for all minorities in the country, and especially for Christians, has been systematically cultivated, imposing a tacit agreement based on an exchange between accepting constraints on political liberties and undoubted loyalty to the regime in power, with the right to practice one's own religion and defend professional interests in the economy (Farha, Mousa, 2015).

Nevertheless, the propensity to prioritize security should not be overstated or considered the sole dimension describing all Christian forms of participation. Christians have also concentrated on their renewal and social activism, advocating for their rights as full citizens of their countries and for those of their Muslim brethren. In this framework, the Christian diaspora has increasingly played an important role in echoing and internationalizing what was and is going on in their country of origins (Longva, Roald, 2012).

The 2011 uprisings, the so-called Arab Spring, drastically denounced the limits of such political pacts on which most regimes have based their legitimacy and power in the region. The protests openly called for the ousting of authoritarian rulers and the development of inclusive and pluralist systems at the political, social and economic levels. Christians looked at protests and demonstrations with a great degree of trepidation. While some Christian leaders initially hesitated to support the demonstrations, most of their faithful actively participated in what seemed to be the winning battle for pluralism (Muasher, 2014). However, it soon became clear that the end of traditional regimes was also producing the severe destabilization of entire state systems. Herein lies the "awakening" paradox. While successful in dismantling old regimes, until today protests have failed to develop new concepts of State and civic relations. At the same time, the instability has politically reactivated primordial ties such as ethnicity, tribalism and religious factionalism. Against this background, religious affiliations proved to be useful mechanisms at the service of international, regional and local elites' interests in pursuing different political agendas. In this regard, the case of Syria is emblematic. In this country, protests soon transformed into a civil war, also becoming the final hotbed, along with Iraq, of the Islamic State. The successful popular revolts calling for pluralism and inclusion quickly gave way to the present regional geopolitical struggle for power and the "global minority crisis in the Arab World or in the Muslim World" (Picard, 2012) produced by growing sectarian rivalries. This situation has fragmented Christian communities in these countries, dividing Church leaders, the local clergy and laity between different positions towards the regime (Fahmi, 2018).

Today, Christians find themselves again confronted with all traditional dilemmas of the past. While it is undeniable that the uprisings seem to have definitively deprived Christians of political influence, marginalizing their position and making them even more subjected to the authoritarian paradox, conflicts have again pushed them to prove their resilience, increasing their activism. Today's Middle Eastern Christians are thus committed to remaining a factor and a voice in the region, resisting the general conviction that they can be solely the victims of Middle Eastern politics, doomed to seek refuge abroad or to accept marginalization and protection from the "new" political regimes. Accordingly, the analysis of the Copts' strategy and position during those events will be illustrative.

3   Sectarianism, Religious Strife and the "Unbreakable Marriage" between the State and the Church under Mubarak (1981–2011)

When Mubarak resigned as president of Egypt, after thirty years of continuous power and as a consequence of the famous "Tahrir's days of wrath", the Copts finally believed, with their Muslim counterparts, that past discrimination was largely over. This belief fostered the vision that the Egyptian revolt of 2011 tried to make possible, only to see hopes wane in the post-revolutionary stage.

For the Copts, the following transition phase and the current presidency of Abd al-Fattah al-Sisi represent the replay of the same dynamics: nowadays as in the past, the Egyptian Orthodox Christian community, the biggest Christian community of Middle East, remains the target of violence and discrimination that neither the revolt nor the establishment of a new post-revolutionary government have been able to stop. As in the past, religious freedom and equality, depending on state institutions that can guarantee all citizens' constitutional rights, are far from putting down roots.

After the collaboration established in the 1960s between Gamal 'Abd al-Nasser and the Patriarch Kirollos VI, relations between the regime and the Coptic community deteriorated in the 1970s under President Anwar al-Sadat, who embraced Islam and Islamists as a tool to carry out the so called "corrective revolution": the aim was to change the ideological and economic theories which supported the Nasserian regime, the secularism and the Egyptian socialism over all, that had failed under the blows of the 1967 defeat. A consequence of this "correction" was the return of Islam in the political sphere and the following conclusion of the golden age for interfaith relations in Egypt which put again the Copts under siege, as a separated and discriminated community. But while attacks by Muslims on Copts have a sectarian element, confessional differences are not the primary source of tension. Egypt's outdated laws and authoritarian institutions have made Copts a target of social conflict.

All analysis and research on the Coptic community in Egypt needs to devote a part to analyze its real numerical size. From an historical perspective, this represents a complex dispute: it is difficult to obtain reliable data from government statistics and from those of the community. The government's will to reduce the relevance of the Coptic community and the fear of the Christians to declare their faith in public has made the official census inaccurate.

The Egyptian census, conducted in 1976 during the presidency of Anwar al-Sadat, reported a total of 2.3 million Copts, or 6.7% of the total population of almost 39 million (McDermott, 1988; Chitham, 1986). This figure met the incredulity of the Copts who threatened to launch their door to door count. This impracticable method was not put into practice and the Copts continue to speak of a much higher figure: Coptic groups in the US talk of 8 million, a figure which has gained wide currency outside Egypt (Pennington, 1982).

The Egyptian official statistics available pointed out that in 1996 the number of Christians reached 3.5 million, 5.7% of the population of 63 million (Courbage, Fargues, 1998; Denis, 2000; Bayoumi, Moriconi-Ebrard, 2005). According to the 2006 census figures, released by the official statistical agency of Egypt, the Central Agency for Mobilization and Statistics, the population, including those living abroad, is estimated to have reached 76.5 million.

A study published in 2011 by the Pew Research Center's Forum on Religion and Public Life states that the Christian population represents the 5.3 % of the Egyptian's one (Pew Research Center, 2011), as opposed to the widely used media figure of 10%. Researchers arrived at the number from Egypt's 2006 census data underlining that "for decades the Christian population in Egypt has been less than 10% of the population". Though there may be some converts in Egypt from Islam to Christianity, "it's unlikely that that number is very large" (Harrington, 2011). According to this research "the highest share reported in the past century was in 1927, when the census found that 8.3% of Egyptians were Christian; in each of the eight subsequent censuses, the Christian share of the population gradually shrank" (Harrington, 2011). In spite of these new data, some others estimate that the number of Copts oscillates between 5 and 6 million, or 8% to 9% of the entire population. The number of Christians in Egypt remains a hotly-debated issue in the country but, looking at the recent figures, the

Copts continue to represent by far the largest Christian community in the Middle East.

Intercommunal conflict during Sadat's presidency prefigured the problems Copts would face under Mubarak (1981–2011), the SCAF (Supreme Council of the Armed Forces, which took power upon Mubarak's ouster in 2011), and the presidency of the Muslim Brother Muhammad Morsi (2012–2013). Since religion has replaced nationalism, matters that should have been governed by the law became to be managed as identity politics.

Religious strife emerged during all of the Mubarak regime, although particularly it started to increase from the end of the 1980s. The "Autumn of fury" that overwhelmed Sadat and his presidency, culminated with the assassination of Sadat the 6th October 1981 by an Islamist militant and the house arrested of the Patriarch Shenuda, after a dramatic period marked by social violence between the Muslims and Christians (Farah, 1986; Murphy, 2002).

One of the first goals carried out by Mubarak after he took power was to fight against the radical Islamic movement in order to isolate and crush the violent extremists: Mubarak's regime remained under severe Islamist pressure for all the 1990s and the beginning of the 2000s. During the 1990s, Mubarak's intelligence and police forces fought an internal war against *al-jama'a al-islamiyya* which become very powerful and had stepped up its violent activities: they started to target regime officials, foreign tourists and Copts.

Radical Islamists were more widespread through the rural immigrants of *Sa'id* although the Cairo suburbs of Ayn Shams and Imbaba also witnessed outbreaks of violent clashes from 1990–1992, typically instigated by routine disputes between Muslim and Christian neighbors that escalated into large-scale riots with numerous injuries and casualties on both sides. The wave of radical Islamist terrorist attacks targeting tourists and foreign businesses beginning in mid-1992 was also a threat to Coptic security. In 1992 alone, thirty-seven anti-Coptic attacks were reported, although national attention was more focused on the threat that Islamist radicals posed to state security rather than addressing the Coptic issue in particular (Ayalon, 1999).

This specific type of answer to the religious issue in Egypt, and the problems linked with it, are rooted in the tarnish nature of the Egyptian authoritarian regime and in the sectarianism concept. Since the beginning of the Republic, Egyptian leaders have defended a rigid hierarchy instead of instituting political equality and the country's military rulers governed granted rights and opportunities as a concession to the population. Under such an authoritarian system, religious identity mattered less than wealth and personal connections to the army and religion has served to fragment a society that is already sharply split between rulers and ruled (Melcangi, 2018).

The capacity and will of the Egyptian authoritarian political system to manage sectarianism as a tool for maintaining their power and for exploiting the religious or communal identity in order to enable the political organization, the gaining of political legitimacy, and the promotion of political change was fundamental (Aras, Bardakcı, 2014). The ideal of *dividi et impera* with a top-down sectarianism strategy was finalized to keep consensus and maintain support for the regime. Although sectarianism was denied and repudiated, informally the Egyptian regimes engaged in a systematic attempt to politicize differences as tools for controlling masses and maintaining power (Ryan, 2001).

As always, the government position moved toward two main paths: denial and repression. The denial, expressed in an insensitive way, became rejection of the existence of tensions. The president tried to cement the President's image as a protector of Muslims and Christians with the "national unity" campaign of the early 1990s, but the claims of the Christians went unheeded.

A perpetual guarantee remained in the form of a shared Egyptian identity and the social intermingling of Copts and Muslims in a single social context, a "unique Egyptian fabric... whether in the cities or in the country" (al-Gawhary, 1996: 21). The use of terms like "national dialogue" and "national unity", trying apparently to break down barriers, did not consider the differences and the real problems of the Christian group. This claim to national unity was for example used by Nasser and Kyrollos VI during all the Nasserian period. National unity is not a new concept, but it started to have an increased political significance: at that time it was used in order to consolidate the government rhetoric and bring together the different groups in support of the regime which depict itself as the only defender of the national unity (Fawzi, 2010; Elsässer, 2014).

This is especially true in particular conditions depending on economic, social and political changes: in the late 1980s, Egypt's economy suffered markedly from falling oil prices and was further weakened by a drop in the number of remittances from its three million workers abroad. In spite of a rising debt burden, the government continued to rely heavily on foreign economic aid, leading to growing interference by the International Monetary Fund (IMF) in Egypt's economic policies; in 1991 the Egyptian government signed the Economic Reform and Structural Adjustment Program with the IMF and the World Bank. The country's currency, the Egyptian pound, had to be devalued several times, interest rates were raised, and subsidies were lowered on food and fuel (Roccu, 2013). These policies especially harmed the poorest Egyptians, who often looked to Islamist groups such as the Muslim Brotherhood for assistance.

On the other side, the Islamic Group, continued to resort to terrorism against political leaders, secularist writers, Copts, and even foreign tourists, the last-named being a major source of Egypt's foreign exchange. So, as for the previous presidents, the official rhetoric and the use of the call to national unity became a mechanism for avoiding a discussion of the challenges inherent to the social, political and economic dramatic situation.

In fact, although the government of Mubarak issued several laws in favor of the Copts such as the "relative" flexibility in the legal procedure for building churches, the establishment of Christmas as an official state holiday, the leadership's intervention to sponsor the development and revival of study centers and of cultural artefacts, especially on the occasion of millennium celebrations, the community emphasized that the government's attempts to fight the fundamentalist current led to its side-lining of Coptic issues and concerns (Melcangi, 2015). When attacks against Copts intensified, Mubarak exploited Coptic insecurity to his own political benefit and the government remained passive and refrained from intervention or action. For decades he and his coterie propagated the narrative that without Mubarak's protection the Copts would fall into the shadow of a zealously Islamist and anti-Christian regime (Ibrahim, 2000).

During the last three decades, polarization between Muslims and Christians has grown. Both groups have become religiously more conservative. Mubarak allowed interreligious tensions to escalate; by the year 2000, random acts of violence against the Copts had become normative. Many state officials, security officers and legislators denied the existence of sectarian violence in Egypt or minimized the extent of the problem. The most dangerous way to deal with the problem of interreligious clashes was based on the conviction that it was a security problem that required the application of the ongoing state of emergency (Mubarak conducted his entire presidency under "emergency law" No. 162 of 1958) which legitimized all types of intervention of the State (Egyptian Initiative for Personal Rights, 2010). Of course, the worsening of the economy, infrastructure and security climate of Egypt dragged Copts down along with all other Egyptians who suffered for a civil society which was marked by permanent government interference and repression (Brownlee, 2013). "This inconsistency has led people to lose faith in the law and to take the law into their own hands, which has caused horrendous crimes" (Al-Aswani, 2011: 131). Under Sadat and his successor, State security agents have been active participants in the violence rather than inept bystanders, a practice that with difficulty has changed during the decades, as the facts of Kosheh[1] in 2000 confirmed. It was

---

1   The al-Kosheh incidents refer to a series of intercommunal riots and strife in an Upper Egyptian small village arising from a murder investigation in the autumn of 1998 in which Copts

clear that the State neglected to protect them, as in the bombing of the Alexandria Church in 2011.

4   Reformation and Resilience: Strategies of the Church *vis-à-vis* Mubarak's Regime

The only way to survive for Church was to reshape the self-image in which it took an important lead, resulting in continuing the reformation of the communal identity towards a religious identity and in the social restructuring of a traditional community. In doing so, the Church, stifling the divergent opinions inside the community, imposed itself as the only voice which had the right to define what it means to be Coptic, underlining the differences and the sameness compared with the other community and defining their way to be Egyptian. Having overcome the polarization born inside the community during the exile of the Patriarch Shenuda, the Church was able again to re-establish its strength enlarging consensus around the notion of Coptic identity and the foundation of philanthropic societies and a reinvigorated patriarchate.

The Patriarchate expanded its services compared with the past three decades through a centralization of church administration and a revival of Coptic culture. In doing so the Church saved Copticness blending it with the Egyptianness by working at the level of religious traditions and everyday activities. The common national sense of belonging was strictly connected with a specific symbolism: e.g. the continuous reference to the Nile river as the common cradle of both Muslims and Christians considered as naturally Egyptians. "Inscribing the Nile in the Christian mythology of sanctity consequently constitutes an effective claim of belonging to the national entity" (Galal, 2012: 51). This reference created a connection to the time when Egypt was Christian, Egyptians were Copts and the Egyptian territory was consequently genuinely Christian. "The pilgrimage to the sites where, according to tradition, the Holy Family lived during its stay in Egypt, can trace an ideal direct line between the nation and the Copts' authentic sense of belonging and the coherence between being Christian and being Egyptian" (Melcangi, 2018: 135). At the same time, Coptic sacred sites where saints and martyrs lived, together with the stories and traditions about their martyrdom, became a fundamental point of reference for Copts in order to show their way of being Egyptian through Christianity. They were used not only to build Christian identity but also to negotiate

---

were disproportionately targeted with severe methods of interrogation and torture by the local police.

the minority status. Obviously, the stories about the saints and martyrs showed the importance of the asceticism and the sacrifice. Suffering became an aspect of the life of Egyptian Copts, the only possible destiny which relegate the Christian to this marginal and passive minority status.

Regarding the ecclesiastic structure, Shenuda tried to enforce parity and uniformity on the dioceses replacing the local privileges and clan loyalties with the loyalty to his person, by placing people close to him in the key positions in the administration throughout the country (Hasan, 2003). The aim was not only to introduce a new morality into the Church, but, more importantly, to control the economic and cultural development of the community. Moreover, a new spread of the Patriarch's monographs regarding all sorts of topics from Christian life was implemented: the Church's newsletter and the illustrated news magazine *al-Kiraza* were published regularly by the office of the patriarchate and projected the image of an active Church and a tool for responding to social concerns and criticisms of the Church leadership (Rowe, 2009). On the other side, we can see how the spread of publications among the Christian group, critical editorials of the community newspaper *Watani*, and Christian television programs contributed in the same way to consolidating the community support for the Church policy. Part of this flowed into the wider project of creating a network of supporting foreign Christian organizations with the final aim of promoting the "internationalization" of the Coptic question. In spite of his advanced age, the Pope continued to visit the Coptic community abroad in order to demonstrate his global leadership at home as it was reported in the patriarchal publications, with the consequent effect of provoking a division inside the community between who consider this as an external interference.

An evident "vibrant and resilient civil society apparatus" (Rowe, 2009: 124) emerged during the last ten years of the Mubarak regime which was boosted by the neo-millet forms of Coptic engagement. As Paul Rowe states, "Christians are unlikely even to pose a security threat to the regime and instead form a convenient pet concern that justifies a strong security State" (Rowe, 2009: 124). This form of social participation which is based on civil society activity strictly connected with the Church became the expression of a "high-impact political participation" which denied electoral challenge and at the same time the absence of participation of the Copts in the political arena, highlighting a change in the way it was expressed. Or, as Samer Soliman states, it cannot be explained just as a reaction to the Islamization of the State and the public space, but as a product of modernity itself (Soliman, 2006) or, as Dina al-Khawaga underlines "elle est une action de moralisation religieuse de la vie publique dépourvue de valeurs et corrompues, (...) la réponse à une crise de valeur et le moyen direct de défendre une minorité dans une société qui perdrait ses références communes et qui tendrait à exclure les coptes de ses repères culturels" (Al-Khawaga, 1992: 347).

"As a result, there are effectively no challenges to the authority of the Church in the spiritual realm" (Rowe 2005: 90) which directly led it to play a more active and defensive role but, above all, to exercise a high power such a mission to minister to all Egyptian Christians, inside and outside the community. And this role had to be played with the support of the President, according the tradition personal collaboration established between Nasser and the patriarch Kyrollos VI, elected in 1959. From the years of Nasser and Kyrollos, these characteristics of the relationship between the Copts and the Egyptian government have remained until today.

In fact, regime-Church relations benefited from a fresh start when Shenuda was released from house arrest in 1985: the Patriarch supported Mubarak politically while the president privileged the Coptic Orthodox Church as the principal channel for handling Copts' concerns. This arrangement, a kind of religious corporatism or a "tactical agreement", amplified Shenuda's authority and let Mubarak address millions of Egyptian Christians through a single proxy (Asher-Schapiro, 2012).

The former started to adopt a low profile, to cooperate with the regime, to avoid confrontation and embrace the rhetoric of national unity publicly supporting Mubarak and consolidate his power within the Church. The President needed the support of the Copts more than ever in order to base its antiterrorism policy and create a magnificent image of interreligious harmony, allowing Coptic independence in community affairs and recognizing Shenuda as the voice of the Church in political matters. This entente fostered the kind of minoritarian discourse. It was in the Church's interest to limit the expression of Copts as individuals.

"The regime was good at window dressing, and public meetings with the Coptic Patriarch Shenuda III cemented the president's image as protector of Muslims and non-Muslims alike. Although it remained difficult for Copts to obtain permits to build or repair churches, he (the president Mubarak) allowed several grand projects, and declared January 7th, Coptic Christmas, a national holiday" (Van Doorn-Harder, 2011). So, the national public sphere started to be based on the relationship between Patriarch Shenuda III and president Mubarak, like what Rowe called a "millet partnership": the historic pattern of the late Ottoman period, known as the millet system, thus gave way to a neo-millet system in which the Church operated as the main filter and representative for the interest of individual Christians under republican system (Rowe, 2009).

As Fahmi states, "the regime also protected the Church's financial indepen-dence, and permitted the Church to ignore court rulings concerning Copts' personal affairs that were not supported by the Church leadership" (Fahmi, 2014). In the wake of this new phase cooperation, the Pope supported Mubarak's policies, discouraging Coptic activists from putting pressure on the regime.

Shenuda and the bishops alone were allowed to petition the regime on a whole range of sensitive issues including sectarian violence, church construc-tion and family disputes. He was also consulted in appointing Coptic govern-ment officials and bureaucrats (Asher-Schapiro, 2012). The only chance for av-erage Copts to improve their lives would have been to take a high-profile position in the government-backed National Democratic Party of Mubarak, not only because religious political parties are not legal, so that even the Mus-lim Brotherhood have had to stand as independents, but also because "it was in the Church's interest to limit the expression of Copts as individuals rejecting the idea of founding a Coptic political party" (Melcangi 2013: 236). The presi-dential and parliamentary elections have highlighted how the government tries to exploit the Coptic votes by making all kinds of promises to the Church and the people, but not offering anything in return after victory. Moreover, the government, supported by the Pope, manipulated the community as a sectar-ian bloc, instead of participating in the political process as individuals: "Indi-vidual political stances based on democratic convictions are the only way to solve ongoing political problems. That is certainly more preferable than de-claring loyalty, *en masse*, to the ruling party only to be met with unfulfilled promises. (...) Maintaining this position Coptic votes have remained a bargain-ing chip between the NDP and political authorities on the one hand, and the Church on the other" (Kamal, 2010).

This provoked the severe reaction of the Coptic elite and young Copts who had repeatedly asked the Patriarch to operate according to his role, accusing him of penalizing the culture and practice of full Egyptian citizenship (Niko-lov, 2008). It was in the Church's intention to make the Copts – once again – into a *millet*, a sectarian community that is largely autonomous, while at the same time, the Church itself was pressing the State to implement the rights of modern citizenship.

By recognizing the Patriarch as the official representative and voice of the Coptic community, the State endorsed this emerging ethno-religious identity, by which Copts are characterized by religion rather than by citizenship. More broadly, the result of the partnership between Patriarch and President is that there exists no secular leadership of the Coptic community untainted by com-plicity with the government – no independent voice willing and able to voice Copts' grievances. Finally, the Mubarak-Shenuda pact hid rather than solved the institutional disadvantages suffered by Coptic communities.

The political, social and economic condition of Christians in Egypt, in fact, remained one of the main reasons for concerns. Whatever their percentages and the State statements according to which the Copts enjoy the same rights of citizenship as the Muslims, the practices governing their public life have not always been equitable. They are politically underrepresented and Coptic political participation remained limited to a number of appointed members of the Parliament and ministers with second-rate portfolios. In the election of 2005, Copts were disappointed when the NDP, despite its pretensions to being the party of national unity, announced that only few Copts would be on its list of candidates (Melcangi, 2013) explaining that Coptic candidates were "less electable" and an obstacle for the aims of the party. Moreover, in 2007, the regime broke a promise reportedly made to the Church that it would allocate a specific number of seats to Copts in the Shura Council elections.

Coptic representation in the last cabinet before the recent Egyptian Revolution consisted of two ministers, Youssef Boutros Ghali in the Ministry of Finance and Maged George in the Ministry of the Environment; in the Shafiq interim cabinet (January 2011) only the Minister of Environment kept his post (Chaillot, 2011). The official regime limits Coptic citizens to a symbolic participation in the political system, which is made most evident by the President's appointment of Coptic representatives in the People's Assembly. In the 2010 elections, prior to the Alexandria Church bombing, former President Mubarak chose to appoint only seven Coptic members of Parliament out of ten that he is constitutionally allowed to select (Ibrahim, 2008).

If we look at the social context, they are drastically underrepresented in a number of fields. There are hardly any high-ranking Copts in the military, police force, judiciary or diplomatic corps. Copts are also marginalized in university presidencies and governorships as well as positions deemed sensitive to national security, from the upper echelons of the security apparatus to the pedagogical front lines where Copts are prevented from teaching Arabic. And furthermore, the issue of the renovation or construction of new churches remained a reason of concern for Copts that the Egyptian governments have failed to address. Copts seeking to build or renovate churches still had to work through a bureaucratic and political morass to obtain permits.

Important state offices are still closed to Egyptian citizens with a Coptic background, and their representation in the judiciary, the official media, diplomatic missions, the army and the police does not exceed 2% of the total. For instance, there are 17 public universities in Egypt, each having one director and three or four deputy directors with a total of 71 positions; not a single Copt occupies one of these seats. In addition, there are 274 deans in Egyptian faculties, none of which includes a single Copt (Guindy, 2010).

However, Copts do obtain leading posts in Egyptian society and have a large presence in civil society associations. The presence of Egyptian Copts is not limited to a specific profession or a cluster of professions; they practice all professions and are active in all economic fields like their Muslim counterparts. Just like Muslims, Copts are represented in all social strata.

A significant number of Copts are concentrated in private and skilled professions; even so a large gap exists between the economic dynamism of Egyptian Christians and their political and legal stature. Such a fact tends not to console the productive and economically successful Coptic man, but increases his frustration instead, for he would expect –with additional vigor– a legal and political treatment that makes him equal to other citizens.

Only at the end of the 2000s, some Coptic youth, believing that the Mubarak regime was the cause of their problems, started to participate to new political movements which called for workers' rights, full judicial independence, and political reform (the April 6 Youth Movement, youth for Justice and Freedom). One of them was the Egyptian Movement for Change, and also known by its slogan *Kifaya* (Enough). This group, born in 2004, led some Copts who opposed Mubarak's policies to act politically and challenge the President's partnership with Shenuda. It was the rising of a new activism among the youth within the community: this group put a distance between themselves and the Church's support for the regime and started to get involved in politics on their own. "Some young Copts, rather than appealing to the respect of human rights, concluded that Christians would only get equal rights within a democratic regime based on the principle of citizenship for all Egyptians" (Fahmi, 2014). These movements from below represented the beginning of a protest march which was able to break the chains of the national ideal, now too narrow and unbearable, questioning the power of Mubarak, his solid alliance with the Church and bringing out all the contradictions of the Egyptian system that would lead to the revolt of 25th January, 2011.

5   Revolution and Beyond: the Long Road for Coptic Rights' Recognition in the Post 2011 Egypt

The revolution of 2011 put a strain on the political role played by the Patriarch within the Coptic community: some tragical attacks on Christians in 2010 led a younger cohort of Copts to distance themselves from the Church's support for the regime. The decisive event happened in 2011, when a massive explosion tore through the midnight mass at the Coptic Church of Saint Mark and Pope Peter (also known as the Church of the Two Saints) in Alexandria. The car bomb killed 23 parishioners, injured dozens, and shattered the regime's pretense of keeping Christians safe. The New Year's attack exposed Copts' continuing vulnerability, despite living in a security State with a powerful chief executive. Egyptians were horrified and outraged while during the investigation some Coptic lawyer accused the Minister of Interior orchestrated the bombing to scare Copts into backing Mubarak out of fear of further sectarian strife (Fadl, 2011; Tadros, 2013).

As a consequence, many young Christians decided to take part in the 25 January uprising, challenged the position of Shenuda, revealing a new political and social rebirth inside the community which emerged from a long political apathy (Casper, 2013). They fought by rallying behind a liberal and civil cause or demonstrated for particular Coptic issues, showing that they claimed an idea of Egyptian nationality while not refusing their religious identity (Guirguis, 2012).

The Church discouraged the Copts to participate in the uprisings, considering the linkage with the Mubarak regime, but despite this, the revolutionary days soon became a moment of unity in Egypt between Muslims and Christians where they agreed and cooperated on the need for democratic reform.

By contrast, after the 2011 revolt, the camaraderie that joined Copts and Muslims lasted only a few weeks and new sectarian strife seemed to start again. Only to quote some examples, on the 4th of March 2011 two men were killed during clashes in Helwan Governorate between Muslims and Christians, which also saw Muslims set fire to a church in the village of Sol, in the south of Cairo; thousands of Christians, joined by many Muslims, have been staging a sit-in in front of the Egyptian TV building on the Nile Corniche in Cairo protesting against the attack on the St. Mina and St. George churches (Habib, 2011). On the 7th of May, 2011 there was a series of attacks that took place against Coptic churches in the poor working-class neighborhood of Imbaba in Cairo; many protesters staged a sit-in in front of the Egyptian Television and Radio Union, known as Maspero (Habib, 2011; Osman, 2011).

The Copts became increasingly fearful as the political and social identities of Islamist groups began to crystallize in the aftermath of Egypt's 25th January revolution (El-Ghobashy, 2011). The first months after Mubarak was deposed revealed that Copts were isolated if not overwhelmed by the rise of Islamist forces which took control of Tahrir Square. During this period of general insecurity for all Egyptians, public security had collapsed across the country and a wave of violent episodes involving Copts showed their acute vulnerability.

Christians in Qena and the nearby governorates of Sohag, Minya, and Asyut, which are home to the country's largest concentration of Copts, became the target for many kidnappings: beginning in 2011, Copts in these regions of Upper

Egypt were frequently abducted and held until their families paid a ransom (Tadros, 2011). Indeed, kidnappings in Minya, where Christians are estimated to make up more than a third of the population, have been a weekly occurrence since Mubarak's ouster (Brownlee, 2013). SCAF's position on sectarian matters suggested the adoption of a policy of tolerance toward sectarian assaults on non-Muslims.

The most tragic attack on Copts occurred the 9th October, when, after the arson of a church in Aswan, a large group of Copts and their Muslim supporters congregated once again in front of Maspero to denounce the SCAF's complicity in anti-Christian violence. Before the protesters could reach the building, army vehicles plowed through the crowd. The day ended with clashes with the army, where in the end, 25 Copts were killed and more than 300 were injured. The Maspero massacre created a real trauma in the memories of the Christians and the Muslims who participated to the sit-in which is still extremely difficult to forget: it represented a critical moment in the history of Egypt's political transition from authoritarian rule because it reflected the single worst assault by an Egyptian ruling authority against a non-Muslim minority in modern Egyptian history. And, moreover, it demonstrated that Copts were as vulnerable as they had been before the revolution and that the SCAF soon showed its violent face (Toma, 2016; Tadros, 2011; Carr, 2013; Eskander, 2016).

The Maspero Youth Union,[2] a political group whom quest for recognition of religious justice has found a receptive audience among Copts across classes, geographic locations, and political orientations, asked immediately for a fair trial to find out what happened in Maspero, why it happened and who ordered the killings of peaceful protesters (Fahmi, 2015). But finally, the court verdict read that three soldiers were found guilty but that nobody had been charged with any crime (Gokpinar, 2012).

The presidential election of 2012 summer gave the final blow to all the Christian's chances for the establishment of a democratic and human rights respectful Egyptian political system; in fact, during the presidential election of 2012, Mohamed Morsi, the official candidate of the Muslim Brotherhood's Freedom and Justice party, edged out Shafiq, 51.7% to 48.3%.

The election victory of Morsi plunged Copts into mourning as they started to feel in danger, more than in Mubarak period. According to Mariz Tadros, and as the National Council for Human Rights (NCHR) highlighted in its report on

---

2   The main ideal of this group was the prevention of conflict and in case of conflict, to compel government authorities to implement the rule of the law rather than hold the more traditional meetings of reconciliation.

the second round of elections, Copts were prevented from going to the voting stations and that assaults were instigated against them: "the use of intimidation against Copts went largely unreported in the media as the focus was on what was happening inside the polling stations" (Tadros, 2013: 232).

In fact, although the Constitution issued at the end of 2012 stated that Christians enjoy full citizenship, they remained marginalized and with Islamist voices dominating the government they were becoming more socially isolated. "While President Morsi's rhetoric indicated a desire to be more inclusive, his actions fail to protect the Christian communities by, for example, curtailing hateful speech and unfounded allegations about them" (Van Doorn-Harder, 2013: 17). Mohammed Morsi and his government have not found an appropriate response to the problems of religious diversity, rights and minorities, and the relations between the religions and the State.

When in June 2014, one year after the new president's election, an anti-Morsi movement gained steam, Copts were among the millions calling for his early removal from office and new elections. The military answered by deposing the President the 3rd of July: they were led by the Minister of Defence and Commander-in-Chief of the Egyptian Armed Forces, General Abdel Fattah al-Sisi.

He was flanked by notables from the country's major religious communities, including the new Patriarch Tawadros II elected in November 2012: the Pope, who has declared his will to return to a spiritual role within the community, soon returned to his political role as a consequence of a more polarized Egypt. Al-Sisi spoke in reconciliatory tones of moving the country forward according to a political route map and a new collaborative feeling between communities: in fact, the new cabinet included three Coptic ministers, one of them assigned to handle the influential trade portfolio. "But displays of national unity at the upper echelons of Egyptians politics did not establish interfaith comity among the population. Further violence followed the coup. Initial reports indicate the attacks were fueled in equal measure by Islamist grievances and State indifference" (Brownlee, 2013: 19). On the 3rd of July, arsonists burned a church in Minya in the south while vandals struck at a church in Marsa Matruh on the northwestern coast. The sectarian clashes arose again and in a violent form. In the middle of August arsonists damaged or destroyed more than 40 churches in Upper Egypt, Beni Suef, and Fayum. In this chaotic context, General Abdel Fattah al-Sisi run for the presidential election in May 2014 winning it with 23.78 million votes, 96.91% a turnout of 47.5%. This market the beginning of the "al-Sisi's reign" and a sort of go back to the past for the Coptic community.

The current Egyptian President al-Sisi wants to renew the covenant of collaboration established with the Church years ago: following in the footsteps of his predecessor Gamal 'Abd al-Nasser, today the new *ra'is* is trying to overcome the criticism of those who accuse the State of not doing enough to protect the rights of Christians in Egypt. On January 6, 2018, on the occasion of the Coptic Christmas, al-Sisi inaugurated with Patriarch Tawadros II the new cathedral that, according to the President's intentions, should become the largest Christian Church in the Middle East.

Built 40 kilometers east of Cairo, on the site that will see the rise of the "New Cairo" (the future administrative and financial capital of Egypt according to a government plan of urban expansion), the cathedral was erected in record time so that the Egyptian authorities could show this goal on a solemn occasion where al-Sisi held a speech restating the call for national unity between Christians and Muslims without divisions or differences. But the churches in Cairo look like fortresses nowadays, because of the enormous security measures stepped up by the government in every place of worship around the country: a consequence of the violence that in recent years has seen the Copts become the new target of ISIS terrorist attacks (Melcangi, 2019).

From the killing and forced evacuation of several dozens of Christians in 2017 in al-Arish, the capital city of the North Sinai governorate –where a vast anti-terrorist operation of the armed forces is now taking place– to the brutal attack of December 11th 2016 at the Coptic cathedral in Cairo, and the double attack on Palm Sunday, April 9th, 2017, in Tanta, in the Nile Delta region, and in Alexandria: these attacks against the Copts suggest that terrorist violence is no longer confined to the Sinai peninsula but is instead moving towards the main urban centers, putting a strain on the validity of al-Sisi's vows to preserve Egypt's security, a pivot of his propaganda especially during the 2018's presidential election.

The security question therefore continues to represent a dangerous *vulnus* in the Egypt of al-Sisi. Despite the terrorist attacks seems to be progressively diminishing, as a sign that the military repression carried out by the Egyptian president mainly on the Sinai produces encouraging results, the country fails to guarantee security, indispensable for the rebirth of international tourism, and to eradicate sectarian attacks against the religious minorities, which always have great echo in international public opinion.

Al-Sisi, re-elected in march 2018 with 97% of the votes for the second term, put security as the fundamental point of his electoral campaign. However, even if diminished, the terrorist attacks continue to threaten two important pillars of the president's stabilization strategy: first of all foreign tourism linked with the economic condition of the country which now is going through a period of economic growth.

The other priority objective is to tackle the jihadist terrorism which targets especially the Coptic Christians: the attacks on churches and Christian institutions are increasing. These actions move in the dual direction of accentuating sectarianism within Egyptian society and undermining the external image of al-Sisi, sanctioning its inadequacy in controlling the jihadist threat present in Egypt.

Acts of violence have a strong emotional and political impact, because they can tear the "Egyptian national fabric" to which the *ra'is* constantly appeals. On the other side the government has thus played the card of terrorism to legitimize the continuation of the state of emergency, to justify the brutality of national security personnel and to silence political opposition.

Al-Sisi's government still represents for the Copts of Egypt a barrier of protection and the guarantee of political stability. And the last presidential elections confirmed the positioning of the Christian community led by the Patriarch faithfully at the side of the al-Sisi, despite the voices of many young Copts and intellectuals resonate with criticism towards the President's authoritarianism.

6   Conclusion

The transitional period, following the Egyptian uprising of January 2011, showed how much the country has a fragile and polarizing political system and an economical sector in deep crisis. In this situation it was very simple for the minorities to look at the regime as the only guarantee for their survival. Especially when the support is proportional to the regime opportunistic claims for democratic or secular values. Or if the risk of being persecuted and considered a target for violent attack is real, as in the case of the last attacks committed by jihadist groups against several Coptic churches, using the minorities support to authoritarian regimes as a justification for their violent attacks against religious minorities. In addition to acts of violence and intimidation, the conditions of political, economic and social discrimination still weigh on the most numerous Christian communities in the Arab world. This condition makes Copts' strategy and position clearly illustrative of the wider challenge that today's Christians are experiencing in the region.

Since the uprising, the complex political situation of Egypt led to an evolution on the activism and political participation of the Coptic community, which confirm these aspects. Beside the claim of some Copts who stand alongside the President, with the Patriarch, afraid of becoming the new martyrs of the "religious war" conducted by jihadists, there is a dissident movement within the community that has long claimed a return of the Church to its original spiritual task. These are the voices of a large group of young Copts who participated in the 2011 uprising and who became the bearer of demands for democracy, freedom and full political participation, freed from identity and sectarian dynamics.

But Al-Sisi's government still represents a barrier of protection and the guarantee of political stability for the Copts of Egypt. And the latest elections confirmed the positioning of the Christian community led by the Patriarch faithfully at the side of the *ra'is*, despite the voices of many young Copts and intellectuals have resonated with criticism towards the President's authoritarianism.

CHAPTER 7

Religious Affiliations and Social Coexistence in the Islamic Middle East Countries

Giancarlo Rovati

1   Introduction

In the contest of our multi-dimensional research on (forced) migrations because of religious reasons, it is particularly interesting to analyze the religious and cultural orientations that characterize Islamic Middle East countries, where several religious minorities are facing heavy difficulties to be accepted and welcomed.

With the aim of focusing on the question of religious tolerance in Islamic countries and understanding how tolerance could be increased, it is particularly useful to consider the information provided by the most recent Arab Barometer surveys, which, since 2006, have been studying Arab people's values, attitudes and behaviors. Among these aspects, careful and close attention is devoted to the relation among religion, civil law, political authorities, and democracy, in addition to the classic religion topics – i.e. beliefs, practices, and sense of belonging.

In this chapter, we will analyze some data collected over the past decade through the third and fourth Arab Barometer survey (carried out in the two-year period 2012–2014 and in the year 2016–17) based on representative samples of the adult population. They involved, respectively, 12 and 7 Arab countries (Table 7.1) (Arab Barometer, 2012–2014 2016–17) but our analysis will focus only on some of them (Egypt, Jordan, Iraq, Lebanon, Palestine), as they can be compared to each other more directly, from a cultural and geopolitical point of view. Unfortunately, Iraq was not included in the 2016 wave, so it is impossible to apply an identical longitudinal comparison to this country.

People living in these five countries have been active subjects and –at the same time– victims of the large and lasting conflicts that have broken out in the Middle East in the last few decades. In the case of Egypt and Iraq, citizens took part in a hopeful democratic experiment –optimistically named Arab Springs (Ghanem, 2018)– based on a pluralistic electoral competition to choose their ruling classes. Despite every optimistic expectation, this democratic

TABLE 7.1   Countries involved in the third and fourth Arab Barometer survey

Third survey: 2012–2014		Fourth survey: 2016–17	
Country	Sample	Country	Sample
Egypt	1195	Egypt	1200
Jordan	1795	Jordan	1500
Iraq	1215	n.p.	n.p.
Lebanon	1200	Lebanon	1500
Palestine	1171	Palestine	1199
Algeria	1220	Algeria	1200
Morocco	1116	Morocco	1200
Tunisia	1199	Tunisia	1200
Kuwait	1021		
Libya	1247		
Sudan	1200		
Yemen	1200		

SOURCE: ARAB BAROMETER DATA

process failed and new autocratic regimes have been established (Alkhatib, 2014; Ceyhun, 2017a, 2017b; Tavana. 2017). The hope of a real new course of political events has been scaled down, as well as the expectations of a more open pluralistic society (Rahman, 2016; Grinin *et al.*, 2019).

2   Religious Belonging and Personal Religiosity

The wide majority of people interviewed in each Arabian country belongs to Islamic religion with the exception of the Lebanese, one third of which (38%) are Christians and in small amount (7%) Druse; also in Egypt and Palestine there is a small minority of Christian believers (4–5%) mainly concentrated in some areas.

The same distribution is confirmed by the fourth Arab Barometer wave (applied in 2016) with a small, but significant, increase in Christians and other minorities, parts of which have been compelled to escape from Syria (Ceyhun, 2017c) (Table 7.2).

TABLE 7.2   Religious belonging of representative samples interviewed in 2014 (3rd wave) and
2016 (4th wave)

	Egypt		Iraq		Jordan		Lebanon		Palestine		Total	
	2014	2016	2014	2016	2014	2016	2014	2016	2014	2016	2014	2016
Muslim	94%	96%	100%	n.p.	100%	98%	n.p.	60%	96%	97%	91%	87%
Christian	6%	4%	0%	n.p.	0%	2%	38%	33%	4%	3%	9%	11%
Other	n.p.	n.p.	n.p.	n.p.	n.p.	n.p.	n.p.	7%	n.p.	n.p.	n.p.	2%
Total	100%	100%	100%	n.p.	100%	100%	38%	100%	100%	100%	100%	100%

SOURCE: AUTHOR'S ELABORATION OF ARAB BAROMETER DATA

It is only in the case of Lebanon that we have specific information on the religion composition of both the Islamic community –with half Sunnis and Scythians, who together represent 56% of the total sample[1]– and of the Christian one that includes a high variety of denominations, mainly Maronite (25%), Orthodox (7%), Catholic (4%), and Armenian (1%). This empirical evidence documents the possibility of a real pluralistic coexistence among different religious and cultural identities, with the support of suitable political institutions.

According the sample composition of each country, the data commented below include the answers by both Islamic and not Islamic people, the large diffusion of Islamic faith and belonging in four out five countries (see 3rd wave) offers the opportunity to make some comparisons among national differences about religion, civil law, politics, and democracy (Bréchon, 2018).

The diffuse sense of belonging to a specific religion is supported by a strong personal commitment, considering that:

– More than 90% declare to be a "religious person", with the highest degree in Egypt and Jordan (94–95%); two years later (2016), Egyptians and Jordanians confirm their primacy, while Lebanese drop 7 percentage points (Table 7.3);

– About 70% declare to pray regularly every day, with values under the average in Lebanon (60%), where there are more unresponsive and indifferent people. These widespread attitudes register some changes in the fourth wave, growing up in Jordan (from 71% to 77%) and decreasing in Egypt (from 69% to 56%), Lebanon (from 60% to 50%) and on the whole (from 70% to 65%) (Table 7.4);

---

1   In the 2016 survey Muslims represent 60% of the total interviewed, 46% of them Sunni and 54% Shia.

TABLE 7.3   Do you consider yourself to be a religious person?

	Egypt	Jordan	Lebanon	Palestine	Total
2014	94%	95%	85%	93%	92%
2016	97%	97%	78%	92%	89%

SOURCE: AUTHOR'S ELABORATION OF ARAB BAROMETER DATA

TABLE 7.4   Do you pray daily?

	Egypt	Jordan	Lebanon	Palestine	Total
2014	69%	71%	60%	77%	70%
2016	56%	77%	50%	75%	65%

SOURCE: AUTHOR'S ELABORATION OF ARAB BAROMETER DATA

- 40% declare to take part regularly in weekly religious ceremonies, with higher percentages among Egyptians (67%) and Jordanians (61%), and lower percentages among Iraqis (18%), for reasons that could be related to insecurity rather than religious disinterest. The irregular ceremony participation is more widespread among Palestinians who, from this point of view, appear to be more secularized.[2]
- The listening and the reading of the Koran (or the Bible) are more diffused, also in this case, among Egyptians (50%) and Jordanians (49%), thus confirming that they are the most faithful and assiduous people. According to the 2016 survey, this behavior declines in each country (especially in Lebanon with 20% vs 38%) and, overall, attesting at 35% vs 42% (Table 7.5).
- The majority of interviewed (39%) assert to apply effectively the teachings of the Prophet (Mahomet) in their daily life and therefore to be good Muslim;[3] on the contrary, only a small minority (3%) consider themselves as completely incoherent and faraway from Islamic commandments.
- It's interesting to underline the strong distance between the Palestinians' and the Lebanese' self-esteem regarding their religious commitment: the former are confident in 46% of the cases, while the latter only in 26%.

---

2   This issue is absent in the 4th wave survey.
3   This issue, too, is absent in the 4th wave survey.

TABLE 7.5   Do you always listen to or read the Quran/the Bible?

	Egypt	Iraq	Jordan	Lebanon	Palestine	Total
2014	50%	26%	50%	38%	46%	42.5%
2016	43%	n.a.	41%	20%	40%	35%

SOURCE: AUTHOR'S ELABORATION OF ARAB BAROMETER DATA

The "self-examination" requested to the interviewed regarding their understanding and their practice of the faith also includes an evaluation of their personal fidelity and coherence towards the teaching of Prophet Muhammed and an evaluation of the same topics from other believers with whom they are in touch.

Generally, the interviewed evaluate themselves as good testimony of the Prophet's teachings, with some kind of over-estimation and self-confidence: 39% declare to be "a good Muslim" and only 21% feel to be "not very" or "not at all" reliable.

The evaluations towards the others is decisively lower, because they are considered as "good" testimony only by 18% of the people and as "bad" by 37%. The general results are differentiated among countries: Lebanese and Palestinians are particularly negative, while Egyptians are very optimistic and confident toward their fellow worshippers.

In summary, we may say that most interviewed have a high self-commitment to the faith they declare, which, in fact, has a great and direct influence on their everyday life (Spierings, 2018).

3   Islam and Civil Law

The relation among the norms ruling the religious community and the secular community has been (and still is) a largely discussed topic, ascribable – synthetically– to the question of "secularity", i.e. the distinction among the religious and the civil spheres in the context of "pluralistic societies", very differentiated in every aspect (Jamal, 2018).

In Europe, the acquisition of this distinction is part of a long-lasting and dramatic historical process, started during the 14th century and proceeded until the 19th century. Indeed, the principle *"cuius regio, eius religio"* (during the Protestant and Catholic Reform) established the primacy of the religious beliefs of the rulers (kings or other chiefs) over the ruled people, with the consequent right to impose their own ideas and principles over the "mass", with an authoritarian approach.

What European culture has considered for many centuries as obvious and mainstream is, however, not accepted inside the Islamic world. There, the distinction between religion and politics –established, from an ideal point of view, from Jesus Christ's sentence "Render to Caesar the things that are Caesar's, and to God the things that are God's"– has never taken root, either for doctrinal and social reasons.

Even if in some Arab Islamic countries secular political regimes arose during 20th century,[4] after the Khomeini revolution (1979) the cultural and political hegemony of religious chiefs was reasserted, with a consequent revival of political-religious conflicts in the whole Middle East, as in the typical case of Shia and Sunni regimes (see Chapter 5).

With the complicity of many economic, national, ethnic cleavages inside the Arab Islamic countries, the religious identities have re-obtained the central role of "cement of the society"; therefore, it is not surprising that religious norms have become the central point of every kind of (moral, legal, economic, political) value and rule. The open question is in which way the coexistence of different religious believers may be regulated, respecting differences and promoting freedom of speech and expression.

According our empirical data,[5] most of the people interviewed in 2012–2014 have assigned to Islamic laws the primacy over popular willing, denying essential value to democratic procedures. This approach is mainly diffused in Jordan, where 40% of the people strongly agree with the idea that "The Government and the Parliament should enact laws in accordance with the Islamic law"; the same idea is more cautiously supported by Palestinians (30%), Egyptians (26%), and Iraqis (16%), but if we add the partial agreement ("somewhat agree"), the consensus reaches 65–80%. This idea is firmly refused by the Lebanese, who prefer the secular primacy of popular consensus.

The opposite idea that "The Government and the Parliament should enact laws in accordance with people's wishes" reaches less consensus (20% on average), even if, in total, agreements (52%) always overcome disagreements (42%). It is important to underline that the Lebanese people confirm their support to the principle of democratic consensus (43%), rejecting "strongly or somewhat" (82%) the principle of Islamic hegemony. In other words, many

---

4   See the regime of Nasser, Gamal Abdel (1918–1970), President of Egypt from 1954 to 1970 and the role of Ba'th party, in Iraq, at the base of the regime of Saddam Hussein (1937–2006), lasted from 1979 to 2006, and supporter, in Syria, of the Arab Republic since 1963. In 1970, the power was achieved by the Assad dynasty.

5   The data here discussed have been collected only in the third Arab Barometer survey (2012–2014).

Lebanese people support the distinction between religion and politics according to the secular approach (see below, §4).

The intermediate solution that tries to combine both the previous principles –assigning different priorities to religious or secular principles, according to the questions to face[6]– gets the maximum consensus among Iraqis (34%) and Egyptians (33%), followed by Jordanians (26%) and Palestinian (16%), who, as we noted before, largely support the monocratic solutions. The dissent of the Lebanese towards the religious principle is confirmed also by means of this variable, considering that 52% of them reject a limited intrusion of religious norms into politics.

The same ideological tendencies get reinforcement when people react to the question of criminal laws, i.e. the branch of law that produces heavy restrictions to personal freedom in the event of behaviors considered as dangerous for the members of society. The most confessional are, again, Jordanians (51%), followed by Palestinians (37%), Egyptians (31%) and Iraqis (28%). Lebanese people confirm their previous attitudes, supporting mainly (60%) the non-religious perspective.

Similar preferences emerge when people refer to the primacy of Islamic laws in the contest of family relations: 60% of Jordanians strongly agree with the idea that "The Government and the Parliament should enact personal status laws (marriage, divorce) in accordance with the Islamic law", while only 12% of Lebanese accept this hypothesis.

Finally, the fundamentalist approach is, once again, clear when people answer to the sentence "The Government and the Parliament should enact inheritance laws in accordance with the Islamic law" by referring directly to tradition and Islamic norms: Jordanians put themselves at the top (63%), followed by Egyptians (56%), Palestinians (50%) and Iraqis (49%). Lebanese are at the bottom, with a very little agreement (14%).

All the answers on these topics have been transformed in a synthetic index named *Islam Law Conformity Index* (ISLC Index) finalized to check how important the Islamic law must (or must not) be in producing and supporting the decision of both Government and Parliament (Table 7.6).[7]

---

6 See the following sentence: "To what extent do you agree or disagree with each of the following principles in the enactment of your country's laws and regulations? The Government and the parliament should enact penal laws in accordance with the Islamic law".

7 For calculating this index, the original variables (q605.1 to q605.6) have been recoded giving:
   – Highest score to options that indicate unconditioned agreement with the primacy of Koranic law in every Government or Parliament decision (see q605.2, q605.4, q605.5, q605.6);
   – Middle score to options that indicate a conditioned agreement with the primacy of Koranic law in every Government or Parliament decision (see q605.1);

TABLE 7.6   *Islamic Law Conformity Index* by sex and age (score: min = 1, max = 6)

		Sex			Age	
	Total	Male	Female	Up to 29	30–45	46 and over
Egypt	4.30	4.32	4.28	4.03	4.42	4.52
Iraq	4.28	4.27	4.28	4.22	4.33	4.30
Jordan	4.51	4.43	4.61	4.55	4.48	4.51
Lebanon	2.43	2.41	2.45	2.71	2.56	2.09
Palestine	4.36	4.27	4.45	4.45	4.32	4.30
Total	4.02	3.99	4.04	4.06	4.11	3.83

SOURCE: AUTHOR'S ELABORATION OF ARAB BAROMETER DATA

On a scale from 1 to 6, the average score reached by all interviewed is 4.02, with higher values in Jordan (4.51) and lower ones in Lebanon (2.43) confirming a well know trend.

In Jordan and Palestine, the ISLC *Index* is higher among young people (up to 29 years old: 4.55 and 4.45), who look more radical, while in Egypt and Iraq this Index is higher among the elderly (4.52, 4.30). The generational change goes in opposite directions in the single countries: it increases traditionalism in Jordan and Palestine, but it contributes to modernization in Egypt and Iraq. Lebanon keeps its originality: it is less sensible to Islamic traditionalism, owing to the relevant presence of Christians; nevertheless the (low) Islamic traditionalism is more attractive for young people (Robbins, 2017).

4   The Influence of Shariʻa

Inside these general trends, largely approving the cultural leadership of Islam in the field of moral and legal regulation of society, specific attention should be paid to the supporters of the direct application of Shariʻa in all private and public spheres – as it is recommended by the radical loyalty to Islamic tradition

---

–   Lowest score to options indicated in the unique variable that establishes no conformity to Quranic law (see q605.1).

and by the fundamentalist political movements (Bell *et al.*, 2013; Ciftci *et al.*, 2018).

Our reference is mainly to the third edition of Arab Barometer employing more questions[8] finalized to understand:

- The expected role of Shari'a in laws regulating marriage and divorce;
- The perception of the effective influence of Shari'a on the laws of each country;
- The divine or human foundation of Shari'a according the theological and cultural debate developed in the last years inside Islam;
- The (effective or potential) conflict among the western vision of democracy and the Islam teachings on the same question;
- The limited concession of political rights to non-Islamic minorities;
- The contrast among the economic Islamic teachings and the application of interests by the bank system.

The idea that Shari'a must regulate marriage and divorce is supported by 69%, mainly in Egypt and Palestine, where people appear to be more orthodox and radical. The existence of a direct relationship (strong or not) among Shari'a and ordinary laws is perceived by 53% of the interviewed, with percentages above 60 points in Iraq, Jordan, Palestine, but very low in Lebanon (23%).

Except for the Lebanon case –where Shari'a influence is limited and, therefore, the opinions expressed by the interviewed probably reflect the reality– it is not easy to distinguish if the evaluations by people reflect a deed (judgment of fact) or a wish (judgment of value).

This ambivalence cannot be observed in the 2016 survey, where people have answered to a clearer question: 33% would like the laws in their countries to be entirely or, mostly, based on the Shari'a. Then, 41% would like an equally balanced system (based on Shari'a and on the will of the people). Finally, only 12% indicate the primacy of the people will, according the rules of liberal-democratic systems. The preference for Shari'a overcomes that for democracy, mainly in Palestine (50% *vs* 11%) and Jordan (44% *vs* 4%), in open opposition to Lebanese attitudes (66% in favor of popular will) (Table 7.7).

According to a fundamentalist interpretation, the primacy of Shari'a gains its support by its divine origin and, thus, it cannot be reformed or disregarded; this approach produces radical consequences, not only at theological level, but

---

8   In the 2016 survey, this issue was not discussed with the same extension, even if some topics had been dealt with.

TABLE 7.7   Which of the following statements is the closest to your point of view? *The laws of our country should be based...*

Fourth wave: 2016	Entirely on Shari'a	Mostly on Shari'a	Equally on Shari'a and the will of the people	Mostly on the will of the people	Entirely on the will of the people	Do not know	Decline to answer	Total
Egypt	23%	10%	50%	4%	7%	4%	0%	100%
Jordan	32%	11%	51%	2%	2%	2%	0%	100%
Lebanon	3%	4%	27%	22%	44%	1%	0%	100%
Palestine	41%	10%	36%	3%	8%	2%	0%	100%
Total	24%	9%	41%	8%	16%	2%	0%	100%

SOURCE: AUTHOR'S ELABORATION OF ARAB BAROMETER DATA

also at a social and political one, therefore generating difficulties as far as a pluralistic and tolerant coexistence is concerned.

Two interviewed out of three extensively agree with the idea that Shari'a is "Word of God", with higher consensus among Palestinians (76%) and Jordanians (71%), but under average percentages among Lebanese people (43%), owing to the presence of many non-Muslim people.

The spread of the ideological radicalism may be further estimated through three other items creating a large debate among Islamic theologians and lawyers and concerning democracy, political rights, as well as the bank system.

On average, 26% think that democracy is a system that contradicts the teaching of Islam. This attitude is more diffused among Jordanians (strongly + somewhat: 37%), Palestinians (31%) and Lebanese (30%) because the Muslim part of the population is highly concentrated on this position. On the contrary, it is less supported by Egyptians (6%), directly involved –in the same period– in a democratic experiment.

These orientations have been confirmed also in the 4th Arab Barometer wave (agreement: 26% *vs* 24%), but with very significant changes in Jordan and Egypt, respectively more and less supportive towards the compatibility Islam-democracy (Jordan: 79% *vs* 54%; Egypt 71% *vs* 77%) (Table 7.8).

Strictly connected to the democratic question is the idea (sometimes, unfortunately, corresponding to a practice) that in a Muslim country, non-Muslims should enjoy less political rights than Muslims: 21% agree, strongly or somewhat, with this hypothesis. Compared with other topics, the consensus is low: only Jordanians exceed the average (39% *vs* 21%) while 65% of Lebanese and 46% of Egyptians strongly refuse it.

TABLE 7.8   Compatibility of Western democracy with Islam teachings: agreement[a]

	Agree (strongly or somewhat)		Disagree (strongly or somewhat)	
	2014	2016	2014	2016
Egypt	5%	12%	77%	71%
Iraq	23%	n/a	55%	n/a
Jordan	37%	18%	54%	79%
Lebanon	30%	34%	61%	60%
Palestine	31%	30%	66%	64%
Total	26%	24%	65%	69%

SOURCE: AUTHOR'S ELABORATION OF ARAB BAROMETER DATA

a   The formulation of the question presents some differences in the two Arab Barometer waves. In the 2014 wave, the question was "Democracy is a system that contradicts the teachings of Islam"; in the 2016 wave, the question was "Democracy is a Western form of Government that is not compatible with Islam".

The agreement goes up, once again, when people answer to the contrast among teachings of Islam and the charging of interest applied by banks: 86% of Jordanians and 81% of Palestinians support this interpretation, but only 53% of Egyptians and Iraqis share the same sentiment. Submitted two years later, the same question has obtained, on average, an increasing agreement (75% vs 69%), due principally to Lebanese answers (77% vs 62%), mainly to engage in controversy with Islamic people than for ideological consensus (Table 7.9).

In conclusion, we must register a very large consensus towards central topics of the Islamic doctrine, which, on many occasions, have relevant political consequences. Even if the majority of people does not directly support the radical Islamic groups that propose to apply Shariʿa "sine glossa" to all the aspects of social and political life, these groups receive, at least indirectly, an ideological legitimization that is difficult to deny.

On the basis of the previous variables, we may elaborate an "Islamic Traditionalism Index" (IST Index) that reaches its maximum agreement (73%) at the maximum level of intensity.[9] This result acquires an emblematic importance when compared between each country: the ideological traditionalism reaches its (relatively) higher degree in Egypt (average score 2.76 on a scale 1 to 3) and

9   By grouping the scores of this cardinal measure at three levels (low, middle, high), the large majority appears to be very traditionalist.

TABLE 7.9   Banks charging interest contradict the teachings of Islam

	Agree (strongly or somewhat)		Disagree (strongly or somewhat)	
	2014	2016	2014	2016
Egypt	55%	53%	21%	30%
Iraq	54%	n/a	29%	n/a
Jordan	86%	85%	9%	13%
Lebanon	62%	77%	25%	19%
Palestine	81%	81%	15%	16%
Total	69%	75%	19%	19%

SOURCE: AUTHOR'S ELABORATION OF ARAB BAROMETER DATA

in Palestine (2.73), while its minimum degree is registered in Lebanon (2.12). By comparing the totals, we can observe that there are no significant differences among male and female sub-groups (2.64). The same trend is registered in each country, with the only exception of Lebanon, where women overcome man in the level of traditionalism – which, in any case, is lower than in other countries.

The orientations of the three different age groups are practically similar, but it is interesting to note that in Egypt, Palestine and Lebanon, the Islam traditionalism is a peculiarity of the youngsters, with probably not positive consequences on social coexistence (Table 7.10).

In opposition to the *Islamic Traditionalism Index* –synonymous of strong conservativism– we have elaborated an index of modernization, named "*Islam Openness Index*" (ISO Index), on the basis of three variables collecting positive agreement towards:

a)   gender-mixed education in Universities;
b)   the possibility for women to wear modest clothes without needing to wear hijab;
c)   the right of religious minorities to practice their religion freely.[10]

---

10   From the calculus of the Index, we have excluded the variable "*To what extent do you agree with each of these statements?*" Difference and variation between Islamic scholars, with regard to their interpretation of religious matters, is a good thing (q6082) because, by

TABLE 7.10   *Islamic Traditionalism Index* by sex and age (score: min = 1, max = 3)

	Total	Sex		Age		
	Total	Male	Female	Up to 29	30–45	46 and over
Egypt	2.76	2.79	2.74	2.79	2.74	2.76
Iraq	2.71	2.72	2.71	2.70	2.72	2.73
Jordan	2.71	2.70	2.73	2.67	2.72	2.76
Lebanon	2.12	2.08	2.16	2.16	2.19	2.00
Palestine	2.73	2.75	2.71	2.75	2.72	2.72
Total	2.64	2.64	2.64	2.64	2.66	2.62

SOURCE: AUTHOR'S ELABORATION OF ARAB BAROMETER DATA

The majority (63%) of the whole sample agrees (strongly or somewhat) that, in universities, young women and men could study together, but the differences among countries are very wide (Robbins, Thomas, 2018): the agreement of Egyptians (49%), Palestinians (55%) and Jordanians (57%) is under average, while 94% of the Lebanese openly support this issue (Table 7.11).

The substitution of the hijab with other modest clothes receives, at a general level, less consensus than before (54% *vs* 63%), because 65% of Iraqi, and 52% of Palestinians are mainly adverse (Table 7.12).

The right to practice freely own religion meets a quite universalistic support (86% agree strongly or somewhat) but in Jordan (79%), the consensus is under the average.

Despite what we could expect on the basis of *Islamic Traditionalism Index* (very high in 73% of the cases), people who are not open-minded are a minority (25%), while people with a positive openness reach 36%. On a scale from 1 to 4, the most open-minded country is Lebanon (3.30 scores), followed by Jordan (2.93) and Egypt (2.90): on the contrary, the countries less open to the innovations are Iraq (2.70) followed by Palestine (2.83) (Table 7.13). Gender differences are generally not relevant, except in Jordan, where women are more innovative than men; young people are not more open than the elderly, as in Egypt and Lebanon.

---

applying factor analysis to the empty array (q6071 to q6073 and q6082 to q6087), it turns out to be not pertinent enough.

TABLE 7.11   Gender mixed education should be allowed in universities[a]

	Agree (strongly or somewhat)		Disagree (strongly or somewhat)	
	2014	2016	2014	2016
Egypt	49%	64%	41%	33%
Iraq	66%	n.p.	30%	n.p.
Jordan	57%	56%	38%	44%
Lebanon	94%	90%	5%	9%
Palestine	55%	56%	44%	43%
Total	64%	67%	32%	31%

SOURCE: AUTHOR'S ELABORATION OF ARAB BAROMETER DATA

a   In the 2017 wave, the question was "Is it acceptable, in Islam, for male and female university students to attend classes together?".

TABLE 7.12   Women should wear modest clothes without needing to wear the hijab[a]

	Agree (strongly or somewhat)		Disagree (strongly or somewhat)	
	2014	2017	2014	2017
Egypt	50%	51%	41%	46%
Iraq	31%	n.p.	66%	n.p.
Jordan	61%	49%	34%	51%
Lebanon	78%	68%	20%	31%
Palestine	47%	44%	52%	56%
Total	54%	54%	42%	45%

SOURCE: AUTHOR'S ELABORATION OF ARAB BAROMETER DATA

a   In the 2017 wave the question was "A woman should dress modestly, but Islam does not require that she wears a hijab".

The indexes that we have constructed to reduce the complexity of the information present direct (and statistically significant) correlations among them,

TABLE 7.13   *Islam Openness Index* by sex and age (score: min = 1, max = 4)

	Total	Sex		Age		
		Male	Female	Up to 29	30–45	46 and over
Egypt	2.90	2.92	2.88	2.86	2.91	2.95
Iraq	2.70	2.73	2.67	2.72	2.71	2.65
Jordan	2.93	2.88	2.98	2.96	2.93	2.88
Lebanon	3.30	3.29	3.31	3.25	3.27	3.36
Palestine	2.83	2.84	2.83	2.81	2.86	2.82
Total	2.93	2.92	2.94	2.91	2.93	2.97

SOURCE: AUTHOR'S ELABORATION OF ARAB BAROMETER DATA

which are sometimes positive and sometimes negative, as in the case of *Islamic Traditionalism Index* and of *Islam Openness Index*.[11]

Thanks to these two indexes, it is possible to identify different ideological subgroups inside Islamic people that create an *Islam pluralistic typology,* not always easy to interpreter in an ideal-type way. The conceptual boundaries among them are sometimes undetermined by an empirical point of view, owing to some contradictory overlapping, as in the case of 1,437 interviewed (23% of total sample) who reach a high score in both the indexes (Table 7.14).

The most numerous group is represented by "opportunist people", i.e. very conformist, but hesitant and open to some changes (27%), followed by those who may be defined as "contradictory people" (23%), as they declare to be very traditionalist as well as very open to some changes, and the effective radical extremist, i.e. very traditional and very close (22%). All the other groups are not very consistent and are composed of: "revisionist" (7%) (traditionalist, but with much openness); "moderate people" (7%) (traditionalist and open-minded at a medium level); "conservative people" (5%) (traditionalist and less open); reformist (5%) (not that traditionalist and very open); in talks people (2%) (not that traditionalist and quite open); apathetic (1%) (neither traditionalist nor open) (Table 7.15).

---

11   The highest positive correlation emerges among *Islamic Traditionalism Index* and *Islam Law Conformity Index* (r coefficient = .448); negative correlations emerge, on the contrary, among *Islam Openness Index* (that indicates distancing from a rigid orthodoxy) and the other ones, respectively with r. coefficient -.190 and -.304.

TABLE 7.14   *Islamic Traditionalism Index* (recorded in three levels) (IST INDEX R3) by *Islam Openness Index* (recorded in three levels) (ISO INDEX R3)

IST INDEX R3	ISO INDEX R3			
	Low	Medium	High	Total
low	89	136	294	519
medium	305	438	446	1189
high	1398	1667	1437	4502
Total	1792	2241	2177	6210

SOURCE: AUTHOR'S ELABORATION OF ARAB BAROMETER DATA

TABLE 7.15   Islam pluralistic typology

	Country					Total	
	Egypt	Iraq	Jordan	Lebanon	Palestine	%	N.
Opportunist	28%	34%	26%	12%	32%	27%	1667
Contradictory	25%	13%	29%	27%	20%	23%	1437
Radical	29%	29%	21%	5%	27%	23%	1398
Revisionist	6%	4%	8%	14%	6%	7%	446
Moderate	6%	9%	7%	7%	6%	7%	438
Conservative	2%	8%	6%	3%	4%	5%	305
Reformist	3%	1%	1%	22%	3%	5%	294
In talks	1%	2%	1%	7%	2%	2%	136
Apathetic	0%	2%	1%	3%	1%	1%	89
Total	100%	100%	100%	100%	100%	100%	6210

SOURCE: AUTHOR'S ELABORATION OF ARAB BAROMETER DATA

The statistical distribution of all these groups inside each country allows to find some new peculiarities, together with some confirmations: in Egypt, Iraq, and Palestine the diffusion of extreme radicalism is confirmed, but positive signals come from the presence of contradictory openness in favor of the abolition of some "taboos".

The contradictory orientations indicated by empirical results reproduce, in a reliable way, the ideological and political uncertainty that has been long characterizing the Islamic countries of the Middle East and their difficulties to promote a transition towards a more tolerant coexistence between majority and minority groups (identified mainly by their religious beliefs) among which Christians are prevalent.[12]

The comparisons by sex and age show less differences inside each ideological group, which are characterized more for their radicalism than for their reformism.

5   Religion and Politics Relations: Towards a Secular Political Approach

In order to understand the cultural trends that are developing in Arab societies, it is important to deal with the relations among religion and politics, by using as reference the polarity "dependence–autonomy" of politics, according to a well-known Western intellectual approach. Without accepting the interpretative frame of the French "laïcité" –based on a radical separation between religion and politics, which in fact aims to submit religion to politics– we assume the distinction among "fundamentalism" (direct interference of religious authorities on politics) and "secularism" (autonomy of politics from religion's influence).

Among the variables regarding this issue, four of them measure the agreement towards a direct interference of religion in the political arena, while the other two measure the opposite vision; on the basis of these variables, we have elaborated two concise indexes, named, respectively "Secular Politics Index" (SECPOL) and "Fundamentalism Index" (FUNPOL).

On a scale from 1 to 4, the total average score of the Secular Politics Index overcomes point 3, documenting –as we will read below– a middle-high disposition to defend the autonomy of politics (and politicians) from religious leaders (imams, preachers, priests). This disposition is less appreciated in Palestine (2.90), but strongly shared in Lebanon (3.62), where each variable reaches the highest average score.

By grouping the scores of Secular Politics Index in three modalities (low, middle, high), most of those interviewed (53%) put themselves at the highest level of agreement, with 82% of the Lebanese vs 29% of Palestinians (Table 7.16).

Gender and age differences are very limited, confirming a large ideological homogeneity and conformism (Table 7.17).

---

12   The contradictory attitudes are less diffused in Iraq (13%) where opportunism is more extensive (34%), while Lebanon confirms its peculiarity with a lot of "reformist" (22%) and "revisionist" (14%).

TABLE 7.16   *Secular Politics Index R3*

	Country					
	Egypt	**Iraq**	**Jordan**	**Lebanon**	**Palestine**	**Total**
Low	15%	17%	21%	7%	26%	17%
Middle	27%	35%	31%	11%	45%	30%
High	58%	48%	48%	82%	29%	53%
Total	100%	100%	100%	100%	100%	100%

SOURCE: AUTHOR'S ELABORATION OF ARAB BAROMETER DATA

TABLE 7.17   *Secular Politics Index* by sex and age (scores: min = 1, max = 4)

		Sex		Age		
	Total	**Male**	**Female**	**Up to 29**	**30–45**	**46 and over**
Egypt	3.27	3.32	3.22	3.19	3.26	3.39
Iraq	3.10	3.14	3.07	3.10	3.11	3.09
Jordan	3.10	3.08	3.11	3.09	3.13	3.05
Lebanon	3.62	3.63	3.60	3.54	3.55	3.73
Palestine	2.90	2.91	2.88	2.87	2.89	2.93
Total	3.19	3.20	3.17	3.15	3.17	3.27

SOURCE: AUTHOR'S ELABORATION OF ARAB BAROMETER DATA

The total average score of the *Fundamentalism Index* is attested at point 2; this result documents a low disposition for the direct control of political organizations from religious authorities. This attitude reaches the highest score in Jordan (2.52), Palestine (2.44), Iraq (2.43), and the lowest one in Lebanon (1.38) confirming the specificity of this country (Table 7.18).

By grouping the scores of the *Fundamentalism Index* in three levels, it emerges that 56% of the people put themselves at a low level, with a primacy of the Lebanese (90%) and the last place of Jordanians (39%) (Table 7.19).

The comparisons by gender underline, in each country, that women are more traditionalist than men; fundamentalism is also more diffuse among the

TABLE 7.18 *Fundamentalism Index* by sex and age (scores: min = 1, max = 4)

		Sex		Age		
	Total	Male	Female	Up to 29	30–45	46 and over
Egypt	1.99	1.90	2.08	1.92	1.98	2.09
Iraq	2.43	2.38	2.49	2.36	2.49	2.47
Jordan	2.52	2.49	2.55	2.47	2.56	2.53
Lebanon	1.38	1.37	1.39	1.45	1.44	1.26
Palestine	2.44	2.37	2.50	2.46	2.44	2.40
Total	2.18	2.14	2.22	2.18	2.24	2.10

SOURCE: AUTHOR'S ELABORATION OF ARAB BAROMETER DATA

TABLE 7.19 *Fundamentalism Index* R3

	Egypt	Iraq	Jordan	Lebanon	Palestine	Total
Low	70%	44%	39%	90%	44%	56%
Middle	16%	23%	20%	5%	24%	18%
High	14%	33%	40%	5%	33%	26%
Total	100%	100%	100%	100%	100%	100%

SOURCE: AUTHOR'S ELABORATION OF ARAB BAROMETER DATA

elderly, except in Lebanon, where they lived the dramatic ethno-religious conflict during the 70s and the 80s of the past century (Table 7.20).

The secular or fundamentalist attitudes toward politics are directly related to the consensus towards secular or religious political parties in each country, which has been evaluated, too. In partial contradiction with the opinions registered through the *Secular Politics Index*, the majority of the interviewed (49%) express their (strong plus positive) preferences in favor of the religious political parties, while only 30% disagree with this eventuality. As usual, the citizens of Palestine and Jordan opt for a fundamentalist approach (supported by 67% and 59% of the people), while the citizens of Lebanon mainly adopt a secular approach (67%) (Table 7.20).

TABLE 7.20   Religious – Not religious political party agreement

	Egypt	Iraq	Jordan	Lebanon	Palestine	Total
Strong preference for a religious political party	26%	20%	35%	8%	43%	27%
Preference for a religious political party	19%	35%	24%	9%	24%	22%
Preference for a not religious political party	27%	17%	10%	27%	14%	18%
Strong preference for a not religious political party	12%	4%	2%	39%	5%	12%
Do not agree with either sentence	16%	24%	30%	16%	14%	21%
Total	100%	100%	100%	100%	100%	100%

SOURCE: AUTHOR'S ELABORATION OF ARAB BAROMETER DATA

Some final evaluations arise from the correlation coefficients between the indexes built during our comparative analysis[13] and from the frequencies of the indexes grouped in three classes.

As might be expected, the preferences for the autonomy of politics from religious authorities (see *Secular Politics Index*) are positively correlated with the *Islam Openness Index* (r= .364) and negatively correlated with the *Fundamentalism Index* (r= -.322). A negative link (even if with lower score) may be observed with some other indexes, such as the *Islam Law Conformity Index* (r= -.158), *Islamic Traditionalism Index* (r = -.148). On the contrary, the *Fundamentalism Index* is positively correlated with the *Islam Law Conformity Index* (r = .461), the *Islamic Traditionalism Index* (r=.216) and negatively correlated with the *Islam Openness Index* (r= -.308) (Table 7.21).

Finally, we may underline that the highest ideological consensus is in favor of the *Islamic Traditional Index* (73%), on the one hand, and of the *Secular*

---

13   All the correlations are statistically significant at .001.

TABLE 7.21   Correlation coefficients between indexes

	Islamic Law Conformity Index	Islamic Traditionalism Index	Islam Openness Index	Secular Politics Index
Islamic Traditionalism Index	.448**			
Islam Openness Index	-.304**	-.190**		
Secular Politics Index	-.158**	-.148**	.364**	
Fundamentalism Index	.461**	.216**	-.308**	-.322**

SOURCE: AUTHOR'S ELABORATION OF ARAB BAROMETER DATA

TABLE 7.22   Frequencies of indexes grouped in three levels

	Islam Law Conformity Index	Islamic Traditionalism Index	Islam Openness Index	Secular Politics Index	Fundamentalism Index
Low	26%	8%	28%	17%	56%
Middle	34%	19%	35%	30%	18%
High	39%	73%	38%	53%	26%
Total	100%	100%	100%	100%	100%

SOURCE: AUTHOR'S ELABORATION OF ARAB BAROMETER DATA

Politics Index (53%), on the other, followed by the *Islam Law Conformity Index* (39%) and the *Islam Openness Index* (38%). Fortunately, the *Fundamentalism Index* –which may be considered as a radical expression of traditionalism – obtains the last position (26%) (Table 7.22).

The positive position gained by secular perspective in the field of politics may be considered as a promising step for the improvement of the democratic dialectics inside Muslim Arab society, even if the past attempts to build secular politics (in Egypt, Iraq, and Syria) have flown into autocratic regimes.

6 Coexistence among Islamic and Christian People

The presence of religious minorities in hegemonic contests meets, in general, a lot of difficulties, not only for legal reasons (that formally could establish fair rules) but, principally, for social reasons, i.e. for the sense of superiority that majority groups express and apply toward "the others", easily considered deviant and dangerous for the establishment. According to the most positive hypothesis, majority groups may be "tolerant" but are rarely "inclusive", i.e. open to mutual relationship.

Lebanon's troubled experiences –marked by bloody conflicts in the 1970s and the 1980s– are the reasons behind the fact that Lebanese are less optimistic about the effective status of the relationship among Christian minorities and Islamic majorities in their country. On the contrary, it is likely that among the most optimistic are Egyptians, Palestinian and Iraqis (in their countries, in fact, Christian minorities are nearly invisible). There is, in practice, a negative correlation among the effective relevance of Christian minorities in each country and the idyllic representation of their acceptance from Muslim majorities (Table 7.23).

In the perspective of our research, it is, in any case, interesting to analyze the sentiment of social distance towards people concerned with a different religion (mainly Christians) or belonging to different Islamic tradition, such as Shia or Sunni (Jihan, 2017).

In the first hypothesis, 27% of interviewed does not like to have people of different religion as neighbors, and 18% like it (the remaining 55% are indifferent). The refusal overcomes the acceptance in Palestine (28% *vs* 19%) and in Jordan (21% *vs* 10%), while the contrary happens in Egypt (47% like it *vs* 14%) and in Lebanon (29% *vs* 14%) (Figure 7.1).

In the second hypothesis, hostility grows up to 39%, while acceptance decreases to 14% (with 45% indifferent) (Figure 7.2). Strong difficulties arise, therefore, inside the Muslim people whose religious and political conflicts affect dramatically the people living outside the Islamic denominations. The hostility is stronger in Egypt (50% *vs* 14%) and in Jordan (41% *vs* 7%), while tolerance is more widespread in Lebanon (31% *vs* 15%), confirming the attitudes and the trends emerged also in the Third Arab Barometer survey.

7 Conclusions

Every reflection on the ideal relation that should exist between religious belonging and the promotion of a renewed social coexistence –built on the

TABLE 7.23   How do you view the relationship between Christians (in Egypt: Copts) and
Muslims in reality?

	Egypt	Iraq	Lebanon	Palestine	Total
A relationship of brotherhood, citizenship and cooperation	80%	73%	39%	77%	67%
A relationship strained as a result of the cumulative mistakes of both officials and the people on both sides	12%	6%	30%	9%	14%
A relationship strained because of the mistakes of officials	3%	7%	16%	5%	8%
A relationship strained because of foreign conspiracy	5%	11%	13%	5%	9%
Do not know	1%	3%	1%	4%	2%
Refuse	-	-	1%	-	-
Total	100%	100%	100%	100%	100%

SOURCE: AUTHOR'S ELABORATION OF ARAB BAROMETER DATA

respect of the different identities and on the promotion of their right of expression at individual and collective level– must be based on the epochal
meeting between Pope Francis and the Grand Imam of Al-Azhar Ahamad al-
Tayyib, which took place in February 2019 in Abu Dhabi, ended with the Document *Human Fraternity for world peace and living together.*[14]

The first apostolic visit of a Pope to the Arabian peninsula, and the long and
intense dialogue with the Islamic religious authorities that made it possible,
established a very fruitful opportunity to explain to all religious believers and
goodwill people the joining value of faith in God and its reconciling consequences on human and interpersonal relationships. The idea of this Document
was itself conceived from a fraternal and open discussion to invite "all persons

---

14   The "Human Fraternity for World Peace and Living Together" document, signed by His
Holiness Pope Francis and the Grand Imam of Al-Azhar Ahamad al-Tayyib (Abu Dhabi,
4 February 2019).

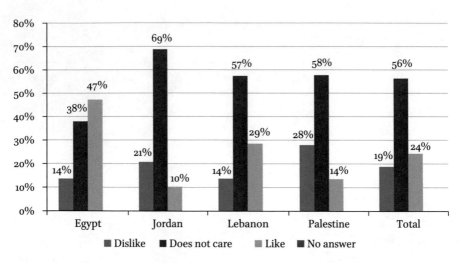

FIGURE 7.1   Having people of a different religion as neighbors, by country
SOURCE: AUTHOR'S ELABORATION OF ARAB BAROMETER DATA

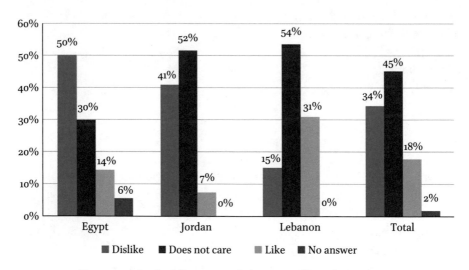

FIGURE 7.2   Having people of a different sect of Islam as neighbors, by country
SOURCE: AUTHOR'S ELABORATION OF ARAB BAROMETER DATA

who have faith in God and faith in human fraternity" to work together for promoting the "culture of mutual respect, tolerance, coexistence and peace".

The foreword of the Document states that "Faith leads a believer to see in
the other a brother or sister to be supported and loved. Through faith in God,
who has created the universe, creatures and all human beings (...) believers are
called to express this human fraternity by safeguarding creation and the entire

universe and supporting all persons, especially the poorest and those most in need."

The Document resolutely declares that "religions must never incite war, hateful attitudes, hostility and extremism, nor must they incite violence or the shedding of blood. These tragic realities are the consequence of a deviation from religious teachings. They result from a political manipulation of religions and from interpretations made by religious groups who, in the course of history, have taken advantage of the power of religious sentiment in the hearts of men and women in order to make them act in a way that has nothing to do with the truth of religion."

The Pope and the Imam invite all the believers "to stop using religions to incite hatred, violence, extremism and blind fanaticism and to refrain from using the name of God to justify acts of murder, exile, terrorism and oppression". In this way, they emphasize the importance of the role of religions in the construction of world peace.

Among the most demanding sentences of the Document –which aim to imprint a turn to the religious and social relations between Muslims and Eastern and Western Christians– we found the solemn obligation to adopt "a culture of dialogue as the path; mutual cooperation as the code of conduct; reciprocal understanding as the method and standard."

The Document is fully aware of the difficulties that prevent the fulfilment of a "bright future for all human beings (the arms race, social injustice, corruption, inequality, moral decline, terrorism, discrimination, extremism and many other causes)." However, it intentionally bets on the deepest desires of every man and woman.

The aim of the Document is very clear, as much as the urgencies and hopes that support it, but it is evident that many efforts should be made to solve the religious, cultural and social conflicts that affect Middle East countries, as we have verified also through the Arab Barometer surveys.

According our empirical data, most of the people interviewed in 2014 and 2016 support the fundamental values at the basis of a pluralistic, tolerant, and democratic political system (freedom of belief, right to practice freely own religion, equal political rights for the religious minorities, same rights of women to education and employment). However, in every country (mainly in Jordan and Palestine), there are significant minorities (well organized and powerful) that do not support a more open society, i.e. a different way to build the coexistence of different identities. In this perspective, also the generational change looks ambivalent: in Jordan and Palestine, many young people are still attracted by Islamic traditionalism more than by its modernization, even if in Egypt and Iraq opposite trends can be observed. Also in Lebanon, that is the most

pluralistic and tolerant country, the (low) Islamic traditionalism is more attractive for young people.

On the whole, people open to introduce positive changes in civil and political society represent a consistent minority (about 35%), but they have to face
a very conservative and reacting people (about 25%) who, in fact, support different kinds of fundamentalism.

From a historical and political point of view, it is evident that in many countries it is impossible to promote and reach a positive coexistence and peace
without a true and affordable cooperation among religious leaders and a faithful belonging to the Christian and Islamic religion. Many ancient and contemporary events document the big importance of this kind of relationships, especially in the Middle East region where Christianity and Islam arose and where,
nowadays, Christians are a small minority with many social troubles, and Muslims are the largest majority, unfortunately divided by strong and large conflicts between Sunni and Shia.

According to our empirical analysis, we may say that the transition to a
more tolerant, civil, and religious coexistence met the largest difficulties
among Muslim people, from whom is expected a decisive contribution to
peace and prosperity – two fundamental conditions also for the right to not
emigrate (Teti, Abbott, 2017).

CHAPTER 8

Women's Rights and *Shari'a* Law in the MENA Region

Vera Lomazzi

1 Introduction

In Muslim-majority societies, women tend to face severe disadvantages and discrimination more than in other countries. As a source of the gender inequalities existing in these countries, the patriarchal tradition is generally linked to the religious roots of legislation and cultural heritage. Despite what most of the Western public opinion believes, the gender cultures that can be retrieved in the Muslim-majority countries differ across societies and the status of women varies. In this contribution, we aim at reflecting beyond the simple readings that equate gender inequality with Islam. With a focus on countries of North Africa and the Middle East (MENA) we intend to provide an overview of the different gender cultures existing in this area. Gender cultures in this region are all somehow affected by the relation between religious norms, political and legislative power, but the extent to which norms and regulations impact on women's right can be different. Similarly, people also can combine their quest for gender equality and the support for the religious influence on legislation and social life in different forms. Furthermore, gender cultures are subject to the country's specific way of coping with the post-colonialist period and implementing reforms. Despite the strong normative effect of these institutional positions, there is not a unique way of living the link between religious faith and women's rights. On the contrary, in the MENA societies some feminist positions challenge the current status quo combining the quest for women's rights with their support for the implementation of laws inspired by Islam in a variety of combinations, which range from secular to Islamist feminisms.

After providing a general overview of the gender cultures in MENA countries, the contribution offers a reflection on the different outcomes for gender equality of the Arab Uprisings occurred in the region in 2011. In order to further explore the current gender cultures in the region, we observed how people combine the quest for gender equality with their support of Shari'a law. To do so, we use data from the Arab Transformations Project, which investigated the social, political and economic transformation after the uprisings in Egypt, Libya, Jordan, Iraq, Morocco, and Tunisia. By using typologies built on the basis of extant literature (Badran, 2001; Fox *et al.,* 2016; Mir-Hosseini, 2011), we identified differences in the distribution of Secular Feminist, Muslim Feminist, Reformist, and Islamist people living in these countries, illustrating a variety of gender cultures in line with the historical developments described by the theoretical literature.

2   Gender Cultures in the MENA Region

Pfau-Effinger (1998: 150) describes the gender culture as the "uniform normative assumptions existing in society about the proper form of gender relations and of the division of work between men and women". These norms and values guide people in their behavior about gender relations and provide gender role expectations. Societies differ in the way they define the proper role for women and men. Gender cultures are in fact situated, that means that they are subject to the characteristics of each society, which can also change over time. The different economic, political, and social historical pathways led societies to develop different gender cultures, which reflect in a variety of gender norms and related expected gender roles, who changed accordingly with the broader structural and cultural change of societies (Inglehart, Norris, 2003; Pfau-Effinger, 2004). The way gender cultures develop is a very complicated process: it refers to the intertwined relation between individual, relational and institutional levels of gender relations (Wharton, 2005). The individual values, showed for example in supporting egalitarian gender roles, cannot be explained only from an individual perspective, because they also result from the socialization process and the daily negotiations (West, Zimmerman, 1987). Therefore, they are not just a matter of individual preference. Furthermore, this ongoing process takes place in a societal context, made of laws, social norms, and institutional structures that are of course part of a society's gender culture and affect the individuals' values and behaviors.

In a cultural context, the mainstreaming ideas about masculinity and femininity as well the prevailing family model determine what in a society can be considered an appropriate role for a man and for a woman. Such gender norms impact on people's life at individual, domestic and social level. They could refer to every aspect of personal and social life. The appropriate way of dressing for a woman or a man at each stage of life, the behaviors considered more or less adequate in private and in public contexts, the "right" roles that a woman or a man should have in society, the distinction of tasks and caring responsibilities between husband and wife and the tasks assigned to sons and daughters, the agreement about a specific share of inheritance between daughters and sons, or the fact the women could or could not be allowed to travel alone – these are all aspects of the gender norms within a particular social context. Following different historical-cultural paths, societies have developed different gender cultures displaying different position between the maintenance of more traditional-patriarchal values and progressive views, with the adoption of values and behaviors more oriented towards reciprocity than complementarity (Inglehart, Norris, 2003; Pfau-Effinger, 1998 and 2004).

In the case of societies in the MENA region, it is impossible to think of gender cultures without including into the reflection two relevant aspects that contribute to defining the value systems of these societies as well their structural organization: the intertwined relationship between religion and politics and the past Western domination.

Islam and post-colonialism are in fact essential elements of the cultural context of this region. In several countries of the MENA region, the Shari'a law disciplines the private as well as the public life. In particular, the personal status codes concern laws and norms about marriage, divorce, custody, inheritance. Because of the impact of such regulation on women's lives, the personal status codes are often recognized as a central issue for women's rights in the region (Fox *et al.*, 2016; Hatem, 1994; Rahman, 2012). Western observers tend to equate Shari'a to patriarchal laws. As Mir-Hossein points out (Mir-Hosseini, 2006, 2011), it is instead necessary to consider the distinction between Shari'a, that refers to the revealed law of God, and *fiqh*, which is the jurisprudence based on the human interpretation of Shari'a. The Sahri'a is an essential source of justice for most Muslims, but its interpretation is a crucial debate in the Muslim world and different traditions exist (Carlisle, 2019; Mir-Hosseini, 2011; Rahman, 2012). As Rahman (2012) explains, regardless of the school of law, the family laws sourced by Shari'a are built on the Quran that describes gender roles according to the natural differences between men and women. Similarly as in other religious traditions, this reflects into the specialization of tasks and responsibilities because of gender. Nevertheless, also in this case scholars' positions can differ. In addition to the quest for women's rights, also reformist views that would encourage reinterpretation and legal changes are emerging (Mir-Hosseini, 2011).

Such a strict link between religion and legislation challenges the traditional conceptualization of Western democracy, based on the separation of religious and political powers (Hashemi, 2009). By assuming this perspective, theocracy has been seen as one of the main causes of unequal rights (in the cases of women and minorities) and of the reinforcement of authoritarianism

(Altemeyer, Hunsberger, 1992; Hunsberger, 1995; Mir-Hosseini, 2006). The current process of radicalization, with the call for a rigid "return to Shariʿa" also in the domain of women's rights, claimed by Islamist forces, is interpreted as an opposition to the Western model of democracy and the attempt of re-affirming an authentic identity as reaction to the colonialist era and orientalism (Fox *et al.*, 2016; Hilsdon, Rozario, 2006; Mir-Hosseini, 2011).

In this general context of complexity, countries in the MENA region developed different gender cultures, which resulted from the specific historical pathways, cultural heritage, the unique ways of coping with the post-colonialist period and of implementing reforms (Abbott, Teti, 2017b; Sarnelli, 2016).

3   CEDAW Acceptance and Shariʿa Law

To consider differences in gender cultures one may consider individual values as well as institutional aspects. To further explore the connections between gender cultures and their relation with religion, it could be interesting to consider to what extent country legislations norm gender relations and define women's right (Branisa *et al.*, 2014). While previous research already explored differences between the institutional aspects of gender cultures in the MENA region concerning issues related to gender-based violence (Kelly, Breslin, 2010), here we consider how the gender cultures can differ in this region by observing the ways countries accepted the Convention on the Elimination of all Forms of Discrimination Against Women (CEDAW).

The CEDAW, adopted by the United Nations in 1979, is one of the most important treaties concerning gender equality. Not only does it define the basis to achieve gender equality, but it also conceptualizes the equal access to, and equal opportunities in, political and public life as a matter of human rights. The Convention describes discrimination against women as

> any distinction, exclusion or restriction made on the basis of sex which has the effect or purpose of impairing or nullifying the recognition, enjoyment or exercise by women, irrespective of their marital status, on a basis of equality of men and women, of human rights and fundamental freedoms in the political, economic, social, cultural, civil or any other field. (Article 1)

The CEDAW is a cornerstone for gender equality legislation. Its strong relevance is due to the fact of defining the forms of gender discrimination in a treaty potentially valid worldwide.

Made of 30 articles, which cover gender equality in several domains (from personal freedom, to family rights, to social and political participation), the CEDAW has been subscribed by 189 countries. However, not all of them accepted it entirely. Some countries ratified the CEDAW with reservations on specific articles that would not be compatible with a nationally accepted interpretation of the Shariʿa provisions. The main aspects of the different degree of acceptance of the CEDAW have been already described in previous studies (El-Masri, 2012; Lomazzi, 2016). Here, a recap of the reservations to CEDAW articles in countries of the MENA region is summarized in Table 8.1.

While Morocco, Tunisia, Djibouti, and Palestine Authority accepted CEDAW without any reservations (Morocco withdrew the reservations in 2011), the other countries differ by their degree of acceptance of the convention, ranging from Yemen, that made a reservation only on article 29 concerning the administration of the convention, to Syria, that displays the highest number of reservations, including the one concerning child marriage. As shown in Table 8.1, articles concerning marriage and family life, and freedom of movement are those that more frequently are considered in contrast with the national interpretation of Shariʿa law. Such reservations are of particular relevance for the interest of this study. Laws implying a subsidiary position of women in society and in family life have a substantial impact on gender role expectations and individuals' opportunity of self-determination. Since these reservations derive from the nationally widespread interpretation of Shariʿa, one could think that gender equality in Muslim majority States is limited because of the influence of the predominant religion and that people living in MENA region are generally against women's rights.

While it is undoubted that the countries in this region display lower levels of gender equality compared to other areas of the world, the generalization of such stereotypes may be misleading.

The World Economic Forum yearly drafts the Global Gender Gap Report.[1] It provides a gender gap index aimed at measuring gender inequality in four domains: economic participation and opportunity, educational attainment, health and survival, and political empowerment. The index ranges from 0 (inequality) to 1 (lack of gender gaps, equality). According to the most recent report (WEF, 2018), countries in the MENA region have low scores and occupy the lowest part of the rank. The most egalitarian is however Tunisia (0.648), followed by United Arab Emirates (0.642); Kuwait (0.630); Qatar (0.629); Algeria (0.629); Bahrain (0.627); Egypt (0.614); Morocco (0.607); Oman (0.605); Jordan

---

1   More information can be retrieved on the Global Gender Gap Report website (https://www
.weforum.org/reports/the-global-gender-gap-report-2018).

TABLE 8.1   CEDAW Convention acceptance

Country	Year of acceptance	Reservations to articles and main topics (the numbers in parenthesis indicate a specific paragraph of the article)
Algeria	1996	2 (policy measures i.e. intention to enshrine gender equality into domestic legislation)15(4) (equal rights to legal capacity and freedom of movement) 16 (equal rights in marriage and family life) 29 (an article related to the administration of the convention; i.e. arbitration in the event of a dispute)
Bahrain	2002	2 (policy measures i.e. intention to enshrine gender equality into domestic legislation)9 (2) (equal rights with men to acquire, change or retain their nationality; equal rights with regard to the nationality of children) 15 (4) (equal rights to legal capacity and freedom of movement) 16 (equal rights in marriage and family life) 29 (1) (an article related to the administration of the convention; i.e. arbitration in the event of a dispute)
Djibouti	1998	No reservation
Egypt	1981	2 (policy measures i.e. intention to enshrine gender equality into domestic legislation)16 (equal rights in marriage and family life) 29 (an article related to the administration of the convention; i.e. arbitration in the event of a dispute)
Iran	-	Even if in 2003, the Iranian parliament ratified the CEDAW, it is still awaiting consideration by the Expediency Council.
Iraq	1986	2 (f) (g) (policy measures i.e. intention to enshrine gender equality into domestic legislation)16 (equal rights in marriage and family life) 29 (1) (an article related to the administration of the convention; i.e. arbitration in the event of a dispute)
Jordan	1992	9 (2) (equal rights with men to acquire, change or retain their nationality; equal rights with regard to the nationality of children)16 Paragraph 1 (c) (same rights and responsibilities during marriage and at its dissolution), (d) (same rights and responsibilities as parents) and (g) (same personal rights, including the right to choose a family name, a profession and an occupation)

Country	Year of acceptance	Reservations to articles and main topics (the numbers in parenthesis indicate a specific paragraph of the article)
Kuwait	1994	9(2) (equal rights with men to acquire, change or retain their nationality; equal rights with regard to the nationality of children)16(f) (equal rights in marriage and family life)
		29(1) (an article related to the administration of the convention; i.e. arbitration in the event of a dispute)
Libya	1989	2 (policy measures i.e. intention to enshrine gender equality into domestic legislation)16 (equal rights in marriage and family life)
Lebanon	1997	9 (2) (equal rights with men to acquire, change or retain their nationality; equal rights with regard to the nationality of children)16 (1) (c) (d) (f) (g) (equal rights in marriage and family life)
		29 (1) (related to the administration of the convention; arbitration in the event of a dispute)
Morocco	1993	2 (policy measures i.e. intention to enshrine gender equality into domestic legislation)15(4) (equal rights to legal capacity and freedom of movement)
		29 (an article related to the administration of the convention; i.e. arbitration in the event of a dispute)
		The reservations were formally withdrawn in 2011.
Oman	2006	9(2) (equal rights with men to acquire, change or retain their nationality; equal rights with regard to the nationality of children)15 (4) (equal rights to legal capacity and freedom of movement)
		16 (1a,c,f) (equal rights in marriage and family life)
		29 (1) (an article related to the administration of the convention; i.e. arbitration in the event of a dispute)
Palestine Authority		Ratification without any reservations as a non-member State
Qatar	2009	2(a) (policy measures i.e. intention to enshrine gender equality into domestic legislation)9(2) (equal rights with men to acquire, change or retain their nationality; equal rights with regard to the nationality of children)
		15(1) (4) (equal rights to legal capacity and freedom of movement)
		16(1a) (equal rights in marriage and family life)

TABLE 8.1   CEDAW Convention acceptance (*cont.*)

Country	Year of acceptance	Reservations to articles and main topics (the numbers in parenthesis indicate a specific paragraph of the article)
Saudi Arabia	2000	9(2) (equal rights with men to acquire, change or retain their nationality; equal rights with regard to the nationality of children)29(1) (an article related to the administration of the convention; i.e. arbitration in the event of a dispute)
Syria	2003	2 (policy measures i.e. intention to enshrine gender equality into domestic legislation)9 (2) (equal rights with men to acquire, change or retain their nationality; equal rights with regard to the nationality of children) 15 (4) (equal rights to legal capacity and freedom of movement) 16 1 (c), (d), (f) and (g) (equality in marriage and family life) 16 (2) (child marriage) 29 (1) (an article related to the administration of the convention; i.e. arbitration in the event of a dispute)
Tunisia	2008	No reservations
United Arab Emirates	2004	2(f) (policy measures i.e. intention to enshrine gender equality into domestic legislation)9 (equal rights with men to acquire, change or retain their nationality; equal rights with regard to the nationality of children) 15(2) (equal rights to legal capacity and freedom of movement) 16 (equal rights in marriage and family life) 29(1) (an article related to the administration of the convention; i.e. arbitration in the event of a dispute)
Yemen	1984	29(1) (an article related to the administration of the convention; i.e. arbitration in the event of a dispute)

SOURCE: OECD/CAWTAR, 2014

(0.605); Lebanon (0.595); Saudi Arabia (0.590); Iran (0.589); Syria (0.568); Iraq (0.551); Yemen (0.499).[2] These situations can be considered as the result of this

---

2   Data on Palestine, Libya, Djibouti are not available.

variety of gender cultures, produced by the intertwined relationship of historical, cultural, political, economic and social processes. Despite the common fact of being a Muslim-majority country, countries in the MENA region differ in several ways. The historical heritages flow into new and different pathways that distinguish political systems and regimes. The degree of influence of religious power on the political processes can profoundly differ and the institutional positions towards human rights, and more specifically towards minorities and women rights, vary as well. In the context of such different cultural and structural frameworks, women's movements developed their action accordingly (Moghadam, 2018; Parashar, 2016). Consequently, also their influence on social change did not impact in the same way in all the countries.

The relation between religion and gender equality is however a central issue (Razavi, Jenichen, 2010), especially in this region. Most of the religions tend to support a traditional and patriarchal view of gender roles (Alexander, Welzel, 2015; Forman-Rabinovici, Sommer, 2018; Inglehart, Norris, 2003; Klingorová, Havlíček, 2015). When religious and political powers are not distinct, their reciprocal influence can establish a strong barrier to gender equality, especially when strictly confessional views are embraced in policy-making processes. On the other hand, the support for patriarchal values is not only due to religion and cultural aspects. In the case of the MENA region, for example, authors also take into account structural factors that contribute to explaining gender inequality in the region (Moghadam, 2003; Rahman, 2012; Ross, 2008), such as oils and gas rent: "Oil production reduces the number of women in the labor force, which in turn reduces their political influence. As a result, oil-producing States are left with atypically strong patriarchal norms, laws, and political institutions" (Ross, 2008: 117).

Investigating gender equality in Muslim-majority countries is not easy because of the degree of complexity that needs to be taken into account (Alexander, Welzel, 2015). For example, as seen earlier, countries in the MENA region display a variety of institutional position towards conservative views. Furthermore, people's opinions in the domain of women's right and of the relation between religious and political powers can deeply differ. Moreover, such individual positions need to be considered in the frame of the historical pathways of gender cultures that, in these countries, have been affected also by the colonialist domination – which, in the long term, may have generated a backlash to traditional values (Fox *et al.*, 2016; Hilsdon, Rozario, 2006). Alongside a dynamic and longstanding scenario of feminist movements quite vivid in some of the MENA countries (Al-Ali, 2003; Moghadam, 2003, 2008), people nowadays combine the support for women's rights with the support for the implementation of laws inspired by Islam in a variety of formulations ranging from secular feminism to Islamist positions.

4   Islam and Feminisms

According to extant literature (Azam, 2018; Badran, 2001; Halverson, Way, 2011; Mir-Hosseini, 2006), four possible ways to combine the support for the religious source of personal status codes and women's rights can be identified.

Based on the idea that only the separation between religious and political power can guarantee the establishment and the development of women's right, the secular feminism follows the Western idea of a division between Mosque and State. According to this view, women's rights should not have their roots in the religious tradition.

People who see this conceptualization as the fruit of the Western colonialist era and refuse the idea of a Westernization of the Arab world tend to criticize the secular position. Two main perspectives can be then assumed according to the degree of support towards gender equality and to what extent people link women's rights to Islam.

The Muslim feminism (Halverson, Way, 2011; Mir-Hosseini, 2011) is a global movement that affirms that gender equality is reconcilable with Islam. "Justice and equality are intrinsic values and cardinal principles in Islam and the Shari'a" (Mir-Hosseini, 2006: 629), and the traditional patriarchal interpretation of the Quran needs to be questioned. This perspective keeps the centrality and authority of the Quran uncontested. Furthermore, the supporters of the Muslim feminism argue that the promotion of women's rights in the Arab world can be effectively pursued only by Islam-centered feminism (el-Husseini, 2016).

Pursuing the centrality of Islam in social and political life, but with a radical twist, Islamists favor a stronger role of religious norms in personal status law. In contrast to Muslim feminism, who asks for a reinterpretation of the patriarchal reading of Shari'a, Islamism views do not challenge the traditional perspective but call instead for a stricter observation of the religious provisions concerning also gender roles. Halverson and Way (2011) define Islamism as the result of the anti-colonial feeling that was widespread in the early twentieth century and that was particularly remarkable in British ex-colonies such as Egypt and India. Such fervor against the dominators led to the establishment in the city of Cairo of the Society of Muslim Brotherhood in 1931. Since its birth, the Muslim Brothers aimed to defend and reinforce the Islamic identity in contrast to Western influence. This intention reflected in the reinforcement of traditional Islamic morality. In more recent times, and not only in Egypt, Islamist forces start opposing the reform processes of law secularization calling for a return to the Shari'a. As reported by Mir-Hosseini (2011), this implied consequences also in the domain of gender equality with the return to patriarchal norms and gender segregation. In the long term, the events connected with the Arab uprising have in some cases exacerbated this return to conservative views and resulted in radicalization.

The case of Islamic Reformism is a fourth theoretically possible combination of the concerns for gender equality and Shari'a. This typology represents the position of those people who refuse the religious source of legislation and norms, but at the same time do not support gender equality. Their possible quest of reforms of Shari'a provisions, considered necessary to deal with social change (when it is not meant for an entirely secular interpretation), is then not related to the support for women's rights.

5 Women's Rights and the Arab Uprisings

The events that developed into the Arab Uprisings made the relationship between gender equality, democracy, and religion even more complex. While initially the public opinion thought that such events would have triggered the quest for democratic values and gender equality, the effective impact of such uprisings on gender equality in the region is still unclear (Fox *et al.*, 2016). This uncertainty in finding a common pattern is due to the fact that the impact of the uprisings cannot be evaluated without considering the particular situation of each country and the women's status before the uprisings and the eventual pre-existing feminist movements. Countries have their own history and expecting similar pathways is a false pre-assumption. Furthermore, while many authors argue that the quest for gender equality should be considered as a relevant part of social change, also wished by the Arab Uprising, which included the challenge to systems characterized by corruption, political and economic marginalization, this did not always meet the expectations (Teti, Abbott, 2017b).

The outcomes of the Arab Uprisings have been deeply different (Abbott, Teti, 2017b; Moghadam, 2018). In some countries, such as Syria, Yemen, and Libya the protests turned into violent civil conflicts, which are still causing a severe humanitarian crisis. Tunisia and Morocco embraced democratic transitions. Protests in Morocco, for example, were very soon followed by promised reforms and amendments. Other countries reverted to authoritarianism. Egypt, which initially approached a democratic transition, turned instead into military authoritarianism. With regard to the impact of the uprisings on gender equality, Moghadam (2018) points out that it is necessary to consider women's status before the rise of the protests because these prior conditions, that differed across the region, help to explain the different outcomes. Compared to other countries in the region, in Morocco and Tunisia women's rights have a longer tradition (Moghadam, 2018). Institutional changes concerning for example the withdrawal of the reservations to CEDAW started quite earlier than the uprisings. Tunisia is considered to be one of the most gender-egalitarian country in the Arab world and the achievement obtained soon after the 2011 protests are considered as part of a long-term process (Charrad, Zarrugh, 2014; Khalil, 2014). As Moghadam (2018) reports, Tunisia's figures concerning female labor market participation, education, literacy and women in the judiciary and politics have been better than elsewhere already in the past. Furthermore, it was the only country with a political party led by a woman (Maya Jribi, leader of the Progressive Democratic Party). After the 2011 protests, the transitional government declared an equal opportunity law. Women largely participated in the public debate that deeply influenced the political processes. The role of women's associations has been particularly relevant in the quest for women's rights and secular law (Charrad, Zarrugh, 2014; Gray, 2012; Khalil, 2014; Moghadam, 2018).

As in the Tunisian case, even in Morocco the achievements in the formal recognition of gender equality rights are part of a gradual process, which started with the acceptance of CEDAW in 1993. In 2004, King Mohammed VI made essential amendments to the Family Code, giving women broader access to family and personal rights. In 2008, he lifted the reservations on CEDAW. Enabled also by the structural changes who favored women participation in public life, women's movements played an important role in addressing issues and assert women into this relevant debate (Moghadam, 2018). In 2011, the mass protest February 20th Movement brought to the adoption of a new constitution, which additionally increased women's rights (Prettitore, 2015), prohibits any form of discrimination and defines the supremacy of the international human rights conventions over domestic law.

In Egypt, the situation took a different pathway. In the first decades of the 20th century, women activism focused against colonial practices and protested alongside men for the liberation of Egypt (Magdy, 2017). As Sorbera describes (2014), this participation did not result in a formal recognition of political rights and women organized themselves in informal networks and later structured through those civil society organizations that led to achieve the right to vote in 1956. However, the patriarchal system remains unchanged and women's rights groups were slowly marginalized (Magdy, 2017; Moghadam, 2018). Nevertheless, the long history of the Egyptian resistance to patriarchy exploded in the protests of 2011 (Sorbera, 2016).

During the protests of 2011, women who participated in the rallies were sub-ject to harassment and sexual abuse. When they were arrested during the pro-tests that they were forced to undergo virginity tests (Hafez, 2014; Moghadam, 2018). Such repression limited even more the potential participation of wom-en. As Magdy (2017) reports, women's quest for equal rights is still generally perceived as an attempt at Westernization and as a threat to traditional family values. Since after the revolution, the Muslim Brotherhood have tried to re-place the women's rights agenda with a "family agenda", reinforcing the oppo-sition to a secular perspective on gender roles and gender equality. Under Al Sisi's regime, women's status did not improve. On the contrary, sexual violence and harassment increased and, in general, human rights were considered un-der threat. Sorbera (2016) reports that only in the first months of 2015 almost 400 Non-Governmental Organizations were obliged to closure, supporters of Muslim Brotherhood were sentenced to death, and activists in favor of human and labor rights were prosecuted. The risk of persecution, torture and death increased also for scholars, as in the terrible case of Giulio Regeni as well as in the recent one of Patrick George Zaki, demonstrating to the international ob-servers the progressive turn of the Egyptian regime into a violent authoritari-anism (Gonzales, 2016; Ryzova, 2017; Teti *et al.*, 2017).

Moghadam's overview of female mobilization in the MENA region (2018) also reports the situation of Libya, Syria and Yemen. In Libya, since 1969, many laws have been implemented to grant women personal rights and to make sec-ondary education compulsory for both men and women. These norms gave formal equality in the public sphere, but family law still relies on the unequal relationship between men and women and put women under the supervision of a male kin. At the same time, the country did not experience any formal women's activism.

Soon after obtaining the right to vote in 1949, women were involved in pub-lic life in Syria. However, the personal status law remained mainly uncontested. The country accepted the CEDAW with a long list of reservation that made it impossible to implement any improvement for the women's legal rights in the domain of family, marriage, divorce, child custody, and protection from gender-based violence (Kelly, Breslin, 2010). In Yemen, one of the poorest countries of the region, women's status worsened after the unification in 1990, which brought the country to stronger Islamism. The constitution declares Shari'a as a source of legislation. In addition, Article 31 affirms that women's rights and duties are assigned by Shari'a and established by the law (Moghadam, 2018). As reported also by the Human Rights Watch (2015), women in Yemen face restric-tion in their freedom of movement, discrimination with regard to access to resources, and they are marginalized in political processes. Gender-based vio-lence is widespread and early marriage is a socially legitimized practice. After the revolts, Libyan Islamist groups start promoting a stricter interpretation of the Islamic personal law as well as gender segregation in the public spaces. Meanwhile, Libya become an unsafe country and a central point for the ISIS activity (Engel, 2015; Moghadam, 2018). The group of Syrian women "Syrian women for the Syrian revolt", emerged during the uprising, has been suppressed by the rising Islamist groups. Women were marginalized by the political life, patriarchal views and gender-based violence, included child marriage, exacerbated during the Syrian war and refugee crisis (Lomazzi, 2016).

So far, the situation of women in Jordan and Iraq after the uprising has not been studied in depth as in the case of the other countries. Among the few studies of this kind, Ferguson reports (2017) that in Jordan women's organization were not able to effectively improve the status of women during and after the uprising, also because of the depoliticization of such organizations.

This brief overview of women's rights in the MENA region suggests that people living in such different societies would express their support to gender equality and Shari'a provisions in a variety of forms, especially in the aftermath of the uprisings. In the next section, we will explore how people combine these two aspects.

6   Islamism, Reformism, Secular and Muslim Feminism in Six Countries

While previous studies mainly focused on the theoretical description of the forms of feminism in the MENA region (Badran, 2001; Halverson, Way, 2011; Mir-Hosseini, 2011; Moghadam, 2001; Parashar, 2016; Winter, 2001), the current contribution aims at empirically identifying the existence of such typologies. To our knowledge, only Fox *et al.* (2016) dealt with this issue by using survey data. They mainly focused on the change of support for women's right in the aftermath of the Arab uprising, but not much information about the different distribution of the forms of supports across countries is provided. Here, we slightly revise their conceptualization of feminism and use a combination of support for Shari'a law and attitudes towards gender roles to describe the distribution of Secular Feminism, Muslim Feminism, Islamic Reformism, and Islamism by using the most recent data available on this issue collected by the Arab Transformations Project in 2014 in Egypt, Iraq, Jordan, Libya, Morocco and Tunisia.

6.1   *Data Description*
To illustrate the forms of feminisms supported by people, we use data collected by the Arab Transformations Project (AT2014).

TABLE 8.2 Sample sizes by country and survey

	Sample size	Fieldwork period
Egypt	1525	05 – 24/11/2014
Iraq	1613	4/05 – 22/06/2014
Jordan	2139	7–18/06/2014
Libya	1540	25/05 – 31/08/2014
Morocco	1777	15/07 – 30/10/2014
Tunisia	1215	01– 31/08/2014

SOURCE: AT2014

The Arab Transformations Project is a European Commission funded project (2013–2016) investigating the root causes of the Arab Uprisings in seven Arab MENA countries. The project carried out also a survey in late 2014 to explore people's attitudes and behaviors. Data collected among representative samples of the population are available for Egypt, Iraq, Jordan, Libya, Morocco and Tunisia.[3] The dataset is freely accessible to users (Abbott, Teti, 2017a). Table 8.2 shows the sample sizes and the fieldwork period for each country.

6.2 *Measurements*
To be able to detect different forms of feminism, we built a typology based on the theoretical literature (el-Husseini, 2016; Halverson, Way, 2011; Mir-Husseini, 2006, 2011) as well on the empirical work proposed by Fox *et al.* (2016). According to such perspectives, it is necessary to consider, on the one hand, the support for women's rights and, on the other, the support for Shari'a law. In particular, the authors stressed the important connection with the support for Islam being the source of legislation of family and personal status laws. We therefore computed two measurements, indicating the support for gender equality and the support for legislation inspired by Shari'a and combined them to define four distinct typologies: secular feminists, Muslim feminists, Islam Reformist, and Islamist.

The support for gender equality is grasped by the agreement of the respondents with the following statements:
a.   A university education is more important for a boy than for a girl*
b.   Women can work outside the home
c.   On the whole, men make better political leaders than women do*

---

3   For more information about the project and survey methodology applied, please consult the project website: https://www.arabtrans.eu/.

These items specifically cover the public dimension of gender ideologies (Davis, Greenstein, 2009) and help understand the degree of support for women's rights in contrast with patriarchal values. The index is obtained by computing the mean of the scores of each item and it goes from 1 (lowest support for gender equality) to 4 (highest support for gender equality). The scores of items indicated with * were reversed in order to achieve the same direction.

As pointed out by Fair *et al.* (2018), the support for Shari'a can be operationalized in several ways. It is a complex and multi-dimensional concept and scholars have used measurements based on different conceptualizations focused on general or specific aspects of Shari'a. While Fox *et al.* (2016), focused on the dimension of family and inheritance laws, alongside other religious provisions concerning gender mixed education and women's dress code, in our measurement we substitute the dimension related to inheritance issues with the support for Shari'a in all aspects of the legislation. In this way we can cover a broader belief concerning the role of Shari'a in regulating social, political, and economic life. The respondents were asked to express their agreement to the statements:

d.   The government should implement only the laws derived from Shari'a

e.   The government and the parliament should make personal status/family law according to Shari'a

f.   It is acceptable in Islam for male and female university students to attend class together*

g.   In Islam women should dress modestly, but Islam does not require that they wear a hijab*

Also in this case, the index is obtained by computing the mean of the scores of each item and it goes from 1 (lowest support for Shari'a) to 4 (highest support for Shari'a). The scores of items indicated with * were reversed in order to achieve the same direction.

Fox *et al.* (2016) were particularly interested in studying the support for Muslim feminism and according to the goal of their study; they operate distinctions only between secular and religious forms of support for gender equality. Here, we wish to explore differences in the distribution of different possible forms of combination of the support for gender equality and support for Shari'a as described in the literature. The scores of both measurements have been then dichotomized and four typologies result from their possible combinations:

– *Muslim Feminists*: people supporting both gender equality and Shari'a. Those belonging to this typology, support women's right but refuse a secular interpretation of gender roles. Gender equality, according to this view, may be achieved through Islam.

- *Secular Feminists*: this typology refers to those respondents who consider theocracy a limit for gender equality. Their support for gender equality goes together with the quest for secular codes ruling family laws, dress code, gender segregation etc.
- *Islamists*: people belonging to this group display conservative views concerning both gender equality and the source of legislation. They support Shari'a as the primary source of regulations and support a traditional separation of roles between men and women.
- *Reformists*: this fourth typology, resulted from the combination of low support for gender equality and low support for Shari'a law, comprises the respondents who have a traditional view of gender roles and, at the same time, may express a secular view concerning the source of legislation and would support reforms in this perspective.

By using such operative definitions, the graph in Figure 8.1 displays their distribution in Egypt, Iraq, Jordan, Libya, and Tunisia.

While in all the countries the different typologies coexist, their distribution profoundly differs. Compared to the other five countries here considered, Egypt displays the lowest share of people supporting gender equality (46.3%). Tunisia and Morocco, instead, show the highest rate of people questing for women's rights (respectively 78.1% and 76.8% of the population sample). However, in all the countries except Tunisia, Muslim feminists are the biggest share of the gender egalitarian supporters. This means that most of the people advocating for women's rights see the roots of women's rights in Islam and challenge the patriarchal reading of Shari'a. About half of the people living in Jordan, Iraq, Libya and Morocco belong to this group.

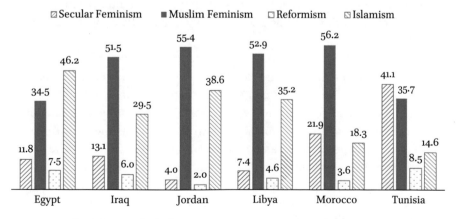

FIGURE 8.1   Feminism typologies by country
SOURCE: AT2014

In all the countries, only a small amount of people question Shariʿa without supporting gender equality. The share of pure Reformists is very small (from 3.6% in Morocco to 8.5% in Tunisia). Islamists, who consider Shariʿa as the essential source for legislation in all aspects of social and personal life and argue that gender roles are defined by Shariʿa, are the biggest group in Egypt (46.2% of the sample). Islamist perspective is assumed by one-third of the Iraqi and by a bit less than 2 people in 5 in Jordan and Libya. In Morocco and Tunisia, people expressing Islamist view are far less 20%.

These distributions result in line with the country characteristics emerged by the literature review (§5), especially in the case of Egypt, Morocco and Tunisia. After the uprising, Egypt reversed into an authoritarian regime with a strong Islamist component and anti-Western feelings. Considering these aspects, it does not surprise that the country displays the lowest support for gender equality, with particular regard to the secular (Western) view, and the highest share of Islamist. Tunisia and Morocco both implemented reforms that increased women's rights as part of a pathway towards gender equality rooted in the past history of women's movements, with Tunisia developing a stronger secular component.

7   Conclusive Remarks

Too often Western observers risk considering countries belonging to the MENA region, and in general, Muslim-majority countries, as similar social contexts characterized by the common denominator of patriarchal gender norms. According to these views, Muslim women are thought in need of being saved (Abu-Lughod, 2013), assuming that they are not able to empower themselves and that the Western way to democracy and gender equality is the only way possible.

In this chapter, we tried to go beyond these perspectives and offered some elements to be taken into account for a more profound study of gender equality in these social and cultural contexts. In particular, we tried to stress the importance of considering the history of the country, with a specific reference to the colonialism and post-colonial framework, as well as the political, economic, and social processes related to the Arab Uprisings that may have accelerated or suppressed the quest for democratic values and gender equality. Furthermore, gender norms and the support for gender equality need to be studied in the context of the relationship with religion, in particular with the Shariʿa provisions concerning family rights and personal status.

We introduced the variety of gender cultures existing in the MENA region by providing an overview of the country's acceptance of the CEDAW, the most important international treaty on gender equality. The topics, as well as the amount, of reservations that each country made to the CEDAW provide valuable insights to start understanding how deeply different the status of women between the countries of this region is. Women cannot access, at least formally, the same rights in all the countries. In most of the countries, women do not have the same rights as men in family matters, such as marriage, divorce, and inheritance. Algeria, Bahrein, Egypt, Iraq, Libya, Qatar, United Arab Emirates, and Syria made reservations to the article requiring countries to include gender equality in the domestic legislation. In addition to these restrictions, women have limited freedom of movement in Oman, Qatar, Syria, Bahrein, United Arab Emirates. Iran never accepted the CEDAW. Saudi Arabia made a reservation only to rights concerning the nationality of children. Djibouti, Palestine, and Tunisia have accepted the CEDAW entirely. Morocco removed all the reservation after the revolts of 2011.

Most of these reservations are due to a strict institutional observation of the Shari'a personal status law. Institutions have an important role in defining gender cultures. They provide the opportunity structure that enables men and women to enact their personal preferences and values. In addition, they contribute to legitimizing gender roles. Despite the strong importance of religion in Muslim-majority countries, people may conceive the influence that religion should have in politics and legislation in different ways. Alongside a secular perspective that considers theocracy as a limit for gender equality, forms of feminisms combining the quest for women's right with the support for the Shari'a law are possible. So far, the different typologies have been discussed in the literature mainly from a theoretical perspective, while in this chapter we attempted an empirical exploration aimed at retrieving four typologies of the combination of support for gender equality and support for Shari'a among representative samples of the population living in Egypt, Tunisia, Morocco, Libya, Iraq, and Jordan in 2014. The distribution of the forms of feminisms differs among societies and reflects the historical pathways of these countries and the different outcomes of the Arab Uprisings. Tunisia, for example, has embraced an explicitly secular perspective since the acceptance of the CEDAW in 2008. But this formal position reflected an already existing social context where the levels of female economic and political participation were higher than in other countries of the region, as well as education and literacy. During the uprising, women had a crucial role in the quest for women's right and secular law (Charrad, Zarrugh, 2014; Gray, 2012; Khalil, 2014; Moghadam, 2018). In the aftermath of the uprising, Tunisians showed the highest share of support for secular feminism among the countries here considered. Also in Morocco, women's organizations were particularly active before the uprisings that, however, pushed for reforms that increased women's rights. Here the religious component is particularly strong and most of the supporters for women's rights also believe that gender equality can be achieved in the respect of Islam and challenge the current interpretation of Shariʿa. Such "inspiration from Sharʿa" to achieve gender equality must not be confused with the wish of a "return to Shariʿa" called out by Islamist groups, which advocate for a stricter observation of Shariʿa provisions also concerning gender roles. In this respect, Egyptian society is a special case. According to our typologies, Egypt displays the highest share of Islamists: about 46% of the sample support Shariʿa as a source of legislation for personal status law and express conservative attitudes towards gender roles. Looking back to the history of Egypt, where anti-Western feelings have always been particularly strong, the refusal of a secular approach to gender roles can be read as a reaction to Western colonialism. The events following the turmoil led the country into violent authoritarianism that strongly supports Islamic radicalization. Taken into account that Muslim feminism challenges the patriarchal approach to Shariʿa, the political processes in Egypt could explain why even the different forms of Muslim feminism, which is quite high in all the other countries, encounter less favor in Egypt.

Rooted in the historical pathways of each country, the question of whether the Arab Uprisings that occurred in several countries of the MENA region in 2011 resulted in democratization processes, and improved gender equality or, on the contrary, led to radicalization cannot therefore have a unique answer.

This chapter provided an introductory exploration of the form of feminism that can be developed in more complex interpretative analyses. A latent class approach, for example, may be particularly helpful to investigate the patterns concerning religiosity, the support of Shariʿa as a source of legislation, and the quest for women's right. In addition, future research may employ time series data to consider the change over time and, therefore, assess better the impact of the Arab Uprisings on social change.

References to Part 2

Abbott, P., & Teti, A. (2017a). *Arab Transformations Project Data Set SPSS Version. DOI: 10.13140/RG.2.2.35058.30408.*

Abbott, P., & Teti, A. (2017b). *Key Findings from the Arab Transformations Project* (https://www.jstor.org/stable/resrep14100).

Abu-Lughod, L. (2013). *Do Muslim Women Need Saving?* Cambridge, UK; New York: Harvard University Press.

Al-Ali, N. (2003). Gender and Civil Society in the Middle East. *International Feminist Journal of Politics, 5*(2), 216–232.

Alexander, A.C., & Welzel, C. (2015). Eroding patriarchy: the co-evolution of women's rights and emancipative values. *International Review of Sociology, 25*(1), 144–165.

Alkhatib W. (2014). *Iraq Public Opinion Survey Report – 2013/2014*, Arab Barometer – Wave III.

Altemeyer, B., & Hunsberger, B. (1992). Authoritarianism, Religious Fundamentalism, Quest, and Prejudice. *The International Journal for the Psychology of Religion, 2*(2), 113–133.

Amnesty International (20 September 2018). *Egypt: Unprecedented crackdown on freedom of expression under al-Sisi turns Egypt into open-air prison* (https://www.amnesty.org/en/latest/news/2018/09/egypt-unprecedented-crackdown-on-freedom-of-expression-under-alsisi-turns-egypt-into-openair-prison/).

Anderson, B. (1991), *Imagined Communities*. London and New York: Verso.

Andezian, S. (2008). Palestiniens chrétiens et construction nationale. *Confluences Mediterranee, 3*, 59–71.

Arab Barometer – Wave III (2012–2014), Technical Report.

Arab Barometer – Wave IV (2016–2017), Technical Report.

Aras, B., & Bardakcı, S. (2014). Egypt's Top-Down Sectarianism. *Pomeas Policy Brief, 1*, 1–8.

Asher-Schapiro, A. (1 March 2012). *Is the Government-Church Alliance a "Coptic Marriage"?.* Carnegie Endowment, No. 1 (http://carnegieendowment.org/sada/2012/03/01/is-government-church-alliance-copticmarriage/aot6).

Al-Aswani, A. (2011). *On the state of Egypt: What Made the Revolution Inevitable.* Edinburgh: Canongate Books Ltd.

Ayalon, A (1999). Egypt's Coptic Pandora's Box. In O. Bengio, & G. Ben-Dor (Eds), *Minorities and the State in the Arab World.* Boulder, CO: Lynne Reiner Publishers, pp. 53–71.

Ayubi, N.N. (1996). *Over-stating the Arab state: Politics and society in the Middle East.* London and New York: IB Tauris.

Azam, H. (2018). Islamic Feminism between Islam and Islamophobia. *Journal of Middle East Women's Studies, 14*(1), 124–128.

Badran, M. (2001). Understanding Islam, Islamism, and Islamic Feminism. *Journal of Women's History; Baltimore, 13*(1), 47–52.

Bahlul, R. (2018). Religion, Democracy and the 'Dawla Madaniyya' of the Arab Spring. *Islam and Christian–Muslim Relations, 29*(3), 331–347.

Baram, A. (1997). Neo-Tribalism in Iraq: Saddam Hussein's Tribal Policies 1991–96. *International Journal of Middle East Studies, 29*(1).

Baram, A. (2003). Saddam's Power Structure: The Tikritis Before, During and After the War. In T. Dodge, & S. Simon (Eds), *Iraq at the Crossroad: State and Society in the Shadow of Regime Change*. London: Routledge.

Bayoumi, H., & Moriconi-Ebrard, F. (2003), *Century Census Egypt 1882–1996/Un Siècle de Recensement*. Le Caire : CEDEJ-CAPMAS.

Beblawi, H., & Luciani, G. (1987). *Nation, State and Integration in the Arab World. Vol II: The Rentier State*. London: Groom Helm.

Bell, J. *et al.* (2013). *Beliefs about Sharia* (Chapter 1). In *The World's Muslims: Religion, Politics and Society*, Pew Research Center.

Bengio, O., & Ben-Dor, G. (Eds). (1999). *Minorities and the State in the Arab World*. Boulder: Lynne Rienner Publishers.

Boulby, M. (1999). *The Muslim Brotherhood and the Kings of Jordan, 1945–1993*. Atlanta, Scholar's Press.

Branisa, B., Klasen, S., Ziegler, M., Drechsler, D., & Jütting, J. (2014). The Institutional Basis of Gender Inequality: The Social Institutions and Gender Index (SIGI). *Feminist Economics, 20*(2), 29–64.

Bréchon P., (2018). Arab Public Opinion: Between Attachment To Islam and Commitment to Democracy. *Futuribles, 425*, 5–19.

Brownlee, J. (2013). *Violence against Copts in Egypt*. Carnegie Endowment for International Peace, 1–26 (https://carnegieendowment.org/files/violence_against_copts3 .pdf).

Carlisle, J. (2019). Muslim Divorce in the MENA: Shari'a, Codification, State Feminism, and the Courts. In J. Carlisle (Ed.), *Muslim Divorce in the Middle East: Contesting Gender in the Contemporary Courts*. Cham: Springer International Publishing, pp. 1–31.

Carr, S. (9 October 2013). Why is Maspero Different?. *Mada Masr* (https://madamasr. com/en/2013/10/09/feature/politics/why-is-maspero-different/).

Casper, J. (2013). *Mapping the Coptic movements: Coptic activism in a revolutionary setting*. Arab West Report, No. 44 (https://www.arabwestreport.info/sites/default/ files/Paper%2044_Mapping%20the%20Coptic%20Movements.pdf).

Central Agency for Mobilization and Statistics – CAPMAS (2015), *Census Info Egypt*. (http://www.censusinfo.capmas.gov.eg/).

Ceyhun, H.E. (2017a). *Jordan five years after the Uprisings*, Jordan Wave 4 Country Report.

Ceyhun, H.E. (2017b). *Lebanon five years after the Uprisings*, Lebanon Wave 4 Country Report.

Ceyhun, H.E. (2017c). *Refugees in Jordan and Lebanon: life on the Margins*, Arab Barometer – Wave IV, Topic Report.

Chaillot, C. (2011). *Les Coptes d'Égypte. Discriminations et persecutions*. Paris: L'oeuvre editions.

Charrad, M.M., & Zarrugh, A. (2014). Equal or complementary? Women in the new Tunisian Constitution after the Arab Spring. *The Journal of North African Studies*, 19 (2), 230–243.

Chitham, E.J. (1986), *The Coptic community in Egypt: spatial and social change*. Durham: University of Durham.

Ciftci, S., Wuthrich F.M., & Shamaileh A. (2018). Islam, Religious Outlooks, and Support For Democracy. *Political Research Quarterly*, 72(2) 435–449.

Collombier, V., & Roy, O. (Eds). (2017). *Tribes and Global Jihadism*. London: C. Hurst & Co. Publishers.

Courbage, F., & Fargues P. (1997). *Chrétiens et Juifs dans l'Islam arabe et turc*. Paris: Payot.

Cragg, K. (1991). *The Arab Christian: A History in the Middle East*. Lousiville: Westminster John Knox Press.

Davis, S. N., & Greenstein, T. N. (2009). Gender Ideology: Components, Predictors, and Consequences. *Annual Review of Sociology*, 35(1), 87–105.

Denis, É. (1999), Cent ans de localisation de la population chrétienne égyptienne. *Astrolabe*, 2, 25–40.

Dodge, T. (2018). 'Bourdieu Goes to Baghdad': Explaining Hybrid Political Identities in Iraq. *Journal of Historical Sociology*, (31), 25–38.

Donabed, S. (2015). *Reforging a Forgotten History: Iraq and the Assyrians in the Twentieth Century*. Edinburgh: Edinburgh University Press.

Dueck, J.M. (2010). *The Claims of Culture at Empire's End: Syria and Lebanon under French Rule*. Oxford: Oxford University Press.

Egyptian Initiative for Personal Rights (2010). *Two Years of Sectarian Violence: What Happened? Where do we begin? An Analytical Study of January 2008–January 2010*, (http://eipr.org/en/report/2010/04/11/776).

el-Husseini, R. (2016). Is gender the barrier to democracy? Women, Islamism, and the "Arab spring". *Contemporary Islam*, 10(1): 53–66.

El-Masri, S. (2012). Challenges facing CEDAW in the Middle East and North Africa. *The International Journal of Human Rights*, 16(7), 931–946.

Elsässer, S. (2014). *The Coptic Question in the Mubarak Era: Debating National Identity, Religion, and Citizenship*. New York: Oxford University Press.

Engel, A. (2015). The islamic State's expansion in Libya. *The Washington Institute for Near East Policy* (https://www.washingtoninstitute.org/policy-analysis/view/the-islamic-states-expansion-in-libya).

Eskander, W. (18 December 2016). Egypt's Copts between terror and discrimination. *Open-democracy* (https://www.opendemocracy.net/en/north-africa-west-asia/battling-culture-of-inferior-copt/).

Fadl, E. (2011). Prosecution Investigates Interior Minister's Alleged Involvement in Church Attack. *Daily News Egypt* (www.dailynewsegypt.com/2011/02/07/prosecution-investigates-interior-min-alleged-involvement-inchurch-attack).

Fair, C. C., Littman, R., & Nugent, E. R. (2018). Conceptions of Shari'a and Support for Militancy and Democratic Values: Evidence From Pakistan. *Political Science Research and Methods, 6*(3), 429–448.

Fahmi, G. (2014). *The Coptic Church and Politics in Egypt.* Carnagie Middle East Center No.18 (https://carnegie-mec.org/2014/12/18/coptic-church-and-politics-in-egypt-pub-57563).

Fahmi, G. (2015). The Crisis of Citizenship in Egypt: Why Did the Youth Movements Calling for s State Based On Citizenship Fail? The Case of The Maspero Youth Union and The Nubian Democratic Youth Union. In *Citizenship and Social Components in the Arab region,* The Arab Forum for Alternatives Think Tank and the Hivos Knowledge Program, pp. 67–88.

Fahmi, G. (2018). The Future of Syrian Christians after the Arab Spring. In Kawakibi S. (Ed.), *Politics of Recognition and Denial. Minorities in the Mena Region, Euromesco Joint Policy Study, 11*(2018), 48–67.

Farah, N.R. (1986). *Religious Strife in Egypt: Crisis and Ideological Conflict in the Seventies.* London: Routledge.

Farha, M., & Mousa, S. (2015). Secular Autocracy vs. Sectarian Democracy? Weighing Reasons for Christian Support for Regime Transition in Syria and Egypt. *Mediterranean Politics, 20*(2), 178–197.

Fawzi, S. (2010). *The Copts of Egypt: Specific Problems and General Tension.* Arab Reform initiative, No. 41 (https://archives.arab-reform.net/en/node/414).

Ferguson, P.A. (2017). The State of Jordanian Women's Organizations – Five Years Beyond the Arab Spring. *Politics and Governance, 5*(2), 59–68.

Forman-Rabinovici, A., & Sommer, U. (2018). An impediment to gender Equality? Religion's influence on development and reproductive policy. *World Development,* 105, 48–58.

Fox, A.M., Alzwawi, S.A., & Refki, D. (2016). Islamism, Secularism and the Woman Question in the Aftermath of the Arab Spring: Evidence from the Arab Barometer. *Politics and Governance, 4*(4), 40–57.

Frisch, H. (2002). Fuzzy Nationalism: The case of Jordan. *Nationalism and Ethnic Politics*, *8*(4), 86–103.

Galal, L.P. (2012). Coptic Christian Practices: Formations of Sameness and Difference. *Islam and Christian–Muslim Relations*, *23*(1), 45–58.

Al-Gawhary, K. (1996). Copts in the "Egyptian Fabric". *Middle East Report* (200), 21–22.

Geertz, C. (Ed.) (1967). *Old Societies and New States: The Quest for Modernity in Africa and Asia*. New York: The Free Press.

Gellner, E. (1983). Tribal Society and its Enemies in Tapper R. (Ed.), *The Conflict of Tribe and State in Iran and Afghanistan*. London: Croom Helm Ltd.

Gellner, E. (1990). Tribalism and the State in the Middle East. In P. Khoury, & J. Kostiner (Eds), *Tribes and State Formation in the Middle East*. Berkeley: University of California Press.

Ghanem H. (2018). *The Arab Spring Five Years Later Volume One: Toward Greater Inclusiveness*. Arab Barometer Paper.

El-Ghobashy, M. (2011). *The Praxis of the Egyptian Revolution*. Middle East Report, 41 (258), (www.merip.org/mer/mer258/praxis-egyptian-revolution).

Gokpinar, A. (2012). Remembering Maspero, *Opendemocracy* (https://www.opendem ocracy.net/en/remembering-maspero/).

Gonzales, R. (2016). Five Years after the Revolutions, this is Egypt's Worst Dictatorship'. *CIDOB: Opinion*, 385(02).

Gray, D.H. (2012). Tunisia after the Uprising: Islamist and Secular Quests for Women's Rights. *Mediterranean Politics*, *17*(3), 285–302.

Grinin, L., Korotayev, A., & Tausch, A. (2019). *Islamism, Arab Spring, and the Future of Democracy. World System and World Values Perspectives*. New York: Springer International Publishing.

Guindy, A. (2010). Symbolic Victims in a Socially Regressing Egypt: The Declining Situation of the Copts. *Middle East Review of International Affairs*, *14*(1), 80.

Guirguis, L. (2012). *Les coptes d'Égypte. Violences communautaires et transformations politiques (2005–2012)*. Paris: Karthala.

Habib, N. (10–16 March 2011). Ablaze with tension. *Al-Ahram Weekly* (http://weekly.ah ram.org.eg/2011/1038/eg401.htm).

Habib, N. (12–18 May 2011). Staying put in Maspero. *Al-Ahram Weekly* (http://weekly. ahram.org.eg/2011/1047/eg51.htm).

Haddad, F. (2017). 'Sectarianism' and Its Discontents in the Study of the Middle East. *Middle East Journal*, *71*(3), pp. 363–382.

Hafez, S. (2014). The revolution shall not pass through women's bodies: Egypt, uprising and gender politics. *The Journal of North African Studies*, *19*(2), 172–185.

Halverson, J.R., & Way, A.K. (2011). Islamist Feminism: Constructing Gender Identities in Postcolonial Muslim Societies. *C*, *4*(3), 503–525.

Harrington, E. (19 December 2011). *Number of Coptic Christians in Egypt Is Far Less Than Media Estimates, Report Says* (http://cnsnews.com/news/article/number-coptic-christians-egyptfar-less-media-estimates-report-says).

Hasan, S.S. (2003). *Christian versus Muslims in Modern Egypt: The Century-Long Struggle for Coptic Equality.* Oxford: Oxford University Press.

Hashemi, N. (2009). *Islam, Secularism, and Liberal Democracy: Toward a Democratic Theory for Muslim Societies.* Oxford: Oxford University Press.

Hatem, M.F. (1994). Egyptian Discourses on Gender and Political Liberalization: Do Secularist and Islamist Views Really Differ? *Middle East Journal, 48*(4), 661–676.

Hibbard, S.W. (2010). *Religious Politics and Secular States: Egypt, India and the United States.* Baltimore: Johns Hopkins University Press.

Hilsdon, A.-M., & Rozario, S. (2006). Special issue on Islam, gender and human rights. *Women's Studies International Forum, 29*(4), 331–338.

Hinnebusch, R. (2016). The Sectarian Revolution in the Middle East. *R/evolutions: Global Trends & Regional Issues, 4*(1), pp. 120–152.

Hughes, E. (2017). Nationalism by Another Name: Examining "Religious Radicalism" from the Perspective of Iraq's Christians. *The Review of Faith & International Affairs, 15*(2), pp. 34–44.

Human Rights Watch (2019). *World Report 2019* (https://www.hrw.org/world-report/2019/country-chapters/egypt).

Human Rights Watch (2015). *Human Rights Watch Submission to the CEDAW Committee on Yemen's Periodic Report, 62th session* (https://www.hrw.org/sites/default/files/related_material/2015_HRW%20CEDAW%20Submission_Yemen.pdf).

Hunsberger, B. (1995). Religion and Prejudice: The Role of Religious Fundamentalism, Quest, and Right-Wing Authoritarianism. *Journal of Social Issues, 51*(2), 113–129.

Ibrahim, I. (20 January 2008), Luring Copts into politics, *Watani International* (http://www.wataninet.com/watani_Article_Details.aspx?A=1555).

Ibrahim, S.E. (13 February 2000). The Road of Thorns from Al-Khanka 1972 to Al-Kosheh 2000. *Watani* (http://www.arabwestreport.info/year-2000/week-7/21-road-thorn-s-al-khanka-1972-al-kosheh-2000).

Ibrahim, S.E., *et al.* (1996). *The Copts of Egypt.* London: Minority Rights Group International Report.

Inglehart, R., & Norris, P. (2003). *Rising Tide: Gender Equality and Cultural Change Around the World.* Cambridge, UK; New York: Cambridge University Press.

Isakhan, B., & Mulherin, P.E. (2018). Basra's Bid for Autonomy: Peaceful Progress toward a Decentralized Iraq. *Middle East Journal, 72*(2), pp. 267–285.

Islamic State Report (2014). Smashing the Borders of the Tawaghit. *al-Hayat Media Center,* (4).

Jamal A.A. (2018). *Islam, Law and Modern State. (Re)imagining Liberal Theory in Muslim Contexts.* London: Routledge.

Johnson, T.M., & Zurlo, G.A. (2015). *World Christian Database*. Leiden, Boston: Brill.

Kamal, K. (19 November 2010). The NDP's manipulation of Egyptian Copts, *Egypt Independent* (http://www.egyptindependent.com/opinion/ndps-manipulation-egypti an-copts).

Kamel, L. (2016a). Artificial nations? The Sykes-Picot and the Islamic State's Narratives in a Historical Perspective. *Diacronie, 25*(1), 1–20.

Kamel, L. (2016b), Reshuffling the Middle East: A Historical and Political Perspective. *The International Spectator*, pp. 132–141.

Kattan, A.E. (2012). Christians in the Arab World: Beyond Role Syndrome. *The Ecumenical Review, 64*(1), 50–53.

Kelly, S., & Breslin, J. (Eds). (2010). *Women's Rights in the Middle East and North Africa: Progress Amid Resistance* (https://freedomhouse.org/report/women039s-rights-middle-east-and-north-africa/womens-rights-middle-east-and-north-africa-2010).

Khalil, A. (2014). Tunisia's women: partners in revolution. *The Journal of North African Studies, 19*(2), 186–199.

Al-Khawaga, D. (1992). L'affirmation d'une identité chrétienne copte : Saisir un processus encours. In C. Décobert (Ed.), *Itinéraires d'Égypte. Mélanges offerts au père Maurice Martin, sj*. Le Caire: Institut Français d'Archéologie Orientale de Caire (ifao), pp. 345–365.

Khoury, P., Kostiner J. (1991), *Tribes and State Formation in the Middle East*. Berkeley: University of California Press.

Khoury, P.S. (2003). *Urban Notables and Arab Nationalism: The Politics of Damascus 1860–1920*. Cambridge: Cambridge University Press.

Khoury, P.S. (2014). *Syria and the French Mandate: The Politics of Arab Nationalism, 1920–1945*. Princeton: Princeton University Press.

Klingorová, K., & Havlíček, T. (2015). Religion and gender inequality: The status of women in the societies of world religions. *Moravian Geographical Reports, 23*(2), 2–11.

Korany, B. (2010). *Looking at the Middle East Differently: An Alternative Conceptual Lens*. Cairo: American University in Cairo Press.

Lindholm, C. (1986). Kinship Structure and Political Authority: The Middle East and Central Asia. *Comparative Studies in Society and History, 28*(2), pp. 334–355.

Lomazzi, V. (2016). Middle East Refugee Response and Gender Equality Challenges. *Journal of Global Faultlines, 3*(1), 56–64 (https://doi.org/10.13169/jglobfaul.3.1. 0056).

Longva, A.N., & Roald, A.S. (Eds) (2012). *Religious Minorities in the Middle East: Domination, Self-empowerment, Accommodation*. Leiden: Brill.

Magdy, R. (2017). Egyptian feminist movement: a brief history. *OpenDemocracy*, 8 March (https://www.opendemocracy.net/en/north-africa-west-asia/egyptian-feminist-movement-brief-history/).

Maggiolini, P. (2015). Christian Churches and Arab Christians in the Hashemite Kingdom of Jordan. *Archives De Sciences Sociales Des Religions*, (3), 37–58.

Maggiolini, P. (2018). The Origin and Development of the Idea of 'Minority' in The
Mena Region: A Multilevel Analysis. In Kawakibi S. (Ed.), *Politics of Recognition and
Denial. Minorities in the Mena Region, Euromesco Joint Policy Study*, 11, 10–47.

Mahmood, S. (2015). *Religious Difference in a Secular Age: A Minority Report*. Princeton:
Princeton University Press.

Mahmood, S. (2012). Religious Freedom, the Minority Question, and Geopolitics in the
Middle East. *Comparative Studies in Society and History*, 25(2), 418–446.

Makari, P.E. (2014). Christians Working for Peace in the Middle East. Efforts and Expectations. In P.S. Rowe, J.H. Dyck, & J. Zimmermann (Eds), *Christians and the Middle
East Conflict*. London: Routledge, pp. 117–136.

Makdisi, U. (2000). *The Culture of Sectarianism: Community, History, and Violence in
Nineteenth-Century Ottoman Lebanon*. Berkeley: University of California Press.

Malak, K., & Salem, S. (2015). Reorientalizing the Middle east: The Power agenda Setting Post-arab Uprisings. *Middle East-Topics & Arguments*, 4, 93–109.

Marx, E. (1977). The Tribe as a Unit of Subsistence: Nomadic Pastoralism in the Middle
East. *American Anthropologist*, 79(2), pp. 343–363.

Massad, J. (2008). Producing the Palestinian as Other. Jordan and the Palestinians. *Collections électroniques de l'Ifpo. Livres en ligne des Presses de l'Institut français du
Proche-Orient*, (25), pp. 273–292.

Massad, J.A. (2001). *Colonial effects: The making of national identity in Jordan*. New York:
Columbia University Press.

McCallum, F. (2010). *Christian Religious Leadership in the Middle East: The Political Role
of the Patriarch*. Lewiston: Edwin Mellen Press.

McCallum, F. (2012). Christian Political Participation in the Arab world. *Islam and
Christian–Muslim Relations*, 23(1), pp. 3–18.

McCallum, F. (2012). Religious Institutions and Authoritarian States: Church–State Relations in the Middle East. *Third World Quarterly*, 33(1), 109–124.

McDermott, A. (1988). *Egypt from Nasser to Mubarak*. London-New York-Sydney:
Croom Helm.

McGahern, U. (2012). *Palestinian Christians in Israel: State Attitudes towards Non-Muslims in a Jewish state*. London: Routledge.

Melcangi, A. (2019). *Al Sisi, la questione copta e la minaccia terroristica*. Ispi (https://
www.ispionline.it/it/pubblicazione/al-sisi-la-questione-copta-e-la-min
accia-terroristica-21963).

Melcangi, A. (2013). The political participation of Copts in Egypt: From the Nasser
years to the sectarian strife of the nineties. In M. Fois, & A. Pes (Eds), *Politics and
Minorities in Africa*. Roma: Aracne, pp. 221–243.

Melcangi, A. (2015). La valorizzazione del patrimonio cristiano copto nell'Egitto repub-
blicano (1952–2011). Tra compromesso e affermazione identitaria. In L. El Houssi

Leila (Ed.), Le politiche culturali nella sponda sud del Mediterraneo. *Giornale di Storia Contemporanea, XVIII*(2), 67–84.

Melcangi, A. (2018). *Statualità e minoranze: meccanismi di resistenza e integrazione in Medio Oriente. Il caso dei cristiani copti in Egitto*. Milano: Ledizioni.

Melcangi, A. (2018). *Divide et impera*: the political application of sectarianism in the Egyptian context. From the Sadat years to the reign of Mubarak (1970–2011). In M. Demichelis (Ed.), *Religious Violence, Political Ends. Nationalism, citizenship and radicalizations in the Middle East and Europe*. Hildesheim: Georg Olms Verlag, pp. 35–53.

Migdal, J. (1988). *Strong States and Weak Societies: State-Society Relations and State Capabilities in the Third World*. Princeton: Princeton University Press.

Milton-Edwards, B. (2017). Grappling with Islamism: Assessing Jordan's Evolving Approach. *Brookings Doha Center Analysis Paper*, (19), 1–33. Online at: https://www .brookings.edu/wp-content/uploads/2017/09/final_9_27_analysis-paper_milton-edwards_english_web.pdf.

Mir-Hosseini, Z. (2006). Muslim Women's Quest for Equality: Between Islamic Law and Feminism. *Critical Inquiry, 32*(4), 629–645.

Mir-Hosseini, Z. (2011). Beyond 'Islam' vs 'Feminism'. *IDS Bulletin, 42*(1), 67–77.

Mitchell, T. (1991). The Limits of the State: Beyond Statist Approaches and Their Critics. *American Political Science Review, 85*(1), 77–96.

Mitri, T. (2012). Christians in the Arab World: Minority Attitudes and Citizenship. *The Ecumenical Review, 64*(1), 43–49.

Moaddel, M. (2002). *Jordanian Exceptionalism: A Comparative Analysis of State-Religion Relationships in Egypt, Iran, Jordan, and Syria*. New York: Palgrave.

Moghadam, V.M. (2001). Feminism and Islamic fundamentalism: A secularist interpretation. *Journal of Women's History; Baltimore, 13*(1), 42–45.

Moghadam, V.M. (2003). *Modernizing women: Gender and social change in the Middle East*. Boulder, CO: Lynne Rienner Publishers.

Moghadam, V.M. (2008). Feminism, legal reform and women's empowerment in the Middle East and North Africa. *International Social Science Journal, 59*(191), 9–16.

Moghadam, V.M. (2018). Explaining divergent outcomes of the Arab Spring: the significance of gender and women's mobilizations. *Politics, Groups, and Identities, 6*(4), 666–681.

Mohammed, J.A. (2017). *Social distance in Iraq and Lebanon*. Michigan State University, Thesis.

Muasher, M. (2014). *The Second Arab Awakening: And the Battle for Pluralism*. New Haven: Yale University Press.

Müller-Sommerfeld, H. (2016). The League of Nations, A-Mandates and Minority Rights during the Mandate Period in Iraq (1920–1932). In S.R. Goldstein-Sabbah, & H.L. Murre-van den Berg (Eds). *Modernity, Minority, and the Public Sphere: Jews and Christians in the Middle East*. Leiden: Brill, pp. 258–283.

Murphy, C. (2002). *Passion for Islam: Shaping the Modern Middle East: The Egyptian Experience*. New York: Scribner.

Nikolov, B. (2008). *Care of poor and ecclesiastical government: an ethnography of the social service of the Coptic Orthodox Church in Cairo*. Baltimore – Maryland: ProQuest UMI Dissertation Publishing.

O'Mahony, A. (Ed.). (1999). *Palestinian Christians: religion, politics and society in the Holy Land*. London: Melisende.

O'Mahony, A. (2004). The Chaldean Catholic Church: The Politics of Church-state Relations in Modern Iraq. *The Heythrop Journal, 45*(4), 435–450.

O'Mahony, A. (2005). Christianity and Jerusalem: Religion, Politics and Theology in the Modern Holy Land. *International journal for the Study of the Christian Church, 5*(2), 86–102.

OECD/CAWTAR (2014). *Women in Public Life. Gender, Law and Policy in the Middle East and North Africa*(https://doi.org/10.1787/9789264224636-en).

Owen, R. (2013). *State, Power and Politics in the Making of the Modern Middle East*. London: Routledge.

Parashar, S. (2016). Feminism and Postcolonialism: (En)gendering Encounters. *Postcolonial Studies, 19*(4), 371–377.

Pennington, J.D. (1982). The Copts in Modern Egypt. *Middle Eastern Studies, 18*(2), 158–179.

Pew Research Center Religion & Public Life (2011). *Global Christianity-A Report on the Size and Distribution of the World's Christian Population*. (https://www.pewforum.org/2011/12/19/global-christianity-exec/).

Pfau-Effinger, B. (1998). Gender cultures and the gender arrangement—a theoretical framework for cross-national gender research. *Innovation: The European Journal of Social Science Research, 11*(2), 147–166.

Pfau-Effinger, B. (2004). Socio-historical paths of the male breadwinner model – an explanation of cross-national differences. *The British Journal of Sociology, 55*(3), 377–399.

Picard, E. (2012). Conclusion: Nation-Building and Minority Rights in the Middle East. In A.N. Longva, & A.S. Roald (Eds). Religious Minorities in the Middle East: Domination, Self-empowerment, Accommodation. Leiden: Brill, pp. 230–255.

Plebani, A. (2018). Iraq: From Fragmentation to (De)Centralization?. In K. Mezran, & A. Varvelli (Eds), *The Arch of Crisis in the MENA Region. Fragmentation, Decentralization and Islamist Opposition*. Milano: Ledizioni LediPublishing, pp. 75–85.

Prettitore, P.S. (2015). Family Law Reform, Gender Equality, and Underage Marriage: A view from Morocco and Jordan. *The Review of Faith & International Affairs, 13*(3), 32–40.

Rabo, A. (2012). 'We Are Christians and We Are Equal Citizens': Perspectives on Particularity and Pluralism in Contemporary Syria. *Islam and Christian–Muslim Relations, 23*(1), 79–93.

Rahman, F.Z. (2012). Gender Equality in Muslim-Majority States and Shari'a Family Law: Is There a Link? *Australian Journal of Political Science*, *47*(3), 347–362.

Rahman, N. (2016). *Democracy in the Middle East and North Africa: five years after the Arab Uprisings*. Arab Barometer – Wave iv, Topic Report.

Rassam, S. (2005). *Christianity in Iraq: Its Origins and Development to the Present Day*. Leominster: Gracewing Publishing.

Razavi, S., & Jenichen, A. (2010). The Unhappy Marriage of Religion and Politics: problems and pitfalls for gender equality. *Third World Quarterly*, *31*(6), 833–850.

Robbins, M. (2017). Youth, Religion and Democracy after The Arab Uprisings: Evidence from the Arab Barometer. *The Muslim World*, *107*(1), 100–126.

Robbins, M., & Thomas, K. (2018). *Women in the Middle East and North Africa: a divide between Rights and Roles*. Arab Barometer – Wave IV, Topic Report.

Robson, L. (2011). *Colonialism and Christianity in Mandate Palestine*. Austin: University of Texas Press.

Robson, L. (2011). Recent perspectives on Christianity in the modern Arab world. *History Compass*, *9*(4), 312–325.

Roccu, R. (2013). *The Political Economy of the Egyptian Revolution*. Basingstoke: Palgrave Macmillan.

Rogan, E. (2009). *The Arabs: A History*. New York: Basic Books.

Ross, M.L. (2008). Oil, Islam, and Women. *American Political Science Review*, *102*(1), 107–123.

Roussos, S. (2014). Globalization Processes and Christians in the Middle East: A Comparative Analysis. *The Journal of the Middle East and Africa*, *5*(2), 111–130.

Rowe, P. (2005). The Sheep and the Goats? Christian Groups in Lebanon and Egypt in Comparative Perspective. In M. Shatzmiller (Ed.), *Nationalism and Minority Identities in Islamic Societies*. Montreal and Kingston: McGill-Queen's University Press, pp. 85–107.

Rowe, P. (2009). Building Coptic Civil Society: Christian Groups and the State in Mubarak's Egypt. *Middle Eastern Studies*, *45*(1), 111–126.

Rowe, P. (2014). In this World You Will Have Trouble. Christians Living Amid Conflict in the Middle East. In P.S. Rowe, J.H. Dyck, & J. Zimmermann (Eds). *Christians and the Middle East Conflict*. London: Routledge, pp. 101–116.

Roy, O. (2007). *The Politics of Chaos in the Middle East*. London: C. Hurst & Co. Publishers.

Ryan, C.R. (2001). Political Strategies and Regime Survival in Egypt. *Journal of Third World Studies*, *18*(2), 25–46.

Ryzova, L. (2017). New Asymmetries in the New Authoritarianism: Research in Egypt in the Age of Post-Revolution. *International Journal of Middle East Studies*, *49*(3), 511–514.

Sabra, G. (2006). Two Ways of Being a Christian in the Muslim Context of the Middle East. *Islam and Christian–Muslim Relations*, 17(1), 43–53.

Salibi, K.S. (1998). *The Modern History of Jordan*. London: IB Tauris.

Salloum, S.A. (2013). *Minorities in Iraq: Memory, Identity and Challenges*. Baghdad: National library and archive.

Sarnelli, V. (2016). After the Arab Uprisings: resilience or transformation? *Journal of Global Faultlines*, 3(1), 70–76.

Sassoon, J. (2012). *Saddam Hussein's Ba'th Party. Inside an Authoritarian Regime*. New York: Cambridge University Press.

Sayigh, Y. (2011). *Policing the People, Building the State: Authoritarian Transformation in the West Bank and Gaza*. Washington, DC: Carnegie Endowment for International Peace.

Smith, A.D. (1989). The Origins of Nations. *Ethnic and Racial Studies*, 12(3), 340–367.

Smith, A.D. (1999). *Myths and Memories of the Nation*. Oxford: Oxford University Press.

Smith, A.D (2003). *Chosen Peoples: Sacred Sources of National Identity*. Oxford: Oxford University Press.

Soliman, S. (2009). The radical turn of Coptic activism. *Cairo Papers in Social Science*, 29(2–3), 135–155.

Sorbera, L. (2014). Challenges of thinking feminism and revolution in Egypt between 2011 and 2014. *Postcolonial Studies*, 17(1), 63–75.

Sorbera, L. (2016). Body politics and legitimacy: towards a feminist epistemology of the Egyptian revolution. *Global Discourse*, 6(3), 493–512.

Spierings, N. (2018). *The Multidimensional Impact of Islamic Religiosity on Ethno-Religious Social Tolerance In The Middle East And North Afric*. Arab Barometer Paper.

Tadros, M. (2011). *Sectarianism and Its Discontents in Post-Mubarak Egypt*. Middle East Report (259), (www.merip.org/mer/mer259/sectarianism-its-discontents-post-mubarakegypt?ip_login_no_cache=3c91272c1d56bc3b03739bb6a3022e49).

Tadros, M. (2013). *Copts at the Crossroads: The Challenges of Building Inclusive Democracy in Egypt*. New York: American University in Cairo Press.

Tavana, D. (2017). *Egypt five years after the Uprisings*, Egypt Wave 4 Country Report.

Teti, A., & Abbott, P. (2017a). *What Drives Migration From The Middle East? Why People Want To Leave Arab State, Working Paper,* University of Aberdeen.

Teti, A., & Abbott, P. (2017b). Against the tide: why women's equality remains a distant dream in Arab countries. The Conversation, April 20 (http://theconversation.com/against-the-tide-why-womens-equality-remains-a-distant-dream-in-arab-countries-74410).

Teti, A., Xypolia, I., Sarnelli, V., Tsourapas, G., Lomazzi, V., & Abbott, P. (2017). Political and Social Transformations in Egypt. *The Arab Transformations Working Paper Series*, 7. (http://dx.doi.org/10.2139/ssrn.2948593).

Toma, S. (2016). My survivor's guilt: coping with the trauma of loss after Maspero. *Coptic Solidarity* (https://www.copticsolidarity.org/2016/10/07/my-survivors-guilt-coping-with-teh-trauma-of-loss-after-maspero/).

Tuastad, D. (2003). Neo-Orientalism and the New Barbarism Thesis: Aspects of Symbolic Violence in the Middle East Conflict(s). *Third World Quarterly, 24*(4), 591–599.

Van Doorn-Harder, N., N. (10 October 2011). Egypt: Does the revolution include the Copts?, *Opendemocracy* (https://www.opendemocracy.net/en/5050/egypt-does-revolution-include-copts/).

Van Doorn-Harder, N. (2013). Betwixt and Between. The Copts of Egypt. *Studies in Interreligious Dialogue, 23*(1), 8–26.

Vatikiotis, P.J. (2016). *Islam and the State*. London: Routledge.

Visser, R. (2005). *Basra, the Failed Gulf State*. Munster: Lit Verlag Munster.

WEF. (2018). *The Global Gender Gap Teport: 2018*. Geneva: World Economic Forum.

West, C., & Zimmerman, D.H. (1987). Doing Gender. *Gender and Society, 1*(2), 125–151.

Wharton, A.S. (2005). *The Sociology of Gender: An Introduction to Theory and Research*. Oxford: Blackwell Publishing.

White, B. (2007). The Nation-State Form and the Emergence of 'Minorities' in Syria. *Studies in Ethnicity and Nationalism, 7*(1), 64–85.

White, B.T. (2012). *Emergence of Minorities in the Middle East*. Edinburgh: Edinburgh University Press.

Wictorowicz, Q. (2006). Anatomy of the Salafi Movement. *Studies in Conflict & Terrorism, 29*(3), 207–239.

Winter, B. (2001). Fundamental misunderstandings: Issues in feminist approaches to Islamism. *Journal of Women's History; Baltimore, 13*(1), 9–41.

Wright, R. (2013). Imagining a Remapped Middle East. *International New York Times*, 28 September.

Wright, R. (2016). How the Curse of Sykes-Picot Still Haunts the Middle East. *The New Yorker*, 30 April.

Zeidel, R. (2007). The Decline of Small-Scale Regionalism in Tikrit. In R. Visser, & G. Stansfield (Eds), *An Iraq of Its Regions. Cornerstones of a Federal Democracy?* London: C. Hurst & Co. Publishers.

Zubaida S. (1993). *Islam, the People and the State, Political ideas and Movements in the Middle East*. London: I.B Tauris.

Zubaida S. (2001). Islam and the Politics of Community and Citizenship. In *Middle East Report*, 221.

Zubaida, S. (2002). The Fragments Imagine the Nation: The Case of Iraq. *International Journal of Middle East Studies, 34*(2), 205–215.

Zubaida, S. (2005). Communalism and Thwarted Aspirations of Iraqi Citizenship. *Middle East Report*, 237.

Zubaida, S. (2011). *Beyond Islam: A New Understanding of the Middle East*. London: IB Tauris.

Zubaida, S. (2012). Iraq: History, Memory, Culture. *International Journal of Middle East Studies, 44*(2), 333–345.

PART 3

The Religious Dimension in the Trajectories of (Forced) Migrants Directed to Italy

∴

The "Place" of Religion in the Italian Asylum Seekers' Reception System: Constitutional, Legislative and Procedural Framework

Paolo Bonetti

1 Religion in the Italian Constitutional System: Every (Italian or Foreign) Person's Right to Religious Freedom

Forced migrations lead foreigners to come into contact with the Italian legal system, which is person-based, as well as built on the principles of democracy, pluralism and secularism, and in which religion plays an open role and has an open discipline, often shaped by very different criteria than those existing in the countries of origin and transit.

In the Italian constitutional system, the religious phenomenon is part of a social dynamic that must be recognized, respected and supported by public authorities through "negative" and "positive" guarantees: exercising religious freedom contributes to the "full development of the human person" (art. 3, par. 2 of the Constitution) and to the "spiritual progress of society" (art. 4, par. 2 of the Constitution) (Troilo, 2008).

Furthermore, the historically predominant presence of Catholics and the presence, on the Italian territory, of the Vatican City State (state entity established in 1929 thanks to the Lateran Pacts and in which the Holy See –i.e. the supreme authority governing the whole Catholic Church– is located) have caused religion in Italy to be perceived differently than in the other States (Ravà, 1963), and have facilitated the preservation of the *de facto* dominant character of the Catholic Church (Botta, 2002).

Indeed, sometimes foreigners enter the Italian territory to participate in the functioning of the central bodies of the Catholic Church (for this purpose, they enjoy free access and a special treatment, as established by the 1929 Treaty between Italy and the Holy See) and the number of foreigners arriving and staying in the Italian State for religious reasons are much higher than in other States. The same provisions concerning immigration and the status of foreign nationals (Legislative Decree no. 286/1998) provide for a specific entry visa for religious reasons (which allows entry to religious people and foreign religious ministers belonging to denominational organizations and who intend to participate in religious events or exercise ecclesiastical, religious or pastoral activity), regulate stays for religious reasons and the right to maintain or regain family unity for holders of this kind of residence permit.

The constitutional principle of equality, established by art. 3 of the Constitution, also applies to foreigners as regards the ownership of the fundamental rights guaranteed to every person by art. 2 of the Constitution. Among the latter, the right to religious freedom is certainly included, regardless of citizenship status (Grosso, 1999; Pistan, 2013; Olivetti, 2018; Curreri, 2018) and is one of the fundamental rights guaranteed to all foreigners present in Italy, also in compliance with the already cited Legislative Decree no. 286/1998. Art. 19 of the Constitution acknowledges the right to freely profess one's religious faith and to exercise it in any form, individually or with others, in private and in public, through rites not offensive to the accepted principles of public morality.

Hence it follows that the religious freedom is guaranteed to all foreigners, including asylum seekers, both during and after the administrative and judicial procedure examining their applications. Moreover, foreigners who are prevented from the actual exercise of these rights in their country of origin are entitled to apply for asylum according to art. 10, par. 3 of the Constitution as enforced by the current legislation. More precisely, art. 19 of the Italian Constitution guarantees three faculties pertaining to religious freedom.

The first is the *freedom to profess one's own religion*. This entails the freedom to declare publicly, either through words or deeds, (or even not to be forced to declare) one's own religious faith, as well as the very freedom to choose to follow one religion first, and then opt for another; or the freedom not to follow any religion or even to stop following it;[1] or, more generally, the right not to be forced to behave in a religious way (Musselli, 1994), with no punitive, discriminatory or persecutory consequences, on both the regulatory and the social level. The refusal or the claim to adopt behaviors that are forbidden or imposed by one's own belief are in fact considered as actual acts of profession (Ricca, 2006). In this respect, freedom of religion also includes the right to conform one's life to the indispensable dictates of one's own conscience, thus respecting the fundamental rights recognized to other people as well as the constitutional duties.

Besides, the freedom to profess one's own religion implies –and implicitly presupposes– the faculty of shaping one's own personal idea regarding religious matters and the faculty of adhering to, or not adhering to, a particular religious doctrine. Thus, the Constitutional Court affirmed that *freedom of*

---

[1]   See Constitutional Court, sentence no. 239/1984.

conscience, referring to the profession of both one's religious faith and of one's opinion in religious matters, is included in the guarantee of art. 19 of the Constitution and must also be included among the inviolable rights of man.[2]

The Italian legal system, which is based on personalist and pluralist principles, cannot remain indifferent to the cases of conscientious objection for religious reasons. Indeed, it has responded by repealing the obligations that were objected to, transforming them into mere faculties or allowing exemptions from them by providing alternative forms of services (for example, civil service as an alternative to the enrolment in the armed or police forces in times of war or serious international crisis). Moreover, the law recognizes forms of conscientious objection to abortive practices and medically assisted procreation (laws no. 194/1978 and no. 40/2004), as well as to animal testing carried out by doctors, researchers and students (law no. 413/1993).

The Italian constitutional system presupposes that "the development of the individual conscience as far as religious matters are concerned (whatever the final decisions are) is part of a more general spiritual and intellectual maturation of the person. Thus, denying or reducing the autonomy of this process of maturation means to deny or prevent the development of the person as such" (Cardia, 1998; Bellini, 1973).

Religious freedom is a perfect subjective right, which can be enforced, within the limits set by the juridical system, in relation to any subject, either public or private, and in any social context or relationship, exactly as all the rights pertaining to freedom: it is, therefore, an inviolable and fundamental right, which does not allow for any repression or restriction by any public administrations.[3]

However, religious freedom is not without limitations, as every fundamental right can be restricted by other principles and precepts expressly stated or deriving from the Constitution,[4] and must therefore be exercised so as not to damage other fundamental rights, both one's own and others' (e.g. personal freedom, freedom of domicile, of communicating privately, of circulation, of residence, of manifestation of thought, of association, of peaceful and unarmed assembly, of trade union and political party organization, of property rights and private economic initiative, and of active and passive electorate) and in order to fulfill constitutional obligations (i.e. economic, political and social solidarity, defending one's homeland, observing the Constitution and

---

2   See Constitutional Court, sentences no. 14/1973, no. 117/1979, no. 239/1984.
3   See Cassation Court in joint sessions, 18 November 1997, no. 11432, in *Quad. dir. e pol. eccl.*, 6, 1998, p. 736.
4   Constitutional Court, sentence no. 100/1981.

the laws, paying taxes, studying, educating and financially supporting one's children).

Religious freedom also includes the right to leave or change one's religious group. This is relevant also in relation to the legal status of foreigners already present in Italy, also to obtain the right to asylum, when in the country of origin such conversion might cause persecutions or discriminations. In fact, it allows the foreigner to be granted the status of refugee *sur place*, in compliance with art. 4 of Legislative Decree no. 251/2007, especially if the conversion is manifested in Italy, but originally happened in the country of origin, without having been manifested in that country for the well-founded fear of being punished.

The conversion of anyone, Italian or foreigner, to a different religion cannot entail any sanction, not even by the abandoned religious confession, so that any impediment to cultivate normal relationships with one's relatives and to use means of communication to prevent the conversion to, or the abandonment of, a religious confession (when it does not integrate the criminal offence of kidnapping or private violence) violate the fundamental rights of freedom of the person, who is given the right to perform the activities necessary for the full restoration of the freedom, either directly or by contacting the judicial or the public security authority. Then, in the event that people within an authoritarian religious structure may lose their autonomous decision-making capacity, either their relatives or the public prosecutor could ask for judicial measures with the aim to ascertain that they are not withheld against their will and that they are not the victim of undue external pressure to remain in the group (Musselli, 1994).

The religious freedom illustrated so far leads at least to four consequences, identified by the doctrine (Cardia, 2010), some of which may have significant relevance for the foreigner, including the asylum seeker:

a) the juridical irrelevance of both the confessional belonging and the religious beliefs of citizens in their public and social life;

b) the right to keep their religious affiliation and their religious convictions confidential;

c) the prohibition of imposing any confessional behavior on people;

d) the prohibition to investigate the personal religious orientation.

In this regard, it is worth looking more closely at the consolidated aspect of Italian jurisprudence and doctrine according to which confessional belonging, sentiments, opinions, and the behavior of people which are the direct expression of religious feelings or inner convictions are protected by a general principle of confidentiality, based on art. 2 and 19 of the Constitution.

This aspect significantly affects the evaluation of the asylum applications that are based on an impediment to the effective exercise of religious freedom.

Said applications cannot be assessed by asking the foreigner to prove his or her religious affiliation or to fully understand the dogmas and the acts of worship of the professed religion, nor can they be rejected for the mere circumstance that, in the country of origin, the applicant did not state his/her religious affiliation or religious conversion in order to avoid negative consequences. In the Italian constitutional system these principles are implicit; on the other hand, these same principles have already been affirmed by the Court of Justice of the European Union in examining the applications for the recognition of international protection (Chapter 4).

The second faculty included in religious freedom is *the right to promote one's own religion*, which comprises the right to spread information and knowledge among others in order to make them appreciate the religion and to try to convert them – this, however, does not stand for conversion practices that undermine the fundamental rights of the converts, i.e. if they are not aware of it, if the conversion involves the use of force, or if it compromises the others' personal integrity, health, and private property (Ricca, 2006).

The right to religious propaganda has some limits, since it must be exercised in such a way as to respect:

a)   the rights of others, so that, for example, no type of religious propaganda legitimizes the violation of a person's domicile or his/her right to rest (when the person is disturbed by songs, calls to prayer or ringing of bells);

b)   the rules governing the means by which propaganda is implemented (for example, the press, radio and television broadcasting, etc.);

c)   the religious freedom of others and also the religious sentiment towards other religions, so that it cannot be exercised through useless contumely which offends the believer (and therefore his/her personality) and insults the ethical values on which the religious phenomenon is based.[5]

After many sentences of the Constitutional Court, the criminal legislation regarding the offenses against religious sentiment has been reformulated by law no. 85/2006, which ensures an equal protection of all religious confessions from the above-mentioned offenses.

The right to religious propaganda includes presenting one's message in a way that turns out to be attractive, but, at the same time, does not allow any mystification – i.e. a manner that prevents the recipient of the propaganda from correctly perceiving the aims of the religious group (Musselli, 1994; Finocchiaro, 1990).

The constitutional protection of the freedom to profess and promote one's religion is relevant both for the reception standards of the asylum seekers

---

5   Constitutional Court, sentence no. 188/1975.

(which will be examined further below), and for the legal qualification of the actual danger to the security of the State deriving from the manifestation of any religious ideas. In particular, the administrative measure for expulsion ordered by the Minister of the Interior on grounds of public and state security, pursuant to art. 13, par. 1 of Legislative Decree no. 286/1998, cannot be applied in the event of mere manifestations of religious ideas, even in the case of Islamic religious fundamentalism, and must instead refer to behaviors that are likely to create an actual danger to public order and to the security of the State (art. 159 of Legislative Decree no. 112/1998).

Indeed, the jurisprudence, faced with a ministerial expulsion based only on declarations made by the foreigner to the press and considered as "simple manifestations of the thought that, because of the blatant ways in which they have been expressed, objectively appear to be incompatible with the will to cause any real damage to anyone", has affirmed that "the need to protect the fundamental good represented by the preservation of the bases of the system that guarantees the orderly development of the entire social life can legitimately involve the compression of other constitutional values" and has therefore expressed the principle of law according to which "the faculties protected directly by the Constitution (such as the expression of thought) can be administratively compressed only if their exercise has proved to be of concrete danger to society".[6] On the contrary, the ministerial expulsion is considered legitimate if it is not only based on an explicit adherence to Islamic fundamentalism, but also on the participation in activities of propaganda or of dissemination of material to incite religious violence in Italy or abroad.[7]

The third faculty consists in *the freedom of worship, both in private and in public, excluding rites contrary to public morality*. This freedom is manifested when performing ritual activities in private or public places, without requiring any authorization from the public authorities[8] and without the prior notice to the authorities required by art. 17 of the Constitution for meetings in public places.[9] It also entails the right not to participate in religious rites (Curreri, 2018). In fact, religious freedom generally excludes any imposition by the state legal system, even when the act of worship belongs to the confession professed by the one to whom it is imposed, because the State does not have to interfere in an "order" that does not belong to it, except for the aims and in the cases

---

6 Lazio Regional Administrative Court, headquartered in Rome, Section I ter, sentence 11 November 2004, no. 15336.
7 See Council of State, Section VI, no. 88/2006.
8 See Constitutional Court, sentence no. 59/1958.
9 See Constitutional Court, sentence no. 45/1957.

expressly mentioned by the Constitution.[10] Thus, it is not only a matter of conscience for non-believers, since they cannot be obliged to perform acts whose meaning goes against their convictions. The very nature of being religious is at stake, and, in the civil order, said nature can only be a manifestation of freedom.[11] While implementing this principle, the Constitutional Court, with the sentence no. 149/1995 and other rulings, has played an important role on the legislation concerning the oath in the civil trial, which no longer contains appeals to the deity. Similarly, with regard to the criminal trial, the legislator intervened directly when the new criminal procedure code was issued.

Moreover, the public worship of one's religion also entails the need to have free access to places where it is possible to perform cult activities and to open new places of worship not because there is a social right to have a place of worship, but because the State does promote its establishment, in compliance with both the rules on land management and of those concerning safety.[12] The only rituals that are not admitted are those against public morality, which the doctrine identifies with the common sense of decency. Therefore, rituals involving sexual or orgiastic activities are considered to be against public morality, as well as practices causing a general sense of repugnance and disgust on the basis of a common ethical sentiment, such as particular initiation ceremonies (Mortati, 1976; Musselli, 1994) – which includes, in the prohibition, the "practices of worship that, due to their violent and aggressive nature, may be reprehensible to the human conscience" (Lillo, 2006).

Freedom of worship must also be exercised in accordance with the rights and freedoms of others. Ritual practices that damage life or personal liberty, and that therefore involve permanent damage to the physical integrity of consenting people (e.g. female genital mutilation), as well as practices that damage the life or the physical integrity of animals are in fact unlawful. In particular, art. 583-bis of the Penal Code defines as a crime, punished by imprisonment from 4 to 12 years, "clitoridectomy, excision, infibulation and every other practice that produces effects of the same type". Besides, art. 544-bis and 544-ter punish anyone who, "out of cruelty or without necessity", kills or injures an animal, or subjects it to torture or distress (even during shows and events). On the contrary, the ritual slaughter of animals (*halal* for Muslims and *kosher* for Jews) is allowed by derogatory provisions of the Ministry of Health, and must be carried out in authorized facilities and under the supervision of local health authorities.

---

10   See Constitutional Court, sentence no. 85/1963.
11   See Constitutional Court, sentence no. 334/1996.
12   See Constitutional Court, sentence no. 63/2016.

2   The Right to Asylum of the Foreign Nationals Who are Prevented
     from Actually Exercising Religious Freedom

Art. 10, par. 3 of the Italian Constitution provides that foreign nationals who, in
their own countries, are denied the freedoms guaranteed by the Italian Constitution, have the right to asylum in the Italian territory under the conditions
established by law. Since religious freedom and the non-discrimination principle towards any religion are provided for by the Italian Constitution, foreigners who have a well-founded fear of being persecuted for religious reasons
should enjoy the right to asylum. They should do so in one of the three forms
provided for by the existing laws, in compliance with international and European standards (Legislative Decree no. 251/2007 and no. 25/2008). Such forms
are the following: *a*) the *refugee status* (providing a 5-year residence permit,
automatically renewable upon expiry); *b*) the status of *subsidiary protection*
(providing a 5-year residence permit, renewable upon expiry and if the situation persists) for those who cannot be granted the refugee status, but who are
afraid of suffering physical harm because of death penalty threats, inhuman
and degrading treatments, tortures, and possible violence against civilians in
situations of internal or international conflict; *c*) the *special protection* (providing a 1-year permit, renewable as long as the situation persists) for those who
cannot obtain the refugee status or the subsidiary protection, but cannot be
expelled because of the chance of persecution or torture in either the origin or
the sending country. This last permit has partially replaced the previous residence permit for humanitarian reasons repealed by Decree Law no. 113/2018
and which used to be issued to those who could not be removed for humanitarian reasons also deriving from constitutional or international obligations.

   Legislative Decree no. 251/2007, in order to enforce the EU directive on international protection (see Chapter 4), defines as "refugee" the foreign national who, owing to the well-founded fear of being persecuted for reasons of race,
religion, nationality, membership of a particular social group or political opinion, is outside the country of nationality and is unable or –owing to such fear–
is unwilling to avail himself or herself of protection of that country, or a stateless person, who is outside the territory of former habitual residence and is
unable or is unwilling to return to it for the same reasons as mentioned above,
without prejudice to the causes of exclusion pursuant to art. 10 of Legislative
Decree no. 251/2007. In order to grant the refugee status, the acts of persecution must be a serious violation of fundamental human rights, including religious freedom. This is violated when it is reduced to freedom of worship alone,
or to worship only in certain places, when it is impeded or sanctioned the freedom to profess or to propagandize (thus prohibiting and punishing any form

of proselytizing or of missionary activity) or to belong or to convert to a particular religion.

However, the refugee status can be granted only if the violation of rights is serious. In fact, when a State guarantees a special condition for a specific religion, there is no persecution if the lives of the believers of other religions are substantially normal. Besides, as of December 2018, protection against religious persecutions may be less effective because –in compliance with the EU directive– the application for international protection in the Italian legal system must be rejected when "in a part of the country of origin, the applicant either has no well-founded fear of being persecuted or is not at real risk of suffering serious harm, or has access to protection against persecution or serious harm, and he/she can legally and safely travel to and gain admittance to that part of the country and can reasonably be expected to settle there" (art. 30, par. 1 of Legislative Decree no. 25/2008). Such notion turns out to be hardly effective if applied to the situation of multi-religious or federal States in which interreligious conflicts are very serious and the legislation of each federated State can adopt the model of confessionalism and religious discrimination.

In order to recognize the refugee status, acts of persecution or lack of protection against such acts must be connected to the reasons indicated by art. 8 of Legislative Decree no. 251/2007, among which is "religion" itself, which includes theistic, non-theist and atheist convictions, participation in, or abstention from, rituals of worship celebrated in private or in public, both individually and in community, other religious acts or professions of faith, as well as the forms of personal or social behavior based on a religious belief or prescribed by it.

It is therefore not necessary to prove that the personal or social behavior that has been persecuted has a strictly religious character. As a result, if in a particular country there are policies specifically implemented to contrast certain religions or certain religious currents of thought (e.g. Islamic fundamentalism) through measures to combat terrorism or conducts against social peace, acts of persecution for religious reasons may occur. For example, they may happen against women who wear the veil in public, without having to demonstrate the anti-Islamic orientation of said political measures, nor the existence of a real intrinsically religious character of that social behavior, e.g. of the veil as prescribed by Islam, since a link with this religion based on experience is sufficient (Codini, 2009). Moreover, there is no persecution for religious reasons if ritual murders are prohibited, as well as any incitement to violence or to any common crimes committed for religious reasons.

Furthermore, there is actual religious persecution even if the religious affiliation of the person or his/her religious acts have erroneously been presupposed by the persecutor. In fact, in examining whether an applicant has a well-founded fear of being persecuted, it is irrelevant that the person actually possesses the racial, religious, national, social or political characteristics that provoke the acts of persecution, as long as said characteristic is attributed to the persecuted person by the author of the persecutions (art. 8 of Legislative Decree no. 251/2007). In practice, for example, the Gorizia Territorial Commission recognized the religious persecution of an Eritrean woman raped in prison while pregnant and forced to have an abortion because of the violence suffered after being accused of belonging to the Pentecostal Christian faith without any evidence (Benvenuti, 2011).

Besides incorporating the EU directive on international protection qualifications (Chapter 4), these legislative norms seem to take over the three notions of religion indicated in the UNHCR guidelines:

a)   religion seen as a belief;
b)   religion seen as identity;
c)   religion as a lifestyle.

The Court of Cassation granted the refugee status to a foreigner who fled his country for reasons connected to religious persecutions, even if said applicant had provided no evidence whatsoever – and that was because the persecution had been attested by documentation from governmental and non-governmental organizations.[13]

Nevertheless, religious persecutions usually affect the right to freedom of religion (for example by prohibiting the worship of certain cults or confessions), as well as other rights, for example by providing for different legal treatment basing on whether one is or is not a member of a particular religion.[14]

Indeed, religious persecution can take different forms. For instance, the prohibition of being part of a religious community or of celebrating the cult in public or in private, the adoption of discriminatory measures against a specific confession, forced conversions (Abu Salem, Fiorita, 2016) or impeded conversions towards religions that are not recognized by the authorities.

During the examination of the applications, in cases of persecution for religious reasons, the personal interview plays a significant role, especially when the reasons behind the persecution are, for example, a conversion to a religion that was not manifested in the country of origin. When there is no supporting

---

13   Court of Cassation I, sentence no. 26056, 1 December 2010.
14   *La tutela dei richiedenti asilo – Manuale giuridico per l'operatore,* curated by UNHCR, ASGI, Central service of the SPRAR, 2016, p. 16 (http://www.unhcr.it/wp-content/uploads/2016/01/1UNHCR_manuale_operatore.pdf).

evidence of the persecutions, the interview has to focus on the details of the conversion, on the contents of the religion that the applicant wants to profess, on the methods of prayer and on all the other elements that prove that his/her statements are well-founded. To this end, information on the punishment imposed, in the country of origin, in the event of a conversion appears to be useful (Benvenuti, 2011).

Besides, it is difficult to provide *evidence demonstrating the persecution* and regarding the *agents of persecution*. According to art. 3 of Legislative Decree no. 251/2007, while examining the application, in addition to the declarations and the documentation presented by the applicant, one must also take into consideration the facts concerning the country of origin and the personal situation of the applicant. In fact, it is important to collect information on the countries of origin through the various databases (including the ones managed by EASO, by UNHCR, and by the National Commission for the right to asylum) even though it is not sufficient.

Judges, in fact, usually nullify the reject of the applications decided by the territorial commissions, especially when they are based on the non-credibility of the applicants, in virtue of art. 3, par. 5 of Legislative Decree no. 251/2007. In compliance with the EU directive, it states that "where some elements or aspects of the statements of the applicant for international protection are not supported by evidence, said elements shall be considered to be truthful if the competent authority recognizes that:

a) the applicant has made all reasonable efforts to substantiate the application;

b) all relevant elements at the applicant's disposal have been submitted, and a satisfactory explanation regarding any lack of other relevant elements has been given;

c) the applicant's statements are found to be coherent and plausible and do not run counter to available specific and general information relevant to his/her case;

d) the applicant has applied for international protection at the earliest possible time, unless he/she can demonstrate good reason for not having done so;

e) the general credibility of the applicant has been established".

Fundamentally, because of the principle of good faith, asylum seekers do not have the burden of proving irrefutably their claims – which would be extremely difficult to fulfill after escaping from persecution or from a conflict, and which would nullify the right to asylum. Any elements of the narration expressed by the applicant, even if not proven, are considered as credible if the circumstances indicated in the article are present.

In this regard, the Court of Cassation makes it mandatory for those who examine the applications to cooperate to ascertain the facts, after having heard the declarations of the foreigner and even if these are incomplete or apparently contradictory. More precisely, the Court of Cassation[15] has decided that the statements that are intrinsically unreliable based on the indicators of subjective authenticity contained in art. 3 of Legislative Decree no. 251/2007, do not require an informal in-depth investigation, when the lack of truthfulness does not derive exclusively from the impossibility of providing evidence on the objective situation from which the described situation of risk arises or when the narration is about strictly interpersonal episodes of violence. Furthermore, the description of a life-threatening situation deriving from unwritten rules imposed with violence towards a gender, a social or religious group, or even an enemy family group (e.g. tribal rules), when it is tolerated or tacitly approved by state authorities, does require an informal in-depth investigation in order to verify the degree of diffusion and impunity of the violent behavior described, as well as the response of state authorities. To sum it up, the assessment of the unreliability of the foreigner's statements cannot be based only on his/her impossibility to provide evidence, as it is formally necessary to evaluate if the representation of situations that allow for subsidiary protection is true in the current situation of the country of origin.[16]

Moreover, the Court of Cassation specified in sentence no. 5224 of 2013 that the presence of a credible version of the facts causing possible life-threatening situations in case of return to the homeland is the necessary condition for the competent judicial body to start an investigation. Therefore, even if the conformity of the documents produced by the applicant with the original ones and the substantial credibility of his/her statements are disputed, the traditional principle of the ordinary civil proceedings does not apply. Indeed, the judge –except in the case of procedural impediments– has the duty to cooperate in ascertaining the relevant facts by carrying out an unofficial preliminary investigation, since it is necessary to counterbalance the asymmetry deriving from the different positions of the parties.[17]

Then, the Court of Cassation[18] clarified that, as regards international protection, the assessment procedure carried out by the judge should firstly consider the subjective credibility of the applicant's version of the life-threatening

---

15   Civil Cassation, Section VI-1, ordinance 10 April 2015 no. 7333.
16   See Court of Cassation, 16 July 2015, no. 14998 and Court of Cassation, 21 July 2015, no. 15275.
17   Court of Cassation, no. 25534 of 2016.
18   Court of Cassation, no. 16925 of 2018; no. 28862 of 2018.

facts. Therefore, if the declarations are judged to be unreliable (on the basis of the indicators of subjective authenticity of art. 3 of Legislative Decree no. 251/2007), an informal in-depth investigation into the situations of persecutions in the countries of origin is not necessary, unless the lack of truthfulness derives exclusively from the impossibility of providing probative evidence.

An example of what just explained is the 22 January 2016 ordinance of the Court of Rome, which granted the refugee status to an Egyptian citizen of Coptic Orthodox religion forced to flee with her family after threats and acts of persecution. In order to support her statements, the applicant presented numerous documents: some aimed at demonstrating her personal condition (e.g. identity documents and baptismal certificates for all her family members), others relating to the socio-political-religious situation of Egypt. However, since the judge has to evaluate the effective protection of the right to religious freedom, changes occurring at institutional level are not enough. In fact, art. 64 of the Egyptian Constitution recognizes religious freedom as an absolute right and allows the Religions of the Book to practice religious rites and build places of worship within the limits set by law. Nevertheless, as confirmed by reports by authoritative international organizations examined by the judge, a progressive and dramatic deterioration in the protection of human rights is taking place in Egypt. Indeed, the ordinance shows that state authorities have not done enough to fight discrimination against religious minorities, especially Shiite Muslims, Bahá'is and Coptic Christians, who, after President Morsi's destitution, were subject to new attacks of sectarian origin and encountered many obstacles in the construction of new places of worship and in the maintenance of the already existing ones. Therefore, the persecutions suffered, the fear of suffering new ones, as well as the information gathered on the country of origin, have led the judge to find concretely proven "the circumstance according to which the applicants, in case of repatriation, would objectively be sent back to persecution", thus recognizing them the refugee status.

On the contrary, the Court of Cassation quashed a decision of the Court of Appeal relating to an asylum-seeker of Christian religion who had stated to have lived in Benin City until the death of his parents, killed by the Muslims of Boko Haram, and to have moved to Abuja in the house of a friend later killed by terrorists. The Court did not specify the reasons why the story was considered to be not credible and contradictory. After the applicant's assertion that violence for religious reasons happened in an area of the country different from the one he was from, the Court did not take into account that he also declared to have tried in vain to escape and find shelter in another area of the country.[19]

---

19   See Court of Cassation, Section 6-1, no. 12135/2013.

In March 2015, the Bari Court of Appeal decided the case of a Pakistani Ahmyahite citizen who had faced persecution along with all of his family members: his father was arrested while an intimidation campaign was going on against his two children. After having already suffered persecution, the fear of having to suffer again increases, except that the circumstances of the individual case indicate the opposite (art. 3, par. 4 of Legislative Decree no. 251/2007). A relevant element to ascertain the validity of such fear (as in the case under examination) is the fact that other subjects of the same environment as the applicant's, or other individuals who find themselves in the same situation, have already been victims of persecution in that territorial context. In that case, in the recognition of the status a key role was played by the ascertainment of a widespread intolerance, which had not been fought by the authorities, and which has affected the life of the whole Ahmyahite community in Pakistan.

The Court of Appeal, in opposition to what was decided by the Court of first instance, states that "considering the situation of the country of origin and the significance of what has been discovered about the risks to the lives of the individuals (the story is coherent and credible, as can been proven by the leaflet reporting a threat of death, as well as the promise of an economic reward for those who would find the applicant and his brother – later on, the applicant would tell the same story without any uncertainties), in reform of the decision under appeal, the applicant must be granted the political refugee status, on the basis of the knowledge that, in the event of a return to the country of origin, he would face discriminations or life threats perpetrated by members of other religions". With reference to this matter, it was also observed that "the threat justifying such protection is not necessarily posed by the State, as it may also come from other subjects when state authorities are unable or unwilling to provide adequate protection, as stated in art. 6, par. 2 of Legislative Decree n. 251/2007".

Similar observations are present in the 11 November 2018 ordinance of the Court of Ancona on the appeal against the rejection of the application for international protection submitted by a citizen of Bangladesh who was being persecuted in his country for religious reasons. We can see how in this case, too, the Court considers that "with reference to the evaluation of the truthfulness of the declarations, the Commission finds lack of credibility to the story – assumption that we cannot support. In fact, the legislative parameters to decide on the reliability of the declarations made by the asylum seeker are established by art. 3, par. 5 of Legislative Decree no. 251/2007. Moreover, the Commission observes a correspondence between what was highlighted by the applicant and the information gathered from the sources (...). In truth, the applicant's story appeared to be credible because it was fully detailed, as well as confirmed by the information collected (...)".

Here is another case concerning a Sunni Muslim coming from Pakistan, who was the subject of persecution by members of his own religious group because of the good relations he used to have with some Shiites. The hostility of the Sunnis towards him precluded him from the possibility of obtaining protection from state authorities and left him without any shelter: shut out by the majority, not belonging to any minority, and neglected by the State. In the absence of further evidence besides his declarations, the Court of Appeal of Palermo (sentence no. 281 of 15 February 2016), in accordance with art. 3 of Legislative Decree no. 251/2007, considered the applicant's effort to substantiate his claim to be decisive. However, as for similar cases, the ruling clarifies that it is not possible to make "any decision that may result in the return to the country of origin of a person who could suffer serious harm there". Besides the fact that the person requesting protection does not have to belong to a persecuted minority, since persecution for religious reasons may arise from many different events, the Sicilian judge stressed the central role of the credibility of the asylum seeker, and drew attention to the subjective opinion of the judge.

Back in 2010, the Court of Cassation, with sentence no. 26056, ruled on similar cases, introducing two criteria. The first case concerned a Nigerian citizen of Catholic faith. His views were considered as contradictory and vague by the Court of Appeal of Turin, which stated that, in this type of disputes, the burden of proof mainly falls on the applicant and any lack of arguments could not be filled by the powers of instructions of the judicial organ. On the contrary, the Court of Cassation reiterated the obligation of the judges to cooperate actively in the investigation phase, and stated that granting of refugee status cannot be based exclusively on the credibility of the applicant and the duty of the latter to prove the oppression suffered. Furthermore, the Court adds, the truthfulness of the persecution can be ascertained thanks to external and objective information concerning the country of origin, and it is the connection of these conditions to the present case that will help verify the asylum seeker's credibility.

Another interesting decision of the Court of Cassation[20] confirms the ruling of the Court of Appeal of Naples rejecting, for lack of requirements, the request for international protection due to religious persecution perpetrated by the parents of the applicant. While reaffirming that, hypothetically, even

---

20   Civil Cassation, Section VI, no. 21612/2018, available at: www.dirittoimmigrazionecittadinanza.it/archivio-fascicoli/fascicolo-2018-n-3/54-rassegne-di-giurisprudenza-n-3-2018/rassegne-di-giurisprudenza-italiana-n-3-2018/88-asilo-e-protezione-internazionale.

parents can be agents of persecution for religious reasons, in this case the applicant's statements were not considered as credible: he, in fact, had reported that he had always lived with his parents and had attended Christian schools, thus leading the judge to believe that it was unlikely that the applicant's father might not approve of the faith that his son had matured in the Christian school the parents themselves had enrolled him at.

There are also cases of religious persecution among the different currents of thought within the Islamic religion. The 15 November 2017 decree issued by the Court of Brescia[21] granted the refugee status to a Pakistani citizen who was the Imam of a mosque and who used to teach the Koran to children. The Court judged the applicant's story to be credible by linking the religious persecution he was facing to his role as a Koran teacher inside a mosque (he belonged to the Barelvi religious group) and to having refused to stop his religious teaching. In the decree, the Court, while exercising its duty of cooperation, allowed the appellant to clarify some aspects that seemed to be unclear during the hearing in the previous administrative phase.

The Court of Rome has recognized a Nigerian citizen the refugee status because of the persecutions of Christians in his country. Thanks to a newspaper article presented to the Court and reporting his story of persecution (he had received threats by a terrorist organization because of his Christian faith), the plaintiff managed to prove the truthfulness of his words. As the Court reaffirms, the fact that the threats are not posed by state authorities does not prevent the recognition of the protection. Indeed: "(...) even if the danger the plaintiff is exposed to cannot be linked to any activity of the State, the third-country national can still consider well-founded the fear of suffering serious damage in case of return to the country of origin, given the context of religious conflicts in many areas of the Country".[22]

What is even more challenging, in relation to religion, is the recognition of the subsidiary protection to the foreigner or to the stateless person who flees from a specific country for the well-founded fear of suffering serious damage resulting from death penalty, torture, inhuman or degrading treatment or generalized violence to civilians in situations of internal or international conflict.

The Cassation has granted the status of subsidiary protection (and not the refugee status) to a third-country national (in this case, escaped from Pakistan not to join the Taliban militias) because the violent pressure he was put under was not dictated by the willingness to impose a religious option, but by the

---

21   Available at: https://www.dirittoimmigrazionecittadinanza.it/allegati/fascicolo-n-2-2018/
        rifugio-2/217-5-trib-brescia-15-11-2017-rifugio/file.

22   Court of Rome, I Civil section, sentence no. 20908 of 21 October 2013.

need to enlarge an armed organization. Besides, his refusal was not due to religious reasons.[23]

It is also worthwhile mentioning both the ruling concerning the recognition of humanitarian protection to a Benin citizen, given the significant danger of enforcement of the Shariʿa against the applicant in his country of origin, and the ruling that granted subsidiary protection to a Pakistani citizen because of the risk of possible persecution linked to his religious faith.

The issues relating to the persecutions of new religions and sects and the persecution in the case of conversion to another religion are of particular importance. The *persecution of sects or "new religions"* is observed especially in countries where the law provides for oppressive conditions to legitimize the action of religious confessions. The term "sect" is often one of the tools used in some countries to discriminate or persecute certain new, non-traditional religious groups, which are not submissive to political power. However, it is not allowed to deny the refugee status only because the creed that is subjected to persecution is considered as a sect or because sects are not religions, but pseudo-religions.[24]

An example of an upheld appeal is the sentence of the Court of Trieste of 2 January 2018. It concerned a Chinese woman who reported having left her country of origin because, due to her religious faith, she was being sought by the authorities – who were persecuting the members of the so-called House Churches by arresting and torturing its followers and its promoters. In particular, the applicant reported being intimidated by the authorities, which led her to flee her country. The Court of Trieste had criticized the territorial commission's rejection of the request because "without consulting specific sources, it estimated that there were no reasonable grounds to believe that if the applicant had returned to China, she would have run the risk of suffering serious harm, pursuant to the provisions of art. 14 of Legislative Decree 251/2007" even if in that case "the intrinsic reliability of the applicant's story (...) is linked to the extrinsic one. The circumstances described are in line with the information acquired; the religiosity of the applicant seems to be deeply convinced: in such a homogeneous context, even the more uncertain circumstances relating to her escape from her country remain credible".

As recalled by the Court of Bari, civil Section II, through the ordinance of 7 April 2016, the *darwishi gonabadi* religious current (of the ascetic and mystic type of Sufi Islam diffused in Iran and Turkey) according to reliable international

---

23   See Court of Cassation, Section 6-1, no. 12075/2014, Rv. 631321-01.
24   General Comment no. 22 of the International Covenant on Civil and Political Rights, 1993, no. 2.

sources has been persecuted for years by the Iranian government. For this reason, it can be stated that its followers have been persecuted by state forces because of their religious affiliation.

Furthermore, it is useful to mention the 22 May 2018 ordinance of the Court of Perugia. In evaluating whether a person has the right to obtain international protection, judges cannot make their decision exclusively on the basis of the personal credibility of the applicant and of the fulfillment of the burden of proof relating to the existence of the *fumus persecutionis* against him/her in the country of origin. The judge, in fact, must verify that there actually is a persecution of opinions, habits, and practices by basing on external and objective information relating to the situation of the country of origin. However, in order to prove the *fumus persecutionis*, the applicant can also use elements of personal evaluation, including the credibility of the declarations of the interested party. The judge, therefore, has a duty to carry out an extensive investigation, obtain all the documentation (even if unofficial) and generally assess the actual situation of the country of origin. The specific case was an appeal against the refusal of international and humanitarian protection of a Chinese woman belonging to the "Church of God Almighty" who was forced to flee her country, since the cult she belonged to was being persecuted (Soryte, 2018).

In this case, the Court states again that "the reasons given in this regard by the commission are not convincing, as (...) the applicant's statements appear to be intrinsically coherent and credible (...) and correspond to the actual characteristics of the cult"; "(...) it must also be noted that the applicant has tried to provide all the elements in her possession in order to prove that she belonged to the cult (...) therefore, for the purpose of recognizing the refugee status to the applicant, the Court must acknowledge that she has a well-founded fear of being persecuted for religious reasons, both from a subjective and an objective point of view, since the applicant's statements in this regard appear to be in line with the latest news on religious freedom in China (...) we must consider that the article 300 of the Chinese Penal Code, which also punishes those who participate in superstitious sects, is interpreted by the jurisprudence in the sense of punishing even those who are active in a superstitious sect; thus, it is sufficient to be identified as a member of a forbidden cult to be arrested and sentenced to prison for even more than seven years, in case of serious circumstances".

The persecution in case of *conversion* has been as well recognized in many cases, both in administrative and judicial cases. In the administrative practice, a decision of the territorial commission of Rome is fundamental, as it recognized the refugee status to all the members of a Christian Egyptian family, in which the mother was sexually harassed and the father was convicted for apostasy, was the subject of discrimination in the workplace, and even received death threats and was abused by the police in order to force him and his children to convert (Benvenuti, 2011). The ordinance of the Court of Bari, II civil section, of 15 March 2017[25] recognized the status of refugee to an Iranian man, whose conversion to the Catholic religion gave rise to religious persecution and to a warrant for his arrest. The Court recalled that his conversion was known to the state authorities, because of his father's (a *Hezbollah*) complaint, as well as because of the discovery of a box containing copies of the Bible (and kept by the applicant, as requested by a friend, inside his computer shop) and after a search carried out by the police in the house of the applicant's family. The judge examined the condition of Christians in Iran also through the consultation of an essay on being Christians in Iran today, published in an Italian magazine, through the reading of passages from the Koran (where the crime of apostasy is unfounded) and in the light of the number of people hanging themselves after President Rouhani took office.

Lastly, today in Italy the effective protection against any form of religious persecution no longer appears to be guaranteed when it concerns either a citizen of a State included in the list of safe countries of origin or a stateless person who legally resides there. In fact, by making use of the faculty provided by the EU directive, art. 2-bis of Legislative Decree 25/2008 (added in 2018) gives the Minister of Foreign Affairs and Cooperation, in agreement with the Ministers of Interior and of Justice, the faculty to approve a list of safe countries of origin. As shown by the information gathered by national, European, and international bodies, in these States the risk of suffering persecution, torture, inhuman or degrading treatment or even general violence during conflicts can be ruled out thanks to their democratic system, their current laws and the effective application of said laws; besides, the rights and the jurisdictional guarantees provided for in the International Covenant on Civil and Political Rights, in the European Convention for Human Rights, in the International Convention against Torture and in the Convention on the Status of Refugees are effectively ensured.

The Decree of the Minister of Foreign Affairs of 4 October 2019 designates as safe countries of origin Algeria, Morocco, Tunisia, Albania, Bosnia, Cape Verde, Ghana, Kosovo, Montenegro, Northern Macedonia, Senegal, Ukraine, and Serbia. However, such Decree appears to be illegitimate since these countries, except for Cape Verde, do not have the required requisites for this qualification. In fact, some of these States have a legal order based on a state religion and the

---

25   Available at: https://www.dirittoimmigrazionecittadinanza.it/allegati/fascicolo-n-2-2017/
        rifugio/90-4-ordinanza-tribunale-di-bari-iran-conversione/file.

people who do not belong to said religion, or stop practicing it, cannot fully enjoy religious freedom and can suffer legal discrimination, criminal sanctions or other forms of persecution for religious reasons (Morocco, Algeria, and Tunisia). Besides, in some of those States, conflict situations are underway for religious reasons and certain sexual orientations are considered as a criminal offense.

This Decree will not only speed up the procedures for examining the applications submitted by the citizens of the States defined as safe and by the stateless persons residing there. Since the applicants coming from those countries have the burden of bringing elements showing that, in their personal situation, their country is not safe, the Decree will also deter the submission of applications and the possible subsequent jurisdictional appeals. Besides, it will cause a decrease in the positive results of the applications.[26]

---

26   In fact, the designation of the safe country of origin produces the following effects on the applications for international protection presented by citizens of the designated State or by stateless persons staying there: 1) The authority examining the application is exempt from the obligation to collect the information on the country of origin *ex officio*, but the applicants have the burden of invoking serious reasons showing that, in their specific situations, their country is not safe (art. 2-bis, par. 5 of Legislative Decree 25/2008); 2) Denying the applications adopted by the Territorial Commission for the recognition of international protection due to manifest groundlessness is justified only when the applicants have not demonstrated that there are serious reasons to believe that, in relation to their specific situations, the designated safe countries of origin are in fact unsafe, thus making them run the risk of persecution or serious damage (art. 9, par. 2-bis of Legislative Decree 25/2008); 3) Upon presentation of the applications for international protection, the police office informs the applicants that the application can be rejected as manifestly unfounded simply because they have not demonstrated the existence of serious reasons for considering the designated safe countries of origin to be unsafe in relation to their specific situations, thus making them run the risk of persecution or serious damage (art. 10, par.1 of Legislative Decree 25/2008); 4) The request for international protection is examined by the Territorial Commission as a priority (art. 28, par. 1, letter c-ter of Legislative Decree 25/2008) and with an accelerated procedure: as soon as the request is received, the police station immediately proceeds to the transmission of the necessary documentation to the Territorial Commission, which makes a decision within five days (the deadline can be extended to ten days or more if the application is deemed manifestly unfounded and needs a more in-depth examination). If the application is presented in the border or transit area, the examination can take place directly at the border or in the transit area (art. 29, par. 1.1-bis, 1- ter and 1-quater, 2 and 3 of Legislative Decree 25/2008); many of the citizens of the countries included in the list of safe countries of origin arrive in Italy precisely in the border areas identified by the Ministry of the Interior Decree of 5 August 2019, that is southern Sardinia and southern Sicily (especially the citizens of Tunisia, Algeria and Morocco, who make up 40% of the average number of irregular entries from the sea and the Bosnian, Kosovar and Montenegrin citizens who enter the border areas of Apulia in southern Italy or of Friuli Venezia Giulia in northern Italy); 5) The rejection of the

3   Persecution for Multiple Reasons: Religion and Sex, Religion and
       Sexual Orientation

Discrimination and persecution can also be based on reasons other than
religion.

For example, the persecution against those who fight to change their State
from a confessional one to a secular one, in which people can freely express
atheistic ideas, is a persecution both for religious and political reasons.

There are also *persecutions and discrimination against women, i.e. for rea-*
sons connected with belonging to the female gender, but which are also motivated
by political and religious reasons. In this regard, it must be highlighted that persecutions could also happen if the persecutor supposes that the person belongs to a particular religion. In the administrative practice, for instance, there
was a case of an Eritrean female citizen who suffered imprisonment and mis-
treatment because of her supposed membership to the Pentecostal Church.
She was granted the refugee status after having verified her credibility on the
basis of her very declarations.

---

application for the international protection by the Territorial Commission due to manifest groundlessness involves, at the end of the term for the appeal (reduced to 15 days by
art. 35, par. 2 of Legislative Decree 25/2008), the obligation for the applicant to leave the
national territory, unless he/she has been issued a residence permit for another reason,
and the adoption in his/her regard of an administrative expulsion order by the prefect,
which is executed by the quaestor who accompanies the applicant to the frontier; if this
is not executable, the quaestor can also issue a detention order to keep the applicant in a
center for repatriation (art. 32, par. 4 of Legislative Decree 25/2008); 6) The enforceability
of the rejection due to manifest groundlessness cannot be suspended by the mere presentation of the judicial appeal to the court, as it can be suspended only for serious reasons
and after having issued a decree motivated by the court judge, pronounced within five
days since the submission of the request for suspension, without the prior call of the
counterpart and, if necessary, after having gathered more general information. The decree that either grants or denies the suspension of the disputed provision is notified to the
parties. Within five days since the notification, the parties can file defensive notes. Within
five days after the expiry of this deadline, replies may be filed and the judge, with a new
decree to be issued within the next five days, can confirm, amend or revoke the measures
already issued. In any case, such decrees are not subject to appeal, and only once the request for suspension has been accepted, the applicant is issued a residence permit due to
the asylum request (art. 35-bis, par. 4 of Legislative Decree 25/2008); 7) When the appellant is admitted to patronage at the State's expense and the appeal concerns a decision,
adopted by the Territorial Commission, that is manifestly unfounded, the judge that rejects the appeal indicates in the decree for the payment of the expenses by the State the
reasons why the claims of the plaintiff cannot be considered as manifestly unfounded (in
the absence of those reasons, the costs of the proceedings are charched to the applicant
and not to the State).

In this regard, another case can be mentioned. By keeping in mind that in such cases judges must exercise their broad powers of instructions and collect all the information useful to reconstruct the narrative context, the Court of Cassation (ordinance no. 24064 of 2013) approved the appeal of a Cameroonian woman, accused of witchcraft in her country. According to the Court, any anthropological analysis would have made it possible to ascertain that the accusations of witchcraft constitute a sociocultural-religious phenomenon that is widespread in the community of origin of the applicant, just as convictions for common crimes that cover up convictions for witchcraft. From such analysis, it could easily have emerged that the applicant had been convicted on the basis of persecution for, in the broad sense, religious reasons (Benvenuti, 2011).

On the contrary, when the condemnations for witchcraft are inflicted by local courts against women to punish serious common crimes, such as murders, these acts are meant to prevent all forms of self-determination and, even if they are not aimed at harming women's religious freedom (therefore not legitimizing the recognition of the refugee status) they can cause the compression of fundamental rights and could thus legitimize the recognition of minor international protection measures (Acierno, 2019), i.e. the status of subsidiary protection or of special protection.

More generally, since any act specifically directed against a sexual gender is considered as persecution (art. 7, par. 2 of Legislative Decree no. 251/2007), in a case concerning a Nigerian citizen, the Cassation has found that a woman, as such, can be persecuted for belonging to a social group and, at the same time, for religious reasons – if she rebels against a code of conduct, against duties and responsibilities, against men (Madera, 2018).

Genital mutilation, as it is performed against the female gender, can also be based on religious motives. In fact, the jurisprudence has observed that since their genesis lies in deep cultural traditions or religious beliefs, women's refusal to subject themselves or their daughters to such practices exposes them to the actual risk of being considered, in their country, as political opponents or as subjects that reject religious models and social values, and are therefore persecuted for this reason. So, they must be granted the status of refugee to stop gender violence as well as the discriminatory treatment that would ensue in case of refusal to submit to the violence (Cattelan, 2013).

More generally, violence against women can also occur because of religious reasons. In this sense, Courts grant subsidiary protection when a female is forced to an unwanted marriage and authorities do not oppose it, thus leaving any decision to the patriarchal family or a religious structure.

Thus, the Cassation includes in the concept of domestic violence (pursuant to art. 3 of the Istanbul Convention of 11 May 2011 on preventing and combating violence against women and domestic violence, enforced in Italy by the law of 27 June 2013, no. 77) a case of restriction on enjoyment of fundamental human rights imposed to a woman, of Christian religion, because of her refusal to abide by the custom of her own village – according to which, after becoming a widow, she had to get married to her brother-in-law. The Cassation decided so even if the tribal authorities, to which the woman had asked for help against her brother-in-law, had allowed her not to marry him – since that was on condition that she left the village, leaving her children and her belongings behind. According to the Court, these acts, pursuant to art. 5, letter c of Legislative Decree no. 251/2007, meet the requirements of persecution pursuant to art. 7 of Legislative Decree no. 251/2007, even if implemented by non-state authorities, if –as in this case– state authorities do not fight them or do not provide any protection, as they are the result of local customary rules. The ruling also refers, at the soft law level, to the UNHCR guidelines of 7 May 2002 on gender-based persecution, whose point no. 25 specifies that persecution occurs even when a woman is prevented from enjoying her rights because of the refusal to conform her behavior in accordance with traditional provisions relating to her gender. In another case concerning a Moroccan female citizen, victim of abuse and violence (which would go on even after the divorce) perpetrated by her husband, who had been punished by the Moroccan justice with a bland criminal sanction, the Cassation[27] (always by referring to articles 3 and 60 of the Istanbul Convention), albeit to the effects of subsidiary protection, links the acts of domestic violence to the issue of inhuman and degrading treatment, asking the judge to verify concretely whether, despite the threat of serious damage by a "non-state subject", pursuant to art. 5, lett. c of Legislative Decree no. 251/2007, the country of origin of the applicant is able to offer adequate protection.

There are also *persecutions and discrimination against people because of their sexual orientation, and at the same time because of religious reasons*. Persecutions for sexual orientation are connected to the fact of belonging to a specific social category, and they can also be considered as religious persecutions when there are religious motivations, too. The persecutor can link religion to homosexuality by using religion to legitimize the persecution and the discrimination or to define homosexuality as a sin, as an abomination or as a form of apostasy (Ferrari, 2018). There are frequent cases of persecution for sexual orientation in the Islamic world, as the social context is marked by values that are hostile to homosexuality, which can be punished with death penalty, with imprisonment, or with other discriminatory and persecutory acts.

---

27   Court of Cassation, Section 6-1, no. 12333/2017, Rv. 644272-01.

The Court of Catanzaro (ordinance of 2 July 2015) recognized the persecution of a Bengali citizen who was having a homosexual relationship and, for that reason, was denounced to the mullah, who issued a *fatwa* against him. He managed to escape, but then he was falsely accused of having caused a fire in a shop – which killed an entire family and for which he was sentenced to death. The same Court (ordinance of 7 December 2015) also recognized the persecution of a Ghanaian citizen who was having a relationship with his cousin and who later fled for fear of being killed by his father – an *imam* who had never accepted his homosexuality (Abu Salem, Fiorita, 2016).

4   The Religious Aspects in the Examination of Asylum Applications and in the Reception System

The religious affiliation of asylum seekers, which is essential for the recognition of one of the forms of protection provided by the legal system, however, appears to be scarcely relevant during the procedures for examining and deciding on applications, although every territorial commission for the recognition of the international protection has also been composed, since July 2018, of four experts on human rights, including religious rights, and gathers information on the situation of the countries of origin (also with reference to the religious rights) from specific databases managed by the National Commission for the right to asylum or by the European Asylum Support Office (EASO).

Every Commission, whenever necessary in order to examine the application, may consult experts on particular topics, such as health, culture, religion, gender and minors (art. 8, par. 3-bis of Legislative Decree 25/2008). Besides, during the personal interview with the commission, the applicant can request not to use the video recording (also for religious reasons) and the decision lies with the Commission, and not with the individual commissioner in charge of conducting the personal interview. The decision cannot be contested (art. 14 of Legislative Decree 25/2008).

Religion is hardly taken into consideration in the effective management of the reception system for asylum seekers and for people granted asylum. In centers where foreign nationals seeking asylum are detained (repatriation detention centers or first aid or reception centers or government reception centers) or in the preliminary reception centers where asylum seekers are initially hosted to be identified and to be allowed to submit the asylum application, applicants are granted the right to speak to ministers of worship (art. 7, par. 2, and 10, par. 3 of Legislative Decree no. 142/2015). In the detention centers for repatriation, the freedom to speak to other people within the center must be guaranteed, as it must be ensured the freedom to talk to visitors, such the ministers of worship, as well as the freedom of worship, within the limits set by the Constitution (art. 21, par. 1 and 2 of Presidential Decree 394/1999). It is not clear if this limit refers to the limit set in art. 19 of the Constitution (which concerns rites against public morality) or if it refers to some other limits (Consorti, 2011). Even inside the governmental centers for asylum seekers, specific spaces must be designated for various activities, including activities of worship (art. 9, par. 3 of Presidential Decree of 12 January 2015, no. 21). Finally, every project to create a reception service for asylum seekers, undertaken by Italian local authorities within the framework of the SPRAR (Protection System for Asylum Seekers and Refugees), for which the local authority asks for funding from the National Fund for Asylum Policies and Services, has to make sure that the people hosted are guaranteed food and the fulfillment of other needs by respecting their cultural and religious traditions (art. 31, par. 2 of the guidelines for the functioning of the protection system for asylum seekers and refugees, attached to the Ministerial Decree of 10 August 2016).

Even if the Legislative Decree no. 113/2018 has reformed the entire reception system, in art. 1, par. 9 of the new tender specifications scheme attached to the Ministerial Decree of December 2018 for the management of preliminary reception facilities, of extraordinary reception centers for asylum seekers activated by the Prefects, and of repatriation detention centers where asylum seekers can be held, it is reiterated that the organization of reception services is based on the full respect of the fundamental rights of the individuals, also in consideration of their religious faith. However, there are no specific details in order to explain the implementation of this principle in the various typologies of centers: first aid and reception centers, governmental preliminary reception centers, hotspots, temporary reception centers for repatriation, and extraordinary reception centers (the Italian CAS, which can be both collective centers and housing units).

Furthermore, the aforementioned norms fail to indicate which ministers of worship are actually allowed in the various centers – which partially limits the effectiveness of the norm, for whose implementation it will be necessary to resort to the unilateral provisions used for other forms of spiritual assistance, even if –so far– no norm inside the various agreements with the religious confessions has yet dealt with such topic (Carnì, 2015).

This gap remains intact for all types of reception centers for asylum seekers, who can freely satisfy any religious need outside, while it is apparently bridged for the repatriation centers, in which foreigners are detained and therefore their personal freedom is restricted, as they are supervised by the police and cannot leave without proper permission. The centers for repatriation have the same rules as the penitentiary institutes as to the indication of the subjects authorized to visit the centers, with particular reference, for example, to the ministers of Catholic worship and other cults, who can visit after being authorized by the director of the center.

The right to profess one's own religion is fundamental to respect the dignity of each individual and, in order to satisfy this need, the legal system has tried to grant religious assistance to all those whose personal freedom is restricted. As a result, the principle of secularity of the State, meant as the protection of each person's religious freedom, requires the State to guarantee the religious freedom of those who are deprived of the possibility of exercising it autonomously, so that the ministers of worship must be allowed into temporary detention centers, specific spaces to pray must be ensured, and other religiously motivated requests concerning food, clothing and the display of symbols must be accepted (Fiorita, 2007). In this regard, the regulation defining the "Criteria for the organization and management of the centers for identification and expulsion", issued by the Ministerial Decree of 20 October 2014, provides that in each CIE (now renamed as Temporary Reception Centres for Repatriation) recreational, social and religious activities must be organized in specific spaces and, to this end, the manager has to prepare a weekly calendar of the planned activities to be shared with all the foreigners living there.

However, the first inspections carried out in February-March 2018 by the national Guarantor of the rights of the detained persons and of those deprived of personal liberty in all the centers for repatriation have shown that, in every center, the rules mentioned above regarding the exercise of each person's religious freedom and the access of the ministers of worship appear to be substantially unobserved. The report issued by the Guarantor[28] is critical: all the centers visited had no space to be utilized as a place of worship (for example, the daily prayers of people of Islamic religion would take place in the corridors, while no space at all was guaranteed to the Christians) and the possibility of religious practice was severely limited because no minister of religion could visit. Therefore, the national Guarantor recommends that a program of activities should be outlined in full compliance with the CIE's single Regulation and, due to a serious lack of said recreational, social and religious activities, it invites the Ministry of the Interior to carry out a strict monitoring of the managing bodies' obligations derived by the contract regulating the supply of

---

28   Italian Guarantor of the rights of the detained persons and of those deprived of personal liberty, *Rapporto sulle visite tematiche effettuate nei centri di permanenza per il rimpatrio (CPR) in Italia* (February-March 2018), available at: http://www.garantenazionaleprivatiliberta.it/gnpl/resources/cms/documents/c30efc290216094f855c99bfb8644ce5.pdf.

the aforementioned activities.[29] However, it seems that only the Prefecture of Bari was willing to push the managing body to use specific spaces in the center of Bari as actual places of worship.[30]

Consequently, it seems that, in order to put security first, the needs connected to freedom and assistance, including the religious and the spiritual ones, are overshadowed: these needs are protected at the highest constitutional level, but nevertheless seem to be relegated to elements of form – which confirms that, in practice, guaranteeing public order turns out to be more important than protecting the inviolable rights (Consorti, 2011).

This notion is confirmed if two particular aspects are taken into account.

On the one hand, it is clear that there is an *underestimation of the religious dimension in the management of the reception centers for unaccompanied foreign minors*. In fact, the Guidelines to apply for financial aid for the National Fund for Asylum Policies and Services for the reception of unaccompanied foreign minors first demand that each center respect the cultural and religious traditions of the guests. Besides, in order to meet the cultural, linguistic and religious needs of minors, they demand the use of linguistic and cultural mediators in every service provided, so that they can bridge the gap between the two cultures, i.e. the one of the welcoming context and the one brought by the minors (Ministerial Decree of 27 April 2015, Annexes 2.1 and 2.5). However, article 18 of Legislative Decree no. 142/2015 does not specify if the exercise of religious freedom has to fall in the category represented by "the living conditions that must be guaranteed to each minor, with regard to the child's protection, welfare and development, including the social one", or that the child's previous religious habits must also be taken into consideration in the evaluation of the minor's best interest; it does not even specify that among the various needs of minors hosted in the reception centers there are also the religious ones. The needs connected to the effective exercise of religious freedom do not even seem to be precisely indicated in the list of fundamental rights of the minor. Moreover, no detail regarding the religious aspects of the child's life is expressly stated in the Ministerial Decree of 1 September 2016, which sets up the governmental preliminary reception centers destined to unaccompanied foreign minors. All this can cause unpredictable effects on how these minors (under

---

29   Italian Guarantor of the rights of the detained persons and of those deprived of personal liberty, *Norme e normalità. Standard per la privazione della libertà delle persone migranti. Raccolta delle Raccomandazioni 2016–2018*, p. 29, available at: http://www.garantenazionaleprivatiliberta.it/gnpl/resources/cms/documents/ef9c34b393cd0cb6960 fd724d590f062.pdf.

30   Italian Guarantor of the rights of the detained persons and of those deprived of personal liberty, *Report to the Italian Parliament 2019*, p. 195, available at: http://www.garantenazionale privatiliberta.it/gnpl/resources/cms/documents/00059ffe970d21856c9d52871fb31fe7.pdf.

the supervision of guardians and managers of the reception centers) relate to the different places of worship, the ministers of worship and the religious education at school and out of school. The constitutionally guaranteed religious freedom requires that, in the "best interests of the child", religious education must be taken into primary consideration, as well as the minor's linguistic needs and the minor's requests for changing or deepening the religious experience.

On the other hand, *an underestimation of the religious aspects in the reception of asylum seekers* is evident, both in everyone's life and in the overall management of each center. In fact, it must be remembered that all reception centers for asylum seekers must adopt appropriate measures to prevent all forms of violence, including gender-based violence, and to guarantee the safety and the protection of both the applicants and the staff working at the centers (art. 10 of Legislative Decree no. 142/2015). Besides, the reception measures take into account the specific situation of vulnerable persons, such as minors, unaccompanied minors, disabled persons, the elderly, pregnant women, single parents with minor children, victims of trafficking in human beings, persons suffering from serious illnesses or mental disorders, persons subjected to torture, rape or other serious forms of psychological, physical or sexual violence or violence linked to sexual orientation or gender identity, and victims of genital mutilation. In fact, people who have suffered torture, rape or other serious acts of violence are guaranteed appropriate medical and psychological assistance or treatment (art. 17, par. 1 and 8 of Legislative Decree no. 142/2015).

At the same time, seriously violent behaviors perpetrated by the hosted people legitimize the revocation of the reception measures (art. 23 of Legislative Decree no. 142/2015). These rules explain why the religious belonging of the guests of the reception centers for asylum seekers always seems to be taken into consideration, in order to prevent any danger to the safety of both the guests and the staff deriving from possible interreligious tensions. These dangers (which are concrete, as they can also be observed in other EU countries welcoming asylum seekers) can affect the lives of the asylum seekers who have fled the persecutions or the religious discrimination occurring in their country of origin. Of course, it could turn out to be potentially dangerous for them to find themselves living in a reception center alongside other foreign guests belonging to a hostile religious confession. The possibility of episodes of intolerance and violence, in these circumstances, could increase and endanger the safety of all the guests at the reception centers.

Moreover, in the projects aimed to build SPRAR centers that have been approved so far, there has been no analysis of the religious aspect, except for the administration of food (in order to respect the dictates required by the different religions) and for the designation of mediators to partially fulfill the need for a cultural and religious integration.

Nevertheless, some calls for tenders for the management of extraordinary reception centers for asylum seekers require that guests be allocated by taking into account their religious affiliation in order to prevent any tension between guests belonging to different religious denominations. For example, in the attachment to the Public notice of call for tenders of the Syracuse Prefecture of 14 January 2016, it is indicated that "the Prefecture maintain the power to manage the reception in the structures of the chosen subjects according to criteria meeting the needs of protection of the dignity, the safety and the physical integrity of the applicants, especially if vulnerable, as well as any need to safeguard public safety. For instance, the same structure will not include at the same time the following: a) guests of different ethnicities or of different religions that are in conflict or in a strong state of tension". This means that, instead of providing guidelines for the management of conflicts that could hypothetically arise within the structure, the Prefecture makes a prognostic judgment, with the aim of preventing possible critical issues.

The failure in preventing difficulties concerning the interreligious coexistence in the reception facilities for asylum seekers appears to be a serious contradiction with reference both to the effectiveness of the protection of religious freedom, and to the safeguard of right of asylum – as these people flee from countries where they cannot exercise their freedom. As a result, the formal recognition of the foreigner's religious freedom is ineffective if it is not ensured even in the person's daily life.

5   The Constitutional Aspects of the Religious Dimension of Foreign Nationals in Italy

Since religious freedom belongs to anyone who lives in Italy independently of their citizenship, it is very important to examine the discipline of the religious dimension of everyone's life, which can also be applied to the foreigners who have been forced to migrate to Italy.

In fact, the religious freedom guaranteed by the Constitution is associated with an equal social dignity and with the equality of each person before the law, without any discrimination based on religion (art. 3 of the Constitution). This has two meanings:

1)   Primacy of the laws in force in the Italian Republic, which everyone must observe, as prescribed by art. 54 of the Constitution, without considering oneself as exempt from the need to observe the norms of one's own

religion. Any conflicts with other religions can be prevented by the rules adopted pursuant to articles 7 and 8 of the Constitution, which regulate the relations between the State and each religious denomination in a specific and differentiated way. This makes it possible to temper the observance of state norms to the religious norms;

2)   Public authorities are prohibited from provide for and implement differential treatment on the basis of religion, unless it is expressly provided for in the Lateran Pacts with the Catholic Church or in the agreements stipulated with other religious denominations (see below).

Therefore, in Italy, any norm contrasting with this fundamental principle of non-religious discrimination is not applicable. Thus, as a result of the prohibition provided by art. 16 of law 31 May 1995, no. 218, norms of foreign legal systems cannot be applied if they cause discrimination based on a particular religious affiliation or a non-religious affiliation – this is the case, for example, of some laws in force in States whose legal order is based on the Islamic Shari'a.

The prohibition of religious discrimination does not mean that every religious confession and that every believer has the right to obtain the same treatments guaranteed to other religions, but it means that every person has the right not to suffer any discrimination based on religious affiliation, on the change of religion, or on atheism. Moreover, art. 3 of the Constitution does not prevent the legislator from introducing reasonably different treatments to regulate "not substantially identical" situations. Besides, in compliance with the "supreme principles of the constitutional order", some norms can be waived by other particular norms which have constitutional coverage – for example, those established by the Concordat with the Catholic Church (referred to in art. 7 of the Constitution) and those found in the agreements with non-Catholic confessions (which are mentioned in art. 8 of the Constitution).

In art. 3 of the Constitution, the prohibition of discrimination is connected to the principle of formal equality and is accompanied by positive obligations for the public authorities, which have to remove the obstacles which constrain equality and freedom. Consequently, the Italian legal system provides for rules that prevent and contrast discriminatory practices implemented both in the relations with public authorities and in the relations between people.

Firstly, incitement to hatred or discrimination for religious reasons are crimes, also because of the international obligations in force in Italy following the ratification of the International Convention on the Elimination of all Forms of Racial Discrimination, adopted by the UN General Assembly on 25 December 1966, which prescribes as punishable under criminal law the dissemination of ideas based on racial hatred, the incitement to commit violence for racial reasons and the participation in associations whose purpose is the incitement to discrimination or violence on racial grounds. By implementing these international standards, Decree Law 26 April 1993, no. 122, converted, with modifications, by law 25 June 1993, no. 205, introduced criminal norms punishing propaganda and instigation to commit crimes on grounds of racial, ethnic and religious discrimination. Said norms ended up in 2018 into art. 604-bis of the Italian Penal Code. Furthermore, any organization, association, movement or group having as its purpose the incitement to discrimination or to violence for racial, ethnic, national or religious reasons is prohibited.

Secondly, many laws provide for measures to prevent and combat discrimination, including any discrimination for religious reasons carried out in the relations between private individuals. In particular, the Consolidated act of provisions concerning immigration (Legislative Decree of 25 July 1998, no. 286) defines the behaviors that constitute discrimination, also for religious reasons. Article 43 defines as discriminatory "any behavior which, directly or indirectly, entails a distinction, exclusion, restriction or preference based on race, color, national or ethnic ancestry, religious beliefs and practices, and that has the purpose or the effect to destroy or compromise the recognition, the benefit or the exercise, in conditions of equality, of human rights and fundamental freedoms in political, economic, social and cultural fields and in any other sector of public life". Article 43 also provides that, in any case, an act of discrimination is carried out by "anyone who illegitimately imposes more disadvantageous conditions or refuses to provide access to employment, housing, education, training and social services and social assistance to the foreigner legally residing in Italy only because of the status of foreigner or because belonging to a specific race, religion, ethnicity or nationality". Article 44 gives those who consider themselves as victims of discrimination perpetrated by a private individual or by a public administration for religious or ethnic reasons, the right to appeal to the judge to stop the prejudicial behavior.

Finally, the same Legislative Decree, with the aim to prevent and combat discrimination, provides that the Italian Regions, in collaboration with the Provinces and each Municipality, and with the associations of immigrants and social volunteers, set up information and legal assistance centers for foreigners who are the victims of discrimination on racial, ethnic, national or religious grounds. In implementing the law, the national fund for migration policies also finances annual and multi-year programs prepared by the Regions for carrying out activities aimed at preventing and removing all forms of discrimination.

Nevertheless, the national Office for the promotion of equal treatment and the removal of discrimination based on race or ethnic origin (UNAR), in its 2015 report observed an increase in the cases of discrimination on grounds of religion. In the following report, it is noted that the reports of discrimination based on "religion or personal opinions" have increased compared to 2015 and that the subtype that mainly originated discriminatory behavior is Islamophobia (5.3%), which consists of "an exaggerated fear, hatred and hostility towards Islam and Muslims, as well as of negative stereotypes that lead to prejudice, discrimination, marginalization and exclusion of Muslims from social, political and civil life". The distinction with other subtypes, such as anti-Semitism (1.1%) and Christianophobia (0.2%), shows a growth in the phenomenon of discrimination against people of Islamic religion or perceived as such. The 2017 report counts 354 cases of discrimination based on religion and personal opinion, and that the highest number of discriminatory behaviors are due to Islamophobia (74.3% of the typology), followed by anti-Semitism (18.9%).

In any case, since the principle of equality before the law without distinctions of religion also means that no one can escape the application of the law on the basis of their religious affiliation, no one can also avoid complying with the criminal law or believe that they can be acquitted of any crime only because their actions or omissions are based on real or alleged precepts of one's own religion.

In fact, no one can claim as an excuse the ignorance of the criminal law (art. 5 of the Italian Penal Code), except in the case of unavoidable ignorance – which, according to the jurisprudence, does not apply for the crimes committed for religious reasons, and therefore the religious factor does not have sufficient relevance with regard to non-liability to punishment.

The Court of Cassation was called upon to assess how relevant the fact of belonging to the Islamic religion was in ascertaining whether all the constituent elements of the crime of family abuse were present. The Court,[31] after having linked the issue to the *cultural offense* phenomenon (which is characterized by the conflict between the precepts of culture, of tradition and –at least in the Islamic world– of the law of a particular country, and of those of the host country) notes that, with respect to this conflict, there are two opposing perspectives. The first is the *assimilationist* one, based on the need for foreign nationals to be incorporated in the legal system of the country of arrival, after having renounced their own ethnic and cultural roots. The other is the *integrationist* one, oriented towards the preservation of identities, as it is based on the recognition of the coexistence of different cultures as a positive value. In most jurisdictions, such conflict is solved by making both perspectives coexist. In the Italian legal system, alongside the aggravating circumstance envisaged by art. 3, par. 1 of Legislative Decree no. 122/1993 for crimes characterized by

---

31   Court of Cassation, sentence of 26 November 2008, no. 46300, with a note by F. Pavesi in
       Giur.it, 2010, 2, p. 416.

ethnic, national, racial or religious discrimination and hatred, inspired by the "integrationist" perspective, there are crimes that punish female genital mutilation (art. 583 bis of the Penal Code) and bigamy (art. 556 of the Penal Code), which can be considered as expressions of the "assimilationist" logic.

The Court continues by observing that, even for cultural or culturally-oriented crimes, the judge has the duty to simultaneously guarantee the protection of the victims (it is irrelevant whether they consent or not to the infringement of their inalienable rights[32]), the respect of the right of the accused to a rigorous verification of the facts and a correct application of the rules, and the delivering of an appropriate verdict for each case. This is because the role of cultural mediator that the doctrine attributes to the criminal judge has to be fulfilled by respecting the rules. In particular, the "integrationist" logic finds a limitation in the respect of the main principles of interpersonal relationships – i.e. in the protection of the fundamental and inviolable rights of the person, as imposed by art. 2 and 3 of the Constitution. On the basis of these premises, the Court of Cassation affirmed that the subjective element of the crime of family abuse could not be ruled out by the circumstance that the offender was of Islamic religion and therefore he would claim a particular power as the "head" of the family unit, because such concepts are in absolute contrast with fundamental rules of the Italian legal system.

These considerations have been even more relevant with reference to the issue of *what to wear*. In this regard, it should be remembered that in personal freedom and in religious freedom, the freedom to decide what to wear is implicit. It can be limited only by law and only when the type of clothing worn or not worn turns out to be against morality, i.e. against the common sense of decency (public indecency), or when clothes make the identity of a person unrecognizable, or when objects that can offend or even weapons are worn as clothing. With regard to the clothes worn by foreigners for religious reasons, the legal questions concerning the Islamic veil and the *Sikh kirpan* are still not resolved peacefully in the absence of an agreement between the State and the two religious denominations.

In the Italian legal system, the *Islamic female veil* does not raise any particular problems if it leaves the face uncovered, since every situation in which the woman (Italian or foreign) receives a different treatment only because she wears an Islamic veil is illegal and punishable with an anti-discrimination action. However, the discrimination against women wearing a veil is considered to be legitimate when hiring at a workplace for which not to wear the veil is a

---

32   Court of Cassation, criminal section, 20 October 1999, no. 3398.

determinant requirement,[33] as stated prior to the preliminary selection for employment, or when employers want to connote their business, directly working with the public, in the most neutral way with respect to religion (a question resolved by the European Court of Human Rights by affirming the legitimacy and the reasonableness of this apparent discrimination).

Instead, the use of a full veil preventing the face from being seen (thus not allowing the identification of the person) can be considered as an offence, since it violates the prohibition to use any means to hinder the recognition of the person in a public place, when it happens with no good reason and during events taking place in a public place – an exception is made for sporting events where such use is necessary (art. 5 of law no. 152/1975). Said violation is punishable as a criminal offence not only in cases of willful misconduct, but also for negligence, and it can lead to imprisonment from one to two years or to a fine from 1,000 to 2,000 euros.

The use of the Islamic veil can also be considered as a violation of the prohibition to appear masked in a public place, provided by art. 85 of the Consolidated act of provisions on Public Security and punished with an administrative sanction.

Nonetheless, the jurisprudence rightfully applies such sanctions in a restrictive way. That is both when the veil is temporarily removed for identification purposes and when the not punishable conduct may be carried out to fulfill a religious prescription (even if the Koranic prescription for women is a mere suggestion and does not require a complete obscuration of the face). As said behavior is displayed in order to exercise the constitutional right to freely profess one's religion, it is not sanctioned, as the Penal Code excludes any punishment for those who have committed a crime with the aim to exercise a right.

On the contrary, the administrative and jurisprudential orientation prohibiting the full veil is more severe. Several mayors have taken specific measures, including contingent and urgent ones, to prevent and eliminate serious dangers threatening public safety and urban security (as permitted by art. 54 of Legislative Decree no. 267/2000), which have prohibited the use of the veil (Caravaggion, 2016). In this regard, the Council of State –by rejecting the appeal that had been lodged against a prefectural provision which had quashed an ordinance, issued by a Mayor, that had forbidden the wearing of the veil in a public place– stated that the use of the veil covering the face (the *burqa*, but especially the *ḥiǧāb*) is not generally aimed at avoiding recognition, as it

---

33   See Court of Appeal of Milan, labour section, sentence of 20 May 2016, no. 579, commented in L. Pedullà, *L'abbigliamento religioso tra identità e compatibilità ordinamentale*, in *Federalismi.it*, no. 24, 2016.

constitutes the implementation of a tradition of certain peoples and cultures. Consequently, the judge does not have to make value judgments on the mere use of such symbols, but just has to verify whether the veil is worn to prevent recognition without any justifiable reason. Article 5 of law no. 152/1975, observes the Council of State,[34] allows that "a person wear the veil for religious or cultural reasons, as public safety is ensured by the obligation for such person to remove the veil, if necessary, to be identified", at the request of an authorized public official. Even criminal judges have always acquitted women who had promptly lifted the veil to allow their identification before entering a courtroom.[35] On the other hand, the resolution no. x/4553 of 10 December 2015 adopted by the Lombardy Regional Council, which prohibited people with covered faces to enter the main regional buildings, was considered as lawful, as it specified that religious traditions could not represent a valid reason to justify exceptions, pursuant to art. 5 of law no. 152/1975 relating to safety inside the regional buildings. The Court of Milan, in fact, considered the measure to be non-discriminatory because the disadvantage for Muslim women was strictly necessary to ensure identification with public security purposes, which are objectively justified and legitimate.

The ruling of the Court of Milan was criticized by the doctrine, according to which the above-mentioned regional provision does not cause a mere disadvantage but, rather, a serious limitation to some constitutional rights. In fact, since hospitals are regional facilities, as well as the headquarters of the Lombardy public housing agency, a Muslim woman who is wearing the veil finds herself forced to choose between two distinct constitutionally-guaranteed fundamental rights, i.e. religious freedom and the rights to health, assistance and housing (Caravaggion, 2018).

Even the carrying of the *kirpan* (the ceremonial dagger of the Sikhs) seems to be forbidden, since it infringes the prohibition (provided by art. 4 of law no. 110/1975) to carry, without any justifiable reason, certain types of knifes perceived as offensive weapons. Besides, this issue has been dealt with in different ways, over time – as the jurisprudence shows.

The judges would initially have dismissed such cases, as the Sikhs could use, as a justifiable reason, the right to freely profess their faith. Later on, instead, the Court of Cassation declared the illegitimacy of this conduct, believing that

---

34 Council of State, Section VI, sentence of 19 June 2008, no. 3076.
35 See Court of Treviso, Office of the Preliminary investigations judge, ordinance of 3 March 2005 and Court of Cremona, sentence of 27 November 2008, on which see G.L. Gatta, *Islam, abbigliamento religioso, diritto e processo penale: brevi note a margine di due casi giurisprudenziali*, in *Stato, Chiese e pluralismo confessionale*, June 2009, pag. 3 et seq.

religious practices should respect the fundamental principles of the Italian legal system, indicated in art. 8 of the Constitution, which includes the protection of people's safety and security ensured by the legislation regulating the use of weapons, and the jurisprudence of the European Court of Human Rights concerning the discretion of the employer to not hire people carrying weapons. The doctrine criticizes these decisions by observing that the limitation within which the fundamental principles of art. 8 of the Constitution can be exercised concerns the internal organization of the various religious confessions – and not the individuals' right to exercise their own freedom of religion, which is limited by art. 19 of the Constitution only in the case of rituals against public morality. Besides, the employer's discretion could lead to paradoxical consequences, as gardeners (for example) could actually carry the *kirpan* to work, without no intention of showing it in public (*ibidem*).

6   The State's Relations with the Various Religious Denominations

The Italian Constitution guarantees the freedom of religion not only in its individual dimension, but also in its collective expression through a diversified system of relations between the State and the various religious denominations, in a context of state secularism.

First of all, it is important to note that the Constitution uses the notion of *religious denomination*, but does not indicate its constituent elements. The issue is essential when it comes to minority religious groups, new groups, groups that are not very well known or that are even secret – and which, because of those characteristics, are sometimes discriminated and persecuted. This is significant also with regard to the religious denominations professed by foreigners forced to leave their own country because of their belonging to sects or to local or new animistic groups. In this regard, doctrine is divided: some demand that every denomination have a normative and organizational structure similar to that of the Catholic Church or other "traditional" Churches (Gismondi, 1975; D'Avack, 1978), while others refer to the autonomous decision of each group to qualify as a religious denomination (Randazzo, 2006).

The Constitutional Court, however, clearly excludes "the unreasonable results of an uncontrollable self-qualification"[36] and believes that the confessional nature of a community of faithful can derive from many factors. Some of them are the following: the possible presence of an agreement stipulated with the State, pursuant to art. 8 of the Constitution; previous public recognition,

---

36   Constitutional Court, sentence no. 467/1992.

such as the attribution of legal personality to a representative body (on the basis of the law on "accepted cults" of 1929); a statute that clearly expresses its main features; or even the common consideration.[37] Moreover, in the absence of an agreement with the State, the criteria indicated by the Court, as part of the doctrine believes (Randazzo, 2006), should be considered as a whole, and not as an alternative. This is to avoid putting self-reference first (through the statutory element) or even the State's point of view (through previous public recognition) or, finally, the sociological aspect (through the common consideration element). In particular, the sociological criterion of the "common consideration", suggested by a part of the doctrine (Barillaro, 1968), is difficult to observe when it comes to both new religious movements (whose distinctive features are not yet known by public opinion) and other religious movements that are present in other countries (even though as a minority) and have been brought to Italy by persecuted foreigner nationals.

The self-definition of the religious group must be in line not only with its external characteristics, but also with the *animus* of its members, i.e. with their willingness to act as an autonomous formation in the pursuit of a religious purpose (Colaianni, 1990). In fact, people who gather under the same religious denomination do so because they embrace a creed that is different from any other – thus organizing themselves within a distinct structure (Long, 1991). They, in fact, have their own specific view of the world, as well as of the relationship with the transcendent – both sustained by an autonomous doctrinal and dogmatic knowledge and by a special organization (which can be minimal, at times, but nevertheless characterized by an independent consistency and a precise identity) (Finocchiaro, 1975; Cardia, 1983; Mirabelli, 2006). However fundamental, the State's evaluation appears to be quite difficult to ascertain. Indeed, it cannot only "acknowledge" the situation, nor can it cast doubts on that doctrinal knowledge (as the Council of State pointed out in opinions relating to the recognition of the legal personality of the Italian Congregation of Jehovah's Witnesses and of the Italian Buddhist Union). Rather, it has to judge the *animus* of the community by examining the purposes pursued and the organizational structure that has been built (Botta, 1994).

Moreover, the established doctrine accepts the notion according to which a religious denomination is characterized by a community united around the elements of crystallization, development and expression of faith. It differs from other social formations because of its collective identity, anchored in an attitude towards a transcendent dimension (Colaianni, 2000).

---

37   Constitutional Court, sentence no. 195/1993.

This being clarified, the first constitutional principle concerning the discipline of the public dimension of religions is the *distinction between the juridical order of the State and the spiritual and religious order of religious denominations*. This principle is derived from both art. 7 of the Constitution, which provides that the State and the Catholic Church are independent and sovereign, each within its own sphere; and from art. 8, which provides that religious denominations other than Catholicism have the right to self-organization according to their own statutes, provided these do not conflict with Italian law.

That principle of distinction between orders has two consequences:

a)   the religious, spiritual and doctrinal area, as well as the internal organization of every religious denomination (statutes, indication of religious authorities, management of places of worship, religious activity, and administrative, financial and territorial set of rules) belong only to the religious groups. Public authorities, in fact, have no power of interference, nor can they use the law to impose to the different religious denominations the timing and the methods to adopt their internal rules or even their contents. Public authorities only have to acknowledge the choices freely adopted by every religious denomination;

b)   the fundamental principles of the Italian legal system must be respected by all religious denominations, which cannot wish to directly influence the republican legal system itself, nor make their rules prevail over state norms.

The second relevant constitutional principle in the relations between the Italian State and the various religious denominations is the equally important freedom of each religious confession, as provided by art. 8 of the Constitution. It does not mean that all confessions are subjected to the same juridical discipline, but rather that their members can freely profess their beliefs and carry out the respective activities with no limitations other than those provided for by the Constitution and by the laws (Del Giudice, 1964).

As for the theme of religion, religious affiliation is of essence, considering that any kind of discrimination based only on the number of members is "unacceptable"[38] as it is the "intensity"[39] of the social reactions that may follow the violation of the rights of the different groups. Since every religious denomination must receive the same juridical treatment, a differentiated treatment is legitimate only if connected to the different needs or organizational peculiarities of a confession and does not derive from a purely discretionary choice of the State.

---

38   Constitutional Court, sentence no. 440/1995.
39   Constitutional Court, sentence no. 329/1997 and no. 508/2000.

The third relevant constitutional principle in the relations between the Italian State and the religious denominations is that of *bilateralism*. The Italian Constitution provides, in fact, for differentiated regimes in the relations between the State and the Catholic Church, and between the State and any other religious denomination, governed by special bilateral agreements.

On the one hand, the relations with the Catholic Church, recognized as independent and sovereign in its order, are regulated by the Lateran Pacts stipulated in 1929, whose amendment agreed by both parties does not require any constitutional revision (art. 7 of the Constitution). Unilateral amendments by the State are allowed, but bilateral ones are preferred. Thus, the agreement revising the Lateran Concordat (signed on 18 February 1984 and approved by law 25 March 1985 no. 121) adapted the rules of the Concordat between State and Church to the republican constitutional system by establishing framework norms on the basis of which other agreements were later concluded. Such agreements focused on the subject of ecclesiastical goods, support of the Catholic clergy, teaching of religion in schools (see also Chapter 21), religious festivities, management of cultural heritage, and ecclesiastical appointments.

However, the relations of the State with any other religious denomination can be regulated by specific agreements that must be approved by law. Today, there are specific laws approving agreements between the Italian State and 12 religious denominations other than the Catholic one. They are the following:

a) the agreement with the *Waldensian Church* and the subsequent amending agreements (signed on 21 February 1984, 25 January 1993 and 4 April 2007 and respectively approved by law no. 449/1994, no. 409/1993 and no. 68/2009);

b) the agreement with the *Union of the Seventh-day Adventist Christian Churches* and the subsequent amending agreements (signed on 29 December 1986, 6 November 1996 and 4 April 2007 and respectively approved with law no. 516/1988, no. 637/1996 and no. 67/2009);

c) the agreement with the *Assemblies of God in Italy* (signed on 29 December 1986 and approved by law no. 517/1988);

d) the agreement with the *Union of Italian Jewish Communities* and the subsequent modification (signed on 27 February 1987 and 6 November 1996 and respectively approved by law no. 101/1989 and no. 638/1996);

e) the agreement with the *Christian Baptist Evangelical Union of Italy* and the subsequent modification (signed on 29 March 1993 and on 16 July 2010 and approved respectively by law no. 116/1995 and no. 34/2012);

f) agreement with the *Lutheran Evangelical Church in Italy* (signed on 20 April 1993 and approved by law no. 520/1995);

g) agreement with the *Sacred Orthodox Archdiocese of Italy* and *Exarchate for Southern Europe* (signed on 4 April 2007 and approved by law no. 126/2012);

h) the agreement with the *Church of Jesus Christ of Latter-day Saints* (signed on 4 April 2007 and approved by law no. 127/2012);

i) the agreement with the *Apostolic Church in Italy* (signed on 4 April 2007 and approved by law no. 128/2012);

j) the agreement with the *Italian Buddhist Union* (signed on 4 April 2007 and approved by law no. 245/2012);

k) the agreement with the *Italian Hindu Union* (signed on 4 April 2007 and approved by law no. 246/2012);

l) the agreement with the *Italian Soka Gakkai Buddhist Institute* (signed on 27 June 2015 and approved by law no. 130/2016).

The agreements reached so far have similar contents, including rules concerning:

a) the spiritual assistance in institutions such as the armed forces, health facilities, and prisons;

b) the right of pupils not to attend Catholic religion classes;

c) the recognition of diplomas conferred by institutes of theological studies;

d) the right to freely establish schools of all levels and other educational institutions (guaranteed also by art. 33 of the Constitution);

e) the recognition of the civil effects to marriages celebrated by the ministers of worship of the respective religious denominations;

f) the tax treatment of the various religious denominations and their financial relations with the State, on the model outlined for the Catholic Church by law 20 May 1985, no. 222;

g) the protection of religious buildings and of assets pertaining to the historical and cultural heritage of each religious denomination, as a guarantee of their own cultural identities;

h) the free exercise of one's own ministry by the ministers of worship appointed by the religious denomination;

i) the recognition of the festivities of each religious denomination.

The agreements that have been stipulated so far offer to the other religious denominations similar guarantees and freedoms as the ones conferred to the Catholic Church by the current Concordat of 1984. They concern, for example, the management of the religious denomination, the religious group's full right of internal jurisdiction and regulation, the freedom of communication, as well as the right to provide religious assistance in particular institutions, such as military bases, hospitals and prisons. Besides, they guarantee certain rights only to the faithful of certain communities: in particular, the right of Adventists and Jews to sabbatical rest, the right of the Jews to respect specific food prescriptions, and the right of Adventists and Buddhists to conscientious objection to military obligations.

The text of an agreement with the *Christian Congregation of Jehovah's Witnesses in Italy* was signed twice (on 20 March 2000 and on 4 April 2007), but it was never approved by the two Houses of Parliament, also because in the parliamentary scrutiny some precepts of that religious group were considered to be against some fundamental principles of the Italian legal system. In fact, the draft law for the approval of the new agreement signed in 2014 was finally never presented to the Chambers.

The draft law approving the agreement with the *Church of England* association (mainly representing the Anglicans) signed on 30 July 2019 has not yet been presented to the Parliament by the Government. Negotiations have also begun for the agreement with the *Romanian Orthodox Diocese of Italy*.

As for the agreement with the *Islamic religious group*, proposals of agreement formulated by various Italian Muslim bodies have so far not led to the start of negotiations with the Italian Government, mainly because of the lack of a unified representation of the Islamic denomination and of a legally approved internal statute. In order to promote a process aimed at filling these gaps, since 2008, the Ministers of the Interior have set up study advisory bodies, also composed of representatives of various Italian Islamic organizations and of Muslim experts.

The negotiation of an agreement with the Sikhs appears to be hindered by two opinions of the Council of State, according to which this religious group has rules that contrast with some fundamental principles of the Italian legal system.

Furthermore, the Constitutional Court has clarified that the agreements do not grant additional privileges to the religious denominations that have concluded them, nor do they prevent the religious groups that have not yet stipulated them from exercising their religious freedom. In fact, since the attitude of the State can only be of equality and impartiality towards all religious groups,[40] these agreements regulate the relations of the various religious denominations with the State as for some specific aspects concerning the individual groups or when exceptions to the ordinary law are needed. Public authorities, in fact, cannot impose such agreements to the different religious groups in order to benefit of the freedom of organization and action guaranteed by the

---

40   Constitutional Court, sentence no. 508/2000.

Constitution, nor to make them take advantage of the favorable norms regarding religious denominations.[41]

Therefore, the State can regulate, in a bilateral and differentiated way, its relations with each religious denomination, as provided for by art. 7 and 8 of the Constitution, in order to fulfill specific needs, to grant particular advantages or impose particular limitations, or to give relevance, in its legal system, to specific acts of the religious denomination in consideration. Consequently, it would be a violation of the constitutional principle of the equality of freedom to grant advantages to one religious group if not connected to its specific needs (Onida, 1978).

In any case, state and regional laws cannot "discriminate between religious denominations on the basis of the sole circumstance that they have, or have not, regulated their relations with the State through agreements". Indeed, "religious freedom is one thing, and is guaranteed to everyone without any distinction, while agreements are another",[42] so that the freedom of religion –of which the freedom of worship is an essential part (art. 19 and 20 of the Constitution)– cannot be subordinated to the stipulation of agreements with the State.[43]

7   Religious Freedom with Reference to Family, Education of Minors, Religious Assistance in Prisons

Numerous practical issues linked to the cohabitation of different religions concern religious aspects that have affected the legal status of foreigners and of asylum seekers. Some issues relate to family formation and to the *celebration of marriage*. First of all, it must be remembered that religious freedom (art. 19 of the Constitution), the prohibition of discrimination based on religion and gender (art. 3 of the Constitution), the juridical and moral equality of spouses (art. 29 of the Constitution), the right and the duty of both parents to educate their children (art. 30 of the Constitution) are fundamental principles of the Italian legal system. Said principles are incompatible with any rule, in force in other States, preventing the marriage –or imposing the dissolution of a marriage– when the partners have different religion, or one of them refuses to convert to a particular religion, or providing a preferential legal treatment to one spouse (e.g. possibility of polygamous marriage, dissolution of marriage

---

41   Constitutional Court, sentence no. 346/2002.
42   See Constitutional Court, sentence no. 63/2016, with reference to sentence no. 52/2016.
43   See Constitutional Court, sentence no. 52/2016 and no. 63/2016.

with unilateral repudiation, exclusive custody of children or exclusive possession of the assets of the other spouse). These rules are against public order, i.e. against the fundamental principles of the Italian legal system, and are therefore inapplicable by the Italian judge –pursuant to art. 16 of law no. 218/1995– who has to apply the Italian regulations and not the ones in force in the country of origin.

Moreover, laws on marriage in force in another State have an indirect effect on the Italian legal system as for the impediments to the celebration of marriage. According to art. 116 of the Italian Civil Code, foreigners who want to celebrate their marriage in Italy must possess the permit issued by the competent authority of their country – thus showing that there are no impediments to the celebration of the marriage, according to the law in force in the country of which the foreigner is a national. This obligation causes at least two potentially prejudicial effects on the right of every person to form his own family. People affected by this are the following:

a) The ones who are seeking asylum or have been persecuted cannot obtain this certification from the diplomatic-consular representatives of the State from which they have escaped, also because they would jeopardize the credibility of their application for international protection. According to art. 25 of the 1951 Convention on the status of refugees, this impossibility can be compensated by the Italian diplomatic representation in the foreigner's State, but also –in Italy– by the United Nations High Commissioner for Refugees.[44]

b) Asylum seekers, holders of subsidiary protection, all those who would never obtain the permit – i.e. people who do not have any identification documents, or fear being identified and persecuted, or must obey to a foreign law establishing, as impediment to marriage, the belonging to a specific religious denomination or conviction for crimes linked to the violation of religious norms, the conversion to another religion, and the expression of religious criticism or atheist convictions. For these people, it is possible to appeal to a faculty envisaged by art. 98 of the Italian Civil Code: the Court, at the request of the two people who want to get married and who declare, in compliance the Italian law, that there are no impediments, can lift them from the mandatory marriage publications.

Another topic concerns the *right to educate one's children according to the dictates of one's religion.*

---

44   See the forms provided by the offices of the UNHCR in Italy to obtain the documentation replacing the marriage permit: https://www.unhcr.it/wp-content/uploads/2018/11/Scheda-NO-new-.pdf.

In respect of people's personal and religious freedom and of minors' right to health, the above-mentioned right to education is guaranteed by international standards and by the freedom of religion (art. 19 of the Constitution), by the parents' right to educate their children (art. 30 of the Constitution) and by the right to build private schools (art. 33 of the Constitution). The implementation of these rights is ensured both by the rules governing relations between the State and the various religious denominations and by the rules on school equality (see Chapter 21). In particular, art. 1 of law no. 62/2000 provides for a balance between religious needs and constitutional principles: "Private schools are guaranteed full freedom with regard to their cultural orientation and their pedagogical-didactic direction. Independently of the specific educational project of the single schools, teaching has to be based on the principles of freedom established by the Constitution. Private schools carry out a public service, as they welcome everyone who accepts their educational project, including pupils and students with disabilities. The educational project of the school has a precise cultural or religious view. However, extra-curricular activities that require the adherence to a specific ideology or to a specific religious denomination are not compulsory for any student".

As far as religious and family matters are concerned, the contrast between foreign laws and the fundamental principles of the Italian legal system has manifested itself also in relation to other themes, relevant for the life of all foreigners in Italy, including asylum seekers, i.e. the care of children and the dissolution of marriage.

With reference to the *responsibility of the parents*, the Court of Cassation[45] stated that, in deciding on the custody of children in case of separation of the parents, the Italian judge cannot apply the Iranian law (national law of the father), which allows the father to gain the exclusive custody of the children, since such law is inapplicable in the Italian system, due to the aforementioned limit represented by public order. This criterion is different from that set by art. 155, par. 1 of the Italian Civil Code, by virtue of which decisions relating to children must be adopted with exclusive reference to the moral and material interest of the minors. Independently of the actual ability of the parent to take care of one's offspring, the Iranian law clearly contrasts with the gender discrimination prohibition (art. 3 and 29 of the Constitution) and with the principle of secularism – which does not allow to use the religious belief of the parents as a criterion for choosing the foster parent.

As for *the foreigners' right to family unity*, the Court of Cassation has stated that the foreign parent can request the reunification with his/her dependent

---

45   Court of Cassation, civil section, 27 February 1985, no. 1714.

children (according to art. 29 of Legislative Decree no. 286/1998) if he/she is able to financially support them. However, in doing so, said parent does not also gain the –exclusive or concurrent– parental responsibility of minors. On this topic, it is worth mentioning a case relating to a Moroccan citizen who was repudiated by her husband in accordance with the Moroccan law and was denied the legal protection of her children, as requested by her husband. Under such circumstances, she could ask for reunification with her children only on condition that she provided them with a suitable accommodation in the Italian territory and that she earned a sufficient income to satisfy this requirement.

Every foreign minor in Italy is subject to compulsory schooling under the same conditions as Italian citizens (art. 38 of Legislative Decree no. 286/1998). Thus, another issue concerning the religious education of foreigners, including asylum seekers, is that of *religious education in public schools*.

Art. 9 of the 1984 Amendment Agreement of the Concordat between the State and the Holy See, affirms that the State, "recognizing the value of religious culture and considering that the principles of Catholicism are part of the historical heritage of the Italian people, continues to ensure, within the framework of school aims, the teaching of the Catholic religion in educational institutions of all types and at all levels". However, it leaves it up to either the students –if aged 14 or over– or their parents to decide whether to attend such classes. Therefore, the teaching of Catholic religion in public schools involves a faculty that the parents (or the students who are 14 years old or older) express at the beginning of the school year. And that even if the teachers of Catholic religion are paid by the State and their grading is an integral part of the student's overall scholastic evaluation. Besides, alternative educational activities must be provided for those who do not attend those classes. The Constitutional Court has specified that it is no "obligation" and that, for this reason, the school workload cannot increase for those who choose not to participate. In fact, alternative activities cannot be made compulsory – otherwise, a primary subjective right is violated, thus causing a compensable damage.[46] Besides, class schedule must be organized in such a way as to avoid any discrimination, even if said class does not necessarily have to be placed in the first or in the last hour of the school day, since the characteristic of non-obligation may also include the choice to leave the school during that hour.[47]

In addition, as stated in the agreements with the religious denominations other than the Catholic one, each religious group has the right to respond to any requests made by the students, their families and the schools, as far as the

---

46   Court of Cassation, united civil section, no. 11432/1997.

47   Constitutional Court, sentence no. 13/1991.

study of the religious facts and their implications are concerned. However, it must be noted the lengthy jurisprudential controversy concerning the exposition of the *crucifix* in the classrooms. Some wanted to have it removed from the walls of the Italian public schools because, as a symbol of a religious group, it was considered an instrument of religious propaganda incompatible with the secular state and potentially offensive for atheists and for those belonging to other religious denominations. With regard to the exhibition of the crucifix in public places (classrooms, courts of justice, electoral offices), the jurisprudence has expressed conflicting orientations. In fact, some have deemed the obligation to be no longer in force, having been provided by secondary rules that have been introduced during the fascist regime in a constitutional system that used to consider the Catholic religion as the religion of State, and are now incompatible with the current constitutional and international norms.[48] Others have affirmed that it cannot offend anyone since it is not the religious symbol of a religious group, but rather a symbol of the historical roots of the Italian people, which expresses "the religious origin of the values of tolerance, mutual respect, enhancement of the persons, promotion of their rights, of their freedom, of the autonomy of their moral conscience towards the authority, of human solidarity, and of rejection of all discriminations. All of this characterizes the Italian civilization". Therefore, the exposition of the crucifix evokes values that "emerge from the fundamental norms of our Charter and, specifically, from the ones mentioned by the Constitutional Court about the secular nature of the Italian State".[49] Besides, some other, by basing on the principle of

---

48   Court of Cassation, criminal Sction IV, no. 439/2000. It stated that the rules on the display
      of the crucifix should implicitly be understood as repealed due to their religious domina-
      tion matrix, also because the presence of this symbol in classrooms used as polling sta-
      tions would risk causing "a serious disturbance to one's conscience" and its imposition, as
      linked to the symbolic value of an entire civilization or of the collective ethical con-
      science, would go against the "clear prohibition" imposed in this matter by the principle
      of equality referred to in art. 3 of the Constitution.

49   Council of State, Section VI, sentence no. 556/2006 and Council of State, Section II, opin-
      ion of 15 February 2006 (issued in the extraordinary appeal to the Head of State proposed
      by the Union of atheists, agnostics and rationalists against the directive of 3 October 2002
      by the Ministry of Education on the display of the crucifix in classrooms). In this opinion,
      it is admitted that, today, the crucifix "must also be seen as a religious symbol", and com-
      mon to several denominations (all Christian ones). However, it would be "in opposition to
      the very origins of our Constitution, as well as to the sentiment of our people, to exclude
      a Christian sign from a public structure in the name of secularism, which also finds one of
      its distant sources in the Christian religion". Nor could the subjective right of religious
      freedom be invoked, because its "protection cannot be extended to the psychological
      sphere, that is, to the dimensions of individual conscience and feelings, which would lead

autonomy of each scholastic institution provided by the Constitution, believe that all classes should decide for themselves.

Finally, the religious dimension of foreigners, including asylum seekers, is especially relevant for people inside Italian *prisons* (in which there are many foreigners). Prisoners must be treated with humanity and respect for the dignity of the person, with absolute impartiality, without discrimination as regards gender, sexual orientation, race, nationality, economic and social conditions, political opinions and religious beliefs, and must follow models that favor autonomy, responsibility, socialization and integration (art. 1 of law 26 July 1975, no. 354).

Furthermore, penitentiary institutions must be equipped with rooms that are suitable for the needs of the prisoners' individual life and, if possible, rooms to carry out religious activities (art. 5 of law no. 354/1975). Prisoners must be guaranteed a diet that respects their religious beliefs (art. 9 of law no. 354/1975), so that in deciding the food to administer to prisoners, which must be approved by a decree of the Minister of Justice, the prescriptions of the different religious faiths must be taken into account (art. 11 of Presidential Decree no. 230/2000).

More generally, prisoners' treatment also involves religion (art. 15 of law no. 354/1975). Indeed, prisoners have the freedom to profess their religious faith and to practice its worship. In penitentiary institutions, the celebration of Catholic rites is guaranteed and at least one Catholic chaplain is assigned to each institute. Prisoners following a religion other than the Catholic one have the right to receive, at their request, the assistance of ministers of their own religious denomination and celebrate their rites (art. 26 of law no. 354/1975). Prisoners, in fact, have the right to participate in the rites of their religious group, provided they are compatible with the security of the institution and not contrary to the law, according to the provisions of art. 58 of Presidential decree no. 230/2000:

a)   prisoners have the right to display, in their room, images and symbols of their own religion;

b)   during free time, prisoners are allowed to practice their religions, provided that they do not engage in dangerous acts for the community;

c)   in order to celebrate Catholic rites, each institute has one or more chapels, according to the requirements of the religious service;

---

to the recognition of a right to a sterile environment, in which we are all preserved from receiving messages against personal sentiments".

d)   for religious education and for the practices of worship by members of other religious denominations, even when in the absence of ministers, the institute's management offers suitable spaces.

The institute's management, in order to guarantee to prisoners religious education and spiritual assistance, as well as the celebration of the rites of other confessions, arranges for the ministers of worship requested by the different religious groups, and always indicated by the Ministry of the Interior, to perform their duties inside the prisons. Finally, the daytime isolation of prisoners sentenced to life does not exclude their admission to religious services (art. 73 of Presidential decree no. 230/2000).

In the 2019 Report to Parliament, the National Defender for the rights of persons whose personal freedom has been restricted has recommended the Government (so far, without any implementation) to promote in "high security" prisons, thanks to specific scientific competences, projects and programs of de-radicalization of the people who have been sentenced for crimes aggravated by the terrorist aim of the so-called religious fundamentalism.

The rules examined so far make us understand why from the principle of equality for any religion (art. 3 of the Constitution), from religious freedom (art. 19 of the Constitution), from the prohibition of special burdens for religious bodies (art. 20 of the Constitution), from the equal freedom of every religious group before the law and from their full freedom of internal organization (art. 7 and 8 of the Constitution), the Constitutional Court has deduced that the Italian legal system is characterized by the principle of state secularity, meant not as indifference of the State towards the religious experience, but rather as the protection of pluralism, in support of the maximum expansion of freedom for all, according to criteria of impartiality.

In this regard, some doctrine (D'Amico, 2008) has developed a method that can be defined as "secular" to resolve conflicts between opposing and apparently irreconcilable rights, which is the resort to constitutional principles. Fundamental aspects of this method are:

a)   the involvement of different institutional actors, i.e. the legislator, the Constitutional Court, the common judges and the citizens, since there is not one unique way to defend the rights;

b)   the rejection of laws that attempt to "moralize" by imposing "values";

c)   the acquisition by the institutional actors of the scientific data and their attention to reality, to be taken into consideration in an objective manner;

d)   attention towards the respect for the rights of minorities, especially if they are "weak". And, of course, these weak minorities include asylum seekers for religious reasons.

On the Role of Religion in the Decision to Migrate

Laura Zanfrini

In this chapter and in the following two, attention will move from the societal to the individual level, focusing on three main topics.

Firstly (Chapter 10), we will concentrate on the role of religion as a push/pull factor influencing the decision to migrate and, consequently, as a factor contributing to the distinction between forced and voluntary migrations. Moving from the current debate about the increasing "porosity" of this distinction, we will discuss how the evidence from the fieldwork can help us describe and understand the role of the two key concepts represented by Religious Identity and Religious Liberty (see Chapter 2).

The second topic is represented by the procedure for the analysis of asylum applications (Chapter 11). Given the legislative framework in force in Italy (as described in Chapter 9), we will discuss how the effective implementation of rules and procedures allows the emergence and the acknowledgment of those aspects variously connected with asylum seekers' religious belongings.

Thirdly, we will discuss (Chapter 12) the space dedicated to the religious dimension and to the spiritual needs of migrants, even during the delicate phase of the first reception and re-elaboration of the migratory trauma, as well as the "functions" and meanings that (forced) migrants for religious reasons attribute to religion, seen both in its individual and collective aspects.

Methodologically, Chapters 10–12 are based on the following sources:

a) A literature review of the topics discussed;
b) Data and suggestions emerged from five focus groups discussion (FGDs),[1] which have globally involved around 40 key informants selected among executives, officials and operators of the reception system for asylum seekers; spiritual leaders and pastoral agents of different religions; representatives of Italian and international organizations and associations involved in the reception of asylum seekers; managers and members of the assessment commissions for asylum applications; local administrators; executives and officials of police stations and prefectures. The FGDs were held in Milan and Rome, from January to July 2017 and subsequently transcribed;

---

1 FGDs were conducted by Laura Zanfrini and organized by Annavittoria Sarli.

c)   Six semi-structured interviews with religious leaders and pastoral opera-
     tors[2] belonging to different catholic organizations involved in the recep-
     tion of migrants and asylum seekers. These interviews were conducted
     from May to October 2017, at the domiciles of the interviewed and subse-
     quently transcribed;

d)   20 in-depth interviews,[3] carried out from March 2017 to December 2018,
     with migrants and asylum seekers who, regardless of the entry channel
     and of their current legal status, have been significantly affected by their
     religious belonging; in other words, religion is a variable that influenced
     both their decision to migrate and the development of migration and in-
     sertion processes. Individuals to be interviewed were selected thanks to
     the suggestions coming from various experts and informants (including
     operators of the reception system, religious leaders, pastoral operators,
     attorneys in charge with asylum seekers assistance, and researchers).
     These interviews have been conducted either at the researchers' work-
     place or at other public places such as cafés, places of worship, and cul-
     tural associations. All the interviewed were clearly informed about the
     aims of the study and gave their verbal agreement once assured that no
     identificative elements would be inserted in the final report of the re-
     search or in any other public release of its results.

Notwithstanding these selective criteria and the large spectrum of informants
activated, the conduction of the interviews proved to be more difficult than
expected, mainly because of the relevant linguistic barriers. Some of the selected interviewed turned out to have a modest knowledge not only of the Italian language (despite in some cases they had been living in Italy for several
years), but also of other languages known by the research team (English,
French, Spanish, Arab). We also tried to involve a translator during the interview or in the process of transcription –particularly in the case of migrants
coming from China– but the quality of the reports proved to be, in many cases,
not adequate, thus making us have to remove them from the sample. Some
other migrants appeared to be reluctant to describe their religious feelings and
experience, despite the strong preparation of the interviewers and the clear
illustration of the object of the study. This attitude could have to do with the
bias already discussed (Chapters 1 and 2), which produces a rather negative
consideration of religion and of religious belongings. As a consequence of
these difficulties, we renounced to recur to a sophisticated methodology for

---

2   Semi-structured interviews were conducted by Silvia Serafini as part of the fieldwork for her
    final master degree dissertation.
3   In-depth interviews were conducted by Francesca Mungiardi and Annavittoria Sarli.

the text analysis, as initially envisaged, and we chose to only transcript parts of the interviews.[4] These, in any case, are particularly interesting and suggestive of the importance of the religious and spiritual dimension.

Finally, despite these weaknesses, remarkable insight emerged from the study, which confirms the general hypothesis of the research and provides new suggestions for their explanation. Furthermore, it is interesting to note that the fieldwork turned out to be quite touching, not only from a professional point of view, but also as human beings. Narratives were always moving, and it also happened that the interviewed would cry and ask for a break to get themselves together. The researchers involved were profoundly hit by these testimonies, which definitely confirmed the awareness of the importance of the discussed topics. In a few cases, the interview marked the beginning of a new friendship between the researcher and the interviewed.

1   Faith-Based Organizations as a Push/Pull Effect in the Migration to Italy

As described in the introductory chapter of this book (Chapter 1), our research has moved from the hypothesis that religion plays a significant role in the decision to migrate, much more than it is usually grasped. More precisely, together with the forms of mobility specifically driven by religious motives –in their multiple declinations–,[5] religion is supposed to play a greater role than usually acknowledged. Within the context of contemporary literature and theories (Massey *et al.*, 1993), the *institutional theory* offers the theoretical framework to capture the role of Faith Based Organizations (from now on: FBOs) as both push and pull factors, as well the *networks theory* highlights the importance of interpersonal links and social capital, possibly based on a common religious belonging, in reducing the costs and risks of migration, and in making the latter more feasible. As far Italy as a destination country is concerned, there is much empirical evidence on the key role played by religious institutions and

---

4   In some cases, we were obliged to adjust the syntactic of the text, in order to make the English translation understandable.

5   Including some forms escluded from the present study, but surely interesting from a sociological point of view, such as that involving Muslim people who left Europe to go to an Islamic country in order to break with a social model which contradicts their puritan aspirations (see Adraoui, 2015). Not to mention the phenomenon of religious radicalization that has caused the expatriation of so called foreign faighters.

religious affiliations in structuring specific migration chains originating from various countries of the world.

The same Italian migratory transition –from being a predominantly emigration to a predominantly immigration country– was announced, during the 1970s, by the influx of young women recruited as house-maids thanks to the presence, in their home countries, of Catholic missions, schools, and hospitals. Their arrival gave rise to various migratory networks doomed to acquire, with the passing of time, an extraordinary self-propelling power (among the most known, the chain linking Italy to the Philippines: Zanfrini, Asis, 2006). Another suggestive example is the influx from Senegal, mostly composed of young men affiliated to the *Muridiyya* Islamic brotherhood, a component of a larger migration system linking the sending communities with the multiple poles of the Senegal's Diaspora (Schmiddt di Firedberg, 1994). This latter offers one of the most impressive examples of how migratory models, migratory cultures, and migratory systems can institutionalize around religious affiliations, thus offering even to very disadvantaged people, coming from marginal regions, the possibility to migrate and participate in transnational networks.

As illustrated by these same examples, religious links and connections help to explain not only the upsurge of specific migratory channels, but also the site and characters of the adaptation process. Finally, some of the subject involved in the study suggested that there can be "vicious" links between migration and FBOS, if not a sort of contamination with the so called "migration industry" and –in the case of "fake" FBOS– with its illegal and criminal components (e.g. those involved in human trafficking, sexual exploitation, drug dealing, or in illegal transfer of remittances). This aspect has not until now emerged from "official" sociological research, but it has been directly denounced by some of our key informants and interviewed migrants:

> In Europe ... (...), most African Churches are just for money, so people go to church and give offers, but there are others that are from God. I'm not surprised about these things, because it's written in the Bible that when the time comes, so many priests act in the name of God, but are not from God. So, I'm not surprised, because it is written in the Bible. (Man – Nigeria – Catholic Christian)

> (...) unfortunately, the immigration channel to request international protection is used by criminal networks, obviously in an inappropriate way, especially for women. I am talking about those who use this channel because they are fleeing from war and then arrive here. Now, I do not know the percentages, but they are certainly not all of those who arrive, and it is a channel used by criminal networks, by networks dealing with

prostitution, and even by those who give alms. Now we are trying to understand ... (Woman – social worker in the reception system)

A particularly representative example is provided by the case of Nigerian women forced to prostitution, many of whom are held hostages by their exploiters through woodo curses threatening their family members at home.

As controversially suggested by an African Catholic priest, encountered thanks to the teaching activity of this chapter's author, together with family members, religious leaders too contribute to shape the path and the course of migration, as they "encourage, advise and direct the course of affairs not only for the would-be migrants but also for their own personal interests and advantages that they hope to share at the end of the successful journey" (Man – Ghana – Catholic Christian religious leader).

> Realizing how desperate many Ghanaians want to migrate to the West, many pastors and religious leaders who are more interested in preaching prosperity than in salvation are now encouraging mass migration by offering endless prayers for prospective migrants. In almost all religious programs in Ghana by the so-called Charismatic Churches, except for the mainstream Churches, such as crusade, all night vigils, conventions, and preaching, pastors pray that the dreams of travelling to the land of the light-skinned man are fulfilled. Some of these are broadcast on radio and on TV. With fake testimonies (...) people are persuaded and believe in them (...) because the "men of God" have spoken. How these poor people make it to their destinations is not the pastors' concern. What they are usually concerned about is the fat monthly "tithe" the would-be migrants would be pumping into their churches' coffers or directly into their pockets once they get there. Out of ignorance, selfishness or greed, they fail to use their commanding position to educate people about the perils and discomfort of migrating to the so-called civilized countries.
>
> Some pastors, quite ridiculously, are ready to pray for the fulfilment of the dreams of someone ignorantly planning to travel to unknown destinations (...). In brief, many pastors have turned into powerful agents of mass migration of Ghanaians to other continents through their prophecies and predictions addressed to people who are weak but ready to go a long way to see "Heaven on Earth". (Man – Ghana – Catholic Christian religious leader)

According to what has emerged during the fieldwork, migrations of Chinese affiliated to the "Church of God Almighty" are suspected to be triggered by "religious" links. Since its establishment –dating back to 1991– this FBOs has been the object of strong persecution by the Chinese government, which has condemned hundreds of thousands of its affiliated to prison, and in a few cases to the death penalty, thus encouraging most of them to emigrate.[6]

> In China, repression is really very strong. I have been persecuted several times. Even now, I have some wounds and scars. For these reasons, I wanted to leave China. Actually, I had no choice, I was forced. Those reasons were enough for me to leave China. (Man – China – Church of God Almighty)

Exactly during the time-span of our study, the presence of migrants affiliated with this Church has become more visible also in Italy through the arrival of a group of people (mostly women); some of them are now assisted by Evangelic churches. Since they are often "hosted" by co-nationals who exploit them as cheap labor force, someone suspects that they arrived through some sort of smuggling organizations specialized in offering to the victims of religious persecutions the possibility to escape. The fact is that some of these women are still very worried about their situation. They tend to avoid any contact with Chinese people (and are therefore reluctant to ask for Chinese translators, despite their lack of linguistic competences), because they fear to be denounced and eventually forcibly sent back to China; at the same time, they are afraid of the possible repercussions on their left-behind family members, thus showing the "transnational character" of the phenomenon of religious-based persecutions, which reverberates, as suggested by this interviewee, also in everyday relations between the faithful.

> I'm always afraid to meet other Chinese people. Sometimes the Chinese of Paolo Sarpi (*author's note: a district of Milan with a strong concentration of Chinese people*) are businessmen and have strong relations with China. They often go to China for work. I also have a family in China and if they know me I do not want this to harm my family in China. Even among us, Christian brothers and sisters, we do not ask personal questions, we do not want to know details. (Woman – China – Church of God Almighty)

As we will describe later, in contemporary Italy, dramatically involved in the management of "mixed fluxes", this kind of phenomena –on which, however,

---

6   https://www/cesnur.org/2017/almighty_china_report.pdf.

accurate and in-depth information is still lacking– contribute to fuel the idea that this kind of actors could encourage the arrival of bogus asylum seekers.

Still, FBOs can exercise a pull effect as well. This is particularly true, once again, in the case of Italy, thanks to the presence of the universal capital of Catholicism –Rome and the Vatican City–, where various pontifical universities and general houses of religious congregations are based and are able to attract different categories of migrants (from the members of the religious communities to the international students). Particularly on the occasion of special events (such as a Jubilee), the Holy See magnetizes the arrival of a huge number of "pilgrims", who sometimes only have a one-way ticket, and who are usually interested in settling in the country, most of the times to rejoin some of their friends or extended family members. Moreover, Italy represents a particularly attractive destination for the so-called *fidei donum*, who are Catholic priests involved in a specific form of "circular migration", which often turns into a permanent settlement. For the priests coming from the "global South", the possibility to complete their education in Rome is sometimes interpreted as the harbinger of a future "career" within the ecclesiastical hierarchy.[7] Finally, many of the religious who go to study in Europe do not return to their home countries, either because they are destined for other tasks, or because they simply refuse to return.

Decidedly more relevant, in quantity terms, is the role played by many Catholic (or other Christian confessions) pro-migrant organizations, since they concur to create a "migrant-friendly" environment, which supports newcomers and vulnerable migrants, including undocumented ones, immediately after their arrival and in their process of adaptation. Just to cite an iconographic example, since the 1980s until today, migrants who have come to Milan have often carried with them a piece of paper with the address of the first aid service managed by the local Caritas, close to the Central Station.

Significantly, this supporting environment proves to be advantageous for all migrants, regardless of their country of origin and of their religious affiliations, and any migrant has the opportunity to directly take advantage from goods and services provided by religious charities and other kinds of FBOs (including the legal assistance offered on a free basis to the asylum applicants and to the denied asylum seekers who decide to appeal for a re-examination of their claim). In order to appreciate the relevance of these kinds of actors in the

---

7   Antwi-Boasiako, B. (AY 2016-17). *The Causes of Migration: The Ghanaian Experience*. Roma: Faculty of Pastoral Theology of Human Mobility, SIMI, Università Urbaniana (work prepared for the exam of the teaching of "Sociology of Human Mobility").

contemporary Italian landscape, it is sufficient to report how, on June 2018,[8] 21,429 asylum seekers/migrants (among which more than 700 unaccompanied minors) were hosted in one of the 2,100 ecclesial structures in the 180 Catholic dioceses involved. 2,589 were hosted directly by the parishes, the remaining part within the Sprar (protection system for asylum seekers and refugees), the Cas (extraordinary reception centers) or the center for minors managed through an agreement with the Ministry. Significantly, about a quarter of the hosting initiatives were entirely financed by their own funds. Furthermore, particularly in the Northern regions, migrants represent a large portion of the beneficiaries of initiatives addressed to the homeless, the poor, and other vulnerable people managed and financed by Catholic institutions. Single parishes, as well as Catholic movements and associations, are largely involved in a range of "pro-migrants" activity, from the help in the search of a job to the learning-support offered to foreign students. The composite landscape of Protestant Christian Churches as well is significantly involved. For example, we can note the commitment displayed in this field by the Waldensian Church. Through the inclusion services managed by the Waldenasian Diakonia, it offers reception services for migrants who are hosted thanks to different programs, which follow the guidelines requested, and which are managed by Sprar services with a "diffused model" of reception (Chapter 9, §4). According to the last available data, in January 2019, more than 700 migrants were hosted in one of the reception services – the majority of which arrived through the "Humanitarian Corridors" program (see later). Moreover, the Waldensian Diakonia has recently partnered with Oxfam Italia and, together, they have opened the so-called "Community Centers" in Turin, Milan, Arezzo, Florence, and Catania, conceived as social meeting places offering consultancy services to the migrants and the local population.

Once again, thanks to the mobilization of some religious organizations (in the framework of an ecumenical initiative), humanitarian corridors were lunched in order to permit the secure travel and the legal entry of asylum seekers coming from unsafe countries. A first pilot project was launched, in December 2015, thanks to a collaboration between the Community of Sant'Egidio (a Catholic organization), the Federation of Evangelic Churches, the Waldensian and Methodist Churches to consider the arrival in Italy, over two years, of a thousand refugees from Lebanon (mostly Syrians who fled the war), Morocco (where most of those coming from sub-Saharan countries affected by civil wars and widespread violence land) and Ethiopia (Eritreans, Somalis and Sudanese). The Corridors are the result of a *Memorandum of Understanding*

---

8 Survey realized by the Italian Episcopal Conference on Dioceses active at 30 June 2018.

signed by the proponents, the Italian Ministry of Foreign Affairs and International Cooperation, and the Ministry of Interior, but are nevertheless funded by the organizations that promoted them, and implemented thanks to the commitment of other non-governmental actors. Beneficiaries have been selected on the basis of their level of vulnerability –regardless of their religious or ethnic background– and are provided with legal assistance for visas, hospitality and accommodation for a reasonable period of time, economic support for the transfer to Italy, and support in the integration process. Following this experience, this approach has been established with the particular engagement of the Migrantes Foundation, i.e. the body of the Italian (Catholic) Episcopal Conference in charge with migrants' pastoral assistance, so as to allow the arrival of new contingents of refugees (Caritas Italiana, 2019). Within the framework of an ecumenical effort, involving both Catholic parishes and Waldensian and Methodist Churches, 4,000 vulnerable people will be welcomed over four years. It is useful to observe that, besides offering a safety migratory route, this experience provides a positive example of how to integrate newcomers through the activation of local communities.

Moreover, FBOs frequently act as advocacy actors, recommending the authorities and civil society to adopt more generous policies and more tolerant practices towards arriving and sojourning foreigners, including the undocumented ones. During the last refugee crisis, this position –embodied by the apex of the Catholic Church, Pope Francis– has translated into various forms of mobilization: from the initiatives aimed to receive and assist asylum seekers to the involvement in the rescue operations, not to mention the large presence of Catholic actors and institutions in the occasion of sensitization marches in support of the right to be welcomed. Various Christian leaders and institutions have yet repeatedly disputed the very distinction between economic and humanitarian migrants, in the face of the deep injustice of the contemporary global regime. Religious organizations have been among the most consistent voices supporting the idea that plight of refugees (particularly from the Middle East) require an ethical and political response emphasizing the centrality of hospitality and solidarity (Petito, 2017). And it is significant to observe how one of the reasons evoked is religious-based, that is a principle of universal brotherhood. The following assertion is just one of the many that we collected during the study.

> One of the main reasons why it is difficult to describe the religious theme as a determining factor for forced or unforced migration is linked to the absence of legal access routes to Europe, unless it is through an asylum request. There is a mix of factors that determine the escape, so when you

find yourself in Italy having to apply for asylum, the religious theme can come out among others. The Geneva Convention can't handle the complexity of the flows. The question of mixed flows should not be resolved in the distinction between economic and political migrants, but in a multiplicity of factors that the same person has in his/her individual capacity. Clearly, in some cases, one factor prevails over the other, but there are also situations determined by accessing Europe in a legal manner. When this is not possible for economic reasons, the religious motivation is the one invoked. (Woman – Pastoral operator – Waldenasian Diakonia)

Without entering in the analysis of their motivations (which can be of ethical, humanitarian, or even of theological nature), the point that must be stressed is that, in this manner, FBOs contribute, more or less consciously, to attract new migrants, if not to institutionalize migration patterns outside the legislative framework in force, including the rules governing the acknowledgment of the status of refugee (such as other statutes of protection). Together with the practical difficulty in rejecting and expelling (irregular) migrants, this position has certainly concurred to the wide tolerance manifested by Italy towards them, notwithstanding their formal status. Moreover, at institutional level, the growing porosity among different "types" of migrants was implicitly acknowledged through the introduction (and the large use of) the "humanitarian protection", that is a third possible outcome of the asylum demand (besides the acknowledgment of the status of refugee and of the subsidiary protection), frequently granted, for "humanitarian" reasons, to those migrants lacking conventional criteria to be acknowledged in need of protection, but who are impossible to expatriate.[9] As a matter of fact, during the refugee crises, all around Europe, not only a high number of asylum seekers received a status that is different from that of refugee, but also different countries recorded very different approval rates and tended to grant different statuses (Eurostat, 2017). In this context, Italy stands out both for the very high number of applicants who were granted humanitarian protection, and for the very high number of appeals and successful appeals.

These trends certainly influenced recent changes to the regulatory framework contained in the so-called "security decree" (see Chapter 9, §2). However, what is interesting to observe is that even after the "restrictive turn" in the government's approach towards asylum seekers, many FBOs (supported by the official voice of the Catholic Church, constituted by the Italian Episcopal Conference) have immediately declared that they will continue to help migrants,

---

9 Decree Law no. 113/2018, so-called "security decree", has drastically reduced the possibility of obtaining humanitarian protection.

TABLE 10.1   Results of asylum applications. Italy, 2016–2018

	Refugee status	Subsidiary protection	Humanitarian protection	Denied applications	Untraceable	Other outcome	Total applications examined*
2016	4,808	12,873	18,979	51,170	3,084	188	91,102
2017	6,827	6,880	20,166	42,700	4,292	662	81,527
2018	7,096	4,319	20,014	56,002	7,740	405	95,576
2016	5.3	14.1	20.8	56.2	3.4	0.2	100.0
2017	8.4	8.4	24.7	52.4	5.3	0.8	100.0
2018	7.4	4.5	20.9	58.6	8.1	0.4	100.0

SOURCE: ISMU ELABORATIONS OF DATA FROM THE NATIONAL ASYLUM COMMISSION, http://www.libertaciviliimmigrazione.dlci.interno.gov.it/it/documentazione/statistica/i-numeri-dellasilo

even when the latter lack the legal requisites to be hosted in the official reception centers. Together with other civil society's actors, FBOs of different Christian denominations have mobilized not only by making their properties available in order to accommodate migrants expelled from the official reception system, but also by checking the availability of private citizens and families to welcome them in their homes. All this proves that not only FBOs certainly contribute to make Italy an "attractive" country, but also that many migrants – notwithstanding their religious belonging and beliefs– find in (Christian) FBOs one of the most important reference actor during the first steps of their adaptation process.

2   Religion as a Belief, Religion as an Identity, Religion as a Way of Life

Above and beyond the role of FBOs and of the migratory chains and migratory systems that they have contributed to establish and strengthen, our study has assumed that religion can be a powerful variable to understand migration choices and trajectories, since it influences both individual (and family) *identity* and individual (and societal) *freedom* (Chapter 1). In this perspective, it has been traditionally deemed in the analysis and management of forced migrations. The main reference on this regard is constituted by the UNHCR *Guidelines on International Protection: Religion-Based Refugee Claims under Article 1A(2) of the 1951 Convention and/or the 1967 Protocol relating to the Status of Refugees* (2004), inspired by the work of J. Gunn (2003), and providing a multi-level definition of religion, on which the procedures of asylum recognition, in different destination countries, are substantially based. The three definition items are the following:

a)   religion as a belief (including non-belief);
b)   religion as an identity;
c)   religion as a way of life.

What is interesting to observe is that, in the narrative of (forced) migrants, these three items turn into special resources when they have to come to terms with their very personal and collective experience. In this perspective, religious affiliations affect the decision to migrate not only because they are the "causes" of violations, persecutions, and discriminations –as we will describe later–; but also because they provide the migrants with the *lexicon* to understand their own (individual and collective) life trajectory, and possibly their migratory trajectory. Finally, they are powerful signifiers to define oneself as a "forced" migrant, largely independently of the migratory channel actually used.

So, religion is a *belief* which provides would-be migrants the force to resist despite the persecutions and, possibly, the reason to see the "opportunity" to migrate, as in the dramatic experience of these two interviewed, both escaped from the threat of being killed:

> In Pakistan, people have a very strong faith, no one can stop them ... but the faith of Christians in Pakistan is too strong, even if there are difficulties, even if there are bomb blasts, even if they are kidnapping people, they keep praying, they keep celebrating Christmas, Easter ... they do not stop. (Man – Pakistan – Catholic Christian)

> How I know that I could escape through Italy? When we are in the church, the fathers would tell us: pray for the people who are in the hospital, pray for the people who went from Libya to Italy and then died, many people, so everybody pray for them and start fasting, so God will help them. I started asking questions: how did these people die? Crossing from Libya to Italy? Why? Then they told me. Then, from that, I understood. So, in the morning, 1st January 2015, I left my country. (Man – Nigeria – Christian Pentecostal Church [former Catholic Christian])

As a belief, religion makes the concept of a person's freedom clear –and, in a certain way, provides a sense to the decision to migrate for religious reasons–. In general terms, this concept refers to both the freedom to believe and the freedom to practice one's faith:

(...) in the Bahá'i faith, the principle is that mankind has the right to choose what to believe, what to do. Instead, in the Islamic faith, everything is decided by the clergy, so the fear is to lose one's .... power. So they are afraid that other people will become Bahá'i or ... have others ... influence other people. (Woman – Iran – Bahá'i)

Perhaps it was made in a different way, because in Iran we do not have a place to see each other, we do not have a very free way to practice our faith. But here it is much easier, much more natural. (Woman – Iran – Bahá'i)

Furthermore, this concept seems to concern the freedom of choosing one's personal way to believe and practice, thus contrasting a misleading conception of religion, where the latter is reduced to an instrument of social control, which exactly denies the very strict association between religion and freedom, as clearly asserted by this Yemeni woman:

It was not a problem that I am a Muslim, the problem is that I am a different Muslim. I'm not the Muslim that they want me to be. They are not Muslims according to one specific model; they are Muslims according to another model. So I told you that religion is a private relationship. I think so: it's a private relationship. Nobody has to tell me that I have to put the veil, or that I have to say the prayer, or that I have to dress this way, or that I have to stay at home and not go out because I am a woman, because God says so. This is what I do not want. (Woman – Yemen – Muslim)

This point is even more palpable in the case of those who choose to not believe, as suggestively expressed, though ungrammatically, by this (ex) Coptic Catholic coming from Egypt. His assertion stresses the right essence of Christianity, made of personal freedom and care for the others:

So if I am an atheist today it is thanks to Jesus Christ. Because I, this gave me freedom. If this person I say are in Italy or in another country, find the clean road because people care so much, even if they are atheists, why? Because they care about their neighbor. (Man – Egypt – former Coptic Catholic Christian)

Secondly, religion is a source of individual and collective *identity*, an identity whose awareness is reinforced exactly through the persecution, and which gives to the latter a theological meaning:

> We, Christians in Iraq, have lost our country, our houses, everything we
> have built. It is very hard, but in this situation we have been able to dis-
> cover that we are truly at home in the faith. (Man – Iraq – Chaldean Cath-
> olic Christian)

Not by chance, it happens that people and communities who share a long-
standing culture of migration and persecution keep an iconographic heritage
of this experience in their collective memory. Coptic Christians in Egypt, for
example, used to engrave their religious roots in the skin, through a little crux
tattooed on the right wrist (Ha, 2017). Almost a metaphor of the function of
resilience carried out by faith and religious identity (see also Part 5). As this
informant reminded us, deciding to get a tattoo of the crux on the skin can also
be a strategy to escape the risk of a marriage with a non-Christian partner, thus
marking the edge beyond which it is not possible to accept any abuse or harassment, when it comes to preserve exactly one's identity.

> This is especially true in Egypt. The Coptic Christians in Egypt have the
> crux tattooed on the hands, while we (*in Eritrea, author's note*) especially
> the women, wore the crux tattooed on our foreheads, and this was born ...
> was born as a form of resistance to the Islamization of the region, to say
> that ... Christianity and Christ is in our blood, in our ... that is, it is not
> separable, so we cannot ... it is a sign of fidelity and of not betraying our
> faith, even in the face of those who force us, so ... because they beheaded
> those who refused to convert, at the beginning of the Ottoman invasion.
>   Interviewer: So centuries ago, anyway...
>   Yes, yes, it was born many centuries ago. For us, for example, it was
> born in 1500, so when Islam saw that it did not work by force, they chose
> to marry the local women to convert them, at least the children would
> become Muslims, so also the fathers, the mothers of these girls have the
> crux tattooed on their foreheads saying that if the Muslim who will marry
> this girl, if he marries her with the concrete crux, then it was a form of
> resistance that they implemented to also say that our daughters are
> Christian in blood and skin, so if they were to marry, then if they had to
> marry, he had to take off her head, to marry her, so she wanted to say that
> it could not be done. (Man – Religious leader – Catholic Christian)

In the bloody scenario of contemporary Eritrea (one of the major countries of
origin of asylum seekers arriving in Italy), it is known that, for many youths,
migration is the only strategy to escape the "life-long" military service imposed
by the regime; however, in the case of certain religious minorities –particularly
Jehovah's Witnesses, often deprived of the same citizenship because of their

refusal to provide military service–, this motivation is strengthened by one of a religious nature, relating precisely to their duty to refrain from taking up arms. Significantly, migrants with very different origins (from Iran to Tibet, from Pakistan to Nigeria) and belonging to different religions have clearly expressed this same concept: *it is exactly the need to preserve one's own (religious) identity that gives sense to the decision to migrate*: an exit strategy –the only available strategy– to protect one's faith even before one's survival:

> (...) We must not be aggressive, but we must continue to fight for our rights. This fight must be very peaceful, no aggression must exist and then the only thing, the only thing we do not accept is when they ask us to falsely declare our beliefs. What we believe we resist. For example, when you put a gun under your throat and you must declare yourself a Muslim, you still say no. My belief, fundamental beliefs must not be rejected. However, secondary things, which are still important, we accept them so as not to create an aggressive atmosphere. (Man – Iran – Bahá'i)

> (...) from Tibet, in 2004 I left my country because there is a problem with the Chinese. Before that, I went to India, when I was little I went to India to study, because in Tibet there is a problem with culture, because the Chinese do not want us to study the Tibetan language, they want us to study the Chinese language too, but we do not want to, because when I do not speak Tibetan I become, I change in Chinese, I study Chinese, Chinese history, everything, so I become a Chinese. (Man – Tibet –Buddhist)
> Interviewer: When you received threats, didn't you think: I will stop my political and religious activity, to be safe? Didn't you have this idea? Or did you want to be free?
> Yes, he said: you stop your activity, stop activity in religion, especially religion. Yes, political, but religious, stop, is not possible, I am a Shiya, I am Muslim man, this is my right, this is not possible to someone, say you: don't pray, and I say: it is OK, I don't pray, this is not, this is not possible. (Man – Pakistan – Muslim)

> They know my problem, that they killed my father, and they tell me to go and worship this ... so they know. They know. People were praying to say: God will protect me. God will protect me. They know. Some people would tell me: you'll better join these people, they will kill you. You'd better join them, even ... they will kill you, they will kill you. I said: I will not join them, I will not join them. I'm a Christian. (Man – Nigeria – Christian Pentecostal Church [former Catholic Christian])

A specular experience is that of people coming from non-religious families and societies, who declare to have "discovered" a religious identity that they did not have the possibility to experience before migrating (or before deciding to migrate). Also in this case, it is exactly the migratory experience that has permitted the emergence of a latent need to believe and to provide the individual biography with an immanent meaning. During the fieldwork, various migrants coming from China have expressed this kind of feeling:

> (...) Only by embracing religion we can truly understand where we come from, the origin of man, we can make sense of our origin, our existence. (Young Woman – China – Evangelical Christian [synthesis provided by the translator])

Actually, in the case of migrants coming from atheistic contexts, religion is an extraordinary and unexpected resource that breaks into a biographical journey marked by sufferance and oppression. Among our interviewed, Chinese who have adhered to various forms of Christianity represent a case in point; not incidentally, in their chronicle, religious freedom –even just the mere fact of being able to freely talk about religious arguments– is often conceptually superimposed on the possibility of living in a democratic society.

> In Italy, I felt the true freedom to believe and practice. I can say with courage that I am a Christian. Christians are respected here. No one will laugh at them. I can boldly enter the church, praise the Lord without worries. I can watch videos of religions online. I could not enjoy all these rights in China. I don't need to hide the Bible, I can sleep peacefully, I'm not worried that the police will come and take me at any time. I can share the experience of the Lord with fellow believers from other countries with Facebook, YouTube (...). In China, because of the monitoring by the Chinese Communist Party, we Christians do not use these means of communication, the telephone cannot be used. We can't even use the computer. There is no Facebook, Internet is impossible. We can only pray for each other. (...) In Italy, everything is different. (Woman – China – Waldensian Christian [former Zhao Hui Church])

Thirdly, religion crystallizes a specific *way of life*. The most reported expression refers to the multiple ways through which this concept translates into a form of mutual support and protection fed by a principle of brotherhood. As emphasized by many interviews, this character is able to reproduce itself in every place, and to overcome the barriers represented by:

– Social classes:

> (...) before I began to believe, I thought that only if a person had a certain social level could have consideration from others. If they did not, they were not worthy of being considered. I really had this idea and for this I was always fighting. When I began to attend the Church of God Almighty, I saw that it was not like that at all. In our community, some were leaders, they had a firm, others had a humbler job, they did the cleaning, others were teachers, but we were the same. In this way, we did not feel suffering, I felt that we lived like real human beings, all equals, in a situation of justice. (Woman – China – Church of God Almighty)

– National borders:

> (...) throughout the Bahá'i community, throughout the world there is a form of system that every Bahá'i, wherever it is, found in the world and will have its supportive community. For example, when we arrived in Italy we were welcomed by the Bahá'i community and for us it was like a kind of community of belonging and support. (Couple (Man and Woman) – Iran – Bahá'i)

> (...) I chose Italy for one reason only: because there is the Vatican. My thoughts ... then I come here, I am protected, because I live inside my Church, because there is the Vatican (...).
> So I was for the first time at Mass celebrated in Italian, I did not understand anything, but I felt everything inside. Then here I made the Communion, I came out of the Church and I cried, and I said: "Long live my Church. This is truly a universal Church. It is not a word, but a fact". (Man – Egypt – Coptic Catholic Christian)

> I was very, very happy to meet them, I'm very, very happy, because they are teaching, it is the same teaching that I had before in Nigeria. It is Bible, we read the Bible, they teach you how to live your life, don't do bad, do good, don't follow bad people, don't smoke, don't do this. So I see them as good people, which is why I follow them, which is why I baptize, and when I entered the church, in the church there are also good people. They are helping me.
> (...) When time come you hear balan-balan (*he imitates the sound of the bells*), then you know it is the time, I attend the evening Mass in Catholic church to pray to God, all the church is the same, because they are

preaching the Word of God, they are preaching the same, to follow Jesus Christ, to do good. As Catholic preach about Jesus, this church is preaching about Jesus, Catholics preach to be good persons, to repent, don't do bad, this church also preaches to be good persons, don't do bad. So, when you see, you will know it is the same. (Man – Nigeria – Christian Pentecostal Church [former Catholic Christian])

– As well as overcoming the distance traced by the passage of time:

There were some Iranian families who went to Greece forty years ago, fifty years ago, or even the Greeks who were Bahá's. So having this Bahá'i community in Greece has helped me a lot, well, even in Italy, because you already had some friends, even if you did not know them (she smiles), but there were these people who could help you, you trusted them, and … it was very easy. [Woman – Iran – Bahá'i]

Finally, as has also emerged from previous studies (see, for example, Levitt, Jaworsky, 2007), religion connects migrants over time, allowing them to remain part of a chain of memory with the coreligionists from the past, present, and future.

3   Religion as a Direct "Cause" of Migration

There is certainly a situation of irregularities in religious freedom in most of the countries of origin of asylum seekers. If we analyze the scenario, there are serious problems of abuse, apologetic interpretation, lack of equal dignity, freedom of worship. (Man – Religious leader – Muslim)

In the previous section we have described how the concepts of belief, identity, and way of life mark the life-trajectories of (forced) migrants, making migration –independently of the specific decisional context– a sort of accomplishment of an existence characterized by the need to affirm one's own (religious) identity and projected to the realization also of the spiritual dimension of the human being.

However, to understand how these elements can influence the decision to migrate, and possibly give rise to a request for protection, it is necessary to take a further step. In this section, we set the goal of classifying, through the evidence gathered with field work, the cases in which religion can become a direct or indirect cause of migration, following a distinction largely employed in the migration studies.

According to the existing literature, the *direct causes* are first of all represented by *a sending context clearly compromised by the presence of religious-
based conflicts and of religious-based persecutions*, which pose an immediate
risk to be murdered, injured or violated. As a matter of fact, since the strong
majority of people in the world live in countries where they experience high
restrictions on religion,[10] democratic nations are expected to become increasingly involved in the arrival of migrants escaping their country for this kind of
reason. Considering the current migration fluxes directed to Italy, the most
patent example is that of Nigeria, where both Christians and non-conformist
Muslims are often perceived as potential victims of Boko Haram. Born in 2002,
this terroristic organization has subsequently joined Isis, subverting the political situation of the country and producing plenty of forced migrants. The following testimony gives us a raw example of how a risk reduced to the rank of
geopolitical data in the analysis of the Italian media, materializes in the concrete life of people who, despite having escaped, will always remember it in
their personal history:

> During the course of the past two years, I lost two colleagues to terrorist
> attacks from Boko Haram and it wasn't even outside the city, it was inside
> of the city. There was one who was involved in the suicide bomb attack
> and he died, and there was another who was shocked to death by a mem-
> ber of Boko Haram in the center of the city. After the second death, the
> company decided to stop operating and they moved to other offices in the
> country and they closed the office in Meiduguri, so I lost my job. (Man –
> Nigeria – now attending an Adventist Church)

However, the fieldwork has provided many other cases in point. Christian migrants, left to the margins of the attention by the Italian media –rather "attracted" by Muslim immigration and by all the connected questions– reappear
here as the unarmed victims of dramatic violence committed against them in
different countries, from Africa to Asia:

> (…) the father told us that they had tried to kidnap one of his children.
> Muslims. They just took the child in motion and he was saved by a neigh-
> bor who threw himself on him, pulling the child away from the motor-
> bike. And he said … then we told him: "Why kidnap him like that? You're

---

10   https://www.pewforum.org/2019/07/15/a-closer-look-at-how-religious-restrictions-have-
        risen-around-the-world/.

not…". And he said that "Muslims kidnap our children or give them back in exchange for a ransom in dollars or there is organ trafficking". Then he, to make us understand, said: "Open them"; we did not even understand because he could not say the word "organ trafficking". (Women – Nuns – Christian Catholic)

So something happened, they were planning, so at one point we started hearing a shout outside, we were hearing because our neighbors are Christians, so we understood their language and they were…

Interviewer: So you heard someone shouting outside?

Yes, they were shouting that my father should go, leave the house, leave the house … and those people were running away … and some people came and they wanted to use the knife so I jumped away … my father was inside but I was the one who jumped outside the window … but my father managed to defend himself … he was the one who cut the hands of the chief's son, so when I jumped outside the window, there I heard they were shouting at Allah … I asked where is my father, where is my father but then I discovered my father was dead too, so they were telling me to go away from the community, so I went to the bus stop, they might cut me and kill me, so I didn't have an alternative, so there were some cars to Niger, so it was one of those cars I was in, so I come to Niger, so that I can show I come to Niger and it was from Niger that I started the journey. (Man – Egypt – Christian)

Interviewer: How is the situation of Catholics in Pakistan? What happens to Catholics?

It is a little bit difficult because when Catholics are going for work or for their jobs it's difficult because Muslims think we cannot live in the same place because they think they are superior. They think that their religion is superior. There are many many things because sometimes they burn Christians in fire; sometimes they cut their head. (Man – Pakistan – Christian Catholic)

We are believers; the other Chinese came here to make money. China is a country with an atheistic government; we grew up with an atheistic education. The books we studied when we were young said that this world is without God; so many people do not know the truth. Later, when we met God we became Christians, but the Chinese atheist party did not allow us to believe in God, to walk on the right path. For this, they were arrested, persecuted and even killed. (Woman – China – Church of God Almighty)

As in the case of Egypt, frequently cited during the fieldwork, open persecution and violence can represent the "evolution" of a situation traditionally marked by discrimination towards minority groups. So, in the case under discussion, the advent of Muslim Brothers has made the country one of the most hostile towards Christians in the world, rendering their condition more and more dangerous. According to the interviewed migrants, persecution towards Christians has spread extensively in society, and has taking on multiple forms. From the humiliation inflicted on Christian students –obliged to study and repeat koranic verses during the school time– to the practice of seducing young female Christians, "just to take their virginity and then abandoning them" (Man – Egypt – Coptic Orthodox), not to mention the repeated terrorist attacks that claimed dozens of victims among the faithful gathered in the Church for the Mass. This context has favored the reactivation of already established migration chains linking Egypt and North Italy (Chapter 17), giving rise to an Egyptian immigration where the share of Christians is largely overrepresented compared with the situation in the origin country:

> (...) we have families, like these Egyptian ones, who have come away for persecution reasons. Another who ... for example, the classmates of a girl ... where the first bomb, that was in Egypt, Christmas Eve, Cairo, Alexandria, where the mother and the three little girls were going out (...)and all the classmates of this little girl, who was then small, now in high school, died. And this is the reason why they escaped, they came to Italy in 15 days, to reach her husband was this. (Women – Nuns – Catholic Christians)

> (...) especially in the period from 2010 to 2014, in Italy there was a migration linked to discrimination; at that time there were the Muslim Brothers in the government ... practically, there was an attack to the Church every week, so at that moment immigration in Italy had a peak. (Man – Pastoral operator – Catholic Christian)

Furthermore, as observed by this key expert, the public perception, largely shaped by the selective attention of the media and of the political debate, often tends to ignore the "production" of asylum seekers due to different kinds of "religious wars".

> The religious wars are the engine of history and today they are also touching Europe. Our time is characterized by "holy" wars of religion. For example, the Chechen conflict, largely ignored by the media, but a reality that continues to exist and produce a large number of asylum seekers. (Woman – Officer of the asylum seekers' reception system)

A second direct cause of migration can be identified in *a sending context characterized by serious violations of religious rights of minority groups*.

These include, first of all, the right to believe:

> (...) after they arrested me, they took me to the secret police, because he said that with my association ... we help the terrorists to get into Cameroon ... that's not well known, because Buddhism is not a bad religion, it's not a religion of violence, but because he has power, he sent the army to arrest me (...).
>
> There is this psychology to make you afraid, every time when you go around, they show you with their fingers: "It's him, there he is, he's a Buddhist, he's the Buddhist, he's the Buddhist". (Man – Cameron – Buddhist)

> Until 2013, when the Chinese government restricted control over Christians, we were spied upon. Within a night, they arrested all those who did the work of "guidance" within the churches in Zhejiang Province. After this fact, the others and I who were still free moved to other provinces, I stayed 14 months, but I was always locked in the house, I could not go out, talk to other people. I was disconnected from the world, I could not call home, I did not hear from my family. At that time, to better control the government, they began to control the residences. Every time someone knocked on the door, I was afraid and, in this context, I began to think that I could not stay in China, that I was always in danger. I kept moving, changing house. I do not even know how many houses I've lived in. So I started thinking about emigrating, coming to a democratic country, to keep on believing. (Woman – China – Church of God Almighty)

With regard to the right to believe, special attention must be given to the topic of conversions. As this testimony illustrates –one of the many that we could bring back– the belonging to an "undesirable" religion is sometimes tolerable when it is a legacy of a family history, but it becomes a fault to be punished when it is the upshot of an individual choice. This is a sort of counter-test of the profound link between religion and individual freedom.

> We have not asked for (international protection) but many Iranians make this request, they are those who (...) have converted to the Bahá'i religion because according to the Islamic rule, if one comes out of the Islamic religion they can kill them quietly and then it is more dangerous for those who convert than for us who were born so. (Woman – Iran – Bahá'i)

Secondly, the right to publicly manifest one's own religious beliefs:

> We cannot even speak as we speak now. Everywhere there are cameras. Not only in the rooms, but also outside, in the neighborhoods. And so the government can come to know anything. Now they are also putting cameras in rural areas. (Woman – China – Evangelical Christian)

> We stayed hidden for a long time, but at some point we decided to go out to serve in a suburb, far from the city. There, sometimes, the soldiers arrived at night to take away the young people. We seminarians were often in the church and the soldiers did not enter here, so we managed to hide. But the situation was heavy and dangerous and the area was on the border. We discussed with each other and we decided to cross the border to go to Ethiopia, rather than go back to the city and keep hiding. (Man – Eritrea – Catholic Christian)

And of course the right to take part to collective celebrations:

> In Libya forget about Christians! (*he laughs*) You can only pray in your room. (Imam – Nigeria – Catholic Christian)

> In China (...) we did these things in the house, secretly, we had to close the windows and the door well. We sang the hymns of the Word of God in a low voice. When we wanted to talk about the Gospel we were arrested, tortured, killed. It was very dangerous, so we had to leave our country, our family. (Woman – China – Church of God Almighty)

A third direct cause is constituted by *a sending context characterized by various kinds of discriminations and abuses towards minority groups.*

One case in point is represented by the presence of (legal) barriers limiting the possibility to enter some sectors of the educational system and/or of the occupational market. According to the testimonies gathered, the impossibility to access the university is one of the most recurrent examples:

> (...) why did we arrive in Italy? Because for reasons based on religion we could not go to university, because university in Iran is exclusively for four main forms of religion and ours does not enter this ranking...
>
> (We are) both of the Bahá'i religion, so we have ... In Iran there is a form of movement in which the Bahá'i boys ... try in some way ... then ... because of the convention, from 2005 if you wanted to enter university you had to enter your name, surname, father's name, identity card

number and religion ... so you are immediately rejected on the admission test ... (Couple [Man and Woman] – Iran – Bahá'i)

There are a lot of difficulties in Pakistan for Christians to go to university. When you go to university the level of difficulties grew up, because in most universities there are a lot of Muslim groups, so sometimes they forced the other students to join them as a groups, sometimes they are terrorism groups, they use drugs, they use guns, they fight and they kill other people ... they are not scared of police because they have too much money, so when the police come to arrest them, they have the money to pay ... (Man – Pakistan – Catholic Christian)

When she embraced religion she (*the interviewee*) involved some friends in reading sacred texts. Then they began to plague posters in which people were discouraged to believe in religion. That's why one of her friends was scared and decided not to continue, and she told the teacher everything. The fact of having religious students at school can be a danger to the students themselves who are precluded from the chance to graduate and job opportunities, but it is also a danger for teachers, because they risk being denied the opportunity to continue teaching. (Woman – China – Evangelical Christian [synthesis provided by the translator])

Another case is constituted by the different kinds of limitations in the exercise of political and social rights, and particularly by the exclusion from certain welfare amenities, including the possibility to attend school:

(...) I was in fifth grade and there was a specific school for talents, a kind of high school, and I passed the entry exam but they did not let me in because I was Bahá'i. It was the first time I had to face this ... because at that age you're hardly still a Bahá'i, you're very little. But they told me: "Since you are Bahá'i, you cannot enter". (Woman – Iran – Bahá'i)

(...) there are many obstacles that the regime also creates to the Catholic Church, especially after the law issued in 1995, where the regime avails all the activities of a social, charitable nature, and the aid to those in difficulty, but also in the field of health care, in education, then all the parts of charity that concern the action of the Church. There are very strong obstacles created by the regime, which a few months ago came to close eight clinics run by the Catholic Church and closed a school in the capital, a school of the Catholic Church which among other things was the school attended by our seminarians from the minor seminary, so there are a number of obstacles; for example, the regime closed all the information, the Catholic Church published different types of magazines, newspapers, and all this was closed by the regime, so in Eritrea today there is freedom of worship, but not religious freedom. (Man – Religious leader – Catholic Christian of Eritrean rite)

Not to mention the recurrence of abuses and injustices, in the form of, for example, a boycott of entrepreneurial or working activity (an example reported during the focus group discussions is that of Hindu fishermen in Bangladesh, who have faced a sudden death of fish), expropriation from their properties, the application of discriminatory methods of evaluation, or even threats to their own safety and that of family members. As evidenced by some individual stories, since their tender age many interviewees have begun to experience the condition of victims of completely unjustified abuses and violence:

(...) the government intelligentsia began to investigate who the pastor was, and they realized it was me. And so the persecution began (...). They come here and tell me: get out of here, out! We'll kill you! The persecution began. We had made 2,400 meters (...) we had the machinery, we had bought it ... I had just committed to it, when suddenly a military commission said that they would expropriate this land. I said no, that they could not do it (...) because I had an ecclesiastical-social project; I wanted to make a church, a technical school, an orphanage and a canteen. They could not do this; I showed them the numbers, the data regarding the situation that was characterizing that area. A young entrepreneur, a profiteer ... they sent the National Guard, they expropriated the land, they hit me, they threw me on the ground, me, my wife, the Christian brothers who were there. The people revolted in the neighborhood. They started pulling tear gas bombs. We resisted, but eventually they took me along with 25 other people, and they took the ground. (Man – Venezuela – Protestant Evangelical Religious leader)

(...) Dad said, "They're not hurting us, but they do not allow us to work. So they do not allow me to be a man and raise my family". So, he came to Italy.
  (...) even xxx, the hairdresser's shop, is from this Egyptian father. He had important cloth shops in Cairo, him and the brothers –who still have them in xxx– and they came away because the Muslims cut their trade relations and brought them to close up. So he came away, even with an invalid brother. (Women – Nuns – Catholic Christians)

This was also a big problem because when a Christian is intelligent they give different scores just because you are Christian. (Man – Pakistan – Catholic Christian)

(…) they wanted us to join them (*the interviewed' mates*) in music, be-cause we were musicians. We studied music in church … when I was 9 years old, after that when I was in college I played different functions, my parents were asking to join them in music but we rejected their offers, and they were jealous because we were good also at sports. I was an ath-lete, I was a runner, so they were jealous and our problem started like this; my Islamic teacher told me to read some Koranic verses, because there is a book of Islamic verses and it is obligatory to read their verses. So my teacher told me to read it but it was a little hard for me because Koran is only in the Arabic language, so I read something that I was not good at, I made mistakes and he was a little bit angry with me and he batted me and he told me not to make mistakes again. He thought I made mistake on purpose … like I know how to read, but I made mistake. After that, it was not a problem, but after three or four lessons it was a break time … three or four students beat me during the break time, they entered the room and started beating me because I had made a mistake.
    Interviewer: When students were beating you, did they have to hide from the teacher or could they beat you without any trouble?
    No, they don't hide because in Pakistan Muslim students can do what-ever they want. They have too much money, so they can do whatever they want. Even teacher sometimes beat students. (Man – Pakistan – Catholic Christian)

After these events I was afraid and therefore I did not go anymore. The director advised me to renounce the faith, so I was forced to leave my job. The manager also told me that if he arrested me again he would not help me out of prison anymore. (Woman – China – Church of God Almighty)

Finally, some interviewees reported to have been victims of discriminations in the access to given occupations and professional roles, due to the presence of "glass ceilings" or to vexatious behaviors. Although certainly not as dramatic as violence and direct persecution, these situations are revealed to us, through the story of those who suffered them directly, as strong obstacles to personal and professional projects, to legitimate career ambitions, or simply to the ex-pectation of enjoying a fair treatment.

(…) the high level must be Muslim, regardless of whether you are capable or not. In fact, the reason I left is because every time I submitted job applications I passed all the possible and impossible exams with a good mark, the only thing that remains ... my surname is xxx, I am a Christian. And on the identity card this is what is written. (Man – Egypt – Coptic Catholic Christian)

(...) most are out of the country, let's say half, because after we graduated it was not ... the situation was not very good even for work. And even for those who wanted to continue studying there were not so many options, so many opportunities. And then, when I finished, I started working in a private company, but after a year they knew that we are Bahá'ís and they expelled me. (Woman – Iran – Bahá'i)

(...) unfortunately, there is also the difficulty that the company supports you up to a certain point. It does not make all the struggles it does against the State. If the State threatens the company saying it cannot have a Bahá'i employee ... it's difficult. For example, the company where I worked for six years had the problem that you could not build your career any further because otherwise you could spread the rumors in the corridor ... and what happened to me was that, at a certain point, I realized that either I had to do the job I was doing as a junior for a lifetime or I had to choose something else ... (Woman – Iran – Bahá'i)

There was no real persecution, there was never a ... a ban to go to Mass, there was nothing like that. For two reasons: he was engaged in many other wars, not in that against us. The second: we could not bring danger to him. He was afraid of the Shiites, who slaughtered them, of the Kurds of the North, who slaughtered them, the Christians were the good ones that ... (...).

So to speak, like sheep (...), because in order to live together you have to do this. So there were no problems, persecutions in that period there, say 10 or 15 years before the war, to enter. On the other hand, discrimination and various things remain, such as the results of school exams, a job, if you present yourself and introduce other Muslims, you always reach the second place. Those are indirect things, but okay, we lived together, let's say. We lived together. (Woman – Iraq – Chaldean Catholic Christian)

In all these cases, the role of religious affiliations can easily be seen as the reason for the persecutions and abuses suffered. It is therefore relatively simple to hypothesize how they can submit a request for protection based on religious motives. However, based on the testimonies gathered during the study, it is easy to grasp how the violation of individual rights and dignity often passes through subtler practices, which hide behind the appearance of legality. In a

very simple manner, this Egyptian man, for example, describes the exposition
to abuses and vexations that marked his everyday life:

> For example, when you present yourself to make documents, they ask
> you: "What's your name?", "My name is R.". But it is not known whether
> you are a Christian or a Muslim. "And what is your father's name?", "My
> father's name is T." But he has not yet discovered whether I am a Christian
> or a Muslim. Up to the fourth, fifth (generation), to great-grandfather, to
> know if you are a Christian or a Muslim. If they find out you're a Christian
> "No, documents are still missing". It is always like this. (Man – Egypt –
> Coptic Orthodox)

In this other testimony, a young girl coming from Iran describes how the awareness of their strong vulnerability is part of the everyday life of some religious
minorities' members, to the point of encouraging a sort of spirit of resignation
and a sense of vulnerability and danger that accompanies daily existence, regardless of whether or not they directly suffered persecution:

> (…) because we are used to living like that, we are used to them every day,
> maybe they come to take us, so the way of life in Iran for the Bahá'ís is like
> that, always waiting for someone who (*she laughs*) comes to the door to
> pick you up. So in the end you're used to living like this. (Woman –
> Iran – Bahá'i)

These testimonies bring us to the next section, in which we will analyze
how religion can become a relevant factor in the genesis of the decision to
migrate well beyond the "codified" situations. In other words, the concept
of religion as the direct cause of a forced migration, today, is challenged by
the growing complexity of human (forced) mobility, in its turn influenced
by the intricacy of the sending countries' scenario. In this context, religions
and religious memberships are a sort of filter through which trying to grasp
the two phenomena.

4   How Religion Intermingles Many Contextual and Personal Variables

The first observation worth making is that, in agreement with the international literature (and with what we have deeply analyzed about specific contexts:
see Chapters 5 and 6), religious factors are by and large intermingled with
ethno-racial, cultural, political, and economic factors, up to the point that it

can be difficult to isolate their relevance. Once again, this aspect finds an immediate –and "suffered"– confirmation in the testimonies gathered during the fieldwork. The following statements made by three "religious" men from three different continents provide a good example. The former explicitly refers to political power and its contamination with terrorist organizations. The second calls into question the links between political authorities and organized crime, by alluding to an instrumental use of religious issues to get rid of any potential dissident. The third concerns the legacy of colonization, as well as the tendency to overlap Christianity and the West, thus making today's Christians pay for the sins of yesterday's Christians.

> This was before my killing problem. Then sometime after I come here, then coming again: where is Sajjat? Where is Sajjat? Looking for me, my account is blocked and everything, this is not for religion, this is political.
>   Interviewer: But is the responsibility always of this terrorist group?
>   No, the Government is the responsible. Terrorists have only tried to kill me, they don't like Shiya.
>   Interviewer: So for your religious issue the problem is with a terrorist group, for your political activity the problem is with the Government…
>   Yes, Government, but the Government is linked to terrorists. Government control … Government is responsible to make everything stop, but Government is … it didn't stop this. (Man – Pakistan – Muslim)

> A dean, a military friend of mine, a dean of the president's escort, told me: "xxx, save your life because they kill you. And your life has a price". Ten days later they kidnapped me. I do not know who he was, I cannot say who he was, but they kidnapped me, they hit me, they put me in a cell, in a place but I do not know if it was a cell … I stayed there ten days, then I did not know anything, then they released me and told me: "if you do not go away, we'll kill you, you, let's kill your wife, your children, and we'll say it was 'el ampa', delinquency". At this point, I had to think for my children, for my wife. A person who lives in Italy, an evangelical, knew about this and sent me the ticket. (Man – Venezuela – Protestant Evangelical Religious leader)

> My starting hypothesis is that somehow religion comes to identify a group of people not so much as a religion, but as a group of people that is uncomfortable, that I do not want, that I hate, that I do not, to which I do not want to allow entry into my community, and this is why the religious aspect, from my point of view, is not persecuted, that is, there will

certainly be cases in which Christ is why he persecuted the Christians, but I think, at least as a working hypothesis, which in most cases is because those people who are Christians constitute a group of former colonizers, that is the disturbing minority group, people who put you in question ... (Man – Religious leader – Catholic Christian)

Another case in point emerged from the study is that of Tibetan Buddhists, victims of the "assimilationistic" policy of the Chinese government. Here, the violation of religious rights and the persecution of the faithful is only an ingredient of a wider long-standing conflict, in which the independence of Tibet and the preservation of its cultural identity is at stake. But even in the famous case of Nigeria, the explosion of violence against Christians and the advent of Boko Haram rank as the pinnacle of an involutionary path. As it emerges from this dramatic testimony, in highly compromised situations, the same distinction between majority and minority gives way to a context of general terror and insecurity. And religion ends up trivially constituting the pretext around which grudges and long-standing conflicts crystallize:

(...) in the Northern part of Nigeria we have a lots of different crisis, different types of problems: ethnic problems, religious problems and so forth and in the Northern part of Nigeria, where I come from, Christians are basically a minority and in the Southern part Christians are the majority, so during my time in Nigeria we normally faced a lot of ... for example, clashes between ethnic groups and between religious groups and usually because the Christians were like the minority in the North they were usually the ones who suffered the most and discussions happened. I got admission to the University of Maiduguri, the University of Maiduguri was part of, is located in the city where the terrorist Boko Haram originated from and is a predominant Muslim city, even the school is a predominantly Muslim students' school and after the rise of Boko Haram in the city, the city was like no longer the same. There were so many incidents of terrorist attacks, suicide attacks, some students have been killed, Christians –not only Christians, but also Muslims and any Muslims who don't agree with the doctrines of Boko Haram were also victims– were killed. (Man – Nigeria – Christian now attending a Baptist Church)

It has not always been like that but it escalated. So I was staying with my father so mainly we attended this Catholic church so that Catholic church is not so far from the Mosque and sometimes when we go for Bible story on Friday evening and the priest always preaches peace and not to fight but at this stage any small thing would become a religious problem. (Man – Nigeria – Catholic Christian)

Moreover, the "simple" contraposition between Christians and Muslims –that is the way in which these situations are often perceived by the Italian public opinion– results in obscuring a very complex state of affairs. As it emerges from the story of this interviewee, the mere fact of coming from a region with an Islamic majority can turn into an unshakable stigma, paradoxically considering as a threat those who flee from the risk of persecution:

> (...) sometimes because of ignorance, many people in the South feel that everybody that comes from the North is a Muslim and they have that stereotype that everybody who is a Muslim or who is from the North is a terrorist, so there is this sort of divide between people from the North and people from the South and it's not easy to really adapt to that way of life. It's not that is not possible, is possible but is something that can take time. For example, when I was trying to relocate and to find another place to live and find a job I was in Lagos which is the commercial capital city of Nigeria and there was a place I went to look for a house and the landlord of the house refused to give me the house because he said I was maybe a Boko Haram member and these are like some of the stereotypes that people from the North can face: you are from the North and the Muslims don't like you because you are a Christian, and in the South people don't like you because they think you are a Muslim, so when people in the North, they share similar cultures, not really identical, but people in the North have a certain way of living that is totally different from the lives of those from the southern part of Nigeria (...) many of them don't even believe that there are Christians who live in the northern part of Nigeria, so this was one of the problems, maybe the major problem that contributed, for me; I wanted to leave Nigeria and find some other place. (Man – Nigeria – Christian now attending a Baptist Church)

Religion, when it takes on the appearance of singular phenomena –such as *Ogboni*, a sect rooted in Nigeria–, crystallizes dramatic widespread violence. Following the chronicle of our migrant informants, it is quite impossible to understand if practices such as persecutions towards unarmed people and sacrifices of every kind of creature (including human beings) obey to religious precepts and edicts or to power strategies; as well if they come from the government's initiative or from anti-system militants. According to some of our key informants, it also happens that these organizations are replicated in Italy, as a way to involve migrants and asylum seekers in deviant activities such as drug dealing and to recruit victims of sex exploitation. In this case, the demand of asylum turns out to be an instrument used by both victims and execution-ers, thus making the relationship between migration and religion even more complex; not to mention the difficulty in examining asylum applications, as we will analyze later.

Another interesting example is offered by a Pakistani interviewee, who ob-tained a status of protection after having provided the Commission proofs of the menaces of which he was victim because of his membership in a reli-gious/political Islamic organization. His case actually demonstrates how dif-ficult it can be to define the concept of "minority group" within a context that does not offer protection, despite the clear exposition to serious risks. In this case, the interviewee declared to have survived after a car-accident caused by his persecutors, in which his brother died and his cousin was seriously in-jured. The accident happened after several threatening letters. According to his interpretation, the reluctance of the police to take his report seriously was due to the strong connection between the political authorities and the Sunni component, traditionally antagonistic to the one to which the interviewee belongs.

> Yes, I am threat, I go to police, Chekoala police, I give letter, and police record everything, I have made application, I said: please, I'm not safe. And I have ... they said they give me help, what they can do, but (...) police don't care, police say ok, ok, I said I have this problem, I have this letter, I have this telephone number, please take it, but they don't.
> Interviewer: Why do you think they didn't care?
> He is Sunni, the Government is Sunni, this Government, Government, No ... So I have myself escort, my cousin, my brother ... (Man – Pakistan – Muslim)

Moving in a different context, the following testimony describes the rapid de-terioration of the situation in Iraq, after the arrival of the US arm. The inter-viewee suggests how the "martyrdom" of Christians has to do with unknown logics of power, evidently hidden behind the rapid materialization of anti-Christian terrorist organizations.

> After the arrival of the Americans in 2003, many attacks against the churches began, they were things referred to internal war, religious war, but in reality it is always guided by some external hands as for example if we come to the present Isis, not Isis itself, there is always a power over Isis,

because Isis is not formed in a day and a night and said: "Here we meet and do something". It is always a programmed thing. Ok, here. And so it was these attacks on churches, so many killings of priests, bishops, in public, on the street, they were beheaded, many lay people were killed, churches were bombed, robberies happened, they entered during the hours of the Mass and threatened people, they exploded bombs. (Woman – Iraq – Chaldean Catholic Christian)

Just to cite another example, a young man who comes from Cameroon, and who has declared to be a Buddhist, has described a sending context strongly influenced by a societal élite hegemonized by French masonry. Strong discrimination suffered by people not affiliated to this organization would have a part, according to his interpretation, in the genesis of migration. Indeed, adherence to this power structure involves strong limitations to personal freedom. It is interesting to note how, in his story, religion can have a different meaning depending on the situation: on the one hand, it can be an instrument of enslavement to the logic of power (a sort of "opium of the peoples" of Marxian memory); on the other hand, a lever that awakens consciences:

Whenever I was at my home for Buddhist meetings, one or two secret agents came to follow the meeting and tried to get some good or bad information, but always to hurt you, because something that is understood, becomes something that he does not get along with the government. They like people who are stupid enough, who do not wake up to the reality of society. Once there is someone who awakens consciences to say that it is useless to wait there and say prayers that do not help you, but it is better to get busy, trying to make money for them is not good. We must have people who always say yes. That's why I did not get along with them. I had to leave this place and I went very far. (Man – Cameron – Buddhist)

Here, again, we can appreciate, in all its ambivalence, the strict relationship between religion and freedom. That is, we can appreciate how the theme of religious freedom –and of its violation– constitutes a litmus test of individual freedom *tout court*; alternatively, as the reflection of our interviewee seems to suggest, a litmus test of the future prospects of an entire country and of an entire generation. This solicits us to re-discuss, in depth, the distinction between voluntary migration and forced migration: should the concept of forced migration be limited to the situations in which individual survival and integrity is seriously in danger? Or should it be extended to every situation of serious limitation of individual freedom and lack of democracy?

So that's where it's done, but I did not accept it. I decided to run away because I did not want to work with him and because they persecuted me so much and followed me to my house in the meetings that took place in my house and ... all this there, I had this feeling of fear while walking on the road I used to take to go to my job because I was afraid ... There, one always feels that one was arrested because he said this ... There is not this freedom of speech, there is not this freedom of thought. And young people do not dream, they do not have this support to say that: "I want to become like this gentleman, that...", No, because if you go to the Cameroon Government website, the Minister, the Director, are all elderly. They are old, all. (Man – Cameron – Buddhist)

Finally, this woman coming from Iraq –who proudly declares that she did not follow the "easier" route to request political asylum, "because if my country does not offer protection, I cannot ask another country to protect me"– illustrates, in turn, as, in a context of insecurity, minority groups are most at risk, even independently of a precise wish to persecute them:

So, indirectly, because when I left the country, the country was in pieces after the entry of the Americans in Iraq the year before, there was total chaos at all levels, social, economic, infrastructure, protection, police, we did not have, still if you have a thief in the house you do not even have a number to call, and still things work like that. And ... I had finished the specialty in 2003 and as a law in Iraq all specialists from one to two years post specialties are assigned to remote places, in the countryside, border, to serve the centers there, because otherwise the doctors are not there, then go back to the city of origin, of the residence. So, in 2004, I fell on the list of distribution, I was assigned a city just in the border with Iran, between Iraq and Iran, then go to that place there was almost impossible, because the attacks, the attacks were almost every day, a tide. But more than this I thought the fact that I'm Christian, I do not wear the veil, so you can already see aesthetically, I'm not dark, I have a fairly clear color, that is, we can see that we are Christians.
     Interviewer: Also from color?
     Even from the color, yes, we are a clearer complexion, us. And then I said...
     Interviewer: Can I ask you what it's called ... ethnicity, your?

No, no, I'm Catholic, Chaldean. Chaldea proper, of the ancient origin of the Christians. And ... so I thought that just to go there by bus takes me a week, makes me go back a weekend at my house, it brings me so many risks. Both internal and external objects because there has already been a bit of guerrilla warfare among the races, then it is always the Christians who go in between, even if we do not get involved, we always enter the middle. (Woman – Iraq – Chaldean Catholic Christian)

Lastly, to augment even further the level of complexity of the issue under discussion, we have to consider how religious-based violations and persecutions often occur also in transit countries, and during the most dramatic phases of the migration journey. Therefore, some respondents reported how, during their travel and in the time spent in the refugee camps, they became victims (or spectators) of different kinds of violence and abuses, because they were identified as members of given religious groups. In the dramatic chronicle of this interviewee, bogus religious beliefs can turn into violent fetishes, transforming victims (the migrants who escape from their country) into executioners, who "immolate" other (impure) migrants as a sacrifice in order to reach their "promised land".

In Africa, you have fetish, you have ghosts that you use to destroy people, or your mission is to come to Europe to destroy, so you are not clean with that. Inside the boat, you start to manifest, you start to confess, you start saying things why you want to go to Europe. So, there's a power in the sea, that you can't ... Maybe you have some medicines in your pocket and take it to Europe to destroy other persons, so you start manifest, maybe rolling on the ground, behaving like a fish, or a snake, and people who are there, know this sort of things, have seen that before, so ... so they will simply take the person and put the person inside the water. So things like this happen. Because in the boat there are more than fifty people, maybe one or two people who have this kind of power, when they get in the middle of this water, they must manifest.

(...) Most of the times you see ladies ... they start falling on the ground and behaving like snakes, or start shouting, so this makes us understand that these people are not clean. And if we don't throw these people in the water, the water, the boat will become full of water, so what they do fast is taking the person and throwing inside the water. (Man – Nigeria – Catholic Christian)

5   The Variety of Religious-Based Persecution's Agents

The muddle of religious factors and political factors does not exhaust the intricacy of the contemporary scenario. Reflecting the growing complexity of the current landscape –on which we will enter in more detail later (Chapter 11, §3.1)–, our fieldwork proves the variety of both threats and persecution's agents which can produce (forced) mobility, well beyond the traditional refugee archetype. As well as the widest range of risks, which can justify the request for protection. Governmental authorities –or the other power structures– are surely a crucial actor, when they directly oppress the members of given religions, limit citizens' religious freedom, encourage or permit a discriminating treatment of minority groups, and impose a climate of suspect and intolerance by means of a radical application or religious rules. Nevertheless, several others may be the persecutory agents. We have already cited the case of Nigerians who escape from the violence perpetrated by Boko Haram: in this example, the persecutor is not the State, but an organization that controls part of the territory of the State (while the latter does not want or cannot offer protection).

It is particularly interesting to note that religious authorities and religious leaders are often referred to as the main cause of the troubles experienced by future migrants. Moreover, in the turbulent context characterizing many of the countries of origin of the current migratory flows towards Italy, the concept of religious authority is often very distant from how it is framed in Europe. The chronicles, often confused and emotionally overloaded, of our interviewees, shed light on forms of "pre-modern" religiosity. Forms that make it rather difficult to trace the boundary between "authentic" religious feelings (although expressed in radicalized ways) and the pretentious use of religious obligations to harass "sacrificial victims". Just to cite an example, one of our interviewees –a young man coming from Nigeria–, reported that he was obliged to escape from his country since he had been selected to succeed, after his death, to the man involved in the worshiping of the "ghost":

> My story is that the reason why I left my country and I come to Italy is that after the man that worships the ghost of our land died on 5th November 2013 they buried the man on 15th November 2013. On January 10th 2014, in the evening by 8 o'clock, three elderly men came to our house and told us that the ghost had chosen me to worship him. And I told them: "Why? Because I am a small boy. How can the ghost choose me, instead of them, that elderly man?" They tell us that the ghost chooses by small age and I told them that I am sorry, that I will not worship those ghosts, because

> I'm a Christian, and they go. And they also come again on 20th January
> 2014 and tell us, they come in the evening by 8 o' clock, the same time,
> and I also tell them that I won't worship this God, because I'm a Christian.
> Then go. They also come on 30; they also come on 30 January 2014 by 8
> o' clock in the evening and tell us the same thing. I tell them that I will
> not worship those ghosts, even my father told them that his son would
> not worship those ghosts, because we are Christians. (Man – Nigeria –
> Pentecostal Christian Church [former Catholic Christian])

Due to his refusal, the interviewee had to watch the murder of his father, who
had opposed to this request. His chronicle is particularly impressive, since it
demonstrates the manner in which religious persecution can suddenly break
into one's life.

> So, since I was born I never participate in their ... idles, worshiping the
> ghost. Even my family were Christians, I attend the Catholic Church in
> my village (...).
>   You know how evil operates? Those are rituals, when they have rituals,
> people from another people come, you don't know them. Even the time
> when this thing happened, they give me the 10th of December, when I'm
> on the way, going to the market, I would see people I don't know, they
> wanted me, I have to obey them, they were threatening my life, I don't
> know the person, but the person is threatening my life, he is not in that
> village, he just met me in the market and he is pointing me...
>   (...) anywhere they see me they would kill me, because I didn't come, I
> didn't follow them in worshipping the ghost. (Man – Nigeria – Christian
> Pentecostal Church [former Catholic Christian])

We have already observed that what is violated is often not the right to believe,
but the right to convert to a different faith, a minority or otherwise opposed
faith. On the contrary, this interviewee offers us a specular testimony. Once
again, in his narrative, considerations pertaining to religion are mixed with
others types of considerations, in this case of an economic nature (the impossibility of inheriting goods for those who do not belong to the "right" religion).
Yet, "formally", it is his refusal to convert that becomes the cause of persecution, giving it a halo of legitimacy.

> So, what happened is that there was a serious crisis in Jos so that I lost my
> dad for that. It was like a war between the Christians and the Muslims and

my mother she is a Christian so we decided to go back to the village and I decided to be a Christian because I don't love Muslims so when the village they were like trying to kill me because I was supposed to be a Muslim since I was the son of my father. We were three, me and my sisters.

We all decided to be Christians, so the problem is that the village say we must be Muslims but we say no, we are not going to be Muslims, but they say we had to and the problem is that my father inherit this property but we cannot inherit it without being a Muslim, so they were trying to kill my parents but I couldn't go with them because I have a family: I have a wife and a daughter, but I had to leave them so that my son and my daughter are with my mum. My wife left me because of the problem. She has to leave me because they were imposing us to be Muslims, she never wanted to be a Muslim so if she was with me she had to be a Muslim so for not being a Muslim she left me. (Man – Nigeria – Christ Church)

Civil society's actors may be another persecution agent, particularly relevant within non-democratic contexts. Here, the threatened subjects are not provided with adequate protection by the authorities. Moreover, these very authorities are the ones who legitimize abuses and discriminations on a religious basis, even rewarding them as expressions of loyalty to the regime. As we have already observed, the school system constitutes, in this regard, one of the most sensitive environments, together with the field of economics, where religious affiliation can become an easy alibi to justify discriminations, abuses, and frauds.

When I was in middle school, my classmates beat me and teachers criticized me, disrespected me, treated me badly because I was a believer and did not respect my beliefs. Once they beat me so much that I ended up in the hospital. (Man – China – Church of God Almighty)

(…) stalking, the fact that a person fires from a business because being a Christian was derided or discriminated against is very subtle. Hence, persecution in interpersonal relationships is important, especially if there is no rule in these countries to protect against this discrimination. In interpreting relationships, persecution can occur, but it is enough for me to ask the public authorities that the matter is resolved. But if there is no such legislation in the countries of origin or it is not intended to be applied, it is again a persecution. (Man – Expert)

Furthermore, even family members and local communities have emerged, during the fieldwork, as frequently involved in imposing, in the name of alleged religious precepts, choices and behaviors contrary to individual will. Arranged (forced) marriages are a case in point, together with the lack of parents' consensus towards a freely chosen nuptial union, particularly in the case of inter-religious marriages.

Finally, as demonstrated by the following examples, the family itself can perpetrate abuses and violations in the name of religion. Once again, it is very easy to understand how reasons of economic convenience, social "respectability", political opportunity, and superstition, often tend to prevail over genuine religious sentiments.

> They insist I became a Muslim because of my father property. So, we don't give you your property without being a Muslim and they were trying to kill my wife, so she left. When my father died, we think the best place to go was to go back to his village, and the problem started in the village, while I think I was safe but I was not. This is a Muslim village and a Christian village ... both. And in my father family they wanted me to be a Muslim and it was the family of my father who insisted me to be a Muslim. But I want to be a Christian. (Man – Nigeria – Christ Church)

> My family, they believe in fetish religion, so from the beginning, when I was young I didn't know all about what it meant to be in a fetish religion, I decided to follow Christ. So it became a problem with my father because I'm the first one of the family. Normally as the first one of the family after my father is dead I'm supposed to take from my father, I'm supposed to continue the fetish religion from my father. But for me I don't like the religion, because it is contrary with Christ, so I decided not to follow up with this religion. Anyway, my father was still alive, so before he died I was supposed to be in this religion called Ogbony. It is popular in Edo State. The majority in Nigeria does not know this religion, because it is with Edo people, who usually have this religion. These people have this religion because they want to be famous, rich...
>
> When I was born, for the first eight years, nine years, my father went to their meetings, to their meetings whenever they meet, all of them came with their sons, their first sons, who will take over from them, we sit down with them, sometimes when they want to do something terrible they go to a place where we cannot go, until we are more than eighteen, then we are fully initiated and we can go to that place where they make these strong, strong sacrifices. When I was young, I used to go with my father, until thirteen years, when I knew the difference between

Christianity and these things, I stopped going. Then when I got to that age when I was supposed to be initiated, at eighteen years, then he started, at the beginning he tried to persuade me peacefully, but when he saw that persuading me was not, that he won't not make me one of them, he decided to make it with force. Then the young ones came, like six of them, trying to force me, to get me to the shrine, because they go to a shrine, where they keep their ghost, but I refused, then they started beating me up, trying to force me, they molested me, and I was able to run away, and I went to my friend's place, but they came to my friend's place and I was so lucky that I noticed earlier that they were coming, so I ran away from there, and I went to Niger, I spent some days in Niger, well I spent some, you know, many years in Niger, before my father's younger brother, he also lives in Niger, so he learned from my father that I was in Niger, then problems started again. (Man – Nigeria – Catholic Christian)

As the reported cases suggest, when acting in the name of religion, the violation of individual rights –be it mediated by political and/or religious authorities, or by an actor of civil society or even by the same family– calls into question the relationship between genders and generations. In other words, besides being influenced by the relations between social classes and between political and religious groups, violations of individual rights often reflect the patriarchal structures of many societies, the gender regimes, the expectations connected to generational roles. Therefore, it is not surprising that to be frequently called into question are matters pertaining to marriage choices (in particular, the choice to marry a partner of a different religion), to the relationships between fathers and children, to the rules that regulate hereditary transmission and the transmission of roles within the community; not to mention the fear to suffer genital mutilation, excision, forced sterilization.

My mother, she is a Christian, but ... she is not able to fully practice a Christian life because she got married to my father, so in Nigeria a woman, it is not like in Europe where a woman can say something, in Nigeria, when you come to my State, a woman does not say, what her husband says, that's what she walks with. (Man – Nigeria – Christian now attending the Adventist Church)

(...) I come from Yemen, from the South of Yemen and I've been here in Italy for almost 5 years, and I came ... I left my country because I had to leave because I do not find my soul there ... Let's say I'm a woman and I'm different I am free, and I want to be as I want ... I have a bit of a Western woman, but let's say in an oriental, conservative environment where women do not have many rights, they have no rights, let's say. That's why I decided to leave. (Woman – Yemen – Muslim)

Once again, it is immediate to grasp, through the testimonies of our interviewees, the close link between religion, individual freedom, and the quality of democracy. The latter intended not as an academic concern, but as something that pervasively affects individual lives and prospects. The same Yemeni woman sums it up well.

In my country, if the man does not accept the divorce then the woman cannot have it. It is not a decision from two sides, it is always man. If he wants to divorce, yes, but if he does not want to leave you like that, half way. You are no longer married but you are not divorced. These are the laws when we do not have civil laws like in Europe. In our Muslim countries, the law is not civil but it is based on religion, what is written in religion, so we do not have this parity between man and woman because they use religion to make law and instead if we use this because we know that religion Islamic is almost 1,400 years ago ... and all that is written inside the Quran is good for that era, there is written of things we say as law, ok there are, but this was fine for that era of 1,400 years ago but not you can apply it now. (Woman – Yemen – Muslim)

Finally, as we will analyze in the next chapter, asylum seekers' reception systems are more and more challenged, today, not only by the "simple" violations of religious rights and religious freedoms. An important share of contemporary migrants –independently of the migration channel for which they opt– wants to escape a radical interpretation of religious prescriptions, such as that imposed by some authoritarian regimes. Here, the concepts of religious identity and religious freedom appear in their suggestively, and not unequivocally, interconnected nature. As argued by these last testimonies, the violation of the principle of personal freedom can assume different forms and degrees, including a persistent sense of oppression. And, as efficaciously synthesized by the second one, maybe migration is not a forced choice, but just a simple wish: it is the best thing to do, an exit strategy to realize those personal goals made unachievable by an oppressive societal context.

(...) I always had so many questions, "Why do we have to cover ourselves? Why do we have to do this? Why?". And then sincerely after a while I grew up I do not know, I felt that ... all day always I had to think, this is right or wrong, so ... life had become too heavy, distressing. Because, I know, maybe you said a little lie, but you already felt guilty because you said "now God is staring at me" (...).

So it's not that you say "Okay, Ok, I do not follow and I do not care and it ends there". At whatever level of your life you arrive there are discussions you have to do. And then if ... like ... if you do not overcome these discussions maybe you lose an opportunity of your life (...).

Then in the field of art it is very difficult, because for example you cannot find the books, the paintings come ... that is, the naked body is forbidden, so maybe, I know, I wanted to study the history of art in Europe ... but I did not found the books, or if you found them they were already all censored. (Woman – Iran – Protestant Christian [former Muslim])

So I thought about it and said: "Now I have three choices in front of me. Or I go and risk my life as a life and as a woman, because there is also the possibility of violence and things that happen ... and they happen! Or I'm at home and I'm a housewife, but I've studied medicine for six years and five years of specialty, if we talk only about medicine it took me eleven years, and I'm at home, which is something ... frustrating. The third choice I escape from this country". So I thought about it, I wrote a little about the three things and I said: "The best one seems to me the third". So it's not a wish, but a ... the best thing. (Woman – Iraq – Chaldean Catholic Christian)

At the end, once put in a humanistic perspective and from the point of view of the people directly involved (Chapter 2), it becomes quite impossible to clearly distinguish between voluntary and forced migration; particularly when this distinction calls into question a dimension such as religion and its strict relationship with personal identity and personal freedom. Correspondingly, it is easy to understand how the extraordinary complexity of contemporary (forced) mobility –as illustrated by the evidence discussed in this chapter– turns out to be quite difficult to process through standardized procedures, such as the procedures regulating the acknowledgment of a status of protection. Besides, it is extraordinarily complex to rightly grasp and recognize the role of religion in the asylum seekers' trajectories and choices. These issues will constitute the object of the following chapter.

CHAPTER 11

The "Space" of Religion in the Assessment of Asylum Applications

Laura Zanfrini

As anticipated in the previous chapter, one of the main purposes of this part of the study is to inquire how the process of asylum applications' assessment leads to the emergence and the acknowledgment of all those aspects connected in many ways to asylum seekers' religious belonging. In Chapter 9, we have illustrated the Italian legislation in force, in its contents and its weaknesses. Here, we will examine the attitude of the various stakeholders involved, with an attempt to provide an answer to the following question: do these aspects constitute a relevant variable in acknowledging the need of protection, possibly even beyond what established by the legislative framework?

This goal implies having to deal with a bigger question regarding the criteria useful to define the "borders" of forced mobility, which helps to distinguish between voluntary and forced migrants. As it is well known, this distinction, on which migratory regimes have been traditionally based, today is strongly challenged from both a political and an ethical point of view. The authors of Chapters 2 and 4 have already analyzed some of the main issues involved, and the manner in which those have been influencing the legislative evolution at both the international and the European level. Here, it is useful to remember that it is exactly because of the progressive inclusion of new categories of people and circumstances into the systems of protection that the line between voluntary and forced migrations has become increasingly porous and disputable, to the point of putting in question its own existence (for a deeper analysis, see Zanfrini, 2019). Our hypothesis is that this trend influences the attitude of all the actors of the reception system, from the commissioners in charge of the asylum demands' evaluation to the operators who "prepare" the asylum seekers for the interview.

1 Religion(s) and the Borders of Forced Mobility

As we have already described (Chapters 3 and 9), unlike other types of migrants, variously defined by the laws of individual countries, the refugee figure is based on a precise –internationally recognized– legal institution, contained in the *Declaration on the Status of Refugees*. However, given the growing complexity of human mobility at the global scale, nowadays asylum seekers resemble less and less the Ideal Type of refugee inspired by the 1951 Geneva Convention. First of all, forced migration has usually a collective, not individual, configuration (Zolberg, 1989), and reflects a shared need to flee from situations of crisis that have unpredictable consequences and evolution. Moreover, the threat from which one may flee is not necessarily the State, but it may be represented by an agent of civil society, or even by a family member, as we have also observed in the previous chapter. Furthermore, the fear of persecution no longer only concerns imprisonment, but it also refers to the widest range of human rights, including, for example: the fear of being subjected to sterilization or excision or of being imposed into forced marriage, violations of the rights of homosexuals, or even survival jeopardized by only announced environmental catastrophes (Black *et al.*, 2011; Kumin, 2007; Pickering, 2011). Migration is sometimes not only forced (i.e. due to the lack of other possibilities of survival and development), but even compulsory, triggered by various forms of trafficking and enslavement. Moreover, because of its circumscribed nature, the Convention's definition of "refugee" is poorly equipped to protect people who cross international borders in the context of wars and civil unrest (IOM, 2017). Finally, protection systems have been built in compliance with a male archetype, a circumstance that makes said systems inadequate to meet the needs and the specific risks posed to female migrants (Pickering, 2011). Not to mention their inadequacy in the face of the growing incidence of minors, sometimes unaccompanied, who are the most vulnerable among the vulnerable (Valtolina, 2014). This complex scenario –amply mirrored in the characters of migration fluxes currently addressed to Italy– must be taken into account in order to apprehend the relevance of various aspects connected to religions, in their interrelation with other variables such as gender, age, family status, sexual orientation, and so on.

Religion is one of the causes of persecution specifically evoked by the 1951 Geneva Convention, together with race, nationality, belonging to a given social group, and political opinions. However, its role must to be contextualized within the complex reality of contemporary human mobility, and particularly within the so-called *migration–asylum nexus*: this expression describes how fluxes due to different reasons and inscribed in different legislative regimes display themselves through similar modes, such as through the same routes and entry channels (including the demand for asylum), within the same international context. Hence, the relations among different religious groups, and their unpredictable evolution, are in the background of many collective arrivals; moreover, they are strictly interconnected with ethnic and socio-economic variables, as we have commented in the previous chapter. As clearly demonstrated by the following statement, this circumstance can result if not in the "omission" of the religion issue, surely in the "temptation" to pre-categorize those asylum seekers whose claims are based on religious reasons according to their gender, country/region of origin, and, paradoxically, right on their presumed religious affiliation:

> In the case of migrants coming from North-East of Nigeria, if Christians are considered refugees for the Geneva Convention, if Muslims are distinguished according to the areas. Women are refugees by themselves. Women in southern Nigeria are Christians, but the problem is the trafficking of human beings. The fear of Islamic fundamentalism as a drive to emigrate has never been connected. A theme to think about, but I think the problem of Nigerians is not religious. (Woman – Official of the asylum seekers' reception system)

This declaration, on the other hand, seems to suggest that the "mere" fact of coming from a potentially risky context can be a reason to become eligible for international protection. In this way, Christians escaping from Nigeria, particularly in the case of women, are offered a special treatment, despite the fact that the same expert had observed that "the problem of Nigerian women is not of religious nature", and despite the fact that most of them come from regions different than those actually under the control of Boko Haram (but where its expansion is dreaded).

Furthermore, protection is envisaged also in the case of those who do not belong to established religions, as in the case of adepts to religious sects. According to the testimonies of our key informants, as we have already reported, an increasing number of Chinese, women in almost all the cases, declare to be victims of various forms of persecution because of their affiliation to "God Almighty", a Chinese sect which sustains that Christ has come a second time, with a female body; he/she is still living, but no one knows where he/she is now.

> (...) girls who need immediate care of souls, a direct relationship with the Pastor or the Pastora (*author's note: the female pastor*), because they need to tell their own story and be directed to those mechanisms that will allow them to have a residence permit. They are asylum seekers for religious reasons (...). Young girls ... from their stories it is clear that they have been persecuted; in China there are Churches of State, the others are out of the norm, so they are persecuted. These girls are part of domestic Churches, tiny churches, which are in homes, but neighbors are spies. The girls are arrested, they try to collect money and they come to

Milan, Turin, Florence, where there are other people who can give that
logistic support that they pay. (Woman – Religious leader – Evangelical
Christian)

However, as pointed out by this executive of the Italian reception system, it is
extremely difficult, not to say impossible, to grasp the contexts of origin of asylum seekers in all their complexity, despite the possibility of consulting the
database made available to them (§2). And adequately classify actors, reasons
and consequences of persecution on a religious basis. While unanimously declaring their adherence to a guaranteed approach, the key experts involved in
the study reveal all their difficulty in dealing with this issue and, at times, the
tendency to be guided by preconceived visions of the importance to be paid to
the different religious affiliations, to the point of crossing the risk of ethnocentrism. Thus, it is interesting to observe how, in the formulation of this expert,
"tribal rites" are downgraded to the role of something that cannot be considered as a "real" faith.

> The situations are varied so it is impossible to make a unitary reading.
> Example: Pakistani boy (Shiite) who had fallen in love with a Pakistani
> girl (Sunni). The Imam refuses to celebrate the marriage because it would
> have polluted the purity of the faith. The boy goes to a civil court, but a
> commando at a checkpoint kills the girl. Today in the Islamic area there
> are phenomena of persecution against the Azeris who are worse than
> those towards the Christians (...). In many countries there are prohibi-
> tions to enroll children in school, to practice trade. There are areas in
> which one is persecuted for being Christian, areas in which there is an
> element of discrimination, or where situations of confrontation occur
> due to animistic phenomena, for which it is not clear whether it is a prob-
> lem of faith or linked to tribal rites. (Man – Officer of the asylum seekers'
> reception system)

It is quite clear how, once confronted with given kinds of narratives, the distinction between forced and voluntary migration becomes even more porous
and arbitrary. What's more, it frequently happens that the same narrative is
repeated in a quite identical manner, thus feeding the suspect of its bogus
nature.

> There are very few credible religious claims. The interviewer's task is to
> investigate not only what is being told, but also to understand if the

person is at risk of persecution regardless of what he tells. (Woman –
Officer of the asylum seekers' reception system)

We will return to this phenomenon later on, since it is one of the most critical
points. What is interesting to note is that it is explicitly denounced by the migrants themselves, as in this testimony where the interviewee observes how
phenomena like human sacrifices do exist in certain African regions, but in a
number surely lower than the one reported to the commissions.

> (...) you know when people come to Europe and seek for asylum or inter-
> national protection, they did something to tell the commission ... for the
> commission to believe in them so if it happens to one person and person
> comes and tells in front of the commission: "This is my story", then the
> next person is like: "Oh, that's what that person said, so I'll go and tell the
> same story" and he goes and tells the same story, and you know it's just
> like my own story when I told my own story, I was told that –not by com-
> mission but by other people– that Nigerians come and they said that left
> Nigeria because of Boko Haram and some of them don't even know any-
> thing about Boko Haram, they don't even live in the northern part of Ni-
> geria, they don't even speak the language that we speak in the northern
> part of Nigeria, so what do you ... they have never been affected by Boko
> Haram, but because they know that other Nigerians have got the permis-
> sion or international protection because of their experiences of Boko Ha-
> ram they feel like, ok I'll tell the same story. So the story of human sacri-
> fices, yes, it's possible that some people have actually faced human
> sacrifices, but if you interview maybe 20 people from Edo State and 15 tell
> you that they left because of human sacrifices then it is a lie. Even the
> chances of you meeting somebody who was involved in human sacrifices
> and escaped is maybe one in two hundred, if you ask me ... it's just that
> everybody needs a story to give ... but I don't think that human sacrifices
> happen like that in Nigeria, no it doesn't, it's very rare. (Young man –
> Nigeria – Christian)

Another Nigerian interviewee is even more drastic when he affirms that Europe is a powerful pulling pole, even independently of effective "true" reasons
to migrate; so attractive to encourage a widespread tendency to lie:

> I don't know about people that go there, tell lies and have documents, but
> I know that people tell lies. Most people lie, everybody lie. So most people

> lie to get the documents, because most of the times, most of us, most Ni-
> gerians, most blacks, they don't leave home because they have problems,
> that's the truth, they leave home because they think that Europe is beau-
> tiful, Europe is free, you can live a free life, you can be happy ... (Man –
> Nigeria – Catholic Christian)

The risk of an instrumental reference to religious arguments, by any "bogus"
asylum seeker who tries in this manner to "confuse" the commissioners, has
repeatedly emerged during the focus groups. The recurrence of narratives
identical to each other is often referred to as a clear symptom of this phenomenon. In any case, despite the different perception of some applicants (who
may fear that this circumstance would negatively influence the commission
approach, making it more suspicious), our key informants have unanimously
concluded that this risk cannot influence the assessment activity.

> The Court of Cassation has clearly said that repetition does not mean
> that there is falsehood. It is up to the one who decides to do the necessary
> investigations. It is not that if the story is repetitive then it is not true.
> Many may have been involved in Boko Haram's village fire. Group perse-
> cution is a true, real phenomenon. (Man – Expert)

In this regard, a point repeatedly underlined is that the commission must always evaluate each single position, and encompass all the possible kinds of
violations, included those quite impossible to prove. One case in point is represented by the declaration of a conversion to a minority religion not manifested publicly because of the fear of becoming a victim of harassment (with
very few exceptions, our informants have excluded the possibility or recurring,
in these situations, to the help of religious authorities in order to obtain some
"proofs" of the feasibility of the conversion).

> Then comes the question that has already been dealt with by the Court of
> Justice of the European Union: whether or not it is obligatory for the for-
> eigner to demonstrate that he has already exercised his religious confes-
> sion in his homeland. And the Court has rightly said: but not even for an
> idea, because in that country a minority confession is persecuted but if I
> declare my membership I will be persecuted. So it is clear, says the Court,
> we cannot force ourselves to submit to the persecution. Religious free-
> dom, like other positive liberties, entails the right to manifest or not to
> manifest, freely to say one's own belonging. And also the right to keep it
> confidential (...).

They can say that the request must be rejected only because if the foreigner remained in his own country without demonstrating, he would not be persecuted. Because, says the Court, it would end up legitimizing persecution and/or legitimizing an abusive restriction of religious freedom that is guaranteed in our legal systems. (Man – Expert)

Finally, the suspect of a "bogus" use of religious arguments is widespread among both the experts and the officers in charge with the applications' assessment. However, even if they are aware that this phenomenon is playing a specific role in delegitimizing the asylum system in the eyes of public opinion, they assert pragmatically that this risk is part of the "rules of the game". Or, as suggested by a UNHCR officer, it is even a further signal of a progressive erosion of the distinction between forced and voluntary migration:

> (...) an expansion of secure migration channels supported by local communities is needed. Where there is a risk of life, those with religious responsibility often become unbalanced and it is delicate to enter the realm of the conversion process. (Woman – UNHCR officer)

Despite the fact that, today, asylum seekers are mainly coming from Islam-majority countries, it is decidedly more frequent to find a reference to the violation of religious rights in the applications of asylum seekers affiliated to other religious traditions, starting from the Christian ones. The most quoted cases concern: Chinese (female) migrants who declare to be victims of persecution because they belong to Christians sects (in particular to the Church of God Almighty), Christians flying from Northern Nigeria, and Coptic Egyptians and Iranians converted to a different religion than the Islamic one.

> (...) we find ourselves managing an emergency in which a series of complex factors exercise their influence. Some religious claims in the pure sense paradoxically at this moment are only advanced by the Chinese. Chinese who adhere to Christian sects. In the office, I have a package of applications presented by women who do not know how to evaluate because they have problems of dialogue and of information on the country of origin. (Woman – Official of the asylum seekers' reception system)

This circumstance does not cause Christian applicants to experience a positive discrimination when they enter the procedure. As we will describe in the following paragraphs, as any other applicant, they have to face a system that, despite a genuine intention to cover all the situations connected to a violation of religious rights and religious freedoms, suffer different forms of bias.

Actually, independently of their religious membership, the interviews with migrants provide considerable evidence, as we have seen in the previous chapter, of the many religious-connected factors that concurred to the decision to migrate, even though only in a few cases these factors are emphasized during the dialogue with the commissioners. Not to mention the fact that most of our sample entered Italy and obtained his/her stay-permit through a procedure different than the request for protection: a further signal of the tremendous gap between contemporary migration trends and established migratory schemes. On the other hand, the personnel in charge with the analysis of the asylum applications seems to be particularly sensitive not only to those situations in which religion appears to be the direct "cause" of migration, but also with those that we can define as indirect religious-connected causes of (forced) migration, even if they could be not easily acknowledgeable from a formal point of view. This is particularly true as far as those situations in which the living conditions turn out to be strongly compromised by the presence of dictatorial or autocratic regimes, based on a fundamentalist view of religious precepts...

> The persecution must be considered in an enlarged dimension. Why do people leave the Middle East? There are fundamentalisms (I think about Syria), but also dictatorial systems that exploit the fear of the Islamist adversary (Egypt: there is no real persecution, but civil war). One can thus see the effect of religious fundamentalism in perpetuating autocratic regimes: migratory flows not to escape persecution, but a religious factor, however, is at the origin. (Man – FBOs leader – Catholic)

...or where, in the name of religious teachings and guidelines, strong limitations to the personal freedom are imposed, particularly upon women and other subordinated groups, thus transforming religion into a mechanism of social and political control:

> We evaluate to investigate the case of Nigerian women. The Islamist fundamentalist presence hostile to women and a growing history of women's migration cannot be by chance. But to what extent are these factors also linked to the unconscious level? The fact is that I want to survive, and it is difficult to survive in a certain country if you are a woman; and if you are Muslim, but not in the way the fanatics want it. (Man – Religious leader – Muslim)

Furthermore, the focus group discussions took in consideration those applications referring to a possible involution of religious minorities' conditions, connected to the current geopolitical context. The most quoted case is that of Nigeria, with reference to asylum seekers coming from geographical areas that are still outside the control of Boko Haram – which they fear will expand its territory even further.

All the key informants have agreed with the conclusion that the mere risk of future persecution is sufficient argument to receive a demand; it is definitely rational to search for protection before it is too late to escape (the many Jews who fled from Europe at the dawn of the Nazi delirium are proof of this, since many others did not have time to seek shelter).

Finally, what has clearly emerged from the study is that the Italian system of protection (including in this expression all the categories of key informants involved) seems to be globally immune from the influence of the present context, where applicants are increasingly perceived as bogus asylum seekers who "use" religion as a pretext to produce false chronicles; besides, said system does not even seem to be prejudiced by the outcomes of previous demands, most of which had been actually rejected (see Chapter 10, §1). The key informants have stated that every kind of persecution and violation, directly or indirectly linked to the applicant's religious profile, must be seriously taken into account, regardless of the risk of a forged chronicle. Since religious freedom is defined as a fundamental human right, every kind of violation (from a violent persecution to the simple fear of declaring one's own religious beliefs) must be covered by the procedures of protection. The same should happen as far as the mere risk of persecution is concerned: as we noted above, many informants evoked the historical antecedent of Jews, remembering that only those who had been welcomed before the mass deportation to concentration camps had the chance to escape from persecution and survive.

Lastly, the commissioners are expected to explore this issue whenever the situation of the country of origin, as well as the "tone" of the account provided by the applicant, make it pertinent and relevant. Very few of the key informants have maintained that, since we are dealing with a very intimate and personal sphere, religious arguments not spontaneously emerged during the interview are not to be solicited by the commissioners. On the contrary, most of the experts involved think that, at least when the situation of the sending country makes it pertinent, it is always advisable to scrutinize the issue of religion. In other words, even if the applicant does not refer to specific facts connected to his/her religious identity and beliefs, the commissioners explore this facet, since it represents an important factor when deciding to approve or deny a request.

> Even if the applicant does not state a religious motivation, because per-
> haps he is not aware that this may be a reason, the commission, which
> has knowledge of the situation in the country of origin, highlights it and
> has a duty to investigate that aspect. (Man – UNHCR Official)

Despite all this, two main critical aspects have emerged from the fieldwork.
The first one, on which we will focus the attention in the next section, is of a
"technical" nature. The second one, object of the following one, has to do with
the political/ideological dimension of the issue and with the manner in which
it feeds back on the evaluation setting.

2 Technical Biases

Given the extraordinary complexity of the current scenario, it is easy to understand how the different actors of the reception system, including the commissioners in charge with the applications' assessment, lack a comprehensive
knowledge of the situations of both origin and transit countries, not to mention the intra-national variety of risks and problems. It is not a coincidence
that they admit their difficulty in talking about subjects that they do not completely master. According to their reading of the subject, the religious landscape of origin countries is not only tremendously complex, it is also "filtered"
by the ambiguous and embellished representations diffused through the media system, which can influence the commissioners' perceptions –despite
their desire to remain neutral– or even induce them to underestimate the risks
to which people coming from given countries were exposed (we will return to
this point in the next section).

First of all, as stressed by this interviewee, Italians' perception suffers from
a strong cultural distance with respect to the sending countries' social
landscape:

> Interviewer: For us, in Italy, it is very difficult to believe that they really
> perform human sacrifices. Because we think that...
> Do you know the reason why it is very difficult for you to believe? Be-
> cause you are far from Africa. Do you understand? You are very, very far
> from Africa. When you watch television and see what is happening in
> Nigeria you will believe! You are in a country that respects the law. If Ni-
> geria respects the law, all these things would not happen in Nigeria. Italy
> respects the law, they respect their law. You can't see Italy fight, I've never
> seen Italy fight. They can talk. But for Nigeria everything is possible there,
> for them to do. To kill somebody is nothing to them. When you watch

television, what is happening in South East, now, for my region, what is happening there, even Italy's Government knows what is happening in Nigeria. (Man – Nigeria – Christian Pentecostal Church)

Another critical point has to do with the manner in which religion and spirituality are understood and experienced across the various socio-cultural contexts. Just to cite a case in point, Catholicism in Armenia is not the same as Catholicism in Italy; rituals, prayers, devotions are deeply embedded in the local history and traditions. Therefore, when the commission puts questions based on the "Italian version" of Catholicism, this can result in understandable confusion for an applicant coming from a different milieu. This kind of "cultural bias", on its turn, is just the first piece of a mosaic of a deeper ideological bias that we will further discuss in the next section.

Technically, the regulations in force offer the possibility of resorting to a cultural mediator with the aim of understanding the gap between the applicant's experience and feelings and the commissioners' mind-set. However, many informants have observed that, despite being indispensable, the use of a cultural mediator (or, quite often, a simple translator) turns into a supplementary problem, since he/she might be considered to be not completely trustworthy when dealing with specific topics. The following testimonies provide some examples of how, in the perception of applicants who are waiting for the interview, current procedures are not reliable enough to protect migrants from given countries who have had to face persecution to the point that they fear they might find it in the destination country too:

I'm still waiting and also nowadays I see the result is negative for so many persons from Pakistan, also Christians, one of my friends went to Commission two times but he was rejected. He was a Catholic Christian.
Interviewer: Did he tell you why? Was he able to tell his story completely or what?
He told his story completely but sometimes there are Muslim translators/mediators so...
Interviewer: Do you think they are Muslims?
Yes, they are Muslims, even when we applied for asylum we asked for a Christian translator but we get our reply that there was no option for us to have a Christian mediator. (Man – Pakistan – Catholic Christian)

I'm worried. Here in Milan, they do not make you tell the story well, they interrupt you, there is little time. Then the interpreters are Chinese and I heard from confreres who sometimes do not translate what you say because they think it is not right and so they interrupt us and do not tell the committee. Some things are not translated. (Woman – China – Church of God Almighty)

Afghan Muslims think that Pakistan's Muslims are not well, but I do not know why, because some time ago, 20, 25 years ago, Afghans came to Pakistan for asylum, when there was war and because sometime before, 25 years back, they came to Pakistan as refugees, but when they were there, they were going to go back to their land, so now we have a problem, so when there are mediators from Afghanistan there are problems for Muslims from Pakistan…

Interviewer: And did you ever talk to a Muslim from Pakistan who had a mediator from Afghanistan?

Yes, I have one friend who had one mediator from Afghanistan about one year back, he was … he spoke a different language so it was difficult for him. (Man – Pakistan – Catholic Christian)

On the other hand, even if reliable, when they lack a specific competence about religious matters, translators may not be able to decode concepts and institutes embedded in a specific religious tradition and milieu. As observed by a key informant (an attorney in charge of assisting asylum seekers), a non-believer translator can encounter many difficulties in decoding religious and theological concepts and in rendering them in a different language, understandable by the commissioners. The same is obviously true when it comes to translating for the applicant the questions posed by the commissioners. An expression such as "Jesus' transfiguration" (which can be used by the commission in order to test the authenticity of a conversion) can be impossible to translate by a non-Christian translator (but also by a Christian translator who is not so familiar with religious matters). Only very professional and trustworthy translators admit their inadequacy in this kind of circumstance, eventually suggesting they should ask for the help of an expert (this possibility is permitted by the legislation, even though it is scarcely used by the commissions, due to the high number of applications that have to be evaluated).

Religious beliefs, identities and ways of life are definitively sensitive topics. As a matter of fact, "religious" variables are in many ways interconnected with ethno-racial, political, and economic ones, as we have amply observed. Unequivocally pertinent, from an empirical point of view, the interconnections between the different variables can turn into a "rational stratagem" to avoid facing any facts, feelings or fears related to religion.

Encouraged to deepen the analysis of this topic, our key informants have described the experience of being questioned about their religion as shaped and structured not only by the political and cultural context of the sending community, but also by the sex/gender of each asylum seeker, his/her age and the specific phase of his/her life cycle, his/her age cohort (since many sending countries have been recently characterized by a significant evolution/involution of their religious landscape), not to mention his/her level of education (only well-educated applicants are normally able to understand complex concepts and expressions).

> Some Syrian refugees, who have a motivation to escape in which there is religious relevance, interpret this cause differently than the previous generation of Syrian refugees. The interpretation of one's right to freedom, one's own religious interpretation, is conceived in a different way. The context of Syria has changed and the type of interlocution must also change. (Man – Religious leader – Muslim)

In an "ideal world" this would imply, for example, the possibility to resort to a "specific" cultural mediator, or to adopt an individualized approach, thus permitting each applicant not only to describe his/her own experience and feelings, but also to elaborate them. Just to cite an example, people coming from specific contexts can find it impossible to discuss sensitive subjects with someone of the opposite sex. For all these reasons, the discussion within the focus groups has reached the conclusion that dealing with religiosity and spirituality would require specific hearing techniques, different from those employed to talk about less sensitive topics.

> Then there is the theme of re-reading the motivations that lead to the problem of persecution. Religious confession is a trait of the person who in some places leads to discrimination, such as ethnicity, lineage, family. But there is difficulty in telling it (...). It is hard to go deep when the motivations are complex. The persecution for religious reasons must be explained, contextualized. Explaining that a moderate Muslim who is persecuted by extreme Islamist fringes is difficult. The theme is there, I do not know if it can be pigeonholed: everyone has his own path. (Woman – Local government official)

Ultimately, this issue seems to be paradigmatic of the challenge of processing an extraordinary variety of human experiences through standardized procedures; not to mention the short time devoted to each interview, which does not offer the possibility of deeply analyzing individual experiences and feelings.

> There are some guidelines, but in Italy we are subjected to an immense logistic challenge for the number of languages and interpreters we need,

for the time, etc. It is not that we do not know what would be better and more appropriate, but we need a balance with what is reasonable and we are able to do in fact. The interpreters, the commission, deal with issues which do not need only geopolitical competences, since they are characterized by a detail of complexity that is not said to be managed. (Woman – FBOs operator – Catholic Christian)

3   Cultural and Political/Ideological Biases

Besides technical biases, our study led to the emergence of other kinds of biases, which are connected to various contextual variables.

First of all, the reception system –starting from the commissioners– does not always possess suitable knowledge of the complex religious scenario of the asylum seekers' origin and transit countries. Testimonies reported in the previous chapter provide ample evidence of this complexity. As we have already discussed, the people involved are commonly aware of this critical issue, which is somehow irremediable, despite significant efforts made in order to enrich the level of knowledge and competence of the commissioners.

However, evidence provided by the study support the hypothesis that we also have to deal with the risk of a "cultural bias". Not only because, as we have already described, it is tremendously difficult to decode highly sensitive experiences and feelings, such as religious ones, in a way that would turn out to be comprehensible even to a foreign examiner. What's more, migrants and asylum seekers sometimes bring with them –or speak about– religious beliefs and practices that differ widely from the Italian experience. As observed by this Cameroonian intercultural mediator, established perceptions about religious problems –such as a supposed conflict between Muslims and Christians– tend to dominate common opinion, thus obscuring many local varieties of "religious" traditions, precepts, and duties.

> (…) everyone thinks in terms of Muslims and Christians conflict, they do not know that in the tribes there are these things that happen, as I for example in my country, if you have been chosen as future king, you cannot run away from that responsibility, they look for you everywhere, so maybe if someone runs away, they come here, they say: "But it cannot be true", instead it often happens that there is also someone who escapes from that responsibility, to be … it is a traditional responsibility and there are perhaps Christians who do not want to go into that too spiritual thing in the village, so they prefer to leave, but they will tell you: "It cannot be true here". So it's a little difficult to understand the type of situation, if

> they do not go right on the field to see ... (Man – Cameron – Intercultural
> mediator in the reception system)

One case in point is represented by those applicants who declare problems connected to belonging to communities devoted to animistic cults. Since the latter can sound "exotic" (if not primitive) to a Western (Italian) mentality, it is easy to understand how this case, if not in the applicants' perception, can be underestimated. It is not a coincidence that in the current anti-migrants' discourse, the applicant who declares they have escaped because of a risk of being sacrificed by his/her community's members (or be obliged to sacrifice someone else) has become a sort of paradigmatic example of the bogus nature of many applications. As a matter of fact, besides having fed the stereotypes about non-Western religious customs and backgrounds, the recurrence of this kind of chronicle has contributed to "devaluate" claims based on religious arguments.

Conversely, various key informants have indicated a second critical phenomenon, by signaling that many asylum seekers would tend to gloss over religion, if not to omit it entirely during the interview. Europe and Italy are actually perceived as secularized societies, to the point that omitting "this part of the discourse" is sometimes conceived as a strategic behavior, one that raises the possibility of the request for asylum to be approved. According to a shared perception, commissioners are stereotypically considered to be unsympathetic towards religious arguments. As stated by this Nigerian man, in the present Italian cultural landscape, other issues –such as homosexuality– encounter much more consideration. According to his testimony, this even involves a sharp discrimination towards asylum seekers whose claims are founded on religious motives. Probably in an unconscious manner, his experience reflects a common trend in democratic societies, where in the name of an "equality paradigm" in social consciousness, religious rights are too often given little weight (Durham Jr., Thayer, 2019).

> I explained to them the reason why I came to Italy. When I talked about
> Christian religion, that I had religion problems, they wouldn't listen, be-
> cause I think they don't know about it, but when you talk about maybe
> lesbian, that sort of things, they give you documents fast, but this is the
> reason why even if I told them they gave me the negative one.
> (...) In my opinion ... They say that when you go to the commission,
> they take some time to investigate, but ... my understanding is that this
> world that we are living in belongs to the devil, so time will come that
> God will come and take his people to Heaven, so if I believe in my own
> understanding that if you have problems that concern God in Italy they

don't, they don't take you seriously. I don't believe they investigate ... if
you say that you want to become Christian and you left your country, this
makes them upset. But if I was homosexual now, I go to the commission
and I tell them I'm homosexual, now, they give me five-year shop, because I have many friends, and also friends when I was in the camp before, because they are homosexuals, they go to commission and most
times they had documents, but when you talk about Christians, and you
come for religion, they don't even want to listen. (Man – Nigeria – Catholic
Christian)

On the other hand, commissioners are sometimes stereotypically perceived as
"Catholics" –since Italy is known as a Catholic country worldwide– and therefore prejudicially deemed as characterized by a potentially discriminating attitude towards people belonging to other religious traditions. As it is easy to
imagine, in the case of Muslim asylum seekers, this kind of feeling is nourished
by a general climate of "Islamophobia", which sometimes encourages applicants to keep their religious sentiments to themselves. This bias definitely has
counterproductive effects, since it fuels the perception of a narrative from
which something is missing, as observed by various key informants, both Muslims and non-Muslims.

The impression is that the asylum seeker, in his complexity and personal
tragedy, in having to find the answers to the questions of his interlocutor,
adapts himself to the perception of the interlocutors. The interlocutors
are mostly Westerners, officials, insensitive to the explicit confessional
dimension, or Catholics. When some representatives of xxx (*an Islamic
FBOs*) happened to visit some centers, in particular circumstances, like
Ramadan, and no, I had the impression that a psychological adaptation
scenario took over: there was the surprise of being in front of me, a Muslim, perhaps Western, and thus discover another type of language and
content, but also the need to let off steam. (Man – Religious leader –
Muslim)

What we have also noticed is that the immigrant too has a distorted view
of the West, on how the Muslim religion is accepted, so sometimes the
immigrant when he enters does not immediately declare himself a Muslim, because he is afraid that maybe there are prejudices or things like
that, and you have to break this difficulty a bit first. (Man – Pastoral
operator – Muslim)

> After the attacks in Paris, the fear of receiving denial as Muslims grew; hence the denial of their religious identity during the interviews. (Woman – Officer of the asylum seekers' reception system)

On this regard, it is significant to observe that many –if not all– of the key informants involved in the study share the opinion that religious-connected factors surely play a role bigger than that recorded by official reports and data. Trying to explain this gap, only in very few cases did our informants refer to the possible inadequacy of legislative and procedural instruments to grasp the role of religion:

> (...) it's just a matter of regulation; they do not fall under this legislation. It is a bit to the conscience of the judge, but of stories like these you hear every day, every day and many are true, many are invented ... In favor of R. we have some documentation, and for this we hope and we trust in the fact that the judge against the documentation brought ... had also brought it to the committee ... I trust that ... R. is always very precise, every question, dates ... is always very precise, does not go into confusion, but unfortunately the judge made us understand that ... there is not really a law in Italy that ... is prepared to evaluate and then give or not the status of refugee for situations of this kind, and unfortunately many refugees arrive here in these circumstances, but (*this kind of law*) does not exist ... I don't know if I explained myself. (Woman – Italian – Social worker of the reception center)

Decidedly more frequently, the focus was on some characters of the contemporary Italian cultural landscape, that unavoidably influence the asylum system's attitude, the interviews' setting included. In general terms, some informants have observed that the contemporary hegemony of economicistic approaches led to understanding migration strategies as guided by an economic rationale, thus producing a harsh under-evaluation of any other dimension involved in the decision-making process, starting from the spiritual-religious one. What's more, according to different categories of informants – from religious leaders to operators of the reception centers, and to the same officials of the asylum system– the celebration of secularism –that is, of laicism–, and the political-ideological instrumentalization of religion, are two key aspects of contemporary European and Italian society which newcomers have to face. Furthermore, these aspects even affect interview settings, within a paradoxical spiral fueled by specular "modesty" to approach this theme. It is not a coincidence that such disregard mainly involves Christian applicants: a paradoxical consequence of the hegemony attributed to Islam in the public and media discourse about migrants and refugees: what has been defined the Islamization of European immigration debates (Papademetriou *et al.*, 2016). This circumstance inhibits, according to some key informants, concern towards other religious traditions (and towards the variety of Islamic traditions as well), through a game of mutual "complicity" between commissioners and asylum seekers. To sum it up, despite its relevance, the religious dimension turns out to be largely "invisible" in this setting, reflecting its invisibility in the public sphere. This circumstance should make us aware of how, if on the one hand it is possible to commit serious persecutions and abuses in religion (and the experience of forced migrants is there to prove this), expelling religion through "secularized" procedures can be just as prejudicial of individual rights.

Finally, this sort of "reluctance" towards religious items –further fueled by a widespread perception of their instrumental use– produces a double counterfactual outcome.

From the asylum seeker's point of view, the fear is of not being understood, and of being eventually rejected:

> I'm worried because I know it is not easy for the commission to accept truly that I left my country for religious conflict and if you see I run out of the country for my life so I would be safe and not killed. (Man – Nigeria – Catholic Christian)

From the asylum system's point of view –or, to be more precise, the most acute members of this system– the awareness that, by doing so, we run the risk not exactly of violating the asylum seekers' rights, but of lending support to a political instrumentalization of the issue, which loses sight of the most important aspect. As the following official says, the instruments of protection, often considered as a threat to "our" Christian identity, or a temptation for possible usurpers, are the seal of our civilization and of our identity:

> Very often, we see the tools that protect the migrants as a threat to our status quo. We lose the message that we also help many Christians ... there is no awareness of the situation, which has become more political than technical. (Woman – Officer of the asylum seekers' reception system)

As a matter of fact, the issue here discussed provides a paradigmatic example of a broader one, related to the protection of individual (religious) rights in multi-cultural and multi-religious settings. In this regard, as stressed by some experts (Mensky, Topidi, 2016), legal empowerment is an interesting approach, since it can provide a solution against the essentialism of religious minorities.

Finally, if you look at the "success" of the process of adaptation, banishing religion is not a good strategy. The procedure of asylum request –from the phase of preparing the interview until the phase of following the possible recognition of a status of protection– can turn into a fundamental occasion to elaborate traumatic experiences, possibly through the "filter" of one's religious beliefs and experiences. This point leads us to the fourth chapter of this part, which is devoted to the (supporting) role that religion and spirituality can play in the welcoming and integration process of (forced) migrants.

CHAPTER 12

On the Role of Religion in the Process of Adaptation of (Forced) Migrants

Laura Zanfrini and Mario Antonelli

As illustrated in Chapter 1, our study has moved from the hypothesis that religiosity, in both its individual and collective expressions, can represent a source of support and of personal and family well-being, to more specifically, it can support lives and integration paths of (forced) migrants, particularly of the migrants whose biographies have been strongly marked by religious belongings and beliefs.

Other chapters of this book focus on the role of religion and spirituality as far as the migrants' psychological well-being is concerned and, particularly, their influence on the primary socialization of children belonging to (forced) migrant families, and their potential in the process of identity's construction (Chapters 19 and 20). In this chapter, we will investigate their role in the first phases of (forced) migrants' adaptation process, as well their acknowledgment by the different actors of the reception system. Finally, in the concluding part of the chapter, we will investigate the role of religious agency in the process of refugees' public space making.

1 Religion as a "Balm for the Soul"

In the previous chapter, we discussed the manner in which the commissions in charge with the evaluation of asylum demands succeed (or do not succeed) in intercepting the role of asylum seekers' religious affiliations. From the applicant's point of view, as suggested by this interviewee in a very stumbling talk, the spiritual dimension can also represent a crucial support in facing such a stressing setting:

> Before I took my interview in the commission I went there (*to the Buddhist temple*), because I do not understand how it works, but fear for them not to give a ... and therefore fear. So I went there, I asked: "Please help me for the ... for the interview, because I need a force". Because when they ask all the history, how to throw up all your problems (I have) inside, who's left behind, you do not want to see, like a book, when you open all

the problems, so I do not want to look at all this, but that is a time you open that all problems, problems that my father, my mother, every problem, because this is all important for them to understand. So, I need an energy to do that ... go with this problem. So I asked for Drawma, ask Tara for that to become strong. (Man – Tibet – Buddhist)

He is echoed by other interviewees who affirm that, by relying on their God, it is possible to overcome any concern about the outcome of the asylum application –or of the appeal, in the case of the second interviewee, when the first application was not successful–. Significantly, the latter interviewee insists on his intention to relieve the commissioners of the responsibility for not accepting his demand, by repeating, almost like a mantra, that he does not blame them; almost as if he wanted to recode a procedural event through a religious *lexicon*.

No, I'm not worried (*about the interview with the Commission*), I'm waiting for that day to come. I speak to the Father ... I feel comfortable because He will give me what I want. I have faith. (Man – Nigeria – Christ Church)

Interviewer: Are you worried about the appeal? Because it is next week...
      I'm not worried, so I believe in God because ... I'm not worried ... I told you, God is the one that has ultimate power, so I believe in God,
      I ... I don't ... they gave me a negative answer. I think maybe ... they want to go to my ... I didn't blame them for the negative that they gave me. I don't blame anybody, for the negative. They know the best.
      Interviewer: But maybe they couldn't understand very well your story?
      Yes. They couldn't understand it, they want the lawyer, maybe they want the lawyer to come, and read the story for them, but I have already told them the truth, and I stand in this that I told them, this that I told you now is where I stand, I don't have anything else to add to it. Tomorrow I stand in this story, it's not changing, it is what I told you, it is what I told them. Maybe the negative is they want ... the story, they want to understand it well. So, I didn't blame them. (Man – Nigeria – Christian Pentecostal Church)

Specularly, in a very fatalistic way, this interviewee considers the denial of his application as coherent with God's will. As we will illustrate later, fatalism is a common character of the migration phenomenon, particularly when the choice to migrate appears to be "irrational" and decidedly unsecure. In this specific case, in order to understand the respondent's paradoxical stance, it is useful to remember how migration is not an easy or cheap choice, but a strong investment involving many family members and which often implies getting into debt. The fact of attributing the last word to an ultra-terrestrial identity can be a psychological stratagem to make such a big failure more tolerable. Curiously, he does not refer to his personal situation or to the elements of his story on which his asylum demand was based. On the contrary, he simply concludes by affirming that it was not the time that God wanted him to get the permit: when God wants it, he will obtain the documents.

> I think, I think it's not the time that God wants me to get ... that they get me the permit. I think ... because Bible makes me understand that man proposes, God disposes. Everything in life gives glory to God, because I can propose, but God disposes, so I believe that God has not disposed my proposition, this is why they didn't give me the documents. But if the time comes that God wants me to have the documents, I will have it. (Man – Nigeria – Catholic Christian)

Lastly, this Pakistani interviewee observes that the same God "who granted him permission to stay" will continue to assist him, helping him to solve the multiple problems with which he has to live. In this case, too, it is curious to note the affirmation according to which it is God who gave him the permit ... a five-year permit!

> I don't care, I have a lot of proofs for my problems, I show, and he knows I have in original, believe me, plus I am sick, but I'm a gentle person, I don't lie too much, I say truth everything, and I thank God he believes me, he gives me permission, he gave me five years, this for me is ... I'm lucky he believes me. (Man – Pakistan – Muslim)

In the face of the exponential growth of suffering, and of unjust suffering, which leads to the abandonment of one's own land, two questions emerge, which are anything but academic: why the suffering of migrating and its dramatic unfolding? What does God want and what does He do for that confession for which I find myself in a situation of extreme tribulation? From the data offered by the interviews, a sort of atheistic protest does not emerge as a result of this double query. The problematization of God and of his actions and, therefore, an abandonment of the related religious practices, does not seem to be a foregone answer. Rather, a feeling and an interpretation of this unjust suffering emerge, according to the imprint of a religious resignation with a fatalistic character.

On the one hand, one is even willing to ascribe to God the sufferance experienced, not because of His arbitrary wickedness, but because of his providential plan which, in view of a correct progression of personal and collective history, devises painful events for me and for others, in order to fix human wickedness and thus correcting the disorder produced by men.

On the other hand, religious feelings and religious practices seem to be based on a widespread understanding, transversal to the various confessions, of the omnipotence of God. The latter is immediately identified in an "absolute power" that ends up lightening human freedom and its "powers". The "direct" action of God in the events of history is so accredited that, correspondingly, the action of the man is discredited: for better or for worse. Personal and collective history appears to be subjugated by the "almighty" God who dominates the world and manages its events in a fatalistic way. The deity acts as an ominously capricious omnipotence, available for a man-made relationship of manipulation. The "divine" appears to be tremendous in its inscrutable omnipotence and fascinating in its seductive immediacy. One's own freedom and the freedom of others are in some way absolved from their very responsibilities and from their right/duty to make history. What happens to me and to everyone is immediately related to the only cause, God; what happens is supinely accepted, as it is what He wants, without any margins for the affirmation of one's own commitment or of others'. In this perspective, the fatalistic contraction of the religious bond makes it possible to think of the divine as being tamed at the price of some propitiatory sacrifices and some prayers. Without saying that the religious man, under the aegis of this religious figure, feels authorized to consistently represent God through the form of despotism and prevarication over others.

A different approach is the one followed by this interviewee. Faced with the failure of the project to obtain a status of protection, he declares that the Church is the only place where one can feel free. In his testimony, the status of "slave" –due to the lack of documents– is opposed to that of a free man who can experience the dignity of every human being.

> (...) when I arrived to Milan, in the camp of the Red Cross, I met with some Nigerians who are Christians, so the very first day I started going to church.
>
> Interviewer: And what was your feeling?
>
> I was feeling happy. I was really happy, because church is the only place I go that I feel happy.

Interviewer: Also in Nigeria before?

Yes.

Interviewer: Is it different to go to church here in Italy and in Nigeria?

No it is not different.

Interviewer: It is the same?

It is the same. The only difference here is that we are slaves.

Interviewer: Why?

We are slaves.

Interviewer: What does it mean?

To be slaves?

Interviewer: Yes. We know what it means, but why do you feel a slave here?

To my understanding, when you are in Europe and you do not have documents, you are not privileged in most things in life. So automatically you are slave, when you are not privileged in most things in life. Here we are slaves.

Interviewer: And do you feel this also in church?

No, this is what I'm saying. That the church is the only place where I feel happy because in church I feel I am free with God. I'm free even though I'm a slave, but I'm not a slave beside of God. (Men – Nigeria – Catholic Christian)

Trying to put in a theological perspective these paradoxical moods, we can observe, following the analysis of this Catholic priest, that it is the very experience of migrating that raises the awareness of human vulnerability. Beyond the most dramatic situations –such as those involving forced migrants– the experience of migrating becomes a sort of paradigm of the "migration" which every human being is expected to follow to get to the "promised land". The fact of turning to God during the most dramatic phases of one's own life is not only coherent with the human condition *tout court*, but also with the most authentic faith experience.

I believe that when a man is put in a condition of particular fragility, he magically rediscovers those values that perhaps are a bit dormant and therefore in some way are the great pillars of our lives. A little like health: as long as one is healthy, he does not notice the gift he has. When he is ill, he realizes that without health it is a mess and therefore he must try to return to health. And so is the theme of faith: many times the seafarers, people who do not attend the church at home, do not practice, but when he climbs a priest on board that for four months they do not go to a church, they hear someone helping them pray etc. the priest celebrates Mass and they all go because it is an important moment, because it is a way to be with the Lord, to be together with others, each one in the name of his own faith. So I think the fragility of distance from home, the uncertainty of the future and so on. In some way, it makes us particularly sensitive to what is precisely the spiritual and religious dimension. When we are, I have experienced in my sailing twice the sea to force 9... And you really think those are your last moments of life, pray. One says: "It's too easy!" No, it is right, the Lord when you need it, as a child thinks of his father and his mother when he needs them, even if only of a caress and therefore, those who are far away are particularly attached to their faith, their own traditions. (Man – Religious leader – Catholic Christian)

In psychological terms, this kind of narrative proves the supporting function played by religion and spirituality along the entire migration route. However, once put in a religious perspective, the search for a peaceful place where to live can easily be superimposed by the search for inner peace. And the stormy sea to cross is not only the one separating Africa from Europe, but also the one that is stirred up in the depths of strongly worn-out people.

Certainly, also a road to reach an inner peace, because we say that precisely they are thirsty for peace. Not only to find a place of peace, but also to find pacification, there is a more peaceful sense of interior, because they come, however, beyond the journey, even from situations of instability. And so ... they are tormented a little bit inwardly. So I think also in the relationship with God, but I think for myself, even just to find some peace in my heart, even moments of silence. For them, a friend of mine, a Nigerian, she tells me that when she asked her what she likes to do in her spare time, she told me: "I love to have spaces of silence to read the Gospel", and she explained why she says: "I feel a lot like a sea moved inside and in those moments of silence in which I read, I try to listen to what the Lord wants to tell me, I calm down". (Woman – FBOs operator – Christian Catholic)

Given these premises, it is not surprising if every step of the migration journey can be "oxygenated" by the spiritual dimension, becoming an empowering factor. This point is even more interesting if we consider that, in many sending countries, religious affiliations (in the case of minority groups' members) and religious obligations (in the case of majority groups' members) often act as "disempowering" factors, as we have illustrated in the previous chapter.

Let us consider some typical examples.

In this moving account of a former seminarian, spiritual assistance is presented as what gives refreshment –where "it was very hot"– and gives hope when, in the darkest moments, one runs the risk of losing his/her strength. The story reported here suggests that, through the pastoral action, religion can help to insert a project's component and a hope for the future –like preparing children for first communion– into the web of those existences suspended in a sort of limbo, such as the existences of people interned in refugee camps.

> Then they helped us get help or to a UNHCR hospital in a small town called Shire. Here my friend healed and we went to a refugee camp where we stayed for a year: to XXX, in the North of Ethiopia. There we began to serve the Catholics, because there were no pastors and we were seminarians close to the end of the studies, so we knew the liturgical service. In this way we have been able to help people without hope, because UNHCR's help was not much. We built a small church in the field and we stayed for about a year. People needed hope so much: it was very hot, they lost their strength. It needed some form of encouragement. Doing service means making people communicate with God, then to empower them. In a short time, the church we had built was filled with believers, including some Orthodox. Some Orthodox deacons have taken an example from us and have begun to imitate our initiative. We got in touch with the Diocese in the Ethiopian capital from which they agreed to send us a priest twice a month for a Mass. We also had catechism classes, to prepare the children for the first communion. Then I went to the capital and I spoke with the Bishop, who came to visit the camp. (Man – Eritrea – Catholic Christian)

Evidence from the fieldwork provides many other interesting examples. As suggested by these testimonies, religion is a sort of "balm for the soul", that is the certainty that Someone is taking care of you. It happens during the most perilous journeys, when one's survival cannot be taken for granted, as in the case of migrants who have tried to reach Italy by boat:

> (…) I believe that in the journey, I know of many stories in the boats, that while the boat was waiting for a safe harbor, whether they were Christians, Orthodox, or Catholics, whatever, they had Mary's medals in their mouths and they prayed. I believe that in those dramatic moments, where you think you can lose your life, it is clear that this is a time when faith plays an important role. (Man – Religious leader – Catholic Christian)

> Interviewer: In what way do you think your faith has helped you?
>
> Because I had this strong decision to overcome, cross the sea, and stay alive, because ... I said that I have this mission to stay alive, I should not die now, and this strong decision in my opinion has brought me here with all this. (Man – Cameroon – Buddhist)

But this also happens during the long periods spent in Libya, waiting to be able to leave for Europe. Let us observe how, in the first testimony reported here, the evangelical promise "where two or more are gathered in my name, I will be there" finds an echo in a story that seems to evoke the dramatic hours that announced the passion of Christ. In the second testimony, instead, the emphasis is on the invincibility of those who entrust themselves to God.

> I pray, even the time I was in Libya, on Sunday we prayed, all of us, in the night we prayed, but we did not go outside the church, where do you go to church? They would come and kill you! (...).
>
> We organized together at home, we pray to God. God is there, God is there, God is there, when he is one, he is there, in the middle of you, he is not afraid. If you are alone, you are not alone, God is with you, because you remember when you want to pray, you are alone, you are praying, you are worshiping God, praising God, when you start praying you see the Spirit of God, you can speak in trance, when the spirit of God comes, you also speak in trance, you will speak the language that you cannot understand, when you ... Your body will be shaking, you will know the power of God is like, I know ... when you are one, or two, or three, in your house, you pray to God, you are not alone, God is there, even if you are in the cave, pray to God, is there, because God is a spirit. (Man – Nigeria – Christian Pentecostal Church)

> They are serving, they cannot kill me, I know the God that I'm serving, it's only God that moves my life, it is not them. The power is in me, the power of God is in me, it is better than the one that is in them. (Man – Nigeria – Christian now attending a Pentecostal Church)

As we have noted above, the emphasis on the omnipotent divine protection mostly generates resignation and fatalism; without saying that a certain sense of invincibility (the relationship with God as a guarantee against evil and death) should be easily dismantled by history, which tells of countless martyrs of every religious confession (and of countless deaths during the migration journey).

On the other hand, the first testimony highlights a constant of the religious dynamic, on which we have already called the attention: the intimate link between precariousness and faith. It is certainly improper to identify migrants with the poor *tout court*. However, the link between the precariousness experienced in the dramatic events –occurred during both the migration and the process of adaptation– and faith –in its most elementary gestures– surely emerges here. Every need relating to the fundamental experiences of living and of living together –especially when it is dramatically disregarded– is a gateway capable of nesting the movement of faith. It is true for the hungry, where the expected food is denied; it is true for the homeless, when there is nothing but the street or, at best, a precarious hospitality; it is true for those who do not have a job or a salary, both expected and absent or not worthy of the man; it is true for those who are alone, when family and social relationships are somehow made inaccessible.

Immediately after landing in the receiving country, as confirmed by the following testimony, God appears to be the only one who can understand those who speak in a different language, the "Italians' *idioma*", and the only one who offers his companionship. A sort of confirmation of the above-mentioned profound vein of religious experience in relation to the drama of solitude, so severely documented by the linguistic strangeness that precludes the relationship:

> Where I live there are all refugees, you do not know anything, you do not even speak the Italian language and they do not speak the language of my country (...). So I found this place to go there some time, when there is a problem, feel bad, it is not a body, but you feel your heart hurting, missing family, country, friends ... even you do not find a person here you say that, all problems ... important just for God. So, I like going there. (Man – Tibet – Buddhist)

> I came to an unknown country, but the Lord did not leave me, I had the company of the Lord. (Woman – China – Church of God Almighty)

God is "here" when the everyday life leaves a large gap to bridge, as far as the dreams that accompanied the decision to migrate are concerned...

> (...) I get up at 4:30 in the morning and talk to God, like talking to a father. God is not in heaven. God is here and listens (...). My son tells me "Daddy I'm hungry". I ask: "Do you believe in God?" If you talk to God, father, father, I need this, I came to Italy because I need you, I do not want to stay

> here but this country supports me ... (Man – Venezuela – Protestant
> Evangelical Religious leader)

... and when something goes wrong, when difficulties or family problems arise,
thus making the sense of nostalgia even more acute:

> (...) certainly, just arrived, because however there is all the talk to elabo-
> rate the detachment, just as M. said before, to be in a very different con-
> text, the nostalgia of home then surely in that phase and then in a mo-
> ment of personal weakness I believe. In a phase in fact maybe a distant
> relative dies, you cannot go to the funeral. Often it is clearly experienced
> as a tragic moment because many cannot come back for matters of docu-
> ments, of money ... so surely when life gets harder or you lose your job, I
> think of all those situations in which you feel weaker and you need to be
> more supported by the religious community and by God. (Woman – FBOS
> operator – Christian Catholic)

This last testimony invites us to consider the value of a religious community of
reference and belonging. Once the migrant has landed in the receiving country, the religious community with its place of worship represents the "promised land" for a lifeless identity: an environment that is favorable to the recognition of oneself, to exorcise the hell of anonymity, to experience freedom.
Through the network of positive relationships and ritual celebrations, a new-
comer can hear his/her name in the religious place; it is heard what is whis-
pered by God, pronounced by his "sacred minister", it is read on the lips of
those who participate in the same cult. All this, in spite of the fact of being
undocumented, which seems to decree slavery, of the dissolution of personal
identity, of the impossibility of fulfilling one's own responsibilities. While one
feels enslaved by being in the hands of others, who do not know your name or
cannot pronounce it, in the sacred space one can express his/her own documented identity and one's freedom can be redeemed while being in God's
hands.

In front of the dramatic persistence of many needs, the sense of religious
community is associated with the sense of God. Numerous testimonies agree
on expressing this connection: the intimate union with God –in listening to his
speech, in the prayers said to ask for something or give thanks– is intertwined
with some community figures who favor that union to the social level that is
also involved in what the faithful seeks – whether it is a home in which to live,
a city to move to, to work and go shopping in, or a school where children can
study. *A fortiori*, this link proving the social depth of the religious phenomenon

is noteworthy in the testimony of migrants who mostly come from cultural contexts in which religion has not known the privatistic depreciation consumed in the West. Contrary to the individualistic involution of the religious phenomenon in Western countries (Chapter 3), in the faith experience of migrants, their "staying in God", in fact, is generally bound by their "being in the community".

> It is (*the need to go to the church*) because I have to go and thank God for his protection. (Man – Nigeria – Catholic Christian)

> I feel, this is my prayer, this is, I feel better, when I pray then I feel better, pray, reading the Koran, this is my belief, this is my belief, so like you, you go to church, you read the Bible, then you feel a little better. (Man – Pakistan – Muslim)

Finally, as efficaciously synthesized by this young Eritrean, on the one hand, religion supports every step of the migratory journey, and permits to "cross the border"; on the other, the migratory journey, with its burden of human suffering, increases migrants' personal faith and makes them much more inclined to religious practices. In his moving testimony, a clear religious sentiment emerges:

> Religion is an important help for us to make this path. Religion is an important help for us to take this dangerous road. Every person experiences difficult stories when they cross the border. Someone remains killed. Some see people dying in front of them. It is because you believe in God that you decide to face such dangerous situations to come to Europe. Believing in God helps to make this decision. Relatives abroad send money that helps to escape, but it is not thanks to the money that you get here. It comes thanks to God. For example, my cousin was not very interested in religion when he was in Eritrea, but crossing the border he saw things so hard that when he saved he wanted to thank God and began to pray. He crossed Sudan, the Sahara, the Mediterranean, and now he is in Germany. Now he thanks God, he has become a very believing Christian. Many people learn a lot along the way: trust in God and have good relations with Him. When they come here they keep their faith, but in Europe they do not have pastors. (Man – Eritrea – Catholic Christian)

In this light, it is also possible to understand the special rank of the sacred minister of the migrant community. In a community recognized as a safe place for storing the few personal belongings in which one's identity and one's memory can still be found, the figure of the religious leader functions as a safe place for one's conscience, when it feels the need to be blessed and reassured. That safe place is at its most vital when the migrant comes from a land and a tradition where a strong sense of the divine entails a deep respect for the religious authority. Staying as close as possible to the minister is a source of joy and satisfaction, as he works in order to let the life of the faithful be blessed by God – which feels even better when the sound of such blessing is in his/her mother tongue. Because of his sacred nature, the minister of the community acts as a mediator between "me" and God's words and actions. He is seen as the most precious safe place for one's troubled conscience, when it is afflicted by everything that it still does not have; he represents God's holiness, God's hospitality and generous blessing.

However, according to a shared experience, as acutely observed in the interview reported below, the prospect that religiosity becomes increasingly tenuous, if only at the level of daily practices, is an epilogue far from impossible. Thus, the link between need and faith is reaffirmed once again, and it is fueled by the troubled events of migration. The dramatic situation of privation concerns the most ordinary forms in which life unfolds and is expressed in that repetition of the word "without": without family, without work, without language, without money. Nevertheless, when "without" becomes "with", the experience of faith predictably suffers an attenuation, at least as far as daily gestures are concerned.

From the interviews that dwell on the "need/faith" connection, the information that we have just highlighted transpires. And also, at least in perspective, a paradox that makes us reflect in a number of ways. As mentioned in the testimony reported in Chapter 10 ("many pastors and religious leaders who are more interested in preaching prosperity than salvation"), the preaching that "strategically" equates salvation in terms of "prosperity" is increasingly widespread in the countries of origin of migrants. However, this kind of preaching, as well as the kind of "theology" that innervates it, now echoes in Italy too. Certainly, it is not only economic prosperity to be in play; more deeply, what is at stake is the general well-being, at the level of psychological harmony, of a peaceful recomposition of the relational network, especially as far as family and marital life is concerned, and of financial success. A sort of paradox can be glimpsed when a religious proposal founded on the "myth" of prosperity promises the achievement, through religious performances, of a well-being that, according to the most notable sacred experiences and texts, should restrict even more "the eye of the needle!"

In this respect, this testimony introduces an argument that will be developed in the final part of the chapter, where we will analyze the manner in which the migrants challenge "our" faith.

(...) then I had moments, ups and downs, and sure that when I arrived it
was a very difficult time for me, I found myself alone in a rented house in
Milan, without family, without work, without language, without money,
without anything and I had moments that I was very down but I have to
say, those moments that made me read the Gospel every day, much much
better than now ... other sides ... now I'm taken by a thousand other
things ... enter the daily life of the West that is not really healthy, it gives
you and takes you ... (Woman – Iraq – Chaldean Catholic Christian)

2   Religious Assistance in the Reception Phase

Another important aspect analyzed during the fieldwork is the "space" that
can/must be given to the religious rights and the spiritual needs of asylum
seekers and refugees hosted within the reception institutional system. In general terms, all the key informants have agreed on the opportunity to include
both of them in daily operations, thus confirming the peculiarity of the "Italian
version" of the European secularized society (Chapter 9). As a matter of fact,
Italian application of secularism is very distant from the French "*laïcité*", and
implies the need to recognize and protect individual religious belongings. Coherently, none of our key informants has raised doubts about the fact that the
religious and spiritual dimensions should also be recognized in the institutional system. Furthermore, almost all of them have confirmed how important it is
to involve spiritual leaders and religious organizations in the reception process, according to a holistic approach, currently judged to be the best one in
order to favor both the overcoming of the displacement trauma and the positive integration in the new society. As suggested by this operator, spirituality
can also have a "therapeutic" impact, when it comes to dealing with traumatized people:

> (...) when we talk about a complex case, we take into consideration reli-
> gious belief or belonging. We would like the involvement of the ministers
> of worship. For a person who is very ill and has that identity structure, it
> may be easier to engage with the minister of worship than the therapist.
> (Man – Operator of the reception system)

At the same time, the solutions adopted are always different, reflecting the heterogeneity of approaches that distinguish the Italian reception system, largely
entrusted with the initiative of the actors of the civil society. What is still

lacking is the formal acknowledgment of the role of the religious leaders within the reception path, besides the indications provided by the legislation in force (Chapter 9, §4). As a consequence, we can record an ample variety of "creative" solutions, together with the tendency to "confuse" spiritual assistance with psychological support or other kinds of empowering interventions, as we will analyze later.

On the other hand, there are many problematic issues and knots that need to be undone. Just to cite some examples, some key issues amply discussed during the focus group discussions are represented by:

- The opportunity to create rooms specifically for prayer inside the reception centers (rather than directing guests to worship in other places present in the local community);
- The preference for confessional worships, rather than for interreligious ones;
- The criteria for the selection of the spiritual leaders authorized to exercise their functions within the reception centers, and how to manage possible risks of circumvention and radicalization;
- The opportunity to promote ecumenical and interreligious meetings and initiatives, also as a way to raise the awareness towards religious pluralism;
- The methods for managing religious conflicts and interpersonal skirmishes due to the conflicting context of the origin countries, while avoiding their reification in the destination ones.

Overall, the issue regarding the "space" of religion within the reception system provides a brilliant example of a more general issue, concerning the need "to determine the boundaries of religion, religious jurisdiction(s), individual autonomy and equality" (Menski, Topidi, 2016: 8), which becomes even more challenging when vulnerable people are involved. On the basis of the study's evidence, the impression is that these issues are surely emerging, but still need to be addressed properly, as they were dealt with in different ways, depending on the sensitivity of the center's operators and managers, as well as on the characteristics of the hosted population. Curiously, the reception centers entrusted with the management of religious (Christian)-inspired organizations are not necessarily those that pay the greatest attention to the provision of religious services. In particular, the choice of some Catholic organizations not to "exhibit" any religious symbol in the rooms used for the reception of asylum seekers, in the name of a universalistic principle and out of respect for non-Christian guests, has been highly debated. On the other hand, some "lay" managers (including the services managed directly by local public bodies) have included religious services among the facilities offered to their guests.

On their part, as we have already observed (Chapter 10), various religious organizations have developed a particular sensitiveness towards migrants and refugees. Here, again, we can note an extraordinary convergence of the positions of the religious leaders of different traditions. Their shared approach is inspired by the following points:

a) the spiritual one is an innate dimension in human nature, shared by people of every religion and also by those who declare to be agnostic;

b) a welcoming system will not be as such if it does not recognize this dimension and is not prepared to respond to spiritual needs as well as to other primary needs;

c) recognizing and taking care of this dimension is fundamental not only because it responds to the need, expressed or latent, of every person, but also because the satisfaction of this need makes the process of integration less difficult and favors peaceful coexistence (on this point see also Chapter 15).

Then rightly we are all pressed by the emergency, by the immediacy of primary needs, but then always missing a piece, people who arrive in difficult situations are first of all also integral people, here, complete people, who also have a religious dimension, sacral, spiritual, which is the one that can actually help. (Man – Pastoral operator – Muslim)

(…) spiritual dimension … all men and women of the world have it regardless of the faith they profess, regardless of religion. The spiritual dimension is that which someone calls only psychological, but in the inherent nature of each one. And this I believe is part of this duty that we have to welcome these people as people … that is, welcoming a person does not mean welcoming a body, it means welcoming a story, a sensitivity, and certainly, in some way, this … when we talk about projects, expectations, hopes, after all we are talking about the spiritual world. So the attention to this means I do not do the practices, I'll give you a job, I'll give you … it's … it is walking near these people, entering for a moment with their life in their lives here.

(…) What does this mean? Whatever necessity one has, it can be a sock rather than a pair of shoes, but it can instead be an outburst or a request, a … even simply a friendly shoulder on which to cry or with which to laugh. Therefore, our operators are called to, I say to "mark a man", these people. These people must really feel … because then everything starts from there, no? Any speech starts from there. (Man – Religious leader – Catholic Christian)

(...) because the care of the spiritual dimension in my opinion leads me out of the person, can bring out from the person the best, the highest, the deepest, the most authentic there can be and therefore can be for this reason a great integration factor: because it improves, it makes us better say that the possibility of living, of expressing our faith, makes us better. So I think it's a great factor of integration. (Woman – FBOS operator – Catholic Christian)

At the same time, our key informants have insisted on the sensitivity of the topic under discussion. It has emerged, in particular, that the respect for the religious rights of both majority and minority groups is not sufficient to solve the challenges of interreligious coexistence. In fact, the tortuous existential and migratory paths have left open wounds that often find in the "religious" issue the reason to flare up. The circumstance of having left behind authoritarian regimes, or even autocratic ones, has indelibly marked the relationship with religiosity and, in particular, with the faithful of other religions. The concept of religious pluralism, which we are inclined to consider as obvious –beyond the resistance that is observed in translating it into the daily practice of the same European societies– is anything but obvious for those coming from confessional States. According to some of the experts involved, the first reception, if not because it often implies the need to cohabit with asylum seekers of other religions, is therefore the right phase during which to set the education to religious pluralism. Regardless of the reasons that led them to emigrate, and of the role that religion played in that decision, it is precisely the context of the incoming countries that shows the relevance of this type of action, also as an antidote to the problems that could arise in the future. As a matter of fact, European receiving societies are today more and more called to manage the expectations of minority groups –avoiding that their requests instrumentally turn into an anti-immigration argument– while also laying the foundations of a cohesive society.

As a matter of fact, it is now widely known that the early stages of reception are made up of crucial moments in which to recover an emotional balance and a working capacity, as well as to lay the foundations of the path of integration. Just as in the context of a holistic approach to integration, there are many dimensions of recovery and of personal well-being that need to be considered. At the same time, some key informants have underlined how the foundations for integration in a secular society based on respect for religious pluralism must also be laid from the beginning of the reception path. It is significant to observe that this very concept was expressed by a Catholic priest, a Muslim Imam, and an expert on migration law. It might seem paradoxical, but precisely those who suffered "because of" religion are not said to be tolerant towards other religions.

> (...) they are very solid people precisely in their spirituality on the one hand and people who are struggling, however, to say how to live that mutual respect precisely because they have not been respected. As a person who has been raped in his own corporeity and then becomes particularly suspicious and then I would say that the two ... when easily either a persecuted Christian or the persecuted Muslim must speak of those who persecuted them for pseudo reasons of faith do not have the condescension and tolerance that we have that in some way we have never been offended by the different parties. (Man – Religious leader – Catholic Christian)

> People who require asylum and the majority of migrants, however, are not coming to Europe for that reason. But anyway they will need a reframing of what religion is, what religious pluralism is, how to integrate into a secularized society ... because they do not know it, whatever religion they may have. We need more an educational scenario than an existential scenario. The motivation to escape is not predominantly that, but this does not mean that civil society and institutions must do not take care of religious acceptance. (Man – Religious leader – Muslim)

> The essential thing is to educate to diversity, to respect, because for many who come from confessional contexts, or with a state religion, it may seem shocking, precisely, but we must bring the reasoning on the opportunity. It becomes a vision of life, the possibility, finally, of conceiving a free public space, free from constraints and free from the impossibility of parrying. (Man – Expert)

Finally, as acutely suggested by this interviewee, the simple existence of a free and pluralistic society is not a sufficient condition to achieve a peaceful coexistence. Freedom is a right, but it is also a "duty" and a responsibility, the awareness of which is not automatically acquired once landed in a free and democratic society:

> (...) here they have freedom but do not understand what it is ... because freedom is not ... sorry I give an example: "Freedom is not I do that fuck I want". It is not true, this is not freedom ... that is, I interpreted it in the first few months, when I went out at 9 pm in Corso Sempione to walk

alone, without being afraid ... now there is the fear, however, to say, I have never been able to do this in my country, this is freedom, freedom that you put on what you want, but not that you have to go naked because you say "I am free" ... respecting the dignity, the place ... to say what you want, to express yourself as you want ... this is freedom, it is not as it is understood by many ... (Woman – Iraq – Chaldean Catholic Christian)

On the other hand, as we will analyze in the following section, it is equally significant to observe how education to religious pluralism is a need that also concerns the host society:

(...) we are Catholics, but we are Catholics of Eastern rite, so we have a different tradition and also a different calendar, our liturgical calendar, so we are a minority ... even among the minorities of other ethnic groups, other Catholic migrants, but that they are of Latin rite, therefore easily inserted, integrable into the Church, also in its liturgical calendar and all. Instead we have a completely different tradition, so we are seen, often then people confuse, for the simple fact that we have another rite, we are confused with the Orthodox, instead we are not Orthodox, we are Catholics, and even there is ... in the calendar the fact that we celebrate Christmas on a different date, Easter on another different date, sometimes creates conflicts with some parish priests, because they do not understand why we do not celebrate Christmas or Easter with them. It is necessary to explain ... some refuse to accept it, but ... there are a number of difficulties, even as minorities in the minorities, which we must face. (Man – Religious Leader – Catholic Christian of Eritrean rite)

3   How (Forced) Migrants Challenge Host Society's Churches

As we will analyze in Chapter 16, through the account of a paradigmatic initiative launched by the Archdioceses of Milan, the issue of religious pluralism particularly challenges the Italian Catholic Church, since it has until recently benefited from a situation of undisputed hegemony within the Italian religion landscape. Despite the historical presence of various religious minorities (Chapter 9), Italian public institutions and private organizations had often operated in an environment reflecting a sort of "invisibility" of religion, basing on the presumption that Italy was a mono-religious country, and this situation also influenced the attitude of many religious leaders and single believers. However, in the last decades, as a consequence of immigration, religious minorities have grown significantly: the issue of interreligious co-existence, tradition-ally underexplored, has emerged, putting the country into a better position for gaining awareness of the unfolding processes by which it is increasingly becoming a multi-faith society. Besides the challenges represented by the pres-ence of minority religions (particularly Islam, which today covers around 5% of the population residing in Italy), and by the huge presence of Christian Ortho-dox (around 2%, mainly migrants coming from East Europe),[1] this has implied the need to confront with different ritual and liturgical traditions, brought by the arrival of Catholic migrants who, as highlighted by the above-reported tes-timony of an Eritrean priest, are often completely unknown by Italian Catho-lics, or even confused with other confessions. In general terms, faithful of non-(Roman) Catholic tradition are today solicited to become more familiar with the concept of religious pluralism, and better equipped to confront with other confessions and religious habits. Before discussing this topic, we have to con-sider the manner in which host society's Churches have been reacting to the arrival of migrants and asylum seekers. More precisely, it is by analyzing their approach towards newcomers that we can grasp the challenging nature of the relationship between migrants and established Italian Churches.

As we have already pointed out (Chapter 10, §1; see also Chapter 14), (Italian) Catholic Churches and faith-based organizations of different inspiration share a common effort in welcoming migrants and refugees. In particular, many reli-gious groups have implemented, independently from the official reception sys-tem, various initiatives specifically addressed to (forced) migrants and refu-gees. This aspect was not among the main topics we planned to investigate within this part of the study, but it has repeatedly emerged during the field-work. Indeed, every time they have been solicited to describe the religious and spiritual needs of refugees and asylum seekers, the religious leaders involved in the study have ended up in depicting their own engagement in this field.

> (…) that is, to meet migrants according to their needs. So, Italian language and culture, promotion and defense of health. How important it is to ac-company migrants and accompany them on a journey of health, because migrants come here to work, as Italians abroad often bring home money, send money home … instead they must be accompanied in health, they are neglected in health. So we have the defense project, the prevention of cancer for women, and I think of the Ukrainian communities, because first-generation Ukrainian women are older in age, they are almost my age or slightly younger. And so the risk of breast cancer is considerable, then

---

1 ISMU estimates on ISTAT and Pew Research Center data.

coming from the Chernobyl area, nearby, etc. but here is the prevention of health that projects together with the local health authorities, both with the diocesan Caritas, the health center of the diocesan Caritas, projects designed together to defend the migrant, for the health of the migrant and therefore the communities, to create in the communities, beyond the study of the Italian language, the places of prevention for health, where nobody is afraid to ask questions, to be oriented to specialized centers, to be invited to take exams ... there is a fear of approaching hospitals from many migrants that is dangerous to their health, so this, the defense of health, language, because language is the first thing, integration is the language ... go to the market and know how to say pepper or eggplant is a different thing. (Man – Religious leader – Catholic Christian)

What's more, in their description, spiritual and religious assistance is often mixed up with different forms of social assistance, empathetic sustain, or "tutoring"/"coaching". As a matter of fact, both the experience of interviewed migrants and of the managers of hosting centers and religious communities prove how the assistance addressed to meet religious sentiments intermingles with the basic everyday needs and expectations. Even the above-reported interview confirms that it is not possible to offer care related to the sacred link with the Deity if not through the answer to these needs and expectations. According to what has emerged, it is only through the latter that the religious sentiment is generated, with all its rituality and living experience. Significantly, the interview contains a specific reference to health and language, body and relationship, rest and feast, motherhood/fatherhood and work; whatever the identity of a person, where does this identity ignite its freedom if not here? Where else can it bow to the transcendent for a "thank you" or for "help"? If not here, in these elementary living experiences? Are there other places where the intuition of a God and the taste for his performing could strike? It is asserted, in these interviews, that the attention for the sacred bond of those who are welcomed and accompanied in integration paths can be seen in the rigorous assumption of those fundamental forms of existence that the experience of migration makes problematic and impractical. There is no cure for the sacred bond in its formally religious expressions without the passionate care of those dimensions of experience and their sacred profile. An Evangelical Christian pastor, who was involved in one of the focus groups, even employed the expression "Christian counselling" to allude to an institutionalized practice based on the use of the Bible in searching the answers to offer to the people in need. This is a model that has already been extensively tested and which should now be adopted to tackle the specific needs of (forced) migrants and asylum seekers.

Coherently with this kind of approach, migrants' spiritual needs are often reduced, in the description made by the religious leaders, to the migrants' need to practice their cult according to their past experience and traditions. This means, first of all, the possibility to attend the celebrations in the migrants' mother tongue, with traditional rituals, songs and liturgies, and to meet and spend free time in spaces provided by their places of worship. A point that has almost inevitably led to the memory of Italian emigrants abroad:

> Who is used to celebrating the liturgy in a very festive, very dynamic way, so we can sing songs, clap hands, etc. our style is a little Genoese that is very sober and therefore risks discouraging many people who come from the Catholic faith but then maybe many have been absorbed in some way or by Evangelicals or Pentecostals, however also seven pseudo Christians because they approach their way of praying more to what was the way of praying in their country. So these communities have chaplains, the term that is not used but I do not know what other term to use, ethnic chaplains, chaplains of their lands, which speak their language, which use their customs and habits just for ... just as there are in the world the missions were called Italian, they are nothing more than Italian priests than in Paris rather than in New York etc. who have accompanied the communities of Italian emigrants in their growth in faith. (Man – Religious leader – Catholic Christian)

> (...) I thought she was crying because she had lost her job, because she was far from her husband, because her daughter was studying and she was missing them, right? She had been treated badly, I do not know. Instead she told me that she could for the first time pray in Romanian, confess in her language, sing with the songs of her tradition. She has confused me, because I had already gone with mine, my mental prejudices: so, the daughter who does not have her, her husband works in France, work is precarious. No, the first generation wants to hear their own languages. So hear your tongue in a foreign land, eat Romanian food. We started this way, but why did the Italians meet in the Belgian, French and German communities and they ate fettuccine?! And it was important that they find themselves. (Man – Religious leader – Catholic Christian)

As a matter of fact, despite our repeated solicitations, many religious leaders have shown a certain difficulty in dealing with the concept of "migrants' spiritual needs"; a specific reflection on this aspect is in fact substantially lacking. For example, in their description of the role of worships in the face of newcomers' arrivals, almost all the religious leaders involved in the study have referred to them as places to meet, to support each other, and as places of "identity compensation". Much emphasis has been placed on the initiatives implemented to support the inclusion process (language courses, matching with the labor demand, social assistance...). As stated by this Catholic priest, the risk could be that of "skipping" spiritual needs, to the point of discovering that they are the very migrants who encourage us to be less materialistic –or, in evangelical terms, "to choose the best part"–:

> (...) in a general sense, I believe that all those who do this kind of welcome do not have particular attention to this dimension. So we are all always very concerned about giving the food, the documents, job opportunities, without taking into account what then is the real engine of our ... the pursuit of happiness that can also come from a job, from a home, which cannot be only that, then the risk is that perhaps we are the very materialistic in the West and therefore easily pretend or do not take into account, even worse, the most spiritual part of each of us, so attentive to practical needs, that we forget the reason why one looks for a home, for a job, then your own happiness. And so this surely would mean that it would take a little bit to return to a culture, to the man in his integrity. (Man – Religious leader – Catholic Christian)

Quite surprisingly –but in line with the study background– within this effort to meet migrants' cultural, social, and economic needs, it is migrants' spiritual needs that risk being unmet. Undoubtedly, the habit to meet religious demand where it emerges, that is through the most elementary needs dramatically perceived, produces the risk of disregarding exactly the very spiritual dimension. The following testimony is typical. Authentic spiritual assistance has to be grounded in a human promotion. However, this circumstance involves the risk of a possible involution of the religious communities: these are so entangled in sophisticated initiatives of "material support" that they are disengaged in that proximity that listens to the expectation of God – an expectation that ends up turning into *the announcement*, as well as into the interpretation of the sacred texts, the exhortation to faith, a blessing and a consolation, and that invites to an intense experience of faith. In the following testimony, a Catholic priest reveals, through a biographic anecdote, how it is precisely the immigrants who do solicit to welcome, besides their own material needs, those of a spiritual nature.

> (...) there were these guys last year in the sports hall, that this AB was a pretty infernal place, in the sense that there were 250 of these on the camp beds, dumped there, when running, with difficulty we managed to

create a structure, we brought them there and these happy ones, finally inside a house, the showers, the towel and so on. It was a Saturday afternoon. At a certain point, about fifteen of them took me aside, put me in the middle of a circle, they told me: "We have to ask you something". And I inside me I said: "But what I want there ... we had done races, fatal labors, what do they still want?" And then one of them advances and says: "We have two requests". Oh well, "Tell me". So a little resigned. Then he says: "The first we are English speakers, we ask you if you can find one or two Bibles in English. The second is this: we are Christians, today is Saturday and we would like to know if tomorrow there is a function to celebrate Sunday". And I am a priest and I said: "Look at what a man of faith you are". These tossed, brought in this new structure etc. they remembered that today is Saturday, because then you lose; I always lost the sense of time on ships. And their two requests have certainly involved two needs that I had not thought about. I thought about them all: towel, phone card, read this one ... and they told me: "Well, thank you, we are happy, but we need these two things". This was one of the many slaps I got in my face! (Man – Religious leader – Catholic Christian)

Indeed, in-depth interviews with a group of people in charge with the pastoral care of migrants have permitted us to better clarify this sort of "overlapping" between spiritual assistance and human promotion, which starts by accompanying the migrants in their first steps into the new society. Inspired by the ancient experience of priests and nuns working with Italian emigrants in the "new world", and then in Northern Europe, pastoral operators have identified migrants as people in need, people to whom address their special care and "to serve". According to their testimony, spiritual assistance cannot be separated from the simple act of taking care of migrants and their basic needs; thus doing –as suggested by one of our interviewees– "you will touch their heart".

Then the "Migrantes" (*The Foundation of the Italian Episcopal Conference in charge of the pastoral care of migrants, authors' note*) is the care, the support, the accompaniment of migrants in the pastoral centers at the service of migrants. It is not a pastoral care ex novo, because it was born from the experience of Italians abroad, when the Scalabrinian missionaries and then priests, following the Italian communities abroad, created this pastoral care and accompanied the Italian migrants to integrate where they were: Canada, United States, Australia, how many problems for the first Italian migrants in the great Australian "farms". There is an interesting book by the Migrantes Foundation on mental illnesses, the mental problems of the first Italians in these lost farms. Then how much the presence of the priest, the presence of the nuns, I think of the Scalabrinian nuns and so on, they have helped and supported the Italian migrants. It's really a human, spiritual accompaniment ... I think of the tragedy of Marcinelle[2] and how much the priests and nuns had been close to those poor women, to their children. For that great tragedy they played a very important role of consolation, of support, of help, not of confrontation but of accompaniment, as important. Here all this is treasured and experienced for the Church and we live it today as a great experience in the reality of the communities present here. (Man – Religious leader – Catholic Christian)

(...) there is a need for an accompaniment just a little ... something that maybe in the reception centers cannot be done, but a little face to face. If you happen to be close, I see that other associations, maybe they can do it less, we have a little more in this DNA, this needs not only to give what you need to survive ... first then to help them find ... but you also know a spiritual need can also be rediscovering dignity. For example, a person who lives on the street and to whom no one has ever said that maybe he could live differently and help him, and it happened, we have several experiences on this and on other things, and help you find your way back home ... Is it not perhaps satisfying a great spiritual need? (Woman – FBOs operator – Catholic Christian)

(...) welcome a family, meet them, answer maybe just at first impact in that way no? But it is precisely to cross that need there, to meet that man there, to be there those gestures through which you then reach the heart. When you called, I said: "What do you mean by spiritual assistance?" Because we do not, in fact I told you, we're not doing spiritual assistance, right? But precisely through our work, no? Our service ... we answer the need of the man who arrives, through whose relationship we get to that spiritual need, of meaning, need of hope, no?

(...) Then we are just certain that serving a need comes to the heart. There is not, how to say: "I'll help you there, but then I want something else". No, no, the experience is also that you are sure that you touch the strings of the heart of man ... (Women – Nuns – Catholic Christians)

---

2   The tragedy occurred in the mine of Marcinelle, in Belgium, the 8th August 1956, in which hundreds of miners died, the majority of those were Italians.

So, yes for me personally the spiritual accompaniment, there is ... if you
can call it that, it goes more through the everyday life of the things of life.
(Woman – FBOs operator – Catholic Christian)

Finally, it is precisely through their physical presence that religious operators
can try to answer refugees' spiritual needs. As described in this eloquent testimony, showing an empathetic attitude toward those who suffered a lot during
the journey, and who continue to experiment solitude and isolation, is the
most immediate way to satisfy their spiritual needs.

(...) this is a discovery that took place after a short time to try to respond
precisely to those that we understood to be the inner, spiritual needs. Because the first need seemed to us to be close to a friendly presence and
someone who could participate in the pain and in some way learn to deal
with those that were wounds of the heart because most live, as xxx said,
the separation clearly from the family, from the figures of reference, from
... ties a little frayed ... the drama of the journey for all is very strong.
I would say that most of our friends told us about the prison in Libya;
however, the period spent in Libya as something that has marked them
forever. In personal terms, they all suffered torture, however harassment,
women in any case ... abuses of all kinds. And even during the crossing
at sea they saw friends die. So they find themselves having to face a very
great pain, a pain that does not make them sleep at night, a pain that ...
and that's why they ask first of all a human proximity and someone who
tries to stay close to them and they say it clearly. I speak ... I have no family, no friends, I need someone close to me. So they look for someone who
listens to them, who listens to their story, without having to evaluate it
in terms of "accepted" or "not accepted", then to receive it and in some
way support it. And then in this sense we organize prayers with the community, we also concretely try to help them to live a spiritual dimension,
both personal and communitarian, by making a bridge with the realities
that are present on the territory, the Islamic realities say, with the communities of the mosques present ... with the prayer rooms ... with which
we are in relationship. And with the Christians instead inviting them to
our prayer and to all the moments of reflection on the Gospel for Christians of course ... and then there is this beautiful prayer we say every year,
which is called "Prayer of hope", in which we remember all the names of
the people who died at sea during the voyage and many of these names
have been given us by them. And this year, for example, a friend of ours
who is an Imam from the Ivory Coast, his name is M.M., he is a Muslim.

They made a moment of prayer with another Imam outside the Church of the Annunciation, then they entered and during the prayer he cried and thanked at the same time why he was reminded of all the people he saw dying on the boat. So, first of all this need for friendship ... This need to live spirituality, because they are also far from the communities with which they lived there. Since religion is also a bond with others, especially not just a private matter, they ask for a community dimension in order to live their religion. (Woman – FBOs operator – Catholic Christian)

On his turn, in this moving testimony, a Catholic priest describes how the ethnic chaplain is the "safe place" which permits to overcome the sense of estrangement experienced by newcomers:

So the Latin American community has a room, if you open it, it is full of suitcases. (...) when they arrive, they do not know where to put the baggage: one thing is to leave it to payment at the Termini station (*the Roma central station, author's note*), another thing is in a safe place, that you feel at home, the community. Then that room for suitcases, and the suitcase in the imagination of the migrant, but it is still so, is certainly more beautiful than that of the Italians of the nineteenth or twentieth century or after the Second World War (...), are perhaps more beautiful but the content is life, there is the whole of the migrant inside. That's what they bring, so it's precious to them, that of photos, memories, computers, cell phones, before there were not now, but there is what you can bring everything. Where do I put it? In a place that welcomes me, the community, so that room is much better than the station terms pay. I give it, I put it in the Latin American community entrusted to the Scalabrinian Fathers and it's like keeping it in my house until I find a place. (Man – Religious leader – Catholic Christian)

Finally, every form of help in the little and big tasks newcomers have to face gain a specific theological meaning once put in a spiritual and pastoral perspective:

(...) if you find a house that welcomes you, that is the Church, that supports you, that helps you to study Italian, that takes care of your soul so try to make you stay at home even if away from home, it helps you to recreate a family even if you do not have a blood family but a family of faith, if it helps you to get better, to live your daily life, share your hard work to find a job, share your hard work to find a home, share your effort for a residence permit, help you find the channels, for a civil lawyer, when you need a criminal lawyer, what you need. It is beside you, it cries with you and smiles with you, makes a feast, embraces you if you were perhaps in reunion, helps you in reuniting your family. Of course it works for integration, damn it! Because you feel welcomed, supported, you do not feel alone. And loneliness leads you then, if you do not find answers, more easily to crime, more easily to do what you would never imagine doing, if instead be welcomed, supported, accompanied by a hug, a smile, that is some advice on how to go to the police station, which is a patronage that helps you for work, that is other families that welcome you when you do not have a home, and of course that helps you live better. And if it helps you to live better, in addition to prayer, which is very important, then better deal with your daily life. Integration is a journey. Of course, yes, we must create welcoming communities, ever more welcoming, ever more attentive to hugs, smiles, to give just directions and even when we have no answers to look for them, not to resign ourselves not to find them, to accompany and if it were just crying, even crying together. (Man – Religious leader – Catholic Christian)

Furthermore, as suggested by this Evangelical pastor, material and psychological support becomes an instrument of evangelization of those people who never patently experienced the presence of God:

The support they receive is linked to the word of God, to the promises that God makes in his word to those who believe in him. There is a God who takes care of them, he loves them. According to Chinese culture, there is no God. The fact that you are someone who takes care of them, who listens to them, who supports them, who cares about them can be very important. (Woman – Religious leader – Evangelical Christian)

To be more precise, many religious leaders and pastoral operators (particularly within the Catholic Church) appear definitely reluctant to the prospect of understanding the reception aids as a means to encourage the conversion of the newcomers. The following testimony is just one of the many proving the extreme "prudence" with which they consider this possibility:

We also had some cases of ... fascinated by the beauty of the Gospel he asked to make a journey of catechesis, of knowledge of the Gospel. Someone asked for the baptism but I said: "We are careful not to confuse

things, not to think that as a welcoming is made by the Church, we are
here to convert them all. We are all thinking of converting ourselves, then
we see, now we see". (Man – Religious Leader – Catholic Christian)

Finally, also linguistic and cultural barriers can be easily overcome when the
newcomers perceive the presence of God through the proximity of His
ministers:

> People for centuries prayed in Latin without understanding anything.
> There have been many saints in centuries, many good people who under-
> stand the Gospel much more than we who are exegetes. So I would dare
> say that precisely for the specifically spiritual part, language is the last
> obstacle because precisely the affection, the welcome, a look, a smile, a
> handshake, a hug that indicate this proximity does not have a different
> language. (Man – Religious leader – Catholic Christian)

Last but not least, as observed by this Catholic nun, by displaying their care for
the newcomers, religious people are simply taking care of their own
spirituality:

> (...) And then, excuse me, it seems that, perhaps I say one thing ... but it
> seems to me that, at least I do not have a concern, when I meet the boys,
> when I meet the families, their spiritual care. I have the concern of my
> spiritual care which is what allows me to look at them and to allow them
> to truly be what I am. (Woman – Nun – Christian Catholic)

Lastly, we will now analyze how the presence of migrants who guard their faith
according to communicative paradigms and celebratory codes originating
from their land challenges the Italian communities, until calling them to a conversion in the resumption of their most authentic traditions and their sacred
texts. Evidently –this aspect has already emerged abundantly– the call for a
reform of experience and religious practice also comes from the communities
encountered in the country that welcomes and radically questions the quality
of the faith of migrants. Thus, integration finds its most convincing fruitfulness
in a kind of reciprocity. On the one hand, through its reading of the founda-
tional texts, its celebratory ways, its style of community life, the faith of migrants comes to "integrate" (that is to make it more mature, but also to move
towards the "whole") the faith of the hosting communities. The first enriches
the second since it reveals and offers aspects of the religious experience that,

due to different traditions and history, were perhaps scarcely lived or even ignored in the indigenous communities. On the other hand, in the same way, the faith of the indigenous communities encountered in the host country manages to integrate the faith of the migrants, revealing and offering them some values of the religious experience which tend to be neglected in the believing practice of migrants.

From this point of view, in the various interviews, we seem to glimpse some major themes in which this mutual integration unfolds. The religious experience of migrants gives back to the religious communities of the host country the primacy of "feeling" as the heart of the faith; mainly, with respect to a "knowledge" and a "doing" that in the West (not only the Christian West) ended up dismissing the feeling, equating it with emotionalism and childishness. This experience ends up questioning about "joy" as an inevitable trait in the authentic relationship with God. Besides, as stated in one of the above-reported interviews, it testifies to a freedom and a frankness in proclaiming and practicing one's faith in a way that knows no timidity or false human respect even in a largely secularized world.

At the same time, the religious experience they have intercepted in the communities of the host country offers them a sense of "religious freedom", with practical declinations both at a family and at a social level – we will return to this point in the following section. Finally, another value particularly appreciated by migrants seems to be the ability to make –with rigor and passion– the connection between the announcement/celebration of faith and the human promotion in every sector of society.

What's more, as captured by this moving testimony, the arrival of migrants who have never found the faith is even more challenging in both human and spiritual terms, since it offers the unique opportunity to listen to the Word of the Lord with the ears of those who have never heard it.

> When xxx asked me to begin a journey of biblical reading, we began to read the Gospel (...). So, at a certain point, I read the parable of the merciful Father (...). And I thought that for thirty years now I have been a Pastor I had never read the parable of the prodigal son to someone who did not already know it. And so, thinking back to that parable that speaks of a merciful God who forgives you, doesn't he? That is, of this celebration of God ... for the first time I listened to this parable with the ears of someone who has never heard it. Simply this thing has impressed me and also moved me. (Man – Religious leader – Protestant Christian)

4   Religious Agency in the Process of (Forced) Migrants' Public Space
     Making

In the previous sections, we have analyzed various aspects connected to the
role played by religion and spirituality in the process of adaptation of (forced)
migrants. In this final section, we will discuss how the evidence collected during
this part of the study can help us to develop the prospect of re-humanization
of (forced) migrants along the four lines of research identified above
(Chapter 2):
a)   identity;
b)   religious freedom;
c)   citizenship;
d)   common good.
As already described (Chapter 10), many of the migrants interviewed have emphasized how religion is a source of individual and collective *identity*, shaped
by the intra-familiar transmission of religious values and beliefs (as we will
deeply analyze in Part 5), but also –and especially– by the experience of discrimination and persecution suffered before emigrating, as well as by the troubles encountered during the migratory journey. Religious identity represents
a source of resistance and resilience, but it is also the limit beyond which it
is not possible to accept any violations. Therefore, the concept of religious
identity provides a meaning to the decision to migrate, even for those who
"did not know they had a religious identity": this concept has been unveiled
only after having migrated to another country, where they first experienced
both a context of religious freedom and the possibility to be helped by religious people. Finally, religious identity is a crucial resource providing (forced)
migrants with an extraordinary ability to face problems and challenging situations, as unanimously asserted by the following interviewees, who are coming
from different countries and have different religious backgrounds:

> (…) it was very difficult, but I remember when I was very young, my par-
> ents always talked about this thing, this sacrifice that we always have to
> make to resist, just to show that we have our identity, and then they gave
> me force to fight these problems. (Woman – Iran – Bahá'í)

> (…) I am right to be Catholic until I die, if I die tomorrow or if I die in fifty
> years … These are my roots, this is my identity. If I remove my identity, it
> means that I have nothing that supports me. (Man – Egypt – Coptic Cath-
> olic Christian)

> Since I was a child, my father told me to read the Bible every day, every morning and, before going to his job, he used to read the Bible for five to ten minutes and he taught me that when you are starting to learn the Bible, your problems will be fewer, Jesus will help you and so you can just relax. (Man – Pakistan – Catholic Christian)

If we consider the collective dimension of the religious identity, we can observe that religious affiliations reinforce the sense of belonging to a community of peers, i.e. a sort of enlarged family that makes its members feel "at home" and loved – a key form of support for those who experience the status of stranger, for those who have to deal with everyday frustrations and who fear a sense of solitude.

> I know the Focolari movement from 1982, in Egypt. Here is something that pushed me to grow, because I felt loved, because a foreigner, when changing places for religious reasons, does not need money, but to feel loved, a sense of family, this is what he is missing. (Man – Egypt – Coptic Catholic Christian)

> There is another reason for the celebration that is, for the Bahá'i people, in addition to participation in the activities and the administrative system, to meet and be aware of the daily life of others. The Bahá'ís to meet only ... that is, a party is organized. Maybe you eat ... all the people are there to increase community solidarity. So the Bahá'i community, at the local, national and international levels, is connected through this 19th century celebration.
>
> (...) therefore, let's say that our community for us is like our family and as members of the community they are also our family. (Couple (Man and Woman) – Iran – Bahá'i)

In this same perspective, religion functions as an identity anchor, and as an instrument of defense for those who perceive the hosting society as an anomic one, to the point of menacing migrants' personal moral integrity and their offspring's socialization (see also Chapter 20). Finally, the migrants' community gathered around the Church offers the possibility to maintain a link with one's past and one's roots, and to safe one's original identity.

> (...) on the one hand, it is a function I think of link to their past because even this I think is an important aspect. There is for many of them a fundamental aspect of their history, of the history of their family, that is, I do

not know a Latin American with its Catholic faith, or today also many that are of Evangelical confession, however it is a link with one's own history. Or a Muslim as we said before. (Woman – FBOs operator – Catholic Christian)

It has been said that the religious community often functions as a social place of "identity compensation" (§3), or better yet, an identity anchoring. It saves from the icy waters of anonymity, since your name resounds in it and, eventually, it becomes the subject of attributions of rights and duties. A second fundamental reason concerns the religious experience as a way of life: the reference or belonging to the religious community are experienced as bastions of resistance with respect to that corruption of moral-religious integrity that the host world seems to foster because of its widespread secularization. Finally, the circulation of words in the same language, the immediacy in cultivating personal and national memory, the custom of celebrating God's providence in the language of the fathers, guarantee the bond with one's roots. A circumstance that certainly seems profitable in terms of identity custody. However, the metaphor of the tree and the roots evokes a rigid and static identity: a pattern that is not absent in the so-called "ethnic communities", where migrants usually meet and celebrate their religious rites (§3). With this in mind, would the metaphor of a river and its springs be more adequate to express the migrants' religious identity? It does evoke a "traditional principle" that is still active and fruitful (the springs) and that feeds a flow open to promising contributions and contaminations – thus concurring to the process of migrants' public space making.

As a matter of fact, religious identity becomes even clearer once compared to the situation of the destination country, where religious affiliation is lived in a much milder way. Quite significantly, this woman, despite a biography strongly marked by her membership to a minority, and persecuted, religious group –which we could expect to have indelibly marked her existence– observes how "religion is always something that you must grow inside of you":

(...) then we have a strength that I do not feel so much in Italy that we try to keep tradition, even religion as a tradition, in the sense that I am Christian and I must be and I have to say it, but here in Italy we say: ah, yes, I am a Christian but I'm not a practitioner; ah, but I'm not ... but I say, but what are you not? But thank God you are in a Catholic country! We, at this point, are very strong, we are very jealous. Then, even after religion is always something that you have to grow yourself, it's not just something

that you inherit from yours, but you also have to work on it, you have to
feel it too, otherwise it will just be ... (Woman – Iraq – Chaldean Catholic
Christian)

Inspired by this kind of feelings, we can grasp a first important contribution
provided by the process of refugees' public space making. As brilliantly described by this FBOs staff-member, migrants' religiosity is "more religious" than
that of the locals. If not for this reason, as discussed in another part of this
volume (Chapter 16), independently of their motive to migrate, migrants challenge European secularized society, and particularly those who demand to be
acknowledged as religious. Fundamentally, as exemplified by the following
statements, this sentiment has emerged from both the "insiders" (the religious
leaders and the pastoral operators) and the "outsiders" (the Catholic migrants
coming from non-Christian countries):

(...) we probably, as a Western society, are a fairly secularized society,
while in other contexts, basically those who leave, come from a context,
there is an economic migrant, migrant who comes here seeking asylum
for humanitarian reasons, leaving a situation a little different even at the
level of society ... so for them, in my opinion, the religious factor is their
own identity. There's ... like ... it's also very providential. That is why it is
not like ... at least from my experience, from what I think, it is not that
they first look for the house and work, and then they go to church. Indeed, they go to church to look for ... there is the paradox is a bit that we
ask the Lord to send us these things and then see ... is a religion very
"religious" in quotes not? At least, I think of the Africans with whom I
had more to do but also them, maybe the Chinese are more discreet
from this point of view ... but if they pray even three hours a day, they
do it, they have always done it because it is probably right of their identity. Is there ... maybe you recognize that too, and then even ... that is
also the identity because often, according to me, religion and their ethnic identity often merge? So ... I do not even know the African community, also Arab, there is the Coptic, there is the Muslim and then, in
short, it is so...
    (...) even if in fact it is they who accompany me as a spiritual guide.
They say: "I have prayed!". All right, good! Maybe there are those who
question me more from this point of view. (...) Then they provoke me,
trusting this Providence, both the Africans to Allah, and they ... probably
we Westerners have lost something, I do not know! So I am constantly
provoked from this point of view, in short. They tell me: "Saturday we

read the Bible for four hours". Saturday I'm going to have a coffee, I see some friends! (Woman – FBOs operator – Catholic Christian)

I'll bring them to church every Sunday; I'll tell them to read the Bible, to join Christian groups, to join Christian culture, because without faith, without religion we are nothing. When Jesus is not in your life, you have nothing in your life. In Pakistan, when children are 3 or 4, they send them to the mosque and to learn, and even children from 4 or 5 learn the Koran orally without reading. But Christian children don't, but I think it is also important to learn the Bible also like this, they should learn the Bible by heart even when they are 4 or 5, before learning to read. (Man – Pakistan – Catholic Christian)

Furthermore, we can note that the migrants' presence and their desire to be acknowledged as (forced) migrants further develop the concept of *religious pluralism*. The example provided by this Eritrean priest is typical. The special identity of Eritrean Catholics is not only mirrored by the shared experience of persecution, but also "embedded" in a singular ritual –the "Gèéz"–, which reinforces the diasporic character of this community. It is quite significant to observe that, once again, the appeal to be recognized as a legitimate component of a pluralistic society seems to be addressed first to other Catholics (see also Chapters 16, 19, and 20).

The number of Catholic Eritreans in Europe is enormous and they are accustomed to a different ritual, even to a different language, the Gèéz. In my congregation, we also celebrate the Latin Mass, but the Gèéz is very important for us. You study it for years, to celebrate the liturgical ceremony in Gèéz you have to be an expert (...). There are some particular prayers in Gèéz that the priests abroad do not know, but we, who did the seminar in Eritrea, we do.

(...) It is very important for Eritreans to participate in the Mass celebrated with their rite, in Gèéz. The problem is not of linguistic understanding: the skeleton of the rite is the same as the Latin Church. The fact is that our prayers are linked to our culture. Culture and prayer are in close relationship. While we pray, we understand what we are praying for, because everything is linked to our culture. It helps us to pray a lot with our ritual, rather than using a language that has no connection with our culture. On the basis of my experience, I can say that prayers are very linked to our way of thinking, to behave, to judge what is good and what is not. All of this is linked to our culture. (Man – Eritrea – Catholic Christian)

As a matter of fact, religious pluralism, intended as a crucial element of the democratic governance, is not only a principle inscribed in the legislation (Chapter 9), but also a goal that is still to be achieved in the Italian society, which has been rapidly passing from a mono-religious to a multi-faith society. Up until recently, the Italian population was fairly homogeneous (or at least perceived as such) in terms of ethnicity and religion. As we have already observed, because of immigration, all religious minorities have grown significantly, and the issue of interreligious co-existence, traditionally underrated, has emerged, allowing the country to gain more awareness of how much religion is encapsulated in allegedly secularized/neutral behavioral and legal patterns (Chapter 3). Besides, as observed by this Catholic priest, the Church itself is challenged by the pluralism that the migrants bring with them; a pluralism made up of different religions, but also of a plurality of traditions within each religion confession:

> (...) if in the end, the right to equality is guaranteed in the communities, what is not sometimes even listened to is the instance of differentiation that sometimes arises from the migrants, and I say in particular from migrants with a Catholic background. The right, the right to differentiation (...).
>
> (A) sacrosanct instance of differentiation that migrants advance precisely because they instinctively want their identity, their singularity to be recognized and therefore also valued in favor of the whole community. (Man – Religious leader – Catholic Christian)

> It is not enough that we go and welcome, we must get involved, and this is the important thing of interculturalism: that is not only to welcome who comes, does not change only what comes, but we also change, in welcoming. Our identity becomes somewhat more fluid and I think this is the richness, but also the fatigue of interculturalism. Because however I have to put into play and I can no longer define myself in a certain way, but I have to expect to change. (Woman – Religious leader – Methodist Evangelical Church)

It is rather superfluous to observe that forced migrants, particularly those emigrated for religious motives, have a crucial role to play in this process. This, however, implies a cooperative stance, that is a cooperative way to intend ones' membership to the new society. In this perspective, we can really appreciate the importance of educating newcomers to the concept of religious pluralism, since –as we have seen (§3)– they often come from illiberal societies and have mainly experienced their religious identity as an antagonistic marker.

It is through the impact with a democratic society –such as the Italian one– that many migrants have had the opportunity to experience, for the first time, the idea of religious pluralism. Once again, it is essential to observe how people of different origins and religious memberships share the same concept according to which living in a democratic State provides a meaning to the very concept of religious freedom and personal freedom, which are based on the principle of the inviolable dignity of each individual.

The social structures of the democratic State enshrine religious freedom as an implication of the freedom of thought and conscience; in fact, it has been within the same substantially dominant religious structure that many migrants have started to get closer to the idea and the practice of religious freedom. At least on paper, the communicative and educational modules in the most widespread religious community in Italy, i.e. the Catholic Church, adheres to the announced God in such a way that it reflects the profound meaning of freedom. Faith is the responsibility of everyone's freedom. Personal freedom is meant as people's freedom to behave independently of both God's teaching and one's family or community tradition (however relevant it may be, it cannot be understood as oppressive and it will not replace one's capacity of judgment and personal decision).

The novelty of this situation changes the parameters of thought and practice of many migrants –especially of those coming from countries that are fundamentally theocratic and/or traditionally characterized by a state religion that suppresses the spaces and the voices of other religious experiences. We have already observed that, for many of them, the need to migrate has arisen precisely because of the overt denial of religious freedom. Now –here is one of the most delicate challenges in the integration process– they find themselves in a social and political context that is certainly democratic, but in a cultural-political situation that does sympathize with various forms of ethnic and religious discrimination. Today, in Italy, the religious group that is most likely to be discriminated against is the one that, in the country of origin of many (forced) migrants, used to be in force in its exclusive and persecutory hegemony. Here, these migrants, while benefitting from this modulation of the Italian democracy, are sometimes inclined to replicate the same exclusive and persecutory forms for which they had found themselves in the need to migrate; in this sense, they sometimes adopt an aggressive attitude towards religious minorities. As showed by the following testimony, when they fail to heal the wounds of forced migration, migrants risk being overwhelmed by resentment, ending up looking for a new emotional balance that would ensure their psychological and relational well-being. In these cases, religious teachings risk being overturned, and religious cleavages absolutized, to the point of erecting impassable barriers:

(...) for me, it would be the ideal that comes another Hitler against Muslims. Because, however, there are always these wounds inside of you. I did not leave my land because I wanted to. I have been forced. This wound always remains, until death, no one can erase it. I did not hurt anyone. But everyone hurt me. Why do I have to accept it? A. (*his wife*) was very Christian and said that we must love one another. Yes, it's true. But Jesus condemned the tree that does not bear fruit. I, for me, they are the fruitless trees. But why do they have to stay? (Man – Egypt – Coptic Catholic Christian)

No, if I have children they will be Christians. They will be born in Europe so they will not even know about the wrong part of religion. They will only know about Christianity. (Man – Nigeria – Catholic Christian)

(...) the things that I do not share very much, even though I'm a foreigner, that I should not say it, really, but I say it anyway, is that there is so much welcoming to other religions here and indeed we take it with such enthusiasm and so much hospitality and admiration, where an Italian may not even admire his own true religion, I do not know if I explained myself and I do not like it so much because I accept how much I am so lucky to accept and accept your diversity ... then I accept you, that you're different, and instead here you try to give the best to this person just because he/she's different, because he/she's different ... okay, he/she's not bad! Not bad! But you are also happy with what you have? And on other side what do Muslims do then? They try to take advantage of it in the sense that they see this thing and try to impose what they are ... maybe they do not wear the veil in their country but try to put it in Italy ... to say look I'm different, I'm Muslim ... that is to impose their things ... mosque that they claim they have it, they have it, how much freedom did they give us in our countries? If you go to Saudi Arabia for example, even if there are millions of Christians, Filipinos working there ... there is no right to a church in Saudi Arabia, but here we have to give all rights ... (Woman – Iraq – Chaldean Catholic Christian)

These considerations lead us to the second main dimension involved in the process of rehumanization of asylum seekers, that is the concept of *religious freedom*.

On an elementary level, this concept can be grasped through the everyday experience, whenever a foreign migrant touches the privilege of living in a democratic society, founded on the principles of universal equality and human dignity. As suggested by the following statements, beyond the principle of equality between all religious traditions –and therefore the prohibition of discrimination on a religious basis– it is precisely the concept of the inviolable dignity of every person, that everyone can claim for the mere fact of being a *person*, which materializes in the daily experience of many migrants:

> Here in Italy, it is not as a religion to ... everyone treats them like humans, they treat well, like a person, alone, like in a family ... (...) In Egypt they have many weapons, we are saying steps ... (Man – Egypt – Coptic Orthodox Christian)

> I see the rule here and for Christians and Muslims are totally the same, because when you go to questura (*police headquarters, author's note*) they don't show any preference for Muslims or Christians, they prefer the rules. (Man – Pakistan   Catholic Christian)

> I feel like if I've saved my life, I feel I found the peace, I feel I'm free to start a new life, I feel so happy, I feel so special, what is special is the way they treat us, and I like the manner they use to approach, the way everything has been done is something a normal human being should emulate.
> Interviewer: Can you make an example?
> Respect, the way of behaving, when you see someone and say: "ciao, ciao come stai? Come stai? Bene?" There is a lot of respect, people leave in joy, nobody wants to kill you ... everybody is equal. In Nigeria is not like this. In Nigeria you have to have absolute respect for people older than you, there is a lot of difference between the young and old but also between the poor and the rich. The poor have always been suppressed ... the gap is too much. (Man – Nigeria – Catholic Christian)

Secondly, the notion of religious freedom directly calls into question the respect for religious rights, including those of minority groups. Migrants with a different religious background share the awareness that only after their arrival in Italy they have had the opportunity to fully experience their faith:

> In Italy, going to church helps us to pray for documents and so on, it's an opportunity to feel free to pray, to go to church, to pray like this, it's totally different from Pakistan where it's difficult also to pray. I remember it was Easter, after praying I come to my home, I see television, there was a blast

in church and almost 82 persons died just because they were Christians. Here there is no fear ... in Pakistan there is no security for this.... (Man – Pakistan – Catholic Christian)

Whenever I can (*I go to the Buddhist center*), because I feel very well here. I had the good fortune to come to a country where there is this religious freedom. Everyone can do what he wants, while not disturbing social serenity, so ... and ... Buddhism being a religion of peace, of ... education and culture, often when I go there in xxx, yes? It is there that the center of the Soka Gakkai is located. I always go there. (Man – Cameron – Buddhist)

I have never had problems (*in Italy*) to express my religious opinion. Neither with colleagues at the university, nor with my current colleagues. I never had problems.... No one has ever offended me or laughed in my face.

(...) (*In Italy*) we learned a lot, but thanks to the very heterogeneous Bahá'i community. Thanks to the exercises we have been able to do here and which we could not do in Iran because the administrative system does not exist there. We knew on paper how it worked but we only experienced it here. (Couple [Man and Woman] – Iran – Bahá'i)

Thirdly, this concept also involves the protection towards the risk of being victims of deviated understandings of religious duties and precepts. In the following excerpt, for example, a Nigerian man says that there is no way that, in Italy, people can encounter any forms of violent and occult religiosity such as those he had known in the context of provenance:

Worshipping ghost here? I don't know. Because, I don't know. Because ... How can they worship ghost here? You can't come here, you start worshiping the ghost. In Italy there are not, I don't see people, I see in Italy people that worship God. I see in Italy people that worship God. Italy's people are good people, because how they do their things, they have fear of God, and they have the law, there is the law, the law in Italy is working, the law in Italy is not as the law in my country. The law in my country is not working. In Italy, the law is working, so they have human sympathy. So ... I didn't see them, I can't ... you understand what I mean. (Man – Nigeria – Christian attending the Pentecostal Church)

He is echoed by this other Muslim interviewee, who notes that in Italy it is possible to live one's faith freely, despite the stern gaze of other immigrants:

> In Italy being a Muslim … I do not think there is any difference, I do not feel different from others. I say that I do not feel different from others when I'm with Italians, I feel good. But when I'm with other Arabs and Muslims, for example, maybe, sometimes, I drink a few glasses of wine and they look at me badly! Because they say: "You are a Muslim and you drink wine"! Because wine is forbidden, but it is forbidden if you have to go to pray, of course, you must not drink, but if you are with your friends, if you are in the party and it is not a time of prayer, excuse me why? Because wine makes you feel high, and when you want to go pray you have to be 100% awake and you do not have to drink wine and so, when I'm with them and I drink a glass of wine, I feel the annoyance, but I do not care, I go on. (Woman – Yemen – Muslim)

Interestingly, the appreciation for religious freedom is shown also by those who were almost unaware of the fact of being subjected to limitations in this field. Almost as if those who migrated for other reasons –mainly economic ones–, at some point realized the importance of living in a democratic context, whose distinctive icon is represented by (religious) freedom and mutual respect.

> We sing a lot in our liturgies. This is felt and therefore it can be risky for those living in contexts like China. For people who have experienced a story similar to those of these two girls, it is a relief to come here and be able to sing, to do something publicly, without having to hide.
> (…) The most important thing found in Italy: democracy, religious freedom. For them, it's the most important thing, they came for this. (Couple of women – China – Evangelic Christians [experience reported by their Pastor in Italy])

Finally, our study proves that religious agency can certainly be an integral part of (forced) migrants' public space making, the latter intended as a process targeted to the invention of new ways to live together. This prospect, as we will describe now, is shared by many of them. However, the harmonious cohabitation of different religious groups is not an automatic outcome of the arrival of people with "non-conformistic" religious backgrounds. As we have already discussed (Chapter 11), providing education about religious pluralism is a fundamental ingredient to build a cohesive society, and to facilitate the process of newcomers' adaptation. At the same time, among the most suggestive insights emerged from the fieldwork there is the fact that religion and spirituality provide the migrants with the *lexicon*, not only to face everyday challenges and troubles, but also to understand personal and community lives and give a meaning to their experiences of sufferance. Once put in a religious perspective, experiences such as those of persecution and exile gain an unusual significance, thus giving the migrants an extraordinary resource at both individual and collective level. Indeed, while offering the opportunity for a personal development, the spiritual re-elaboration of these traumas breaks down the logic of revenge and rancor, and lays the foundation for a generative attitude, oriented towards the construction of the *common good*. This point leads us to the third dimension that is implied in our reasoning.

The concept under discussion is brilliantly expressed by this couple of Bahá'i spouses, who trace a direct relationship between the following four factors: the experience of discrimination, individual empowerment, the reinforcement of personal faith, and the engagement for the common well-being.

> (...) there are unmotivated people, but we can generally say that all the Bahá'ís are examples of how not to demotivate and not to commit any act of aggression! How can I say ... perseverance. Bahá'ís are examples of perseverance. You could also look it up in the websites, there are many testimonies. Then I wanted to say that we have grown up with discrimination, so in our life there is something called discrimination, which exists from our parents who first suffered it and then it comes to us...
>
> (...) we ended up here, but basically there is a reason ... global and profound that is to resist discrimination to get ... To grow, to take this crisis as an opportunity for growth and understand that these discriminations are for our beliefs, our religion. So it's their problem, it's not my problem. They discriminate against me but the problem is theirs. If I get depressed, I have a double problem with myself. They are wrong but I do not have to be aggressive with them, I have to be peaceful because it does not work. We believe that aggression is not useful for any reason, so I can grow and understand that my faith and belief is more important than anything and so it is important that I find something for the growth of my study, my skills and then give service to the same community that discriminated against me. (Couple [Man and Woman] – Iran – Bahá'i)

In the same line of reasoning, a Pakistani man and a Chinese woman provide two other interesting testimonies. They both suggest that it was religion that, through the testimonies of other believers who took care of them, instilled in them the motivation to help others.

> In Italy, I learned to help, so I was not good in Italian ... but I see some Italian people helping me; so, now, when I see some Pakistani people not

> able to speak Italian, I start helping them ... so this is like a circle of help.
> (Man – Pakistan – Catholic Christian)

> (...) coming here, I lost things, my father, my sisters. I came here with my
> mother, I lost my home, my education, the university; but I do not care,
> it's not important to me. Maybe it's important to live. Religion is more
> important to me. Even working to make money is no longer important, I
> want to volunteer, to help. If you want to do something, it is enough to
> have some people; I want to have God in my life, to have Love and to
> share it with other people. (Woman – China – Church of God
> Almighty)

Other testimonies as well highlight that a liberal society is the natural humus
which permits religiosity to widespread all its potential for the common good.
This young woman coming from Iran, for example, stresses that it is the faith
which, in principle, has provided a meaning to her life; but it is a liberal context
which has permitted to caught this meaning, through the choice of helping
people in need and contributing to the prosperity of society:

> (...) having my faith has given me a way of ... a purpose of life, a way of
> life, how to live and how to help people, how to have a life of service for
> others. Because in the Bahá'i faith this goal is very important to help oth-
> ers, to serve, to educate the younger generations, so my religion, my faith
> has given me an instrument to live a life of service, not just going to uni-
> versity, wake up, go to university, go to work, come back and do nothing,
> instead of being useful for society. And this thing abroad helped me a lot,
> because it is freer, everything is freer than in Iran, so I could do all this
> activity with the kids, with the kids who had problems, with so many dif-
> ferent people, so I was helped to be useful for society, also to have this
> feeling that I have a purpose in my life. (Woman – Iran – Bahá'i)

Another example is provided by this Iranian woman. In her testimony, the experience of conversion –in this specific case from Islam to Christianity– seems
to mark, in a metaphoric manner, a transition to a liberal-democratic way of
life, as well as to a more conscious and mature personal approach to
religiosity:

> (...) especially when you live in a country where you are still alone ... you
> feel much more this need, so ... If, for example ... it happened that ...
> when in Islam they say that God decides on all destinies. So, I thought

that God had taken my mother away from me, so I should have had it
with God (*she laughs*). So, for a while, I did not even want to talk, that is
... about subjects that concerned God I did not even want to hear them
because I was saying "How is this possible? Do you have fun playing with
it?" And then you know, changing this point of view helps you to live
more peacefully (...). So, changing point of view helps you a lot to accept
things, to have more serenity, this is important.

   (...) That is in the sense that before you saw God in a higher point,
looking at us, from above, from above ... always just looking at you to
see what sin you're making, or maybe, I know, you're always on trial ...
So, seeing God who stands next to you, who helps you on your journey, is a very big change. (Woman – Iran – Protestant Christian [former
Muslim])

To sum it up, the interviews disclose a flowering of religious experiences among
virtuous practices oriented to the common good. Small gestures or public commitments in favor of the *polis* and of those inhabitants who are in a precarious
condition and suffer from a lack of linguistic competence and from having no
house, no job, no social relations, and no documented identity. The democratic
configuration of the socio-cultural framework encountered in Italy facilitates
the fruitfulness of religious practices in behaviors of commitment to the common good. Besides –it should never be forgotten–, the migrant is encouraged
to translate his/her faith into good practices precisely because of a "contagion",
that is as a form of "restitution" of the services offered by the public administration as well as of the care and assistance from the religious community and
its members. When they perceive the proximity of God, thanks to the benevo-
lent and beneficent proximity of the other, migrants are activated in the benefited logic of emulation/participation in which the solidarity potential of the
religious experience is released in doing to others what has been done to him/
herself.

   Significantly, help is offered without any kind of selection or hindrance
based on the religious affiliation. This experience, which is marked by a broad
sense of gratitude, fuels the attitude to "give back" the good that one has been
given, in the form of commitment to the common good – which, in turn,
should move away from corporatist models. If the religious experience feeds
on the intimacy with God, in the sense that the believer acts according to God's
will, what is considered to be its ultimately authenticating trait can be found in
the act of "giving something to someone" – i.e. giving back what one has been
given for free, without expecting anything in return, and starting to "assist" instead of just "being assisted".

(…) I think it is a great spiritual need for their desire to move from the condition of being assisted, namely being people who only receive help, to living that dimension which, for us, is strongly evangelical and spiritual, where "there is more joy in giving than in receiving", that is, giving support to a weaker person, and therefore they have become involved in a discourse of closeness with the elderly, with the children of the suburbs who voluntarily give us a helping hand with the poor. And it is a contagion, a truly very fruitful alliance, positive for all we say. Imagine an old man in the institute, however, who also lived through difficult times in Italy, at the time of fascism … then he finds himself immersed in a difficult culture, a culture that tells you that you must be afraid of the different, you have to look at the world with anxiety and fear, the meeting with a refugee who loves you, helps him to reassure himself, to open up to the other, to the future, and even the elderly are mines for the fact that refugees are far from the family, they also need words of comfort. (Woman – FBOs operator – Catholic Christian)

Finally, we have to consider the manner in which (forced) migrants build their role in the public space also by soliciting a new understanding of the concept of *citizenship* and of its different components. Coherently with our initial assumptions, interviews provide evidence of how (forced) migrants, through their citizenship's practices, are producing a *multi-religious social capital* which, in its turn, can contribute to the creation of a common good. More in detail, we can consider three different kinds of practices that, following the well-known Hirschman's trilogy (1970), can be identified as, respectively, *voice, exit,* and *loyalty*.

The first practice is exemplified by the chronicle provided by this Nigerian man, who directly experienced the cruel violence perpetrated by terrorist groups in the name of religion. His suffered testimony –in which it is not easy to distinguish the content of reality from the metaphorical one– speaks about a shared mobilization of Christians and "authentic" Muslims, united in the *protest* (voice) towards Boko Haram and its illegitimate claim to be recognized as an Islamic troupe:

(…) it's just the … like ignorant people, it's like stereotypes and things like that. And so, when Boko Haram came, it came and they were an Islamic group but they also killed Muslims so people were like: no, Boko Haram is not an Islamic group, some people like many Christians, especially Christians from the South, they felt that Boko Haram was just like an Islamic terrorist group but people from the North, people like me who have

Muslim friends and know what a real Muslim is, I wouldn't say Boko Haram are Muslims, we know Boko Haram are not Muslims; Muslims knew that Boko Haram are not Muslims, they are just a terrorist group and the way they use is not as something to give them support or something to give them credibility. So, I was there like when Boko Haram came and the real Muslims and the real Christians were able to unite and face Boko Haram and said: "No, this one is a war just against terrorism". (Man – Nigeria – Christian now attending an Adventist Church)

This kind of experience can be observed in the many cases in which believers of different religions and with different migratory backgrounds promoted public demonstrations, in Italy and all around Europe, in order to contrast both the criminalization of (Muslim) migrants and the ideological use of religious motives to justify terroristic attacks (see, for example, the mobilization "Not in my name",[3] rightly after the terrorist attacks in Paris). It can also be seen in the many cases where advocacy coalitions were formed with the aim of supporting a "post-national" idea of citizenship (Soysal, 1994), based on porous States' borders, and of progressively expanding the systems of protection. In the end, once experienced as an obstacle to achieve rights and opportunities, religion turns out to be a vehicle to conquer them, through individual and collective action.

A second example of citizenship's practice is offered by this Yemeni woman, who declared to have left her country because of the deviant understanding of religious precepts by the religious authorities, and because of their attempt to control both women's "brains" and women's "bodies". During the interview, she insisted on the need to respect the principle according to which religious authorities must not exercise political power. According to her, religion cannot be reduced to an instrument of social control, or a means to harass the most vulnerable people; on the other hand, no one –neither the political authorities, nor the religious authorities– has the right to invade the private relationship between God and the single believer:

I am a Muslim and, as we all know, Islam now, as a religion, is not true Islam. Now, Islam has become politics, an ideology. Some people, certain regimes use religion because of their interests, so religion has become a hard thing, a rigid thing, a soulless thing and then religion is influencing

---

3 A campaign, launched in the aftermath of the terrorist attacks, through social media, by young Muslims (often second-generation immigrants) intent on taking a decisive distance from the terrorists who call for a holy war.

women and children more and more because those are the weakest parts
of society, it was always like this, even before in Europe, when Christianity went through hard times, like us, times of darkness. Because they use
religion to control people and the same thing happens now in the Arab
world, they use religion, they did not live it like in Europe that now religion has become something else and they understood it after years of
wars, of battle, of death of so many people, they have come to the point
that religion should be left in peace and you must not mix religion with
politics, understood? You must not. Religion is just religion and politics is
another thing. You cannot put both things together. Because this is dangerous. It is not only in Yemen, you can be in other countries; I speak of
the Arab world in general, the Arab world. You can be the Imam of a
mosque, like a priest, you can be a Muslim Imam and you can also work
with politics, you can work ... this is not good. You can be an Imam and at
the same time you are a member of the parliament, or a member of the
military. It's all mixed up, all a mess. So religion is all ruined, and therefore
this ugly figure of the Muslim, I am sorry because Islam is not so, the religion is not so, it is not this bad thing. Religion is a simple thing, it is a
simple relationship between us and God, privately. No one must enter
into this relationship. Nobody has the, let's say ... permission to intervene
in this relationship. Everyone has one's own relationship with God and
that's it, nobody has to control you or block him with the name of God or
the name of religion. This is what happens in the Arab world. I say it sincerely ... (Woman – Yemen – Muslim)

In front of the gap separating her conception of "true" religion and the misleading interpretation made by many religious leaders –"motivated by non-
religious aims"–, this Muslim woman chose to abandon her origin country.
Once in Italy, she decided, once more, to adopt an *exit* strategy –she gave up
attending the mosque–, intended as a line of action (the only possible one)
useful to affirm her own distance from people who "are not able to represent
our religion". In Simmelian terms (see Chapter 3, §4.1), this behavior could be
described as the choice to take a distance from religion as a way to affirm one's
religiosity.

No, I do not go to any mosque here, I do not like it because I went once
and I did not like to go because there are people there ... you do not feel
at peace, there is discrimination against women, they put women in a
room and men in another. We are not together ... I do not like it that way.
Then people, those who run mosques are people ... I cannot be, to

represent our religion. I'm sorry but this is the truth, I'm sorry. Because even with an Imam from the mosque I went with my husband to take a picture in the mosque and the Imam did not allow us to take a picture. But can you imagine this thing? He said God said it was forbidden. But what is this God? Because I cannot hear lies and shut up, this is my character. So I arrived in Italy at the age of 44, it's not easy, because they cannot mess with me at this age; they messed with me when I was young and I did not understand anything. But with my age I now have open eyes and I understand everything, so here ... "Sorry but who said that we cannot take pictures?" And he said: "God!" And I said: "So, why do we have direct transmission from Mecca? Why is that not forbidden?" And he was silent, he could not answer me. On the contrary, he told me that since I thought I knew everything, I could go and become the Imam. He made this joke. Those are the people who control Italy here ... lousy people. (Woman – Yemen – Muslim)

In the same line of reasoning, we can see that the very presence of migrants, who suffered the violation of their religious rights and of their freedom, challenges European "tired" democracies, since through their experience they could regain the awareness of the importance of religious rights, intended as an archetype –as we have already commented– of both individual rights and the quality of a democracy. At the same time, through their presence, (forced) migrants challenge established religions, and could turn into an extraordinary source of revitalization for European Churches and for European "believers": as observed by a young woman coming from Iran, for many European young people, who live in a democratic and secularized society, the relationship with religiosity could not be so different than that experienced in an illiberal or autocratic society.

And do you know what the first thing is for them? Being able to freely express faith without fear of losing your life. Does it seem trivial? Look is essential. It is ... I saw the Albanians again after years of persecution, being able to express the faith where the only thing they did, they could secretly do the sign of the cross, an Albanian woman said: "P. has taken away everything, but this is not me, they could remove it secretly". They could not have any religious signs; they could not have anything, the Albanians. Under the dictatorship and in short ... they were certainly persecuted very seriously until 1994. But there is the only thing that remained for me, before going to bed, secretly, nobody saw me; it was the sign of the cross. Then you can freely express your faith without incurring in serious risks. Is it trivial? No, it's vital. It is the first thing: to be able to go to a church, to be able to confess, to pray, to make the sign of the cross, to freely express, to put a rosary on the finger, to be able to show Christians simply, without fear of the risk of life. Is it trivial? (...). Because the right to faith must be defended for all, must be protected for all, everyone has the right to express faith in the respect of their traditions, their culture, their faith. And we must help those who are all free to express in faith, to welcome Christians who in many parts of the world today find it hard to express faith. And then we try to express the closeness to all ... in a network like I told you before, but above all to allow him to pray and then the celebrations with them really become a source of emotion, to be able to return to celebrate the Eucharist, not in the basements, not secretly, but with the open doors of the church. (Man – Religious leader – Catholic Christian)

(...) in my opinion, a kind of brainwashing, which actually has an opposite effect, in the sense that they do this to force you, but you overcome it only as an exam, afterwards you do not remember what you had studied. And ... then nothing. Instead I do not know a thing that ... I found a lot in common here, then when I was studying at the academy, I saw my friends who were mostly Catholic. Then they did all these paths of the Catholics, like communion ... then, when it was enough, they no longer went to church ... that is, it seems to me, I do not know, maybe I'm wrong, maybe not, but it seems to me that they were like me, maybe I did all these things in my Islam, I did things because I had to do them ... (Woman – Iran – Protestant Christian [former Muslim])

On the other hand, as suggested by this pastoral operator, it is by welcoming newcomers that established religious communities lay the foundations of a peaceful coexistence, inspired by the values of humanism, which are the same that gave life to the European democracies:

(...) the custom, for example, of welcoming, sharing the same churches (*with the Orthodox, author's note*) is the best way to actually transmit the kind of attitude we have, so the bishops themselves remain open-mouthed to hear the description of what happens here and this, in my opinion, is one of the signs that we distribute and that we will see how they will flourish, but the reception is something that never remains fruitless. (Man – Pastoral operator – Catholic Christian)

Finally, moving on to considering the third paradigmatic pattern of citizenship's practice, this young Bahá'i offers a brilliant example of an approach based on the concept of *loyalty*. Her personal engagement with (Italian) children, independently of their religion, reflects an authentic desire to participate in the settlement society, and to contribute in the creation of a common good.

> This particular activity that I do is a group that is called Youths' Group for middle school kids; we give a space for them. It does not matter what religion they come from, what background, what origin, it matters just to have a space together and try to pull out the virtues and the positive things that they have within them and put them into practice to help others. So, channeling positive energy that these kids have, put them into practice to be useful for society, to improve the environment they live. So every week we see each other and read a book that is a storybook of children of their age and then we talk about different concepts, such as justice, peace, unity, these things, and then we also have a moment of practice, then do something for our environment – for example, going to clean the park, going to visit the elderly center, to give them a way to serve, to do something for their environment. And I like this a lot, because I live with them and it's a lot of fun, they have lots of energy and then you can see how you can help these kids, because society considers them ... that they are very ... they are in an age that is very difficult, let's say ... instead, when you trust them, they can do everything and this thing is very beautiful. (Woman – Iran – Bahá'i)

This kind of stance is the most coherent with a *generative idea of citizenship*, that is a citizenship able to embrace multiple identities, aimed at supporting the empowerment of people who mainly risk to be excluded, and fueled by participative practices oriented toward the common good (Martinelli, 2013). As a matter of fact, citizenship is a process: for everyone, but particularly for those who suffered from a sense of strangeness in their own land, and then have been experiencing the concept of hospitality. Several of our interviewees spoke about their path from a condition (and a feeling) of parasitic presence, of marginality with respect to the *polis* and its social plots, towards forms and practices of social protagonism. What's more, some interviews show that it is religious experience and belonging to a religious community that promotes a generative virtue in relation to the common good, since they activate and encourage training in practical forms of citizenship: from the education of children to the care of the environment, from responsibility for a working activity to the tax contribution for the well-being of the country in which "you feel at home". As a matter of fact, as we have already mentioned, this stance is strongly favored by a spiritual understanding of one's own life-experience, including the experience of suffering and of (forcibly) migrating. At the same time, as suggested by this pastoral operator, it represents the accomplishment of the most authentic (migrants') spiritual need: the need to give something to those in need; more particularly, to share, with those who have not yet discovered it, the true meaning of life:

> (...) I saw it just as a satisfaction of her spiritual need: that of giving something to those who have less than her. This is already a person ... she does not work, but the fact that she felt ... and told us: "But, you are really precious, because you give us the idea, the support, the support, but also the cue to throw us out. And do us too, because we are a little hesitant in another city. We are not rooted, no?". Here, and this seems to us the most satisfying ... of the greatest spirituality because to teach people or not to teach, I have nothing to teach, but to tell them how life must be lived well. (Woman – FBOS operator – Christian Catholic)

It is almost superfluous to observe that this type of posture is not the natural result of living in a democratic context. Numerous variables influence the relationship between religiosity and the attitude towards the host society and its well-being: from the values transmitted by the parents to the personal way of elaborating the migratory experience; from the behavior of the people met in Italy to the attitude of religious leaders. Their singular combination explains the multiplicity of possible individual feelings and behaviors. However, our study allowed us to grasp the importance of certain societal conditions and actions. Among them, the contrast to the widespread "religious illiteracy" and the education to religious pluralism. In particular, regaining the awareness of "our" –i.e. the Italian one, strongly shaped by Christianism– cultural and religious identity constitutes the indispensable premise for the construction of a society founded on authentic religious pluralism oriented towards the common good. We will analyze this point in Chapter 16, through the illustration of the synodal experience conducted in the Diocesis of Milan. Here, it must be observed how this premise represents, in its turn, a supportive condition to let migrants and refugees contribute to the creation of a multi-religious social capital.

References to Part 3

Abu Salem, M., & Fiorita, N. (2016). Protezione internazionale e persecuzione per motivi religiosi: la giurisprudenza più recente. *Stato, Chiese e pluralismo confessionale*, n. 37, 21 novembre.

Acierno, A. (2019). Il diritto del cittadino straniero alla protezione internazionale: condizione attuale e prospettive future. In P. Morozzo Della Rocca (Ed.), *Immigrazione, asilo e cittadinanza*, IVᵃ ed. Santarcangelo di Romagna: Maggioli editore, pp. 65–124.

Adraoui, M. (2015). Partir au nom de Dieu? Islam er migration. *Migrations Société*, 27(159–160), 13–28.

Barillaro, D. (1968). *Considerazioni preliminari sulle confessioni religiose diverse dalla cattolica*. Milano: Giuffrè.

Bellini, P. (1973). Nuova problematica della libertà religiosa individuale nella società pluralistica. In Various Authors, *Individuo, gruppi, confessioni religiose nello Stato democratico*. Milano: Giuffrè, pp. 1095–1151.

Benvenuti, M. (Ed.) (2011). *La protezione internazionale degli stranieri in Italia*. Napoli: Jovene.

Black, R., Adger, W.N., Arnell, N., Dercon, S. Geddes, A., & Thomas, D.S. (2011). The effect of environmental change on human migration. *Global Environmental Change, 21*: S3–S11.

Botta, R. (1994). Confessioni religiose, I) Profili generali. In *Enc. giur.,* vol. VIII. Roma: Treccani.

Botta, R. (2002). *Tutela del sentimento religioso ed appartenenza confessionale nella società globale*. Torino: Giappichelli.

Caravaggion, G. (2016). Gli enti locali e le limitazioni del diritto alla libertà religiosa: il divieto di indossare il velo integrale. *Stato, Chiese e pluralismo confessionale*, n. 28, 19 settembre.

Caravaggion, G. (2018). *Diritti culturali e modello costituzionale di integrazione*. Torino: Giapichelli.

Cardia, C. (1983). Pluralismo (diritto ecclesiastico). In *Enc. dir.*, vol. XXXIII. Milano: Giuffrè, pp. 983–1003.

Cardia, C. (1998). Religione (libertà di). In *Enc. giur.*, Aggiornam., vol. II. Milano: Giuffrè, pp. 919–936.

Cardia, C. (2010). *Principi di diritto ecclesiastico. Tradizione europea, legislazione italiana*. Torino: Giappichelli.

Caritas Italiana (Ed.) (2019). *Oltre il mare. Primo rapporto sui Corridoi Umanitari in Italia e altre vie legali e sicure d'ingresso*. Roma: Caritas Italiana.

Carnì, M. (2015). I ministri di culto delle confessioni religiose di minoranza: problematiche attuali. *Stato, Chiese e pluralismo confessionale*, n. 19, 1 giugno.

Cattelan, B. (2013). Mutilazioni genitali femminili rilevanti per status di rifugiato. *Quest. Giust.*, 28 maggio.

Codini, E. (2009). I presupposti della protezione internazionale. In E. Codini, M. D'Odorico, & M. Gioiosa (Eds), *Per una vita diversa. La nuova disciplina italiana dell'asilo*. Milano: FrancoAngeli, pp. 41–60.

Colaianni, N. (1990). *Confessioni religiose e intese. Contributo all'interpretazione dell'art. 8 della Costituzione*. Bari: Cacucci.

Colaianni, N. (2000). Confessioni religiose. In *Enc. Dir.*, Agg., IV. Milano: Giuffrè, pp. 363–380.

Consorti, P. (2011). Pacchetto sicurezza e fattore religioso. *Stato, Chiese e pluralismo confessionale*, febbraio.

Curreri, S. (2018). *Lezioni sui diritti fondamentali*. Milano: FrancoAngeli.

D'Amico, M. (2008). *I diritti contesi*. Milano: FrancoAngeli.

D'Avack, P.A. (1978). *Trattato di diritto ecclesiastico italiano*, Parte gen., second ed., Milano: Giuffrè.

Del Giudice, M. (1964). *Manuale di diritto ecclesiastico*. Milano: Giuffrè.

Durham Jr., W.C., & Thayer, D.D. (2019) (Eds). *Religion, Pluralism and Reconciling Differences*. London: Routledge.

Eurostat (2017). *Asylum decisions in the EU Member States granted protection to more than 700000 asylum seekers in 2016*, Eursotat newsrelease, 70, April 26.

Ferrari, D. (2018). Protezione internazionale, orientamento sessuale e religione. Un bilancio tra stato dell'arte e nuove prospettive di ricerca. *Quad. dir. e pol. eccl.*, n. 2, 493–498.

Finocchiaro, F. (1975). Art. 8. In V. Branca (Ed.), *Commentario della Costituzione*, vol. I. Bologna: Zanichelli, pp. 383–434.

Finocchiaro, F. (1990). Libertà: VII) Libertà di coscienza e di religione. In *Enc. Giur.* Roma: Treccani.

Fiorita, N. (2007). Immigrazione, diritto e libertà religiosa: per una mappatura preliminare del campo d'indagine. *Stato, Chiese e pluralismo confessionale*, marzo.

Gatta, G.L. (2009). Islam, abbigliamento religioso, diritto e processo penale: brevi note a margine di due casi giurisprudenziali. *Stato, Chiese e pluralismo confessionale*, giugno.

Gismondi, P. (1975). *Lezioni di diritto ecclesiastico. Stato e confessioni religiose*, III ed. Milano: Giuffrè.

Grosso, E. (1999). Straniero. In *Dig. Disc. pubbl.*, vol. XV. Torino: UTET, pp. 156–179.

Gunn, T.J. (2003). The Complexity of Religion and the Definition of "Religion" in International Law. *Harvard Human Rights Journal, 16*, 189–215.

Ha, H.I. (2017). Emotions of the weak: violence and ethnic boundaries among Coptic Christians in Egypt. *Ethnic and Racial Studies, 40*(1), 133–151.

Hirschman, A. (1970). *Exit, voice, and Loyalty: Responses to Decline in Firms, Organizations, and States*. Cambridge, MA: Harvard University Press.

International Organization for Migration (IOM). (2017). *World Migration Report 2018*. Geneva: International Organization for Migration.

Kumin, J. (2007). In-country "refugee" processing arrangements: a humanitarian alternative?. In M. Jandl (Ed.), *Ten Innovative Approaches to the Challenges of Migration in the 21st Century*. Amsterdam: Amsterdam University Press, pp. 79–87.

Levitt, P., & Jaworsky, B.N. (2007). Transnational Migration Studies: the Longue Durée. *Annual Review of Sociology, 33*, 129–156.

Lillo, P. (2000). Libertà religiosa. In S. Cassese (Ed.), *Dizion. dir. pubbl.*, vol. IV. Milano: Giuffrè, pp. 3547–3556.

Long, G. (1991). *Le confessioni religiose "diverse dalla cattolica". Ordinamenti interni e rapporti con lo Stato*, Bologna: Zanichelli.

Madera, A. (2018). Quando la religione si interseca con la tutela di genere: quale impatto sulle dinamiche dell'accoglienza? (prime osservazioni a margine di Cass., sez. I, 24 novembre 2017, n. 28152). *Stato, Chiese e pluralismo confessionale*, n. 14.

Martinelli, M. (2013). Cittadini e nuove forme di appartenenza: esperienze in discussione. *Studi Emigrazione/International Journal of Migration Studies, 50*(189), 172–183.

Massey, D.S., Arango, J., Hugo, G., Kouaouci, A., Pellegrino, A., & Taylor, E. (1993). Theories of International Migration: A Review and Appraisal. *Population and Development Review, XIX*(3), 431–466.

Menski, W., Topidi, K. (2016). Introduction. Religion as empowerment?. In K. Topidi, & L. Helder (Eds), *Religion as Empowerment. Global Legal perspectives*. New York: Routledge, pp. 1–18.

Mirabelli, C. (2006). Confessioni religiose. In *Dizion. dir. pubbl.*, vol. IV. Milano: Giuffrè, pp. 1239–1250.

Mortati, C. (1976). *Istituzioni di diritto pubblico*, vol. II, IX ed. Padova: Cedam.

Musselli, L. (1994). Libertà religiosa e di coscienza. In *Dig. disc. pubbl.*, vol. IX. Torino: Utet, pp. 215–231.

Olivetti, M. (2018). *Diritti fondamentali*. Torino: Giappichelli.

Onida, V. (1978). Profili costituzionali delle intese. In C. Mirabelli (Ed.). *Le intese tra Stato e confessioni religiose. Problemi e prospettive*. Milano: Giuffrè, pp. 25–47.

Papademetriou, D., Alba, R., Foner, N., & Banulescu-Bogdan, N. (2016). *Managing Religious Difference in North America and Europe in an Era of Mass Migration*. Washington: Migration Policy Institute.

Pedullà, L. (2016). L'abbigliamento religioso tra identità e compatibilità ordina mentale. *Federalismi.it*, n. 24, 14 dicembre.

Petito, F. (2017). *Policy Dialogue*. Concept note draft prepared on the occasion of the international workshop "The Refugee Crisis and Religious Engagement: Widening

Routes to Legal Protection" ISPI-Italian Ministry of Foreign Affairs, Milan, 13–14 March.

Pickering, S. (2011). *Women, Borders and Violence. Current Issues in Asylum, Forced Migration, and Trafficking*. New York: Springer.

Pistan, C. (2013). La libertà religiosa. In L. Mezzetti (Ed.). *Diritti e doveri*, Torino: Giappichelli, pp. 445–488.

Randazzo, B. (2006). Art. 8. In R. Bifulco, A. Celotto, & M. Olivetti (Eds), *Commentario alla Costituzione*, vol. I. Torino: Utet, pp. 139–216.

Ravà, A. (1963). *Rilevanza dei presupposti storico-politici nell'interpretazione della legislazione ecclesiastica*. Milano: Giuffré.

Ricca, M. (2006). Art. 19. In R. Bifulco, A. Celotto, & M. Olivetti (Eds), *Commentario alla Costituzione*, vol. I. Torino: Utet, pp. 420–440.

Schmidt di Friedberg, O. (1994). *Islam, solidarietà e lavoro. I muridi senegalesi in Italia*. Torino: Fondazione Giovanni Agnelli.

Soysal, Y. (1994). *Limits of Citizenship*. Chicago: University of Chicago Press.

Soryte, R. (2018). Persecuzione religiosa, profughi e diritto di asilo: il caso della Chiesa di Dio onnipotente. *The Journal of CENSUR*, suppl. 2, XLIX–LXXIII.

Troilo, S. (2008). La libertà religiosa a sessant'anni dalla Costituzione. *Forum dei Quad. cost., Rassegna*, 21 dicembre.

Valtolina, G.G. (Ed.) (2014). *Unaccompanied Minors in Italy. Challenges and Ways Ahead*. Milano: McGraw-Hill.

Zanfrini, L., & Asis, M.B. (2006). *Orgoglio e pregiudizio. Una ricerca tra Filippine e Italia sulla transizione all'età attiva dei figli di emigrati e dei figli di immigrati*. Milano: FrancoAngeli.

Zanfrini, L. (2019). *The Challenge of Migration in a Janus-Faced Europe*. London: Palgrave Macmillan.

Zolberg, A.R. (1989). *Escape from Violence: Conflict and the Refugee Crisis in the Developing World*. New York: Oxford University Press.

PART 4

Religion, Faith-Based Organizations, Integration and Social Cohesion

∵

CHAPTER 13

Religion and Integration: Issues from International Literature

Annavittoria Sarli and Giulia Mezzetti

The available literature on the relationship between migration and integration can be divided in two research strands that are based on opposite sets of assumptions developed mostly on the two sides of the Atlantic, namely in Western Europe and North America (Alba, Foner, 2015; Kivisto, 2014; Lewis, Kashyap, 2013; García-Muñoz, Neuman, 2012; Zolberg, Woon, 1999).

The North American literature on migration –particularly the US one– tends to see religion as a factor fostering integration, by playing a role in addressing migrants' social needs. Religious identity and participation in public religious life are thought to facilitate the Americanization of recent migrants and of their descendants, strengthen their sense of belonging *vis-à-vis* the host country and increase the level of acceptance of minorities by the dominant group (Foner, Alba, 2008).

On the contrary, in Europe the literature sees migrants' religion as a problem and a potential source of conflict, in line with a social attitude widespread across the continent. In particular, the relationship between religion and integration tends to be framed in a negative way as religious affiliation, especially with Islam, is considered to be a marker of wide social distance and a factor of disadvantage in the interaction with the native population (Fiddian-Qasmiyeh, Qasmiyeh, 2010).

These distinctive, opposite perspectives about the link between religion and integration derive from significant divergences in the two social and cultural contexts, which generated two different public discourses on the issue. In fact, we are here dealing with contextual discrepancies of cultural, institutional, and demographic nature (Kivisto, 2014). These differences, in turn, have produced diverging influences on social research, in terms of assumptions, of topics to be investigated, and, hence, of findings. Indeed, as Weber (1922 (2003)) authoritatively pointed out, social sciences are always rooted in and produced by the culture where they unfold.

The present chapter sets to examine these contextual differences and their influence on the research questions and approaches that have animated the study of the relationship between religion and migrant integration, across the two sides of the pond. In §1 and §2, describing respectively the North American and the European contexts, we follow a similar structure: we start by presenting the context and institutional arrangements characterizing the two areas and we reconstruct the different public discourses that developed in the two public arenas; subsequently, we discuss how this impacted social science research on these topics. In light of the comparison outlined, in §3 we propose some conclusive reflections that put these two "traditions" into perspective by tracing recent tendencies that are actually making the two contexts more similar in their approach to migrant religion in integration processes. On the one hand, public discourse in the US started framing migrant's religion as problematic when it comes to Muslim migrants and communities; on the other hand, across European countries, both institutions (at different levels) and civil society started considering religious leaders and communities as potential allies in facilitating integration and in promoting social cohesion, thus possibly getting past the idea that religion is intrinsically an obstacle to integration. This, in turn, may open further directions for research.

1　　　Religion and Integration in North American Social Sciences

1.1　　*Salient Contextual Factors*

In North America, and particularly in the US, social sciences tend to describe religion in positive terms, as a major facilitator of integration and a source for overcoming social exclusion. This view has been crucially influenced by a series of historical processes.

In the US, the institutionalization of religion took place on the basis of the religious diversity featured among colonies and then States. Such a diversity made it impossible to create a single "State Church" in the newly-formed federal State. This has led to constitutional fundamentals being codified to enshrine essential principles such as religious freedom, substantial equality among all faiths, neutrality or equidistance between the State and all confessions, with a clear separation between Church and State. Kuru (2009:11) defines this institutional setting as "passive secularism", whereby such a neutrality on the State's side allows for the public visibility of each religion. Undeniably, until the end of the Second World War, the Catholic and Jewish minorities enjoyed little acceptance among the Protestant majority and were forced to relegate their religion to the private sphere. However, such an institutional framework has allowed religious groups to put forward religiously-based demands, which have become a common feature of American life, laying the foundations for a multi-religious nation from the very beginning (Foner, Alba, 2008). Based on these assumptions, by the mid-1900s Jews and Catholics could be integrated into the American pluralistic system. This process has shaped the religious pluralism that many migrants with different religious backgrounds still experience once they move to the US–including the more recently settled Muslim minority, whose incorporation in the American religious landscape presents significant differences as compared to Europe.

Indeed, the evolution of religious pluralism in the US must be seen in the context of the nation-building process. Since its creation, the US have labelled itself as a country of immigration, and have made migration a founding myth underpinning its national identity. As a result, the permanent settlement and naturalization of migrants tended to be promoted, which facilitated both the migration and the integration process at the earliest stage by strengthening migrants' emotional bond with the receiving society. While the country has promoted the "Americanization" of newcomers, it has also recognized the legitimacy of multiple identities – the so-called "hyphenated identities". Religious identity has therefore often been perceived as a distinctive feature to be combined with a common sense of belonging to the American nation, thus playing a key role in the incorporation of migrants into the dominant society (Papademetriou et al., 2016; Alba, Foner, 2015).

The passive secularism (Kuru, 2009) featuring Church-State relations in the US is at the basis of the central role played by religion in integration dynamics. According to this setting, the State allows the public visibility of religion. This has been conducive of a positive view of religion, generally conceived as a civic value and highly acknowledged in the public sphere. Even if in the US religiosity has been declining over successive cohorts (Voas, Chaves, 2016), in the US religiosity tends to be exhibited and being religious is considered as the social norm: surveys concerning religious beliefs and services attendance demonstrate high levels of religiosity among Americans (e.g. PEW, 2011; Gallup, 2009). As Alba and Foner note (2015), Americans tend to overstate their church attendance and degree of religious practice; however, this very tendency testifies to the perceived importance attributed to religion on the American public ethos. Hence, the religious engagement of migrants ends up favoring their social inclusion (Kivisto, 2014; Niebuhr, 2007).

This is the institutional and socio-cultural environment where North American social scientists have conceived their research questions, and the ground they have explored to formulate their research outcomes. It is easily conceivable that, within this framework, religion has generally been observed as a source for integration and research has investigated how this facilitating role is played.

There are also demographic contextual factors that account for this tendency in North American social sciences: in the US, the majority of migrants identify as Christians, a feature that is in line with the one of the dominant society. Therefore, viewing religion as a catalyst of integration has been favored by the perceived "low" *religious* distance between natives and migrants. On the other hand, the predominantly Christian group of Mexican migrants face serious integration issues (Papademetriou, 2016; García-Muñoz, Neuman, 2012). Subsequently, in the American context, the main dividing line marking social distance between native and migrants tends to be language and cultural belonging (Zolberg, Woon, 1999). On the contrary, religion and religiosity are generally seen as a potential bridge between different ethnic groups and this common perception is mirrored in the approaches adopted by social researchers.

Nonetheless, even such a "religion-friendly" context has not been immune to the expression of concerns towards religions that are depicted as more "distant" – and particularly towards Islam, which has been framed as the "enemy of the West". In the US, a negative construction of Islam had been taking place in the immediate post-Cold War era, when Islam started being cast as the new threat for Western powers: indeed, Huntington's theses (1993) about the existence of a "clash of civilizations" between the West and Islam have been gaining currency in most public debates worldwide (Nielsen, 2013). This could not but be reinforced by the 9/11 events and by the following string of jihadist attacks perpetrated in Western countries. However, paradoxically, for a long time such concerns have only marginally regarded Muslim migrants living in the US. In fact, they could benefit from the institutional arrangements that favor the accommodation of new religions (Alba, Foner, 2015). This has also been facilitated by the fact that they constitute a small minority and that, contrary to the majority of Christian migrants, they have reached a high degree of socio-economic integration, with levels of education even higher than the national average. Rather, the perception of threat has long been imputed to Islam as an *external enemy* within the realm of international relations, which led to frame this religion in securitarian terms (Foner, Alba, 2008; Frisina, 2010).

However, as we will discuss in the final section of the present chapter, recent analyses have highlighted how this tendency is taking on a more culturalist flavor, with Islam –and more precisely American Muslims– being subjected to forms of cultural racism, which parallel similar, more rooted attitudes that characterize the European context more profoundly. This does not mean that manifestations of this type of racism were completely absent in the American context in the past decades; however, they concerned fringes of American society (Council on American-Islamic Relations, 2016). How this has become a more mainstreamed trend will be discussed in §3.

1.2 *Religion as a Catalyst of Integration in US Social Sciences*

In the preceding pages, we have analyzed the socio-cultural and demographic features that have generated, within US society, positive perceptions of migrants' religious belongings and their function for social cohesion. As has already been hinted at, this orientation in collective representations and public discourse has undoubtedly played an influential role in shaping the assumptions and perspectives of social researchers in exploring the link between religion and integration. Indeed, the view of religion as a resource in integration dynamics can already be traced in classics of the American literature on migrants' religious life, such as the contributions by Herberg (1960) and Handlin (1951) that highlight the particular role religion played in the assimilation of Catholic Europeans and Jews who had come to the US –a predominantly protestant society– after World War II. In this regard, Herberg (1960) observes that having found greater social acceptance of religious diversity, rather than ethnic diversity, these migrants saw the religious sphere as a privileged space for the construction of their own American identity (Herberg, 1960).

Gordon (1964) and Smith (1978) reiterate this consideration by noting that the religious connotation of migrants' identity allows them to maintain their cultural specificity while blurring their ethnic and national differences. As a component that is not necessarily linked to a specific place, religious identification offers the possibility to settle in a new territory without losing ties with one's origins and traditions. Kurien's "Becoming American by becoming Hindu" (1998) illustrates this idea very clearly, as it presents the mechanism by which Indian migrants leverage on their Hindu identity, or rather its updated version, resulting from the adaptation to the new context, to claim their position within the American pluralistic society, while maintaining ties with the Hindu tradition. Similarly, Ebaugh and Chafetz (2000) define religious institutions as physical and social spaces where the adaptation to the new environment can develop along with the cultural continuity needed by migrants.

This approach to religion, which took shape at the time when Judaism and Catholicism were being embedded into the US pluralistic system, has characterized all relevant North American literature, and continued to permeate US social sciences, even after new waves of migration from non-European countries have greatly expanded the religious diversity of the American society, especially since the Immigration and Naturalization Services Act was passed in 1965 (Portes, Rumbaut, 2006; Casanova, Zolberg, 2002; Warner, 2000a, 2000b).

Thus, drawing on this scientific tradition, which mirrored a "religion-friendly" social and cultural context, North American social scientists have been tending to observe religion as a source of tangible and intangible assets – a "spiritual capital" that promotes the integration of migrants (Hagan, 2008; Stark,

Finke, 2000). As we will see, most of their investigations on the link between religion and integration aim at exploring the various components of this "spiritual capital", shedding light on their function in favoring integration dynamics, with reference to several domains of social life.

As thoroughly explained in Chapter 17, individual and collective identities are process-based and multi-dimensional, as they are constantly re-shaped according to the historical and social context, and are composed of multiple aspects that are more or less coherent with each other (Ajrouch, 2004). The very process of migrating produces deep changes in the migrant's socio-cultural context of reference, thereby generating the migrant's need to redefine oneself in relation to the new environment. North American literature widely shows how religion can provide valuable tools in this sense (Talebi, Desjardins, 2012), both for maintaining one's own identity in the new context of emigration, and for adapting to such a new context, even across different generations.

US scholars observe that, when building their identity, migrants draw on their religious sphere by activating several mechanisms. For instance, religious organizations are used to replicate major aspects of the culture of origin in order to keep the ethnic identity alive and pass it on to second generations. As a result, different aspects of the culture of origin are often incorporated into religious ceremonies. For example, rituals can be performed in the language of the place of origin and be accompanied by traditional music (Ebaugh, 2010; Foner, Alba, 2008; Carnes, 2004; Ebaugh, Chafetz, 2000; Warner, Wittner, 1998; Min, 1992).

Min's work (2005) shows, for example, how groups of Hindu Indians and Christian Koreans preserve their ethnic traditions by overlapping and combining ethnic and religious rituals together. With reference to second generations of Christian Koreans born in the US, Chai (1998) illustrates that religious organizations contribute to the reproduction of ethnic identity through the sacralization of traditional values. In other words, people reinterpret their traditional culture in the light of the values of a conservative Christian morality.

Another aspect of religion that was studied by North American scholars in connection with identity construction is religious conversion. The latter are an increasingly frequent phenomenon – in general terms and not only among migrants, in a cultural context that is characterized by a growing subjectivism in religious orientations (as illustrated in depth in Chapter 3 of the present volume). Conversion has been conceptualized as the adoption of an identity that has been chosen independently and consciously for its role in responding to existential needs (Hervieu-Léger, 2003). Several studies on migrant conversions in the US highlight that people's agency plays a crucial role in shaping new religious identities and in combining them with other aspects of identity, such as the ethnic or national one (Ebaugh, 2010). For instance, in exploring the reality of some Chinese Churches in the US, Ng (2002) notes that, by converting to Christianity, these migrants bring with them their own cultural categories, their own symbols and their own practices, which are all incorporated into a religiosity that is both a distinctive trait of a minority culture and a trait shared with the dominant society. In focusing on a similar context, Yang (1999, 2000) shows that conversions drive people to renegotiate the very meaning of "belonging". By redefining what being Chinese, American and Christian means and by identifying and combining the elements of each of these multiple identities that are most functional to the new context, migrants perform selective processes in both assimilating to the host society and preserving ethnicity.

Smith-Hefner (1994) also notes that, among Cambodian Khmer refugees in the US, the conversion to Christianity addresses the need to abandon the previous identity and acquire a new one, thus leaving the pain, the grief and the guilt experienced behind. At the same time, however, Smith-Hefner highlights a further function: conversion offers opportunities for social mobility, by enabling people to access positions of authority and prestige within religious organizations. Several authors stress that religious participation can address the need to build a positive social identity. The roles available within religious communities allow migrants to obtain the social recognition that is denied in the hosting community. Both on a personal level and in the eyes of members of the religious group, the position reached through religious practice enables people to cope with the sense of subordination experienced in emigration, namely in the social and occupational sphere (Warner, 2000). Smith-Hefner (1994) takes the analysis of the functions of religious conversion among Khmer refugees even further. According to the author, by becoming Christian, many young Khmers get involved in activities and organizations that socialize them to a new system of values. As a result, by distancing themselves from their own tradition, they have the possibility to reduce the barriers that separate them from the mainstream American society. Hirschman (2004) has efficaciously synthesized the workings of these processes by arguing that religious organizations in the US provide immigrants with psychological solace from discrimination, hostility and, in general, from the traumatic experience of emigrating (*refuge*), access to opportunities for economic mobility (*resources*) as well as social recognition (*respectability*).

So far, the analysis has focused on how some of these resources are activated through an identity building that is able to provide migrants with value systems, relationships and opportunities for social mobility. Religion, however, can also mediate other adaptive processes, as it represents a cultural institution that helps humans make sense of everyday life and of the challenges it poses (Bankston, 1997). Religious involvement and practice constitute an individual and collective process that can enable the maintenance of emotional balance. This is particularly true in situations of trauma or stress, both factors being often associated with the migration experience. For this reason, several US authors underline the importance of the spiritual resources made available by religions and underline their positive psychological effects on migrants' ability to cope with uncertainty and difficulties (Kyoung Ok, Lee, 2012; Connor, 2012; Suárez-Orozco *et al.*, 2012).

These resources consist first of all of the consolidated and rich symbolic heritage that people can draw from to give sense to the pain experienced in the process of migration (detachment from motherland, orientation in a new context, racism...). Religious organizations often support people in these processes of creation of meaning through a set of activities that Schiffauer (2006) defines as spiritual welfare, ranging from purification exercises to spiritual assistance. Furthermore, through these organizations, migrants can build social networks that provide them with psychological support in times of hardship.

By analyzing data on the mental health of migrants in Australia, the US and Western Europe, Connor (2012) notes a positive correlation between regular participation in religious activities and emotional well-being in the three contexts. According to his analysis, a close relationship between religion and migrants' inner balance exists independently of the contextual elements, which leads the author to suggest that this aspect be taken into account when designing integration policies, as involvement in religious organizations appears to be more effective than participation in other types of ethnic associations.

In the case of migrants who have escaped from situations of mass violence, persecution, war or natural disaster, the comforting power of faith is often crucial. Religious values and rituals, indeed, provide a sense of peace and inner salvation (Fox, 2012). Populations that have lost their original geographical bound and that are now scattered across regions can regroup around religious organizations. The latter help them activate social practices that, in turn, give a new meaning to people's life (Talebi, Desjardins, 2012; Zhou *et al.*, 2002).

While spiritual capital encompasses a series of intangible resources, such as the strength of faith and its "curative" power, North American literature also highlights a series of tangible advantages that, for the most part, are accessible through participation in religious organizations. Religious organizations offer tools to overcome the initial hardship of integration and draw a path of upwards social mobility over time. They promote social support services and, thanks to the trust established among fellow believers, they facilitate the flow of information on housing, education, entrepreneurship or employment opportunities (Cadge *et al.*, 2013; Munshi, 2003; Guest, 2003; Campion, 2003; Ebaugh, Pipes, 2001; Menjivar, 2001; Bankston, Zhou, 2000). In some cases, religious institutions become a source of information and social support even for migrants with different religious affiliations. For instance, in some contexts, the Church plays a crucial role in promoting migrants' rights, as well as their political and social inclusion, thanks to its transnational presence and the activism of its members (Kim, 2011).

Several US researchers see religious communities of migrants as places where second generations can acquire the social and cultural capital needed to succeed at school and get a sound position in the receiving society (Ebaugh, 2010; Bankston, Zhou, 1996; 1995). In some cases, they do so by organizing educational activities, such as language courses, to maintain the language of origin and learn about the language of the hosting country (Lopez, 2009). In other cases, they run private schools that second generations see as an important opportunity for social mobility (Smith-Hefner, 1994). Several North American authors underline the protective role played by religious organizations *vis-à-vis* migrant children. By promoting various recreational and educational activities for children while their parents are working, they often manage to prevent them from falling in deviance (Foner, Alba, 2008; Zhou, Bankston, 1998). For all these reasons, Cao (2005) and Guest (2003) describe religious communities as places where second generations can find social, financial and parental support.

In addition, many US scholars describe how religious groups provide migrants with a first opportunity to learn about participatory democracy (Foley, Hoge, 2007; Eck, 2001). Through religious activism, migrants have the opportunity to take part in elections and steering committees or learn how to chair meetings and organize public events (Foner, Alba, 2008). Religious institutions often encourage volunteering, also by opening it up to people of other faiths (Ecklund, 2006; Ebaugh, Pipes, 2001; Ebaugh, Chafetz, 2000; Wuthnow, 1999; Cnaan, 1997; Min, 1992).

North American literature widely shows that religion may become a resource for engaging migrants civically, but also for mobilizing them politically (Kurien, 2014; Levitt, 2008; Ecklund, 2006; Ramakrishnan, Viramontes, 2006; Lien, 2004; Menjivar, 2003; Chen, 2002; Kurien, 2001). Some religious groups promote courses on active citizenship, support citizenship programs and encourage the participation of naturalized migrants in elections (Ebaugh, Chafetz, 2000; Min, 1992).

Some US authors highlight that different religious ideologies have a different influence on how organizations support migrants' civic engagement and political participation. Chen (2002), for example, shows that a Buddhist temple and an evangelical organization, both run by Taiwanese migrants, can have very different approaches to civic engagement, with the Buddhist temple tending to promote the organization of charity activities for the community with greater intensity than the Evangelical Church. One of the main reasons motivating this difference lies in the more heightened perception of "foreignness" associated to Buddhist immigrants, who feel pressured to prove their "Americanness" through acts of public relations more than Christian immigrants do.

As illustrated by some North American scholars, religion can also have an important impact on how naturalized migrants are positioned in the political landscape of the hosting country, by encouraging new ideological alliances. Ethnic and religious identity often determines what forms these political coalitions take (Ebaugh, 2010; Lien, 2004; Leal *et al.*, 2005; Espinosa *et al.*, 2003). The country of origin sometimes has an influence on the political life of the hosting country through migrants' transnational relations within the religious domain (Levitt, 2002). Moreover, religion can lay the foundations for global citizenship by encouraging forms of transnational activism, for example on themes such as education, work and health (Levitt, 2008).

This literature review testifies to the multifarious perspectives in which religion has been described as a facilitator of integration by social scientists in the North American context, in line with research questions and designs that intentionally set to explore the role of religion as a resource in the process of settlement. However, as we will see in the following section, the peculiarities of the European context produced a completely different perspective, which interrogates the relationship between religion and integration in opposite terms, as it frames religion as an obstacle for the incorporation of newcomers, rather than as a potential resource.

2   Research on the Religion and Integration Nexus in Western Europe

2.1   *The European Context: Secularization, State-Church Relations and the Public Discourse about Migrants' Religion*

While the cultural landscape of the US allows for a more generalized acceptance of religion, some core and deeply entrenched traits of Western Europe's cultural, social and political identity make it impossible to view religion as a facilitator of migrants' integration processes, which cause an extremely different consideration and treatment of religion as compared to the US. These core features result from two main historical developments: on the one hand, "secularization" and the continuously diminishing levels of religiosity of Western European populations; on the other hand, long-established institutional arrangements governing State-Church relationships, which make the enjoyment of religious rights almost exclusive for "old", mainstream religions. As divergent and unrelated as they may seem, these two tendencies are strongly intertwined: in fact, scholars in this field widely agree in tracing both of them to the Peace of Westphalia (1648) and its effects.

That Treaty put an end to bloody and violent conflicts between and within Protestant and Catholic reigns by sanctioning that the religion of a territory would be that of its ruler. That had considerable consequences in two directions. First, it established an official, direct linkage between modern European States and their respective rulers' religion, thereby creating the ground for establishing a State Church. Second, it identified a clear condition for the maintenance of peace – that is, the expunction of religion from public and political affairs, as religion, from that moment on, was not to be made a matter of contention or a reason for waging war between and within States. This paved the way for a gradual "banning" of religion from what we now define "the public sphere": the issue lied not so much in religion *qua talis*; rather, it was represented by its public dimension and manifestation, with its possible consequences at the geopolitical level (May *et al.*, 2014). Religion was then gradually confined to the private sphere: faith was assigned a limited –and limiting– space. As explained by Introini (2017), this meant positing the very possibility to distinguish between what is private and public in religion, by judging the latter as particularly dangerous for social order. Therefore, while establishing almost exclusive relations with one main confession, the State "obliged" religious institutions to recognize that there were two separate entities: the State, having the monopoly over the management of political affairs, and the Church, that ought to deal only with religious affairs, within the space delimited by the State. These institutional arrangements regulating the "boundaries" of religion are therefore co-essential with the genesis of the modern nation State, based as it is upon the "taming" of religion. This is the reason why the Peace of Westphalia sowed the seeds of secularism, as primarily understood as an intentional separation between "the political" and "the religious".

Today, we can distinguish the consequences and implications of these historical developments for our object of study in two main domains. Firstly, the institutional settlements regulating the presence of the "nation's" Church in every European nation-State entailed that there would be no –or very limited– religious pluralism within each of them (Kivisto, 2014). Contrary to the US, where no single state Church could (and can) be established, allowing for a gradual pluralization of the religious landscape, every European nation-State would accord special privileges to the Church (be it Protestant or Catholic), which entailed a substantial religious homogeneity in each of them, with one dominant, prevailing confession. These privileges seem to be unattainable by the "new" religions brought by newcomers – which accounts for substantial inequalities in the possibility to enjoy religious rights. For instance, representatives of migrant religious communities may find it practically impossible to obtain funds to construct places of worship, or to establish religious schools, across Western European countries, or had (and still have) to go through very lengthy processes for being acknowledged as interlocutors by local and national-level authorities (Laurence, 2012; Joppke, Torpey, 2013; Alba, Foner, 2015). The reluctance of European States to accommodate migrants' religions institutionally –and to acknowledge the religious plurality now characterizing their societies– is linked to the peculiar economism that has traditionally been marking the European migration regime. By importing manpower in the form of "temporary migrants" or of "guest workers" in the post-war decades, Western European countries have followed a model by which migrants' presence was conceived as purely momentary, aimed as it was at filling labor market's contingent demand for work force. In such a perspective, migrants have been viewed only as workers, which entailed a long disregard for the social, cultural and religious components of their identities – and a consequent institutional neglect of these aspects in the process of migrants' incorporation (Zanfrini, 2019). Although this model typically characterized post-war immigration, its effects are still persistent, as the example of States' (absent or belated) recognition of religious pluralism clearly shows.

Secondly, and even more importantly, political secularism (separation between Church and State, and erasure of the Church from political affairs) stimulated cultural secularism (gradual diminution of personal levels of religiosity among individuals). According to May *et al.* (2014), the division between the political and the religious, superimposed on the distinction between the public and the private, entailed that less and less value would be attributed to the religious, because the public/political was considered to be much more important (Introini, 2017). In other words, the progressive devitalization of the public dimension of religion (necessary to contain its potential as a source of conflicts) caused a progressive loss in importance of religion even in the private sphere. Incidentally, this would lead to consider those faiths in which the believer is encouraged to cultivate an extremely privatized practice (read, the Protestant confessions) as better compatible with the public *ethos* – something that affects the way research is conducted in this domain, as we will see below.

This process was also significantly reinforced by the diffusion of Illuminist ideals, whose trust in the human's reason and rationalism would free men from the obscurantist conditionings of tradition and superstition – and, ultimately, of religion. Countless sociological accounts explain how the European experience of the "project of modernity" is co-essential with the process of secularization. Admittedly, contemporary Europe is characterized by a coexistence of secularized attitudes and different forms of religious beliefs and practices (see Chapter 3), whose vitality is also meaningfully linked to the cultural transformations generated by globalization and migration. Therefore, while religion has all but disappeared, neither in public life nor in private lives (Pollack, Rosta, 2017), factual evidence points to a prevailing decline in "traditional" religious attendance and behaviors (Hunt, 2005). Indeed, for the majority of Western Europeans, it is commonsensical to represent themselves as non-religious, with religious symbols of major, traditional denominations simply being perceived as elements of the cultural heritage. Surveys well illustrate this trend: according to a PEW study (2018), only 22% of interviewed Western European Christians declared to attend a place of worship regularly. Only a fifth –or less– of the population of France, Germany, the United Kingdom and the Netherlands would affirm that religion is very important in their lives, as reported by another survey conducted by PEW (2011).

In light of the above-described cultural setting, it is not surprising that Europeans tend to view religion as the most problematic aspect of immigrant integration. In nations characterized by religious uniformity (rather than by the coexistence of different faiths as in the US), and by increasingly marked secularist attitudes, public discourses across European countries inevitably fixated on migrants' religiosity and degree of practice of religion as the most prominent "features" incarnating the "difference" between receiving societies and migrants, ascribing to religion all of what most distinguishes Europeans from "the Other". As Alba and Foner (2015) point out, immigrant religion in Europe has become a significant marker of social divide and a source of conflict as "race" is in the context of the US. In recurrent debates about migration-related anxieties, the religious affiliation of immigrant populations has come to represent a dividing line to the extent that it is deemed the main obstacle in their process of integration.

However, it is safe to affirm that this does not refer to "any" religious affiliation, as these tensions concern most exclusively Islam. Indeed, as many scholars have amply demonstrated (e.g. Césari, 2004, 2013; Modood et al., 2006; Massari, 2006; Bowen, 2007; Celermajer, 2007; Foner, Alba, 2008; Fredette, 2014; Beaman, 2017; Alba, Foner, 2015; Bowen et al., 2015; Pickel, 2018) Western societies, and particularly European ones, have developed a terribly fraught relationship with Muslims migrants and the practice of Islam over the past decades. The reason why this is the case partly lies in the fact that Muslims constitute (and will continue to constitute) a large part of the overall population with an immigrant background in Western Europe[1] –much more, both in relative and absolute terms, than in the US, where immigrants are mostly Christians (PEW, 2012)– as anticipated above. In other words, whilst the population of migrant heritage in the US presents high degrees of diversification in terms of ethnicities and migratory backgrounds, in various European countries migrant populations mostly originate from Muslim-majority countries. In fact, other non-Western religions (Buddhism, Hinduism, etc.) represent extremely low percentages of the immigrant population residing in European countries (*ibid.*). This facilitated the perception of Muslims as quite a "neat" bloc of "foreigners", and gradually induced an automatic association between "immigrant" and "Muslim" (Allievi, 2005; Brubaker, 2013).

A significant factor that motivated the singling out of immigrants with a Muslim background or affiliation as a distinctive "socially distant" group is their socioeconomic profile, which is quite low in all European countries (Césari, 2011; Zanfrini, 2019). For the most part, when they started settling in Europe, they had poor levels of education and were employed in jobs at the bottom of the labor market; after decades since their settlement, relatively high levels of unemployment have affected these groups and patterns of inequality and of socio-economic disadvantage still significantly concern their Europe-born descendants; lastly, they often find themselves segregated in deprived neighborhoods and housing conditions.

However, this perception of "distance" with "Muslims" is not just based on demographic characteristics. Actually, it results from a tendency to view Muslims, in "Orientalistic" terms, as the enemy of the West, which is rooted in centuries-long confrontations, form Crusades to colonialism, as described by Said (1978). More recently, a "revival" of this process of "Otherization" took place in the context of the gradual settlement and visibilization of Muslim migrants in European societies during the second half of the 20th century. This further reinforced a constructed image of Islam in negative and oppositional terms as the "West's Other" – an image that, by now, has become deeply ingrained in European countries' public opinions. The first patent manifestations of this uneasy relation with migrants' Islam date back to the late 1980s,

---

1 According to the data collected by PEW (2012), the share of immigrants coming from Muslim-majority countries and the share of Christian immigrants are very close, as the former account for 39% of the total immigrant population residing in the European Union, while the latter represent 42% (these figures refer only to immigrants from non-EU countries). On the contrary, in the US, Christian immigrants (74% of the total immigrant population) largely outnumber Muslim immigrants (5 % of the total immigrant population).

when the polemics aroused by the "Rushdie affair"[2] in the UK and by the *affaire du foulard*[3] in France marked the beginning of heated and enduring controversies that brought to light the gradual rooting of Islam in European countries.

In the public debates that ensued these two sets of incidents, the behavior of the Muslim immigrant population was deemed to be challenging core "Western" values: in particular, freedom of speech, gender equality (with the veil being considered as a sign of oppression towards women), and the separation between State and religion, allegedly threatened by the request of a separate regime of religious rights. Therefore, these events seemed to question the very nature and narrative of secular States and of secular societies (Nielsen, 2013:168). In this sense, they paved the way for an increasingly distrustful depiction of Muslims, who have been regarded with suspicion as potentially nonintegrable citizens ever since.

Similar discussions surrounding Muslims repeatedly take place in other European countries.[4] In addition, the centuries-old, exclusive systems of Church-State relations existing in all European countries made it quite impossible for a new religious group, such as Muslims, to be treated on an equal par with mainstream religion, meaning that the accommodation of their religious demands have always been objects of heated contentions, as illustrated above. In fact, a malaise in accepting the increasing diversification of societies concretely manifests itself in controversies over those symbols that would definitively mark the presence of Islam in the European cultural landscape – as testified by the numerous recurring local conflicts over the establishment of mosques

---

2   Muslim leaders, communities and organizations organized demonstrations across Britain – but also in India and Pakistan– in response to the publication of Salman Rushdie's novel "The satanic verses" by a British publisher, as the book was considered blasphemous and offensive towards Muslims. Some of these protests culminated with the burning of the book, a violent action bearing a strong symbolism, which sparked harsh criticism. The polemic and the spiral of reactions and counter-reactions reached their peak when ayatollah Khomeini of Iran issued a *fatwa* ordering Muslims to kill Rushdie.

3   In this case, the controversy evolved around the gradual refusal of some headmasters to accommodate the demand of some female Muslim teenagers to wear their *hijab* in public schools, with the explanation that this would allegedly endanger the principle of *laïcité* of the State.

4   Specious controversies about the respective limits of freedom of speech and minorities' rights aroused again in Denmark, with the publication of a series of cartoons featuring the Prophet Muhammad on the newspaper "Jyllands-Posten" and the following protests that took place in many countries across the world. Debates on an alleged intrinsic impossibility of gender equality in Islam recur, especially when a country considers the possibility to ban – partially or completely– the full veil, or *niqab* (Belgium, France, Denmark, Germany, and the Netherlands). A constantly updated review of the issues and the debates about Islam in Europe is available on the website www.euro-islam.info.

(Allievi, 2009) or by the Swiss ban on minarets voted through a referendum in 2009.

More generally, the point of departure of debates on these issues is the superiority of the West's "secular normality", on the basis of which migrants from Muslim-majority countries are assigned an *a priori* negative, "Muslim" identity, as if they constituted a threatening, monolithic and undifferentiated Other by virtue of their "problematic" religion – something which makes them radically different than the "secular us" (Jeldtoft, 2013:26–27). As a result, any debate about the integration of Muslim immigrant populations in Europe is framed in culturalist terms (Frisina, 2010; Césari, 2011), as will be developed below. All negative trends in this domain are easily attributed to Muslims' alleged lack of will to integrate, *due to their backward religion*, which, because of its very tenets, would make Muslims "disloyal citizens", intrinsically incapable of ever being "truly" modern or European (Kivisto, 2014). For example, where Muslims are ghettoized and concentrate in urban, peripheral and more disadvantaged areas, Islam is perceived as responsible for their "failed" integration and their presumed desire to live "parallel lives", separate from and in opposition to the rest of society.[5] Or, jihadist radicalization of disenfranchised youths was explained only with their belonging to Muslim "enclaves" at the margins of society: while it is true that religious movements such as Salafism are on the rise in Europe, and especially in poor, more deprived areas (although this phenomenon remains strongly minoritarian in absolute terms), the debate tends to exaggerate or generalize towards all Muslims these mistrustful depictions.

2.2   *Migrants' Religion –and Islam– in European Social Sciences*
Having analyzed the general consideration of religion in the European context, as well as today's public discourse about immigrant religion –i.e. Islam– we can now examine how social scientists approached the study of religion in migrant integration processes in Europe.

Concerning the topic of religion in general, we may affirm that social sciences have not been quite neutral, as they contributed to and enthusiastically espoused the cause of secularization since the very beginning: the triumph of

---

5   In the case of French *banlieues*, even events that were not connected to religious demands have been tellingly interpreted under the prism of Islam: the riots that took place in the peripheries of French cities during autumn 2005 were initially linked to a supposed "Muslim rage". While the riots certainly channelled rage at and contestation against discriminatory institutions, they did not express any demand concerning Islam or religion: actually, they represented a massive demand for citizenship, recognition and inclusion (Kepel, 2012; see also the special issue of the *Journal of Ethnic and Migration Studies*, n. 5. vol. 35, 2009 entirely devoted to this topic).

"science" over "superstitious beliefs" was seen as key in global the emancipative project of rationalization and modernization (Introini, 2017; Chapter 3 in
the present volume). This means that any investigation of "the religious" in
Europe is framed within the hermeneutic "principle" of secularization, with a
"secularist bias" affecting the study of these topics.

This had a first fundamental consequence: social sciences in Western Europe have been much less "sensitive" to treating religious matters and much
more incapable to grasp their many shades. This obviously impacted the study
of migrants' religion, as such a secularist bias caused a "structural" blindness in
research assumptions (Introini, 2017; Kivisto, 2014), whereby the potential of
religion for integration, or its role as facilitator of the process of incorporation
into receiving societies are hardly taken as research questions, almost taking
for granted that it represents a stumbling block.

A subtle –but highly significant– impact of the "secularist bias" is illustrated,
for instance, by how research about the religiosity of Muslim migrants and of
their descendants in Europe has tended to study religiosity through the prism
of an often-wished-for privatization (Mahmood, 2005; Barylo, 2017; Introini,
2017; Celermajer, 2007). In other words, there has been a tendency to test
whether trends of "protestantization" were in place among religious migrants,
starting from a viewpoint that looks at the extent to which the West has been
able to "tame" religion and Islam (Sunier, 2014). However, when it comes to Islam, this approach appears profoundly inappropriate and unfruitful. Indeed,
the study of Islam seems all the more to challenge the conceptual framework
with which the West and social sciences have "domesticated" the religious
sphere, because its orthodoxy, belief system and trajectory cannot be assimilated to that of Christian traditions, meaning that distinctions between private
and public, religious and non-religious do not work in the same way for Islam
as they do for Christian denominations. Therefore, while these studies were
important in sketching some significant issues and trends, they nonetheless
run the risk of offering an incomplete picture of Muslims' relation to religion
and self-identifications –one that wittingly or unwittingly tends to consider
Muslims as "misfits" whose "incomprehensible" religiousness deviates from
the West's (supposed) secular normality. For instance, Sunier (2014) argues
that surveys conducted among people of Muslim affiliation in Europe on identity and religiosity suffer the problem that they mainly aim at showing that
Muslims, *despite their religion*, become integrated –read, are assimilating– to
presumed homogenous and "superior" Western cultures and values. To put it
differently: even with the best of intentions, these studies are designed to address the question of whether Muslims' integration into society proceeds –
thus, always from the standpoint of Islam's "domestication".

However, it is not just a secularist bias that impedes to formulate research questions aiming to investigate the potential resources offered by religion for integration. Indeed, the way migrants' religion was framed and studied inevitably reflected the above-described negative dominant discourse about Islam. It is true that studies which deconstruct negative prejudices and stereotypes concerning migrants' religion and particularly Islam abound in scientific literature. Indeed, as documented by Nielsen (2013) and Jeldtoft (2013), the life of Muslims and of their descendants in the West has come to represent a compelling object of study. In the past three decades, a consistent quantity of research has been conducted across European countries, enquiring about the actual conditions of Muslim immigrants, the levels of discrimination they endure, the accommodation of Islam in State's institutions, the significance of religion and its social consequences, the positioning and the discourse of Islamic religious actors, and the like. These research endeavors did contribute to dismantle the Hungtinonian view of Islam as an immutable, incommensurable and problematic religion. Nonetheless, there remain issues concerning the hermeneutic premises of these studies, not only because, to a lesser or greater extent, they are marked by the above-described secularist bias, but also as they partly mirror the anxieties and fixations of public discourses on this topic: it is precisely because the assumptions and starting points of these studies aim at deconstructing the negative stereotypes of public discourses, that they have the unintentional consequence of contributing to legitimize such negative images.

There is nothing strange or wrong in the fact that researchers have busied themselves with issues circulating in public debates – it is precisely the duty of social sciences to explore societal questions. However, there should also be awareness of the contexts that shape and inform epistemologies, determining research questions and who, and how, is to be investigated.

There are some overt examples of how public debates have influenced how research has been designed and conducted, possibly generating questionable results. Césari (2013: 29–39) denounces how, in many surveys, the religiosity of "Muslims" is compared to that of an undifferentiated group clustering all "non-Muslims", as the latter were homogenous. Not only does this reiterates an ideological bias by which Muslims are depicted as "something different" than "us", but is also poorly informative: Muslims should be compared to other religious groups, i.e. people who practice religion, not to "non-Muslims", who may also include non-religious people.

Other examples are represented by studies which isolate the investigated group on the basis of its religious –Muslim– affiliation, thus running the serious risk of adopting an "ethnic" or a "cultural lens", and, therefore, of offering a culturalist reading of how they fare in their process of integration into the receiving society (Thomson, Crul, 2007). It is certainly true that many Muslims do encounter disadvantage and marginalization; however, these should be primarily studied as problems pertaining to class, social stratification, access to education:

> the social processes governing the socio-economic status of populations of immigrant origin, for example, have more to do with the social origins of migrant populations and the dynamics of labor markets, schools, neighborhoods than with religion. (...) Grouping populations of immigrant origin under a religious rubric in studies of urban marginality is (...) potentially distracting and possibly misleading; it risks suggesting a cultural explanation for a primarily socio-economic phenomenon. (Brubaker, 2013: 5)

A further example concerns the way in which scholars, too, have contributed to the social construction of the meaning of the term "Muslim": "researchers have adopted the focus on Islam across ethnonational origins, ironically often because they wish to deconstruct and counter (...) crude generalizations" – about, for instance, "Pakistani immigrants" in the UK or "*les algériens*" in France (Nielsen, 2013:170). Even if such research was precisely animated by the positive –and often attained– goal of myth-busting stereotypes about Islam as "an enemy", and considerably added to our knowledge about the condition of Muslims in the West, it is argued that it nonetheless concurred, wittingly or unwittingly, to stress the image of Islam as "something different", thus having the potential paradoxical consequence of ultimately legitimizing and reinforcing the public discourse.

This is the case of studies that focused on Muslim visibilities or on Muslim visible actors. Since "public representations (...) share an imaginary of Muslims that enhances the ways in which they are visible –vocal and involved in social conflict– to the West" (Jeldtoft, 2013:29), the majority society grants legitimacy only to those who correspond to its stereotypes and selects its Muslim "counterparts" on the grounds of their patent "Muslimness". As a consequence, Muslim actors who present themselves as "especially Muslim" in more visible ways gain a sort of monopoly, or are given a chance to impose their hegemony, in the public realm. This had important consequences also on scholarly work, as the portrayal of Muslims only as Muslims inevitably influenced the way researchers have conceptualized their object of study, with research ending up privileging visible manifestations of Muslimness as sites of observation – which, again, resulted in the reinforcement of the dichotomous relationship between "us" and "them" (Jeldtoft, 2013:27).

Indeed, just as public discourses concentrated only on more visible Muslim actors, who would frame their presence and demands in more conflictual terms, so research has over-focused on forms of Muslim life that are constructed as subordinate or antagonistic *vis-à-vis* the majority, and by choosing its interlocutors among visible, practicing, vocal, devout, pious, active, even militant, Muslims. As a result, countless studies concern *visibilities* such as the *hijab*, Muslim organizations and groupings, Muslim places of worship, Muslim's claim-making and relationship with authorities, youth groups, Quran classes, transnational religious movements, and so on. Indeed, much of the existing literature has focused on organized forms of Islam, in which a substantial effort was concentrated on investigating how "these" Muslims challenge their minority status by leveraging primarily on the "Muslim component" of their identity in order to put forward demands for recognition *as Muslims* (to name just a few, see Mandaville, 2001; Silvestri, 2005; Klausen, 2005, 2009; Kepel, 2012; Bolognani, Statham, 2013).

Moreover, it has been underlined that research regarding young Muslims has concentrated almost exclusively on the most visible and conspicuously devout –frequently neo-orthodox– ones (Selby, 2016; Jeldtoft, 2013; Brubaker, 2013; Woodhead, 2013; Jeldtoft, 2011; Jeldtoft, Nielsen, 2011). Whilst this has been motivated by the need to "make sense" of the "sudden" –and visible– re-Islamization of young western-born Muslims (Roy, 2004; Laurence, Vaisse, 2006; Kepel, 2012), who were showing to be increasingly interested in a revivalist neo-orthodox Islam (Kibria, 2008), this actually translated to a heightened focus solely on them.

Focusing on organized Muslims or on these Muslim visibilities was not only easier for scholars – as the field is more accessible when investigating identifiable, visible organizations and associations (Dessing, 2013; Schimdt, 2011). It was motivated by the fact that precisely Muslims' organizations were "attracting attention", due to their very visibility and their claim making, which was transforming Islam in a public (and sometimes political) identity. While these research endeavors sought to challenge the negative dominant discourse about Islam, at the same time they inevitably reflected such discourse, with the risk of "becoming hegemonic "evidence" of political and public understandings of Muslims as particularly (and dangerously) religious" (Schmidt, 2011:1217).

In this sense, denouncing these risks represents an invitation to an increased reflexivity in the definition of objects of study and to a heightened awareness of the never-completely-neutral role that researchers have, as any other social agent, in producing public representations. Indeed, the study of only more "visible" Muslims might end up focusing too narrowly on religion, by interpreting everything through the prism of Islam and overemphasizing the religious component of identities. While there are vocal Muslims who identify primarily as "Muslims" and wish to show their "Muslimness" in daily lives as their first defining feature, this might not be true for the rest of Muslims –and extending these observations to them would be artificial and simplistic. In other words, studying only visible Muslims might result in a reification of Muslims and Islam, thus falling into the pitfall of essentialization and culturalization and playing into the very hands of the dominant discourse, which portrays Muslims, in their entirety, as being "all about religion", and more importantly, their religion as an obstacle to integration.

In response to this trend in research, an opposed approach which gained ground in the relevant literature is to be welcomed, as it focuses on those Muslims who do not visibly appear as such and who escape from the discursive construction of Muslimness, which sees "Islam" as an invariable, master status and the only relevant identifier for Muslims. In seeking to counterbalance the tendency to study only the most pious and vocal Muslims, who are often found in religious organizations, this second approach has "looked for" Muslims outside religious institutions and organizations –i.e. removed from the sites of production of "visible Muslimness"– with the aim of exploring how these "non-obvious" Muslims make sense of religion in their daily lives and what meanings they attach to the practice of religion in their own right, "far" from possibly taken-for-granted (self-)representations of Islam. In response, these same researchers have pleaded for studying Muslims *outside* of visible or obvious Muslim visibilities (Selby, 2016; Jeldtoft, 2013; Brubaker, 2013; Woodhead, 2013; Jeldtoft, 2011; Jeldtoft, Nielsen, 2011).

Lastly, a final example of how contextual factors influenced research is represented by the broader spectrum of studies that analyze the Islamic presence in the West from the point of view of security issues. Here too, debates evolve around the role of religion as a "threat", particularly when jihadist radicalization is under scrutiny. In this case, the "secularist bias" plays out differently at the public discourse level and in research approaches. In the first case, the public discourse tends to blame the very essence of Islam for radicalization, due to its "backward" and "intrinsically violent" tenets, resorting to the Hungtinonian refrain which posits a superiority of the West's civilization over such a "barbaric religion". In the second case, the "secular lenses" explained jihadist radicalization not by resorting to religion as the "root cause", but by pointing to other factors, such as today's culture of violence (Roy, 2016) or political claims (Burgat, 2016). These have been considered extremely valid explanations; paradoxically, this research stance was precisely animated by the commendable intention to not offer culturalist explanations of this phenomenon, by not reducing it only to religion. However, this also meant that some specific religious shades of the phenomenon could not be grasped, which, on the contrary, need to be somehow taken into account in the analysis of the rise of jihadism in Europe (Introini, 2017; Bichi *et al.*, 2018).

More generally, these examples show how, by foregrounding religion in our studies, social sciences may run the risk of unintentionally reinforcing negative representations about Muslims. This is why Brubaker (2013) urges scholars to exert a heightened reflexivity when approaching this object of study, in order to not consider "Islam" as a black-boxed *explanans*. In other words, research should not treat the categories of "Islam" and "Muslim" as *tools* of analysis, as this can predictably lead to use cultural lenses. Rather than as tools of analysis, "Islam" and "Muslim" should be treated as *objects* of analysis (*ibid.*). This means taking up Allievi's invitation (2005) to walk the thin line between avoiding the risk of reductionism on one hand –i.e. downplaying the importance of religion and the specificities of the religious experience– and avoiding the risk of essentialization on the other hand – i.e. overemphasizing religious and cultural aspects and explain all that concerns Muslims in light of Islam.

3   Recent Developments and Issues at Stake in the European and North American Contexts

As explained in the previous sections, there are meaningful differences in the ways Northern America and Western Europe perceive immigrant religion. In Europe, religion has traditionally been considered a bright boundary, a central dividing line separating native from immigrants and their offspring, who, due to their religion, cannot be considered to be "like the mainstream". On the contrary, immigrant religions in the US have never represented a serious basis for contention in the same terms as in Europe – on the contrary, in many cases, immigrant religions worked as bridges rather than barriers to inclusion in the American context, as illustrated by Foner and Alba (2008), among others. As previously discussed, these diverging perceptions and attitudes have inevitably affected the way research has been conducted on both sides of the pond, with religion being considered more as a resource for integration in the North American tradition, or being problematized (and deconstructed) as an obstacle to integration in European social science.

However, we believe that some recent tendencies that have been developing in these two contexts over the most recent years have decreased the differences between them, if not enhanced possible resemblances, making them actually more similar than what it used to be the case. These trends are linked to a series of historical circumstances – particularly the jihadist attacks perpetrated in the US and in Europe in the past few decades, and the so-called refugee crisis reaching its peak in Europe in 2015–2016. This conclusive part addresses their role in rendering the two contexts now more akin, and sketches possible advantageous implications for future research.

3.1   Culturalization and Racialization of Muslims in the US

The first trend that is enhancing the resemblance between the US and European context regards changes in the perception and framing of Muslims in the North American public discourse. In the US, the Hungtinonian view of Islam as the enemy of the West has long been framed in securitarian terms. As illustrated above, the related perception of threat has only marginally been referred to Muslim migrants living in the US. Rather, it has been attributed to Islam as an external player in contemporary geopolitics and as a danger within the sphere of international relations. In Europe, by contrast, Muslim migrants have traditionally undergone processes of cultural racialization, by which they have been interiorized not so much on the basis of a biological characteristic, but rather of their anti-modern culture and religiosity (Modood, 2018; Alba, Foner, 2015). Since the beginning of the 2000s, however, this difference between the European and the North American contexts has been gradually disappearing, with Muslim migrants living in the US being progressively racialized and seen as inherently culturally inferior to the mainstream, white society.

Mostly following the 9/11/2001 terrorist attacks, this demonization of American Muslims, previously limited to fringes of public opinion, has reached wide layers of society. This has normalized anti-Muslim narrative and led to the setup of structured, well-funded Islamophobic movements. Several authors highlight how, within the framework of the war on terror, anti-Shari'a legislations were proposed and enacted by many American States: such Islamophobic politics has fueled, across the country, anti-Muslim attitudes, generating discrimination of Muslim migrants on the basis of religious/physical signifiers (Nagel, 2016; Garner, Selod, 2015; Cainkar, 2009) – which most detrimentally affects Muslim communities that are exposed to intersectional discrimination, such as Black Muslims living in impoverished urban areas (Beydoun, 2017). Particularly, Trump's anti-Muslim rhetoric and policies –such as the so-called "Muslim ban" and his proposal to create a Muslim registry– had a decisive role in these ongoing processes (Yukich, 2018), especially because this rhetoric was skillfully supported and amplified by the alt-right movement, through a website such as Breitbart (Lean, 2017).

Hence, even in such a "religion-friendly" context as the US, migrants' religiosity has started to be unwelcome and seen, like in Europe, as a barrier to pacific coexistence when the social construction of Islam as a diametrically different cultural reality has come into play. This trend has attracted the attention of US social scientists, who have underlined the utility of concepts such as racism and racialization for understanding Islamophobia in the US and have highlighted the need to deepen, through fieldwork-based studies, the impact of anti-Muslim sentiment, rhetoric, and behaviors on the everyday life of American Muslims with migratory background (Husain, Howard, 2016; Garner, Selod, 2015; Cainkar, 2009).

Interestingly, literature also highlights the dialectic relationship between islamophobia and general anti-migrant attitudes in the US, and reveals the impact of anti-Muslim politics on anti-refugee sentiment across the country (Nagel, 2016). For instance, Islamophobia and the fear of terrorism, fed by the attacks in Paris and the mass shootings in San Bernardino, California (December 2015), or in Orlando, Florida (June 2016), had a meaningful role in fueling the support for the strong republican opposition to the resettlement plan for 10,000 refugees from Syria eventually carried out by the Obama administration in 2016 (Nagel, 2016). Such an interrelation between anti-Islamic and anti-refugee sentiment, along with the intensifying racialization of Muslim migrants, represent a further tendency that makes the US context increasingly similar to the European one, where reactions of refusal towards the recently-arrived refugees and migrants are also based on their religious affiliation, as we will show in §3.2. This constitutes a significant shift in a context where religion, as explained in §1, hardly represented a serious basis of contention in the processes of incorporation of newcomers in North America in the past.

However, in the US, this view of migrants as problematic and unwelcome due to their religious affiliation gains center stage only in the case of Muslim migrants: indeed, the present polemics concerning irregular migration flows from Latin America through the border with Mexico do not contemplate their religion at all. This does not mean that, since they are mostly Christians, or in any case non-Muslims, they are easily welcomed. However, the social and cultural distance between them and mainstream society is constructed on elements other than religious affiliations.

In sum, in the US migrants' religion is perceived as problematic for the cohesion of American society only when it comes to Muslims. This has happened only recently, and it is hard to foresee what effect this will have on US social sciences. What is certain, as has amply been illustrated in §1, is that North American social research, having concentrated on faiths and on communities different than the Islamic one for a long time, could focus on the integrative aspects of religion. This led to establishing a proper tradition of research in this field that highlighted the positive role played by religion in migrant integration processes.

On the other side of the pond, migrants' religion has long been considered exclusively in negative terms, because it has always been equated with Islam (although this does not reflect the reality of figures, as shown in §2). The negative consideration of *this* religion implied that research had to overcome the widespread attitude of considering religion as an obstacle to integration, but, in doing so, it ended up unwittingly reinforcing or legitimizing this preliminary assumption, even if it aimed at deconstructing it, for the simple reason that it constituted its starting point.

This comparison leads us to underline, once again, that it is precisely the social construction of Islam as the monolithic, paradigmatic Other the filter that has made it difficult for research to avoid the conundrum of the circular and mirroring dynamics between public perceptions and social investigation. It may be safe to argue that, when the "threatening", "radically different" Other is out of the focus of research, the potential beneficial contributions of religion to social life and the inclusion of migrants can be investigated much more easily and more fruitfully. When Islam is not the object of research, approaches to the study of religion yield research results that seem to provide a more complete picture of the often-beneficial role played by religion in migrants' processes of settlement, which may possibly go unnoticed when research focuses on "the problematic religion".

3.2   *Migrant Religion as a Category of Practice in Integration Measures Across Europe: a New Attitude?*

The other shift that, in our view, is gradually making similarities appear between the North American and the European context concerns subtle changes occurring in the perspective generally adopted in Europe in looking at the "religion and integration" nexus. This development –with its controversial aspects and implications– is the object of the conclusive pages of the present chapter.

As discussed by a number of authors, the traditional negative consideration of Islam and the perceived difficult inclusion of Muslim migrants in society that, as described above, developed in the European public sphere led to treating religion –read, Islam– as a category on its own of migrant integration policies. Through this process, "Islam", and, subsequently "religion", have been framed as pivotal policy areas in the steering of migrant integration (as hinted at also in Chapter 3 of this volume). This has typically concerned religion-related measures aimed at meeting the claims of Muslim minorities and the institutional establishment of their religion –mosque-building, *halal* butchery, or teaching of religion in schools... (Brunn, 2012; Joppke, 2009). Such measures, usually very contentious, have been generally framed so as to primarily meet aims of control and of assimilation. In line with a view that has uniformly cast religion as an obstacle to integration across European countries, it is not surprising that the inclusion of "religion" within the realm of migrant integration policies bears the mark of the centuries-old consideration of religion as a potentially dangerous "force" to be "tamed".

Whilst in the past migrants from Muslim-majority countries were mostly identified through their legal status (e.g. foreigners, third-country nationals, guest-workers), or through their nationalities, this has progressively shifted to "Muslim" as a religious group (Mattes, 2018; Yılmaz, 2016; Brubaker, 2013; Nielsen, 2013; Bleich, 2009). Needless to say, the choice of policy categories is tightly interconnected with problem formulation and has a decisive influence on the proposed measures and their implications. In this case, the underlying assumption is that, in order to reach integration goals, the religion professed by migrants becomes as relevant as –or even more meaningful than– for instance, socio-economic aspects or ethnic-national ties. This approach is marked by meaningful criticalities: if the very concept of migrant integration assumes that some "others" are to be integrated within the supposedly uniform nation-State, then a political practice that targets "Muslims" categorizes these "others" based on their religious belonging and risks reinforcing an exclusionary effect, linked to this specific component of their identity, conceived of as a collective attribute (Mattes, 2018; Korteweg, Yurdakul, 2009).

However, recent developments that occurred in Europe in the mid-2010s triggered some partial changes in the public policies or in the initiatives developed by a number of European countries with reference to the treatment of migrant religion. As is known, Western European countries have been the target of deadly and vast jihadist attacks between 2014 and 2017. The fear of Islamist terrorism could not but sharpen the perceptions of social and cultural distance from Islam and Muslim migrants. A further circumstance took time in the same unfortunate period – i.e. the so-called "refugee crisis". The growing number of people seeking asylum in Europe has caused widespread public anxieties, with refugees' religion frequently becoming the main focus of these concerns (Buber-Ennser *et al.*, 2018; Zanfrini, 2019). This was clearly reflected by the reaction of the self-defined "Visegrad group" (Poland, Slovakia, Czech Republic, Hungary) to the policy of redistribution of migrants among EU Member States designed by the European Commission. These Central and Eastern European countries explicitly and repeatedly expressed their refusal to accommodate quotas of migrants, on the grounds that their religious affiliation, mostly Islamic, would pose a threat to their societies.

In this case, the difference that was stressed was not so much along the fault line dividing "the secular us" and "the backwardly religious them"; rather, what was highlighted was the Christian identity of the receiving countries, put in danger by the arrival of Muslim asylum seekers (Krotofil, Motak, 2018; Brubaker, 2017). This adds a problematic shade to the already negative consideration of the relationship between religion and integration spread in the European culture. Furthermore, it offers the opportunity to develop a provocative reflection, as one might reasonably ask whether these asylum seekers would have been welcomed, had they been Christian.

What is certain, in any case, is that in Europe jihadist violence and the so-called "refugee crisis" had the indirect consequence of renewing the role of religion as a symbolic boundary, that is, as a category marking perceptions of self and otherness (Krotofil, Motak, 2018). The occurrence of the two phenomena at the same point in time further reinforced the tendency to identify migrants with Muslims and Muslims with migrants, in conjunction with the assumption that Islam and terrorism are inextricably interwoven (Pickel, 2018) or that "jihadism" represents the "quintessence" of "real Islam" (Geisser, 2015). This distortive overlapping, defined by Schiffauer (2007) as a "muslimization of migrants", expands the perceived social and cultural distance between "us" and "them". Whilst invisibilizing both natives of Islamic faith and migrants professing other credos –despite their conspicuous presence– this served the logic of promoting a Christian identity narrative especially in Eastern European countries – which worked as a marker of "internal" unity (Mattes, 2017; Mavelli, Wilson, 2016; Johansen, Spielhaus, 2012). Indeed, in the context of a social reality characterized by plurality and complexity, religious identity, when taken in its cultural contents more than in its strictly spiritual meanings, risks assuming a reactive connotation (Brubaker, 2017), being utilized to affirm "reassuring", essentialized differences between an "ingroup" and an "outgroup" (see Chapter 3).

At the level of policy-making, this renewed focus on religious identities translated into a renovated interest in transforming religion into a "cornerstone" of integration measures – however, with some ambivalent attitudes. Certainly, the attempt to "control" and "contain" religion continues to significantly characterize many of these measures. For instance, it is through the development of "Muslim" as a category of integration that the prevention of radicalization has become a primary objective of integration policies. One of the most famous examples in these domains is represented by the approach developed by the UK government, with its "Prevent" strategy – a national plan aimed at countering jihadist radicalization, which has explicitly targeted "Muslims". Many observers have highlighted the strongly stigmatizing effects of this strategy: by targeting leaders of Muslim communities, or by encouraging school teachers and healthcare officers to report about possible "suspect" cases of radicalization, this caused Muslims to be increasingly viewed by the public opinion as a homogeneously dangerous, suspect group, thus eroding trust and social cohesion (Qureshi, 2017; Open Society Justice Initiative, 2016). In this sense, the exclusionary framing of the link between religion and integration policies continues a well-established pattern in policy-making, whereby migrant integration policies feature "migration-security" and "religion-security" nexuses, aimed at addressing the perceived security threat represented by Muslim migrants (Mattes, 2018). Such a political agenda keeps serving the interests of political parties that rely on the social construction of juxtaposed "us" and "them" identities for gaining electoral consensus.

At the same time, however, the potentials of religion for facilitating migrants' social inclusion start to be taken into account across European countries. The involvement of faith-based organizations is increasingly acknowledged as a fruitful way for promoting integration, as religious communities are recognized in their function of single point of contact for State actors, and their organizational structure is seen as a strategic basis for the implementation of integration measures (Mattes, 2018). For instance, in the National Integration Plan for Beneficiaries of International Protection launched by the Italian Government in 2017,[6] interreligious dialogue is counted as one of the four pillars for the promotion of integration. In Germany, the "German Islam Conference" has been explicitly conceived as an integration device: while at the beginning it can be said to have served more the interests of the State in "domesticating" Islam, its efforts have increasingly concerned Muslim's needs, with a recognition of the welfare provided by German Muslims communities – e.g. in childhood and elderly care. Moreover, the Conference has also officially acknowledged and supported the role played by Muslim organizations in the provision of aid and assistance to the refugees who arrived in Germany at the peak of the "refugee crisis" in 2015[7] (Chbib, 2016).

Again, these approaches may be problematic, as they continue to apply a "group" label and essentializing its religious dimension, while risking subduing

---

6   See the version of the Plan translated into English: http://www.interno.gov.it/sites/default/ files/piano_nazionale_integrazione_eng.pdf (last accessed: 05 July 2019).

7   See https://www.bmi.bund.de/EN/topics/community-and-integration/german-islam- conference/german-islam-conference-node.html; https://www.deutsche-islam-konferenz. de/SharedDocs/Anlagen/DE/Ergebnisse-Empfehlungen/20170314-la-3-umsetzungsbericht- wohlfahrt.pdf?__blob=publicationFile&v=6; https://www.an-nusrat.de/suem-dik/ (last accessed: 05 July 2019).

religion to control aims (Stålsett, 2018; Tezcan, 2012). Nonetheless, these developments represent a meaningful innovation in the European landscape and in its perspective on the link between religion and integration, as they may open up a new field in integration policies, possibly creating further, novel opportunities which, if properly harnessed, may fruitfully bring about positive consequences. For instance, while the prevention of radicalization has more often the exclusionary effects described above, it also represented the starting point for experiences of cooperation between State institutions, practitioners and religious leaders, as documented in the collection of practices constantly updated by the Radicalization Awareness Network (RAN), coordinated by the European Commission (RAN, 2017; 2016).

Other interesting cases, in this regard, are offered by Italy and Denmark. In Italy, the State signed an agreement with the largest federation of Islamic associations (UCOII – Unione Comunità Islamiche Italiane) giving the possibility to Islamic religious guides –four women and four men– to access eight prisons in order to provide spiritual assistance and religious instruction to Muslim detainees (Angeletti, 2018), with the aim of countering the possible spread of the "jihadist" message in jails – i.e. contexts that have been identified as breeding grounds for radicalization phenomena across European countries. In Denmark, the model for preventing radicalization and for reintegrating so-called returnees (i.e. individuals who had joined the jihadist insurgency in Syria and have returned to their home country), developed by the city of Aarhus, envisages a rehabilitation and mentoring program involving family networks, social workers, teachers *and* religious communities and places of worship (Bertelsen, 2015). The person who was actively involved in jihadist networks, or is likely to get involved, is assigned a mentor, who engages in sustained dialogue efforts also of religious and theological nature.[8] It is out of the scope of the present contribution to assess the premises and the effects of these measures from the point of view of the prevention of radicalization. What is of great interest, for the purposes of this analysis, is that, in these practices, precisely religious-cultural proximity gets valued, with religion being considered as an *ally* in promoting social cohesion, rather than as an obstacle.

---

8   See Hanna Rosin, "How A Danish Town Helped Young Muslims Turn Away From ISIS", NPR, 15 July 2016 (https://www.npr.org/sections/health-shots/2016/07/15/485900076/how-a-dan-ish-town-helped-young-muslims-turn-away-from-isis?t=1564408937981) (last accessed: 05 July 2019); Tim Mansel, "How I was de-radicalized", BBC, 2 July 2015, (https://www.bbc.com/news/magazine-33344898) (last accessed: 05 July 2019); David Crouch, "A way home for ji-hadis: Denmark's radical appraoch to Islamic extremism", The Guardian, 23 February 2015 (https://www.theguardian.com/world/2015/feb/23/home-jihadi-denmark-radical-islamic-extremism-aarhus-model-scandinavia) (last accessed: 05 July 2019).

That religion is gradually being framed as a resource to tap into for fostering integration and inclusion is also demonstrated by an array of pragmatic, promising initiatives and practices realized by local administrations and civil society, which often seem to be animated by a genuine belief in the role of religious organizations as fully-fledged actors able to play a potentially meaningful and positive role in the integration of migrants. For instance, several civil society organizations promoting migrants' social inclusion are putting in place multidimensional interventions considering religion as a key factor to properly consider. For instance, the KAICIID[9] organization for interreligious and intercultural dialogue, which gathers high-level representatives from major world religions, has initiated a "Program for the social inclusion of people seeking refuge in Europe", with the explicit aim of bringing together representatives from faith-based and secular organizations at various levels (local, national, and international), for providing capacity-building for the integration of people seeking refuge and migrants in Europe,[10] based on the assumption that "because all mainstream religious traditions promote inclusion and care for poor or marginalized people, integration provides a fantastic opportunity for coordinated interreligious cooperation". So far, this initiative has concretely resulted in a pilot project carried out in Vienna, in which dialogue features as "key" to integration: with the aid of four dialogue facilitators having a migrant background (Syria and Afghanistan), thirteen dialogue sessions with refugees have been organized between 2018 and 2019, in order to help refugees "deepen their understanding of Austrian systems, services, and culture". Moreover, the initiative is creating a Network with other European grassroots organizations for promoting interreligious dialogue for social inclusion, and has produced a Toolkit for refugee integration.[11]

This kind of approach has also been encouraged by EU institutions through their soft-steering instruments, and has been adopted by international organizations or by third-sector entities operating in Europe. For instance, the International Organisation for Migration (IOM) implemented several projects in Germany: i.e. the "Integration: A Multi-faith Approach" (IAMA) project, the "Dialogue for Integration: Engaging Religious Communities" (DIRECT) project,

---

9   KAICIID stands for "King Abdullah Bin Abdulaziz International Centre for Interreligious and Intercultural Dialogue" - https://www.kaiciid.org/who-we-are (last accessed: 05 July 2019).

10   See https://www.kaiciid.org/what-we-do/programme-social-inclusion-people-seeking-refuge-europe and https://www.kaiciid.org/news-events/news/network-dialogue-work shop-takes-place-bologna-defines-way-forward-and-membership (last accessed: 5 July 2019).

11   See https://www.kaiciid.org/publications-resources (last accessed: 05 July 2019).

and the "Pilot multi-faith and interfaith fora for religious leaders of third coun-try migrant communities" (REKORD) project. They were co-funded by the Eu-ropean Commission (European Fund for Integration) and supported by the German Federal Office for Migration and Refugees (BAMF), with the aim of enhancing the role of religious communities in the integration process.

These recent trends are likely to have implications on the conceptualization of the integration and religion nexus, that could be fruitfully explored through research. More broadly, the new tendency featuring both civil society and EU and national-level institutions to conceive religion as a key resource in integra-tion offers scholars a rich ground of investigation. In fact, the linkage between religion and integration has started to be the subject of some recent contribu-tions by European researchers, who, more in the vein of the American tradi-tion, analyze the potentials of religion and of FBOs for promoting social inclusion processes, thus deviating from the European tradition, which tends to look at religion as an obstacle to social inclusion (Khallouk, 2018; Andrej, 2018; Ager, Ager, 2016; Mavelli, Wilson, 2016; Snyder, 2012).

One could argue that, through the fears generated by the Islamist terror at-tacks and the refugee crisis, European societies have (re)discovered religion as a meaningful ingredient in social life: while, on the one hand, this continues to be framed as a dividing line, drawing on its symbolism to justify "fortification" processes (Schmiedel, Smith, 2018), there has also been a re-evaluation of reli-gion as a dimension of migrants' life, which should not be neglected for the purpose of facilitating their process of settlement.

The attention recently expressed by civil society and some State's actors for religion as a dimension of migrants' integration undeniably offers rich and promising investigation paths to researchers – as some contributions com-prised in this volume will start to explore. Studying the plurality of migrants' religion with a view to analyzing how the dimension of faith interacts with in-tegration processes certainly represents an innovative perspective in the land-scape of European social sciences. In the light of the considerations developed in this chapter, we hope that research on these themes will be able to adopt, as compared to the past, a more neutral approach to the study of religion –and certainly of Islam– in order not to run the risk of beginning investigation endeavors by having to deconstruct religion as an obstacle to social inclusion.

CHAPTER 14

Religious Persecution, Migrations and Practices in Faith-Based Organizations: Some Recommendations from a Qualitative Study

Lucia Boccacin and Linda Lombi

1 Introduction

The chapter focuses on the findings from a qualitative empirical study into the degree of visibility of the religious dimension in hospitality offered to migrants by Faith Based Organizations (from now on FBOS) operating in Italy.[1]

The departure point of this reflection is the relationship between belonging to a FBOS and the public thematization of the religious dimension. This relationship is characterized in contemporary society by a strong ambivalence. In fact, *believing without belonging* appears be the motto connoting the individualized religious experience of Western society today (Terenzi, 2010: xvii), an experience where religion remains limited to an intimate, psychological and emotional dimension, lodged to a much lesser extent in the social and rational dimensions (see also Chapter 3).

On the other hand, the opposite phenomenon is also present in contemporary postmodernity, and may be expressed as *belonging without believing*. It allows a "rediscovery of the traditional majority religion as a symbol of cultural identity" (Ambrosini, 2014: 1) in the West, and permits the identification of religious symbols as an expression of Western culture, even from people and social components who do not declare a belief or an explicit religious practice. Religion thus becomes a way to give form to a cultural tradition that it is felt should be defended.

This ambivalence does not lack an almost fanatical tendency to reconfigure the social and political structures through a kind of re-sacralization of social ties, offering dramatic examples of fundamentalism.

Under the sociological profile, therefore, the wide and articulated debate on the role of religion in contemporary society (see among others Colozzi, 1999;

---

1 The chapter is the result of a joint investigation between the two authors. Lucia Boccacin was responsible for sections 1, 5 and 6, and Linda Lombi for sections 2, 3 and 4. Sincere gratitude is expressed to Sara Nanetti for her operative support in the analysis of the empirical material.

Casanova, 2000; Kurtz, 2000; Bass and Pfau-Effinger; 2012 and the famous dialogue between Habermas and Ratzinger, 2005) tends to indicate, particularly in Western societies, a focus on the religious dimension which, however, demonstrates signs of ambiguity and a marked imbalance against an individualistic drift in which membership in associations and communities tends to become evanescent and irrelevant to the religious experience.

It is in this context that the issue of religious freedom becomes a theme, both for the individual, in particular in the case of forced migration, and for associations and their ability to act in the public space, according to the social citizenship view.[2]

However, which kind of public space for associative membership does exist in today's social contexts, where the fragmentation of the subject reflects dramatically on their relationships?

According to relational theory (Donati, 1991, 2011), it is within the relationships themselves that the possibility must be found to legitimize both the personal religiosity and, in support of the former, the associative experience in the public space. All this in a perspective that understands the distinction between immanence and transcendence, not as antithetical or with a predominance of one over the other, but as the search for interconnection between the two dimensions. Overcoming contrapositive visions allows us to observe how the religious dimension affects the social sphere in people's lives and communities.

The theme of the relationship between associational membership and the religious dimension is at the intersection between the sphere of civil society and that of value orientations, assuming that social ties dictated by membership association produce social integration[3] and, at the same time, transcendent values of religion, made accessible in everyday life, attribute that intersubjective and social sense and meaning to personal life, which alone are able to constitute the fertilizing substance of integration processes.

In this perspective, there are significant similarities with the concept of common good presented in Chapter 2 with particular reference to the specific role that FBOs may play, through the interpersonal relationships and social memberships that these involve,[4] so that "an active tolerance and promotion of fundamental human values" (Donati, 2010: 102–103) based on individual and intersubjective religious freedom can be pursued. Hand in hand with this concept of religious freedom is that of a secularism understood as a value

---

2   On religious freedom and citizenship at the micro level, see Chapter 2; on the issue of social citizenship, see Donati 2000.

3   The relationship between the religious dimension and integration in the international literature is discussed in Chapter 13.

4   On the concept of the common good, see also: Archer, Donati, 2012.

originating from the recognition of a common world and combining diverse cultural and ethnic groups as an expression of human society (Donati, 2008a).

Through their actions among their members, but also the recipients and the surrounding social context in general, FBOs can make a distinctive contribution in promoting *civicness* (Putnam, 2003) by stimulating political and social empowerment attitudes and the development of relationships based on trust and cooperation within a tolerant and intercultural perspective (Donati, 2013). The latter is based on the acknowledgment of the relationality between cultures, rooted in the principles of fraternity, solidarity and reciprocity. Promoting interculturality means, in other words, recognizing that men and women, although they belong to different ethnic groups and cultures, have more in common than they have differences, a fact which leads to the recognition of the Other as a person with dignity and respect (Meda, 2016).

2   Research Objectives and Design

The research presented in this chapter aims to make a first and not systematic survey of the complex relationship between forced migration and the religious dimension within the environment of FBOs in order to shed light on a theme that has been, to date, the subject of scarce attention. Particular attention will be paid to the forms of persecution and religious discrimination that may have led to the migration choice. This limited thematic relevance is rooted in cultural diversity highlighted in the previous section on the public place of religion in the West, the most common point of arrival for migrants, and other contexts.

The difficulties encountered in general in giving voice to the issue must be underlined at this point, both on the side of leaders of FBOs, and the migrants themselves. The reasons for these difficulties are numerous. Among FBOs there is a consensus to provide services, interventions and practices to anyone in need, regardless of religion and the culture of origin. However, it is this "global offer" that limits, in some aspects, the ability to trace the various root causes of the migration in its distinctive forms, especially if forced, and, in particular, the possibility of pinpointing departures prompted by religious persecution.

In addition to contingent problems such as linguistic barrier, migrants are reluctant to emphasize the religious dimension among the reasons that led to the choice to emigrate because of the fear that this may lead to possible reprisals on family members still in the country of origin. The ability to indicate religious persecution as the reason behind migrations rarely occurred, as it rarely occurred with other motivations too, during the first phases of the reception process (on this point see also Chapter 11). It was only later, after having established an interpersonal relationship between the contact person from reception organizations and the migrant, that the migrant admitted the real reason for the departure.

A qualitative approach was applied to the research data. Four case studies were conducted, investigated through the administration of eight semi-structured interviews with representatives of FBOs who participated of their own free will. The interviews were held between April and June 2017. Interview grid was divided into three main sections:

a) the first section attempts to reconstruct the history and characteristics of the organization (founding and transformations, major assets, any stipulation of partnership, resources, goals, norms and values held);[5]

b) the second section investigates the issue of religious persecution, exploring the reference scenario (context analysis of origin, flows, data, religious groups involved, etc.);

c) the third section analyses the intervention strategies put in place by organizations, and the outcomes such as in-field projects, results and good practices.

The interviews were transcribed *ad verbatim* and the content analyzed through a hermeneutic methodological approach structured to fully exploit the information gathered and to propose an exploratory analysis guided by the facts and oriented to an understanding and attribution of sense. Subsequently, on the basis of content, an initial system of flexible categories was outlined which made it possible to build a taxonomy of useful concepts and categories for the construction of a coding grid coherent with the interview texts. This preliminary analysis did not intend to capture aspects of similarity and difference between the interviews. Instead, it was geared to the observation of the distinctive aspects of the texts. Following the formulation of the coding grid, the interviews having a congruent coding were grouped in a single case study. Commencing with the initial eight interviews, four case studies were identified as respectively addressing actions of advocacy and dialogue with public institutions (*Observatory on Intolerance and Discrimination against Christians in Europe, Religions for Peace*), integration and training services (*Sant'Egidio Community* in Rome and Milan), reception services and response to needs (*Opera San Francesco* in Milan), and proposals for interreligious dialogue (*Service for Ecumenism and Dialogue* of the Archdiocese of Milan and the *Italian Hindu*

---

5   The AGIL scheme from Talcott Parsons revised through a relational approach (Parsons, 1951; Donati, 1991, 2011) was applied.

TABLE 14.1   The empirical reference group: case studies and interviews

Case studies	FBOS	Qualification	Identifying code
First	Observatory on Intolerance and Discrimination against Christians in Europe (OIDCE), Vienna	Representative	Interview no. 1
	Religions for Peace Rome	Representative	Interview no. 2
Second	Sant'Egidio Community, Rome	Voluntary Manager of Agents for Peace	Interview no. 3
	Sant'Egidio Community, Milan	Language Teacher, voluntary	Interview no. 6
Third	Opera San Francesco for the Poor (OSF), Milan	Contact person	Interview no. 4
	San Francesco for the Poor (OSF), Milan	Specialized operator	Interview no. 8
Fourth	Ecumenism and Dialogue Service, Archdiocese of Milan	Representative	Interview no. 5
	Italian Hindu Union – Milan Section	Representative	Interview no. 7

SOURCE: AUTHORS' PERSONAL ELABORATION

Union).[6] Table 14.1 summarizes the list of interviews conducted and the allocation to the various case studies.

The analysis of the individual cases, by applying the codification previously carried out, identified co-occurrences among the various thematic areas,

---

6   The authors would like to thank the participating organisations and their representatives for generously donating their assistance and time, not inconsiderable, to the survey.

which in turn define the mutual relations between phenomena, concepts and categories. After the registration of co-occurrences, summarizing schemes of the process of analysis and narrative expressions present in the texts were produced.[7]

Through an additional coding phase, the most relevant semantic terms in the text were revealed. A *Greimas* or *semiotic square* was constructed, allowing the observation of the elementary structure of signification presented by the various narratives (Greimas, 1974).[8]

The overall results of these analyses will be illustrated here in the following order: §3 provides basic information related to the FBOs involved in the study. §4 will present the findings with respect to the relationship between religious freedom, identity and the response to needs. The relationship between migration and religious persecution in the reception practices of FBOs is the focus of §5. Lastly, §6 illustrates the findings, with particular reference to the type of common good generated by FBOs and specificities related to the religious dimension that have emerged.

3   Case Studies

The first case study involves two FBOs, the *Observatory on Intolerance and Discrimination against Christians in Europe* (OIDCE), headquartered in Vienna, and *Religions for Peace*, based in Rome.

The OIDCE is a non-governmental, non-profit organization engaged in the research and analysis of episodes of intolerance and discrimination against Christians in the European context. The organization produces an annual report aimed at documenting discrimination and religious intolerance against Christians. The discrimination of Christians involves limits in the freedom of conscience and freedom of speech. In some European countries, these limits extend to the freedom to wear religious symbols in the workplace, to pray or to ensure the sexual education of their children according to religious values. Recent reports published by the OIDCE have also noted the presence of numerous occasions of social intolerance towards Christians fueled by a marginal or

---

7   For reasons of space, this contribution will not present the analysis of co-occurrences detected in the interview materials. If further details are required, please refer to the research report available from the authors of this chapter.

8   The semiotic square enables a definition of the general pattern of the articulations of a semantic category, giving form to the sense within a micro-universe of meaning, one composed of the content of the analysed texts.

stereotypical representation of Christians during public debates proposed by the media.

The association *Religions for Peace*, also present at the European transnational level, is instead directed more specifically to interdialogue. The aim of this organization is addressed to create a virtuous relationship between inter-religious and international groups involving the representative personalities of the various religions. Through an open attentiveness, the diverse religious beliefs attempt to identify those common and universal elements able to promote a compatibility between differences and a lessening of conflict tensions. Supported by this value model, the initiatives promoted by the organization act on several fronts, ranging from the purely religious aimed at dialogue between the different communities to the more sociocultural, which includes multi-religious assistance in hospitals or in prisons. An initiative that in part sums up the values and actions undertaken by the association is the drafting and dissemination of a multi-religious calendar highlighting the festivals of all religions and including citations from different traditions. The willingness to support the interfaith integration process and to contribute to the development of a multi-cultural society is also demonstrated through the promotion of leisure or recreational activities.

Despite the heterogeneous interventions proposed and the different recipients involved, both the *OIDCE* and *Religions for Peace* contribute to enhancing the scope of religion within the social context, firstly in a perspective of protection and then promotional. The identification of religiosity as a qualifying component is for the two organizations an ideal reason and value on which to base their actions.

The second case study includes interviews administered to two volunteers of the *Community of Sant'Egidio* from the centers in Rome and Milan. Among the various services offered by the organization, mention should be made of the canteen, the initiatives for dialogue, appeals and signatures collected for social and humanitarian causes, educational activities and the activities of the Peace Agents. In particular, the *Community* offers Italian language school services for foreigners. Learning the language can establish a first point of contact in society, aiding the inclusion processes. The classes offered have over time improved in quality and recognition, and now provide a verifiable linguistic certification for the students. The *Community's* language school is an instrument allowing the full realization of the values woven into the organizations structure, affirming the dignity of every person and establishing personal relationships between operators and migrants.

The volunteers in the Agents of Peace movement offer free services for the elderly connected with the organization. The Italians and foreigners who work

TABLE 14.2   A summary of the first case study

	OIDCE – Interview no. 1	Religions for Peace – Interview no. 2
History		➢ Association founded in 1970 (international context) ➢ World Assembly in Kyoto (relationship between religions as related to international relations)
Activities	1. *Information* ➢ Provide information to institutions regarding episodes of intolerance and discrimination against Christians in Europe 2. *Reception* ➢ Support Christians victims of intolerance or discrimination to tell their story 3. *Research* ➢ Collect data about vandalism against Christian symbols	
Partnerships	➢ EU- Fundamental Rights Agency ➢ European institutions ➢ UN ➢ Religious institutions	➢ Public entities (Ministry of Education, City of Rome) ➢ Associated groups (national and international)
Target	4. *Institutions* ➢ Religious ➢ Public	➢ Companies (health service clients, workers, prisoners, students, associations) ➢ Religious communities (Christian, Jewish, Muslim, Hindu, Buddhist)

TABLE 14.2   A summary of the first case study (*cont.*)

	OIDCE – Interview no. 1	Religions for Peace – Interview no. 2
Methods	➢ Annual reports ➢ Newsletter ➢ Newspaper articles	➢ Limited financing (Calendar, City of Rome) ➢ 5×1000 tax donation receiver
Scope	➢ Improve institutions' awareness about appropriate intervention measures ➢ Improve general awareness about the situation of fleeing from persecution and genocide	➢ The relationship between religion and peace ➢ Preventing tensions and conflicts ➢ Promoting tolerance ➢ Promoting religious freedom
Norms Values	➢ Freedom of religion	➢ Commonalities between the different religious traditions (mutual attention) ➢ Sacred respect of life
Critical issues	➢ Ill-treatment and discrimination of Christian refugees and asylum seekers in some European countries ➢ Vandalization of churches ➢ Stigmatization of Christians through the media	➢ The relationship between religion and modernity ➢ Modern individualism and idealism ➢ Social anxiety caused by increases in migratory flows
Effects and best practices	➢ Identification of regular patterns of discrimination (predictive) ➢ Enunciation of effective measures to combat discrimination and intolerance	➢ Attention paid to suffering and to freedoms ➢ Enhancement of sport as an alternative to violent confrontation

SOURCE: AUTHORS' ELABORATION

in the movement, in gratitude, return the reception and attention they have received from the *Community* back to the wider social environment and senior citizens in particular through their volunteer services.

The activities focusing on interreligious dialogue include prayers for peace and participation in a panel of representatives of different religions. The values of humanitarianism, civic, solidarity, hospitality, peace and sharing that guide the work of volunteers within the *Community* derive from a common religious faith and are transversely promoted in favor of the Other, without distinction of creed. The initiatives are defined according to a predominantly relational register, and in fact the quality of the events is measured through the relationship and mutual confidence established between the participants, allowing a real and symbolic exchange of ideas and values aimed at overcoming ethnicism.

If the process of integration occurs through the relationship created between volunteers and migrants, then in the same way a recognition of the cultural and religious identity of the migrants will require the same relational and personal formula. The *Community* attempts to establish a genuine reciprocal relationship through the recognition of the person's identity, commencing with being completely open to a person's needs. The religious sphere is the point of reference for the principle values of the organization's activities, and by proactively promoting this openness to all religious identities, their commitment is fulfilled. In this sense, religion is never presented as a reason for division and exclusion, but as an open answer to the needs arising from societies.

During the interview with the Rome volunteer, it emerged that the recipients of *Community* services included persons who had fled their country of origin because of religious interventions, including in the areas of origin, through. These included Christians from Nigeria, Egypt or Iraq, and also Afghani Shiite Muslims. In responding to the religious persecution reported by migrants, the *Community* implements specific interventions, including in the areas of origin, through dialogues between religious representatives, appeals and peace initiatives.

The third case study involves interviews with a representative of a reception center and a specialized operator of the *Opera San Francesco for the Poor* (OSF) in Milan.

The *Opera San Francesco for the Poor* is a reception center characterized by services that have expanded gradually from the initial canteen to more complex structures dedicated to social integration. This evolution is linked, from an operational point of view, to user requests to meet new and advanced needs prompted largely by the migration flows of the Nineties. The traditional

TABLE 14.3   A summary of the second case study

	Community of Sant'Egidio – Rome – Interview no. 6	Community of Sant'Egidio – Milan – Interview no. 4
History	➢ Active for over 35 years ➢ Evolution over time conditioned by the flow of migrants	➢ Active from 1997 ➢ Evolution from the lower levels of language training to higher ones (L2–C2)
Activities	1. *Education* ➢ Language or vocational training ➢ Insertion into mainstream education systems ➢ Relationships with the certifying authorities 2. *Social cohesion* ➢ Peace Agents ➢ Catering services ➢ Political asylum applications/ appeals 3. *Religious identity* ➢ Religious path ➢ Interventions in prisons ➢ Aid for religious professions ➢ Shared prayer periods ➢ Memorials ➢ In-class lessons ➢ Mutual respect for celebrations 4. *Combating persecution (the points of departure and destination)* ➢ Dialogue initiatives ➢ Signature collection ➢ Peace initiatives ➢ Prayer in public places	1. *Teaching* ➢ Language learning school (Olivetani – Garibaldi) ➢ Insertion into mainstream education systems ➢ Language certification exams 2. *Social cohesion* ➢ Peace Agents (elderly, cultural initiatives, fundraising through dinners and light meals) 3. *Religious identity* ➢ Shared prayers for peace (Assisi) ➢ Discussion panels (Muslims, Christians)
Partnerships	➢ Religious associations ➢ Prison ➢ Caritas ➢ Evangelical Churches ➢ Municipality of Rome ➢ Prefectures	➢ University for Foreigners Perugia (exams for language certification) ➢ Refugee camp ➢ Institute Panagarola ➢ Schools

	Community of Sant'Egidio – Rome – Interview no. 6	Community of Sant'Egidio – Milan – Interview no. 4
	➢ Foreign minister ➢ Tavola Valdese dialogue group for State relations	
Target	1. *Origin* ➢ Romania, Morocco, the Philippines, Georgia 2. *Migration due to religious persecution:* ➢ Christians (Nigeria, Egypt, Iraq) ➢ Afghan Shiite Muslims	1. *Origin* ➢ Latin America, Sri Lanka, Eastern Europe, Peru, Ecuador, El Salvador 2. *Reason for migration* ➢ Economic, political, defense of values i.e. flee forced abortion
Methods	➢ Operator/migrant relationship	➢ Free labor from volunteers ➢ Teacher/migrant personal relationship ➢ Meetings, prayer, discussion panel
Scope		➢ Social cohesion and interpersonal relationships ➢ Social justice, help and support for others ➢ Growth of the sense of belonging to Italy, social and cultural inclusion ➢ Interfaith dialogue and overcoming of ethnicism
Norms Values	➢ Free Access Policy (need-based) ➢ Religious, humanitarian, civic ➢ Solidarity, hospitality, peace, sharing	➢ Christians, recognition of Christ in the poorest ➢ Hospitality, loyalty, dignity, social contact

TABLE 14.3   A summary of the second case study (*cont.*)

	Community of Sant'Egidio – Rome – Interview no. 6	Community of Sant'Egidio – Milan – Interview no. 4
Critical issues	➢ Citizenship, *jus soli* complications ➢ School integration, the gap between foreigners and Italians ➢ Cultural mediator	➢ Early abandonment of schools
Effects and best practices	➢ Use of recycled material ➢ Perception of foreigners ➢ Attention to social media ➢ "Adoptive" integration model promoting familiarization with foreigners	➢ Agent of Peace reach-out meetings with the elderly ➢ Positive, productive relations with schools

SOURCE: AUTHORS' PERSONAL ELABORATION

recipients of the *Opera*'s works were the homeless. However, the migration phenomenon has resulted in a series of new requirements for assistance, quite different from the previous services. The operators, mostly volunteers, offering service in the centers have diverse professions, including medical doctors, nurses and cultural mediators.

The combination of the religious elements characterizing the *Opera* as an institution and the respect for other religious and cultural traditions are complementary elements of the service. This respect for different religions, beginning with an absence of pork on canteen menus, coexists with the religious nature of the association. The recognition and respect for different identities is visible, in operational terms, in the quality of the services and the enhancement of the personal dignity of every person.

The ambulatory activities of the *Opera San Francesco* are addressed to recipients of medical services suffering extremely fragile socio-economic conditions, complicated by psychic fragility and the inability, in some cases, to benefit from the National Health Service. The ability to intercept these problems is ensured by the complete accessibility to the basic services, coordinated by a freely available psychological counselling contact point where decisions are made during the first contact regarding the most suitable cure and treatment path to be undertaken by the specialists in responding to the recipient's needs.

The fourth case study is based on interviews with representatives of two FBOs, the *Service for Ecumenism and Dialogue* of the Archdiocese of Milan, and the *Italian Hindu Union* of Milan.

TABLE 14.4   A summary of the third case study

	Opera San Francesco – Interview no. 4	Opera San Francesco – Interview no. 8
History	➢ Foundation of Opera San Francesco in the 80s as a canteen service for homeless	➢ Active since 2008
Activities	1. *Social area:* ➢ Reception service ➢ Canteen ➢ Showers and wardrobe 2. *Healthcare division:* ➢ Polyclinic ➢ Dentistry ➢ Pharmacy	1. *Health services:* ➢ Psychology and psychiatry clinics ➢ Pharmacy ➢ Canteen facilities
Partnerships	➢ Municipality ➢ Juvenile Court ➢ Schools	➢ Municipality (CELAV) (Local Employment Mediation Centre) ➢ Caritas (SAI) (Immigrant Reception Service) ➢ Mangiagalli Polyclinic (SED) (Female Services) ➢ Somaschi Foundation (Segnavia women's reception center) ➢ Onlus Farsi (planned)
Target	1. *Status* ➢ The homeless, migrants, third country nationals 2. *Origin:* ➢ Eritrea, Tunisia, Mali, Ivory Coast, Nigeria, Sudan, Algeria, Morocco, Egypt, Eastern Europe, Pakistan, Bangladesh, Sri Lanka	1. *Status* ➢ Socio-economic and psychological fragility, persons without residence permit/homeless/valid documents 2. *Origin:* ➢ *Previously* South America, Eastern Europe, Italy

TABLE 14.4   A summary of the third case study (*cont.*)

	Opera San Francesco – Interview no. 4	Opera San Francesco – Interview no. 8
		➣ *Currently* South America, Italy, Iran, Pakistan, Bangladesh, Sri Lanka, North Africa, China
		3. *Migration for religious persecution:*
		➣ Somalia, Eritrea, China, Pakistan, Mauritania, Bangladesh, Sri Lanka
Methods	➣ Interviews in person to interpret the user's needs ➣ Cards for service access ➣ Increased professionalism in services ➣ Employees (50) and volunteers (780)	➣ Psychological counselling contact point ➣ Personal appointments ➣ Cultural mediation and teamwork
Scope	➣ Integration through the use of the Italian language ➣ Cultural mediator support ➣ Re-education	➣ Personal integration of recipients into society
Norms	➣ Registration of recipients with document ➣ Quality of services and spaces (canteen, showers)	➣ Registration of recipients ➣ Appointment-free access to services ➣ Free services
Values	➣ Dignity ➣ Relationality	➣ Promotion of human dignity ➣ Meeting between cultures and religions

	Opera San Francesco – Interview no. 4	Opera San Francesco – Interview no. 8
Critical issues	➤ Decreased numbers of occasional users and increase in chronic users ➤ Repeat service users ➤ Language problems ➤ Responsibilities towards minors	➤ Problems with waiting times before social integration related to political asylum requests
Effects and best practices	➤ Ability to meet the needs through the evolution of services ➤ Relationship with external local services	➤ Teamwork involving several professionals working in contact with the patient, e.g. psychologist, physician, employer, in order to bolster the recipient's dignity

SOURCE: AUTHORS' PERSONAL ELABORATION

TABLE 14.5 A summary of the fourth case study

	Service for Ecumenism and Dialogue (Archdiocese, Milan) – Interview no. 5	Italian Hindu Union (Milan branch) – Interview no. 7
History	➤ Reorientation of services as a result of the changes imposed by migration	➤ Italian Hindu Union founded in the early nineties ➤ Religious authority recognized with a Presidential Decree Law in 2002 ➤ Understanding signed with the Italian State in 2012

TABLE 14.5   A summary of the fourth case study (*cont.*)

	Service for Ecumenism and Dialogue (Archdiocese, Milan) – Interview no. 5	Italian Hindu Union (Milan branch) – Interview no. 7
Activities	1. *Ecumenism:* ➢ Relationship with the faithful of other religions ➢ Identify and assign the Churches to share with representatives of different religious communities 2. *Education and training:* ➢ Parish assemblies and meetings between the followers of different religions ➢ Teaching the history of religions involving representatives of all religions ➢ Training of prison guards and operators of prisons on the theme of religious pluralism ➢ Healthcare professionals course entitled *Taking care of yourself*	1. *Religious:* ➢ Worship ➢ Teacher training ➢ Yoga 2. *Cultural:* ➢ Lessons of Hinduism in schools ➢ Conferences and studies in universities ➢ Hindu-Christian Table 3. *Integration:* ➢ *We care*, Hindu communities engaged in the care of nature, the environment and social realities ➢ Preservation and enhancement of the natural environment ➢ Assistance for persons who have suffered ill-treatment (women and children) ➢ Italian language lessons for women ➢ Education of men cultivating a less macho approach ➢ National Day for Hindus
Partnerships	➢ Municipality of Milan ➢ Lombardy Regional Administration ➢ Representatives of various religious organizations ➢ Parishes in the area	➢ Municipality of Milan ➢ Gregorian University, the Pontifical Office ➢ Forum of Religions, Diocese of Milan ➢ *Nare non-profit* ➢ Buddhist community

	Service for Ecumenism and Dialogue (Archdiocese, Milan) – Interview no. 5	Italian Hindu Union (Milan branch) – Interview no. 7
Target	1. *Religious communities:* ➤ Orthodox Christians, Sikhs, Muslims, Jews, Copts, Hindus, Buddhists 2. *Host communities:* ➤ Pastors, pastoral council, the community of believers	1. *Origin* ➤ 50,000/60,000 Italians and 100,000 foreigners from India or from Mauritania 2. *Persecuted for religious reasons:* ➤ Bangladesh
Methods	➤ Offices responsible for ecumenism and relations with Islam, Judaism and other Eastern religions ➤ Office coordination ➤ Section collaborators ➤ Contact meetings with political institutions ➤ Research into the potential needs of the faithful of other religions ➤ Religious communities	➤ Self-financing ➤ 8×1000 tax donation receiver ➤ Temple (place of worship and assembly)
Scope	➤ Relationship with Christian Churches, active interreligious dialogue ➤ Create citizens without reference to religious affiliation ➤ Model of distributive interreligious commencing with the reception ➤ Diversity understood as a positive contribution to society ➤ Support in institutional activities, register of religions, through the involvement of religious communities	➤ Support for the practice of Hinduism ➤ Personal integration of recipients into society ➤ Celebration of religious ceremonies and weddings ➤ Promoting knowledge of the principles of Hinduism

TABLE 14.5   A summary of the fourth case study (*cont.*)

	Service for Ecumenism and Dialogue (Archdiocese, Milan) – Interview no. 5	Italian Hindu Union (Milan branch) – Interview no. 7
Provisions		➤ Free ➤ Assembly of Ministers of worship
Values	➤ Hospitality ➤ Religious identity	➤ The oneness of God ➤ A complete coming together and unity among the people under the motto "you and I are one", non-discrimination ➤ Every living thing, animate or inanimate, is divine consciousness ➤ Religion is a way of life ➤ Secularity of the State
Critical issues	➤ Tensions between the host community and other religious communities ➤ Persecution of those who convert ➤ Lack of State guarantees for religious freedom	➤ Lack of a national law under municipal administration on freedom of religion ➤ Difficulties in opening places of worship
Effects and best practices	➤ Redevelopment of neighborhoods in a state of disrepair ➤ Overcoming prejudice of identity and discrimination ➤ Prevention of religious radicalism	➤ Social integration through reciprocal knowledge ➤ Italy is the only country in the world where Hinduism is recognized as a religion

SOURCE: AUTHORS' PERSONAL ELABORATION

The interview conducted with a manager of the *Service for Ecumenism and Dialogue* in Milan clearly demonstrates the operational approach of the Church to interreligious dialogue. The organization's activities are based on understanding the local religious composition revealed by surveys, as well as the collaboration formulas established between the various religious communities involved in the services for the weak. The purpose of the actions promoted by the Archdiocese is to establish a citizenship that precedes religious affiliation, giving new meaning to both identities and differences. Ecumenism, which characterizes the main intervention ambit, is aimed at fostering relations with the Christian Churches and interreligious dialogue. Among the range of activities supported by the *Service for Ecumenism and Dialogue* in partnership with the Municipality of Milan are several training initiatives in local elementary schools where the history of religions is presented by members of the various faiths, including Christians, Hindus, Muslims, Buddhists and Jews. The main purpose of this project is to help pupils see religious diversity in terms of an asset, not as a problem.

The second religious body in the third case study is the *Italian Hindu Union* representing Hindus in Italy. The association was formed in Italy by devotees of Hindu traditions who over time have established a stable center for the State-recognized religion. The main purpose of this FBOs is the promotion of integration processes between cultures and of initiatives to spread both historical and theological knowledge of Hinduism. Operationally, these objectives are achieved in the opening up of numerous collaborations with public and religious organizations. The *Hindu Union* is a participant in the initiative promoted by the Municipality of Milan and the Archdiocese and offers a lesson in Hinduism as part of the history of religion project. One of the main tools supporting the integration process between religions is in fact mutual knowledge and awareness.

4   Religious Freedom, Identity and the Universal Response to the Needs of Forced Migrants: Indications from the Construction of the Semiotic Square

As with the first case study, an analysis of the interviews demonstrated how both groups address the relationship between religion and society, presenting a comparison between possible models of interaction and integration between the secular and religious spheres. The crucial issue of this report presents a twofold semantics detectable with the Greimas square.

The first binary opposition detected in the interview conducted with a representative of the OIDCE is seen when comparing the American and European models. For the former, religion appears as a factor serving the public debate, one able to enhance social integration. The assumption of religion as a

constitutive component of the social dynamics visible in the public arena allows American secularism to apply a concrete form of *religious freedom*. On
the contrary, the prevailing European approach interprets the separation between public and religious spheres in exclusivist terms, when not oppositional
or alienating. The impossibility for the Church to have a voice in the public
debate fosters a new European secularism based on the byword freedom from
the religion.

The interview with the President of *Religion for Peace* in Rome notes secularism as a component of modernity, and the relationship between religion
and modernity can be clearly summarized by applying the Greimas square.
The *golden rule* proposed by the organization intends to focus on the mutual

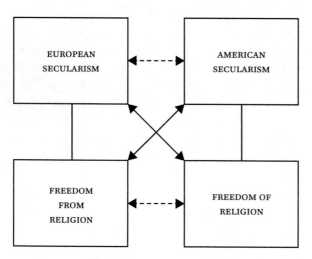

FIGURE 14.1   The Greimas square applied to interview number 1

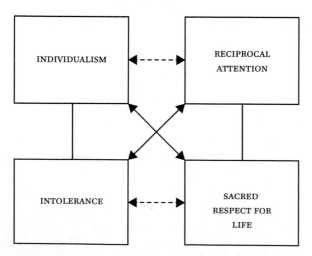

FIGURE 14.2   The Greimas square applied to interview number 2

relationships between different religious traditions, a counter-position to the existential loneliness and the separation processes offered by modern individualistic and idealistic philosophies. Modernity has led to a general mistrust of the main human fulcrum of intolerance and mutual foreignness. In contrast, the great religious traditions agree that a point of convergence may be a sacred respect for life. By means of a growth process within religions, oriented to comparison, to a respect for diversity and the desire to locate a universalist profile, it is possible to act to prevent social tensions and conflict as well to work toward a reconciliation between the multiple identities.

A Greimas square analysis of the second case study involving the two interviews with the *Sant'Egidio Community* allows us to highlight how religious persecution represents the most complete manifestation of intolerance, and

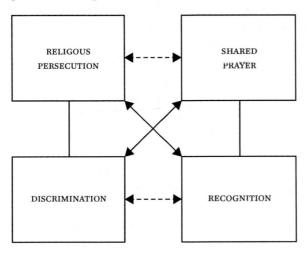

FIGURE 14.3   The Greimas square applied to interview number 6

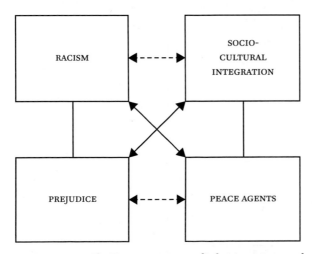

FIGURE 14.4   The Greimas square applied to interview number 3

how this negative factor may be opposed through shared prayer, encounters based on respect for the identity of other religions.

Where religious persecution involves conflict and results in discrimination against a religious component, shared prayer addresses the diversity through a meeting and mutual recognition of the various religions.

A further application of the Greimas semiotic square to the interviews allows the definition of the opposition between racism and socio-cultural integration through two predictors, prejudice and the initiatives promoted by the Agents of Peace, which are revealed as fundamental to the actions undertaken by the organization.

The activities carried out by the migrants as Agents of Peace give and return an image of the foreigner as someone familiar to the social fabric, while attributing a positive value to the membership of the foreigner to the community. Through concrete actions, the prejudice is transformed into knowledge, a prerequisite for genuine socio-cultural integration.

The analysis continues by commenting on the third case study and the two interviews involving the *Opera San Francesco for the Poor* (OSF), an organization of religious inspiration. Applying Greimas square to the content proposed by the manager of the reception services makes the profound and qualifying importance of the organization of *hospitality* clear. This operating mode is notable in the act of acceptance, understood as the immediate passage from user registration to offer of service. The norms regarding the reception proposed by the OSF do not require the validation of the identification documents presented by users. The first contacts with the recipients are not geared exclusively to allow the use of the organization's services. There is also a willingness to accept the complete gamma of personal needs and provide the functional tools needed to meet them.

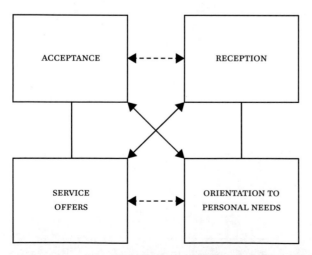

FIGURE 14.5   The Greimas square applied to interview number 4

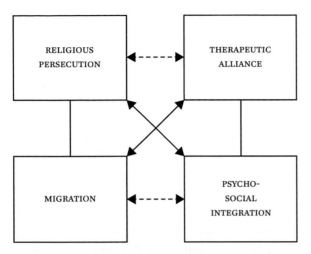

FIGURE 14.6   The Greimas square applied to interview number 8

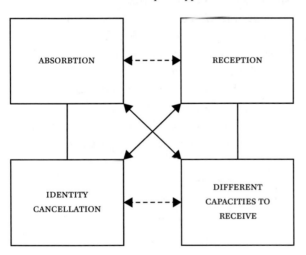

FIGURE 14.7   The Greimas square applied to interview number 5

The interview conducted with the specialist engaged in the organization's Polyclinic revealed even more clearly the personal narratives and life stories of the service users. The semantic category of religious persecution in its physical and psychological implications is very clearly outlined.

The mode of intervention, in these cases, is divided according to the transverse channels of medico-legal, legal, and psychological. The importance of the therapeutic alliance emerges at the center of the care process as a counterresponse to the traumatic experience of persecution. A timely response to the needs of the person, in its concrete and psychic expressions, makes it possible to arrive at a complete integration of the subject.

The last analysis concerns the fundamental features of the interreligious approach promoted respectively by the Archdiocese of Milan and the *Italian Hindu Union*. Once more, the salient features offered by the two institutions may be understood by applying the Greimas semiotic square. The two models of interreligious dialogue, although different in what they assume, display a converging social orientation.

The *Service for Ecumenism and Dialogue* proposes a model involving an integration, allowing for the increase in migratory flows, of the different religious identities present in the social fabric. This is a trend in contrast to the absorption model and to an indifference in identifying differences,[9] which has resulted in the failure of integration models, therefore producing a clear stigmatization of any reference to identity. The interventions promoted by the Archdiocese of Milan, in dialogue with the Municipality of Milan, aim instead at boosting a distribution model geared to reception and inclusion, one able to develop differences while respecting reciprocal identities.

The interview with the President of the *Italian Hindu Union*, in introducing the institution's religious training and the main features that characterize it, indicated the presence of important factors of integration inherent in the Hindu religion. Hinduism is characterized by the coexistence of a multiplicity of cultures, traditions and languages, which can lead to ethnic discrimination. However, these divisions can also act as a binding agent and an integration tool through the religion's recognition of the oneness of God. This perception of the existence of a single God and its manifestation in every person establishes

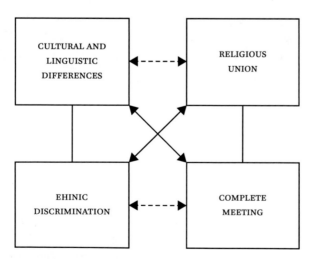

FIGURE 14.8   The Greimas square applied to interview number 7

---

9   See Chapter 2.

an immediate connection with every other person, disallowing any form of conflict.

5   Is It Possible to Reveal any Relationship between Migration and Religious Persecution in the Reception and Acceptance Practices of FBOS?

The phenomenon of persecution for religious reasons assumes a plurality of facets in the content of the interviews, which refer in part to the *mission* peculiar to each organization involved in the study as well as to the different political and cultural realities of the origins of the persecution.

In the interview with the representative of the OIDCE, persecution for religious reasons is identified as a phenomenon having its geographic-political position within an Arab context in Africa and Asia, with persecution addressed mainly to the Christian faith groups. This form of persecution recurs in several European states with violence and threats against Christian refugees or asylum seekers, where it is perpetrated by other migrants. The incidence and extent of these events has led the Observatory to recognize a central theme for the future: the protection of the most vulnerable asylum seekers, namely the Christians fleeing from persecution and genocide.

Religions for Peace has detected the widespread presence of a persecution that is not defined as strictly religious, as it mainly involves minority groups that cannot be categorized according to a religious belief. The centrality of the persecution in this case moves from the religious register to the social and political one, with the identification of the presence of a significant element of difference and diversity in the group persecuted. ("It is a persecution towards religious groups as different groups, not so much for the content... because where there are these situations of extreme violence, regimes or attempts to impose regimes etc., the problem is the diversity", interview 2). In response to these situations, the organization supports those who are persecuted by maintaining stable contacts with minorities, by raising public awareness regarding situations of violence and by telling about the presence of humanitarian corridors. Examples of the groups aided are the Christian Coptic community present in the Middle East and the movement of authentic religiosity in Turkey.

Specific data about the origin of migrants because of religious persecution emerge from the interview conducted with a volunteer from the *Sant'Egidio Community* in Rome. These migrants are generally Christian groups from Nigeria, Egypt or Iraq, or Afghan Shiite Muslims, all minority groups in the country of origin. Religion turns out to be, just as in the case of ethnicity, a persecution factor. However, it is difficult to define the classificatory limits of the phenomenon. Within the context of persecution, religion and ethnicity do not exhibit features that can clearly mark a clear distinction between the two spheres ("often, it has more to do with ethnicity than religions, but here things are mixed, it is difficult to make distinctions", interview 3). In many cases, the reasons for migration remain hidden or unexpressed. In reporting the experiences of those affected by religious persecution, the volunteer stressed that to enable migrants to reveal their religious background and their experience, it is imperative that a trust relationship with the operator be established.

The Copts from Egypt show a similar form of discrimination, which interweaves economic, political and religious factors. They are discriminated for two main reasons: on the one hand, because they are followers of a minority religious community, and on the other hand because of the fact that they belong in many cases to the upper class due to their professional status (they are often the professional contact privileged by embassies or Western commercial reality) ("They suffer a double discrimination: (...)... you are a Christian and rich, that's why you are doubly discriminated", interview 6).

The manager of reception services at the *Opera San Francesco* noted a low percentage of people who had fled religious persecution, and the centrality of political and social component was highlighted. The religious factor is added as a contributory cause ("The migrants come from countries where there are on-going civil wars, the political and social conditions are grave. Religion is an additional factor", interview 4). However, as pointed out by the interviewee, the issue of religious persecution rarely arises during the organization's first contact with and acceptance of the migrant, emerging only after the processes of acquaintance and mutual trust are established, which is a time-consuming process. The interview conducted with a specialized operator in the same organization was able to reveal aspects of the socio-religious interrelationship and the persecution experienced in the countries of origin – and, in fact, it was the depth and intimacy of health interventions which allowed the detection of cases, not particularly numerous, of migration due to religious persecution. These cases require a dual therapeutic approach. The effectiveness of the intervention, in view of the intense suffering that the persecution experience has produced, relies on a personal and intimate integration of the patient within the social context. On the other hand, the interventions reveal the forensic documentation necessary for the acquisition of refugee status.

According to the specialist operator interviewed (interview 8), the main states of origin of migrants who have encountered social and religious persecution and who turned to the OSF Health Services are Somalia, Eritrea, China, Pakistan, Bangladesh and Sri Lanka. These migrants are, from a clinical point of view, marked by visible injuries related to torture or beatings, and invisible psychological wounds. The experiences of patients show that the religious factor is often inseparable from the economic and socio-political components. The existence of violent clashes between groups belonging to different ethnic groups is often the root cause of abuse towards minority groups. The religious identity is then part of the ascriptive characteristics of their communities and represents a decisive factor in the balance of power in the area.

A form of circularity between the political, ethnic, religious and social dimensions is shown, also thanks to a combination of these dimensions, which renders each one of them indistinguishable within the total of the various factors contributing to sparking the migration process. The reticular nature of these elements is confirmed in the case of Iranian women married to Italian non-Muslim men. These women cannot return to the country of origin because they would be subject to discrimination. The condition of these women is aggravated when divorced because they face an exclusion from the activities necessary for the conduct of an independent life. The example underlines once again the close connection between social, economic and religious factors.

Further geographical and social information related to persecution emerged during the interview with the *Service for Ecumenism and Dialogue*. In their experience, the Sub-Saharan Africa is the area where most episodes occur, and the victims are mainly female. However, the religious factor is not identified as an underlying cause of migration and arrival in Italy. The main reasons for an ebb and flow in migratory processes in these cases are economic or political. A previously unrecognized element revealed in the interview relates to the migrant conversions. Although this does not represent a specific persecution in the strict sense of the word, it is in fact retaliation against the subject and their primary relationships, particularly family.

Again, women are the main victims of such incidents.

The representative from the *Italian Hindu Union* provided evidence of religious persecution present in Bangladesh, where Hindus are a minority dominated by violence exercised by Muslim fundamentalists. However, the emigration in this case is once again mainly attributed to economic and social causes.

Table 14.6 summarizes the main findings from the case studies with respect to religious persecution as a migration push factor.

In conclusion, while accepting the diverse points of observation in the survey, the data that emerge from the interviews as a whole demonstrate the prevalence of a migration with a composite of causes and irreducible to a single motive. The religious factor, although present as a contributory cause, is often inseparable from the given socio-political and economic context.

The interconnection between multiplicities of factors appears as the most prevalent interpretation in the interview's texts. In fact, even in cases where it

TABLE 14.6   Religious persecution and migration paths: a summary based on the case studies

Case study	FBOS	Type	Country of origin	Reason for migration	References
First	*Observatory on Intolerance and Discrimination against Christians in Europe*	Representative	Africa Asia	*Explained:* social political *Latent:* religious	Persecution is what our brothers and sisters in the Arab world, Africa or Asia face (FBO n. 1)
	Religions for Peace	Representative	Turkey Egypt	*Explained:* social political *Latent:* religious	It is a persecution of religious groups as *different groups,* not so much for the content ... there are these extremist violence situations, regimes or regime attempts (FBO n. 2)
Second	*Sant'Egidio Community (Rome)*	Manager of Agents for Peace	Nigeria Egypt Iraq Afghanistan	*Explained:* ethnic religious economic-political	Often it is more of *ethnicities* than *religions* but here things are mixed, *it is difficult to make distinctions.* Very often, the religious factor is behind the granting of asylum. As they slowly gain courage, they tell us the reasons for the trip. At first no ... they need to trust you (FBO n. 3)
	Sant'Egidio Community (Milan)	Language teacher, volunteer	China Egypt	*Explained:* parties political *Latent:* religious	It's a *difficult subject.* Perhaps they don't want to tell you, perhaps it is intertwined with other migration factors... Many tell us about the *political* problems, many others

Case study	FBOS	Type	Country of origin	Reason for migration	References
					talk about the *economic* issues... but they don't talk about these things (religious persecution) with a Christian woman (FBO n. 4)
Third	*Church*	Specialized operator	Somalia, Eritrea, China, Pakistan	*Explained:* religious social political	For religious persecution there are the signs... *invisible wounds* and more *visible* ones related to the *persecution* of Christians, Muslims ... because they are not of the same religion or of a lower caste. Because even there the social and religious system breaks down (FBO n. 5)
		Reception service aide		*Explained:* political social *Latent:* religious	It is very unlikely that such a difficult and internalized subject emerges... The migrants come from countries where there are on-going civil wars, the political and social conditions are grave. Religion is an additional factor (FBO n. 6)

TABLE 14.6   Religious persecution and migration paths: a summary based on the case
studies (*cont.*)

Case study	FBOS	Type	Country of origin	Reason for migration	References
Fourth	*Ecumenism and Dialogue Service, Archdiocese of Milan*	Manager	Sub-Saharan Africa Nigeria	*Explained:* political parties *Latent:* religious	For whoever *does not want to convert*, to travel, a trip that may be one towards death is the only possible choice. However, not a large number of people affected by discrimination arrive in Italy. There are other causes: *economic, politics,* or sometimes there is a combination of factors (FBO n. 7)
	Italian Hindu Union – Milan Section	Manager	Bangla-desh	*Explained:* economic *Latent:* religious	There was a gentleman in tears, desperate, saying that they returned a *relative one piece at a time* ... these are frightening things, things that *we know nothing of* ... But I wouldn't say that there is a strong migrant flow towards Italy for persecu-tion reasons. The migration is more *economic* in origin (FBO n. 8)

SOURCE: AUTHORS' PERSONAL ELABORATION

is themed as the direct or manifest reason for the choice to migrate, religion never occurs as an isolated element but is always combined with socio-political and economic factors. This constant feature underlines above all the differences in the context in which persecution takes place and that of the culture of the host countries. The conceptual categories allowing a clear distinction between the religious sphere and the social, political and economic one in the Western context help to ensure freedom from any religiously motivated persecution. As noted by the representative from the *Observatory for Intolerance and Discrimination against Christians in Europe*, it is not possible to speak of persecution in the European context. Although there are episodes of discrimination and intolerance, the substantial characteristics of persecutory actions do not find expression. The public affirmation of violence and the denial of any right of any citizen on the basis of religious affiliation are in complete opposition to the principles of law and secularism on which coexistence and social order in Europe are based and stabilized. This framework, both conceptual and practical, allows to understand the difficulties encountered in defining the identity of a religious factor that manifests itself in the migrant population according to codes that are not only religious, but also political, social and economic. As a result, the cross-factor, which occurs in all the analyzed interviews, is given by the mixture between the religious, political, social and economic, and only a small number of cases clearly present religion as a distinctive and qualifying factor in migration. Narratives that did qualitatively designate religion as a manifest cause of migration were recorded in interviews conducted with the manager of the Peace Agent movement of the *Community of Sant'Egidio* in Rome and the specialist operator of the *Opera San Francesco*. In each case, a single migrant person was referred to. By resorting to the previously described AGIL scheme, it emerges that the operating code of both services is defined in terms of an *interpersonal relationship* (A) regulated by *temporal continuity* (I), characterized by *attention/care for the other* (L), encouraging *trust* (G):

> *trust* is needed (G) ... also through a fundamental key, the *personal relationship* between the operator and the migrant (A), the possibility to *express oneself* is created (L). The recipient always has one or two aid personnel in the organization as a point of reference. *Time* is required, sometimes even years (I). (interview 3)
>
> We have to work with the *person* (L) ... at first we worked on practical things, the concrete needs, "*how do you feel*" (A), an alliance first, *then* the therapy, *then* we pursue the person's needs (I) ... perhaps *trust* follows (G). (interview 8)

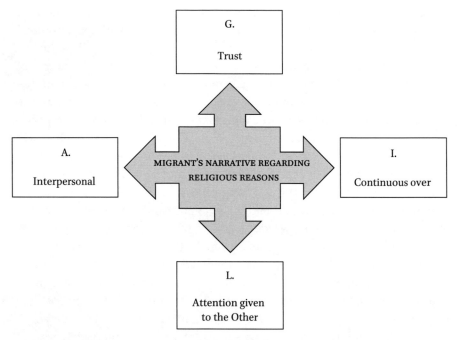

FIGURE 14.9   Migratory processes and the religious dimension in migrant narratives

The application of AGIL (Adaptation, Goal attainment, Integration, Latent pattern maintenance) in the interpretation of the content allows an observation of the constituent categories of the narratives where religion is detected as the manifest cause of the migration process. The media (A) indicate the opening to a deep dialogue with the migrants, the interpersonal and direct relationship. This contact follows the historical path of sharing and mutual growth between subjects, and it is dependent on (I), the temporal continuity of the exchange between the subjects. The value (L), which supports the relational structure, is represented by the person-centered attention and the care demonstrated towards the other. Finally, the precise purpose (G) is the establishment of a trust relationship with the migrant (Figure 14.9).

The time variable in relational continuity is therefore crucial in detecting the emergence of religious data and for the accounting of experiences and stories articulated on several levels.

The reading of this specific relational structure, able to identify the underlying causes of migration in relation to religious identity, makes the definition of those contextual aspects possible, thus allowing the transmission of intercultural motivations – a definition that would otherwise remain submerged. The analysis of the complete body of the interviews highlighted the difficulty the interviewees have in delimiting the field of religion due to the clear discrepancies between their own pragmatic and conceptual references and those projected by migrants. The texts highlighting religion as the direct cause of migration choice do not deny the plurality of factors involved but, at the same time, they recognize the particular gravity of the religious factor. This recognition identifies a twofold process of opening between the migrant and the operator. On the one hand, the migrants manifest their experience as a result of the establishment of a personal and trusting relationship with the operator. On the other hand, the operator involved in the same relationship learns of the other's reality and understands it more and more. The reciprocity of what is understood as an exchange generates trust towards the host context and at the same time a familiarity of foreigners.

6 Pursuing the Common Good through Interreligious Dialogue: a "Good Practice" Instituted by FBOS

Although religion as a motive for migration is scarcely supported by the direct statements in the texts, its interpretation as a defining element of the integration process between different confessional traditions is demonstrated not only transversally throughout the interviews; it also assumes its own specific connotation and articulation. The semiotic squares identified for each case study, in denoting the profound significance of narratives, capture the focus of the interviews in the interweaving of different religious identities and their social recognition. Table 14.7 specifies the values and actions characterizing the interreligious dialogue and those relating to religious integration.

The texts that make up the first case study recognize religion as a constitutive element of human beings and of social life. Both organizations have a critical attitude towards European secularism and the individualistic and idealistic profile prevalent in modernity. The two interviews paint a highly complementary picture regarding the position of religion within the social context. The *Observatory on Intolerance and Discrimination against Christians in Europe* aims to protect religious freedom within the European context through the observation of the dialogue with public institutions, whereas the *Religion for Peace* proposes new growth areas for religion through an open dialogue and an exchange of ideas with the different traditions.

The identification of a public space for association memberships highlighted in the first section of this chapter is sometimes problematic, as seen clearly by the OIDCE protection of religious presence in the public sphere. Potential risk factors include the possible exclusion of the organization from the social

TABLE 14.7 Values and actions in the interreligious dialogue and religious integration

Case studies	FBOS	Interreligious dialogue		Religious integration	
		Values	Actions	Values	Actions
First	*OIDC*			Freedom of religion	Transmission of information and data
	Religions for Peace	Sacred respect of life	Dissemination, training and meetings between religious communities		
Second	*Sant'Egidio Community (Rome)*			Socio-cultural integration	Peace Agents
	Sant'Egidio Community (Milan)	Recognition	Shared prayer periods		
Third	*Opera San Francesco*	Dignity of the person	Hospitality	Promotion of human dignity	Therapeutic alliance
Fourth	*Service for Ecumenism and Dialogue*	Ability to accept differences	Ecumenism		
	Italian Hindu Union			Complete union with each other	Training

SOURCE: AUTHORS' PERSONAL ELABORATION

context, and the emerging of social aspects of intolerance and discrimination unfavorable to the co-construction of common public spaces.

Important and parallel to these difficulties are the experiences in which religion assumes a specific social function, that of peace and of understanding of social complexity, such as in the case of *Religions for Peace*. By means of dialogue and a mutual recognition of the various denominations, religion becomes the form through which a common sacred respect for life is asserted, a respect shared by all the great traditions, as well as by the principle eliciting a common concern for the particularities of the other. The place occupied by religion in the public sphere is therefore crucial in confronting major global crises.

The creation, maintenance and promotion of public spaces for the religious dimension does not produce situations that, once acquired, remain stable. The spaces require continuous attention, defense, as in the OIDCE action, and promotion, such as that undertaken by *Religions for Peace*.

The second case study addresses the issue of religion by following a trajectory in part superimposed on the reading of the preceding case study. It can on the one hand be identified in the founding value of the *Sant'Egidio Community* and its services ("For Sant'Egidio, service is the concrete expression of what our faith is ... you are a Christian, you're a believer when you recognize Christ in the poor", interview 6). On the other hand, the policy of dialogue and respect for all religious traditions pursued by the organization helps to establish greater social integration, avoid conflict, alleviate mistrust and improve the social climate.

Religion is therefore the point of origin for the *Community's* activities, and the point of arrival in the implementation of a relationship between the different religious beliefs. Interreligious dialogue is presented as an important step in reaching an understanding of the social context ("We pray alongside each other, each according to their faith ... taking advantage of the time of prayer as a spiritual nourishment in order to develop a vision of dialogue which in our view is the only one that makes sense when you are faced with the great tragedies of the world") and a mutual recognition of identity.

The religiosity proposed by the *Community* is not geared to proselytism and does not preclude access to operators or users of different faith. It establishes a direction towards shared values based on solidarity, hospitality, peace and sharing. In this sense, the *Community* "constructs" an open space for multiple identities, which, however, orient towards each other by adopting the same symbolic code.

The issue of identification of a public space for religion is in this case subject to the placement of the religious identity, or rather, the religious identities, at the meso level. This placement is adequately symbolized by the work of the *Peace Agent* movement, where the free services received by the recipients is returned to the social context through services performed in aid of others in fragile conditions. This interchange establishes a double and non-denominational bond between the religious values proposed by the body and the migrant integration process. The integration is carried out through the opening up of an interreligious dialogue, which brings the faithful of the

different communities together. In addition, the foundations and services offered by the *Community* contribute to the integration of foreigners into
society.

The religious dimension in the third study is present by inference and is not
made obvious by a direct relationship between religion and the services offered
by the organization. Instead, the identification of a public space for the religious dimension is latent, perceived rather through the articulated range of
interventions achieved.

The Opera San Francesco is a Franciscan religious institution. Its many services and aids offered to a mainly foreign recipient group belonging to a variety
of religious confessions contribute to the creation of a public space located
within the folds of the broad range of operative units characterizing this FBOs.
These spaces at once public and internal may generate an interreligious dialogue between the operator and the migrant, which can in turn lead to existential paths of social integration. The presence of consecrated personnel and religious symbols is not imposed as a qualifying element of the services offered.
The choice to professionalize the services and make them available to foreigners has influenced the establishment of an environment devoid of religious
connotations. The religious element is reflected, however, in the mode of implementation of the interventions, in particular in clinical activities where the
required personal exchange with the patient inevitably opens an interreligious
and intercultural dialogue ("You have to enter the culture ... then you realize
that you have to keep a distance. With the presence of the mediator we can
help ... very quickly it is we who become the stranger", interview 8).

The last case study allows us at this point to address the issue of religion in
more detail by examining the theme of dialogue between the different faiths
and the relationship between religion and social integration. The point of observation of the religious phenomenon in this study assumes a different perspective. The interview conducted with the manager of the *Service for Ecumenism* in Milan demonstrated existing opportunities to establish a dialogue with
other religious traditions, contributing to the integration of these communities within the social fabric. The aims of the service reside in the research and
development of interreligious dialogue, which results in a practical sense in a
direct relationship with the faithful of other religions. To this end, a model is
proposed of public space geared to the reception of migrants and respect for
different cultural and religious identities.

What emerges from the interview conducted with the representative of the
Italian Hindu Union, however, is a more direct correlation between the religious dimension and the social integration process, which establishes porous
borders between the two spheres. The element qualifying integration is in fact

identified in the recognition of a divinity in the other ("I see God in you ... so it is nothing other than you yourself, so therefore this relationship means that if you really see the other as such you cannot be violent, you cannot do anything to the other person, because it would mean harming yourself, you would be harming God himself", interview 7). The relationship with the different religious traditions is marked by the same identification process ("We all believe in the same reality ... if we are asked "Do you believe in God?" we answer "(We believe in the God) in which you also believe", interview 7). Such mingling, while not infringing on the boundaries of the secular state, is demonstrated through a lifestyle, one intrinsically oriented towards both religious and social integration. The public space for the religious dimension in the *Union* seems better constructed at the micro level in relations between the members of different religions and less at the State/institutional level ("Hinduism has the concept of integration in its DNA, we do not discriminate against other religions, we see God in everything. It has its natural vocation to participation", interview 7).

The Hindu religious process of identification of faiths and of all life does not preclude other forms of interreligious dialogue present among the activities promoted by the body.

While conceptualizing the mutual relationship between the various confessional traditions from different points of departure, both organizations agree on the importance of religion as a social glue and as an integration factor in the presence of multiple cultural, ethnic and national identities. They also both recognize the possibility of creating a more complete integration of foreigners, which accepts the specific differences of identity within the social context. The dialogue between religious communities supported by the *Service for Ecumenism* is a first step in creating an atmosphere of respect for differences in identity and a recognition of the gains this exchange brings both in the formation of an integrated religious knowledge of different confessional traditions and by contributing to the coexistence of different communities within the same religious or social context. The teaching of the history of religion in schools, undertaken by the organization, is supported by representatives of all religions and contributes to the formation of a conscious understanding of diversity and its positive aspects. At the same time, the sharing of worship spaces between religious communities, as well as the establishment of new religious communities within the broader social context, promotes a mutual understanding and acceptance process.

Basing on their recognition of one God and the divinity that unites all human beings and living organisms, the Italian Hindu Union incorporates the integration of religious and social differences within their religious orientation.

They represent two implementation forms of this combination: the socio-
cultural reality of India and the adaptability of Hindu migrants. India is a State
deeply divided socially and politically and marked by strong internal ethnic
discrimination. The binding element making social integration possible is contained in the common religion and the sharing of places of worship. The Hindu
migrants tend, however, to express their faith within the context in which they
live through participation and integration into society ("There are 20,000 people in the Hindu community ... in Lombardy. But they are not such an obvious
presence because they are inserted into society, they work ... they are therefore
a very integrated group of people", interview 7).

The theme of a common good pursued through specific activities and practices based on the recognition of the religious dimension as an inalienable
right emerges clearly in both organizational practices.

This trait is the red thread connecting the actions of the FBOs considered.
Through specific actions of voice and loyalty (Hirschman, 1970), via interventions linked to the initial reception of persons forced to migrate, through the
provision of medium and long term services intended to achieve an acceptable
quality of life, and the implementation of educational and cultural services,
the organizations contribute to the realization of a common articulated good
in which the religious dimension is not expunged but rather contributes to the
building up of specific public spaces.

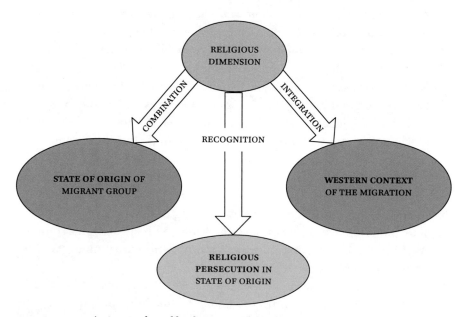

FIGURE 14.10   Action conducted by the FBOs and the explication of the religious dimension

Overall, from the qualitative investigation conducted and the interpretation of the relationship between the religious dimension and action taken of FBOs from a meta-reflexive perspective, three articulations of the religious factor emerge. The first focuses on the singular and unique blends of religious, political and social spheres present in the countries of origin. The second is related to migratory cases linked to religious persecution, and the last is the extension of the relationship between religion and social integration in the Western context represented by the organizations.

Religious identity is thus defined in relation to the culture of the migrant population as an element inseparable from the broader social, political, ethnic and economic contexts. The organizations are active promoters of a social integration mode, which sees the religious dimension as an important reception tool as well as a connecting factor for intercultural dialogue, a clear contributor to the creation of specific public spaces. A very particular approach is useful in allowing experiences of religious persecution to be revealed. Close contact with the migrant and the establishment over time of a lasting and stable interpersonal relationship characterized by attention and care on the part of the operator may lead the migrants to trust the operators enough to be able to express themselves. The operators, on their part, gain a closer familiarity with the cultural and symbolic codes of the migrant.

The triple articulation of the religious dimension described above (see Figure 14.10) allows the emergence of a *relational semantic* in the meeting of the different cultures and religious traditions (Donati, 2008). The *recognition* of the Other and their identity is the point of departure for the description of the religious matrix borne by the migrants. Similarly, the establishment of a relationship of *reciprocity* between different identities enables integration of the differences in the context of hospitality (Zanfrini, 2019). This integration recognizes the *real otherness* between the subjects, one rooted in an authentic symbolic and instrumental *sharing*. "The sharing is not between two reflections (two similar entities mirroring each other) but between two unique entities which, while retaining their impenetrability without losses (because they continue to live their memberships in other social and cultural worlds), reveal themselves as different in reference to a reality they have in common, for example, the human race" (Donati, 2008: 84). Finally, the *reflexivity, which* allows the detection of those very intimate cases of suffering and discomfort, caused by episodes of religious persecution, gives body to a morphogenetic relational form, one that evolves gradually through the establishment of a relationship of trust and familiarity between *ego* and *alter*.

CHAPTER 15

Interreligious Dialogue in the Governance of Migration and Interethnic Cohabitation

Fabio Baggio

Without the acknowledgement of his spiritual being, without openness to the transcendent, the human person withdraws within himself, fails to find answers to the heart's deepest questions about life's meaning, fails to appropriate lasting ethical values and principles, and fails even to experience authentic freedom and to build a just society (Benedict XVI, 2010).

∴

The words of Pope Benedict XVI are a perfect *incipit* for this chapter, with which we propose to highlight the importance of interreligious dialogue in the governance of contemporary migration flows and multi-ethnic cohabitation.

According to data gathered by the *Pew Research Center*, in 2010, 83.7% of the global population said they adhered to a religion (Pew Research Center, 2012a). Based on this statistic alone, it is evident how the religious dimension represents an important aspect in the life of the great majority of people. Consequently, every act of government that wants to be oriented to the good of people cannot be exempted from this essential consideration. Also, the governance of migration flows and multi-ethnic cohabitation, as a political exercise, must include the religious dimension among the areas of greatest interest, promoting interreligious dialogue.

Before moving to the real discussion, we think it is appropriate to present some methodological clarifications. A large part of the considerations expressed further below are the fruit of a personal reflection based on first hand experiences in different regions of the world. The spiritual dimension discussed in this article is, by its very nature, difficult to measure in scientific terms: this represents at the same time a challenge and a limit of my study. Considering my Catholic faith, we will make frequent reference to the teaching of the Church, particularly its universal teaching, without failing to mention thought developed in other religious contexts.

© FABIO BAGGIO, 2020 | DOI:10.1163/9789004429604_016

1   The Essentiality of the Religious Dimension

At the historical level, it is undeniable the role that religions –and the values proclaimed by them– have had in the construction of the different civilizations which have marked the continuous progress of humanity in the various regions of the world. The opening to the transcendent, considered in its multiple forms, has profoundly characterized human evolution in ages and places that are so different that it is hard to believe it is not primarily constitutive to the human being. Its dogmatic and cultural structuring and its different institutionalizations, while developing over time, have resisted attacks of all kinds, often becoming a reason for resilience and survival. There are also considerable and widely documented contributions from the various religions in the moral, political, cultural and artistic spheres in all regions of the world. And in addition to what is expressed above, it cannot be denied that a large part of humanity adheres to a religion and that, again according to the *Pew Research Center*, a significant percentage of people who say they are not part of any religion in fact also confess to having some religious belief (Pew Research Center, 2012a).

What has been presented above should be sufficient to demonstrate how religiosity –or spirituality– makes up a substantial dimension of human realization that cannot be omitted in any debate that regards the human according to Terence (*Heautontimorumenos*, I, 1, 25). In other words, promoting the realization of this dimension of human existence contributes to the full realization of the human being. As Pope Benedict XVI affirmed, "The religious dimension is in fact intrinsic to culture. It contributes to the overall formation of the person and makes it possible to transform knowledge into wisdom of life" (Benedict XVI, 2009). The pope explains a conviction of Christian doctrine that is rooted in the Jewish tradition, which considers the denial of the existence of God as foolishness, with ominous consequences in moral life: "The fool says in his heart, 'There is no God'. They are corrupt, they do abominable deeds, there is none that does good" (Psalm 14:1.). According to Islam, the human being has two series of essential needs: spiritual and material. The first are satisfied through faith in Allah; the second by using the resources that Allah has created for that purpose in the best way (Ahmad Kausar *et al.*, 2013). Regarding the Hindu, Jainist and Buddhist traditions, human realization consists in the capacity to elevate oneself from the material sphere to the spiritual sphere, through a process of personal purification.

In the contemporary age, two trends have affirmed themselves that have contributed to challenging the essentiality of the religious dimension in human realization: the acclamation of the superiority of secularism and the political-ideological abuse of religion.

It is evident how in some environments a hostile attitude toward religions has spread widely, with religions standing accused of conditioning and inter-ference in the management of the *res publica*. Starting from the principle that religiosity belongs to the private sphere and has to be kept that way in every political exercise, many moral values, which find their reason for being in reli-gious traditions, have been banned from public debate. In the name of a sup-posed superiority of being a-religious in the secular sphere, political discourse has disappeared, eliminating any reference to spirituality and transcendence, leading to the view that religious affiliation in fact makes up an impediment to the good exercise of government, and that beliefs are irrational, fruit of super-stition and anti-modern. All of this has contributed to increasing disaffection toward the traditional religions, which have already been tested by processes of secularization. Deprived of its collective and moral value, religion has ended up among the "optional" aspects of human realization: an elective –and pri-vate– hour in the calendar of life.

Regarding this, in 2005, Pope John Paul II warned on the threats of secular-ism to religious freedom:

> A mind-set inspired by a secular outlook is spreading in society. This ideology leads gradually, more or less consciously, to the restriction of religious freedom to the point that it advocates contempt for, or igno-rance of, the religious environment, relegating faith to the private sphere and opposing its public expression. (...) A correct concept of religious freedom is incompatible with this ideology that is sometimes presented as the only rational voice. Religious freedom cannot be curtailed with-out depriving human beings of something fundamental. (John Paul II, 2005)

The second trend, which is just as widespread currently, is the exploitation of religion for ideological and political aims. Even if history is rich in episodes of this kind, it was thought that this sort of "abuse" could not "take root" in con-temporary societies. Unfortunately, the news reveals the opposite, as the *Par-liament of the World's Religions* underlined some years ago: "Time and again we see leaders and members of religions incite aggression, fanaticism, hate, and xenophobia – even inspire and legitimize violent and bloody conflicts. Reli-gion often is misused for purely power-political goals, including war" (Parlia-ment of the World's Religions, 1993).

Abused for personal interests, retaliation or revenge, religions are used to mark out differences, counterpose civilizations, oppress the most vulnerable, and justify wars. But "wars of religions" often become "wars against religion" due to the fact that they contribute to perverting the nature of religious affiliation, depriving it of its aspect of being transcendent, mystic and an instigator of good.

Faced with these challenges, the necessity arises to re-establish the essential role that corresponds to the religious dimension, restoring the inspiring principles of religions and reinstating the great ideals of truth, justice and solidarity. The necessary first step is the recognition of religious freedom. In 2001, John Paul II wrote:

> Basic to all human rights is the freedom of religion, which includes the right to be instructed in the faith. (...) This requires that governments and school authorities ensure that this right is effectively respected. (...) Men and women religious, lay people and clergy have labored to achieve this end, often with prodigious effort and many sacrifices. Their work needs to be consolidated and extended to ensure that all the baptized grow in faith and in understanding of the truth of Christ. (John Paul II, 2001: 22)

As a corollary to the recognition of freedom of religion, with a view to a peaceful and enriching cohabitation in multi-cultural societies, John Paul II (2001) encourages all stakeholders to commit themselves to an ecumenical and inter-religious dialogue, seeking to avoid any type of fundamentalism.

2   The Religious Dimension in the Migration Process

As it is logical to suppose, migrants are worthy representatives of the people of their countries at the religious level. Their religious affiliation generally corresponds to the percentages observed in their homeland. With regard to international migrants, some estimates already exist that we find useful to consider when examining this point.

According to data gathered by the already-cited *Pew Research Center* (2012b), in 2010, of the 210 million international migrants estimated by the United Nations, 106 million were Christians (49%), 60 million were Muslims (27%). The rest were made up of Hindus (5%) Buddhists (3%), Jews (2%), other religions (4%) and unaffiliated believers and non-believers (9%).

In the 27 countries of the European Union, again according to data elaborated by the *Pew Research Center*, in 2010, the religious composition of migrants who were citizens of non-member countries was the following: 42% Christians, 39% Muslims, 8% unaffiliated or atheists, 3% Buddhists, 2% Hindus, 1% Jewish and 4% of other religions.

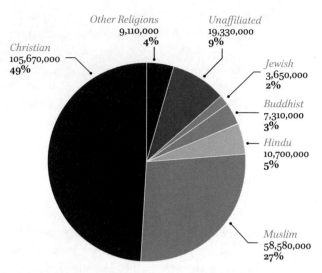

FIGURE 15.1   Religious composition of international migrants, 2010
SOURCE: PEW RESEARCH CENTER, 2012B: 11

These numbers, however, only give an idea of the importance of religiosity for migrants, which very frequently is not limited to a mere declaration of affiliation. The religious dimension, in its symbolic and cultural expressions, is essential for many migrants in the various phases of the migration process: departure, journey and arrival/residence.

In recent decades, scientific production on this theme has been enriched thanks to contributions from anthropologists, sociologists, theologians and religion experts, who have formulated interesting theories, often starting from the observation of specific cases. These theories can be classified in three big groups based on their main subject: those that regard personal faith as a spiritual and social resource for migrants, those that refer to the role of religious communities for immigrants, and those that concentrate on transnational dynamics of migrants in the religious sphere (Frederiks, 2016).

In the large part of cases, the analysis of researchers has focused on immigrant communities. Some studies have gone into depth also on other phases of the migration process. This is the case of J. Hagan and H.R. Ebaugh, who studied the role of religion in the whole migration process of the Maya population of San Pedro, Guatemala, to Houston, Texas. The people who intend to depart usually turn to ministers of the Pentecostal Church to obtain advice in their decision process. The same people participate in large numbers in moments of fasting and prayer (*ayunos*) in which qualified pastors prophesize, indicating God's will for each person. Once the decision is made, the migrants, along with

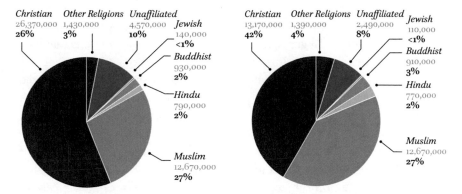

FIGURE 15.2   Religious composition of international migrants in the EU, 2010
SOURCE: PEW RESEARCH CENTER, 2012: 54

their families, refer to the ministers again for the necessary preparations. Often, the ministers are requested to check the honesty of the guides (*coyotes*) who lead the migrants in the long and dangerous journey (Hagan, Ebaugh, 2003). Again J. Hagan, this time along with H. Straut Eppsteiner, underlines how particularly in the cases in which the migration is ventured through irregular channels, and for this reason, is set to be risky, the departing –often with their relatives– turn to divinities to obtain strength and protection. This is the case for many Catholics in Guatemala and Mexico who make pilgrimages to sanctuaries, carry out devotional practices and offer *ex voto* objects in exchange for "spiritual travel permits" (Straut Eppsteiner, Hagan, 2016). Already in 1980, P.A. McAllister explained how the *Gkaleca*, an indigenous group of South Africa, practiced special propitiatory rites before the departure of migrant workers, with the aim of obtaining protection and guarantee of return from the spirits (McAllister, 1980).

During the second phase of the migration process, or the journey, religion continues to be important for many people on the move. In a study published by L.J. Dorais in 2007, the interviews with Vietnamese refugees of different religions (Buddhists, Catholics and Caodaists) revealed how each person had found comfort, hope, consolation and strength of spirit in prayer and in religious practices (Dorais, 2007). From the testimonies that I could gather personally, I was able to glimpse the same faithful abandonment and confident recourse in many migrants and refugees who braved the Sahara Desert and the waves of the Mediterranean Sea. After the adventurous crossing of the Mediterranean, for many migrants the path continued toward the North, and with it the trust in the transcendent, which was also manifested in the construction of real places of worship. This is how it was for Orthodox Christian and Muslim migrants in the so-called "jungle" of Calais, who wanted to entrust their dreams to divine providence in a church and a mosque built with their own hands ("Corriere della Sera", 9 August 2015). These are the same convictions that lead many Central American migrants to build sanctuaries along the "vertical border" that is Mexico, to jealously guard pictures of the saint they have entrusted themselves to in their pockets, to wear miraculous medallions around their neck and to sculpt sacred images in stones along the way (Straut Eppsteiner, Hagan, 2016).

The importance of the dimension in the third migration phase, made up of the arrival and residence in the country of destination, is surely that which has been the most common subject of studies in recent decades. In the case of Maya migrants in the United States, studied by Hagan and Ebaugh, communication with relatives who remained in the homeland is kept alive also thanks to religion. The migrants send photos to families in Guatemala so that they can be taken to the *ayunos*. The pastors commonly show hundreds of photographs to indicate that the propitiatory rites had their effect. On the other side, the pastors of the "sister" Churches in the United States hang photographs on the walls of reunited relatives who were prayed for, in this way closing a spiritual circle of divine protection. Furthermore, the Pentecostal communities in US cities offer immediate social support networks for the new arrivals and contribute to maintaining the feeling and the religious practices of the country of origin among immigrants (Hagan, Ebaugh, 2003). Proof of the importance of the religious dimension in the migrant settlement process is provided by the intensification of the religious practice openly declared on the part of some ethnic groups, like in the case of Indians of the Hindu religion in the US interviewed by P. Kurien, many of these said they had rediscovered their religiosity in the land of emigration, also introducing expressions of regular collective worship which in their homeland were relegated to a few big celebrations (Kurien, 2002). Moreover, contemporary history is rich in similar examples; you only have to think of the religious vitality of the Italian Catholic immigrants in Argentina between 1800 and 1900 (Baggio, 2000), the robust community structuring of Hindus from Surinam in the Netherlands between 1970 and 1990 (van der Burgin, 1991), the cultural and institutional development of Muslim immigrants in Germany in the last 50 years (Troll, 2003), and the extraordinary adherence to evangelical Christian communities on the part of Korean and Chinese immigrants in the United States in the third millennium (Ambrosini, 2007).

It should also be noted how, in the residence phase, the religious practice of migrants usually produces a significant impact also on the religiosity of host societies, as shown by several pieces of research on the subject. R. Henkel and

H. Knippenberg sustain that, thanks to the religiosity of immigrants, in Europe there has been a slowing in the process of secularization and religion has regained a space in the public sphere (Henkel, Knippenberg, 2005). In certain geographical areas, some religious confessions are today present only thanks to the mass arrival of immigrants, who have caused profound change in the religious landscape of some countries. This is the case of Christianity in the Gulf countries, brought by Philippine immigrants and Indians from Kerala. This is the case also for Hinduism in Britain and Canada (Frederiks, 2016). The most recent flows of Christian immigrants into the United States brought with them a new way of living and celebrating faith, which is obliging local communities to invent, along with the latest arrivals, new forms of praying, announcing and serving (Levitt, 2007).

3   Religions in Dialogue

The big religions, even in their diversity, offer a priceless common heritage of principles and values if meeting and dialogue is encouraged between them. As the *Parliament of the World's Religions*, underlines: "A common set of core values is found in the teachings of the religions, and (...) these form the basis of a global ethic" (Parliament of the World's Religions, 1993).

Some scholars say that the definition of a universally accepted ethical platform should be free from any religious consideration. Only a neutral –or rather purely philosophical– series of principles could overcome the divisions that exist between various faiths and beliefs (Nielsen, 1990). The development of this thought has led to three different philosophical orientations: the modern doctrine of natural law,[1] normative hedonism[2] and moral contractualism.[3] The French philosopher Jacques Maritain was strongly opposed to the total secularization of ethics, advancing the theory of integral humanism. This theory

---

1   "A philosophical-juridical current founded on two principles: the existence of natural law (corresponding, that is, to the nature of man and therefore intrinsically right) and its superiority over positive law". "Giusnaturalismo", Treccani - Enciclopedia On Line, http://www.treccani.it/enciclopedia/giusnaturalismo/ (accessed October 5, 2018).

2   Normative hedonism says that pleasure is a value and suffering is a disvalue regardless of the value of anything they can cause or prevent. See. "Hedonism", Stanford Encyclopedia of Philosophy, http://plato.stanford.edu/entries/hedonism/ (accessed October 5, 2005).

3   Moral contractualism defines as right the action that can be rationally justified by the individual and approved on the part of other members of the social group of reference. See P. Marrone, "Contrattualismo morale e intellettualismo etico in T. Scanlon", Etica & Politica / Ethics & Politics, 2, 2010, 2, 369–370.

founds itself on the conviction that the human person is at the same time material and spiritual and for this reason the religious dimension, understood beyond any confessional sense, cannot be excluded from ethical debate (Maritain, 1996). And it is worth adding that, considering the large part of humanity defines itself as religious, it would be unreasonable to exclude the spiritual dimension from the start from the determination of the ethicality of human behavior.

In the world of today, strongly marked by questionable truths and random interpretations, an inclusive approach could better respond to contemporary ethical challenges. This does not therefore involve the search for universality of principles "beyond" religions, but "together" with them, to reach the point of being able to define the rules of a common wisdom, which integrates the moral paradigms of the different philosophies and faiths. For this reason, in the ethical debate –and at the same time in every public debate– no one should renounce one's own religiosity (Carter, 1993).

Some attempts in this direction are worthy of mention. In the 1990s, a process of interreligious reflection resulted in the document *The Declaration Toward a Global Ethic* that was adopted by the *Parliament of the World's Religions* in 1993. The global ethics proposed in the declaration are founded on common values advocated by the different religions that took part in the process. More recent is the proposal by Darrell Fasching and Dell Dechant, who suggest a comparative narrative approach to the different religious ethics, of which the result is structured in a normative ethics of human dignity and liberation, in conformity with the Universal Declaration of Human Rights (Fasching, Dechant, 2001). A third attempt, named "ethics through cultures" proposes a purely descriptive approach to morality, with great consideration for cultural and religious differences, without any kind of judgement (Brannigan, 1998; Guptara, 1998). Even in their diversity, these efforts made toward the definition of a universally accepted ethical paradigm coincide in the need to make different cultures and religions converse to obtain a result that is globally significant.

In the last few years, I have dedicated myself to going into more depth on this issue, making use of the study and meeting opportunities that my missionary experience has offered me. I managed to highlight some principles that the big religious and philosophical traditions concur on. The first of these refers to the existence of principles beyond human contingency. For many religious traditions, these are fruit of a divine revelation and respond to the will of a superior and transcendent being. For other traditions, these principles are registered in the cosmic order and can be understood through a process of enlightenment and purification. For many philosophical traditions, universal values exist that can be understood by all human beings beyond their spatial-temporal condition (Baggio, 2007).

A second principle that many religious and philosophical traditions have in common is that of the primacy of the common good over that of the individual. As the Lucca-based Group of the Ecclesial Movement for Cultural Commitment (MEIC) underlined in 2008:

> In fact, all religions, through varied means, spur their own faithful to collaborate where they live, with all those who make efforts to ensure respect for the dignity of the human person and of their fundamental rights, to develop the sense of fraternity and of solidarity, to be inspired by the savoir faire of the community of believers that, at least once a week, bring together millions of people, of the utmost differences, in an authentic spiritual communion, and to help the men and women of this time to not be slaves of fashions, consumerism and profit. The believers are therefore called upon to contribute concretely to the common good, to an authentic solidarity, to the overcoming of crises, and to intercultural dialogue: they have to participate in public dialogue in societies they are members of. (MEIC, 2008: 38)

The coincidence with the big philosophical traditions of the East and West made itself evident in firstly the drawing up and then the application of the international conventions that protect human rights and promote their dignity.

The third principle of universal destination of goods on the earth, the first foundation of the "duty" of solidarity, finds the different religions and philosophical ethics in the world in agreement. The concept of a common wealth to share, overcoming historical divisions, can be justified by an explicit will of the divine creator or by respect for a cosmic order, which guides human history. Following on is a moral obligation of charity and sharing which in all cases responds to the full realization of one's own humanity according to a superior design. In an immanent philosophical perspective, many currents of thought consider philanthropy and solidarity as excellent virtues, even if these do not always reach the point of constituting a moral obligation for individuals (Baggio, 2014). It should anyhow be noted that, also in the secular sphere, there is no lack of people who advocate for the equal allocation of common resources as a duty for all, based on the principles of equality, non-discrimination and equal access to development (Atuguba, 2013).

A fourth principle is codified in the duty of hospitality toward the other, the stranger or in any case the person who does not belong to the group of reference. The major religious traditions coincide in situating that obligation in the sphere of the sacred; some justify it with the fact that the guest is specially protected by divinity due to their vulnerability; others base it on the mysterious presence of God himself in the guest; others furthermore see a way toward ascension and purification in the practice of unselfish hospitality (Baggio, 2007). In secular ethics, the offer of hospitality is generally a sign of civility, a demonstration of magnanimity, even if it does not reach the point of constituting a moral imperative. Cases exist, however, in which humanely reception cannot be denied. This is the case of those who escape war and persecution, for whom the duty of hospitality is set forth by international and national law (Gil-Bazo, 2015; see also Chapter 4).

Many religious traditions affirm the principle of the global management of the earth, from which springs a common duty to the whole of humankind around the correct administration, the healthy use and the harmonious development of environmental and natural resources. Some of these, such as Judaism, Christianity and Islam, base that duty on an explicit divine disposition since the beginning of the world; others, like Hinduism and Buddhism, justify it with the need to maintain cosmic harmony through a profound respect and meticulous nurturing of every element. Shared management translates into co-responsibility to be implemented with respect for the principle of subsidiarity (Baggio, 2014). Also within the secular sphere, this principle is generally accepted, to the point of becoming a foundation of the international agreements related to questions of common interest. In this sense, the preamble of the Paris Agreement on climate change is emblematic, affirming as fundamental "the principle of equity and common but differentiated responsibilities and respective capabilities, in the light of different national circumstances" (UN, 2015a, Preamble).

A sixth principle can be deduced from the sense of transnational belonging advocated by different religious traditions. Some of these affirm the existence of a "universal citizenship" founded on the adherence to a specific faith rather than national belonging. In a transcendent perspective, every earthly country in any case is transitory compared to the real celestial land, which you reach after death. Other religions more simply consider nationality as a spatial-temporal accident in the cycle of rebirths, which reveals the cosmic belonging of each being. It should also be underlined that these religions teach respect for the existing political constructions but push believers to look beyond every historical structuring. Some philosophical traditions coincide with this vision of citizenship, underlining the precariousness of every spatial-temporal juridical determination and they insist on the concept of "global fraternity". On the other side, one has to admit that, if nationality can be given or taken, it cannot constitute a real source of personal identity (Baggio, 2014).

These six principles do not in any way exhaust the wealth of common heritage of global religious and philosophical traditions. However, they represent a concrete example of how an approach that is inclusive of religions in the public debate can contribute substantially to identifying and sharing essential principles and values for a convivial cohabitation, which is particularly necessary in an age that has rightly been defined by some scholars as the age of migration (Castle *et al.*, 2014).

4   Religion and Multi-Ethnic Cohabitation

Even if we mentioned above the importance of the religious dimension in the phase of arrival and residence, we consider it is worthwhile to go into more depth at this point on the role that religions often play in the process of integration with a view to a mutually enriching multi-ethnic cohabitation. In 2016, D. Nagy and M. Frederiks observed that this particular argument had not been especially studied by researchers, probably based on the unfounded assumption that in the integration process religion was being progressively relegated to the private sphere, in this way becoming uninfluential in the dynamic of identity reconfiguration (Nagy, Frederiks, 2016). A more attentive bibliographical research, however, reveals that there is no lack of studies that have tackled this topic in recent years. Many of these highlight the positive contribution of religion in the process of integration, dwelling on very varied aspects (Lyck-Bowen, Owen, 2018). As a methodological choice, we limited to analyzing the studies that refer directly to the European reality.

Firstly, religion contributes generally toward the conservation of migrants' original identity, which is necessary to start a constructive dialogue in the integration process, without easy concessions to assimilation pressures. In 2008, Annemarie Dupré underlined how in the case of Christian communities in Europe, for many migrants, religion represented an essential element for the maintenance of their ethnic or national identity and, at the same time, a source of "transnational" identity, which facilitates moving beyond the former (Dupré, 2008). In 2011, Jørn Borup and Lars Ahlin, after having studied the case of Catholic Vietnamese migrants in Denmark, observed how religion had played a crucial role in the maintenance of the identity of a minority group, even if it had not in fact encouraged a subsequent step toward integration (Borup, Ahlin, 2011). In 2012, some Spanish researchers, analyzing the migration reality in the Castile and León region, concluded that migrant communities originally from Morocco, Sub Saharan Africa and Latin America consider religion –and above all religious practice– an important element for their collective and individual identity redefinition (Valero Matas *et al.*, 2012). In 2013, Claudia Diehl and Matthias Koenig noted how for two different groups of migrants in Germany, Turkish Muslims and Polish Catholics, religious practice, initially reduced upon contact with a largely secular society, was then recovered to rediscover their own identity which had been "diluted" in the initial years (Diehlm, Koenig, 2013). A recent study on the reality of Muslim migrants in Europe concludes that, despite the many prejudices and the hostility of the native population, religion can encourage significant links between minority groups and between the minority groups and the majority group; this can contribute to mitigating the stress of the process of adaptation, foster a sense of collective belonging in second generations and offer refuge from discrimination experienced in host societies (Papademetriou *et al.*, 2016).

A second aspect highlighted by the studies consulted refers to the positive effect of religion on the willingness of migrants to collaborate in the construction of integrated communities in the countries of immigration. In her analysis, Dupré underlines two elements: on the one hand, the importance of the positive experience of inclusion of migrants in religious communities in the host societies, which often reproduces a climate of fraternity experienced in one's home country; on the other, the recognition of common religious values which, translated in ethical terms, serve to promote peaceful and convivial cohabitation (Dupré, 2008). In 2013, presenting the results of research on integration of citizens from third countries in the European Union, Jocelyne Cesari underlined how active and structured religious participation generally represents an element encouraging the political participation of migrants (Cesari, 2013). Religion can function also as a driving force for the emancipation of minority migrant groups from particularly stringent political, social and economic structures in immigration countries, like in the case of the Sri Lankan Tamil community in Britain studied by Donald Taylor (Taylor, 1991).

A final element worthy of consideration is that underlined by Majbritt Lyck-Bowen and Mark Owen in a very recent article, which is the contribution of cooperation between religions to the process of integration. According to the authors, a multi-religious approach can be of benefit for the improvement of services supporting the integration process, and the intensification of collaboration between religious organizations and communities, with positive consequences on dynamics of inclusion, and the creation of a social fabric that is more open and respectful of differences (Lyck-Bowen, Owen, 2018).

There are many cases in which religion has been fundamental for the creation of *ad hoc* structures and the organization of services for migrants and refugees. In 2004, Charles Hirschman stated that religions play a triple role in the life of migrants, codified with the formula of the three "rs": refuge, respect and resources. And it was to obtain one of these "rs" that migrants decided generally to affiliate themselves with this or that religious group (Hirschman, 2004). This interpretation, while with all its limitations, is reflected in that which many religious organizations and communities tend to offer their faithful in the various phases of the migration process (see on this point Chapter 12).

In my missionary experience, I have had the chance to get to know numerous associations, organizations and foundations of declared religious inspiration, which have made assistance to migrants and refugees their main reason of being. In the origin countries, they dedicate themselves to providing useful information on emigration, preparing the departing and their relatives who remain in the homeland, demanding more protection of migrants on the part of accountable institutions and assisting migrants and their families in making the migration experience a real development opportunity. In the transit countries, they usually offer refugees and migrants assistance and refuge, seeking to satisfy their fundamental needs. In the destination countries, they offer a wide range of services both in the spiritual as well as in the social sphere, in many cases promoting integration between migrants and native peoples, active participation, with respect for differences, as well as the reinforcement of transnational dynamics with positive effects on development of origin communities.

Summing up the conclusions of various studies on the issue, in 2004 Alejandro Portes and Josh DeWind observed that in the US, religious institutions contributed in a significant way to the integration process of migrants through the support of a positive reception, the mitigation of any negative attitudes, collaboration with the accountable authorities toward inclusion, the protection of minority groups from exclusion, support toward the incorporation of new arrivals and equally of their transnational practices and help to migrant parents toward ensuring a positive integration of their children (Portes, DeWind, 2004) (Chapter 20).

In his 2003 article, Christian Troll noted that from the 1970s in Germany, Muslim associations in which the first aim was to guarantee places of worship to the migrant faithful had multiplied, but also noted that, over the years, they had widened their range of action, elevating themselves to official representatives of their members in the public sphere and, in this way, offering learning courses and going into more depth on the Koran. From the 1980s, many of these associations came together in federations, often with a strong national connotation, to ensure better religious assistance to members, guarantee a greater political weight to Muslim communities, initiate dialogue with

Christianity, educate young generations in the doctrine of Islam and create
and manage Islamic cultural centers (Troll, 2003).

A report published in 2016 by the *Churches' Commission for Migrants in Europe* and by the *World Council of Churches* illustrated in detail the ministry carried out by some Christian communities in Europe to the benefit of migrants
and refugees, underlining as spheres of specific commitment their inclusion in
the life and apostolate of local Churches, the accompaniment of young people,
social assistance and the work of *advocacy* (Jackson, Passarelli, 2016).

5   Valuing Religion and Interreligious Dialogue

From what has been presented above, we believe we can affirm that the importance of the religious dimension in the migration experience appears evident.
Since it constitutes an important aspect in the life of the great majority of migrants, it has to be considered in all its potentiality in the governance of migration and multi-ethnic cohabitation. Interreligious dialogue represents a privileged instrument to increase and release that potential, inasmuch as the
participation of many actors, all authoritative and animated by common principles and values, is already a guarantee of success.

In 2014, Pope Francis affirmed that

> Religious freedom (…) is a shared space (…) an atmosphere of respect
> and cooperation that must be built with everyone's participation, even
> those who have no religious convictions. (Francis, 2014)

For the construction and the maintenance of this shared space, it is essential
to promote dialogue and meeting between the different religions and between
them and institutions with every means.

Those meetings should be favored both at the level of religious leaders as
well as at the level of the faithful, so as to harmonize theoretical exchange on
principles and values with dialogue on concrete questions of day-to-day life. It
is appropriate for them to be organized in neutral spaces, guaranteeing the
participants the possibility of expressing themselves in utmost liberty. It is
convenient also to foresee moments of informal, recreational, sportive and artistic meeting, to widen the opportunities of expression beyond the knowledge
of language. Ecumenical and interreligious prayer meetings, furthermore, represent the highest expression of reciprocal recognition and respect, inasmuch
as the communication takes place in the sphere of the sacred.

Sincere dialogue and the enriching encounter between religions and be-tween religions and institutions can prepare the ground for the development of shared initiatives and programs, characterized by a multi-religious ap-proach. The already-cited study of M. Lyck-Bowen and M. Owen (2018) pres-ents five concrete examples of that collaboration at the European level.

Refugee Support is a psychological and social assistance program for asylum seekers and refugees in Britain. Managed by the British Red Cross, it relies upon the cooperation of different religious, interreligious and secular organizations.

The second project, entitled *Goda Grannar* (good neighbors) sprang from a spontaneous collaboration between a Christian Church and a mosque in the offering of temporary lodging and food to migrants in transit at Stockholm sta-tion. In 2015, the collaboration was structured in a common program that add-ed among its services teaching of the language, legal assistance and the direct-ing of those assisted to the competent public offices.

With the objective of accompanying migrants in the integration process in Germany, the project *Weisst Du Wer Ich bin?* (Do you know who I am?) brought together Muslims, Christians and Jews of good will. This project is supported financially by the Federal Government.

Dialogue for Integration–a Multi-Faith Approach is a program promoted by the Afryka Connect Foundation to improve relations between African mi-grants and the local population in Poland. This program foresees a series of training seminars for leaders of different religions and representatives of institutions.

The last project studied by the two researchers is that of the "Humanitarian Corridors" through which hundreds of particularly vulnerable refugees and asylum seekers are rapidly relocated in Italy. The initiative, promoted jointly by the (Catholic) Community of Sant'Egidio and by the Waldensian Church (see Chapter 10), saw the effective informal collaboration of some Muslim commu-nities and mosques on Italian territory.

Interreligious dialogue is a privileged vehicle for valuing the religious di-mension of natives and migrants, and every political exercise aimed at the gov-ernance of migration and multi-ethnic cohabitation should consider it. Start-ing from my experience, I would like to highlight five concrete ways of valuing the religious dimension, without any claim of being exhaustive in my proposal.

1)   The first way of valuing religion in the governance of migration is guaran-teeing its freedom, both in its profession as well as in its practice. In 2017, the Migrants and Refugees Section of the Dicastery for Promoting Integral

Human Development of the Vatican encouraged states to "adopt policies and practices that guarantee the freedom of religion, in both belief and practice, to all migrants and refugees regardless of their migratory status" (Migrants and Refugees Section, 2017, 17).

2) The reason for the encouragement is due to the observation that in some countries, by law, it is not permitted to affiliate oneself with or publicly practice a religion that is different from that of the majority of citizens. In that sense, migrants, who often make up a large percentage of religious minorities in these countries, find themselves prevented from freely expressing their faith, above all when this requires collective participation (Chapter 10).

3) It is not enough to recognize freedom of worship as an individual and collective right. It is also necessary to ensure its exercise. For this reason, States have to concede to the use of appropriate structures of worship, so that spaces and things that belong to the sacred sphere that many faithful turn to with devotion can be treated with the due respect. This concession would serve to guarantee the dignity of different cultural manifestations and contribute likewise to eliminating all forms of religious "secrecy" that usually stoke suspicions and fears among the local population.

4) Guaranteeing the exercise of the right translates also in the "political" consideration of the special times, celebrations and traditions of each religion. The faithful should be put in a condition to be able to carry out the devotional practices considered as a duty in the doctrine of the professed faith, with all those elements considered "obligatory" (rests, fasting, food etc.) with the aim of religious compliance, always and when these do not violate local laws and do not undermine the fundamental rules of peaceful and respectful cohabitation.

5) For an effective exercise of freedom of worship, the competent authorities have to eliminate or prevent every form of discrimination of a religious origin. This can be achieved through a relentless pursuit of every discriminatory attitude and specific awareness-raising campaigns that have mutual tolerance and respect as their aim. Focusing on the medium to long term results, it would be all the more opportune to introduce teaching modules in educational curricula of primary and secondary schools that allow students to get to know different religions, seeing as ignorance is frequently the source of prejudices, which in turn produce fears and conflicts.

The guarantee of the exercise of religious freedom, both in its profession and its practice, undoubtedly makes up a first step toward the valuing of religion, but it does not determine in itself any proactive commitment on the part of the state. The real appreciation of the value of the religious dimension is demonstrated by its inclusion in the formulation of policies and programs targeted at the departure, transit, entrance, residence and return of migrants.

In the Message for the World Day of Migrants and Refugees 2018, entitled "Welcoming, protecting, promoting and integrating migrants and refugees", Pope Francis explained how the four verbs of the title were the summary of the pastoral action of the Church for migrants and refugees. In the section dedicated to "promoting", the Holy Father underlined how religion makes up an essential dimension of integral human development, the search for which represents the main cause of the large part of contemporary migration flows.

> Promoting essentially means a determined effort to ensure that all migrants and refugees –as well as the communities that welcome them– are empowered to achieve their potential as human beings, in all the dimensions that constitute the humanity intended by the Creator. Among these, we must recognize the true value of the religious dimension. (Francis, 2017)

It would be interesting, as a scientific exercise, to encourage an objective assessment of the consideration of the religious dimension in migration policies and programs of the countries of departure, transit, and destination. The privileged observatory in which I find myself working today has allowed me to draft a few attempts in this direction. Rarely have I managed to find significant references to religion in the policies and programs that I have analyzed. Often, those references were motivated either by the will to prevent every form of discrimination toward minority religious groups, or by the concern about maintaining a neutral attitude toward each faith (or not to consider it in political practice) or by the need for greater control over who professes this or that religion.

The inclusion of the religious dimension in the formulation of migration policies and programs of the departure countries means the acknowledgment of the role of religions in the discernment process leading to the decision to migrate and to the immediate preparation for the departure. It also means the recognition of situations where the impossibility of confessing and practicing a specific religion is the cause of a forced migration. Such situations highlight the need for promoting appropriate measures toward resolving this problem.

Migration policies and programs in transit countries cannot ignore the influence of the religiosity of migrants on their capacity of resilience and on the conservation of hope beyond any logical reasoning. Considering the religious dimension, "politically" means ensuring places of worship and prayer to all itinerant people and encouraging their referral, when possible, to local ministers of the same religion.

With regard to the destination countries, the religious dimension has to be included in initial reception policies and programs, in those of integration in the medium to long term and those of returning. Above, we have already highlighted the positive potential of religion in this migration phase – potential that has to be opportunely released through appropriate and far-sighted normative and institutional interventions. We would like to underline the transnational significance of the religious dimension of migrant communities, which requires special attention and a considered appreciation when elaborating bilateral or multilateral agreements on migration questions.

The inclusion of the religious dimension in the formulation of migration policies and programs also regards the international community, which for some years has inserted migration among the main issues of its common agenda. Unfortunately, it seems that this has not yet happened. In the document of the United Nations entitled "Transforming our World: the 2030 Agenda for Sustainable Development", we find just two very short mentions of religion to say that this cannot ever be an element of discrimination (UN, 2015b: 19). The same applies for the New York Declaration for Refugees and Migrants from 2016 (UN, 2016: 13–14). Neither the word "religion" nor the word "faith" ever appear in the text of the report by the United Nations Secretary General entitled *Making migration work for all* and published at the end of 2017 (UN Secretary General, 2017). The final drafts of the "Global Compact on Refugees" (UN, 2018a: 9) and the "Global Compact for Safe, Orderly and Regular Migration" (UN, 2018b: 31a) are situated on the same line as the "New York Declaration".

All of the studies analyzed highlight the fundamental role that religious organizations are playing in the maintenance of "faith" among migrants and refugees, offering cultural services and guaranteeing appropriate spaces and spiritual counselling. They are often committed to the maintenance of original identity, promoting the richness of different cultures. Many have widened the range of services offered, responding to the most varied needs of their faithful. Even with different ways and with different motivations, the large part of them has in any case contributed positively to the process of integration of migrants and refugees in the host communities.

The enormous role played by religious organizations in favor of migrants and refugees has to be appropriately recognized and appreciated on the part of institutions. That appreciation has to translate in terms of legislative, political and financial support. In the first place, it is essential that national and/or local legislation consider and order their legal existence through clear regulation and simple procedures for inclusion in public registers. Religious organizations, then, have to be appropriately considered in the formulation of policies on emigration, entrance, integration and return, with a view to the activation of useful synergies toward a better governance of the migration phenomenon and the construction of intercultural and plural societies. Institutions, finally, have to insert the financing of those synergies in their public spending estimate, guaranteeing religious organizations the possibility of participating actively in activities and programs in favor of migrants and refugees, as well as cover for expenses generated by that participation. The authorities in charge have to equip themselves with mechanisms of monitoring and checking of the work of religious organizations with the aim of guaranteeing maximum transparency.

Between 2008 and 2010, I directed research into the relationship between Philippine migrant associations and Philippine institutions, entitled *Migrant Associations and Philippine Institutions for Development* (MAPID). The large part of the migrants interviewed said they had lost their faith in homeland institutions, considered "to blame" in some way for their emigration (Baggio, 2010). On the other hand, the same migrants showed they placed much faith in the Catholic Church and in other religious organizations (Asis, Roma, 2010; Villarroya Soler, 2010; Zanfrini, Sarli, 2010). I had the opportunity to personally note similar situations related to other groups of migrants and in other geographical contexts. With regard to refugees, the loss of faith in authorities of their own country made up one of the main reasons of their forced migration. In many cases, the mistrust is not limited to countries of origin, but extends as a consequence also to those of the countries of immigration. Collaboration between institutions and religious organizations can favor the re-establishment of a relationship of trust between migrants and public authorities, generating fertile ground for an open and constructive dialogue. The opportunity to institutionalize that collaboration therefore appears evident, inviting representatives of the different religious organizations to participate in the committees and round tables on migration questions and integration processes.

Considering the presence of a considerable number of highly diversified stakeholders, it is appropriate for States to promote an inclusive and effective cooperation between the different religious organizations. It would be useful to entrust the institutions that are responsible with the task of coordinating the actions of religious organizations in favor of migrants and refugees, always with respect for the relative prerogatives and autonomies.

The importance of collaboration with religious organizations is clearly affirmed in the final draft of the "Global Compact for Safe, Orderly and Regular Migration": "We will implement the Global Compact in cooperation and partnership with migrants, civil society, migrant and diaspora organizations, faith-based organizations, local authorities and communities, the private sector, trade unions, parliamentarians" (UN, 2018b: 44). The final text of the "Global Compact on Refugees", after having included religious organizations among the "relevant stakeholders" in the division of responsibility for aid, at point 41 affirms that: "Faith-based actors could support the planning and delivery of arrangements to assist refugees and host communities, including in the areas of conflict prevention, reconciliation, and peace-building, as well as other relevant areas" (UN, 2018a: 41).

The same text also underlines the commitment of States to make the most of the potential of civil society, religious organizations and communications means "in fostering respect and understanding, as well as combating discrimination" (UN, 2018a: 84). Echoing that emphasis is the final draft of the "Global Compact for Safe, Orderly and Regular Migration", which indicates among the commitments foreseen by the agreement to:

> Engage migrants, political, religious and community leaders, as well as educators and service providers to detect and prevent incidences of intolerance, racism, xenophobia, and other forms of discrimination against migrants and Diasporas and support activities in local communities to promote mutual respect, including in the context of electoral campaigns. (UN, 2018b: 33)

For this reason, it is important that institutions make efforts to offer religious leaders and directors of religious organizations accessible training opportunities, aimed at the acquisition of the necessary skills for far-sighted guidance, conscientious teaching and a significant functioning in the migration sphere. Every investment in this sense will be generously repaid by results in the field. These offers of training, when they are capable of attracting representatives from different religious groups, could also ensure spaces of shared planning and favor the creation of operational networks.

The multiple services offered by religious organizations beyond the purely spiritual area are often entrusted to volunteers, whose generosity is not always matched by adequate training. To bridge this gap, institutions could create courses of certification and professionalization of skills for workers of religious organizations. These courses could also provide the same workers greater information on existing regulation around the services offered and on the possibilities and/or opportunities to redirect cases.

The inadequate consideration of the religious dimension in the provision of services on the part of institutions can produce serious problems, such as the formulation of judgements tainted by ignorance of the limits imposed by religious traditions, discrimination in access to services and the generation of hostile sentiment in some minorities. For this reason, it is appropriate for public officials to be educated on the essential elements of different religions, in particular on beliefs and religious practices that can have a strong impact on the social life of the faithful.

CHAPTER 16

The Multi-Ethnic and Multi-Religious Transformation of the Largest Diocese in the World: The Church of Milan and the "Synod from the Peoples"

Laura Zanfrini and Luca Bressan

Held in the middle of the largest refugee crisis of our time since the end of World War II, while the city of Milan was dealing with the arrival of thousands of desperate –yet filled with hope– people, the minor Synod was immediately regarded as an initiative with prophetic meaning.[1]

The Synod is the instrument through which the Catholic Church enables each Diocese, convened in a formal gathering under the rule of the respective Bishop, to better define its mission to both announce and be a witness to the Christian faith. The recently appointed Archbishop Mons. Delpini chose to start the highly challenging rewriting process of the previous Diocesan Synod (the 47th) with the chapter on the Pastorale degli Esteri[2] (literally "Pastoral of the Abroads", that is Pastoral of Foreign People) and took the occasion to remind the Church of its daily duty to be a witness to the Gospel. Through this Synod, the Church was reminded of the importance of practicing hospitality – "we can find ourselves welcoming angels without even knowing it"[3]– and was further encouraged to become a "Church *from* the People", thus fulfilling the ultimate aim of Catholicism.

This Church, as we will illustrate in this chapter, reflects the transformation of a city that has been changing considerably since the previous Synod, which dates back to the 1990s. In fact, both the Church and the city of Milan are facing the urgency to *find their own identity*. In this search, it is safe to say that the

---

1   This chapter is a translation, with minor changes, of an essay already published in an Italian version: Zanfrini L., Bressan L., 2018.

2   The previous Synod that took place in Milan was convened by Cardinal Carlo Maria Martini and was concluded in 1995. While the latter was meant to outline the general characteristics of the local Church, the one launched by Mons. Mario Delpini aimed at redefining every single trait of it. Such redefinition began with the examination of the trait that, in the past few decades, has been undergoing the most changes, due to the arrival in Milan of many people from very different places of the world.

3   Letter to the Hebrews, 13, 2.

Christian roots preserved by the Ambrosian rite –some kind of "Oriental echo in the West" (SC[4]: Focus group of Professors from the Faculty of Political and Social Sciences of Milan's Università Cattolica del Sacro Cuore, 22 February 2018)– can offer all the interpretation and communication tools that will help them find their place in today's global society and inside the universal Church.

The present chapter, authored by two members of the Coordinating Committee, is based on the information and suggestion collected through a public consultation launched at the beginning of the synodal process (started 15 January 2018 and continued until 1 April 2018).

1   On the Eve of a New Era: Milan as a Cultural and Religious
        Melting Pot

It is safe to say that the Church, through its many articulations –from parishes to Caritas facilities spread all over the diocesan territory, from religious congregations to Catholic movements, from the various associations to the numerous charismatic figures of the Catholic world– has been, in the past few years, one of the main actors on the Italian and Milanese reception scene (Chapter 10). It is surely thanks to the valuable experiences and competences gained over time that the local Church has managed to be actively helpful, despite a social climate marked by the aftermath of the economic crisis and by the growing concern towards migration and its impact on local communities. As proof of the Church mobilization, we can observe that the asylum-seekers hosted by parishes and accommodated in facilities associated with religious organizations, at the beginning of 2018, account for as many as 2,360. Besides, Catholic aid centers are also offering sanctuary to those who are officially denied asylum but who remain in the country of arrival illegally and have no other access to essential goods. Both newly arrived and long-time foreign nationals are today the main group of people who look for help in centers providing assistance to the poor – which is paradigmatic of the different needs of a society that is dealing with the consequences of an instability affecting not only the labour market, but social relations too.[5] Finally, the Church has always been there for people in need, even during the recent refugee crisis, in both formal and informal spontaneous ways. For example, by arranging Italian language courses in

4   From now on, we will use the acronym SC (Synodal Consultation) when referring to the documents either written or collected by the Synodal Coordinating Committee between 15 January and 1 April 2018. When available, the exact date was indicated.
5   Caritas Ambrosiana – Osservatorio diocesano delle povertà e delle risorse, *La fatica del fare comunità di cura. Un'indagine presso i centri di ascolto della Caritas Ambrosiana.* 16th Report on poverty in the Diocese of Milan, November 2017.

the local parishes, by organizing collections to help immigrant families, and by encouraging private citizens to either welcome migrants in their own houses, or –just to give an example– accompany them to their doctor's appointment or to the offices of the public administration, whenever they have to go.

As many observed during the synodal Assembly, it was the Ambrosian Church's hard work, as well as its pragmatism, that actively inspired the whole Catholic Church in its constantly prompt and generous responses to the different issues that need to be tackled. Moreover, all the Christian believers and all the members of the clergy who volunteer to take care of refugees and migrants act on behalf of the Church as they follow the example of the "good Samaritan" who helps strangers regardless of who they are. However, a corollary of this somewhat extraordinary capability to cause mobilization is a substantial lack of awareness of the profound changes that the migration issue is also introducing to the Church.

It is worth noting that, long before the refugee crisis started dominating the reception system, as well as the public debate on the short- and long-term impact of migration, Milan had become one of the main cultural, linguistic and religious melting pot in Italy and in contemporary Europe, too.[6] The sharp rise in the number of foreign nationals –an eightfold increase over the course of thirty years, i.e. 800,000 foreign residents as of today– has led to irreversible transformations in the ethno-cultural composition of Milan's population, as well as to the creation of many national and religious minority groups. Their considerable size has indeed modified the city's "public" profile, even if integration models –such as those dealing with occupational segregation– often make them quite invisible in social contexts. For instance, the first foreign community in the rankings in terms of presence on the metropolitan territory is the Filipino. As it is a very large community, it can be compared to a medium-sized Italian city, with over 40,000 residents only in the municipality of Milan. Besides, the beginning of the Filipino immigration process can be traced back to many years ago (the average migratory seniority is twenty years) – which is reflected in a large second generation and in an incipient third one. The same kind of observations can be made about many other national groups, as they are crucial in the outlining of Milan's current and future configuration, also because of their different migration patterns. In fact, some are largely male-dominated, some others have a clear prevalence of women; some are

---

6   In order to further examine this phenomenon, see the documentation available on the Synod website. Cf. especially: *Come l'immigrazione ha cambiato la Diocesi ambrosiana interpellandone la capacità di guardare al futuro*. In this document, you can also find the sources of the data discussed above.

characterized by temporary and circular migration, some others by long-term settlements sometimes ending up with the acquisition of the Italian citizenship, which, in the province of Milan, reached in 2016 an amount of over 16,000.

Reflecting the high transformative potential that migration has, there are data documenting how advanced its stabilization process is, with a migrant presence configuration becoming more and more family-based, a large proportion of migrants' children attending schools (i.e. over 160,000 foreign pupils) and, most notably, a high incidence of newborns with a migratory background (28% of babies born in Milan have foreign parents, and 37% have at least one foreign parent) – which is crucial in determining the generative potential of a Diocese that is somewhat growing older and older. However, there are also data showing how migrants leaving their countries either alone or with their families finally enjoy a fair amount of "success" (e.g. through the achievement of employment stability, the purchase of a house, or the start of a small-sized business) and reach relevant roles in the cultural and economic spheres. Indeed, the international students enrolled in the universities of Milan amount to no less than 12,000, while thousands of foreign professionals, managers and high-skilled workers find employment in industries such as finance, fashion, design and healthcare. It is safe to say, in fact, that Italians tend to forget that migration is characterized not only by people moving away from the southern countries of the world to look for a better life, but also by the so-called transnational hyper-bourgeoisie, i.e. a population that is part of an international network and whose behavioral and consumption patterns –along with its lifestyle, expectations and needs– are paradigmatic of a global interconnected society and are the result of social relations and changeable personal/professional life choices.

2 "The Church acts through the power of the Holy Spirit, not by law": Challenges and Opportunities Posed by the Religious Pluralism

By focusing our attention on religious affiliations, we can see that migration flows have not only provoked *a growth of all minority religions*, but have also triggered three phenomena, which have all proven meaningful for the future of Milan and the Ambrosian Church.

2.1 *An Identity Challenge and an Opportunity for Interreligious Dialogue*

The first phenomenon, which is the most emphasized in the political and media debate, is the *growth of Muslim residents*, who are an estimated 270,000 over the Diocese territory.

Such phenomenon, as observed during the consultation phase, has crystallized both the concern –with reference not really to security issues and *jihadist* fanaticism (which many do not consider as a high risk), but mainly to the identity issue– and the opportunity for an interreligious dialogue, as expected by Cardinal Scola (the predecessor of the current archbishop), who centered its episcopal ministry on how to reach this goal.

Muslims, in a way admired for the diligence with which they observe fasting and offer the daily prayers during Ramadan, are nevertheless typical of how hard interethnic coexistence can in fact be. To some, they represent the threat of a potential "clash of civilizations": the relationship between men and women –and especially the role of women in the Islamic culture–, is one of the most critical aspects affecting the perception of a social and cultural divide, or even incompatibility, between the Italian society and the apparently integrated Muslims.

On top of that, it is the presence of Islamic immigrants that fuel people's hostility towards immigration –hostility that must be explained from the broader point of view of the transformations occurred in the Italian society (SC: Focus with Movimento Terza Età, 16 March 2018). First of all, an ageing population; then, a large-scale unemployment, which affects most of all young people (who sometimes end up leaving Italy or being exposed to the "unfair competition" of newly-arrived migrants); a public debt accumulated over the years and subtracting resources from redistribution policies; the transformation of values and lifestyles, as well as the undermining of the local religious identity, which turns out to be inadequate to deal with other religious traditions (such as, first of all, the Islamic one), often interpreted by their followers in a more orthodox way. Some also act on the paradox according to which

> it is easier to recognize and respect the traditions of other religions (...) than the Christian one. Today, this happens because of an overall false sense of decency that somehow compels people to choose not to seem racist over looking like devout observant Christians. (SC: Young and Adults Group AC, Deanship of Missaglia)

Furthermore, if we move from a collective level to a more private one –for example, when it comes to dealing with our[7] children's marital and friendship choices or, more simply, with the "excessive" presence of Muslims in schools or in our neighborhoods–, the aspiration to behave in compliance with the dictates of the Christian doctrine collides with a widespread concern for the

---

7   In this text we use the terms "our" / "us" to refer to the indigenous (Catholic) long-term resident population.

possible problems that any relationships with those who are "too" different from us can cause.

However, these exact circumstances can become fruitful opportunities to "measure" our own faith and rediscover its contents. It is crucial to underline, in particular, the opportunity to search for connections, such as some specific aspects and values of a religion that are considered as to be universal and that, for this reason, can also be shared by those who originally have different religious traditions (see also Chapter 15). In order to find those connections, in fact, we have to focus on what unites, and not on what divides –and such aim is achieved by cultivating ecumenical dialogue, by helping the needy, by praying at the same time or in the same place (SC: Marceline Sisters of Albania, 1 March 2018), and finally by promoting those figures who, because of the "universal" character of their spirituality, can attract other cultures and religions (SC: Friars Minor Capuchins of Varese). It also fundamental to point out that dealing with people who show a great attachment to their original religious traditions, also because of their migrant status, can be a stimulus for Catholic believers.[8] Lastly, it is important to remind us all that only through a direct interpersonal relationship we can fight prejudice:

> If you do not want to meet the other people and you do not move away from your personal disinformation, you will express your judgment on the "types of religion", but you will not be able to really see the people behind them. (SC: Focus group with students from Università Cattolica, 22 March 2018)

2.2   A Spiritual Challenge and a Chance for the Development of Ecumenism

The second phenomenon is the "appearance", on the Milanese scene, of the *Orthodox Christianity* (whose followers are estimated to be over 100,000), most of all thanks to a large presence of women from Eastern Europe.

---

8   See, for example, the testimony of this religion teacher: "Once, in the classroom, I asked Catholic and Muslim children to discuss the traditional festivities of their religions. To my great surprise, this emerged: Muslim children talked with joy, pride, and sometimes nostalgia, about the typical festivities of their country, also recounting the profound meanings behind each festivity; Italian Christian children, who represent the Christianity of the West, showed a warm faith and barely expressed the profound meaning of Christmas and Easter, boiling Christmas down to receiving gifts". Also see the testimony of a university professor: "I must say that, on several occasions, some questions posed by the brothers and sisters of other religions made me feel ignorant about my faith and pushed me to fortify my ability to "justify" my belief".

As a reflection of the concentration of Orthodox (female) immigrants in definitely *sui generis* jobs (especially home-care assistants), this minority has long remained in the shadows until some caregivers (who, in Italian, are usually referred to as "*badanti*", which is a term that has a rather stereotypical connotation) started showing up for Mass, discreetly and silently, usually to accompany the elderly they assist or because there are no Orthodox churches in the surrounding area. The Italian term "*badante*" (from the verb "*badare*", to care for/to tend to) on the one hand intends to evoke the gratitude of the Catholic community for the carer's precious contribution (which can also be found in the choice of dedicating one of the meetings conducted by the Archbishop in the Cathedral during the 2018 Advent Sundays specifically to them); but on the other reveals the tendency to consider them not for who they are, but for what they do, in both the social and the religious space. As a result, they are stripped of their own individuality, as well as of their own faith, in order to place them in a specific professional category and therefore making Orthodox immigrants who do not share the same work destiny even more invisible.

Finally, the initiatives promoted to cultivate ecumenism –in particular the Week for Christian Unity– do not manage to be organized properly and end up being attended by very few people, thus becoming completely irrelevant to the pastoral practice of each parish community. With very rare exceptions, there are no significant relationships either with individual believers or with the organized communities.[9]

And yet, the awareness of the contribution that the Orthodox presence can bring to the rediscovery of a more authentic spiritual dimension of faith has emerged several times during the consultation; for the benefit of all the faithful and, in particular, as many observed, for the benefit of the clergy, "meeting other Christian Churches, such as the Orthodox Church, and start an ecumenical dialogue with them can make the consecrated people rediscover the essence of their lives" (SC: Daughters of the presentation of Blessed Virgin Mary in the Temple).

2.3   *A Pastoral Challenge and a Chance for Learning How to Engage in Self-Reflection*

The third phenomenon that we are going to discuss is the *arrival of Catholic migrants*. It is in fact on them –who are the living testimonies of the new

---

9 Among these exceptions, we can mention the initiatives undertaken by the Ecumenical Group of the Cantù Deanship, the fruitful work of the Council of Christian Churches of Milan, and the various initiatives promoted –in collaboration with the Orthodox Church and other Christian Churches– by the Community of Sant'Egidio.

Church from the people– that the attention must be focused, in order to grasp the ambivalence –which sometimes becomes indifference– of the attitudes towards migrants.

Thanks to immigration, there are about 233,000 "new" Catholics either gathered around the so-called ethnic chaplaincies or included in the everyday religious activities of the parishes of the Diocese or practicing their religion more sporadically.

The first observation that can be made after the consultation is that, despite the statistics documenting their conspicuous number, many parish communities do not really seem to notice the presence of Catholic immigrants, probably because of the different lifestyles and the different places of worship they attend, as immigrants either prefer liturgies and places reserved for them or manage to go to church without really being noticed – except in specific moments, such as the baptism of a newborn. However, even on these particular occasions they are unlikely to affect the life of the community in which they live.

Called upon on the occasion of the Synod, various parishes and deanships realized that they did not know much about their parishioners of foreign origin, and for this reason decided to conduct a "census" to estimate their number and better understand their situation. So far, in fact, the interest towards migrants has been shown especially in relation to their needs, without any distinction between Christian immigrants, agnostics or people of other faiths (see Chapters 10 and 12). Indeed, they are seen as the recipients of a "special" pastoral care –the "pastoral care of migrants"– a sort of "compensatory" pastoral care (to draw a parallelism with the compensatory pedagogy once used in schools) for those who have some "deficits" (at least of a linguistic nature) to tackle. It has also been noticed that some people tend to adopt attitudes of superiority towards them, or even feel annoyed by them, or suspicious, when for example their behaviors are considered to be unsuitable for holy places. One of the most striking case is that of an immigrant who used to help collect the offers during Mass and who was accused of trying to profit by it. Finally, we also need to mention the tendency to dismiss their religious manifestations as folkloristic.

As can be noted, there is some sort of resistance and a general sense of mistrust when considering giving tasks and responsibilities to the Christians coming from other nations, consequently recreating within the Church that subordination process that takes place in the labor market. Migrants' sense of inferiority, caused by their social role, is expressed in their propensity to self-ghettoization and gives rise to stereotyped expectations also as far as their roles in parochial activities are concerned. On top of that, not only are common believers not valorized; consecrated people, too, find themselves "filling the holes" in the religious orders that are short of vocations, and are appreciated only in relation to the tasks that their accomplish, especially if they are in the field of assistance.

The suburban areas, however, are significantly affected by the problems caused by an either poor or marginal immigration, and for this reason are deeply aware of how migration flows are indelibly transforming the composition of the neighborhoods, of the school populations, of the needs of the inhabitants, and of the ecclesial community. We can cite the parishes of via Padova, of the Barona neighborhood, and of the deanery of San Siro, which are areas where it is easy to observe situations of hardship, along with a few episodes of "interracial" conflict, but where, at the same time, it is possible to record experiences of mobilization from below, as well as practices of neighborliness and projects promoting the inclusion of newcomers and the construction of the common good. In many respects –and with a prophetic meaning– it is the "suburbs" (in a sociological rather than a geographical sense) that turn out to be authentic laboratories of interethnic coexistence in which the future of the Ambrosian Church is being written. As stated in one of the documents received,

> (...) the most intense context where the dialogue takes place is the one involving the most socially disadvantaged Italians, as immigrants find themselves in their life contexts. The care-givers deal with the elderly; workers find jobs in the least qualified areas of work, such as construction or manual work; students attend schools on the outskirts of the city; and the buildings are public housing buildings. (SC: Deanship of Gallarate)

Contrary to the threat of a "war between the poor", it is precisely in this context that the concern to not relegate foreigners to the margins of the community is manifested, along with the concern to not disregard their forms of popular piety. It is always in this context that, to quote the words of a priest, the focus is on overcoming formal "liturgical languages and styles, not limiting ourselves to proposing our traditions and celebratory forms, but being willing to be contaminated" (SC: Priests of the San Siro Deanship). It is not by chance, in fact, that it is more usual, here, for immigrant traditions to find space in the liturgy, for foreigners to sit in pastoral councils and among educators in the oratory, for catechesis to be "multi-ethnic".

Very often, however, immigration is not perceived in its transformative quality, and not even as an opportunity for self-reflection, i.e. an encouragement to reflect on both the present and the future of the local Church. In describing the evolution of interethnic relations, the assimilation solution is frequently used in order to indicate a non-problematic coexistence, where foreigners –who are not many and who are, at times, barely visible in the public space– are not considered as such anymore (as it used to happen during the internal migrations of the past decades), except in some critical situations when people are looking for someone to blame. To cite just a few examples, the extraordinary linguistic richness that immigration creates –easily seen in the Milanese cultural industry– cannot be found in the liturgy of the Ambrosian churches, which are basically still monolingual (and mono-cultural) –if we do not take into consideration the celebrations held specifically for foreign communities. In fact, Milanese Catholics are still not fully aware of the evangelization potential of immigration,[10] and that is because they tend to focus more on issues such as the violation of human rights or religious persecutions. Also, many migrant parents are not happy with the idea of raising their children in a society they perceive as "morally neutral" and, for this reason, different from what they had imagined when they were planning their journey to the cradle of Christianity. Besides, we can see how "old" and "new" Milanese (especially those who have left fundamentalist and oppressive regimes behind) need to be educated in the values of secularism –conceived in its deepest form– and of religious pluralism (see in this regard Chapter 11). We finally have to note that the needs, the skills and the potential of the aforementioned hyper-bourgeois are only partially recognized by the structures of the local Church. And that the same can be stated for the contribution of dozens of priests and other religious people coming from all over the world who are members of religious orders or work in diocesan institutions or in local parishes.

3   It Is Sowing Time: The Reasons behind the "Church from the People" Synod

To break the inertial mechanism with which the ecclesial body was responding to the many stimuli described above and, at the same time, to make the Christian communities, as well as the whole Diocese, become a reflection of their ongoing transformations, the new archbishop Mons. Mario Delpini decided to

---

10 In this case, too, there are some significant exceptions. For example: "The evangelization of the poor through charity is one of the clearest signs of the Kingdom of God. When this is achieved, it creates a dimension of positive and joyful proclamation that generates hope" . (SC: Community of Sant'Egidio, 30 March 2018)

use an instrument that was typical of periods of major change (such as in St. Charles Borromeo's times or, more recently, in Cardinal Schuster's). That instrument was the Diocesan Synod.

The Archbishop's declared aim for the "Church from the people" Diocesan Synod was to help the Diocese recognize the changes that are taking place in its *corpus* in order to remain faithful to the task that defines its identity – and that is serving as the instrument through which the Christian faith and God's message of love for everyone is announced.

3.1   *Inside a Tradition*

The Synod has not been created out of the blue. It was in fact the result of a process of dialogue started in the immediate post-war period. The Ambrosian Church has always paid attention to any changes taking place in the world around it, and has always tried to understand them and adapt to them, or even criticize them in an attempt to correct them. Cardinals Montini, Colombo, Martini, Tettamanzi and Scola have always done everything they could to keep the Christian faith alive in the urban context of Milan, which has always been marked by profound transformations. With the help of many Christians, they used to listen to every question they were asked, they tried the best to respond to all the requests for help they would receive, and they would do anything in their power to fulfill the hope of those wishing for a happy life – starting from the poorest and the marginalized.

The "Church from the people" minor Synod is part of this tradition. The Ambrosian Diocese participates in the synodal journey in order to remain faithful to a specific trait of the Church, which is the will to be there for those who look for help and for those who feel alone or struggle to decipher the meaning of every major change. The Ambrosian Church sets out on this synodal journey also to discover more about the Holy Spirit's plans inside these changes, and to offer everyone the fruit of this comprehension exercise, as it strongly believes that a more mature and incarnated Christian faith will create a brighter future not only for the ecclesiastical institutions and its pastoral bodies, but also for the people living in Milan and the institutions contributing to the development and the governance of the city.

3.2   *An Intense and Quick Journey*

The Synod was defined as "minor", since it focused only on a chapter of the text to be updated. It was active for a relatively short period time, as it began in November 2017 and ended on St. Charles Borromeo'day, 4 November 2018 – the connection with this holy pastor is deliberate: he was in fact the one who gathered the first synods to keep the ecclesial body up to date with what had been introduced by the Council of Trent. It activated an articulated and well-planned process that focused on listening and on dialoguing, thus leading the ecclesial body to a better understanding of the changes it has been experiencing, as it knows that the destiny of grace that God has in store for us must be sought inside those changes.

Many thought that such a short time would be not enough to complete such an important task, i.e. understanding and interpreting all major changes. In truth, the appointed time frame is perfectly in line with the code of communication typical of our contemporary culture: a longer time frame would in fact let the synodal theme fall behind many other urgent issues characterizing the life of individuals and communities; on the contrary, a shorter time can help focus more on what is really at stake. The Synod is conceived as a moment of awareness based on the idea that the changes the Christian communities need to make are above all cultural. It will take years to really put into action the insights and the signs of openness that the minor Synod has been showing within the Diocese.[11] With this in mind, everyone was welcomed to participate: women and men, lay people and clergy, individuals and families, people living a consecrated life and the new ecclesial realities, members of the Ambrosian Church for generations as well as newcomers, Christian believers and anyone else who is willing to take part in the construction of the Milan of tomorrow. The theme on which the Ambrosian Church has to express itself was well defined: as the title "Church from the people" clearly suggests, we must observe how, in a time of social and cultural changes, the operation of gathering of people that has been carried out for centuries by the Holy Spirit here in Milan is undergoing significant transformations.

3.3   *Milan, Church from the People*

For this mission to be successful, a Synod was certainly necessary. As it had been necessary in 1995, at the time of the 47th Synod promulgated by Cardinal Martini – although it is fair to say that the evaluation of its results did not concern such a wide scope as today. The Ambrosian Church was invited to go back to a particular chapter of that Synod, the one dedicated to Pastoral of Foreign People. As the reader can easily guess from the title, there was a clear need for this text to be adapted to the changes that have been taking place in the world around. The Ambrosian Church was asked to reinterpret this section of the Synod by focusing on a more specific dimension of its life and of its actions, i.e. the one that expresses its catholicity. This means understanding that, because

---

11   At the beginning of 2019, a special commission was established in order to implent the Synod's indications.

of the arrival of new people, the Ambrosian Christian communities have not only activated reception services and integration paths, but have also tried to encourage a fraternity among different people.

The purpose of this synodal path is eminently pastoral. Every Christian community and every ecclesial reality was invited to react to the questions posed by the synodal path. As a result, the Church was expected to become more aware of its catholicity and to do its best to translate this awareness into pastoral choices that are agreed upon across the diocesan territory. A Church from the people that, day by day, will be able to spread more serenity and more hope for the future even to the rest of the social body. The Ambrosian Christian communities will in fact have tools to better comprehend the very complex social and cultural situation that many tend to define, in a quite simplistic way, as "the phenomenon of migration". A Church from the people, a Church gathered in a Synod with the aim of remaining faithful to its Ambrosian identity – that is, as in the days of Saint Ambrose, in continuity with its spirit.

4   "The Church is bigger than our fences"

Migration scholars are very fond of the "mirror" metaphor. Indeed, if many themes and problems raised by the multi-ethnic and multi-religious transformation of Milan had already been outlined during the 47th Synod, we need to point out that although the immigrant population, today, has dramatically grown (and, with it, its incidence on the demographic profile of a city with an aging population), there is an increased awareness –at least among the "experts"– of the fact that the destinies of the city and of the Ambrosian Church are indelibly intertwined with that of immigration (if this is the word that we want to keep using when referring to it). Taking into consideration this mirror function is therefore a precious opportunity for a Church –and for a society– that wants to reflect on its own future.

To evoke one of the themes that has already emerged, but that we will not be able to discuss any further here, we will not be surprised to hear that the "good" integration (and the good coexistence) will not be built by migration policies (or, at least, not only by them), but rather by "good politics" itself, with both a government and a governance system truly oriented towards the common good. In this context, immigration helps lay bare the problems, bring a different perspective from which to look at things, and show the risk of "wars between the poor", especially where the social protection systems are flawed and where a sense of insecurity is more widespread: "The presence of people who migrate creates issues that must be faced" (sc: Focus with students from

Università Cattolica, 22 March 2018). As some explicitly claim, and as seen in many other documents, a renewed spirit of evangelical testimony displayed by Christians will not however be enough to solve the many problems that are affecting all the communities. For this reason, it is necessary to develop the idea of a society that is able to meet the need for more sustainable processes, and it will be in this framework that the management of new arrivals and the enhancement of the contribution of migrants will be placed (sc: Focus with Movimento Terza Età, 16 March 2018). Catholics will have to do their part in order to achieve this goal.[12]

In this light, the consultation has produced, we believe, some significant results. We will refer to them in a necessarily brief form, without further discussing the richness of the contributions received, and we will try to clarify some crucial matters, which indicate the emergence of the awareness of how Milan is, and must learn to think of itself as, one of the focal points of a truly universal Church, a reflection of a globalized society and, at the same time, the expression of catholicity at its deepest. Such awareness cannot help but make the Church come to terms with some implications regarding the various dimensions of its identity: its everyday life, its organization, its pastoral care, and its theology.

4.1   The Dimension of the Everyday Life

From the everyday life point of view, it is above all the young people who are confronted with this reality. They naturally live their destiny as global citizens, growing side by side, in a city that has become cosmopolitan, with peers who are more and more distant from the myth of ethnic, cultural and religious homogeneity on which our state communities had been founded. This reality, however, sounds less familiar and less "natural" to the adults and to the older generations, although they are more prone to religious practice and to participation in Catholic associations, therefore being more exposed to the values of Christianity.

This generation gap clearly suggests that the need to keep the traditions alive, the reluctance to include the novelty brought by immigration, and the issue of cultural identity, end up hiding the Church's effort to renew itself, to propose a liturgical and pastoral offer that is able to intercept the expressed and latent needs of the diversified population of the Diocese of Milan, with its variety of individual and family lifestyles. The decrease in the number of

---

12   An indication that was first taken into account after the establishment of the Commission for the common good that will support the Archbishop in the analysis of "social matters".

faithful who regularly attend Mass (particularly true for younger age groups), and an even more dramatic reduction in the amount of people who receive the Sacraments (especially baptism) is the most eloquent sign of this problem that, if not addressed, can become a real risk.[13] Nevertheless, this problem is also a providential warning:

> In our pastoral condition of parishes built in suburban areas and full of different people and cultures, it is clear to all of us that if we (*authors' note: the Western Church*) shut ourselves down we will surely disappear. The phenomenon of the drastic reduction in baptisms and marriages among Italians is well known. Further discussions on this interesting phenomenon could be carried out during the Eucharistic assemblies or while taking catechism classes. (SC: Priests of the San Siro Deanship)

The coincidence in time between the diocesan minor Synod and the world Synod dedicated to young people is perhaps a prophetic sign, which tells us of a Church –and of a society– called to renew itself, to "regenerate itself", through the activation of channels of dialogue, exchange, mutual fertilization between different generations. On the one hand, we can see that young people, as "exiles of the real meaning", have at heart the desire to overcome every inadequate behavior or language, and feel inevitably close to foreign people for being on the margins of a Church that they would like to be able to

> walk "with" them and to be more close to reality; a Church that is a "home" for everyone, and not just a club of friends; a Church that is open to the risk of encountering others. (SC: Focus group with students from Milan's Università Cattolica, 22 March 2018)

On the other hand, we have the elderly who, in order to fully play their role as witnesses/educators and as guardians of the values of humanism and catholicity, express the need to be the recipients of the "care" of the diocesan Church and of a project designed and created specifically for them (SC: Focus group with Movimento Terza Età, 16 March 2018).

---

13   "Our communities run the risk of becoming self-referential and closed in on themselves; their traditions could end up being excessively glorified to the detriment of a true Christian experience, continuously kept alive by the Holy Spirit; our habits, our order, our certainties could finally prevent us from "being fertilized and enriched"". (Pastoral Council of the Pastoral Community Paul VI, Paderno Dugnano)

4.2 *The Organizational Dimension*

At the organizational level, the Church's universal feature manifests itself in the numerous ethnic chaplaincies that welcome the faithful who come from other places, in the increasingly heterogeneous composition of the religious congregations present in the area, and in the presence of foreign priests who support the Diocese and the various parishes in their daily work. As stated in one of the contributions received, today the Church from the People is outside the door (SC: Presbyteral Assembly, Varese, 6 March 2018) and is linked, not only ideally, to the Ambrosian Church by a story of reciprocity.[14] However, the potential of this transformation still remains largely unexpressed.

Certainly, the most attentive observers can understand the precious role that foreign religious people play in all those areas where the presence of foreign users is increasing and, in particular in places of suffering, such as hospitals and prisons. They also make everyone more aware of the conditions of people living in other continents, showing us that we are actually "fortunate faithful". Besides, we can observe that the testimony of foreign religious people can attenuate the frenetic activism of the Ambrosian Catholicism, asking for more meditative and internalized ways of living one's faith:

> The sisters who have come from the Asian continent, who are more inclined to meditation and prayer than to activities, remind the people of the Ambrosian God, who is active and frenetic, to the foster the values of interiority, of relations and of Christian creativity. (SC: USMI Council, Archdiocese of Milan integrated by two non-European sisters, 22 February 2018)

In this regard, the presence of the Eastern-rite Catholic believers, such as the wide presence of the Orthodox Church in its various national declinations (Romanian, Russian, Bulgarian, Serbian, Greek, and also Coptic), make the Western declination of the Christian faith –very intellectual and very simple from a liturgical point of view– wonder how the gift of a God who reveals himself and who makes himself present by entering into a relationship with all dimensions of the human person should be lived today, in the current culture.

---

14   SC: "It is with affection and gratitude that we want to remind you that some of PIME (the pontifical institute for foreign missions) missionaries who came to us were from this parish: since they helped us learn more about the Christian faith, today we, too, would like to give our contribution to the local Church". (Sister Giustina Kalko, Shanti Rani Community, Valmadrera, 25 March 2018)

Once again at an organizational level, we can see that the missionary orders present in Milan, and their communities, carry in their *imprinting* a desire for openness that makes them inclined to collaboration as well as capable of "inhabiting change", as they reflect on the different ways that migrants have to live their religion. We can also observe that the Milanese missionaries scattered around the world can show the sensitivity of a Church that is a minority and that cannot impose itself, but that can still do little things that will not make it to the news, "but that will make a difference for those who live next to me" (SC: Father Paolo Ceruti, PIME missionary of Hong Kong); a Church that can become an intermediary between believers of different cultures and societies, as the Church really knows what it means to feel like a stranger (SC: Marcelline Nuns in Albania). Finally, the ethnic chaplaincies, often accused of contributing to the self-segregation of immigrant communities, start to be seen in a different light, thanks to the Synod, as they become important actors in the construction of the new "Church from the People", linking not only the immigrant communities and the Ambrosian Church, but also –and above all– the Ambrosian and the universal Church. Together with other religious orders, they "pose to the Ambrosian Church the challenge to achieve a universal opening" (SC: Community of Comboni Missionary Nuns).

However, as it is evident in this testimony, the universality of the Church is measured, first of all, by the ability to see in each person a Son of the only Father. It is precisely in this context that much still needs to be done, even within the boundaries of the Church:

> There is much to be improved even within the ecclesial community, which sometimes is not aware of the fact that acting on behalf of the Church means to act on behalf of the Spirit and not just by the rule of law; that being part of the Church means catholicity and openness to the world. Even though officially proclaimed, there is no real perception of the absolute equality of men as children of God in the Son – children who all carry, deep down, the image of the Father, who all wish to love and to be loved, who all have the same needs and the same feelings, and who are able to think and make decisions. (SC: Italian Conference of Secular Institutes)

4.3   *The Pastoral Dimension*

Moving on to the pastoral plan, as many have stressed, it is a matter of changing from "doing for" to "doing with" the migrants. Of course, we are not at year zero. The consultation was also an opportunity to measure the richness of the initiatives "generated" by the territories (from intercultural theater workshops to Italian language courses – which became, over time, places of confrontation and mutual re-evangelization). The opportunity offered by the Synod to make these projects known to a larger audience was much appreciated and managed to trigger a process of mutual fertilization. However, as we mentioned above, it is not easy for many to make room for immigrants and for their ways of living the faith and the liturgy – thus preventing their potential for evangelization and regeneration from being exploited. "Doing for" is certainly an expression of altruism and generosity, but when it turns into paternalism "it hinders the achievement of an authentic human relationship" (SC: Lay volunteers of the Missionaries of Charity, Baggio, 3 March 2018).

In any case, we can list a number of specific suggestions. Some are quite "obvious" and recurrent, like the hope that during the liturgical celebrations more space could be granted to migrant believers, for example by choosing them as readers (even if their linguistic competences are not perfect); by saying prayers in a foreign language; by introducing songs from their tradition; by presenting "their gifts" during the offertory; by sharing the celebration of the typical festivities of their countries of origin; by including some contributions in foreign languages in the parish bulletin; and by translating the leaflets for Mass and the various notices. Besides, it would also help if there could be a less ethnocentric approach during catechism classes; a mutual explanation of the meaning of the respective devotional practices; an effort to rethink the language and cultural patterns of the basic pastoral care; a more punctual reference (for example in homilies) to the Christian values and their concrete declination in the relationship with others (which must always be inspired by the principles of respect and equity); a valorization of the Pentecost events as tools to understand the current Church in the paths of education to the faith; the inclusion of non-European Saints in the liturgical calendar; greater appreciation of the foreign priests of the Diocese; preaching by using narrative and experiential dynamics; choosing prayers that are universally comprehensible and that actually give voice to what is happening in the world; implementing international mobility schemes (on the model of the Erasmus project) for new priests and religion teachers; promoting the study and the teaching of African and Latin American theology, as well as the Orthodox theology; offering courses on the different religious and liturgical traditions, inside and outside the Christian world, to pastoral workers and to all the faithful; and finally rethinking the ways in which

Catholicism has expressed itself: the Western modality, exported as the best one by the European missions of preservation during the colonial expansion, should be open to the changes historically brought by the different cultures. (SC: Diocesan pastoral Council, 24–25 February 2018)

As summarized by another contribution,

> we need to go from choosing to receive to choosing to meet; when receiving people, the relationship between those who welcome and those who are welcomed is not equal; on the contrary, when we meet people, our differences are recognized and valued as a gift and we all walk together carrying each other's burdens. (SC: Deanship of Cagnola, March 2018)

4.4   *The Theological Dimension*

Finally, as for the theological dimension, the challenge is to learn to reread the experience of faith, at the personal and at the community level, in light of the presence of Christians coming from other places and of believers of other religions, as well as in view of the growing number of agnostics and other people seeking alternative ways to express their spirituality. The importance of this challenge is effectively summarized by this testimony:

> The initiative of the Feast of the Christian Peoples helped us reinvigorate our faith; despite all the limitations encountered, it helped us understand that we are not superior, and that the Church is greater than what expected by its boundaries – which can be affirmed not directly for sociological reasons, but because of the original plan of God who wants all peoples to participate equally in the communion with his Son, Jesus Christ. (SC: San Siro Deanship)

As we have already pointed out, it is first of all the "suburbs" that will grasp the regenerative scope of this challenge. Conversely, by virtue of their experience marked by precariousness, many immigrants represent the "existential peripheries", namely the places where the Lord primarily manifests itself, according to the theology enunciated by Pope Francis.[15] In this perspective, there are many reasons behind immigration's potential for evangelization, especially if we consider that many of its protagonists have dramatic stories to tell, all marked by a lot of suffering and persecutions – thus encouraging us to seek a new socio-demographic, economic, political and democratic balance, as well

---

15   To further read about Pope Francis' theology, see: Cozzi, A., Repole, R., & Piana, G. (2016). *Papa Francesco. Quale teologia?*. Assisi: Cittadella.

as to deal with the ethical aspects of political choices, of the relations between countries, and of our daily behavior. In broader terms, there is a strong need to promote an intercultural approach, which invites us to put people and their relationships with other people at the center of attention, with each person meant as the "flesh of Christ". "We must not forget that the Church's task is first and foremost that of taking care of human relationships" (SC: Lay volunteers of the Missionaries of Charity, Baggio, 3 March 2018). In its most authentic meaning, inter-culture should give us the chance to look beyond people's countries of origin, on which we tend to focus too much, and

> to simply favor human relationships: we are all different persons, and we know it, but we can try to get to know each other and get together as human beings in order to enrich ourselves. (SC: Families of different nationalities from the Migrant Pastoral, Baggio, 24 February 2018)

It is only at this point that the authenticity of the Christian message can be grasped:

> We need to see people just as God sees them; therefore, the main focus should not be on immigrants, but on how we look at people, which should be in the same way as God does. (SC: Pastoral Council of the Deanship of Vimercate, 19 February 2018)

A message that, by its very nature, does not involve any distinction between migrants and non-migrants:

> Like the first Christian community in Ephesus, we have the opportunity to discover an even greater value to our faith, which is true when there is an authentic sharing and a felt reciprocity. This practice of a more attentive catholicity starts from the awareness that speaking of "foreigners" and of "migrants" is deeply improper (as it emerges in the Old Testament, the whole Church was born from the Jewish-Christian announcement) and creates what can be defined as the population "of the people", which is determined by God's plan for all humanity. It is in fact the universal Church that will be able to seize the new opportunities for enrichment and for an authentic evangelization that will come along, and it will do so through the creation of new relationships, which will closely follow the Christian message and which will be strongly inspired by the commitment of the incarnate Word. (SC: Pastoral Council San Vittore Martire parish)

5   "Seeing people as God sees them": Implications for the Pastoral
        Care and the Future of the Ambrosian Church

A first fundamental declination of this perspective is the way in which the Ambrosian Church should deal with migrants, in particular when it comes to the theme of spiritual accompaniment. The logic of interculturality, to which the Synod has further attributed the concept of "hybridization", can help the single Christians and all the communities remember that at the heart of the Church's birth and growth there is a true encounter between people. This allows them to see the presence of Christ in other people, as well as the gift that the Spirit offers to their faith, together with the need that they all have to support each other in the search for the only Father and in the understanding of God's plan for everyone. Thanks to the Synod, several Christian communities found out they had not been offering what migrants need the most: a spiritual accompaniment and support, as well as the possibility for them to feel in communion with God and "at home" even here, where they often feel in a foreign land. Such discovery manages to solve many problems concerning the relationships between natives and newcomers, thus preventing the latter from being considered as simple users of the services provided by the Catholic parishes and communities:

> Helping these brothers grow humanly and spiritually means to make them aware of their potential ability to offer a service to others. (SC: USMI Council, Archdiocese of Milan integrated by two non-European sisters, 22 February 2018)

> The Church can consider itself as open to the people not only if it manages to make these people feel accepted, but also if it helps them keep in contact with their place of origin, their culture, their language, their traditions and their religions. (SC: Father Paolo Ceruti, PIME missionary of Hong Kong)

A second, and even more important, declination of this perspective is the encouragement to recognize, and realize, the connection between unity and variety, as well as the idea of the "body of Christ as a unity in diversity", both in history and in the Church's life.[16] The Synod allows to decline the principle of "pluriformity in unity", taught in recent years by the Magisterium of Cardinal Scola. It is a matter of interpreting the differences in celebrating, in praying, and in bearing witness to one's faith as many different ways of expressing the

---

16   1 Cor 12, 19–20, 27.

same faith, the one that has been given to humanity, and that has been nourished by the Holy Spirit. Out of all the contributions from the consultation,
many of them go in this direction:

> We could also mention other examples drawn from the same narrative:
> people who, despite belonging to different cultures, feel united by the
> common Catholic Faith and by the wish that this Faith will not remain
> closed in a tabernacle, but will instead inundate every aspect of our life.
> (SC: CL Varese)

However, it is in particular the field of consecrated life that leads the way in
this experience:

> The communities that live a consecrated life, made up of people of differ-
> ent ages and of different social and cultural backgrounds, all throughout
> history have tried to embody the Father's plan to let all human beings be
> part of one big family united in love, without erasing any of their differ-
> ences. Moreover, it is in the care of the weakest that we can see the inclu-
> sive and missionary nature of the Christian faith. (SC: Daughters of the
> presentation of Holy Mary in the Temple)

> Our community life in itself is a sign of an inclusive and unconditional
> mutual acceptance that speaks of a single family with a single Father.
> Through community life, through a spirit of acceptance for all and by
> praying with everyone and for everyone, we can show people that we are
> the sons of the same Father (...). Our charisma brings the experience of
> other rites to the Ambrosian Church (...) and can help welcome other
> ways of praying and behaving, bearing in mind that, in the Church, there
> is room for everyone. (SC: Community of Comboni Missionary Nuns)

> The daily "effort" of our communities to experience interculturality as an
> opportunity to grow in love and trust is one of the gifts that the conse-
> crated life can offer to the Church, especially today. We feel the encour-
> agement to build a communion in communities made up of sisters from
> different cultures, thus showing that a conviviality of differences is com-
> pletely possible. (SC: Consecrated of the Forlanini Pastoral Unit, 22 March
> 2018)

As we notice by another testimony, it is from the orders of consecrated (and
cloistered) life that a precious –yet unexpected– teaching is passed on to the
Diocese:

> The efforts that we make day by day –all together as a choir or in silence–
> when we have to blend our voices in one single song of praise, is what we
> believe to be our contribution to the journey that the Diocese is making
> in the search for a spirit of communion among any cultural, social and
> ecclesial differences. (sc: Observation by the Benedictine Nuns of the
> San Benedetto Monastery)

Finally, a third declination of this perspective is the encouragement to question ourselves, to reflect on the profound meaning of being a Christian today in
the city of Milan, which is a city that is constantly changing. At this point, we
can really grasp the deep intention of the Synod, the fundamental reason behind its proclamation: when confronted with the social and cultural changes
around them, the only adequate response that Christians can give to themselves as Christians is that they, too, have to change; they have to change their
institutional subject and they have to create (by asking the Holy Spirit) new
ways to be part of the Church today. As cleverly observed by some from the
world of education:

> Living in a plural society, characterized by the coexistence of different
> faiths and cultures does not have to be a problem neither for Christianity
> nor for the Catholic Church. It used to be that way for the very first com-
> munities of believers, and it still is in many nations of the world. At times,
> it may even be seen as a providential opportunity, as it encourages Chris-
> tians to deepen their faith: this is what Peter used to suggest by warning
> about the importance of always being ready to give reason for one's faith.
> (sc: Catholic religion teachers of the Besta Institute of Higher Education
> in Milan)

Significantly, one of the most recurring aspects is the awareness –either acquired or strengthened when facing the "different"– of the need to regain "our"
Christian identity through the attempt to deepen the faith and to define the
personal and the collective identity of local believers. As stressed by many participants, only through dialogue can the local culture survive and open up to
change.

Many have observed, or at least perceived, that the re-appropriation of one's
own Christian identity is the first step towards an authentic dialogue with otherness; conversely,

> the difficulty of starting a dialogue is not necessarily due to the diversity
> of cultures; it rather depends on the weakening of our Christian values. In

> our society we tend to hide any possible reference to our faith, and that starts being true ever since our children's early education (...). Therefore, people should be braver when it comes to living and bearing witness to their faith in the world. (sc: Deanship of Carnago)

Finally, as a result of the encounter with other people, Ambrosian Catholics' faith becomes stronger and more aware of its universality. Contrary to what is usually believed, a dialogue is possible not only when one tries to acquire or broaden his/her knowledge of other faiths:

> I think that Catholics can really open up to others if they do become more aware of their own Catholic identity – which has nothing to lose (but much to gain) if compared with the other faiths, as they encourage us to further understand the reasons for our faith. (sc: Observation by a Religion teacher)

As it appears, the most tangible –and perhaps the most profound– result of the minor Synod is the acknowledgment of the need for a process of re-Christianization of the Ambrosian Diocese, namely the need for the Ambrosian Church to keep up with the present time in order to remain a friendly face of Christianity, close to the people's hopes and needs, in line with the model of popular Catholicism inherited from the past. As some priests and some paro-chial realities have pointed out, in order to achieve this goal, Catholics from other cultures and nations can be extremely helpful: from some communities of foreign Catholics, in fact, indigenous people could learn "a more authentic faith, a deeper devotion and a more lively liturgy" (sc: Deanship of Legnano, 14 February 2018), "the same careful attention to the liturgy and the Eucharistic celebra-tions, as well as a true sense of fraternity" (sc: Cassina de' Pecchi Pastoral Councils). Ultimately, to quote the words of a group of priests, it is necessary to

> focus more on that essential, on the Gospel and on the Eucharist, and therefore on the basics of our faith, in order to catch sight of the afore-mentioned openness towards "the others". (sc: Meeting of priests in San Pietro Cusico di Zibido San Giacomo, 15 March 2018)

We can finally observe that the Synod has strongly promoted the need for a re-Christianization, that is a re-appropriation of the past through a path of self-reflexivity, always with an eye towards the future and towards the new age that the current surge in migration flows is powerfully announcing. The Synod has in fact encouraged the adoption of a *dialogical style*, which –as the results of the consultation phase clearly demonstrate– can help raise awareness of the multiple implications of the transformations taking place around us. Finally, by supporting the adoption of a *participatory approach*, the Synod has given the communities a chance to reflect on their plans for their future, as well as on the future of the next generations and of the Ambrosian Church –a Church made up of people where there is, indeed, "room for everyone".

References to Part 4

Ahmad, N.N., Bhatti, K.A., & Arshad, M.U. (2013). Economic Growth and Human Development in Islam. *Al-Qalam*, December, 68–76.

Ajrouch, K.J. (2004). Gender, race, and symbolic boundaries: contested spaces of identity among Arab American adolescents. *Sociological Perspectives, 47*(4), 371–391.

Alba, R. & Foner, N. (2015). *Strangers No More: Immigration and the Challenges of Integration in North America and Western Europe.* Princeton: Princeton University Press.

Allievi, S. (2005). How the immigrant has become Muslim. Public debates on Islam in Europe. *Revue Européenne des Migrations Internationales, 21*(2), 135–163.

Allievi S. (2009). *Conflicts over mosques in Europe: Policy issues and trends* – Eurobarometer & Network of European Foundations for Innovative Cooperation, Alliance Pub. Trust.

Ambrosini, M. (2007). Gli immigrati e la religione: fattore d'integrazione o alterità irriducibile. *Studi Emigrazione, XLIV*(165), 33–60.

Ambrosini, M. (2014). Credere senza appartenere? O appartenere senza credere? interview with V. Premazzi, *Oasis*, December http://www.oasiscenter.eu/it/articoli/religioni-e-spazio-pubblico/2014/12/05/credere-senza-appartenere-o-appartenere-senza-credere.

Angeletti, S. (2018) L'accesso dei ministri di culto islamici negli istituti di detenzione, tra antichi problemi e prospettive di riforma. L'esperienza del Protocollo tra Dipartimento dell'Amministrazione penitenziaria e UCOII. *Stato, Chiese e pluralismo confessionale, 24* (https://www.statoechiese.it/images/uploads/articoli_pdf/Angeletti.M_Laccesso.pdf?pdf=laccesso-dei-ministri-di-culto-islamici-negli-istituti-di-detenzione-tra-an).

Archer, M., & Donati, P., (2012). Pursuing the Common Good: How Solidarity and Subsidiarity Can Work Together. In Sharkey, S.R. (Ed.). *Sociology and Catholic Social Teaching: Contemporary Theory and Research*, The Scarecrow Press, Lanham, Md., pp. 187–192.

Asis, M.M.B, & Roma, G.M. (2010). Eyes on the Prize: Towards a Migration and Development Agenda in the Philippines. In F. Baggio (Ed.), *Brick by Brick. Building Cooperation between the Philippines and Migrants' Associations in Italy and Spain.* Quezon City: SMC, pp. 35–137.

Atuguba, R.A. (2013). Equality, non-discrimination and fair distribution of the benefits of development. In OHCHR (Ed.), *Realizing the Right to Development*. New York: United Nations, pp. 109–116.

Baggio, F. (2000). *La Chiesa argentina di fronte all'immigrazione italiana tra il 1870 e il 1915*. Roma: CSER.

Baggio, F. (2007). Migrants on Sale in East and Southeast Asia: An Urgent Call for the Ethicization of Migration Policies. In M.C. Caloz-Tschopp, & P. Dasen (Eds), *Mondialisation, migration et droits de l'homme : un nouveau paradigme pour la recherche et la citoyenneté. Globalization, migration and human rights: a new paradigm for research and citizenship*, Vol. 1. Bruxelles: Bruylant, pp. 716–764.

Baggio, F. (2010). Introduction, In F. Baggio (Ed.), *Brick by Brick. Building Cooperation between the Philippines and Migrants' Associations in Italy and Spain.* Quezon City: SMC, pp. 1–33.

Baggio, F. (2014). Reflections on EU Border Policies: Human Mobility and Borders – Ethical Perspectives. In M. van der Velde, & T. van Naerssen (Eds), *Mobility and Migration Choices. Thresholds to Crossing Borders.* Surrey: Ashgate Publishing, pp. 167–181.

Bankston, C.L., & Zhou, M. (1995). Religious participation, ethnic identification, and adaptation of Vietnamese adolescents in an immigrant community. *The Sociological Quarterly, 36*(3), 523–534.

Bankston, C.L., & Zhou, M. (1996). The ethnic church, ethnic identification, and the social adjustment of Vietnamese adolescents. *Review of Religious Research, 38*(1), 18–37.

Bankston, C.L., & Zhou, M. (2000). De facto congregationalism and socioeconomic mobility in Laotian and Vietnamese immigrant communities: a study of religious institutions and economic change. *Review of Religious Research, 41*(4), 453–470.

Bankston, C.L. (1997). Bayou lotus: Theravada Buddhism in southwestern Louisiana. *Sociological Spectrum, 17*(4), 453–472.

Barylo, W. (2017). *Young Muslim change-makers. Grassroots charities rethinking modern societies.* London: Routledge.

Bassi, A., & Pfau-Effinger, B. (Eds) (2012). Lo spirito del welfare. *Sociologia epolitiche sociali, 15*(3).

Beaman, J. (2017). *Citizen outsider: Children of North African immigrants in France.* Oakland, California: University of California Press.

Benedict XVI (2009). *Address of his Holiness Benedict XVI to the Catholic Religion Teachers.* April 25.

Benedict XVI (2010). *Message for the Celebration of the 2011 World Day of Peace.* December 8.

Bertelsen, P. (2015). Danish preventive measures and deradicalization strategies: The Aarhus model. In Konrad Adenauer Stiftung (Ed.), *Panorama: Insights into Asian and European Affairs*, pp. 241–253 (http://www.kas.de/wf/doc/kas_42032-1522-2-30.pdf?150714075727).

Beydoun, K.A. (2017). Muslim Bans and the (Re) Making of Political Islamophobia. *University of Illinois Law Review* (5), 1733–1774.

Bichi, R., Introini, F., & Mezzetti, G. (2018). L'escalation jihadista in Europa: genesi e contromisure da una prospettiva ecologica. In Fondazione ISMU, *XXIII Rapporto ISMU sulle Migrazioni 2017.* FrancoAngeli: Milano, pp. 199–222.

Bleich, E. (2009). Muslims and the State in the Post-9/11 West: Introduction. *Journal of Ethnic and Migration Studies, 35*(3), 353–360.

Bolognani, M., & Statham, P. (2013). The changing public face of Muslim associations in Britain: coming together for common 'social' goals?. *Ethnicities, 13*(2), 229–249.

Borup, J., & Ahlin, L. (2011). Religion and Cultural Integration: Vietnamese Catholics and Buddhists in Denmark. *Nordic Journal of Migration Research, 1*(3), 176–184.

Bowen, J.R. (2006). *Why the French don't like headscarves: Islam, the state, and public space.* Princeton, Oxford: Princeton University Press.

Bowen, J.R., Bertossi, C., Duyvendak, J.W., & Krook, M.L. (Eds). (2013) *European states and their Muslim citizens. The impact of institutions on perceptions and boundaries.* Cambridge: Cambridge University Press.

Brannigan, M.C. (2005). *Ethics across Cultures: An Introductory Text with Readings.* New York: McGraw-Hill Education.

Brubaker, R. (2013). Categories of analysis and categories of practice: A note on the study of Muslims in European countries of immigration. *Ethnic and Racial Studies, 36*(1), 1–8.

Brubaker, R. (2017). Between nationalism and civilizationism: the European populist moment in comparative perspective. *Ethnic and Racial Studies, 40*(8), 1191–1226.

Brunn, C. (2012). *Religion im Fokus der Integrationspolitik: Ein Vergleich zwischen Deutschland, Frankreich und dem Vereinigten Königreich.* Wiesbaden: Springer VS.

Buber-Ennser, I., Goujon A., Kohlenberger, J., & Rengs, B. (2018). Multi-Layered Roles of Religion among Refugees Arriving in Austria around 2015. *Religions, 9*(5), 154.

Burgat, F. (2016). *Comprendre l'islam politique. Une trajectoire de recherche sur l'altérité islamiste, 1973–2016.* Paris: La Découverte.

Cadge, W. Levitt, P., Jaworsky, B.N., & Clevenger, C. (2013). Religious Dimensions of Contexts of Reception: Comparing Two New England Cities. *International Migration, 51*(3), 84–98.

Cainkar, L.A. (2009). *Homeland insecurity: the Arab American and Muslim American experience after 9/11.* New York: Russell Sage Foundation.

Campion, P. (2003). One under God? Religious entrepreneurship and pioneer Latino immigrants in southern Louisiana. *Sociological Spectrum, 23*(2), 279–301.

Cao, N. (2005). The church as a surrogate family for working class immigrant Chinese youth: an ethnography of segmented assimilation. *Sociology of Religion, 66*(2), 183–200.

Carnes, T. (2004). Faith, values, and fears of New York City Chinatown seniors. In T. Carnes, & F. Yang (Eds), *Asian American Religions: The Making and Remaking of Borders and Boundaries.* New York: New York University Press, pp. 223–244.

Carter, S.L. (1993). *The Culture of Disbelief.* New York: Basic Books.

Casanova, J., & Zolberg, A. (2002). *Religion and Immigrant Incorporation in New York.* Paper presented at the conference on Immigrant Incorporation in New York, The New School.

Casanova, J. (2000). *Oltre la secolarizzazione*. Bologna: Il Mulino.

Castle, S., de Haas, H, & Miller, M. (2014). *The Age of Migration*. New York: Guilford.

Celermajer, D. (2007). If Islam is our other, who are 'we'? *Australian Journal of Social Issues, 42*(1), 103–123.

Césari, J. (2004). *When Islam and democracy meet. Muslims in Europe and in the United States*. New York; Basingstoke: Palgrave Macmillan.

Césari, J. (2011). Islamophobia in the West: A Comparison between Europe and the United States. In J.L. Esposito, & I. Kalin (Eds), *Islamophobia. The Challenge of Pluralism in the 21st Century*. Oxford: Oxford University Press, pp. 21–43.

Cesari, J. (2013). *Religion and Diasporas: Challenges of the Emigration Countries*. San Domenico di Fiesole: European University Institute.

Césari, J. (2013). *Why the West fears Islam. An exploration of Muslims in liberal democracies*. New York: Palgrave Macmillan US.

Chai, K.J. (1998). Competing for the second generation: English-language ministry at the Korean Protestant church. In R.S. Warner, & J.G. Wittner (Eds), *Gatherings in Diaspora: Religious Communities and the New Immigration*, Philadelphia: Temple University Press, pp. 295–331.

Chbib, R. (2016). *Muslim Perspectives on the Immigration and Integration Debate in Germany Today*. American Institute for Contemporary German Studies (AICGS) (https://www.aicgs.org/publication/muslim-perspectives-on-the-immigration-and-integration-debate-in-germany-today/).

Chen, C. (2002). The religious varieties of ethnic presence: a comparison between a Taiwanese immigrant Buddhist temple and an evangelical Christian Church. *Sociology of Religion, 63*(2), 215–238.

Cnaan, R.A. (1997). *Social and Community Involvement of Religious Congregations Housed in Historic Religious Properties: Findings from a Six-City Study*. Philadelphia: Program for the Study of Organized Religion and Social Work.

Colozzi, I. (1999). *Lineamenti di sociologia della religione*. Padova: Cedam.

Colozzi, I. (2001). "Matrice teologica" e società civile. In P. Donati, & I. Colozzi (Eds), *Religione, società civile e stato: quale progetto?* Bologna: Edizioni Dehoniane, pp. 13–50.

Colozzi, I. (2016). Laicità. In P. Terenzi, L. Boccacin, & R. Prandini, (Eds), *Lessico della sociologia relazionale*, Bologna: Il Mulino, pp. 147–151.

Connor, P. (2012). Balm for the Soul: Immigrant Religion and Emotional Well-Being. *International Migration, 50*(2), 130–157.

Corriere della Sera (2015). *Calais: la speranza dei migranti che fa sorgere chiese, moschee, scuole* (http://www.corriere.it/foto-gallery/esteri/15_agosto_09/francia-giungla-calais-migranti-costruiscono-chiese-moschee-scuole-di-fortuna-4ce9f7b2-3ec2-11e5-9ebf-dac2328c7227.shtml).

Council on American-Islamic Relations (2016). *Confront Fear: Islamophobia and its Impact in the United States.* Washington: Council on American-Islamic Relations.

Dessing, N.M. (2013). How to study everyday Islam. In N.M. Dessing, N. Jeldtoft, J.S. Nielsen, & L. Woodhead (Eds), *Everyday lived Islam in Europe.* London: Ashgate, pp. 39–52.

Diehl, C., & Koenig, M. (2013). God Can Wait. New Migrants in Germany between Early Adaptation and Religious Reorganization. *International Migration, 3*(51), 8–22.

Donati, P. (1991). *Teoria relazionale della società.* Milano: FrancoAngeli (English translation: (2011). *Relational Sociology. A New Paradigm for the Social Sciences,* London-New York: Routledge).

Donati, P. (2000). *La cittadinanza societaria, II edizione riveduta e ampliata.* Rome-Bari: Laterza.

Donati, P. (2008). La laicità in una società multiculturale: declinare le differenze con "ragione relazionale". In P. Donati (Ed.), *Oltre il multiculturalismo La ragione relazionale per un mondo migliore.* Rome-Bari: Laterza, pp. 141–203.

Donati, P. (2013). From Multiculturalism to Interculturality through the Relational Reason. *Memorandum,* 24, pp. 133–167.

Donati, P. (Ed.) (2010). *La matrice teologica della società.* Soveria Mannelli: Rubbettino Editore.

Dorais, L.J. (2007). Faith, hope and identity: religion and the Vietnamese refugees. *Refugee Survey Quarterly,* 2(26), 57–68.

Dupré, A. (2008). What Role Does Religion Play in the Migration Process?. *Mozaik* (1), 7–11.

Ebaugh, E.R. (2010). Transnationality and religion in immigrant congregations: the global impact. *Nordic Journal of Religion and Society, 23*(2), 105–119.

Ebaugh, H.R., & Chafetz, J.S. (Eds) (2000). *Religion and the New Immigrants: Continuities and Adaptations in Immigrant Congregations,* Walnut Creek, CA: AltaMira Press.

Ebaugh, H.R., & Pipes P. (2001). Immigrant congregations as social service providers: Are they safety nets for welfare reform?. In P. Nesbitt (Ed.), *Religion and Social Policy.* Walnut Creek, CA: AltaMira, pp. 95–110.

Eck, D. (2001). *A New Religious America.* New York, NY: HarperCollins.

Ecklund, E.H. (2006). *Korean American Evangelicals: New Models for Civic Life.* New York, NY: Oxford University Press.

Espinosa, G., Elizondo, V., & Miranda, J. (2003). *Hispanic churches in American public life: summary of findings.* Interim Report n.2, Notre Dame, IN: Institute for Latino Studies, University of Notre Dame.

Fasching, D, & Dechant, D. (2001). *Comparative Religious Ethics. A Narrative Approach.* Malden: Wiley-Blackwell.

Fiddian-Qasmiyeh, E., & Qasmiyeh, Y.M. (2010). Muslim Asylum-Seekers and Refugees: Negotiating Identity, Politics and Religion in the UK. *Journal of Refugee Studies*, 23(3), 294–314.

Foley, M., & Hoge, D. (2007) *Religion and the New Immigrants: How Faith Communities Form Our Newest Citizens*. New York, NY: Oxford University Press.

Foner, N., & Alba, R. (2008). Immigrant Religion in the U.S. and Western Europe: Bridge or Barrier to Inclusion. *International Migration Review*, 42(2), 360–392.

Fox, N. (2012). "God Must Have Been Sleeping": Faith as an Obstacle and a Resource for Rwandan Genocide Survivors in the United States. *Journal for the Scientific Study of Religion*, 51(1), 65–78.

Francis (2014). *Meeting with the leaders of other religions and other Christian denominations*. September 21.

Francis (2017). *Message for the World Day of Migrants and Refugees 2018*. August 15.

Frederiks, M. (2016). Religion, Migration, and Identity. A Conceptual and Theoretical Exploration. In M. Fredericks, & D. Nagy (Eds), *Religion, Migration and Identity. Methodological and theological explorations*. Leiden: Brill, pp. 9–29.

Fredette, J. (2014). *Constructing Muslims in France. Discourse, public identity, and the politics of citizenship*. Philadelphia: Temple University Press.

Frisina, A. (2010). Young Muslims' everyday tactics and strategies: Resisting Islamophobia, negotiating Italianness, becoming citizens. *Journal of Intercultural Studies*, 31(5), 557–572.

GALLUP – The Coexist Foundation (2009). *The Gallup Coexist Index 2009: A Global Study of Interfaith Relations* (https://ec.europa.eu/migrant-integration/librarydoc/the-gallup-coexist-index-2009-a-global-study-of-interfaith-relations).

García-Muñoz, T., & Neuman, S. (2012). *Is Religiosity of Immigrants a Bridge or a Buffer in the Process of Integration? A Comparative Study of Europe and the United States*. Discussion Paper no. 6384, Bonn: Institute for the Study of Labor (IZA) (http://ftp.iza.org/dp6384.pdf).

Garner, S., & Selod, S. (2015). The racialization of Muslims: empirical studies of Islamophobia. *Critical Sociology*, 41(1), 9–19.

Geisser, V. (2015). Éduquer à la laïcité, rééduquer au "bon islam" ? Limites et dangers des réponses culturalistes et misérabilisties au terrorisme. *Migrations Société*, 157, 3–14.

Gil-Bazo, M.T. (2015). Asylum as a General Principle of International Law. *International Journal of Refugee Law*, 1(27), 3–28.

Gordon, M.M. (1964). *Assimilation in American Life*. New York: Oxford University Press.

Greimas, P.C. (1974). *Elementi per una grammatica narrativa*. Milan: Bompiani.

Guest, K.J. (2003). *God in Chinatown: Religion and Survival in New York's Evolving Immigrant Community*. New York: NY Univ. Press.

Guptara, P. (1998). Ethics across Cultures. *RSA Journal*, 5485(146), 30–33.

Habermas, J., & Ratzinger, J. (2005). *Ragione e fede in dialogo*. Venice: Marsilio.

Hagan, J. (2008). *Migration Miracle: Faith, Hope, and Meaning on the Undocumented Journey*. Cambridge, MA: Harvard University Press.

Hagan, J., & Ebaugh, H.R. (2003). Calling upon the Sacred: Migrants' Use of Religion in the Migration Process. *International Migration Review, 4*(37), 1145–1162.

Handlin, O. (1951). *The Uprooted: The Epic Story of the Great Migrations that Made the American People*. Boston: Little Brown and Company.

Henkel, R., & Knippenberg H. (2005). Secularisation and the Rise of Religious Pluralism: Main Features of the Changing Religious Landscape of Europe. In H. Knippenberg (Ed.), *The Changing Religious Landscape of Europe*. Amsterdam: Het Spinhuis, pp. 1–13.

Herberg, W. (1960). *Protestant, Catholic, Jew*. New York, NY: Anchor Books.

Hervieu-Léger, D., (2003). *Il pellegrino e il convertito. La religione in movimento*. Bologna: Il Mulino.

Hirschman, A.O. (1970). *Exit, Voice, and Loyalty: Responses to Decline in Firms, Organizations, and States*. Cambridge, MA: Harvard University Press.

Hirschman, C. (2004). The role of religion in the origin and adaptation of immigrant groups in the United States. *International Migration Review, 38*(3), 1206–1233.

Hunt, S. (2005). *Religion and everyday life*. London: Routledge.

Huntington, S. (1993). *The Clash of Civilizations and the Remaking of World Order*. London: Simon and Schuster.

Husain, A., & Howard, S. (2017). Religious Microaggressions: A Case Study of Muslim Americans. *Journal of Ethnic & Cultural Diversity in Social Work, 26*(1/2), 139–152.

Introini, F. (2017). *Religione e radicalizzazione. Un nesso che sfida l'Occidente*. Paper ISMU, (http://www.ismu.org/religione-e-radicalizzazione-un-nesso-che-sfida-loccidente/).

Jackson, D., & Passarelli, A. (2016). *Mapping Migration, Mapping Churches' Responses in Europe. Belonging, Community and Integration: The Witness and Service of Churches in Europe*. Geneva-Brussels: WCC.

Jeldtoft, N. (2011). Lived Islam: Religious identity with 'non-organized' Muslim minorities. *Ethnic and Racial Studies, 34*(7), 1134–1151.

Jeldtoft, N. (2013). The hypervisibility of Islam. In N.M. Dessing, N. Jeldtoft, J.S. Nielsen, & L. Woodhead (Eds), *Everyday lived Islam in Europe*. London: Ashgate, pp. 23–37.

Jeldtoft, N., & Nielsen, J. (2011). Introduction: Methods in the study of 'non-organized' Muslim minorities. *Ethnic and Racial Studies, 34*(7), 1113–1119.

Johansen, B.S., & Spielhaus, R. (2012). Counting Deviance: Revisiting a Decade's Production of Surveys among Muslims in Western Europe. *Journal of Muslims in Europe, 1*(1), 81–112.

John Paul II (2005). *Address of Pope John Paul II to Spanish Bishops on their Ad Limina visit*. January 24.

John Paul II (2001). *Post-Synodal Apostolic Exhortation Ecclesia in Oceania*, November 22.

Joppke, C. (2009). Limits of Integration Policy: Britain and her Muslims. *Journal of Ethnic and Migration Studies*, 35(3), 453–472.

Joppke, C., & Torpey, J. (2013). *Legal Integration of Islam*. Cambridge, MA: Harvard University Press.

Kepel, G. (2012). *Quatre-vingt-treize*. Paris: Gallimard.

Kim, R.Y. (2011). Religion and Ethnicity: Theoretical Connections. *Religions*, 2(3), 312–332.

Kivisto, P. (2014). *Religion and Immigration: Migrant Faiths in North America and Western Europe*. Hoboken, NJ: John Wiley & Sons.

Klausen, J. (2005). *The Challenge of Islam: Politics and Religion in Western Politics*, Oxford: Oxford University Press.

Klausen, J. (2009). Muslims representing Muslims in Europe: parties and associations. In A. Sinno. (Ed.). *Muslims in Western Politics*. Bloomington: Indiana University Press, pp. 96–112.

Korteweg, A., & Yurdakul, G. (2009). Islam, Gender, and Immigrant Integration: Boundary Drawing in Discourses on Honour Killing in the Netherlands and Germany. *Ethnic and Racial Studies*, 32(2), 218–238.

Krotofil, J., & Motak, D. (2018). Between Traditionalism, Fundamentalism, and Populism: A Critical Discourse Analysis of the Media Coverage of the Migration Crisis in Poland. In U. Schmiedel, & G. Smith (Eds), *Religion in the European Refugee Crisis*. Basingstoke: Palgrave Macmillan, pp. 61–85.

Kurien, P. (1998). Becoming American by Becoming Hindu: Indian Americans Take Their Place at the Multicultural Table. In R.S. Warner, & J.G. Wittner (Eds), *Gatherings in Diaspora: Religious Communities and the New Immigration*. Philadelphia, PA: Temple University Press, pp. 37–70.

Kurien, P. (2001). Religion, ethnicity, and politics: Hindu and Muslim Indian immigrants in the United States. *Ethnic and Racial Studies*, 24(2), 263–293.

Kurien, P. (2002). We are Better Hindus Here: Religion and Ethnicity among Indian Americans. In P. G. Min, & J.H. Kim (Eds), *Religions in Asian America. Building Faith Communities*. Walnut Creek: Altamira Press, pp. 99–120.

Kurien, P. (2014). Immigration, community formation, political incorporation, and why religion matters: Migration and settlement patterns of the Indian Diaspora. *Sociology of Religion*, 75(4), 524–536.

Kurtz, L.R. (2000). *Le religioni nell'era della globalizzazione*. Bologna: Il Mulino.

Kuru, A.T. (2009). *Secularism and State Policies toward Religion: The United States, France, and Turkey*. Cambridge: Cambridge University Press.

Kyoung Ok, S., & Lee R.M. (2012). The Effects of Religious Socialization and Religious Identity on Psychological Functioning in Korean American Adolescents from Immigrant Families. *Journal of Family Psychology*, *26*(3), 371–80.

Laurence, J., (2012). *The emancipation of Europe's Muslims. The state's role in minority integration*. Princeton, N.J.: Princeton University Press.

Laurence, J., & Vaisse, J. (2006). *Integrating Islam. Political and religious challenges in contemporary France*. Washington, D.C.: Brookings Institution Press.

Leal, D.L., Barreto, M.A., Lee, J., & de la Garza, R. (2005). The Latino vote in the 2004 election. *PS: Political Science & Politics*, *38*(1), 41–49.

Lean, N.C. (2017). Mainstreaming Anti-Muslim Prejudice: The Rise of the Islamophobia Industry in American Electoral Politics. In N. Massoumi, T. Mills, & D. Miller (Eds), *What is Islamophobia? Racism, Social Movements and the State*. London: PlutoPress, pp. 123–136.

Levitt, P. (2002). Two nations under God? Latino religious life in the U.S. In M.M. Suárez-Orozco, & M. Páez (Eds), *Latinos: Remaking America*. Berkeley: University of California Press, pp. 150–64.

Levitt, P. (2007). Rezar por encima de las fronteras: cómo los inmigrantes están cambiando el panorama religioso. *Migración y Desarrollo*, 8, 76–77.

Levitt, P. (2008). Religion as a path to civic engagement. *Ethnic and Racial Studies*, *31*(4), 766–791.

Lewis, V.A., & Kashyap, R. (2013). Piety in a secular society: Migration, religiosity, and Islam in Britain. *International Migration*, *51*(3), 57–66.

Lien, P. (2004). Religion and political adaptation among Asian Americans: an empirical assessment from the Pilot National Asian American Political Survey. In T. Carnes, & F. Yang (Eds), *Asian American Religions: The Making and Remaking of Borders and Boundaries*. New York, NY: New York University Press, pp. 263–286.

Lopez, D. (2009). Whither the Flock? The Catholic Church and the Success of Mexicans in the United States. In R. Alba, A. Roboteau, & J. De Wind (Eds), *Religion, Immigration and Civic Life in America*. New York, NY: New York University Press.

Lyck-bowen, M., & Owen, M. (2018). A multi-religious response to the migrant crisis in Europe: A preliminary examination of potential benefits of multireligious cooperation on the integration of migrants. *Journal of Ethnic and Migration Studies*, 1 (45), 21–41.

Mahmood, S. (2005). *Politics of piety: The Islamic revival and the feminist subject*. Princeton, NJ, Oxford: Princeton University Press.

Mandaville, P. (2001). Reimagining Islam in diaspora: The politics of mediated community. *International Communication Gazette*, *63*(2–3), 169–186.

Maritain J. (1996), *Integral Humanism: Freedom in the Modern World, and A Letter on Independence*. Notre Dame: University of Notre Dame Press.

Massari, M. (2006). *Islamofobia. La paura e l'Islam*. Roma-Bari: Laterza.

Mattes, A. (2017). Who We Are Is What We Believe? Religion and Collective Identity in Austrian and German Immigrant Integration Policies. *Social Inclusion*, 5(1), 93–104.

Mattes, A. (2018). How religion came into play: 'Muslim' as a category of practice in immigrant integration debates. *Religion, State & Society*, 46(3), 186–205.

Mavelli, L., & Wilson, E. (Eds) (2016). *The Refugee Crisis and Religion: Secularism, Security and Hospitality in Question*. London: Rowman & Littlefield.

May S., Wilson E.K., Baumgart-Ochse C., & Sheikh, F. (2014). The Religious as Political and the Political as Religious: Globalisation, Post-Secularism and the Shifting Boundaries of the Sacred. *Politics Religion and Ideology*, 15(3), 331–346.

McAllister, P.A. (1980). Work, Homestead and the Shades: The Ritual Interpretation of Labour Migration Among the Gcaleka. In P. Mayer (Ed.), *Black Villagers in an Industrial Society*. Cape Town: Oxford University, pp. 205–252.

Meda, S.G. (2016). Interculturalità e multiculturalismo. In P. Terenzi, L. Boccacin, & R. Prandini (Eds). *Lessico della sociologia relazionale*. Bologna: Il Mulino, pp. 137–142.

MEIC (2008). *Materiali sul Dialogo Interreligioso discussi nel Gruppo di Lucca* (http://www.meic.net/allegati/files/2011/07/18682.pdf).

Menjivar, C. (2001). Latino immigrants and their perceptions of religious institutions: Cubans, Salvadorans, and Guatemalans in Phoenix, Arizona. *Migraciones Internacionales*, 1(1), 65–88.

Menjivar, C. (2003). Religion and immigration in comparative perspective: Catholic and evangelical Salvadorans in San Francisco, Washington D.C., and Phoenix. *Sociology of Religion*, 64(1), 21–45.

Migrants and Refugees Section (2017). *20 Action Points for the Global Compacts*. Vatican City: LEV.

Min, P.G. (1992). The structure and social functions of Korean immigrant churches in the United States. *International Migration Review*, 26(4), 1370–1394.

Min, P.G. (2005). Religion and the maintenance of ethnicity among immigrants: a comparison of Indian Hindus and Korean Protestants. In K.I. Leonard, A. Stepick, M.A. Vasquez, & J. Holdaway (Eds), *Immigrant Faiths: Transforming Religious Life in America*. Walnut Creek: AltaMira Press, pp. 99–122.

Modood, T. (2018). *Islamophobia: A Form of Cultural Racism*. A Submission to the All-Party Parliamentary Group on British Muslims in response to the call for evidence on 'Working Definition of Islamophobia, 1 June.

Modood, T., Triandafyllidou, A., & Zapata-Barrero, R. (Eds) (2006). *Multiculturalism, Muslims and citizenship: A European approach*. London: Routledge.

Munshi, K. (2003). Networks in the Modern economy: Mexican Migrants in the U.S. Labor Market. *Quarterly Journal of Economics*, 8(2), 549–597.

Nagel, C. (2016). Southern Hospitality? Islamophobia and the Politicization of Refugees in South Carolina During the 2016 Election Season. *Southeastern Geographer, 56*(3), 283–290.

Nagy, D., & Frederiks, M. (2016). Introduction. In M. Fredericks, & D. Nagy (Eds), *Religion, Migration and Identity. Methodological and theological explorations.* Leiden: Brill, pp. 1–8.

Ng, K.H. (2002). Seeking the Christian tutelage: agency and culture in Chinese immigrants' conversion to Christianity. *Sociology of Religion, 63*(2), 195–214.

Niebuhr, G. (2007). All Need Toleration: Some Observations about Recent Differences in the Experiences of Religious Minorities in the United States and Western Europe. *Annals of the American Academy of Political and Social Science, 612,* 172–186.

Nielsen, J.S. (2013). Concluding reflections: Everyday lived Islam and the future of Islamic studies. In N.M. Dessing, N. Jeldtoft, J.S. Nielsen, & L. Woodhead (Eds), *Everyday lived Islam in Europe.* London: Ashgate, pp. 163–177.

Niclsen, K. (1990). *Ethics Without God.* New York: Prometheus Books.

Open Society Justice Initiative (2016). Eroding Trust: The UK's PREVENT Counter-Extremism Strategy in Health and Education. New York: Open Society Foundations. (https://www.justiceinitiative.org/publications/eroding-trust-uk-s-prevent-coun ter-extremism-strategy-health-and-education).

Papademetriou, D.G., Alba, R., Foner, N., & Banulescu-Bogdan, N. (2016). *Managing Religious Difference in North America and Europe in an Era of Mass Migration.* Washington DC, Migration Policy Institute.

Parliament of the World's Religions (1993). *Toward A Global Ethic* (https://parliamento-freligions.org/sites/default/files/Global%20Ethic%20booklet%20final.pdf).

Parsons, T. (1951). *The Social System.* New York: Free Press.

PEW (2011). *The American-Western European Values Gap.* Pew Global Attitudes & Trends Project. (https://www.pewresearch.org/global/2011/11/17/the-american-western-european-values-gap/).

PEW (2012). *Faith on the Move: The Religious Affiliation of International Migrants.* Pew Religion & Public Life Project. (https://www.pewforum.org/2012/03/08/religious -migration-exec/).

PEW (2018). *Being Christian in Western Europe.* Pew Religion & Public Life Project. (https://www.pewforum.org/2018/05/29/being-christian-in-western-europe/).

Pew Research Center (2012a). *The Global Religious Landscape.* Washington: Pew Templeton.

Pew Research Center (2012b). *Faith on the Move. The Religious Affiliation of International Migrants.* Washington: Pew Templeton.

Pickel, G. (2018). Perceptions of Plurality: The Impact of the Refugee Crisis on the Interpretation of Religious Pluralization in Europe. In U. Schmiedel, & G. Smith (Eds),

Religion in the European Refugee Crisis. Basingstoke: Palgrave Macmillan, pp. 15–37.

Pollack, D., & Rosta, G. (2017). *Religion and Modernity. An International Comparison.* Oxford: Oxford University Press.

Portes, A., & Rumbaut, R. (2006). *Immigrant America* (3rd edition). Berkeley, CA: University of California Press.

Portes, A., & DeWind, J. (2004). A Cross-Atlantic Dialogue: The Progress of Research and Theory in the Study of International Migration. *International Migration Review, 3*(38), 828–851.

Putnam, R.D. (2003). *Better together. Restoring the American Community,* New York: Simon & Schuster.

Qureshi, A. (2017). The UK Counter-terrorism Matrix: Structural Racism and the Case of Mahdi Hashi. In N. Massoumi, T. Mills, & D. Miller (Eds) *What is Islamophobia? Racism, Social Movements and the State,* London: PlutoPress, pp. 74–96.

Ramakrishnan, K., & Viramontes, C. (2006). *Civic Inequalities: Immigrants Volunteerism and Community Organizations in California.* San Francisco, CA: Public Policy Institute of California.

RAN (2016). *How to cooperate with religious organisations and communities within the local approach to radicalisation?* Ex Post paper - RAN Local. Radicalisation Awareness Network - European Commission, DG Home (https://ec.europa.eu/home-affairs/sites/homeaffairs/files/what-we-do/networks/radicalisation_awareness_network/about-ran/ran-local/docs/ran_local_how_to_cooperate_with_religious_organisations_08122016_en.pdf).

RAN (2017). *The role of religion in exit programmes and religious counselling in prison and probation settings.* Ex Post paper. Radicalisation Awareness Network - European Commission, DG Home (https://ec.europa.eu/home-affairs/sites/homeaffairs/files/what-we-do/networks/radicalisation_awareness_network/about-ran/ran-p-and-p/docs/ran_pp_role_of_religion_in_exit_programmes_10-11_10_2017_en.pdf).

Roy, O. (2004). *L'Islam mondialisé* (Nouv. éd.). Paris: Seuil.

Roy, O. (2016). *Le djihad et la mort.* Paris: Seuil.

Said, E.W. (1978). *Orientalism.* London: Penguin.

Schiffauer, W. (2006). Migration and Religion. A Special Relationship. *Fikrun wa Fann/ Art and Thought, 83,* 29–34.

Schiffauer, W. (2007). Der unheimliche Muslim - Staatsbürgerschaft und zivilgesellschaftliche Ängste. In L. Tezcan, & M. Wohlrab-Sahr (Eds), *Konfliktfeld Islam in Europa.* Baden-Baden: Nomos, pp. 111–134.

Schmidt, G. (2011). Understanding and approaching Muslim visibilities: Lessons learned from a fieldwork-based study of Muslims in Copenhagen. *Ethnic and Racial Studies, 34*(7), 1216–1229.

Selby, J.A. (2016). "Muslimness" and multiplicity in qualitative research and in government reports in Canada. *Critical Research on Religion, 4*(1), 72–89.

Silvestri, S. (2005). The Situation of Muslim Immigrants in Europe in the Twenty-first Century: The Creation of National Muslim Councils. In H. Holger (Ed.), *Crossing Over: Comparing Recent Migration in Europe and the United States.* Lanham, MD: Lexington, pp. 101–129.

Smith, T. (1978). Religion and Ethnicity in America. *American Historical Review, 83*(5), 1155–1185.

Smith-Hefner, N.J. (1994). Ethnicity and the force of faith. Christian conversion among khmer refugees. *Anthropological Quarterly, 67*(1), 24–37.

Stålsett, S.J. (2018). Fearing the Faith of Others? Government, Religion, and Integration in Norway. In U. Schmiedel, & G. Smith (Eds), *Religion in the European Refugee Crisis.* Basingstoke: Palgrave Macmillan, pp. 105–120.

Stark, R., & Finke, R. (2000). *Acts of Faith: Explaining the Human Side of Religion.* Berkeley: University of California Press.

Straut Eppsteiner, H., & Hagan, J. (2016). Religion as Psychological, Spiritual, and Social Support in the Migration Undertaking. In J. Saunders, E. Fiddian-Qasmiyeh, & S. Snyder (Eds), *Intersections of Religion and Migration. Religion and Global Migrations.* New York: Palgrave Macmillan, pp. 49–70.

Suárez-Orozco, M.M., Singh, S., Abo-Zena, M.M., Du D., & Roeser, R.W. (2012). The Role of Religion and Worship Communities in the Positive Development of Immigrant Youth. In A.E. Alberts Warren, R.M. Lerner, & E. Phelps (Eds), *Thriving and Spirituality among Youth: Research Perspectives and Future Possibilities.* Hoboken, NJ: John Wiley and Sons, pp. 255–288.

Sunier, T. (2014). Domesticating Islam: Exploring academic knowledge production on Islam and Muslims in European societies. *Ethnic and Racial Studies, 37*(6), 1138–1155.

Talebi, M., & Desjardins, M. (2012). The Immigration Experience of Iranian Baha'is in Saskatchewan: The Reconstruction of Their Existence, Faith, and Religious Experience. *Journal of Religion and Health, 51*(2), 293–309.

Taylor, D. (1991). The Role of Religion and the Emancipation of an Ethnic Minority: The Case of the Sri Lankan Hindu Tamils in Britain. In W.A.R. Shadid, & P.S. van Koningsvelt (Eds), *The Integration of Islam and Hinduism in Western Europe.* Kampen: Kok Pharos Pub. House, pp. 201–212.

Terenzi, P. (2010). *Introduzione. Sociologia e trascendenza: oltre i paradigmi tradizionali.* In P. Donati (Ed.), *La matrice teologica della società,* Soveria Mannelli: Rubbettino Editore, pp. vii–xxv.

Tezcan, L. (2012). *Das muslimische Subjekt: Verfangen im Dialog der Deutschen Islam Konferenz.* Paderborn: Konstanz UnivPress.

Thomson, M., & Crul, M. (2007). The Second Generation in Europe and the United States: How is the Transatlantic Debate Relevant for Further Research on the European Second Generation?. *Journal of Ethnic and Migration Studies*, *33*(7), 1025–1041.

Troll, C. (2003). Christian-Muslim Relations in Germany. A Critical Survey. *Islamochristiana*, *29*, 165–202.

UN Secretary General (2017). *Making Migration Work for All* (https://refugeesmigrants.un.org/sites/default/ files/sg_report_en.pdf).

United Nations (UN) (2015a). *Paris Agreement* (https://unfccc.int/sites/default/files/english_paris_agreement.pdf).

United Nations (UN) (2015b). *Transforming our world: the 2030 Agenda for Sustainable Development* (https://sustainabledevelopment.un.org/post2015/transformingourworld).

United Nations (UN) (2016). *New York Declaration for Refugees and Migrants* (http://www.un.org/en/ ga/search/view_doc.asp?symbol=A/RES/71/1).

United Nations (UN) (2018a). *Global Compact on Refugees. Final Draft. 26 June 2018* (http://www.unhcr.org/events/conferences/5b3295167/official-version-final-draft-global-compact-refugees.html).

United Nations (UN) (2018b). *Global Compact for Safe, Orderly and Regular Migration. Final Draft. 11 July 2018* (https://refugeesmigrants.un.org/sites/default/files/180711_final_draft_0.pdf).

Valero Matas, J.A., & Miranda Castañeda S., & Romay Coca J. (2012). La identidad religiosa de la inmigración en España: el caso de Castilla y León. *Journal of the Sociology and Theory of Religion*, *1*(1), 1–16.

van der Burgin C.J. (1991). The Structural Conditioning of Identity Formation. Suriname Hindus and Religious Policy in The Netherlands. In W.A.R. Shadid, & P.S. van Koningsvelt (Eds), *The Integration of Islam and Hinduism in Western Europe*, Kampen: Kok Pharos Pub. House, pp. 218–226.

Villaroya Soler, E. (2010), Filipino Migrants' Associations in Spain as Potential Agents of Change. In F. Baggio (Ed.), *Brick by Brick. Building Cooperation between the Philippines and Migrants' Associations in Italy and Spain*. Quezon City: SMC, pp. 255.335.

Voas, D., & Chaves, M. (2016). Is the United States a Counterexample to the Secularization Thesis?. *American Journal of Sociology*, *121*(5), 1517–1556.

Warner R.S., & Wittner, J.G. (Eds) (1998). *Gatherings in Diaspora: Religious Communities and the New Immigrants*. Philadelphia: Temple University Press.

Warner, R.S. (2000a). Religion and the New (post-1965) Immigrants: Some Principles Drawn from Field Research. *American Studies*, *41*(2/3), 267–286.

Warner, R.S. (2000b). The new immigrant religion: an update and appraisal. *Epicenter*, *5*(2) 1–7.

Weber, M. (1922) (2003) *Il metodo delle scienze storico-sociali*. Torino: Einaudi.

Woodhead, L. (2013). Tactical and strategic religion. In N.M. Dessing, N. Jeldtoft, J.S. Nielsen, & L. Woodhead (Eds), *Everyday lived Islam in Europe*. London: Ashgate, pp. 9–22.

Wuthnow, R. (1999). Mobilizing civic engagement: the changing impact of religious involvement. In T. Skocpol, & M.P. Fiorina (Eds), *Civic Engagement in American Democracy*. Washington, DC: BrookingsInst. Press, pp. 331–364.

Yang, F. (1999). *Chinese Christians in America: Conversion, Assimilation, and Adhesive Identities*. University Park: Pennsylvania State University Press.

Yang, F. (2000). Chinese Gospel Church: the Sinicization of Christianity. In H.R. Ebaugh, & J.S. Chafetz (Eds), *Religion and the New Immigrants: Continuities and Adaptations in Immigrant Congregations*, Walnut Creek, CA: AltaMira Press, pp. 89–107.

Yılmaz, F. (2016). *How the workers became Muslims. Immigration, culture and hegemonic transformation in Europe*. Ann Arbor: University of Michigan Press.

Yukich, G. (2018). Muslim American activism in the age of Trump. *Sociology of Religion*, 79(2), 220–247.

Zanfrini, L., & Sarli, A. (2010). *What are the Opportunities for Mobilizing the Filipino Diaspora in Italy? Lessons from the MAPID Project*. In F. Baggio (Ed.), *Brick by Brick. Building Cooperation between the Philippines and Migrants' Associations in Italy and Spain*. Quezon city: SMC, pp. 139–253.

Zanfrini, L. (2019). *The Challenge of Migration in a Janus-faced Europe*, London: Palgrave Macmillan.

Zhou, M., Bankston, C.L., & Kim R.Y. (2002). Rebuilding Spiritual Lives in the New Land: Religious Practices among Southeast Asian Refugees in the United States. In P.G. Min, & J.H. Kim (Eds), *Religions in Asian America: Building Faith Communities*. Walnut Creek, Ca.: AltaMira Press, pp. 37–70.

Zhou, M., & Bankston, C.L. (1998). *Growing Up American*. New York, NY: Russell Sage Foundation.

Zolberg, A., & Woon, L.L. (1999). Why Islam Is Like Spanish: Cultural Incorporation in Europe and the United States. *Politics and Society*, 27(5), 5–38.

PART 5

Migrations, Intergenerational Relations and Families

∵

Migrations and Intergenerational Religious Transmission: Issues from International Literature

Donatella Bramanti, Stefania Meda and Giovanna Rossi

1 Introduction

The aim of this chapter is to provide an overview of international literature about the importance of religion in family migration histories, with a special focus on how religious values are transmitted between generations.

The significant presence of migrant families having a clear religious identity, which they keep nurturing in their host country (USA, Canada, France and the Netherlands), for at least the last thirty years has brought about the need to explore the issue of religion, in order to understand its significance within the processes aimed at integrating migrant minorities. Today, we are facing one further issue, which has been investigated by research less extensively and which is the focus of this analysis, concerning the fact that the reason behind migration is a specific religious affiliation.

Giving consideration to the connection between religion and migrant families seems quite arduous in our highly secularized society, where the topic of religion appears to be in the background and is often regarded as playing a barely active role in guiding choices and strategies to face the challenges and risks related to families' and individuals' migration.

The following critical issues tend to overlap in this topic:

a) The phenomenon of religious persecution of Christian minorities in their home countries, which affects several families migrating to Europe and to Italy in particular, shifts the focus back onto the debate about religious belonging, which has gradually been playing a secondary role with the advent of the secularization process. This process is now apparently suffering a setback, and religious belonging is once again playing a primary role (Rizzi, 2016; see also Chapter 3).

b) On the other hand, the secularization process (Eberstadt, 2013) –which has been present, at least so far, to some extent in Western Europe, as well as in the English-speaking world, since the second half of the 20th century– has been documented by several studies in Europe (Pollini *et al.*,

DOI:10.1163/9789004429604_018

2012). These studies underline how religiousness has suffered a steady decline in its role as a pillar of the transmission of values, in general, and also of the importance of the family.

c)   But what is the outcome of secularization? The advent of a post-secular society, which is the outcome of the morphogenetic process of the previous secularized society. This process implies "a further differentiation between the essential values (let us say religious, for the sake of simplicity) that inspire the variety of cultures appearing in it" (Belardinelli *et al.*, 2009: 110). In the Western world, where the phenomenon of migration is increasingly important, a process of differentiation from a cultural and religious point of view has been taking place over the last few decades. Today, the post-secular society is expressed by a multi-cultural society (Donati, 2008).

d)   The post-secular society includes elements of paradoxicality as it incorporates both the unexpected effects of secularization (lack of meaning, deviant behaviors that can be classified as discomforts of modernity) and direct effects (need for transcendent meanings in irrational forms or forms of new rationality) (Donati, 2009). As for Europeans, on the one hand there is a progressive decrease in the importance of religious belonging, and, on the other hand, there is a sort of re-sacralization of social bonds (sometimes required by non-Christian religions) and of new forms of religious participation.

e)   The behavior of migrant families having a clear religious identity can be explained in the same perspective of paradoxicality. Two different processes emerge: a sort of theologizing experience (Connor, 2009; Massey, Higgins, 2011) –which is a sign of a higher level of personal awareness, but will not always affect the communal religious participation–, and the disaffiliation from religious practices and beliefs.

f)   It is also necessary to avoid any generalization when referring to the word *generation*. What do we mean by it today? Generation is a group of people sharing one relationship (Boccacin, 2005), that is the one linking their position within one's progeny in the family-relatives sphere (i.e. child, parent, grandparent, etc.) with the well-defined position in the societal sphere depending on the *social age* (i.e. depending on the relevant age group: young, adult, elderly, etc.) (Attias-Donfut, 2000; Rossi, 2012).

g)   Lastly, what do we mean by religion? Religion differs from culture (rituals, myths, sacred, etc.) when "it becomes the relationship with the entirely other than me (transcendence) that is within me and outside of me at the same time" (Donati, 2009: 304). However, differences between religions can be observed by considering the idea of transcendence. This produces social effects that can be very diverse; in particular, "the difference of Christianity lies in referring to a theological matrix that uses a relational semantics of difference" (Donati, 2010: 218) thus not limiting religion to a series of practices and/or ritual obligations (Pace, 2013).

2   Intergenerational Transmission of Religious Values: the Main Issues Emerging from Italian and International Studies

The transmission of values falls within the realm of socialization processes and –from a relational sociology perspective– can be seen as a process aimed at "transmitting the ethos of a culture, which expresses a normative, i.e. interpretive, view on life and on the world that individuals have despite not being their own only makers" (Donati, 1989: 98). Values and norms are part of a story, a memory, and are constantly comprehended, endorsed and modified within relationships, thus eventually becoming an interpretive project (Donati, 1991). Socialization is virtuously achieved when shifting from a unidirectional model to a transactional model implying reciprocity between individuals (in this case, adults-grandparents, parents-children, grandparents-grandchildren).

The intergenerational transmission of values, which plays a crucial role in the socialization process (Pontalti, Rossi, 1995; Cigoli, 1995; Barni, 2009), includes two logs, the first one recording what lies between generations and which can be defined as intergenerational transmission, and the second one concerning what goes beyond, what crosses and transcends generations, by exceeding them – which has been defined as transgenerational transmission in psychosocial literature (Cigoli, Scabini, 2006). The intergenerational transmission of values refers to the system of moral principles that previous generations pass down to the following ones (whether they pass it down and how) and to what the latter, in turn, perceive, accept, or refuse to pass down (Scabini, 2006). The transmission of religion has specific features that have long been underestimated and appear significant in relationships between generations.

One of the issues that several studies on migration, families and religion focus on is linked to the question whether religion is a bridge or a barrier to the inclusion of families (Foner, Alba, 2008). The findings of the study conducted on Coptic families and their children in the following chapters provide interesting elements on this matter.

The act of *thinking by generations* involves a significant heuristic ability: this approach actually allows to observe relationships between generations and the symbolic content that is generated through them and is transmitted within families and society. *Thinking by generations* implies bringing into focus a different, mutual responsibility: previous generations actually play a crucial role in favoring or hindering the chances that the following generations could be or not be generative. In our opinion, the meaning of the whole generation concept lies in the bond, in the significance that such bond assumes on a personal level for those who engage in it in everyday life, and in the significance, within a social context, that the intergenerational bond, engaged both inside and outside the family, assumes in the surrounding context (*meso* level) as well as in a wider, or social, context (*macro* level). In this perspective, the concept of generation is based, on the one hand, on the historical-biological age, in terms of descendant/ancestor relationships (family axis), and, on the other hand, on the mediation that society, and welfare systems in particular, provides to these bonds (social axis).

The concept of generation, thus, appears as a synthesis between the family and social spheres, and allows to place generations within the complex dynamics of resource and general exchange allocation.

Through the relational approach, it is possible to go beyond the previously quoted and predominantly monosemic interpretations of the concept of generation, which, despite helping to clarify the various meanings of the word, prevent us from reaching a comprehensive and multi-dimensional understanding of it.

Focusing on relationships between generations also implies considering their ambivalence, which is generated by the considerable variety and fragmentary nature of the elements at stake in relationships, and is related to their elements of risk.

One way to deal with this ambivalence in family relationships between generations is favoring elements of obligation/subjection and keeping the marked cultural differences between generations in the background. The emancipation strategy stands at the other end of the spectrum; within this strategy, balance in family life and possible innovations are based on the convergence of all family members' cultural patterns and values (Lüscher, 2011).

The elements of risk in intergenerational relationships do not seem to be considered in most postmodern analyses and reflections. However, we know that relationships between generations are not immune from ambivalence and can therefore be either generative or degenerative.

2.1   *Is Religion a Dependent or Independent Variable in Generational Transmission?*
Let us now explore the main issues emerging from the most recent studies on the transmission of values in immigrant families, with a special focus on

religious values, which have been carried out in Italy and other European and non-European countries.

The relationship between religion and family has been extensively studied by sociologists, who have provided religion with a role of both a dependent and an independent variable in socialization processes within families.

The following are the areas explored by researchers who have embraced the first hypothesis (religion as a dependent variable):

a)   the intentional religious education provided by parents;
b)   the family atmosphere, i.e. relationships based on trust and mutual respect;
c)   the family structure, with reference to the presence of the marital dyad;
d)   the group of peers, i.e. the community.

A second line of research identifies religion as an independent variable. In this case, the main focus for researchers is to determine whether and when religion is a crucial factor in how families work.

Notably, researchers have analyzed the impact of parents' religiousness on the strength of family bonds, especially couple relationships; religious practices as a strengthening element in the educational project; and the parents' religiousness as a strong predictor of juvenile religiousness.

Both these perspectives provide very interesting clues to understanding the dynamics of the transmission of values between generations and allow to develop a complex picture.

3   The Transmission of Religious Values in Immigrant Families: Some Empirical Evidence

The main empirical evidence emerging from research can be regarded as a reflection of two macro topics: *the relationship between family and society* and *the dynamics within generations*.

As for the relationship between *family and society*, a key issue is the place that religion holds in the transmission of a sense of ethnic belonging and identity (Chen, 2002; Min, Kim, 2002; Rumbaut, 2006). It is actually one of the most important indicators of group identity (Verkuyten *et al.*, 2012). Moreover, religions provide certainty of belonging, but also the support for many beliefs and lifestyles, such as intergenerational obligations, or family rituals. One key issue concerns the contribution that religious values can offer in the transmission of the most salient features of a cultural heritage (Warner, 2000). In intergenerational relationships, the issue of cultural reproduction arises when children start going to school.

3.1   The Relationship between Family and Society

In general, the connection between family, cultural identities and religious in-stitutions is a crucial element in the processes through which migrants seek to forge a system of meanings and to find a way of life for themselves and their children. Scholars (Ambrosini, 2007) have noted that, for Catholic families during the first migration flows to North America, aggregation around religious institutions was a way to preserve their languages and cultural traditions, while trying to adapt to an obscure and often hostile environment.

Catholic schools often represented an ideal place to help children avoid discrimination. Besides, Churches represented more than just a place of worship: they were places where people could meet, socialize, and form associations or informal groups. These religious environments also provided the chance to take on leadership roles and experience civic participation, which otherwise would not have been accessible in the surrounding society. To quote a classic text on this matter: "Church was the first line of defense behind which immigrants could preserve their group identity" (Warner, Srole, 1945: 160). In other words, for years Churches and religious associations have repre-sented a clearinghouse that allowed immigrants to adapt to the new social context without losing their roots and social networks (support). This role has proven long lasting and capable of passing from one generation to another. Nowadays, this applies to a certain number of communities, not only to Catholics.

Sometimes, these forms of belonging lead individuals and families to strengthen their religious sentiment. The title of a study about religion and ethnicity among Indian immigrants in the United States (Kurien, 2002) is: *We are better Hindus here.* And actually most of the people who were interviewed reported that they had become more religious after arriving in the new coun-try, as they started to ponder the meaning of their religious identity (see also Chapter 12), which they gave for granted in their home country, for the first time. Besides, while the traditional Hindu religious activity is not generally practiced in groups except for some celebrations, religious gatherings provide community support in a context of migration.

3.2   Social Integration

According to several scholars (Hirschman, 2004; Reitz *et al.*, 2009), religion can act as a vehicle for a good level of integration into society, despite the fact that, after what happened on 9/11/2001, Islam is regarded as a barrier to the integra-tion process, especially in Europe (Foner, Alba, 2008), because the values it fosters are considered in stark contrast with the values fostered by the society of the host country.

The widespread phenomenon of conversion to Christian Churches among Asian immigrants in the United States is a sign of the importance of faith for families that are trying to redefine their identities in a new environment.

It is more difficult to detect this kind of experience in a secularized context like the European one, in which, conversely, the loss of religious practices by migrants (and especially by second generations) is seen as a positive event, an indication of a full and successful assimilation (Tribalat, 1995).

Religious belonging appears to be a rather important factor according to the chances of social integration and to the cultural differences with the host country (see also Chapter 13).

Foner and Alba (2008) addressed the issue of differences in the importance of religion in Western countries. The assumption is that, in the United States, studies tend to focus more on religion as a factor in integration, whereas in Europe religion (and Islam in particular) is regarded as a barrier to immigrants' integration. These polarized perspectives reflect the different social dynamics that characterize the United States and Europe.

American literature highlights the role of religion in responding and catering to the immigrants' social needs, which can be summarized, by borrowing Hirschman's (2004) formula, by the three Rs: refuge, respectability, and resources.

Religion has been analyzed as a socially acceptable way for American immigrants to express, reformulate and convey their cultures and ethnic identities. Immigrants learn that Americans are more willing to accept religious diversity that ethnic diversity, and therefore use religion as a socially tolerated tool to build their culture and identity (Herberg, 1960; Karpathakis, 2001).

In churches and temples, immigrants "can (…) pass on their religious and cultural heritage to the following generation" (Ebaugh, Chafetz, 2000: 141). The act of going to church or a place of worship, which is often encouraged by families, seems to have a positive effect on young generations, also limiting the risk of situations of social exclusion (Zhou, Bankston, 1994). Moreover, religious organizations can increase upward mobility in second generations (Zhou, Bankston, 1998).

In the United States, religion helps transform immigrants into Americans and gives them and their children a sense of belonging. In other words, religious institutions are places where immigrants can formulate their requests to be included in the American society (Portes, Rumbaut, 2006).

3.3   *Religion as a Barrier to Integration*
In Western Europe, religion is generally perceived as an issue associated with immigrant minorities. When analyzing immigrants' religions, the focus of

academic researchers is almost exclusively on Islam, which is regarded as a barrier or as a challenge to integration, and as a source of conflict with local customs and institutions. Some social scientists have more radical views suggesting or explicitly stating that Islam is hindering the integration of immigrant minorities and threatening the liberal values of European countries. Another topic in the social sciences literature concerns the discrimination against and restrictions on Muslims in Western Europe (religion as a vehicle for discrimination and prejudice).

Islam can become a place where to build an opposing identity: a progressive growth of a religious conscience among members of the younger generation more and more often refers to a globalized Islam, rather than to their parents' *Islamic family*. This process has been called *re-islamization* (Laurence, Vaisse, 2006). Some scholars and researchers claim that loyalty to Islam has had positive effects, such as helping young people keep away from criminality and juvenile delinquency, but there is also growing concern about the role of Islam in second-generation *cultural isolationism*, which may lead to acts of violence and terrorism.

An interesting perspective is the one relating to the theory of *segmented assimilation* (Portes, Zhou, 1993; Portes, Rumbaut, 2006): after migration, the various generations in the family pursue continuity with the culture of their home country in very different ways. Therefore, there are several possible outcomes of this:

- *Consonant* acculturation: it occurs when the parents and children are acculturated at the same time and speed, both in learning the culture of the host society, and in abandoning their native language and cultural traditions; in these situations there are few intergenerational conflicts;
- *Dissonant* acculturation: it occurs when children learn English and adopt habits and lifestyles of the host society faster than their parents do. Differences in the acculturation processes can lead to intergenerational conflicts;
- *Selective* acculturation: it may occur when parents and children, who have been acculturated together, preserve ties with their culture of origin. This can lead to socialization with the lifestyles of the host country without losing the most important cultural values of one's home country, in both the first and second generation.

There is another perspective in the analysis of intergenerational transmission that highlights the conflict between generations.

There is a conflict between generations when children are exposed to the new cultural inputs from the society of the country where they live and from global cultures (Caneva, 2011), while their parents want to teach them the values and behaviors from their homeland. Besides, sometimes parents have an embellished version of the values from their homeland, which might have changed since they left it (Foner, 2009).

Often, at the heart of this intergenerational conflict, there is some difficulty in accepting one's paternal authority (Fass, 2005), or even the discomfort and shame caused by the customs and traditions typical of one's home country (D'Alisera, 2009).

However, this conflict is not the only option in intergenerational relationships: admitting the possibility of cultural hybridization (Gomarasca, 2009) is also possible. Moro *et al.* (2009) remind us that the real challenge of migration is indeed that of hybridization: "...integrating into the world here, with the support of one's parents' world of origin, leads to a dynamic mix of women and men, thoughts and their evolution. Saying hybridization means saying that all forms are possible ... in an ever-changing configuration, which sometimes varies according to internal needs and in the various stages in life" (Moro, Baubet *et al.*, 2009: 14).

By adopting their first-generation immigrant parents' point of view, children, who are surrounded by new lifestyles, can also change some cultural patterns and social customs. Adults can try and negotiate new family rules with their children, accept new norms and soften their parenting styles (Zhou, 2009). This approach shows a sort of reciprocity between generations.

The big picture thus appears to be quite articulate and complex, and it is precisely within this marked differentiation, which sometimes can be extremely ambivalent, that the transmission of values takes place in families experiencing migration.

3.4   The Dynamics within Immigrant Families

If, on the one hand, emigration is always an event involving the whole family, and in which the whole family changes (Gozzoli, Regalia, 2005; Valtolina, Colombo, 2012), different generations will implement different strategies to *preserve-while-changing*.

In Vatz-Laaroussi's study (2001) –whose suggestive title is *Le familial au cœur de l'immigration*–, family is once again at the center both in migration trajectories and in integration dynamics. In her book, the author duly relates that not only migration, but also social participation and exercising one's citizenship are a *family affair*.

Sociologists studying the transmission of values claim that, in various fields such as religion, politics, or relationships between the sexes, family is what affects the most young people's socialization, whereas parents' educational methods –be they authoritarian or permissive, autocratic or democratic– only have a mild influence on the level of transmission of values within the family (Percheron, 1991). Coherence, persistence, visibility and the social acceptability of the message appear crucial; these are the essential dimensions for the transmission between generations, and family is the privileged place for transmission. For a long time, immigrant families have been described as a place of cultural contradictions, in which the parents' coherence and persistence is opposed to the social invisibility and unacceptability of the supported values. Observing real-life experiences in both Quebec and France, a dynamic transmission may be identified in migration trajectories. Although it does not transmit a fixed set of values and customs from one generation to another, this transmission transforms "containers, contents, transmitters and receivers" (Percheron, 1991: 94).

Migration favors a two-way (bidirectional) transmission between children and parents. Everybody must adapt to and increase knowledge and expertise. And therefore, the transmission of values involved in immigration is never linear, but is more often multi-faceted and can be understood by analyzing it at different levels.

3.5 Semantic Transmissions

Their aim is to transfer a meaning and an orientation within the family (such as, for instance, the importance of helping each other out). The vast majority of immigrant families describe this as a spiritual value, connected with religion or a form of cultural humanism, which is quite distant from the idea of obligation that we tend to associate it with.

3.6 Hybrid Transmissions

These transmissions are the strongest indicator of the family's tendency to change.

It can be noted that, in hybrid transmissions, parents', as well as children's, customs are less and less formal and automatic, and more and more contextualized and dynamic, justified on a spiritual or social level. Both the effort and the progressive re-orientation of younger generations range from the need to conform to one's family to the ability to make personal decisions (e.g. Ramadan for Muslims), without the support of the surrounding social context.

Some relevant strategies seem quite significant: for example, Catholics from Latin America join specific religious groups (Adventists or Seventh-Day Christians) as there they find an environment that looks more appropriate to the transmission of their faith and beliefs.

3.7 Transmissions by Keywords

The semantic meaning given to values that can have multiple meanings deserves special attention. A key concept becomes the center of, and a catalyst to, family transmission: it is often polysemous and multi-dimensional, and allows for several interpretations and multiple updates depending on the family members who use it –young or adults, men or women–, and on the context. An example of this is *the value of respect*. It is one of the key concepts of immigrant families' transmission in both Quebec and France, precisely because of its polysemy. Through nuances and contextualization, respect allows each family member to find their place within the family, and to interact with other generations, sexes, as well as society and institutions.

The transformation of the contents of the transmission often leads to switch from values to skills, due to the need to survive in an unfamiliar setting (e.g. the value of patience of Arab Muslim women in the relationships with their husbands can, in turn, become a skill for their husbands in their social relations with the Public Administration, in the labor market, or in neighborhoods).

In another survey (Helly *et al.*, 2001) conducted by the same research team, the focus is on the transformation process of values and customs by Moroccan and Salvadoran immigrants who, in the 1990s, faced different stabilization conditions than people from previous migration flows. Four are the reasons why such processes are observed within families: the importance of families in socialization processes as well as in processes of production and reproduction of models and customs; their intermediate position among the macro- and micro-sociological (individual) levels of analysis; their key role in emigration as a meeting and stabilization place for homeland cultures; and the promotion of family solidarity for most immigrants.

The research focuses on the project of transmission of values and customs and allows to identify three types of pivot (i.e. *element that eases the transfer*) in transmission: 1) grandparents, who are the symbolic and actual actors of this process; 2) the home country, which is sometimes idealized and unwelcoming, and towards which parents develop an ambiguous relationship, which they communicate to their children to justify their emigration and offer them a potential identity; 3) networks, mainly informal ones, including members from one's home country community and from the immigrant community, which allow to recreate value-based social relations and to speak one's native language.

In a more recent article, Vatz-Laaroussi (2007) emphasizes how important family (*us as a family*) and social networks are. This *us as a family* –carrying a strong migration project, acting as a vehicle for integration into the new social life, and mediating participation in new social institutions– is also a catalyst to resilience and, at times, almost the only element of continuity in disruption and change trajectories for those who emigrate. The featured analysis follows the three dimensions that run through and make up the dynamics within immigrant families: the processes of intergenerational transmission, family

memories and history, and resilience. This study is based on a number of surveys conducted on foreign families with children in Quebec. Its results show
that neither the home country nor the parents' level of education were the
single determining factors affecting the processes of intergenerational transmission or children's resilience. However, these factors lead to a range of modes
of transmission of the family's history, and of children's school performances.
The author's analysis allows to redefine the axes that run through family issues
and immigration: family transmission is here associated with the creation of
new reference points and meanings, family memories refer to a contextualized
construction of the family's history within immigration, and resilience allows
for each individual's re-integration into transnational networks crossing space
and time boundaries. If we observe intergenerational relationships from these
complicated processes, they appear as a turning point in the family's and society's transformation, which establishes a continuity that is essential to resilience, social integration and the creation of a new Self, within a different and
multiple *Us*, and possibly also to the birth of a new reality.

While immigration has altered the religious structures in French society, the
opposite process, i.e. the transformation of immigrants' religiousness in their
new living environment (Simon, Tiberj, 2014), can also be observed. In this
context, how does immigrants' religiousness evolve and differ from that of the
mainstream population? How does intrafamilial religious transmission occur?
And to what extent does being raised in a family where religion was important
determine people's current religiousness? Is the religious sentiment more often maintained in religious minorities, particularly in the context of migration? The authors of the recent Survey on the Diversity of the French Population (Beauchemin *et al.*, 2016) have tried to answer these questions through
data analysis.

Before being a matter of personal choice, religion is transmitted by parents
through socialization or, more in general, *religious belonging*: in other words,
children are regarded as the heirs to their parents' religion. The survey reveals
which religions the parents belong to, and emphasizes the importance of religion in the education people receive. Being raised in a family where religion is
very important influences the formation of religious feelings: transmission
happens in 85% of cases, even though with a marked decrease in the intensity
of religiousness. Conversely, almost everyone who was raised in an agnostic or
atheistic family claims to be equally agnostic or atheist, and less than 7% reports some degree of religiousness. Religious-mixed families, i.e. where one of
the two parents has no religion, represent 10% of cases and are even rarer
among immigrant families. The decrease in religion intensity from one
generation to the following one is clearly expressed by this comparison: 24% of

people between 18 and 50 living in metropolitan France were raised in a self-declared religion-less family, and today 44% of people claim to have no religion.

This disaffiliation trend varies according to the religion that the parents practice. Religious disaffiliation is apparently more frequent for people raised in a Buddhist (30% of disaffiliation), Christian and Jewish (26%) family than for those who have Muslim parents (11%). Intergenerational transmission can be divided into three categories:

– Secularization: religious disaffiliation from the religion of one's parents, or lower level of religiousness compared to that of one's family;
– Reproduction: same level of religiousness, including absence of religion;
– Reinforcement: higher level of religiousness than that of one's parents (including agnostics).

According to this categorization, slightly more than a quarter of people between 18 and 50 living in metropolitan France followed a secularization trajectory and consider themselves less attached to religion than their parents, two thirds maintain continuity with their families' religious feelings, and only 7% consider themselves more religious than the previous generation.

3.8   The Relationship between Parents and Children in Transmission

Observing the dynamics of intergenerational transmission of values in immigrant families from the mother-child relationship perspective is the aim of the research conducted in Italy by Caneva and Pozzi (2014). Through the design of qualitative interviews with immigrant mothers and children, the research analyses how mothers and children negotiate styles of transmission of values, as well as the importance of language and religion.[1] The survey provides different results for Muslim and Christian women. Muslim women perceive religion as a key factor in personal identity, whereas Eastern-European Christian women perceive religious belonging as a private matter and generally attach little importance to participation in religious celebrations and Holy Scripture reading. For Muslim women, though, the little chance they have to take part in religious celebrations and their long stay in Italy lead them to distance themselves from religious practices, and this impacts their children's socialization. This distancing from rules is especially present in the younger generations and determines a sense of discomfort and shame in mothers, in so far as they have

---

1   The interviewees were 23 children between 14 and 20 who came to Italy to be joined with their parents again (10 Pakistanis, 9 Romanians, 2 Ukrainians, and 2 Moldovans), and 58 women (26 Bangladeshi, 7 Pakistanis, 21 Romanians, 3 Ukrainians, and 1 Moldovan) who had emigrated before, or had arrived in Lombardy through processes of family reunification.

not been able to maintain interest in a religion. Children feign interest only when their parents are present.

For Eastern-European immigrant women, the importance of religion does not lie in regular attendance, but in its supporting and guiding role. This allows children to feel independent and autonomous, and mothers to not feel a sense of shame or defeat (the transmission of religion is regarded as a transmission of values rather than of customs).

For children, knowing and speaking their parents' native language is essential to preserve their connection with their origins and define their identity. Language is a symbolic boundary through which children define themselves and differentiate themselves from others. As for the transmission of religion, some of the young interviewees state that they go to church or the mosque and perform religious rituals (e.g. they pray). In particular, Muslim children state that religion is part of everyday life in their families. For some, religion is a way of life, a set of rules that are useful in everyday life to provide a guide to solve problems. Children feel that faith and religious practices are part of their identity and want to transfer them to their children in the future.

Despite some differences with their mothers, conflicts do not occur over religion and religious practices. This behavior is common to a lot of young people who claim to be religious, even though they go less often to church or the mosque and pray less than their parents. The decrease in religious practice is partly due to the duration of their stay in Italy. Young people who are born in Italy or who came when they were still babies are less devoted to beliefs and religious practices, whereas those who have been socialized in their homelands and have arrived in Italy in their teenage years are more devoted.

Children with Easter-European origins state that their families are not religious, and that religion is not a part of the education they receive from their parents. For these children, the transmission of values is related to other cultural issues (like, for instance, the importance of showing adults respect, or the importance of the nuclear family), which are not closely related to religion.

In conclusion, Asian Muslim families show a stronger attachment to religion, whereas Easter-European families seem less interested in religious aspects.

For Muslim women and their children, religion is still a fundamental issue. Both parents and children see the transmission of religion as a way to preserve values and moral integrity, even though second-generation children attach less importance to customs, thus creating a conflict with their parents.

However, this sense of belonging to a religious community clashes with a lower attendance at the mosque. This could be a consequence of an absence or shortage of places of worship, but also of a change in habits in a context of migration, or a strategy to avoid discrimination. For Eastern-European women and younger generations, religion is not closely related to identity issues and attachment to origins issues: it can be seen at most as a moral guide.

Also a recent study conducted in the Archdiocese of Milan on two generations of Muslims (Bramanti, Meda, 2016) highlights a different degree of adherence to Islam related to gender and generation. As for gender, women get predominantly higher scores in the adherence to Islam index (Closeness–Distance between self and Islam (Graphical Display); Attendance at religious practices; Orientations–Values) (49% high modality versus 42.3% for men), whereas, in terms of difference between generations, older people show higher levels of identification with Islam. Those who were born in Italy (second generation) actually appear in definitely lower numbers within the higher level of adherence to Islam (about 17% versus 49% of those who were born abroad or are first-generation), almost as if a secularization process is already underway for second generations.

In terms of willingness to get to know the host culture, the level of adherence to Islam seems to be neither a hindering nor an enhancing factor: both those who appear to be relatively more distant from a strong identification with religious values and those who are conversely totally devoted are actually *willing to dialogue*, whereas bridging social capital availability proves crucial.

3.9 *The Importance of One's Native Language*

Language, particularly one's mother's language (Medvedeva, 2012), is definitely a unique tool to transfer values within families. Language is closely related to the chance to express religious contents and preserve a sense of belonging to one's original community, especially for Muslims. Using one's native language, effectively combined with the new language, is crucial for a successful integration process (Esser, 2006; Jiménez, 2011; Ambrosini *et al.*, 2013). However, parents and children show different abilities in learning the language of the host country: children tend to learn it faster than their parents. And this can lead children to become their parents' parents: the result is a dissonant acculturation and, eventually, a weaker parental authority, or even conflict (Choi *et al.*, 2008).

3.10 *Generational Differences*

The author (Saint-Blancat, 2004) analyses the cultural and religious socialization of young Muslims who were born or socialized in Europe, through the generation category. The family's religious socialization, the pluralism of Islam re-affiliation paths followed by young Muslims and their current attempts at re-orientation towards faith are then examined. Lastly, identifying changes in the transmission process (contents and practices) highlights the queries new generations have: claiming a sort of gender identity for women through the prism of religion, a new need of citizenship, and the issue of "religious" authority. All these progresses help Islam emerge and drift away from a social construction of exception.

3.11   *Gender Differences*

This paper (Flor, Knapp, 2001) is interesting for the interpretive categories used and the final discussion highlighting the paradoxical effects related to the children's gender.[2] The first introductory part proposes an open discussion about the unidirectional model (parents to children) versus a dialectical model (transactional). In these models, both parents and children are perceived as active agents in the internalization process.

Some of the parents' transmission methods are unidirectional, such as, for instance, the parental desire for the child to be religious, but there are also more dialogical methods.

In this research, the child's religiousness is regarded as a dependent variable of the parents' religiousness. In short, parents appear to have a direct influence over children, but transactional elements can also be noted. There are some interesting paradoxical effects about gender. Despite the occurrence of dialogical discussions about faith between fathers and daughters, the latter see religion as decreasingly important; a similar paradoxical, although less marked, effect was evidenced in the mother-son dyads.

3.12   *Memories*

According to Amadini (2012), in reprocessing one's obligations, heritage and sense of belonging, new generations can discover that there is a system of models, rules and values that convey the reassuring feeling of not having to start from scratch. This takes us back to memories, a topic included in the broader topic of transmission.

Among the records of the past, Assman distinguishes cultural memory from communicative memory, which includes memories from the recent past that human beings share with their peers: a typical case is generational memory. Assman underlines that this memory is built on the interaction in everyday life which is transmitted between generations by witnesses, and is less institutionalized than cultural memory, which has fixed objectifications (Assman, 2002). In religious transmission, everyday life within the family and living in the

---

2   Participants in this study were a subgroup of 171 Caucasians living in families with two parents and one pre-adolescent child (84 women, 87 men).

family's house help build an incorporated memory that can be described as communicative memory. Leccardi (2009) argues that, in family relationships, experience is incorporated as a *natural behavior*, which generations are a *living memory* of, a *long memory* that is present in families below the threshold of awareness.

According to Pace, the act of transmission indicates a constant movement in time: in the transfer from one generation to the other, not only do external conditions vary, but also different and somehow opposite ways of understanding and interpreting the contents of the beliefs being transmitted alternate (Pace, 2008).

This structuring of beliefs has a social, cultural and political nature. It can be interpreted as a search for new meanings of everyday life in spite of diversity as a continuous negotiation process to extend the symbolic boundaries of faith, a constant symbolic (and generational) renovation to adapt to the surrounding environment.

According to Campiche (2010), religious transmission shows a personal history building up through a relationship between the evolution of personal freedom, management of one's heritage and integration into a specific socio-historical context.

Barrera Rivera (2001) argues that transmission is a religious language dynamics in the making, and describes it as being inseparable from the concept of group-approved memory, and here a connection between transmission and exercise of religious authority is inevitably established. According to the Brazilian author, the aim of transmission is ensuring socialization to individuals and groups within this institutional framework, by also integrating, in a balanced way, community, ethical, emotional end cultural records of identification with the religious traditions. Thus, transmission continues to be a process on which religious identities, which are temporary and partial, are built and rebuilt, based on individual experiences.

3.13   *The Role of Elderly People*

Elderly people are the leading actors in the exercise of memory. Aggoun (2003) described their (the grandparents') place in Algeria and France. Immigrant grandparents can combine their individual memory of the past –which includes a collective identity– with the present and future of the host society. They build their identity through a selective memory (a collage of elements from the homeland and host societies in a dialectical and non-dichotomous way) and by trying to find consistency and plausibility in their present and past. In doing so, the sense of belonging to their community, as an element in their personal identity, is lost in their transition from one society to the other.

However, religion is still an element that ensures a connection between the living and the dead.

This analysis allows to explore the continuity and discontinuity of roles and functions and the transmission of memory in migration situations.

As for references to the past, the concept of *generation of post-memory* refers to the transmission of family memories across generations, and specifically to second generations' ties with their religious past in "an (...) oscillation between continuity and rupture" (Hirsch, 2008: 106). This is a particularly interesting concept for the generations of Jewish families' children who have not experienced the Holocaust; of Armenian descendants who have not experienced the genocide; of Catholic younger people (e.g. Focolare Movement) who have neither experienced World War II, nor taken part in the 1970s youth revolution, nor known the pre-conciliar Church or the birth of ecclesial movements.

Hervieu-Léger (2003) argues that what matters the most is not continuity itself, but the fact that continuity is the visible expression of a filiation, which is explicitly claimed by the single or collective believers and makes them members of a spiritual community including past, present and future believers.

4   And Finally ... Breaking the Silence

Studies on the transmission of religious values among people who have suffered religious persecutions in their home country are missing from this analytical presentation of the main studies on the transmission of religious values in immigrant families.

This absence highlights a significant gap and also a sort of collective removal.

The findings that we have presented are obviously of enormous value and importance. This is what guided us in designing the study of persecuted groups, as the following chapters in this part will illustrate. However, the almost total lack of this specific focus highlights that, in the Western scientific community, attention has only recently been turned to this issue, which has not been thoroughly examined yet.

For immigrants, the religious persecutions that they suffered in their homeland and that have forced them to emigrate are, of course, an element of severe distress, and shed a sad light on their homeland, even though the sense of belonging to it is a major factor in the immigrants' identity. Therefore, as the interviews with the members of the Coptic community emphasize (see Chapters 19 and 20), those who have suffered discrimination or violence in their home country struggle to talk about that.

The religious freedom that immigrants experience in host countries is thus a key factor in supporting integration and re-socialization paths for both adults and youth, provided that it does not imply that religion is a totally irrelevant fact. On the one hand, removing all the pain suffered because of religion can make the role that religion has in Western countries incomprehensible to immigrants; on the other hand, it can reduce immigrants to a sort of forced silence in order to live up to social expectations.

To this effect, the integrated model of transmission of values gains a special heuristic significance: it is a common thread running through several studies, and it combines the vertical axis (generations), horizontal axis (the group of peers) and diagonal axis of social transmission (Maliepaard, Lubbers, 2013). In particular, vertical transmission refers to the role that parents play in explicit socialization, cultural education, norms and values, and in the everyday practice of behaviors that children interiorize by observing and imitating their parents' actions. Horizontal transmission is fundamental during adolescence, when friends and peers have a growing influence on them. The diagonal axis refers to extra-familial socialization: individuals are also influenced by the social context in which they grow up, notably school (Berry et al., 1992), working environments and associations or non-profit organizations.

The present chapter hypothesizes that religious values and beliefs are a valid support in integration and cohesion processes for migrant families. The framework within which this hypothesis can be verified refers to the four key concepts presented in Chapter 2.

Based on the empirical evidence provided, it can be stated that the families' commitment in the transmission of religious values is definitely aimed at building an individual and family identity in the contexts of origin. It can also be stated that this effort tends to persist at least in first-generation immigrants even in the host country.

If it is true that religious values are mainly conveyed within family relationships, it is also true, as research has found, that they are challenged by the social background of the host country, which is new to immigrants.

In European host countries and in Italy in particular, migrants experience freedom of religion, as a formal right, which, however, plays a barely active role in defining a new right to *citizenship* and making *places of public life* accessible.

This condition poses a threat: leaving families alone in their efforts to pass down values. However, on the other hand, it adds value to ethnic communities, as well as to local Christian Churches and Parishes, by investing them with a supporting role to families in this task.

Unfortunately, in Italy, there is still no adequate empiric research about these dynamics, due to the complexity of the investigation (as the first findings presented in the chapters about the Coptic families and their children who were targeted in this study will illustrate), and also to a sort of removal of the religious issue as a cause of migration.

This silence is dangerous and has to be purposefully tackled and studied, in order to prevent the courage and self-sacrifice of the many people who have risked or given up their lives from crashing into a wall of silence and denial.

CHAPTER 18

The Copts in Italy: Migration and Generosity

Beatrice Nicolini

1 The Coptic Church and Italy

The term *copt*, initially without any confessional connotations, derives from the Arab term *qutb, quft, qift*, and more precisely from the Arab translation of the Greek term *aiguptios* imported through the Latin term *cophti, cophtitae*. At the beginning of the Arab domination along the Mediterranean African regions, this term indicated Egypt's original inhabitants in order to distinguish them from *rum*, which was referred to those Egyptians of Greek-Byzantine origins.[1] Copts were simply thought as Egyptians.

The Copts once formed a large Christian community, from the Nile to the Middle East to the Horn of Africa. They became a minority after the Muslim occupation of Egypt in the seventh century; they remained an integral part of the Egyptian world.

The relationship between Italy and the Coptic community in the Middle East is ancient and intense. Coptic recorded history ended around the fourteenth century (Ayad, 2016). In the fifteenth century, the Council of Florence, held between 1438 and 1445, decided to invite the first official delegation to Europe. The first Coptic manuscripts were introduced in Italy and soon the Copts were persuaded to submit to the papacy. In 1630, there were Copts in Italy although, on the whole, they were very reluctant to travel to Europe or, indeed, to travel at all (Hamilton, 2006). Nevertheless, the Coptic Diaspora showed that upward mobility could be achieved without loss of heritage identity (Mahmood, 2012). Until the nineteenth century there have not been many sources. Occasional sources from Arab authors or from Western travelers or pilgrims were the only available information. Gian Battista Brocchi (who visited Egypt in 1822–26), Alessandro Ricci (1817–22) and Ippolito Rossellini (1828–19) visited Egypt and reported about the Copts. These explorers, through their adventures, described the Coptic Churches they visited and explained the main theological differences between the Coptic Orthodox, the Coptic

---

[1] A special thanks to L. Zanfrini, G. Valtolina, A. Melcangi, R. Bottoni and P. Schellenbaum for their precious comments. Transcriptions and transliterations are here simplified and as in consulted sources and texts.

© BEATRICE NICOLINI, 2020 | DOI:10.1163/9789004429604_019

Catholic and the Roman Catholic Churches. It must be remembered that the three Italian explorers were driven by prejudice typical of their epoch and, in their reports, wrote about the Copts as "heretics", "schismatics", "ignorant", "intolerant", "extremely poor"; besides, monks were believed to have permission to get married. In 1824, Vatican City opened a parochiality for the Catholic Copts, but it remained a theory and was never realized. On March 15, 1895 Pope Leo XIII (1810–1903) appointed vicar apostolic G. Makarios who took the name of bishop Cyril. Once elected, Cyril guided a delegation to Rome asking for the realization of the parochiality. Pope Leo XIII agreed to this request through the apostolic letter "Christi Domini" of 26 November 1895, which officially restored the Coptic patriarch of Alexandria of Egypt. Catholic Coptic priests can get married except for the bishops; the majority of them lives in Egypt and in Sudan; and, as stressed above, very few migrated to other countries.

2   Migrations and Presence

The migration fluxes in Italy were historically mainly from Egypt due to the persecutions and the violence against the Coptic community. Today, the presence of the Copts in Italy is supposed to be around 70,000 people scattered along the territory (International Congress of Coptic Studies, 2016; Ambrosiana Community Report, 2018). The majority is centered around the Milan area. The total number of the Copts in Italy remains quite obscure also because of the non-compulsory religious identity clarification in Italian censuses (Bottoni, 2019). In France, there are about 250,000 Copts, and in Great Britain 20,000. In total, Egyptian migrants in Italy are estimated to be around 119,000 (Istat, 2018), with the Copts representing almost one third of this total. The role of this religious community is very important: the Copts not only give to their parishioners, but they offer shelter to local communities, thus valorizing the churches and the places where they pray and live. Violence hits but does not prevail. The religious structure facilitates positive assimilation. Copts Churches are present on the Italian territory as follows: in Tuscany, Florence, St. Mina Coptic Orthodox church in Scandicci; in Lazio, St. George, and St. Mark in Rome; in Lombardy, monastery Anba Shenouda in Lacchiarella, St. Mary & St. Antonius in Cinisello Balsamo, St. Mark in Milan; in Piedmont, St. Mary, Turin.

The recent presence of the Copts in Italy dates back to the 1970s; pastoral activities started in those years, too. In 1973, the historical meeting between Pope Paul VI (1897–1978) and Shenuda III, Pope of the Copts, marked the conclusion of a route that lasted fourteen centuries. Since 1982, the Copts have not increased their presence in the Milan area, where today there are two bishops, one monastery, the Episcopal seat in Lacchiarella, close to the city of Milan, and twenty parishes and other communities are growing quickly. Moreover, in 1995, a second reality organized by the Coptic community in Italy, in collaboration with the Patriarch Tawadros II (Waqih Sobhi Bakky Suleiman, born in 1952), 118th Pope of the Copt Orthodox Church, did appear in Turin, Rome, Florence and its surroundings. It was divided into some main areas: Rome, Florence, Perugia, Bologna and Reggio Emilia, Turin (plus the other centers of Genova, La Spezia and Bari), with the central seat in Rome under the guide of the bishop Barnaba El Soryany. The Coptic diocese of Rome has some 7,000 worshippers. The Coptic Church found a welcoming environment in Italy, where it was possible to show all the vitality of a Christian reality that survived centuries of persecution, an intense liturgical life focused on the radical experience of the monasticism of the desert, and an active interest for the mutual support of the faithful in various aspects of social and family life. The Coptic Church is in favor of the theological dialogue between Christians and supports many initiatives for Christian realities in the Middle East. Cinisello Balsamo, Milan, is the Episcopal seat with Anba Kirolos, metropolitan bishop of Europe, who died in 2017 and strongly contributed to the construction and realization of ten churches in the Milan area. Today (2019), the new bishop is Anba Antonius. Visiting the Episcopal seat is very instructive to try to understand the Coptic world. From outside, it looks like a former factory that remained as it used to be. Inside, it has been totally renovated: in the main corpus, today, there is a beautiful Coptic church that can seat up to 500 people. All around there are buildings for parishioners' gatherings after the celebrations, for catechism, priests' residential houses, and the bishop residence. Joining a Coptic Mass is a fascinating experience; the whole community sings and dialogues with the priest in Coptic, in Greek and in Italian. The community is very young, with many families with more than three children; this is one of the main reasons of the great attention to the religious education of the young Coptic generations. Furthermore, it is interesting to note the new positive experiences of the open oratories during summer. Here, the children join the priests, as the Coptic structures remain open during summertime, while others usually close. Among the nine Coptic churches in Milan, only one is Catholic in origin, which is the one in Senato Street, in the very center of Milan, dedicated to St. Mark. The other churches have been restored from abandoned buildings, such as the one in Gorla and in Saronno. In Gorla, a dismissed industrial area has been bought through a judicial action and two industrial sheds were united so that it could host all the parishioners. In Saronno, instead, a formerly abandoned gym became a place to deal drugs and created many problems to the local inhabitants. The Copt community helped Saronno through the acquisition of this degraded space. The proof of this positive initiative was that the *Via Crucis* celebrated by Cardinal Angelo Scola through the pastoral zone 4 during the route between the two stations saw the alternation in carrying the Cross of St. Charles containing the Saint Nail of a Coptic exponent, a Romanian, and a Russian: important signs of the multi-religious reality. The commitment to redevelop abandoned spaces is among the main tasks of the Coptic Church in Italy. This is the answer of a migrant community in touch with its identity, which never stops dialoguing with the surrounding communities and attempts to solve many troubled situations in order to set constructive examples to many people.

3   Terrorist Attacks and the Coptic Church in Italy

Since 2011, hundreds of Egyptian Copts have been killed in sectarian clashes, and many homes and businesses have been destroyed. In just one province (Minya in Egypt), 77 cases of sectarian attacks against Copts between 2011 and 2018 have been documented. Copts migrated to Italy from Egypt between 1952 and 1975 because they could not find jobs due to discrimination. Their wives could not go to a Coptic gynaecologist because Coptic gynaecologists could not practice – and this is just one of the examples of daily discrimination faced by Copts in Egypt. Equality did not exist at work or in the streets. If a woman was seen walking around wearing a cross, she would have to face harassment. It was forbidden to park cars outside of any church. Copts have been, and still are, strangers in their own country. In Egypt, rarely are documents released to Copts, and they prohibit people from converting to Christianity by putting them in jail. The terrorist attacks against Copts in Egypt during these recent years were all firmly condemned by the Italian governments and by the main religious communities. According to bishop al-Soryani, all Christians expressed their grief in the demonstration against the terroristic attacks in 2000 in Kosheh, where 21 Copts died, and on 7 January 2010 in Naga Hammadi, where eight Copts were shot dead in the Upper Egyptian city of Naga Hammadi, right in front of the cathedral. On that occasion, Italy condemned violence against Coptic Christians in Egypt, with Foreign Minister F. Frattini during his second mandate (2008–11) saying he would personally take up the matter with his Egyptian counterpart on a visit to Cairo. The violence perpetrated against the Christian Copt community in Egypt was horrific and outrageous after six Copts and one Muslim police officer were killed, apparently by Muslims, in the south of the country. At least nine more Copts were wounded, two of them seriously, when drive-by attackers raked a crowd of shoppers in a southern Egypt town with gunfire, on the eve of their Christmas celebrations. Rome and Milan's Coptic community organized demonstrations in various parts of the country to express support to Coptic Christians in Egypt after the New Year's Eve bomb attack on a church in Alexandria in 2017 (Cucca, 2018). Milan saw a sit-in in front of the Egyptian embassy in Porpora Street, with some demonstrators blocking the road for a few hours. Tensions increased when Muslim citizens arrived, and police intervention was required. No demonstration received the support of the Coptic diocese of Milan, which consists of about 12,000 Copts guided by Anba Antonius. The bishop did not approve of the sit-in from a spiritual point of view since he disagreed with the idea of priests leaving the church to demonstrate in the streets. There were two main reasons. First, it must be noted that the Coptic Church is not a political entity; second, the way to support the Copts in Egypt is through prayer and sending aid to the affected families. This is why Coptic churches of the diocese of Milan held a mass prayer on 8 January 2018 for the dead and the wounded of the Alexandria attack. The diocese agreed to meet Egypt's ambassador to Italy and the consul general in Milan at the monastery of Anba Shenouda in Lachiarella to express condolences and discuss the current situation of the Copts in Egypt. They stressed the urgency of an education reform, the spread of the concept of citizenship regardless of religious affiliation, changing the rules for church construction, upholding the rights of non-Muslim families, and other measures aimed at eliminating inequality between Copts and Muslims. The Coptic Church asked them not to make any comments so as not to make the situation worse and endanger the lives of the Copts in Egypt. Fear pervaded in the Milan demonstration. All those interviewed were reluctant to give their names, afraid of endangering relatives in Egypt. They denounced the Egyptian government's conspiracy of silence, which, they said, failed to put an end to the discriminations against the Copts, though it had been stipulated in the Constitution. Interviewees cited the need to obtain a presidential decree to build a church and pointed out the low number of Copts in parliament, as well as the fact that key positions remain inaccessible to Copts. Many of the Egyptians who joined the sit-in had emigrated because of religious discrimination, which had prevented them either from finding a job or from advancing in their careers.

Rome was also ripe with Coptic reactions to the incident. Unlike Milan, the Rome diocese organized a January 2018 demonstration in support of Coptic Egyptians and against terrorism and religious discrimination. Criticism started before the event, when al-Soryani asked Muslims and Jews not to take part in the Repubblica Square sit-in, saying it was the wish of the Copts to mourn within their community. He invited them to organize a different demonstration.

About 1,000 Copts from different areas, including Turin, Florence, and Reggio Emilia, gathered amid massive security measures. Prayers in Arabic and Italian were recited by bishop al-Soryan and priests from all over the Diocese. Another recent attack was in Minya, in Egypt, on 2 November 2018. A prayer in St. Peter's Basilica preceded the Rome demonstration, and Catholics could show solidarity with the global Christian community. Common requests to the Egyptian government by Copts from both Milan and Rome were cancelling the field of religion in identity cards, changing regulations on the construction and restoration of churches, changing the school curriculum to include the pre-Islamic period, which used to be omitted, and other reforms aiming at eliminating religious discrimination. On 9 July 2018, the President Sergio Mattarella received at the Quirinale Tawadros II, Pope of Alexandria and of San Mark. Pope Tawadros II, Pope of the Copts, came from Bari, and then he went in the Basilica of St. Paul Outside the Walls in Rome with Anba Barnaba, Anba Antonius and Anba Wisa. Ambassadors of Rome and of Vatican City, Hisham Badr and Mahmud Sami with a diplomatic delegation with Wael Selim. During the celebration, Anghelos Bisha became the new bishop of Florence, beloved by his parishioners when he was in Rome. Pope Tawadros II appointed the new Coptic bishop of Milan, Anba Antonius, as successor of Anba Kirolos. He graduated in medicine at Assiut University and at Ain Shams University in Cairo. He chose the monastic life and he lived in the Anba Shenouda monastery in Milan serving many churches of the Coptic community. Anba Antonius is the new bishop of Milan and its surroundings, with the Venice exemption.

4   Conclusions

While the Coptic tradition and presence constitutes an ancient and strong reality in Italy, today the majority of Italians are substantially ignoring Copts' lives and activities. The striking lack of recent sources and information, compared to the richness of Middle Eastern sources of such a lively religious reality in Italy, is a symptom of the deep necessity for further research on this important topic. The history of religious and political persecutions and violence is a tragedy that affected all Copts, most of all in Egypt. Throughout their Diaspora history, the principle of unity as a nation represented Copts' only hope, and it was only within the context of the nation-state that the point of unity could be possible across all the religious and cultural differences. The creation and the necessity for the definition of religious minorities was a dramatic passage in Christian Copts' history. They refused to be classified as a religious minority and claimed the recognition of their identity not on a religious basis but on a national one. This topic is so vast that it could represent a further issue of research alone. Moreover, the Coptic presence in Italy, as described above, can surely be seen as positive, since the Coptic Church not only takes care of its parishioners, but is also very generous with the whole environment and the surrounding communities. Coptic migration and generosity are positive and potential issues to a future communication and a future understanding between religious as well as between social communities in Italy.

CHAPTER 19

Religious Belonging and (Forced) Migration: a Study on Migrant Coptic Families in Italy

Cristina Giuliani and Camillo Regalia

1 (Forced) Migrants and Post-migration Processes

Within the extant psychology scientific literature, the epidemiological and psychiatric perspectives for a long time have been predominant in research on (forced) migration processes. The latter approach aims at assessing the typology and severity of pre-migration traumas (including war-related violence, exposure to persecution for religious and/or political reasons, injustice and oppression) as well as their effects on the mental health of adult and under-age migrants (Hussain, Bhushan, 2009; Jović *et al.*, 2005; McGregor *et al.*, 2015; Reading, 2009; Wilson, Tang, 2007).

Recently, such theoretical models have become richer and more complex in two respects:

a) firstly, the focus has shifted from the pre-migration to the post-migration phase; this is characterized by numerous stressors related to resettlement and acculturative processes, which increase long-term risks of mental health issues (Betancourt *et al.*, 2015; Laban *et al.*, 2008);

b) secondly, the identification of risk factors and protective processes capable of moderating the link between cumulative trauma and psychosocial well-being has become richer.

Overall, although psychological/psychiatric diagnoses and comparisons are at times difficult, research on (forced) migrants, refugees and asylum seekers confirms the groups' high rates of psychological suffering, as well as increasing psychic pathologies in the post-migration phase. Indeed, this phase is likely characterized by a vicious cycle featuring the disruptive effects of traumas and difficulties prior to migration and of the multiple losses and stressors faced in the respective resettlement countries, ultimately leading to a shift from an "actual exile" condition to a "psychological exile condition" (Ellis *et al.*, 2008; Jović *et al.*, 2015; Salvatore *et al.*, 2014).

As noted by a growing body of scientific literature featuring empirical studies mostly conducted in the United States, Canada and Israel on refugee groups that are relatively homogenous as for geographical provenance (Sudan, Eritrea,

Iraq) as well as religious faith (Christian), several variables appear to be correlated to migrants' processes of psychological adjustment and mental health.

Although laden with expectations of safety and hope, (forced) migrants' arrival in their respective resettlement country engenders delusion and suffering. This sharpens the condition of psychological "exile". Amongst the most frequently noted risk factors during the resettlement phase, there are the lengthiness of juridical asylum procedures, the uncertainty of living conditions, prolonged stays in immigration detention centers (Kronick *et al.*, 2015; Laban *et al.*, 2008); the feeling of being discriminated in the resettlement country due to ethnicity or religion, aggravating the experience of migrants which have already suffered from oppression in their country of origin and injustice; the accumulation of stressful circumstances such as poverty, loss of social roles and status, unemployment, social isolation, identity and culture loss, precariousness of dwelling, discrimination, separation from family members (Betancourt *et al.*, 2015; Ellis *et al.*, 2008; Weine, 2008, 2011).

In addition to the aforementioned stressors, acculturation implicates further difficulties, such as the encounter with a new society and being faced with other cultural models. These experiences cause acculturation stress, intra- and extra-familiar cultural clashes (i.e. couple conflicts, intergenerational acculturative gaps) (Betancourt *et al.*, 2015; Nakash *et al.*, 2015; Yako, Biswas, 2014).

Within the extant research, post-migration stressors and adversities faced by migrants have received considerable attention. However, few studies have considered the role of resilience and protective processes in influencing post-migration adaptation among (forced) migrants and refugees from a salutogenic point of view. According to the Conservation of Resources Theory (COR – Betancourt *et al.*, 2015; Hooberman *et al.*, 2010; Silove, 2013), migrant individuals and families face multiple traumatic losses during migration but they are also able to conserve, use and enhance many types of resources (individual, familiar, and collective). According to this framework, the impact of (forced) migration transition is linked to a deeper understanding of the interplay between cumulative pre- and post- resettlement stressors and protective processes on the individual, family and community level (APA, 2010; Bottura, Mancini, 2016; Kramer, Bala, 2010).

Overall, the few quantitative studies conducted on refugee families highlight the presence of positive resources capable of supporting families through this difficult life stage. Resources include family cohesion, community support and the support granted by formal institutions, the relationship with one's country of origin, a parental investment and the stability of children's upbringing (parenting styles, school support, and parental investment), transnational relationships and spiritual beliefs. The stronger one's cultural identity, the better such families seem to cope with the difficulties they encounter. On an individual level, religious faith and a strong sense of belonging to a religious community play an important protective role as migrants resettle in new societies. Religious identity is a strong feature of cultural identity and it acts as a spiritual resource as individuals accept and process events (Betancourt *et al.*, 2015; Bottura, Mancini, 2016; Laban *et al.*, 2008; McGregor *et al.*, 2015; Yako, Biswas, 2014).

The well-being of younger generations, which experienced (forced) migration, is also strongly linked to some relational resources within their family (cohesion, supportive relationship with parents, parental monitoring, maintenance of cultural and collective identity, effective use of external resources and services) and school (e.g. positive feeling about school, sense of school belonging) (McGregor *et al.*, 2015; Trentacosta *et al.*, 2016).

Within the scenario described above, religion and belonging to a religious community deeply affect migrant people's lives. As previously noted in the present book (Part 1 and Chapter 17), the rebuilding of community and faith-based organizations in their respective resettlement countries has a significant impact on integration processes for religious minorities that have suffered from marginalization and violence in their country of provenance. A body of historical-anthropological as well as sociological literature corroborates this, as it aims at exploring and understanding the experience and history of the so-called migrant Christian Churches, also named Diasporic Churches, well established in several Western countries.[1]

It is worth bearing in mind that within the psychology literature on (forced) migrations reviewed in the present book, for a long time, religion has been exclusively considered as a category to identify pre-migration traumas linked to religion-related persecution. Indeed, few studies have explored the interplay between religion and ethnicity in post-migration identity redefinition process (Eid, 2003; Van Dijk, Botros, 2009). This seeming lack of research is remarkable, especially when considering that transnational religious groups and institutions constitute a resilient resource in supporting members' resettlement and

---

1   As described in Chapter 18, two terms are used to indicate Egyptian Copt migration, namely "Coptic diaspora", phrase promoted by secular activist Copt organizations in the West, and "Copts/Coptic Churches in the lands of immigration", promoted by the Egyptian Church. The double terminology is symptom of two competing narratives and transnational strategies: the former focuses on human rights and Coptic persecution at the hands of Muslims, the latter focuses on religion and on efforts to persuade Copts to preserve their religious identity in their lands of immigration (Galal, 2012a, 2012b; Haddad, 2013). On the complexity of the concept of diaspora, see also Karoui, 2012.

acculturation experiences (Bottura, Mancini, 2016; Connor, 2012; Gozdziak, 2002).

As thoroughly illustrated in the first part of the present work, there are several reasons for the limited research interest taken into the variety and diversity of migrant groups' religious experiences, especially regarding Christian (forced) migrants. Psychological research, too, has prevalently described migrant people based on their ethnicity (country of origin). In turn, this has prioritized the focus on ethnic identity whilst blurring other components of identity, thus neglecting the importance of further cultural, religious and language differences amongst migrant groups from the same country. On the contrary, in Western countries, scientific literature and research have looked at religion almost only when the latter is perceived as a problematic issue for how immigrant minorities and the local majority interact in resettlement countries (Sparre, Galal, 2018). As a consequence, in Europe and in other Western countries with a long-standing history of immigration (US, Canada, Australia), attention has mostly been paid to Islam and to integration processes of first- and second-generation immigrant Muslims (Giuliani *et al.*, 2018).

However, over the last decade, it is worth noting that scholars have indeed taken interest in the adjustment process of immigrant Eastern Christian Churches in North America (Canada, US) and in some North-European countries. Next to historical-political perspectives (Chapter 18), studies have been observing the complexity of Middle Eastern Christians' migration experiences to the West, as well as the prominent role played by religious institutions in the lives of their members (Diez, 2017; Marzouki, 2016; Sparre, Galal, 2018).

A recent multi-site fieldwork project conducted in Sweden, Denmark and UK (DIMECCE, 2015; https://arts.st-andrews.ac.uk/dimecce) has explored identity formation processes of three *Middle Eastern Christians* groups (Iraqi, Assyrian/Syriac, Coptic Orthodox Christians) migrated to European countries and the distinctive traits of their post-migration resettlement experiences. Generally, marginalization and *double minority status* seem to characterize the experiences of immigrant Middle Eastern Christians in Europe. They are a religious minority in their Muslim-majority country of origin *and* in their new countries of residence, resulting in their frequently being an invisible minority within a mostly Muslim immigrant group. Galal *et al.* (2016) suggest that this double minority status is nevertheless displayed in different ways in the three case study countries and that such display is dependent on several factors (specific location, community size, diversity and minority position). In London (UK), where Middle Eastern Christians are one group among others without an apparent majority, they present themselves as a visible minority within a multi-cultural and multi-ethnic setting. In Taastrup (Denmark), Middle

Eastern Christians are an invisible minority within a visible Arab Muslim immigrant minority. In Södertälje (Sweden), the high concentration of Assyrian/
Syriac Christians living around their churches makes them a visible majority (a
"Little Assyria" or "Little Babylon") within an immigrant minority. The diasporic identity of these communities requires careful apprehension of their specific resettlement experiences and relative cultural encounters (Sparre, Galal,
2018).

A few recent studies –mostly carried out in North America– confirm migrant Coptic Churches' will to remain separate and distinct from mainstream
society (Van Dijk, Botros, 2009). Said choice seems to be due to both the recent
migration history of these communities and to their efforts to retain a strong
and distinct ethnic-religious identity in the countries of immigration. Furthermore, these works highlight the prominent role played by migrant Churches
and faith-based institutions in preserving a strong connection to the Mother
Church and homeland Egypt, replicating religious rituals, negotiating an
ethno-religious identity within immigrant societies and supporting adaptation
of their members (Botros, 2006; Brinkerhoff, 2009, 2014, 2016; Galal, 2012b;
Saad, 2010; Sparre, Galal, 2018; Van Dijk, Botros, 2009; Westbrook, Saad, 2017).

Lastly, a recent quantitative research carried out in United States (Brinkerhoff, 2016) comparing different generations of Coptic immigrants shows that
second and third generations are experiencing a selective acculturation pattern, characterized both by a selective retention of their heritage culture and
by efforts of positive socioeconomic assimilation in mainstream society. Thus,
younger generations' positive assimilation efforts do not seem to prevent the
preservation of a strong heritage identity.

Given the extant literature outlined above, and considering the scarcity of
psychological studies taking into account Middle Eastern Christian immigrant
families' narratives and subjective experiences of migration, the aim of the research illustrated in this chapter has been to explore the post-migration experience of Coptic Orthodox families immigrated from Egypt to Northern Italy,
comparing perception and narratives of two different family generations (first-
generation parents and their second-generation children).

2   The Present Study

The present study aims to explore post-migration experiences among Coptic
Orthodox families immigrated from Egypt to Northern Italy. Specifically,
we explored and compared parents and children's narratives about family

migration history and projects, negotiation processes of their identity within the Italian society, intergenerational transmission of values and practices, role played by religious communities and institutions in their lives, social and community support network.

As previously described (Chapter 18), the Egyptian immigrant community in Italy numbers 119,513 individuals (67.7% of them living in Lombardy, a region in Northern Italy) officially residing in Italy on January 1, 2018 (ISTAT, 2018) and it is amongst the largest Muslim minorities in the country. For this immigrant group, the first migration wave was male-dominated. Although this trend was gradually counterbalanced by the arrival of women and children within the scope of family reunification, even today, female Egyptian immigrants in Italy are fewer than male immigrants (33% versus 67%) (ISTAT, 2018). Within the Egyptian immigrant community, it is estimated that the number of Orthodox Copts ranges between 18,000 and 40,000 (https://www.chiesadimilano.it/news/chiesa-diocesi/vivacita-e-fermenti-dei-cristiani-copti-a-milano-146112.html).

From April to June 2017, ten Coptic Orthodox families coming from Egypt participated in the study. Members of Coptic Churches located in Milan suburban area were contacted to inform families about the possibility to take part in the research project and recruit them. For every recruited family, both parents and a preadolescent/adolescent child were interviewed, for a total of 30 interviewed participants: 10 first-generation fathers, 10 first-generation mothers, and 10 second-generation children. Fathers were aged between 37 and 51 years (M=44.9) and they had lived in Italy on average for 19.4 years (range: 17–27 y.). Mothers had immigrated to Italy from Egypt through family reunification, were aged between 34 and 43 years (M=38.4) and had lived in Italy on average for 15 years (range: 9–18 y.). Pre-adolescent and adolescent children (5 males, 5 females) were aged between 13 and 16 years (M= 13.5), mostly born in Italy (only 2 had been reunified with their families before they were two) and attending secondary school.

After being informed of the general aim and scope of the research, interested adult participants with their children were invited to sign a consent form and interviewed individually by a researcher with extensive experience in qualitative interviewing and (forced) migration-related topics (Pernice, 1994).

Upon having granted anonymity to participants, the in-depth interviews took place at the respondents' Church. The interview aimed at gauging interviewees' perceptions of the changes occurred in their lives following migration (only for adult respondents), of the challenges and hardships faced in Italy, comparisons between homeland and resettlement country, personal and family immigration history, identity construction process, intergenerational communication of values, family relationship and community context (family, school, work, leisure), activities and role of the Coptic Church in their lives.

All interviews were conducted in Italian. Adult and young participants differed in their fluency in the Italian language, with some linguistic difficulties encountered whilst interviewing adult participants.

The interviews were recorded and transcribed verbatim in order to carry out a thematic analysis of the transcripts. Thematic analysis was conducted utilizing Atlas.ti 7.0 (Muhr, 2004); the transcripts were uploaded on the database and subsequently coded independently by two researchers. External team members who were not directly involved with the analysis reviewed the transcripts, methodology and analytic strategy to increase the study's credibility and validity.

3   Results

The thematic analysis carried out on the interview transcripts has allowed to identify several themes, revealing the complexity that characterizes Coptic families' post-migration experience in Italy. The choice to interview first generation parents and children from the same family has allowed to highlight parallelisms and similarities emerging from their stories.

Firstly, the *separation from the home country because of migration* has been a recurring theme amongst interviews conducted with first-generation parents – which have directly experienced the migration journey, unlike their children. Although they migrated many years ago, separation from the country of origin and the feeling of estrangement upon arriving in Italy is a strong, vivid memory especially for women.

> (...) it's that after you've come here with no job, no language (...) no identity (...) you are very very painful because one is not recognized like, like in Egypt (...) and maybe this is something we all suffer without distinctions, without one taking the skin off ... language ... look, waving hello in the street, what can you say? All these ... without ... naked. (Mother 1)

In the long run, the disorientation experienced upon arrival is coupled with the difficulties and stressful conditions caused by the encounter with another culture and by the acculturation process. Interviewed parents mostly recall the challenging redefinition of gender roles. This has shown both forms of defensive closure towards the new environment to preserve heritage culture (mostly for men) and bi-cultural approaches striving to combine heritage culture and new culture (mostly from women). The starkest perceived difference with the new culture concerns the deeply cultural range of gender roles identity within family and society – strict and traditional gender roles can clash with Western, more egalitarian gender roles definition within families.

> Most things I cannot, I don't understand because the culture is different (…) Let's say, if before there was something they shouldn't do because it is not possible for females to do this, that … like in Egyptian culture. (…) For me, all this I still cannot accept because it is an evil thing. (Mother 2)

> I, like before, haven't changed anything … Everything is the same … same, even though the society was new to me, the culture was new but I have stayed like I was born until now. (Father 1)

> I like it as, as a way of living in general, let's say … as I said earlier Egypti-talian. I take the good from this and the good from that, too, I cannot be pure Italian and pure Egyptian, too (…) now, I am a bit stronger, I manage to do many things, let's say because it's a mum responsible of a house and children. I have to make decisions about many things. This has changed, it wasn't like this before, I was not like this. But now I've become like this, I want to choose, to think things through. (Mother 3)

Memories of pre-migration experiences come to live in both parents and children's stories – although they have never lived in Egypt, children speak about marginalization of and discrimination against their parents in several areas of Egyptian social life, especially the work environment (see also Chapter 20). If, on the one hand, the choice to migrate is linked to a need and a desire for personal and professional emancipation, on the other hand migrant people's high-profile education background was seemingly not adequately matched by the work environment upon arrival. Thus, comparison with the Muslim majority in Egypt is mostly explicitly recalled in terms of discrimination.

> Well, my father was like a lawyer in Egypt, but he was Christian anyway, so when compared with Muslim lawyers … it was more likely that they would hire them instead of him and so … he came here essentially for work, then essentially from what I remember he started working at a restaurant first, then at a garage and in places like this, then he opened a cleaning company and now he goes, well he works with … he has a van with which he works with those who make advertisements. (Son 7)

Look, there are many reasons in Egypt, for us even finding a job is too difficult, as us, as Christians, even in the middle of Egypt, too much effort. (Father 4)

About every aspect of life, even when you are to go to the hospital, when you are at the hospital, all folks are the same, no? No, instead, it's not like that in Egypt for them. (Mother 9)

Episodes of violence against Christians remain in the background. Only two of the men interviewed address it very carefully and prudently; as they recall, episodes happened in the distant past, they mention the Christians' centuries-long martyrdom in Egypt. As far as discrimination is concerned, the comparison with the Muslim majority is explicit, whereas as far as religion-based persecution against Christians is concerned, the theme is treated with greater prudence and awareness of the situation in Egyptian society – mentioning violence suffered by Christians does not imply that Islam or Muslims are generally enemies, but it refers to extremists or jihadists.

The Churches of Egypt have paid with so much blood, since the early days up to now. (Father 2)

In the old generations, grandfathers of grandfathers of grandfathers, we come from a city, from a town where everybody was Christian and half of them were killed. And others fled and others have been killed because they were Christians ... (...) This is something like they have killed more than 3,000 people just because they were Christians, and we're talking about 350 years ago. (Father 1)

I have experienced them. From the beginning of the 1980s until 1986 – I have seen my brother jumping from the second floor, running away from jihadists who wanted to kill him because somehow at the time he had let his beard grow, and let his hair grow longer. They said: "You look like your Christ in movies", so they had to kill him. Jumping off, he broke his leg, but other friends brought him to the station and managed to escape. (Father 1)

There have also been terrible moments, in 1997 here in Italy, I heard of my 27 years old brother killed whilst he was praying in church with groups of young people, reciting the vespers, it was Wednesday 12th February, an extremist had gone to the church and made all these young people die as they were praying ... my brother was the leader of the group and I went back to Egypt to be close to my family until this bad moment went away, but we consider him as a martyr because we was dead only for this reason, nothing else, then my family mourned a little, but faith grows anyway. (Father 1)

More than religion-based persecution, the theme of *martyrdom* is recurring amongst interviewed adults, both mothers and fathers. Telling dramatic events about Christians' persecution asserts one's faith's strength and courage and strengthens the feeling of belonging to the millenary history of the Coptic community, scattered with martyrdoms. As they speak of Christians who were killed in Egypt, interviewed mothers claim and repeat together that "No one is afraid to die" – martyrdom is "not a bad thing"; rather, it is a destiny, evidence and message of faith.

> Interviewer: but maybe it is harder to be religious when ...
> No, no, no, that is not the case because even when it happened on Palm Sunday ... even after Holy Week there were even more people, for example inside a church there were 3,000 people, there were even 5,000 people inside. They go more often, they go to church even if something happens, my brother. No, no, no, no one is afraid of that.
> Interviewer: One needs to be strong, when these things happen
> Eh, yes it is not a problem at all, on the contrary, they say next time we all go to church, we must be martyrs ourselves ... even the Gospel that is always in church and this, no one, no one is afraid to die. (Mother 5)

> No one is afraid to die, that also becomes martyr because it is not a bad thing. Because all these martyrs is not (...) prayer because ... we are close to them ... yes but, I'm saying that we are also happy, we are not that afraid ... this never happens. (Mother 8)

Martyrdom conveys the same spiritual strength that animates Coptic migration (according to others, Diaspora) and thus the destiny of all migrants and immigrant Coptic Egyptian families. Migration and all its related suffering find a meaning in being testimony to faith, in serving Christ and in the mission for others. "That's why they are scattered" claims a woman, valuing migration as a choice at once of sorrow and glory – "our pain is our glory". Interviewees' narratives confirm and make apparent that attributing spiritual meaning to one's suffering is amongst the most effective and positive resilience strategies to cope with persecutions (Betancourt *et al.*, 2015; Laban *et al.*, 2008; McGregor *et al.*, 2015; Yako, Biswas, 2014).

> I had to leave family behind to go to a place where you don't know where you're going to stay, what to eat, but this is why there is faith within us,

that we serve Christ this is why there is not fear to go far away and serve like this, my family gave me the courage to serve like this ... (Father 1)

(*being Coptic*) is the most beautiful thing in the world even if suffering is a part of our glory as a Church. This is our core teaching. The martyrs of the Coptic Church and the suffering in the Middle East, the whole Church, especially us because the Christian majority in the Middle East has taught me our bishop, he has always taught me that our pain is our glory ... this is part of their cross also for us. If you are Christian in Egypt, you are not Muslim, this has been our identity and this to nurture oneself. (Mother 2)

Coptic means that the Coptic Church has always ... been persecuted, it has ... they have offered to their sons, as martyrs do, so I'm happy ... uhm ... I'm Coptic, uhm ... and so our Church ... let's say ...we were few in our country ... (Father 5)

Like the presence of the Lord in Egypt and Christians in Egypt keep on until the last day on Earth and they proclaim his presence here, (...) They are scattered because of this, because it is a very honorable thing ... not for us to be the only ones to keep his Kingdom, we need to give it for others, too (...). None of us wanted to leave Egypt because it is the most beautiful country in the world for us, but with all these bombs, with all these martyrs he has urged of us to go and bring the mission to others. (Mother 1)

As far as identity is concerned, and especially when comparing themselves to Italians, the deep spirituality and the belonging to the Coptic Community are central elements. Comparison with Italian peers –and with the Italian society more generally– emerges from interviews conducted with second-generation children. Such a comparison is instrumental to claim the positive in-group's distinctiveness related to spirituality and assiduous religious practice in a largely non-religious context.

(*Being a member of an Egyptian Coptic family*) is something that surely makes us different from the others ... because everyone is used to one way of living, whilst I am used to a very different one. Nowadays, I see that the religious sphere shrinks in Italian families, whereas it grows a lot in Egyptian families where it is always increasing because of the persecutions, the suffering, and the suffering of Christians worldwide and most of all in the Middle East and in the East and most of all in Egypt. (Son 1)

Very few Italians go to church ... some (of their Italian peers) are Christians and they have no faith at all, they are Christians, but they do not even believe in Jesus ... (Daughter 6)

Those are not duties, because we love the Church ... (...) yes, it is part of my identity, something specific of our life and Church, Mass, and prayer always! (Mother 6)

I wanted to say that the most important thing about Egypt is that people are more attached to the Church here than in Italy. (Father 1)

Interviews show the efforts of parents and religious institutions to pass down values, practices and religious beliefs to young generations. The aim of such an intergenerational communication of values is twofold: firstly, it aims at granting adults' continuity of individual churchgoing experiences; secondly, it aims at ensuring obedience to what is preached by the Mother Church to diasporic Churches. The relationship with homeland Egypt and Mother Church is very deeply-rooted – indeed, religious identity references and features an ethnic dimension acting as a strong bond with homeland Egypt.

No, faith hasn't changed our Church, here it is the same as the one in Egypt, nothing changes. Even there, all my life I was like him (points at her son) always at church and always at Catechism with parents always for us. (Mother 1)

We are Christians, we have been used to it since we were born, we are always in church and do a lot of things we grew up like this and then I want that my children, too, grow up like we have lived, always growing up here in church and become children of God, not children of the world, that is what we want to be, children of God. (Mother 1)

Because most of all my dad and my mum are very devoted to the Church, to Christianity, they never let I go, my dad always prays for anything and most of all my dad, and my mum a bit less, she's very Christian compared to me and my sister and even for the little things for example, the computer breaks and instead of calling she prays and it's all good, then she calls the technician who fixes it in no time then Mass everyday my dad my mum sometimes after she's taken me to school then she goes, too, otherwise she stays home and is the housewife. (Son 1)

My parents even at catechism they always tell me, when you don't manage to do something ... let's make an example, during a school test, you know that you have studied a lot, say that you've been studying that book for three hours, to pass the History test and then you can't remember anything and then you recall the teaching of your parents at catechism and you make the sign of the cross and maybe then you calm down, you trust in Jesus and then maybe you can also hope that the school test goes well. (Son 2)

For both children and parents, praying, rites and activities at the Coptic Church in Italy are crucial.

Faith is fundamental in my life, everything I do is related to faith … during the day there is Mass, a specific prayer, and I attend it every day and every week I go to the Sunday Mass and on Saturday, too, on Saturday morning, then there are the afternoon prayers and the vespers at night which I always attend … (Son 1)

Religious structures and Coptic communities in Italy greatly support and strengthen religious identity. Regarding the post-migration experience, interviewed families acknowledge the centrality of attachment and the role played by Churches in countries of immigration. Coptic Churches support believers in several ways, ranging from providing religious support, to social, affective, material support, too.

No one manages to live here in Milan without the Church, because the Church is just too important … important to live, to pray, to meet someone who is a priest and maybe confess, the chance also to be in church that is a quiet place, far away from life, from the stress of the outside world and so church is simply too beautiful a moment. (Mother 5)

No, I can't see the difference. Here the Church does everything … all Masses, the Holy Week, Christmas, Easter, everything, everything … in summer they have camps, maybe, they do something that … the church is always open to everyone. (Mother 5)

The Churches and those who work for them (priests, bishops, and metropolitans) are a guide and a fundamental point of reference for families coping with an outside world perceived as "threatening" and "negative". Interestingly, interviewed children born here acknowledge said role as guides to navigate a threatening and dangerous world, thus showing a great degree of similarity between how parents and children perceive the world.

I have learned a lot ...sharing other things than games, experiences and fun. (...) I mean, they teach you a lot about how to behave outside, when somebody is unkind to you, I mean from the lives of Saints you learn how to react outside. (...) Well since I pray and since all the friends I have, I have been knowing them since I was a child, let's say that it's a second family. (Son 2)

The outside world is also ugly, boys outside, what happens in schools. I think I gave everything, the right path and the wrong path. So, the Church is always important (...) that children are born like my son, young, so young until they marry her inside the church (...) otherwise even children outside get lost. I mean, the Church is our mum, a mother ... which is also our very own mum. (Mother 5)

(...) so about friendships only at church, there is not friendship at school ... girls have many friends they attend catechism together and afterwards they play together, there is quite a few friends, the churches for us I cannot live without churches. (Father 3)

Priests, bishops and metropolitans participate in families' daily and extraordinary decision-making, striving to concretely help families but also, seemingly, to underline their distance from the external society and its institutions (school and young people's gathering places).

For Coptic people, the priest is a very important figure, then always rely on this priest when they don't know where to come, for me with my community there are always meet-ups, when they have problems they call me, always some ... and ...strength ... joy to gather together. (Father 1)

We followed advice from metropolitan A. who even before becoming priest, for us he was always a father, a father for everything, and he tried to give the right advice, put people on the right path and, I mean, has always passed on that who does good, finds good, a right path is always right, so, I mean ... we have, we have that he has pointed in the right direction, so let's hope that we did very few mistakes, or almost none at all. (Father 5)

I have to answer all, all questions. I am not used to it and I find difficult. The Church has helped me with this. When I cannot answer certain questions, fathers, the Church and the bishops ... because we have a wonderful bishop, really like a father. He lives with us the difficulties that I find with my children ... well ... M., my daughter, in her 5th year of primary school she wanted to go on a school trip for three days. It was the first time because her school usually doesn't bring children to nature camps and I have said, worried: "No M.". Mad, she said "How? Why? All my classmates go apart from me why?" Because I was not used to go on school trips. In Egypt, even at school, boys and girls were apart. Here not, boys sleep ... and I have said no M., and she got mad. I've spoken with our bishop and he said: "Alright, I solve this problem". He called M. and said: "M., we are spending three days in Venice, are you coming with us?" (laughter). (Mother 7)

4   Conclusions

The aim of this study was to explore migration experiences of Coptic Egyptian families migrated to Italy and living around Milan. More specifically, the study aimed at understanding the families' efforts and resources in the context of both their pre-migration experience as a religious minority in their country of origin and of their encounter with a new culture. Adopting the family-based scope whilst designing the study has allowed to explore processes of adjustment and identity redefinition by combining the voices of several members from the same family – namely, first-generation parents and second-generation children. The 10 families interviewed for the present study belong to and regularly attend Coptic Churches located in Milan's suburban area.

Since the earliest stages of research, including the reaching out phase and the recruitment phase, participants showed a strong ethnic-religious identity, corroborating previous studies (Van Dijk, Botros, 2009); the reaching out phase and the first point of contact was mediated and supervised by the local Coptic Church's priest and all interviews took place at the church the families regularly go to. Therefore, the results allowed us to deepen the understanding of the experience of a group of families that share a strong ecclesial belonging as well as a keen involvement in the activities promoted by their Church. Given the potential bias in our sampling processes, we cannot know the extent to which these findings may be generalized to other Egyptian Coptic immigrants living in Italy.

Parent and children's narrations feature several common elements, and this seems to validate the joint efforts of first-generation parents and religious leaders to pass heritage values and practices onto younger generations (Botros, 2006; Saad, 2010; Saad, Westbrook, 2015).

A strong sense of belonging to the religious community and a deep, rooted link with the Mother Church and country of origin characterize the experience of interviewed Coptic families. Interviews have highlighted the all-encompassing reach of the decision to migrate for men and of family reunification processes for women. The feeling of estrangement experienced upon arrival and the grieving loss of one's homeland are extremely vivid. From the interviews, it emerges that religious identity is strongly connected to an ethnic nuance of the link with the country of origin and with the Mother Church in Egypt (see Chapter 18). The interviews also express the efforts and fatigues brought about by the acculturation process, by the perception of cultural differences –unreconcilable, for some– and by feeling threatened and endangered by the outside world.

The cultural encounter with the *Other* recurring across the interviews designates only the encounter with "Italians". Interactions with Italian people often acquire negative connotations, because Italian society is essentially considered non-religious and distant from faith. Such difference with the Italian majority underscores the religious and spiritual distinctiveness of the group one belongs to. It also underlines the distinctive features of the Coptic Church since its formation and its mission for Christianity.

The focus on difference –both religious and ethnic– acts as an intergenerational social glue and it is present in parents *and* children's perceptions of reality and worldviews. Said focus is also the target of great efforts on the part of the parents and the Church to pass on religious faith, to preserve practices and rituals, to maintain a strong link with the Mother Church, in Egypt.

All interviewees (both adolescents and adults) are very proud of the heritage of which they bear witness to the world, as well as about the sorrow and "glory" awaiting Coptic Churches and their believers.

Interviewed individuals –including the second-generation children born in Italy– talk about the difficult situation of Christians in Egypt, where they are marginalized and widely discriminated against by the Muslim majority. Although they do denounce discriminatory behaviors against Christians, interviewees do not talk at length about the acts of violence against Christians in Egypt, nor about Egypt's socio-political situation.

Overall, they do not seem willing to endorse narratives framing them as victims. There is no place for fear, be it fear of the *Other*, fear of suffering or fear of the disintegration of the community. Although one could see a shared psychological mechanism of denial of reality at work, but the latter should not be regarded as dysfunctional. Indeed, Terror Management Theory (Greenberg *et al.*, 1997) points at the stronger adhesion to one's own cultural worldviews as one of the most effective strategies –for individuals and groups– when facing death. Attachment to one's cultural roots and history allows to develop and maintain feelings of symbolic immortality, which counter anxieties and sorrows derived from one's mortality.

Furthermore, interviewees distance themselves from stereotypical representations of Islam as an enemy and of Muslim people as terrorists. Thus, they appear –consciously or unconsciously– to reject the demonizing narratives that are so common in Western countries and illustrated in the introductory part (Chapter 2). For interviewees, the religious theme of martyrdom (in Egypt) and of the migration/diaspora (in Italy) characterize the millenary history of the Coptic Church and as the migration mandate much more decidedly than the theme of violence and persecution against Christians. By praying, interviewees take part in dramatic events unfolding in Egypt, too.

Themes emerged from the interviews are in line with the collective memory and the ethnic-religious identity promoted by the Coptic Orthodox Church on the transnational level (Botros, 2006; Galal, 2012b). As previously noted, the aims and language of such narrative contrast with the narrative promoted by secular Coptic Organizations in immigrant societies (Galal, 2012b; Van Dijk, Botros, 2009). Within the Coptic Churches' narrative, immigrant communities are communities of memory which ensure continuity between the past and the present (Botros, 2006). As highlighted in Chapter 18, several elements from this Coptic narrative are meant to underline the uniqueness and distinctiveness of Coptic communities as regards the outside society; these include the Pharaonic heritage, the twenty centuries of Christianity, the apostolic foundation in Egypt and the glorious early era, up to the latest 14 centuries, which show this Church's resilience, its strength and spirituality, as well as the "miracle of survival". Interviews with parents and children seem to suggest that migration strengthens the celebration of the group's distinctiveness. The theme of migration as a destiny and as a mission conveys the strong link between immigrant Churches and the Mother Church in Egypt, as well as the transnational role of the Mother Church in supporting and guiding immigrant Churches.

In this regard, interviewees greatly value the role played by the community's religious leaders, as they become very dependable in many respects. This applies to migrant parents as well as to young generations, which fulfill their spiritual, material, friendship- and school-related needs within the religious community.

At the same time, interviewees treated the stories of violence against Christians and the issue of relationships between Muslims and Copts in Egypt with great caution. It seems to echo the Mother Church's message and warning to avoid issues that may have an impact on Egyptian society, on relationships between Egyptian Muslims and Christians living in Egypt, as such issues run the risk of easing foreign influence into Egypt's socio-political scenario.

Numerous psychology studies have widely emphasized how the intergenerational transmission of a strong ethnic-religious identity is a key protection factor for migrants who often experience distress and fatigue due to immigration (discrimination, status loss, social isolation). Thus, the focus on the history of the Egyptian Coptic Church and its distinctive traits meet the needs of immigrant communities living in Western countries where they face marginalization (Van Dijk, Botros, 2009). However, the emphasis on the distinctiveness of the Coptic identity raises doubts and questions the risks that could arise from such a stark juxtaposition to –and separation from– Italian people and the Italian society as stereotyped in the interviews. The Coptic minority is often an invisible minority within the resettlement country's society (Galal *et al.*, 2016); consequently, choosing to remain separate from it does not seem to promote cultural contacts with the local majority and its communities (Christians, other immigrant communities). In the long run, the gap may become challenging especially for younger generations born and raised in Italy, as they are expected to be loyal to a migration mandate requiring them to protect and preserve their cultural and religious heritage, prioritizing the latter over an opening towards the new culture. Indeed, a strong commitment to the values passed down from their parents and the Coptic community is a strong protection factor. It is nevertheless worth questioning whether this tendency leaves space for intergenerational negotiation, if the choices of the younger generations deviate from prescribed norms and rules. Furthermore, even if younger generations fully endorse the cultural and familial value system, the relationship with the outside world based mainly on defensive or utilitarian behaviors would be problematic. It is a common bias across immigrant communities to underscore their distinctiveness and positive uniqueness compared to the new context they live in. The main issue concerns the extent to which the Coptic Community intend to maintain this separated acculturative orientation or to pursue a more integrative perspective, enabling their members to be open to the new society and culture, while maintaining their cultural roots (Berry, 1997; Phinney *et al.*, 2001) On the long run, integration is widely recognized as the better solution for immigrants and host society in terms of personal and social well-being. However, in order to achieve this goal, both the Coptic community and the Italian society need to accept the challenge of trespassing the borders they live in and dare to start interacting with each other. The shared Christian faith may help bridge the gap, allowing for mediation and personal contacts.

In line with the prospect of an ethics of hospitality presented in the first part of the present work (Chapter 2), the experiences of the Coptic families interviewed corroborates the crucial role of religion in the post-migration phase, as well as the complexity of (forced) migrants' identity redefinition process.

The religious sphere is intrinsically connected to the history of this community and to the collective memory passed down from one generation to the next. However, the religious sphere necessarily faces the challenges derived from the narratives and counter-narratives that inform the Western gaze on migrants, refugees and asylum seekers. In our study, interviewed families' difficulties with the encounter with the *Other* is conveyed through the perception of the outside world as threatening, a world one needs to be cautious of; yet, at the same time, it is a world in which it is possible to reaffirm the distinctiveness and strength of one's Church. The risk of an introverted tendency and of displaying reactive solutions and behaviors is apparent. As such behaviors risk creating an extreme gap between immigrant communities and the Italian society, they make it more complicated to individuate the *common good* that human migration can promote.

CHAPTER 20

Religious Belonging and (Forced) Migration: a Study on Migrant Coptic Minors in Italy

Giovanni Giulio Valtolina and Paola Barachetti

1 The Effects of Forced Migration on Children

In recent years, a growing number of migrant children have been seeking psychological assistance or mental health treatment in European Union countries. Many of these minors, of different origins and cultural backgrounds, are victims of persecution, ethnic conflict, war or political troubles, and come to Western Europe in search of a better future. However, the condition of migrant is often burdensome, especially in the case of forced migration, and the combined effects of these experiences can lead to problematic consequences for the mental health of boys and girls, bringing additional complexity to their psychological well-being and having negative effects on parent-child interaction (Wiese, Burhorst, 2007).

The literature on the consequences of forced migration for children's health can be summarized in two groups: studies focusing on the immediate effects of forced migration and studies examining long-term effects (Avogo, Agadjanian, 2010). As far as the very short term is concerned, the research significantly demonstrates the disadvantage of children of displaced populations compared to the host population. Thus, a study of mortality rates from 37 conflict zones (Guha-Sapir, Gijsbert, 2004) showed the increase in vulnerabilities among children, especially under the age of five. In the longer term, the results of research on the effects of forced migration on children's mental health are less conclusive, but the high probability of a disadvantaged development seems evident. The results of the long-term impact of forced migration are also documented for their consequences on children's health (Saarela, Elo, 2016; Pavli, Maltezou, 2017; Santavirta, 2017).

Among the factors that induce stress in the persecution, there are some – such as wounds and death threats– that directly affect the child, and others that are more indirect, such as the disintegration of the family and the separation or loss of the parents (Terr, 1988; Yurtbay *et al.*, 2003). The enormous impact of violence –seen or directly experienced– seriously deteriorates the child development. However, according to many child psychologists (i.e. Jensen,

Shaw, 1993; Garmezy, Rutter, 1985), the cognitive abilities of the children, who are still immature, and therefore very flexible and easily malleable, as well as their ability to develop adaptive strategies for self-protection, frequently cover the impact of violence to a certain extent. For example, research report that the children's reactions to stress and behavioral changes were less severe than expected (Masten *et al.*, 1990).

The degree of influence of terrorist attacks and similar violent events on children depends on many factors (Wiese, 2010). The level of expectation of such episodes in the society where the child lives in, the range and time of the violence, the preparation of the society for the attack expected (or not expected), the value of the judgments and of the attitudes of society towards terrorists are considered among these factors. Almost certainly, the personality of the children, their levels of cognitive development, the broad circumstances they live in, the changes that these events cause in their lives and their ages are decisive factors, too. Garmezy and Rutter (1985) highlight that the qualities of the accident that causes stress must be fussily examined: physical and emotional deprivation, hunger, physical injury, loss of loved relatives and friends, as well as being taken away from the dangerous area.

Adolescents, whose physical integrity is very important, tend to perceive wars and terrorist attacks as threats against their bodies. It is generally accepted that those who have previously suffered serious losses within their families or among their friends are much more harshly affected by violence and persecution (Pynoos, Nader, 1990; Wiese 2010).

Furthermore, it has been suggested that not only people directly exposed to traumatic events are affected by long-term damage to mental well-being, but also their significant others, such as their offspring (Dekel, Goldblatt, 2008; Jelinek *et al.*, 2013). The process by which the symptoms associated with trauma are transferred from one person to another is named "*secondary traumatization*" (Rosenheck, Nathan, 1985). Considering a meta-analysis by Bakermans-Kranenburg *et al.* (2003), in non-clinical populations such a transgenerational transmission is unlikely, meanwhile an increased risk to develop mental disorders, particularly PTSD, has been detected in the offspring of individuals with post-traumatic stress disorder (from now on PTSD) (Roberts *et al.*, 2012; Yehuda, Bierer, 2008; Shrira *et al.,* 2011). Furthermore, the processing of biased information is implicated in the adult offspring of parents with PTSD (Suozzia, Motta, 2004; Wittekind *et al.*, 2010).

Since World War II, there has been a growing awareness of children's psychological vulnerability in persecution and in the discriminatory context. Studies on stress reactions related to war in children (Freud, Burlingham, 1973), which identified the mother-child relationship as a protective shield for the psychological well-being of preschool children, and which found out that the separation between mother and child in preschool age has negative effects, have been of great importance.

More recent studies, however, have shown that intimacy to a responsible mother does not fully protect the preschool child from the traumatic effect of the persecution. Studies on children exposed to government persecution have highlighted an improved prevalence of behavioral disorders in the form of social withdrawal, sleep disorders, clinging and over-dependent behavior, chronic fear, depressive moods (Allodi, 1980; Lustig *et al.*, 2004), regressive symptoms, such as separation and stranger anxiety, repeated bed-wetting, tetchiness, loss of learned abilities (Arroyo, Eth, 1985; Thomas *et al.*, 2004), psychic indifference (Dodge, Raundalen, 1987; Craig *et al.*, 2009), and behavior problems such as struggling and insubordination (Baker, 1990; Fazel *et al.*, 2012). Even refugee children, previously exposed to persecution, have been described as showing symptoms such as difficulty in concentrating, sleep disturbances, anxiety, addiction, and depressed mood (Hjern *et al.*, 1991; Schottelkorb *et al.*, 2012).

Since 1980, when PTSD was included as a diagnosis in DSM-III,[1] knowledge of psychological reactions in children exposed to violence and in hazardous backgrounds has been growing significantly. There has been a number of studies on post-traumatic stress reactions in children following violent incidents and disasters, such as witnessed acts of personal violence in countries where minority groups are persecuted (Eth, Pynoos, 1985; Schwarz, Kowalski, 1991). A shared trait of most of these studies is the uniqueness of the traumatic event, whose circumstances are known to researchers by journalists, adult eyewitnesses or police reports. When families flee from war and persecution and move to another country, they are the only sources of information on the traumatic stress they suffered.

Most studies about the reactions of preschool children to danger and ferocity are based on interviews with the parents of children, and sometimes with their teachers, and the results show that parents and teachers tend to underestimate the post-traumatic problems of the children (Almqvist, Brandell-Forsberg, 1995). Furthermore, children can try to protect their parents from knowing the full extent of the traumatic event (Yule, 1991). It is known that traumatized children do not tell what happened until they are asked the right question, and usually do not do it in front of their parents (Eth, Pynoos, 1994). However, there is evidence that even very young children are able to talk about

---

1   The Diagnostic and Statistical Manual of Mental Disorders is the taxonomic and diagnostic tool, published by the American Psychiatric Association (APA), worldwide considered the primary authority for psychiatric diagnoses.

traumatic experiences or to dramatize "malignant memories" in the right conditions, for example in play therapy (Eth, Pynoos, 1994; Terr, 1988).

Studies on refugee children were generally based on samples in which the age differences were wide, or on samples restricted to more mature kids, who are easier to talk to. This makes it difficult to compare different developmental ages, in particular in light of the results that post-traumatic stress reactions take different forms depending on the age of the child (Eth, 1990; Eth, Pynoos, 1985).

2   Egyptian Christianity and Discrimination

As for our study, the background of the Coptic boys and girls we interviewed is Egypt, a country that has several ethnic and religious groups with a dominant Islamic religion and a majority of Sunni Muslims. Among the Christian population, Coptic Orthodox Christians are the largest group, while other ethnic and religious groups include Iranian Jews, Buddhist and Bahais (Pew Research Center, 2010) (see also Chapters 5 and 6).

The history of Egyptian Christianity precedes that of Islam, as we saw earlier (Chapter 6). However, due to the seventh century Islamic conquest, Egypt became Islamized and Arabized; many Coptic Christians converted to Islam to sidestep religious persecution and extra taxes under Islamic law, and Arabic gradually replaced Coptic language with the implementation of state norms at the beginning of the eighth century, which meant a ban on Coptic language (Swanson, 2010). After the long history of Islamization, the Egyptians who remained Christians today proudly consider themselves "true" Egyptians of Pharaonic origin (Cragg, 1992). And religion is a fundamental social marker for Coptic Christians.

Christianity is deeply rooted in the history of the Coptic families; thus, religious conversion and interfaith marriages are infrequent in order to preserve the Coptic identity. While religious symbols are a means of identity expression for the Copts, the cultural development that distinguishes them from Egyptian Muslims has also built Coptic ethnic group (Rowe, 2017). For example, veils are associated with Muslim women and silver rings are associated with married Muslim men, while Christian women wear crucifix necklaces and married Christian men wear gold rings. Only Coptic Orthodox Christians often have cross tattoos on their right wrists. In addition to these visible indicators, the names mainly differentiate the Copts from the Muslims. Although there are some names for both Christians and Muslims, many Copts are likely to appoint their children with biblical figures, Coptic saints and martyrs. Furthermore, although both Egyptian Christians and Muslims use the same language – Egyptian Arabic–, Coptic Christians have developed several specific expressions for their religious faith.

Sometimes these religious signs become reasons for discrimination, perpetuating a religious hierarchy that privileges Muslims over Christians in Egypt. For example, the Copts are not only significantly underrepresented in politics and the media –only a few Copts currently occupy positions of political, military and educational leadership (Bayat, Herrera, 2010; TIMEP, 2018)– but they have also limited employment opportunities and promotions, compared to the Muslim majority. This underrepresentation of the Copts has gradually progressed through discriminatory policies and state-sponsored violence against them, led by radical Islamists in all areas of Egyptian society (McCallum, 2012; Bosmat, 2017) (see also Chapter 10).

Experiences like terrorist attacks, but also indirect violence, discrimination and micro-aggression generate collective emotions within an ethnic group. The collective emotions contribute to the "ethnic affinity", while creating symbolic boundaries along ethnic lines. Emotions are therefore not only social, but also political and collective, and further strengthen the sense of belonging to a minority group, such as the Coptic Christians (Ha, 2017).

Studies on religious minorities in Egypt have paid attention, so far, mainly to two topics with a clear focus on the Coptic Orthodox Church: State-Church relations and revival movements of the Church's identity. This second issue concerns the politics of the revival of the identity of the Coptic Church. For example, McCallum (2007) explores the political function of the Patriarch (the Head of the Church) to reinforce the Coptic identity during national crisis and others focus on the Coptic formation of identity within the Egyptian political structures (Ibrahim, 2015; Rowe, 2007; Sedra, 1999[2]). Current studies indicate more unlike issues such as the conceptualization of citizenship based on religious identity (Pizzo, 2015); the double-edged consequences of new media on the Coptic issues (Elsässer, 2010) and the importance of religious dialogue in the understanding of Muslim-Christian relations (Hansen, 2015).

While most studies on Coptic Christians have provided historical analysis and identity formation within the Coptic Orthodox Church, they have paid much less attention to common Coptic lay people and their daily lives. Therefore, the focus on the Coptic laymen in place of the Coptic Orthodox Church as the main actor in the Coptic community is very important to fill the gap in the current literature.

---

2 The interesting study of Sedra (1999) highlights a "class cleavages" in national identity among Copts.

3   The Present Study

The study aimed to investigate –using a qualitative methodology– factors and processes promoting or hindering the integration process of Coptic minors migrated to Italy with their parents. The main aims were to identify the acculturative challenges faced by these minors, the role played by Churches in sustaining heritage identity and faith across generations, by paying special attention to the significance of the persecution of Christians and martyrdom.

We adopted a salutogenic perspective (Antonovsky, 1987) that focuses on the resources of individuals and families, as well as on the resources of the social context, rather than focusing on the unavoidable critical issues, typical of the migration process.

The main strategy to reach our goals was to encourage the young Copts of the sample to tell their stories and standpoints, and to ponder about their past experience and their lives in Italy. In order to do this, 4 focus groups have been carried out, with Coptic minors, living in Milan, some of them Orthodox and other Catholics. 18 minors have been involved, 12 females and 6 males, aged 12 to 18. Almost all the Coptic teenagers who participated in the focus groups were born in Egypt and arrived in Italy as children, except one. Most of them attended primary schools in Milan, almost all of them –except one– the lower secondary schools. All the minors interviewed for the present study regularly attend Coptic churches located in the Milan area.

The focus groups have been audiotaped and entirely transcribed. Afterwards, using the methodology of the content analysis, the text has been segmented into codes created by the researchers; thenceforth the codes have been reassembled, thus leading the researchers to work on the meaning attribution (the code-and-retrieval logic). The analysis was computer-aided, by means of the software ATLAS.ti (Muhr, 2004) and based on the principles based on the grounded theory: we started from the participants' accounts and debates, and from the meanings they constructed during the interactions, trying to avoid selecting information and data on the basis of pre-existing categories.

The required criteria for the selection of participants were the following: a) being part of a family with Coptic belonging only (no bi-cultural families); b) living in Italy for at least two years; c) speaking fluently the Italian language.

Coptic minors have been contacted through multiple channels, such as local Coptic associations, Coptic communities, and the Archdioceses of Milan and third-sector associations.

Coptic minors' experience and adaptation to the Italian context have been investigated considering some main topics: the (forced) migration process, that is a reason why families leave their home country, with special attention to the migratory mandate; the difficult phases of family separation and reunification; the efforts to keep ties and create new relationships; stereotypes and prejudices, which have a great influence on the relations between Italians and Egyptians, and which can negatively affect the contact between the two social groups and their cultures and traditions. For each topic, we tried to highlight critical issues and resources.

The research work focused on the (forced) migration caused by religious persecution, seen through the eyes of the offspring of migrant families: preadolescents and adolescents, mostly arrived in Italy very young, some born in Italy, children of Coptic Orthodox and Coptic Catholics Christians, forced to leave their country of origin due to harassment, persecution, and violence suffered as Christians. The perspective of the minor sons and daughters was adopted to gather what they know, what they lived, what they were told about the persecutions their families had suffered.

The set-up of the work, the methodology and the tools used have had the purpose of favoring the rise of memories, thoughts and issues, in a climate of protection and trust, and guaranteeing total respect for privacy. All the minors seemed to be very motivated in debating and showed very high involvement. The data and the elements detected allowed to collect stories, directly experienced or "inherited" by their parents. We have chosen to deal with some issues, such as the persecution experienced and remembered, with the tools of verbal narration and without the use of mediums – such as writing– in front of which minors often show resistance. All the boys and the girls have freely brought memories, data, images, feelings and emotions, declaring themselves happy to participate in the research, and above all happy to have the chance to speak about their condition. In fact, they stated that no one had ever been interested in their history of religious persecution before, no one ever asked them what they had lived and seen.

4 The Results

After the content analysis of the transcriptions of the focus groups, five words came out as the most important for the participants: *violence, fear, freedom, religious freedom, future*. These words were the most frequent and the most meaningful among those used by the interviewees to describe themselves, to tell about the violence suffered by them or their parents, and to tell about the freedom found escaping from Egypt. The results are presented according to the outcomes of the content analysis and according to the elements already described (§2). The words will be commented in three different groups: two word pairs (violence-fear and freedom-religious freedom) and one single word (future). The reason is that, in the narratives, the two pairs of words were strictly interconnected and very often verbalized together.

4.1   *Violence and Fear*

Violence and fear are two different words –and concepts– repeatedly encountered in the narrative that the Coptic boys and girls have proposed in a sort of link of meaning and experience. The first one –*violence*– is harsh and focused on contacting the outside environment; the second one –*fear*– is emotional and focused on the inside world. In the stories narrated by the Coptic minors, the two concepts are strictly connected, linked to each other, interdependent and consequential.

Violence is perceived as a form of abuse of power and control, which manifests itself through physical and social dimensions. The use of the term in the collected narratives mainly concerns physical violence, understood as actions aimed at hurting or frightening. In this sense, the Coptic minors reported the episodes that characterized their brief life in the country of origin –Egypt– as experiences of great violence against Christians and women. A violence expressed through public and private aggressions, consumed at home, but also on the streets, in public places. A violence with the purpose of intimidating and frightening, and, for this reason, necessarily manifest, visible, and close to the everyday life.

> My mom, dad and grandparents were going to church in Egypt and a few minutes before they arrived, the church exploded; they were waiting for a taxi that arrived 5 minutes late and those minutes saved their lives. It was 2012 and it was one of the many attacks against Christians.[3] I also witnessed an act of extreme violence against Christian children. We were playing football in our parish center, in Cairo. Suddenly, some men on motorbikes came in, they were driving very fast; they shot randomly and killed three children; then they left. (...). I also remember Christian boys, at school, playing football. They broke a window and the teacher forced them to collect the glass with their bare hands, hurting their hands so badly ... (M., 12 years old, Male)

> (*Whispering*) When I was in Egypt, two little girls, twin sisters ... they were my friends ... one day they were sent to blow themselves up: one did

---

3   He is describing the attack against the church of Holy Mary of Zeitoun, a place of worship and visit for the apparitions of Saint Mary.

it, but the other one didn't have the courage. I don't know what happened to her after that .... (A., 13 years old, Female)

A quarrel between two people, in Egypt, ended in a firefight that struck two innocent men who were chatting in the street: the bullets entered our house and we witnessed the scene. The people of the house helped the man who had been shot to escape because the dead persons were Christian and the killer Muslim. The law imposes the death penalty if a Muslim kills another Muslim or if a Christian kills a Muslim, but not if a Muslim kills a Christian; nothing happens to him ... (F., 14 years old, Female)

Besides, the violence they experienced has also a psychological dimension, which grows up in the continuous lack of respect, in the offenses that humble the dignity of Christians, in a relentless devaluation that aims to bend Christians by humiliating, disqualifying and intimidating them overtly.

The young Copts interviewed reported several episodes of adults chastened in public because of their Christian faith, hampered in their professional career because they were identified by a Christian name. They also reported episodes of children humiliated and denigrated by peers –or older children– in school courtyards.

In Egypt, Christians cannot have a job in the police, in the army, as judges and often die during military service. The media call it "misfortune" –e.g. while cleaning a weapon, while doing something in very difficult situations–, but these are not reliable stories! The truth is that they send Christians to carry out very dangerous actions, which put their lives at risk as if they had no value ... (G., 16 years old, Female).

Religious violence and the following persecutions strike the spiritual life of Christians by not allowing them to practice their religious duties or by imposing conversion to the Islam.

(...) In Egypt, when girls are 16, they take them away, they take them somewhere else –even with violence– and they try to convert them to Islam until they turn 18 (...). They do it with girls but also with women living in the country ... and then they say they became Muslim ... (D., 16 years old, Male)

I saw the same things! I come from Alexandria of Egypt. Over there, the girls were kidnapped in order to convert them. In other places in Egypt it is not so common. (...) Only girls, no women. At 16 and before they turn

18 ... because then they have an identity card and the religious choice is considered complete and official. It is scary, always ... (S., 14 years old, Male)

All the Coptic teenagers reported strongly discriminatory acts and behaviors acted in public schools in Egypt by Muslim adults and pupils. Acts of physical violence of groups of Muslim children against single Christian child in the courtyards, but also assaults approved by adults and even by teachers, who very often "turned away".

When I attended school in Egypt, at the age of 6, a classmate was asked –from the group of peers in the schoolyard– which religion he was practicing. As soon as he said "I am a Christian", the other classmates began to throw stones against him with violence. The adults that were in the schoolyard intervened after a long time, but that delay was intentional and punitive ... the Christian child suffered serious injuries. In Egypt, I had to suffer violence too, in primary school; violence perpetrated by the teacher, who put me in the middle of the class so that the other classmates could insult me because of my Christian faith ... I remember the pain and the sense of powerlessness, the tears ... (G., 16 years old, Female)

There was a ritual practiced at school. If you are a Christian in Egypt, at school, you have to say: "I am a bad person"... in front of everyone ... You feel terrible ... I felt offended and abashed ... it's not fair ... (M., 18 years old, Male)

I remember that the bus driver often mistreated Christian girls by grabbing their hair, for no other reason but their Christian belief. (A., 12 years old, Female)

Many Coptic minors reported violent practices such as abduction, torture and murder in Egypt, in Cairo as well as in Alexandria: 16-year-old girls kidnapped by Islamic extremists and forced to convert to Islam before their 18th birthday; Christians killed by firearms while walking in the streets –with the murderer never being stopped–; children threatened, mocked and beaten in the classrooms and courtyards of Islamic public schools.

Nevertheless, if in the collective image of Islamic extremism, what attracts and seduces adults and children is a sort of "aesthetic of violence" and if the identity of the groups finds an effectual way of expression in violence, when it comes to the persecutions of the Coptic Christians, the Islamic violence aims to generate distress and fear. This fear, however, instead of intimidating and questioning their faith, straightens the awareness that being a "true Christian" also means bearing discrimination and violence, without losing faith. Being a good Copt Christian is part of their identity, since it is what parents have passed on to them and it is a very important value that is considered as a priority. Many of the interviewed teenagers reported phrases stated by their parents throughout their lives (if they ask you if you are Christian, you answer "yes" and defend your faith until you die). The relationship between violent and discriminatory acts and the fact of being Christian is grounded on real facts – situations they memorized because they experienced them directly or because of the constant reminder from their parents: burnt churches, children killed with firearms while playing in the church square, cars and buses blown up.

The relationship between violence, death and faith and the practice of the Christian faith appears in its terrifying consequentiality: being Christians in Egypt, bearing a Christian name, and professing the Christian faith leads to the risk of death, to the certainty of being a target of denigration, persecution and violence.

The parents of Coptic children have transmitted religious values to their offspring, who have made them their own, as distinctive elements of their identity. Most parents have told and continue to tell their children about the persecution of Christians by Muslims, often showing them photos and videos of the acts of violence that continue to be perpetrated in Egypt. Daughters and sons are very conscious of the reality of being Christian in Egypt: they talked about it as if it were part of their everyday life. They contrast the beauty of Christian faith to these narratives of violence: several times, they talk about Christianity as a tolerant and peaceful religion; they say that their behavior must always be respectful and tolerant because they are Christians and Christians do not discriminate, do not misbehave, and do not lie. These are values that these minors re-propose with strength: tolerance, respect for others, acceptance, brotherhood, sincerity and righteousness.

Fear is a second facade of the Janus-faced concept emerged by the analysis, directly linked to violence. We have considered fear in its psychological meaning, as an emotional response of an adaptive system, an active defense mechanism against the dangers to people's survival. In this sense, the function of fear is both individual and social but, in the minors' narratives, fear was mainly used in connection with personal experience, as the consequence of threats, persecutions and violence, and in situations of danger or in the case of possible interaction with people who were truly dangerous. They express a fear that comes from direct experiences –the narration of violence experienced directly by children and remembered with the same emotional intensity that has left the inheritance of fear– and experiences frequently narrated by parents, rooted through videos and photos and kept alive as they are continuous and condition stimuli.

Fear, for these minors, occurred at different times in their lives, triggered by the perception of a threatening and potentially harmful presence for their survival. A threat certainly aimed at the expression of religious freedom, but also at their own lives. For most of the interviewed teenagers, the response to fear is to claim a denied right, the right to live free from fear.

In the narratives of some Coptic minors who came to Milan around the age of 4, fear takes on the anxious tones of an alarming conundrum: the memories of burned churches or of killed children are mixed with the stories told by parents, with what they see on television and with the images that come from Egypt.

> I have never liked living in Egypt; when I was in Egypt, I wished to go away, to America or Europe. I was afraid. (…) In Egyptian public schools, Muslims have far more rights than Christians. I was lucky enough to go to a Franciscan school in Egypt, but when my parents started thinking about coming to Milan, they sent me to a public school to save money for travel and a new life in Europe. In Egypt, Muslims pupils did not want to be with their Christians peers, so Christian children were isolated, even by professors, treated badly, threatened. I have always lived with fear in Egypt … (S., 14 years old, Male)

For many Coptic teenagers, fear had the outlines of anxiety, with negative predictions about all the events that are perceived as dangerous or only potentially dangerous. In the tones of the voice, in the modalities chosen to speak, and in the very words of the minors, it was clear that the feeling that the persecutions suffered in Egypt by their parents and their relatives are shaping up their existence and their projects for the future. None of them, in fact, plans to go back to Egypt one day.

> In Egypt, girls can never go out alone; they cannot leave their heads and arms uncovered. If they do, boys and adults males pull their hair violently or use a sort of electric baton to shake their arms. I was always afraid! (P., 17 years old, Female)

The stories of the Coptic boys and girls expressed a fear that, in many moments, seemed tied to traumatic events, reactivated as the narration proceeded. Because of the violence they witnessed, their accounts were emotionally intense: Christian children abused and killed in front of them, and people beaten in the street before their eyes, only because they were Christians. In general, the fear is perceivable in almost all the interviewed teenagers, thus producing a negative image of the life in Egypt.

However, it must be noted that the fear brought by these minors is the result of a sort of "parental contagion". That is anxiety and fears for the relatives still living in Egypt and in constant contact with these teenagers, along with the fears that those living in Italy pass on to their offspring, thus generating or amplifying their anxieties and fears both by imitation and by sharing the same environment, which is particularly demanding and distressing.

> The arrival in Milan was difficult at the beginning, but now we are free and I'm fine. Now I know that I can trust people here in Milan. At the beginning, I couldn't, because when in Egypt some called me: "Come here a second!". I was scared that he could kidnap me ... Even in kindergarten, Islamic children managed to beat Christian children. I was always afraid! (M., 12 years old, Male)

Yet, this intense fear does not stop them from acting as Christians, as newspaper documented over the years. In the aftermath of the double Islamic attack on 9 April 2017, for example, an article by a major national newspaper titled: "The Copts do not seem to know the fear. Armored churches between metal detectors and soldiers: this is how we live in the Coptic community after the long wave of fundamentalist attacks. But fear has not emptied the churches" (ANSA Magazine, 2017).

The interviewed Coptic teenagers have reported stories of Coptic Christians, victims of terrorist attacks, who died invoking the name of Christ, in preventing terrorists from accessing churches. They talked passionately about having learned from their parents and from their own faith that being a Christian is a value that goes beyond life, which must be defended from everything and everyone. They said they were ready to die for the faith and proud to be Christians.

> We learned from an early age. Our parents have always told us: "If they kidnap you and try to convert you, you have to say no until death. Rather die". We learn this from an early age. (G., 16 years old, Female)

4.2   *Freedom and Religious Freedom*

The questions that explored whether and how the religious factor represents a constraint or a resource for the interviewed minors revealed good levels of integration, openly declared by boys and girls that "feel Italian and Milanese", while maintaining a constant and significant link with the country of origin. The profile that emerges –with a minimum variance– describes them as boys and girls who, above all, feel "free" in Italy, free to join peers, Italians or Egyptians, classmates, but also friends from the parish. For the Coptic teenagers interviewed, the religious practice is also lived through the attendance of Catholic youth centers and churches in Milan, where they have no difficulty in adapting to the Ambrosian rite (the rite of the Milan Archdioceses). In particular, almost all the Coptic minors interviewed attend the Coptic Church – Orthodox or Catholic– at least once a week (often even twice a week) and, in addition, the Catholic Churches in Milan.

A constant religious commitment brings together Coptic boys and girls, as it is considered a value transmitted by parents and internalized, reached by a careful and constant practice. The religious practice links and allows to know and meet peers of the same ethnic origin. If attending school opens up opportunities for integration and freedom, it is in religious practice that they all rediscover the values of their own origins. The two things seem to fit perfectly into almost all the experiences reported in the focus groups.

> (...) The others must know that you are a Christian, and you must prove it with facts. You must prove it in practice. You don't have to ruin Christianity's reputation for what you do. On the contrary ... you have to improve it. All of us must be like this. Our values have been passed on to us by our parents thanks to what they do and say. They are our guide and our freedom. (P., 17 years old, Female)

> Our mother always tells us that if there is the possibility of going to church we must go there. My mother says I shouldn't be afraid to talk about our religion. That we should let it be known, talk about it ... (A., 13 years old, Female)

They are teenagers who recognize that they have more opportunities in Italy than in Egypt and recognize the sacrifices made by parents to offer them a future of freedom, as well as the chance to practice their religion. Some of them, the majority, have managed to go along the difficult path of integration by sharing and living the two worlds that are part of their identity: Egypt and Italy.

> Being in Milan is much better than being in the city where I was born, in my home country, because the school in Italy welcomes everyone,

regardless of the religion they have ... In Egypt, Christians are separated from others, ridiculed, abused. In Milan, there is space to play safe, free – which there was not in Egypt ... (M., 12 years old, Male)

Being able to live in a State where you are free to practice your religion, to dress in many different ways, to be yourself ... this is what freedom is to me. Like in Milan. In Egypt, we could not do anything. Anything ... (F., 13 years old, Female)

For all Coptic minors, the values transmitted by the family, and by the parents in particular, are very important as they have become a primary part of their identity and are also taken into consideration in relationships with adults and peers. In Italy, they feel "free": free of being Christians and of being able to practice their religion, free to proclaim themselves to be Christians without any fear of discrimination or violence. They also feel they can be free to live their lives by connecting the present to the past, which means being Egyptian and Italian at the same time. Being able to say what they think, dress like their Italian peers, and have the same opportunities as Italians have without being discriminated is recognized as the result of a sacrifice made by their parents, who –in most cases– deprived themselves of that higher socio-economic status they had in Egypt and which was not possible to achieve in Italy.

I know my parents made great sacrifices to take us to Italy, giving up their social position in Egypt and accepting to have jobs in Italy they didn't like, just to make me and my brother feel comfortable and give us a better future. In Egypt, we were not free. I was trained to protect myself in case I was kidnapped and forced to convert to Islam. Our parents told us that we should oppose to that, that we should continue to say that we are Christians and that we want to remain Christian. We lived in a constant state of anxiety, with the fear of going out and being kidnapped. We learned from an early age that, if they kidnap you and try to convert you, you have to say no, until you die. You'd rather die ... we learned this from an early age ... (G., 16 years old, Female)

The issue of the persecutions suffered in Egypt is part of the chapter on religious freedom. The boys and girls who participated in the focus groups believe that values are fundamental and essential. And among these values, there certainly are the religious values, transmitted by the family through the generations, along with the narration of the denied liberties in the home country. All the Coptic teenagers interviewed know their family history and the persecutions lived by their parents when they were in Egypt, and consider those persecutions as inhuman and unacceptable. They think that their parents have made a choice for them, which is important, as much as it is painful, and tiring, in order to offer them a better future. They call themselves "lucky" for having had the opportunity to live in Italy, which they consider as a country in which they can really be free.

> We Christians make no difference between Christians and Muslims: we make friends with everyone and our parents educate us in this. I had Muslim friends in Egypt. Not everyone is like that, but the majority are. They know that there is a difference between religions, but ... people are people ... We can be together, play and do things together, and then everyone goes back to his/her religion. On the contrary, in public schools in Egypt, everyone is forced to study the Koran. Pupils must recite some parts by memory. If they do not know those parts and do not recite them, they do not pass the exam and they just flunk out ... (D., 20 years old, Male)

> The values our parents have taught us are to be honest, to respect others and to treat everyone well, to help without expecting compensation. Do everything possible. Try to stick to religion. When my mom has to teach me something, she tells me: you are Christian, you cannot tell lies .... (M., 13 years old, Female)

Almost all the Coptic teenagers tell stories of discrimination, intimidation, aggression and violence perpetrated by Muslim children, teenagers and adults against Christians. Some of them attended private Catholic schools in Egypt: very expensive institutions into which parents have enrolled them in order to protect them and allow them to exercise their religious freedom despite Islamic pressures and violence. In private schools, the students actually felt protected and had the opportunity to study in a context that is described as positive and respectful. However, friends, neighbors, relatives and other children in their neighborhood, who could not afford the high cost of private schools, continued to go to public schools, in a climate of terror and overwhelmed by constant humiliation and harassment.

> In Egyptian public schools, Muslims had far more rights than Christians. I was lucky enough to go to a Franciscan school in Egypt. My parents made many sacrifices to find the money they needed to send me and my sisters to a private school. (S., 14 years old, male)

The narratives about school describe institutions in which children and young people, instead of finding a room for growth and education, found teachers ready to taunt them, to ridicule them by isolating them publicly, humiliating them precisely because of the Christian name they had or because they were defenders of their religion. Touching and delicate stories, which are surprising mainly because of the depth and the maturity showed in the opinions and beliefs of these teenagers. Freedom for Coptic minors is made up of the possibility of having behaviors that are not admitted in Egypt, but which belong to the set of what "a good Christian should do", in line with rigorous values. Freedom, for them, is the possibility to go to school and stay with classmates; to go out on Saturdays; to go shopping or to a football match; to go to Mass and to church whenever they feel like it.

> In Egypt, we were used to spend a lot of time indoors. We couldn't go out. In Italy, I feel free, I feel really free. It was painful, however, to abandon a piece of the family in Egypt. Because one of the most important values, for us, is family. (L., 17 years old, Male)

> To me, it is very easy to live in Milan. People welcomed us, (...) and the language was not a problem: we learnt it in three months. We are very comfortable here and we only have to be good people and good Christians. We are free, now. (F., 14 years old, Female)

All teenagers go to Mass on Sundays either with family or with friends. They do not seem to perceive great discrepancies between the practice of the Orthodox rite and the Catholic one; certainly, they attend their own church and their own ritual, but they also attend other churches, even with a local rite, different from the Copt one.

> I do not see any striking differences between the Ambrosian rite and ours. Few things are different: the language and Palm Sunday, which is much more beautiful here. The ritual is beautiful both in the Arabic and in the Italian language. (V., 15 years old, Male)

Some Coptic teenagers reported a problem they experienced in Italy: they said that their schoolmates in high school, but also some professors, label them as "Muslims" in a negative way, or even call them "Islamic extremists", since they are Egyptians. The minors participating in the focus group interpreted this misjudgment as a lack of knowledge, as a consequence of the Italians' ignorance about the very existence of Christians in Egypt. It is a not discussed topic, unlike Islamic extremism, and therefore it is not known. Narratives of Muslim–Coptic unity have played an important role in the collective imagination of the nations, and these narratives have effects that are distinct from that of formal legislation. Although these narratives are often advocated and supported by the State, they are not reducible to the actions of state officials. Rather, they rely on popular rhetoric, repeated and performed as part of the imaginary of a modern plural Egypt. The perpetuation of this national unity performance has led to the "invisibility" of the Copts in the contemporary political landscape, with minority rights being subjugated to national needs (Ibrahim, 2015) (see also Chapter 6).

4.3   *Future*

"Future" is a word emerged many times from the narratives of the Coptic teenagers and –in most cases– it is strictly connected with the idea of freedom, which is what pushed them and their families to migrate to Italy.

> My parents came to Italy to live better together, to have a quieter life and to give us more opportunities for our future; also, to let us have a peaceful life in which we can do what we want to do. I am well aware of my parents' sacrifices and I know what they had to give up on for my future …
> (G., 16 years old, Female)

For Coptic minors, the future is a possibility determined by freedom and by the sacrifices made by their parents. The qualitative level of the narratives –for the breadth and richness of the vocabulary and for the wide use of a hypotactic syntax– expresses a maturity that is usually more present in young adults than in teenagers: the minors who participated in the focus groups are preadolescents and adolescents who know very well the moods and the emotions that accompanied the choice of their parents, but also of their grandparents, their uncles, their cousins and the relatives they left behind in Egypt. Their future is the consequence of the freedom they have today to study in Milan, which tomorrow will allow them to find the job they want, without any discriminations or abuse of power. Almost all the interviewed minors want their studying or working future to be in Milan, the city that welcomed them in Italy, or somewhere else in the world, but without forgetting to maintain solid roots in Milan. Milan seems to have become the "secure base" from which to start and to which go back in the journey of life.

> My father wanted to find something better than what we had in Egypt and he was afraid for us. (….) He wanted to offer our lives a new possibility. He saw the future in Egypt and understood that there was

nothing for us. He was afraid for us, who were alone in Egypt. (L., 17 years old, Male)

The Coptic boys and girls, who project their future mainly in Italy, as we saw before, are strongly focused on the "doing", on achieving something that can lead them to a profession. The future is linked to freedom in a very decisive way, as if the experience of having been deprived of their own freedom and of the possibility to think of a future in their home country had led them to the idea that living in a nation allowing you to be free already means to have a future ahead of you. Most of them attend technical or professional institutes. They have concrete goals in the short term, such as passing school exams and gain a diploma. Their goals are so pragmatic that none of them even envisages attending university. Their aims seem to be a job, a home, and a future in Milan.

Being in Milan is much better than being in the city where I was born. (…) It is in a free country where you can imagine living your life. (C., 17 years old, Male)

The future can be built on today's integration process, on the ability to keep together, and in balance, both the identity of the country of origin and the new one, acquired thanks to the migration to Milan. In fact, Coptic teenagers continue to maintain constant relationships with their community of belonging, which many visit continuously, going back to Egypt on a yearly basis. All the interviewed minors claim to have a constant relationship with the country of origin; most of them go there every year, others every two or three years. From their narratives, in fact, we can see that there is a "double bond", one with the host country, Italy –to which they feel they belong and in which they dream to live their future– and one with the home country, to which they are still emotionally tied and which they continue to visit, valuing family ties with relatives left behind (grandparents, uncles, cousins), to whom all the boys and girls claim a strong attachment.

As far as I'm concerned, it has been very useful to come to Milan: here I studied and I started working, but I miss family and friends and sometimes I have to visit them. I have to endure two more years, and then I want to go to Egypt to see them. But I wouldn't go back to living there. No, I really wouldn't … (M., 18 years old, Male)

They are clearly aware that freedom is fundamental to even think of a possible future. They have learned by their parents that the choice to go to Milan has involved many sacrifices, but at the same time, it has allowed them to live in a country where they can be themselves, and where they can freely practice their religion, dress as they wish, and make the choices they think are best suited to them.

> I felt good coming to Milan, I felt the peace, which was very different from Egypt; the cleaner air and a sense of security. (…) I was constantly being afraid, in Egypt. I would not go back to live in Egypt ever again; now, I feel very good here in Milan … (S., 14 years old, Male)

> My father in Egypt had a shop and my mother was an accountant. They arrived in Italy separately: first, my father and then my mother and I reached him when I was 3 and a half years old. In Egypt, I attended a Christian private kindergarten. My father found it hard to recognize us, since he was seeing us after a very long time. My parents made massive efforts in Italy at the beginning. But they did it for us and today we are grateful to them, because in Egypt a Christian can only die. Here, on the contrary, we have a future. (F., 14 years old, Female)

While they really appreciate the variety of values and cultural proposals of Milan, they do not renounce the values and the distinctive elements of their culture: they listen to Egyptian music, along with the Italian ones; they all speak the Arabic and the Italian language with no difficulties; they have eating habits that mix food and traditions of both countries; they follow different habits and rituals linked to the Coptic tradition; they profess and practice the values of their home country. They have ways of dressing that are identical to those of all the adolescents in Milan and –an element of primary importance– they have a pigmentation and a physiognomy that does not make them particularly different from their autochthonous peers.

A girl wanting to explain how important it was for her parents to pass on their native language to their children, in order to preserve it besides the Italian language, said:

> When I came home from kindergarten and I spoke Italian, my parents pretended not to understand me: so I had to learn Arabic too … (*smile*)… but now I like it! (A., 12 years old, Female)

5   Final Remarks

The purpose of the present study was to investigate factors and processes promoting or hindering the integration process of Coptic minors, migrated to Italy along with their parents. More specifically, the main aims were to identify the acculturative challenges faced by these minors, the role played by religion in sustaining heritage identity and faith across generations, paying special attention to the significance of the persecution of Christians and martyrdom. By adopting a salutogenic perspective, which focuses on the resources of individuals and families, we wanted to help Copt boys and girls to report their opinions, and to reflect on their past experience and their lives in Italy.

As already highlighted in the previous section, the focus group participants revealed a strong ethnic-religious identity, differently from their autochthonous peers, as also highlighted by several studies on Copts (Brinkerhoff, 2016; Henderson, 2015; Ibrahim, 2010; Smith, 2005).

The thoughts and the feelings expressed by the young Copts during the focus group seem to be an endorsement of the effectiveness of efforts made by their parents and by the religious leaders in order to pass heritage values and practices to second-generation Diaspora.

Even if they are still adolescents –and adolescence is notoriously a tumultuous age– they clearly have a deep sense of belonging to their religious traditions and their community.

In the focus group, it became evident that religious identity is strongly connected to the home country, even though they had left it when they were very young and have little memories of that time. Nevertheless, the teachings of their parents and the frequent visits to Egypt have managed to make the link become stronger and deep-rooted. Many migrant groups are worried that their cultural tradition will not survive in the following generations living in the Diaspora – a feeling that has developed most intensely in faith-based or faith-centered Diasporas, such as the Coptic Diaspora. An important member of the Coptic Diaspora in the USA, after having lived fifty years in the US, wrote: "One of the serious challenges has been the age-old tension facing immigrant communities: maintaining a strong communal identity while dealing with the pressures of "compromise" associated with assimilating into a new society. An associated challenge is keeping most –if not all– second and third generations within the church" (Saad, 2010: 220). As for our sample, up to now this challenge has been faced successfully, through a wise strategy of narratives and personal relationships with the family left behind in Egypt. These Coptic teenagers were very proud of the legacy of their history and their culture, along with the awareness of the "hard time" that Christians in Egypt have to endure. They have a clear picture of what it means to be living in Egypt as a Christian, also because –besides the narratives of their parents–, most of them witnessed cruel terroristic actions and institutional discriminatory behaviors in the home country. During the focus group, they spent a lot of time describing the acts of violence against them as Christian children in Egypt, the pressure of the discriminatory laws on their parents, and the fear characterizing the everyday life at school and in the streets. It is surprising to see as these young Copts talk about violence and terroristic actions with equilibrium, not showing evident signs of PTSD or of the traumatic background due to having witnessed people being stubbed or dying. Further research should focus on a follow-up study, maybe in 10 years, to see what would happen to these second-generation offspring entering the adult life.

According to the remarks on the ethics of hospitality presented in Chapter 2, the experiences of the Coptic minors we met in the focus groups uphold the key role of religion in the host country, as well as the importance of a *"cross-cultural institutional folder"* in order to maintain strong roots and develop new sprouts.

As far as one of our main aims is concerned –the role played by religion and the Church in sustaining heritage identity and faith across generations– we can observe, from the narratives of the participants in our focus groups, that the Coptic Church turns out to be, as Brinkerhoff writes, "a transnational arena, linking the single Christian to churches and to the Mother Church in Egypt" (p. 483). In this way, the link across generations is assured. The Coptic Church tries to provide facilitative mechanisms to keep in touch with the home country, for example through philanthropy, helping Christian families in Egypt (Ebaugh, Chafetz, 2002). The Church's fostering of philanthropy betokens a positive link between the later generations in Diaspora –not willing to go back to their home country, as clearly stated by the interviewed teenagers– and the Egyptian society. Early studies about such phenomenon showed that this experience likely lead to such participation in adulthood (Perks, Haan, 2011). Another observation that can be made out of the analysis of our focus group is that the role of the Coptic Church implies a dimension of cross-culturalism, because it stresses the Coptic identity and its legacy and –at the same time– it promotes the adaptation to the way of living in Diaspora, outside of Egypt, including the fact of being proud of one's non-Egyptian citizenship. According to some scholars, this attitude of the Coptic Church shows that selective acculturation processes do not automatically hinder ascendant mobility, and that acculturation itself does not have to imply a loss of the heritage culture and of the religious values and practices associated with it.

The Coptic Diaspora is probably one of the few that supports selective acculturation. The Coptic Church gives the impression of underlining the great importance of keeping Egyptian and Coptic identity alive in Diaspora and that –to do so– suppleness and adaptation is fundamental to many host societies, which are very different in terms of values, practices and customs.

Given the potential bias in our sample, we cannot know the extent to which these strategies for transnationalism and selective acculturation influence Diaspora members who are not active in the Coptic Church, but it is possible to say that very few Coptic Egyptians living abroad have no link to the Church, being the Copt identity so in-deep rooted, as we saw in our focus groups. Acculturation with upward mobility does not require substitution of one culture for another. This study highlights some issues and, at the same time, raises several questions. The human capital legacy of the Coptic second generation is noteworthy and liable not only to help its upward mobility but also to support an insight in exploring and enacting the Coptic identity. Sharp and fuzzy borders may change according to life events and to subjective dynamics. In a faith-based migrant community, does religion play a mediating role in the network mechanisms that can facilitate acculturation? More generally, how important are institutional structures, such as those provided by the Coptic Church, in facilitating transnationalism and selective acculturation? What other types of structure might proffer similar advantages?

Certainly, these remarks would need to be re-examined after a long period of time, through third and fourth generations, to evaluate whether or not this cross-cultural approach, adopted by the Coptic Church, works.

Further research can begin to answer some of these questions. Keeping cultural legacy –while reaching upward mobility– is possible, and this process can be eagerly supported. Preserving roots and not "selling off" one's legacy are aims that are as crucial as socio-economic achievements. The issue is how to pull all of them together.

References to Part 5

Various Authors. (1937). *L'antischiavismo organo della Società antischiavista d'Italia e dei comitati antischiavisti nazionali.* Roma: Società antischiavista d'Italia.

Aggoun, A. (2003). Immigration, grands-parents algériens et mémoire : entre la transmission et l'oubli. *L'Homme et la société*, 1(147), 191–207.

Allodi, F. (1980). The psychiatric effects in children and families of victims of political persecution and torture. *Danish Medical Bulletin*, 27(5), 229–232.

Almqvist K., & Brandell-Forsberg M. (1995). Iranian refugee children in Sweden: effects of Organized Violence and Forced Migration on Preschool Children. *American Journal of Orthopsychiatry*, 65(2), 225–237.

Amadini, M. (2012). Di generazione in generazione: il passaggio delle eredità in famiglia. *La Famiglia*, 46(256), 30–45.

Ambrosiana Community Report (2018). *Milan.*

Ambrosini, M. (2007). Bonds Across Borders: Migrant Families in a Global World. In *Charity and Justice in the Relations among Peoples and Nations.* Vatican City: Pontifical Academy of Social Sciences, Acta 13.

Ambrosini, M., Bonizzoni, P., & Pozzi, S. (2013). Donne ricongiunte. I dilemmi dell'integrazione. In ORIM, *Gli immigrati in Lombardia – Rapporto 2012.* Milano: Regione Lombardia, Eupolis Lombardia, Fondazione Ismu, Orim, pp. 261–295.

Antonovsky, A. (1987). *Unravelling the Mystery of Health. How people manage stress and stay well.* San Francisco: Jossey-Bass.

APA-American Psychological Association (2010). *Resilience and recovery after war: Refugee children and families in the United States.* Washington, DC: American Psychological Association.

Arroyo, W., & Eth, S. (1985). Children traumatized by central American warfare. In S. Eth, & R.S. Pynoos (Eds), *Posttraumatic stress disorder in children.* Washington DC: American Psychiatric Press, pp. 103–120.

Assman, A. (2002). *Ricordare. Forme e mutamenti della memoria culturale.* Bologna: Il Mulino.

Attias-Donfut, C. (2000). Rapports de générations. Transferts intrafamiliaux et dynamique macrosociale. *Revue française de sociologie*, 4(41), 643–684.

Avogo, W.A., & Agadjanian, V. (2010). Forced migration and child health and mortality in Angola. *Social Science and Medicine*, 70(1), 53–60.

Ayad, M.F. (Ed.) (2016). *Studies in Coptic Culture. Transmission and Interaction.* Cairo: American University in Cairo Press.

Baker, A.M. (1990). The psychological impact of the intifada on Palestinian children in the occupied west bank and Gaza: an exploratory study. *American Journal of Orthopsychiatry*, 60(4), 496–505.

Bakermans-Kranenburg, M.J., Van IJzendoorn, H., & Juffer, F. (2003). Less is more: meta-analyses of sensitivity and attachment interventions in early childhood. *Psychological Bulletin*, *129*(2), 195–215.

Barni, D. (2009). *Trasmettere valori. Tre generazioni familiari a confronto.* Milano: Unicopli.

Barrera Rivera, P. (2001). *Tradicão, transmissão, emocão religiosa.* São Paulo: Olho d'Água.

Bayat, A., & Herrera, L. (2010). *Being young and Muslim: new cultural politics in the global South and North.* New York: Oxford University Press.

Beauchemin, C., Hamel, C., & Simon, P. (Eds) (2016). *Trajectoires et origines. Enquête sur la diversité des populations en France.* Collection: Grandes Enquêtes. Paris: Éditions Ined.

Belardinelli, S., Allodi, L., & Gattamorta, L. (Eds) (2009). *Verso una società post-secolare?* Soveria Mannelli: Rubbettino.

Berry, J.W. (1997). Immigration, acculturation, and adaptation. *Applied Psychology*, *46*(1), 5–34.

Berry, J.W., Poortinga, Y.H., Segall, M.H., & Dasen, P.R. (1992). *Cross-Cultural Psychology: Research and Applications.* Cambridge: Cambridge University Press.

Betancourt, T.S., Abdi, S., Ito, B.S., Lilienthal, G.M., Agalab, N., & Ellis, H. (2015). We left one war and came to another: Resource loss, acculturative stress, and caregiver–child relationships in Somali refugee families. *Cultural Diversity and Ethnic Minority Psychology*, *21*(1), 114–125.

Boccacin, L. (2005). Le generazioni nell'ottica della teoria relazionale. In P. Donati, & P. Terenzi (Eds), *Invito alla sociologia relazionale. Teoria e Applicazioni.* Milano: FrancoAngeli, pp. 95–109.

Boëdec, F. (2007). *Cristiani d'Oriente: un futuro di dubbi e angoscia.* Milano: Vita & Pensiero.

Borruso, P. (2013). Église et État en Éthiopie pendant le Règne du dernier Négus Haïlé Sélassié (1916–1974). *Revue d'Histoire Ecclesiastique*, *108*(3–4), 908–930.

Bosmat, Y. (2017). The Coptic diaspora and the status of the Coptic minority in Egypt. *Journal of Ethnic and Migration Studies*, *43*(7), 1205–1221.

Botros, G. (2006). Religious identity as an historical narrative: Coptic Orthodox immigrant churches and the representation of history. *Journal of Historical Sociology*, *19*(2), 174–201.

Bottura, B., & Mancini, T. (2016). Psychosocial dynamics affecting health and social care of forced migrants: a narrative review. *International Journal of Migration, Health and Social Care*, *12*(2), 109–119.

Bramanti, D., & Meda, S. (2016). I differenti percorsi delle generazioni migranti: verso possibili forme di meticciato? In C. Regalia, C. Giuliani, & S. Meda (Eds), *La sfida del meticciato nella migrazione musulmana. Una ricerca sul territorio milanese.* Milano: FrancoAngeli, pp. 93–118.

Brinkerhoff, J.M. (2009). *Digital diasporas: Identity and transnational engagement.* New York: Cambridge University Press.

Brinkerhoff, J.M. (2014). Diaspora philanthropy: Lessons from a demographic analysis of the Coptic diaspora. *Nonprofit and Voluntary Sector Quarterly, 43*(6), 969–992.

Brinkerhoff, J.M. (2016). Assimilation and heritage identity: Lessons from the Coptic diaspora. *Journal of International Migration and Integration, 17*(2), 467–485.

Brownlee, J. (2013). *Violence against the Copts in Egypt.* Washington D.C.: Carnegie Endowment for International Peace.

Buzi, P., Camplani, A., & Contardi, F. (Eds) (2016). *Coptic Society, Literature and Religion from Late Antiquity to Modern Times: Proceedings of the Tenth International Congress of Coptic Studies,* Rome, September 17th – 22th, 2012 and *Plenary Reports of the Ninth International Congress of Coptic Studies,* Cairo, September 15th - 19th, 2008. Leuven: Peeters Publishers.

Caffulli, C. (2010). *I Cristiani con la valigia nella Penisola Arabica.* Milano: Vita & Pensiero.

Campiche, R. (2010). *La religion visible.* Lausanne: Presses polytechniques et universitaires romandes.

Caneva, E. (2011). *Mix generation. Gli adolescenti di origine straniera tra globale e locale.* Milano: FrancoAngeli.

Caneva, E., & Pozzi, S. (2014). The Transmission of Language and Religion in Immigrant Families: A Comparison between Mothers and Children. *International Review of Sociology/Revue Internationale de Sociologie, 24*(3), pp. 436–449.

Cannuyer, C. (1994). *I Copti.* trad. it. Schio: Interlogos.

Chen, C. (2002). The Religious Variety of Ethnic Presence: A Comparison between Taiwanese Immigrant Buddhist Temple and Evangelical Christian Churches. *Sociology of Religion, 63,* 215–238.

Choi, Y., He, M., & Harachi, T.W. (2008). Intergenerational Cultural Dissonance, Parent-Child Conflict and Bonding, and Youth Problem Behaviors among Vietnamese and Cambodian Immigrant Families. *Journal of youth and adolescence, 37*(1), pp. 85–96.

Cigoli, V. (1995). Transizioni familiari. In E. Scabini, & P. Donati (Eds), *Nuovo lessico familiare.* Studi interdisciplinari sulla Famiglia, 14. Milano: Vita e Pensiero, pp. 107–116.

Cigoli, V., & Scabini E. (2006). *Relazione familiare: la prospettiva psicologica,* in E. Scabini, & P. Donati (Eds), *Le parole della famiglia.* Studi interdisciplinari sulla Famiglia, 21. Milano: Vita e Pensiero, pp. 13–46.

Clermont Coptic Encyclopedia (1991). Clermont Digital Library: Macmillan.

Connor, P. (2009). International Migration and Religious Participation. *Sociological Forum, 4*(24), 779–803.

Connor, P. (2012), Balm for The Soul: Immigrant Religion and Emotional Well-Being. *International Migration, 50,* 130–157.

Cragg, K. (1992). A tale of two cities. Helping the heirs of Mecca to transform Medina. *Mission Frontiers, 12*(21), 21–22.

Craig, T., Mac Jajua, P., & Warfa, N. (2009). Mental health care needs of refugees. *Psychiatry, 8*(9), 351–354.

D'Alisera, J. (2009). Images of a Wounded Homeland: Sierra Leonean Children and the New Heart of Darkness. In N. Foner (Ed.), *Across Generations. Immigrant Families in America.* New York: New York University Press, pp. 114–134.

Dekel, R., & Goldblatt, H. (2008). Is there intergenerational transmission of trauma? The case of combat veterans' Children. *American Journal of Orthopsychiatry, 78*(3), 281–289.

Diez, M. (2017). *Christians in the Middle East: A Guide.* Retrieved from https://www.oasiscenter.eu/en/christians-middle-east-guide.

DIMECCE (Defining and identifying Middle Eastern Christians Communities in Egypt) (2015). *Research findings presented at "Middle Eastern Christians in the Diaspora: Past and Present, Continuity and Change".* Conference, University of St. Andrews, 26–27 May.

Dodge, C.P., & Raundalen, M. (1987). *War violence and children in Uganda.* Uppsala: Norwegian University Press.

Donati, P. (1989). *La famiglia come relazione sociale.* Milano: FrancoAngeli.

Donati, P. (1991). *Teoria relazionale della società.* Milano: FrancoAngeli.

Donati, P. (2008). *Oltre il multiculturalismo. La ragione relazionale per un mondo comune.* Roma-Bari: Laterza.

Donati, P. (2009). *La società dell'umano.* Genova-Milano: Editrice Marietti 1820.

Donati, P. (2010). *La matrice teologica della società.* Soveria Mannelli: Rubbettino.

Ebaugh, H.R., & Chafetz, J. (2002). *Religion across borders: Transnational religious networks.* Walnut Creek: Altamira Press.

Ebaugh, H.R., & Chafetz, J.S. (2000). *Religion and the New Immigrants: Continuities and Adaptation in Immigrant Congregations.* Walnut Creek: AltaMira Press.

Eberstadt, M. (2013). *How the West Really Lost God: A New Theory of Secularization.* West Conshohocken: Templeton Foundation Press.

Eid, P. (2003). The Interplay between Ethnicity, Religion, and Gender among Second-Generation Christian and Muslim Arabs in Montreal. *Canadian Ethnic Studies, 35*(2), 30–62.

Ellis, B.H., MacDonald, H.Z., Lincoln, A.K., & Cabral, H.J. (2008). Mental health of Somali adolescent refugees: the role of trauma, stress, and perceived discrimination. *Journal of Consulting and Clinical Psychology, 76*(2), 184–193.

Elsässer, S. (2010). Press liberalization, the new media and the "Coptic question": Muslim-Coptic relations in Egypt in a changing media landscape. *Journal Middle Eastern Studies, 46*(1), 131–150.

Erlich, H. (1994). *Ethiopia and the Middle East.* Boulder: Lynne Rienner Press.

Esser, H. (2006). *Migration, Language and Integration.* AKI Research Review 4. Berlin: Social Science Research Centre.

Eth, S. (1990). Post-traumatic stress disorder in childhood. In M. Hersen, & C.G. Last (Eds), *Pergamon general psychology series, 161. Handbook of child and adult psychopathology: a longitudinal perspective.* Elmsford. New York: Pergamon Press, pp. 263–274.

Eth, S., & Pynoos, R.S. (1985). *Post-traumatic stress disorder in children.* Washington, DC: American Psychiatric Press.

Eth, S., & Pynoos, R.S. (1994). Children who witness the homicide of a parent. *Psychiatry Interpersonal and Biological Processes, 57*(4), 287–306.

Fass, P.S. (2005). Children in Global Migrations. *Journal of Social History, 38*(4), 937–953.

Fauri, F. (2015). *Storia economica delle migrazioni italiane.* Bologna: Il Mulino.

Fazel, M., Reed, R.V., Panter-Brick, C., & Stein, A. (2012). Mental health of displaced and refugee children resettled in high-income countries: risk and protective factors. *The Lancet, 379*(9812), 266–282.

Flor, D.L., & Flanagan Knapp, N. (2001). Transmission and Transaction: Predicting Adolescents Internalization of Parental Religious Values. *Journal of Family Psychology, 15*(4), 627–645.

Foner, N. (Ed.) (2009). *Across Generations. Immigrant Families in America.* New York: New York University Press.

Foner, N., & Alba, R. (2008). Immigrant Religion in the U.S. and Western Europe: Bridge or Barrier to Inclusion? *International Migration Review, 42*(2) (Summer), 360–392.

Freud, A., & Burlingham, D.T. (1973). *War and children.* New York: Greenwood Press.

Galal, L.P. (2012a). Coptic Christian practices: formations of sameness and difference. *Islam and Christian–Muslim Relations, 23*(1), 45–58.

Galal, L.P. (2012b). Guardians of contested borders. Transnational Strategies for Coptic Survival. In L.K. Rasmussen, & L.P. Galal (Eds), *Transnational Experiences. Europe. Middle East.* Denmark: Kvinder, Køn & Forskning, (2–3), 63–74.

Galal, L.P., Hunter, A., McCallum, F., Sparre, S.L., & Wozniak-Bobinska, M. (2016). Middle Eastern Christian spaces in Europe: multi-sited and super-diverse. *Journal of Religion in Europe, 9*(1), 1–25.

Garmezy, N., & Rutter, M. (1985). Acute reactions to stress. In M. Rutter, & L. Hersov (Eds), *Child and Adolescent Psychiatry: Modern Approaches.* London: Blackwell Scientific Publication, pp. 152–196.

Giuliani, C., Tagliabue, S., & Regalia, C. (2018). Psychological well-being, multiple identities, and discrimination among first and second generation immigrant Muslims. *Europe's journal of psychology, 14*(1), 66.

Gomarasca, P. (2009). *Meticciato. Convivenza o confusione?* Venezia: Marcianum Press.

Gozdziak, E.M. (2002). Spiritual emergency room: the role of spirituality and religion in the resettlement of Kosovar Albanians. *Journal of Refugee Studies, 15*(2), 136–152.

Gozzoli, C., & Regalia, C. (2005). *Migrazioni e famiglie. Percorsi, legami e interventi.* Bologna: Il Mulino.

Greenberg, J., Solomon, S., & Pyszczynski, T. (1997). Terror management theory of self-esteem and cultural worldviews: Empirical assessments and conceptual refinements. *Advances in Experimental Social Psychology, 29*, 61–139.

Guha-Sapir, D., & Gijsbert, W. (2004). Conflict-related Mortality: An Analysis of 37 Datasets. *Disasters, 28*(4), 418–428.

Ha, H.J. (2017). Emotions of the weak: violence and ethnic boundaries among Coptic Christians in Egypt. *Ethnic and Racial Studies, 40*(1), 133–151.

Haddad, Y.J. (2013). Good Copt, bad Copt: competing narratives on Coptic identity in Egypt and the United States. *Studies in World Christianity, 19*(3), 208–232.

Hamilton, A. (2006). *The Copts and the West, 1439–1822: The European Discovery of the Egyptian Church.* Oxford: Oxford University Press.

Hansen, H.L. (2015). *Christian-Muslim Relations in Egypt: politics, society and interfaith encounters.* London: I.B. Tauris.

Helly, D., Vatz-Laaroussi, M., & Rachedi, L. (2001). *Transmission culturelle aux enfants par de jeunes couples immigrants.* Montréal: Sherbrooke.

Henderson, R.P. (2005). The Egyptian Coptic Christians: the conflict between identity and equality. *Islam and Christian–Muslim Relations, 16*(2), 155–166.

Herberg, W. (1960). *Protestant, Catholic, Jew.* New York: Anchor Books.

Hervieu-Léger, D. (2003). Pour une sociologie des modernités religieuses multiples. *Social Compass, 50*(3), 287–295.

Hirsch, M. (2008). The Generation of Postmemory. *Poetics Today, 29*(1), 103–128.

Hirschman, C. (2004). The Role of Religion in the Origins and Adaptation of Immigrant Groups in the United States. *International Migration Review, 38*, 1206–1233.

Hjern, A., Angel, B., & Hojer, B. (1991). Persecution and behavior: a report of refugee children from Chile. *Child Abuse & Neglect, 15*(3), 239–248.

Hooberman, J., Rosenfeld, B., Rasmussen, A., & Keller, A. (2010). Resilience in trauma-exposed refugees: The moderating effect of coping style on resilience variables. *American Journal of Orthopsychiatry, 80*(4), 557–563.

Hussain, D., & Bhushan, B. (2009). Development and validation of the Refugee Trauma Experience Inventory. *Psychological Trauma: Theory, Research, Practice, and Policy, 1*(2), 107–117.

Ibrahim, V. (2010). *The Copts of Egypt: The Challenges of Modernisation and Identity*. London: I.B. Tauris.

Ibrahim, V. (2015). Beyond the cross and the crescent: plural identities and the Copts in contemporary Egypt. *Journal Ethnic and Radical Studies, 38*(14), 2584–2597.

ISTAT (Istituto Italiano di Statistica) (2018). *Immigrati e nuovi cittadini* (Report Monitoring Unit of Immigration). Retrieved from http://www4.istat.it/it/ archivio/208951.

Jelinek, L., Wittekind, C.E., Moritz, S., Kellner, M., & Muhtz, C. (2013). Neuropsychological functioning in posttraumatic stress disorder following forced displacement in older adults and their offspring. *Psychiatry Research, 210*(2), 584–589.

Jenkins, P. (2016). *Chiese d'Oriente crepuscolo inevitabile?* Milano: Vita & Pensiero.

Jensen, P.S. & Shaw, J. (1993). Children as victims of war: current knowledge and future research needs. *Journal of the American Academy of Child & Adolescent Psychiatry, 32*(4), 697–708.

Jiménez, T.R. (2011). *Immigrants in The United States: How Well Are They Integrating Into Society?* Washington DC: Migration Policy Institute.

Jovic, V., Opacic, G., & Speh-Vujadinovic, S. (2005). Refugees and mental health-implications for the processes of repatriation and integration. *Goran Opacic/Ivana Vidakovic/Branko Vujadinovic (Hg.): Living in post-war communities, Belgrad: International Aid Network*, 149–181.

Kamil, J. (2013). *Christianity in the land of Pharaons. The Coptic Orthodox Church*. London: Routledge.

Kaoues, F. (2011). *Cristiani d'Oriente l'emergenza continua*. Milano: Vita & Pensiero.

Karoui, D.P.E. (2012). Égyptiens d'outre-Nil : des diasporas égyptiennes. *Tracés. Revue de Sciences Humaines, (23)*, 89–112.

Karpathakis, A. (2001). Conclusion: New York City's Religions. In T. Carnes, & A. Karpathakis (Eds), *New York Glory: Religions in the City*. New York: New York University Press, pp. 388–394.

Khairallah, M. (2014). *Un cupo futuro per i cristiani in Medio Oriente*. Milano: Vita & Pensiero.

Kramer, S., & Bala, J. (2010). Intercultural dimensions in the treatment of traumatized refugee families. *Traumatology, 16*(4) 153–159.

Kronick, R., Rousseau, C., & Cleveland, J. (2015). Asylum-seeking children's experiences of detention in Canada: A qualitative study. *American Journal of Orthopsychiatry, 85*(3), 287–294.

Kurien, P. (2002). 'We Are Better Hindus Here': Religion and Ethnicity among Indian Americans. In P.G. Min, & J.H. Kim (Eds), *Religions in Asian America. Building Faith Communities*. Walnut Creek: AltaMira Press, pp. 99–120.

Laban, C.J., Komproe, I.H., Gernaat, H.B., & de Jong, J.T. (2008). The impact of a long asylum procedure on quality of life, disability and physical health in Iraqi asylum seekers in the Netherlands. *Social Psychiatry and Psychiatric Epidemiology*, *43*(7), 507–515.

Laurence, J., & Vaisse, J. (2006). *Integrating Islam: Political and Religious Challenges in Contemporary France*. Washington DC: Brookings Institution Press.

Leccardi, C. (2009). *Sociologie del tempo*. Roma-Bari: Laterza.

Levi Della Vida, G. (Ed.). (1984). Documenti intorno alle relazioni delle chiese orientali con la S. Sede durante il pontificato di Gregorio XIII. (Including correspondence between Pope Gregory XIII, Ignatius XIV, Patriarch of the Jacobites, and John XIV, Patriarch of the Copts). Vatican City: Biblioteca Apostolica Vaticana.

Lüscher, K. (2011). Ambivalence: A "Sensitizing Construct" for the Study and Practice of Intergenerational Relationships. *Journal of Intergenerational Relationships*, *9*(2), 191–206.

Lustig, S.L., Kia-Keating, M., Knight, W.G., Geltman, P., Ellis, H., Kinzie, J.D., & Saxe, G.N. (2004). Review of child and adolescent refugee mental health. *Journal of the American Academy of Child & Adolescent Psychiatry*, *43*(1), 24–36.

Mahmood, S. (2012). Religious Freedom, the Minority Question, and Geopolitics in the Middle East. *Comparative Studies in Society and History*, *54*(2), 418–446.

Maliepaard, M., & Lubbers, M. (2013). Parental Religious Transmission after Migration: The Case of Dutch Muslims. *Journal of Ethnic and Migration Studies*, *39*(3), 425–442.

Marongiu Bonaiuti, C. (1982). *Politica e religioni nel colonialismo italiano (1882–1941)*. Milano: Giuffrè.

Marzouki, N. (2016). The US Coptic Diaspora and the Limit of Polarization. *Journal of Immigrant & Refugee Studies*, *14*(3), 261–276.

Massey, D.S., & Higgins, M.E. (2011). The Effect of Immigration on Religious Belief and Practice: A Theologizing or Alienating Experience? Office of Population Research, Princeton University. *Social Science Research (Soc Sci Res)*, *40*(5), 1371–1389.

Masten, A.S., Best, K.M., & Garmezy, N. (1990). Resilience and development: Contributions from the study of children who overcome adversity. *Development and Psychopathology*, *2*(4), 425–444.

McCallum, F. (2007). The political role of the patriarch in the contemporary Middle East. *Journal Middle Eastern Studies*, *43*(6), 923–940.

McCallum, F. (2012). Christian political participation in the Arab world. *Islam and Christian-Muslim Relations,* *23*(1), 3–18.

McGregor, L.S., Melvin, G.A., & Newman, L.K. (2015). Differential accounts of refugee and resettlement experiences in youth with high and low levels of posttraumatic stress disorder (PTSD) symptomatology: A mixed-methods investigation. *American Journal of Orthopsychiatry*, *85*(4), 371–381.

Medvedeva, M. (2012). Negotiating Languages In Immigrant Families. *International Migration Review*, *46*(2), 517–545.

Melcangi, A. (2018). *I Copti nell'Egitto di Nasser. Tra politica e religione (1952–1970)*. Roma: Carocci.

Min, P.G., & Kim, J.H. (Eds) (2002). *Religions in Asian America. Building Faith Communities*. Walnut Creek: AltaMira Press.

Moro, M.R., De la Noé, Q., Moukenich, Y., & Baubet, T. (2009). *Manuale di psichiatria transculturale. Dalla clinica alla società*. Milano: FrancoAngeli.

Muhr, T. (2004). *Atlas.ti 5.0* (Computer software). Berlin, Germany: Scientific Software Development.

Nakash, O., Nagar, M., Shoshani, A., & Lurie, I. (2015). The association between acculturation patterns and mental health symptoms among Eritrean and Sudanese asylum seekers in Israel. *Cultural Diversity and Ethnic Minority Psychology*, *21*(3), 468–476.

Pace, E. (2008). *Raccontare Dio. La religione come comunicazione*. Bologna: Il Mulino.

Pace, E. (Ed.) (2013). *Le religioni nell'Italia che cambia*. Roma: Carocci editore.

Pavli, A., & Maltezou, H. (2017). Health problems of newly arrived migrants and refugees in Europe. *Journal of Travel Medicine*, *24*(4), 1–8.

Percheron, A. (1991). La transmission des valeurs. In F. De Singly (Ed.), *La famille: l'état des savoirs*. Paris: La Découverte.

Pérennès, J.J. (2016). *Cristiani d'Egitto fiaccole nella tormenta*. Milano: Vita & Pensiero.

Perks, T., & Haan, M. (2011). Youth religious involvement and adult community participation: Do levels of youth involvement matter? *Nonprofit and Voluntary Sector Quarterly*, *40*(1), 107–129.

Pernice, R. (1994). Methodological issues in research with refugees and immigrants. *Professional Psychology: Research and Practice, 25*(3), 207–213.

Pew Research Center (2010). *Global Religious Futures*. (http://www.globalreligiousfuturesorg/countries/egypt/religious_demography#/?affiliations_religion_id=0&affiliations_year=2010).

Phinney, J.S., Horenczyk, G., Liebkind, K., & Vedder, P. (2001). Ethnic identity, immigration, and well-being: An interactional perspective. *The Journal of Social Issues, 57*(3), 493–510.

Picard, E. (2012). Nation-Building and Minority Rights in the Middle East. In A.N. Longva, & A.S. Roald (Eds), *Religious Minorities in the Middle East. Domination, Self-empowerment, Accommodation*. Leiden: Brill, pp. 325–350.

Pizzo, P. (2015). The "Coptic question" in post- revolutionary Egypt: citizenship, democracy, religion. *Journal Ethnic and Racial Studies, 38*(14), 2598–2613.

Pollini, G., Pretto, A., & Rovati, G. (2012). *L'Italia nell'Europa: i valori tra persistenze e trasformazioni*. Milano: FrancoAngeli.

Pontalti, C., & Rossi, G. (1995). Legame intergenerazionale. In E. Scabini, & P. Donati (Eds), *Nuovo lessico familiare*. Studi interdisciplinari sulla Famiglia, 14. Milano: Vita e Pensiero, pp. 69–82.

Portes, A., & Rumbaut, R. (2006). *Immigrant America*. Berkeley, US: University of California Press.

Portes, A., & Zhou, M. (1993). The New Second Generation: Segmented Assimilation and Its Variants. *The Annals of the American Academy of Political and Social Science*, *530*(1), 74–96.

Pynoos, R.S., & Nader, K. (1990). Children's exposure to violence and traumatic death. *Psychiatric Annals*, *20*(6), 334–344.

Raineri, O. (1996). *La spiritualità etiopica*. Roma: Studium.

Reading, R. (2009). Long-term effects of organized violence on young Middle Eastern refugees' mental health. *Child: Care, Health and Development*, *35*(2), 281–281.

Reitz, J.G., Banerjee, R., Phan, M., & Thompson, J. (2009). Race, Religion, and the Social Integration of New Immigrant Minorities in Canada. *International Migration Review*, *43*(4), 695–726.

Rizzi, M. (2016). *La secolarizzazione debole*. Bologna: Il Mulino.

Roberts, A.L., Dohrenwend, B.P., Aiello, A., Wright, R.J., Maercker, A., Galea, S., & Koenen, K.C. (2012). The stressor criterion for posttraumatic stress disorder: Does it matter? *Journal of Clinical Psychiatry*, *73*(2), 264–270.

Rogan, E. (2011). *The Arabs*. New York: Basic Books.

Rosenheck, R., & Nathan, P. (1985). Secondary traumatization in children of Vietnam veterans. *Psychiatric Services*, *36*(5), 538–539.

Rossi, G. (2012). La famiglia tra le generazioni. *La Famiglia*, *46*(256), 46–63.

Rowe, P.S. (2007). Neo-Millet systems and transnational religious movements: the humayun decrees and Church construction in Egypt. *Journal of Church and State*, *49*, 329–350.

Rowe, P.S. (2017). *Who are the Coptic Christians?* The Conversation, April 17 (https://theconversation.com/who-are-the-coptic-christians-76273).

Rumbaut, R.G. (2006). *Severed or Sustained Attachments? Language, Identity and Imagined Communities in the Post-Immigrant Generation*. In P. Levitt, & M.C. Waters (Eds), *The Changing Face of Home. The Transnational Lives of the Second Generation*. New York: Russell Sage Foundation, pp. 43–95.

Saad, S.M. (2010). The contemporary life of the Coptic orthodox church in the United States. *Studies in World Christianity*, *16*(3), 207–225.

Saad, S.M., & Westbrook, D.A. (2015). Copts, scripturalization, and identity in the diaspora. In V.L. Wimbush (Ed.). *Scripturalizing the Human: The Written as the Political*. New York: Routledge, pp. 233–252.

Saarela, J.M., & Elo, I.T. (2016). Forced migration in childhood: Are there long-term health effects? *SSM – Population Health*, *2*, 813–823.

Saint-Blancat, C. (2004). La transmission de l'islam auprès des nouvelles générations de la diaspora. *Social Compass*, *51*(2), 235–247.

Salvatore, S., Gennaro, A., & Valsiner, J. (Eds). (2014). *Multicentric identities in a globalizing world*. Charlotte, NC: Information Age Publishing.

Santavirta T. (2017). The long term impact of forced migration during childhood on adult health. *SSM - Population Health*, 2, 914–916.

Scabini, E. (2006). Rapporto tra le generazioni e trasmissione dei valori. In A.C. Bosio (Ed.), *Esplorare il cambiamento sociale*. Studi in onore di Gabriele Calvi. Milano: FrancoAngeli, pp. 17–34.

Schwarz, E., & Kowalski, J. (1991). Malignant memories: PTSD in children and adults after a school shooting. *Journal of the American Academy of Child & Adolescent Psychiatry*, *30*(6), 936–944.

Schottelkorb, A.A., Doumas, D.M., & Garcia, R. (2012). Treatment for childhood refugee trauma: A randomized, controlled trial. *International Journal of Play Therapy*, *21*(2), 57–73.

Sedra, P. (1999). Class cleavages and ethnic conflict: Coptic Christian communities in modern Egyptian politics. *Journal Islam and Christian-Muslim Relations*, *10*(2), 219–235.

Shrira, A., Yuval, P., Menachem, B.E., & Shmotkin, D. (2011). Transgenerational effects of trauma in midlife: evidence for resilience and vulnerability in offspring of holocaust survivors. *Psychological Trauma: Theory, Research, Practice, and Policy*, *3*(4), 394–402.

Silove, D. (2013). The ADAPT model: a conceptual framework for mental health and psychosocial programming in post conflict settings. *Intervention*, *11*(3), 237–248.

Simon, P., & Tiberj, V. (2014). *Religions : Documents de travail de l'INED 2010* (http:// spire.sciencespo.fr/hdl:/2441/eu4vqp9ompqllro9hi642i8gn/resources/dt-teo-embargo-2.pdf).

Smith, C.D. (2005). The Egyptian Copts: Nationalism, Ethnicity, and the Definition of Identity for a Religious Minority. In M. Shatzmiller (Eds). *Nationalism and minority identities in Islamic societies*. Montreal: McGill-Queen's University Press, pp. 58–84.

Sparre, S.L., & Galal, L.P. (2018). Incense and holy bread: the sense of belonging through ritual among Middle Eastern Christians in Denmark. *Journal of Ethnic and Migration Studies*, *44*(16), 2649–2666.

Suozzia, J.M., & Motta, R.W. (2004). The relationship between combat exposure and the transfer of trauma-like symptoms to offspring of veterans. *Traumatology*, *10*, 17–37.

Swanson, M.N. (2010). *The Coptic papacy in Islamic Egypt 641–1517: the popes of Egypt*, 2. New York: American University in Cairo Press.

Terr, L. (1988). What happens to early memories of trauma? A study of twenty children under age five at the time of documented traumatic events. *Journal of the American Academy of Child & Adolescent Psychiatry*, *27*(1), 96–104.

Thomas, S., Nafees, B., & Bhugra, D. (2004). 'I was running away from death' – the preflight experiences of unaccompanied asylum seeking children in the UK. *Child: Care, Health and Development, 30*(2), 113–122.

TIMEP (2018). *Christians in Egypt.* https://timep.org/wp-content/uploads/2018/10/Christian-Issue-Brief-10-9-18option1-with-hyperlinks.pdf.

Trentacosta, C.J., McLear, C.M., Ziadni, M.S., Lumley, M.A., & Arfken, C.L. (2016). Potentially Traumatic Events and Mental Health Problems Among Children of Iraqi Refugees: The Roles of Relationships With Parents and Feelings About School. *American Journal of Orthopsychiatry, 86*(4), 384–392.

Tribalat, M. (1995). *Faire France. Une grande enquête sur les immigrés et leurs enfants.* Paris: La Découverte.

Valtolina, G.G., & Colombo, C. (2012). La ricerca sui ricongiungimenti familiari: Una rassegna. *Studi Emigrazione/International Journal of Migration Studies, 48*(185), 129–144.

Van Dijk, J., & Botros, G. (2009). The importance of ethnicity and religion in the life cycle of immigrant churches: A comparison of Coptic and Calvinist churches. *Canadian Ethnic Studies, 41*(1), 191–214.

Vatz-Laaroussi, M. (2001). *Le familial au cœur de l'immigration.* Paris: L'Harmattan.

Vatz-Laaroussi, M. (2007). Les relations intergénérationnelles, vecteurs de transmission et de résilience au sein des familles immigrantes et réfugiées au Québec. *Revue internationale électronique Enfances, familles, générations, 6*, Printemps.

Verkuyten, M., Thijs, J., & Stevens, G. (2012). Multiple Identities and Religious Transmission: A Study among Moroccan-Dutch Muslim Adolescents and Their Parents Multiple Identities and Religious Transmission. *Child Development, 83*(5), 1577–1590.

Warner, R.S. (2000). The New Immigrant Religion: An Update and Appraisal. *Epicenter, 5*(2) (Spring), 1–7.

Warner, W.L., & Srole, L. (1945). *The Social System of American Ethnic Groups.* New Haven: Yale University Press.

Weine, S. (2008). Family Roles in Refugee Youth Resettlement from a Prevention Perspective. *Child and Adolescent Psychiatric Clinics of North America, 17*(3), 515–532.

Weine, S.M. (2011). Developing Preventive Mental Health Interventions for Refugee Families in Resettlement. *Family Process, 50*(3), 410–430.

Westbrook, D.A., & Saad, S.M. (2017). Religious Identity and Borderless Territoriality in the Coptic e-Diaspora. *Journal of International Migration and Integration, 18*(1), 341–351.

Wiese, E.B.P., (2010). Culture and Migration: Psychological Trauma in Children and Adolescents. *Traumatology. 16*(4), 142–152.

Wiese, E.B.P., E., & Burhorst, I. (2007). The Mental Healt of Asylum-seeking and Refugee Children and Adolescents Attending a Clinic in the Netherlands. *Transcultural Psychiatry, 44*(4), 596–613.

Wilson, J.P., & Tang, C.C.S.K. (Eds) (2007). *Cross-cultural assessment of psychological trauma and PTSD*. New York: Springer Science & Business Media.

Wittekind, C., Jelinek, L., Kellner, M., Moritz, S., & Muhtz, C. (2010). Intergenerational transmission of biased information processing in posttraumatic stress disorder (PTSD) following displacement after world war II. *Journal of Anxiety Disorders, 24*(8), 953–957.

Yacoub, C., & Yacoup, J. (2015). *Dall'Iraq alla Siria l'estinzione dei cristiani*. Milano: Vita & Pensiero.

Yako, R.M., & Biswas, B. (2014). "We came to this country for the future of our children. We have no future": Acculturative stress among Iraqi refugees in the United States. *International Journal of Intercultural Relations, 38*, 133–141.

Yehuda, R., & Bierer, L.M. (2008). Transgenerational transmission of cortisol and PTSD risk. *Progress in Brain Research, 167*, 121–135.

Yule, W., & Udwin, O. (1991). Screening child survivors for post-traumatic stress disorders: experiences from "Jupiter" sinking. *British Journal of Clinical Psychology, 30*(2), 131–138.

Yurtbay, T., Alyanak, B., Abali, O., Kaynak, N., & Durukan, M. (2003). The psychological effects of forced emigration on Muslim Albanian children and adolescents. *Community Mental Health Journal, 39*(3), 203–212.

Zhou, M. (2009). Conflict, Coping, and Reconciliation: Intergenerational Relations in Chinese Immigrant Families. In N. Foner (Ed.), *Across Generations. Immigrant Families in America*. New York: New York University Press, pp. 21–46.

Zhou, M., & Bankston, C.L. (1994). Social Capital and the Adaptation of the Second Generation: The Case of Vietnamese Youth in New Orleans. *International Migration Review, 28*(4), 821–845.

Zhou, M., & Bankston, C.L. (1998). *Growing Up American*. New York: Russell Sage Foundation.

Websites

https://arts.st-andrews.ac.uk/dimecce.

http://www.diocesicoptamilano.com/la-sede-di-san-marco.html.

http://www.integrazionemigranti.gov.it/Areetematiche/PaesiComunitari-e-associazioniMigranti/Pagine/mappatura-associazioni.aspx.

https://ifg.uniurb.it/static/lavori-fine-corso-2008/dimatteo_roberta/lavoro_di_fine_corso/pagine/lacomunita.htm.

https://www.chiesadimilano.it/news/chiesa-diocesi/vivacita-e-fermenti-dei-cristiani-copti-a-milano-146112.html.

https://www.tuttitalia.it/lombardia/provincia-di-milano/statistiche/cittadini-stranieri/egitto/.

PART 6

Religious Diversity in Italian Schools

∴

The Religious Dimension in Plural Schools: Institutional, Relational and Strategic Issues

Maddalena Colombo

1 Introduction: Cultural Change and the Role of Religion in Public Schooling

This chapter is focused on religion as an element of the schooling process and aims at enlightening the main changes occurring in public schools as a consequence of the increasing pluralism and multi-ethnicity (Colombo, 2013), overall among students and their families, and the "new" consideration of religion (and religion education) within the school environment (Hobson, Edwards, 1999). The change is mainly due to a two-fold pushing factor:

- *A demographic change,* in all Europe the second-generation immigrant population brings into the school environment the reality of a multitude of faiths and worships, with more or less attachment in comparisons to their parents or to peers with a native background;
- *A cultural change*, the organization of public education in many countries lies on the secularization principle – which means that, when it comes to student's religion, it tends to be as neutral as possible. This goes along with an increasing "indifference" of young people to the family religious traditions and belonging, and the growth in the number of youngsters who are not believers, agnostic or religious recusants (Garelli, 2016). It is widely acknowledged that secularization brings about a privatization of the religious choice and observance, and an increase in religious illiteracy (Melloni, 2014; Cadeddu, Melloni, 2018).

Here, we want to discuss two consequences of this on public schooling. At an institutional level, pluralization through migration –especially after the last decade, with its threatening issues about religious fundamentalism and radicalization among people with an immigrant background– may have led many educators to change the focus of their discussions on religion at school; i.e. from a form of single faith religious teaching to a "non-confessional", inclusive, multi-faith approach, including learning *about* the religions of relatively newly established minorities such as Hindus, Sikhs and Muslims, as well as about Christianity and Judaism. Or, from a casual and mostly improvised reference to faith into the Human Studies curriculum, to a more structured inclusion of learning objects concerning religions as historic expressions of mankind, modern institutions and set of lively rituals that feature different people and States, etc. (Jackson, 2014 and 2016).

At a relational level, instead, the resurgence of religion (as "identity specific") among immigrant students and parents may have generated various kinds of reactions, both by majority and minority school agents, from discomfort to curiosity, from intolerance to intercultural solidarity. As sociologists of education, we have been interrogating about how this mixed educational landscape is going to be designed, as regards the main issues at stake when students' religion is visible: equity, integration, diversity management, citizenship and values education. Questions, such as "Are we in an equal, not discriminating, and peaceful environment because of the disappearance (or neutralization) of religion(s)?" and "Are we in a conflict arena, where religious worships, communitarian belonging and perception of social discrimination generate discussion, tensions and fight among students, teachers and parents?" become urgent. As well as the question about the strategy that schools with multi-ethnic groups of learners may adopt to reach their purposes better: "Must the public school teach more about religions, with the aim of making students aware of their own cultural roots and religious belongings? Or must it practice more laicism, avoiding to pervade teaching about religious contents and pursue the objective to give students tools for choice and identity building, across a neutral, non-religious, universalistic, curriculum?". In evidence, the response to such questions shows if a school can represent a "neutral space" for students, where diversities can respect one another independently of their roots or, instead, if it becomes a "common house", where students background is reciprocally questioned and recognized as a tool for growth.

Recently, Benadusi *et al.* (2017) stated that teaching religions in public institutions is still an open issue, because of the main associated risks of ideologization and "functionalization" of religion in mixed schools – facing interfaith conflicts, misunderstandings and negative stereotypes that are likely to rise where religious speech and practices take place. Although the majority of state school principals (elsewhere in Europe) seem to recommend to keep out from religious disputes and show the "secular self", many school professionals feel distress facing the negative externalities of the neutral school, and claim for better preparation to cope with cultural and religious clashes among students or with immigrant parents (Laborde, Silhol, 2018).

Taking religions as a fundamental part (among others) of the public debate on education is thus unavoidable today for plural schools, even if this will lead to take over the traditional reluctance to engage schools in "private issues". In fact, if religion is a "pending question" for young people, education must provide some replies. As Meuret (2015) argued, in order to contrast young people's fascination for ideological and religious radicalism, democratic education, as well as the republican one, have the specific task to teach students tolerance and civicness facing multi-religiosity. Youngsters can profit mainly from the school experience, if they want to learn how to gain (and not to lose) from religious diversity and how (and why) to avoid the main inconvenient of xenophobia, religious phobia and intolerance. Education in multi-religious settings can really open students towards a "non-relativistic view" and create in them a "value-sensitive attitude" (Pace, 2004: 279).

In the next sections, after a brief overview on the secularized school environment in Europe, we will emphasize the role of religious education in the institutional frame (§2). Then, we will mention the state of religious education (RE) in Italy, both in socio-demographic (what kind and how many students ask for RE) and in normative terms (how the access to RE in public schools is regulated) (§3). Afterwards, we will discuss the different approaches to inter-ethnic dialogue in the Italian mixed schools (§4). We will close the chapter by presenting the main theoretical and methodological assumptions of an empirical study focusing on the religious dimension of interethnic relationships in public education system, which was carried out during s.y. 2016/17 in lower secondary state schools in Northern Italy (§5).

2 The Secularized School Environment in Europe: What Is Religious Education Expected To Do?

The transformation of school environment in an increasing secularized setting (see Chapter 3) has to do with the reciprocal implications between state, education and religion, three fundamental institutions of the European civil society. Although with diverse *nuances*, at the turn of the millennium the process of de-institutionalization affected every organizations: the consequence has been a widespread suspicion and mistrust by people towards all kinds of formal guarantee –in the domain of social, economic and cultural or religious right's protection, the strongest opposition being against the political institutions. Since religion and education have a political side (although it may be non-visible to users), they could not avoid to be affected by this "institutional crisis".

Secularization began to be a feature of the modern education system long before the creation of a European space for education, as it is rooted in the Enlightening period. Anyway, it was during the 20th century that the rationalistic school systems were established, and they regulated the spaces devoted to religious education, according to every national history and religious or cultural tradition.[1] As Schreiner argues (2009; 2013), there are different religious landscapes in Europe. The South tends to be dominated by Catholicism (Austria, Italy, Spain, Portugal, Malta and to some extent France, as well as Poland, Ireland and Lithuania), whereas the North is more Lutheran-Protestant (Scandinavia). Central European countries tend to have mixed religious landscapes (Germany, Hungary, the Netherlands, etc.), while Orthodoxy dominates most countries in Eastern Europe, including Greece and Cipro. Finally, Islam is the major religion in countries like Turkey, Albania and Bosnia-Herzegovina.

Of course, the way in which the majority religion is followed, and taught in public schools, depends on the relation between state and religious authorities, state and education system and, finally, on the characteristics of education offer. It is not the case to compare all these elements. It is worth remembering, however, that multi-religiosity has had, and still has, different impacts on Member States, with direct implications on the cultural phenomena that I will analyze: secularization and resurgence of religions (de-secularization or post-secularization).[2]

According to many, secularization has different ways to be embodied and expressed by both institutions and lay people. On the institutional side, keeping the public school system as an example, secularization implies not only adopting a non-religious (or secular) curriculum, but also having looser relations with religious authorities (at a local and larger scale) and avoiding to let students practicing worships or celebrating religious ceremonies in the school space (including to forbid to wear religious symbols and clothes). On the personal side, secularization goes hand in hand with the decline of religious service attendance among youngsters (a sort of disaffiliation from religion) (Bertrand, 2015) and, more generally, the tolerance towards who is non-believer, or the idea that the condition of a believer is not necessarily superior to that of a non-believer. Both stand at the same level of importance and have the capacity to cope with the fundamentals in life (Garelli, 2016), provided that they are free to choose their beliefs.

---

1   As Casanova wrote: "Internal differences notwithstanding, Western European societies are deeply secular societies, shaped by the hegemonic knowledge regime of secularism" (Casanova, 2007: 62).

2   In the Humanities and Social Sciences field, many scholars advocate that religion has gained a new role in the globalized and plural society; after the "dogmatic secularism" imposed by the Enlightening, and after refusing the State religion, contemporary men still need a system of beliefs to follow, which justifies all the efforts to progress. Thus, for many, faith and religious observance become the response to this post-secular need, if chosen in a free and private regime (Berger, 1999; Habermas, 2006; Rosati, Stoeckl, 2012; De Kesel, 2017).

Without doubt, in all Western countries the separation between state and church authorities, along with the affirmation of universalism of rights as a basic principle for the nation, have reduced the public role of religion in many spheres, i.e. in public education. This had some consequences, as religion may be a neglected and controversial topic, and laicism or neutrality may affect the way in which students, teachers and parents construct the discourse about religion in education. At the same time, in a liberal society public education does not derogate from its civic mission: promoting religious literacy and tolerance, and protecting individual and minority religious liberty, which are among the greatest challenges facing pluralism. How do public schools afford this dilemma on the ground?

In USA and Canada (two good examples of secularized and multi-cultural nation), schools typically adopt two different and extreme solutions: (1) making schools hyper-secular and potentially hostile to religion and religious believers, or (2) promoting either flagrantly or subtly the dominant religion of the local community, by adopting curricula that give the impression that any religion is inherently good (Bindewald *et al.*, 2017). Nevertheless, none of the solutions have been successful: although they act within "a solid legal framework to protect the rights of students, the reality on the ground is that many schools are failing to live up to their obligations to students" (*Ibidem*: 18). The middle-path between the two extremes would be what the provinces of Ontario and Quebec, for example, carried out: "Enhancing students' religious literacy and engagement with the religious/cultural other – paying heed to warnings about not allowing majority groups to take advantage of religious education programs (...) or discriminating against minorities in the public schools" (*Ibidem*: 28).

In Europe the effects of secularization are deep and differ according to each country. A range of approaches to provide religion education have been adopted thanks to the initiative of different providers (religious communities, or the state or both). According to Schreiner (2009) and Ferrari S. (2013), the main distinction must be drawn among the following formula:

1) *Learning from religion*: countries where no teaching of one or more specific religions is offered, because references to religion are part of the corpus of other disciplines; this secular teaching is organized by state authorities exclusively (like in France, Czech Republic, Sweden, Belarus and Hungary);

2) *Learning religion* (or *into religion*): in many countries there is a confessional/catechetical approach, where RE is provided by religious communities that have the exclusive responsibility for teachers, textbooks and curricula: this is called "denominational" teaching of religion,

(as in Austria, Poland, Spain and Italy); it is compulsory but in some cases students can opt out;

3) *Learning about religion*: RE is taught as a voluntary and/or mandatory subject in state schools and provides knowledge and information about a number of different religions from a point of view that is external to each of them; activities are fully in charge of the State, which pays for teachers, organizes curricula and checks for textbooks (i.e. in Slovenia: Kodeljia, 2012). RE is called "non-denominational" education and sometimes is taught collaboration with religious authorities (for instance, in the UK and Denmark).

Beyond the single pedagogical strategy, all kinds of RE find their legitimation in the attempt to respond to the new needs of young generations by facing multi-culturalism and secularization. This becomes more urgent in the countries where RE is denominational. In a "Europeanized" curriculum (Bekemans, 2013), Religion Education (even the denominational one) must be rooted not only in an academic and theological justification, but also in the search for a common understanding of religion as a social fact, mixing historical and philosophical elements of knowledge. This is the only "antidote against the threats of fundamentalism, on the one hand, or the 'big blank' of the laicism, on the other" (Pajer, 2009). The same purpose has been expressed by the Council of Europe in the Recommendation no. 1720 (*Religion & Education,* 2005): "By teaching children the history and philosophy of the main religions with restraint and objectivity, and with respect for the values of the European Convention on Human Rights, it will effectively combat fanaticism. Understanding the history of political conflicts in the name of religion is essential". This document addresses some issues previously emphasized by the Parliamentary Assembly in 1999 (see *Religion & Democracy*),[3] which recommended that all State members provided in public schools any sort of religion education, both denominational and non-denominational, on a mandatory basis.

Strong support to this approach comes even from ODIHR-OSCE, whose Expert Group on Freedom of religion set up an important list of recommendations in 2007, the Toledo Guiding Principles (ODIHR-OSCE, 2007). They stated that: *a*) there is a positive value in teaching religion that must emphasize respect for every religion and belief; *b*) teaching about religions and beliefs can reduce misunderstandings and simplifications in facing the beliefs of others.

The traditional way to teach religion subjects, as doctrine transmission and preparation to worships, has been hardly discussed and reformed in many

---

3   Resolution adopted by the Assembly on 27 January 1999 (5th Sitting). See: http://assembly
    .coe.int/nw/xml/XRef/Xref-XML2HTML-en.asp?fileid=16672&lang=en.

countries. What is urgent now is to give people of the globalized 21st century not only reasons to reinforce one's identity and choice, but also the widest cognitive and ethic potential to "get" a religious culture with freedom and awareness. The perspective to assume is thus interdisciplinary and intercultural: religious education embodies both religious and moral convictions; these are gradually taken from the subject along the life course, and are based more on real social and personal experiences than on the family heritage; the school approach must integrate spiritual, moral, ethical and civic values (Council of Europe, 2006).

In conclusion, the role that RE is expected to play in the European secularized and multi-cultural landscape is multiple: *a*) to give pupils a religious literacy in their own and others' religion; *b*) to instill the rational and critical thinking facing religious issues; *c*) to reinforce social cohesion by recognizing that belonging to a religion is a fundamental "identity marker" among others; *d*) to offer exemplary patterns of social coexistence among diverse people.

As a matter of fact, these are very challenging objectives in many countries. RE still remains a "slippery arena of education" (Benadusi *et al.*, 2017: 476) because of the implicitness of many issues that it raises up: equality and right of difference; visibility and invisibility of one's religious belonging; school autonomy and need of extra-school partnerships with confessional representatives, only to mention some of the main dilemmas.

3 The State of Religious Education (RE) in Italy

Italy has greatly been affected by cultural diversity and plural religiosity as well, especially since the turn of Millennium. The country has a long tradition in RE, for the teaching of one religion, i.e. Roman Catholicism, which is the majority religion. The teaching of the Catholic religion is called IRC (*Insegnamento della religione cattolica*). Despite the nation has strong Catholic roots, education is by 90% provided by the State; in addition, 7.5% of private schools are coordinated by the Catholic Church with the support of the State.[4]

According to the agreement signed in 1922 by Italy and the Holy Church and renewed in 1984 (Chapter 9), in all state schools, IRC is guaranteed from the

---

4 Law n. 62 of 2000 establishes that private schools can be recognized on an equal basis with State schools, in accordance with Article 33.4 of the Italian Constitution, if they comply with some requisites (about programs, teachers, etc.). In this case, they are called *scuole paritarie*. They are publicly subsidized; they also have the authority to issue certificates with the same legal value as qualifications from State schools. Most of the Catholic schools in Italy are classified as "*paritarie*".

infant school to upper secondary education for one hour per week (two hours only in kindergarten and pre-school services) and it is funded by the State. The IRC is taught by class teachers, if they are available and considered appropriate by the Catholic Church authority (CEI – *Conferenza Episcopale Italiana* – Italian Episcopal Conference), or by special teachers, selected and prepared by the CEI itself.

Until the 1980s, IRC was a "compulsory discipline, from which parents were allowed to withdraw their children" (Giorda, 2015: 80) in case they disagreed with a confessional education or they were non-believers. In other words, as Coglievina says (2017: 2): "As Catholicism shaped Italian national identity, the presence of Catholic religion lessons in the state-school system has been regarded as something 'normal'". Nonetheless, in 1984, after a strong and confrontational debate developed in many political and cultural environments, the renewal of the Concordate introduced a new type of student's engagement: parents were requested to subscribe IRC at the beginning of school cycle. For those who do not opt for IRC, the regulation offers several options: an "alternative activity" (AA) established by the school itself, which should address topics concerning ethics, values, tolerance and peace.[5] This activity should be imparted by any teacher who is, at the time, available. Another option is tutoring (revision, in-depth studying) or, for high school, a study activity without the presence of any teacher, within the school premises; lastly, an often selected option is the early exit from school (or delayed entry).

Due to the history of the country as mono-confessional, the opening of an alternative education to teaching of one religion represents an official acknowledgment of religious pluralism: in public and state schools, there is an amount of children coming from families with different views or practices concerning religion. Thus, RE is asked to meet the challenge of secularization and religious plurality and the multiple needs of a secularized and multi-faith student body.

As a consequence of the new choice regime, the number of students who followed IRC during the ordinary school time has decreased, even if the vast majority still opt for it (the provision of IRC is guaranteed in every school no matter of how many students subscribe). The Catholic Church office for IRC (Servizio Nazionale CEI per l'IRC, 2016; 2015) shows this trend: in s.y. 2015/16, the subscribers to IRC in the state school system (all degrees) were 87.9% out of the total (81.5% in upper secondary education). Since s.y. 1993/94, this proportion has decreased by -5.6%. In the private school system, the participation to IRC is much higher than in the public one, being most of private schools

---

5   See the Ministry of Education Circular Letters, No. 128, 129, 131 (1986).

run by Catholic organizations: 97% of the private school population opt for IRC and only 3% for alternative activity (AA).

As a matter of fact, AA have been little and badly organized so far, even because they have been optioned by a minority of students (12.1%); someone argues it is still an "invisible education" because, by ministerial rules, it is not requested to be planned and included in the PTOF (the 3-year general education plan of one school). This explains its inferior status in comparison with the rest of school subjects and, consequently, it reduces the legitimation of the student's choice between RE or AA (Bossi, 2017). If a non-choice could be a little problem for natives (whose majority opt for IRC), it can be considered as a falsification or a lack of freedom of choice by immigrant students (amongst whom, almost 20% are Catholic). As shown by the Istat research on Religious belonging and practice among foreign citizens (2011–12), 60.4% of immigrants in Italy between 6 and 17 years old attending Italian schools do not belong to the Catholic religion (Istat, 2015). The majority are Muslim (30%), followed by Catholic (23.2%), Orthodox (19.6%) and, at a distance, Buddhist (3.6%) and Protestant (2.4%) and others.[6]

Therefore, the multi-ethnic composition of the classrooms (especially in the North of country) radically changes the "religious profile" of a school or group of students: not all are believers; not all believers are observant; not all believers have a mono-religion family background, etc. In a past study on low secondary multi-ethnic schools in Lombardy (Colombo, Santagati, 2017; Santagati *et al.*, 2019), with 39% average rate of non-Italian students), the sample was distributed as follows: 11% were not believers; 89% believers; within believers, ¾ were Catholic and ¼ minority religions; ¾ were observant but ¼ (both Catholic and non-Catholic) were non-observant.

Thus, in the last decade, a fundamental reforming process of the IRC teaching has been activated, both by the CEI and the whole body of IRC teachers. They have become aware of the multi-faith change of school population, which affects the attendance of IRC both quantitatively and qualitatively. The challenge of secularism is also becoming day by day more acute.

From the one side, students of foreign origin bear a religious belonging and a family tradition (according to which religion must be respected as a belief, a worship, and a concrete authority performed by parents or community representatives) and emphasize the identity meaning of religion. If non-Catholic,

---

6 For distribution of non-Italians according to their religion, see also Idos, 2018: 196, and Ismu Foundation, 2018. Idos estimates that among foreigners 33% is Muslim; 30% Orthodox; 18% Catholic; 4.5% Protestants; 3% Induist: 2.5% Induist; 0.1% Hebrew; 1.6% Sikh and other Eastern faiths; and 5% atheist or agnostic.

they do not attend IRC, because it is considered as "an hour of other people's religion" (Frisina, 2011: 275). In this way, they reinforce the religious and cultural divide between believers of different origins: seen as a narrow confessional education, IRC ends up going far from the article 9 of the Concordat, which states that the teaching of Catholic religion in state schools (according to the secular nature of the State) must be "part of the aims of the education system" and consequently cannot coincide with catechism, but it must be open to pluralism and take a cultural-historical perspective.

From the other side, native students attend IRC for a range of motivations, not always spiritual or authentically religious, but often practical, opportunistic, and superficial – which tends to diminish the importance and seriousness of IRC itself.[7] This is due to the increasing secularism, or laicism, or "flexible Catholicism" among Italian population, as Garelli (2011, 2012) pointed out, that is a widespread affiliation to Christianity associated to a secular behavior and discontinuous presence in ecclesial settings. Among Italian young people, a "cold" attitude towards religion and personal engagement in worship is very common, and it is called "occasional Catholicism" (Grassi, 2006: 60).

To remark the weakness of the IRC (Canta, 1999), it is also worth mentioning that IRC teachers are considered by students and parents as less authoritative than other professors; moreover, their professional status is more precarious in comparison with the rest of the teaching staff (Silhol, 2017).

To sum it up, as of today, IRC must meet a double-face challenge:

a)   to reinforce and legitimate its status, balancing believer and non-believer students' needs in the light of a "national way to secularism" (Garelli, 2011; Canta *et al.*, 2011), and

b)   to help any religion to take voice in public spaces according to ecumenism and post-secular societal needs (which requires that a discourse on God must be carried out and not bypassed, even in affluent and fully secularized societies[8]).

In particular, RE is a sensitive and "heated" matter in the everyday life of school. The initiatives introduced by IRC teachers outside the classroom (i.e. celebrations, projects, campaigns etc.) meet the disagreement of atheist representatives, who claim for a secular education according to the Constitutional right of freedom of belief and nurture a long-standing debate with many political repercussions on the status of RE in public schools (Giorda, 2015). However, the presence of religions other than Catholicism among the student

---

7   Mentasti and Ottaviano (2009: 243) spoke about a "lukewarm" participation to IRC in a sample of upper secondary students surveyed in 2006.

8   On the post-secular societal needs, see: Rizzi, 2016.

population is not easy to manage and, often, it is up to IRC professors to deal with it. Generally speaking, multi-religiosity is not emphasized or stigmatized in Italian public schools: rather it's ignored and minimized.[9] There is very limited room for minority religions (Ferrari A., 2013b), so that sometimes non-Catholic migrant pupils do attend IRC (especially those coming from an Orthodox, Protestant, and sometimes even Islamic family), when parents agree if their children get some information about religion instead of no religious information at all (or they attend classes against their parent's wishes) (Frisina, 2011: 276). In these cases, IRC becomes a "space of presentation and mediation" between diverse habits, beliefs and traditions.

Because of these facts, the need to renew RE in public schools has become urgent in order, firstly, to cultivate a type of education, which renews the sense of RE for dubitative or superficial Catholic offspring. Secondly, to give room to other narratives of God (and spiritual positions) coming from minority believers, whose sense of belonging to their own religion is often stronger than the one Catholics have. RE addresses both minority and majority followers (and atheists too) in order to raise awareness of the risks of fundamentalism and to educated in the practicing of dialogue. Consequently both IRC and secular curricula, in the last few decades have begun to focus on active citizenship, communication about religion and interreligious dialogue (Vacchiano, 2013), as new fields of engagement for RE scholars and teachers (Bradford Local Authority, 2016; Salvarani, 2006).

4   Different Approaches to Interreligious Dialogue in the Italian Mixed Schools

On the future of RE in Italy within the frame of intercultural education, an intensive cultural debate has been developed in the last decades, involving politicians, Church representatives, academic experts, etc. An even higher number of Italians ask for a change in denominational RE in public schools, despite they do not want to delete IRC (Garelli, 2011: 171–4). Giorda (2015: 91) states that "This country offers a special and original focus to consider the ambiguity of unsolved tensions between the authority and the Constitutional privilege of one Church, the secularism of the juridical frame and the plural and super-diverse reality". It is not surprising, then, if at a national and institutional level,

---

9   For example, non-Catholic students can opt out from IRC, but they cannot have a parallel confessional education during the school time.

the public debate brought about only few concrete consequences.[10] However, in many local realities affected by this debate and moved by a spirit of renewal, new pluralistic strategies have been adopted in RE provision – some temporary and experimental, some more structured.

Many providers agree on two fundamental principles, useful to bypass prejudices and discriminations among students of different beliefs: *a*) knowledge about religion is necessary for anyone, believers and non-believers; *b*) confrontation among different beliefs must occur in a free and democratic educational setting (Pinto Minerva, 2012). By consequence RE, no matter if denominational or non-denominational, must be rooted on the universal values of men and women, drawn from the European Union Chart of Values, and must train the basic citizenship competences in every (future) citizen (Halász, Michel, 2011).

In fact, RE helps to reach a European integration, and must refuse any method or content that could end up separating, isolating, or segregating individuals on the basis of their religion, or that creates intergroup conflicts. Knowing one's own religion, or others' religion, is considered to be fundamental for a full maturation of the person and for a peaceful coexistence between diverse people. On the contrary, ignorance and illiteracy, neglecting and neutrality facing religion issues are considered as factors of social disorder (Council of Europe, 2008;[11] Wierzbicki, 2016). This kind of preparation to diversity must occur in a secular environment, based on freedom of thought, conscience and religion, in which diverse religious beliefs are welcome, but none should have the prominence on others. This is the necessary premise facing the risk that –among immigrant people– Islam would become the first minority religion by number of followers and take advantage of other faiths, limiting the freedom of expression of other beliefs.[12]

---

10   For example, from about 2000 to now, a heated debate has been developed on the laicity in Italian schools, that is, the correctness of exposing religious signs in state schools (i.e. Crucifix), or imposing food regimes or religious celebrations to minority students (this echoed the laicism adopted in France with the "no-veil legislation" in 2003). See the mention to "Ofena case" in Ottaviano, 2010. The issues at stake were: *a*) the way in which the secular nature of public institutions would be guaranteed, and *b*) the safeguarding of the right of free expression for every religion. At the end of a large debate, legislative changes have taken place.

11   Intercultural and interreligious dialogue, as a means to foster democracy and prevent social conflicts, is an idea emphasized by the *White paper on Intercultural dialogue in Europe* (Council of Europe, 2008: 4): "It contributes to strengthening democratic stability and to the fight against prejudice and stereotypes in public life and political discourse and to facilitating coalition-building across diverse cultural and religious communities, and can thereby help to prevent or de-escalate conflicts – including in situations of post conflict and "frozen conflicts"".

12   Although Islam is the majority faith followed by foreign citizens, in Italy the risk of "Islamization" is far from the truth. Nevertheless, many authors report that native parents

Several authors and studies report experimental activities of interreligious dialogue, carried out both within and outside IRC in Italian multi-cultural schools. All attempts are embodied in one of the three landscapes, designed by Canta (2006, 2013b).

1) *Religious Pluralism:* beyond IRC (which remains unaltered, addressed to Catholics), other denominational teaching of religions could be offered to non-Catholic students as a curricular activity, according to specific agreements signed by the State and the single Churches. An alternative activity (AA) for atheist and agnostic students must be provided as well, to guarantee equity in the school offer, teaching "religious issues", such as ethics, history of religions, religious culture.

2) *Interreligious curriculum:* with the compliance of ecclesial authority, IRC could addresses all learners (who opt for IRC and who do not), teaching the basic elements not only of Christianism but also of other faiths; i.e. the three monotheisms (Christianism, Hebraism and Islam) or some of Mediterranean faiths, or those religions that are represented in the school population.

3) *"Understanding Islam" Laboratory:* within IRC curriculum, Catholic religion teachers can be prepared to teach some learning modules devoted to understanding Islam (of course, this module cannot be confessional). The aim of this proposal is multiple: to make Catholics aware of the historical and cultural contribution given by the Islamic religion to Europe; to prevent the diffusion of religious prejudices towards Muslims (islamophobia) among native students; to prevent the formation of radicalized visions of Islam among children of Muslim immigrants; to involve Muslim students in participating at IRC as witnesses of their own religion; and to implement a "laboratory" of interreligious dialogue, although this cannot universalistic (and participation of IRC remains optional).

To mention only a few exemplary experiences, the first scenario is underpinned by what Giorda (2013) reports: in a Waldesian Lyceum (Torre Pellice, Piedmont), since 1984, a 5-year mandatory course of History of Religions, associated to that of Local History,[13] has been carried out. Both have been considered as complementary subjects to general history, and attended by both Waldensian and non-Waldensian pupils, believers and non-believers. "The

---

express an increasing islamophobia (especially after the 11th of September 2001), associating Islam to fanaticism, fundamentalism, intolerance and ethnocentrism, and this prejudice look higher towards Muslim Middle Eastern people (Santerini, 2008; Branca, Cuciniello, 2014).

13   This course was activated in collaboration with the local archive and library of Waldensian Society of Studies.

course, which features a historical approach and integrates the normal course of history, aims to teach the principal founding elements of the ancient religions of the Mediterranean (...) and of the religions of the present-day world; there are presentations of the Bible and the Koran (Giorda, 2013: 185). Learners are expected to understand "the main differences between religions, and to learn about the relationship between religion and culture of people throughout history" (*Ibidem*).

Within the second landscape, a number of experimental curricula of RE based on historical and comparative approach has been put in place in many Italian high schools (i.e. in Bari, Turin, Verona and Rome), often in collaboration with Departments of Religious studies and academic staff of the local universities, local ministerial offices, NGOs and municipalities. Salvarani (2008) reports the experience named *Bible Educational,* aimed at widening the knowledge of the Bible beyond the Catholic students; it is a project carried out in many secondary schools (in 2006–2008) with the aid of the Ministry of Education and several private foundations.[14]

However, before introducing an interreligious curriculum, there is the need to compensate the low preparation of ordinary teachers with external competences (which must come from both university and confessional agencies) (Rispoli, Giorda, 2016; Naso, 2013). When teachers are not prepared enough, or they have no textbooks and bibliography updated with the extracts from the Sacred texts of all religions, the experiment ends up being too specific and the school as a whole does not change, does not learn from the didactic innovation (Mentasti, Ottaviano, 2008). The main tendency, monitored in Italy, is the minimization of religious plurality: the majority of teachers underestimate the influence of religions in the classroom (Daher *et al.*, 2016), and the potential of conflict underpinning the tacit non-consideration of other religions. In this way, the interreligious dialogue cannot proceed and teachers have to cope with the interfaith or intrafaith conflicts without appropriate tools (Daher *et al.*, 2017).

One other interesting innovation in IRC provisions is the activity aiming at understanding Islam (third landscape). Since 2005, several NGOs and experts in Islam-Christianity Dialogue have been committed to preparing didactic materials in order to provide teachers with correct information about Islam, even in collaboration with the Faculties and Departments of Islamology (Bargellini, Frascoli, 2005; Bargellini, Cicciarelli, 2007; Canta, 2013b; Cuciniello,

---

14   See: www.bibbiaeducational.org. Other projects are reported in: Clementi, 2008.

2017a). The first purpose is to lead Catholic students not to perceive Islam as an "archaeological" and uninvolved civility (according to a "synchronic approach") and to transmit a more adequate representation of Islamic culture and societies, as: *a*) connected with the European history, and *b*) embraced by a multi-segmented, non-monolithic population. A wider and modern view of Islam should include not only historical and territorial conquests, but also scientific and cultural innovations. Thus after a deconstructive analysis of traditional textbooks a re-construction of what is said and written about Islam in regular lessons has become a fundamental part of the new way to "understand Islam".

5 The Study: Theoretical and Methodological Assumptions

In the previous sections we described how RE, multi-religiosity and secularism set up in Italian public schools. To sum it up there is a contradiction between the institutional and the "relational" school life:

- *At institutional and formal level*, almost all religious issues are attributed and regulated within the IRC frame (that is, teaching of one religion), as the rest of the subjects taught are "secular" or "neutral";
- Instead, *at relational and informal level*, religious issues are lived and questioned by pupils, teachers and parents in the ordinary school life, being the majority of school staff almost uniformed and non-prepared to manage them.

When religious bullying arises or even happens, the high level of tension among peers reveals the difficult management of multi-ethnic classes (Bergamaschi, 2016; Colombo, Santagati, 2017). Even the recent violence and radicalism within the second generation of immigrants tells us the same (Gambetta, Hertog, 2016), although this violence does not always occur *within* the school, as much as *outside* the school (Santagati *et al.*, 2017). The persistence of the juvenile need to be identified (and distinguished) not only by name, family background, local and cultural roots, but also by the religious community the children/youngsters belong to, is a push for deep reflection for sociologists of education (Cipriani, Costa, 2015). It requires exploring:

a)   the student's point of view,
b)   that of parents/teachers, and
c)   the public/institutional perspective (Rowe, 2016).

Because of this, an empirical study has been carried out with the aim of exploring the religious dimension of interethnic relationships in public schools. The analysis of religions in public schooling is associated to both the presence of second-generation immigrants (who can get citizenship by law only at 18, unless their parents have naturalized thus transmitted Italian citizenship to their minor-aged children) and the perspective of interreligious dialogue, that is, religious pluralism is seen as a push factor for RE renewal (Halafoff *et al.*, 2015).

The major aim of the field enquiry is *analyzing how (and in which forms) religion is a relevant dimension within the interethnic dynamics in the school context, both in vertical relationships (teacher-students) and horizontal relationships (among peers).*

The theoretical frame of research embeds religion in a system of interdependency between *four key dimensions*: Identity (I), Freedom (F), Citizenship (C) and Common good (CG) (see Chapter 2). For native and immigrant population, the religious belief has an impact on each of these dimensions, affecting both the individual and the collective life. Thus it is worth wondering: does the religious faith influence the process of Self-shaping? (I); how much can people practice a given religion freely within an institution or a social group? (F); how does a given religion affect the access to legal citizenship for the group of followers? (C); what is the contribution of religiosity to the civic consciousness (religion as a cultural heritage)? (CG), and so on.

In the school environment, the four key dimensions lead to more specific questions, such as:

- How does pupil's and adult's religion become an element for self-identification, self-expression and affirmation in intergroup exchanges? What kind of frictions or conflicts do the different cultural and religious identities bring about in the school environment?
- (F) Are teachers and students feeling free to express their own religious beliefs at school? How much is the attendance of IRC classes freely chosen or, instead, imposed by parents among both majority and minority students? Are the religious prohibitions of school activities (among immigrant students) an expression of their freedom of choice or a parent imposition? Is the freedom of expression about one's own religion limited or negatively affected by prejudices, jokes, teasing or bullying among peers?
- (C) Is religion conceived by both young people and adults as a private or public matter? Are the non-Italian nationals affected by minority status, also due to their religious faith, as far as their sense of belonging and their school integration are concerned?
- (CG) Are the minority religions represented enough in the school curriculum? Can the whole school population correctly understand the contribution of a single religion to the current national and European common identity?

Our general *hypothesis* says that, despite religion is often considered as a reason for social conflicts and xenophobia in secularized society, in the school environment students' religious beliefs and values (if expressed in a regulated, welcoming and accommodating institutional setting) could be positive factors for the social integration process as a whole. In fact, religious socialization provided by family, school and confessional community might reinforce one's own sense of identity and the will of integration by enlarging the social capital necessary for the growing process of pupils (Coleman, 1988). This applies both to native and immigrant children.

Through the medium of self-reports, collected by pupils, teachers and parents, we can observe, *firstly* (Chapter 22), how (and in which forms) the religious belonging of the different social actors is visible and expressed in the school environment, rather than hidden and neglected. In particular, we want to verify if the "freedom of choice and expression" (as a Constitutional principle) applies to the religious needs and sensitivity of people who attend public education in a multi-ethnic and multi-cultural situation. We expect to draw findings about:

a) Existence (or non-existence) of an open debate around the minority pupils' rights in schooling according to their religious convictions;
b) Different ways by which religion (or atheism) affects students' behavior and attitudes;
c) Different patterns in the school-family link about religious matters, possible impediments or discriminatory behavior towards minorities (put in place by either teachers or peers), chances and opportunities generated by interreligious dialogue;
d) Different ways in which the school curriculum, and particularly the IRC curriculum, deal with multi-religiosity the classroom.

Secondly (Chapter 23), we want to analyze religion as a triggering factor of interethnic exchanges in schools, by wondering:

– Does religion play the role of "precipitating factor" of conflicts, being a source of problems and tensions, generally seen as the marker of diversity and social divide (Foner, Alba, 2008)?
– Or, on the contrary, is it a bridge for inclusion, a "facilitating factor" of the adaptation process of immigrant offspring?

Previous European studies on the same topic came to different conclusions: someone found out that educational integration is facilitated by the disappearance of religious identity (Esser, 2010); someone else stated that, in some cases, religiosity is compatible with integration, if the receiving school contexts are welcoming enough and try to accommodate religious diversity (Flieschmann, Phalet, 2012). In our study, we expect to draw findings about:

a) Different kinds of conflict (on the basis of religion) among peers and between teachers and students, or teachers and parents, in multi-cultural classrooms and how they generate, develop, spread with specific attention paid to words, attitudes and behavior adopted by social actors;

b) Different narratives on religious tensions, made by teachers, native and foreign students, native and foreign parents;

c) Ways to manage religious conflicts from the perspective of school institution and professors;

d) Explanations of religious-based conflicts from the different point of views of adults and preadolescents.

Of course, we will consider the backdrop of the possible conflicts in multi-cultural classroom, that is, the wider social disadvantage of immigrant children, due to the economic and cultural divide with native population, in which the religious difference covers only a part of the problem (Santagati, 2015; Ricucci, 2017). Several studies highlight the combination between multiple constraints and factors of disadvantage (the so-called intersectionality) (Crenshaw, 1989), such as age, race, ethnicity, gender, sexuality, class, cultural capital, living place, etc. According to the intersectionality framework, the interplay between structural and cultural factors brings about boundaries and hierarchies in social life, mostly beyond the individual efforts. Thus an empirical study on disadvantage categories and subjects should have the sensitivity for the issue of power and it should locate the social practice within given spatial and temporal contexts (Anthias, 2013).

As far as the methodology is concerned, the field enquiry was carried out in spring-summer 2017 in lower secondary state schools (compulsory education) located in Lombardy (Italy): Milan, Brescia, and Bergamo.[15] The target population was made up of a sample of low secondary students (11 to 14 years old), some of their parents, and a selected group of secondary school teachers and principals. 14 focus groups have been carried out (7 groups with students and 7 with adults) for a total of 74 students and 69 adults. Groups

---

15   The schools participating in the research are: IC Calcio (Province of Bergamo – BG); IC Ovest 2 Tridentina Brescia; IC Pralboino (Province of Brescia – BS); IC Polo EST Lumezzane (BS); IC Terzani Abbiategrasso (Province of Milan – MI); IC Palestro Abbiategrasso (MI); IC Aldo Moro Abbiategrasso (Mi); IC Borsi-Ojetti Milano; IC Primo Levi Baggio Milano. We are grateful to all participants and their school representatives for the serious and precious engagement in the study.

were composed of believers of different religions and non-believer persons (atheist or sceptical): see Tables 21.1–21.2 for the participants' composition.

A semi-structured grid of questions has been administered to each group of discussion (lasting 1.30 to 2.30 hours), based on similar inputs. All questions addressed to students and adults referred to the four key dimensions of the study (see above) and they tried to be as "two-fold" as possible: the same item was administered to both targets (youngsters and adults), with the necessary adjustments due to different languages and status. In Table 21.3, one can read the comparative list of questions.

All focus groups have been conducted and recorded by the same research staff. All transcripts have been processed by N-Vivo 11.0. Chapters 22 and 23 will present some of the research findings about the main objectives of enquiry.

After these, two concluding chapters will host the analysis of the multi-religiosity schooling link respectively in France (Chapter 24) and Spain (Chapter 25), two European countries whose history of migrations and public education systems are of interesting comparison with Italy. From a cross-national comparison, the reader will learn how much Italy differs on:

a) the implementation of secularization (which in France is part of the national identity) in public education;

b) the cultural diversity management within the earlier stages of public education, included the RE curriculum which in Spain is under revision, due to the multi-religious composition of the classrooms in many places of immigration.

TABLE 21.1   Focus groups with students – participants' composition

FG	N.	Females	Males	Italian	Non-Italian	Catholics	Muslims	Orthodox Christians	Sikhs	Hindus	Buddhists
1 BS	14	8	6	7	7	7	6	1	0	0	0
2 BS	7	4	3	2	5	2	1	0	2	2	0
3 BS	12	4	8	6	6	6	3	1	0	1	1
4 BG	11	7	4	6	5	6	3	0	1	1	0
5 MI	10	4	6	5	5	8	0	1	0	0	1
6 MI	10	5	5	6	4	7	2	0	0	0	1
7 MI	10	5	5	4	6	4	4	0	0	0	2
TOT	74	37	37	36	38	40	19	3	3	4	5

TABLE 21.2   Focus groups with adults – participants' composition

FG	N.	Females	Males	Parents	Teachers	Principals	Italian	Non-Italian	Catholics
1 BS	13	13	0	7	5	1	9	4	10
2 BS	8	6	2	3	4	1	8	0	8
3 BG	13	6	7	5	7	1	11	2	11
4 MI	9	7	2	3	5	1	9	0	9
5 MI	9	6	3	4	4	1	7	2	8
6 MI	8	8	0	2	4	2	8	0	6
7 MI	9	7	2	0	6	3	9	0	9
TOT	69	53	16	24	35	10	61	8	61

SOURCE: AUTHOR'S PERSONAL ELABORATION

TABLE 21.3   Items for focus group interview – reference to 4 keywords and comparison between targets

Prevailing dimensions	Students	Teachers–Parents
Identity	What is their religious consciousness and "literacy"? What do they do to make their religion visible/invisible?	Agreement on "religion as identity factor" (collection of opinions)
Freedom	Which feelings are associated to the expression of the minority or majority's religion in the school context (I-F): Muslim veil, Catholic crucifixes …? (collection of episodes) How do they feel when coping with religious pluralism in the school?	How/how much are religions expressed (or not) in the school context?In which forms? (collection of episodes) How do they feel when coping with religious pluralism in the school?
Citizenship	What religion-based conflicts do they cope with and how do they manage them (pro and against who?)? (collection of episodes)	How does pupils' religion take part or intervene in their educational relationships (collection of episodes)?

Prevailing dimensions	Students	Teachers–Parents
Common good	Do they think religion must be more or less considered in the curriculum? How do they practice dialogue with other religion observants?	What kind of religion-based conflicts do they cope with (if rights and duties are at stake)? How do they manage them? Do they think religion must be more or less considered in the curriculum? How do they practice dialogue with other religion observants?

SOURCE: AUTHOR'S PERSONAL ELABORATION

In conclusion, we are convinced that the sociological look at the religion-immigration relationship in the school environment should develop a sensitivity about the main patterns of religious-based behavior in multi-cultural schools (including symbols usages). If school professionals would become competent to detect religious frictions and "religious bullying" among peers (along with a specific preparation in conflict management), they could recognize the multiple nuances of religious pluralism and the ways it can increase or hinder integration of minority pupils. In this way, there would be room to enhance the effectivity of their efforts towards civic and religious education in a frame of intercultural dialogue.

CHAPTER 22

Religious Belongings in Multi-Cultural Schools: Freedom of Expression and Citizenship Values

Rosangela Lodigiani

1 Introduction

This chapter is aimed at presenting and discussing the main findings of the qualitative research illustrated in Chapter 21. Deepening the research findings by focusing on the basic concepts of religious freedom and citizenship rights, the chapter explores youth religious beliefs, spirituality and atheism in a context of "weak secularization" (Chapter 3) and illustrates how the school can be deemed as a public space to test religious pluralism. Religious diversity deeply and increasingly challenges the school intended as a secular and open place, by producing different, when not fully opposite, reactions: from neutralization of religion to the promotion of its cultural dimensions. However, the interreligious and intercultural dialogue developed within the school turns out to be a training ground for democratic citizenship, at least when aimed at fostering mutual knowledge, respect, acceptance of differences, and at sheltering from the temptation to reject different memberships because of a certain idea of secularism.

The chapter is organized as follows: §2 briefly draws the theoretical framework and the research's aim and hypothesis. The subsequent sections arrange the research findings around four main themes, by deepening:

a) the freedom of expression of religious belonging (that is, religious freedom and the worship of one God, of another God or of no God at all) in the school context –through the use of religious symbols too–, where there may be either ease, caution, indifference or lack of awareness (§3);

b) the relation between religious plurality and the development of different "world visions", which calls into question the citizenship values and the differentiation of public and private spheres (§4);

c) educational students' and families' choices affected by religious beliefs, which show that issues that were thought to have been secularized – finding a peaceful solution in the differentiation of private, civil and religious spheres– are coming back in the school debate (e.g. how to protect the right to freedom of expression, and what the boundaries of parental authority over children's education are) (§5);

d) the space for religious issues through and beyond the curriculum and in the daily school life: by enhancing different religious cultural heritage (§6, 7), the school becomes a "laboratory for dialogue", in which different voices co-operate for finding ways of living peacefully together (§8).

2 Scenario Outlines, Theoretical Framework, and Study's Aims

As described in the previous chapter, multi-ethnicity is becoming a structural and fundamental feature of Italian public schools. Actually, schools experience –and reflect– in a specific way what happens in society.

2.1 A Brief Outlook on the Italian Context

Since the beginning of the Seventies, Italy has started to record a positive net migration, reversing its traditional role and turning from an emigration to an immigration country. However, the increase of the foreign population, speeded up especially since the Nineties, began to be felt in the school system, due to the growing of migrants' offspring born in Italy to foreign parents or re-joined with members of their own family already settled in Italy. Some figures are useful for drawing the trend.

In the last two decades, the increase of students with an immigrant background has been exponential, and Italy reported immigration rates of foreign student, calculated on the total amount of students, close to the ones recorded in the European traditional immigration countries (Santagati *et al.*, 2019): from 0.7 % in the 1996/1997 school year, the rate has been rapidly increased to 7.9% in the 2010/2011 school year and to 9.4% in the 2016/2017 school year. Particularly in the last five years, there has been a surge of new migrant students, which can be partly explained by the significant rise in the arrival of unaccompanied minors, asylum seekers and refugees (Azzolini *et al.*, 2019). Therefore, in the 2017/2018 school year, about 826,000 foreign students have been enrolled in the different educational levels of the Italian school system, which is characterized by an inclusive approach. The rate reaches 10.7% in pre-school, 10.8% in primary school, 9.7% in lower secondary school, 7.1% in high school, respectively (MIUR, 2018). Moreover, alongside the second generations of foreign immigrants, a second generation of "Italians with migratory background" is growing, born to –or re-joined with– foreign parents who have completed the naturalization process, and who, together with the children of mixed couples, are legally indistinguishable from Italians students, except for some specific points of view –e.g. language, religious confession or other features– which make them fully belong to the second-generation "universe" (Molina, 2014). As the latter is a plural and diversified universe, we should speak about "second generations of immigration" instead of "second generations of immigrants"[1] for a better understanding of the phenomenon.

The national outlook does not allow to appreciate the territorial differences that are relevant at the regional and, especially, at the local level: among cities of the same region or districts, or single schools of the same urban area. Foreign population is distributed unevenly along the peninsula and the highest number of students with non-Italian citizenship does not necessary result in the highest rates. Lombardy is the region with the highest number of foreign students (207,979), equal to about a quarter of the total foreign students in Italy, while Emilia Romagna has the highest percentage of students' regional populations. Milan leads the cities ranking considering the absolute numbers, but it is not even among the top 10 in relative terms; however, in some districts and in some institutes, the percentage of students with non-Italian citizenship exceeds the majority, so as to have triggered –in some cases– the so-called "white flight" phenomenon (Pacchi, Ranci, 2017).

Beyond the statistics, Lombardy and the main urban centers of the region are interesting contexts to observe with regard to intercultural (and interreligious) dynamics in multi-cultural schools because of the long-lasting attention to this issue witnessed by the large number of studies carried out on education and on social inclusion of foreign students, ethnic inequalities in education etc. (Santagati, 2015). In line with this type of studies, as explained in Chapter 21, the research here presented focuses on 7 lower secondary schools (ISCED 2) in the Lombardy Region: 3 in Milan, 3 in Brescia and 1 Bergamo.[2] These three cities gather about 37%, 17% and 12%, respectively, that is almost two-thirds of the total amount of foreign student enrolled in the Lombardy schools; and Brescia is the fourth largest city in Italy as for the foreign students' rate.

---

1 As claimed by the youngsters with a migratory background. See, for example, "Rete G2" (G2 Network), a non-party national organization, founded –in connection with the International G2 Network– by children of immigrants and refugees born or arrived in Italy as children (http://www.secondegenerazioni.it/).

2 For more details about the schools and the persons included in the research, see Chapter 21 Focus groups' quotations reported throughout this chapter have been codified as follows: participants' gender, nationality, religious affiliation (if any), FG number, school province and typology of participants (students or adults, that is: teachers/school manager/school assistant or parents-mother/father).

Due to the growth and expansion in the number of students with a foreign and migratory background, multiple cultural roots and religious belonging meet with each other in everyday school life, as in the whole society. The structural and stable changing in the ethnic composition of the classrooms underlines (in Lombardy as in Italy) the need to deal with the multi-cultural education issues and takes back to the very center of the educational debate the question of how to treat the students' different cultural and religious belongings in order to promote school integration (Colombo, Santagati, 2017).

2.2 Beyond the School as a Secular Space

As deeply discussed in Chapter 21, the revival of the role of religion inside and outside the school environment contrasts with the idea that religion belonging must be shut in the private sphere and should not interfere with the understanding of the public schooling as a secular, "neutral" space, with respect to different religions.

The core idea of a secular education in public schooling took shape in a scenario of increasing secularization, pluralization and "disenchantment" of the world (in Weberian words) of Western countries, Italy included. In this scenario, according to secularization theory, at the collective (political and institutional) level, the separation between State and Church authorities/religious communities became a central pillar of the "modern State", intended as "a non-denominational State", and of liberal democracies grounded on the fundamental rights of universal human dignity and equality and freedom of expression. That is, freedom of thought, conscience and religion, as affirmed by the European Convention on Human Rights (1950, art. 9), but firstly stated by the Universal Declaration of Human Rights of the Unite Nations (1948, art. 18). As for religion, this means: freedom to choose among different religions and between believing or not in any religion. It is worthy to add that, although the freedom of conscience, religion and worship is an inviolable right of the person, to be guaranteed to all citizens, the freedom to manifest and practice one's religion is not absolute whereas it is subject to the political legitimation within the framework of democratic laws and citizenship, as we can read –for example– in the above-mentioned European Convention (art. 9). All these statements, principles and liberties are clearly expressed and guaranteed by the Italian Constitution (particularly at art. 8 and 19) too, and are today acquired and recognized as fundamental part of the European legal and legislative culture (Chapter 4).

In this wake, in accordance with the process of functional "differentiation and specialization" of modern society –which represents the basic assumption of the secularization theory (Luhmann, 1982)–, Churches and religious communities increasingly confined their function to pastoral care by renouncing their competencies in other areas of society, schooling education included, while the State protects and promotes the rights and the general welfare of its citizens, without interfering in matters of faith. Simultaneously, at the individual level, religious believing and behaviors have undergone a process of privatization as there is a link between the functional differentiation of the religious system within the whole society and the individualization of religious practice (Habermas, 2014).

In other words, as argued by Ferrara (2009; 2014), secularism refers both to: (*i*) *a political dimension*, since the Churches and the State are clearly separated; all citizens can freely exercise their religious freedom and worship (or atheism), and the Church religious faiths are protected by the State, which maintains its "neutrality"; and (*ii*) *a social dimension*, since religious communities cease to influence law, politics, education and public life in general and become functionally specialized sub-groups, while religious rituals, symbols and boundaries of faith diminish their role in marking significant moments of people's lives, in shaping their thoughts, commitments, loyalties and their main concerns. As the author affirms, this distinction "allows us to pinpoint asymmetries and unbalances in complex processes of secularization. In some countries, at a certain time, political secularization may proceed at a faster pace than societal secularization" (Ferrara, 2014: 68).

Within this framework, the implications of public schooling are supposed to be clear: the school has to focus mainly on its role of public and secular institution, by teaching civic and democratic citizenship values and competences, thus giving all students the same opportunity to access education regardless of their religious belief. Religion neutrality is assured through a curriculum that tends to expel "religion education" (RE) (whatever the solution adopted by the organization, in order to ensure religion literacy alongside the curriculum itself): religion should not interfere with people behavior outside their very private sphere, in school life as well in public. From this point of view, the French case represents a meaningful example, since it theorized and then applied the so-called "Republican model of integration", which turned into the "Republican model of indifference (to ethnic, but also cultural and religious) differences" (Ichou, van Zanten, 2019: 519–520; see also Chapter 24).

However, in the last few years, the scenario has dramatically changed, and the complexity and misalignment evoked by Ferrara has come to the fore.

As Habermas –among others– argued, not only "the loss of function and the trend towards individualization (did) not necessarily imply that religion (has lost) influence and relevance either in the political arena and in the culture of a society or in the personal conduct of life", and "quite apart from their numerical weight, religious communities can still claim a "seat" in the life of societies that are largely secularized", but even the awareness about the persistence of religion in the public arena is becoming "common sense" to the point that the awareness of living in a "post-secular society" is widely spreading (*Ibidem*: 63–64). In the author's thinking, three overlapping phenomena are moving in this direction: (*i*) the rise of international and local conflicts connected to religious issues (terrorism and fundamentalism); (*ii*) the revival of the public role of religions in pluralist national contexts (as the Western ones), where a growing number of ethical dilemmas (i.e. abortion, voluntary euthanasia, bioethical new frontiers) needs a political regulation, which is hardly attained by ignoring Churches and religious organizations voices that push to enter and influence the public arena; (*iii*) the intensification of global migration flows that obliges to face the pluralism of religions, cultures and ways of life and the consequent challenges for social integration. As a result, not only people's awareness of the relevant role still played by religion in the public space rises but, more radically, the secularization theory itself ends up going under profound scrutiny (Rizzi, 2016; Chapter 3).

Public school –as the whole society– is put to the test of religious plurality, expected to be a secular and, at the same time multi-religious, context (Fabretti, 2013), and is called to reach two different aims: because of its status of public institution, being a secular place, not conditioned by norms and values of a specific religion; and because of its status of education institution, promoting religious education within a framework of mutual respect and tolerance about different religions. As highlighted in Chapter 21, due to the increasingly multi-cultural and multi-religious character of contemporary societies and schools, this twofold purpose becomes more challenging, turning into a "dilemma":

(i)   being anchored to the "modern" idea of secularism (e.g. renouncing to delve into religious contents, ensuring that the school is recognized as a neutral space, a "free-zone" in which personal convictions and religious belongings are substantially ignored);

(ii)   opening the door to the dialogue between different cultural roots and religious belongings, by teaching about different religions in a climate of mutual respect and reciprocal understanding.

2.3   Study's Aims, Hypotheses and Questions

Against this backdrop, this chapter seeks to explore how the Italian public school deals with these challenges; more in detail, the chapter aims at investigating what place is given to religion in school life and in the curricula, assuming that the capacity of enhancing (respecting, knowing) the (religious) differences as an essential part of personal identity can be a lever promoting school (and social) integration. In fact, through the research outcomes here discussed, we will shed a light on interethnic and interreligious dynamics in the school context, considering both vertical (between teachers/parents and students) and horizontal (among peers, and between teachers and parents) relationships, by scrutinizing if and how (in which forms and circumstances) religion affects them.

In our hypothesis, students' religious belongings (beliefs and values) –if dialogue is encouraged and adequately accompanied– promote social integration in the multi-cultural school context. Although it cannot be excluded that conflicts and xenophobic attitudes may arise inside and outside the classroom, we assume that when conflicts are properly managed, they may represent an opportunity to foster social cohesion and build bridges between cultures.

Following the whole project's theoretical framework, we can maintain that for both migrant and native students, personal belonging to a religion faces at least four cultural and social, individual and collective spheres of experience, here identified through the four keywords/lines of research outlined in Chapter 2: Identity, (Religious) Freedom, Citizenship, and Common good. These four spheres of experience are mirrored by the school context in a specific way.

The first term, *identity*, focuses the attention on the individual and collective processes of (re)shaping self-definition, based on religious beliefs and values, in the school environment. More precisely, it pushes for considering religion belonging as a fundamental "identity marker" (among others) in school relationships: among students, between students and teachers, between teachers and parents.

The second term, *religious freedom*, draws the attention to the legitimization of the pluralistic involvement of religious identities and affiliation in the school life, by guaranteeing the right to freedom of religious choice and expression. Many questions arise around the actual exposure of one's religion belonging through symbols and/or decisions and behavior, which clearly depend on it.

The third term, *citizenship,* concentrates not only on the normative (regulative and legislative) framework of religious freedom –in the Italian school protected by the Constitution and regulated through specific agreements between the State and different Churches, denominations and religious communities (Chapter 9)– but also on the contrasts that may arise among the multiple identities and loyalties deriving from the affiliation to a certain religion and connected to the specific place where one has grown up (in our case, Italy).

The fourth term, *common good*, directs the attention to the school (students, teachers, parents) strategies (if there are any) to enhance RE as a cultural heritage for the curriculum enrichment, to consider interreligious dialogue as a laboratory of "civicness" and participation.

Within this framework, the field research aimed at:

(i)   analyzing school life and school curriculum to see if, and to what extent, religion is "at stake", and which role it plays towards school integration;

(ii)   describing the main patterns of religious-based behavior in multi-cultural schools (including symbols' usages);

(iii) gathering empirical evidences about the role of religion diversity in school integration;

(iv)   deepening the issue of interreligiouss conflict in the classroom (see Chapter 23, specifically focused on interreligious conflicts and integration processes in multi-cultural schools).

The focus groups and the chances for a progressive deepening that this method entails allowed us to delve into three main themes: spontaneous outpouring of religious belonging; when and why (in which circumstance) the presence of different religious affiliations arises; how schools cope with religious plurality.

3   Religious Identity and Freedom: Lights and Shadows from an "opaque prism"

The issue of *religious identity*, explored through the spontaneous declarations of belonging at the very beginning of each focus group, shows, along with some elements of convergence, interesting differences between what students and adults think.

At first, consistently with other research carried out in the Italian multi-cultural school (Ottaviano, 2010), the presence of different religions in the classroom is perceived as something that tends to remain in the shadow and that is generally a-problematic, since it is considered neither a relevant matter of interpersonal relationships nor a lever for conflicts. By examining the issue more in depth, however, the picture becomes more complex.

Thanks to the preliminary content analysis carried out with Nvivo software, it is worth noting the sizable difference in the most frequently-mentioned words recoded during the students' and adults' focus groups. Selecting the only words with a minimum length of four letters and excluding religion(s)/religious, school(s), student(s), teacher(s) –which, due to the guideline provided for discussion, are necessarily continuously utilized in every focus group– we find that students largely utilize the terms freedom and friend/friendship, while the adults' narratives revolve around the concepts of differences/diversities, and especially gender and cultures differences (See Table 22.1).

The uneven distribution of the most recurrent words reveals students' and adults' different concerns regarding the presence of religion plurality at school: as we will examine below, the former certainly have been influenced by the students' age (11–14 years) and the transition into adolescence that they are experiencing; the latter have been influenced, on the one hand, by their specific role –as teachers or parents–, and, on the other hand, by the composition of the adults' sample, in which female teachers and people belonging to the national and religious majority were over-represented. Beyond the frequency, however, it is more interesting to understand the semantic context in which the most recurrent words have been used and the meaning given to them. To understand these aspects, we need to go in-depth into the analysis.

3.1   The Students' Point of View

In the students' opinion, religious belonging remains in the backdrop of their identity until something happens and brings it back to the surface. They declare that religion is not influential neither in their interpersonal relationships nor, in more in general, in their daily life, both inside and outside the school. According to them, religion pertains to the individual, to the "private and emotional sphere", and certainly, it is not relevant in forging the bonds of friendship. It is therefore not important to talk about it, to address the issue openly.

On the one hand, there is a strong (idealistic) recall to the shared values of friendship and "common humanity": religion belonging is not important –they say– since friendship goes further, as all people are equal. "Friendship has no religion. Friendships are always friendships without religion. Friendship is not based on religion or nationality" are the most used phrases at the beginning of every focus group.

> I don't care about religion or nationality because, actually, even if we belong to different religions, we are all brothers and sisters ... hence, we are all bonded together, nothing and nobody can divide us. (Female, Moldova, Orthodox Christian, FG 1 BS, students)

On the other hand, the issue –as the students assert– simply does not concern them as young people, more precisely as adolescents with many interests but with no interest for religion.

> Religion ... it's more for adults. Indeed, it's just for adults! As teenagers, we don't care so much about religion, because then it depends on what you like ... I like football and when we talk, we talk about hobbies and not

TABLE 22.1   Most frequently mentioned words during the focus groups

Students' FG		Adults' FG	
Words	Frequency	Words	Frequency
Friend/Friendship	227	Woman/girl	350
Person	234	Differences	332
Family/Parents	225	Family/Parents	291
Christians/Christianity	180	Culture/cultural	165
Differences	158	Conflict	156
Conflict	149	Italy/Italian	143
Muslim	148	Catholic	143
Freedom	125	Male	136
Nationality	109	Children	132
Italian	93	Muslim	125

SOURCE: AUTHOR'S PERSONAL ELABORATION

about religion, which is a bit more of an adult thing. (Female, Egyptian, Muslim, FG 7 MI, students)

It is not by chance that friendship is positioned at the top of students' concerns and thoughts. During the adolescence transitional phase, finding one's own place in the world and the process of identity formation require peer confrontation, from which depends one's own self-esteem (Jounisse, Hanye, 1992).

Beneath the surface, however, students' points of view differ. Once called to reflect on concrete experiences, on their actual relationships at school with peers of other religions, they reveal to be aware of their own (and other students') religious affiliation and the role that it actually plays in different situations. Religion may facilitate friendships among students affiliated to the same religion or hinder friendships with students that "are perceived" as belonging to a different religion. In other words, religion may connect students to each other or may bring differences to light.

In the first part of the discussion, however, religion is seen by students as any other personal feature that they may, or may not, have in common. As studies on adolescents have long been demonstrating, friendship is nourished by reciprocal and consensual validation: "reciprocity" lies at the root of friendship, thus giving to this bond a symmetric feature (in contrast with the asymmetry that characterizes parents-children relations). Moreover, adolescent friendship is based on a process of "co-construction of reality" that emerges through debates, discussions, compromises and negotiations, and that permits to participate in the "construction of each friend's life story" (*Ibidem*, 1992: 60). In this perspective, religion may affect friendships firstly because "you do the same things, you go to the same places, you have the same school hours, you schedule the same activities...", and secondly because you share the same values and ideas, as many students concurred.

Going in-depth into the analysis, students admit that religion is a "sensitive" issue, which should be handled with care. It is something one can talk about freely, but with caution, as one can fear to be misunderstood or even teased about; something that makes you think of the other as an "unknown world", even when looking at the choices he/she makes at school, which are not always transparent.

Although students unanimously declare they feel free to show their religious beliefs, and part of them clearly recognize that religion freedom is one of their rights which are protected by the Italian law in public schools (see also Chapter 9), various participants show they worry about being teased and misunderstood because of religion and report that similar circumstances occurred to some of their classmates. This kind of worries could be an unavoidable implication of the typical adolescent's overriding concern –the inner personal need of being accepted/included as a boy/girl by the peer group– rather than an effective anxiety relating to religion diversity. However, many students' narratives converge on it within the majority (Catholic students) and the minority groups (with different religious belonging and/or ethnic origin): both recall circumstances in which they (or some friends of theirs) have endured sarcastic jokes or even religious bullying.

> This should be a public school; hence we should take the fact of being free for granted! If one is a Muslim or a Buddhist, there is no problem! For example, I'm a Christian, thanks to my parents, even if I do not profess very much ... I do not really mind about it. It might be a problem for someone else, but that's the society's feature today, so ... (Female, Italian, Christian, FG 6 MI, students)

> I feel free to express my religion, it's my right. That is all. The others could be against me, but I don't care. The only thing is that sometimes I have a problem in sharing my opinion with my classmates: they keep on bullying me most of the time. (Female, Egyptian, Coptic Christians, FG 6 MI, students)

> I am Christian, I believe and I like religion. However, my classmates often say unpleasant things about my religion: I feel free to profess it, but sometimes they hurt me. (Female, Italian, Christian, FG 7 MI, students)

Actually, freedom of expression seems to be an acknowledged and proclaimed right more than a fact experienced at first hand. However, the scarce ability to identify moments and contexts in which they benefited from religious freedom hides the fact that it is generally taken for granted. This is true especially for the Italian students who claim to be Catholics: there is little awareness that religious belonging may represent a means for their self-affirmation or self-definition, while the awareness arises among minority students and those who proclaim themselves to be atheists. Among the minority groups, however, there could be the habit to keep religion belonging to the foreground, as any other diversity markers, in order to reduce contrasts and possible stigmatizations. The fear of being excluded tends to prevail.

The classmates' religious affiliation is generally deduced from external behavior and personal choices: in this perspective, what they eat at the cafeteria, their behavior during gym time, their participation (or not) in educational trips, and –particularly– their use of some religious symbols (such as the Islamic veil and headscarf, the Sikh uncut-hair, or the Christian cross) are considered as relevant markers that bear witness more than any spoken word. Furthermore, consistently with some research carried out in other countries (Jackson, 2014), the students interviewed firmly support the right to wear religious symbols as an expression of their own faith. It is perceived as something compatible with the school (and society) multi-culturalism.

However, in mixed classrooms, religious symbols sometimes are misunderstood and thus inappropriately used to label classmates. They are even worn and utilized without being fully aware of their meaning, just as ethnic fashion accessories mirroring a style of clothing, hence it is not always possible to presume the religion belonging of a classmate by only observing the external symbols he/she wears. "There are girls with veils: thus, one understands that they are Muslim, but then there are also Muslims without a veil" is the laconic gloss of a Muslim male student from Pakistan (FG 1 BS). Another student echoes: "… it depends because … maybe you can understand if a person is Indian from the traditional clothes he/she wears, but … you don't recognize it … that is, you cannot say yes, he/she belongs to that religion because … one can be Moroccan or Indian … and wear western clothes … so it's difficult to understand" (Male, Indian, Sikh, FG 2 BS, students).

From the students' narratives, the idea that the veil (or other symbols) may be in profound relation with one's identity, as an external signal for self-affirmation and subjectivation – or even, as some research pointed out (Fassari, Pompili, 2017) for combating the stereotype that wearing the veil is an imposition suffered by girls and women, due to unavoidable family or community traditions – does not emerge. Few students try to understand whether the veil is a symbol of fundamentalism or just of cultural diversity: the curiosity to grasp their deepest meaning, or to wonder about it, remains latent.

Actually, students tend to simplify and stereotype classmates' affiliations, often confusing religious affiliation with physical appearance or ethnic origin with nationality. In their mind, Italian corresponds to Christian, or white-skinned, by default, likewise dark-skinned corresponds to Muslim, to the point that discovering that there are Italian Muslims or white-skinned Muslims has been reported as something still astonishing.

The students' low familiarity with religion within the educational settings does not mean that the religious matter is expelled from school lessons, rather it is both a proper object of the RE lessons and an occasional object in other disciplines of study (we will further examine this issue below: §5). However, students complain that teachers rarely give room to a deeper reflection and that teachers' religious belonging (if there is any) remains generally hidden from their eyes.

As wondered by a Catholic, Italian male student (FG 1 BS): "We never speak about religion at school. Maybe this matter is something that teachers want keeping as private".

In a nutshell, religious identity and freedom of expression through symbols and daily actions emerge among students with different nuances: ease for someone; caution and distress for others; and indifference or lack of awareness for others. In any case, the sensitivity of teachers and school managers, together with a cooperative family-school relationship, can be decisive to let religious plurality enter the school as an issue to treat openly. To delve into the point, it is worth highlighting how adults deal with religious belonging at school.

3.2   *The Adults' Point of View*

In the same way as students/children, the largest part of teachers and parents involved in the focus groups (excluding the answers of the teachers of RE) initially declared that religion belonging should remain confined to the private sphere: teachers do not want to create barriers that hinder an open dialogue with students, and parents do not want to be misunderstood and prejudicially labelled.

According to some teachers, keeping religious identity into the private sphere is necessary to properly exercise their role in compliance with their own commitment to a secular education in the public school, for being *super partes*, tolerant and respectful towards the different beliefs of students (and their families), and avoiding to construct "walls" and barriers. Disclosing it –someone adds– could be counter-productive since exposing or talking about one's own religion and beliefs, or simply showing one's belonging through religious symbols, can produce frictions with students and their families.

(*Our own religion*) is something personal ... so it isn't something to show off and it doesn't really concern school. It can, by the way, come out and you can talk about it and make the most of it in a specific context, in connection with a topic or something happening, otherwise it can't be useful. (Female, Italian, School assistant, Catholic, FG 2 BS, adults)

At school it is not relevant. Maybe because religion is something spiritual (...) something very personal, which we have inside. (Mother, Tunisian, FG 1 BS, adults)

Being Catholic, Muslim, Evangelical, it's a form of choice to be the unique human being one can be, who lives as a Catholic, as a Protestant and so on (...) people can't be categorized, because the truth, for me, has got lots of different sides, it can't be kept within bounds, only in one field. In this world, (...) we can't categorize, because if we do that, we withdraw; instead, opening to the others as individuals means to be universal, to be open towards anybody, towards differences, towards meeting and dealing with others. (Male, Italian, School manager, FG 5 MI, adults)

I'm an Evangelical, but I don' like labels, because behind a label there are a lot of prejudices and a lot of judgment, which prevents any dialogue. I don't do that, even if I'm deeply convinced, I'm observant and everything, but I prefer when people notice, thanks to my actions, my way of living and dealing with others and being an open-minded person. (Mother, Italian, FG 5 MI, adults)

Not surprisingly, unlike the students, teachers are more aware of the importance of religious belonging in the process of identity formation. According to some of them, religious beliefs and affiliations represent a habit that concerns a person's daily actions and relationships, and since they –the habit and the person– are one, the former does not need to be explained.

First of all, we all have something in common with the others, as human beings. (Father, Albanian, FG 3 BS, adults)

Generosity, for instance, is an aspect of the religion I belong to and that I usually practice (...), generosity is something I have been taught for all my life, by the people who witness it, or anyway indirectly by the meeting I have had with God, so I bear it as my main characteristic ... In this way, I think I witness my religious belonging without saying it openly; even if I openly say I'm a Catholic to my students. (Female, Italian, Teacher, Catholic, FG 3 BS adults)

It is an identity element which is part of our way of being, if I am like that it is also thanks to my religious faith, my education and so on. (Mother, Italian, Catholic, FG 3 BG, adults)

Well, I'm a church-going Catholic (…) I don't see that as something I wear on the surface, but it must be your way of being; well, I'm a Catholic, but I don't play the Catholic, I believe, but I don't play that role. And my way of being a Christian Catholic has to be visible through my daily actions, through my way of acting and speaking, thanks to the choices I make. Besides, I'm convinced that every religion, the Catholic one, the Jewish one and the Muslim one must focus on the idea of meeting and on a constructive debate. (Male, Italian, School manager, Catholic, FG 5 MI, adults)

Called to reflect upon their actual freedom to express religious belonging, teachers and parents feel that they are completely free and are convinced that their students do feel the same.

I express my religious affiliation in an extremely free manner (…). For me, there is no such thing as not being able to freely express one's religious affiliation. (Mother, Italian, FG 4 BS, adults)

When it happens during my lessons, I express my idea, my religious creed, without any problems. We often face the subject during our school activities, so, since I talk about it, even my students do the same (….) In practice, we often face subjects which lead to the religious aspect and to a constructive debate. (Male, Italian, Teacher, Catholic, FG 3 BS adults)

We don't have to put up barriers, I am (…) free, free, because I'm open-minded, I'm Muslim, I pray, but I'm even open to talk about my religion … (Mother, Macedonian-Albanian, Muslim, FG 3 BS, adults)

However, two *caveats* are worth noting:
- On the one hand, adults, and particularly teachers, are fully aware that speaking about their own religion may create difficulties to students which are sometimes afraid of being teased or simply are less self-aware or their own convictions and beliefs, given their young age.
- On the other hand, teachers and parents agree that students have little knowledge about religion. In this regard, our research seems to confirm

what mentioned above (§2.2): religion privatization and individualization tend to produce religious illiteracy and trigger religious indifference, especially among young people, among which those who declare themselves to be atheist and agnostic are growing in number. This phenomenon is increasingly visible in Italy too (Cadeddu, Melloni, 2018; Garelli, 2016; Melloni, 2014). Although the religious affiliation remains higher among the Italian population, compared with the average of the Western European countries, and Catholicism is still the first religion of the Country, a "flexible Catholicism" is emerging, making room for personal interpretations of religious precepts and for critical positions towards the Church (Garelli, 2012).

> Maybe, there are more people who don't feel like sharing their religious experiences with Italian students, sometimes they feel ashamed or simply a bit afraid ... they are discrete ... sometimes it is hard to let their characteristics come out ... well, we need to follow some paths ... where they can feel welcomed and free to talk about it, to bring out their peculiarities. (Female, Italian, Teacher, FG 2 BS, adults)

> The general trend is that students don't get to know other people's religion, because it is not an aspect that comes out at first. (....) I'm thinking about my classes, there are a lot of religions and students ... who find it difficult to get the right time to talk about their faith, their religion, and to express it through their way of being, so sometimes, they are, maybe, I beg your pardon for my words, "crashed by that aspect" (...). It is not something that comes out positively, it only ... comes out in a very superficial way ... I tease you because you wear a veil or because you don't eat this and that, so, well, I really don't think that what concerns the religious sphere is a bed of roses, I really don't think so; on the contrary, in my opinion, at school, they don't show their religious belief so much. (Female, Italian, Teacher, FG 3 BS, adults)

> I feel that they don't give great importance to their religion (Catholic). What I notice, on the contrary, is that they have a great curiosity towards the Muslim religion. I notice that when we face the subject from a historical point of view, they keep asking questions to their schoolmates. Yes, they have a sort of curiosity but, in my opinion, it is not connected to the religious belief itself, but to their habits, which are so different from theirs, and they want to know why. (Female, Italian, Teacher FG 4 MI, adults)

> We have freedom of worship, but it's superficial, young people don't think about religion; as I see it, teenagers and children, since we are talking

> about lower secondary school, don't talk about religion when they are
> together, even Catholic teenagers don't do that, common topics are: the
> way you dress, what music you listen to, what sort of mobile you have, so
> I underline it, well … I don't even see it as a form of division. Just when
> they start to observe "the way they dress" then they wonder about it.
> (Mother, Italian, FG 3 BG, adults)

What is more, teachers are persuaded that parents generally acknowledge that
the school can be a favorable place for their children to fully express themselves and their religious affiliation. At the same time, they seem deeply aware
that a reciprocal trust can be reached only step by step. It's a long way to, a sort
of learning path featured by open dialogue, commitment, willingness to listen
to each other without prejudice.

> I believe we have basic confidence in our school: families know their chil-
> dren are safe here at school and the message is, or at least I believe it is (a
> lot of mothers come to our school, well the general opinion is that, at
> school, children are at ease and teachers look after them). (Female, Ital-
> ian, School manager, FG 2 BS, adults)

> I sometimes have perceived that foreign parents –as long as you respect
> their children and they understand you are there to do the right thing for
> their children, and you devote to that– accept your decisions and are
> aware that all that you do is for their children's good education, they re-
> spect you. So, the basic choice is: I respect you and when I understand this,
> I accept any action or decision you make. (Mother, Italian, FG 2 BS, adults)

Besides a deep confidence in the school's ability to be a "common place for
everyone", the awareness that conflicts and frictions may arise is widespread as
well. When solicited to push forward their analysis, going beyond the abstract
principles to describe what happens during and between the lessons in the
school environment, the picture outlined by the adults becomes multi-faceted
and some criticalities –concerning the school-family/teachers-parents' relationships, especially– are pinpointed. It is not by chance that, at this level, the
parents' voice emerges more clearly.

4   Religious Beliefs and Citizenship Values: the Blurring Boundaries
between the Public and the Private Spheres

Generally speaking, public school is perceived as an open and inclusive space,
capable of assuring freedom of religious expression to all its members and

stakeholders. However, even the huge complexity of the issue emerges, together with the need to be better scrutinized within the daily school life practice, where ideal precepts and concrete actions intertwine, and where the secular feature of the school demands to be preserved.

Religious belonging, in many ways, concerns citizenship rights and religious freedom, as defined above, that is: (*i*) freedom to *believe,* as an inviolable right for the human person; and (*i*) freedom to *express* one's faith within the given framework of rules and norms for a democratic coexistence (Bychawska-Siniarska, 2017). In other words, the full enjoyment of the right goes hand in hand with the fulfilment of the corresponding duties. Indeed, the multi-faceted feature of this relationship clearly emerges when we also consider the right to *practice* one's own faith.

The many dilemmas that may arise from the struggle due to the coexistence in the same public arena of different religious values and prescriptions, possibly contrasting some democratic values, have found a solution across the ages in the separation between the public and the private sphere. As mentioned above (§2.2), while it seems relatively easy to outline the relationship between the State and the Church (Churches) –which are two institutions– as the paradigm of secularization theorizes, it is much harder to trace the relationship between citizenship (human) rights and religious rights. The latter, in the name of a religious belonging, recall the need for religious practices to comply with the rules (and limits) of the democratic, liberal society.

According to Max Weber's lesson in *The Protestant Ethic and the Spirit of Capitalism*, for some aspects still unsurpassed (Rossi, 2002), any religion embeds ethical and moral principles as well as (what any religion considers) "civic virtues", values and norms, that is, an idea of what constitutes a good citizen, of how it should be the "right order" of society (together with the affirmation of the truth and of the universality of their assumptions). This occurs even if the relationship between the religious doctrine and a moral code does not follow a unique model, since it is defined in a specific (and differentiated) way for each religion. Therefore, religious affiliation affects individual and collective life-conduct and coexistence. Consequently, human rights (and the relating universal and internationally protected legal code) and "God's rights" (specific religious law of the diverse religious communities and Churches) may collide with each other (Ferrari, 2017). Following the author, we may mention three main areas of possible ethical conflicts:

– The first area concerns *religious practices* expressing the right of parents to transmit their religious faith to their children, but potentially crashing with individual rights. A meaningful example is neonatal male circumcision, a fundamental practice both for Judaism and Islam. Practiced in the first few weeks after birth, therefore necessarily disregarding the individual consent,

it leaves an indelible physical mark, which may be considered as a violation of the individual integrity of one's own body;
- A second area relates to the *juridical status of women*: human rights conventions prohibit any discrimination based on sex, whereas many religions prohibit ordaining women to the priesthood, prevent them from accessing other leadership positions in the religious community or gaining access to certain functions or jobs;
- A third area concerns the *right to convert*, that is to replace one's current religion or belief with another (on none), protected by the UN Declaration of Human Rights, but strictly banned (and even punished) from some religion systems (*Ibidem*).

Without further exploring these extremely controversial debates, these few hints offer a suitable framework to understand to what extent, in the contemporary plural society, it is difficult to establish, once and for all, the boundaries between different orders of law, and between beliefs and practices.

These arguments are breaching the wall among the scholars who reflect on the "post-secular turn", questioning the supposed religions irrelevance in politics and in public life. As argued by May *et al.*, religion "is not simply concerned with supernatural entities and the nature and existence of a transcendental realm. It is also, crucially, a framework through which interpreting and responding to immanent contexts, events and experiences. Through symbolism, rhetoric, images, narratives, histories, myths, values and experiences, religious ideas and influences continue to intervene in, and unsettle, the supposedly ordered rational nature of secular politics" (2014: 339).

Clearly, the aforementioned controversies do not directly pertain to the school domain, but to the awareness that the relevance of these issues should be reminded in the school debate. As stated by Benadusi *et al.* (2017: 478), the debates concerning the multi-ethnic and multi-cultural schools tend to switch "from the religions (viewed as spiritual and pragmatic systems for "ordering" the world) to religious beliefs (seen as systems of values and moral guidance for conforming to institutions and adhering to established religious practices)". The relationship between religious beliefs and power is particularly "circumvented or suppressed in the public discourse on religious teaching in schools and in educational curricula" (*Ibidem*), but its relevance deserves much attention. In fact, the school mirrors similar sets of problems and, in a way, allows us to focus on them better, as the separation between the public and the private spheres is daily challenged by the students', families' and teachers' behaviors and choices. The legal protections of religious freedom, while providing a crucial leverage for social integration, triggers claims for the recognition of the legitimacy of each religious belief and practice within the school life, by asking for a definition of borders between religious and civic loyalties – borders that no longer seem easy to identify.

As highlighted above, the different ethnic, cultural, and religion affiliations, burst into the school daily life mainly through external symbols and customs, like some peculiar eating habits observed in the school cafeteria (e.g. not eating pork meat, fasting, eating halal food) or some religious symbols worn by students (e.g. the Islamic veil). However, both students and adults agree that it is when these external symbols and customs start to influence people's behavior that they need to be handled in some way. The cases reported by focus groups' participants concern some "typical" circumstances, such as:

- The request –from some students (and their families)– not to be enrolled in the Catholic religion lessons or to be enrolled in them despite admittedly adhering to another religion or despite being atheist/agnostic;
- The request –from some female Muslim students (and their families)– not to attend two-days (or more) long school trips, and not to have male classmates seated next to them;
- The request –once again from some female Muslim students (and their families)– for a derogation to the dressing code, e.g. the request to wear only long pants during gym class or other special clothes for attending sports activities (e.g. swimming) or to skip swimming lessons.

Evidently, these are very different examples. However –although with different intensity– they all prove how much the distinction between the private and the public spheres at school is blurred. Furthermore, these examples prove the inner "power dimension" of school relationships and the religion's role in shaping people's (in this case, students') "world vision". Consequently, they reveal how thorny the recognition of religious rights at school is, not only from a cultural and religious point of view (pertaining values and beliefs) but also from a political one, *lato sensu*. Ethical and moral principles, as well as "civic virtues" (as intended above), are –more or less implicitly– fundamental matters of the religious socialization that students undergo within their families, and surface in some of the family's choices, preferences and prohibitions imposed to them in the school contexts, as well as in some students' behaviors, challenging the school's ability to properly answer as a public, secular, and plural space, and bringing the school-family relationship to the foreground.

5 The School–Family Interface as a Keystone for Religious Socialization

In a certain sense, the aforementioned requests brought to the fore what Charles Taylor theorized about the effects of secularism on religion, in his highly-influential book *A Secular Age*: "Believing in God is no longer axiomatic. There are alternatives. And this will also likely mean that at least in certain *milieu*, it may be hard to sustain one's faith. There will be people who feel bound to give it up, even though they mourn its loss" (Taylor, 2007: 3). Religious belief has become a "social contingency". This assertion does not imply that believers experience their own faith with the sense of contingency or value-relativity, but that our social world is now sufficiently pluralistic regarding faith-commitments, to the point that we no longer consider religion as what provides us with the default normative foundations for collective action (Gordon, 2008: 665).

Religion interpretation of the world cannot be longer taken for granted, since it is a possibility among others. The gradual loss of a fully shared common sense –that is, the "social imaginary" (…), the "common understanding, which makes common practices possible, and a widely shared sense of legitimacy" pushes forward for a "radical reflexivity" (Taylor, 2007: 171–2). In other words, in post secular society, religion turns into a system of beliefs that is both self-reflexive and aware of the pluralistic scenario in which it is definitively inserted. As underscored by Ferrara (2014: 70), Taylor's argumentation allows us to pinpoint a *third dimension of secularism* (together with the political and social ones, mentioned above), a phenomenological and "experience-near" dimension: "from the standpoint of this third variety of secularism, belief and non-belief, theism and atheism are not to be seen as rival *theories*, in cognitive terms, but rather as different ways of being in the world, of living one's life". As a consequence, the experience of believing has undergone a deep transformation: from being the unquestioned framework shared by everybody in a natural, unreflective way, to being one among other options available, and which can no longer be lived in an unreflective and naïve way.

Keeping this background, it is worth noticing that this self-awareness seems to be shared by all focus groups' participants. The major part of the narratives underlines the importance of reciprocal exchange of views on religious issues and related practices, even if this exchange may lead to some disagreement.

In this regard, two macro-issues deserve our attention: the process of religious socialization and school-family dialogue.

Not surprisingly, family is acknowledged as the main agent of students' religious socialization, even if the school and the peer group certainly contribute to it, considering that school is the place where the youngsters spend most of their time and build friendships. The opinions of students, teachers and parents converge in it: family plays a fundamental role in the transmission of values and religious heritage. Not by chance, family, mother, father, parents were among the most-frequency words counted by the Nvivo Word Frequency

Query. The socialization role of the family is considered as pivotal, especially for families with a migratory background and their offspring. As some research has proved, it is an ambivalent role since it may favor or hinder the children's integration process inside and outside the school (Bichi *et al.*, 2018; Ricucci, 2017).

Parents are seen as the legitimate custodians of the religious knowledge transmitted to children. Hence, they are also responsible for the quality of the religious education offered to them. The educational and socialization role of the family is considered to be so influential that, according to many narratives, students' behavior should be interpreted as a "direct consequence" of the teaching received at home, consistently with a "over-socialized" vision of the children that does not recognize neither the dynamic and relational nature of socialization process nor the active involvement of children themselves (Klingenberg, Sjö, 2019). What is more, this vision does not take into account that religious socialization is a process occurring in several different settings simultaneously, since there are many different ways in which young people encounter religion (*Ibidem*).

By the way, recognizing the family as a fundamental agent of religion socialization leads to highlight the responsibility that falls on parents' shoulders, and the controversial aspects that may arise from the clash between, on the one hand, their influential role in children's identity formation and, on the other hand, the peers' and school's (and media's) influence that increases during the adolescence, thus eroding parents' authority.

Approaching the issue, both youngsters and adults participating in the focus groups somehow "theorize" that all the families shape children choices, behavior, and beliefs regarding, for instance:
- Which religion to follow (and whether or not to follow one);
- Which choices and behavior to adopt at school: attending religion lessons or opting for alternative activities;
- Asking to skip some school activities (gym, journey, etc.) or to receive a "different treatments" (e.g. to dress differently, to choose who can be sitting by one's side),
- How to judge other religions and cultures, (power) relationships between people, teachers' and families' respective roles and boundaries of authority, currents events, etc.

However, moving on from this common "theoretical" vision, when narratives refer to personal experiences, both students' and adults' attention focus on two main issues:
- Freedom of religious choice;
- Role of women according to religion beliefs.

Notwithstanding these similarities, their opinions diverge for some aspects that we need to mention, considering: *a*) students' and *b*) adults' voice separately.

5.1 The Students' Point of View

On the students' part, attention is paid to the *freedom of religious choice*, that is as a matter of possible controversy within the family relationships.

Students belonging to the majority (Italians and Catholics) generally consider their experience of freedom of religious choice as something just acquired and a-problematic. Being aware that religion affiliation is a relevant family's heritage, they feel free to change religion if they want to. They generally express gratitude for family education, for the values passed on to them and for their religion's legacy, as well as for the freedom of choice, thought and act that they admit to benefit from. At the same time, they firmly criticize what happens to some of their classmates belonging to other religions, who –in their eyes– are conditioned and limited by family impositions that they cannot bypass and that can hinder their personal freedom and their transition to adulthood. Indeed, some students with a migratory background –mainly girls professing Islam, but also a couple of Catholic non-Italian native students– reported to having to endure family impositions. However, this is a controversial issue and no generalization can be applied to the relating narratives, as the following few ones show.

> I would like to live on my own ... I want to have two dogs, not just one. I don't know ... I feel under the control of my parents. (Female, Italian, Catholic, FG 1 BS, students)

> I'm Muslim too, but I'm not like her, they don't oblige me to stay at home, I go wherever, whenever I want! (Male, Senegalese, Muslim, FG 1 BS, students)

> We are free, but we are on probation, because our freedom is also limited by some factors. For instance, I would like to be Buddhist, but I'm influenced by the others, what my friends and relatives think about me. (Female, Italian, Coptic Christian, FG 6 MI, students)

> We are oriented since our birth: our parents influence us a lot. When you have Christian relatives, it is difficult (to change), because you are used to specific habits. (Male, Italian, Atheist, FG 6 MI, students)

> I agree, there are religions and religions ... Maybe there are stricter parents who, according to their beliefs, tell their children they must do what their religion says, that's it; on the other hand, other parents may say that ... their children can dress as they like and believe in what they want ... they are free. (Male, Moldavian, Coptic Christian, FG 3 BS, students)

> In religion they cannot oblige you, because if you don't wear a veil you are not doing anything wrong. (Female, Kosovara, Muslim, FG 3 BS, students)

> In her religion there is no law which states: you must wear a veil, it's a tradition which has been passed down. She says: "I wish I could take it off, but ... my dad actually obliges me to keep it on". According to her, that's wrong, because nowhere it is mentioned that we must wear a veil and she told me that, actually, it just happens because men oblige women to do that. (Male, Italian, Catholic, FG 5 MI, students)

What is more, students debate on the *role of women in the family*, at school and in society, as an issue considered to be strictly connected to some religion beliefs and visions of the world. Here, the narratives become even more controversial, enriched by both personal experiences and (above all) stereotypes, prejudgments and hearsay, particularly dealing with:

- Restrictions that (in the Catholics' opinion) some female classmates suffer because of their family's religious beliefs concerning especially the duty to wear the Islamic veil, the prohibition to participate in school journeys or to attend some sports lessons, etc.
- The idea that girls/women have to play a subordinate role in some "traditional" families and are subjected to specific restrictions at school due to religion prescriptions.

The example provided by the above-reported students mainly revolve around Islamic religion, but narratives often overlap and confuse religion affiliation and nationality, without being capable of distinguishing between migrant, cultural and national backgrounds. A meaningful example is represented by the narratives focused on some Pakistani or Egyptian girls and families, whose religious belonging to the Islamic religion is presumed, but not really known by participants. Although the students consider this issue as a potential source of conflict, their discussions tend to remain on the surface, simplified and polarized upon few circumstances in which they assume the passive role of the girls as an unavoidable outcome of parents' impositions on daughters. The "asymmetric vision" in the participants' narratives (between what, generally positively, happens to oneself and what, negatively, may happen to the others) can be due to the composition of the focus groups (too many majority students). However, it can also reflect the students' difficulty in revealing situations personally experienced as problematic: it is easier to talk about yourself in the third person than being exposed to collective judgment. To "break the circle", there is the testimony of a young Pakistani and Islamic girl, who tells her experience in first person.

> For instance, Muslim people treat women in a peculiar way, while the Christians or people from other religions treat them in a different way. In my family, we only have one woman: my mother; we are all males because I have two brothers and a father and, obviously, we treat her well, but our Muslim neighbors, I don't want to say, they treat women badly, but they don't have the same rights as men ... I hear them (...) Well, it happened once that the Muslim family had to go somewhere, but the woman couldn't do that ... so she had to stay at home for two days, because, as I figured out, the family was on a 2-day trip; on the contrary, we always take my mother with us ... I mean, there are some differences. To tell the truth, there are some Muslim families that are more open-minded and others that are stricter, my neighbors are open in comparison with others I know, some other friends of mine ... (Male, Romanian, Orthodox Christian, FG 4 MI, students)

> When we go to school we don't care about our different religions, we are all together and we are used to living together, even if we have different religions ... we know everything about each other. However, when we are with our parents, Muslim people have more problems –at least this is what I have noticed– while Christian students don't have this many problems, if they want to talk with their parents about what they want to do. It's harder for Muslim students because we live in a prison ... believe me, my house is a prison! Up to a few months ago, I could not even get out of my house, except for going to school or to the mosque, nowhere else (....). Over the last few months, I only have been to the library twice, nowhere else. They don't let me go out so much. On Saturday they take me to the supermarket, otherwise they leave me at home ... I feel like living in a prison and I want to go out more often, I want to run away from home because I don't like it, I don't like to live there ... I want to live like the other students, but if I say so, they get angry, the only thing they can do is to force me ... (Female, Pakistani, Muslim, FG 1 BS, students)

5.2   *The Adults' Point of View*

On the adults' part, the role of family in children's religious socialization is ac-knowledged as particularly influential as it is the first agent that instils cus-toms, values, social norms, social roles, etc. For better or for worse, hence, family is considered to be responsible for students' behavior at school, behav-ior that "certainly reflects" –as it is said– "what they 'breath' at home".

> I think that teenagers and pre-teens, in general, at a religious level have more freedom of expression. I think that one of the limits is given both by their parents' culture and by the culture in the school educational orien-tation, which may have been more or less evident according to their dif-ferent religions. (Father, Italian, FG 4 BS, adults)

> The question is that in dogmatic families (not necessarily Arabian fami-lies, there may even be some very integralist Catholics, who despite the very inclusive message of the Gospel, show suspicion) there may be an impact on teenagers, thus, their behavior reflects what they hear at home (…). In my opinion, students are inclusive with other young people, but the influence from their families may cause a sort of cultural resistance, which leads them to be more suspicious. (Female, Italian, School man-ager, FG 4 BS, adults)

> I sometimes see mothers wearing a veil and daughters without it and the other way around. I even met two sisters, one was wearing a veil the other one was not; their mother wasn't wearing it either … I see, you under-stand, they perceive in their families a sort of approach that, according to their personality and growing-up process, leads them to choose to wear it or not, despite their mothers. Well, you can really feel the difference … I've noticed that change over the past few years. (Female, Italian, Teacher, FG 1 BS, adults)

> For the two Muslim girls who wear the veil, who are attending their last year here and are about to move on to the secondary school, the choice has been conditioned (…). (It would be necessary) to free them from a situation of "closure", in that case, really, because of the father … They do the school that the father decided for them. (Female, Italian, School man-ager, FG 4 MI, adults)

Teachers and parents agree that the issue of *freedom of religious choice* is gener-ally easy to be addressed at school. Besides being quite sure that their children can freely express their religious belonging at school, parents declare that they can make their choices about their children's participation in religion lessons, or in other activities, peacefully and, even if not Catholic, they are often open to a better understanding of the Catholic religion teaching, which is provided by every Italian public school within the curriculum (see Chapter 21 and §7). In some cases, IRC teachers reported to have had (and still have) Muslim (or belonging to other religions) students attending their lessons with the consent of their parents, or to argue with parents about the desire of their children to attend IRC against their opinion. All the reported controversies, however, came to a positive solution. Similarly, some parents say they have had to discuss with their children the choice of attending IRC because their children wanted to attend it against their will; even in this case, their experiences have been generally positive. On the other hand, it is interesting to notice that teachers stress its importance to let students and families know more about the "non confessional" aim of IRC, so that these classes can be shared by students from different religions and different cultures in a better way.

Compared with the students' focus groups, the adults' ones revolve more on *the gender relations, differences, inequalities and even conflicts*. To the adults' eyes, these are very critical issues to address. Teachers' comments are largely negative on this, by reporting examples of parents (especially the fathers) impeding daughters from participating in some school activities, obliging them to wear the veil, and prevent mothers to talk with teachers. In this regard, however, we must remember that the adults' focus groups are mainly composed by women, Italian teachers who turned out to be particularly sensitive to these issues.

Although adults are generally more able to think critically than youngsters, their narratives are sometimes affected by stereotypes and simplifications (e.g. by considering people/students with the same ethnic/religion/cultural background as a homogeneous group) as well. Unlike the students, the adults consciously try (and hardly succeed in) distinguishing the reasons of gender disputes. For someone, these are rooted in a specific religion background and for someone else they are connected to the personal mentality or to a system of cultural beliefs rather than to a religion. Indeed, they think that prohibitions to girls and women are a "radical" and "betraying" way of interpreting religious precepts or a heritage of a patriarchal mindset and household.

> It is a cultural problem and it relates to a religious vision ... it is useless to bury our heads in the sand, well ... beyond some sorts of integralism relating to religion, there is also a vision connected with (women's role). May be inside the family the woman has some freedom, but outside she is not allowed to do much ... It is especially true with Pakistani people: they have a more restricted vision of religion. I'm talking about the Muslim

one, which creates troubles for us, even as teachers, because starting from the swimming pool for girls and other stuff there is a prohibition and that's it (...). We can even talk about Jehovah's Witnesses and other situations ... I mean, when the cultural and religious vision is very restricted, or anyway when religion becomes an alibi even for some cultural choices, it is clear that it is hard for us with our students, but also for students too ... (Mother & teacher, Italian, FG BS 1, adults)

I would like to focus on the gender difference, because, according to my own experience, not only as a school manager in a school for one year and a half, but also as a teacher, I have faced some episodes which made me wonder about it. Once, it happened with a Senegalese student ... let's say a very "lively" student ... I told him "Well, I want to talk to your father» and he answered "My father is not interested at all in what you say because you are a woman". As a matter of fact, his father was only in contact with the School manager who was a man, at that time, and the ICT teacher who was a man as well. Anyway, I think this relates to some people, rather than to their religion (...). I think it's a cultural question, rather than a religious one. (Female, Italian, School manager, FG 7 MI, adults)

They say they are subjugated, but ... religion has nothing to do with it. I'm a Muslim, I know the Quran and I know what I'm saying ... really, it has nothing to do with it, it is not mentioned anywhere that you have to be subjugated to men and that they are supposed to decide for you ... (Mother, Tunisian, Muslim, FG 1 BS, adults)

6 School–Family Dialogue: Boundaries of Responsibilities and Religious Reflexivity

On the whole, the teachers' efforts are aimed at addressing the demand for recognition of different cultural and religious backgrounds through a "family-friendly approach" that needs to be "child-centered", geared towards the full respect of each child's identity. By asking for the recognition of religious identity at school –and, hence, asking for different ways to handle some aspects of school life in order to meet the values, the customs, and the practices relating to religion affiliation– families request that teachers (and school managers) opt for an intense dialogue, negotiations, argumentations.

Apart from an overall positive appraisal of school-family relations, teachers neither diminish the difficulties met to carry on a constructive debate nor hide the failures suffered. At the same time, they also point out the crucial relevance of such an effort, since it proved to be a profitable way to overcome barriers and to build reciprocal trust in the long run, even creating new chances for emancipation for some foreign mothers, once asked to be involved in their children's school life.

> (*it is difficult*) especially with young girls, for instance when we have to go away for a couple of days ... Two years ago, for the first time, a girl was allowed to come with us (on a school trip). Her family had accepted, because they trusted us, it's just a question of trust, we had built that trust, otherwise they would have said "no" for sure ... (Mother & Teacher, Italian, FG 1 BS, adults)

> (...) On another occasion, a young girl wished her mother could come to talk to her teachers at the general school meetings, she really wished she could, so this lady in a burka came and told the teacher: "If my husband finds out I'm here I may have consequences". So, we got worried and said: "Madam, go home right now to avoid any kind of consequences". That lady was a newcomer, she had just arrived. Now, let's say, we still have contacts with this family and things have changed a lot, as they have been living here for a while ... (Female, Italian, School manager, FG 3 BG, adults)

> The Pakistani experience is very strong here, in my opinion ... It is the result of the typical narrow-mindedness of this nation, with its habits and customs, which are strictly controlled and tied to religion. We have had boys in our school institute who went home and "tipped off", if I may say so, that the girls in their neighborhood or the daughters of some friends were not wearing a veil or just wore it on their shoulders rather than on their heads ... A young girl had been badly told off by her family because of that ... but some other things have improved a lot. I have seen Pakistani women who were very proud because they had come to school meetings and could sign documents: then, sometimes, they asked "Could you write down the things you are telling me? So, my son will not tell my husband that what I'm saying is not true..." Can you understand that? (Female, Italian, Teacher, FG 1 BS, adults)

> Together with the local intercultural contact, we have been organizing meetings with parents, actually Indian mothers ... We had a meeting last year and one at the beginning of this year and we noticed some confidence in our school. A lot of mothers come to our school, and the message

we get is (or at least I believe so) that at school (their children) are at ease and their teachers look after them. (Female, Teacher, Italian, FG 2 BS, adults)

Foreign mothers come to the general school meetings and apparently this is, let's say, a way to get their revenge ... my impression is that some foreign mothers take a sort of revenge because they come to school as if they were "fathers" who want to know about their children's school life, and this is something typical here ... Well, it is not that widespread because it is usually the fathers' task to come to the school meetings, isn't it? But actually, a lot of mothers have come to our school meetings (Female, Teacher, Italian, FG 2 BS, adults)

What is more, the teachers recognize the need to consider carefully the ethical dilemma concerning the "boundaries of responsibilities" between school and family: to what extent can teachers discuss families' decisions? Which are the limits of parental authority over children's education? How to protect the freedom of expression with regards to religious plurality, in compliance with the school's "laïcité"? As a matter of fact, issues that were thought to have been overtaken by the secularization process –finding a peaceful solution in the separation of private, civil and religious spheres– can be found again in the school debate.

In addition, teachers underline that generalizing may lead to wrong conclusions. Circumstances are complex and implications relate to the personal attitude of people who experience them: the religious belonging is not at all "predictive" of a specific kind of behavior.

On the one hand, there are minorities, with a culture different from the Italian one and a religion different from the Catholic one, in which there may be frictions and reasons for disagreements – never easy to handle effectively. As this story witnesses:

We had the case of a Muslim student, a girl who lived her religion as an imposition, she wanted to integrate, but could not because of his extremist father. She was always accompanied to school, walking a step behind, she could not walk side by side, she could not attend the gym, she could not remove her veil in the classroom, she could not play music, watch movies ... The nice thing was that she had found solidarity among the classmates. Whenever she entered the school, she took of her veil asking them not to tell outside ... At a certain point, we fought because her father no longer sent her to school ... and had arranged a marriage: she had

> to go to her country of origin to get married. She used to say "I don't want
> to get married and with a man older than me". We managed in some way,
> involving the Social Services, to let her conclude lower secondary school
> with the final exam. But, unfortunately, after that she disappeared. (Male,
> Teacher, FG 5 MI, adults)

On the other hand, some minority families are actually eager to encourage
their children to deepen their cultural and religious roots, and to open up
to a constructive debate with others. This behavior, which is characterized
by "willingness to know", appears even at school: the students with a migration background, from another culture and religion, are often more "experienced" when it comes to religion and more curious about other people's
religions.

> The foreign student is always called to reflect on ..., so he/she has a great-
> er awareness. (Male, Teacher, FG 5 MI, adults)

> We sometimes feel embarrassed, it has happened several times, even
> with a colleague of mine and her pupil, when the teacher of the alterna-
> tive subject to the study of Catholic Religion was absent, the pupil had
> stayed in class and before the following lesson he said: "I want to stay
> because I'm interested in what the teacher says ... and I want to attend
> this class as well". (Female, Teacher, FG 1 BS, adults)

The parents participating in focus groups do not reveal much about the matters of these subjects, but some of them say that their children's school experience, their willingness to follow (or not) religion classes and other school activities, encourage them to get utterly informed, to explain the deep-rooted
reasons behind their choices to their children.

In any case, the coexistence of different religious belongings (including the
non-believers) both at school and in society, may lead adults and young people
to develop reflection, self-awareness and reciprocal dialogue. Indeed, these
forms of understanding can favor integration, due to the capability of transforming such attitudes into an effective, constructive debate.

7   **Religion as a Transversal Content of the School's Curriculum and
         Cultural Heritage**

Within the given theoretical framework, the last issue that is worth being
considered concerns the strategies enacted by schools to cope with students'

religious diversities through and beyond the curriculum and the corresponding consequences. Besides RE (whose teaching is guaranteed in Italian public schools for those who select that option; see Chapter 21), the different subjects offer several opportunities to speak about the religious diversity.

Students and adults agree with the idea that the school –as far as it is described as an inclusive space, where everyone feels free to express his/her religious belonging– is not always capable of meeting students' need to delve into the religion knowledge and to discuss it. A number of narratives underline that there are many chances to speak about religion offered within the several disciplines –e.g. literature, history, art and music– but few are the circumstances that allow teachers to develop an in-depth debate. Despite this, teachers try to take advantage of the school curriculum, of the religious festivities and of the daily news that in some way regard religion, to solicit the attention of students for religion issues.

> I don't talk about my religious beliefs at school, but as a Geography, History and Italian teacher, I really like to explore the historical root of someone who practices one religion or another. And I should say I have always had positive experiences, even with religion teachers who aimed to avoid catechesis at school, and rather focused on the history and culture of the country we live in. For instance, we can reinforce that with the "Divina Commedia" or with art history ... (Male, Teacher, FG 3 BG, adults)

Consequently, by grasping only the anthropological and cultural dimension of religion, the subject focuses more on habits, customs, folkways, and religious traditions rather than, strictly speaking, on religious faith. It does not tackle the main issues that each religion deals with, such as the "ultimate questions" and the corresponding answers, nor does it explore the transcendent dimension and the claims to truth, which are at the basis of every religion. The connection between faith and culture is dialectic and unavoidable, and even mutually beneficial (we may say that religion is a "cultural fact"). However, the distinction between the two fades out in the perception of the interviewed people. Furthermore, some of them see the risk of reducing religion to a mere type of culture, losing the connection with the transcendent dimension, which instead represents the distinctive contribution that religions may give in the contemporary society (Magatti, 2018).

> Culture and religion are not separated, because culture develops together with religion and religion turns into culture, they are strictly connected. (Male, Religion Teacher, FG 3 BG, adults)

This is, maybe, something inevitably related to the above-mentioned third dimension of secularization (phenomenological and "experience-near" dimension), which reduces the experience of faith to one of the possible points of view coexisting in the common life.

Actually, thanks to the teachers' narratives, we can grasp that RE is not fully exploited for adequate insight because of the lack of suitable didactic means. Moreover, even though RE does not follow a dogmatic approach and cannot be identified with a confessional teaching (catechism), students, who do not attend it, have a limited knowledge of the contents they deal with.

Religion teachers especially want to emphasize that in their lessons they focus on the dialogue, by carefully taking into consideration different religions; moreover, they concentrate on developing ethical and universal issues.

> Actually, they say it is a Catholic religion class, but we teach the history of religions, it depends on the (school) program we have. During the third year, we teach all the values ... Life as a gift, from the beginning to the end, so we consider all the issues regarding procreation, abortion, euthanasia, all those things, which do not concern Catholic religion only. (Female, Religion Teacher, FG 3 BG, adults)

> For years, I have been encouraging foreign parents to be curious and to come and talk to a Religion teacher because we don't teach catechism, we don't teach any doctrine. (Female, Teacher, FG 1 BS, adults)

> At school, we experience humanity. (Male, Teacher, FG 3 BG, adults)

> There is a Muslim boy who always wants to stay in the classroom and have religion lessons with me, I sometimes let him stay with me and he doesn't leave for the alterative activity ... but his parents told me not to do so, at present ... but he told me that next year he will come. (...) In my opinion, it is also a question of information, maybe they don't know what we do during Religion classes ... teaching Catholic religion is not teaching catechism, catechism teaches you to believe in one God, but the IRC is not only that ... I teach you some values and it's up to you to stick to them or not. (Female, Religion Teacher, FG 3 BG, adults)

Although some scholars critically assert that the Italian public school still remains Catholic-centric[3] (e.g. it affects the annual school calendar), over time,

---

3   So that, Pace (2005) spoke about a "Catholic model of secularism" to underline the persistence of Catholic Church's influence in the public school and, more widely, in the public sphere.

the changes introduced have been huge, due both to the acknowledging of public schools as secular and plural spaces, and to the growing number of students with different cultural and religious background. As a matter of fact, within the secular setting of the Italian State, the acknowledgment that the Catholic religion is no longer the only religion of the country, and that the latter is increasingly becoming a pluralistic (multi-cultural, multi-religious and multi-ethnic) society, have pushed to renew both the historically privileged and exclusive relationship set between the Italian State and the Catholic Church and the regulation and content of RE (Giorda, 2015; see Chapter 21). Regarding to the IRC, these changes –reinforced by the increasing numbers of foreign students (Catholic or not) attending the lessons– have pushed to rethink its content, opening it to the religious pluralism and adopting a "cultural perspective" (Frisina, 2011).

Despite this, the research shows that some contrast may persist between two opposite ways of understanding IRC: one more pluralistic, the other more conservative and confessional. Indeed, the translation in practice of this "new deal" appears to be uneven across the education system, "depending partly on the training and sensitivity of the RE teachers and partly on the local (social, scholastic, ecclesiastic) context", also resulting from the school autonomy (*Ibidem*: 267). Likewise, the right to freedom of choice –formally proclaimed– is hardly guaranteed as equally on the substantive level, since it may happen that no alternative activities (or only low-quality ones) are arranged for students who would attend them (Giorda, 2015). However, these criticalities remain in the background of the narratives collected though the focus groups.

Students seem to appreciate the "new deal" of IRC, underlining that it is an opportunity to understand the differences (not only the religious ones) they find at school. Simply considering the fact that there are students who do not attend IRC, in fact, encourages reflection. Those who attend Religion classes assess them positively and more than once suggest that everybody should attend them (whatever religion they belong to, including non-believers), since it is a precious opportunity for debate. Because of this, students agree that a Religion class should be called, in a more explicit way, "the class for religions".

> Something that disturbs me relates to the students who abandon the Religion classes because they belong to another religion ... In our school program, next year we will deal with Buddhism and all the other religions, so, as we learn about other religions, the other students from different religions can attend our Religion classes; because, by the way, it's an opportunity for discussions. (Male, Italian, Catholic, FG 4 MI, students)

> Religion classes are not only important for one religion, but for all of them because students can learn a lot in any case. (Male, Romanian, Orthodox Christian, FG 4 MI, students)

Indeed, religious pluralism at school may be restrained by two facts: firstly, there are almost only Catholic students attend IRC, and secondly there are only Catholic teachers who have the task to speak about other religions – hence, from a point of view which is (more or less implicitly) mono-confessional.

> We lack places and time for discussion, because even when I teach my subject, that is to say the IRC, well, very often the group is only made up of few Christian Catholics. So, starting a dialogue with different religions is really complicated. Even if we should deepen the study of other religions, we would do it exactly as we do with all the other school subjects ... There is no close relationship with the students who live and belong to a different religion ... So, well, according to me, that class, that is to say the Religion one, would be a "good" one, in order to talk and go deeper and deeper into details about different festivals, ways of dressing, eating habits and so on, but in my opinion we hardly ever use Religion classes for that purpose. (Male, Religion Teacher, FG 3 BG, adults)

> In the first year, according to the school program, I always deal with the Jewish roots, so we study the Torah, the Jewish Bible and then Islam, the structure of the Quran, we read something ... Then in the third year, we go on with Buddhism, Confucianism ... to show that ... the man who is behind that can express himself in different contexts ... As a Catholic religion teacher, I am not worried about talking about my religion, so ... When you teach a subject, you cannot separate it from its essence. (Male, Religion Teacher, FG 5 MI, adults)

> Maybe, in order to open up to a more constructive debate, we might decide to make Religion classes compulsory, on a State level, not as Catholic Religion classes but as the classes about the history of religions based on constructive debate. That might be interesting. (Male, School manager, FG 4 MI, adults)

Recalling the seminal Eisner's work (1985) on the different levels and types of school curriculum, which weave together in the school[4] – we may conclude

---

4 The *explicit* curriculum is the formal one, intentionally communicated; it refers to what is designed to teach, to the contents, goals, resources, documents etc. that are included in a

that no teaching and no curriculum can be considered as "neutral" choices. Teachers' narratives confirm that teaching is intertwined with socialization processes and that, especially through the *hidden* and *implicit* curriculum, socialization's formal and informal dimensions penetrate each other (Besozzi, 2017). As a consequence –with reference to the Religion teaching –as to any other subject– teachers implicitly convey their expectations and preferences to students. Moreover, when you teach something, you deliberately choose not to teach something else (actually, by giving shape to a *null* curriculum): you cannot teach everything, obviously, but what you choose to teach does not reflect only a specific vision of the discipline and of the "state of the art", but also what the school (on the teacher) believes should be taught/neglected in light of its own vision of the world.

8   Giving Citizenship to Religions at School: a Training Ground for Democracy

Although public education has totally taken over its role as a secular and free context, we still have to consider the issue about religious differences. How does the "*laïcité*" of its mandate can be observed, together with a correct consideration of pupils' religious identity? The adults involved in the focus groups complain that this mandate might be misinterpreted, often resulting in a total denial of the different religious belongings and, thus, limiting opportunities for dialogue and critical thinking.

> For instance, I'm against professing a sort of laicism as anti-religion, that is to say "State school: let's stay without symbols and crosses". On the contrary, I believe in people's spontaneity, which can be expressed without showing it off, anyway having something that refers to our religious belonging cannot be considered as bad if this is used to launch a sort of crusade. I find the attempt to cut off differences to be negative, because it

---

(written, official and public) lesson plan and teaching programme. The *implicit* or *hidden* curriculum consists of all the messages that are conveyed indirectly, without being stated explicitly, which regards teachers' attitudes, preferences, values, and expectations not included in the formal curriculum (e.g. meta-messages and "implicit theories" embedded in every teaching style), as well as the school setting (organization structure, physical characteristic etc.). The *null* curriculum is what schools do *not* teach, which may be as important as what they teach, since schools teach much more –and much less– than they intend to teach; it regards "the options students are not offered, the perspectives they may never know about –much less be able to use–, the concepts and skills that are not part of their intellectual repertoire" (*Ibidem*: 107).

forces human beings to suppress one of their inmost parts, which –
because of culture or nature– may on the contrary be important. (Male,
School manager, FG 4 MI, adults)

There is a misleading idea that laicism does not favor a constructive debate
or the presence of the Catholic religion at school. We should remind everybody that the 1984 Concordat recognizes the presence of the Catholic religion because it is part of the Italian cultural heritage. By the way, at present,
the discussion (even online and on social media) aims to limit this aspect as
if it was a threat to people's freedom. On the contrary, I would say that, from
this point of view, we need to protect the sense of belonging, because if
people cannot express their innermost essence, well, in that case there will
be no debate at all. (Male, School manager, FG 5 MI, adults)

This is what actually happens in some European societies: the trend is to
remove and ban any religious symbol. But this doesn't mean more freedom, it means less freedom for everybody. The question then is not to
remove religious symbols and signs of religious belonging. The question
is to accept differences (...). We should focus on the way we use the word
"different". If we use it as a synonym of "other than/unlike", as the Latin
"divertere", it means something characteristic, but also something which
takes us far from the others. On the contrary, if we use "different" with the
same meaning as the Latin "differo", that is to say that is typical of me, of
you, personal and peculiar, this means I can transfer something which is
personal in my relationships with others and the others can do the same.
In this case, "differences" become something valuable, and of course,
they can only be valuable if we consider them as peculiar and unique
aspects that we have and that we want to share with the others. If we
consider the word "different" as a synonym for other than/unlike, this vision, because of its meaning, will tear us apart and lead to conflict. (Female, Teacher, FG 5 MI, adults)

Other teachers state that the school's *laïcité* is not problem-free, and the risk
that a secular education can pose is not considering differences at all, and then
denying them together with one's own identity. The fear of triggering conflicts
or not having the suitable means to cope with religious contrasts, or establishing which differential treatments can be accepted or not, leads many teachers
to remove the problem, reframing it as non-pertinent. The consequence is that
"neutrality" turns into "neutralization", with two consequences.

On the one hand, the concerns about extremism, and the strategies to face
it, could put an end to classroom debates. On the other hand, managing

classroom discussions requires specific skills, taking into consideration what is appropriate to discuss in the classroom within the legal and educational systems and cultural context of reference, and with due regard to the age, maturity and aptitudes of students (Jackson, 2019). Teachers feel not prepared to it.

Instead, as seen above, also in the national and the European public debate, in the school public debate carried out by teachers, students and their families, issues that were considered to have been sorted out peacefully (such as tracing the boundaries of freedom of expression, of parental authority, and of religion authority) are regaining the center of attention.

The *laïcité* implies, besides the duality between private and public spheres, the distinction between the civil and religious spheres. The latter implies the existence of a "religious authority", which succeeds in transforming its absolute truth into dialogue (Rizzi, 2016). This is properly what matters. Then, for schools, the challenge is not to implement cultural divisions, but to encourage the knowledge of all religions, so that each student can learn how to use critical reflection upon one's own religious identity and tradition. Otherwise, no dualism is either applicable or believable (*Ibidem*: 89).

If we assume that "reflexivity" is a typical feature of Christianity –a religion historically open to reflexivity and to the hermeneutic exercise (*Ibidem*; Magatti, 2018)–, the RE and mainly the IRC have an extraordinary learning potential. In other words, the cultural heritage of Christianity may be a lever for curriculum enrichment and for promoting constructive dialogue skills among pupils.

In the wake of the European Recommendations, particularly the *Recommendation on the Dimension of Religions and Nonreligious Convictions within Intercultural Education* (Council of Europe, 2008a), both adults' and students' narratives suggest that the school may represent a privileged space for learning what it means to live in a multi-cultural, multi-religious and multi-ethnic society, that is, learning to become a citizen who peacefully and actively participates in such society. To accomplish this mandate, at least, two more steps need to be taken.

First, the recognition of diversity –and, eventually, agreeing to different treatments– needs to be linked to the *fight against the disadvantages related to it*. The studies on educational inequalities still give evidence to this phenomenon, with particularly reference to migrants' offspring and pupils' lower education attainment (Ambrosini, Pozzi, 2018; Colombo, Santagati, 2017). In this regard, the school mirrors what happens in the wider society. In Italy, as well as in the rest of Europe, migrants' offspring is affected by the intergenerational transmission of disadvantages in the labor market outcomes, with a higher concentration in low-skilled and "ethnicized" jobs, and in the social mobility process, with little capacity to benefit from the opportunity structure because of both the inequalities constrains and the families' legacies (Zanfrini, 2019).

All of this, as Zanfrini clearly pointed out, calls into question the prevailing (and "ambivalent") model of integration. The latter is featured by the persistent tension between two opposite aims –on the one hand, recognizing (and managing) the diversity "embedded" in the population with a migrant background, on the other hand, accomplishing the request for equality and uniformity; moreover, it still appears to be incapable of "exploiting" the migration-related diversity, despite many attempts (*Ibidem*).

Secondly, under the same tension, *the school needs to find its way for giving value to diversity*. This is a priority, as it is for the whole society. Indeed, for society, the enhancement of (migrant-related) diversity may represent a lever to "renew the integration model", thus linking economic competitiveness to social cohesion, viewing migrants as active citizens able to mobilize distinctive potentialities and resources and contributing to the common good (Zanfrini, 2015). For the school itself the intercultural approach that characterizes the Italian educational system represents the best choice to move forward, providing that theoretical principles are translated in classroom practices. Although the Italian intercultural education policies are seen as quite advanced in Europe, the literature underlines the weak correlation between policies, organizational and institutional practices, teaching strategies and educational experiences (Santagati, 2016). As our research suggests, the need to recognize, manage and value religious diversity represents a "test bed" for the intercultural approach and an opportunity to overcome those weaknesses. Acknowledging religion beliefs (as well as atheism) as a fundamental part of one's personal identity, gives to religions "citizenship in the school" and paves the way for an effective interreligious and intercultural dialogue.

When it calls to reflect on the freedom of expression, on the boundaries of responsibilities and limits of claims for different treatments, school becomes a training ground for democratic citizenship and active membership. Beyond the contradiction and difficulties highlighted by focus groups, the participants outline the profile of a public school that is "on the way" to cope with this challenge. The final goal is still far to reach, but it is clearly defined: instead of being a "neutral space", the school will ensure a "safe space" for dialogue (Jackson, 2014). As European Recommendations demand, this is a space where –with appropriate ground rules for constructive discussions in a given normative framework– inclusion and mutual respect are promoted. It is a space in which positive relations with students and parents are daily cultivated, in which students are helped to deal with a plurality of visions, ideas, cultures and religions, to develop critical thinking, to learn how to debate in an atmosphere of mutual tolerance, when they confront each other, and so on (*Ibidem*). Surely, renewed learning tools, teachers' competences and environmental conditions need to be developed, but first steps have already been taken.

Religious Conflicts in Multi-Cultural Schools: a Generational Divide between Students and Adults

Mariagrazia Santagati

1   Introduction: the Ambivalence of Conflict within the Integration Process of the Immigrants

For several decades, European countries have been undergoing a transformation towards greater cultural and religious pluralization: in the public debate, religious diversity –deriving from the growing presence of immigrants– has generated concern, misunderstanding, and has been perceived as a threat to the cultural identity of host societies (Foner, Alba, 2008; Wieviorka, 2001).

One of the most consolidated approaches to explain the diffusion of these negative attitudes toward immigrants and their diversities, in the field of social sciences, is the Group Conflict Theory, that predicts that increased ethnic diversities exacerbate in-group/out-group distinction and foster a state of perpetual conflict and competition for limited resources (Blumer, 1958; Blalock, 1967). Hostility toward immigration is considered a defensive and collective reaction to perceived inter-group competition for scarce goods: from the one hand, in a realistic perspective the immigrants are considered competitors in the labor market and in the Welfare system (Zanfrini, 2019). From the other hand, in a symbolic perspective the most violent conflicts arise in the cultural sphere and assume the shape of an identity fear, since the increase of cultural diversity weakens the national identity and could cause a growing clash between civilizations (Huntington, 1996; Bergamaschi, Santagati, 2019).

From a sociological point of view, however, we have to point out that conflict is not necessary negative *per se,* but is a fundamental element of social life, corresponding to the coexistence of contradictory orientations about motivations, goals, representations, world view, etc. Conflicts include existential, personal, relational, political controversies (Hirschberger *et al.*, 2016), and represent the constitutive dynamics of the individual and collective, material and symbolic dimensions of societies. Undoubtedly, conflict has an ambivalent function, it could be disruptive and violent, but at the same time fruitful and transformative (Simmel, 1968; Dahrendorf, 1959). Within multi-cultural societies, conflict has not a univocal meaning; it does not necessarily coincide with violence, but it can play different roles in the relationship between the host society and immigrants, affected by the different political visions and integration models.

Research findings confirm this interpretation of the ambivalence of conflict, remarking that cooperation and conflict are not alternative outcomes of intergroup relations, as they are constitutive and inextricably linked dimensions of the integration process (Pastore, Ponzo, 2012). In this perspective, the literature has also dealt with the role of intergroup contacts in reducing the prejudices towards immigrants. Hostility will be supplanted by positive and supportive attitudes if contacts and relations between the majority and the minority groups develop under specific situational and structural conditions that facilitate mutual respect (Allport, 1954; cf. Zanfrini, 2016). Hereafter, in its evolution, Contact Theory has focused more on interethnic relationships of friendly nature that will reduce prejudices and xenophobic manifestations and will improve empathy toward members of minority groups (Pettigrew, 1997; cf. Valtolina, 2015). More recently, interculturalism, recalling the Contact Theory and its developments, has proved to be the main pragmatic strategy to promote positive and friendly relationships, thanks to the social proximity between natives and immigrants and considering diversity as an individual and public resource (Zapata-Barrero, 2015).

What happens, however, in the educational field? This chapter deals with the appearance, the development, and the management of religious-based conflicts in multi-cultural schools: this is an interesting sub-topic of our research on educational integration in Northern Italy, already presented in Chapters 21 and 22. After a review of the international and Italian research on this topic in the sociological field, we will present some research results concerning the emerging conflicts in Italian multi-cultural schools, in order to describe, analyze, and interpret the role played by religious affiliations. We will do so through a comparison between the points of view of the adults and of the students involved in the focus groups.

2 From Religious Bullying to Interreligious Friendships in Education: the Contribution of the International Literature

The *Palgrave Handbook of Race and Ethnic Inequalities in Education* (Stevens, Dworkin, 2014) identifies a key tradition on interethnic relationships including an analysis focused on the religious issues. Within this research tradition, since the Nineties the issue of school violence in multi-cultural schools has received an enormous attention, especially in French studies. According to Debarbieux

(1998), the growing concern for violence at school coincides with the collapse of the ideology of progress, and with the crisis of both educational institutions and liberal democracies. In this scenario, the process of "ethnicization of school violence" occurs: ethnic minority groups begin to be considered as naturally aggressive, violent, and dangerous for school environments. Other scholars, however, consider school violence as a type of urban violence, since schools with large proportions of children of immigrants are often located in poor areas, where delinquency and violence are part of everyday life (Dubet, 1987). Research emphasizes the impact of social and ethnic segregation as well as the effect of disorganization of these schools on an emerging culture of drift, deviance, and delinquency (Blaya, 2006). These interethnic tensions risk penalizing the school career of students with minority religious background, thus exacerbating a situation of school distress and causing bad performance, educational failures and early school leaving (Bergamaschi, 2013a, 2016).

Recently, in European and North American literature, the new topic of bullying has emerged, although research has focused more on general forms of bullying than on ethnic and religious bullying. This phenomenon refers to bullying that targets another person's ethnic background or another person's cultural or religious identity (Peguero, Williams, 2011). Ethnic bullying (and ethnic/peer victimization) involves a wide range of aggressive behavior, such as verbal (i.e. taunts and slurs) and indirect (i.e. exclusion from a peer group). A definition of religious bullying was introduced by the Beatbullying's Interfaith Project and created by young people participating in the project (2008: 3):[1] "being taunted, excluded, or abused physically, emotionally or verbally on the grounds of one's own religious beliefs, affiliation to a given religion, perceived religious identity, or sectarian view by others, including those of other religious groups or belief systems". The survey findings indicate that one in four young people of the UK sample are being bullied, often violently, because of their religious affiliation or because they are perceived by peers as members of a specific faith community. Almost half of the young people involved do not talk about religious or faith issues: they have in fact little support, if they want to talk about their faith. The fact of being bullied, moreover, made many adolescents feel ashamed of their religion, made them question their faith and made them stop talking about their beliefs. Many bullied youngsters could not concentrate in class, would lose confidence and would become scared or angry. Those who have a faith experience denounce verbal abuse, harassment

---

1   The project was promoted by the UK's leading bullying prevention charity in different waves, reaching in the last editions (2008) a sample of nearly 1,000 students aged 11–16.

and stereotyping. They are also physically attacked, made feel isolated, and beaten because of their faith.

Other potential tensions are highlighted in the REMC study (*Religious Education in Multicultural Europe: Children, Parents and Schools*), a European comparative research on the way school and family face religious and moral education of new generations (Smyth *et al.,* 2013). The study shows that some parents are critical toward schools that do not provide religious education for minority faith children, claiming an overemphasis on majority faith culture. Minority faith parents are also more likely to criticize the faith educational approach adopted by schools. A common theme among some minority faith/secular parents is the fear that teachers would isolate or differentiate their children from their peers: some interviewed parents report specific incidents where teachers display lack of sensitivity to minority religious beliefs. Schools tend to avoid the use of explicit religious symbols, but some explicit tensions emerge between Muslim and other faith/belief groups, in relation to the use of religious symbols and to participation in specific festivities.

There has not been, until recent times, an explicit reference to religious diversities in the education research traditions, with exception for school violence and religious bullying. REDCo *Religion in Education. A Contribution to Dialogue or a Factor of Conflict in transforming societies of European countries?* (Weisse, 2010; Jackson, 2019) can be considered the first comparative research project on religion and education.[2] The project concerns young people's views about religion, religious diversity and possibilities for dialogue; it involves classroom interactions and conflicts, and it shows teachers' strategies to deal with religious conflict in educational settings. Many surveyed students appreciate the religious heterogeneity in their classrooms, although some prejudices are expressed, too. Students are generally open towards peers with different religious background. However, they tend to socialize with peers from the same background, even when they live in areas characterized by religious pluralism. Moreover, students often express a tolerant attitude more abstractly than practically. The tolerance expressed in classroom discussions is not always replicated in their daily life. Students generally wish to avoid conflict on religious issues, and some of the religiously committed students feel especially vulnerable. Dialogue is the favored strategy for teachers to cope with diversity

---

2   The project was funded by the European Commission (2006–2009), promoted by the Warwick Religions and Education Research Unit (WRERU). It has carried out a qualitative and quantitative research in eight countries (Germany, England, France, The Netherlands, Norway, Estonia, Russia, and Spain), focusing on religion in the lives and schooling of students aged 14–16.

in the classroom, but students are more ambivalent about the importance of it since, in practice, not all students are comfortable with the way diversity is managed in schools.

In the studies mentioned above, interreligious relationships in multi-cultural schools appear two-fold: interreligious dialogue is not always possible in a highly diverse school environment in which different groups of students inevitably have conflicting interests and worldviews. Interethnic and interreligious friendships and conflicts coexist. Conflict does not exclude the mutual recognition of and respect for the other's legitimate presence in a shared social space. Schools are obviously not the only social site for cross-cultural engagement, but they are a perfect illustration of how this respect for others' presence can work in practice (Ho, 2011). In the already quoted Beatbullying's Interfaith Project (2008), many young people interviewed have friends from all religions. Many young people are tolerant and interested in each other's religion. The majority of them have never been bullied because of their faith; their families encourage them to mix with young people from all religions and they feel comfortable discussing about religion with their peers in schools.

3 Religious Diversity in Italian Educational Studies: an Emerging Tradition

In Italian studies, a recent research tradition on interethnic relationships can be identified, including studies aiming at analyzing relationships, contacts and conflicts among peers by focusing on immigrant children's relational experiences as an important asset of immigrants' well-being and a crucial dimension of school integration (Azzolini *et al.,* 2019). Within this research line, the focus on religious diversity and school integration is quite underdeveloped and less consolidated in comparison with the other topics.

On the one hand, these studies highlight a condition of relational disadvantage for immigrant students, without clarifying the role of religious background. The loss of social capital due to recent migration may produce distress and tension among peers, and interethnic conflicts (Colombo, Santagati, 2010). These phenomena, however, are ascribed to variables such as social class or gender, but are rarely explained in ethnic, cultural, or religious terms. Pioneering research on this topic affirms that the religious issue is not explicit and is not dealt with in multi-cultural schools (Ottaviano, 2010).

On the other hand, research shows that students with an immigrant background also experience good-quality relationships with classmates and teachers, and they often do not declare relational difficulties within the classroom

(Besozzi *et al.,* 2009): in general, immigrant students place greater importance on the cognitive dimension of educational integration, whereas they are less concerned with schools as an arena for socialization.

The issue of discrimination and interethnic violence emerges in a couple of studies conducted in schools in Northern Italy (Delli Zotti, 2014). Although peer violence is a common problem, pupils see schools as safe places, since violence mostly happens outside school grounds. The comparison between teachers and students' perceptions of violence reveals the underestimation, on the adults' part, of the ethnic-racial motivations for bullying and other acts of prevarication, as well as the role of gender (males) and (low) social class as catalysts for episodes of school violence. Other studies confirm the diffusion of relational closure towards immigrants among natives, young males, disadvantaged or isolated students, students who have relational difficulties or are unsatisfied with their school environment (Barberis, 2016).

As in French studies, also in Northern Italy tensions among peers are more frequent in classes with a strong multi-culturality and many social problems, where there are low levels of peer exchange and reciprocal support. Specific measures against highly conflictual climates have been created by observing the offensive language used during instances of peer conflict, the development of negative attitudes towards diversity, and the presence of aggressive and violent behavior (Colombo, Santagati, 2014). The same studies also identify "the best school experiences", in which positive classroom climates seem to be characterized by the development of intergroup friendships. In this perspective, the highly multi-cultural institutes can also be interpreted as social contamination labs, multipliers of interethnic social capital, and spaces defining a mixed model of coexistence, in an atmosphere based on openness to diversity (Santagati, 2016).

Schools often offer spaces of (implicit or explicit) exchange in which identities, worldviews, similarities and diversities–also based on religious traits–play a crucial role, depending on the institutional, organizational, historical-cultural conditions (Benadusi *et al.,* 2017): the contradictory Italian frame is featured by the lack of awareness among teachers in managing controversies and dilemmas related to different religious traditions (Daher *et al.,* 2017). Moreover, religion and migration represent an ambivalent mix within the educational pathways of immigrant students (and not only for Muslims), and, at the same time, a stigma and a capital independently of the specific religious background (Ricucci, 2017).

A positive experience emerges from a research on the role of students' religiosity in school integration (Santagati *et al.,* 2019): this study shows that religiosity does play an important role as an integration factor, mainly because it fosters students' well-being, thus improving their relationships with peers and teachers and promoting their openness to interethnic exchanges. Religiosity appears as a lever to improve tolerance, respect, and intercultural sensitivity. These intercultural competences are experienced through everyday religious practices and lifestyles and are shared by pupils with different origins in schools with a high percentage of immigrants. In addition, religiosity positively affects school integration both for Italian and non-Italian students.

Other analyses reveal that young believers from different faiths appear quite open to religious diversities and are able to interweave interreligious relationships featured by pragmatism, reciprocity and respect between majority and minority groups: this attitude seems to be more difficult for non-Catholic students than it appears to be for Catholic ones, but it is not impossible (Bichi *et al.*, 2018).

4   The Religious Nature of Conflicts at School: Research Questions

An overview of the international and Italian studies highlights that religion is still neglected in educational and migration studies, and its role is scarcely considered to analyze the integration process of students with an immigrant background. Especially in Italy, school failure and interethnic conflicts are phenomena that are rarely explained or interpreted by religious factors. However, as pointed out before, religion is often considered a black box of phenomena that are socially and culturally constructed, and it is important to avoid any simplification of the religious issues, considering the effects of the intersection of class, gender, ethnicity, religion, and other factors on educational trajectories (Farris, de Jong, 2014).

The lack of studies invites scholars to examine the role of religion in multicultural schools, especially in producing conflicts or fostering dialogue, affecting relational well-being of students, influencing or preventing violence in the school environment. Our study, based on 14 focus groups involving adults (teachers, school leaders, and parents) and students attending lower secondary schools (as presented before in Chapter 21), try to deepen these issues, in order to describe, analyze and interpret the effect of religious backgrounds on classroom interactions in terms of intergroup tensions and friendships characterizing the school climate.

The research aims at deepening the issue of religious conflict in the classrooms and gathering empirical evidence about the role of religion diversity in educational integration in multi-cultural Italian schools:

a)   exploring the relevance of religion within interethnic relationships in public schools;

b)   mapping the religious conflicts within multi-cultural schools, through students' and adults' narratives;

c)   facilitating the punctual narration of conflictual events and episodes in order to distinguish motivations, actors, evolving dynamics, and identify words, attitudes, behaviors emerging in conflictual situations, analyzing more in-depth elements which define conflictual and contrasting situation;

d)   examining if religion is a triggering factor of interethnic conflicts; observing the religious differences in classrooms and the reactions of adults and students to conflicts;

e)   collecting explanations of religious-based conflicts from the different points of view of students and adults.

In the following sections, we are concentrating on the third part of the focus group grid dedicated to religious conflict at school, regarding the discussion on narratives, feelings, and opinions about religious-based disagreements or tensions. The items used in the focus group are three. From the point of view of pupils, the discussion takes in consideration:

a)   the reconstruction of a list of religion-based conflict involving themselves or classmates;

b)   how they react and cope with conflicts, how they manage such conflicts or how they would like to;

c)   the collection of narratives about religion fights, remembering and sharing words, attitudes, gestures.

From the point of view of adults, the focus group includes:

a)   the (in)direct observation or the knowledge of religion-based conflicts at school;

b)   the way they react and behave facing conflictual situations, what duties they have and what choices they make or would make;

c)   the collection of negative school memories and stories of fights for religious affiliations, considering teasing, bullying, and mentioning verbal and physical fights and their evolution.

Finally, the dimensions of the theoretical scheme used in this book (cf. Part 1 and Chapter 21) help us to reconnect the analysis to some key questions:

–   How the claim for the expression of the religious minorities' *identities* become a matter for religious school conflict?

–   Are religious frictions and tensions among students with different religious backgrounds connected to different degrees of *freedom* and autonomy of students from adults' control?

- Could religion-based conflict and religious discrimination be linked to majority-minority group contrasts, to power disparity, and unequal opportunities in terms of *rights of citizenship*?
- Are conflictual dynamics compatible with tolerant and civil coexistence in multi-religious school environments? How schools become a *common space* in which diversities are combined, shared and transformed in the integration process?

These important questions lead us through the presentation of the results of the research, pointing out the differences and the similarities in the narratives of people from different generations with different cultural and religious backgrounds.

5 Research Results: the Point of View of Students, Teachers, School Leaders, and Parents on Religious-Based Conflicts

In the following sections, we are going to present some results deriving from the content analysis realized by the software Nvivo. We have carried out an *initial coding* of the discussions deriving from the 14 focus groups (§5.1), basically by looking for the description of the school conflicts and the main characteristics of these events narrated by students and adults (map/list of mentioned conflicts; actors involved and their role; kind of conflicts, such as among peers, teacher-student conflict, parents-teacher conflict, etc.; space-time coordinates; religious identities emerging during school conflicts).

Then, we will summarize this analysis through a process of *focused coding*, more precisely by identifying the kind of narratives developed to describe conflicts (§5.2), the variability of conflicts (escalation from verbal to physical harassment, gradation, duration, etc.), the level of importance attributed to religion, the three components of conflicts (words, attitudes, behaviors), the reaction to and the management of conflict.

Finally, we arrive at an *interpretative coding*, elaborating the idea of religion as one of the core variables (mean or end) of school conflicts, identifying material/realistic and cultural/symbolic explanations (cf. Stephan, Stephan, 2000) that underpins the previous in-depth analysis of religious tensions (§5.3).[3]

---

3 For the different types of coding in qualitative research, cf. Charmaz (2006).

TABLE 23.1   Number of conflicts mentioned in focus groups by students or adults

FG students	No. conflicts mentioned	FG adults	No. conflicts mentioned
1 BS	10	1 BS	2
2 BS	3	2 BS	3
3 BS	3	3 BG	2
4 BG	3	4 MI	4
5 MI	3	5 MI	1
6 MI	1	6 MI	2
7 MI	0	7 MI	1

SOURCE: AUTHOR'S PERSONAL ELABORATION

5.1   *The Description of Conflict*

Thanks to the open coding realized through Nvivo, we can observe that each focus group (hereafter FG[4]) involving students or adults has a 15–16% coverage of the total discussion regarding school conflicts. The attention dedicated to exploring conflicts is not similar, in terms of time and mentioned examples, among FGs with adults or students. Moreover, there is not a correspondence between FGs conducted in the same schools with adults or students with respect to the importance given to the issue of religious conflicts. For example, the part about conflict is quite developed in FG4-BG-st, and it is particularly important in FG2-BS-ad, 4-MI-ad, and 5-MI-ad.

Students mentioned a list of 23 examples of conflicts, while adults referred to 15 cases. FG1-BS-st is featured by a very high number of episodes of conflicts, with respect to the other FGs with students and adults: we have to take in consideration that it is the most participated FG (with 14 students) and that it has the highest number of Muslim participants (6 students) among all FGs. We have to remember that FGs with students are multi-religious and multi-cultural in the participants' composition, while adults' FGs are more homogenous with a majority of Italian, Catholic (and females) participants.

Most conflicts mentioned by students are peer conflicts (19), while few other actors seem to be involved in religious-based tensions in the narratives of students: there are only some cases of a discussion between a Muslim student and a teacher; a friction between a Muslim father and the teacher of his

---

4   Focus groups have been codified in the following quotes by number (i.e. FG1), school province (i.e. FG1-BS), kind of participants (i.e. FG1-BS-st for students, FG1-BS-1-ad for adults).

daughter; two cases of religious conflicts are reported from news on television and concern the opposition parents-sons or conflicts among adults. In FG 7-MI-st no conflicts are mentioned.

Almost all the religious conflicts narrated by the students are conflicts that they have witnessed directly (21): in 5 cases, Muslim students reported cases in which they have been victims of religious bullying. Even if these mentioned episodes occurred mainly within school environment and classrooms, in 6 cases students referred to extra-scholastic contexts (oratory, neighborhood streets, television). In 14 cases of the 21 mentioned episodes, students deal with events that take place in the present, while past conflicts are narrated especially by Muslim students, victims of negative religious-based events occurred at school: referring to the past represents a way to make a narrative distance from painful situations.

Students provide a differentiated description of religious identities emerging during school conflicts: although, in most cases, conflicts are developing between Muslim students and the other classmates with no specified religious identity (12 cases), there are individual identities and affiliations that appear, indicating: interreligious conflicts (Muslims-Catholics; a case of Muslim Pakistani *versus* Indian Sikh) as intra-religious conflicts (among Catholics, Muslims, Protestants), majority-minority conflicts (Catholic students –majority faith group– *versus* a classmate with a different religious-minority identity); conflicts between atheists and believers; integralist and soft believers (among Catholic, Protestant, Muslim students); practicing and non-practicing students.

Although the religious majority identity of the classroom is not always explicit, there are different cases in which classmates identify a single student representing the religious alterity in the classroom as a victim of teasing and joking: i.e. the case of a Hindu student or a Jehovah's Witnesses student. In some episodes, this hetero-attribution of a religious identity does not correspond to truth and is used only to hurt a weak classmate: a student, son of a Muslim father and a Catholic mother, which is defined Muslim although he is Catholic; a Thai girl teased as Buddhist, even she is Catholic.

The list of conflicts mentioned by adults during the focus groups is more differentiated, if we consider the actors involved: 6 cases consist in peer conflicts involving students; 5 are conflicts between female teachers and Muslim students (only in one case we have a disagreement between a teacher and a Jehovah's Witnesses student); 3 frictions in the school-family relationship concern the fact that teacher perceive Islam as an impediment to gender equality, reporting experiences with Muslim fathers that prevent girls from participating in school activities or impose the veil. It is also mentioned a case of a mediatized contrast among school leaders of the same territorial area about religious symbols and ceremonies (Crib, Christmas party, Crucifix, etc.).

TABLE 23.2   Religious-based conflicts emerging from FGs with students

N.	Quotes from students' FGs[a]
1	When I arrived in Italy, my Italian classmates did not say anything. After a while they started making fun of me. First, I didn't say anything, but they continued … One day, there were four, but I was bigger than them: I beat them up. (Male, Senegalese, Muslim, FG1-BS-st)
2	I don't remember when it happened, I remember that two classmates and friends were involved, a Muslim and a Christian. They wanted to go out, but the Muslim said "No, I have to go to the mosque" and then the quarrel started. "Come on, you don't care about it", said the Christian, and the Muslim reacted. (Female, Italian, Catholic, FG1-BS-st)
3	One day I went out with my cousin and a friend, they didn't know each other. My cousin wants to become a priest and my friend is an atheist. I don't remember what happened, but my friend cursed, and my cousin got angry. They started fighting, almost slapping each other. (Male, Italian, Catholic, FG1-BS-st)
4	Two Christian classmates started arguing and fighting: one usually does not go to church, while the other goes. The non-practicing student told the other not to go to church anymore. (Female, Italian, Catholic, FG1-BS)
5	Last year there was a student who was half Thai and half Italian, she was Christian. Three or four classmates made fun of her, they told her she was Buddhist. (Male, Italian, Catholic, FG1-BS-st)
6	There was a boy who has a Muslim father and a Spanish mother. One classmate told him "You are a mix" and has continued naming him so. Maybe he teased him because he has parents of different origins, but he is baptized. (Female, Italian, Catholic, FG1-BS-st)
7	Often my classmate makes signs with his hands … he also used to swear (Male, Senegalese, Muslim). I saw some of my classmates who made the sign like ISIS, dressed like ISIS, they put here (points at the face) a kind of band and started doing so: TRRR (machine-gun noise). TRRR (laughter). Against the whole class usually, to tease students from different religions. One of my friends is Pakistani, they point towards her. (Female, Moldovan, Orthodox, FG1-BS-st)
8	That atheist friend of mine, when he sees my cousin or other very Christian people, does this to them (simulates a gesture of prayer). If he sees Muslims, he lies down. He looks at them with contempt. (Male, Italian, Catholic, FG1-BS-st)

N.	Quotes from students' FGs[a]

9   In our classroom, there was a boy who teased a girl because she was a Muslim. He continued for a long time, so the teacher made him feel like the girl, she teased him about his Christian faith. He said a swearword and the teacher repeated it, saying "how would you feel if I told you this bad word?" (Male, Italian, Catholic, FG1-BS-st)

10   Last year there was a Muslim girl in our classroom. She was always silent, a good girl, but everything would happen in the classroom, like stolen things or disappeared, the classmates accused her that it was her religion that told her to do those bad things. She was shy, closed, she didn't know how to defend herself, sometimes she cried. (Male, Italian, Catholic, FG1-BS-st)

11   In primary school, a girl got angry with me, maybe for something I hadn't even done. She said to the others: "You don't have to talk to her, because if you talk to her, I will not be your friend anymore". I said nothing and I continued staying with the ones who loved me. Slowly they understood that I had done nothing wrong and they forgot everything. (Female, Indian, Hindu, FG2-BS-st)

12   Some guys are bullies. I wanted to play with them, but they stayed away from me because I was a Muslim. Once, one of them shoved me and I punched him. There were problems, he got hurt: however, he was weaker than me and I couldn't resist. (Male, Senegalese, Muslim, FG2-BS-st)

13   Once I heard in the TV that someone had hurt a person because they were Muslim (Female, Italian, Catholic). Yes ... Moroccans who kill people, just because they are of another religion and not Muslim.
     Q: But where happens? Among Moroccans, ISIS ... they say they are Muslims. (Male, Senegalese, Muslim, FG2-BS-st)

14   In the oratory, a friend spoke in a negative way of my religion and I got angry.
     Q: And what was he telling you? I won't tell you, bad things. (Male, Senegalese, Muslim, FG3-BS-st)

15   In the classroom, when we talk about religions, there is a Muslim classmate who says that Muslim women must wear a veil by force. The teacher always expresses her disagreement. (Female, Italian, Catholic, FG3-BS-st)

16   In primary school, there was a Muslim boy who beat another who was a Sikh. Someone told me about them, but I knew they used to beat each other frequently, because one was from one religion and the other from another.

TABLE 23.2   Religious-based conflicts emerging from FGs with students (*cont.*)

N.	Quotes from students' FGs[a]
	Q: Were they of the same nationality? No, one was Pakistani, one Indian. There were always religious hostilities between them. (Female, Italian, Catholic, FG3-BS-st)
17	In my case, we argued about religion. A classmate told me "Moroccan with this veil made of sh…". She teased me because I put the veil and because I am Moroccan. I was in primary school; it was not such a happy past. This classmate and others made fun of me, but I pretended not to hear, and I ignored them, waiting for them to stop. (Female, Moroccan, Muslim, FG4-BG-st)
18	My dad wanted me to put the veil, but my teacher in primary school was against this idea and then there was a quarrel between her and my dad. When I was six years old, I was not able to choose, but after I had understood … my dad didn't insist. (Female, Moroccan, Muslim) Perhaps the teacher wanted to take her defenses … about the veil, on the TV news sometimes we heard about girls who don't want to put the veil on and their parents hurt them. (Male, Italian, Catholic) I also agree with him: the choice of religion is a personal choice and it should not be imposed by parents. (Female, Italian, Catholic) But my parents didn't impose me anything. It was my choice, my mom explained to me it was a choice I had to make … certainly it is not a decision of my parents. (Female, Moroccan, Muslim, FG4-BG-st)
19	I have never seen a dispute between parents and sons about religion, maybe on TV I heard something about this … On the TV news, you hear about Muslims more than Christians … I never hear about Christian parents that order their son to go to Mass, and if he does not go, they beat him up. (Male, Italian, Catholic, FG4-BG-st)
20	My friends tease me because I must go to Mass, because it is important for me as it is for my parents. I have to go to Mass; I have to go to catechism class and my friends insult me: "What are you going to do? It is a waste of time". My friends come to the oratory, but mostly for fun and to be troublemakers. (Male, Italian, Catholic, FG5-MI-st)
21	First, that guy came, and I pushed him away. Later he came back, with their friends. He threatened my friend, telling him not to talk about his religion anymore. When my friend wasn't there, I told him that he didn't have to discriminate other people for their ideas because sometimes the religion we profess comes from our parents. (Male, Romanian, Orthodox, FG5-MI-st)

N.	Quotes from students' FGs[a]
22	We have discriminated a girl, a Jehovah's Witnesses. I have a classmate: he is a hacker ... he took videos where she sang and put them on YouTube ... and then we removed her from our WhatsApp group. Many of our classroom laughed. When the fact came out, we were in trouble. We discussed it at school even with our teacher and she and we were uncomfortable. (Male, Italian, Catholic) Q: Before, you said that we excluded her because she is the only one of another religion. Right? Yes ... she is Italian. She is not a very nice girl, her behavior is not so good, moreover she belongs to another religion. (Male, Italian, Catholic, FG5-MI-st)
23	There is a classmate who is a bit stupid, he teased and made fun of our Muslim classmate ... I don't know what he said to him. (Female, Italian, Catholic) He made jokes playing with the word Muhammad. (Male, Italian, Atheist) And obviously our Muslim friend got offended ... (Female, Italian, Catholic) We were going back to the classroom and we saw the Muslim classmate holding the other by the neck and dragging him for the whole class. (Male, Italian, Atheist). Because he is an impulsive boy. (Female, Italian, Catholic, FG6-MI-st)

a   Each quote from FG is ended referring to the main characteristics of the speaking participant: for students gender, nationality, religious belonging, FG code; for adults, gender, role (Parent, Teacher, School Leader), religious belonging and nationality in the case of foreign parents, FG code. In the FG quotes, sometimes we used the letter Q that stands for Question posed by the FG moderator.

SOURCE: AUTHOR'S PERSONAL ELABORATION

The religious conflicts are narrated mainly by teachers and by some school leaders; only in one case a mother reported an experience lived by her daughter. Adults referred only to recent school conflicts, in which they are not directly involved (except for few cases): they told about fights among students, episodes narrated to them by students, negative experiences of colleagues, disagreement with Muslim parents. In general, they are not the main actors of these conflicts.

Adults do not give, as students do, a differentiated Religious identities emerging during school conflicts: in many cases (10 out of 15), conflicts are developing between Muslim students (or parents) and the other classmates, students, teachers with a not-declared Catholic identity. Often, the division is between "we" (probably Catholics, the majority, autochthonous, non-immigrants, etc.) and "they" (mainly Muslims, the minority, foreign-born, immigrants, etc.). Only in few cases do adults refer to other religious identities (Orthodox, Sikh, Jehovah's Witnesses): no reference to intra-religious conflicts between practicing and non-practicing believers, no reference to spread atheism appear (see Garelli, 2016). The adults' view seems a simplified and dichotomist vision of religious diversities at school: majority and minority faith groups, religion of autochthonous and religion of immigrants.

The results of the "Word Frequency Query" carried out by Nvivo have provided a first description of conflicts and have shown that students have a wide vocabulary to discuss conflict: in their FGs, they use words that refer to the form of the conflict (bad words, curses, discussion, insult, etc.) and words concerning feelings and emotions experienced at the beginning and during the controversies (anger, fear, antipathy, etc.). Students also mention some distinctive elements that appear relevant in the context of conflict (i.e. veil, skin color, etc.) and explicit some phenomena that influence negatively the interreligious relationships (prejudice, racism, terrorism and violent radicalism). We can also underline that "freedom" and "woman" are words that are used very often and that turn out to be significant for describing the conflict dynamics from the students' point of view.

As far as adults are concerned, they use words that refer more generally to the form of the conflict (such as problems, difficulties, discussion, etc.); for them, the issues of "woman" (and "veil") and "freedom" are particularly connected to conflict mechanisms; they also introduce a special attention to "integration", while negative attitudes and behaviors are used very few times (i.e. annoyance, mistrust, violence, contempt).

The difference between students' and adults' narratives about conflict can be seen in a relevant gap in the frequency of the use of the words: "freedom" (125 times among students versus 59 among adults) and "woman" (227 among adults versus 33 among students). In the in-depth analysis that will be developed in the following sections, we will see that these are two different interpretative perspectives of the conflict adopted by two different generations:

– The youngest, whose discussions are focused on the issue of freedom to choose one's religion, central in the construction of their own identity, of their educational projects, and of their life plans. In the students' narratives about conflict, the crucial question is the possibility of a free choice of one's religious belonging, independent of the control, the constraints and the imposition of adults;

– The adults' perspective, on the other hand, is mainly focused on the "women" issues, namely gender gap, gender inequality, gender violence (we know that among the adults participating in the FG, as already mentioned,

TABLE 23.3 Religious-based conflicts emerging from FGs with adults

N.	Quotes from adults' FGs

1   Her classmates started to make fun of my daughter, because they heard of Muslims, of ISIS ... a boy said to her "Hey, shut up, you Orthodox!" My daughter replied: "Look, my religion and yours are the same, Christian religions. The boy fell silent. When she came back home, I asked her why the discourse about Orthodox came out. She said that this boy said: "I send Isis to your home" and she answered. (Mother, Moldovan, Orthodox, FG1-BS-ad)

2   Once I scolded a boy for his indiscipline. He told me: "You say that words to me because you are Italian and Catholic". I fell silent, but a girl of Moroccan origin rose up. He also said: "I swear by the Koran", she said to him: "First of all, you don't have to swear because right now you don't deserve to approach to the Koran. In this classroom, do not address in that way to the teacher, who has never given proof of treating us as foreigners or of having anything against us because we are foreigners. In this moment she scolds you because you are rude and that's it. (Female, Italian Teacher, FG1-BS-ad)

3   There was a Muslim boy who always wanted to stay in the classroom during the Religion hour with me. Sometimes I accepted him, but the parents told me they did not want him to be there ... Now he told me that they decided that he could stay, next year. (Female, IRC Teacher, FG2-BS-ad)

4   It is annoying to hear teachers who say "we and them", talking about their students. It means that there are still barriers, they are not all your students, but there are Italian students and the others. I repeat, there are isolated cases, I am not generalizing, but it happens. In the case I remember, the religious identity of the teachers was very strong, so it was precisely "we Christians and Catholics and they who are not". These are not serious things, but I perceive a mental closure. (Female, Teacher, in charge of intercultural activities, FG2-BS-ad)

5   Last year I had a perfectly integrated Muslim pupil born in Italy, without linguistic problems, with a good family. But he was very problematic in terms of behavior, heavy to bear even for his classmates. One day he said to me: "My classmates don't want to play with me because I'm Muslim!". All his classmates turned towards him and one reacted: "What are you saying? I don't remember if you are a Muslim ... you are a nuisance, for this reason we don't want you!" (Female, Teacher, in charge of intercultural activitsies, FG2-BS-ad)

TABLE 23.3   Religious-based conflicts emerging from FGs with adults (*cont.*)

N.	Quotes from adults' FGs
6	I had two Indian pupils belonging to different castes in the same classroom. They could not talk together. It was very difficult to distinguish the religious factor from the cultural factor, but this was the situation. (Mother/Teacher, Italian, Catholic, FG3-BG-ad)
7	This year I witnessed some quarrels but, in my opinion, these were not religious-based conflicts. Some students told me: "But this girl has offended my God, she has insulted Him". But it was a quarrel born out of other reasons and, after that, the religious factor intervenes. (Female, Italian Teacher, FG3-BG-ad)
8	In this case, we can talk about a generational conflict. For the two Muslim girls who wear the veil, the choice was conditioned by the parents. From my point of view, there was also a conflict between the father and the teaching staff, that pointed out the potential of these girls in the educational field ... Regarding the veil, the two girls accepted it. Instead, the youngest sister, also attending our school and with a strong character, said to a colleague that the veil bothered her. (Female, IRC Teacher) She does not bear it. Every five minutes she goes to the bathroom, I think she wants to take it off. (Female, Italian teacher, FG4-MI-ad)
9	I would give you an example of my experience, when I was a teacher myself. It was not a problem linked to immigration, but to religious differences. I remember a girl who was a Jehovah's Witness, I was explaining the Greek mythology and she wrote me a note asking if I could exonerate her because she was against polytheism. I obviously explained to her the difference between a mythological tale and a religious indoctrination ... Her classmates made fun of her, because they considered it a bit naïve. (Female, School Leader, FG4-MI-ad)
10	A Catholic boy says: If they are here, we should remove the crucifix from the classrooms; but if we go there, they do not do so. They have freedom here, if we go there, we don't have the same freedom. We must adapt to their life style and therefore they too must adapt ... if we go there, we must follow their rules, while we leave them free not to follow them. (Male, Italian Teachesr, FG4-MI-ad)

N.   Quotes from adults' FGS

11   Last year there was a controversy because a school principal in this area had decided to boycott the Christmas party. The fact was reported in the newspaper and I remember that a journalist had interviewed me. I think it is not a question of making a crusade for the maintenance of religion, but there are simply symbols of the tradition that have to be respected and preserved. It is sad also to see those who make the crusades to remove all the symbols that distinguish us, as if neutrality was the solution. Instead neutrality per se does not exist ... I am also amazed by those who, facing this wide immigration especially from Muslim lands, want to make a crusade for their own religion. (Female, School Leader) ... In my opinion whoever removes the symbols, does this choice to provoke. We do not make the crib, we do not do the Christmas party, this is a provocation. (Male, Italian Teacher, FG4-MI-ad)

12   We had the case of an Islamic student, who lived her religion as an imposition, she wanted to integrate but could not, because she had an extremist father. He accompanied her to school, she took a step behind him, she could not be equal, she could not do physical education, she could not remove the veil in the classroom, she could not play music, she could not watch movies. The nice thing was that he had found solidarity because she took off her veil in her classroom. She couldn't do homework because she had to study the Koran two or three hours, then she had to do housework. We fought because her father decided to fix the marriage of his daughter. She had to go to her country of origin to get married. She said "I don't want to get married and with a man older than me". We managed in some way, in collaboration with the social services, to conclude lower secondary school with the exam, but unfortunately after she disappeared. (Male, IRC Teacher, FG5-MI-ad)

13   An Italian-Brazilian student, who lives alone with his father, abandoned by his mother asks a Maghreb girl of Islamic origin for her vote. There is a certain frustration with respect to school results and, perhaps, mutual competition. The girl does not answer to him, so the boy begins to insult her heavily: "you are a terrorist", "you have it black because you give it to everyone", "you Muslim, have to stay in your country". The girl replies: "you tell me so, you who are son of a Brazilian woman?" (Male, School Leadesr, FG6-MI-ad)

TABLE 23.3   Religious-based conflicts emerging from FGs with adults (*cont.*)

N.	Quotes from adults' FGs
14	In my school there was a conflict between a teacher and a Muslim girl, with mutual recriminations about religious practices, way of dressing, reciprocal intolerance. The teacher declared to be openly intolerant towards other ethnic groups and acted to defend her idea. The behavior of the teacher and the student seemed inappropriate. The student, though insulted, reacted with the same violence. The group class has taken the defense of the girl, seen as a victim and discredited the teacher who was a substitute teacher. (Female, School Leader, FG-6-MI-ad)
15	An Italian student has targeted a Muslim classmate, until the point of tear off her veil with contempt. (Female, Italian Teacher, FG-7-MI-ad)

SOURCE: AUTHOR'S PERSONAL ELABORATION

women are overrepresented). Religion, by the adults' groups, is represented, in the gender conflict, as an instrument of domination by men over women and as a justification of women's submission to men's power and control.

5.2   *The Analysis of Different Kind of School Conflicts*

From the point of view of adults, religious-based conflicts are collocated in continuum, from "light conflicts" (verbal conflicts, as joking, teasing), often corresponding to problematic attitudes (intolerance, contempt, etc.), to even more "serious conflicts" (bullying, physical violence, etc.). Considering the different kinds of conflict, peer conflicts through adults' words are an escalation of teasing, provoking, offending, silencing, not bearing, insulting, getting angry, exasperating. The violence is mainly a verbal violence and harassment, expressed through shouted words, strong and intolerant language. Among the narrated episodes, only one includes a violent behavior (tearing off the veil of a Muslim classmate, cf. Table 23.3 n. 15).

Between students and teachers, we can observe some disagreements concerning the influence of religious belief on the lifestyle and study choices of Muslim girls (as we have previously commented in the analysis of word frequency query results (§5.2). (Female) teachers report stories of reciprocal accusation, insinuation, rudeness, delegitimization, and lack of respect by students and parents of different religious background (mainly Muslim) towards them. In one case, there is a distinction between "we Catholics" – teachers

TABLE 23.4   Word frequency query concerning conflict and problems in relationships

Word – FG students	Word count	Word – FG adults	Count
Conflict	149	Woman	227
Freedom	125	Conflict	156
Word, Swearword, Curse	59	Problems	122
Veil	46	Difficulties	79
Problems	39	Veil	67
Anger	39	Freedom	59
Woman	33	Integration	48
Discussion	27	Discussion	39
Color	23	Words	35
Prejudice	23	Color	9
Racism	23	Annoyance	9
ISIS / Terrorism	22	Mistrust	8
Antipathy	20	Violence	8
Fear	18	Insult	7
Insult	15	Contempt	6

SOURCE: AUTHOR'S PERSONAL ELABORATION

with closed religious identities –and "them"– students of other religions. In school-family conflicts, dilemmas on religious symbols appear (whether to hang crucifixes or not; whether to put up Nativity scenes at Christmas or not; whether to celebrate Christmas with a party or not, etc.). In these cases, the discussions often concern religion as an imposition by Muslim fathers to daughters, with negative implications for school and life choices: female teachers remark their negative opinion and aversion toward these behaviors. At stake there are different world views, different ideas about the role of women in school and society, sometimes a different treatment at school of students with a different migrant or religious background (Dronkers, Kornder, 2015).

From the analysis of the three main components of religious-based conflicts narrated by adults (Table 23.5), we can point out that there is a correspondence between words and attitudes emerging in conflictual situation (Santagati, 2014: 197). Conflicts appear mainly as verbal quarrel or dispute (see conflict

TABLE 23.5   Words, attitudes, behaviors emerging in religious-based conflicts from FGS with adults

N. Conflict	Words	Attitudes	Behaviors
1	Teasing, insults, quarrel	Simplification, stereotyping	Go home (look for parent support)
9	Teasing, misunderstanding	Prejudice, misinterpretation	Dedicated lesson
11	Discussion, quarrel, dispute	Provocation	Boycott Christmas party
7	Quarrel, curse	Aggressiveness	Look for teacher support
4	Distinction "we and them"	Closure toward religious diversity	Physical distance
2	Scolding, complaint, blame	Playing the victim	Discriminatory treatment
5	Complaint, quarrel	Playing the victim	Unbearable, problematic behavior
8	Complaint, disagreement	Resistance, patience	Wear or not the veil
10	Complaint, dispute	Provocation, lack of reciprocity	Repeated discussion
3	Refusal	Closure of parents	Attend or not IRC
12	Refusal	Extremism, control	Support to conclude Sec School
6	Not talking together	Prohibition, traditionalism	Remain astonished
13	Verbal violence, sexist language	Frustration, competition	Educational failure
14	Recrimination, dispute	Intolerance	Students against substitute teacher
15	Verbal violence	Arrogance, prevarication	Tear off her veil

SOURCE: AUTHOR'S PERSONAL ELABORATION

nn. 1, 4, 7, 9, 11), including teasing, naming, insults (and sometimes curses), controversies, linked to specific ways and attitudes towards religious diversity. In these quarrels, adults discuss:

- Dynamics of simplification and stereotype use concerning religious belonging and identity;
- Provocations triggered by the (ab)use or the refusal of religious symbols and signs;
- Misunderstandings/misinterpretation, confusion between cultural contents of subjects of study and religious indoctrination;
- Presence of close-minded adults that behave differently towards people and pupils depending on other religious background;
- Mental, discursive and physical barriers created to foster insiders-outsiders distinction also in the educational field, as in the access to relevant social knowledge (Merton, 1972).

The analysis of "words" expressing conflict in the narrative of adults, reveal various cases of complaint, disagreement, recrimination and disputes (conflicts no. 2, 5, 8, 10, 14), especially in wide dynamics involving students, classmates, teachers (and sometimes other adults). Some students, in these situations, decide to "play the victim" in order to look for justifications and legitimization of their bad behavior, accusing classmates and teachers of discriminating and treating them unjustly and unequally because of their different religious background. Other verbal disputes refer both to attitudes of resistance to family control and religious impositions on daughters, and of acceptance of conditioned choices concerning school, life, social participation of women; and to challenging attitudes of provocation concerning reciprocity, reciprocal adaptation, religious freedom in Italy and in the countries of origin of students with an immigrant background.

In the last group of conflicts mentioned by adults (no. 3, 6, 12–15), we have listened to and read the description of episodes of verbal violence including offenses, recrimination, verbal attacks, sexist language, ethnic and religious prohibitions and refusals. Insults often intersect and mix multiple offenses concerning religion, color, nationality, gender, etc. (recalling the interpretative intersectionality approach: Anthias, 2013). These are cases in which words are used as "guns" to hurt someone for his/her intolerable religious diversity. This violent language could be interpreted as a consequence of mental closure, violent extremism and radicalism linked to a traditionalist and conservative vision (Santagati *et al.,* 2017), which justifies unequal treatment of diversities, intolerance, frustration and competition among disadvantaged and low-performer students, arrogance and prevarication corresponding to forms of religious bullying (Beatbullying, 2008).

Adults briefly refer to the (real, imagined, wanted) reactions to face conflictual situations. Although they desire to demonstrate that school conflicts are under their control, in different cases teachers stay in silence, watching the reactions of peers in order to stop the conflicts in the classroom. In most cases, teachers intervene by starting open discussions during their lessons, by trying to facilitate dialogue among classmates, by proposing an exchange of views about religious diversity, clarifications in controversies and disputes, and by looking for cooperation with other educational agencies to prevent early school leaving of students discriminated or conditioned from their religious belonging (Bergamaschi, 2016).

In their aspirations, adults think it could be important to intervene to promote and defend respect for everything (people, culture, religion, etc. FG2-BS-ad), since the parents perceive this respect, and consequently can trust schools and teachers more. However, religion is not always considered crucial by teachers in the FGs: the idea they have of conflict prevention is to educate students from all the points of view, including the religious dimension (Cuciniello, 2017), stimulating the expression of specific religious identities, especially during their construction and definition (FG3-BG-ad), working on tolerance, openness to diversity, non-violent communication and emotional intelligence (FG 7-MI-adults). The ideal for teachers is to face conflict with adequate authority and punishment (bad conduct notes on their permanent record, suspension in more serious cases, etc.), restore order, listen to everyone's reasons, teach lessons on the conflictual matter (Sclavi, Giornelli, 2014): teachers will be conflict mediators working at school (Santagati, 2004) and this will give the two sides of the conflict the opportunity to listen to each other and listen to the reasons that led to a certain behavior, in order not to repeat it (FG-7-MI-ad).

From the students' point of view, the different type of conflicts depends on the insult gradation – "if they insult me a little, I don't react, but if they insult me a lot, I get angry" (Male, Pakistani, Muslim, FG-1-BS-st) or/and on the time duration – "if someone is teasing me, at the beginning I'm not angry, but if he continues for a long time I get angry" (Male, Senegal, Muslim, FG-1-BS-st). Students are very good at describing the escalation of conflicts, giving detailed tales of words, attitudes, behaviors emerging in conflictual situations.

Analyzing the three main components of religious-based conflicts narrated by students (Table 23.6), we can find several pronounced (and not pronounced) words that mark and characterize the conflictual climate among peers or the student-teacher interaction. Most conflicts are based on teasing a student with a different religious background (no. 1-5-6-8-9-22): teasing becomes more irritating when it includes verbal insults, attribution of false names and religious identities, laughs. The "perpetrators" do not seem to know that they are dealing with a delicate subject that can hurt the classmate designated as the "victim" very much. In fact, these verbal strategies refer to superficiality, antipathy, but also to contempt and harassing attitudes: practicing students or students from a minority faith group are victims of derision of their religious practice. Their

TABLE 23.6 Words, attitudes, behaviors emerging in religious-based conflicts from FGs with students

N. Conflict	Words	Attitudes	Behaviors
1	Teasing	Superficiality, derision	(Criticized) religious practice, fight
5	Teasing, false naming	Superficiality	Emphasis on diversity aspects
6	Continuous teasing, false naming	Superficiality	Emphasis on diversity aspects
8	Teasing, offense	Contempt	Simulation of gesture of prayer
22	Teasing, laughs, discussion	Harassing attitude	Exclusion, cyberbullying
9	Continuous teasing, bad words	Disrespectful attitude, no empathy	Scold of the teacher
3	Curse, offense	Provocation, aggressiveness	Fight, slaps
7	Swearwords	Provocation, harassing attitude	Simulation of terroristic action
10	Blame, false accusations	Provocation	Cry, inability to defend herself
17	Quarrel, swearwords	Provocation	Negative reaction to veiled girl
23	Quarrel, curse, offense	Group-centrism	Fight
20	Quarrel, insults	Group-centrism	(Criticized) religious practice
4	Quarrel	Group-centrism	(Criticized) religious practice, fight
2	Quarrel, dispute	Group-centrism	Aggressive reaction
15	Quarrel, dispute	Control, resistance	Wear or not the veil
18	Quarrel, dispute	Control, resistance	Restriction of women autonomy
11	Threat, refusal of interaction	Aggressiveness, sense of injustice	Exclusion from the classroom
21	Threat, refused communication	Arrogance, sense of injustice	Move and get away

TABLE 23.6   Words, attitudes, behaviors emerging in religious-based conflicts from FGs with students (*cont.*)

N. Conflict	Words	Attitudes	Behaviors
13	TV news: religious-based murders	Prejudice, stereotyping	Religious-based violence
19	TV news: parent-children dispute	Control, resistance	(Possible) religious-based violence
12	Unrepeatable words	Arrogance, prevarication	Physical distance, shove, punch
14	Unrepeatable words	Arrogance	Aggressive reaction
16	No words	Hostility	Fight

SOURCE: AUTHOR'S PERSONAL ELABORATION

religious diversity is stressed, diminished and criticized; phenomena of religious bullying (also in the version of cyberbullying occurring over digital devices like cell phones, computers, and tablets, in social media or in chats, etc.) take place (cf. Agirdag *et al.*, 2011; Llorent *et al.*, 2016). The exclusion of some students from the classroom because they are excessively different from the other classmates, as well as physical contrasts and fights, also happen as complements to quarrels, arguments, and negative attitudes. In this conflict, unfortunately, "some teachers do not even try to listen, and some others pretend to understand, even if they haven't understood and end up punishing who is in the right" (Female, Italian, Catholic, FG1-BS-st).

Sometimes, in conflicts described by students, teasing is associated to swearwords, curses and blasphemies, verbal offenses, insults, bad words, false accusations (no. 3-7-10-17-20): dynamics of provocation, aggressive and harassing attitudes, absence of empathy towards the teased victims, as well as provocative inclinations aimed at sparking conflicts appear. These negative orientations, on the one hand, often turn into fights, physical violence, worrying simulations of weapons' use (and terroristic attacks), as well as disrespect and disobedience to the teacher's authority. On the other hand, they also create the feeling of being defenseless, sad, isolated and lonely in the classroom.

Quarrels and disputes narrated by students (conflicts no. 2-4-15-18-20-23) introduce the interesting topic of group-centrism (Kent, Burnight, 1951), that is the idea that one's own culture is better than any other culture. This inclination, emerging from students' FGs, consists of evaluating other religious beliefs, practices, and affiliations from of one's own personal perspective, on which is based both the belief in the superiority of one's own group and the contempt for outsiders.

We call this attitude group-centrism, since it is exercised not only on an ethnic, religious, cultural (etc.) basis, but also by some groups towards other groups (Catholics *versus* Muslims; Atheists *versus* Catholics or Muslims; practicing *versus* not-practicing believers; etc.). Group-centrism is a crucial attitude to interpret continuous controversies in which at stake there is the inclusion of "one student" in the majority group of classmates (who are seen as similar, united, and strong). Such inclusion can be attained by avoiding causing the student to feel isolated, weak, or different because of his/her religious, ethnic and cultural belonging, identified as "strange" because of his/her behavior or their way of dressing.

By observing from the point of view of the younger generation, among the various disputes we can see some discussions about the controversial issue of autonomy and control on girls and women exercised by fathers and men through religious traditions and practices. This discourse adds further elements about how adolescents perceive themselves as a group (experimenting youth-centrism) in front of the group of adults (Maassen *et al.*, 1992). Students agree on the fact that the religious choice should be made freely and underline the importance of accepting and recognizing other religions. Accordingly, they are against adults who want to impose (sometimes in violent ways) choices concerning religion and highlight the need of being independent of adults and parents and of resisting to their impositions, with consequences on the physical and mental restriction of women's autonomy.

In conflicts no. 11 and 21, we can find verbal threats and accusations deriving from aggressive, provocative and arrogant attitudes. These episodes are characterized by an explicit refusal of the interaction with the "others" by members of the majority group, driven by the adoption of self-centered attitudes during the construction of a social act, which leads to conflict (in the constructionist view of Mead (Athens, 2012)). These classmates, sometimes, also refuse to communicate with a "super-diverse" victim, often fragile, and seen as not able to defend him/herself, or even not able to participate in the classroom relational dynamics because of his/her religious belonging. Among these last students, we can observe an increase in their perception of being treated unjustly by their classmates, of being discriminated for their religious ideas (without having done anything wrong). Sometimes they are beaten from the majority group, they suffer physical violence and harassment (almost absent in the stories of conflicts as told by adults), other times they experiment the exclusion from the classroom, with the indifference or the cruelty of the whole group.

In the last group of conflicts (no. 12-13-14-16-19), finally, the violence of religious-based conflicts increases even more in the narratives of students. In fact, because of the seriousness of those conflicts, they discuss the news broadcast on television (religious-based murders, parent-children violent disputes about religion choices) and they consider the verbal dynamics of conflict in which they are involved as controversies made of "unrepeatable bad words", hostile words, offenses to God or to the prophets (cf. Lipperini, 2018, about the project "Parole ostili" (hostile words)). We would like to point out that, in this kind of conflicts, a sort of religious-based violence is described. A violence motivated by or in reaction to religious belonging, practice or belief, a violence involving adults and young people caused by some religious aspects, a violence triggered by some religious features of the victims or of the attackers (Hall, 2013).

What are the reactions and the strategies used by students to face a conflictual situation? As in some other studies (Van Praag *et al.*, 2016), students tend to withdraw from classroom discussions and conflicts about religion where they feel that their values are different from those commonly expressed. As these young people from minority groups do not appear to receive a great support from peers or adults, they tend develop their own strategies of coping and survival, through silence, indifference and immobility, trying to hide their religious identity to stop the conflict, through passive waiting. In several cases, students show different emotional reactions: anger, sadness, annoyance, fear, irritability, displeasure, violence. Rarely do they talk about the mediation or the intervention of peers or teachers. In general, students think that sometimes it is necessary to involve teachers in the conflict management, while parents have to stay out of the conflict not to complicate the situation. Teachers have to talk to students trying to mediate and to explain the importance of the respect of others and the injustice of religious offense. Then, sometimes, to punish physical violence, they have to use the appropriate measures, such as school suspension, and most of all they have to give comfort to the victim.

> Teachers have to intervene without scolding those who made the insult and by giving comfort to the victim ... Maybe the student feels under pressure and does not want to profess his religion any longer ... Maybe the teacher's intervention can lead him fight the anxiety he has inside. (Male, Italian, Catholic, FG1-BS-st)

5.3   *Realistic or Symbolic? The Conflict Interpreted by the Focus Group Participants*

The last part of our analysis of school conflicts concerns the explanation and the interpretation that FG participants directly attribute to the role of religion in conflicts, and it takes in consideration different interpretative perspectives emerging from each FG.

For students, religious-based conflicts and disagreements are an important and personal matter, since it is linked to the construction and the definition of their cultural identity, in relation to their familiar history and to the migration experience. In this perspective, religion represents an important cultural dimension *per se*, since it deeply affects the development of the students' identity.

The importance of one's religion belonging appears from the fact that religious issues are used during conflicts to hurt students with a different religious background. In FG1-BS-st, we can clearly observe a vision of religion as a way of life or lifestyle (Berzano, 2011), a way to identify oneself. For this reason, religious-based threats and violence deeply hurt the personal identity: these offenses hit students in their most fragile and intimate dimension, targeting a (super)diversity sometimes considered as socially inassimilable or unacceptable. Religious belonging seems to represent, for students, the weakest point in their inclusion pathways: curses or insults, and other negative attack strategies on religious topics, mark a real distance and create a dramatic rupture in peer relationships. Religion is considered as a weapon that increases the chance of harassment and of suffering for vulnerable victims, implying the feeling of a perceived exclusion, especially when an attitude of contempt towards the other's religion emerges.

> My classmate makes fun of her because she belongs to a different religion. (Female, Moldovan, Orthodox)

> He was pointing at me, saying to the teacher that it was my fault, surely because I belong to another religion, they hit more those who are not Italian and who are not Catholics. (Female, Moldovan, Orthodox)

> I think the people who tease about religion don't really want to make fun of religion, they don't care. Religion is seen as a weapon to tease you even more with contempt. (Male, Italian, Catholic, FG 1-BS-st).

The description of the conflict dynamics provided by the adolescents, in fact, reflects the functioning mechanism of an apparently homogeneous group (in terms of religion, culture, language, clothing style, skin color, etc.: cf. FG-6-MI-st) that exercises its cruelty against a single student because of his/ her difference in religious terms. The majority group attacks students who appear distant and different from the group, expressing either indifference or ability to deny, exclude and reject this religious diversity. Classmates end up turning into "a pack of wolves that attack a vulnerable pray": this opposition between a group of students apparently similar in the religious background and one single student with a clear religious (Muslim) identity, gives evidence of the imbalance in relations crossing a multi-religious classroom, in which power disparity and majority supremacy is expressed and confirmed, identifying a target excluded by the group.

> Q: But what is the origin of this quarrel?
> This quarrel was born from the stupidity of people. (Female, Italian, Catholic)
> No, I think the cause of the quarrel was the religion, because they were friends. Given that religion is a way of identifying oneself, being teased about that topic can be annoying and I know well me too. I am an atheist and, in the classroom, they make all the stupid jokes and I can say that it is very irritating. I have never reacted to these things because I am not an impulsive boy. I must say, however, that there is a lot of aggregation of my classmates to the group of those who made fun of. They are like wolves that run in a pack, if you come off the pack then you are the target too. (Male, Italian, Atheist, FG6-MI-st)

Religion in some cases (FG-2-BS-st) is considered the primary cause of difference, difficulty (and deficit) of immigrant students, therefore provoking conflicts and religious bullying, given the spread of negative prejudice according to which immigrant pupils of other religions (especially Muslims) are naturally incapable and sometimes also intolerant, violent, extremist and terrorist.

> Q: What were these arguments about?
> They depend on my religion, sometimes on my color ... teachers divided us into groups to do something and if I wasn't able to do that, they would start telling me "she's not able to because she's Indian".
> Q: But to what did they refer?
> More to religion than nationality. Before, I couldn't really understand, now I understand. (Female, Indian, Hindu, FG2-BS-st)

Sometimes (i.e. FG-4-BG-st), religious and immigrant backgrounds are confused and mixed, thus representing together the usual issues used to create division and peer conflicts. The positive rhetoric of classrooms as united and cohesive groups, in which religious differences are not taken into account, seems to apply mainly to the majority faith group (of Catholics), while the students belonging to minority groups are discriminated do not have many friends.

> The quarrel started not because of religion, I do not talk about religion, I do not tease, I do not insult the religion of one of my classmates. It happened to me more because of the nationality issue. (Male, Italian, Catholic)

> In my opinion, as he said, there is no quarrel over religion or nationality, but afterwards there are people who always bring up those topics together and use religion, origin, nationality. (Male, Italian, Catholic, FG4-BG-st)

The discussion developed in the same FG-4-BG-st, however, points out the seriousness of religious-based conflicts, as they concern family identity, including religious, social, ethnic, cultural belonging. Religion, in fact, appears as a crucial and substantial element linked to familiar and collective identity. Religious conflicts are, for students, mainly identity conflicts, based on an identity divide involving the position of families towards religion. As we have previously discussed (§5.2), religious belonging is important because it concerns a central question in the growth of new generations: autonomy/independence from parents through a free acceptance or a refusal of religious identity of the family, on the one hand; religious impositions and control from parents in religious beliefs or practices, on the other. Indeed, the dichotomies continuity-discontinuity, tradition-innovation, conservation-change are constitutive of the social dynamics of socialization and education of new generations, of intergenerational relationships, of cultural and religious transmission, dilemmas which continue to accompany the evolution of social life (Arendt, 1972).

> Her parents made the right choice because it is her decision, in my opinion the religion must not be imposed. (Male, Italian, Catholic)

> As far as religion is concern, they must not force you because if you do not wear the veil, you do not do anything wrong. (Female, Kosovar Muslim)

> I also agree, the choice of religion is one's own choice and it should not be imposed by parents. (Female, Italian, Catholic, FG4-BG-st)

The link between religion and family is clarified even more in FG5-MI-st: students reiterate that discriminating for religious ideas is considered to be particularly unfair by new generations, because it is seen as a choice made by parents, just like the choice to immigrate. In general, we can state that students want to represent themselves as active and free in the transmission process of religious belief.

Do not discriminate other people for their religious ideas, because sometimes the religion we profess comes from our parents. For example, I am
an Orthodox, but I would like to become a Catholic as soon as possible. I
like being Orthodox, but I like more Catholic ideas ... do not discriminate
against people for their ideas and their religion because many times it is
not because they choose this religious, but their parents did. (Male, Romanian, Orthodox, FG5-MI-students)

As seen before, adults tend to minimize school conflicts, which are latent, not
very dangerous, temporary and not problematic: they affirm that the religious
issue does not seem to be very important and relevant at school; conflicts are
mainly a personal, intimate, relational, extra scholastic or eventually ethnic
matter that is connected to the adolescent dynamics of like-dislike or inclu-
sion-exclusion from a friends' group. From the point of view of adults, unim-
portant conflicts happen because it is all under adults' control.

For adults, moreover, religion is mainly a pretext and a justification for conflicts. Conflicts that are more dangerous are especially linked to immigration,
to a negative view of the immigrant and the problem they bring, to a non-
acceptance of migrant people, and to the fear of the Otherness. Diversity is
perceived as more static, strong, divisive and excluding, where it is based on
religious dogma (FG4-MI-adults).

In my opinion, there are conflicts linked to non-acceptance of the immigrant. So, in this frame, there have been and there are conflicts. Not in the
sense of non-acceptance because you are Muslim. Because if you are a
Muslim, I accept you, but if you are an immigrant, I begin to make a distinction. The strong conflict is that of immigration because of what students hear in their families. The climate is totally contrary to immigration
and therefore these guys, here, have these attitudes of difficulty ... the
immigrants come here to Italy and take something away from us. This is
a conflictual perspective, but I'll say more. Because of a personal experience, I had fights with colleagues since their idea was: "Couldn't they stay
at home instead of coming here to create a lot of problems?". (Male, Italian Literature Teacher, Italian, Catholic)

Q: But ... what about the religious factor?
In general, I believe the problem is the fear of difference and diversity
is probably perceived as more static where it has a religious dogma behind it. Perhaps it is this. (Female, Italian, School leader, Catholic)

Going back to the religious discourse, it depends on how much a boy feels or doesn't feel to be religious, and, consequently, he defends his idea based on this feeling ... I have not seen among boys any conflicts for religious reasons because I think that religion is a bit personal, there could be a discussion linked to the need of knowing the religion of the other; but this does not lead to a conflict. The religious difference does not generate a conflict ... The cultural diversity generates conflict. When I stop doing what I'm doing with you and I start praying somewhere else, excluding the others in the world. He is strong in other religions; he is much less strong in the Catholic religion, because I have never seen a Catholic say: "I will not go to school tomorrow morning because I must confess ... I have to go to Mass ... etc". (Father, President of parents' association, Italian, Catholic)

As we have seen before, conflicts from adults are mainly between individuals, but some collective identities are mentioned (Muslim identity or majority faith identity): conflicts arise especially when it is possible to identify visible aspects and religious symbols of the others (veil, traditional clothes, hat, etc.). A dilemma appears when extreme attitudes are shown: someone decides to make "a crusade" for the maintenance of the traditional/majority religion and its symbols; someone else tries to remove all the symbols that distinguish the national religious identity (FG-4-MI-ad). In both cases, religious neutrality seems impossible to reach, as a neutral attitude seems unreal, because religious differences need space to express themselves.

In general, for adults, cultural diversity generates more conflicts than religious diversity (FG-5-MI-ad): undoubtedly, a religious practice can affect relationships, having social/relational implications, namely excluding someone who does not share the same religious practices and create links with similar believers. However, when the religious belief is extreme and radical, it causes violent rejection of people with other religious background, and then it becomes a source of conflict. Religions lived as totalizing and closed ideologies create a social and cultural divide: in this perspective, more religion corresponds to less social integration.

When a religious belief becomes extreme, then it is a source of conflict. (Mother, Switzerland/African origin, Protestant)

More religion, less integration, because religion prevails over the main goal of creating a human community with shared human values. If religion presents a partial point of view, then there is the clash of civilizations, closure, religions become theocracies, become a modus vivendi and operandi, an obstacle for the formation of a true human and educational community. (Male, School leader)

Where there is extremism and radicalism there is no integration. (Male, IRC Teacher)

It's true. If religion is lived as a religion with all the symbols, with a brand, as a way of thinking, there is no dialogue. (Mother, Switzerland/African origin, Protestant, FG5-MI-ad)

In FG2-BS and 3-BG-ad, adults confirm a cultural explanation of school conflicts, which depend on the attitude of each student or teacher or parent. Often, the ethnic diversity in intergroup interactions led to the explosion of the conflict; later, religious diversity intervenes to increase the conflictual climate. Religion is an instrument (and not the cause) for school conflict, but the ideological manipulation and exploitation of religion make the conflict worse. Adults repeat that conflicts are generated mainly by group dynamics of sympathy or antipathy, majority-minority interactions, family habits, ethnic factors, etc. At the end of this list, teachers put the religious topic as a conflict generator in adult dynamics.

It is not the religion that creates barriers; in my opinion, religion is often exploited. This year, I have witnessed some quarrels that were not religious based. Students sometimes tell me: "My classmates have offended my God or have insulted him", but it was a quarrel born for other reasons, and only after that the religious factor intervensses. (Female, Italian Teacher)

The ethnic factor certainly intervenes in the conflict first; often, the religious factor intervenes only later, to make it even harsher. The students give that explanation, but the theme is not that. (Mother, Italian, Catholic)

If students ask not to be close to each other, the reasons are very different, it is not for religious reasons; it is more for sympathy or antipathy. (Male, Italian Teacher)

Perhaps, it is more for ethnicity than for religion. (Female, School leader)

Perhaps, this happens more among adults than among adolescents. (Male, Italian Teacher, FG3-BG-ad)

Finally, we give evidence to some considerations emerging in the discussion of FG6-MI-ad and FG1-BS-ad: non-religious causes are considered by the FG participants as the most important explanation of school conflicts. Conflicts are generated by competition for scarce resources, non-acceptance and recognition of the others, incommunicability and intolerance. This interpretation confirms that religion is only a pretext, a spark that makes the conflict explode. Religion diversity represents the most visible aspect of the conflict, but the triggering causes are based on the socio-economic divide between rich and poor people.

From the point of view of adults, the conflict is mainly a material and power conflict; teachers also recall the idea of a political and cultural colonization, based on the use of religions to justify oppression and abuses. The majority-minority contraposition, the native-immigrant divide, the gender gap, all the disparities can be explained in terms of unequal distributions of economic, social and power resources among the population, from the views of adult participants to FGs. Therefore, religion is seen as a cultural instrument to exacerbate the conflict in contexts marked by inequality and disparity.

> Religion is only the tool of insult and abuse. Religious difference could be a pretext. We have seen an ideological conflict that has developed in a verbal crescendo that becomes increasingly heavy. The cause is the non-acceptance of the other and his/her difference. Religious affiliation makes everything explode. It is a pretext, but the cause is another. (Male, School leader, FG6-MI-adults)

> During History and Geography classes, especially during the last year of lower secondary schools, when we face exploitation problems and conflictual perspectives, it is important to look for historical causes and to help students understand how religion has been exploited for political ends. It is also important to reconstruct the history of the Christian religion and other religions, to analyze the attempts of abuses and to carry forward the discourse of imperialism. (Female, Teacher, Italian, Catholic, FG 1- BS-adults)

6   Open Conclusions: Overcoming the Generational Cleavage, Recognizing Material and Identity Claims

Although students and adults agree with the opinion that religious identity is not very important in the school environment (Chapter 22), religious diversity is normally experienced, expressed, taken for granted, or hidden in multicultural

TABLE 23.7   Religious divide among generations

Students' narratives	Adults' narratives
Protagonists of conflict	Spectators in front of conflicts
Peer conflicts	Peer, teacher-student, teacher-parent conflicts
Verbal and physical violence	Verbal violence
Teasing, superficiality, derision	Dispute, controversies
Variety of bad words, offense, curses, provocation	Quarrel, verbal disagreement
Expression of feeling and emotions	Complaint and playing the victim
Religious-based bullying	Words as weapons
Group-centrism	Closure, insider/outsider distinction
Focus on degree of religious freedom from parents	Focus on the control of men on women through religion
Reference to prejudice, racism, extremism	Reference to integration
Strategy of ignoring conflict and hiding religious diversity	Representation of conflict under adults' control
Rare intervention and mediation of conflicts by adults	Silence or dedicated lessons as main strategies
Religious issue, important identity component	Religious issue as unimportant question at school
Cultural, religious and identity divide	Socio-economic and gender divide
Religion as independent dimension to express personal and collective identity	Religion as an instrument to exacerbate the conflict in contexts marked by inequality and disparity

SOURCE: AUTHOR'S PERSONAL ELABORATION

schools, and affects the educational process. Religion seems to become an educational and public matter, especially when conflicts appear. In this conclusion, it is interesting to synthesize briefly the different point of view of students and adults, in the description, analysis and interpretation of the religious-based conflict in classrooms. We try to summarize this analysis proposal in the following table.

First, the FGs' analysis highlights that the role of students is mainly that of *protagonists* of their narratives. They tell concrete and detailed stories, quite adherent to reality, offering a description of differentiated kind of conflicts in which they are directly involved. Moreover, students identify more cases of religious-based conflict than adults do. Adults give a simplified version of conflicts, referring to single episodes, to experiences told by colleagues or students, and to isolated and non-generalizable cases: they are mainly *spectators* in these events, while observing something considered to be not very dangerous or important.

The students' list of school conflicts includes a broader and a more differentiated series of conflicting experiences, above all referring to experiences between peers (intra and interreligious). They report detailed stories, highlighting verbal and physical violence, a religious-based violence motivated by religious belonging and belief of victim and/or perpetrators, violence that is almost absent from the stories of adults, who mostly talk about the use of "words as weapons". Conflicts are interpreted by students as a result of superficial attitudes and habits to make fun of classmates with a different religious background, using a large variety of provocative expression, curses, and blasphemies. The victims, often, refer to negative feelings and emotions, experienced during the conflict, shown a total and direct involvement.

Adults refer mainly to conflicts among students, but consider also teacher-student, teacher-parents' conflicts. They highlight, above of all, examples of verbal violence and lack of respect for their role. They describe a lot of disputes, controversies, quarrel and verbal disagreement, for example between Catholic teachers and Muslim students, female teachers and Muslim fathers, etc. In the conflictual situation, moreover, adults discuss cases of complaints and (false) accusation made by students, which are often "playing the victim": for adults, in fact, students cannot always be considered as victims of religious bullying or excluded or discriminated basing on their religious belonging. Perhaps, students use this issue looking for justification and excuses for their negative or problematic behaviors.

The conflictual situations are interpreted by students as group dynamics and attitudes that looks at the religion of others from the perspective (and the superiority) of their religion of belonging, while adults point out the closure of the majority (Catholic) group, making a clear distinction between insiders-outsiders.

It must be added that the main issue of the arguments, from the students' point of view, concerns freedom (and autonomy) in religious choice from their parents (as confirmed by the Word Frequency Query (see §5.1)), while for the adult participants in the FGs, mainly women, teachers belonging to the national and religious majority, the object of the dispute often concerns women's role in school and society. In the Word Frequency Query, moreover, students make several references to negative phenomena that affect interethnic and interreligious conflicts at school (such as prejudices, racism, extremism, radicalism, etc.); at the same time, teachers among adults refer mainly to the positive goal of integration in multi-cultural schools, which is a word that does not appear in any students' discussion.

Last but not least, to young people, religion represents an important cultural dimension *per se*, since it deeply affects the construction of students' identity. The religious component of the personal, social, and cultural identity is fundamental since it is connected to the story of the immigrant families and to the collective experience of transmission and socialization of culture and values from one generation to another. Instead, adults think that the religious issue is not so important and relevant, especially in the school environment.

Young people tend to distance themselves from an excessive and painful involvement in conflicts, using the strategy of ignoring religious attacks or fighting when they are stronger than classmates, but the main strategy is to stay (im)mobile and resist, waiting for the conflict to end, in a scene where adults are not very present or active. On the other hand, adults tend to minimize school conflicts, conflicts that are always represented under the control of teachers, adults, and educational institutions, with the illusion of playing an important educational role in preventing conflictual situations.

Finally, a sort of generational divide emerges from the different ways to read and interpret religious-based conflicts at school. For adults, the socio-economic issue (inequalities) relating to immigration (and to women's condition) provides the main reason: religion is a pretext for the conflict, as well as the most visible and manifest aspect, legitimized and culturally accepted, to justify the division between groups. Religion is the fuse that bursts the conflict, transforming an already incandescent situation marked by disparities and scarce resources. In fact, these adults grew in a political era in which the main reference was the class or gender conflict and, for that reason, it is quite normal for them to refer mainly to the material socio-economic nature of the conflicts.

For students, instead, the question of identity and belonging to the group is the most important, in a contemporary era in which conflict is interpreted mainly by cultural, ethnic and religious categories (Santagati *et al.,* 2017): they emphasize the cultural nature of conflicts, thus suggesting not only the ethnicization, but also the culturalization and religiouzation of politics. The religious dimension is the bullet that deeply hurts identity dimensions linked to personal, family, communitarian elements.

On the one hand, adults underestimate the question of the religious identity, considering it as a controversial and public issue; on the other, students underestimate the socio-economic issue, which will probably become more important in the transition to adulthood. Although they give different interpretation to the conflicts, adults and students use a similar strategy: they refuse to address topics that are considered to be very contradictory and problematic, i.e. religious and spiritual questions in a material and consumerist era (Kristeva, 2016), work socialization and career opportunities in the jobless society (Lodigiani, Santagati, 2016), etc. Overcoming this generational divide in the interpretation of conflict, and nurturing the possibility of a good life together in schools and inside the society, means that religion is an important element *per se* for individuals and groups, an independent aim and sphere of life. At the same time, it is important to deconstruct the role played by religion, as a dependent dimension and an instrument affected by other dimensions of social life (such as politics, economics, etc.).

Our study, therefore, re-draws the attention to the challenge of working on disparities, not forgetting cultural identities and preserving religious identity, without the fear of being excluded in terms of relationships and educational pathways when this identity is expressed. The challenge –clearly underlined by Zanfrini (2019)– consists in facing socioeconomic inequalities, accepting and recognizing religious identities, promoting cultural exchange and contaminations among peers – a combination of different dimensions that has long been characterizing the Italian vision of educational/social integration in multi-cultural environments (Colombo, Santagati, 2017). Once again, it is time to better combine the cognitive learning with the relational inclusion, by experimenting in schools (and not only there) a space for a "normal experience" of expression of religious minority identities; by promoting the freedom to (not) continue with the familiar tradition in terms of religious belonging, without any imposition or violence, but rather with the family's guidance and support. Other efforts have to be done, in terms of research, in order to recognize the overlap of the disparity deriving from religious belonging with other social, economic and cultural divides, analyzing the intersection of these disadvantage factors and tracing routes to combine equal opportunity in education with guarantee of rights and solidarity (Zanfrini, 2019). It is time to inhabit, accept, and manage the conflict within the democratic frame of the interculturalism (Santagati, Zanzottera, 2018) basing on the idea of dealing with controversies (Cavalli, 2016), transmitting the capability to listen, discuss and face the controversial issues that divide public opinion, and find in democracy a way to make decisions in this controversial world.

CHAPTER 24

Religions and *Laïcité* in the French Republican School

Alessandro Bergamaschi and Catherine Blaya

1   Introduction

The status of religion in Western societies is an issue that constantly comes to the fore in European public debates, especially when the issue is to "go beyond the ordinary, or that regarding social dysfunctions and incidents"[1] (Campiche, 2010: 27). Despite the current relevance of these debates, whenever the question of the capacity of religion to impact daily life is raised, "the hidden assumptions are often found in a narrative of loss – loss of privilege, loss of authority, perhaps loss of vitality and influence" (Ammerman, 2010: 155). This loss of influence appears to be confirmed by various European surveys, especially concerning young people (Lambert, 2000; Galland, 2008, 2009). In any case, a counterweight to the steadily declining influence of religion on individual lives can be observed in the widespread popularity of certain social issues which, either directly or indirectly, question the institutions of religion. In France, the most vivid debate is about wearing visible religious symbols in public spaces or about school lunch specific menus, mainly within schools. This apparent paradox is likely based on the assumption that modernity doesn't allow enough space for religion to act as a means for interpreting reality. Yet closer examination backs up the idea to deal the thesis about the loss of influence cautiously. Even Berger (1999) didn't seem particularly convinced that the impact of religion on daily life was likely to decline inexorably, though he did uphold the hypothesis of its relegation to protected enclaves in order to ensure that it would overcome the effects of the continuing process of rationalization.

The present chapter questions the status of religion in contemporary French society. Throughout the chapter, religion is conceived as a transversal dimension of the constitution of French society. We will see that although it is strongly characterized by the opposite phenomenon, namely secularism, religion

---

1   All the translations are made by the authors.

"exerts its impact both actively and passively, explicitly or implicitly, in every corner of social, cultural and psychological reality" (Hervieu-Leger, 1999: 19).

First, we focus on the relationship between religion and French society. We lay out that the foundation of the principle of secularism is the cornerstone of the French social and political philosophy and its ambition is to be a key element of social cohesion. Then, as this ideological architecture needs a specific actor to be implemented, the following section is devoted to the role played by the school system. We highlight the role of the education system as an actor in charge of the socialization to the Republican creed, widely based on the principle of secularism. The second part of this chapter presents findings from a survey completed in several secondary schools in the South of France. This survey about the factors of social cohesion among teenagers, shows that religious belonging is related to the school experiences and the feeling to belong to the French national community.

2 The Separation of Church and State and the Implementation of Secularism in France

Secularism is a key element of the institutional and political dimensions of French society and has been used as a model for public space management since the French Revolution. This was later strengthened under the Third Republic (1875–1940). At that time, religion was considered as some kind of enemy for two different reasons. First, it claimed to have the monopoly of social knowledge throughout the entire nation or even at a universal level. This was unbearable for the spirits from the Age of Enlightenment (18th century) since France is a nation of which culture was built upon a strong contribution from the intellectual class –namely Auguste Comte and Emile Durkheim– who have worked long and hard to design the core values of the nation that would be freed from the legacies of religion and that should be transmitted and disseminated through the education system. As characterized by the French sociologist, Durkheim (1858–1917) schools are to fulfill a socialization role and teach the children, future of the nation, the way they should behave as citizens in accordance with the rules and norms of the society as a whole. As a consequence, education was a key element of the ideological state apparatus. On the other hand, fears regarding religion were fed by religious authorities who attempted to set up constituencies of local authorities through their diocese and parishes. Aristocrats and revolutionaries were at the roots of suspicion towards any form of local association that were considered as potentially plotting against the project of one dominant national culture at that time. As such, Church and its leadership and convening capacities at the local level could be perceived as a potential counter-power and as the bastion of reaction. This historical background leads to the designing of secularism over three aspects:

a)   the fight against the monopoly of Church over knowledge;
b)   the setting up of a dominant collective culture of which ethics would not be informed by religion;
c)   the strong will for the country to be ruled and the decision power to be held by one actor, the government, and to not be shared with religious authorities, simultaneously neutralizing any local specificity (Duru-Bellat, van Zanten, 2012).

The 1905 law performed a complete separation of Church and State but also set up the principles of freedom of conscience and freedom to exercise any faith. Church was to remain outside any political activity at the national level. This law officialized that schools were to become free from any religious influence and education was about the inculcation of Enlightenment principles and dominated by the collective culture of the French nation in search of unity.

There was a return to religion after the establishment of the July Monarchy in 1830 and a controversy over the freedom of education in 1843 rooting in the 1830 Charte that opened up the possibility of the creation of "public instruction and freedom of education". In 1833, Guizot designed a law including the possibility to create publicly funded elementary schools that could be run by the Church and the creation of Church primary and secondary schools. At that time, secondary schools were not under the supervision of the State. Ten years later, the Church claimed the right for "freedom of education" in secondary education, that is the right of parents to choose the school of their children (private, religious or state schools) and to offer national qualifications. They lost their claim and it was not until 1848 that the Falloux law restored some of the power that the Church had over secondary education and exempted religious schools from delivering state certifications.

The Third Republic was paramount in the creation of modern French society and the strengthening of the Republican ideals, among which the transfer of religious issues into the private sphere. If Church had been marginalized, the education system did not fully manage to offer education to masses and it was not until the end of the nineteenth century that there was a genuine impetus on popular education when primary schooling became compulsory for all. Tensions between the supporters of state education –the new Republican elite– and those of private education, that is anti-Republicans, started to emerge over the content of textbooks. These tensions lasted until after the second world war, when the State became the one actor of the democratization of education and secularism entered the French constitution in 1946. Since the year 1959, the two systems (state education and private religious education) have co-existed, and there has been an increase in state-subsidized private Catholic schools. The private and state system tend to be seen as complementary, since the State has recognized the private education sector as a "private service for public utility", as stressed by Tanguy (1972), considering that private schools are often used as "second chance" schools by parents of students at risk of dropping out (Ballion, 1986).

Although secular education remains dominant, the partisans of secularism have grown less inflexible since the 1970s and some new developments were based on scientific research (Duru-Bellat, van Zanten, 2012). For instance, the sociological analyses of Bourdieu and Passeron (1964, 1970) were influential in highlighting that although education was transmitting knowledge based on rationality versus ideology, it was reproducing social inequality and contributing to inequalities in educational attainment. On the other hand, the emergence of claims for the assertion of identity from ethnic minorities and religious groups in the sake of individual identity and authenticity (Honneth, 1996) have jeopardized the transmission of a national cultural unicity. Private education and more specifically Catholic education have been attracting intakes from more and more various cultural backgrounds and the Savary law project that intended to merge the state and the private system failed under the pressure of public opinion that considered that having the possibility to choose between different systems was a guarantee for quality and even freedom.

In the 1980s there was a turn in the use and understanding of secularism. Until then, secularism was opposed to religious power. Things changed with the long-term immigration of Muslims in France. The issue of diversity and the way to manage it in a society growing more and more plural became vivid. The confrontation of populations with different cultural and religious backgrounds raised new challenges. The growing presence of Muslim background students in schools destabilized the partisans of a homogeneous nation fearing a loss of cultural identity. These fears have been the cause of tensions and originated new laws that were meant to protect national identity and to preserve school from specific identity and religious influences. The ban on wearing conspicuous religious symbols in schools by the law of 2004 is part of these new measures. Since the early 2000s, the issue of secularism has taken a new turn in French society. In 1999, the political project to promote the public recognition of the Muslim faith emerged. The French Council for the Muslim Faith was created in 2003. It is a national elected body under the impulsion of Muslim students who claimed for better representation in the political life of the country and it serves as an official interlocutor with the French State in the regulation of Muslim religious activities. Created by Nicolas Sarkozy, it was at the time criticized as being the tool for social control reinforcement by part of the State. The very same year, President Chirac created the Stasi commission to reflect upon the principle of secularism and the way it was implemented. One of the issues under discussion was the wearing of the Hijab (Muslim scarf) in state schools (Bergamaschi, 2013) and that originated the ban on wearing conspicuous religious symbols in schools. Cherifi (2005) argues that this measure was counterproductive in the sense that it concerned a small number of individuals and that it contributed to revive the faith of millions of people who were initially moderate but who felt insulted in an important aspect of their religious identity. In 2009–2010, the Ministry for immigration and national identity promoted and organized a huge debate on national identity. This debate took the form of a survey completed throughout France including overseas territories and served two major objectives. The first one was to identify the constitutive elements that make up national identity. The second was to question immigration and more precisely the conditions of residence and the conditions for access to nationality. The purpose was to identify ideas that would help to strengthen the sense of pride for being French (Portail du Gouvernement, 2009). In 2010, the prohibition of face-veiling in public spaces was ratified (French Concealment Act of 11 October 2010) and the debate on alternatives to pork in canteen meals for Muslim children emerged again in the public debate.

All of these measures were widely covered by media and monopolized public debates. The relations between secularism and cultural or religious pluralism are still to be explored. Decision-makers rely on the notion of "positive secularism" to argue that one of the missions of the State is to manage religious pluralism (Campiche, 2015). This is considered as potentially facilitating compatibility between secularism and cultural diversity. Secularism serving to assure neutrality in the public sphere where all individuals could cohabitate happily, provided they do not expose their religious specificities or claim some kind of acknowledgment of their difference. The question "who am I?" then becomes a recurrent refrain among the so-called ethnic minorities for which the concept of "diversity", which results from peaceful and respectful cohabitation of the Other, becomes "difference" and creates a situation where alterity is the target of resistance and identity-related oppositions and even leads to hostility between groups.

To understand how the principle of secularism has become one of the key elements of republican life, it is necessary to look at the role played by the school in perpetuating the political philosophy of the République.

3   The French School: a Passionate Link with the République

As we have seen in the first part of this chapter, school in France is willing to neutralize differences and to convey the idea that all people are equal, regardless of their particular characteristics. This is the quintessence of the Republican identity. Conversely, it must fundamentally disseminate the idea that if one wishes to benefit from the protection of the State, including a relatively flexible procedure for acquiring nationality that, still today, is inspired by jus soli, one must abandon one's peculiarities upon crossing the threshold of its institutions – in this case, school. This seemingly perfect sociological architecture leaves no space for cultural particularisms, because such attachments would deeply contradict the universal interpretation of egalitarianism. This recognition would be to the detriment of a national community that sought to be highly integrated. For example, De Gaulle's cultural levelling policies (Narbonne, 1994) aimed to prohibit the use of dialects in institutional spaces and have been broadly implemented, particularly in the educational system. Thus, at the beginning of the 20th century, for a student to speak one's one dialect during classes or break times could mean very strict sanctions. In French society there is therefore no room for identity manifestations other than the Republican identity and school is the institution that has been tasked with instilling this idea. It is a very special role that has led some education specialists such as Eric Debarbieux (2008) to suggest that school and the Republic "have a passionate relationship".

It goes without saying that the French society and its educational system have always had a controversial relationship in relation with the issues of "ethnicity" – namely the result of an identity dialectic between groups endowed with unequal economic and cultural resources and whose consequences are variable in contexts (Poutignat, Streiff-Fenart, 2008; Bertheleu, 2007). However, since the foundation of its modern nation, the French society has experienced a major migration influx, which has led to an exponential growth of cultural diversity. France's challenges are, on the one hand, the fact that it has adopted a political philosophy that leaves no space for multi-culturalism and, on the other hand, the fact that it is one of the main European destinations for waves of international migration. Indeed, France was the first country in Europe to use foreign labor, mainly from its (former) colonies, to meet economic and even military requirements (Noiriel, 1988). How can one expect the millions of foreigners who have settled on French soil, and their descendants, to so easily forget their cultural background? How can one believe that the French society is really "indifferent to differences" (Bourdieu, 1966), such as those that are generated by such migratory flows? How can all its members thrive in the education system, the labor market and in the urban space? The latest PISA data (2015) are rather stark: among industrialized countries, France is the country where the social origin of individuals has the greatest influence on the educational careers of its students. It is obvious that social origin and migratory origins are two variables that are often closely linked. Despite growing social tensions, where the principles of the Republic are confronted by integration deficits, growing social inequalities and urban segregations lead sociologists to talk about "urban ghettos" (Lapeyronnie, 2009), French institutions continue nevertheless to behave in accordance with the Republican philosophy. Instead of opening up to minimal forms of recognition of cultural diversity and its social implications, measures such as the prohibition of wearing religious symbols in the primary and secondary levels of the school system (Law of 15 March 2004) are designed. In 1989 a student was excluded from high school for the first time due to the wear of Muslim veil. The Minister of National Education at the time, not wishing to face the issue directly, had recourse to the Council of State which reaffirmed the principle of secularism in schools without extending this principle to students. In 1994, wearing ostentatious religious symbols was banned from schools by a ministerial decision. From 2004, school principals have had the right to exclude students wearing headscarves. The dominant position of the politicians and intellectuals were in favor of this measure for three main reasons:

a)   to defend the neutrality of the education system;
b)   to protect Muslim women from male's domination and patriarchalism;
c)   to fight against any religious fanaticism.

Although exclusions from schools were scarce, following this measure, the side effect was to encourage families to lodge complains with the High Authority for Discrimination and Equality (Ichou, van Zantent, 2014).[2]

However, the school system oscillates between taking diversity into account and attempting to neutralize any differences. Some intercultural pedagogy interventions aimed at bringing value to cultural diversity have been implemented since the early 1980s. There has been a movement that was sporadically diffused under the impetus of teams of very active teachers who strongly believe in the value of diversity. However, this logic of valorization is not without ambiguities since, in the same period of time, there used to be an appointment of non-teaching staff (supervisors, educators, leadership personnel, etc.) according to ethnic criteria (Rinaudo, 1998; Rayou, van Zanten, 2004; Doytcheva,

---

2   The High Authority for Discrimination and Equality was an independent authority created in 2005 that was dissolved in 2011.

2007). Thus, an institution that has a high concentration of Maghreb or Black African students would recruit staff who belonged to the same cultural/ethnic groups. The basic idea was that similarity should have helped to manage situations perceived as difficult by the school staffs. However, the problem was that the results obtained were often contrary to expectations and tensions and mistrust between minority students and school staffs increased (Zefir, 2010).

This issue of ethnic diversity is one of the problems that grips the Republican education system, which, like the society that it serves, prefers to adopt the "politics of the ostrich" (De Rudder *et al.*, 2000) rather than rethink its fundamental principles in light of the social changes. However, since the 2000s we have been witnessing a timid dialogue, starting with the inclusion of secular issues in the training of teachers and principals, and particularly the approach of the inclusive school with the establishment of a Charte de la Laïcité in 2012, followed by a mobilization around the values of the Republic following the terrorist attacks in January 2015 and July 2016. The problem is this idea of secularism is not interpreted in the same way by everybody, and its implementation is oscillating between social hypercontrol of any form of religious expression in the school and a position of dialogue and tolerance. As emphasized by Dubet (2016), secularism is not a disembodied concept that is inculcated. If we promote the idea of shared values, these values must be put into practice by those who contribute to their spreading and therefore be part of their convictions. To think that this is a value shared by all the representatives of the education system remains a utopia and the children who attend the school of the Republic are not socio-cultural idiots.

4   The Complex Relation between Religion, Schools and Secularism

As we have just seen, the relationship between religion, secularism and school is particularly complex. The French nation was built in opposition to religion and education is the actor in charge of transmitting and perpetuating a shared and unique national identity. As Schnapper states (2008: 133), given the nation's need to adapt to Republican principles, cultural and religious particularisms are not to be taken into consideration in the public sphere. The French model of integration therefore only recognizes free and equal individuals and "it is in this sense that it can be called universalist and every individual is to acquire their self-worth, independently of the community they belong to" (Hervieu-Léger, 1999: 258).

The high number of people from different ethnic backgrounds in French society and in the educational system questions the relevance of a political philosophy rooted in old realities. In particular, as demonstrated by various studies, ethnic minorities are often reminded of their origins –real, supposed, hetero or self-attributed– in several social domains such as labor markets (Silberman, Fournier, 2006; Beauchemin *et al.*, 2010), real estate (Bonnet *et al.*, 2011; Dietrich-Ragon, 2017) and, of course, the education system (Brinbaum, Primon, 2013; Felouzis *et al.*, 2015). In concrete terms, it becomes a form of discrimination that relegates ethnic minorities to underprivileged jobs and neighborhoods and towards educational careers that open up restricted future perspectives. Any attempt from part of these individuals and their communities to reverse the situation and to improve social emancipation is a genuine challenge.

As for education only, the impact of belonging to an ethnic minority on school achievement has been studied expansively in France.

On the one hand, some studies have found that the impact of the ethnic background vanishes once controlled by the socio-economic background of students (Vaillet, Caille, 2001); however, it is also true that the correlation between socio-economic characteristics and ethnic origin is strong and that students, children of immigrants, come mainly from socio-economically deprived backgrounds. On the other hand, more qualitative surveys draw attention to the fact that a significant proportion of these pupils complain of having been victims of some forms of discrimination related to their migratory or cultural origins (Santelli, 2007; 2012). According to Roussier-Fusco (2003) who completed a study in schools in the outskirts of Paris, some teachers' attitudes and behaviors towards students are influenced by the ethnic origin of the latter. In a similar way, other variables are likely to moderate that finding, that is the proportion of ethnic minorities in the class as well as the socio-economical background of the teachers (Perroton, 2000; Rayou, van Zanten, 2004; Sanselme, 2009).

Some other research based on questionnaire surveys and big databases *Trajectories and Origins*, have recently showed evidence that the ethnic origin of certain groups such as those from the Maghreb, Turkey and sub-Saharan Africa are associated with more problematic schooling experience (e.g. year repetition or school dropout) even after checking on the socio-economic characteristics of the respondents (Brinbaum *et al.*, 2012).

These findings question the capacity of the French universal citizenship model to approach ethnic diversity management without creating hostility and conflicts between the different groups. In order to illustrate the concrete way schools manage diversity, we present the findings of a survey completed in secondary schools in the South of France. The survey aimed to analyze the construction of social relationships among adolescents. More specifically, we studied the effect of religious belonging and the way it impacts on the process of developing a sentiment of collective national identity as well as on their school experience.

5 The Present Study

Our survey was completed with 2,907 students from junior and high school in the fall of 2017 in south-eastern France. The average age of the respondents was 13.4 for junior students and 16.2 for high school students. There was an equivalent proportion of males and females. We asked the participants to answer questions on their belonging to a religion, if it played an important role in their life, and if they practiced. Our questionnaire also included questions meant to assess their feeling of belonging to the French nation which were drawn from the TEO survey and questions on their school experience in terms of sanctions (how many of them and the perceived reasons behind them, such as skin color, religion, ethnic origin, language spoken). Finally, we tried to assess what their projects were in terms of further education (Blaya, 2019). In our analyses, based on research about the relationship between intolerance and intergroup friendships (Pettigrew, Tropp, 2008), various control variables have been introduced: gender, school level, parents' education level.

5.1 *Descriptive Findings*
We first completed a descriptive analysis of the religious practices of the participants to the survey. Quite a few students answered they did not follow any religion (37%), one third stated they were Catholics and one out of five students said they were Muslims. The other potential religions were indicated by under 2% of the respondents.

The effects of social stratification, measured by the parents' level of education, on belonging to a religion are as follows: young people who declare themselves to be either Christians, or of another religion or without a religion, are more likely to come from families with high educational capital, whereas Muslim youth are concentrated mainly in culturally poorer families where parents gained their compulsory school certificate, vocational certificates or, at best, their diploma from secondary studies (p. 000 – V .18). The effects of gender are not significant. The importance of religion obtained an average score of 4.1 out of ten points but we noticed differences according to worship: Muslim respondents granted significantly much more importance to religion than the Catholics or the members of other religions (*M*=8,6 *vs M*=5,1 *vs M*=5,1). Religion proves to be more important for girls (p .000 – F 11,3) and for the younger students (p .000 – F 99,2). As for practicing, half of the students who declared themselves as Muslims reported to be attending a religious service at least once a month, while Catholics were 40.1% and 10% from the other religions. The most involved students are the younger ones (p. ≤.001 – phi .13), and gender does not make any difference.

The belonging and practice of a religion both depend upon the school capital of the family.

The vast majority of students reported feeling French (87.3%) and that the others considered they were French (78.9%). The sentiment to be French is stronger among the high school respondents (p. ≤.001 – F 55,2) and depends on the level of education of their parents (p. ≤.001 – F 11,6). However, this feeling is weaker among the Muslim respondents (p. ≤.001 – F 115,7), among those who think that religion is important (p. ≤.001 – F 44,9) and who practice more (p. ≤.001 – F 212,2).

As for sanctions in school, boys are more involved than girls (p. ≤.001 – F 88,7) as well as the students of which parents have low educational background (p. ≤.001 – F 6,9). In the wake of previous studies, we found that Muslim students reported more sanctions than the other students (p. ≤.001 – F 21,3) as well as the importance they granted to religion (p. ≤.001 – F 6,1) and their level of practice (p. ≤.001 – F 22,1). Many students consider these sanctions reflect discrimination (M=5,8) mostly Muslim students (p. ≤.01 – F 5,7). The more the students feel religious (p. ≤.05 – F 2,9) and the more they practice, the more they feel they are discriminated (p. ≤.01 – F 6,9). We also analyzed the relationship between further education ambitions and religion through a linear regression analysis and our findings show that students who belong to a religion have greater ambitions that the others (p ≤.05).

5.2   *How Much Do the Young People Feel French?*

It is now interesting to look at the interactions between the factors we have just described in a global explanatory model. More precisely, we have tried to verify how the feeling of being French is affected by, on the one hand, religion and, on the other hand, by school experiences. In that purpose, we ran a multiple linear regression model with stepwise method (Table 24.1). As our study is mainly exploratory, we thought more relevant to identify progressively what were the variables that lead to the model through regressive equations. (Howell, 2006). Our dependent variable is "the feeling of being French", which has been analyzed by mobilizing three sets of independent variables:

a)   religion, the importance of the feeling of religiosity, the frequency of participation in religious services;

TABLE 24.1   The feeling of being French according to the religion and school experiences - linear regression, stepwise method (*N*=2 625)

Model		Standard error	Bêta	p.
1P ≤.001	(Constant)	,032		,000
R² .105	Muslim religion *vs* any	,075	,309	,000
Δ R² ≤.001	religion			
2P ≤.001	(Constant)	,032		,000
R² .126	Muslim religion *vs* any	,078	,248	,000
Δ R² ≤.001	religion			
	Frequency of participation in rites (practicing *vs* non-practicing)	,085	,186	,000
3P ≤.001	(Constant)	,060		,000
R² .138	Muslim religion *vs* any	,077	,243	,000
Δ R² ≤.001	religion			
	Frequency of participation in rites (practicing *vs* non-practicing)	,085	,176	,000
	School level (lower second-ary school *vs* high secondary school)	,066	-,092	,000
4P ≤.001	(Constant)	,060		,000
R² .150	Muslim religion *vs* any	,078	,255	,000
Δ R² ≤.001	religion			
	Frequency of participation in rites (practicing *vs* non-practicing)	,085	,168	,000
	School level (lower secondary school *vs* high secondary school)	,065	-,094	,000
	Other religion *vs* any religion	,129	,080	,000
5P ≤.001	(Constant)	,096		,000
R² .165	Muslim religion *vs* any	,078	,245	,000
Δ R² ≤.001	religion			

TABLE 24.1   The feeling of being French according to the religion and school experiences -
linear regression, stepwise method (N=2 625) (*cont.*)

Model		Standard error	Bêta	p.
	Frequency of participation in rites (practicing *vs* non-practicing)	,085	,166	,000
	School level (lower second-ary school *vs* high secondary school)	,065	-,097	,000
	Other religion *vs* any religion	,129	,078	,000
	Frequency school convoca-tions / exclusions	,023	,069	,000

b)   the frequency of sanctions and temporary exclusions, the feeling of discrimination it may generate;
c)   sex, the education capital of the parents, the grade level attended by the
student.

Findings show there are five explanatory models, all providing a supplementary and significant explanation compared to the previous model. The first
model is based on a single variable that influences the "feeling of being French",
namely belonging to the Muslim religion: young people who belong to this religion feel less French compared to peers who reported no religion (p ≤.001).
The second model includes religious practice and young people who attend
religious service at least once a month, are characterized by a weaker "feeling
of being French" than the students we have defined as non-practicing (p ≤.001).
In a third model shows high school students have a stronger feeling compared
to junior school respondents (p ≤.001). Students who reported they belonged
to another religion that is neither Muslim nor Catholic i.e. religions that in our
sample are very small, such as the Jewish (1.3% of participants) or the Protestant (1.2% of participants), show a lower feeling of being French compared to
young people without religion (p ≤.001).

Finally, the more being told off and temporary exclusions are frequent, the
weaker is the "feeling of being French" (p ≤.001). The feeling of discrimination
as a result of school sanctions and the school capital of parents are not significantly associated to feeling French, nor being Catholic.

6   Discussion

By reading the findings of this survey, the thesis of the "loss of influence" does not seem to be in tune with the picture that is looming. At first, we have seen that the effects of social stratification are consistent with studies that have taken into account the relationship between the ethnic origin, the cultural and religious affiliations, the sense of identification with the national community, and school careers. There is a clear gap between, on the one hand, young people who reported being Muslim and, on the other, young people of other faiths or without any confession at all. This gap can be explained at different levels as fewer cultural resources available within the family, an indicator of minor economic affluence, greater intensity of the feeling of religiosity and a bigger involvement in the religious practice. Secondly, Muslim respondents reported more often being in conflict with the school authority and feeling discriminated. Despite these findings, when analyzing academic ambitions, young people who claim to belong to one of the religions mentioned in the questionnaire, whichever those are, have higher school expectations than the young people who reported being "without religion". Finally, the effects of belonging to the Muslim religion are also apparent in the "feeling of being French", which is weaker compared to young people of either Christian religion, of another faith or without religion. In the same way, this feeling is weaker among the young people for whom religion occupies an important place in life and who participate in religious services at least on a monthly basis. Simon and Tiberj (2012) in the *Trajectories and Origins* survey showed that the "feeling of being French" fluctuates according to the migratory experiences and the cultural communities. They stress that it would be unfair to conclude that a weak feeling of being French necessarily corresponds to a withdrawal from the mainstream community. According to the authors, it is rather a sign of a society that "is challenging for immigrants and their descendants, to be considered as French". This consideration raises questions and opens the door to a second point from our study, which is the lack of impact of belonging to the Christian religion on the "feeling of being French". In other words, belonging to the Christian faith does not seem to collide with the feeling of belonging to the French identity. We wonder why the membership to the Catholic religion does not trigger the same tensions as the belonging to the Muslim religion, as far as the French identity is concerned. We believe this result deserves a specific analysis throughout history.

As stated in the introduction to this study, it is essential to bear in mind that today "religion plays a role of capital importance in public life and in public action (...) and sheds the perception of it as a vestige from the past" (Moore,

2007: 413). Thus, religion can be seen as the cultural expression of a given context, allowing it to be presented as one of the elements that contribute to defining identity. It follows from this reading that the notion of the low status of religion in France on the basis of the principles of laity formalized under the Law of 1905 must be reformulated. In order to do this, the historical and anthropological aspects that led to the European process of nation-building should be considered. Jolly (2005) showed that the French sense of laity was paradoxically based on the "confessional grounds" represented by the Catholic faith, which imposed itself over the course of centuries as the "dominant cultural sub-stratus" (Jolly, 2005), overshadowing other minority religions. In France, even more than in other nations, the State was born by staking a clear, official distance from religion. But as Detienne affirms, it is difficult to deny that in the course of contemporary history, Catholicism contributed to consolidating its identity by consecrating the idea of Nation built around a precise cultural memory (Detienne, 2010). According to this perspective, therefore, religion may be the one underlying elements of the social landscape and, though it may not be manifestly vindicated, it can be felt implicitly at precise social conjunctures.

In the last few years, one of the characteristics marking the French political debate and particularly useful to promote France's own sense of identity has been the tacit mobilization of the cultural sub-stratus generated by Catholicism, in its role as one of the constituent elements of "Republican living". Tacit mobilization in this sense refers to the observation that belonging to the Catholic religion emerges only indirectly and, in particular, in negative and contrasting terms with the intention of re-stating what one is not. In this sense, the emphasis on the respect for Republican ideals leads to "identity policies" with manifest effects, like the institution of the *Ministère de l'Immigration et de l'Identité Nationale*[3] under Sarkozy's presidency, which promoted the *Grand Débat sur l'Identité Nationale*[4] in 2009. One of the consequences of this accent on identity has been to stigmatize groups that have distanced themselves from the principles of the *République* as a result of their cultural specificity or behavior in the public sphere (Bergamaschi, Santagati, 2019). The group which most often comes "under fire" in these identity policies are Muslims as the results of our study underlined in a sharply way. The incompatibilities in the worldviews characterizing Islam and the Republican model are in fact among the main

---

3   This Ministry was removed, however, during the government reshuffle in November 2010.
4   The history of the *Grand Débat sur l'Identité Nationale* can be found on the French Government's web portal: http://www.debatidentitenationale.fr/.

nodes of French political integration, especially in the last few years. According to Lapeyronnie (2008: 527), the core of the "fight" against Islam involves all sectors of public opinion, since it is associated with "the non-modern or anti-modern world of the Other".

In the Fifties, Gordon Allport emphasized the ambivalent role of religion in the process of forming prejudice and stereotypes: "while Faith in the world's major religions is universal and emphasizes the brotherhood of all mankind, in practice it often engenders divisions, which can sometimes be brutal" (Allport, 1954: 609). More complex results emerged from Valasik's (2010) analysis of a French sample from the Welfare and Values in Europe survey. In this case, the effects of religion on social and ethical questions appeared to be multi-dimensional. Depending on the topic under discussion, religion "appears simultaneously as a factor of solidarity and/or discrimination, of tolerance and/or intolerance, integration and/or xenophobia" (Valasik, 2010: 199). The contours of a multi-dimensional image of religion have become more clearly defined, and the effects appear to take on the guise of a mental map which, according to Willaime (2010: 122), helps to "express a certain conception of man and the world in a given society".

Given these contextual factors, what are the resources French schools have in order to avoid contributing to widening the social gap among young people? We have seen that religious affiliation and the importance attached to it are associated with more chaotic school careers. At the same time, we also know that religious denominations are associated with each other's social hierarchy and, as we have seen, the PISA data point to the difficulties of the Republican school in neutralizing the effects of social stratification on the school experience of students from the most socio-economically deprived backgrounds.

Moreover, young people often consider school difficulties as the result of unequal and discriminatory treatments due to their cultural-religious background. The education system seems to be at the service of one unique and dominant national culture in a perspective of egalitarianism. Nevertheless, the French nation and its education system continue to widen the gap between a so-called majority population –whose profile is in perfect harmony with its principles, even to the point that, in this case, religious affiliation is not a source of tension– and a so-called minority population, increasingly marginalized, and whose basic cultural traits are singled out as the difference *par excellence*.

CHAPTER 25

Religious Education in Schools as a Necessity in a Secular State: the Perspective in Catalonia

Núria Llevot-Calvet, Olga Bernad-Cavero and Jordi Garreta-Bochaca

1   Introduction

The international migrations of the end of the twentieth and beginning of the twenty-first centuries have generated fundamental changes in the social reality of Spain and Catalonia. The latter was one of the first of the Autonomous Communities of Spain to receive, and have to respond to, foreign immigration from a greater diversity of origins from the earliest years of this phenomenon. The inclusion of new cultures and religions into the pre-existing Catalan social fabric and the guarantee of good reception for the new communities by Catalan society have been the two most important axes of the policies of the Catalan autonomous administration (Generalitat de Catalonia) in recent years.

In this context, schools have found themselves faced with the necessity to transform and innovate (Sanuy *et al.*, 2017a), both in their theoretical approaches and in their teaching methodology, with the aim of dealing with this new reality in the schools. In this sense, since the mid-1990s, pre-schools (people aged 3–6) and primary schools (6–12) have become a fundamental tool to manage cultural and religious diversity in Catalonia from a local setting within the working framework established by the Generalitat de Catalunya (Garreta, 2006; Llevot *et al.*, 2016 and 2017). This has meant relative experience in drawing up discourses and designing policies regarding cultural and religious diversity within the Spanish framework.

Education has become one of the capital elements of modern society. The process of training deals with educating people in becoming part of a complex and changing society; the latter needs to be prepared to assimilate the novelties of cultural, social and technical evolution. Education is also a tool that can be very useful for generating understanding, respect and coexistence and for favoring social cohesion among people and groups with different cultural and religious traditions. It must be borne in mind that, throughout its history, Catalan society has been enriched by the reception of various migratory flows. However, in recent decades, the nature of this influx of immigrants has

changed. The fact that they come from varied origins implies the incorporation of a cultural, linguistic and religious diversity that was unthinkable a few
years ago (Garreta, 2011; Garreta, Llevot, 2011; Llevot *et al.*, 2017). Thus, the education system has had to respond, with a positive outlook, to the increase in
diversity and its political and social recognition (Garreta, 2003; Bernad, 2016;
Giró, Andrés, 2018).

In Spain, educational decentralization has led to policies in this field developing in diverse ways. However, the results are not very different, given that
these are always in the framework of the idea of interculturality and under the
general directives of the ministerial educational administration (see CIDE,
2005; Fernández, García, 2015; Santos, 2017). J. Garreta (2003 and 2006) showed
that, at the start of the new century, the dynamics of implantation of intercultural education (a dominant focus in that moment principally through the influence of the European Union) was slow. Consequently, it was not easy to put
the discourse into practice as there was no general proposal or specific focus
on how to do it (the teaching staff were not given adequate orientation or resources, nor were they obliged to define themselves and act accordingly). Despite this, one can state that important steps had been taken (even though
more should have been done) to incorporate the students and families of foreign origin or gypsies into the education system. The few studies that have
compared different Autonomous Communities (especially the work of the
CIDE (2005)) have shown the following. Work has been done to incorporate
students at different moments of their school path and the academic year; the
teaching of the school's vehicular language (in some cases, support has also
been given to the learning of the languages of origin) has been taken into consideration; plans have been drawn up for the reception of families and students; the training of the teaching staff has been enhanced; initiatives for
translation and/or intercultural mediation have been set up; specific materials
have been prepared and included in the curriculum; etc. It is also true that it
was not until very recently that the aspect of religious diversity started being
given consideration when dealing with cultural diversity. It seems to us that,
after being scarcely considered, the discourse and the actions regarding cultural diversity have been consolidating; relevant issues are now emerging, such
as the afore-mentioned mediators and translators, the specific materials, the
adaptation of the curriculum to cultural diversity, etc. However, despite this
development, the research still indicates that it is necessary to better articulate
the necessities through actions and the discourse through practice, as well as
to provide a more advanced training for everyone involved in the schools (see,
among others: Llevot, 2006; Aguado, 2011; Márquez-Lepe, García-Cano, 2014;
Escarbajal, Leiva, 2017). Moreover, it is common to believe it is necessary to

continue to study in order to better know, in a comparative and methodologically plural way, what has been done, what evaluation this has received by the
different agents involved and how this could be improved. As shown above,
Spain has taken steps in the valuation of cultural diversity in the classroom and
has evolved, in just a few years, from a centralized educational system (where
cultural diversity, focused on gypsies, was undervalued) to a decentralized autonomous system, much closer to an intercultural pedagogical model (Essomba, 2014) and in which the cultural pluralism of the State has been accentuated.
This intercultural education has gradually incorporated a more general approach to seeking social cohesion and inclusion.

Thus, the growing cultural and religious diversity in Catalan society has
highlighted the limitations of a social and educational model. These have
become more notable with this demographic evolution (Griera, 2016). In
fact, this debate has been ongoing since the start of the democratic transition
and has placed the school at the center of attention, as a microcosm of what
the society produces (Sanuy *et al.*, 2017b). In this line, one of the challenges
the school faces is how to respond to not only the cultural diversity but also to
the religious diversity in our society and in schools – a debate from which the
teacher-training faculties are not excluded (Bernad, Llevot, 2018a).

Focusing on the religious question, the Spanish Constitution recognizes the
right of families to choose the religious and moral training for their children in
accordance with their own beliefs. This right has been upheld by the successive education laws that have been implemented since the advent of democracy. Thus, in the Spanish educational system, the subject of religion is mandatory for the school and optative for the students. When the latter opt to study
religion, they can choose between those religions that have signed cooperation
agreements with the State (Catholic, Evangelical, Muslim and Jewish). However, various studies (Tarrés, Roson, 2009; Viñao, 2014; Llevot *et al.*, 2017) show
the hegemonic role of the Catholic religion and the scant implantation of the
other three.

In this general setting, we present what happens in the pre-schools and the
primary schools of the Catalan territory; specifically, how religious diversity is
dealt with, and which actions are being carried out in the schools. To this end,
we use two approaches.[1] First, we present the results of a survey of representatives of the management teams from 380 public schools in Catalonia. This is

---

1   The data used are from the Proyecto Recercaixa 2015 and the subvention of the RELIG pro-
    gramme of the Generalitat de Catalunya for university research projects in the field of reli-
    gious diversity. To extend this, one can consult Garreta *et al.*, 2018.

complemented with in-depth interviews (qualitative methodology) of a sample from 16 schools who stand out in the survey for their actions and management regarding the treatment of cultural and/or religious diversity.[2]

2   The School and Cultural and Religious Diversity

The survey is useful for a first approach to the schools, and it shows that the average number of pupils of foreign origin is 19.76%, the largest proportion of whom are of Maghrebi origin. A characteristic of the education system is that despite having a general framework –established by the legislation– within which educational action is developed, each school adapts the elements it has available to its circumstances. Regarding the arrival of pupils with characteristics initially not envisaged by the legal framework, the schools have had to adapt their resources and seek other new ones to tackle these necessities. Teachers have been impelled to prepare new strategies to involve the students and their families, and have prioritized transversal work and, in short, have had to improvise and experiment faced in an unexpected situation.

The survey shows that the cultural diversity in society is analyzed with the pupils in many centers. Specifically, only 15.5% do nothing about this. As could be expected, the response that said they acted was more frequent in schools that have a higher presence of foreign-origin students. The most common actions are working on cultural diversity in the curriculum (60.3%) and organizing intercultural days (32.6%). Other less frequent actions are (in this order) the adaptation of menus, projects and activities in the classroom, specific actions of communication and training of family members, and work on religious diversity.

In more detail, we can see that, among those surveyed, the ones responding that they take cultural diversity into consideration in the curriculum indicate that this is mainly introduced in the subjects of social and natural environment (42.9%), also in tutoring (12.2%), ethics/values (25.3%) and religion (22%). It is true that 36.3% of the schools receive external support to act on cultural diversity (from the Generalitat de Catalunya, especially from the Department of Education's teams of Language and Social Cohesion (ELIC), see: http://xtec.gencat.cat/ca/serveis/sez/elic/), a percentage that increases in line with the rise in the proportion of foreign-origin students in the school.

---

2   Taking the concept of good practices proposed by Ritacco (2011) as a reference, these good practices could be understood as convex and convergent actions within the same framework of action (Sanuy et al., 2017b).

TABLE 25.1　Actions/activities carried out while working on cultural diversity

Actions mentioned spontaneously	Percentage
Working on the curriculum	60.3
Intercultural days	32.6
Training of teachers	4.7
Training for the families	14.2
Specific communication activities	16.1
Adaptation of menus	27.1
Reception	6.6
Reception class	6.1
Support	3.7
Curricular adaptation	1.1
Human rights' days	5.8
Projects specific center	8.4
Working on religious diversity	10.5
Tutoring	6.8
Classes language of origin	2.1
Intercultural mediation	1.6
Organization groups	7.4
Specific to classroom	16.8
Activities for foreign families	8.7
Others	4.2
None	15.5

SOURCE: PROYECTO RECERCAIXA 2015; GARRETA ET AL., 2018.

On focusing interest on the presence/absence of cultural and religious diversity in the documents from the schools, we can observe that cultural diversity receives more attention than religious diversity (and is taken more into consideration as the number of foreign origin pupils increases) in the Centre Curricular Projects (PCC)[3] and Centre Educational Projects (PEC).[4] A minority does

---

3　The PEC is made up of the pedagogical and organisational principles that should run all the educational actions, while the PCC is an eminently pedagogical document that constitutes a basic instrument for defining the approaches developed in the educational project respecting the prescriptions of the official curriculum.

4　Document that defines how the school works: guiding principles that differentiate it from other centres, actions for adaptation to the surroundings; lines of attention to diversity and

not contemplate cultural diversity in its plans – the *Plan for coexistence* being where these themes are most frequently reflected. In contrast, when we refer to religious diversity, the reality is different. Moreover, in the majority of schools, no one is responsible for managing religious diversity. Although 28.4% claim there is someone in charge of this, they are often referring to the teacher of Catholic religion and, to a lesser degree, to the management team or the commission for coexistence.

Regarding the teaching of religion, in primary schools, "the areas of religion and education in social and civic values are mandatory for the schools and optative for the families" (Departament d'Ensenyament, 2015). In other words, when enrolling their children, families can choose whether their offspring study the subject of religion or an alternative. Currently, in line with the Organic Law for the Improvement of Educational Quality (LOMCE in its Spanish initials, 2013),[5] the latter option means social and civic values. Previously, the alternative subject had a wider spectrum according to the criteria of the school (another change introduced by the LOMCE is that both subjects are evaluable and have the same teaching hours). Regarding the area of religion, the Law stipulates there is a choice between the Catholic, Evangelical, Jewish and Muslim religions. However, in practice, as the results of the survey show, in public schools, possibly conditioned by the demand of the families, alternative educational attention and Catholic religion are taught mostly, the presence of the Evangelical religion being almost imperceptible and the other two religions, null. However, in some centers, on their own initiative, the Catholic religion teachers introduce a view of other religions into their subject as religious culture (see Garreta *et al.*, 2019). On the other hand, and for various reasons, either due to the ideas of the center or the choice of the families, we also find centers that only teach the subject of religion and others that only teach the alternative subject.

However, the answers from those surveyed mainly indicate that religions should be taught outside the school (75%). 85.5% of the people interviewed consider that it is important to work with the religious diversity of pupils that exists in society (approximately half of the schools indicate that they have opted for a transversal approach, focusing on objects other than religion/values, such as social environment, music or tutoring). However, only a minority

---

the mid-term objectives; breakdown of the main lines of organisation that are defined in the curricular project, etc.

5   For more details about this law, consult http://www.educacionyfp.gob.es/educacion/mc/lomce/lomce.html.

of centers (1.8%) have received external support to work on it, and this is mainly in those that have a higher presence of foreign-origin pupils.

The representatives of the management teams surveyed indicate that cultural and religious diversity has become "normalized" nowadays. Does this mean, perhaps, that it has ceased to be a "problem" in their schools? Do they now have enough experience and training to know how to deal with it and respond adequately to the needs of their students? Do they work on and respect the differences? According to our study, professionals' knowledge about pupils of foreign origin, their countries and their cultures of origin, the different religions (one of the training requirements in the early years of this immigration (see Garreta, 2003 and 2006)) is no longer a priority in the training plans. However, coexistence in the centers, among pupils from different cultural and ethnic groups and their scholarly and social integration, continues to be an evident necessity. Some of the new demands for training are education in values, management of emotions, organization of the classroom, and, especially, practical resources (like a "recipe book"). In general, they think they have already received sufficient theoretical training, and what is needed now are strategies and practical activities to be able to implant in the classroom immediately. In fact, 21.8% of those surveyed believe they need strategies for conflict resolution to improve their response to cultural diversity.

Thus, the training of teachers to work on cultural and religious diversity is considered sufficient, but less so when referring to religious diversity (77.9% consider their training adequate for cultural diversity and 50% for religious diversity). In some cases, they allege that, since they do not have diversity in the school, they do not consider this necessary. This option is in line with what has already been pointed out: the opinion, shared by many professionals, that it is the level of cultural diversity in the classroom (presence of foreign-origin students or gypsies) that justifies initiatives in this field. In other words, the greater the presence of foreign-origin pupils (or gypsies), the more the actions that are put into movement and the more it is frequent to believe that it is not necessary to take them in schools without diversity, where the idea that society is diverse culturally is taken less into consideration, and where this question has to be dealt with for all the pupils.

3   Experiences Regarding Religious Diversity in the Schools

As indicated above, Catalan schools nowadays have much experience in the reception of pupils from other cultures and in the treatment of cultural diversity, but do not have the same degree of experience as far as religious diversity is concerned. Probably because of that, this subject is not considered as a priority in the training plans or among the necessities expressed by the management teams. Factors like the training received, the teaching experience, the school culture, the organization, the context, the resources and the materials they have, play an important role in the school's micro-politics, and they are reflected in the way this topic is approached in the projects and actions.

The influence of socio-economic and educational factors is highlighted, especially in the schools in depressed neighborhoods. These factors imply great social differentials in a group labelled uniformly as of "immigrant origin". In this sense, differentiated responses are designed to contemplate the multiple realities. Thinking that their function must go beyond the purely instructive aspects, and faced with the evidence of some families' serious socio-economic difficulties, teachers are impelled to seek solutions to palliate the necessities manifested by the children – needs that greatly hinder normal schooling. Given the fall in financial and human resources from the educational administration (especially due to the economic crisis), the schools request financial support from some foundations and also undertake synergies by working with entities in their surroundings. As a differential trait, some privately owned schools with grant-aid agreements with the public administration (known as "*concertadas*" in Spain) receive help and resources from their own foundations and from other schools. Therefore, besides requesting resources such as grants, they implement actions such as opening the school library after school hours to facilitate the children in doing their homework, or organize summer camps and activities. Generally, they do so with the support of volunteers or associations, including *Save the Children*.

The models of management relating to diversity does not follow uniformed models valid for all cases, as each school has to build its own model, adapted to its specific situation. Diversity is considered a "normal" trait in the school, where equality is built from the recognition of differences. Some schools that have transformed their way of being, doing and relating to others, seek a defining trait that brings together and gives sense to the different activities, curricular or not, that are carried out, and choose to create a great school project shared with the community as a "stamp" of identity. In contrast, other centers opt to weave a network of small actions and of small projects that give sense to what they do from day to day, thus creating a school culture.

Other schools with a trajectory of community work seek the involvement of the community by networking with the neighborhood entities. They undertake participative processes to convert the school into a space for learning, participation and communication, where everyone learns and at the same time teaches the other and feels to be listened to. However, the grant-aided schools that have been visited (which belong to a religious order with a number of schools scattered around Catalonia) have a shared project ideal for all the centers, which dictates (and unifies) the guidelines that must be followed and includes the peculiarities of each center. All these schools define themselves as inclusive, but some work more on the aim of extending the equality of opportunities to all the families that make up the community. They work basing on the understanding that we are different and that this difference makes the reality as rich and complex as it is.

To encourage mutual respect, cooperation and knowledge of the other cultures present in the school, as well as to choose the most adequate teaching activities, it is common for them to work in cooperation with each other (with the help of volunteers or family members and having established the same objectives) on other aspects that characterize the everyday life of the school. For example, the cleaning of the dining room, the attention for the school vegetable garden, and other extra-scholar reinforcement activities.

Generally, families do not get involved with the education of their children, as indicated by the interviewees from the schools that carry out the cited good practices regarding the cultural and religious diversity. On the other hand, various studies indicate the involvement of parents (which mainly covers these three aspects: school-family communication, participation of the families in the school and participation of the families at home) as one of the determining factors for success at school (Bernad, 2016). Given the pressing need to improve this aspect, all the centers visited have implemented actions to improve school-family communication, incentivize the participation of families in the school's activities and facilitate the follow-up of their children's progress in the school. Among others, the families are invited to enter the classrooms to see what the children do and to attend workshops designed to show how the school works and what the methodologies used are. They are also encouraged to participate in such teaching-learning activities as class projects or interactive groups. Lastly, some schools offer the families the possibility of participating in running the center through mixed commissions, besides making the mothers and fathers class delegates, creating a family council, scheduling meetings with teachers, etc. These actions relate to the working dynamics of the centers and the attitudes of the professionals who work in them.

The mentioned interviews enable us to analyze what teachers think about the issue of cultural and religious diversity, and what is their position regarding the official curriculum. When the focus is on education policies regarding these themes, reference is quickly made to what they believe to be conditioning their work, namely the series of education laws in Spain, parallel to the changes in the ruling parties, as the application of each of these laws implies curricular changes in different subjects. Secondly, the interviewees focus on religious diversity in schools, which they currently place in a multi-cultural and globalized context in which cultural and religious diversity is managed depending on a wide range of factors, as shown below.

Although the law states that teaching the subject of Religion is mandatory for the centers and optional for the pupils, in public schools we can detect a wide spectrum (possibly conditioned by the choice of the families) of school provisions that range from schools that only teach Catholicism to schools that only offer an alternative subject, while some others offer both options. The majority of the public schools that have been visited, given their successful experiences, often do not work on the religious component besides the subject of Religion. In contrast, the question of values and ethics is dealt with transversally or through various specific actions such as the the 3–12 philosophy program or in tutorials. If the subject of religion is not taught, religious culture is dealt with transversally in other subjects like social environment and tutoring.

One must be more specific, given that when looking at Catholicism (which, we recall, is the most habitual of the optional religions in the survey presented above) and although the curriculum for religion is established at the state level by the Spanish Episcopal Conference, most have adapted the program to the current situation by including knowledge of other religions, emphasizing values and relegating religious practices to the family sphere. At this point, it is notable that, despite their Catholic confessional ideology, the grant-aided centers visited tend to offer a mandatory subject called Religious Cultures to all pupils. It has its own specific content, it includes the study of the other majority religions and the study of the values shared by the different confessions (based on universal human rights).

Independently of whether they choose to attend the Religion class or the alternative, a good part of the foreign-origin pupils tends to go to places of worship after school hours or at the weekend. There, as well as following the religious practices, they can attend classes of religion and culture. Even if the legislation contemplates that it is possible to teach four religions in educational centers, in practice only Catholicism is taught (or religious culture in another case) and, in a few centers, the Evangelical religion. One of the reasons adduced for this is the lack of teachers who fulfill the requisites regarding training (especially the need to have a teaching qualification).

4   Open Discussion and Conclusions

The response to cultural and religious diversity in schools in Catalonia shows a diversity of answers and approaches – a fact that reaffirms that we are witnessing a process of defining and situating these subjects, which have to adapt to the changing laws and to the context and actors who intervene, as Garreta (2006 and 2011) and Rey (2012) indicated previously. The analysis of these data shows a set of paradoxical aspects, which are detailed below:

- The legal framework of the education system provokes certain tensions. In a way, the preferential treatment of Catholicism in a non-denominational State is contrary to the teaching of religious diversity and intercultural dialogue. Besides the policies that can evolve with the changes in educational legislation, this preferential treatment converts the subject of religion into an "anomaly" within the school curriculum, and even more so bearing in mind the cultural and religious diversity that has entered into our school environment (Llevot *et al.*, 2016 and 2017). Nevertheless, the efforts made by Religion teachers, in consonance with the school management teams, in order to incorporate cultural and religious diversity into their subject, sometimes even contravening the guidelines of the bishopric, must be recognized.

- Religious diversity is covered by the legislation of the educational administration. However, in reality, this is never really complied with (Llevot *et al.*, 2017). This is partly due to the lack of specialist teachers that meet the established training requisites to teach other religions (Tarrés, Rosón, 2009). We can also observe that the concept of religious diversity is assimilated to the fact of differentiating the subject according to the different recognized religious confessions (Griera, 2016). This favors religious freedom but, at the same time, hinders interculturality and the interreligious dialogue.

- It must also be added that, as a consequence of this legislation that frames the application of religions in schools, it is often the teachers of Catholic religion who attempt to incorporate knowledge of other religions and shared universal values into their subject (of course, from a clearly Christian viewpoint). This initiative, which should be valued as positive and innovative for the religion that is taught this way, inevitably produces a filter that limits the visibility of other possibilities when religious diversity is reduced to this (Llevot *et al.*, 2017). In summary, we cannot have religious diversity if we only teach the subject of Catholic religion.

Public school faces a great challenge regarding cultural diversity, and that is why this diversity is approached as a joint task and projects are undertaken from the schools and the parents' associations (Garreta, 2003; Garreta, Llevot, 2011; Bernad, Llevot, 2016 and 2018a; Sanuy *et al.*, 2017b). Here, we highlight the extraordinary efforts made by the teaching staff to incorporate these aspects into their everyday routines. The study by Garreta (2003) highlighted the organization of intercultural days above all else. However, this activity has now fallen by almost half in this present study. In fact, there is now a high response

(60.3%) about working on the curriculum, which indicates that the legacy of performing specific actions (special meetings) without modifying anything else is being overcome. Teachers have had to prepare new strategies to involve the pupils and families, transversal work has been prioritized and in short, they have had to improvise and experiment when faced with an unexpected situation. From this initial process, which starts from a positive professional attitude, new experiences applicable to the working of the schools are accumulated, and these undergo a process of constant revision (Garreta, 2011; Llevot *et al.*, 2017; Giró, Andrés, 2018).

It must not be forgotten that education in cultural and religious diversity does not depend only on the centers, on the families or on the teaching staff. It is unthinkable that themes involving the differences and the coexistence of cultures and religions can be dealt with in the schools idyllically, without any problem, when these are in a context of an increasingly conflictive growing world, in the midst of administrative cutbacks, with a greater or lesser understanding between governments (State and autonomous region) and the different options of public and grant-aided schools, and in situations of injustice and poverty. In this scenario, education in diversity is currently one of the greatest educational challenges, for which the responsibility must necessarily fall on the different social agents. If the problems are generated in relation to movements and conflicts, both local and global, it is unlikely that the solution to these will depend on the values and dynamics of an isolated school or community, although some values and some policies can help more than others to facilitate a good coexistence (see actual experiences in Bernad, Llevot, 2018b). However, given that coexistence is not a synonym for harmony or easiness, rethinking the meaning of this term will help us understand some attitudes that express the willingness to avoid involvement in this debate.

All these are aspects that must be re-thought in the training of future teachers (Bernad, Llevot, 2018a). It is not possible to envisage diversity in schools without taking into consideration the globalized society in which they are rooted, nor the tensions that the subject of differences can originate. One of the most tenacious uncertainties of our times, the one studied by De Sousa (2016), is the difficulty of combining the right to equality and the right to difference.

Returning to the concept of good practices proposed by Ritacco (2011), this is precisely in the common framework of action that our study emphasizes. It is also the will to integrate the existing diversity into the projects, bearing in mind aspects such as cohesion and interculturality, as well as the functionality of the learning. A school "for everyone", that is democratic, open to the community, and which works in a network where teachers, families and pupils feel recognized as participants, are other defining aspects. Some factors to take into account are the leadership of the management team, the intercultural climate, the role of religion, the channels of communication and participation, the attitudes of teachers and families and networking, among others. The type of response to religious diversity that has been carried out in schools shows a diversity of reactions and approaches, which reaffirms that we are in the process of defining and locating this subject, one that must adapt to changing laws and the context and actors who intervene (Llevot *et al.*, 2017).

A certain contrast is observed between the experience of religiosity among many recently arrived groups and the increasingly agnostic manifestation of the indigenous population. We believe that the gap that opens in this sense hinders intercultural relations and dialogue and, at the same time, the dynamics inside the educational community and society as a whole. However, some cases have managed to turn the school into a space for understanding and mutual recognition.

A basic premise is actively listening to the necessities and demands, together with sharing one's own, and a shared design and application of the initiatives. The atmosphere in the center cannot be unlinked from mutual trust and the feeling of belonging to the community. To create a real link, it is necessary to make it very strong, solid and, for that reason, the center cannot ignore the social and economic needs of the families, nor even the problems of dislocation and rootlessness. In truth, the school cannot solve many of the social problems that affect them, but they can listen to them and accompany them, and a way to do so is to understand the importance that learning the religion of origin has for some communities. To this end, beyond the single mind-set, it is essential that the school allows the differences to arise and be expressed. It must be given space and time to learn how to think about them, and especially to converse in a space inside the school, which allows to be open to philosophical questions, to religious themes, etc.

Lastly, we have to mention Carlos Skliar (2010), who invites us to consider education as the place that opens a possibility and responsibility towards the existence of the other, of all humankind. Education consists of meeting the specific other, face to face. This meeting is with a specific and singular face, name, word, language, situation, emotion and knowledge. This must be the way to be open to what is different and to learn from each other.

References to Part 6

Agirdag, O., Demanet, J., Van Houtte, M., & Van Avermaet, P. (2011). Ethnic school composition and peer victimization: a focus on the interethnic school climate. *International Journal of Intercultural Relations*, 35(4), pp. 465–473.

Aguado, T. (2011). El enfoque intercultural en la búsqueda de buenas prácticas escolares. *Revista Latinoamericana de Inclusión Educativa*, 5(2), 23–42.

Allport, G.W. (1954). *The Nature of Prejudice*. Cambridge-Massachusetts: Addison-Wesley Publishing.

Ambrosini, M., & Pozzi, S. (2018). *Italiani ma non troppo? Lo stato dell'arte della ricerca sui figli degli immigrati in Italia*. Genova: Centro Studi Medì.

Ammerman, N.T. (2010). The Challenge of Pluralism: Locating Religion in a World of Diversity. *Social Compass*, 57(2), 154–167.

Anthias, F. (2013). Intersectional what? Social divisions, intersectionality, and levels of analysis. *Ethnicities*, 13(1), pp. 3–19.

Arendt, A. (1972). *La crise de la culture*. Paris: Gallimard.

Athens, L. (2012). Mead's Analysis of Social Conflict: A Radical Interactionist's Critique. *The American Sociologist*, 43(4), 428–447.

Azzolini, D., Mantovani, D., & Santagati, M. (2019). Italy: Four Emerging Traditions in Immigrant Education Studies. In P.A.J. Stevens, & G.A. Dworkin (Eds). *The Palgrave Handbook of Race and Ethnic Inequalities in Education*. Cham: Palgrave Macmillan, Volume 2, pp. 697–747.

Baillon, R. (1986). Le choix du collège: le comportement "éclairé" des familles. *Revue Française de Sociologie*, 24(7), 719–734.

Barberis, E. (2016). Figli dell'immigrazione a scuola. Forme della discriminazione. *La rivista delle politiche sociali*, 2, 81–98.

Bargellini, C., & Cicciarelli, E. (Eds) (2007). *Islam a scuola*, Quaderni ISMU, 2.

Bargellini, C., Frascioli, D. (Eds) (2005). *I tanti volti di una religione: l'Islam in classe*, Quaderni ISMU, 1.

Beatbullying (2008). *Interfaith Report*. UK: http://www.beatbullying.org/indexhtm.

Beauchemin, C., Hamel, C., Lesné, M., Simon, P., & l'équipe de l'enquête TeO. (2010). Les discriminations: une question de minorités visibles. *Population et Société*, 466, 3–5.

Bekemans, L. (2013). *Globalisation vs Europeanisation. A Human-centric Interaction*. Brussels, Bern, Berlin: Peter Lang.

Benadusi, M., Fabretti, V., & Salmieri, L. (2017). Dealing with religious multiple belongings and beliefs. *Scuola democratica*, 3, 467–485.

Bergamaschi, A. (2013a). Adolescents and prejudice: A comparative study of the attitudes of two European adolescent populations regarding the issues that are raised by increasing cultural and religious pluralism. *International Journal of Intercultural Relations*, 37(3), 302–312.

Bergamaschi, A. (2013b). *Jeunes Français et Italiens face à l'immigration. Deux facettes d'un même préjugé*. Paris: l'Harmattan.

Bergamaschi, A. (2016). The academic problems of immigrant students by the prism of the ethnicization of peer relations. *International Journal of school climate and violence prevention.* 2, 37–64.

Bergamaschi, A., & Santagati, M. (2019). When friendship is stronger than prejudice. Role of intergroup friendships among adolescents in two distinct socio-cultural contexts of immigration. *International Review of Sociology*, 29(1), 36–57.

Berger, P. (1999). *The desecularization of the world. Resurgent religion and world politics*. Michigan: William B. Eerdmans Publishing Co.

Bernad, O. (2016). School and immigrant origin famílies. In J. Garreta (Ed.), *Immigration into Spain: Evolution and Socio-Educational Challenges*. Bern: Peter Lang, pp. 169–176.

Bernad, O., & Llevot, N. (2016). El papel de las AMPA en los centros escolares: actuaciones y retos. *Revista de la Asociación de Sociología de la Educación (RASE)*, 9(3), 359–371.

Bernad, O., & Llevot, N. (2018a). La escuela y las familias de origen minoritario: retos a abordar en las escuelas y en las facultades de educación (cap. 3). In A. García Manso (coord.), *Aportaciones de vanguardia en la investigación actual*. Madrid: Editorial Tecnos, pp. 127–134.

Bernad, O., & Llevot, N. (Eds) (2018b). *New Pedagogical Challenges in the 21st Century, Contributions of Research in Education*. London: IntechOpen.

Bertrand, R.L. (2015). The limits of secularization through education. *Journal of Religion & Society*, 9(17), 1–43.

Berzano, L. (2011). Religious lifestyles. In G. Giordan, & W.H. Swatos (Eds). *Religion, Spirituality and Everyday Practice*. London: Springer, pp. 467–486.

Besozzi, E. (2017). *Educazione e società*. Roma: Carocci.

Besozzi, E., Colombo, M., & Santagati, M. (Eds) (2009). *Giovani stranieri, nuovi cittadini. Le strategie di una generazione ponte*. Milano: FrancoAngeli.

Bichi, R., Introini, F., & Pasqualini, C. (Eds) (2018). *Di generazione in generazione. La trasmissione della fede nelle famiglie con background migratorio*. Milano: Vita e Pensiero.

Bindewald, B.J, Sanatullova-Allison, E. & Hsiao, Y. (2017). Religion and Public Education in Pluralist, Democratic Societies: Some Lessons from the United States and Canada. *Religion & Education, 44*(2), 180–202.

Blalock, H.M. (1967). *Towards a Theory of Minority Group Relations*. New York: Wiley.

Blaya, C. (2006). *Violences et maltraitances en milieu scolaire*. Paris: Armand Colin.

Blumer, H.G. (1958). Race Prejudice as a Sense of Group Position. *Pacific Sociological Review, 1*(1), 3–7.

Bonnet, F., Safi, M., Lalé, E. & Wasmer, E. (2011). À la recherche du locataire «idéal»: du droit aux pratiques en région parisienne. *Regards croisés sur l'économie, 9*(1), 216–227.

Bossi, L. (2017). L'ora invisibile. Le alternative all'insegnamento della religione cattolica in Italia. *Scuola democratica, 3,* 531–550.

Bourdieu, P., & Passeron, J-C. (1970). *La Reproduction: éléments pour une théorie du système d'enseignement.* Paris: Editions de Minuit.

Bourdieu, P., & Passeron, J-C. (1964). *Les Héritiers: les étudiants et la culture.* Paris: Editions de Minuit.

Bradford Local Authority (2016). *Bradford Agreed Syllabus for Religious Education 2016–2020.* Bradford (UK). https://bso.bradford.gov.uk/schools/CMSPage.aspx?mid=2039.

Branca, P., & Cuciniello, A. (2014). *Scuola e Islam.* In A. Melloni (Ed.). *Rapporto sull'analfabetismo religioso in Italia.* Bologna: Il Mulino, pp. 282–300.

Brinbaum, Y., Moguérou L., & Primon, J-L. (2012). *Les enfants d'immigrés ont des parcours scolaires différenciés selon leur origine migratoire.* INSEE, pp. 43–59. Retrived at: http://www.insee.fr/fr/ffc/docs_ffc/ref/IMMFRA12_d_D2_scol.pdf.

Brinbaum, Y., & Primon, J-L. (2013). Parcours scolaires et sentiment d'injustice et de discrimination chez les descendants d'immigrés. *Économie et Statistique, 464–465–466,* 215–244.

Bychawska-Siniarska, D. (2017). *Protecting the Right to Freedom of Expression under the European Convention on Human Rights.* Council of Europe.

Cadeddu, F., & Melloni, A. (Eds) (2018). *Religious Literacy, Law and History. Perspectives on European Pluralist Societies.* London: Routledge.

Campiche, R.J. (2015). Les laïcités suisses. *Choisir,* février, 12–16.

Canta, C.C. (1999). *L'ora debole. Indagine sull'insegnamento della religione cattolica,* Caltanissetta-Roma: Sciascia.

Canta, C.C. (2006). *Fare scuola in epoca di pluralismo religioso.* In M. Colombo, G. Giovannini, & P. Landri (Eds), *Sociologia delle politiche e dei processi formativi.* Milano: Guerini, pp. 218–238.

Canta, C.C. (2013a). *La pratica del dialogo in Italia.* In P. Naso (Ed.), *Religioni, dialogo, integrazione.* Vademecum a cura del Dipartimento per le libertà civili e l'immigrazione Direzione Centrale degli fari dei Culti Ministero dell'Interno. Roma: Idos, pp. 71–79. http://www.interno.gov.it/sites/default/files/allegati/vademecum_religioni_dialogo_integrazione.pdf.

Canta, C.C. (2013b). *Scenari per l'insegnamento della cultura religiosa in Italia.* In B. Salvarani (Ed.), *Perché le religioni a scuola?* Bologna: EMI, pp. 85–92.

Canta, C.C., Casavecchia, A., Loperfido, M.S., & Pepe, M. (2011). *Laicità in dialogo. I volti della laicità nell'Italia plurale.* Caltanissetta-Roma: Sciascia.

Casanova, J. (2007). *Immigration and the New Religious Pluralism. A European Union/ United States comparison.* In T. Banchoff (Ed.), *Democracy and the New Religious Pluralism.* Oxford: Oxford University Press, pp. 59–84.

Cavalli, A. (2016). Perché l'educazione politica non ha trovato spazio nella scuola italiana (e cosa si può fare per riempire la lacuna). *Scuola democratica,* 3, 791–800.

Charmaz, K. (2006). *Constructing Grounded Theory.* London: Sage.

CIDE (2005). *La atención al alumnado inmigrante en el sistema educativo en España.* Madrid: Ministerio de Educación y Ciencia.

Cipriani, R., & Costa, C. (2015). Preface to the Special Section Socialization and religion. *Italian Journal of Sociology of Education,* 7(3), 1–9.

Clementi, M. (Ed.). *La scuola e il dialogo interculturale.* Milano: Quaderni Ismu, 2/2008.

Coglievina, S. (2017). Religious education in Italian public schools: what room for Islam? *Stato Chiese e pluralismo confessionale,* 29, 1–15 (https://www.statoechiese.it/ images/uploads/articoli_pdf/Coglievina.M_Religious.pdf).

Coleman, J.S. (1988). Social Capital in the Creation of Human Capital. *The American Journal of Sociology, 94,* 95–120.

Colombo, M. (2013). Introduction. Pluralism in education and implications for analysis. *Italian Journal of Sociology of Education,* 5(2), 1–16.

Colombo, M. (2018). The impact of Ethnicity on school life: a cross-national post-commentary. *Italian Journal of Sociology of Education,* 10(3), 187–200.

Colombo, M., & Santagati, M. (2010). Interpreting Social Inclusion of Young Migrants in Italy. *Italian Journal of Sociology of Education,* 2(1), 9–48.

Colombo, M., & Santagati, M. (2014). *Nelle scuole plurali. Misure di integrazione degli alunni stranieri.* Milano: FrancoAngeli.

Colombo, M., & Santagati, M. (2017). School Integration as a Sociological Construct: Measuring Multiethnic Classrooms' Integration in Italy. In M. Espinoza-Herold, & R.M. Contini (Eds), *Living in Two Homes: Integration, Identity and Education of Transnational Migrants in a Globalized World.* Bingley: Emerald Publishing, pp. 253–292.

Council of Europe (2006). *Religious diversity and Intercultural education in Europe: a reference book for schools* (Comm 2006)14.

Council of Europe (2008a). *Recommendation CM/Rec (2008)12 of the Committee of Ministers to Member States on the Dimension of Religions and Nonreligious Convictions within Intercultural Education,* https://wcd.coe.int//ViewDoc.jsp?Ref=CM/Rec(200 8)12&Language=lanEnglish&Ver=original&BackColorInternet=DBDCF2&BackCol orIntranet=FDC864&BackColorLogged=FDC864.

Council of Europe (2008b). *White Paper on Intercultural Dialogue. Living Together As Equals in Dignity.* Strasbourg.

Crenshaw, K. (1989). Demarginalizing the Intersection of Race and Sex: A Black Feminist Critique of Antidiscrimination Doctrine, Feminist Theory and Antiracist Politics. *University of Chicago Legal Forum*, *1*(8), retrieved from http://chicagounbound.uchicago.edu/uclf/vol1989/iss1/8.

Cuciniello, A. (2017a). Contesti educativi di fronte all'alterità religiosa: l'Islam e i musulmani a scuola. *Oppinformazioni*, *44*(123), 38–49. http://oppi.it/wp-content/uploads/2018/06/oppinfo123_038-049_cuciniello.pdf.

Cuciniello, A. (2017b). Religioni e scuole nell'Italia che cambia. In F. Caruso, & V. Ongini. *Scuola, migrazioni e pluralismo religioso*. Todi: Fondazione Migrantes, Tau Editrice, pp. 135–142.

Daher, L., Gamuzza, S., & Leonora, A.M. (Eds) (2016). *Multicultural Schools. Enhancing Cultural and Linguistic Treasure of Europe through Teachers*. Report 01. Project n.: 2015-1-PL01-KA201-016963. http://www.multicultural-schools.eu/description/.

Daher, L., Gamuzza, S., & Leonora, A.M. (2017). Bisogni e competenze degli insegnanti in una società multireligiosa. *Scuola democratica*, 3, 569–588.

Dahrendorf, R. (1959). *Class and Class Conflict in Industrial Society*. CA: Stanford University Press.

De Kesel, J. (2017). Un nuovo ruolo per le religioni nella società post-secolare. *Vita e Pensiero*, *100*(6), 15–22.

De Sousa Santos, B. (2016). La incertidumbre, entre el miedo y la esperanza. *El viejo Topo*, 346, 49–53.

De Venden, V.C. (2011). The case of France. in G. Zincone, R. Pennix, & M. Borkert (Eds), *Migration Policy Making in Europe. The Dynamics of Actors and Context in Past and Present*. Amsterdam: Amsterdam University Press, pp. 61–94.

Debarbieux, E. (1998). Violence et ethnicité dans l'école française. *Revue Européenne des Migrations Internationales*, *14*(1), 77–91.

Delli Zotti, G. (2014). *Children's Voices: etnicità e bullismo nella scuola*. Roma: Bonanno.

Departament d'Ensenyament (2015). *Enseñanza de la religión de la serie Documentos para la organización y la gestión de los centros para el curso 2015/16. Enseñanza de la religión*. Barcelona: Generalitat de Catalunya, Departament d'Ensenyament.

Detienne, M. (2010). *L'Identité nationale, une énigme*. Paris: Gallimard Folio-Histoire.

Dietrich-Ragon, P. (2017). Aux portes de la société française. Les personnes privées de logement issues de l'immigration. *Population*, *72*(1), 7–38.

Doytcheva, M. (2007). *Une discrimination positive à la française? Ethnicité et territoires dans les politiques de la ville*. Paris: La Découverte.

Dronkers, J., & Kornder, N. (2015). Can Gender Differences in Educational Performance of 15-Year-Old Migrant Pupils Be Explained by Societal Gender Equality in Origin and Destination Countries? *Compare: A Journal of Comparative and International Education*, *45*(4), 610–634.

Dubet, F. (1987). *La galère. Jeunes en survie*. Paris: Fayard.

Duru-Bellat, M., & van Zanten, A. (2012). *Sociologie de l'école*. Paris: Armand Colin.

Eisner, E.W. (1985). *The Educational Imagination: On the Design and Evaluation of School Programs*. New York: Macmillan Publishing Co. (2nd edition).

Escarbajal, A., & Leiva, J.J. (2017). La necesidad de formar en competencias interculturales como fundamento pedagógico: un estudio en la región de Murcia (España). *Profesorado. Revista de Currículum y Formación de Profesorado, 21*(1), 281–293.

Esser, H. (2010). Assimilation, Ethnic Stratification, or Selective Acculturation? Recent Theories of the Integration of Immigrants and the Model of Intergenerational Integration. *Sociologica*, 1, 1–29.

Essomba, MA. (2014). Políticas de escolarización del alumnado de origen extranjero en el estado español. *Revista electrónica interuniversitaria de formación del profesorado, 17*(2), 13–27.

Fabretti, V. (2013). Learning from religions. Post-secular Schools and the Challenge of Pluralism. *Italian Journal of Sociology of Education, 5*(3), 46–66.

Farris, S.R., & de Jong, S. (2014). Discontinuous intersections: second-generation immigrant girls in transition from school to work. *Ethnic and Racial Studies, 37*(9), 1505–1525.

Fassari, L.G., & Pompili, G. (2017). On the Learning Process to Be Italian Muslim Women. *Scuola democratica*, 3, 589–606.

Felouzis, G., Fouquet-Chauprade, B., & Charmillot, S. (2015). Les descendants d'immigrés à l'école en France : entre discontinuité culturelle et discrimination systémique. *Revue française de pédagogie*, 191, 11–28.

Fernández, J., & García, F.J. (2015). El desarrollo normativo que regula las aulas para escolares de nacionalidad extranjera. *Profesorado, 19*(1), 468–495.

Ferrara, A. (2009). The separation of religion and politics in a post-secular society. *Philosophy & Social Criticism, XXXV*(1–2), 77–91.

Ferrara, A. (2014). *The Democratic Horizon. Hyperpluralism and the renewal of Political Liberalism*. New York: Cambridge University Press.

Ferrari, A. (2013a). *La libertà religiosa in Italia. Un percorso incompiuto*. Roma: Carocci.

Ferrari, A. (2013b). Religious Education in Italy. In D.H. Davis, & E. Miroshnikova (Eds), *The Routledge International Handbook of Religious Education*. London: Routledge, pp. 175–180.

Ferrari, S. (2013). Religious education in the European Union. In D.H. Davis, & E. Miroshnikova (Eds), *The Routledge International Handbook of Religious Education*. London: Routledge, pp. 100–103.

Ferrari, S. (2017). Diritti dell'uomo e diritti di Dio. Una tensione ineliminabile?, *Rivista di filosofia del diritto, VI*(1), 165–180.

Foner, N., & Alba, R. (2008). Immigrant religion in the US and Western Europe: Bridge or barrier to inclusion? *The International Migration Review, 42*(2), 360–392.

Frisina, A. (2011). The Making of Religious Pluralism in Italy: Discussing Religious Education from a New Generational Perspective. *Social Compass*, 58(2), 271–284.

Galland, O. (2008). Les jeunes et la société: des visions contrastées de l'avenir. In A. Stellinger, & R. Wintrebre (Eds), *Les jeunesses face à leur avenir. Une enquête internationale*. Paris: Fondation pour l'Innovation Politique – Kairos Future.

Galland, O. (2009). *Les jeunes*. Paris: La Découverte.

Gambetta, D., & Hertog, S. (2016). *Engineers of Jihad: the curious connection between violent extremism and education*. Princeton: Princeton University Press.

Garelli, F. (2011). *Religione all'italiana. L'anima del paese messa a nudo*. Bologna: Il Mulino.

Garelli, F. (2012). Flexible Catholicism, Religion and the Church: The Italian Case. *Religions*, 4(1), 1–13.

Garelli, F. (2016). *Piccoli atei crescono. Davvero una generazione senza Dio?* Bologna: Il Mulino.

Garreta, J., & Llevot, N. (2011). Immigrant families and the school in Spain: dynamics and factors that influence their relations. *Journal of Educational, Cultural and Psycological Studies*, 4, 47–67.

Garreta, J. (2003). *El espejismo intercultural. La escuela de Cataluña ante la diversidad cultural*. Madrid: Centro de Investigación y Documentación Educativa (CIDE).

Garreta, J. (2006). Ethnic minorities in the Spanish and Catalan educational systems: From exclusion to intercultural education. *International Journal of Intercultural Relations*, 30(2), 261–279.

Garreta, J. (2011). Atención a la diversidad cultural en Cataluña: exclusión, segregación e interculturalidad. *Revista de Educación*, 355, 213–233.

Garreta, J., Macià, M., & Llevot, N. (2019). Religious education in state primary schools: the case of Catalonia (Spain). *British Journal of Religious Education*, 41(2), 145–154.

Giorda, M.C. (2013). *Religious Education in Italy. Themes and Problems*. In J. Ansgar (Ed.). *Religious Education Politics, the State, and the Society*. Würtzburg: Ergon-Verlag, pp. 177–197.

Giorda, M.C. (2015). Religious Diversity in Italy and the Impact on Education: The History of a Failure. *New Diversities*, 17(1), 77–93.

Giró, J., & Andrés, S. (2018). Profesorado y familias. Actores sin guión. *Contextos educativos*, 22, 29–44.

Gordon, P.E. (2008). The Place of the Sacred in the Absence of God: Charles Taylor's A Secular Age. *Journal of the History of Ideas*, 69(4), 647–673.

Grassi, R. (2006). *I molti volti della religiosità giovanile*. In R. Grassi (Ed.), *Giovani, religione e vita quotidiana*. Bologna: Il Mulino, pp. 25–85.

Griera, M. (2016). El mapa religiós i els nous imaginaris espirituals. In S. Giner (Ed.), *Raó de Catalunya. La societat catalana al segle XXI*, Barcelona: Institut d'Estudis Catalans & Enciclopèdia Catalana, pp. 377–396.

Habermas, J. (2006). On the Relations Between the Secular Liberal state and Religion. In H. de Vries, & L.E. Sullivan (Eds), *Political Theologies. Public Religions in a Post-secular World*. New York: Fordham University Press, pp. 251–260.

Halafoff, A., Arweck, E., & Boisvert, D.L. (2015). Education about Religions and World-views: Promoting Intercultural and Interreligious Understanding in Secular Societ-ies. *Journal of Intercultural Studies, 36*(3), 249–254.

Halász, G., & Michel, A. (2011). Key Competences in Europe: interpretation, policy for-mulation and implementation. *European Journal of Education, 46*(3), 289–306.

Hall, J.R. (2013). Religion and Violence from a Sociological Perspective. In M. Juergens-meyer, M. Kitts, & M. Jerryson (Eds). *The Oxford Handbook of Religion and Violence*. Oxford: Oxford University Press.

Hervieu-Leger, D. (1999). *Le pèlerin et le converti*. Paris: Flammarion.

Hirschberger, G., Ein-Dor, T., Leidner, B., & Saguy, T. (2016). How Is Existential Threat Related to Intergroup Conflict? *Frontiers in Psychology, 7*, 1877 (1–18).

Ho, C. (2011). Respecting the Presence of Others: School Micropublics and Everyday Multiculturalism. *Journal of Intercultural Studies, 32*(6), 603–619.

Hobson, P.R., & Edwards, J.S. (1999). *Religious Education in a Pluralist Society*. London: Woburn Press.

Honneth, A. (1996). Reconnaissance. In *Dictionnaire d'éthique et de philosophie morale*. Paris: Presses Universitaires de France.

Howell, D.C. (2006). *Statistical methods for psychology*. Boston: Wadsworth Publishing.

Ichou, M., & van Zanten, A. (2019). France: The Increasing Recognition of Migration and Ethnicity as a Source of Educational Inequalities. In P.A.J. Stevens, & G.A. Dworkin (Eds). *The Palgrave Handbook of Race and Ethnic Inequalities in Education*. Cham: Palgrave Macmillan, Volume 1, pp. 328–364.

Idos (2018). *Dossier Statistico Immigrazione*. Roma: Idos.

Institut National d'Etudes Démographiques (2010). *Trajectoires et Origines (TeO)*. En ligne: https://teo.site.ined.fr/.

Ismu Foundation (2018). *The Twenty-third Italian Report on Migrations 2017*. Milan: Fon-dazione Ismu.

Istat (2015). *Appartenenza e pratica religiosa tra i cittadini stranieri. Anno 2011–2012*, Roma, October https://www.istat.it/it/files/2015/10/Religione-tra-gli-stranieri.pdf?t itle=Religione+tra+i+cittadini+stranieri+-+02%2Fott%2F2015+-+Testo+integrale .pdf, 16/11/2018.

Jackson, R. (2014). *Signposts – Policy and practice for teaching about religions and non-religious world views in intercultural education*. Strasbourg: Council of Europe. https:// www.academia.edu/29035890/Signposts_Policy_and_practice_for_ teaching_about_religions_and_non-religious_world_views_in_intercultural_ education.

Jackson, R. (2016). Inclusive Study of Religions and World Views in Schools: Signposts from the Council of Europe. *Social Inclusion, 4*(2), 14–25.

Jackson, R. (2019). *Religious Education for Plural Societies: The Selected Works of Robert Jackson.* NY: Routledge.

Jolly, C. (2005). Religion et intégration sociale. *Cahier du Plan*, 8, retrived at: http://www.cicns.net/sociologues-nouvelles-spiritualites-15.htm.

Jounisse, J., & Hanye, D.L., (1992). Friendship in Adolescence. *Journal of Developmental & Behavioral Pediatrics, 13*(1), 59–66.

Kent, D.P., & Burnight, R.G. (1951). Group Centrism in Complex Societies. *American Journal of Sociology, 57*(3), 256–259.

Kivisto, P. (2014). *Religion and Immigration: Migrant Faiths in North America and Western Europe.* Cambridge: Polity press.

Klingenberg, M., & Sjö, S. (2019). Theorizing religious socialization: a critical assessment. *Religion, 49*(2), 163–178.

Knauth, T., Joza, D.P., Bertram-Troost, G., & Ipgrave, J. (Eds) (2008). *Encountering Religious Pluralism in School and Society. A Qualitative Study of Teenage Perspectives in Europe.* Münster: Waxmann.

Kodeljia, Z. (2012). Religious Education and the Teaching about Religions. *Šolsko polje, XXIII*(1–2), 253–280.

Kristeva, J. (2016). Come si può essere jihadisti? A proposito del male radicale. *Vita e Pensiero, 99*(1), 9–18.

Laborde, V., & Silhol, G., (2018). The Intertwining of Laïcité and Ethnicity: Observations from Teachers' Practices in State Schools in Provence. *Italian Journal of Sociology of Education, 10*(3), 58–81.

Lambert, Y. (2000). La renaissance des croyances liées à l'après-mort les évolutions en France et dans plusieurs pays européens. *Recherches Sociologiques, 32*(2), 9–19.

Lapeyronnie, D. (2008). *Ghetto urbain. Ségrégation, violence, pauvreté en France aujourd'hui.* Paris: Robert Laffont.

Lipperini, L. (Ed.) (2018). *Parole ostili. 10 racconti.* Roma-Bari: Laterza.

Llevot, N. (2005). Del Programa d'Educació Compensatòria al nou Pla per a la Llengua i la Cohesió Social. *Revista Papers, 78*, 197–214.

Llevot, N. (Ed.) (2006). *La Educación intercultural : discursos y prácticas.* Lleida: Edicions de la Universitat de Lleida.

Llevot, N., & Bernad, O. (2016). La mediación gitana: herramienta performativa de las relaciones entre escuela y familia. *Revista electrónica Interuniversitaria de formación del profesorado, 19*(1), 113–125.

Llevot, N., Bernad, O., & Molet, C. (2017). Diversidad cultural-religiosa y formación del profesorado. In E. Martínez, P. Raya, & X. Martínez (Coord.), *Investigación, desarrollo e innovación universitarios.* Madrid: Ediciones Mc Graw-Hill, pp. 355–367.

Llevot, N., Garreta, J., Mata, A., Julià, R., Molet, C., Domingo, J. & Bernad, O. (2015). Diversità culturale e religiosa nei centri scolastici della Scuola Primaria in Catalogna. *Civitas Educationis. Education, Politics and Culture*, *4*(2), 85–101.

Llevot, N., Molet, C., Garreta, J., & Bernad, O. (2017). Análisis de la diversidad religiosa en el sistema educativo catalán (España). *Orientamenti Pedagogici, rivista internazionale di scienze dell'educazione*, *64*(368), 323–342.

Llorent, V.J., Ortega-Ruiz, R., & Zych, I. (2016). Bullying and Cyberbullying in Minorities: Are They More Vulnerable than the Majority Group? *Frontiers in Psychology*, *7*(1507), 1–9.

Llorent-Vaquero, M. (2018). Religious Education in Public Schools in Western Europe. *International Education Studies*, *11*(1), 154–165.

Lodigiani, R., & Santagati, M. (2016). Quel che resta della socializzazione lavorativa. *Sociologia del lavoro*, *141*(1), 141–157.

Lorcerie, F. (2002). *Musulman de France et institutions scolaires. Impacts du 11 septembre*, CNRS Editions.

Luhmann, N. (1982). *The Differentiation of Society*. New York: Columbia University Press.

Maassen G.H., & de Goede, P.M.M. (1992). Intergenerational and Intragenerational Perception of Adolescents and Adults. *International Journal of Adolescence and Youth*, *3*(3–4), 269–286.

Magatti, M. (2018). *Oltre l'infinito. Storia della potenza dal sacro alla tecnica*. Milano: Feltrinelli.

Márquez-Lepe, E., & García-Cano Torrico, M. (2014). Condiciones de posibilidad y desarrollo para una educación intercultural crítica. Tres estudios de caso en el contexto andaluz. *Revista Española de Investigaciones Sociológicas*, *148*, 157–170.

May, S., Wilson, E.K., Baumgart-Ochse, C., & Sheikh, F. (2014). The Religious as Political and the Political as Religious: Globalisation, Post-Secularism and the Shifting Boundaries of the Sacred. *Politics, Religion & Ideology*, *15*(3), 331–346.

Melloni, A. (Ed.) (2014). *Rapporto sull'analfabetismo religioso in Italia*. Bologna: Il Mulino.

Mentasti, L., & Ottaviano, C. (2008). *Cento cieli in classe. Pratiche, segni e simboli religiosi nella scuola multiculturale*. Milano: Unicopli.

Mentasti, L., & Ottaviano, C. (2009). *Appartenenze religiose, fragilità e aperture*. In E. Besozzi (Ed.). *Tra sogni e realtà. Gli adolescenti e la transizione alla vita adulta*. Roma: Carocci, pp. 227–248.

Merton, R.K. (1972). Insiders and Outsiders: A Chapter in the Sociology of Knowledge. *American Journal of Sociology*, *78*(1), 9–47.

Meuret, D. (2015). School and the Contrast to Students' Fascination with Religious Terrorism. *Scuola democratica*, *3*, 499–520.

Ministero dell'Istruzione dell'Università e della Ricerca (2018). *Gli alunni con cittadi-nanza non italiana a.s. 2016/2017.* Statistica e Studi marzo 2018 (http://www.miur.gov .it/documents/20182/0/FOCUS+16-17_Studenti+non+italiani/be4e2dc4-d81d-4621 -9e5a-848f1f8609b3?version=1.0).

Molina, S. (2014). Seconde generazioni e scuola italiana: come procede l'integrazione dei figli degli immigrati? In Confindustria-Centro Studi, L. Paolazzi, & P. Sylos La-bini (Eds). *People First. Il capitale sociale e umano: la forza del Paese.* S.I.P.I., pp. 73–97.

Moore, L. (2007). Laïcité et persistance de la croyance religieuse. In M. Wieviorka, (Ed.), *Les sciences sociales en mutation.* Auxerre: Éditions Sciences Humaines.

Naso, P. (Ed.). *Religioni, dialogo, integrazione.* Vademecum a cura del Dipartimento per le libertà civili e l'immigrazione Direzione Centrale degli affari dei Culti, Ministero dell'Interno. Roma: Idos. http://www.interno.gov.it/sites/default/files/allegati/va-demecum_religioni_dialogo_integrazione.pdf.

Ottaviano, C. (2010). Schools and religions: experience, symbols and practices. *Italian Journal of Sociology of Education,* 2(1), 192–207.

Pacchi, C., & Ranci, C. (Eds) (2017). *White flight a Milano. La segregazione sociale ed et-nica nelle scuole dell'obbligo.* Milano: FrancoAngeli.

Pace, E. (2004). La ricreazione è finita. L'insegnamento delle religioni nella scuola itali-ana. In R. De Vita, F. Berti, & L. Nasi (Eds), *Identità multiculturale e multireligiosa. La costruzione di una cittadinanza pluralistica.* Milano: FrancoAngeli, pp. 274–281.

Pace, E. (2005). L'insigne faiblesse de la laïcité italienne. In J.-P. Willaime, & S. Mathieu (Dirs), *Des Maîtres et des Dieux. Écoles et Religions en Europe.* Paris: Belin, pp. 59–70.

Pajer, F. (2009). *Educazione religiosa e cittadinanza. L'insegnamento scolastico della reli-gione in Europa.* Torino: Centro Studi religiosi della Fondazione Collegio San Carlo.

Paletha, U. (2012). *La domination scolaire. Sociologie de l'enseignement professionnel et de ses publics.* Paris: Presses Universitaires de France.

Pastore, F., & Ponzo, I. (Eds) (2015). *Concordia Discors. Convivenza e conflitti nei quart-ieri di immigrazione.* Roma: Carocci.

Peguero, A.A., & Williams, L.M. (2011). Racial and Ethnic Stereotypes and Bullying Vic-timization. *Youth & Society,* 45(4), 545–564.

Perroton, J. (2000). Les dimensions ethniques de l'expérience scolaire. *L'Année soci-ologique,* 50(2), 437–468.

Pettigrew, T.F. (1997). Generalized intergroup contact effects on prejudice. *Personality and Social Psychology Bulletin,* 23(2), 173–185.

Pinto Minerva, F. (2012). Intercultura e dialogo interreligioso. *Pedagogia oggi.* 1, 11–18.

Poucet, B. (2009). *La liberté sous contrat. Une histoire de l'enseignement privé.* Paris: Fabert.

Prost, A. (1981). *Histoire générale de l'enseignement et de l'éducation en France* – tome IV. Paris: Nouvelle librairie de France.

Rayoua, P., & van Zanten, A. (2004). *Les nouveaux enseignants: changeront-ils l'école?* Paris: Bayard.

Rey, F. (2012). ¿Es constitucional la presencia del crucifijo en las escuelas públicas? *Revista jurídica de Castilla y León, 27.*

Ricucci, R. (2017). *Diversi dall'Islam. Figli dell'immigrazione e altre fedi.* Bologna: Il Mulino.

Rispoli, F., & Giorda, M.C. (Eds) (2016). *Scuola&Religioni.* Atti del Convegno a Montecitorio, 26 January. Roma: Fondazione Benvenuti in Italia.

Ritacco, M. (2011). El liderazgo de los centros educativos y las buenas prácticas ante el fracaso escolar y la exclusión social en la comunidad autónoma de Andalucía. *Revista de Investigación en educación, 9*(1), 157–167.

Rizzi, M. (2016). *La secolarizzazione debole.* Bologna: Il Mulino.

Rosati, M., & Stoeckl, K. (2012). *Multiple Modernities and Postsecular Societies.* Farnham: Ashgate.

Rossi, P. (2002). Introduzione. In M. Weber, *Sociologia della religione.* Torino: Edizioni di Comunità.

Roussier-Fusco, E. (2003). Le modèle français d'intégration et les dynamiques interethniques dans deux écoles de ta banlieue parisienne. *Revue française de pédagogie, 144,* 29–37.

Rowe, E. (2016). Politics, religion and morals: the symbolism of public schooling. *International Studies in Sociology of education, 26*(1), 1–15.

Salvarani, B. (2006). *Educare al pluralismo religioso. Bradford chiama Italia.* Bologna: EMI.

Salvarani, B. (2008). *Le esperienze del pluralismo.* In M. Clementi (Ed.). *La scuola e il dialogo interculturale.* Milano: Quaderni Ismu, 2, pp. 141–148.

Sanselme, F. (2009). L'ethnicisation des rapport sociaux à l'école. Ethnographie d'un lycée de banlieue. *Société contemporaines, 4*(76), 121–147.

Santagati, M. (2004). *Mediazione e integrazione.* Milano: FrancoAngeli.

Santagati, M. (2014). Verso le scuole plurali. Dilemmi e proposte per le politiche. In M. Colombo, & M. Santagati, *Nelle scuole plurali. Misure di integrazione degli alunni stranieri.* Milano: Franco Angeli, pp. 185–205.

Santagati, M. (2015). Researching Integration in Multiethnic Italian Schools. A Sociological Review on Educational Inequalities. *Italian Journal of Sociology of Education, 7*(3), 294–334.

Santagati, M. (2016). Interculturalism, Education and Society: Education Policies for Immigrant Students in Italy. *Australia and New Zealand Journal of European Studies, 8*(2): 6–20.

Santagati, M., Argentin, G., & Colombo, M., (2019). Religiosity and school integration among italian and non-italian students. Results from a survey in multi-ethnic classrooms, *Studi di Sociologia*, 47(1), 197–210.

Santagati, M., Giorda M.C. & Cuciniello, A. (2017). Immigrazione in Europa e attrazione giovanile per il radicalismo violento. Concetti chiave per l'analisi. In G. Lazzarini, L. Bollani, & F. Rota (Eds), *Aggressività e violenza*. Milano: FrancoAngeli, pp. 123–144.

Santagati, M., & Zanzottera, C. (2018). Education: A Challenge for Intercultural Cities. In Villa M. (Ed.), *Global Cities and Integration. A Challenge for the Future*. Milan: Ledizioni, pp. 77–104.

Santelli, E. (2007). *Grandir en banlieue. Parcours et devenir des jeunes français et d'origine maghrebine*. Paris: CIEMI Editions.

Santerini, M. (2008). *Islam e islamofobia in classe*. In P. Branca, & M. Santerini (Eds), *Alunni arabofoni a scuola*. Roma: Carocci, pp. 66–78.

Santos, M.A. (2017). La educación intercultural y el pluralismo religioso: Propuestas pedagógicas para el diálogo. *Educación XXI, 20*(1), 17–35.

Sanuy, J., Bernad, O., & Llevot, N. (2017a). Nuevos retos educativos: el Programa Escuela 21 en Cataluña. *Orientamenti Pedagogici: rivista internazionale di science dell'educazione, 64*(368), 323–342.

Sanuy, J., Bernad, O., & Llevot, N. (2017b). El Programa Escuela Nueva 21 en Cataluña (España): Prácticas de Éxito para Combatir el Abandono Escolar Prematuro. *Civitas Educationis. Education, Politics and Culture, 6/2*.

Schnapper, D. (2008). Les enjeux démocratiques de la statistique ethnique. *Revue française de sociologie, 49*(1), 133–139.

Schreiner, P. (2009). *Religious Education in Europe. Situation and Developments,* paper presented at Institute of Education, University of London, March 13.

Schreiner, P. (2013). Religious education in the European context. *ERJ Hungarian Educational Research Journal, 3*(4), 5–15.

Sclavi, M., & Giornielli, G. (2014). *La scuola e l'arte di ascoltare*. Milano: Feltrinelli.

Scott, C.L. (2015). The futures of learning 1: why must learning content and methods change in the 21st century? *Education research and foresight*, Working papers: www.unesdoc.unesco.org.

Servizio Nazionale della Conferenza Episcopale Italiana per l'Insegnamento della Religione Cattolica (2015). *Insegnamento della religione cattolica nelle scuole statali italiane*. Annuario 2015. A.s. 2014/2015. OSReT (Osservatorio Socio-Religioso Triveneto). Vicenza.

Servizio Nazionale della Conferenza Episcopale Italiana per l'Insegnamento della Religione Cattolica (2016). *Insegnamento della religione cattolica nelle scuole statali italiane*. Nuova serie. Sintesi essenziale dei risultati a.s. 2015–2016, OSReT

(Osservatorio Socio-Religioso Triveneto). Vicenza (https://irc.chiesacattolica.it/annuario-irc-2016/).

Silberman, R., & Fournier, I. (2006). Les secondes générations sur le marché du travail en France: une pénalité ethnique ancrée dans le temps. Contribution à la théorie de l'assimilation segmentée. *Revue française de sociologie, 47*(2), 243–292.

Silhol, G. (2017). La religione come professione e come vocazione. Costruire competenze e legittimare gli insegnanti di religione cattolica. *Scuola democratica, 3,* 551–568.

Simmel, G. (1968). *The Conflict in Modern Culture and Other Essays.* New York: Teachers College Press.

Simon, P., & Tiberj, V. (2012). *Les registres de l'identité. Les immigrés et leurs descendants face à l'identité nationale.* Paris: Institut National d'Etudes Démographiques – documents de travail 176, série Trajectoires et Origines (TeO) Enquête sur la diversité des populations en France.

Skliar, C. (2010). Los sentidos implicados en el estar juntos de la educación. *Revista Educación y Pedagogía, 22*(36), 101–111.

Smyth, E., Lyons, M., & Darmody, M. (2013). *Religious Education in a Multicultural Europe: Children, Parents and Schools.* London: Palgrave Macmillan.

Stephan, W.G., & Stephan, C.W. (2000). An integrated threat theory of prejudice. In S. Oskamp (Ed.), *Reducing Prejudice and Discrimination.* N.J.: Lawrence Erlbaum Associates, pp. 23–45.

Stevens, P.A., & Dworkin, G.A. (Eds) (2014). *The Palgrave Handbook of Race and Ethnic Inequalities in Education.* London: Palgrave Macmillan.

Tanguy, L. (1972). L'Etat et l'école privé en France. *Revue Française de Sociologie, 3*(13), 325–375.

Tarrés, S., & Roson, F.J. (2009). La enseñanza de las religiones minoritarias en la escuela. Análisis del caso de Andalucía. *Revista de ciencias de las religiones, 2*(14), 179–197.

Taylor, C. (2007). *A Secular Age.* Cambridge, Mass.: Belknap Press of Harvard University Press.

Vacchiano, F. (2013). *Culture, religion and civilization in selected UN documents on cultural dialogue.* Policy Report No. 01/04. Barcelona: United Nations University Institute on Globalization, Culture and Mobility (UNU-GCM).

Valasik, C. (2010). Le social et l'éthique comme réponse de la religion face au pluralisme religieux. *Social Compass, 57*(2), 168–179.

Vallet, L-A., & Caille, J-P. (2001). La scolarité des enfants d'immigrés. In A. Van Zanten (Eds), *L'école. L'état des savoirs.* Paris: La Découverte, pp. 293–301.

Valtolina, G.G. (2015). Il pregiudizio etnico nella prima infanzia: i programmi di contrasto. *Studi Emigrazione/International Journal of Migration Studies, 52*(197), 50–60.

Van Praag, L., Agirdag, O., Stevens, P.A., & Van Houtte, M. (2016). The perceived role of Islamic religiosity in minorities' educational success in Belgium. A cure or curse? *Social Compass*, *63*(4), 529–546.

Viñao, A. (2014). *Religión en las aulas. Una materia controvertida*. Madrid: Morata.

Weisse, W. (2010). REDco: A European Research Project on Religion in Education. *Religion and Education*, *37*(3), 187–202.

Wierzbicki, M.S. (2016). L'insegnamento della religione cattolica nel contesto europeo: profili e competenze, *Seminare*, *37*(3), 73–84.

Wieviorka, M. (2001). *La différence*. Paris: Les Éditions Balland.

Willaime, J-P. (2010). *Sociologie des religions*. Paris: Presses Universitaires de France.

Zanfrini, L. (2016). *Introduzione alla sociologia delle migrazioni*. Roma-Bari: Laterza.

Zanfrini, L. (2019). *The Challenge of Migration in a Janus-Faced Europe*. London: Palgrave Macmillan.

Zanfrini, L. (Ed.) (2015). *The Diversity Value. How to Reinvent the European Approach to Immigration*. Maidenhead, UK: McGraw-Hill Education.

Zapata-Barrero, R. (Ed.) (2015). *Interculturalism in Cities: Concept, Policy and Implementation*. Cheltenham: Edward Elgar.

Index

Page numbers in **bold** refer to tables; page numbers in *italics* refer to figures; 'n' after a page number indicates the footnote number.

Printed in the United States
By Bookmasters